Biblica

THE BIBLE ATLAS

Biblica

THE BIBLE ATLAS

A Social and Historical Journey Through the Lands of the Bible

CHIEF CONSULTANT

Professor Barry J. Beitzel

This edition for the United States and its territories published by Barron's Educational Series, Inc., 2007.

First published in 2006 by Global Book Publishing Pty Ltd.
This publication and arrangement

All inquiries should be addressed to:
Barron's Educational Series, Inc.
250 Wireless Blvd.
Hauppauge, NY 11788
www.barronseduc.com

ISBN-13: 978-0-7641-6085-1
ISBN-10: 0-7641-6085-0

Library of Congress Control No.: 2007927687

CAPTIONS FOR THE PRELIMINARY PAGES, PART OPENERS, AND COVERS

Page 1: God creating the waters, detail from folio 4V of the late twelfth-century C.E. Souvigny Bible

Page 2: *The Guardian Angel* by Antonio Zona

Pages 4–5: City of Jerusalem, detail from *Christ's Agony in the Garden* by Andrea Mantegna

Pages 6–7: God the Father, detail from *The Last Judgement* by Jean Cousin the Younger

Page 9: *Jacob's Dream of the Ladder* by Luca Giordano

Pages 10–11: *Bethlehem Village, the Holy Land* by David Roberts

Page 12: *Allegory of the Creation* by Jacopo del Zucchi

Pages 14–15: Umbraculum or bower, mosaic from Saint Apollinare Nuovo, Ravenna, Italy

Pages 28–29: *View of Jerusalem from the Valley of Jehoshaphat* by Count Auguste de Forbin

Pages 90–91: Patriarchs, detail from *The Glorification of the Virgin Mary* by Franghias Kavertzas

Pages 182–183: *Samson and Delilah* by Joanna Vergouwen

Pages 214–215: Tree of Jesse painting from Sucevita Monastery, Moldavia, Romania

Pages 268–269: Jonah ejected by the big fish, mosaic from Basilica of Aquileia, Italy

Pages 312–313: Seventh-century B.C.E. Assyrian relief showing the Battle of Til-Tuba

Pages 404–405: *Crucifixion with Dio Padre and Saint Ignatius of Loyola* by Domenico Fontebasso

Pages 452–453: *Saint Stephen Preaching in Jerusalem* by Vittore Carpaccio

Pages 494–495: Detail from *La Généalogie de la Vierge* by Gerard David

Front cover: *God the Eternal Father* by Giovanni Francesco Barbieri Guercino

Back cover: *Jerusalem* by Karl Friedrich H. Werner

Printed in China by SNP Leefung
Color separation by Pica Digital Pte Ltd, Singapore
9 8 7 6 5 4 3 2 1

119180

MANAGING DIRECTOR	Chryl Campbell
PUBLISHING MANAGER	Sarah Anderson
ART DIRECTOR	Stan Lamond
PROJECT MANAGER	Dannielle Doggett
CHIEF CONSULTANT	Professor Barry J. Beitzel
CONTRIBUTORS	Dr. Barry Bandstra Professor William H. Barnes Professor Herbert Basser Dr. Margaret Beirne RSC Professor Gideon Biger Ian Boxall Dr. Tim Bulkeley Dr. Mark W. Chavalas Dr. Eric H. Cline Dr. Katharine Dell Dr. Peter Edwell Professor J. Keith Elliott Rev. Dr. Anna Grant-Henderson Dr. James R. Harrison Janet Healey Dr. Richard S. Hess Robert V. Huber Rev. Dr. James M. Lindenberger Dr. Kevin McGeough Dr. Scott Morschauser Dr. Mark A. O'Brien Dr. Sharon Pace Dr. Kim Ian Parker Dr. Duane Smith Dr. Lawson G. Stone Dr. Kevin Sullivan
EDITORS	Loretta Barnard Kate Etherington Stephanie Goodwin Heather McNamara Janet Parker Marie-Louise Taylor Michael Wall
CARTOGRAPHER	Laurie Whiddon
JERUSALEM MAPS	Suzanne Keating
MAP COORDINATOR	Irene Mickaiel
PHOTO LIBRARY	Alan Edwards
PICTURE RESEARCH	Irene Mickaiel
COVER DESIGN	Bob Mitchell Stan Lamond
DESIGNERS	Cathy Campbell Alex Frampton Stan Lamond Jacqueline Richards
INDEX	Jon Jermey
PRODUCTION	Bernard Roberts Ian Coles
CONTRACTS	Alan Edwards
FOREIGN RIGHTS	Dee Rogers
PUBLISHING ASSISTANTS	Cara Codemo Katie Holmes

Photography credits appear on pages 572–575

Contributors

Dr. Barry Bandstra was trained in Ancient Near Eastern languages and literatures at Yale University, where he studied under Marvin Pope, Franz Rosenthal, Brevard Childs, and William Hallo, and from which he received his PhD. He also has a ministerial degree from Calvin Theological Seminary. He is the author of *Reading the Old Testament: An Introduction to the Hebrew Bible* (Wadsworth, 2004) and does research and writing on biblical Hebrew discourse linguistics. He is the Evert J. and Hattie E. Blekkink Professor of Religion at Hope College in Holland, Michigan, United States, and chairs the Religion Department of the College.

Professor William H. Barnes received his BA from the University of Wisconsin–Milwaukee, his MA from Trinity Evangelical Divinity School, and his ThD from Harvard University. His doctoral dissertation on the subject of the chronology of the divided monarchy of Israel was published in the *Harvard Semitic Monograph Series* in 1991. His research interests include biblical chronology and history, as well as narrative and poetic structure and sequencing in the Hebrew Bible and the New Testament. William H. Barnes is currently the Professor of Old Testament and Hebrew at North Central University in Minneapolis, Minnesota, United States.

Professor Herbert Basser received his PhD from the University of Toronto in 1983 and teaches Religious Studies at Queen's University in Kingston, Ontario, Canada. He frequently contributes reviews and articles to a variety of Bible journals. His latest book, *Studies in Exegesis: Christian Critiques of Jewish Law and Rabbinic Responses 70–300 C.E.* (E. J. Brill: Leiden and Boston), appeared in paperback in 2002. He has been a visiting professor at the University of Toronto, the University of California in Berkeley, and the Hebrew University of Jerusalem, and has been a fellow at Harvard. He lives in Toronto and is the father of ten children.

Dr. Margaret Beirne RSC has, for several years, taught Religious Studies and Mathematics in Sisters of Charity secondary schools, completing ten years as Principal of St. Vincent's College in Potts Point, Sydney, Australia, in 1993. She also ministered with young adults and on the Ignatian Spirituality team at Pymble. Since 1994 she has been involved in tertiary education as student, lecturer, and Principal. Having spent the first semester of 1995 at the École Biblique in Jerusalem, she subsequently completed her doctoral thesis on the Gospel of John and, in 2003, published it under the title *Women and Men in the Fourth Gospel: A Genuine Discipleship of Equals.* She is currently Congregational Councillor of the Sisters of Charity of Australia.

Professor Barry J. Beitzel is Professor of Old Testament and Semitic Languages at Trinity Evangelical Divinity School in Deerfield, Illinois, United States. He holds a PhD in Ancient Near Eastern Studies from the Dropsie University (Philadelphia), he obtained a postdoctorate in Ancient Near Eastern Geography from l'Université de Liège (Belgium), and he has engaged in postdoctoral archaeological work through UCLA in eastern Syria. Beitzel's publications on Near Eastern geography have appeared in a variety of journals, from *Biblical Archaeology Review* to *The British Schools of Archaeology in Iraq.* His maps appear in *National Geographic, the Logos Electronic Atlas of the Bible, the Holman Bible Atlas, The Life Application Bible*, and in several monographs. He is the author of *The Moody Atlas of Bible Lands* (Moody Press, 1985).

Professor Gideon Biger is a professor in the Department of Geography at Tel Aviv University in Israel. He obtained his PhD in Historical Geography from the Hebrew University in Jerusalem in 1979, and joined Tel Aviv University in 1980. During 1986–1988 and 1991–1992 he was Chairperson of the Department of Geography at Tel Aviv University. He has been a visiting professor at University College in Maryland, United States; the University of Melbourne, Australia; and the University of Arizona in the United States. As well as writing more than 100 articles for various journals, he has published several books, including *An Empire in the Holy Land* (St. Martin Press, 1993) and *The Boundaries of Modern Palestine* (Routledge, 2005). He was head of the boundary section during the peace talks between Israel and Syria in 2000.

Ian Boxall is Senior Tutor and Tutorial Fellow in New Testament at St. Stephen's House, University of Oxford, United Kingdom. Born in Folkestone, Kent, he studied Theology at the Franciscan Study Centre, Canterbury, and Oriel College, Oxford. He was previously Tutor in New Testament at Chichester Theological College. He is a member of the Theology Faculty of the University of Oxford, and serves on the Executive Committee of the Catholic Biblical Association of Great Britain. He is the author of *Revelation: Vision and Insight* (SPCK, 2002) and *A Commentary on the Revelation of St John* (Black's New Testament Commentaries; Continuum/Hendrickson, 2006).

Dr. Tim Bulkeley has taught the Old Testament at Carey Baptist College and the University of Auckland since 1993. Before this he was head of Old Testament and Vice-recteur in the Protestant Faculty of Theology in Kinshasa, Congo (ex-Zaïre). His teaching focuses on biblical narrative (especially Genesis, Ruth, and Jonah), and the prophets. He is the author of *Amos: Hypertext Bible Commentary* (www.bible.gen.nz) and numerous journal articles. His websites on Old Testament themes include *Images of Archaeological Sites in Israel* (www.ebibletools.com/Israel). He received a University of Auckland distinguished teaching award in 2001. He edits the Hypertext Bible Commentary series (for which *Amos* is a prototype), and is on the board of the *University Bible Dictionary* and other publications.

Dr. Mark W. Chavalas has been Professor of History at the University of Wisconsin–La Crosse, United States, since 1989. He received his PhD from UCLA in Ancient Near Eastern history. He has had fellowships from Harvard, Yale, Cal-Berkeley, Brown, and Cornell, among others, and has had nine seasons of archaeological fieldwork in Syria. His most recent books include *Mesopotamia and the Bible* (2002) and *Life and Culture in the Ancient Near East, Bible Background Commentary* (2000). He is a past president of the American Oriental Society Middle West, and formerly on the Board of Directors of the American Oriental Society, and the Board of Trustees for the American Schools of Oriental Research.

Dr. Eric H. Cline, a former Fulbright scholar and award-winning teacher and author with degrees from Dartmouth, Yale, and the University of Pennsylvania, is Associate Professor of Classics and of Anthropology (Ancient History and Archaeology) and Chair of the Department of Classical and Semitic Languages and Literatures at The George Washington University in Washington DC, United States. A prolific writer with seven books and more than 60 articles to his credit, he is perhaps best known for *The Battles of Armageddon: Megiddo and the Jezreel Valley from the Bronze Age to the Nuclear Age* (2000) and *Jerusalem Besieged: From Ancient Canaan to Modern Israel* (2004).

Dr. Katharine Dell is a Senior Lecturer in the Faculty of Divinity at the University of Cambridge, United Kingdom, specializing in Old Testament studies. She lectures on wisdom literature, the prophets, and on the development of monotheism in the Old Testament. She is a Fellow of St. Catharine's College. Her research interest is mainly in the wisdom literature of the Old Testament, and she has written three books on Job and two on Proverbs as well as an introduction to the wisdom literature entitled *Get Wisdom, Get Insight* (2000).

Dr. Peter Edwell is a lecturer with the Department of Ancient History at Macquarie University in Sydney, Australia. His research and teaching interests focus on the lands of the eastern Mediterranean and Mesopotamia from the conquests of Alexander to the late Roman period. Dr. Edwell completed a PhD thesis in 2005, which focused on the expansion of Roman power in the Near East. He has traveled extensively throughout Syria and the Near East and is presently writing a book on the Romans in Syria and Mesopotamia.

Professor J. Keith Elliott is Professor of New Testament Textual Criticism at the University of Leeds in the United Kingdom, where he has been lecturing since 1967. His research interests include New Testament textual criticism and noncanonical early Christian literature. He is Secretary of the British committee of the International Greek New Testament Project and editor of *The Apocryphal New Testament* (Oxford, 1993). He is co-author (with David R. Cartlidge) of *Art and the Christian Apocrypha* (Routledge, 2001).

Rev. Dr. Anna Grant-Henderson was born in Glasgow, grew up in South Wales, and migrated to South Australia after she was married in the early 1960s. She was the first woman ordained in the newly formed Uniting Church in Australia in 1978 and spent six and half years in the Happy Valley/Reynella Congregations. She thought it was time there was a woman teaching in the theological college and was successful in obtaining a position teaching pastoral care in 1984. Over the next 20 years she taught Old Testament and completed her PhD, becoming the Lecturer in Old Testament Studies in 1997 at Parkin-Wesley College and Flinders University.

Dr. James R. Harrison is Head of Theology at the Wesley Institute in Sydney, Australia, and teaches New Testament and Greek. He is also an Honorary Associate of Macquarie University's Ancient History Department. He is author of *Paul's Language of Grace in its Graeco-Roman Context* (Mohr Siebeck, 2003), as well as articles in international journals and book chapters. His book won the biennial *Biblical Archaeology Society Publication Award* for "Best Book Relating to New Testament" published in 2003 and 2004. He is a New Testament social historian interested in the intersection of early Christianity with Greco-Roman culture.

Janet Healey is a writer and editor with an honors degree in literature and philosophy from the Australian National University in Canberra. To *Biblica* she brings a background in the Anglican and Catholic communions. Her interest in theology and the nature of religious belief has been sharpened by her reading of spiritual texts, from the Bible itself to the twentieth-century defense of Christianity by C. S. Lewis and the novels of Iris Murdoch. Janet has contributed to publications on subjects ranging from political theory to Australian wildlife. Music is one of her passions; she writes regularly for Australia's flagship company, Opera Australia.

Dr. Richard S. Hess (PhD Hebrew Union College) is Professor of Old Testament and Semitic languages at Denver Seminary in Littleton, Colorado, United States. He is the editor of the *Bulletin for Biblical Research* and the *Denver Journal.* He was a lecturer in Old Testament and Hebrew at the International Christian College, Glasgow, and Reader in Old Testament studies at the Roehampton University, London. Hess has edited ten books, including collections of studies on *The Family in the Bible* and *Israel's Messiah,* and he has authored volumes on Ancient Near Eastern subjects *(Amarna Personal Names)*, Genesis *(Studies in the Personal Names of Genesis 1–11)*, and commentaries on Joshua and the Song of Songs.

Robert V. Huber is co-author of *The Bible: A History,* an award-winning volume that has been translated into six languages. Now a freelance writer in New York City, United States, Robert spent 22 years as an editor for the Readers Digest General Books Division and five years for Encyclopedia Americana. At the Digest he worked on a wide variety of books, including *Jesus and His Times, Who's Who in the Bible,* and *The Bible Through the Ages,* for which he was project editor. Robert holds an MPhil in American and English Literature and an MA and a post-Master's certificate in biblical studies.

Rev. Dr. James M. Lindenberger was ordained by the Presbyterian Church in the United States in 1974 and received by the United Church of Canada as a minister in 1978. He holds a Bachelor of Arts from Southwestern at Memphis (Rhodes College), Bachelor of Divinity and Master of Theology degrees from Union Theological Seminary in Virginia, and a Doctor of Philosophy in Near Eastern Studies from Johns Hopkins University, with further study at the Hebrew University in Jerusalem and at Heidelberg University in Germany. His research interests focus on ancient Aramaic and Hebrew texts. He has recently completed work on an expanded edition of his anthology of ancient letters in the *Writings from the Ancient World* series of the Society of Biblical Literature.

Dr. Kevin McGeough is an archaeologist and historian of the Ancient Near East. He has a BA in History from the University of Lethbridge in western Canada (where he now teaches), a Masters of Theological Studies from Harvard Divinity School, and a PhD in Near Eastern Languages and Civilizations from the University of Pennsylvania. Kevin's dissertation concentrated on economic relationships in ancient Syria, although his scholarly interests are much more broadly focused. He has participated in archaeological excavations in Israel, Jordan, Turkey, and Egypt, and is currently affiliated with the Khirbet al-Mudayna al-Aliya excavations in Jordan. Kevin is also the author of *The Romans: New Perspectives.*

Dr. Scott Morschauser received his MA and PhD in Ancient Near Eastern Studies from Johns Hopkins University. He also has a Master of Divinity degree from Princeton Theological Seminary, and a BA in Classics and Religion from Gettysburg College. He is the author of *Threat Formulae in Ancient Egypt: A Study of the History, Structure, and Use of Threats and Curses in Ancient Egypt;* and co-editor of *Biblical and Related Studies Presented to Samuel Iwry.* He has written numerous journal articles on the Hebrew Scriptures, New Testament, and Ancient Egypt. He has taught at Johns Hopkins University, Princeton Seminary, the Smithsonian Institute, and is currently an Assistant Professor of Ancient History at Rowan University in Glassboro, New Jersey, United States.

Dr. Mark A. O'Brien, born in 1945, is an Australian Roman Catholic priest of the Dominican Order (order of preachers) and has studied in Australia, Ireland, Italy, and the United States. He lectured for many years on the Old Testament/ Hebrew Scriptures at the Melbourne College of Divinity and has recently moved to Sydney where he currently lectures at the Catholic Institute of Sydney, a member institute of the Sydney College of Divinity. He has published several books on Old Testament Narrative (with co-author Antony F. Campbell) as well as a number of articles in local and international journals.

Dr. Sharon Pace, PhD, is Associate Professor of Hebrew Bible at Marquette University in Milwaukee, Wisconsin, United States. She is the author of articles in the *Bulletin of the International Organization for Septuagint and Cognate Studies, Biblical Theology Bulletin, Biblical Research,* and *The Bible Today*. She published *The Old Greek Translation of Daniel 7–12* (The Catholic Biblical Association, 1988) and *The Women of Genesis: From Sarah to Potiphar's Wife* (Fortress, 1990). She wrote the Biblical Commentary for *Women's Stories* (Abingdon, 1993). Her forthcoming works include *Daniel* (Smyth & Helwys) and several entries in *The New Interpreter's Dictionary of the Bible* (Abingdon).

Dr. Kim Ian Parker is a full professor who has taught at the Memorial University of Newfoundland in Canada since 1985. He is the author of four books, three correspondence manuals, over a dozen peer-reviewed articles, and numerous book reviews, and he has given several conference papers. He teaches in the area of Biblical Studies, including courses on the Bible and literature, the Bible and culture, and the Bible and politics. He is currently working on a project dealing with the relationship between political thought and the Bible in the Enlightenment. Dr. Parker resides on Prince Edward Island and is married with three children.

Dr. Duane Smith is currently Associate Professor of Religion at Berea College in Berea, Kentucky, United States. He teaches Hebrew, Introduction to the Old Testament, Introduction to the New Testament, Old Testament Studies in the Prophets, New Testament Studies in Paul, and Introduction to Islam. He worked as the Chaplain at the Hospice of the Bluegrass during the spring of 1986. Ordained in the United Church of Christ in 1986, he is currently pursuing ordination in the Episcopal Church of the United States (through the Diocese of Lexington, Kentucky). He received his MDiv at Earlham School of Religion in Richmond, Indiana, and his PhD in Near Eastern Studies at Harvard University.

Dr. Lawson G. Stone is Professor of Old Testament at Asbury Theological Seminary in Wilmore, Kentucky, United States, having joined the Asbury faculty in 1987. In addition to serving at Asbury, he has taught at Yale Divinity School and Asbury College, and has also taught public school in rural Kenya. He received his PhD in Old Testament Studies in 1988 from Yale University. Dr. Stone has worked as a translator for the *New Living Translation*, has written a commentary on the book of Judges for the *Asbury Bible Commentary*, and has provided articles for the *Dictionary of the Old Testament Historical Books*. He is currently preparing commentaries on the books of Joshua and Judges, and a book on the theological problem of violence in the Bible.

Dr. Kevin Sullivan is an Assistant Professor at Marquette University in Milwaukee, Wisconsin, United States. He specializes in the development of early Christianity. He is the author of a monograph entitled *Wrestling with Angels: A Study of the Relationship between Angels and Humans in Ancient Jewish Literature and the New Testament* (Brill, 2004). He has written numerous reviews for *Catholic Biblical Quarterly* and *Expository Times*. He recently received the Catholic Biblical Association Fellowship Award for 2006. He will use this to work on his next monograph entitled *Spreading the Word: The First Christian Missionaries*, which will be published by Liturgical Press.

C O N T

Introduction

Part One
Geography and History of the Bible Lands

Part Two
Genesis and the Patriarchal Period

Part Six
The Conquest of the Kingdoms

Part Seven
The Life of Jesus of Nazareth

Part Eight
Spreading the Word

E N T S

OMNIA
IN
SAPIENTIA
FECISTI
ET
SVBIECISTI
SVB
PEDIBVS
EIVS

FOREWORD

B*iblica: The Bible Atlas* bridges the conceptual, cultural, chronological, and geographic gap that separates the modern reader from the biblical world. In some sense this atlas adheres to the aphorism of Dean Inge: "Unworldliness based on knowledge of the world is the finest thing on earth; but unworldliness based on ignorance of the world is less admirable."

It is quite common for modern Westerners to fail to ask the question of "Where?" when reading or studying the Bible. This is unfortunate, since biblical narratives are often driven by the notion of space. Particularly in the Old Testament (or Hebrew Bible), an incident may be said to have occurred on a certain hill, in a particular valley, on a discrete plain, or at a given town. At times the name of the location itself becomes an important part of the revelation, frequently with a wordplay or pun on the name to reinforce the locale of the event in public consciousness. Occasionally an aspect of geography becomes a theological axis around which an entire biblical book revolves, or a large block of a book is particularly rich in geographic metaphor: fertility and the book of Deuteronomy, forestation and the book of Isaiah, hydrology and the book of Psalms, and agriculture and the book of Joel.

But perhaps even more profoundly, Jewish faith in the Old Testament was itself inextricably tied to space, and "land" became the prism of this faith. After all, God had repeatedly promised the patriarch Abraham that his descendants would come to occupy and own a particular parcel of real estate. It is not an overstatement to declare that, over its years of recorded biblical history, Israel's quintessential rootage in this "Promised Land" provided its faithful their foundational identity, security, and even prosperity. Conversely, when they were not in possession of their land, Israelites were described dozens of times as "resident aliens" (someone who does not belong and cannot settle, but must survive because of a promise), "wanderers" (someone who is en route to nowhere, who has no specified destination), or "exiles" (someone who has been forcibly uprooted from land, clan, and family and relocated to another "place"). In other words, Israel's covenantal faith was very much based on and grounded in events that transpired in this world. And whether removed to Egypt, Babylon, or elsewhere, landlessness was tantamount to hopelessness.

Similarly, in the New Testament Gospels, much of the teaching of Jesus may be related to where he was situated at the time: Jesus talks about "living water" while at Jacob's Well; he calls himself the "bread of life" while at Capernaum, where basaltic grain mills were manufactured; and he talks about faith that can move a mountain while on the road to Bethphage, from where his disciples could easily have looked southward and physically seen evidence of a mountain that had been moved by Herod the Great in order to construct his fortress site of Herodium. In fact, there are occasions when Jesus appears to go out of his way, and takes a somewhat circuitous course, in order to give a teaching at a particular location.

And for Christians too, many critically important aspects of biblical history have transpired in very precise places on earth—not just in empty space nor in heaven. If the Christian gospel was simply a matter of otherworldliness or concerned only with spiritual or moral values, gaining an appreciation of the spatial dimension of the Bible would hardly matter. But it is neither of these. Central to the kerygma of the New Testament is the claim that God became Man at a definite moment in time and at a definite point in space. To be unaware of or to neglect the geographic DNA of the Bible or the biblical world will therefore often mean that one may run afoul of the biblical argument or that reality may dissolve into sentimentalism.

Biblica: The Bible Atlas takes the reader on a fascinating journey through the landscapes, cultures, and history of the Bible lands. It has been produced by an international team of Jewish, Catholic, and Protestant scholars, across a wide theological spectrum, each with a special skill in bringing the world of the Bible to life. The atlas includes engaging text and informative maps, plus feature boxes, tables, a glossary, and a bibliography, and it is particularly rich in the use of artistic representations of biblical events, enabling the reader to better visualize and appreciate the incidents and narratives within the biblical text.

Barry J. Beitzel
PROFESSOR OF OLD TESTAMENT AND SEMITIC LANGUAGES
TRINITY EVANGELICAL DIVINITY SCHOOL

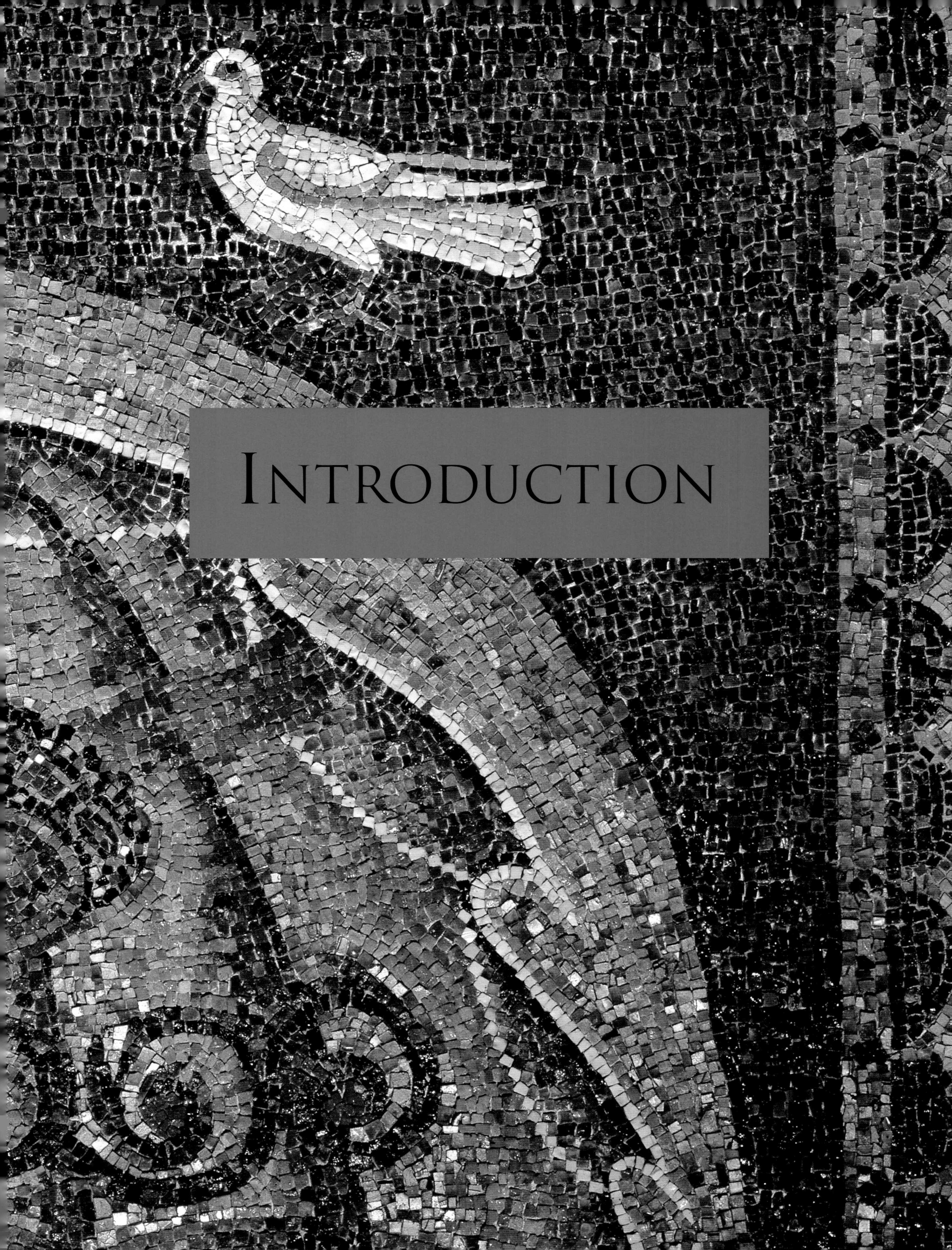

Introduction

DEVELOPMENT OF THE BIBLE

BARUCH WROTE ON A SCROLL AT JEREMIAH'S DICTATION JEREMIAH 36:4

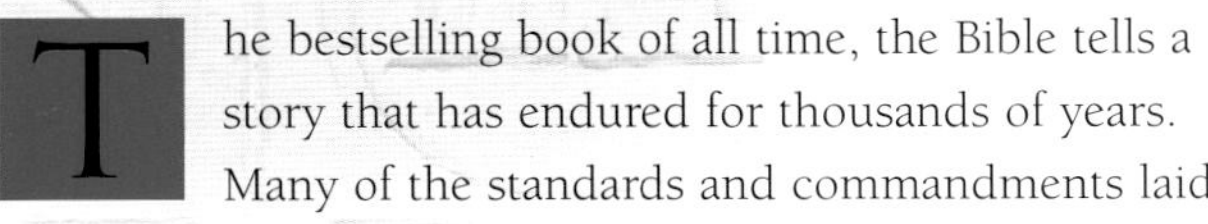

The bestselling book of all time, the Bible tells a story that has endured for thousands of years. Many of the standards and commandments laid down in the Bible form the foundation of the moral values and laws of Western civilization.

RIGHT: CUNEIFORM TABLET WITH CASE, BAKED CLAY, FOURTEENTH–TWELFTH CENTURY B.C.E. AT FIRST CUNEIFORM WRITING WAS ARRANGED IN VERTICAL COLUMNS. LATER, HORIZONTAL ROWS WERE USED.

It all began with storytelling. Long before anyone had learned to read or write, stories about God and his people were passed along by word of mouth from generation to generation. Some stories told how God created the universe. Others related the history of the Hebrew people, beginning with Abraham, a prosperous shepherd who, at the bidding of God, left his home in Mesopotamia to settle in the land of Canaan. Although these stories were dramatic and colorful, they were not told merely to entertain. Rather, they were carefully fashioned to preserve the Hebrew culture and explain how God worked in the people's lives.

The Hebrew people were not unique. Their neighbors in the Ancient Near East had their own tales of primeval times, though they were generally stories about warring gods and superhuman heroes. In contrast, the histories recounted by the Hebrews recognized a single, true God who holds all of creation in his grasp. The characters in the Hebrew sagas were very much of flesh and blood.

BELOW: *MOSES WITH THE TABLETS OF THE LAW* BY CLAUDE VIGNON (1593–1670). MOSES BROKE THE FIRST STONE TABLETS WITH THE LORD'S COMMANDMENTS, BUT THE LORD GAVE THEM TO HIM AGAIN.

While all these stories were still being circulated, the world's first writing systems evolved. In about 3200 B.C.E. the people of Mesopotamia developed cuneiform, a type of writing in which symbols were pressed into clay tablets or chiseled into stone. At about the same time, the Egyptians developed hieroglyphics, writing with pictographs. Both Mesopotamia and Egypt were to play important roles in the Bible. Abraham first heard God's call in Mesopotamia; his 12 great-grandsons migrated to Egypt. But it is unlikely that most of the early Hebrews were literate. Because cuneiform and hieroglyphics utilized thousands of symbols, reading and writing were left to trained scribes. However, by the end of the Hebrews' time in Egypt, Moses, a man with an Egyptian education, began to lead them. It is quite likely that Moses was able to read and write in the Egyptian manner.

IT IS WRITTEN

God directed Moses to free his people from bondage in Egypt and lead them back into the land of Canaan, where they would become the great nation of Israel. Along the way, on the slopes of Mt. Sinai, in the wilderness that lies between Egypt and Canaan, God gave Moses the Ten Commandments, inscribed on stone tablets. By the time the people reached Canaan (40 years later), alphabets were being used there for writing, and the Hebrews soon developed their own alphabet. As they settled into the land, they began to write down the stories and laws that had been handed down by word of mouth.

In about 1011 B.C.E. the heroic young David became King of Israel and initiated a period of literary expansion. David himself is credited with writing many of the Bible's psalms. He also appointed scribes to keep chronicles of his reign, and later kings followed suit. When Solomon, David's son, became king he built a great Temple and commissioned psalms to be sung there. Solomon himself is said to have personally "composed three thousand proverbs, and his songs numbered a thousand and five" (1 Kings 4:32).

When Solomon died in 931 B.C.E. the kingdom split into the northern kingdom of Israel and the smaller southern kingdom of Judah (with Jerusalem as its capital). In the period of the Divided Kingdom that followed, a number of prophets brought God's word to the people, admonishing them for straying away from God and neglecting the poor. If such behavior persisted, they warned, heathen enemies would overthrow them. And so it happened. By 722 B.C.E. the Assyrians had completely conquered the northern kingdom of Israel and scattered the people. The kingdom of Judah survived a little longer. Then, in 587 B.C.E., the

Babylonians swept down, destroyed Jerusalem and its great Temple a year later, and took many of the people (the Jews) to live as captives in Babylon.

PUTTING IT ALL TOGETHER

Stranded far from home, many of the exiles were tempted to follow the exotic customs and rites of idol worship that surrounded them. Worried that their own precious culture would be lost, devout Jews made concerted efforts to organize earlier writings about their heritage and make sense of why they had lost all that God had given them. What emerged were many of the final compositional forms of the texts that constitute the Hebrew Scriptures.

Chief among them are writings covering the period from the creation of the universe to the death of Moses. They are often called the Five Books of Moses because, according to a long-standing tradition, Moses was their author.

Today, however, many scholars doubt that Moses actually wrote these books as they presently appear. Close examination of the texts, they hold, show that several ancient traditions are intertwined. One of those traditions emphasizes heroes associated with the north (the former kingdom of Israel). Another makes Jerusalem's Temple and priests more prominent. According to some scholars, the main traditions were eventually combined, and during the years of captivity in Babylon (or even later), some person or persons (no one knows who) edited them, adding records of religious practices, including those that had been observed in the Temple before its destruction. The five books that resulted were soon considered the Jewish Law and respected as Sacred Scripture. They are also known as the Torah (teachings) or Pentateuch (five scrolls, or books).

Editors also put together final versions of the history of their people in the land of Canaan: the books of Joshua, Judges, Samuel, and Kings. In reflecting on how they lost their land, they could also have gathered the works of royal scribes and some of the writings in which prophets had predicted the fate of the people. Generally, prophets spoke or chanted their messages, but scribes often copied the words for later publication. For example, in the book of Jeremiah we read how Baruch copied the words of the prophet Jeremiah and brought them to the king. When the king burned the writings in anger, Jeremiah dictated the prophecies to Baruch again. The results form a major part of the book of Jeremiah.

ABOVE: *SOLOMON DICTATES THE PROVERBS, C.* FOURTEENTH CENTURY C.E., HELD BY THE BRITISH LIBRARY. THE BOOK OF PROVERBS INCLUDES MATERIAL FROM MANY DIFFERENT SOURCES, INCLUDING EGYPT.

RIGHT: *THE PROPHET JEREMIAH* BY MICHELANGELO BUONARROTI (1475–1564), SISTINE CHAPEL CEILING, VATICAN CITY. JEREMIAH WAS THE PROPHET FOR THE LAST DAYS OF JUDAH, WARNING THAT PAST SINS WOULD CAUSE ITS FALL.

BELOW: *THE JOURNEY TO EMMAUS* BY PAUL BRIL (1554–1626). ACCORDING TO LUKE'S GOSPEL, THIS APPEARANCE IS THE FIRST JESUS MAKES AFTER HIS BURIAL.

COMPLETING AND TRANSLATING THE JEWISH SCRIPTURES

In 539 B.C.E. the great Persian king Cyrus II overthrew the Babylonians and soon permitted the Jews to return to Jerusalem and rebuild their Temple. The words of the prophets from that postexilic period were subsequently grouped together, and this collection came to be known as the Later Prophets. The earlier historical books containing prophetic writings were assembled together and called the Former Prophets by the Jews, and in these books the prophets attempt to form the conscience of the nation.

The books of the Former and Later Prophets were eventually combined. Known simply as The Prophets, these books were soon considered part of Jewish Scripture and are second in importance only to the Torah. (Christians group the so-called Former Prophets along with some others as historical books; they also divide the books of Samuel and Kings into two books each, following the Septuagint.)

All the remaining books in the Jewish Bible are known as the Writings. They include Psalms, Proverbs, and other wisdom writings (including Job and Ecclesiastes), books that update the history of the Jews to just after the rebuilding of the Temple, and a few others (Daniel, Ruth, and Esther among them). This was the last group of books to be accepted by Jews as Holy Scripture.

After Alexander the Great swept across the Near East, amassing his gigantic empire, Greek became the common language, and a Greek translation of the Jewish Scriptures was begun in the third century B.C.E. The translation is known as the Septuagint (from the Greek for 70) because

according to legend 70 (or 72) Jewish scholars each made independent translations, but came up with the same wording. In time, all the books of the Jewish Scriptures were included in the Septuagint, as well as a number of books that would later be excluded from the Protestant canon (authorized collection of sacred writings). These extra books, written between 300 B.C.E. and C.E. 70, came to be known as the Apocrypha.

THE CHRISTIAN SCRIPTURES EMERGE

Like the Jewish books of the Bible, Christian tradition developed first by word of mouth and then was written down. Even though Jesus' disciples had the means to put things in writing from the start, they delayed doing so because they expected Jesus to momentarily return in his full manifestation as Messiah. And so, after Jesus' time on earth, his followers spread the good news of his coming by telling stories about him.

The Gospel of Luke gives us a hint of how such storytelling may have taken place. On the Sunday after Jesus' crucifixion, two disillusioned disciples are walking from Jerusalem to the nearby town of Emmaus. When they meet a stranger they tell him all about Jesus, but add that Jesus has been put to death and cannot be the Messiah as they hoped. Though they have heard that Jesus had risen from the dead, they do not believe it. The stranger scolds them for their disbelief and explains how the Messiah's death was predicted in the Scriptures. Then, at supper, the stranger reveals who he is: it is Jesus himself. Overjoyed, the two disciples hurry back to Jerusalem to share their experience with the others (Luke 24:13–35). This pattern of passing on stories was repeated over and over, incorporating even more of Jesus' words and deeds. All Jesus' followers repeated them, but greater credence was given to those who had known Jesus personally.

As time went on, it became obvious that Jesus' return was not imminent and that the people who had known him personally were dying off. In order to preserve what was known about Jesus, some Christians began to write down accounts of his ministry, death, and resurrection. Consequently, during the second half of the first century the four Gospels were written, as was the Acts of the Apostles, an extension of Luke's Gospel, about the early spread of the Church.

LEFT: *SAINT ATHANASIUS*, 1728, ICON, FROM GREEK ISLAND OF ZANTE (ZAKYNTHOS). DESPITE HIS TURBULENT CAREER AS BISHOP OF ALEXANDRIA, ATHANASIUS PLAYED AN IMPORTANT PART IN THE CHURCH'S HISTORY.

But even before the Gospels were written, the Apostle Paul traveled throughout Greece and Asia Minor (now Turkey), founding communities of believers. During his travels, Paul kept in touch with these communities, or churches, by writing letters. These are the earliest Christian writings to survive. Letters from other Christians followed, and toward the end of the century Revelation, a book of visions about the end of time, appeared. Other Christian works were written as well, including allegories, books of prophecy, and stories about the child Jesus, his mother, and Mary Magdalene. However, none of these was to be accepted as Scripture.

In fact, Christians were slow to characterize any of their writings as Scripture. The Hebrew Scripture was their only Bible, though worshippers did read from Christian writings. In describing services at Rome in the mid-second century, the theologian Justin Martyr reports that "the memoirs of the Apostles" were read to the assembly.

Still, no authorized collection of sacred writings was adopted. Finally, in C.E. 367, Athanasius, bishop of Alexandria, named 27 books (which do not include the Apocrypha) that he believed to be inspired by God and rooted in the teachings of the Apostles. Later Church councils confirmed the books as Sacred Scripture, and they came to be known as the New Testament, complementing the Hebrew Scriptures, or Old Testament.

In establishing the canon, Athanasius wrote: "In these [books] alone is proclaimed the doctrine of godliness. Let no one add to or take anything from them."

BELOW: *SAINT PAUL GIVING HIS WRITINGS TO THE APOSTLES*, THIRTEENTH CENTURY, MOSAIC ON APSE, CATHEDRAL OF MONREALE, SICILY. ST. PAUL BROUGHT THE STORY OF CHRIST TO GENTILES AS WELL AS JEWS.

Spread of the Bible

GO THEREFORE AND MAKE DISCIPLES OF ALL NATIONS MATTHEW 28:19

Early Christians suffered sporadic persecution, but in C.E. 313 Constantine the Great established religious tolerance with the Edict of Milan, and Christianity soon became the official religion of the Roman Empire. Soon missionaries began carrying the Bible and its message throughout the Western world.

Although peoples in the far reaches of the empire had their own languages, they had no way of writing them. In order to reach these people, missionaries not only had to supply translations of the Bible, but they also had to devise alphabets in which to record them. In this way, the early missionaries also spread literacy.

RIGHT: *ST. PATRICK SHOWING THE PEOPLE OF IRELAND THE FOUR GOSPELS, FROM THE TRIAS THAUMATURGA, OR THREE WONDER-WORKING SAINTS OF IRELAND* (C. 1890S) BY MARY CUSACK. POPE CELESTINE I SENT PATRICK TO CONVERT THE IRISH IN C.E. 433.

In the fourth century Ulfilas, a bishop from Cappadocia (now part of Turkey), carried Christianity to the Visigoths, inventing an alphabet and translating Scripture into Gothic. In the fifth century Mesrop, an Armenian monk, created no less than three alphabets that were then used to translate the Bible into Armenian, Albanian, and Georgian.

In the ninth century Cyril and Methodius of Greece traveled to Moravia (now Slovakia), created an alphabet, and translated the Bible into Old Slavonic. From there the Bible was carried into the regions that are now Bulgaria, Serbia, Montenegro, Romania, and Russia. Without the alphabets forged by tireless missionaries, the peoples of Eastern Europe may not have learned to read or write for a long while.

MONKS MAKE A DIFFERENCE

By the fourth century, Latin had replaced Greek as the language of the empire, and so a good Latin Bible was needed. An irascible Italian monk named Jerome accepted the challenge and produced a translation that came to be known as

Spread of Christianity Across the Globe

Arctic Circle
NORTH AMERICA
EUROPE
ASIA
Azores
Bermuda
Canary Islands
Tropic of Cancer
The Bahamas
Hawaii
Puerto Rico
Barbados
Cape Verde
AFRICA
Equator
Kiribati
Galapagos Islands
Seychelles
Comoros
Ascension
SOUTH AMERICA
French Polynesia
Mauritius
Reunion
St. Helena
Tropic of Capricorn
Falkland Islands
South Georgia
Antarctic Circle
ANTARCTICA

- Predominantly Roman Catholic
- Predominantly Protestant
- Predominantly Eastern Orthodox
- Tribal and Christian
- Non-Christian

The Apocrypha

In translating the Old Testament, Jerome had considered the books found in the Septuagint but not in the official Hebrew Canon to be extra-biblical, and he labeled them Apocrypha in the Vulgate Bible. Nevertheless, at the time of the Protestant Reformation, the Catholic Church decided to include the Apocrypha in their Bibles because they regarded the Septuagint as sanctioned by the apostles. Protestants disagree over their status as Holy Scripture, but many of today's Protestant Bibles include the Apocrypha in a separate section (a practice initiated by Martin Luther).

the Vulgate because it was in the vulgar (common) tongue of Latin. Jerome translated most of the New Testament from the original Greek and the entire Old Testament from the ancient Hebrew texts—instead of working from the Greek Septuagint version, which had been used by Christians from the beginning. The Vulgate Bible, completed in C.E. 405, remained the major biblical text for more than a millennium.

As a result of barbarian incursions, the Roman Empire fell and intellectual life in Europe suffered greatly. However, from the late sixth century on, communities of monks worked diligently throughout the West to preserve and copy biblical texts. These meticulously copied manuscripts are amazing in their accuracy and prized for the high quality of their ornamentation. And the monks' endless hours of tireless copying led to a major innovation in handwriting.

In the late seventh century, Alcuin, an Anglo-Saxon monk, perfected a new style of writing known as miniscule script, in which letters were connected rather than printed individually in block form. This free-flowing script, which made it possible to write much more quickly, soon became the standard throughout Europe.

For centuries monks were also the chief educators, teaching in their monasteries or cathedral schools. Then, early in the thirteenth century, the first universities emerged in Paris, Bologna, and England. Theology was still the predominant subject, but for the first time, thanks to a new movement called scholasticism, students were urged to seek knowledge in texts beyond those of Scripture, especially in the works of the Ancient Greek philosopher Aristotle. Scholasticism resulted in the emergence of some of the greatest Christian thinkers of all time, including Thomas Aquinas, whose *Summa Theologica* (1267–1273) remains a masterpiece of Christian theology.

REFORMERS EMERGE

Meanwhile, many Church leaders had moved far away from the spirit of Jesus, becoming more interested in wealth and power. As a result, reformers attempted to turn back to the time of the apostles, when Christians shared their possessions. Among these reformers was a twelfth-century French merchant, Waldes, who acted on Jesus' invitation to "go, sell your possessions, and give the money to the poor ... then come, follow me" (Matthew 19:21).

Waldes and others like him were suppressed by the Church for defying its leaders, but one reformer, Francis of Assisi, took a different approach. Seeking only to imitate Jesus, Francis lived in strict poverty, attracting others by the simplicity of his life. Unlike other reformers, he won papal permission to organize his followers as a religious order, the Friars Minor, or Franciscans. Francis also established an order of contemplative women and an immensely popular Third Order of lay Christians, who followed his example without leaving their families. Because the peace-loving Third Order members refused to take up arms under their feudal overlords, they contributed to the collapse of the feudal system. The Church improved for a time, but soon fell back into decline, spurring on more reformers. One of these was John Wycliffe, a fourteenth-century English theologian who urged the Church to give up its wealth and power.

BELOW: *ST. JEROME TRANSLATING THE BIBLE* (FIFTEENTH CENTURY). ALTHOUGH JEROME WAS A GREAT SCHOLAR, PROFICIENT IN LATIN, GREEK, AND HEBREW, HIS TRANSLATION WAS NOT UNIVERSALLY ACCEPTED AT FIRST.

ABOVE: *JOHN WYCLIFFE READING HIS TRANSLATION OF THE BIBLE TO JOHN OF GAUNT* (1847–48) BY FORD MADOX BROWN. WYCLIFFE WAS THE FIRST TO TRANSLATE SOME OF THE BIBLE INTO ENGLISH.

Wycliffe held that God's decrees were not to be found in Church directives, but in the Bible, and that all Christians should be able to read Scripture in their own language. He was soon silenced.

The next major reformer had help from an unexpected source—the printing press. In 1456 Johannes Gutenberg printed a Bible, revolutionizing the way in which books were produced. Soon Bibles and other books were being printed in large numbers, making them readily available to the people. When Martin Luther initiated his own reforms, he used printed leaflets to spread his message, and in 1534 he translated the Bible into the everyday language of the German people. Luther's translation made the Bible widely accessible and had a lasting impact on the German language.

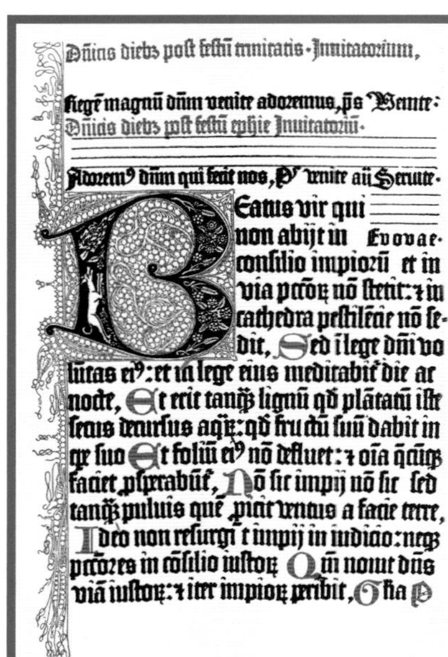

Dñicis dieb3 post festū trinitatis · Inuitatoriū,
Regē magnū dñm venite adoremus, ps Venite·
Dñicis dieb3 post festū ephie Inuitatoriū·
Adorem⁹ dñm qui fecit nos, ps venite aiī Seruite·
Beatus vir qui
non abijt in Euouae·
consilio impiorū et in
via pctōr nō stetit: ɀ in
cathedra pestilēcie nō se-
dit, Sed ī lege dñi vo
lūtas ei⁹: et in lege eius meditabit die ac
nocte, Et erit tanq̄ lignū qd plātatū ē
secus decursus aq̄r: qd fructū suū dabit in
tp̄e suo Et foliū ei⁹ nō defluet: ɀ oīa q̄cūq
faciet, psperabūt, Nō sic impij nō sic sed
tanq̄ pulvis quē pĳcit ventus a facie terre,
Ideo non resurgūt impij in iudicio: neq
pctōres in cōsilio iustor Qm̄ nouit dñs
viā iustor: ɀ iter impior peribit, Gl̄ia P

ABOVE: THIS EXAMPLE FROM *THE ART AND PRACTICE OF TYPOGRAPHY* BY EDMUND G. GRESS SHOWS THE GUTENBERG BIBLE. IT HAD 300 PAGES, EACH WITH 42 LINES.

THE BIBLE IN ENGLISH

In 1523 William Tyndale, a priest and linguist, was denied permission to translate the Bible into English because his Catholic bishop associated such activity with Protestantism. Undaunted, Tyndale sailed to Germany, where he translated the New Testament and parts of the Old. He was later executed as a heretic for the Protestant tone of his biblical notations.

The climate in England soon changed. After King Henry VIII split from the Catholic Church, numerous English translations of the Bible followed. The first, by Miles Coverdale (1535), relied heavily on Tyndale, Luther, and the Vulgate. The popular Geneva Bible (1560) was criticized for being too Protestant and the Bishops' Bible (1568) for not being Protestant enough. Meanwhile, Catholics published their own English Bible from exile in the French cities of Douay and Rheims (in 1582 and 1609–1610 respectively).

In 1604 King James I of England commissioned a new translation of the Bible for use in the churches. A committee of 47 scholars undertook the task, basing their translation on the Bishop's Bible, but also consulting other versions, including the Catholic translation. To avoid theological bias, marginal notes were used only to clarify Hebrew and Greek words and point out parallel passages. The King James, or Authorized, Version of the Bible was published in 1611, and is regarded as one of the greatest translations of all time. The color, richness, and fluidity of the language, which makes the ancient texts seem fresh and lively, had a major impact on the English language.

OPPOSITE: *JOHANNES GUTENBERG* BY JEAN-ANTOINE LAURENT (1763–1832). GUTENBERG'S FIRST BIBLE TOOK THREE YEARS TO PRODUCE, IN A PRINT RUN OF ABOUT 180 COPIES, AND LEFT HIM IN DEBT. HIS WORK CHANGED THE WORLD.

THE PAST FOUR CENTURIES

The Bible was soon brought to the Americas and translated into Native American dialects. In the Age of Enlightenment, skeptics sought to replace the Bible with science, which initiated a backlash of pietism. Bible societies sent missionaries throughout Africa, the Orient, and the South Seas, where they created new alphabets and translated Scripture into the languages of the people as earlier missionaries had done.

Meanwhile, innumerable new English translations appeared, ranging from strictly literal to simple paraphrases. But such was the power and popularity of the King James Version that four updated versions appeared. The English Revised Version (1881–1885) and American Revised Version (1901) made use of more accurate versions of the original texts. The Revised Standard Version (1952) was considered the closest of all English versions to the original languages. Finally, the New Revised Standard Version (1989) drew from still older and more reliable manuscripts and endeavored to eliminate much gender bias in the sound of the language. All biblical citations in *Biblica* are taken from *The New Oxford Annotated Bible, New Revised Standard Version with the Apocrypha*, Third Edition (2001).

RIGHT: *LIVINGSTONE READING THE BIBLE* (NINETEENTH CENTURY). SCOTSMAN DAVID LIVINGSTONE WAS A MISSIONARY AS WELL AS A FAMOUS EXPLORER OF AFRICA.

Archaeology of the Bible

THE FOUNDATIONS OF THE WORLD WERE LAID BARE 2 SAMUEL 22:16

RIGHT: *NOAH'S ARK* (SIXTEENTH CENTURY), CHURCH OF ST. ANIETUS, ST. NEOT, CORNWALL, UNITED KINGDOM. THE STORY OF A MASSIVE FLOOD WAS THE FIRST BIBLICAL ACCOUNT TO BE VERIFIED BY OTHER SOURCES.

On December 3, 1872, George Smith presented a remarkable find to the Biblical Archaeology Society in London, in a meeting attended by the high society of Victorian England, including Prime Minister Gladstone. On that night, Smith displayed a translation of an ancient Mesopotamian tablet that was part of the British Museum's collection. What made this tablet so remarkable was that it was another account of a deluge, perhaps the same flood for which Noah built his ark.

The response cannot be described as anything but a sensation. Archaeologists and historians were sent out in droves, looking for other similar tablets as well as actual evidence of the deluge. Scholars tried to use archaeology as proof that the flood had actually happened as per the biblical account; the University Museum of the University of Pennsylvania has numerous boxes filled with so-called "flood soil" (dirt that archaeologists in their overexcitement had mistakenly attributed to the ancient deluge). Biblical archaeology truly took off as a full-fledged scientific endeavor, as opposed to the haphazard expeditions that had gone before.

PROVING THE BIBLE?

In actual practice, something akin to biblical archaeology had already been going on for centuries, although never as a formal academic discipline. Since ancient times, Jewish, Christian, and Muslim pilgrims had been searching for the actual sites where biblical events had taken place. Monuments such as the Church of the Nativity in Bethlehem and the Church of the Holy Sepulchre in Jerusalem are remnants of this tradition. In the late nineteenth century, however, archaeology had developed into a scientific discipline in its own right, and it was not long before scholars thought to use archaeological methods (as developed for the study of Mesopotamia, Egypt, and ancient American civilizations) to prove (or in some cases attempt to disprove) the Bible.

In its early phases, biblical archaeology was dominated by British and American teams, who, it is said, dug with the Bible in one hand and a trowel in the other. After the formation of the state of Israel in 1948, Israeli archaeologists entered the discipline, wanting concrete evidence of the ancient borders of Israel and Judah. Until the 1970s, this remained the dominant focus of biblical archaeology, and scholars argued vehemently about what constituted actual archaeological proof of the Bible's veracity.

BELOW: ALTAR OF THE INVENTION OF THE CROSS, CHURCH OF THE HOLY SEPULCHRE, JERUSALEM, ISRAEL. ST. HELENA (MOTHER OF CONSTANTINE THE GREAT) IS BELIEVED TO HAVE FOUND CHRIST'S CROSS HERE IN C.E. 326.

In the 1970s, archaeologists and biblical scholars began to rethink the situation. Could archaeological evidence ever prove or disprove the biblical accounts? So far, only limited success had been achieved. For the parts of the Bible that dealt with a larger state-level government (such as the books of Kings and Chronicles), archaeology had been fairly successful in finding ancient buildings and inscriptions associated with the ancient monarchy. But attempts to use archaeology to find traces of the patriarchs or the route of the Exodus had been less than successful. Archaeology is just not well suited for finding the remains of a single family or a group of people. Even if the specific material from a particular family was preserved (and was not obliterated by the natural processes that cause artifacts to decompose), the odds against archaeologists finding the material are astronomical.

Today, biblical archaeologists (more commonly called Syro–Palestinian archaeologists) look for more general information about the people and society of the Bible. They no longer look for evidence about Abraham, but rather look for direct evidence about the daily life of people who lived at the time of Abraham. Take for example the work of Lawrence Stager. An archaeologist from Harvard University, Stager has successfully used archaeology to better understand the story of Jephthah and his daughter, from Judges 11.

Jephthah was one of the Judges sent by God to help deliver the Israelites from their enemy, the Ammonites. During the war between these peoples, Jephthah made a vow to the Lord (see Judges 11:30–31) that if God allowed him to win the battle against the Ammonites, then he would sacrifice whoever came out of his doors first when he returned home. When Jephthah returns home, it is his daughter who first comes out to greet him, and because of his promise to the Lord, he is forced to sacrifice her. This is a very troubling narrative, for a number of reasons.

Stager, after studying the archaeological evidence for houses in ancient Israel, made an important realization that helps us comprehend Jephthah's actions. In ancient Israel, animals and livestock lived in the home, on the ground floor. Jephthah probably assumed that an animal would have been the first to come out to greet him, and it never occurred to him that he would have to sacrifice his daughter. This is a good example of how archaeology can better help us to understand the Bible. Rather than trying to find the remnants of particular individuals, archaeologists look to better interpret the world in which biblical people lived.

The Ketef Hinnom Amulets

While archaeology can frequently shed new light on biblical customs and traditions, on rare occasions it can actually bring to light new (or more accurately "older") copies of the biblical text itself. This was the case when Gabriel Barkay discovered what are now known as the Ketef Hinnom amulets in burial caves near Jerusalem. The two small silver amulets are beautiful in their own right. But it is the inscriptions that make them truly remarkable, since they are word for word the priestly benediction from Numbers 6:24–26. Based on the style of tombs they were found in and the date of the handwriting used in the inscriptions, the amulets could be safely dated to the sixth century B.C.E., making them the oldest-known preserved copy of a section of the Bible.

BELOW: *THE SACRIFICE OF JEPHTHAH'S DAUGHTER* BY GIOVANNI BATTISTA PITTONI (1687–1767). THE STORY OF JEPHTHAH'S DAUGHTER HAS PROMPTED MUCH DISCUSSION AMONG BIBLE SCHOLARS.

BULGARIA
MACEDONIA
ALBANIA
GREECE
TURKEY
Aegean Sea
Ionian Sea
Philippi
Thessaloniki
Troy
Hattusha (Boghazkoy)
Gordion
Pergamum
Sardis
Smyrna
Beycesultan
Antioch in Pisidia
Lake Tuz
Corinth
Athens
Ephesus
Miletus
Catal Huyuk
Tarsus
Mersin
Crete
CYPRUS
Salamis
Paphos
Mediterranean Sea
Tyre
ISRAEL
Alexandria
Tanis
Bitter Lakes
Giza
Memphis
Ezion-geber (Tell el-Kheleifeh)
EGYPT
Gulf of Suez
Gulf of Aqaba
Tell el-Amarna
Nile
Abydos
Nag Hammadi
Luxor (Thebes)
N
Mediterranean Sea
Hazor
GOLAN HEIGHTS
Capernaum
Sea of Galilee
Dor
Megiddo
Taanach
Beth-shean
Tel Zeror
Samaria (Sebaste)
Tirzah
Gerasa
Shechem
Jordan
Jabbok
Aphek (Antipatris)
Tell Qasile
Joppa
WEST BANK
Amman
Bethel
Ai
Mizpah
Araq el-Emir
Gezer
Gibeon
Jericho
Heshbon
Jerusalem
Tuleilat el-Ghassul
Tell es-Safi
Beth-shemesh
Khirbet Qumran
Tel Zayit (Zeitah)
Lachish
Dead Sea
Tell el-Ajjul
Tel Nagila
Dibon
En-gedi
Tell Beit Mirsim
GAZA STRIP
Masada
Tell Sharuhen
Tel Arad
International border
Disputed international border
Golan Heights ceasefire line 1974
0 20 km
0 20 miles

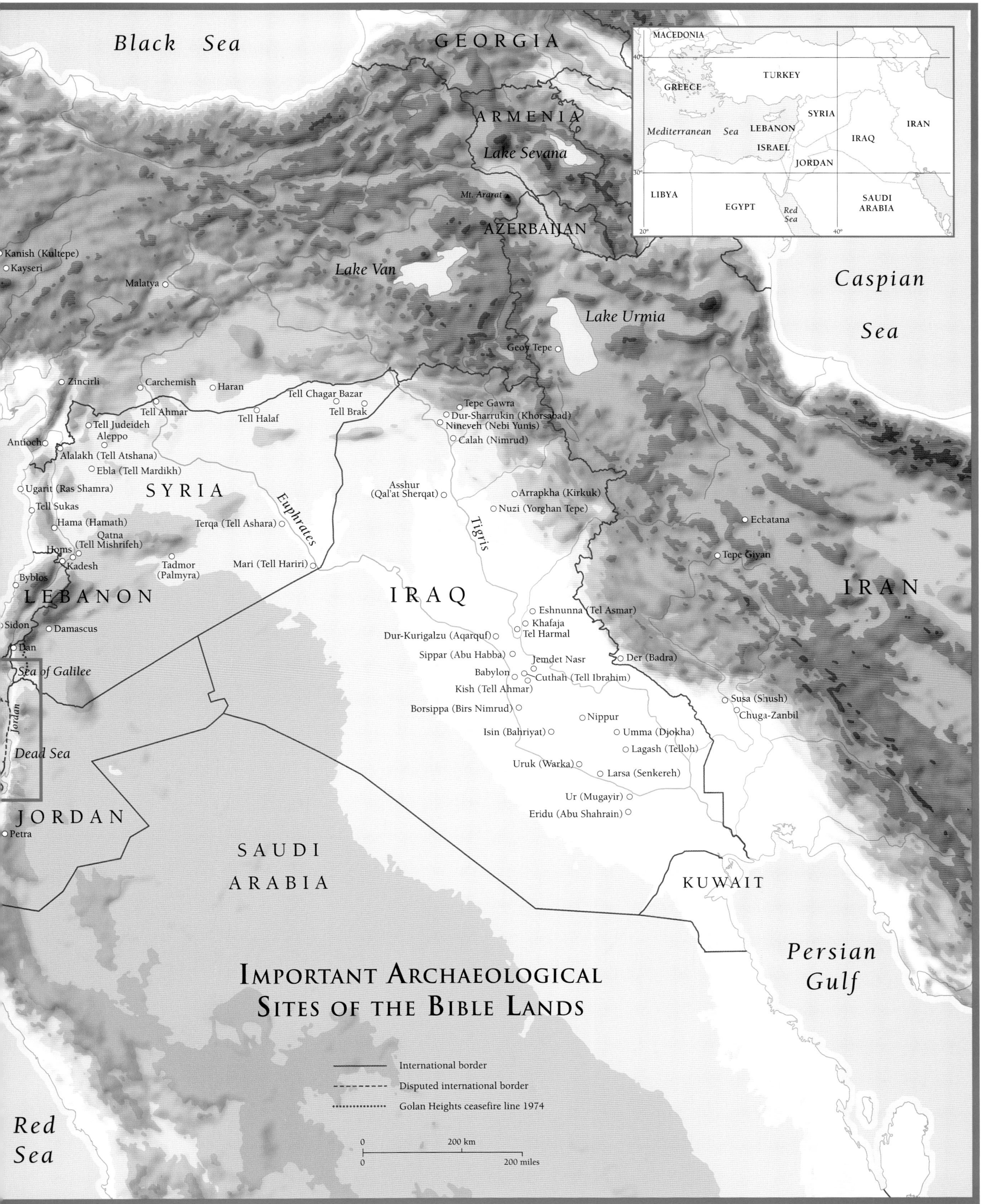

Black Sea
GEORGIA
ARMENIA
Lake Sevana
Mt. Ararat
AZERBAIJAN
Caspian Sea
Lake Van
Lake Urmia
Kanish (Kultepe)
Kayseri
Malatya
Geoy Tepe
Zincirli
Carchemish
Haran
Tell Chagar Bazar
Tell Brak
Tell Ahmar
Tell Halaf
Tepe Gawra
Dur-Sharrukin (Khorsabad)
Nineveh (Nebi Yunis)
Calah (Nimrud)
Tell Judeideh
Aleppo
Antioch
Alalakh (Tell Atshana)
Ebla (Tell Mardikh)
Ugarit (Ras Shamra)
SYRIA
Euphrates
Asshur (Qal'at Sherqat)
Arrapkha (Kirkuk)
Nuzi (Yorghan Tepe)
Tigris
Ecbatana
Tell Sukas
Hama (Hamath)
Qatna (Tell Mishrifeh)
Terqa (Tell Ashara)
Homs
Kadesh
Tadmor (Palmyra)
Mari (Tell Hariri)
Tepe Giyan
Byblos
LEBANON
IRAQ
IRAN
Sidon
Damascus
Dan
Sea of Galilee
Jordan
Dead Sea
JORDAN
Petra
Eshnunna (Tel Asmar)
Khafaja
Tel Harmal
Dur-Kurigalzu (Aqarquf)
Sippar (Abu Habba)
Jemdet Nasr
Der (Badra)
Babylon
Cuthah (Tell Ibrahim)
Kish (Tell Ahmar)
Borsippa (Birs Nimrud)
Nippur
Susa (Shush)
Chuga-Zanbil
Isin (Bahriyat)
Umma (Djokha)
Lagash (Telloh)
Uruk (Warka)
Larsa (Senkereh)
Ur (Mugayir)
Eridu (Abu Shahrain)
SAUDI ARABIA
KUWAIT
Persian Gulf
Red Sea
MACEDONIA
TURKEY
GREECE
SYRIA
IRAN
Mediterranean Sea
LEBANON
ISRAEL
IRAQ
JORDAN
LIBYA
EGYPT
Red Sea
SAUDI ARABIA
IMPORTANT ARCHAEOLOGICAL SITES OF THE BIBLE LANDS
International border
Disputed international border
Golan Heights ceasefire line 1974
0
200 km
0
200 miles

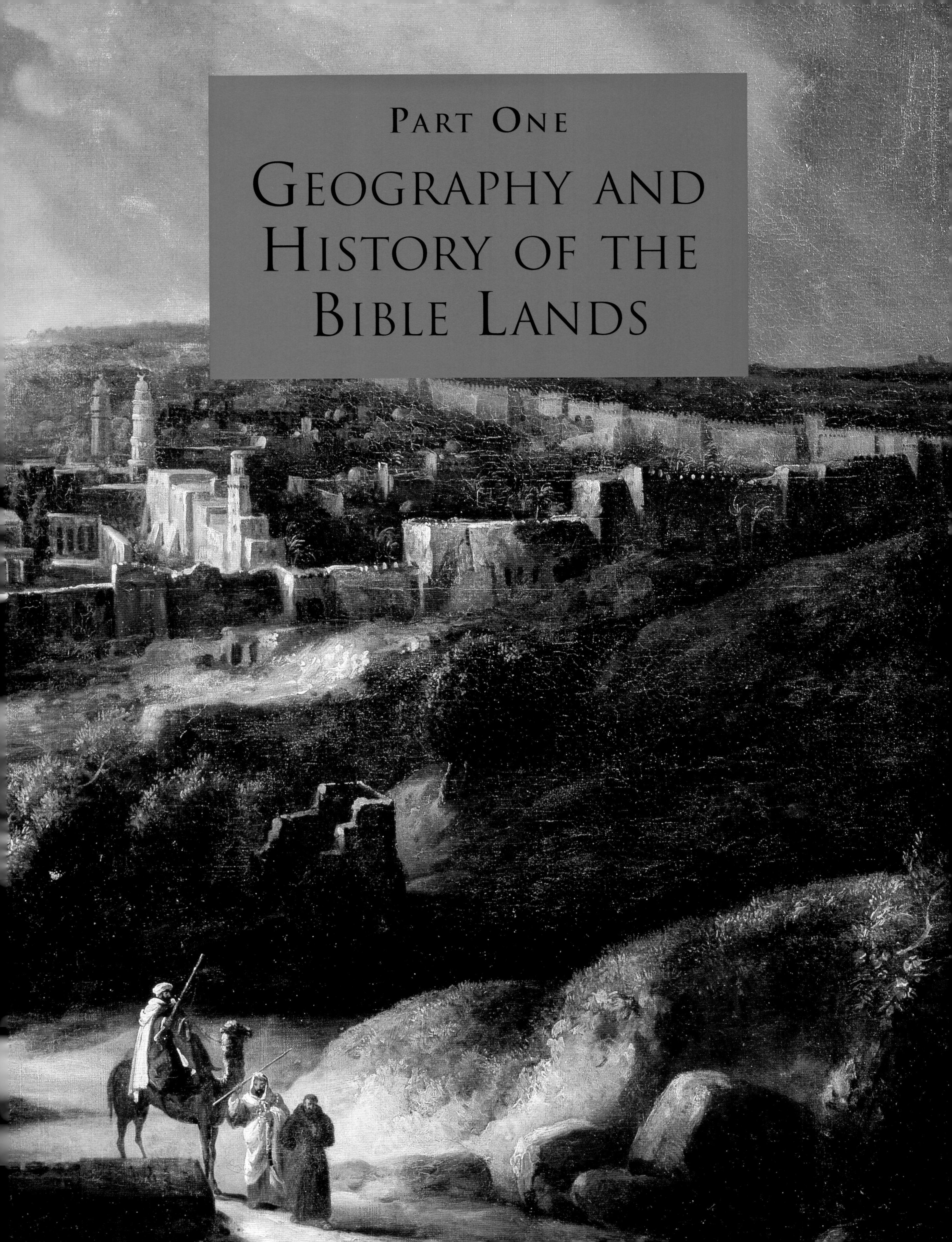

Part One

Geography and History of the Bible Lands

THE PROBLEM WITH PLACES

THE HEAVENS ARE TELLING THE GLORY OF GOD; AND THE FIRMAMENT PROCLAIMS HIS HANDIWORK PSALMS 19:1

Our lives are inextricably bound to our environment, which provides resources for our use, and places constraints on our behavior. People living in harsh landscapes, such as the arid regions found in the majority of the Bible lands, are forced to think deeply about their world in order to formulate unique techniques to survive their surroundings. This interaction with the environment is the basis for social, cultural, and religious development. To truly understand other cultures and their history, we must have a thorough knowledge of the environmental context of those cultures. This is particularly true of our attempts to understand the lives of people in biblical times. So, we begin by looking at the environmental setting of the Bible—the Near East, the Mediterranean world, and Egypt and the Sinai Peninsula.

There are some major problems that face biblical scholars working with extrabiblical historical data, archaeological data, and geographic data. These issues underpin our work and lead to controversies in the field. Biblical scholarship has been going on for thousands of years and the more we learn about the Bible, the more questions arise. Before delving into an overview of the geography and archaeology of the Bible lands, it is important to be aware of some of the major controversies facing biblical historians and geographers. Working with ancient data is rarely straightforward!

HISTORICAL GEOGRAPHY

One challenge for biblical scholars is identifying places mentioned in the Bible with known archaeological sites and modern cities. Sometimes identification is easy—cities like Jerusalem, Damascus, and Rome have been continuously occupied for centuries, and have always had the same name. Other cities, like Ephesus, were abandoned long ago, but its traditions have not been lost. Many cities and places mentioned in the Bible have been otherwise forgotten, so it is up to specialists in historical geography to identify such sites.

So how do historians determine the location of lost cities mentioned in the Bible? It is a painstaking process, but the Bible provides the most important clues, and even the most skeptical scholars recognize that the Bible is very accurate about geography. Careful

BELOW: EXCAVATIONS IN EPHESUS, TURKEY, DURING THE 1980S REVEALED THESE ROMAN-STYLE HOUSES ON MT. CORESSOS. SUCH EXCAVATIONS ASSIST IN THE VERIFICATION OF BIBLICAL ACCOUNTS.

study of the descriptions of locations of places in the Bible is the starting point. Often, extra geographic information is provided, such as ancient itineraries or descriptions of the local region (perhaps hills are nearby, or a source of water is mentioned) to roughly identify the location. If we read that someone visited a place on a journey between two cities with known locations, it is safe to assume that the place must be situated somewhere between the two cities. Then, it is up to the scholar to visit the possible sites in the area. Using scientific dating techniques, it is possible to discover whether the site was inhabited during biblical times. This makes identifying the site of the biblical place reasonably simple.

The Philistine city of Ekron is an example of an historical geography success story. The five major Philistine cities (the Pentapolis in the Old Testament) are written about at length in the Bible. The cities of Ashkelon, Gaza, and Ashdod had never been lost, and archaeological excavations confirmed that these were Philistine cities. But the cities of Ekron and Gath were lost. Archaeologists interested in Ekron identified a possible candidate—Tel Miqne on Kibbutz Revadim in Israel. Excavations there showed that it was a Philistine city, and in the final year of excavation certain proof was found—an inscription stating the name of the city as Ekron. Scholars digging at Tell es-Safi in Israel think they have located Gath, and as excavations continue, the answer will become clearer.

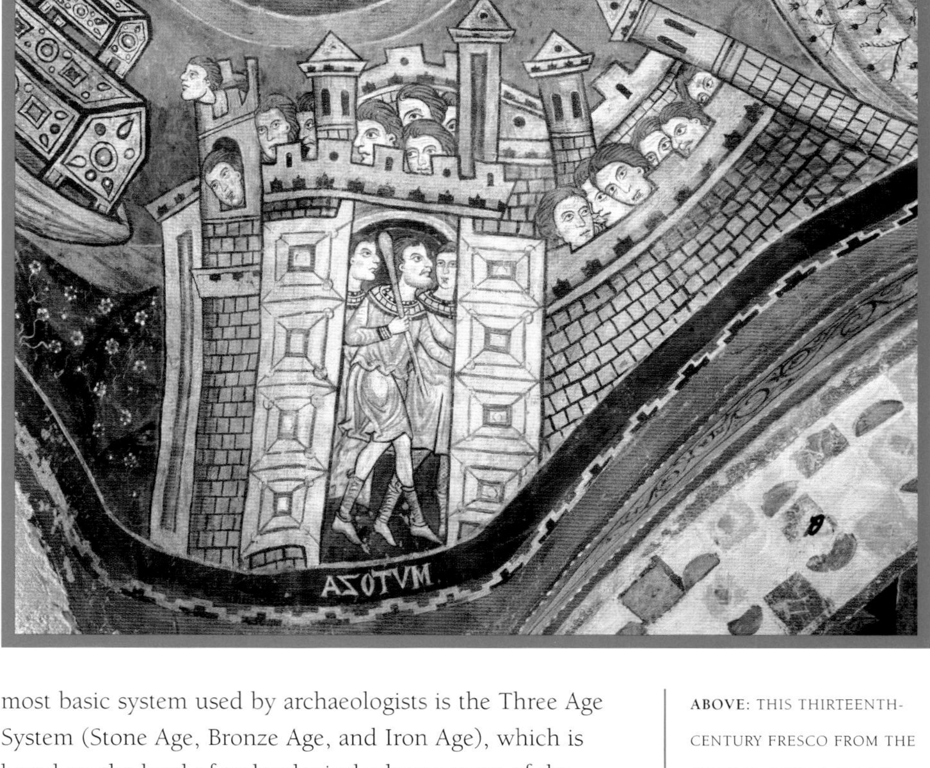

ABOVE: THIS THIRTEENTH-CENTURY FRESCO FROM THE CRYPT OF ITALY'S ANAGNI CATHEDRAL DEPICTS THE LAMENT OF THE PHILISTINES WITHIN IN THE CITY WALLS OF ASHDOD.

PROBLEMS WITH CHRONOLOGY

Chronology is a very difficult subject in the study of biblical history. For the New Testament, we are on fairly safe ground since this was the time of the Romans, who kept accurate and easy-to-understand records. Old Testament chronology is far more challenging. The Old Testament itself frequently refers to periods of time in terms of years, rounding off the months and days. At first this does not appear to be problematic, but if you start to count backward through the lengths of the reigns of the kings of Israel and Judah, this rounding off can lead to a substantial margin of error. So, working backward, we believe that Jerusalem was destroyed in around 586 B.C.E. (but note the uncertainty already). By the time we have counted back to Solomon's and David's reigns, we can no longer be certain about when they ruled.

Years were also reckoned by different means. Since these cultures were unaware that the earth rotated around the sun, their methods of calculating time are difficult to reconcile with our own. Even the chronologies of Mesopotamia and Egypt, which took fairly accurate astronomical observations, are beset with problems, and we are uncertain how to convert their dates into our own. So when Egyptian or Mesopotamian people are mentioned in the Bible, the chronologies of these regions are not necessarily helpful to us.

There is also a problem in corroborating archaeological dating schemes with historical ones. The Old Testament refers to time mainly in historical terms—in relation to important political events, such as the reigns of kings. Archaeological chronologies are based on changes in material culture. The most basic system used by archaeologists is the Three Age System (Stone Age, Bronze Age, and Iron Age), which is based on the level of technological advancement of the society. This does not always match up with historical chronology, since the appearance of a new king does not necessarily mean that a new type of technology is also introduced. Beware of scholars who claim to have solved problems in Old Testament chronology! The situation is very complex and not likely to be fully resolved any time soon.

PROBLEMS IN RECONSTRUCTING THE PAST

The study of history is not merely the study of a series of facts. It is an attempt to understand the past in all its complexity and variation through the written documents of past people. Archaeology is also the study of the past, but through the material culture of ancient peoples. In all facets of scholarly analysis, we are dealing with scientific arguments as well as our beliefs about the past. Since our information about the past is incomplete, our accounts of the past must be uncertain. This uncertainty is why there are so many historical controversies and mysteries, and why there never seems to be full consensus about what happened in the past.

The Bible is a detailed account of the people and places of the time. Its earliest readers were familiar with the geography, cultural practices, and history referred to, but modern readers lack this familiarity. The historical and archaeological study of the people and places of biblical times can help us to better comprehend the Bible itself and give us a fuller context in which to understand it.

What follows is an introduction to the people, places, and environmental constraints of biblical times. The Bible lands were very diverse, and there were vast environmental and cultural differences. Looking to this wider context will enrich your understanding of the Bible and the history that it preserves.

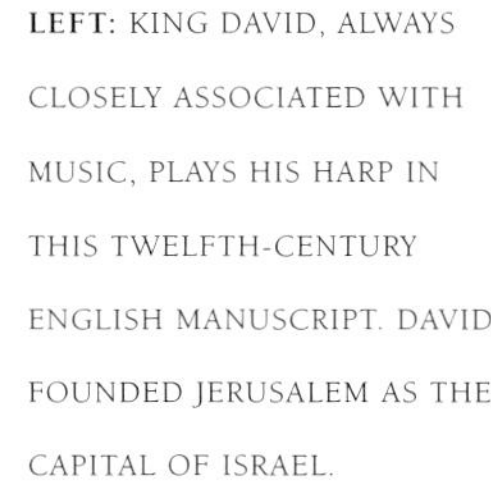

LEFT: KING DAVID, ALWAYS CLOSELY ASSOCIATED WITH MUSIC, PLAYS HIS HARP IN THIS TWELFTH-CENTURY ENGLISH MANUSCRIPT. DAVID FOUNDED JERUSALEM AS THE CAPITAL OF ISRAEL.

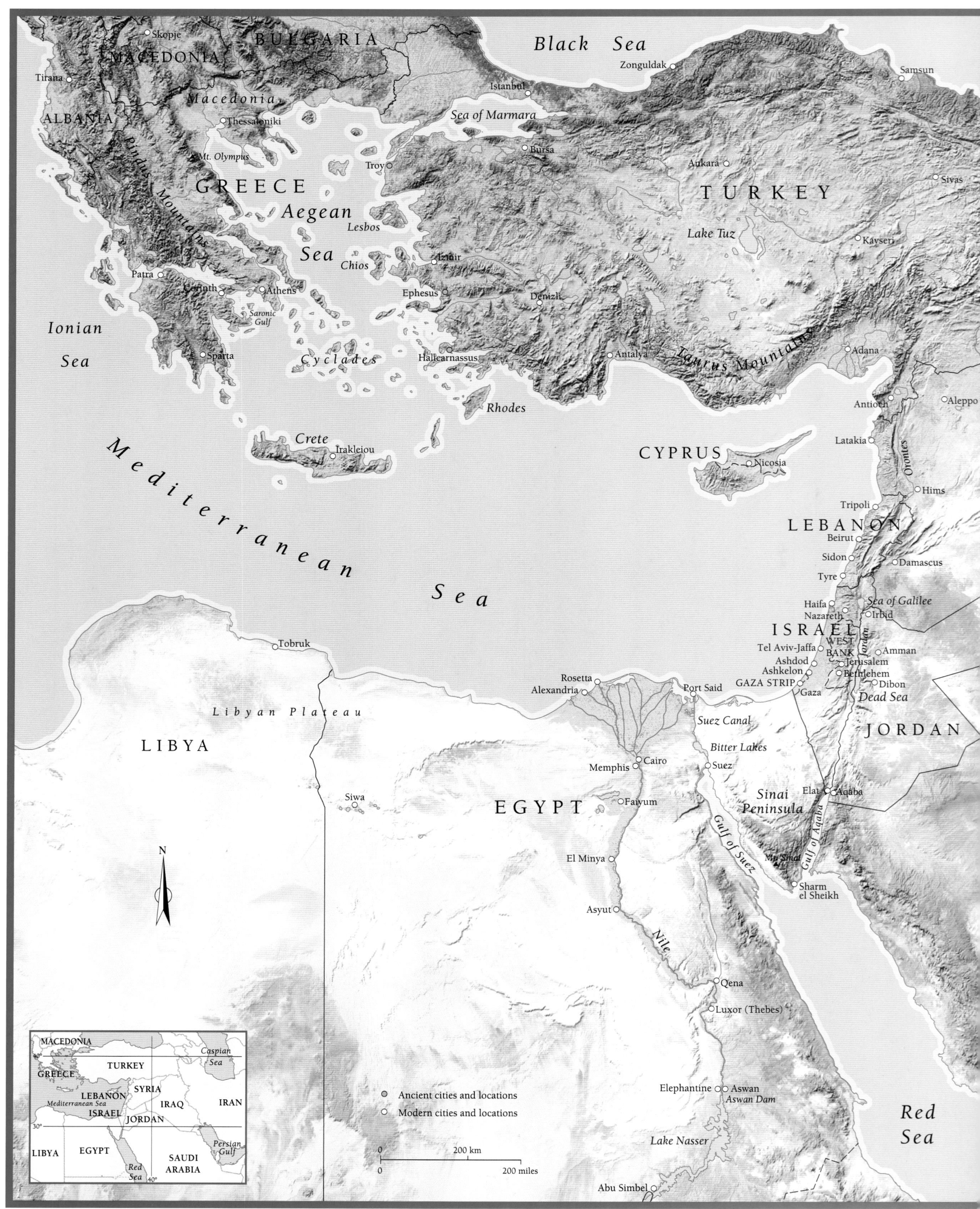

Black Sea
BULGARIA
MACEDONIA
Macedonia
ALBANIA
GREECE
TURKEY
Skopje
Tirana
Thessaloniki
Mt. Olympus
Pindus Mountains
Zonguldak
Samsun
Istanbul
Sea of Marmara
Bursa
Troy
Ankara
Sivas
Aegean Sea
Lesbos
Chios
Lake Tuz
Kayseri
Izmir
Ephesus
Denizli
Patra
Corinth
Athens
Saronic Gulf
Ionian Sea
Sparta
Cyclades
Halicarnassus
Antalya
Taurus Mountains
Adana
Rhodes
Antioch
Aleppo
Crete
Irakleiou
Mediterranean Sea
CYPRUS
Nicosia
Latakia
Orontes
Hims
Tripoli
LEBANON
Beirut
Sidon
Damascus
Tyre
Haifa
Sea of Galilee
Nazareth
Irbid
ISRAEL
WEST BANK
Jordan
Tel Aviv-Jaffa
Amman
Ashdod
Jerusalem
Ashkelon
Bethlehem
GAZA STRIP
Gaza
Dibon
Dead Sea
Tobruk
Rosetta
Alexandria
Port Said
Libyan Plateau
Suez Canal
JORDAN
LIBYA
Bitter Lakes
Cairo
Memphis
Suez
Sinai Peninsula
Elat
Aqaba
Siwa
EGYPT
Faiyum
Gulf of Suez
Gulf of Aqaba
Mt. Sinai
El Minya
Sharm el Sheikh
N
Asyut
Nile
Qena
Luxor (Thebes)
MACEDONIA
Caspian Sea
TURKEY
GREECE
SYRIA
LEBANON
Mediterranean Sea
IRAQ
IRAN
ISRAEL
JORDAN
40°
30°
LIBYA
EGYPT
Persian Gulf
SAUDI ARABIA
Red Sea
40°
Ancient cities and locations
Modern cities and locations
Elephantine
Aswan
Aswan Dam
Lake Nasser
Red Sea
0
200 km
0
200 miles
Abu Simbel

GEORGIA
Batumi
T'bilisi
Trabzon
ARMENIA
Lake Sevana
Yerevan
Baku
AZERBAIJAN
TURKMENISTAN
Erzurum
Mt. Ararat
AZERBAIJAN
Caspian Sea
Elazig
Lake Van
Tabriz
Lake Urmia
Assyria
Nineveh
Mosul
Nimrud
Elburz Mountains
Tehran
Euphrates
Asshur
Kirkuk
SYRIA
Tigris
Qom
Dura-Europas
Samarra
Salt Desert
IRAN
IRAQ
Baghdad
Khorramabad
Syrian Desert
Mesopotamia
Babylon
Esfahan
Susa
Zagros Mountains
Nippur
Larsa
Ur
Basra
Pasargada (Pasargadae)
Persepolis
Shiraz
KUWAIT
Kuwait
Arabian Desert (An Nafud)
SAUDI ARABIA
Jubayl
Buraydah
Strait of Hormuz
Al Manamah
BAHRAIN
Persian Gulf
Doha
QATAR
Medina
Riyadh
Abu Dhabi
TOWNS AND CITIES OF THE BIBLE LANDS
UNITED ARAB EMIRATES
OMAN

GEOGRAPHY OF THE BIBLE LANDS

A GOOD AND BROAD LAND, A LAND FLOWING WITH MILK AND HONEY EXODUS 3:8

RIGHT: THIS RITUAL CUP DECORATED WITH AN ANIMAL RELIEF WAS FOUND AT URUK, NEAR UR IN MESOPOTAMIA (THE LAND OF ABRAHAM), AND IS DATED FROM 3000 B.C.E.

When scholars talk about the geographic regions of the Bible lands, they use a bewildering array of terms and expressions that can be quite difficult to follow. The names scholars use for these regions change over time, and some names fall in and out of fashion. Region names are based on political ideologies or issues of cultural sensitivity, and sometimes they reflect distinct geographic regions, based on particular natural features or climate patterns. At other times, the names refer to political entities, and given the instability of the region, you can imagine how diverse those names are. In this atlas, we use three broad designations for the different regions of the Bible lands: the Near East, the Mediterranean World, and Egypt and the Sinai Peninsula. (Egypt and Mesopotamia are considered cradles of civilization.) These labels well reflect ancient political, geographic, and cultural boundaries. As some of these names are derived from historical situations and some are based on geography, there is significant overlap in their use, so Turkey and Israel could be considered either Mediterranean or Near Eastern. In this atlas the most common scholarly uses have been followed, but you may come across different uses of these terms elsewhere.

THE NEAR EAST

The Near East is the accepted scholarly classification for the region that includes the modern states of Israel, Syria, Jordan, Lebanon, Iraq, and the Persian Gulf states. This region is known in common parlance as the Middle East, and most journalists and modern political commentators refer to it as such. The reason for this discrepancy is simple. When European archaeologists first began to work in this part of the world, it was the time of the British Empire. This area was considered part of "The East" (in the way that Britain and Europe were considered "The West"), and "The East" spanned from Israel to China and Japan (the Far East). Since this was the part of the east that was closest to the British Empire, it was referred to as the Near East. Following World War I, the world political map was substantially redrawn, and the region that used to be known as the Near East came to be called the Middle East. Both archaeologists and historians are conservative by nature, and they kept calling the region the Near East. Politicians and journalists prefer the later designation, the Middle East.

Numerous other names have been used for this region. The area that borders the eastern side of the Mediterranean Sea

LEFT: KING DAVID, THE SECOND KING OF ISRAEL, SHOWN HERE IN A THIRTEENTH-CENTURY FRESCO FROM THE CRYPT OF ANAGNI CATHEDRAL, WAS THE GREAT-GRANDSON OF BOAZ AND RUTH. HE MADE ISRAEL AN INDEPENDENT STATE.

(encompassing modern Turkey, Lebanon, Syria, and Israel) is often called the Levant. Sometimes Jordan is included in this, even though the use of Levant for Jordan is not technically accurate. Other names for the region are based on political or historical events. Palestine can refer to the entire area of the southern Levant, in keeping with the ancient use of this term. But Palestine also refers to a modern political entity, so confusion is possible. More often, the Levant is called Syro–Palestine, based on ancient denominations of the northern half as Syria and the southern half as Palestine.

The term Israel can be very confusing, especially for people studying biblical times. Israel, in its broadest sense, refers to the descendents of Jacob (who took the name Israel in Genesis and early Exodus) and, as such, refers not to a geographic region, but to a group of people. Israel also refers to the kingdom of Saul, David, and Solomon. After Solomon's reign, the northern part of the kingdom revolted, and from that point, the description Israel refers to the northern kingdom and the description Judah refers to the southern kingdom (with its capital in Jerusalem). Judah should not be confused with Judea, the name of the region when it was a Roman province. And of course, Israel also refers to the modern state of Israel. In actual practice, the context of the use of these terms will be clear and it is highly unlikely that anyone will be in any confusion about which "Israel" is being referred to.

Archaeologists and historians have long noticed common cultural patterns among the peoples of the Ancient Near East. The languages spoken in this region are very similar to one another and the laws and customs also bear striking parallels. The peoples of the Old Testament came from this cultural milieu (remember, Genesis tells us that Abraham came from the city of Ur in Mesopotamia), and the archaeological investigations of the Near East have shed much light on Old Testament practices. That is not to say that these cultures were identical—there is much that was distinct about the people of Israel, especially their worship of one God, but it is useful to examine the relationships between Israel and its neighbors.

TELLS: ANCIENT MOUNDS AND FORGOTTEN CITIES

Archaeologists working in the Near East and Mediterranean have no problem finding sites. It is not just because the region has been inhabited for so long, although that helps. The way in which sites develop in this region is distinctive, and impossible to miss. Most Ancient Near Eastern and many Mediterranean cities are built on large hills, known as tells. Ancient people liked building in places that had already been inhabited, so rather than building cities on virgin soil, they would build their cities on top of the ruins of older cities. Usually there were logical reasons for doing so—most cities had stable water sources, ruins had plenty of building equipment that could be salvaged, and strategically it was safer to build on elevated ground. So most ancient sites, such as the foundations of the Hanging Gardens of Babylon (below), are actually large hills consisting of centuries of accumulated deposits.

THE MEDITERRANEAN WORLD

Technically, the Mediterranean refers to all of the land masses that surround the Mediterranean Sea and that have a Mediterranean climate. In biblical scholarship, Mediterranean is used more frequently to refer to the area that makes up the northeastern coast of the sea and the nearby islands. In other words, it includes what is now Italy, Greece, Turkey, and

BELOW: THE BIBLE LANDS WERE, AND ARE, INCREDIBLY VARIED—FROM THE LUSH PASTORAL LANDS OF THE MEDITERRANEAN TO THE UNFORGIVING LANDSCAPE OF THE EGYPTIAN DESERT.

Ancient Maps

Archaeologists have uncovered many ancient maps of the Bible lands. One of the best comes from the ancient Mesopotamian city of Nippur, where someone had sketched a fairly accurate map of the city onto a tablet. Another ancient map is the Medeba Map (part of which is shown at right), a large mosaic of the Holy Land found in an ancient church in Jordan. The exact date of the mosaic is debated, but it played a decorative role in the church where it was found. The map shows the Jordan River, Jerusalem, and other important Christian sites. Based on these finds, as well as from references in the Bible, it is clear that ancient people oriented their directions differently from the way we do. When we look at a map, unless stated otherwise, we assume that north is at the top. For Ancient Near Eastern cartographers, the top of the map was east. So when we are told in Genesis 42:3, "So ten of Joseph's brothers went down to buy grain in Egypt," this reflects an ancient orientation where the western trek across the Sinai Peninsula from Israel would have looked like going down on a map. Likewise, when Joseph's brothers return in Genesis 45:25, it is said that "they went up out of Egypt," reflecting the same orientation.

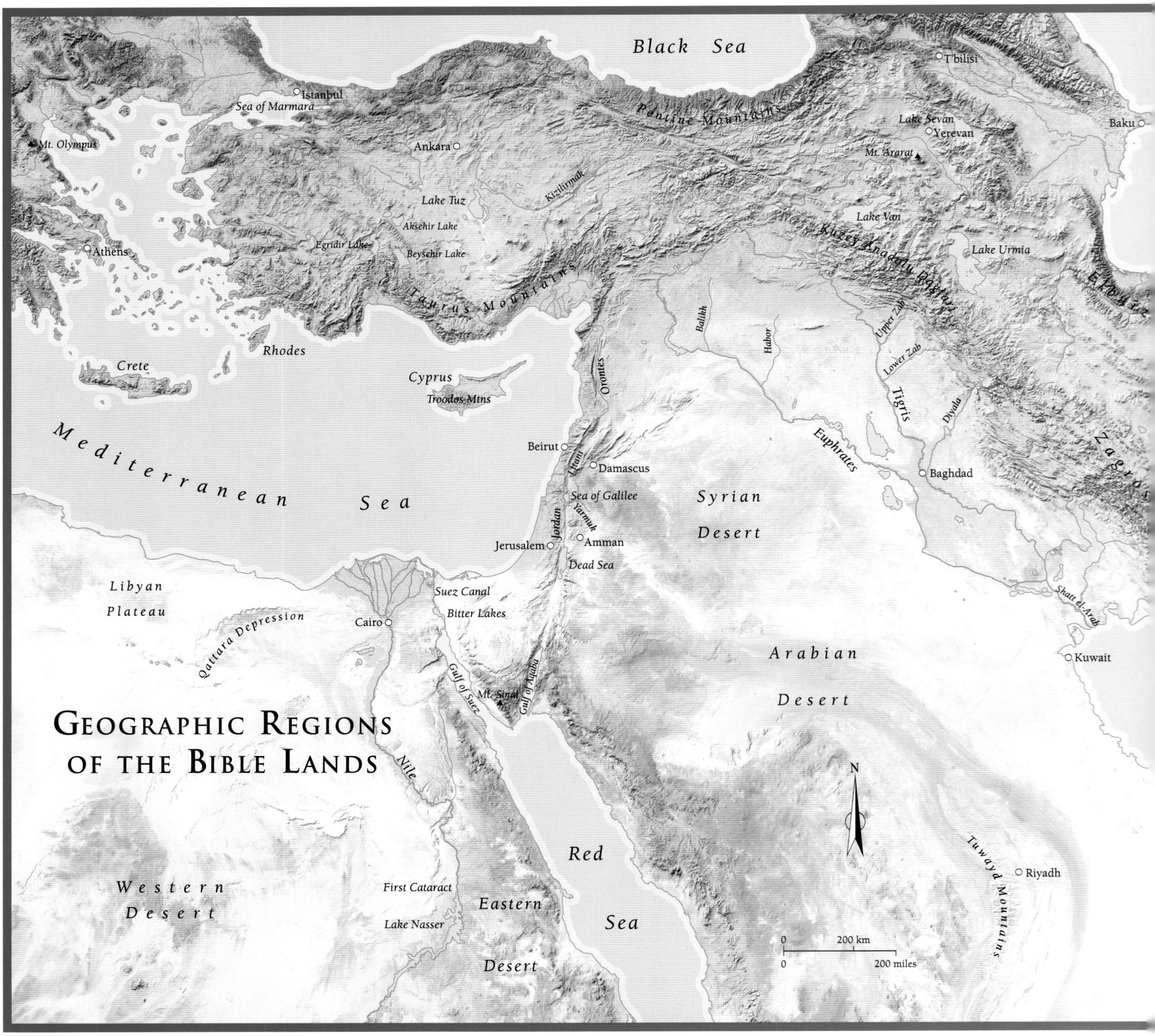

Geographic Regions of the Bible Lands

Black Sea
Tbilisi
Istanbul
Sea of Marmara
Pontine Mountains
Lake Sevan
Yerevan
Baku
Mt. Olympus
Ankara
Mt. Ararat
Kizilirmak
Lake Tuz
Akşehir Lake
Lake Van
Athens
Egridir Lake
Beyşehir Lake
Kuzey Anadolu Dağlari
Lake Urmia
Taurus Mountains
Elburz
Balikh
Habor
Upper Zab
Rhodes
Crete
Lower Zab
Cyprus
Troodos Mtns
Orontes
Tigris
Diyala
Mediterranean Sea
Beirut
Euphrates
Zagros
Litani
Damascus
Baghdad
Sea of Galilee
Syrian Desert
Yarmuk
Jordan
Jerusalem
Amman
Dead Sea
Libyan Plateau
Suez Canal
Shatt el-Arab
Qattara Depression
Cairo
Bitter Lakes
Kuwait
Arabian Desert
Gulf of Suez
Mt. Sinai
Gulf of Aqaba
Nile
N
Red Sea
Tuwayd Mountains
Riyadh
Western Desert
First Cataract
Eastern Desert
Lake Nasser
0 200 km
0 200 miles

islands such as Crete and Cyprus. The similar topography and climate in the Mediterranean has meant that many of the customs, cuisines, and economic practices of people in these areas have developed along comparable lines.

This is an extremely important region for Bible scholars. During the period of the Old Testament, the people of the Near East were in frequent contact with the people of the Mediterranean. Most of this contact was through trade, but in some cases (as with the Philistines, Goliath's kinsfolk) Mediterranean populations actually settled in the Near East. The Mediterranean region is even more important for scholars of the New Testament. Jesus was born in the Roman province of Judea. By his time, Greek culture had heavily influenced the cities of the Levant, and Rome directly controlled the region. Paul's letters, preserved in the New Testament, were mostly written to Mediterranean cities (like Ephesus in Turkey and Corinth in Greece). Paul was concerned with issues facing the local churches, so a greater understanding of these regions can better inform those interested in learning from Paul today.

EGYPT AND THE SINAI PENINSULA

Arguably, "Egypt and the Sinai Peninsula" are the most transparent terms used in this atlas. These words have rather limited ranges—Egypt has always been Egypt and the Sinai has always been the Sinai. Egypt's relationship to biblical peoples was complex. Sometimes, as with Joseph's travels, Egypt acts as a deliverer for the people of Israel, providing food in times of famine. At other times, as in the accounts of the Exodus, Egypt and the Egyptian government are at odds with the best interests of Israel. This well reflects the relationship between the Levantine states and Egypt more generally. Egypt was relatively isolated, with the Sinai the only land route connecting Africa and Asia. So the Levant has always been important for Egypt's security and economic life. Having control of the Sinai meant that Egypt had access via land to the wealthy regions of the Near East and could also easily protect itself from foreign invasion by land.

In the books of Kings and Chronicles, relations between Egypt and the kingdom of Judah are constantly shifting as the Judahite kings try to negotiate their place as intermediaries between the Mesopotamian and Egyptian superpowers. Simple geography explains the precarious political position of the kingdom of Judah, and the region in general is often caught in the middle of these larger political conflicts.

BELOW: THE MONASTERY OF ST. CATHERINE, AT THE FOOT OF MT. MOSES (ALSO KNOWN AS JEBEL MUSA) IN THE SINAI, WAS BUILT BETWEEN C.E. 527 AND 565 BY THE ROMAN EMPEROR JUSTINIAN.

RIGHT: THE PROMISE OF RAIN IN THE BIBLE LANDS IS A MIXED BLESSING—THERE IS EITHER TOO LITTLE OR TOO MUCH, WHICH CAN RESULT IN WIDESPREAD DEVASTATION.

CLIMATE PATTERNS OF THE BIBLE LANDS

The climate of the Bible lands does not appear to have changed dramatically since the first appearance of permanent human villages in the region. There has been significant environmental change, mostly due to human overuse, and global warming has become an increasing problem in recent times, but for the most part, the people of the Bible experienced similar climatic fluctuations as people experience in the region today. Local variations were present and a few isolated periods of drought have been identified. That being said, not much work has been done to study the climate from 3000 B.C.E. to C.E. 100, so our impressions could change dramatically as more evidence is recovered.

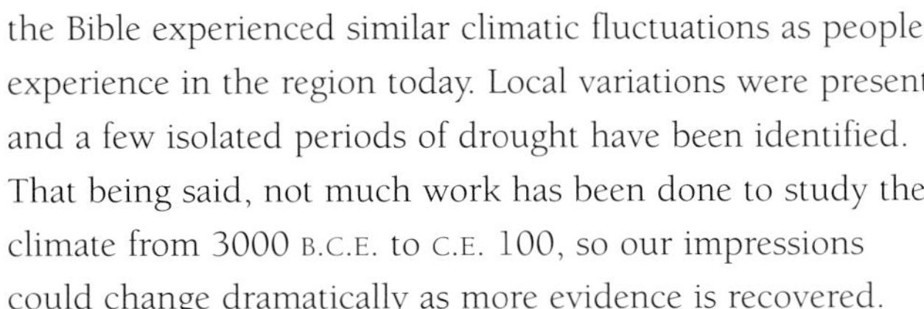

MEDITERRANEAN CLIMATE

Mediterranean climates are typical of all of the land that surrounds the coast of the Mediterranean. In fact, Mediterranean climate refers not just to climates in the region, but also to climates of this type all over the world: in Southern California, Western Australia, and even Vancouver Island in Canada. Technically the Mediterranean climate is a subtropical climate, with typically moderate temperatures. Usually regions with this climate are heavily populated because of the desirable weather conditions.

Generally the Mediterranean has two major seasons. The winter is cool and wet, usually peaking from October to May. The summer (peaking from June to August) is quite dry and rainfall is very unusual. Although the temperatures in summer get incredibly hot, it often does not feel this way. Cool breezes are typical in all Mediterranean lands, making the summers very pleasant, especially in areas directly on the coast or on the higher slopes of the hills. During the Mediterranean summer, the sky is almost always cloudless and sunny. In modern times, direct sunlight poses quite a significant environmental hazard, since when nitrogen oxides mix with pollutants in sunlight, smog forms.

Rain is directly dependent on the patterns of the seasons, and it is brought to the Bible lands by frontal storms that move westward. Throughout the summer, rain cannot fall because of the dominance of high pressure zones in the area. Even during the winter months, precipitation is variable, and never particularly plentiful. It can, however, be extremely destructive. Rain can come suddenly, in torrential downpours. This provides challenges for farmers, who had to develop special methods for trapping water during the brief but intense periods of rainfall in some years. It also creates problems for people living on hill slopes, as landslides are unpredictable and destructive. In other years, rain may fall consistently, in small amounts, throughout the winter months. In some of the outlying areas with a higher altitude, snow is a possibility, and even the city of Jerusalem is known to have the occasional snowfall.

BELOW: IN ANCIENT EGYPT, FIELDS WERE IRRIGATED USING A SAQIYYA, A DEVICE CONSISTING OF POTS FIXED ALONG A STURDY BRANCH ATTACHED TO A WHEEL, AND DRAWN BY OXEN.

THE MESOPOTAMIAN CLIMATE

The climate of ancient Mesopotamia is much like the climate of Iraq today. In the summer months (from June to September), temperatures can exceed 120°F (49°C). Though technically it is a dry subtropical climate similar to the Mediterranean region, but without the cool breezes and with minimal rainfall, it is perhaps better characterized as a semiarid climate. By all standards, the climate of Iraq feels substantially hotter and drier than anything in the Mediterranean region.

These extremes in heat are well matched by the intense aridity—for eight months of the year, Iraq receives almost no rainfall at all. The mouth of the Persian Gulf is an exception, as it does produce scattered precipitation at times. For the most part, by the end of summer, many of the riverbeds in Mesopotamia have dried up and are parched. Because of this lack of precipitation, the Mesopotamians were forced to rely on irrigation agriculture. Indeed, Mesopotamian civilization lies almost exclusively beneath the isohyet (marking the southern limit of rainfall agriculture), and in some ways the civilization is defined by its dependency on irrigation.

Winter in Iraq runs from December to March and never gets particularly cold. Dust storms are a frequent problem in the winter, lasting from 24 to 36 hours at a time. Storms and the subtropical jet stream bring extensive cloud cover in the winter, and Iraq seems relatively dark and gloomy compared with the summer months. This is also the season when some precipitation can be expected and the rivers (especially the tributaries of the Tigris) usually flood.

DESERT CLIMATES: EGYPT AND THE SINAI

Egyptian civilization developed in the midst of one of the most substantial deserts in the world. The environment of the Nile Valley, however, is drastically different from the surrounding desert. The Egyptians themselves distinguished between these two regions. The Nile Valley was referred to as the Black Land, and the desert as the Red Land, based on the different soil colors. The desert is obviously extremely arid. Parts of the Nile Valley feel overwhelmingly humid. Especially in the Delta region in the north, the air can seem hazy and filled with moisture.

The climate of Egypt is quite uniform, especially in comparison with the climates of the other Bible lands (some

PALYNOLOGY

Archaeologists and environmental scientists have many sources that they can use to reconstruct the ancient climate. One of the most productive methods for studying ancient climate is the study of ancient pollen. Pollen, as many allergy sufferers are all too aware, is virtually indestructible. It lasts for centuries and is preserved in easily dated deposits of soil. Scholars can take a sample of the soil from a particular period and study the proportions of pollen in a particular layer. From this, they can draw conclusions about the climate (how cold it was, how much rainfall there was) as well as conclusions about the nature of human interaction with the environment. If one period has large amounts of forest pollen and the next period does not, it is safe to conclude that there was heavy deforestation. Likewise, the appearance of domesticated wheat pollen can help us determine the earliest dates of agriculture.

BELOW: CAMELS FLOCK TO AN OASIS TO QUENCH THEIR THIRST. INCREDIBLY HOT IN THE DAYTIME, THE DESERT CAN BE SURPRISINGLY COOL IN THE EVENINGS.

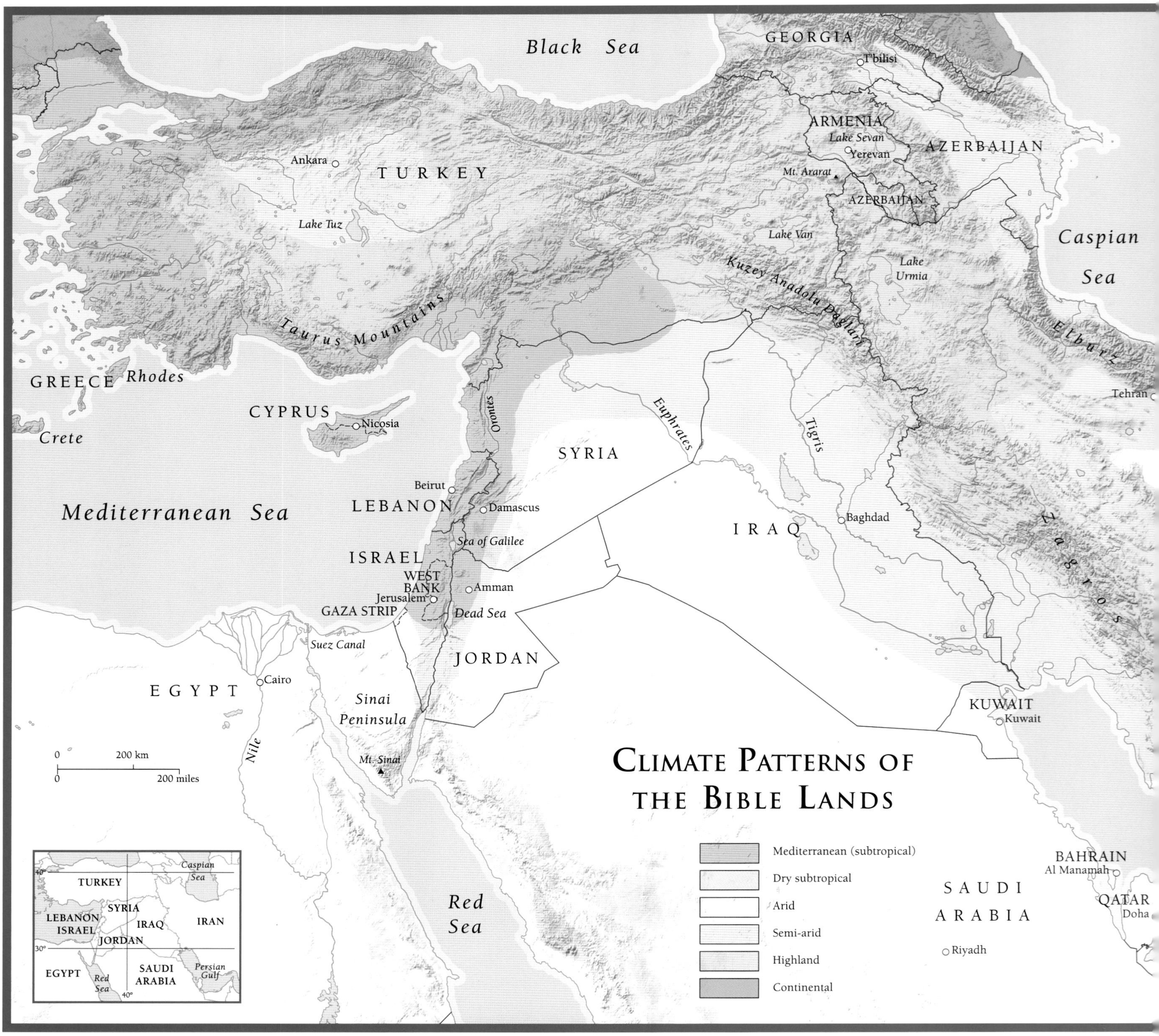

Climate Patterns of the Bible Lands

Mediterranean (subtropical)
Dry subtropical
Arid
Semi-arid
Highland
Continental

Black Sea
GEORGIA
Tbilisi
ARMENIA
Lake Sevan
Yerevan
AZERBAIJAN
Mt. Ararat
AZERBAIJAN
Ankara
TURKEY
Lake Tuz
Lake Van
Caspian Sea
Lake Urmia
Kuzey Anadolu Dağları
Taurus Mountains
Elburz
GREECE
Rhodes
Tehran
CYPRUS
Nicosia
Crete
Orontes
Euphrates
Tigris
SYRIA
Beirut
Mediterranean Sea
LEBANON
Damascus
Baghdad
IRAQ
Zagros
Sea of Galilee
ISRAEL
WEST BANK
Amman
Jerusalem
GAZA STRIP
Dead Sea
Suez Canal
JORDAN
EGYPT
Cairo
Sinai Peninsula
KUWAIT
Kuwait
0 200 km
0 200 miles
Nile
Mt. Sinai
BAHRAIN
Al Manamah
SAUDI ARABIA
QATAR
Doha
Red Sea
Riyadh
TURKEY
Caspian Sea
SYRIA
LEBANON
ISRAEL
IRAQ
IRAN
JORDAN
EGYPT
Red Sea
SAUDI ARABIA
Persian Gulf
40°
30°
40°

scholars have gone so far as to suggest that this led to an Egyptian worldview that nothing ever changed, and a desire to preserve the status quo). There really is not a rainy season or a winter, although there are some changes in temperature. Archaeologists prefer to work in Egypt from December to March, when the air is slightly cooler and quite cold at night. Novice archaeologists often find that they wished they had brought blankets and warmer clothes for the cool Egyptian mornings.

The rest of the Egyptian year is quite hot. From the middle of February to June, hot winds can blow through the land, bringing sudden extremes of heat. During the rest of the hotter months, breezes and winds tend to cool down the Nile Valley. The sun in Egypt is particularly striking. Even in

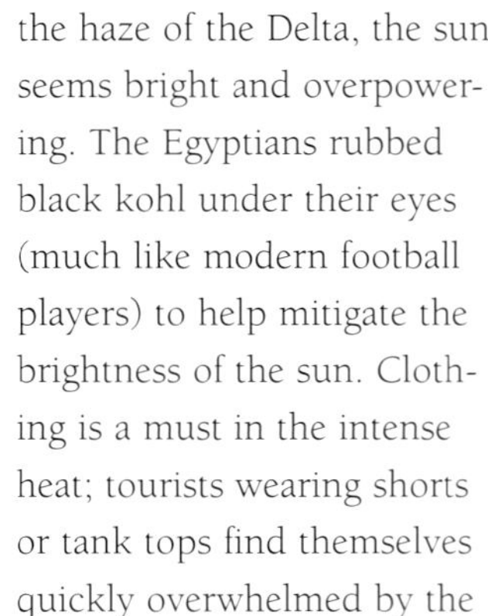

the haze of the Delta, the sun seems bright and overpowering. The Egyptians rubbed black kohl under their eyes (much like modern football players) to help mitigate the brightness of the sun. Clothing is a must in the intense heat; tourists wearing shorts or tank tops find themselves quickly overwhelmed by the

RIGHT: THE JORDAN RIVER HAS ALWAYS HAD A SPECIAL SIGNIFICANCE. IN MEDIEVAL TIMES, PILGRIMS CAME TO THE RIVER TO BATHE AND TO SYMBOLICALLY WASH AWAY THEIR SINS.

glaring sun. Linen or cotton clothes, and some sort of head covering, usually help minimize the effects of the sun, as does the constant drinking of water.

The Sinai Peninsula is also a desert environment, but there is much more diversity in climate given the topographical variation. Coastal temperatures stay relatively consistent year round, with hot air and clear skies the norm. The mountainous areas are more diverse climatically. Visitors to the Monastery of St. Catherine's at the foot of Mt. Moses in the Sinai can be surprised by the very cold morning temperatures in the winter months (November to March). In very ancient times, the Sinai may have been more lush, since numerous dried waterbeds have been identified, but this subject has not been well studied. Winter in the Sinai today is still a dry season with next to no precipitation (less than 4 inches [100 mm] a year), except in the highest elevations.

DESERT CLIMATES: SOUTHERN ISRAEL AND JORDAN

As one travels south in Israel, the favorable Mediterranean climate gives way to an intensely arid environment. Likewise, after one crosses the Jordan River into the modern nation of Jordan, the subtropical environment is soon replaced by a stark desert. The desert in these regions, however, is not at all like the deserts of Egypt and the Sinai. Sand is less common than the hard fragments of broken flint and volcanic stone. As one moves further east into Jordan, the landscape develops into the inhospitable Arabian Desert, filled with massive sand dunes.

Rainfall is also more prevalent in these desert zones than it is in Egypt and Iraq. Rain falls from November to April, and these are also the coldest months of the year, with the temperatures reaching as low as 45°F (7°C). The rainy season brings much of the landscape to life: dry riverbeds fill with water, and vegetation develops in the immediate vicinity. By August though, many of these water sources have already dried up and the vegetation in the outlying areas seems to simply vanish. Some springs remain beautiful oases all year round. In Israel, En-gedi is one of these springs, and it has been transformed into a national park.

THE TOWER OF THE WINDS

Still standing in Athens today is the Horologion, or Tower of the Winds. This beautiful Hellenistic sculpture is constructed of marble and stands about 46 feet (14 m) in height. It encloses a water clock, and sundials on each outer wall also helped keep the time in ancient Athens. The most striking features of the tower are the carvings of the eight winds, one from each major direction. Each wind is personified and is accompanied by an image of the type of weather associated with the particular wind plus an inscription preserving the Greek name of the wind.

BELOW: ISRAEL'S EN-GEDI WATERFALL IS ON THE WESTERN SHORE OF THE DEAD SEA. IN BIBLICAL TIMES, IT PROVIDED A RELIABLE SOURCE OF WATER FOR THE LOCAL PEOPLE.

ABOVE: THIS FIFTEENTH-CENTURY MAP SHOWS TURKEY, THE BLACK SEA, AND MESOPOTAMIA. THE MOUNTAINS AND RIVERS ARE CLEARLY VISIBLE.

VEGETATION AND GEOLOGY OF THE BIBLE LANDS

The Bible lands are as volatile geologically as they are politically. Earthquakes and volcanoes have plagued the region for millennia; most recently Iran has been devastated by successive earthquakes. Numerous plates lie beneath the surface of the region, and it has been the interaction of these plates that has both created the landscape as it is known today and left it geologically unstable. The movements of the plates onto and up against one another resulted in the formation of the region's diverse topography, from the high Zagros mountain ranges that border Mesopotamia on the east, to the largest and lowest valley in the world, the Rift Valley.

The mineral resources of the Bible lands are unevenly distributed. One of the earliest Mesopotamian stories, known to scholars as "Enmerkar and the Lord of Aratta," suggests that writing was developed to facilitate communication between traders of precious stone with Iran. While this is not likely the true origin of writing, the story does accurately reflect the disparity in access to mineral resources that typified the economic history of the region. Most of the surface rocks are sedimentary, with limestone and sandstone being particularly common. Turkey has a wealth of mineral resources, with aboveground deposits of igneous rock in its mountain regions. Volcanic rock (such as basalt and obsidian) is also available in the region and was quickly utilized by many of the earliest human inhabitants.

Although the popular image of the Bible lands is one of flat desert landscapes, most of the region is, in fact, better described as mountainous (or at least hilly). Turkey has many mountain ranges: the Pontine running east to west near the Black Sea, the Taurus likewise running east to west near the Mediterranean Sea, the Elburz near the Caspian Sea, and the Zagros in the far east of the country. Mountain ranges run through the Levant, from Syria and Lebanon in the north to Israel in the south. This whole area should be understood as a succession of hills and valleys. With the predominance of mountains and hills comes a high degree of ecological diversity, especially in vegetation.

FORESTS

The types of vegetation present in particular areas are greatly dependent on two main factors: topography and rainfall. The combination of these two natural attributes determines what kinds of plant life can grow in a particular area. The mountainous regions of the Bible lands can support a wealth of biota, since most of these regions are above the isohyet and thus receive substantial annual rainfall. These regions were heavily forested in antiquity, but now many areas have been clearcut by human inhabitants. Indeed, the most substantial changes in vegetation over the past 10,000 years have come from humans cutting down forests.

Some areas can be labeled as primarily deciduous or coniferous forest. Most of the Bible lands, however, are mixed forests. Within these forests are uneven combinations of oak, pine, cedar, and juniper. Highly prized throughout the Bible lands, especially in Egypt where timber is almost entirely lacking, the cedars of Lebanon are still famous today. The foothill regions have equally varied vegetation: oak, pine, and terebinth were the most common trees. Oak has now mostly vanished from the area. Wild shrubs also grow in the foothills, and these areas are the original homes of the wheat plants first domesticated for farming. The rivers that run through these mountains allow the growth of riverine plant species. Rushes, cattails, and willows all thrive and were made into mats, baskets, and roofs.

The slender bands of forested areas along the coast of the Mediterranean Sea are called Mediterranean forests, although the trees there rarely grow thickly enough to constitute a true forest. Dotted with small pine and oak trees, Mediterranean forests are typified by a distinct type of vegetation, called "maquis." Probably caused through overgrazing and deforestation in these regions, maquis consists of dense, wild, evergreen shrubs, such as juniper and sage. It is particularly drought-resistant and grows well in rocky environments.

These forested regions produced many trees and plants that were exploited by humans. Timber was a major resource in the region. Wild herbs that grew in these forested areas were converted into spices, desired throughout the Bible lands. Thyme and marjoram were probably the most commonly exploited herbs. Nuts of various types also grow in this region, and southern Turkey is still one of the best producers of pistachios in the world. Gums and resins were also harvested from these forests. Harvesters would make small cuts into the trees and collect the resin that oozed out. Sometimes this was chewed, but most often it was manufactured into incense or perfume.

ABOVE: CATTAILS ARE A COMMON SIGHT ALONG THE RIVERBANKS OF THE BIBLE LANDS. THEY PROVIDE A WELCOME HABITAT FOR A VARIETY OF WILDLIFE.

FLOODPLAINS

The two cradles of human civilization, Mesopotamia and Egypt, were located in low floodplains. The geography and vegetation of these regions certainly facilitated the development of complex civilizations—the first large-scale states and the first urban populations. The plentiful resources of these areas allowed the population to grow in large numbers within a limited area, and the means of exploiting these resources required direct human intervention in the environment. With the substantial labor needed to subsist in these floodplains, people were compelled to settle permanently in villages.

The floodplain in Mesopotamia lies between the Tigris and Euphrates rivers. The alluvial lands between these two rivers are well watered, mostly from the twin rivers, but also from the meager rainfall each year. The sediment carried by the rivers is light brown silt, with a high salt content. This high salt content was particularly problematic, since the water channels are much higher than the plain. So instead of immediately running off, the salt-filled water would sit for weeks at a time with salt gradually leaching into the soil.

The Nile Valley had fewer challenges for human settlement. Surrounding the Nile is an alluvial valley, consisting

LEFT: *OVERFLOW OF THE NILE,* PAINTED IN 1842 BY THE RUSSIAN ARTIST GRIGORY TCHERNEZOV, SHOWS THE RICH DARK SOIL THAT IS CHARACTERISTIC OF THE NILE VALLEY.

RIGHT: THIS 1857 ENGRAVING BY J. BENWELL SHOWS A PALESTINIAN SHEPHERD TENDING TO HIS FLOCK. THE STEPPES PROVIDE SUFFICIENT GRAZING LAND FOR LIVESTOCK TO THRIVE.

primarily of dark clay soils. The channel bed of the river was higher than the surrounding valley, meaning that the Nile River would flood its banks only at particular times of the year. In the north of Egypt (the Delta) the relative elevation of the banks to the plain is less severe. This meant that more water would overflow the banks consistently, making the Delta a marshy, swampy area.

Both Mesopotamia and Egypt are part of the Saharo–Sindian region, because of the vegetation that grows there. Vegetation growth patterns are very diverse, since the ability for plants to grow is dependent on local topography. Given the low annual rainfall, the topography must be such that it can trap water for extended periods. Because of this, plants like drought-resistant shrubs, tamarisk, wild date palms, and acacia are unevenly distributed throughout the desert.

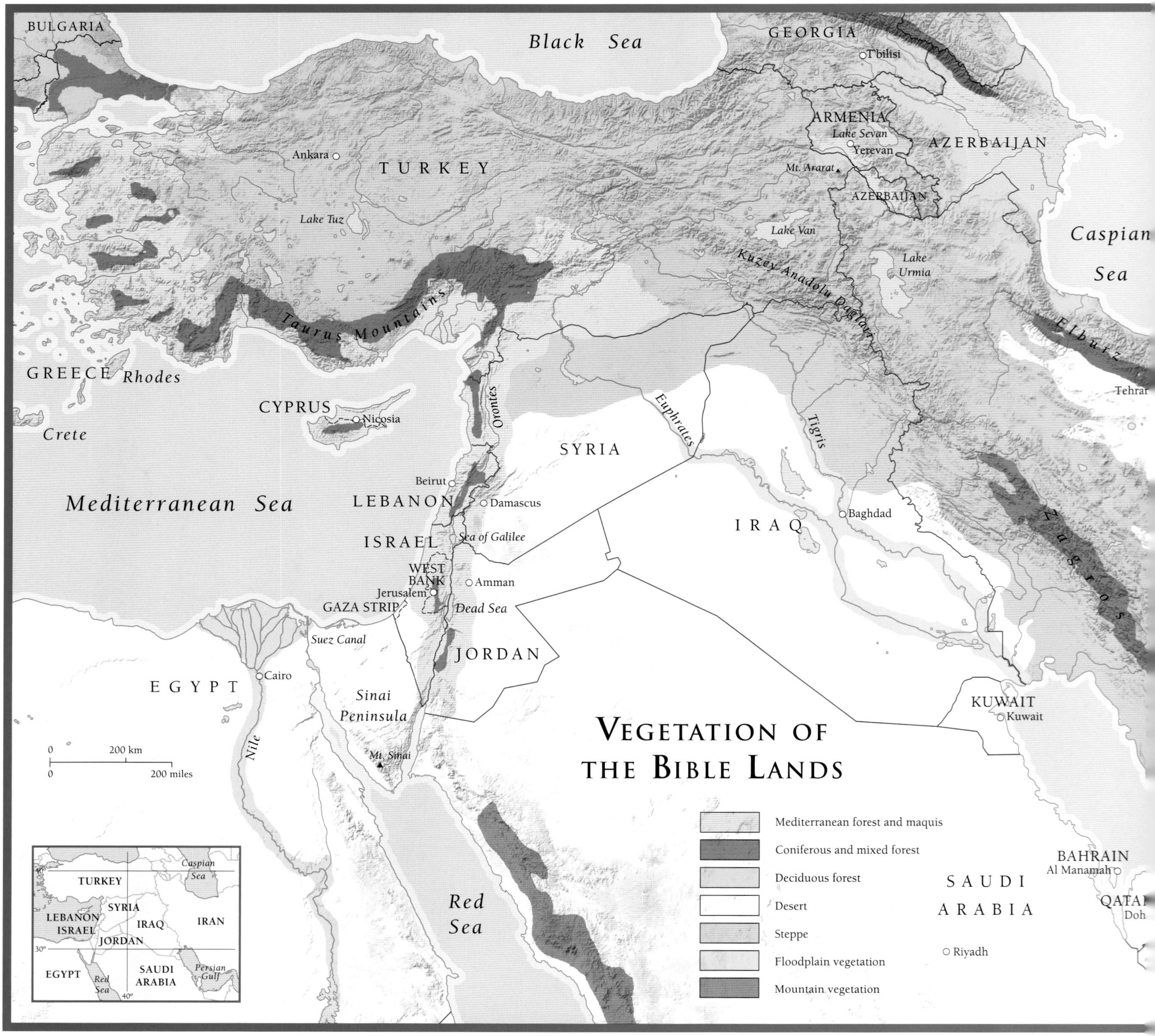

VEGETATION OF THE BIBLE LANDS

Mediterranean forest and maquis
Coniferous and mixed forest
Deciduous forest
Desert
Steppe
Floodplain vegetation
Mountain vegetation

0 200 km
0 200 miles

The major difference between agricultural crops in Mesopotamia and Egypt is related to the salt content of the Mesopotamian floodplain. Because of the highly salinated fields, Mesopotamian crops had to be salt-resistant, so barley was cultivated there successfully. Wheat, which is not as salt-resistant, was the more common Egyptian crop. One reason for this is that wheat does not have to be as thoroughly processed to make edible (and tasty) food products.

DESERTS AND SEMIDESERTS

Between the foothills and the encroaching deserts are the steppes—areas filled with low shrubs and wild grasses. By definition, steppes are plains that are devoid of trees, and the Bible land steppes are no exception. The steppes are particularly good regions for shepherding and animal husbandry, providing ample grazing land. There is not quite enough moisture to truly support the development of forest, but there is enough water to allow the grasses to grow to over a foot (30 cm) high. At many times of the year, the steppes are better considered as semidesert, although technically this is the type of vegetation zone that lies between a desert and a steppe. The exact position of steppes is consistently shifting, interplaying with the deserts that they border.

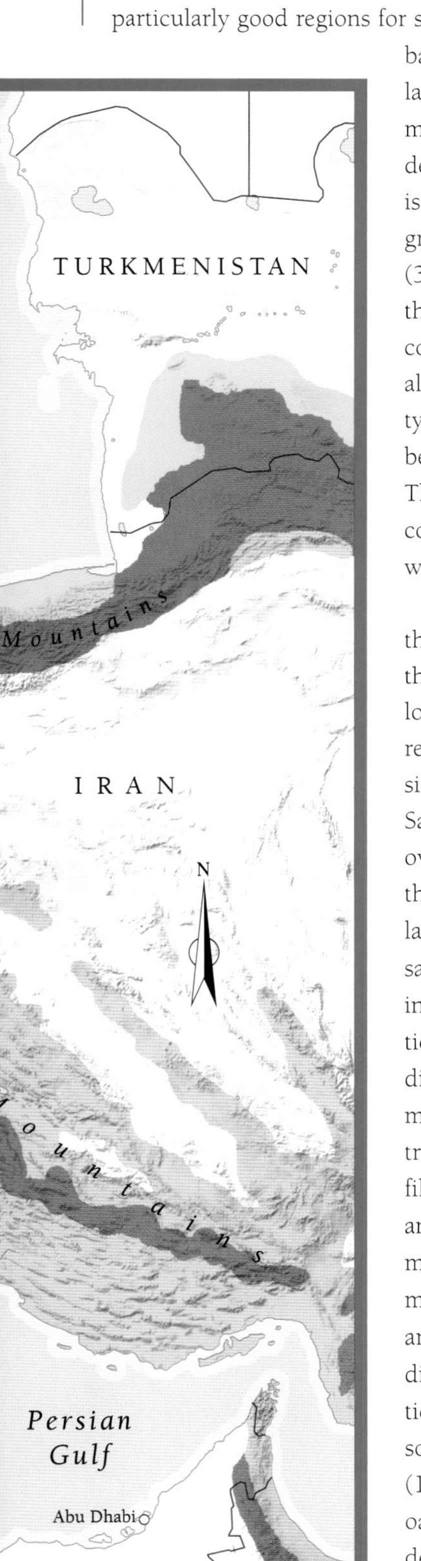

Desert vegetation (or the lack thereof) typifies much of Egypt, the Sinai, and Saudi Arabia. The location of these deserts has remained relatively consistent since ancient times. Unlike the Sahara, which has grown much over the past 4,000 years or so, the desert areas of the Bible lands are pretty much in the same locations now as they were in biblical times. Human habitation in these areas is extremely difficult, and large-scale settlements are impossible. These are true desert regions, which are filled with sand dunes that shift and change like the tides. This makes it extremely difficult to map and navigate through these areas, although caravan traffic did thrive after the domestication of the camel, which was sometime during the Iron Age (1200–586 B.C.E.). Sporadic oases and lakes break up the desert landscape; in these areas, wetland plants are the predominant form of vegetation.

ABOVE: OASES USUALLY OCCUR NEAR A SPRING OR OTHER WATER SOURCE. THE PLANTS AROUND OASES DIFFER MARKEDLY FROM SURROUNDING VEGETATION.

THE TREE OF LIFE—LITERALLY

Archaeologists excavating Herod's Palace near the Dead Sea saved seeds from a plant called the Judean date palm (or "Tree of Life" in ancient Hebrew), long considered extinct. The excavators of the Roman period complex put the seeds into storage, never imagining the request they would get 30 years later. In 2004 scholars from California requested a sample of the seeds so they could plant them, and in 2005 a seedling germinated; scholars appropriately named the seedling Methuselah. So far the plant has thrived in its laboratory environment, promising scholars new opportunities to study the properties of this ancient plant.

THE NEAR EAST

THE WATERS WEAR AWAY THE STONES; THE TORRENTS WASH AWAY THE SOIL OF THE EARTH JOB 14:19

From the sixth century B.C.E., the Near East was ruled by large empires—the Persians, the Hellenistic Empires, the Roman Empire, and the Christian Byzantine Empire. During the Middle Ages, an Arabic empire stretched from Spain to India. After a period of Christian rule during the Crusaders' period in the twelfth and thirteenth centuries C.E., the area was again under Muslim rule. The Mamluks ruled it from 1255 until 1517, and from then until World War I, it was ruled by the Turkish Ottoman Empire.

MODERN POLITICAL DIVISIONS OF THE NEAR EAST

The Near East comprises modern Israel, Lebanon, Syria, Jordan, Iraq (including the ancient area of Mesopotamia),

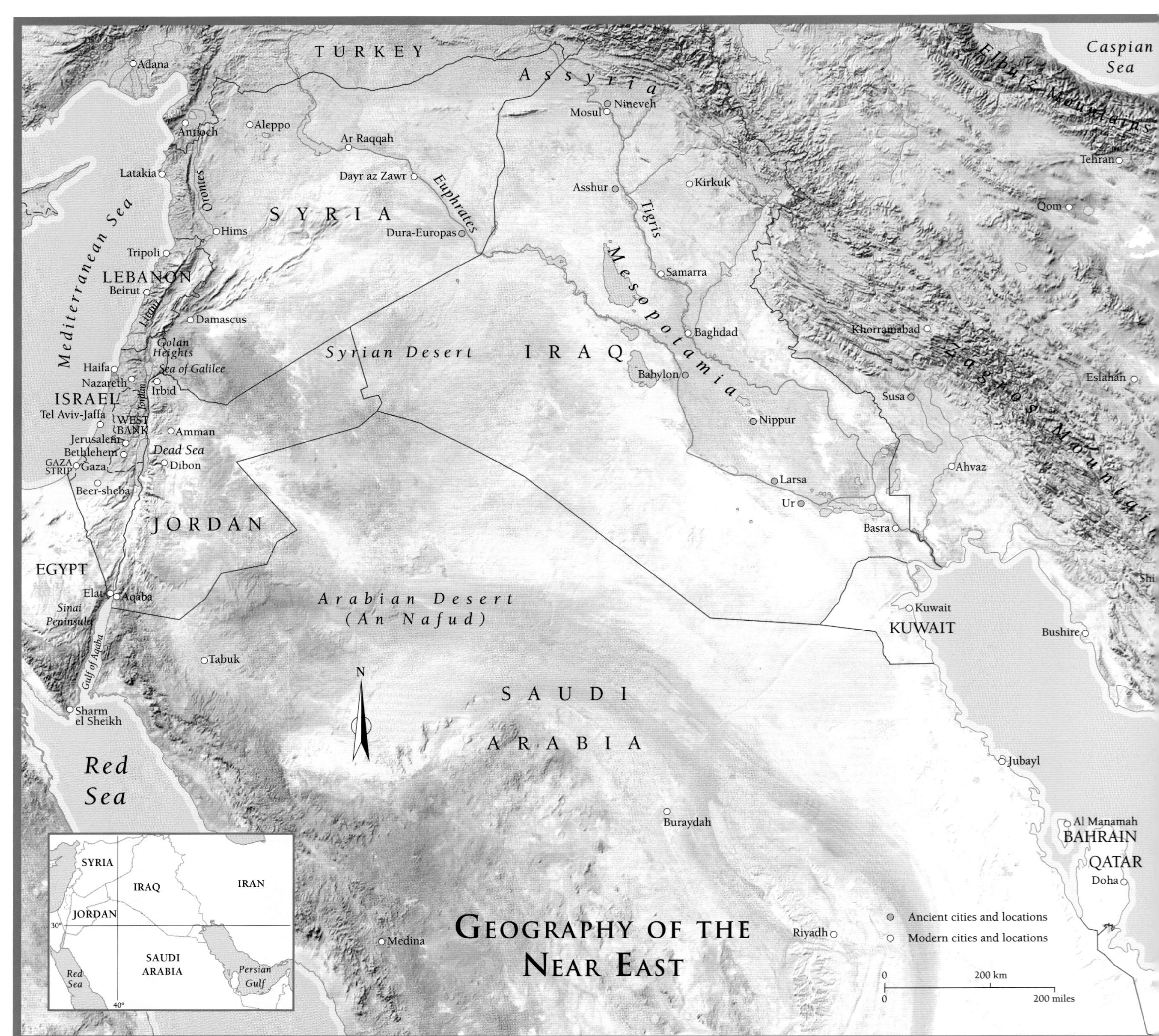

and Iran. The modern division of the Near East is the outcome of the division of that area between Britain and France, after the collapse of the Ottoman Empire in 1917. In May 1916, Britain and France signed the Sykes-Picot agreement, in which France was given the north-eastern shore of the Mediterranean Sea, and Britain was given the lower part of Mesopotamia, from Baghdad to the Persian Gulf, as well as the Acre–Haifa area in Palestine. The whole area east of the Syrian–African Rift was allocated to two Arab states, the one north of the Yarmuk River under French protection, while the one south of it was placed under British protection. The area of Palestine became an international entity.

ROLE OF THE LEAGUE OF NATIONS

After World War I, the League of Nations allocated the Near East to Britain and France, giving them a mandate to rule there and to develop the area for the benefit of its local population and to lead them to independence. On April 24, 1920, Britain was awarded the Mandate for Mesopotamia and Palestine while France was given the Mandate for Syria and Lebanon. Britain and France concluded an agreement, signed on December 23, 1920, in which a line from the Mediterranean Sea in the west, all the way up to the Persian border in the east, divided their areas in the Near East. Later on, after some modification, this line became the boundary line between Palestine, Jordan, and Iraq on one side, and Lebanon and Syria on the other side. France, which ruled Syria and Lebanon, divided the two Mandate areas in 1920, with a line that created the boundaries of modern Lebanon, by adding to the Christian area of Mt. Lebanon the Muslim area of Tripoli, the Baqa'a, and the area of Tyre and Sidon. Syria was cut from the area of Antioch, which was handed to Turkey by the French in 1939. In 1946 both Syria and Lebanon obtained their independence from France.

Britain, which was given the Mandate for Palestine, established two political entities in that area. West of the Jordan River, they established modern Palestine, while east of the river, they established the Emirate of Transjordan. This was a newly established entity, which had no political past, and was created in order to fulfill a British promise to the Hashemite Arab family, who fought alongside it during the War. The British ruled Transjordan up to 1946, during which time they established its boundaries with Syria, Iraq, Saudi Arabia, and Palestine. In 1946 Transjordan became independent, under the rule of King Abdullah.

The British held Palestine until 1948. On November 29, 1947, the United Nations decided to terminate British rule over Palestine and establish two independent states—a Jewish one and an Arab one. The Jewish state was formed in 1948 while the Arab state still fights for its independence.

The British Mandate for Mesopotamia was established in 1920 and the area was called Iraq, a new name, which had never been the name of a country in the past. The British installed another member of the Hashemite family as the ruler of Iraq, which obtained its independence in 1932. Its boundaries were established by the British, without any connection to its history.

Thus, five modern states were created from the ruins of the Ottoman Empire without any connection to the past; the motives were solely to fulfill the needs of European powers to rule the Near East. At the time of writing, the sixth country, that of Arab Palestine, is on its way to independence.

ABOVE: PALESTINIAN FARMERS IN THE GAZA STRIP IN 1956 CARRIED THEIR PRODUCE FROM THE FIELDS TO THE MARKETS. TRANSPORT FOR AGRICULTURAL WORKERS AT THAT TIME WAS EITHER BY DONKEY OR ON FOOT.

LEFT: CRUSADERS, FROM THE PAVEMENT OF ST. JOHN THE EVANGELIST, A THIRTEENTH-CENTURY BYZANTINE MOSAIC. THE CRUSADERS FOUGHT MUSLIM FORCES FOR CONTROL OF JERUSALEM.

BELOW: A CONTEMPORARY DEPICTION OF THE 1936 PALESTINIAN REBELLION AT NABLUS AGAINST THE BRITISH MANDATE. SUCH SCENES WERE ALL TOO COMMON IN THE LATE 1930s.

THE STRUGGLE OVER PALESTINE

Palestine, with its many names and titles—Holy Land, Eretz Israel, Terra Santa, Filistin—was well known in the early years of the nineteenth century, but the name did not signify a defined area. There were no boundaries and there was no demarcated location for Palestine. The area had been ruled by the Ottoman Empire, which conquered the whole Near East in the early sixteenth century. Even then, Palestine was never defined as a separate province or district. The confusion about Palestine's delimitation prevailed among Europeans and Americans as well. Some scholars follow the biblical terms, which describe Palestine as situated from the sea to the desert and from Mt. Lebanon to the southern desert. Others adopted the Ottoman administrative boundaries. The *Encyclopedia Britannica* of 1911 told its readers that "Palestine is an abstract geographical name." Its definition puts Palestine as the area "from the Litany's mouth in the north to Wadi [dry stream] Gaza mouth in the south, the eastern boundary is located on the pilgrimage route from Damascus to Mecca." French publications reflect a slightly different image that extends the southern border to the mouth of Wadi El-Arish. Spanish writers set the line further south. In every publication—American, Russian, Polish, Italian—Palestine delimitation was different.

During the nineteenth century many European powers, including Britain, France, Russia, and Germany, were interested in Palestine but no one would let the others get hold of it. Britain occupied Egypt in 1882, setting its boundary with the Ottoman Empire in 1906 along a line running from Rafa, on the southeastern shore of the Mediterranean Sea, to Taba, on the shore of the Gulf of Aqaba.

THE POST-WORLD WAR I PERIOD

The cultural struggle was transformed into political struggle during World War I. Britain, which fought Turkey in the Near East, looked for allies. The Arabs joined Britain, which promised them an independent country in the Near East, but excluded Palestine from that promise. Later on, in 1916, Britain and France signed the Sykes–Picot agreement in which Britain was given the Haifa Bay area, France was given the northern part of Palestine, while the rest of the Holy Land was to be ruled by Britain, France, Russia, and Italy through Muslim Arab representatives. In November 1917 Britain promised the Jewish Zionist Organization assistance in establishing a Jewish national home in Palestine. All these promises had to be fulfilled when the War was over, after the conquest of Palestine by the British in 1917–18.

The League of Nations allocated Britain the Mandate to govern Palestine in order to establish a Jewish national homeland there. Britain ruled Palestine between 1918 and 1948 but never succeeded in fulfilling its promises to the Jews, as the Palestinian Arabs refused to accept any kind of Jewish regime in Palestine. During the 30 years of British rule, many violent attacks were conducted by the Arabs against the Jews and the British, especially in 1920, 1921, 1929, and during the Arab revolt between 1936 and 1939. In 1937, a British royal commission suggested the establishment of two states in Palestine, a Jewish one and an Arab one, leaving the holy cities of Jerusalem and Bethlehem and a corridor to the Mediterranean Sea in British hands. The Arabs refused to accept the proposal and Britain ruled Palestine for the next 10 years. In 1947 Britain gave back the Mandate over Palestine to the United Nations. In November 1947 the United Nations General Assembly accepted Resolution 184 in which

Palestine was divided between the Jews and the Arabs, leaving Jerusalem and Bethlehem under a separate international regime.

LEFT: YASSER ARAFAT (ABU AMMAR), THE EGYPTIAN-BORN CO-FOUNDER AND LEADER OF THE PALESTINE LIBERATION ORGANIZATION FROM 1969 UNTIL HIS DEATH IN 2004.

JEWISH INDEPENDENCE

The Arabs again refused to accept that resolution and began to conduct a war against the Jews in Palestine. In May 1948 the British left Palestine and the Jews declared their independence at the same time. The State of Israel was born, but no Arab State of Palestine was born by its side. The Arab countries, which surrounded Israel, conducted a war against it. The War of 1948 ended in the spring of 1949 as Israel signed armistice agreements with Egypt, Jordan, Lebanon, and Syria. By these agreements the so-called "Green Line" was established, giving Egypt the Gaza Strip. Jordan got hold of half of the city of Jerusalem with the Old City and the Christian holy site of the Mount of Olives, which in 1950 it named the "West Bank," while Israel got the Christian holy sites in the Galilee area, including Nazareth.

In 1967, alarmed by the Egyptian threat, Israel fought against Egypt and Syria, and some elements of the Jordanian army, occupying the Sinai Peninsula, the West Bank, the Gaza Strip, and the Golan Heights. In 1973 Syria and Egypt tried to recover their losses in another war but failed to do it.

A SHAKY PEACE

The Palestinian Arabs, who up until 1967 were under the occupation of Jordan and Egypt, were united by the Israeli conquest of the whole area of Palestine. They had established the Palestine Liberation Organization (PLO) and started a guerrilla war against Israel, demanding the establishment of a Palestinian state in the West Bank and Gaza. In 1979, Israel signed a peace agreement with Egypt, giving back the Sinai Peninsula to Egypt but still holding the Gaza Strip. In 1993, after several rounds of fighting, Israel and the Palestinian authority signed the Oslo Agreement in which the Palestinians gained some autonomy. In 1994 Israel signed a peace agreement with Jordan but talks in 2000, which were aimed at bringing peace between Syria and Israel, failed. The Palestinians, who were not satisfied with the progress of their autonomy, once again raised an "Intifada" against Israel, using suicide bombings in Israeli cities.

Israel withdrew from the Gaza Strip in 2005, and a free election, which was held in January 2006, gave the majority to the Hamas Movement, over the Palestinian Authority. The struggle still continues.

BELOW: A DIVIDING WALL, MADE OF CONCRETE SLABS, IN THE PALESTINIAN VILLAGE OF ABU-DIS. MANY ISRAELIS AND PALESTINIANS AGREE THAT THE WALL CAUSES MORE PROBLEMS THAN IT SOLVES.

ABOVE: A CLAY CUNEIFORM TABLET FROM THE PALACE AT UR, CONTAINING LEGAL TEXT. CUNEIFORM TABLETS RECORDED IMPORTANT INFORMATION ON RELIGION, GOVERNMENT, AND BUSINESS.

MESOPOTAMIA

With its towering ziggurats and elaborate art, Mesopotamia was one of the foremost civilizations of the ancient world. The first people to develop a writing system, the ancient Mesopotamians were highly sophisticated architects, engineers, astronomers, artists, writers, and scientists. For more than 4,000 years, their kings ruled the region now known as Iraq. Yet after its conquest by the Persians in 539 B.C.E., Mesopotamia gradually disappeared beneath the sands of Iraq, remembered only through biblical accounts, until rediscovered by archaeologists in the nineteenth century.

Mesopotamia is actually a Greek word meaning "the land between two rivers," probably referring to the Tigris and Euphrates. Mesopotamia was situated within the borders of modern Iraq, but at various times, expanded beyond. The people of this area never thought of themselves as Mesopotamians; the region was a melting pot for diverse groups of people, with different cultures and traditions. Yet these groups were united in their adaptations to the environment of southern Iraq (bounded on the east by the Zagros Mountains and on the west by the Arabian Desert), and their utilization of a common writing system called cuneiform.

RIGHT: A STONE RELIEF OF THE MESOPOTAMIAN HERO GILGAMESH, OR THE LION SPIRIT, FROM THE PALACE OF SARGON II (721–705 B.C.E.) IN KHORSABAD, IRAQ.

Geographically, the north is substantially different from the south. Most of the southern region is an alluvial plain, dry other than where the rivers run. The extreme south used to be marshy and wet, filled with reeds and lakes, until the 1980s when Saddam Hussein drained the area. The north is mostly steppe land, well suited for shepherding. The north receives significantly more rainfall, allowing agriculture without extensive irrigation projects. This geographic difference mirrors a cultural contrast and through most of Mesopotamian history, the north and south were politically distinct.

THE FIRST CITIES

Mesopotamia is often credited with having the first cities in human history. Although this is technically not true (the first true cities actually appear in the Levant, in modern Turkey, Syria, and Israel), it is probably safe to say that Mesopotamia was the first civilization dominated by urban environments. The earliest cities were centers of a variety of activities; living in close proximity to others allowed people to develop specialized skills. Instead of farming to acquire food, an urban dweller could craft metal objects or pottery and trade them with somebody who grew crops or kept animals. The houses were made of mud brick and were small, varying between 328 to 1970 sq ft (100 to 600 sq m). When excavated, most of the houses had very few goods left within them. At the center of city life was the temple, usually much larger and more ornately furnished than the houses of everyday people. Surrounding the cities were protective walls, called fortifications, that kept invaders out and limited the ability of people (especially slaves) to leave without being noticed.

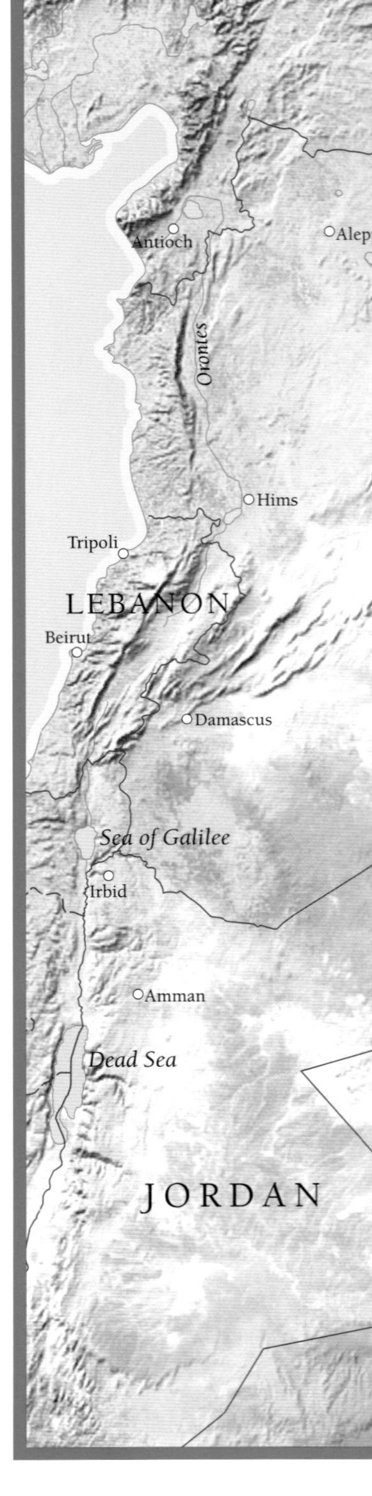

THE EPIC OF GILGAMESH

Perhaps the best-known cultural achievement of the ancient Mesopotamians is the Epic of Gilgamesh. Preserved in a number of versions and traditions, the epic tells the story of Gilgamesh, the King of Uruk (biblical Erech), who is so devastated by the death of his friend Enkidu that he goes on a quest to find the secret of immortality. Failing in this, he realizes that even though he will die, he can still live on in people's memories.

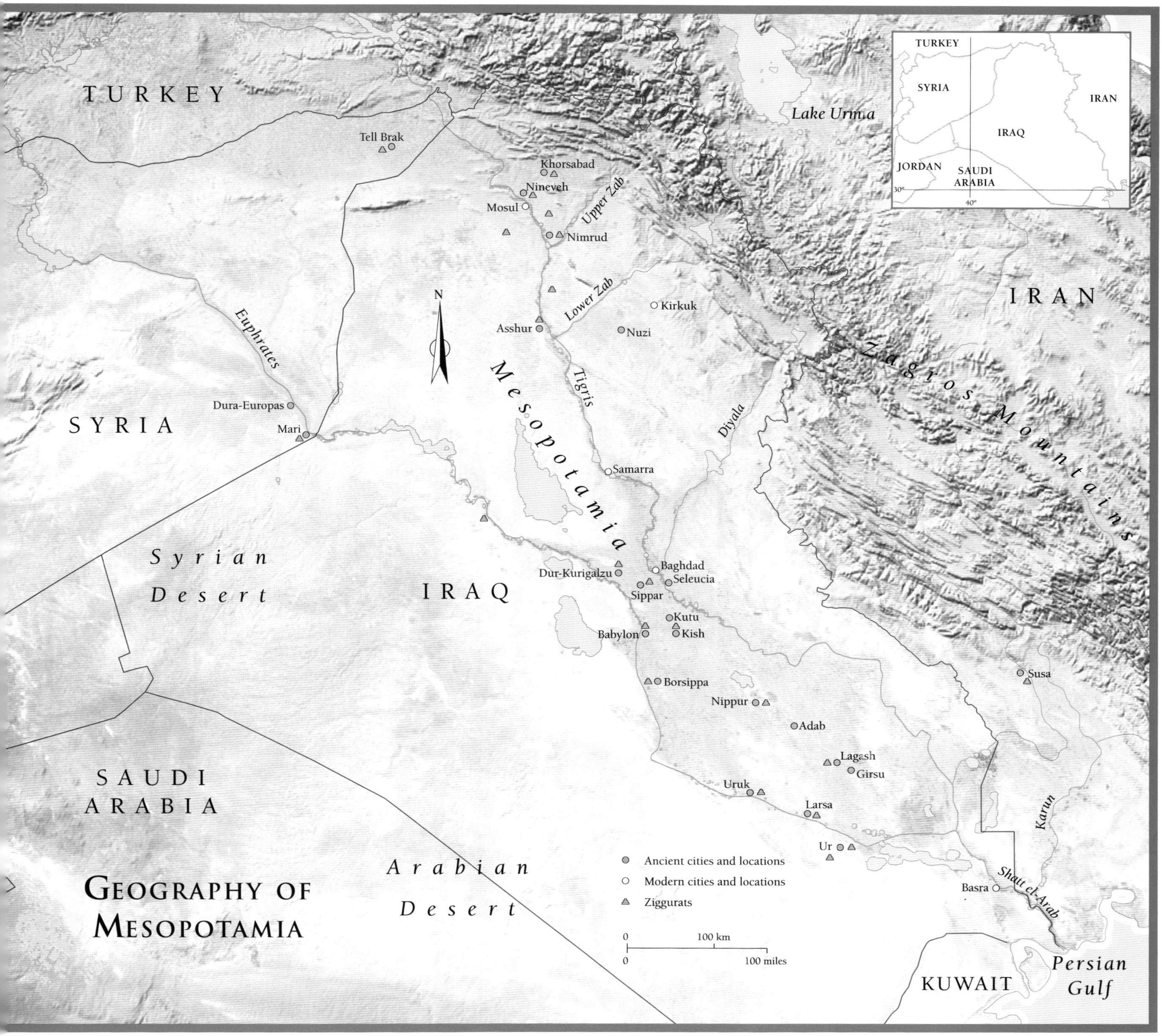

Geography of Mesopotamia

- Ancient cities and locations
- Modern cities and locations
- Ziggurats

0 100 km
0 100 miles

Ziggurats

From about 2100 B.C.E. and well through the Persian Period, the skylines of the major Mesopotamian cities were dominated by stepped, pyramid shaped structures known as ziggurats. The interior of ziggurats were solid mud brick; the exterior usually consisted of glazed mud bricks and architectural flourishes. The exact layout of each ziggurat differed as did the function. The ziggurat was primarily a religious structure, sometimes incorporated into a larger temple complex, and usually containing smaller temples on its exterior platforms. The Greek historian Herodotus claimed that ziggurats were astronomical observatories. While such activities may have taken place, the primary role of the ziggurat was as a monument to the god to whom it was dedicated.

THE DEAD SEA AND OTHER IMPORTANT BODIES OF WATER IN THE REGION

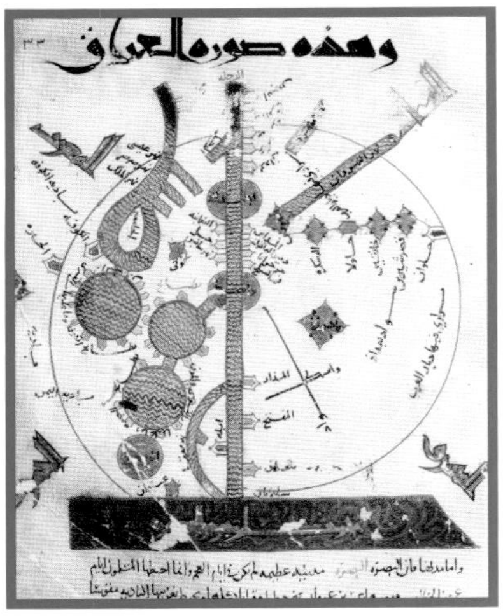

RIGHT: THIS ELEVENTH-CENTURY MAP, PROBABLY COPIED FROM A TENTH CENTURY ATLAS COMPILED BY ARAB SCHOLAR AND GEOGRAPHER AL-ISTAKHRI, SHOWS THE COURSE OF THE TIGRIS RIVER.

Water sources are scarce in the Near East, so much so that *National Geographic* has suggested that the next war in the Middle East will not be over oil, but rather water. Through most of the region, inhabitants are extremely dependent on rain and dew for water, and from the earliest times, technology has been used to assist in the gathering of moisture. Most of southern Mesopotamia falls under the isohyet (a meteorological marker that measures where enough rain falls annually to support agriculture), so there, human manipulation of water sources is more crucial. Israel, Syria, and Lebanon depend on brooks (wadis) that run from the highlands into the Mediterranean Sea or Jordan River. In some parts of Jordan, water is delivered to outlying villages in tanks pulled by tractors, because in the summer, many of the riverbeds dry out completely.

THE DEAD SEA

One of the most unique experiences one can have is to visit the Dead Sea, located in the Rift Valley (the deepest natural fissure in the world). Traveling from Jerusalem to the Dead Sea, the climate becomes more and more inhospitable; the temperature there becomes extremely hot, and minimal vegetation is evident. Since this is the lowest point on earth, subtle changes in pressure are apparent. The Dead Sea is the most mineral-laden body of water on earth and the huge salt content makes it quite impossible to sink! Most tourists to the Dead Sea have a photograph taken of them lying in the water, floating, reading a book or relaxing. Any open wounds burn from the salt, but are found remarkably cured after getting out of the water. The Dead Sea is too salty to sustain life, but the curative powers of the water have been recognized since antiquity.

THE JORDAN RIVER

Running into the Dead Sea from the north, and also part of the Rift Valley, the Jordan River is a natural boundary between modern Israel and Jordan. It is approximately 198 miles (320 km) long, and incorporates the Sea of Galilee, Lake Hula, and the Yarmuk River system, as well as many other smaller tributary systems. It originates at the junction of four streams in the Hula Plain and runs continuously south from there. Modern exploitation of the Jordan (and its associated tributaries) has meant that in recent years the amount of water carried has significantly decreased. In parts, the river looks more like a stream. Yet, in other sections, especially near the Sea of Galilee, the river remains majestic and impressive.

SEA OF GALILEE

One of the most important Christian holy sites, the Sea of Galilee (also known as Lake Tiberius, Lake Kinneret, and the Sea of Gennesaret) is located in the north of Israel, on the Jordan River. The sea is about 103 sq miles (166 sq km) in size, and is located in one of the most beautiful places in the Near East. The sea is not large at all—its deepest point is only about 150 feet (46 m). Yet in antiquity, a busy fishing industry thrived here, exploiting mostly sardines, barbels, and musht (better known as St. Peter's fish).

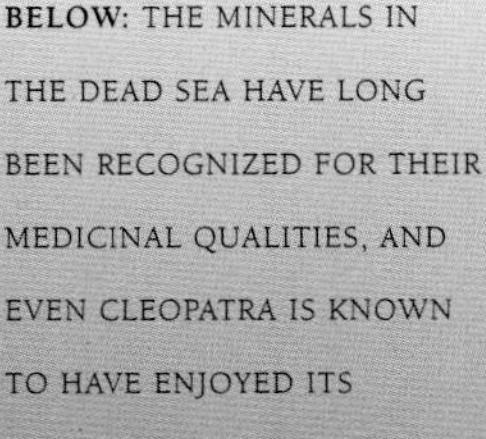

BELOW: THE MINERALS IN THE DEAD SEA HAVE LONG BEEN RECOGNIZED FOR THEIR MEDICINAL QUALITIES, AND EVEN CLEOPATRA IS KNOWN TO HAVE ENJOYED ITS THERAPEUTIC WATERS.

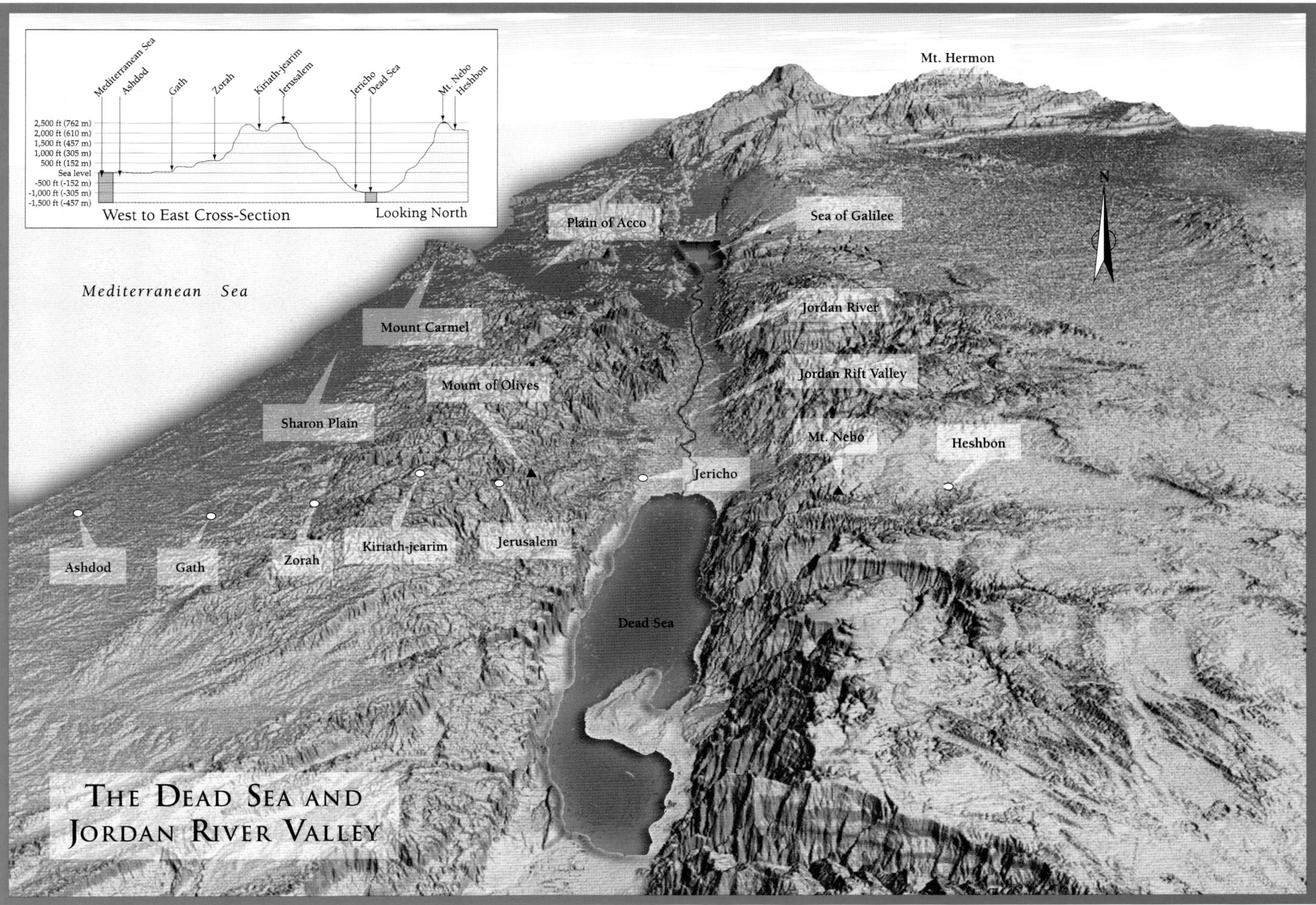

LAKE HULA

The northernmost lake on the Jordan River is Lake Hula. Located in the Hula Valley, the whole region is swampy and in antiquity the terrain was difficult to cross. The decaying vegetation surrounding the lake has gradually reduced its size over the centuries. More extreme alterations came in the 1950s when the lake was drained, transforming the landscape from what it would have been like in biblical times and killing off numerous local species. In recent times it has been artificially refilled, and restocked with fish.

OTHER RIVERS IN MODERN ISRAEL

A long, central mountain plain divides Israel in half. To the west of this range lie the foothills (the Shephelah) that lead down into a coastal plain. Rivers that originate in the mountains cut the coastal plain longitudinally, dividing Israel into natural subsections. Between these rivers are very productive valleys, making these regions the "breadbasket" of Israel, and traditionally the most heavily populated area.

THE TIGRIS AND EUPHRATES

The Tigris and Euphrates Rivers are the defining boundaries of Mesopotamian civilization and the sources of water that make life possible in the brutal environment of Iraq. What is truly shocking for visitors is how painfully ice cold the water is compared with the hot temperatures of the surrounding area. Both rivers originate in Turkey. The Euphrates, about 1,727 miles (2,780 km) long, runs from Lake Van through Turkey, Syria, and Iraq. The much shorter Tigris (1,211 miles [1,950 km] long) begins near Mt. Ararat and runs straight down through Iraq. While the Euphrates is predictable and easily navigable, the Tigris is wild and difficult to manage.

The rivers, as found today, would not be recognizable to the ancient Mesopotamians. The rivers seem to have moved slightly (mostly due to natural causes), since many archaeological sites are significantly farther away from water sources than logic would suggest. Now the Tigris and Euphrates meet close to Baghdad, and join together into the Shatt-'al-Arab River before emptying into the Persian Gulf. In ancient times, the two rivers possibly never met, flowing into the Gulf at separate points. A controversial issue is whether or not these two rivers have been gradually pushing the mouth of the Persian Gulf farther and farther away, through the deposition of massive amounts of silt over the years.

ANCIENT BOAT FROM THE SEA OF GALILEE

Visitors to the Sea of Galilee can view a reconstruction of an ancient wooden boat recovered from the northwestern banks of the sea in 1986. Archaeologists carefully removed the remains of a boat from the shore of the sea, after it had been exposed due to dropping sea levels. Made mostly of oak and cedar, the boat has been radiocarbon-dated to the period between 100 B.C.E. and C.E. 70. The boat could have carried up to 15 people, and was likely used as a fishing vessel in New Testament times.

ABOVE: HANNIBAL, THE CARTHAGINIAN GENERAL (247–183 B.C.E.) WHO LED POSSIBLY THE GREATEST MILITARY POWER OF THE TIME, WAS A PHOENICIAN.

PEOPLES AND CULTURES OF THE REGION FROM ANCIENT TIMES TO THE PRESENT

Any casual reader of the Old Testament will be struck by the diversity of ethnic groups that lived in the Near East. Genesis is filled with offhand allusions to these various groups of people, references that ancient readers would have had no difficulty in understanding. Modern readers have a more difficult time with these citations, since most of these peoples have long since disappeared. The people of the Ancient Near East mostly thought about themselves in relation to their tribe or extended family, so genealogical lists were one of the most important ways of keeping track of who was related to whom. The genealogical lists in Genesis may be some of the more challenging sections for modern people to read. Yet these lists contain very important information about who lived where in biblical times. Perhaps the easiest approach to understanding the various groups who lived in the Near East in biblical times is to think in terms of geographic setting.

WEST OF THE JORDAN RIVER

Much of the Old Testament concentrates on the region to the west of the Jordan River. This is the land promised to Abraham by God and the location of the kingdoms of Judah and Israel. As we are told in Joshua, this region was first inhabited by the Canaanites. The Canaanites lived in large cities with extensive defensive walls and elaborate temple complexes. There was no overarching government between the cities, but for a 200-year period (before the Israelites arrived) the whole region was controlled by Egypt. Often in the Bible, Canaanites refer to themselves by whichever city they came from (i.e., the Shechemites), as opposed to calling themselves Canaanites.

After the formation of the states of Israel and Judah, the only remaining vestige of the Canaanite population was in the north, outside Israel's boundaries. At this stage in history, scholars stop using the Hebrew term "Canaanite" to refer to this group and start using the Greek term "Phoenician." The Phoenicians had fairly good relations with Judah, and in fact it was a Phoenician architect, Huram of Tyre (not to be

RIGHT: THE URN TOMB AT PETRA IN JORDAN, BUILT BETWEEN THE THIRD AND FIRST CENTURIES B.C.E. PETRA WAS THE CAPITAL CITY OF THE NABATAEANS, WHO WERE ORIGINALLY DESERT NOMADS.

confused with King Hiram), who is credited with building the Temple of Solomon. The Phoenicians became expert seafarers and some left Asia Minor for North Africa, settling in Carthage. Hannibal, who crossed the Alps to attack Rome, was arguably Carthage's most famous citizen.

Also to the north of the kingdom of Israel were the Aramaean kingdoms, from whom the Aramaic language comes. These were relatively small city-states that were sometimes friend and sometimes foe to Judah and Israel. The book of Kings discusses these groups in passing. Also troublesome for the Israelites were the Philistines, who settled along coastal Israel. Goliath was the most famous member of this group.

EAST OF THE JORDAN RIVER

Biblical traditions describe the people who lived east of the Jordan River as cousins of the Hebrews. As with any large family, relations were often strained, and this history is well reflected in the Old Testament, especially in the book of Kings. The Moabites, Ammonites, and Edomites developed into state-level societies at approximately the same time as the Israelites and spoke languages very similar to Hebrew.

The Moabites are perhaps the best-known people archaeologically. Exploration at the ancient Moabite capital city of Dibon led to the discovery of one of the most important historical texts relating to Old Testament history—the Mesha Stele. Written on behalf of King Mesha of Moab between 849 and 820 B.C.E., the text recounts a conflict with King Omri of Israel, providing interesting extrabiblical evidence about the kingdom of Israel, but from the perspective of the enemy!

One of the most fascinating groups living in the region of modern Jordan during New Testament times was the Nabataeans. The Nabataeans were originally a nomadic people from Arabia who eventually settled into an urban lifestyle. They are best associated with the site of Petra, where their kings carved elaborate tombs into the sides of canyon walls. Petra was an important trading city; there, precious goods from Arabia were brought to be sold to merchants from all over the Near East and Mediterranean.

MESOPOTAMIAN PEOPLE

Within the biblical text are numerous references to different groups of people who lived in Mesopotamia. It can be quite difficult to keep these groups straight, since they all lived in Mesopotamia and all used the cuneiform writing system.

The earliest people in the region were the Sumerians, who lived in southern Mesopotamia in the region known as Sumer. By about 2300 B.C.E. the Sumerians had been conquered by people who spoke a Semitic language, known as Akkadian. From that point on, Mesopotamian civilization is dominated by Semitic-speaking people, and Akkadian becomes the dominant language in Mesopotamia. Politically, however, the region was rarely unified.

To the north were the Assyrians, who destroyed the kingdom of Israel in 722 B.C.E. The Assyrian capital shifted frequently, but always remained within the region between Assur and Nineveh. To the south were the Babylonians whose capital was the city of Babylon, and who, under the leadership of King Nebuchadnezzar II, conquered Jerusalem and destroyed the First Temple in 586 B.C.E.

ABOVE: THIS NINETEENTH-CENTURY C.E. ENGRAVING BASED ON SEVENTH-CENTURY B.C.E. ASSYRIAN RELIEFS SHOWS FOOD AND OTHER SUPPLIES BEING TRANSPORTED BY RIVER AND WAGON.

THE CUNEIFORM WRITING SYSTEM

Cuneiform is not a language, but a writing system used for rendering many languages. No matter which language is being written, the characters used are shaped like wedges (hence the Latin name "cuneiform," which translates as "wedge-shaped"). The wedges are formed when the scribe impresses a clay tablet with a reed stylus. Sumerian was the first language that used the cuneiform script; it was spoken in the southernmost parts of Mesopotamia. Much like modern Japanese, cuneiform included hundreds of symbols that stood for syllables, words, or grammatical markers. Eventually the cumbersome system was abandoned in favor of a writing system that required the memorization of fewer signs—the alphabet.

RIGHT: WHEN ALEXANDER THE GREAT (356–323 B.C.E.) DEFEATED THE PERSIANS IN 331 B.C.E., GREEK BECAME THE DOMINANT LANGUAGE OF THE NEAR EAST.

A SUCCESSION OF CONQUERORS

The Near East is a crossroads for three continents—Europe, Asia, and Africa. This small region, now more commonly referred to as the Middle East, had as much strategic importance in ancient times as it does today. Because of this, the history of the Near East after biblical times is largely a history of successive invasions, with each new invasion bringing new peoples and cultures.

ANCIENT CONQUERORS

In 539 B.C.E., Cyrus the Great, King of Persia and Media (what is today called Iran) conquered the Babylonians, and incorporated most of the Near East into the Persian Empire. The Persians were tolerant of foreign religions and customs, and unlike the Babylonians, allowed the Jews to return to Israel and rebuild the Temple that had been destroyed (as discussed in the books of Ezra and Nehemiah). Under the Persians, the Aramaic language became the dominant language of the Near East, even though this was not the native Persian tongue.

The Persians held power over most of the Near East for around 200 years, but were eventually defeated by Alexander the Great and his Macedonian Army in 331 B.C.E. Life in the Near East altered drastically after Alexander's conquest. Greek culture (referred to as Hellenistic in this period) was brought to the region. Greek was the language of government and society, although Aramaic and Hebrew were preserved as religious and local languages. After Alexander's death in 323 B.C.E., the Near East was divided up among a number of families, including the Ptolemies (whose most famous member was Cleopatra VII) and the Seleucids.

Eventually the Near East was incorporated into the Roman Empire. The Romans were welcomed to varying degrees—from open arms to armed revolt. The military and economic might of Rome was strong, and they were able to establish a relatively stable regime within the region. This is the world into which Jesus was born and in which the New Testament was written. While Latin was the Roman language of governance, Greek remained the language of commerce, literature, and probably everyday speech. Cities were restructured along Roman lines—so much so that some of the best Roman sites tourists can visit are located in Israel and Jordan!

The Romans held sway over the Near East for centuries, and much of the region's history is tied directly to Rome's. Christianity was eventually transformed from a persecuted, fringe religion to the official state religion of Rome. With that, most of the residents of the Near East became officially Christians, although there were some exceptions. Eventually, Roman power began to fragment, and in C.E. 455, the Roman Empire was permanently split into two halves, with the eastern half (incorporating the Near East) ruled from Constantinople (modern Istanbul). This Greek-speaking, Christian Empire located in the Near East is known as the Byzantine Empire.

MEDIEVAL CONQUERORS

In C.E. 634, the followers of a new religion, Islam, set out from Medina to conquer the Near East. By 640, only Anatolia remained in Byzantine Christian hands. The rest of the region had fallen to the Arab conquerors and Islam had become the dominant religion in the land. While unable to make significant gains in Anatolia or on the other side of Persia, the Islamic Near East still became the cultural center of the world, far eclipsing Europe in terms of literature, science, and wealth.

In the eleventh century, Arab control of the Near East came to an end when a Muslim group from Central Asia, the Seljuk Turks, invaded. The Turks successfully conquered all of the Near East, including Byzantine-held lands. These Turks did not remain unchallenged for control of the region. Christian forces briefly regained parts of the Holy Land in the Crusades, followed by a short-lived resurgence of Arab forces from Egypt, led by Saladin. The Mongols sacked Baghdad in 1258, weakening the region even further, and the Turkish Empire broke into smaller political groups. This chaotic state of affairs was brought to an end in 1453 when one of these groups, the Ottoman Turks, captured Constantinople. For the next 400 years, the Ottoman Empire would provide stability to the region and lurk as an ever-present danger to the neighboring Christian world.

MODERN CONQUERORS

The Ottoman Empire began to show signs of weakness in the nineteenth century. After the Napoleonic conquest of Egypt at the turn of the century, increasingly indebted to European nations, it became a target of colonial aspirations in Europe. In 1882, the British formally occupied Egypt and the French moved into Syria and Lebanon. The collapse of the Ottoman Empire came at the end of World War I. Having sided with Germany, the vestiges of the once great empire were partitioned between France and Britain and became mandate countries of these nations. Throughout the 1920s and the 1930s the former Ottoman nations became independent and the Middle East of today became recognizable.

THE PEOPLE OF MODERN IRAQ

As in ancient times, modern Iraq is populated by diverse groups of people, although almost all are Muslim. The dominant population in Iraq is Arab, which makes up somewhere between 70 percent and 80 percent of the population. There is significant tension among the various Arab groups. Shi'a are the largest Muslim group (about 60 percent), but Sunni Muslims are a close second (about 30–35 percent). The division of Islam into these groups dates to a political conflict in C.E. 632, and since then these two groups have developed separately with periods of intense conflict. Another Arab group is the so-called "Swamp Arabs," who lived in the southern marshes of Iraq until Saddam Hussein allegedly engaged in genocide, killing most of that population in the 1980s. Kurds are a non-Arab group who make up 15–20 percent of the population of Iraq. They are a seminomadic people who live in the mountain ranges of Iraq, Iran, and Turkey. Other groups, like Turkomans, make up a substantially smaller proportion of the population.

OPPOSITE: CRUSADERS ON THE WAY TO THE HOLY LAND IN C.E. 1177, WHEN KING BALDWIN IV OF JERUSALEM WON CONTROL OF THE WHOLE PALESTINIAN COAST, IN A PAINTING BY FRENCH ARTIST CHARLES-PHILIPPE LARIVIERE.

ABOVE: *LEADING THE FLOCK TO PASTURE* BY FREDERICK GOODALL DEPICTS A BEDOUIN PASTORALIST. BEDOUINS MOVED AROUND THE COUNTRYSIDE IN RESPONSE TO THE CHANGING SEASONS.

ECONOMY AND AGRICULTURE FROM ANCIENT TIMES TO THE MODERN ERA

Most residents of the Ancient Near East lived from hand to mouth, barely making ends meet with their small agricultural yields and part-time craft production. While the rich were exceptionally rich, the poor were exceptionally poor. There would have been no middle class and minimal opportunity for social mobility. Almost everyone would have engaged in some type of agriculture, and many small-scale farmers would have been saddled with tremendous debt. In fact, many laws set forth in the Old Testament are intended as remedies for the overwhelming debts that farmers living in biblical times must have accrued.

AGRICULTURE

Agriculture varied from region to region in the Near East, depending on the types of soil and amounts of precipitation. In southern Mesopotamia, extensive irrigation projects were necessary to support agriculture. Local people constructed dams and canals from the Euphrates (and less frequently the Tigris) to water their fields. This irrigation process heavily salinated the land, eventually making it useless. Crops that could be planted had to be resistant to salt, making barley the most common crop in Mesopotamia.

In Israel, farming was much easier and much more varied. Since annual rainfall levels were sufficient for non-irrigation farming, much less organization was required. The richness of the land allowed for a huge variety of crops: cereals, fruits, and vegetables of all sorts were produced here. From an ancient perspective, and compared with the relative aridity of the rest of the Near East, this truly was a land flowing with milk and honey.

Two of the major crops in the Near East were grapes and olives. While some of the yield would have been eaten raw, most of these crops would have been transformed into wine and olive oil. Since the production of wine and olive oil involved the use of expensive equipment, it is likely that neighborhoods shared these tools and communally produced these goods. Wine would have been very sweet, and while the grapes would have been fermented, the alcohol content would have been quite low. Wine was the major drink, other than water, and a major source of income for some farmers. Olive oil was used in food preparation and as lamp fuel. Its

THE GEZER CALENDAR

One of the earliest Hebrew inscriptions is a limestone palette, discovered at the site of Gezer. The calendar consists of seven lines, each line describing different agricultural jobs for each month of the year. Based on this, historians have been able to reconstruct the agricultural year in ancient Israel. An Israelite farmer would farm the whole year round, working with different types of crops, based on seasonal weather patterns.

STONE, MINERAL, AND OTHER RESOURCES

Mesopotamia was almost completely bereft of resources in ancient times. The land lacked stone, wood, and mineral resources, forcing the Mesopotamians to look to other parts of the Near East—mostly Persia and Anatolia—to gain these resources. Both these regions had rich deposits of stone, and ancient texts detail the conveyance of large amounts of stone across the Zagros Mountains into Mesopotamia proper.

BELOW: METALWORK FIT FOR A KING. THIS ELABORATE SUMERIAN GAMES BOARD WAS RECOVERED FROM THE ROYAL CEMETERY AT UR IN MESOPOTAMIA, AND IS DATED TO C. 2250 B.C.E.

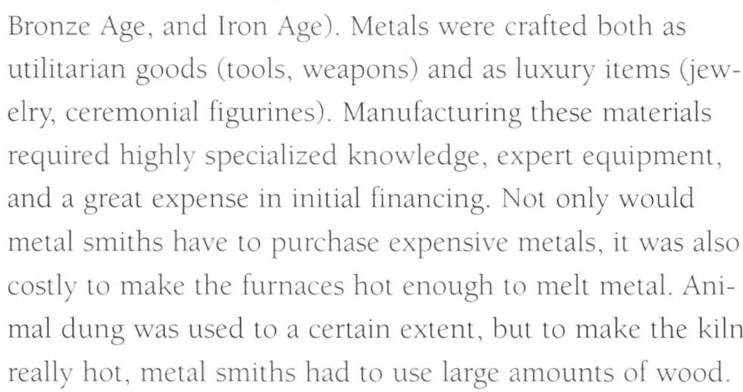

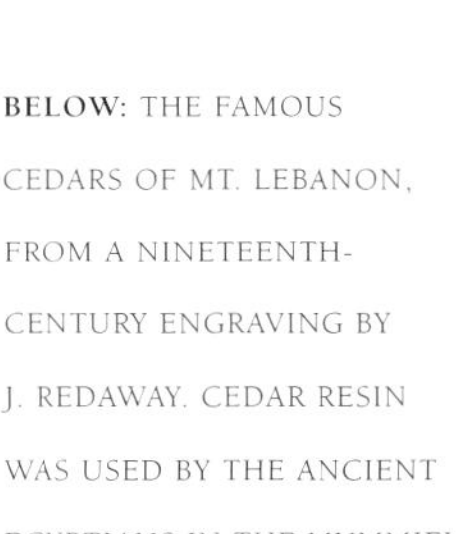

One of the most important industries in the Near East was metallurgy. It was so prominent, in fact, that archaeologists use types of metals as the basis for their understanding of the chronology of the region (i.e., Copper Age, Bronze Age, and Iron Age). Metals were crafted both as utilitarian goods (tools, weapons) and as luxury items (jewelry, ceremonial figurines). Manufacturing these materials required highly specialized knowledge, expert equipment, and a great expense in initial financing. Not only would metal smiths have to purchase expensive metals, it was also costly to make the furnaces hot enough to melt metal. Animal dung was used to a certain extent, but to make the kiln really hot, metal smiths had to use large amounts of wood.

Syro–Palestine was also wealthy in mineral resources, and copper was particularly prominent in the southern regions. Starting around 3000 B.C.E., Egyptian mining expeditions in what would later become southern Israel are evident. The Old Testament hints that Solomon may also have exploited the copper resources in this region.

Due to the lack of forests in Mesopotamia and Egypt, the cedars of Lebanon were highly regarded. Foresters in what are now Syria and Lebanon traded timber and tree products for international goods. Records survive of Egyptian maritime expeditions to the region to gain much-needed wood.

BELOW: THE FAMOUS CEDARS OF MT. LEBANON, FROM A NINETEENTH-CENTURY ENGRAVING BY J. REDAWAY. CEDAR RESIN WAS USED BY THE ANCIENT EGYPTIANS IN THE MUMMIFICATION PROCESS.

use as fuel made it a necessary commodity for all people and it was probably a major expense for most families.

PASTORALISM

The other major subsistence strategy in the Near East was animal husbandry or pastoralism, an industry still apparent in modern settings. The hills of Israel provide ample pasture land for large flocks of sheep and goats, which would have been primarily utilized as sources of wool and milk (and only occasionally as a source of meat). Goat's milk was used extensively, usually processed into a form of yoghurt, but sometimes consumed directly as milk or made into cheese.

Pastoralists would only spend a small portion of the year with their community. For the rest of the time, they would herd their flocks to various pastures dotted around the countryside. Modern-day Bedouin still practice pastoralism much in the same way as their ancestors did in antiquity. They spend the wetter months of the year in the desert fringes with their flocks. As the vegetation is consumed by the grazing animals and scorched by the changing seasons, these nomadic people move their flocks into the less extreme environments, making the most of any available resources.

RIGHT: POTTERY, SUCH AS THIS COLORED TERRACOTTA VESSEL FROM JERICHO, DATED 3000–2100 B.C.E., IS AN IMPORTANT SOURCE OF INFORMATION FOR HISTORIANS AND ARCHAEOLOGISTS.

ENVIRONMENTAL CONSTRAINTS AND PROSPECTS

What is truly striking to visitors of the Middle East is the mixture of ancient and modern economic activities. Your tour bus may have to yield for Bedouin driving sheep across the road. Certainly you will see donkeys pulling carts in urban regions of the Near East. Air-conditioned skyscrapers dominate the urban landscape, yet mud-brick complexes are common in rural areas, not much different from those present thousands of years ago. The very wealthy live alongside the extremely impoverished. Although oil has made many parts of the Near East relatively wealthy, much of this wealth has not trickled down, and unemployment remains one of the major socio-economic problems in many areas of the Near East.

MUD: AN ENDLESSLY RENEWABLE RESOURCE

From ancient times to the present, mud has been the most important economic resource in the Near East. Especially in Mesopotamia, where stone and timber are rare, most buildings are constructed of mud brick. Builders collect wet clay, usually mixing it with some sort of temper (chaff, reeds, manure) to strengthen the material. The mud is shaped with wooden brick molds and then left to bake in the hot, Near Eastern sun. After the bricks have dried, they are used in construction (often without any sort of mortar). In some ways this is a difficult material to build homes from—it is susceptible to the ravages of the weather (especially rain), does not hold up well in natural disasters, and

BELOW: MUD BRICKS DRYING IN THE SUN. ANCIENT METHODS OF MAKING MUD BRICKS HAVE CHANGED LITTLE OVER THE CENTURIES, AND THEY ARE STILL IN USE IN THE NEAR EAST.

is easily destroyed by fire or earthquakes. However, mud brick is well suited to the climate. It keeps the house cool and dark during the day, but retains heat in the cold desert nights. In many parts of the Near East, mud brick is still commonly used because of its eminent suitability for the temperature and the relatively inexpensive nature of this material.

The most common find in any archaeological excavation is pottery, a commodity made primarily of clay. The frequency of ceramic finds is due to the fact that pottery preserves well in the archaeological record—a pot can be smashed, but its constituent materials do not break down. Because of this, archaeologists commonly use ceramics to date sites. An archaeologist can easily tell the difference between Islamic, Roman, and Israelite pottery. In fact, it is usually possible to date a site to within roughly 50 years based on the types of pottery found. The frequency of pottery in the archaeological record also attests to the importance of ceramics in Near Eastern cultures. Used as utensils, for storage, for transport, and for ritual purposes, ceramics are ubiquitous with Near Eastern economy.

DEFORESTATION AND LAND DEGRADATION

Human mismanagement of the environment of the Near East has led to severe deforestation, land degradation, and desertification in the region. The modern conditions of the environment in the region are very different from the conditions in which biblical peoples would have lived. Overuse of farm land and overexploitation of forests, without giving sufficient mind to replacing and managing these resources, have led to a situation where forests are permanently destroyed and farm land can only be reclaimed with extreme human intervention. When forests are cut down too quickly and land is overgrazed or overfarmed, natural processes of wind and water erosion are heightened. Mixed with the variability of rainfall and the frequency of droughts, a land flowing with milk and honey can be transformed into a desert wasteland in a matter of centuries.

Agriculture in the Near East is no longer possible without intense water and soil management. The efforts of modern Israeli governments have been quite successful, and now Israel has a thriving agricultural economy—so much so that many of the fruits and vegetables eaten in Europe actually come from Israel. Grain, however, is still very difficult to cultivate in Israel, and must be imported. Other countries in the region have not been so successful. Perhaps Iraq is in the most difficult situation, where farming is no longer a feasible industry. Before the United Nations trade embargoes in the 1990s, Iraq imported more than 70 percent of its agricultural goods. The sanctions limited this, and the Iraqi people were forced to turn to those crops that can still be grown in the region—such as dates, grapes, and cereals (in only some locations). Unfortunately, this is insufficient for the large population, so agricultural reform will be a key challenge for post-Saddam Hussein Iraq to grapple with.

OIL

Perhaps the most important economic event in Near Eastern history was the realization that petroleum is a dependable fuel resource and the concomitant realization that the Near East has one of the largest, most easily accessible reserves of this fuel. For the first time, Iraq (and its neighbors) had a local natural resource that was desired elsewhere. Crude oil exploitation began first in Persia, but spread in earnest to the Middle East in the 1930s. Western oil companies were the first to tap these reserves and the first to make huge profits from them. Local elites also profited from this newfound wealth, with tribal leaders and political leaders becoming the main beneficiaries. A huge disparity in wealth developed between those who were involved in the petroleum industry and those who were not. The local elites who benefited from this wealth had a stake in preserving the status quo, and many of the social problems in the Middle East region can be traced back to this fundamental divide between the haves and the have-nots. In terms of global politics, the region has now become a location of strategic importance, not just as a crossroads of three continents but because of its position in world economic development.

ABOVE: POOR FARMING METHODS AND INCREASING PRESSURE ON SURROUNDING LANDS BY PEOPLE AND LIVESTOCK CAN RESULT IN DESERTIFICATION, MAKING AGRICULTURE DIFFICULT.

BELOW: THE COUNTRIES OF THE PERSIAN GULF CONTAIN APPROXIMATELY TWO-THIRDS OF THE WORLD'S OIL RESERVES. IRAQ ALONE PRODUCES ABOUT 10 PERCENT OF THE WORLD'S OIL.

ABOVE: JERUSALEM'S CHURCH OF THE HOLY SEPULCHRE SITS ON THE HILL OF CALVARY, OR GOLGOTHA, THE PLACE WHERE JESUS DIED AND WAS REPORTEDLY BURIED.

RIGHT: THE FAMILY TOMB OF JOSEPH OF ARIMATHEA IN THE CHURCH OF THE HOLY SEPULCHRE, JERUSALEM. ACCORDING TO TRADITION, IT WAS HERE THAT JESUS' BODY WAS LAID TO REST.

ARCHAEOLOGY AND THE BIBLE IN THE REGION: IMPORTANT SITES FOR THE STUDY OF BIBLICAL TIMES

Archaeology has been extremely productive in enhancing our knowledge of the world of the Bible and the general Near Eastern context of the Bible. At times, archaeology has revealed structures and cities that are directly mentioned in the Bible. More often, however, archaeology's application to biblical studies is most informative about daily life in biblical times, information that is not readily available from the study of the biblical texts alone.

JERUSALEM

As Jerusalem has been continuously occupied since ancient times, the archaeological remains from the city have been relatively unexplored (it is quite difficult for archaeologists to convince a homeowner to give up their house for archaeological research!). Even more problematic is the fact that Jerusalem is home to sites that are holy to Judaism, Christianity, and Islam. Scholars assume that the most ancient areas of Jerusalem are located beneath these holy sites, making archaeological investigation impossible. It is very unlikely, for example, that scholars will ever find Solomon's Temple, since its remains are likely buried underneath the remains of the Second Temple (the Western Wall) and the Muslim holy site known as the Dome of the Rock.

Yet, there have been some significant finds within the city of Jerusalem that date to biblical times. Archaeologist Kathleen Kenyon, in excavations at the City of David (which is located on a narrow ridge immediately south of Jerusalem's Old City), uncovered what may have been the fortification walls for the city at the time of the United Monarchy and a stepped stone structure that many identify with the biblical Millo. More substantial remains are the intricate water systems, dating to the period of the Divided Monarchy, which supplied the city of Jerusalem with fresh running water. Visitors to Jerusalem can walk through Hezekiah's Tunnel, where an inscription on how the tunnel was constructed was discovered. This tunnel leads from the Gihon Spring outside of the City of David to a pool within the walls, which allowed residents of ancient Jerusalem easy access to water. Recently, archaeologists working in Jerusalem have announced the discovery of David's Palace. This material has not yet been published and it remains to be seen whether or not the excavated structure has been rightly identified with King David.

'AIN DARA AND TELL TA'YINAT

In 1 Kings 5, we are told that King Solomon commissioned a Phoenician architect to design and construct the Temple in Jerusalem. So while it may be impossible to excavate the Temple in Jerusalem, archaeologists have looked to Syria and Lebanon for examples of other ancient temples that were built by Phoenician craftsmen, along the same lines as Solomon's Temple. This has been successful—temples that have layouts similar to the Temple layout described in 1 Kings 6 have been found in this region, at the sites of Tell Ta'yinat and 'Ain Dara. While both temples were probably built for the worship of Phoenician gods, as opposed to the God of Israel and Judah, excavations confirm that the Jerusalem Temple was built according to Phoenician standards.

The temple at 'Ain Dara is the most spectacular. Probably larger than the Jerusalem Temple, it has an otherwise nearly identical layout—a tripartite structure with a rear area isolated like the Holy of Holies in Solomon's Temple. At the entrance are two monumental columns, seemingly similar to the two monumental columns that flanked the entrance to the Jerusalem Temple, known in scripture as Joachin and Boaz (1 Kings 7:19). Where it differs from Solomon's Temple is in the gigantic footprints (each about 3 ft [1 m] long) carved directly into the floor of the temple. Probably meant to represent the Phoenician deity, such carvings would have been considered blasphemous to the ancient Israelites so would not have been included in Solomon's Temple. The layout of the temple at Tell Ta'yinat is similar to that at 'Ain Dara, but is not nearly as well preserved. It, however, was built right next to a palace, like Solomon's Temple was.

QUMRAN

Visitors to the Dead Sea are well served to stop and visit the Roman Period site of Qumran. Most scholars presume that this isolated desert site was the home of the Dead Sea Scrolls community, since the scrolls were found in caves nearby and date to roughly the same period. Most of the buildings at Qumran were constructed of rough-hewn stone, and are in relatively good condition, so the visitor can stroll through the ancient buildings and get a feeling for the lifestyle of the people who lived there. Given its isolated location, it is hardly surprising that the community was almost completely self-sufficient. An extensive aqueduct and water-management system is quite undamaged, as are workshops and food processing areas. One room designated the "scriptorium" by the excavator, Father Roland De Vaux, contained the remains of a burnt map, two tables, and two inkwells. While there is no evidence that the Dead Sea Scrolls were written in this room, it did contain materials typically associated with scribal activity. Other theories about the identity of Qumran and the Qumran community have been put forth—that it was a Roman fort or a Roman villa, for example. Most scholars, however, believe that this was the location of the Essene community mentioned in the New Testament, the authors of the Dead Sea Scrolls.

UR OF THE CHALDEES

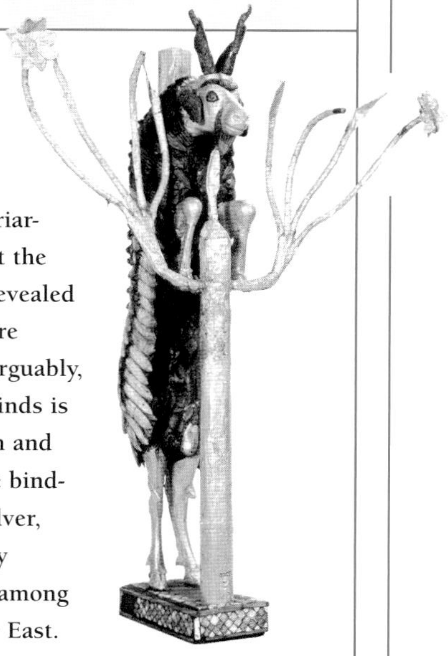

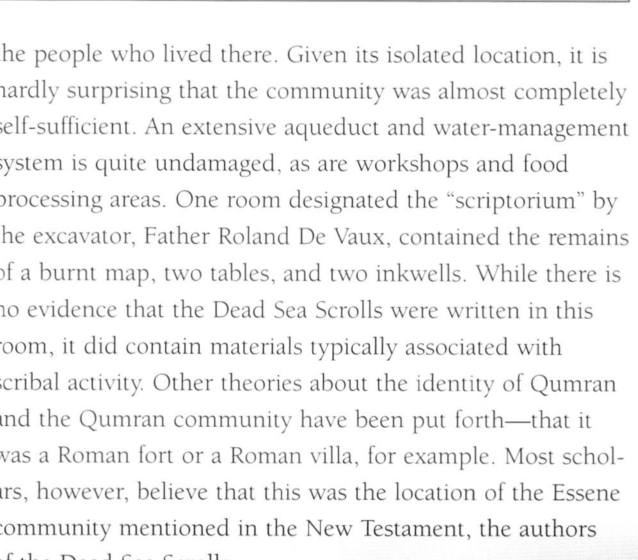

According to Genesis, Abraham originally came from the city of Ur in Mesopotamia. Excavations there have not revealed much about patriarchal life, but investigations at the Royal Cemetery of Ur have revealed a spectacular horde of treasure dating to about 2500 B.C.E. Arguably, one of the most remarkable finds is the sculpture called "the Ram and the Thicket" (right), after the binding of Isaac. Made of gold, silver, and lapis lazuli, this is a truly astonishing piece of art, and among the greatest finds of the Near East.

BELOW: EXCAVATIONS CARRIED OUT IN QUMRAN IN THE 1950S UNEARTHED OVER 1,000 UNBROKEN VESSELS, INCLUDING CUPS AND BOWLS. THE DEAD SEA SCROLLS WERE FOUND IN CAVES NEARBY.

THE JAMES OSSUARY—A BIBLICAL FORGERY?

Perhaps the most controversial recent "find" was a Roman Period ossuary that came to light in a private collection. An ossuary is a small coffin, often made of limestone, where the bones of the deceased were stored; these artifacts are typical of New Testament era Judaism. The James Ossuary is not exceptional in this regard. What is exceptional is the inscription, which reads: "James [right], son of Joseph, brother of Jesus." Scholars generally agree that the box itself and the first half of the inscription are legitimate. The reference to Jesus, however, is more controversial. If this is a legitimate inscription and not a forgery, then this may have been the actual coffin of Jesus' brother. It seems likely, however, that the second part of the inscription was added in modern times. Scientific investigations suggest that modern tools were used to carve it, and ancient handwriting experts believe that the name Jesus was written by a different person. It is unlikely, however, that the controversy over the legitimacy of this inscription will be resolved any time soon.

EXTRABIBLICAL INSCRIPTIONS

Arguably, the archaeological finds that have had the greatest impact on our understanding of the Bible have been inscriptions. The amount of written material found in the Near East is remarkable. In Mesopotamia, where writing was done on clay tablets and stone monuments, inscriptions number in the millions. Unfortunately, the people of ancient Israel wrote on papyrus (a type of paper made from certain reeds found in Egypt). Papyrus does not survive well in Israel's climate, so our record of writing from this region is much smaller.

HEBREW INSCRIPTIONS

Our record of early Hebrew inscriptions continues to grow as excavations reveal the remnants of ancient writing. The most frequent finds are ancient stamp seals. These are small objects, usually made of stone or bone, with an inscription (or symbol) carved into the bottom. When impressed into clay, these stamps leave behind written words or images and were used in ancient times as signatures are used today.

Longer Hebrew inscriptions tend to be letters or remnants of economic documents. These are usually preserved on fragments of pottery, called ostraca, probably the rough drafts used before scribes transferred the information to more expensive papyrus. Perhaps the most important inscription so far uncovered has been a royal inscription, revealed during the excavations of Tel Dan. Usually referred to as the Tel Dan Inscription, it preserves the earliest reference to the "House of David" and has been invaluable in the scholarly study of King David and the United Monarchy.

BELOW: DETAIL FROM THE BLACK OBELISK, SHOWING THE TRIBUTES BEING BROUGHT TO KING SHALMANESER III, WHO REIGNED OVER MESOPOTAMIA IN THE NINTH CENTURY B.C.E.

MESOPOTAMIAN ROYAL INSCRIPTIONS

One of the most exciting archaeological confirmations of the accuracy of biblical traditions has been the various Mesopotamian historical inscriptions about events that are described in the books of Kings and Chronicles. The Neo-Assyrian and Neo-Babylonian kings kept excellent records of their conquests, including descriptions of battles against Judah and Israel. The Neo-Assyrian King Shalmaneser III left numerous records of his dealings with the kinsmen of Israel kings. Most notable is the Black Obelisk, where King Jehu (described inaccurately as a son of Omri) is depicted bowing in obeisance to the Mesopotamian king.

King Sennacherib of Assyria also left records of his conflict with biblical peoples. Recovered from Sennacherib's palace at Nineveh was a huge relief depicting in stunning visual detail the Neo-Assyrian siege of Lachish (preserved in 2 Kings 18:13–16). The scenes carved on the wall depict the Assyrian attack on the city and the subsequent carrying away of captives from Lachish. His written accounts bear a close resemblance to the biblical account, although it is told from the enemy's perspective. Archaeological investigations have subsequently confirmed the accuracy of the written and

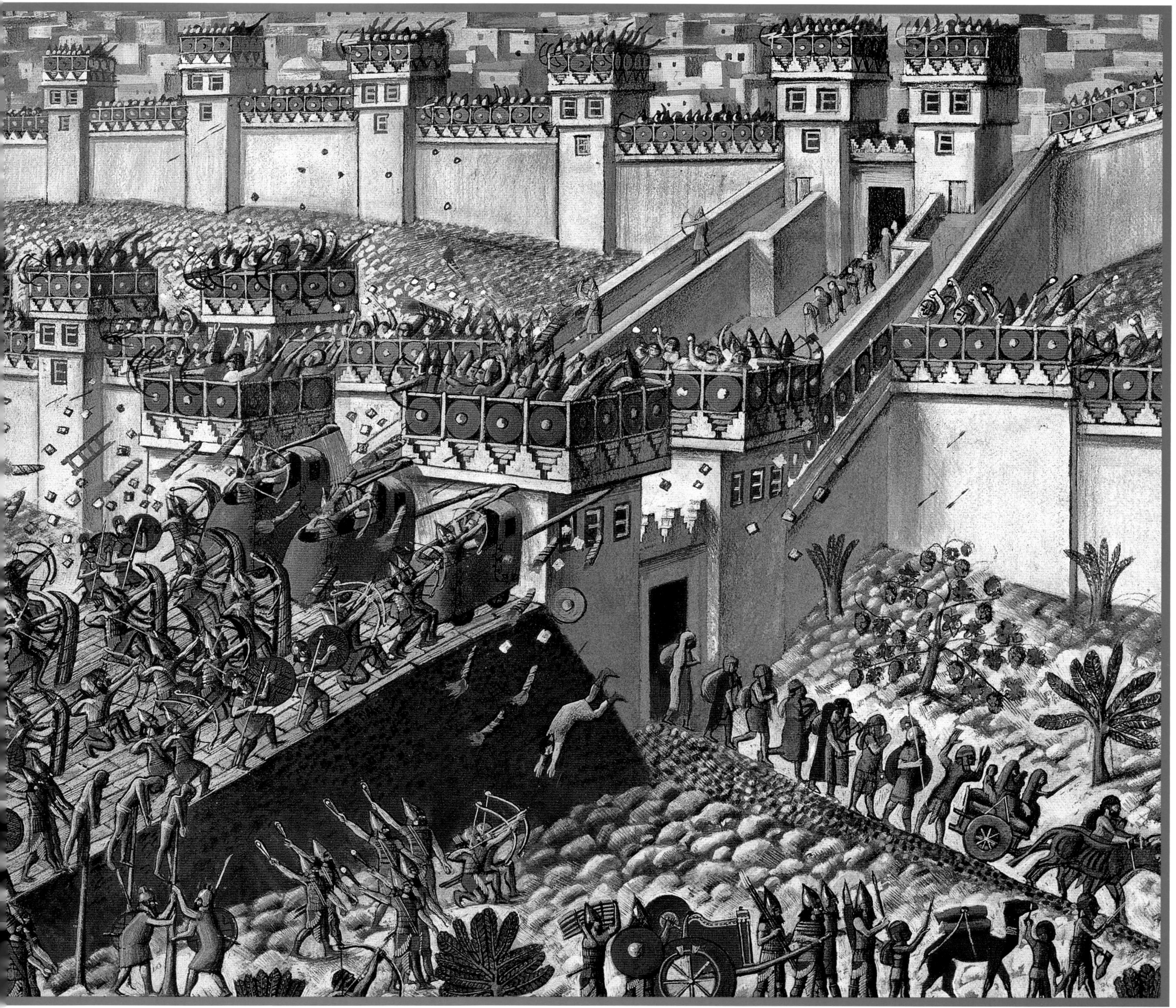

artistic accounts; the Neo-Assyrian siege ramp has been uncovered, as have numerous remnants of the battle—used weapons and the bodies of those who fell in battle.

CUNEIFORM ARCHIVES

The abundance of writing in Mesopotamia goes beyond mere royal inscriptions; cuneiform archives provide scholars with a wealth of insight into daily life. One of the most productive sites for the study of daily life in biblical times has been Nuzi, in northeastern Iraq near modern Kirkuk. Although the material remains of the site were not particularly spectacular, the more than two dozen private archives recovered were unique, as they were the records of families spanning generations. Scholars traced the history of various families (one as long as five generations), providing insight into the daily lives of ancient people. These archives, which roughly date to the fifteenth century B.C.E., have been of great interest to biblical scholars as family law documents are not attested in this much detail elsewhere. At first, scholars assumed that the social organization and customs reflected the practices of the biblical patriarchs, and suggested that the patriarchs lived in the second millennium B.C.E. This argument has been abandoned, as archaeological discoveries have progressed. As more and more family law documents have been unearthed, it has become apparent that this aspect of civilization was relatively conservative throughout the Near East, and the Nuzi evidence does not necessarily date the patriarchs to this period. More productive use of Nuzi scholarship in biblical studies has been in better understanding the socioeconomic background of the patriarchal narratives. Some of the relationships in Genesis that may seem unusual to us (like the complex relationship between Jacob and Laban), while not exactly analogous to practices at Nuzi, can be seen as relatively normative for the Ancient Near East.

ABOVE: THE SURRENDER OF THE CITY OF LACHISH AFTER THE ATTACK BY THE ASSYRIAN KING SENNACHERIB IN 701 B.C.E. THIS PRINT WAS BASED ON THE RELIEF FOUND AT THE PALACE IN NINEVEH.

THE MEDITERRANEAN WORLD

YOU CAST ME INTO THE DEEP, INTO THE HEART OF THE SEAS; AND THE FLOOD SURROUNDED ME JONAH 2:3

The Mediterranean world, when discussed by biblical scholars, mostly refers to the regions of Turkey, Greece, Italy, and the islands located nearby. The similar climate and the close proximity of these regions to one another have helped foster the development of a distinct Mediterranean culture, which still persists in these regions today. And even though most of the events described in the Bible took place in the Near East, the Mediterranean still has much significance for the Bible. The New Testament especially demonstrates this influence: at the time that Jesus lived, the Romans controlled most of the Near East. Equally notable is the fact that the New Testament was originally written in Greek, further pointing to connections between Christianity and the Mediterranean world.

TURKEY

Modern Turkey is a geographically diverse region, home to some of the world's most captivating and unique landscapes. It is bounded by seas on three sides: the Black Sea to the north, the Aegean Sea to the west, and the Mediterranean to the south. To the east are large mountain ranges, which act as a natural border for the country, with the highest peak being Mt. Ararat at 16,948 ft (5,166 m) above sea level. Turkey is strategically located at a crossroads between the Near East, Europe, and the interior of Asia. From an ancient perspective it was also resource-rich, filled with productive farmland, areas of heavy forest, and many mineral resources.

GREECE

Greece encompasses the southernmost portion of the Balkan Peninsula, and, like Turkey, is home to a diverse population, most of which lives in coastal areas. Mainland Greece is surrounded by water on three sides: the Aegean Sea to the east, the Mediterranean Sea to the south, and the Ionian Sea to the west. The southern mainland is separated from the rest of Greece by the Isthmus of Corinth and the Isthmus of Saranikos. It is further isolated by the Peloponnese Mountains, which break up the entire southern region into a series of high rises and low valleys. Across the Saronic Gulf, in the southeast of mainland Greece, is Attica, which has been the culturally dominant region since the fifth century B.C.E. The city of Athens, the capital of modern Greece and the birthplace of democracy, is located in the center of Attica. North of Attica, Greece is dominated by mountains and hills. The largest are the Pindus Mountains, running north to south. Northeast of this range is Mt. Olympus, Greece's highest peak and the legendary home of the gods in antiquity. Macedonia, the homeland of Alexander the Great, is located to the north. The designation "Greece" also extends to numerous islands in the region, including the Cyclades and the island of Crete. The island of Cyprus is still contested by the modern nations of Greece and Turkey.

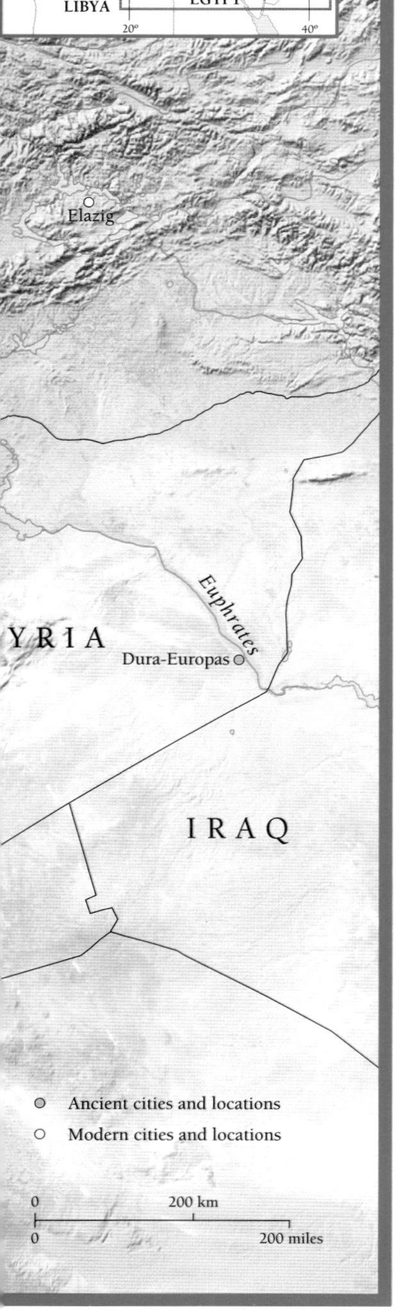

ITALY

Italy is set off from the rest of Europe by the Alps, a natural northern border. South of the Alps, Italy really consists of two distinct geographic regions—Northern Italy and Peninsular (or Southern) Italy. In Northern Italy, lowland plains dominate. This is distinct from Peninsular Italy, where mountains and hills are typical. To the east of Peninsular Italy is the Adriatic Sea, to the south is the Mediterranean Sea, and to the west is the Tyrrhenian Sea. The Tyrrhenian side has many natural bays and gullies and supports maritime travel. The easily navigable rivers in the west allowed easy transportation. The city of Rome is here, on the left bank of the Tiber River. No doubt Rome's position inland (safe from naval attacks) and position on a stable river system helped it grow to dominance. The Adriatic side of Italy is more difficult to travel through, given the lack of dependable river systems and the absence of natural harbors. Only the area around Venice provides suitable ports for seagoing vessels. In the south, Italy borders the Mediterranean Sea, with the Gulf of Taranto separating the "toe" and "heel" of the "boot" of Italy.

ABOVE: HELLENISTIC COINS DEPICTING ALEXANDER THE GREAT AND HIS FATHER PHILIP OF MACEDON. IN HIS SHORT LIFE, ALEXANDER (356–323 B.C.E.) CONQUERED MOST OF THE KNOWN WORLD.

BELOW: TURKEY BOASTS SOME SPECTACULAR SCENERY, INCLUDING THESE "FAIRY CHIMNEY POTS," NATURAL ROCK FORMATIONS IN THE KIZILCKUR VALLEY.

RIGHT: A NINETEENTH-CENTURY PAINTING OF THE BATTLE OF NAVARINO IN OCTOBER 1827, A DECISIVE BATTLE IN THE GREEK WAR OF INDEPENDENCE.

PEOPLES AND CULTURES OF THE REGION FROM ANCIENT TIMES TO THE PRESENT

Turkey, Greece, and Italy are relatively new countries with long histories. Both Greece and Turkey were once part of the Ottoman Empire. In 1821, the Greeks rebelled against the Ottomans, succeeding in gaining their independence in 1829. The modern state of Turkey arose in the aftermath of World War I, following the dissolution of the Ottoman Empire. Greece and Turkey still have a relatively hostile relationship, observable in their conflict over the island of Cyprus. Modern Italy's origins can also be seen in the nineteenth century, when what had been a series of independent city-states since the collapse of the Roman Empire were unified into a larger state. All of these countries, though home to diverse people and cultures, draw inspiration from their ancient cultures and traditions. Archaeology and history play important roles in the nationalism of all of these regions.

TURKEY

Depending on your point of view, the region of Turkey can be considered both Mediterranean and Near Eastern. Before and during Old Testament times, the cultures of what is now Turkey had more in common with the Ancient Near East. By the end of the Old Testament and certainly throughout the New Testament period, the people of Turkey were essentially Greeks. In fact, much of what we think of as Classical Greek literature was actually written in what is now known as Turkey. Troy, the setting of Homer's *Iliad*, is located on the western shores of Turkey, and some of the most famous Greek cities are likewise located in this region.

The Hittites were one of the earliest distinctly Anatolian cultures and were very well known to the people of the Bible (Abraham, for example, purchases the Cave of Machpelah from a Hittite in Genesis 23). The Hittites shared a great deal in common with the people of Mesopotamia, including customs, legal traditions, and the cuneiform writing system. The Hittite language, however, is Indo-European, and thus closer to Greek than to Hebrew. Likewise, the artistic and religious traditions of the Hittites are quite distinct. Hittite culture wanes over the period covered in the Old Testament, and by the time of the New Testament, Greek culture is the dominant culture of the region.

GREECE

Ancient Greek (or Hellenistic) culture comprises more than just the people living in what is now known as Greece. Generally, when scholars talk about Ancient Greek culture, they are referring to people who spoke a dialect of the Greek language, had some shared religious and cultural values, and were familiar with the stories that were written down by Homer. Ancient Greek cities can be found in modern Turkey, Greece, and many of the islands of the Mediterranean. However, Greek culture was spread to the Near Eastern and Egyptian world by Alexander the Great, King of Macedon. By 332 B.C.E., Alexander had conquered much of the known world. He did not simply bring with him new political leadership; with him came new institutions, new types of material culture and cityscapes, and the Greek language, which quickly became the dominant language of the biblical world. However, tensions between the new Hellenistic culture and local cultures persisted. This tension is quite evident in the apocryphal book Sirach (Ecclesiasticus), where the writer, usually called Ben Sirach by Bible scholars, complains about Jewish youth embracing Greek culture.

ROMAN PERSECUTION OF CHRISTIANS

The Romans were generally tolerant of non-Roman religious traditions. At various times, however, this tolerance was suspended as recorded in the many accounts of Christian martyrs. Ironically, these persecuted Christians (shown above in a painting by Giuseppe Mancinelli) were not always persecuted on the charge of being Christians but on the charge of being atheists. Because they refused to worship other gods, or acknowledge the divinity of the Roman gods, these early Christians were put to death. Of course they were not atheists, but their belief in God, and their adherence to his commandment to worship no other God, forced them to stand up to Roman religious demands.

THE ROMANS

Mediterranean culture was further spread through the known world by the Romans, who conquered the lands once held by Alexander the Great. Rome refers both to the city and the larger political entity of the empire. Rome began as a small village in Italy, but through a series of political alliances and military conquests, soon defeated most of Italy. Conflicts with the Carthaginians, most notably with General Hannibal (who brought his army into Italy across the Alps), led Rome on a path of conquest through the Mediterranean and into the Near East.

LEFT: A FIRST-CENTURY RELIEF OF FIGHTING ROMAN GLADIATORS. GLADIATORIAL GAMES WERE MAJOR PUBLIC EVENTS, THE SPECTACLE PROVIDING ENTERTAINMENT FOR BOTH THE EMPEROR AND THE MASSES.

The culture of Rome was a culture of contrasts. On one hand, the Romans valued civic virtue, participation in government, and emotional restraint. On the other hand, this is the civilization where gladiatorial combat was one of the most popular spectacle sports, where a Republican democracy gave way (relatively peacefully) to a dictatorship under an emperor, and where stories of the lewd behavior of the nobility are shocking even to modern sensibilities. This was the dominant culture when Christianity arose, and the first to embrace Christianity as a state religion, so the development of the church has been greatly influenced by Roman institutions.

What caused the fall of Rome is uncertain, although most scholars generally agree that there was not one single reason. Eventually, Rome was overrun by barbarian hordes from Europe. By medieval times, Roman Europe had disintegrated into a number of smaller countries and city-states. The last vestige of the Roman world remained stable in the Byzantine Empire, centered in Constantinople, until it was sacked by Muslim forces. Europe, however, took a very different path, with the rise of regional Christian kings and the development of countries that would eventually become modern England, France, and Spain.

BELOW: A DEBAUCHED END TO A ONCE GREAT EMPIRE? *A BANQUET IN NERO'S PALACE* BY ULPIANO CHECA Y SANZ, SUGGESTS THAT THE ROMAN RULING CLASSES LIVED LIVES OF LUXURY AND DECADENCE.

RIGHT: THE MEDITERRANEAN CLIMATE IS IDEAL FOR WINE-MAKING. IN TUSCANY, ITALY, CHIANTI GRAPES ARE GROWN FOR BOTH THE LOCAL AND INTERNATIONAL MARKETS.

ECONOMY AND AGRICULTURE FROM ANCIENT TIMES TO THE MODERN ERA

Located in one of the most economically productive regions in antiquity, the Mediterranean countries in modern times have faced some tremendous economic problems, both from the mismanagement of resources and a failure to keep in step with changing economic conditions. Perhaps the most evident economic problem in the region is the unevenness of development. There is a huge difference between economic life in the urban landscape of northern Italy and economic life in the underdeveloped south. Turkey and Greece likewise continue to face problems in regional developmental disparity. Perhaps the most significant divide is between wealthy urban areas and poorer rural regions, an economic situation that has been apparent since ancient times.

AGRICULTURE

Given the predominance of hills and valleys in the topography of Mediterranean countries, ancient farmers employed terraces to make the land more suitable for agricultural production. Step-like terraces were built into the sides of hills, and crops were grown on top of these terraces. This was an effective solution to the problem of soil erosion, since it decreases the slope of the hill. The terraces also help to trap water on the terrace (instead of running down the hill), making better use of irrigation schemes and scarce water resources. In recent times, farmers, especially in Italy and Greece, have been abandoning this system of land management. This has led to severe soil degradation and poor crop yields, limiting the agricultural self-sufficiency and economic growth of local regions.

While terracing and Mediterranean agricultural techniques have remained relatively constant from ancient times to the present, deforestation (especially in the medieval and modern periods) has facilitated a decline in the quality of soil. Scarcity of water is another real problem for farmers in the region. Mediterranean regions have substantial annual amounts of rainfall. Unfortunately for farmers, rainfall patterns are extreme, ranging from torrential downpours that wash away crops and soil, to droughts that do not provide enough rain for the crops to grow. So water management is of the utmost importance for agriculture in the region.

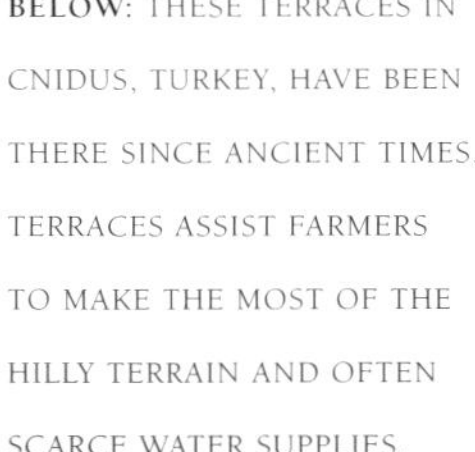

BELOW: THESE TERRACES IN CNIDUS, TURKEY, HAVE BEEN THERE SINCE ANCIENT TIMES. TERRACES ASSIST FARMERS TO MAKE THE MOST OF THE HILLY TERRAIN AND OFTEN SCARCE WATER SUPPLIES.

SLAVERY

Slavery was a fact of economic life for the people of the Mediterranean. The Old Testament contains many laws regarding the proper treatment of slaves (for example, in Exodus 21). Paul's letter to Philemon, in which he tells Philemon to take back into his service the emancipated slave, Onesimus, makes no critical comments about the institution of slavery itself. These sections of the Bible were used as justification for the slavery of African-Americans, with figures such as Jefferson Davis arguing that the Bible actually explicitly sanctioned slavery. This is a considerable misreading of the Bible; ancient Mediterranean slavery and slavery in the United States were very different.

The most important difference was that ancient slavery was not based on race or racist ideologies, although there were African slaves. People became slaves in the ancient Mediterranean because of extreme poverty or debt, not because of the color of their skin. In cases of extreme debt, an individual could sell himself (and/or his wife and children) into slavery to another. In return for service in the master's household, the slave would be the responsibility of the master, who had to clothe, feed, and house his slaves. For many slaves, this was a temporary economic solution, and they would leave their master's service after their debts had been repaid. For others, especially children, it became a permanent situation. Slaves were prominent in Greek and Roman times, where prisoners of war were also enslaved. Many slaves in Rome lived essentially independently of their masters, running businesses and living a fulfilling family life. Other Roman slaves were not as lucky, being forced to engage in gladiatorial combat or other dangerous activities for the amusement of their masters. While there are without a doubt moral and ethical problems regarding ancient slavery, these are very different problems from those posed by the legacy of slavery in the United States.

ABOVE: *THE SLAVE MARKET AT AK-HISSAR, TURKEY* BY THEODORE LEBLANC. THE PRACTICE OF SLAVERY IN THE MEDITERRANEAN REGION CONTINUED WELL INTO MEDIEVAL TIMES.

COINS: THE BIRTH OF MONEY

In the Old Testament, trade and exchange are discussed in terms of "shekels." While shekels are the currency of modern Israel, in the Old Testament the word "shekel" actually refers to a unit of weight. So, ten shekels of silver refers to a specific weight of silver, not a specific amount of money. This was a cumbersome system where, in order to trade with someone else, you needed to have something that the other person wanted. Trade was made somewhat easier by the use of metals as an abstract medium of wealth, but in order to be certain what one was getting, one would still have to weigh the metal, test its purity, and have a good knowledge of metals. By New Testament times, however, trade was done much like it is today, using abstract units of wealth known as currency.

The earliest type of currency was the coin. The use of coins differs from the use of different weights of silver because the amount of metal (and probably its purity) is guaranteed by the issuing authority. The first coins appear in the archaeological record of Greek cities, in the seventh century B.C.E. Their use spread quickly throughout the Mediterranean, and they were soon adopted across the biblical world. In Greece, each major city minted its own coins; inscriptions stamped onto the coins told where, and often when, they were minted. Coins from Athens were called "owls" as they featured a picture of an owl on one side, the symbol of the city's patron goddess, Athena. In Roman times, images of gods on coins were replaced by portraits of the emperor or other leading citizens and historical figures. Since then, this has been the trend for most world currencies, which usually depict the current leader (like the Queen of England) or historical figures (like George Washington).

LEFT: A SILVER COIN, OR "OWL," FROM ATHENS, GREECE, DATED 490–49 B.C.E. THE VALUE OF THE FIRST COINS WAS BASED ON WEIGHT—THIS ONE WEIGHS 0.6 OUNCES (17 G).

THE INFLUENCE OF THE MEDITERRANEAN SEA ON TRADE AND DEVELOPMENT IN THE REGION

In 1949, Fernand Braudel published his masterpiece, *The Mediterranean and the Mediterranean World in the Age of Philip II*, where he argued convincingly that the history of the Mediterranean region cannot be seen as separate from the Mediterranean Sea itself. Until the nineteenth century, when power shifted to the countries of the North Atlantic (especially the United Kingdom and the United States), the countries surrounding the Mediterranean Sea were the dominant decision makers and centers of power in the Western world.

Much of this power developed out of the peculiarities of the Mediterranean Sea itself. The Mediterranean Sea is about 2,237 miles (3,600 km) in length, and is connected to the Atlantic Ocean only at the Strait of Gibraltar. This makes for very calm tidal patterns, and on a local scale, the currents are quite predictable. Differences in local currents are partly due to the massive undersea ridge that separates the sea into two separate basins. The ease of transport on this sea, and its central position between Europe, Asia, and Africa, allowed frequent contact between diverse groups of people. In the Bible, this is very apparent in the Acts of the Apostles, which chronicles Paul's missionary work, traveling by sea to spread the message of the early Church.

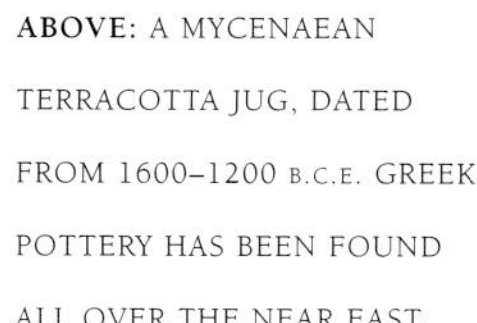

ABOVE: A MYCENAEAN TERRACOTTA JUG, DATED FROM 1600–1200 B.C.E. GREEK POTTERY HAS BEEN FOUND ALL OVER THE NEAR EAST.

INTERREGIONAL TRADE

During biblical times, the Mediterranean Sea was one of the most important locations of interregional trade. The predictability of the currents and relatively safe sailing conditions made this the primary route of trade between Europe, Asia, and Africa. Archaeologically, it is possible to identify periods of high economic prosperity and high levels of international contact. When Greek pottery is found in Israel, or Roman pottery in Egypt, it can be concluded that it is likely that some sort of exchange occurred. By tracing the proportional frequency of the appearance of foreign goods at sites, the economic history of the ancient world can be reconstructed.

Archaeological evidence for trade on this scale is apparent in the period preceding the emergence of the United Monarchy in Israel, the Late Bronze Age (1550–1200 B.C.E.). In this period, goods from all over the Mediterranean are found at sites across the region, indicating that a substantial amount of maritime trade went on. Textual evidence for this trade has been found at Ugarit, on the coast of Syria. During this period, Ugarit was a port city controlled by the Hittites. Archaeologists recovered treaty tablets from the site that included rules for foreign traders visiting Ugarit. These laws limited the rights of merchants to do business at the site: foreign merchants could trade, but could not be paid in real estate, nor could they allow locals to incur any debts

RIGHT: AN EXCAVATED SIXTEENTH-CENTURY B.C.E. ROYAL TOMB FROM THE ANCIENT HITTITE CITY OF UGARIT, NEAR RAS SHAMRA IN MODERN-DAY SYRIA.

to them. Foreign merchants were also only allowed to visit the city during certain seasons, probably so that they would not be trapped in the city during the seasons when unfavorable currents made nautical travel more dangerous. These laws protected foreign merchants from property theft and acts of violence. If crimes were committed against them, the local government at Ugarit was responsible for punishing the offenders and restoring any lost property.

THE PHOENICIANS: PIONEERS OF THE SEA

Phoenician culture is inextricably connected with the Mediterranean Sea. Even their name is connected to the sea. It is derived from the Greek word for purple, because of the purple dye they harvested from murex shells found along the coast. The Phoenicians were expert sailors, and much of their wealth derived from nautical trade conducted around the eastern Mediterranean. Around 800 B.C.E., Phoenician settlers set out from their traditional home in coastal Syria and Lebanon and settled in North Africa at the site of Carthage. From then until Roman times, the Carthaginians ruled the Mediterranean, monopolizing trade and dominating the seas. Phoenician naval primacy did not wane until the arrival of the Romans, who in their earliest history seemed to avoid sea travel, until they developed the *corvus*, a type of grappling weapon that they used to board Carthaginian ships. With this change in technology, the Carthaginians succumbed to the Roman navy, and Carthage was burnt to the ground.

TRAVEL

The Mediterranean Sea allows easy travel throughout the regions bordering the sea. Europeans started exploring the area during the Christian Crusades to the Holy Land, which began in the eleventh century. Crusaders typically traveled to a port city in Spain or Italy and went by ship to the Levant. Large numbers of travelers to the region meant the Mediterranean Sea was filled with traffic. After the crusades, many sea routes and port cities thrived as travelers journeyed via the sea for reasons of trade, pilgrimage, and curiosity.

THE ULU BURUN SHIPWRECK

In 1982 a shipwreck dating to the Late Bronze Age was found off the coast of Turkey. Underwater archaeologists from Texas A & M University retrieved much of the ship and its cargo. Investigation of the cargo has determined that it was a merchant ship, carrying raw materials (including metal ingots) for sale at the ports on the Mediterranean. A spectacular find, the shipwreck is further evidence for the important role the Mediterranean Sea has played in the economic development of the region.

ABOVE: A PHOENICIAN TRADING SHIP ARRIVING AT PHAROS, EGYPT, IN A NINETEENTH-CENTURY PAINTING BY ALBERT SEBILLE. PHOENICIAN EXPORTS INCLUDED TIMBER, LINEN, AND METALWORK.

RIGHT: THE BAPTISM OF CONSTANTINE I BY ST. SYLVESTER, FROM A ROMANESQUE FRESCO IN SANTI QUATTRO CORONATI CHURCH IN ROME, ITALY.

ARCHAEOLOGY AND THE BIBLE IN THE REGION: THE EARLY CHURCH

Archaeology in the Mediterranean has been particularly fruitful for the study of the earliest Christian communities. Archaeologists interested in the New Testament are usually trained in the study of Roman archaeology. The analysis of Roman remains is very helpful in better understanding the context of the Gospels and the later writings. For the period from the end of the New Testament to the conversion of Constantine to Christianity, archaeological discoveries have been one of our primary sources of information about Christianity during these important formative years.

BELOW: CATACOMBS SERVED AS BOTH MEETING PLACES AND TOMBS. THIS THIRD CENTURY C.E. CRYPT IS PART OF THE CATACOMBS OF ST. CALLISTUS IN ROME, ITALY.

CHRISTIAN CATACOMBS IN ROME

During the late fifteenth and early sixteenth centuries, Antonio Bosio systematically explored, mapped, and publicized a long forgotten section of the city of Rome—the Christian catacombs that lay beneath the city. Since then, scholars and tourists have continued to walk in these underground caverns, one of the oldest remnants of the early Church. The catacombs themselves are quite extensive. Some wind in labyrinthine fashion for over 12 miles (20 km) and are located more than 65 ft (20 m) below ground.

The catacombs are essentially Christian cemeteries. As Christianity became more and more popular in Roman times and more people converted to the faith, there came a growing desire to bury Christians in cemeteries separate from the rest of Rome. Some Roman families had already been burying their dead in family tombs below the city; as these families converted, they allowed any Christians to be buried beneath, not just those from their immediate family. During periods of persecution, Christian populations could meet in relative safety in these underground chambers, safe from the policing of the Roman army. Christian wall art and graffiti from these meetings are still preserved in the catacombs.

THE HAGIA SOPHIA

Located in Istanbul, the Hagia Sophia is one of the largest structures remaining from the ancient world, and a spectacular monument to the Christian faith of the Byzantine people.

Consecrated in C.E. 537, by the Byzantine Emperor Justinian, the Hagia Sophia replaced a basilica that had been burnt to the ground five years earlier. The building itself is considered one of the greatest architectural achievements of the ancient world, because of its huge size, opulent design, and creative approach to the management of interior space. Perhaps most spectacular is the domed roof, with a diameter of 101 ft (31 m). The building itself has suffered through many earthquakes and thus many restorations. In 1453, the church was turned into a mosque (and minarets were added) after the Muslim Ottoman Turks conquered the city. In 1935, the building was once again converted, this time into a museum. While most of the Islamic features have been preserved, tourists can see the Christian mosaics that have been recovered and restored by archaeologists.

LEFT: A MASTERPIECE OF BYZANTINE ARCHITECTURE—THIS PART OF THE INTERIOR OF THE HAGIA SOPHIA (OR CHURCH OF HOLY WISDOM) IN ISTANBUL SHOWS SOME OF ITS ORNATE DECORATION.

AN EARLY SYNAGOGUE AND CHURCH AT DURA-EUROPAS

Dura-Europas was a Roman garrison town (in what is now Syria), a relatively unimportant town in the grand scheme of the Roman Empire. It was destroyed in C.E. 256 and never rebuilt. This is one of the most important Roman sites for biblical scholars since preserved in its ruins are one of the oldest synagogues and the oldest-known Christian church. Scholars assume that there would have been older synagogues and churches at other sites, but these were usually reused and rebuilt over time. Since Dura-Europas was destroyed and never inhabited again, the remains of the religious structures were preserved.

The building that housed the synagogue was originally a large private home. In its first phase of use as a synagogue, some architectural features (such as a Torah niche) were added to the sitting room. Around C.E. 244, the building was extensively renovated and transformed into a more formal synagogue. The interior layout of the building was totally redesigned and sectioned into two main parts: a large Hall of Assembly, where the community would come together, and a large main entrance. Artists painted the walls of the Hall of Assembly with many different images from the Bible, and benches were built along the walls so that visitors could sit during the service or meeting.

The church is far less elaborate, and it is even arguable whether or not the designation "church" is appropriate. As with the synagogue, the church was built into a preexisting private home. Most likely a private home owner donated or dedicated his house for Christian meetings. Graffiti in the building may preserve some of the names of the early Christian leaders of the community, but it is difficult to read. One of the long halls had a dais at one end, probably a focal point for worship. Another room of the house functioned as a baptistery and contains the oldest-known baptismal font. Around the font were paintings of biblical scenes (from the Old and New Testaments). While no copies of the Bible have been found in the building, a fragment of Tatian's *Diatesseron* (an attempt to merge the four Gospel accounts) was found.

BASILICAS

The term "basilica" has come to refer to a certain type of church that is rectangular-shaped with a central nave. This is the most common architectural layout of a medieval cathedral, and St. Peter's Basilica in Rome (left) is probably the archetypal example. The term basilica more properly refers to a type of Roman building, shaped along these lines. For the Romans, basilicas may have included temples within them, but were essentially large meeting areas. Civic events took place within, and sometimes permanent shops were housed within the walls of a basilica, giving them an appearance much like modern malls.
As Christianity came to be the dominant religion, many of these large structures were taken over by church authorities and converted into houses of worship.

ABOVE: A MYCENAEAN CIST GRAVE IN IOLKOS, GREECE. SUCH STONE-LINED GRAVES HAVE YIELDED A WEALTH OF ARTIFACTS FOR ARCHAEOLOGICAL STUDY.

A Remnant of a Crucifixion

Crucifixion is a particularly brutal method of execution and fairly typical of Roman punishments. The accounts of Jesus' crucifixion in the Gospels match well with what we know of Roman practices. According to the Jewish historian Josephus, crucifixion was an especially common tactic used against the Jewish people, and during the siege of Jerusalem in C.E. 70, commemorated in the Arch of Titus, mass crucifixions were particularly widespread. In 1968, three burial caves near Jerusalem were excavated that bore evidence of the Roman propensity for this kind of execution. One of the bodies recovered was of a man who was killed around the age of twenty-four. His skeleton showed clear evidence that he had been crucified: his legs were broken, and his right heel was pierced by a nail; and one of his wrist bones had a scratch that may have been caused by another nail. This grisly discovery highlights how common crucifixion was in Judea under the Romans.

CLASSICAL ARCHAEOLOGY

Given Western cultural roots in Greek and Roman times, it is no surprise that Classical archaeology is one of the most thriving archaeological disciplines. Most Classical archaeologists are not excavating sites for the sole purpose of better understanding the Bible; they are usually more interested in Greek and Roman culture. Still, many of their finds and insights have influenced our understanding of the Bible, occasionally bearing directly on questions asked by biblical scholars. The people of the New Testament lived in a predominantly Greco-Roman civilization; because of this, any insight into Greco-Roman culture provides important and relevant information about the people and institutions that are mentioned in the Bible.

THE GREEK ORIGINS OF THE PHILISTINES

Archaeologists studying Bronze Age Greece in the early part of the twentieth century probably never would have guessed that they would help to solve one of the great mysteries of the Bible—the origins of the Philistines. In fact, excavations at Mycenae and elsewhere have provided archaeologists with the proof that the Philistines originally came from Greece, but moved to the Levant at approximately the same time that the Hebrews arrived.

Archaeologists can trace the movement of the Philistines through their material culture. At the end of the late Bronze Age (*c.* 1200 B.C.E.), many Greek sites were destroyed or abandoned. The pottery used at these sites, known to specialists as Mycenaean pottery, stopped being used there and started appearing in Philistine cities in the Levant. The sheer quantities of this type of pottery at these Philistine cities (and the lack of similar pottery at sites known to be Israelite) show that this was not merely trade, but an actual settlement of people. Other evidence, like the use of typical Greek architectural styles, further demonstrates that the roots of Philistia must be in the Greek world. After a few centuries of living in the Levant, the Philistines gradually lost touch with their Greek traditions and their material culture started to look more and more like that of the Israelites.

THE CITY OF EPHESUS

Ephesus, located in western Turkey, has been inhabited since the Bronze Age, but is perhaps most famous for two reasons. First, it is the site of the Temple of Artemis (also called the Artemision), a temple that was so large it was considered one of the seven wonders of the ancient world. Modern visitors to the site will be disappointed in the Artemision: all that remains are the stone foundations of the temple. In the courtyard of the Artemision is one of the oldest Christian churches, erected long after the Temple of Artemis had fallen out of use. Secondly, the city is also famous for the letter Paul wrote to its inhabitants that has been preserved in the New Testament. The city itself is a typical Hellenistic and Roman settlement. Greco-Roman Ephesus is laid out in an orderly grid pattern, characteristic of Roman cities outside of Italy. The city also had many of the institutions common in Greco-Roman cities. It had a gymnasium (exercise yard) and baths. Aqueducts brought water directly into the city. Wealthy inhabitants had water delivered directly to their homes.

Poorer residents could get water from any of the numerous baths that dotted the urban landscape. Many ancient churches have been preserved at Ephesus, including the Church of Holy Mary, which scholars assume was used for the council of Ephesus in C.E. 431.

THE ARCH OF TITUS

In C.E. 81, the Roman Emperor Domitian erected a monumental arch to commemorate the reign of his predecessor (and brother) Titus. The arch is almost 46 ft (14 m) high, and located in the Roman Forum. The arch that visitors to Rome see today has been heavily reconstructed. In 1822, the entire arch was dismantled and put back together in an effort to restore it to its former glory and remove the numerous extraneous structures that had accumulated around it over the medieval period. What makes this arch so interesting for biblical scholars are the reliefs carved into it. In the vault of the arch is an image of Titus being carried up to the heavens on an eagle—which is a fairly typical image of a Roman emperor's deification after death. The marble reliefs in the passage, however, commemorate Titus's sack of Jerusalem and the Second Temple. One particular scene shows Titus riding his chariot in victory, in the triumphal procession after the battle. Another scene shows Roman legionnaires carrying off the spoils from the Temple, including a large menorah.

LEFT: WHEN MYCENAEAN POTTERY WAS FOUND IN MANY PHILISTINE CITIES IN THE LEVANT, SCHOLARS CONCLUDED THAT THE PHILISTINES HAD THEIR ROOTS IN GREECE.

BELOW: *THE ARCH OF TITUS* BY BERNARDO BELLOTTO. AMONG OTHER THINGS, THE ARCH COMMEMORATES THE DESTRUCTION OF THE TEMPLE IN JERUSALEM.

Egypt and the Sinai Peninsula

THERE WILL COME SEVEN YEARS OF GREAT PLENTY THROUGHOUT ALL THE LAND OF EGYPT GENESIS 41:29

RIGHT: EGYPTIAN SCRIBE NEBAMUN, ACCOMPANIED BY HIS WIFE HATSHEPSUT AND HIS SON, ON A PAPYRUS BOAT ON THE MARSHES, IN A TOMB PAINTING DATED 1390 B.C.E.

Egypt is surrounded by a sea, deserts, and difficult river passages—natural geographic barriers that have acted as de facto political borders over the past 5,000 years. Even when controlled by external powers, Egypt remained a stable political and geographic concept. Since the formation of the first state of Egypt, natural boundaries have continued to act as political boundaries as well. The defining feature, symbolically and economically central to Egypt, is the Nile River. Almost all of Egypt's population lives in the Nile Valley, the rich strip of fertile land watered by the inundation of the Nile. To the north, Egypt is bounded by the Mediterranean Sea. Egypt's southern border has been more flexible. The First Cataract on the Nile marked Egypt's southern border at its smallest extent, the rapids of the cataract making the Nile difficult to pass. Egypt's current border ends near the Second Cataract, with the state of Sudan (ancient Nubia) to the south. Desert surrounds the land to the east and west. Traditionally, Egypt has always controlled the Eastern Desert, which runs up to the Red Sea. To the west, borders have been less stable given the largely nomadic population that makes this region home.

BELOW: A NINETEENTH-CENTURY PAINTING OF THE SUEZ CANAL BY ALBERT RIEGER. THE SUEZ CANAL IS APPROXIMATELY 118 MILES (190 KM) LONG AND WAS COMPLETED IN 1869.

UPPER AND LOWER EGYPT

In ancient times, Egypt was viewed as two separate lands that had been unified in a grand act of state formation. The conception of two lands reflects a significant geographic difference between the Delta in the north (Lower Egypt) and the Nile Floodplain in the south (Upper Egypt). The difference in environment between these two regions is extreme. Lower Egypt, where the Nile splits into numerous branches, is humid, lush marshland. The land mass here has been created through the interaction of mud deposited by the Nile and the actions of the Mediterranean Sea, and without a doubt has shifted tremendously over Egypt's history. Upper Egypt is as predictable as Lower Egypt is ever-changing, essentially incorporating the river valley of the Nile and the surrounding deserts. In modern times, the region that connects Upper and Lower Egypt is now called Middle Egypt. Spanning the distance from the Gebel Abu Foda Mountains north of Asyut to the Faiyum, Middle Egypt was in ancient times thought of as an extension of Upper Egypt, even though the swamps and terrain seem more like the environment of the Delta.

THE FAIYUM AND THE DESERT OASES

Besides the Nile, there are a few water sources in the Western Desert that break up the arid expanse. Perhaps the largest water source other than the Nile is Lake Moeris, in the center of the Faiyum Basin in Lower Egypt. Due to its rich farmland and stable source of water, the Faiyum has been inhabited for 8,000 years and bears evidence of the earliest farming in Egypt. The Western Desert is dotted with oases—the most notable being the Siwa Oasis, where the Valley of the Golden Mummies was discovered in the 1990s.

THE SINAI PENINSULA

The Sinai Peninsula connects Egypt to Asia and is the main land route between Asia and Africa. Now split by the Suez Canal, the land crossing between these continents was intersected in the north by a route linking ancient Memphis with Gaza and points north. The Sinai itself is mostly mountainous desert in the south and hills and depressions in the north. The peninsula is bounded on the east by the Gulf of Aqaba and on the west by the Gulf of Suez, both extensions of the Red Sea. The Sinai was well populated in biblical times. Archaeological surveys have identified hundreds of temporary campsites. Other than in a few monasteries and military outposts, the inhabitants of this region have generally been nomads, a lifestyle choice suited to the desert. The Sinai became part of Egypt again in 1982, after the Israeli withdrawal from the peninsula.

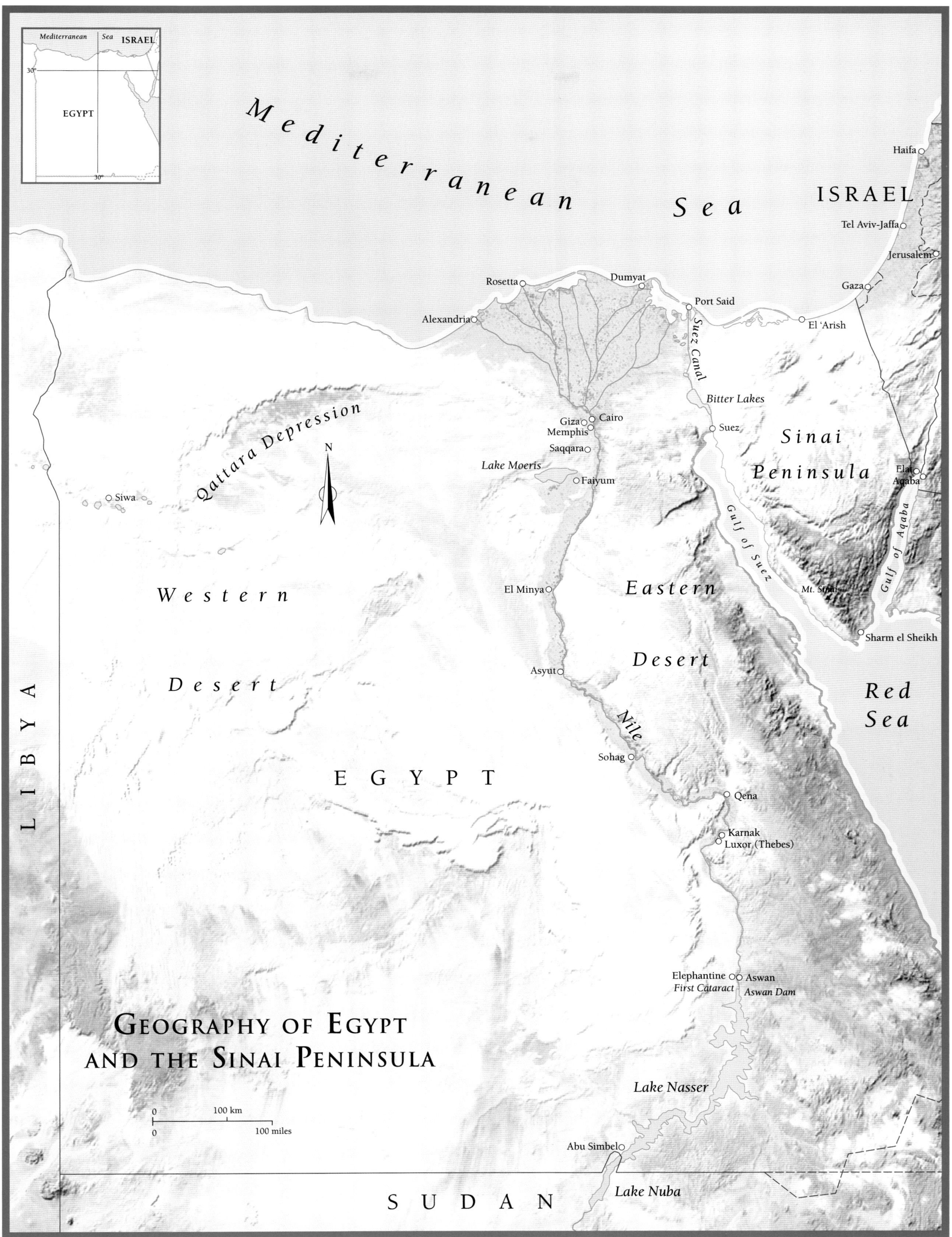
Mediterranean Sea
ISRAEL
30°
EGYPT
30°
Mediterranean Sea
ISRAEL
Haifa
Tel Aviv-Jaffa
Jerusalem
Gaza
Rosetta
Dumyat
Port Said
El 'Arish
Alexandria
Suez Canal
Bitter Lakes
Qattara Depression
Giza
Cairo
Memphis
Suez
Sinai Peninsula
N
Saqqara
Lake Moeris
Faiyum
Elat
Aqaba
Siwa
Gulf of Suez
Gulf of Aqaba
El Minya
Western Desert
Eastern Desert
Mt. Sinai
Sharm el Sheikh
Asyut
Red Sea
Nile
LIBYA
Sohag
EGYPT
Qena
Karnak
Luxor (Thebes)
Elephantine
Aswan
First Cataract
Aswan Dam
Geography of Egypt and the Sinai Peninsula
Lake Nasser
0
100 km
0
100 miles
Abu Simbel
SUDAN
Lake Nuba

RIGHT: THIS PAINTED LIMESTONE STELA SHOWS RAMESES II (1279–1213 B.C.E.) HOLDING NUBIAN, LIBYAN, AND SYRIAN PRISONERS BY THE HAIR.

PEOPLES AND CULTURES OF THE REGION FROM ANCIENT TIMES TO THE PRESENT

Tracing the movements of people into and out of Egypt is a complex and difficult task. Modern scholarship has shown that for the most part there are not significant enough genetic differences between people to make the category of "race" particularly useful in reconstructing past population groups. So archaeologists and historians have looked to "culture" as a more meaningful ancient category, one that can be located in the archaeological or historical record. Culture can manifest in any number of ways—the most readily apparent for earliest Egypt are the languages people used and the artifacts that they possessed.

EARLIEST EGYPTIANS

Despite the very best efforts of modern scholars, the origins of the earliest Egyptians are still obscured in mystery and academic controversy. The evidence so far unearthed suggests that people lived in Egypt long before the appearance of the first Egyptian state. The language of ancient Egypt is very closely related to other languages spoken in northeastern Africa, but beyond this not much can be said about the origins of the earliest group, the builders of the pyramids and worshippers of the sun.

Throughout the ancient period, the Egyptians saw themselves as a unique human culture. They considered themselves distinct from the people who lived outside the Nile Valley and a distinction was made between native Egyptians and foreigners (even if those "foreigners" had lived in Egypt for centuries). The geography of Egypt kept the population relatively isolated and safe from invasion from other regions, and only in a few isolated instances has mainland Egypt been invaded or conquered by an opposing force.

BEDOUIN, NUBIANS, AND LIBYANS

Numerous other groups did live within the borders of Ancient Egypt. Chief among these were nomadic groups, subsisting off the desert fringes and moving from oasis to oasis. Known as Bedouin today, the Ancient Egyptians knew these groups by many names. In historical inscriptions, these nomadic groups are usually described as a thorn in Egypt's side—ungovernable marauders who threatened travelers and generally would not submit to the yoke of pharaoh's rule.

The people to the south of Egypt, the Nubians, were at times friends and at other times foes of the Egyptians. In the Egyptian Middle Kingdom (2016–1786 B.C.E.) the Egyptians built forts to protect their southern frontier from possible Nubian attacks. By the New Kingdom (1550–1070 B.C.E.), Nubian mercenaries were a regular component of the Egyptian military contingent and even formed something of a police force in some Egyptian communities. Nubian power in Egypt reached a high point when a Nubian dynasty ruled over Egypt from 780–656 B.C.E.

BELOW: THE BEDOUIN, SUCH AS THIS ONE IN A PAINTING BY NINETEENTH-CENTURY ARTIST EUGENIO MORETTI, ARE NOMADIC PEOPLE WHO HAVE LIVED IN THE DESERT SINCE ANCIENT TIMES.

ABOVE: AMERICAN ARTIST FREDERICK BRIDGMAN PAINTED *CLEOPATRA ON THE TERRACES OF PHILAE* IN 1896. CLEOPATRA HAS BEEN THE SUBJECT OF MANY WORKS OF ART.

To Egypt's west was Libya. Already a desert by the time of the first Egyptian state, the border between Libya and Egypt proper was probably informally marked by a series of oases that run north-south, roughly near the modern border of the states. To the Ancient Egyptians, Libyans were anyone who lived in this Western Desert region. Generally nomadic pastoralists, the Libyans lived in relative peace with the Egyptians, trading with them and occasionally acting as mercenaries in the army. This harmonious state of affairs changed in the New Kingdom, when a coalition of Libyan tribes (along with tribes from Greek regions of the Mediterranean) attempted to invade Egypt. While these raids did not succeed in toppling the pharaoh's government, it is clear that many Libyans permanently settled in the Delta at this time.

THE ARRIVAL OF ISLAM

As the power of the pharaohs waned, Egypt fell first under the sway of Alexander the Great's Empire (and his successors, the Ptolemies) and then under the control of the Romans. The most notable of these foreign rulers was Cleopatra VII. Actually a Greek woman who did not speak Egyptian, she is usually considered the last pharaoh. While Egypt was ruled by these foreign powers, the internal demographics of Egypt did not change much. Egyptian life continued much as it always had. Yet the arrival of Islam in C.E. 639 brought lasting change to Egypt. An army of Islamic Arabs invaded Egypt, and the region was brought under Muslim control. Most of the population of Egypt converted to Islam in later years, although the Christian Egyptians (known as Copts) resisted and remain a thriving community in present-day Egypt. Islamic Egypt has been under the sway of many rulers since the Islamic invasion, most notably the Ottoman Turks, beginning in 1552, and then the French and British in the nineteenth century. In the 1920s, Egypt gained its independence for the first time since antiquity.

RACE AND ANCIENT EGYPT

In the 1990s, Martin Bernal published a controversial two-volume work called *Black Athena*, in which he alleges that scholars have systematically attempted to undermine the African basis of Western traditions by ignoring the African roots of Egyptian civilization. To some extent he is correct: most scholars have emphasized Egypt's connections to the Near East and downplayed its connections to Africa. Yet Bernal's equation of the Ancient Egyptian population with modern racial categories is inappropriate. "Race" is a relatively modern concept, and we do not have much evidence that the Egyptians themselves considered skin color as a marker of biological distinction. In Egyptian art, skin color is mostly used to differentiate men and women—men are painted in darker colors (from red to black) and women are painted using lighter colors (especially white). Given Egypt's location at a crossroads between Asia, Europe, and Africa, there is no proof of what ancient skin colors would have looked like, nor is there any proof that this would have mattered to the Ancient Egyptians.

RIGHT: THE SKILL OF GOLDSMITHS AND OTHER ARTISANS IS EVIDENT IN THIS GOLD RING, WHICH IS DECORATED WITH HORSE FIGURINES. IT BELONGED TO THE PHAROAH RAMESES II.

BELOW: WHEN ENGLISHMEN HOWARD CARTER AND LORD CARNARVON EXCAVATED THE TOMB OF TUTANKHAMUN IN 1923, IT HERALDED A HUGE REVIVAL OF INTEREST IN ALL THINGS EGYPTIAN.

ECONOMY AND AGRICULTURE FROM ANCIENT TIMES TO THE MODERN ERA

For most Egyptians, from ancient times to the present, farming of some sort or another has been the basis of economic life. Either farming for food or farming for cash-crops and textiles, Egyptians have a long tradition of working the land. Up until modern times, most Egyptians would have been small-scale subsistence farmers, eking out just enough to feed their families and pay their taxes. This situation was in contrast to the small percentage of the population that lived in extreme luxury.

MANUFACTURING FABRIC: TEXTILE PRODUCTION IN EGYPT

Cotton and flax plants have been harvested since antiquity in Egypt in order to produce cotton and linen textiles. While animal skins were also used in the manufacture of Egyptian clothing, the lighter fabrics were more useful in the hot, humid environment of Egypt. The process of transforming cotton plants and flax into textiles is time-consuming and probably the bulk of the work done in poor Egyptian households. First, the plants were harvested and retted (soaked in water until the fibers separated). Once the fibers had dried out, they were spun together to make long, continuous threads. The threads were then woven together, usually on a loom, until a rectangular piece of fabric was formed. Until the Industrial Revolution (which dramatically increased the pace of these initial stages of production), the fabrics would normally have been left in their rectangular shape to be folded and draped to match the desired style. These days, the Egyptian textile manufacturing industry is mostly mechanized, but carpet factories still make Egyptian rugs according to these traditional methods.

GOLD, ART, AND LUXURY GOODS

Since antiquity, Egypt has been a center of highly skilled artisans and metalsmiths, although most Egyptians do not accumulate enough wealth to enjoy it themselves. Working with gold from the south and precious stones and metals from the desert regions, the Egyptians created artistic styles that are distinct and easily recognizable. The popularity of things Egyptian has exploded periodically throughout world history. During the Bronze Age, Egyptian-made items were highly prized throughout the Near East and Mediterranean. For those who could not afford Egyptian-made items, local craftsmen in Phoenicia and Syria made imitation Egyptian goods. In the period when Egypt was a province of Rome, Egyptian goods were in high demand throughout the empire. In the 1920s, the discovery of King Tutankhamun's tomb by Howard Carter led to a revived craze for things Egyptian, called Egyptomania, that brought Egyptian stylistic influence into European and North American homes, perhaps most notably in art-deco design.

ROYAL ECONOMIC POWER

Concomitant with the rise of the Egyptian state was the rise of Egyptian royal economic power. In contrast to the generally minimal wealth of the everyday Egyptian was the extreme wealth of the pharaoh. The king was the dominant landholder, and along with the temples, had the right to tax the population (paid in goods or in service to the state). While much of the royal wealth was spent on living in the heights of luxury, a high proportion went to financing the funerary structures of the royal family. The Egyptians believed that the afterlife was much the same as earthly life. They believed that whatever was buried with them they could bring into the afterlife. This meant that the kings and their families were buried along with massive amounts of luxury goods, in lavishly designed tombs, well furnished to function as an eternal home. Perhaps the most obvious monuments of this type are the pyramids. Although

ABOVE: THE VALLEY OF THE KINGS IN A NINETEENTH-CENTURY LITHOGRAPH BY DAVID ROBERTS AND LOUIS HAGHE. TODAY TOURISTS CAN VISIT A NUMBER OF TOMBS IN THE AREA, INCLUDING ONE THAT HAS BEEN RECENTLY EXCAVATED.

there are hundreds throughout Egypt, the most splendid are the pyramids at Giza, located near modern Cairo. The Great Pyramid is the only human-built structure visible from space and involved an incredible expenditure of resources and labor to construct. It functioned as a burial place for the king and (since the king was seen as an incarnation of the Egyptian sun god) as a platform for his ascendance into the heavens. Associated with the pyramid were large temple complexes, established to provision the dead king with what he needed in the afterlife. Modern scholars are not certain exactly why this type of monument was abandoned, but it seems likely that pyramids were too expensive and too easy a target for tomb robbers. Eventually burial sites for Egyptian royalty moved to the Valley of the Kings and the Valley of the Queens, near the modern city of Luxor. There, kings and queens were buried in secret tombs, filled with all sorts of treasures and goods to be used in the afterlife. This is where King Tutankhamun's tomb was located. While King Tut (as he is better known) was not an important king, the discovery of his tomb was a significant find since most of the other kings' tombs had long ago been found and pillaged by tomb robbers. His tomb was relatively well preserved, and so filled with objects that scholars are still studying the finds today!

Tourism

Since the 1920s the Egyptian economy has become almost entirely dependent on tourism. This is one of the most important industries in the country (perhaps superseded only by textile manufacture and food processing) and a major source of employment for the citizens of Egypt. In 1997, Muslim fundamentalists attempted to undermine the Egyptian economy by destroying the tourist industry. At Deir el-Bahri (below), 58 tourists and four Egyptians were killed as armed gunmen opened fire in a courtyard. Since then, the Egyptian government has taken steps to safeguard visitors to the monuments, but the increasing hostility and the perceived threat of violence in the region continues to keep tourists away, in spite of the relative security of the country.

ABOVE: SINCE ANCIENT TIMES, EGYPTIANS HAVE CHANNELED THE NILE. THIS FARMER IS USING A SHADUF, A HAND-OPERATED LEVER, TO RAISE THE WATER.

BELOW: *THE OVERFLOW OF THE NILE* BY ITALIAN ARTIST AND ARCHAEOLOGIST GIOVANNI BELZONI SHOWS THE EFFECT OF THE NILE'S INUNDATION ON THE SURROUNDING FARMLAND.

THE INFLUENCE OF THE NILE AND ITS INUNDATION ON TRADE AND DEVELOPMENT IN THE REGION

Most introductions to the geography of Egypt begin with Herodotus's assertion that Egypt is "the gift of the Nile." Nothing could be more true of Egypt's geography. The Nile River provides the most important source of fresh water for the whole region. Its predictability allows agriculture on a large scale without much human intervention. And, until recently, the Nile has been the major transportation route through Egypt, with land transport (until the construction of the railroad) being of importance on only a local scale. Egypt's past, present, and future are completely interconnected with the Nile.

THE NILE

About 4,160 miles (6,695 km) in length, the Nile is the longest river in the world. It runs north from equatorial Africa into the Mediterranean. Until it reaches the Sudan, the Nile actually consists of two branches, the White Nile and the Blue Nile. The sources of both are large mountain lakes that collect precipitation during the rainy season. The amounts of water that usually fall during the rainy season are substantial, so Egypt is subject to an annual spike in the influx of water. This rise in water levels forces the Nile to overflow its banks every year, effectively watering the nearby farmland and making the strip of desert land beside the Nile fertile. The difference between land that is in the floodplain and land that is beyond its extent is quite extreme. Visitors to Egypt can literally have their photograph taken with one foot in the desert and one foot in the fertile valley. The Blue Nile waters (collected in Ethiopia) determine the force and volume of water that makes its way into Egypt. The shifting volumes of water have affected Egypt's economic viability throughout its history, and until the construction of the Aswan High Dam, left Egypt heavily dependent on the extent of the annual rains to the south. In the years when the Nile floods were very low, Egypt could be racked with famine.

AGRICULTURE

Harnessing the power of the annual inundation of the Nile lay at the heart of Ancient Egyptian agriculture. This meant managing the flow pattern of the Nile, and controlling where the water went when the Nile overflowed its banks. The water of the Nile would run off into various channels running parallel to the banks of the river. Water from these areas was then forced into irrigation reservoirs through a series of dikes and channels, and then into the agricultural fields. Each year, when the Nile levels began to rise, officials who had been tracking the levels (using measuring instruments called Nilometers) would warn the farmers to prepare.

The crops grown in Egypt were diverse. The most important crops were cereal crops. Emmer was grown for use in bread, and barley was grown to be used in beer making. Vegetables, fruits, and chickpeas (along with other pulses) were also major crops. Dates have always been a major crop in Egypt, and many other plants were grown for non-food purposes, such as flax for textiles or sesame for oil production. Gardens and orchards were also areas of food production, but these needed more intense labor throughout the year. Wheat was introduced to Egypt during Greco-Roman times, only then becoming a major agricultural crop.

The Aswan High Dam

In the 1960s, the Egyptian government began construction of a monumental dam near Aswan to control the flooding of the Nile, increase the amount of arable farmland, and to develop a dependable source of electricity. The construction of the dam involved the creation of an artificial reservoir (Lake Nasser) and a complete transformation of hydrological cycles that had existed in Egypt for centuries. The threat the construction of this dam brought to the antiquities of the region was immense, as most were destined to be destroyed or submerged by the changing water system. A major UNESCO project from 1964 to 1968 managed to save the colossal statues at Abu Simbel. A large international team dismantled the four statues that make up the Great Temple at Abu Simbel (built by Rameses II). The dismantled pieces were moved to a new location (right), and the statues were reconstructed. Visitors to Egypt can take a flight from Luxor to Aswan to visit the preserved monuments in their new location.

TRANSPORTATION

The importance of the Nile for transportation in Egypt cannot be overstated. Evidence for ship construction comes from the Predynastic Period, the period just before the development of the first unified Egyptian state. The types of ships the Egyptians used were diverse, but can be broadly categorized as ships for use on the Nile and ships for use on the Mediterranean. The Nile was Egypt's "highway" and until the rise of cars, was the central hub of Egyptian economic life. Given the difficulty of wheeled transportation over sand, land transport was only used locally.

EGYPT: THE BREADBASKET OF ROME

The combination of stable agriculture and easy transportation provided by the Nile made Egypt an important exporter of agricultural goods to the Mediterranean world. In ancient times, transportation was a major concern in the trade of agricultural goods, since these goods would perish over the course of a long voyage. As the city of Rome grew, it became more and more difficult to feed the urban population with the agricultural commodities produced locally. While Italy was very agriculturally productive, it was difficult to quickly and cheaply transport agricultural goods produced in other parts of Italy to Rome. So the Romans turned to Egypt. Crops could be easily conveyed from the fields after harvest to the Nile, and from there to the port of Alexandria. Cereals, especially wheat, could be shipped in bulk (very cheaply and in huge quantities) across the Mediterranean, so most of Rome ate Egyptian bread!

ABOVE: THE PYLON OF THE MORTUARY TEMPLE OF RAMESES III AT MEDINET HABU. RECORDS FOUND IN THE TEMPLE HAVE PROVIDED VALUABLE INFORMATION ABOUT THE PHILISTINES.

THE CAIRO GENIZAH FRAGMENTS

Visitors to Cairo can visit one of the oldest synagogues in the world, which has been much renovated since ancient times, but is still in use. There, a remarkable find was made in the genizah of the synagogue. A genizah is the section of a synagogue where old manuscripts are kept until they can be disposed of properly. According to Jewish tradition, any documents that contain the name of God cannot be disposed of without proper ceremonial care, and they are kept in a genizah until such time as the ceremonies can be performed.

In the genizah of this synagogue in Cairo, Rabbi Solomon Schechter found fragments of very old copies of some of the books of the Old Testament and the Apocrypha. The documents were soon removed from the genizah, but instead of being ceremonially destroyed, were moved to Cambridge University in England where they could be preserved and studied. In total, about 140,000 manuscript fragments were removed from the genizah, dating from the eleventh to the nineteenth centuries. Some of these were copies of biblical texts; other documents were the remains of the day-to-day administration of the synagogue. Their study has been remarkably profitable for scholars of Judaism. They have provided a valuable insight into the social history of a synagogue over time, new material for the study of some of the most important Jewish thinkers, and evidence for the grammar of the ancient Hebrew language.

ARCHAEOLOGY AND THE BIBLE IN THE REGION

Egyptian archaeology is one of the most exciting and romantic fields of study. Ancient Egypt is inherently interesting—hidden tombs filled with treasure, majestic pyramids looming over the desert, and ancient mummies preserved in mystical funerary rites all awaiting discovery. The Egyptian climate is well suited to archaeological preservation, so the amounts of materials recovered are truly tremendous. Given the prominence of Egyptians and Egyptian civilization in the Bible, the archaeology of Egypt has much to offer biblical readers.

MEDINET HABU

Perhaps the most fruitful use of Egyptology to better understand the Bible has been in the analysis of Egyptian historical records, like those found at Rameses III's memorial temple, located at Medinet Habu near Thebes. On parts of the walls of this temple, Ramses III commemorated his fight with the Sea Peoples, a coalition of forces that attacked Egypt and its holdings in the Levant. One of the groups in this coalition was the Philistines of biblical fame. The Bible never discusses the origins of the Philistines or how they arrived in the land of Canaan. Based on the artistic reliefs and poetic inscriptions at Medinet Habu, archaeologists can confirm that they settled in the land of Canaan shortly before the emergence of Israel. Archaeological investigations at Philistine cities in Israel (such as Ashkelon, Ashdod, and Ekron) have confirmed this and further demonstrated that the Philistines originally came from the Greek islands.

SHISHAK'S BATTLES IN PALESTINE

While the reliefs at Medinet Habu provide background information about events that are not described in the Bible, other Egyptian monuments attest directly to accounts preserved in the Bible. In 1 Kings 14:25–28, we are told that Shishak attacked the kingdoms of Judah and Israel, in the aftermath of the rebellion of Israel against Judah. Shishak (the Hebrew name for the Egyptian king Shoshenq) defeated both kingdoms in 925 B.C.E., and recorded the names of the towns that he destroyed at the Temple of Amun at Karnak. Archaeological investigations in modern Israel have shown that numerous cities were destroyed in 925 B.C.E. and so the biblical and Egyptian accounts are quite accurate. Furthermore, given some of the difficulties of equating ancient sites with ancient place names, comparison of destruction layers in these archaeological excavations with place names from Shishak's inscriptions can better help us identify these sites. Likewise, these destruction layers help date the material from these sites. Anything before the destruction must date to prior to 925 B.C.E. Anything after (or in archaeological terms, above) the destruction layer must date to later than 925 B.C.E.

LEFT: ELEPHANTINE IS AN ISLAND IN THE NILE NEAR MODERN-DAY ASWAN. ITS NAME POSSIBLY DERIVES FROM THE FACT THAT IVORY TRADING WENT ON THERE.

ELEPHANTINE

For biblical scholars, one of the most interesting sites that has been excavated in Egypt is Elephantine. Located on an island in the Nile River opposite the modern city of Aswan, the site has a long and varied history. Of interest here is the portion of the city that was settled by a Jewish group, who lived there (along with the native Egyptian population) from about 525 B.C.E. to about 399 B.C.E. For biblical scholars, this was a remarkable find. The Bible mentions Jewish groups having moved from Judah and Israel into Egypt, and we are told that the prophet Jeremiah moved to Egypt after the conquest by Nebuchadnezzar. But the Bible gives us only these tantalizing hints.

Excavations at the site have revealed not only the buildings that these people lived in, but also many Aramaic papyri attesting to their everyday life. Many of these texts are legal agreements, marriage contracts, court settlements, and wills, and are invaluable for reconstructing the social history of early Jewish groups. Even more remarkable are the documents that preserve this group's political history. It seems that there was some conflict between the Jewish community and the local worshippers of the god Khnum. Because of this conflict, in 410 B.C.E., the local governor ordered that the temple to Yahweh (the Hebrew name for God) be destroyed. So the local Jewish community wrote to Jewish authorities in Samaria and Jerusalem, asking permission to rebuild their local temple. Permission was granted, and we assume that the temple was rebuilt (although archaeologists are not certain which building in Elephantine was the temple to Yahweh).

BELOW: THE PROPHET JEREMIAH WARNED JEWISH REFUGEES IN EGYPT THAT THEY COULD NOT FEEL SECURE THERE, AS NEBUCHADNEZZAR'S DESTRUCTIVE ZEAL WOULD SURELY FOLLOW THEM THERE.

EGYPTIAN LANGUAGES

Ancient Egyptians spoke a unique Afro-Asiatic language, known as Egyptian. Related to African and Semitic language families, this was the dominant language until Alexander the Great's conquest of the region and the subsequent adoption of Greek. Egyptian was written in a number of forms. Hieroglyphs were the formal writing system. Hieratic was the handwritten version. Demotic (shown in the papyrus fragment, right) is a later form of the language using essentially Greek characters. Coptic, a mix between the Greek and Egyptian languages, is spoken by Egyptian Christians. After the Muslim conquest, Arabic became the most important language in Egypt, and it is the official language of the country today.

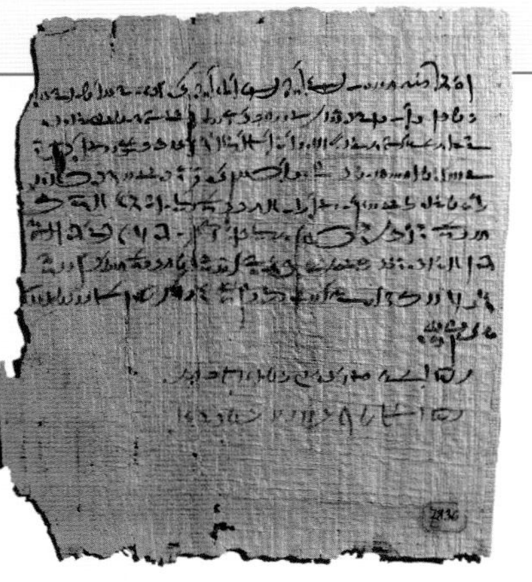

ANCIENT EGYPTIAN WRITINGS AND THE BIBLE

Ancient Egyptian writing is very well preserved. The climate of Egypt is perfect for preserving papyrus, the type of paper used in Egypt. The Egyptians also believed that architectural space should be covered with as much writing and art as possible, so most archaeological investigations in Egypt uncover as much writing as they do buildings. While most of the writing recovered from Egypt does not bear directly on biblical studies, the occasional find is striking in its references to biblical people or themes.

THE TALE OF TWO BROTHERS AND THE TRADITION OF SEVEN LEAN YEARS

Familiar to most Bible readers is Joseph's journey to Egypt and subsequent rise to power there, recorded in the last third of the Book of Genesis. Probably not familiar to biblical readers are two Egyptian stories that bear a remarkable similarity to the narratives about Joseph. In a story known to scholars as "The Tale of Two Brothers," an incident of attempted adultery is recounted, that is often likened to Potiphar's wife's attempts to seduce Joseph. In the Egyptian story, however, a man is accused of adultery with his older brother's wife, even though he rejected her propositions. Another papyrus, dated much later, records an account of the Nile having seven low years and subsequently causing a famine. It seems that the biblical account of Joseph's prediction of seven fat years followed by seven lean years is consistent with general observations about the behavior of the Nile.

THE HYMN TO THE ATEN

One of the oddest periods in Egyptian history is typically referred to as the "Amarna Age." In this period (1350–1334 B.C.E.), the pharaoh Amenhotep IV changed his name to Akhenaten, moved the capital from Thebes to Amarna, and banned the worship of the many Egyptian gods in place of the sole worship of the Aten, the physical disk of the sun. Scholars debate the motives behind Akhenaten's reform, and much of what occurred is not well understood. But it is clear that Akhenaten acted out of religious beliefs in the primacy of Aten.

Sigmund Freud, in his famous work *Moses and Monotheism*, argued that Moses himself learned of God from the pharaoh Akhenaten. While this is unlikely (Akhenaten is far older than Moses is thought to be), there does seem to be some connection between biblical religion and Atenism. This is strikingly apparent in a beautiful Egyptian poem, known to scholars as "The Hymn to the Aten." This 13-line poem, written in Egyptian, was found in the tomb of Ay, Akhenaten's chief courtier and later king of Egypt. The poem is a hymn of praise to the god Aten, praising him as the creator of the world and the pharaoh as sole intermediary between Aten and humanity. Scholars immediately noticed similarities between this poem and Psalm 104, which is a hymn of praise to God. Certain themes are very similar, but, more importantly, particular lines seem like Hebrew translations of the same poem. The poems are not identical, but certainly some sections are very close, both in content and expression. The exact connection between these two works and their relationship to one another remain a mystery of biblical scholarship.

THE MERNEPTAH STELA

Archaeology in Egypt has also uncovered the earliest extra-biblical reference to Israel, although the reference is puzzling. Around 1208 B.C.E., pharaoh Merneptah engaged in campaigns in Canaan, before the people of Israel would have returned to the land. After his campaign, he erected a commemorative stone (called a stela) describing what he had accomplished by his military activities in Canaan. The inscription is fairly typical of an Egyptian king—it is a bombastic account of how successful he was and how easily he destroyed his enemies. What is unusual is the statement, "Israel is laid waste, his seed is not," implying that he had completely destroyed Israel. Now, it is not surprising that an Egyptian king would claim to have totally destroyed a people that he in fact did not (Egyptian kings typically exaggerated their victories). But, whatever battle he did engage in with Israel happened before Israel had taken the land from the Canaanites, and the battle is not mentioned in the Bible. So the challenge for historians is how to understand this passing reference when reconstructing the history of Israel, especially those parts of the history that are not discussed in the Bible.

OPPOSITE: THE PHARAOH AKHENATEN OFFERS LOTUS FLOWERS TO ATEN, THE SUN GOD, IN A COLORED LIMESTONE STELA FROM THE ROYAL TOMB AT AMARNA.

RIGHT: JOSEPH, WHO WAS PURCHASED AS A SLAVE BY POTIPHAR, THE CAPTAIN OF THE GUARD, REJECTING THE ADVANCES OF POTIPHAR'S WIFE, IN A PAINTING BY ESTEBAN MURILLO.

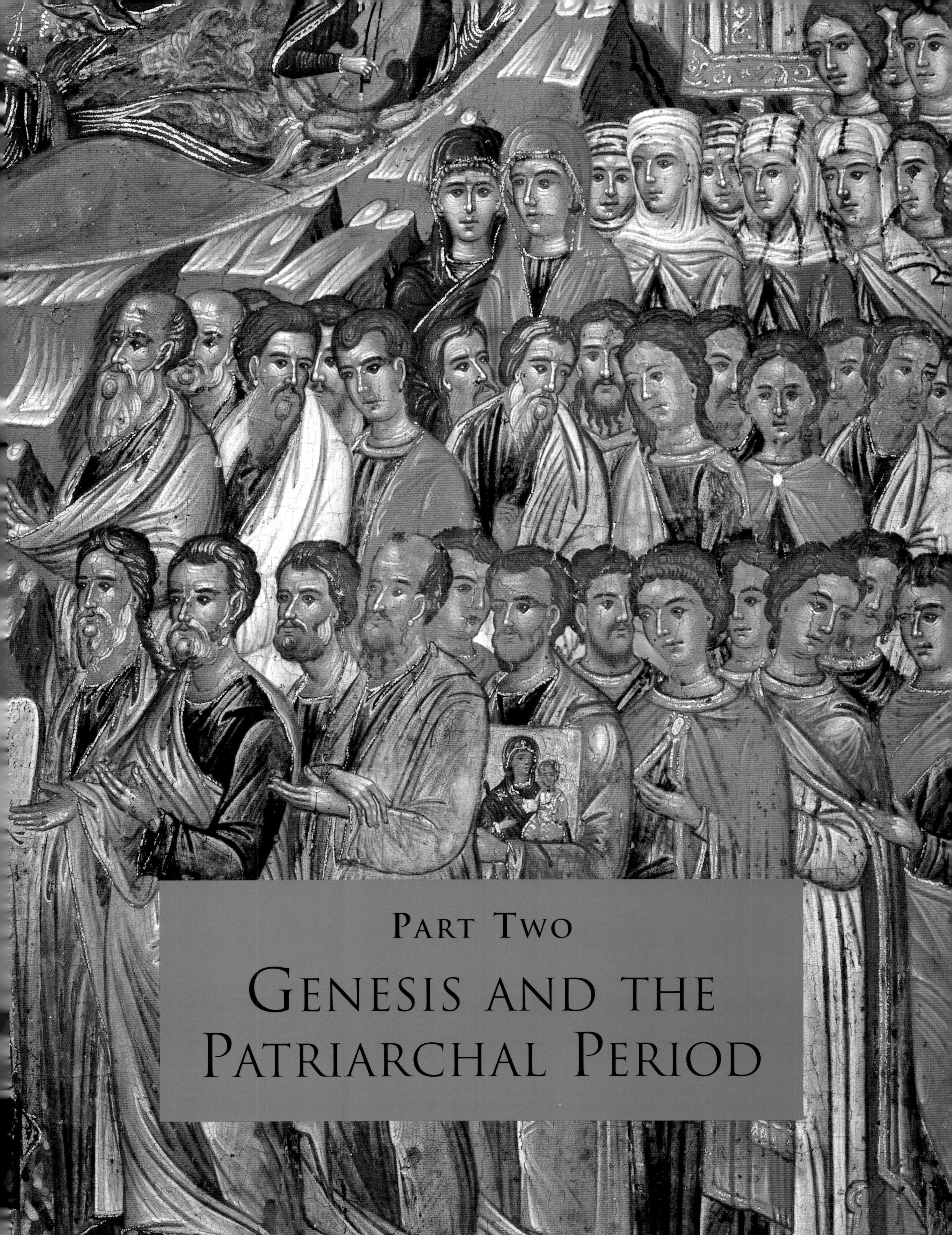

Part Two

Genesis and the Patriarchal Period

THE COVENANT OF THE LORD

IN YOUR STEADFAST LOVE YOU LED THE PEOPLE WHOM YOU REDEEMED ... TO YOUR HOLY ABODE EXODUS 15:13

RIGHT: THIS SIXTEENTH-CENTURY C.E. STAINED GLASS WINDOW FROM EGLISE SAINTE MADELEINE DE TROYES, FRANCE, SHOWS THE STORY OF CREATION.

BELOW: THE SEQUENCE OF EVENTS FROM THE CREATION TO THE FALL OF HUMANKIND FROM GOD'S FAVOR ARE SHOWN IN THIS ORNATE BULGARIAN PAINTING FROM THE NINETEENTH CENTURY C.E.

The first five books of the Old Testament—the Pentateuch—relate a version of the early history of humankind, from the creation of the world to the arrival of the Israelites in the Promised Land.

At one level, it is the story of the wanderings of a group of nomadic tribes under a succession of patriarchal leaders, culminating in their settlement in Canaan under Moses' successor, Joshua. The details of the story are sometimes muddled, but it is clear enough in outline: it records the birth of humankind in the Fertile Crescent; the proliferation of the descendants of Adam and Eve; the migration of the Israelites southwest to the rich land of Egypt; their flight eastward to escape slavery and oppression; and their 40-year journey northward through the wilderness of Sinai toward Canaan.

At a deeper level, however, it is the record of a spiritual apocalypse through which God revealed himself to his people after the fall from innocence and the punishment of sin through the great flood. It is rich in a symbolism that links natural phenomena with the experience of the individual soul. The Passover sacrifice of lambs is a practical expedient, but it is also an image of the death of the Lamb of God on the cross. The manna and water that sustain the Israelites in the wilderness are earthly nourishment, but they are also a foretaste of the spiritual body and blood of Christ.

The Exodus is a factual account of a migration, but it is also significant as a prefiguration of Satan's temptation of Jesus during his 40 days in the desert.

THE SPIRIT OF GOD

This intermingling of history and faith is apparent in the first words of the Old Testament. In a few brief verses, the opening of Genesis gives an account of the prehistoric era, from the emergence of the first life forms to the appearance of the earliest humans: "while the spirit of God swept over the face of the waters ... then the Lord God formed man from the dust of the ground, and breathed into his nostrils the breath of life; and the man became a living being" (Genesis 1:2–2:7).

The word spirit comes from the Latin *spiritus*, meaning "breath," and the imagery of God's breath pervades the early history of the Israelites. Before the flight out of Egypt, God raised a east wind that brought the plague of locusts. He summoned an east wind to open the Red Sea for the Israelites to pass into the desert, and caused the wind to drop so that the pursuing forces of the Egyptian pharaoh were drowned in the surge of water. He took Elijah up to heaven in a whirlwind, and spoke to Job out of a whirlwind. And the wind was not always benevolent; as the prophet Jeremiah foretold, it could be a manifestation of God's anger when his people failed to observe the law.

THE HOLY MOUNTAIN

Central to the adventures of the Israelites in the wilderness was God's handing down of the law—the Ten Commandments—to the Israelites through the patriarch Moses. According to Exodus, this revelation took place on Mt. Sinai, situated at the southern tip of the Sinai Peninsula. God came down to the mountain in cloud, thunder, and lightning, "while the whole mountain shook violently" (Exodus 19:18).

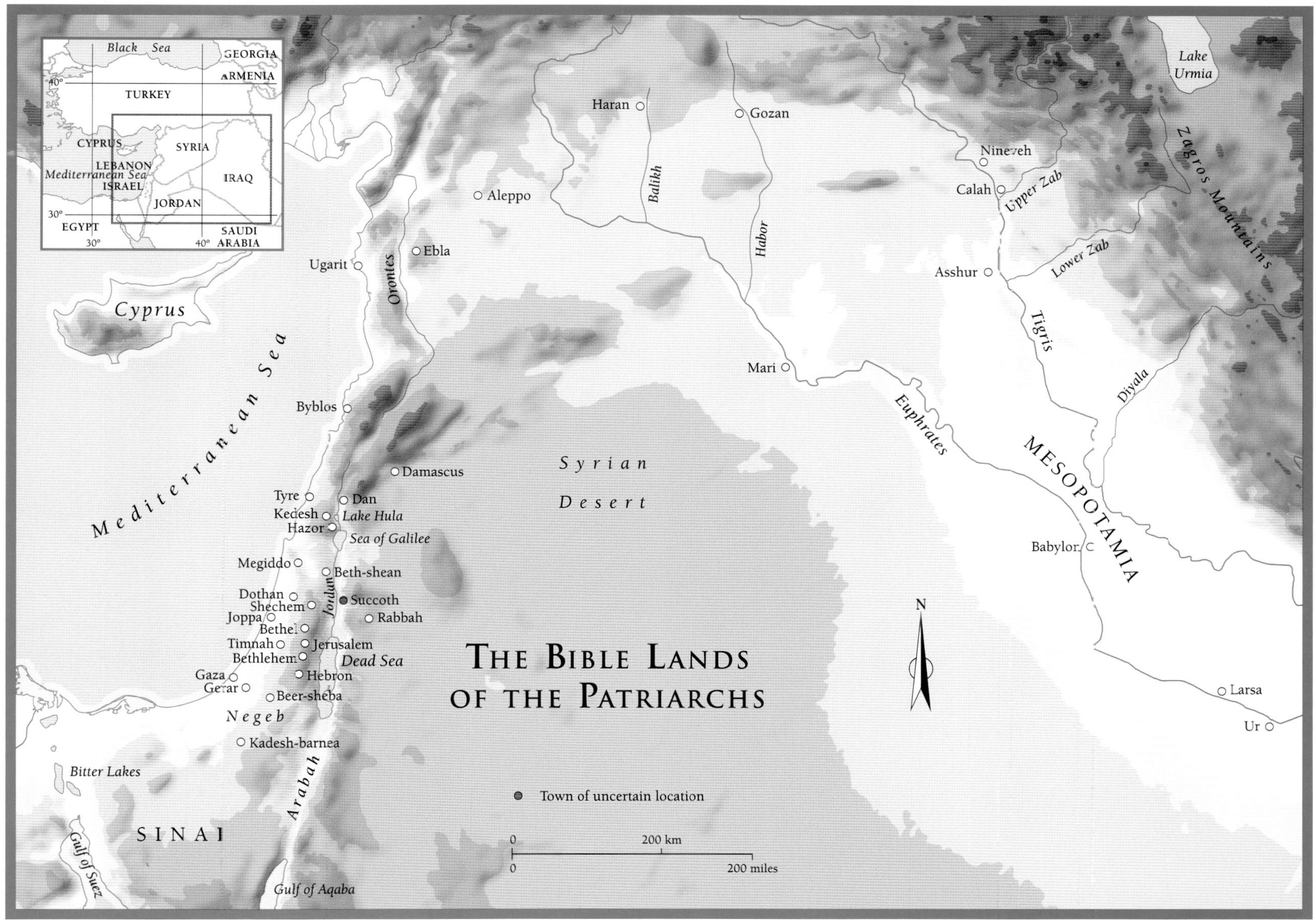

Mt. Sinai and its fire and smoke transcend mere metaphor—they are a manifestation of God himself, and of his awesome power. Like the wind that is the breath of God, tempests and volcanoes are not just poetic images but the authentic voice of God.

In almost every ancient culture, gods dwell on mountains and deploy the forces of nature in their dealings with humans, but the religion of the Israelites stands apart. In the polytheistic mythologies of Greece and Rome, the gods are cruel—in Shakespeare's *King Lear*, Gloucester remarks: "As flies to wanton boys, are we to the gods; they kill us for their sport" (Act IV, scene i, line 36). For the Israelites, however, God is One, both just and merciful, and they stand in a direct relationship to him; human joys and sorrows are the consequences of virtue and wickedness, not of fickle deities playing games with lesser beings.

THE PROMISED LAND

The Israelites completed their long trek northward to the land of Canaan (modern-day Palestine) in around 1190 B.C.E., though there would be years of skirmishing with hostile Gentile tribes before the anointing of Saul as the first king of the Israelites in around 1051 B.C.E.

Here, too, the historical account is interwoven with symbolic representations of God's care for his people. During their 40 years in the wilderness, the Israelites frequently broke God's covenant, failing to keep the faith and worshipping images of false gods. But God, through his prophets, brought them back into the Way of the Lord and kept the promise that he had given them: "And I have come down to deliver them … to a good and broad land, a land flowing with milk and honey" (Exodus 3:8). The promise of earthly prosperity becomes a promise of spiritual sustenance. The pattern of sin, retribution, and repentance would continue, but so would the pattern of divine justice and mercy.

The authorship of the Pentateuch is traditionally attributed to Moses himself, but most biblical scholars agree that in their present form they date from between the ninth and the fourth centuries B.C.E., making them a written record of earlier traditions. The facts as they are presented may be questioned, but the story they tell of a journey toward nationhood rings true. More importantly, its true significance lies in its account of a unique spiritual quest—the human need to explain the vicissitudes of life in terms of something other than chance.

LEFT: A HIGHLY DETAILED PIECE, THIS TWENTIETH-CENTURY C.E. JEWISH RUG SHOWS MT. SINAI—A SIGNIFICANT LANDMARK IN BIBLICAL HISTORY—AMID A LANDSCAPE OF DESERT AND TAMARISK TREES.

CREATION AND FALL

GOD SAW EVERYTHING THAT HE HAD MADE, AND INDEED, IT WAS VERY GOOD GENESIS 1:31

RIGHT: ARTWORK PROVIDES A VISUAL RECORD OF THE SPREAD OF CHRISTIANITY. THIS ELEVENTH-CENTURY C.E. FRESCO—DEPICTING THE CREATION OF THE WORLD—IS FOUND IN HYLLESTAD STAVKIRKE IN NORWAY.

The Creation narratives relate the divine origin of the universe, but also skillfully anticipate the future story of Israel, with the events in Eden foreshadowing the life, travails, and hopes of the historical biblical community.

THE SIX DAYS OF CREATION

Ancient readers would have recognized that the neat division of creation into six divine days signified that the world was carefully designed and imbued with order. The literary pattern of "command, fulfillment, inspection, and approval" amounts to a royal building inscription. God, acting as sovereign, consecrates a virginal spot from which to construct a shrine (Genesis 1:1–3). Replete with dome (1:6–8), floor (earth), sacred pool (seas), supplies (1:11–12, 20–25), ritual calendar (1:14–19), and a "staff" (1:26–31), architecturally, the cosmos is a temple, whose human personnel are consecrated to be its priests.

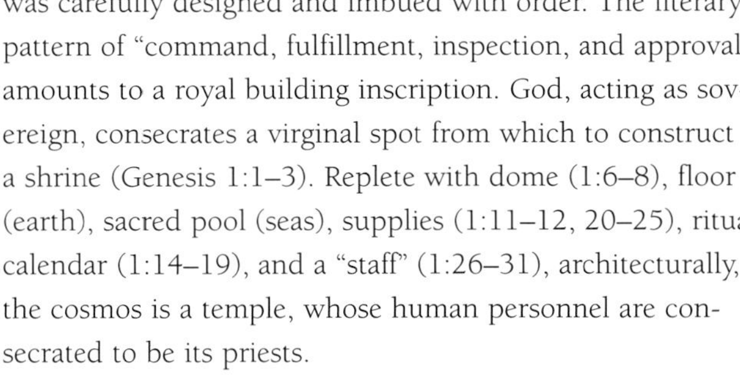

GOD SETS APART THE SEVENTH DAY AS A DAY OF REST

On the seventh day, God rested (Genesis 2:2), representing his "enthronement" as Divine Sovereign, accompanied by the pronouncement of a holiday. In parallel to state festivals, the Sabbath is the time in which the respective members of Creation are exempted from labor to celebrate the Author of Life's granting them a role within his sacred territory and to render him proper gratitude for his gift.

THE GARDEN OF EDEN

The description of the Garden of Eden continues to employ royal imagery. Around the Fertile Crescent, a "garden" with its lushness evoked the exclusive domain of a palace, whose access was limited only to the most trusted personnel. Similarly, the box-like description of the land, bounded on its sides by precious gems and metals, points to the Garden of Eden as being the inner-sanctum or private chapel of a king. Correspondingly, its human inhabitants are accorded the highest privilege within the created order.

ADAM AND EVE

Initially, humankind is described as made "in the image of God" (Genesis 1:26–27). In the Near East, an image served as a boundary marker for its owner. This indicates that the male and female were to advertise and uphold the claim of their Divine Sovereign over the world. Yet, the taking of man "from the dust of the ground" (2:7) also stresses elevation from lowly status to a position of honor: the breathing of the breath of life signified the establishment of a covenantal relationship. Thus, the role of Adam (meaning "the one from the earth" [*'adamah*]) is to be a deputy for God—a task to be shared by the woman designed to be the man's ally (2:18). Strikingly, the term "rib" (*tsela'*)—the material from which Eve is created—can refer to a shrine's annex. God builds the woman to complement her partner, with both functioning as a portable tabernacle to glorify God wherever they go.

BELOW: SECTION OF THE *MADONNA OF VICTORY* BY ANDREA MANTEGNA. THIS EXQUISITELY DETAILED IMAGE DEPICTS "THE FALL OF MAN," AS ADAM AND EVE GIVE IN TO TEMPTATION.

THE TREE OF THE KNOWLEDGE OF GOOD AND EVIL

The creation of Adam and Eve (Genesis 3:20) further represents their commission as vassals of their Divine Sovereign. Befitting their office, they are provided land, sustenance, and freedom to exercise benign dominion. There is one exception: " ... of the tree of the knowledge of good and evil you shall not eat" (2:17).

In biblical Hebrew, the admonition can also be read as "to not partake in the deciding of what is permissible and what is prohibited."

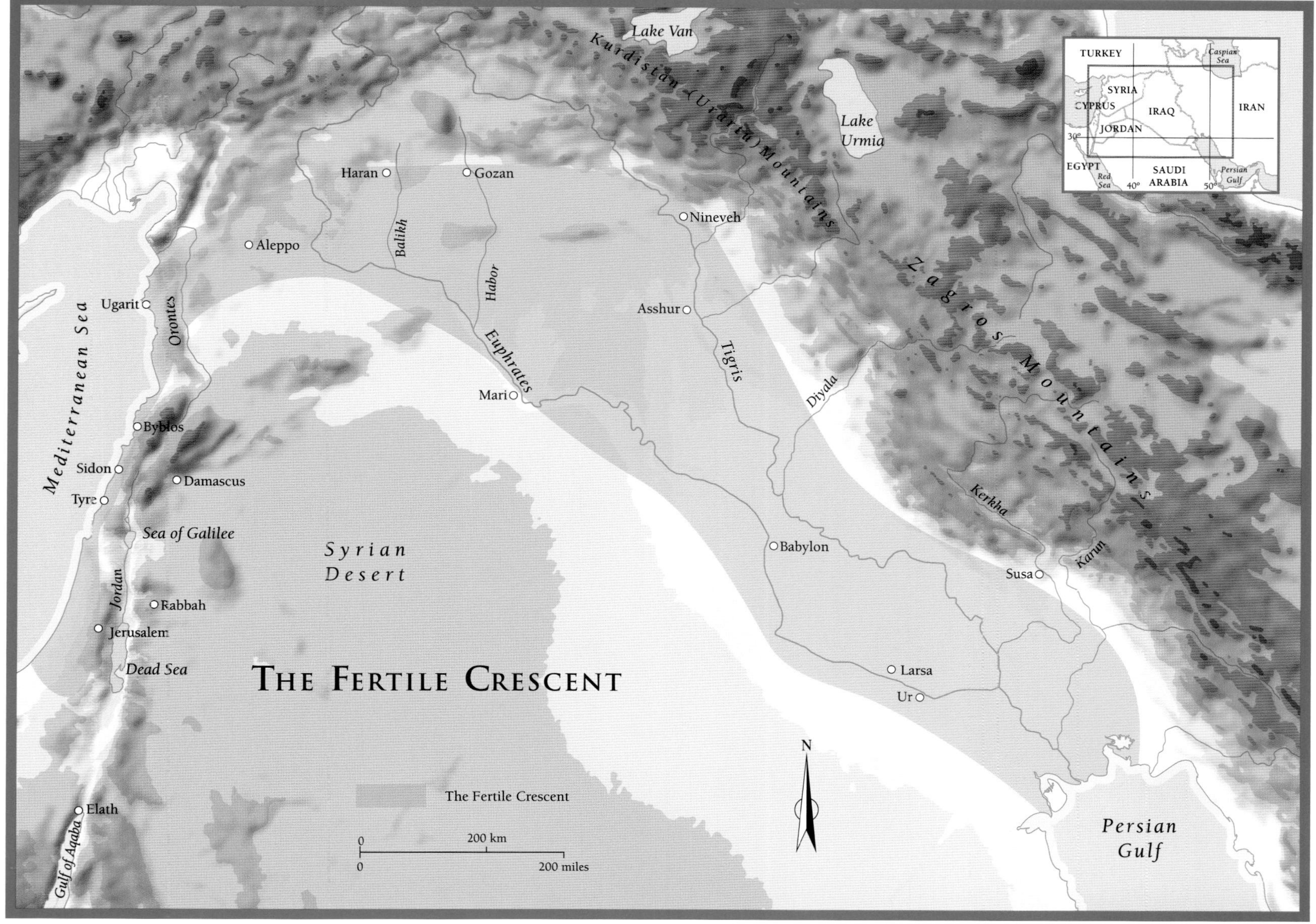

The pair is warned for their own welfare that only God is Lord of his Creation. With its position set squarely within the most holy ground, "the tree of the knowledge of good and evil," is nothing less than the Divine Covenantal Commandment by which there can be meaning and purpose to human existence.

THE TEMPTATION

The introduction of the serpent intrudes upon humanity's pleasant view of the garden (Genesis 3:1). Sometimes identified as the devil, here the serpent is simply more crafty than any other animal. However, in Hebrew, the word "serpent" is a pun for "one who practices divination," indicating efforts to access the divine will for self-advantage. This dynamic will be at the center of the enticement of the woman "to eat of the tree of the garden" (3:4), as the snake ("the diviner") tempts Eve to challenge God's ultimate rule.

THE BIRTH OF SIN AND SHAME

Technically, Adam and Eve's sin is breach of covenant, in other words, rebellion. Incited by an agent provocateur, the couple on its own conspires to revoke its terms of office and seize power during a secret meal—a classic act of revolt (Genesis 3:6–7a). The pair's concealment with loincloths is not just embarrassed shame over nakedness (3:7), but rather, outrage upon realizing its frailty and dependence upon God.

THE CONTEMPORARY LOCATION OF THE GARDEN OF EDEN

The verb from which "Eden" derives never occurs itself in the Old Testament, and the inability to ascertain the precise nuance of a given noun has given rise to a number of geographic misconceptions. The word "Eden" may derive from a Sumerian root *(edinu)* that defines the steppe land of the Mesopotamian valley. The word also appears in Ugaritic literature, where it denotes a place that is fertile and well-watered, a connotation the Bible sometimes also attaches to it. The garden was said to have been located "in Eden, in the east" (Genesis 2:8), and an initial observation suggests a possible location for the garden—somewhere in the Mesopotamian valley.

THE BANISHMENT

The attempted coup is revealed when God is heard walking in the garden (Genesis 3:8). Called to account, the pair seeks to shift the blame for their deeds. But the consequences of Adam and Eve's covenantal violation are far-reaching and severe—Creation's harmony has been shattered, and an oppressive hierarchy will replace human equality and cooperation. The pair loses its original post, and is reduced to the status of hirelings. Driven from their tenured positions, they are to face an uncertain future in exile beyond Eden's confines (3:23–24).

ABOVE: GRABOW ALTARPIECE BY MASTER BERTRAM OF MINDEN. THIS PANEL SHOWS ADAM AND EVE'S LIFE OF TOIL AND HARDSHIP ONCE THEY HAVE BEEN BANISHED FROM THE GARDEN OF EDEN.

ADAM AND EVE'S LIFE OF HARD LABOR

God's threat that "the tree of the knowledge of good and evil you shall not eat, for in the day that you eat of it you shall die" (Genesis 2:17) is not fulfilled right away. However, this language is quite comprehensive, entailing covenantal status, not just biological existence. Accordingly, "meaningful life" is "to be in relationship with another," whereas "death" is "separation from one's partner." It is this latter, depressing sense of alienation that will mark Adam and Eve's immediate years outside of Eden. Regardless, the Scriptures also show that God continues his benevolence to humanity. Despite their demotion or fall, the pair is provided with clothing (3:21). Divine sponsorship does continue, but only at a cost—Creation itself is now sacrificed for Adam and Eve's sustenance.

CAIN AND ABEL

One of the emphases of the Creation story is that all life has been endowed with the ability to reproduce (Genesis 1:22–28). Notwithstanding their transgressions, Adam and Eve fulfill this task, signified by Eve—the mother of all living (3:20)—bearing two sons. The ensuing fraternal conflict between the two has been compared to a Sumerian account about the competition between farmer and shepherd. More probable is that "pastoral" Abel and "agricultural" Cain are demonstrating their obedience to the commands "to have dominion" (1:28) and "to till" (2:15) the land. For the time being, the emerging human family—through its bringing forth and naming of life, accompanied by its care of flora and fauna—musters enough discipline to carry out its divinely ordained tasks.

BELOW: SIBLING RIVALRY SPARKS THE BIBLE'S FIRST MURDER, WHEN CAIN KILLS HIS BROTHER BECAUSE ABEL'S GIFT TO GOD WAS FAVORED OVER HIS OWN OFFERING, AS SEEN IN THIS SIXTEENTH-CENTURY C.E. MAJOLICA PLATE FROM RIMINI, ITALY.

THE FIRST MURDER AND EAST OF EDEN

Tragically, friction occurs as the siblings bring offerings to the Lord (Genesis 4:3–4), although it is only Cain who is disgruntled. Whatever the character of God's reception of their respective offerings, the older brother interprets the divine action as rejection—he has decided "good and evil" on his own. Cautioned by God to mind his own business, Cain's enmity reaches a boiling point. On a pretext, he invites his perceived rival to join him: "Let us go out to the field" (4:8). The irrational killing of Abel drives home the deadly consequences of eating of the tree of knowledge and presuming to be like God. Like his parents, upon discovery of his crime, Cain, too, seeks to avoid responsibility. Pleading ignorance—"Am I my brother's keeper?" (4:9)—he repudiates his duty to "keep" Creation (2:15). Guilty of desecrating the land by murder, Cain is reduced to the most wretched status in the ancient world—a fugitive (4:12). Unfit for the Divine Presence, and without home, family, or patronage, he makes his way east to the land of Nod, or "the Place of Wandering" (4:16)—the gates of Eden have faded completely from sight. Cain's "mark"—a kind of legal brand—is sometimes regarded as an act of God's forbearance. But it is also a warning that his sentence is not to be alleviated by human intervention. Cain is to be disgraced in perpetuity.

THE DESCENDANTS OF ADAM AND EVE FROM SETH TO METHUSELAH AND NOAH

Following Abel's murder, the Bible provides genealogical tables, which move our attention from Eden to the flood. Crucially, the birth of Seth (Genesis 4:25) introduces the idea of the "remnant"—God preserves a seed to allow the "tree of life" to continue. Regardless of the tragedy of human sin, God providentially supplies a line to serve his ultimate purpose. This will be fulfilled by Noah (5:28–29), who assumes the role of a savior of a Creation run amok.

Not surprisingly, the other feature of these lists, extreme human longevity—most notably, Methuselah and his record 969 years (Genesis 5:27)—has prompted much debate.

Modern scholars note parallels in ancient king-lists, where centuries, even millennia, are ascribed to rulers' lengths of reign, suggesting a similar practice for Genesis. Others theorize better immune systems untouched by disease, or a more pristine environment enjoyed by humanity in a world free of industrial toxins and pollutants, or even unknown methods of dating to rationalize the extended chronologies. Among the latter adherents, suggestions range from seeing the Hebrew word for year as referring instead to shorter liturgical periods, making the numbers more manageable; while some have argued that the figures represent the aggregate of all the members of a generation. That is, the patriarch's chronological existence is the total of all the years of his family unit, including various side-branches of siblings and in-laws. Yet, as incredible as these spans are, they illustrate a crucial theological point.

Long life and offspring were obvious signs of divine favor. The post-Eden generations are, therefore, extraordinarily blessed, but their accomplishments are woefully limited! The exception to this pattern is Enoch, who "walked with God" (Genesis 5:18–24). In his relatively limited time on earth—365 years—Enoch is obedient to divine guidance. The notice that "he was no more, because God took him" (5:24) lent itself to the belief that Enoch was transported directly into heaven, escaping death. In time, he will go on to become important in both Judaism and Christianity, with numerous visions being ascribed to him in apocryphal and apocalyptic literature.

ABOVE: THE BEAUTIFUL STAINED GLASS WINDOWS AT SELSLEY CHURCH IN ENGLAND WERE CREATED BY WILLIAM MORRIS AND HIS TEAM OF CRAFTSMEN. THIS WINDOW DEPICTS ENOCH STANDING IN THE HEAVENS.

THE WRATH OF GOD ON SINFUL HUMANITY

The scandalous interaction of "the sons of God" with the "daughters of humans" (Genesis 6:1–4) prompts the eventual reduction of mortal life span to 120 years. Although seemingly mysterious, in the ancient world, "son of god" was often used as a royal title referring to the king as guardian of justice. If the present idiom is being utilized in this manner, what is going on is, that instead of protecting the innocent, these predatory rulers crassly exploit their subjects, claiming the right to sleep with any female they desire. The identification of the "warriors of renown" born from these couplings with the "Nephilim"—literally, "the fallen," or "damned"—presents the Bible's sober assessment of these heroic figures and their exploits. Symptomatic of the escalating decay of morality, humanity's insistence on ruling itself unleashes all-pervasive evil (6:5). The decline set off earlier by Lamech's boast of unlimited vengeance merely for insult (4:23–24) eventually turns into an avalanche of wickedness—human beings have remade themselves entirely over into the image of Cain. Painfully, God turns away from a world gone mad: "I am sorry that I have made them" (6:7). There is only one who is to escape the coming wrath—Noah (6:8).

LEFT: *CAIN'S FIRST CRIME* BY CHARLES NAPIER KENNEDY. BEYOND THE GARDEN OF EDEN, ADAM AND EVE START A FAMILY. FIRSTBORN, CAIN, WILL GROW TO WORK ON THE LAND, WHILE SECOND SON, ABEL, WILL TEND SHEEP.

NOAH AND HIS DESCENDANTS

SO THE LORD SAID, "I WILL BLOT OUT FROM THE EARTH THE HUMAN BEINGS I HAVE CREATED" GENESIS 6:7

RIGHT: EXQUISITELY CRAFTED, THIS ILLUMINATED MANUSCRIPT DEPICTING NOAH'S ARK DURING THE 40 DAYS OF FLOOD IS FROM THE FIFTEENTH-CENTURY C.E. *BOOK OF HOURS* BY THE MASTER OF SIR JOHN FASTOLF.

BELOW: *THE FLOOD* BY HANS BALDUNG GRIEN. TO OVERCOME THE WICKEDNESS THAT PERVADED THE LAND, GOD SENDS A FLOOD TO CLEANSE THE EARTH, SAVING ONLY A CHOSEN FEW.

The terrible pronouncement "to blot out" Creation amounts to a declaration of war. The "temple of the world" is to be swept clean of its violent invaders and usurpers and purified anew by a great flood. So desperate is the earth's condition, that God risks the destruction of his beloved sanctuary to reestablish his righteousness.

GOD COMMANDS NOAH TO BUILD THE ARK

Noah is a prime example of the faithful servant. Because of his unique loyalty in a wayward and apostate generation (Genesis 6:9), God not only warns him of disaster, but also promises to preserve Noah's life through a covenant of grant (6:18, 7:1), providing him with the means of deliverance. Noah will become the biblical prototype of the righteous individual who enjoys a special pledge of divine faithfulness in the face of impending peril.

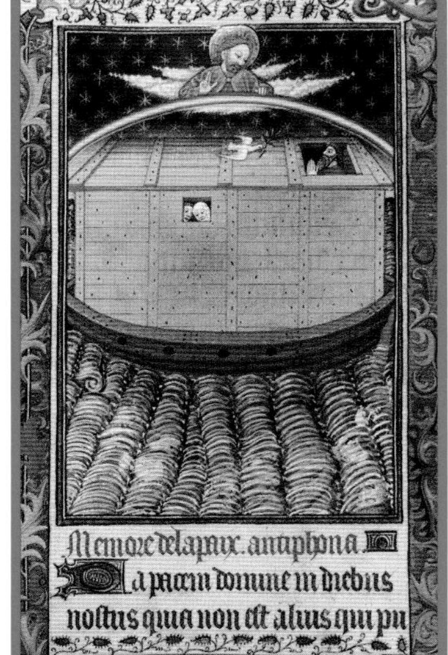

THE DIMENSIONS AND DESIGN OF THE ARK

Noah's "rescue vehicle" was approximately 450 ft long by 75 ft wide and 45 ft high (about 137 m × 23 m × 14 m), and resembled a submarine.

However, an ark was also a piece of sacred furniture. It held the most precious assets of a temple—images dedicated to a deity. When sanctuaries were threatened with destruction, an ark and its treasures were transported to a safe locale. In a similar fashion, Noah and his family are "the images of God," which are carefully preserved by their owner until they can be restored to their place of honor.

THE ARK'S PASSENGERS

To repopulate the earth, God's pledge includes Noah's relatives as well as a portion of Creation. The Bible seemingly contains different traditions about the ark's cargo. Genesis 6:19–20, with its "two of every kind" of living thing, recapitulates the language of the first chapter. By contrast, Genesis 7:2–3 stresses ritual characteristics, narrowing the list down to "seven pairs of all clean animals ... and a pair ... that are not clean." Significantly, "seven" in the Scriptures expresses "completeness," essentially indicating all of Creation in abbreviated, poetic fashion. Clearly, both biblical strands emphasize God's intention to keep alive what he has made (6:19, 7:3), with this remnant providing hope for the future.

THE DELUGE

The flood represents the systematic scouring away of the earth's corruption. Battle imagery is deliberately employed, as God dismantles the barriers that hold back watery chaos, much as ancient armies would hack up dikes and sluice gates while on campaign.

MT. ARARAT

Noah's vessel eventually moors "on the mountains of Ararat" (Genesis 8:4). Known from Assyrian documents as Urartu, the place broadly described mountainous terrain in Armenia. Contrary to Genesis's allusion to a range, later tradition centered on a single peak for the ark's place of repose. The most popular site is the 17,000-ft (5,182-m) Agri Dagi (Mt. Ararat) massif in Turkey. Other locales have been identified in Armenia, southern Turkey, and even as far away as Arabia (Jebel Judi), based on much later Qur'anic (Koranic) tradition.

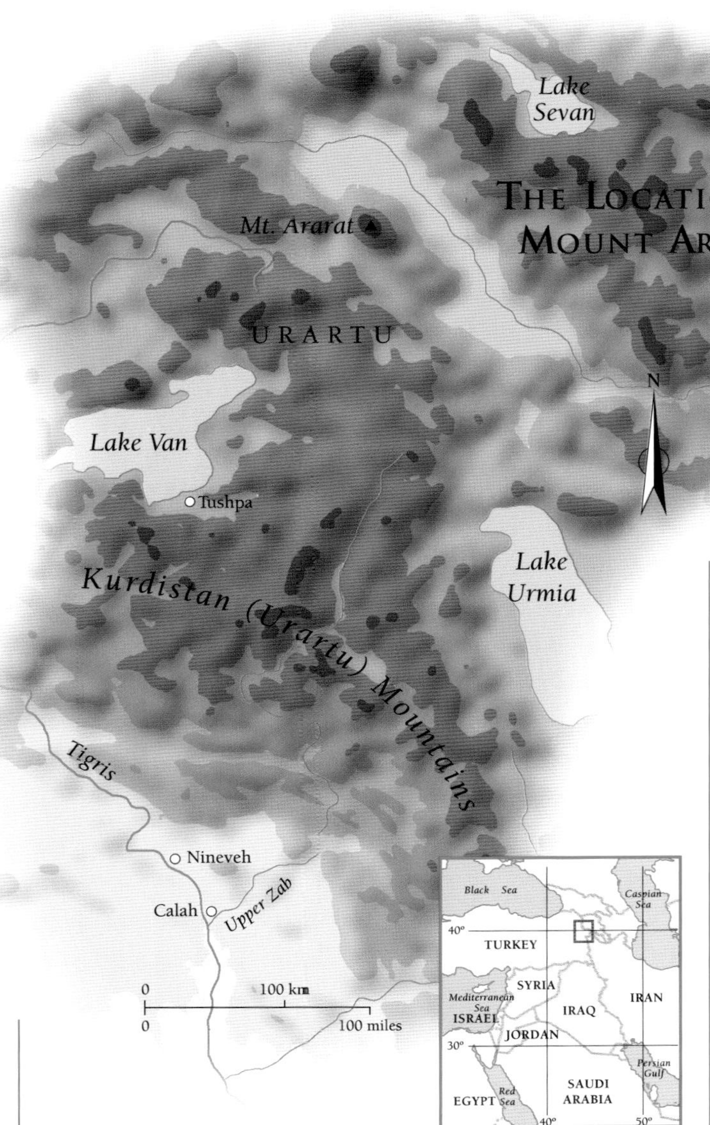

THE RAINBOW

The flood story climaxes in a covenant with all Creation. This covenant is sealed by a powerful symbolic act, to which nature is to bear perpetual witness. Like a victorious warrior, God literally hangs up his weapon from the "ceiling" of his "palace." The king has rescued his subjects, who had been held captive—peace has been restored. The original blessing of Creation is reasserted, while the divine pact on a mountain—accompanied by ethical and ritual stipulations—directs us to look ahead to Horeb/Sinai.

On Mt. Ararat, God promises never to "curse the ground because of humankind" (Genesis 8:21). Despite the hopeful tone, included is a sobering acknowledgment of the human capacity for evil (8:21b). Sadly, the assessment is borne out, as Noah's family—saved from catastrophe—splits apart and splinters across the earth.

THE DOVE AND THE OLIVE BRANCH

Buffeted about, Noah releases in turn, a raven, then a dove, to ascertain the conditions outside the ark. This reconnaissance exercise is analogous to Moses' dispatch of spies prior to Israel's entry into Canaan and their return after 40 days with its vegetation (Numbers 13:17–25). The dove's retrieval of an olive branch demonstrates both the retreat of the waters, as well as the viability of the countryside for settlement. Moreover, the survival of an olive tree in flood-swept terrain indicates that divine blessing has descended upon the land once more.

Archaeological Evidence for the Great Flood

There are indications of flooding at ancient sites near the Tigris and Euphrates rivers, but mud deposits are restricted to these locales. Thus far, proof for a global deluge is inconclusive. By contrast, there is considerable written evidence for flood traditions from the Fertile Crescent and elsewhere. These materials do contain parallels to the biblical story, but unlike the Scriptures, an ethical cause for the disaster is lacking. It is noteworthy that "flood-language" also referred to cultural and societal breakdown, rather than simply hydrological conditions. This dramatic usage is well attested in the Old Testament, where Isaiah and Jeremiah later warn Israel of a coming tide of invaders to punish the people for their sins.

SHEM, HAM, AND JAPHETH

Noah—very much a restored Adam ("the one from the earth" [*'adamah*])—begins the earth's rehabilitation. He nurtures a vineyard, from which he gets deservedly intoxicated, and falls asleep in his tent unclothed (Genesis 9:21). Replaying the tragic past, Noah's youngest son, Ham, "saw the nakedness of his father" (9:23), and assumes the serpent's role. He attempts to draw his brothers, Shem and Japheth, into a cabal to usurp their vulnerable parent's authority. But unlike Adam and Eve, his older siblings refuse to join the coup. Regaining sobriety, Noah denounces Ham for his act of rebellion. The solidarity of the family that had huddled through the storm is shattered, with the brothers' descendants eventually moving farther away from one another. On those occasions when they do draw near, relations will be exceedingly stormy—leading to near-fratricide.

BELOW: VENICE'S SAN MARCO BASILICA IS HOME TO THIS FRESCO DEPICTING NOAH'S RELEASE OF THE ANIMALS. THE DOVE'S RETURN BEARING AN OLIVE BRANCH, AND THE RAINBOW, ARE SIGNS TO NOAH THAT THE FLOOD HAS EASED.

THE REPOPULATION OF THE EARTH

God decrees that the world be populated anew, restating the Creation blessing to "be fruitful and multiply" (Genesis 9:1). But the original benediction is tempered by a necessary prohibition: "Whoever sheds the blood of a human, by a human shall that person's blood be shed; for in his own image, God made humankind" (9:6). Life can only flourish when the murderous anarchy of a "Cain" is placed under restraint. For the first time, human beings are empowered to enact justice against those who would harm God's representatives. Noachian law introduces the concept of *lex talionis*—an eye for an eye—at the same time asserting a divine universal right to life.

NOAH AND HIS DESCENDANTS

Noah's sons provide the rootstock from which humankind will spring. The so-called "Table of Nations," taking us from the flood-soaked world to the verge of the Patriarchal Age, is itself a biblical ethnogeny—or map of humanity's origins. Peoples are roughly grouped geographically—the descendants of Shem are situated in Mesopotamia and Arabia; those of Ham are linked to the Nile Valley, North Africa, the Arabian peninsula, and the Levantine coast and its interior; and the offspring of Japheth are located across Asia Minor and in the Aegean islands.

Importantly, these genealogies are not strictly ethnic in their outlook, but also express developing political alliances, best illustrated by Egypt's patronage of the Caphtorim—the ancestors of the Philistines (Genesis 10:14)—who were of Hellenic (Greek), not African background.

BELOW: NOAH PREDICTS THAT THE DESCENDANTS OF SHEM WILL ULTIMATELY DO BATTLE WITH THE CANAANITES AND TAKE CANAAN AS THEIR OWN—DEPICTED IN THIS FIFTEENTH-CENTURY C.E. ILLUSTRATION BY JEAN FOUQUET.

CANAAN AND THE CANAANITES

"The Table" also introduces important players in the subsequent drama of Israel. Most prominent in this cast list, as it unfolds, is Canaan. The name is literally dropped to the reader, when Noah relegates to servile status this descendant of the upstart Ham. Actually, the target of such cursing was not just the offspring, but the original offender who prompted the act. Scions—rendered helpless by misfortune—would be prevented from honoring the memory of their reviled ancestor, amounting to the latter's extinction.

Still, Noah's prediction hints at events that are yet to come, when the future children of Shem, seeking their divine patrimony, will dispossess the Canaanites of their land.

NIMROD, THE MIGHTY HUNTER

An important theme running throughout the Genesis ethnologies is that "the apple does not fall far from the tree." Among those who would agree with this sentiment were the Assyrians, who will proudly emulate their forebear, Nimrod, known as "a mighty warrior" (Genesis 10:9) and a builder of cities (10:11).

The king's distant kin will show themselves to be his true "sons," imitating their legendary ancestor in every respect. In fact, lion hunting becomes a dominant theme in Assyrian art, vaunting their power over nature, while their raising—and razing—of cities proclaimed their fierce rule over nations.

THE TOWER OF BABEL

If Nimrod produced the seed for Assyrian brutality, then the construction of "a tower with its top in the heavens" (Genesis 11:4) anticipates the arrogance of the Babylonians—a people who were also sired by the famed athlete and ruler.

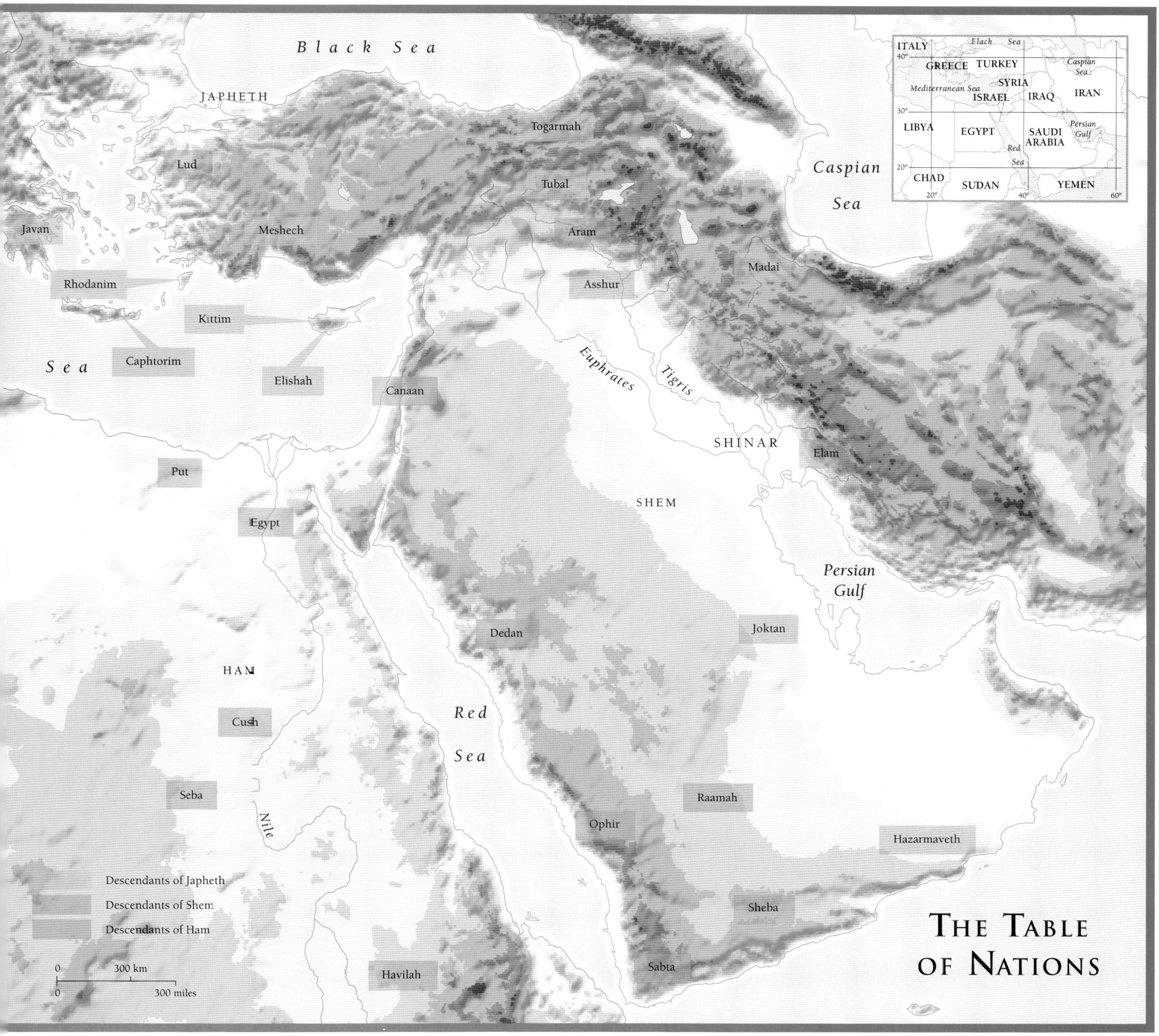

THE TABLE OF NATIONS

Black Sea
JAPHETH
Togarmah
Lud
Tubal
Caspian Sea
Javan
Meshech
Aram
Madai
Rhodanim
Asshur
Kittim
Sea
Caphtorim
Elishah
Canaan
Euphrates
Tigris
SHINAR
Elam
Put
SHEM
Egypt
Persian Gulf
Dedan
Joktan
HAM
Red Sea
Cush
Seba
Raamah
Nile
Ophir
Hazarmaveth
Sheba
Sabta
Havilah

ITALY, GREECE, TURKEY, Black Sea, Caspian Sea, SYRIA, Mediterranean Sea, ISRAEL, IRAQ, IRAN, LIBYA, EGYPT, SAUDI ARABIA, Persian Gulf, Red Sea, CHAD, SUDAN, YEMEN
40°, 30°, 20°, 20°, 40°, 60°

Descendants of Japheth
Descendants of Shem
Descendants of Ham

0 — 300 km
0 — 300 miles

Shockingly, the inhabitants of Shinar—Mesopotamia—speak in tones reserved for God: "Come, let us make … come, let us build … let us make a name for ourselves" (Genesis 11:3–4). The sharing of a common language and distinctly imperial outlook results in a plot to storm heaven, via a step-pyramid, or ziggurat, which serves the function of a siege-engine.

Upon discovery, the conspirators are scattered, their unity of speech destroyed. The locale for this thwarted ambition will be named "gate of/to gods" or Babel by its later denizens. On the other hand, the Scripture unmasks it as "blasphemous babbling"—a place leading not to God but only to separation and alienation from the Divine Will.

LEFT: *THE TOWER OF BABEL* BY LUCAS VAN VALCKENBORCH. GRANDIOSE PLANS TO BUILD A TOWER UP TO THE HEAVENS INCURRED GOD'S WRATH, AND HE SCATTERED THE PEOPLE ACROSS THE LANDS.

ABRAHAM

YOU SHALL BE THE ANCESTOR OF A MULTITUDE OF NATIONS GENESIS 17:4

RIGHT: FAITHFUL SERVANT ABRAHAM IS CHOSEN BY GOD TO FULFILL HIS COMMAND. THIS MOSAIC FROM THE SAN MARCO BASILICA IN VENICE, ITALY, FEATURES THE HEAD OF ABRAHAM.

Abraham, model of faith and trust in God, is the ancestor of three religions. Abraham's story forms a hinge between the two sections of Genesis. The prolog, in chapters 1–11, tells of creation, the first sin, and the subsequent corruption of all humanity. We move from one couple to a multitude of nations spread across the earth (Genesis 11:9).

ABRAHAM'S BIRTH AND EARLY LIFE

The prolog closes by introducing us to Abraham son of Terah. Abraham has two brothers, Haran and Nahor. However, Haran dies in his birthplace Ur, leaving his son, Lot, an orphan. Telling us that Sarah, the wife of Abraham, is barren foreshadows an important factor in the chapters that follow.

Terah leaves the family home in Ur and—taking Abraham, Sarah, and Lot—sets off for Canaan, but on the way settles in Haran (in present-day northern Syria) and dies there. Often in Genesis family stories (genealogy) narrow to focus on the significant branch. Here the story ends with both Abraham and Lot in focus.

BELOW: EXCAVATIONS AT UR IN PRESENT-DAY IRAQ REVEAL MUCH ABOUT THE CULTURE AND SOCIETY OF THE CIVILIZATIONS THAT HAVE INHABITED THE CITY—POSSIBLY THE BIRTHPLACE OF ABRAHAM—OVER THE GENERATIONS.

ABRAHAM'S ORIGINS

The Bible is often sparing with the details it gives us. We want to know where Abraham and Sarah were from, and we expect to identify "Ur of the Chaldeans" with a particular location. But since ancient times, scholars have been unable to decide between several very different locations: from the major Sumerian city in the south of Mesopotamia to Urfa in the north. Actually, though Bible stories are very sparing with detail, they tell us what we need to know, and so help direct and focus our thoughts. Thus, while the point of origin of Abraham's journey is unclear, the destination is very specific—Canaan (Genesis 11:31) or "the land that I will show you" (12:1). Abraham's destination matters more than his starting point, because it is the place God chose.

NAMES

Sarah and Abraham are among the best-known names in the Bible, so it often comes as a surprise to Bible-readers to discover people called Sarai and Abram. Their names are changed, by God, in Genesis 17. While the change in Sarai's name does not seem to change its meaning (Genesis 17:15), the move from Abram (meaning "exalted father") to Abraham (meaning "father to many") no longer looks back to a human ancestry, but forward to a divinely given destiny (17:5). The change of names marks a change of status: they are now covenant-partners of God.

ABRAHAM'S CALL

By the end of Genesis 11, Terah's family has narrowed alarmingly. Haran is dead in Ur, and only one son, Lot, survives him; Sarah is childless, and Terah himself dies.

Chapter 12 begins strikingly. For the first time since Noah, five chapters earlier, God speaks to a human being. His instructions are stark: "go from your country and your kindred and your father's house to the land that I will show you" (Genesis 12:1), in effect telling Abraham to leave everything that makes him who he is—family, place, and people—for an unknown destination.

The threefold demand gets harder and harder, moving from general "land" to specific "household." It is followed by a threefold promise: descendants, blessing, and reputation. Later God's promise will become more specific, as the land of Canaan replaces "reputation" as the third element. For now it is the purpose that is stressed, Abraham is to be blessed so that he may be a blessing. An outworking of this

LEFT: *THE DEPARTURE OF ABRAHAM* BY JOSEPH MOLNAR. THOUGH HE HAS LIVED FOR MANY YEARS IN HARAN, ABRAHAM FAITHFULLY FOLLOWS GOD'S COMMAND TO LEAVE BEHIND ALL HE KNOWS AND TRAVEL TO A NEW LAND.

is that others will seal their fate according to how they respond to this chosen person: bless Abraham—God blesses you, curse him—you are cursed.

In Jewish tradition, this section of the Torah is called (after its first words in Hebrew) *lekh lekah*, meaning "get up and go!" This is just what Abraham does. The Lord's call may come out of the blue, but Abraham went. He takes Lot, his nephew, and Sarah, his wife, with him.

The God who demands this of Abraham seems to have no particular record of special relationship with this family (the Lord was last mentioned simply as the one who scattered humanity in Genesis 11:9), and later we discover Abraham's brother's family in Haran has "household gods" (31:19). This unquestioning obedience to an absolute demand, which comes from a God who will later be called (Genesis 24:12) and call himself (26:24) the "God of Abraham," is the start of the long tradition (Jewish, Christian, and Muslim) of Abraham—the archetype of faithful obedience.

THE MIGRATION TO CANAAN: MIDDLE BRONZE AGE CANAAN AND EGYPT

Pinning down just when Abraham lived is difficult. The biblical evidence is divided: some ancient manuscripts say "Israel" was in Egypt for 430 years, but others imply 215 years. Archaeological evidence has been used to support dates from Early Bronze Age III (2600–2300 B.C.E.) to the Late Bronze Age (1550–1200 B.C.E.). However, the Middle Bronze Age (2100–1550 B.C.E.) seems most likely.

GENEALOGIES IN GENESIS

Genesis is a book of genealogy. The story is punctuated by sections with headings using the word *toledoth*. (It is translated by expressions like "descendants of," though in Genesis 2:4, for the *toledoth* of heaven and earth, other expressions are often used by Bible translators!) These sections contain long, and to many modern readers, boring lists of ancestors.

For other readers though, these genealogies are not dull, but tell us where people come from. A person's origin can explain the quirks that make them who they are. Genesis contains the genealogy of the people of God. The illustration (right) from the Souvigny Bible shows the generations in the bosom of Abraham. For Jesus, and other Jewish hearers of these chapters, these people were their ancestors. Even non-Jewish readers will often find "bits of themselves" not only in Adam and Eve, but also in the faithfulness/faithlessness of Abraham and Sarah, Rebekah's resourcefulness, or Isaac's passivity.

RIGHT: SUNLIGHT STREAMING THROUGH THIS STAINED GLASS WINDOW AT ALL SAINTS CHURCH, SELSLEY, UNITED KINGDOM, ILLUMINATES THE FIGURES OF ABRAHAM AND HIS SON, ISAAC.

This was a time of relative peace and prosperity; cities grew and thrived from trading. Farmers in smaller settlements and nomadic herders supplied their basic needs. Egyptian power was weaker, and balanced by the newer Hittite Empire (located in Asia Minor). So Canaan was composed of city-states, each ruled by a king owing somewhat nominal allegiance to the Egyptian pharaoh.

Later, a letter from one of these kings to Pharaoh—found at Tell el-Amarna in the Nile Delta—describe *'apiru* (who some identify with the "Hebrews") as a threat. An ivory plaque from Megiddo shows an Egyptian king reviewing Semitic prisoners, illustrating this period.

HARAN TO CANAAN

From Haran, near the headwaters of the Euphrates, a well-traveled trade route led through Canaan. Mesopotamia, though a center of civilization, was poor in metals, so copper and tin (to make bronze) were imported (and later, iron was imported from Lebanon or Greece). Imports of cloth, precious stones, perfumes and dyes, wine, honey, and various other luxury goods were also recorded.

Many of these goods from the south and west arrived at Carchemish or Imar (west of Haran) to be shipped downstream to cities like Mari, Babylon, and Ur. South of Carchemish the route is by land, through Damascus, where the road branched, either via Hazor (Upper Galilee) and Megiddo before following the coast (the Great Trunk Road), or a hilly inland route east of the Jordan (the King's Highway, Numbers 20:17). Several cities in Canaan associated with the patriarchs, such as Shechem, Bethel, and Beer-sheba are on a third, less used, route down the spine of hills through Canaan.

When, in Genesis 14, Abraham leads his followers to recapture the booty taken by the eastern kings, he acts like a princely merchant. Yet in other respects the patriarchs seem more like semi-nomads, settled near cities but moving on periodically to pasture their flocks.

BELOW: THESE RUINS IN MARI (IN PRESENT-DAY SYRIA) HARK BACK TO A TIME WHEN THE TOWNS ALONG THE EUPHRATES RIVER WERE BUSTLING CENTERS SUPPLIED BY VESSELS PLYING THE WATERWAY.

PATRIARCHAL RELIGION

The Bible contrasts the patriarchs' religion with the later religion that comes from God's self-revelation to Moses (see Exodus 6:3). Indeed, descriptions of the patriarchs' behavior are interesting. They do not always conform to the laws proclaimed later in the Pentateuch. They set up altars wherever they wish, even under trees (see Deuteronomy 12:1–5). Abraham offers a tithe to the pagan priest-king Melchizedek (Genesis 14:20). Yet alongside this are signs that the last teller of the story lived much later than the patriarch's time, such as calling Terah's home town "Ur of the Chaldeans," for Chaldeans did not arrive there until hundreds of years after Abraham. This way of identifying which Ur is meant made sense for later hearers, but is not a phrase Abraham would have used!

Biblical religion after Moses is monotheistic (or at least focused on one God, maker of all), but patriarchal religion is less obviously exclusive. God is sometimes named with respect to a patriarch: "God of Abraham and the God of Nahor," and different nouns are used: the "fear" of Isaac and the "shield" of Abraham (see also Genesis 31:53 with 15:1). For some, this feels more like the polytheistic world of the Bronze Age Near East than the faith of Moses: "The Lord is God; there is no other besides him" (Deuteronomy 4:35).

ABRAHAM AND HISTORY

Scholars recognize that the Pentateuch was written much later than the events described. Anachronisms suggest this, such as mentioning Philistines (Genesis 21:32), who only arrived in Canaan around 1200 B.C.E. Nineteenth-century C.E. literary studies claimed that Genesis comprises several strands woven together, sometimes retelling a story with small differences, for instance a patriarch in a foreign land identifies his wife as his sister three times (12:10; 20:1; and 26:1). However, archaeology sharpened this debate. Letters, accounts, and laws have been recovered from ancient city sites (Tells) around Haran that illuminate the life and cultures of the region in the Middle Bronze Age. We can compare accounts of Abraham in the Bible with this new information. Often the details fit well. Knowing about a form of marriage there, giving wives the legal status of sisters, may help explain these stories. Interestingly, some early texts mention Bible names not found in later texts outside the Bible.

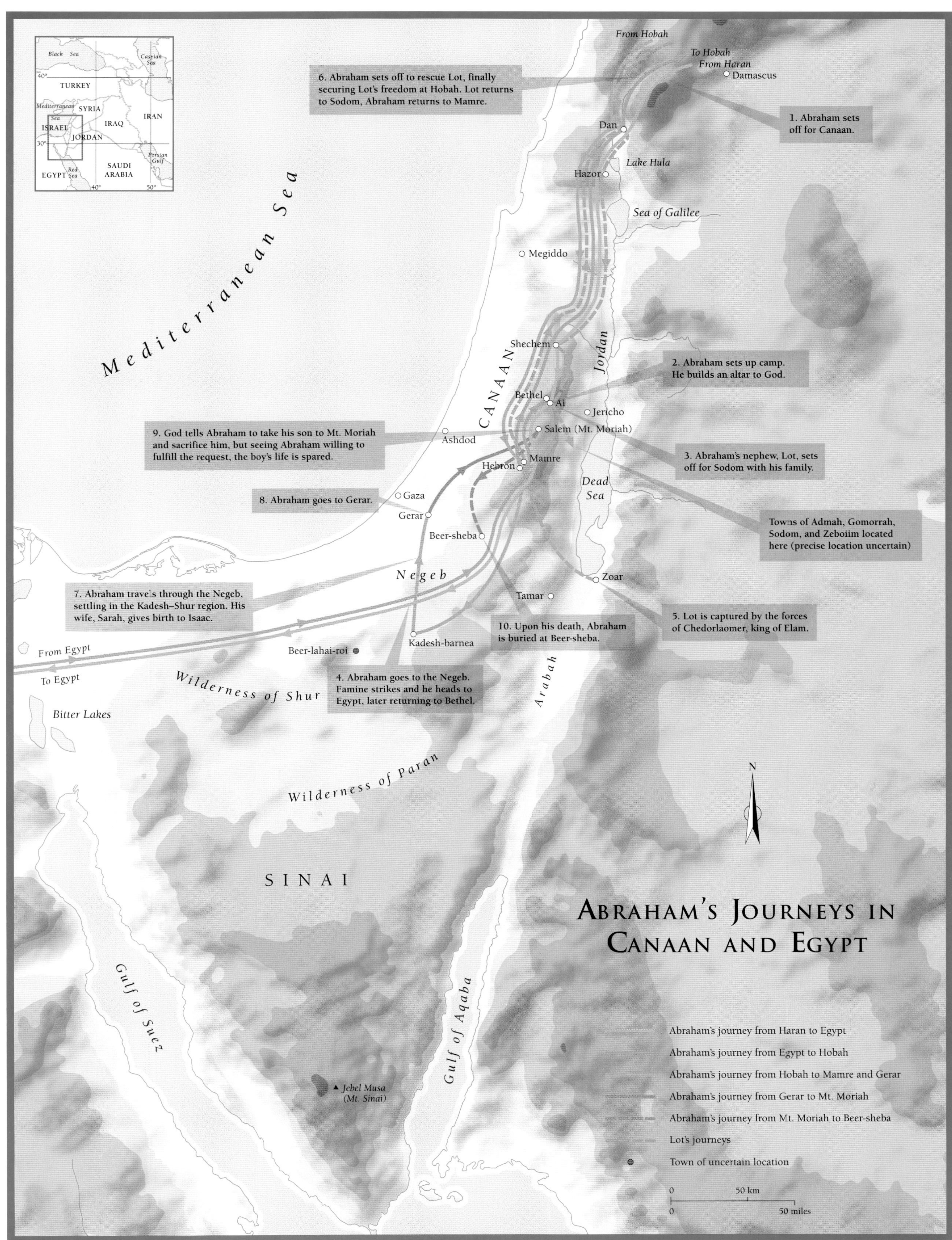

Abraham's Journeys in Canaan and Egypt
1. Abraham sets off for Canaan.
2. Abraham sets up camp. He builds an altar to God.
3. Abraham's nephew, Lot, sets off for Sodom with his family.
4. Abraham goes to the Negeb. Famine strikes and he heads to Egypt, later returning to Bethel.
5. Lot is captured by the forces of Chedorlaomer, king of Elam.
6. Abraham sets off to rescue Lot, finally securing Lot's freedom at Hobah. Lot returns to Sodom, Abraham returns to Mamre.
7. Abraham travels through the Negeb, settling in the Kadesh–Shur region. His wife, Sarah, gives birth to Isaac.
8. Abraham goes to Gerar.
9. God tells Abraham to take his son to Mt. Moriah and sacrifice him, but seeing Abraham willing to fulfill the request, the boy's life is spared.
10. Upon his death, Abraham is buried at Beer-sheba.
Towns of Admah, Gomorrah, Sodom, and Zeboiim located here (precise location uncertain)
From Hobah
To Hobah
From Haran
Damascus
Dan
Lake Hula
Hazor
Sea of Galilee
Megiddo
Shechem
Jordan
Bethel
Ai
Jericho
Salem (Mt. Moriah)
Ashdod
Mamre
Hebron
Dead Sea
Gaza
Gerar
Beer-sheba
Zoar
Tamar
Negeb
CANAAN
Kadesh-barnea
Beer-lahai-roi
From Egypt
To Egypt
Wilderness of Shur
Bitter Lakes
Arabah
Wilderness of Paran
SINAI
Mediterranean Sea
Gulf of Suez
Gulf of Aqaba
Jebel Musa (Mt. Sinai)
N
Black Sea
Caspian Sea
TURKEY
SYRIA
IRAQ
IRAN
Mediterranean Sea
ISRAEL
JORDAN
EGYPT
Red Sea
SAUDI ARABIA
Persian Gulf
40°
30°
50°
Abraham's journey from Haran to Egypt
Abraham's journey from Egypt to Hobah
Abraham's journey from Hobah to Mamre and Gerar
Abraham's journey from Gerar to Mt. Moriah
Abraham's journey from Mt. Moriah to Beer-sheba
Lot's journeys
Town of uncertain location
0
50 km
0
50 miles

RIGHT: *ABRAHAM'S MEETING WITH MELCHIZEDEK* BY LAURENT DE LE HIRE. MELCHIZEDEK GREETS ABRAHAM WITH REVERENCE AND IS REWARDED WITH A TENTH OF THE GOODS SEIZED DURING ABRAHAM'S RAID ON THE EASTERN KINGS.

ABRAHAM AND LOT

Abraham's story is told as a series of short discrete episodes, about a chapter in length. This differs from Joseph's story, which forms a continuous narrative that cannot be read out of sequence; even Jacob's story contains longer episodes. Abraham's nephew, Lot, features prominently in some episodes, and his story progresses. At the start he seems wholly dependent—in Genesis 11:31 and 12:5, simply being taken along, firstly by his grandfather, Terah, and then by his uncle, Abraham. Interestingly, Lot is not mentioned in the next episode (12:10), which tells of the family's time in Egypt, but by the time he returns from there, Lot owns "flocks and herds and tents" (13:5). The time has come for him to form his own family unit.

Genesis 13:9 tells of Abraham offering his nephew first choice of land. This is generous, as the elder Abraham should have chosen first; though we wonder if Abraham has really trusted God's instruction and promise, to go to and possess "the land I will show you." Fortunately (and in Bible stories, good fortune is always the hand of God at work), Lot chooses territory east of the Jordan, leaving Canaan for Abraham. God immediately (13:14) reiterates the promise—our clue that providence is at work, as well as a reminder of the central importance of the patriarchal promises in God's purposes.

BELOW: FRESCO IN THE DUOMO AT SAN GIMIGNANO, ITALY, BY BARTOLO DI FREDI. LOT AND ABRAHAM DIVIDE THEIR WEALTH AND PART COMPANY. LOT MOVES TO THE PLAIN OF JORDAN.

ABRAHAM AND MELCHIZEDEK

Genesis 14 changes the pace—and the presentation of Abraham. Instead of a nomad, Abraham now appears as a warlord engaged in regional geopolitics. Some call this the first Middle East War—the name is not accurate, as other texts tell of earlier wars in the region, but it does capture the flavor of this change of pace.

Transjordan and the Dead Sea area had been offering tribute to Chedorlaomer, king of Elam, but they rebel. Chedorlaomer and his allies mount a raid, and retreat with booty and prisoners. They make the mistake of including Lot "and his goods" (Genesis 12:12). Abraham is told of these events, and with his allies pursues the eastern kings. He defeats them "north of Damascus" (14:15) and recovers both people and goods.

This chapter may already have alluded to God's promise that others will be blessed or cursed according to how they treat Abraham (Genesis 12:3), for when Chedorlaomer takes Abraham's nephew, Lot, his successful raid turns to disaster. The different responses and destinies of the two local kings underline this. Melchizedek, king of Salem, welcomes Abraham with a feast, and a blessing in the name of "God Most High, maker of heaven and earth" (14:19). The king of Sodom, by contrast, speaks rudely and tries to buy off Abraham.

Here, Melchizedek is typical of those who find blessing in blessing Abraham. Later, in Psalm 110, as king and priest, Melchizedek is the model of the later God-appointed kings of Jerusalem. In the New Testament, the writer of Hebrews (7:3) takes this reference to the Messiah (anointed) as "priest forever according to the order of Melchizedek" (Psalms 110:4) and the fact that Melchizedek's ancestry was not mentioned in Genesis to present him as a type of Christ, the eternal priest-king.

SODOM AND GOMORRAH

The story of the destruction of Sodom and Gomorrah has echoed in the imaginations and nightmares of people across time. In Deuteronomy (29:23; 32:32), and prophets from Amos (4:11) to Zephaniah (2:9), the fate of these two cities serves as an chilling example to communities who, full of human greed, pride, and oppression, fall under divine condemnation. In the New Testament too they serve as warnings, and the theme recurs in later art.

The story in Genesis 18 and 19 begins with Abraham welcoming three passing strangers. Abraham's welcome is lavish—best quality meat, curds, and milk—but understated, "a little bread" (Genesis 18:5). This welcome and the revelations that follow prompt readers to hear another level in Abraham's polite greeting "My lord, if I find favor with you, do not pass by your servant" (18:3). Indeed, Genesis 18:13 seems to suggest that one (or all) of the visitors is, in fact, a divine being. After some debate about the propriety of revealing or concealing his intentions from Abraham, God reveals his purpose, to see if Sodom's sin is indeed as bad as the outcry suggests.

Abraham points the men toward Sodom, while himself remaining with God, and haggling for the city's reprieve. The result is that if ten righteous people are found in the city, God will spare the rest for their sake. Bargaining with God seems strange to modern Westerners used to philosophical ideas stemming from Greek and Roman thinking. However, it is typical of the Bible. God talks not in the cool precise language of science, but like a family member, and in such relationships both parties adapt. So Abraham, Moses, and the prophets (see, for example, Amos 7:1–6) can plead successfully with God—indeed this is the equivalent of Christian claims for the efficacy of prayer!

BELOW: *THE DESTRUCTION OF SODOM* BY JULES A. LAURENS. ANGERED BY THE EVILDOING AND SINFULNESS OF THE INHABITANTS OF SODOM AND GOMORRAH, GOD RAZES THE TWO CITIES TO THE GROUND.

ABOVE: GIOVANNI MUZZIOLI'S OPULENT ARTWORK PORTRAYS ABRAHAM AND SARAH IN EGYPT. SARAH'S BEAUTY WILL NOT GO UNNOTICED, AND SHE SOON CAPTURES THE PHARAOH'S ATTENTION.

SARAH AND HAGAR

God promised Abraham he would become a great nation, possess the land, and know God's own presence. Fulfillment depends on Abraham having an heir. The land remains a future hope at the end of the Pentateuch. Genesis closes with the death and burial of Joseph in Egypt (outside the Promised Land). The patriarchs own the grave site at Machpelah where Sarah, Abraham, Rebekah, Isaac, Leah, and Jacob are buried (see Genesis 23).

So, Sarah's childless state is an ongoing motif and theme. In Genesis 12, when God has barely pronounced the blessing for the first time, Abraham and Sarah are in Egypt (fleeing a famine) and Abraham passes Sarah off as his sister. Sarah is so beautiful that she comes to Pharaoh's attention, and hearers of the story worry that she will bear his children rather than Abraham's promised offspring.

In Genesis 16, Sarah tries to overcome the problem her own way. (Though strange and offensive to modern readers of the Bible, her approach follows the customs of northern Mesopotamia where she grew up.) She tells Abraham to sleep with her Egyptian slave Hagar, who will bear children for Abraham and Sarah (16:2).

We remember Abraham as the model of faith in God, but here he meekly accepts his wife's attempt at a human solution to the problem of descendants. Abraham "went in to Hagar, and she conceived" (Genesis 16:4). Instantly there is conflict between the two women. Abraham abdicates authority, and permits Sarah to abuse the pregnant Hagar, who runs away.

God's angel, however, talks to the abandoned Egyptian slave girl and tells her to return. Hagar is further instructed to name the child Ishmael upon his birth, and both she and her child receive a blessing (16:10–12).

RIGHT: THE SLAVE GIRL, HAGAR, BEARS ABRAHAM'S SON, ISHMAEL—A CHILD WITH A MIXED FUTURE AHEAD OF HIM. THIS ELEVENTH-CENTURY C.E. ANGLO-SAXON ILLUSTRATION SHOWS THE BATHING OF ISHMAEL AFTER HIS BIRTH.

ISHMAEL

Ishmael's God-given name means "God hears," because God heard his exploited mother's cries. Ishmael's status is problematic. He is circumcised with his father Abraham, marking his share in the covenant with God (Genesis 17:26). God repeatedly promises him numerous descendants (16:10; 21:18). Yet God also says: "He shall be a wild ass of a man, with his hand against

LEFT: THIS EIGHTEENTH-CENTURY C.E. ILLUSTRATION SHOWS ABIMELECH AND ABRAHAM. ABIMELECH ABDUCTS SARAH, BELIEVING SHE IS ABRAHAM'S SISTER, NOT HIS WIFE. WHEN HE LEARNS THE TRUTH, HE RETURNS SARAH TO HER HUSBAND.

everyone, and everyone's hand against him; and he shall live at odds with all his kin" (16:12), and he is not the heir who bears God's promise to Abraham into the future.

Abraham seems to alternate wildly in his treatment of Ishmael, sometimes—at Sarah's urging —rejecting him and his mother (Genesis 16:6), even though abandoning his son distresses him (21:11), but he also pleads with God on Ishmael's behalf and treats him as an heir (17:18 and 23).

ABRAHAM AND ABIMELECH

In Genesis 20, Abraham and Sarah move to live as resident foreigners, this time in Gerar. Once again, Abraham says only that Sarah is his sister, and once again the local monarch, Abimelech, takes her into his household (Genesis 20:2). Abraham may be the Bible's archetype of faith in God, but he is no superman; he is all too human, repeating earlier mistakes. God appears to the pagan foreign king, and averts disaster. In doing so God underlines (20:7) that he will treat others in the light of their treatment of Abraham (12:3).

Often in the Bible outsiders behave better than God's chosen people. Here again, as before, Abraham reveals a lack of trust in God's promises. Yet his little faith is sufficient, as God's covenant does not depend on the recipient being worthy, strong, good, or even faithful.

THE BIRTH OF ISAAC

Abraham is one hundred years old and Sarah is ninety years old (Genesis 17:17) when their son is born. This birth has been desperately desired for such a long time. Yet the account is spare and brief, just 20 words in Hebrew, over half of which underline that God is doing just what he promised: "The Lord dealt with Sarah as he had said, and the Lord did for Sarah as he had promised. Sarah conceived and bore Abraham a son in his old age, at the time of which God had spoken to him" (21:1–2).

As so often occurs in the Bible, God is responsible for both conception and birth. His promises are fulfilled. Isaac's name, meaning "he laughed," and Sarah's comment that God had brought laughter into her life (Genesis 21:6), underline her own and Abraham's earlier lack of belief (17:17; 18:12) that God could fulfill the promise of offspring to two such long-married and childless people!

Abraham is an exemplar of faith. However, he is not at all the perfect "man of faith" that we might have expected. He exemplifies a real human who trusts God, despite his own failures and weaknesses.

THE GENEALOGY OF ISHMAEL AND THE ISHMAELITES

According to Genesis 25:12–18, Ishmael was the father of 12 sons: Nebaioth, Kedar, Adbeel, Mibsam, Mishma, Dumah, Massa, Hadad, Tema, Jetur, Naphish, and Kedemah. Each son became the head of his own Ishmaelite tribe, and the tribes "settled from Havilah to Shur" (Genesis 25:18).

The Old Testament refers to the Ishmaelites several times. In Genesis 37:25–39:1, Joseph is sold to the Ishmaelites, who then take him to Egypt and sell him to Potiphar; in Judges 8:24, Gideon receives Ishmaelite jewelry; and in 1 Chronicles 27:30, an Ishmaelite is said to have been in charge of King David's camels.

It is a matter of scholarly dispute whether "Ishmaelite" is attested outside the Bible, although it is known that the sons of Ishmael (except Kedemah) are mentioned in Assyrian literature, and the Qur'an (Koran) makes an explicit equation between the term "Ishmaelite" and "Muslim Arab" (and therefore a link to land ownership). It is interesting to note that neither the word "Arab" nor anyone identified in the Bible as "Arab" is found in a biblical genealogy.

BELOW: THIS ITALIAN FRESCO BY GIAMBATTISTA TIEPOLO PORTRAYS AN ANGEL APPEARING TO SARAH. THOUGH SHE BELIEVES SHE IS TOO OLD TO HAVE CHILDREN, SARAH IS TOLD SHE WILL CONCEIVE AND WILL BEAR A SON.

ISAAC

ALL THE NATIONS OF THE EARTH GAIN BLESSING ... BECAUSE YOU HAVE OBEYED MY VOICE GENESIS 22:18

RIGHT: INTRICATELY INLAID WITH MOTHER-OF-PEARL, THIS SCENE OF ABRAHAM'S SACRIFICE OF A GOAT, AFTER THE NEAR-SACRIFICE OF ISAAC, WAS CRAFTED BY FRANCESCO ANTONIO CORBERELLI FOR THE ALTAR AT VICENZA'S CHURCH OF SANTA CORONA.

The figure of Isaac looms very large in biblical tradition. His very birth to aged parents is shrouded in wonder and disbelief, which accounts for his name, signifying both joy and laughter at the absurdity of Isaac's life, beginning with his birth. Isaac's father, Abraham, had received a strange vision in which he was assured that he would have children and these children would inherit the land because Abraham had passed down his spiritual legacy. However, as events unfold, Ishmael, Isaac's half-brother, is sent away and Isaac remains to become the second of the three Israelite patriarchs.

THE NEAR-SACRIFICE OF ISAAC

One day, God tests Abraham's loyalty and commands him to go to an unnamed mountain and sacrifice Isaac upon it. Although the Bible does not indicate how Abraham identifies the proper mountain, other works claim that a cloud or light appeared above Mt. Moriah; the writers of many of these works identify this as the site of the future city of Jerusalem. Abraham ascends this mountain with Isaac and does not tell him the purpose of their ascent. Abraham makes no appeal to God to be released from this harrowing task—such is his faith in God. As he binds Isaac upon an altar the biblical account is brief, but others have speculated in writing and art on the dialog between Abraham and Isaac. Abraham, torn between his love for his promised heir Isaac and his unflinching trust of God, proceeds to steel himself to offer his son to God. Isaac calmly submits. The profound pathos of the scene has inspired writers such as Philo of Alexandria to consider Isaac as born of the divine spirit and emblematic of a deep mysticism.

BELOW: *THE SACRIFICE OF ISAAC* BY CARAVAGGIO. DRAMATICALLY CAPTURED IS THE MOMENT OF ABRAHAM'S REPRIEVE FROM THE ULTIMATE SACRIFICE—THAT OF THE LIFE OF HIS SON ISAAC.

Throughout the centuries, much has been written on this scene, and early thinkers wondered where mother Sarah was while this event took place. Since the account of her death follows this scene, it is thought that perhaps she discovered the truth and died from shock.

As Abraham prepares to carry out God's command, suddenly the Angel of the Lord demands that he cease the sacrifice because his faith is clearly established. The promise of progeny and land remains in place. Still, the trip is not over, and Abraham is able to sacrifice a goat that has been caught in the thicket.

The biblical account takes due note that the mountain is the one where it will be said that the Lord appeared and saw Abraham's faith. And indeed, it is said that three times a year, to affirm their own faith and devotion, males will come to the Temple where God appears and be seen.

ABRAHAM SEEKS A WIFE FOR ISAAC

As Abraham grew older the pressing need for an heir to continue his legacy had to be addressed. The latter part of the life of Abraham shows us a man deeply connected to God through covenants, promises, and visions. The passage in Genesis 15:2–3 relates that Abraham, apparently following the prevalent custom, was prepared to pass over his material and spiritual legacy to Eliezer, since he had no son of his own at that time. By associating this man with the servant who was later sent to find a wife for Isaac, most commentators assume Eliezer managed Abraham's estates, and even his name informs us of his role in the founding of the nation of Israel. His name means "my God is the helper." Much after God's promise had been fulfilled to give Abraham and Sarah a son, Abraham sent his trusted servant, likely none other than Eliezer, to search out a suitable bride who could not be a Canaanite (Genesis 24:2–4). Abraham's own roots and family ties to his native Aram-naharaim made it fertile ground to visit to find an ideal wife for Isaac, Abraham's son and seed.

Abraham was worried that someone attached to local deities and loathsome practices might lead his son astray, whereas a foreigner would not have local reinforcement for her native belief system, and she most likely would know of Abraham's own God and his faith. Abraham administers an oath to his servant to follow his orders strictly. The presumption is that this servant is the aforementioned Eliezer, although the Bible omits his name. It is agreed that Isaac will not be taken to visit the foreign country to meet the prospective bride, rather the servant will come back to Isaac with the bride in accompaniment. In Genesis 24, we learn that Eliezer is told that an angel will accompany him to assure the success of the venture. Eliezer takes with him the customary bridal gifts and sets out for the area where Abraham's relatives live. As he approaches a well, he devises a test to find a bride of exceptionally high character—kind, hospitable, and intelligent.

Eliezer asks for divine assistance in bringing his plans to fruition. The young woman is to bring well water for him at his request and, on her own initiative, water his animals—and immediately Rebekah appears on the scene and passes

ABOVE: PEDRO ORRENTE'S ARTWORK DEPICTS THE SERVANT ELIEZER SWEARING AN OATH TO ABRAHAM, HIS MASTER, TO SEARCH FOR A SUITABLE WIFE FOR ISAAC.

LEFT: *REBECCA AND ELEAZER AT THE WELL* BY GREGORIO LAZZARINI. RESPECTFUL AND DUTIFUL REBEKAH IMMEDIATELY MEETS THE STRINGENT REQUIREMENTS SET DOWN FOR ISAAC'S BRIDE-TO-BE.

ABOVE: *LABAN PRESENTING ELIEZER TO HIS FATHER* BY MARTEN DE VOS. ELIEZER'S UNFALTERING FAITH IN GOD AND HIS DEVOTION TO HIS MASTER, ABRAHAM, WIN OVER REBEKAH'S FAMILY AND THEY CONSENT TO HER MARRIAGE.

the test perfectly. She was indeed a model of the very sensitivity that characterized Abraham himself. So the match was ideal and was guided by providence. It turned out that she was a close relative of Abraham—he was her father's uncle. If we recall that Abraham fathered Isaac at the age of one hundred years, the age span between Rebekah and Isaac may not be as great as one might think. Still, the difference was significant and in various religious traditions this difference is maximized and not minimized. The generation gap between husband and wife may account for their different expectations from their children.

The faithful servant, Eliezer, manages to clinch the marriage arrangements with the family. He recounts to them the details of Abraham's life and his own part in finding the ideal wife for Isaac. His words betray a deep belief and trust in the God of Abraham that the marriage had been destined. Eliezer gives opulent presents and in due course the family consents to the marriage. The family bestows a traditional blessing upon Rebekah by asking for abundant fertility and the survival of her offspring. Then Eliezer, Rebekah, and her maids set out on their journey to meet Isaac at Abraham's home.

BELOW: *ISAAC AND REBECCA* BY SIMEON SOLOMON. WHEN ELIEZER RETURNS HOME WITH REBEKAH, ISAAC MEETS THEM ON THE WAY. HE AND REBEKAH ARE AN IDEAL MATCH AND FALL IN LOVE.

As they near their destination, the traveling party meet up with Isaac. This chance meeting of the future bride and groom, at a well on the road to Abraham's home, echoes the earlier meeting of Rebekah and Eliezer. Rebekah covers herself with her veil, a practice that is also enshrined in modern marriages, and Eliezer tells Isaac who she is and how he knows she is the intended one for him. After she is married to Isaac, Rebekah lives in Isaac's mother's abode, as his mother had died some time before. In biblical times, people had separate dwellings, and various episodes in Genesis indicate that Abraham and Sarah had separate tents.

REBEKAH

Rebekah's life can be divided into two main sections: the time spent in her family home before her marriage, and the time after her marriage. Focusing on her life as Isaac's wife and the mother of twins, the Bible tells that Rebekah, like her mother-in-law Sarah, had trouble conceiving. She and Isaac prayed fervently for 20 years that God would bless them with a child. When the prayers were answered and she conceived, her pregnancy proved difficult and unbearable. Her faith was such that she realized God would not have given her such a turbulent pregnancy had he not expected her to ask for an explanation. When she does ask he answers her query, but attention here is focused on the fact that Rebekah is the only matriarch to be addressed by God (Genesis 25:23).

Commentators have wondered about this unique occurrence, when Isaac could have received the message just as easily. Some suggest she received an oracle from other holy people, who were followers of the Abrahamic faith, whom she consulted. On the other hand, it must be realized that Rebekah was very special and worthy to receive the oracle, which she revealed to no one. It is not beneficial for parents to know their children's future. Abraham had been told to listen to Sarah, and later, knowing God's plans, Rebekah will command her younger son to listen to her voice (Genesis 27:8). Her place as a matriarch assured her, according to tradition, of a burial plot next to Sarah in the Cave of Machpelah.

ISAAC AND REBEKAH

The marriage of Isaac—at the age of forty years old—to Rebekah begins on a romantic note (Genesis 24:67). After many years, they are finally blessed with twin sons—Rebekah favors Jacob, while Isaac favors Esau. Genesis 25:28 relates that "Isaac loved Esau, because he was fond of game; but Rebekah loved Jacob." The firstborn of the twins, Esau, should be Isaac's heir, but Rebekah will have none of that—Jacob must be the heir. Rebekah carries the secret of a prophecy given to her to the effect that Esau will serve Jacob. She must manipulate matters so that Jacob will succeed, and she sets out to deceive Isaac to facilitate Isaac's blessing of Jacob as heir (27:5–17). When the ruse is later discovered, Rebekah manipulates matters so that Isaac sends Jacob away to her brother, the wily Laban (28:1–5). This is the background in which to examine the dynamic of the Isaac–Rebekah relationship.

Isaac symbolizes self-sacrifice and humility. His life mirrors certain episodes of his father and foreshadows others of his son. We hear of him episodically regarding Sarah's concern that his half-brother Ishmael would corrupt him. Isaac's name signifies joy and laughter and his attitude shows him to be unsophisticated and easily duped. When, as a young boy, he was placed on the altar to be sacrificed, we do not hear a word of complaint, and his simple faith has made him the emblem of resurrection in both the Jewish and Christian faiths; he is the triumphant bearer of the covenant despite trial and tribulation.

It would appear that Isaac was dominated by his mother and his wife, who had deeper insight into the destiny of the Abrahamic family than he did. Yet, it would be a mistake to consider him as weak. Indeed, the covenant of land and destiny is renewed with him, and he is the only patriarch not to have sojourned in Egypt. As such, he represents the stable fulfillment of divine promises and is able to appreciate his hunter son. Perhaps he held Esau as the model of what he lacked: strength, physical power, and deep emotion. This bond between the father and his eldest son ultimately saves Jacob from death at the hands of his twin. Esau honors his father too much to murder while his father is alive. Isaac enjoys watching his warrior son and prefers Esau's game to farm livestock. The weakness of Isaac's domestic role is

BELOW: *THE WEDDING FEAST OF ISAAC AND REBECCA* BY PEDRO ORRENTE. ABRAHAM'S WORRIES THAT ISAAC MAY FIND A CANAANITE WIFE ARE RESOLVED WITH THE JOYFUL UNION OF ISAAC AND REBEKAH.

RIGHT: THIS FOURTEENTH-CENTURY C.E. VELLUM MANUSCRIPT FROM THE *BIBLE HISTORIALE* OF GUIART DES MOULINS DEPICTS THE BIRTH OF JACOB AND ESAU.

compensated by the vicarious wish fulfillment inherent in Esau's power and prowess as a hunter. These skills are part of Rebekah's legacy—traits she also exhibits through her wily skills. More than Jacob, she plays the part of the trickster, an important role in ancient family narratives. She furthers the aim of God in subtle ways by moving behind the scenes, much as God does in the natural world. Together, Isaac and Rebekah develop the tension in the family that brings to the fore the question of who is the heir and bearer of the covenant, a theme that runs through both testaments. The biblical narratives have given rise to lengthy commentaries and continue to perplex readers and most likely always will.

THE BIRTH OF JACOB AND ESAU

The wondrous birth of Jacob and Esau parallels the birth of Isaac himself. Sixty years earlier, his own mother had been barren and Isaac was conceived when she was ninety years old. Rebekah's painful pregnancy foretells the future of the belligerent relationship of her twin sons. An oracle given to her reveals that the struggle between her two sons is the struggle that will ensue between them and their progeny—the nation of Israel and the nation of Edom. In the end, the latter will succumb to the former. Indeed, she gives birth to twins, the first born being Esau and the second Jacob.

Since Esau is of a ruddy complexion and has an affinity for red foods, we realize he is the progenitor of the nation of Edom, which also means ruddy. Jacob is born hanging on to Esau's heel while trying to displace him and be born first. The two boys could not have been less alike. Esau was a skilled hunter accustomed to blood, while Jacob was a sedentary person who stayed close to home. Genesis 25:25 tells that Esau was the first born, but later, it is stated that "Esau despised his birthright" (25:34). However, the circumstances of this transfer of birthright are far from clear. Esau was starving and Jacob had cooked his favorite dish of red food, so Jacob gave him the food on condition that Esau would swear to forsake his birthright (25:29–33). Since the transfer was made under duress and not of free will, we do not know if this transfer was binding. Esau, it turns out, always considered himself the rightful heir and plotted to kill Jacob, especially after Jacob duped Isaac into blessing him.

The oracle of the struggle between Esau and Jacob reverberates throughout Israelite history. Nevertheless, the heritage belongs to Jacob, and the Bible often refers to the God of Jacob. Later, Jacob's name is changed to Israel, and so it is that the nation of Abraham and Isaac and Jacob retains only the name of the last of the patriarchs, Jacob or Israel. The name of Jacob (meaning "to hold by the heel" or "to supplant") has implications that he tried to side-step his older brother. Esau notes that Jacob had done this twice (Genesis 27:36). Hosea the prophet recalls that this struggle had already begun in the womb (Hosea 12:3), and the prophet Jeremiah likewise takes note of this struggle (Jeremiah 9:4). Esau's name denotes hairiness in ancient Semitic language and so the country inhabited by Esau and his descendants is known variously as Seir (meaning "hairy") and Edom (meaning "ruddy").

THE JOURNEY TO GERAR

Isaac's sojourn to Gerar is not unlike Abraham's or Jacob's journeys. All three had to leave their homes when famine ravished the land. However, Isaac was warned by God not to go to Egypt, but to a safe place shown to him by the Lord (Genesis 26:2). As his father Abraham had obeyed God's commands, God renewed the patriarchal covenant with Isaac, promising him land and many descendants (26:4–5). Isaac therefore went to the Philistine city of Gerar, which was located toward the southern end of Canaan not far from the Mediterranean coast.

Like Abraham during his sojourns in the very same place, Isaac hides the fact that Rebekah is his wife, but this is soon discovered (Genesis 26:7–11). He prospers in Gerar, but is asked to leave when it is feared that he is becoming too

THE CONFLICT BETWEEN EDOM AND ISRAEL

It is worthwhile to note the history of enmity between the nations of Edom and Israel. When the Israelites left their Egyptian bondage under the leadership of Moses, the Edomites refused passage and humanitarian aid to them as they sought to enter the Promised Land, where they would have to engage the Canaanites in battle. Edom, in what is present-day south Jordan (pictured below), shut its doors to the Israelites out of spite and hatred and sent a huge army to seal its borders. Kings David and Solomon also had strife with Edom. The enmity and struggle between the two nations was constant and relentless.

Many prophets had spoken of the ultimate destruction of Edom. Jeremiah 49:7–22 describes the doom and desolation that will be visited on the Edomites. Isaiah 34:1–17 describes how their land will be turned to waste and jungle rotting away forever. The prophets Obadiah (chapter 1), Ezekiel (25:12–14, 35:1–15), and Malachi (1:1–14) spelled out the horrific punishment that would befall Edom for its senseless treachery, hatred, and enmity of Israel.

Edom—called Idumea by the Romans—was conquered and destroyed in 125 B.C.E. According to the Jewish tradition and found in the writings of Flavius Josephus, the Hasmonean ruler of Judea, John Hyrcanus I, forced the small kingdom to become a slave class. Within a century, Herod the Idumean—better known as Herod the Great, the ruler who played a pivotal role in Jesus' early life—murdered the royal family of Judea, including one of his own wives and a number of his children, and forged alliances with Rome. From this time on, Jewish tradition saw Rome as the embodiment of the continuing struggle between Jacob and Esau as foretold to Rebekah.

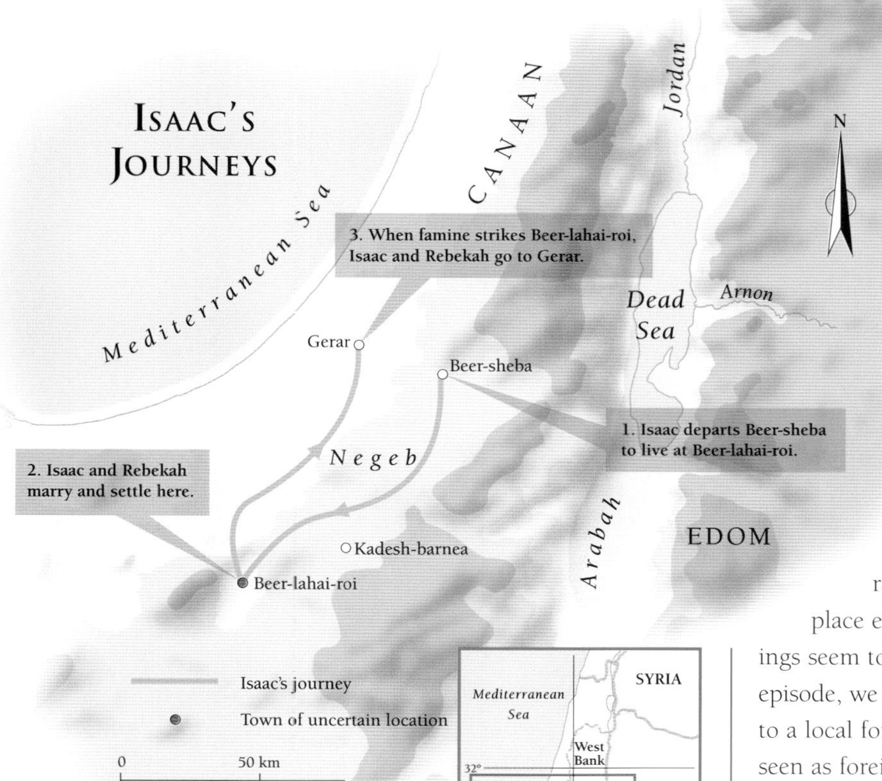

powerful. Isaac departs after concluding an agreement concerning water rights with Abimelech, the king of Gerar. Again, God assures Isaac that he will prosper and not to be afraid—God will protect him on account of his father's commitment to God's ways (26:24). It would seem that the word Abimelech that is found in these narratives concerning Gerar is not really a proper name but rather the term used to designate the king of the city-state.

Isaac's sojourn in Gerar interrupts the narrative of the birthright of Esau and likely took place even before Rebekah was pregnant. The wanderings seem to be an indication of patriarchal history. After this episode, we are told how Esau's parents mourned his marriage to a local foreign woman—the Philistines and Canaanites are seen as foreigners and now Esau has merged with them. It will remain for Jacob and his sons to sojourn in Egypt and carry on the legacy of Abraham and Isaac. Esau's marriages and progeny not only cast him as a foreigner or outsider, but also as a dangerous enemy of the people of Israel.

BELOW: CRAFTED BY LORENZO GHIBERTI FOR THE BAPTISTERY DOORS AT THE FLORENCE DUOMO, THIS GILDED PANEL SHOWS SCENES FROM THE STORY OF THE TWINS JACOB AND ESAU.

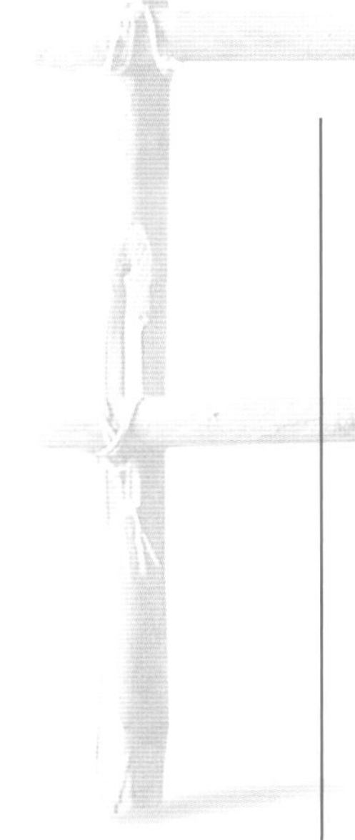

JACOB

YOU HAVE STRIVEN WITH GOD AND WITH HUMANS, AND HAVE PREVAILED GENESIS 32:28

As ancestor of all Israel, Jacob is the first and only patriarch who is not also the ancestor of other nations—the 12 tribes spring from his sons and grandsons. Jacob's significance to the Old Testament is revealed in the fact that this name is mentioned more often in the Bible than even Abraham's. Yet, when God gives Jacob a new name—Israel—it becomes the name of the nation itself.

By the time Jacob's story begins, the Bible has already established some important principles of how God relates to humanity. For example:

- God communicates with men and women alike: already in dealing with Adam and Eve, and later in appearing to Hagar and making promises to her (Genesis 16:10, 13).
- Though human societies give precedence, God does not favor the firstborn: remember Cain and Abel (Genesis 4), and that Abraham is not Nahor's eldest son.
- God sees "rightness" in people who are not perfect by human standards: unlike the rest of humanity, "Noah found favor with God" (6:7–8), yet he was the first recorded drunkard (9:20–21); Abraham, the model of faith in God, often reveals a lack of confidence that God can fulfill his promises unaided.

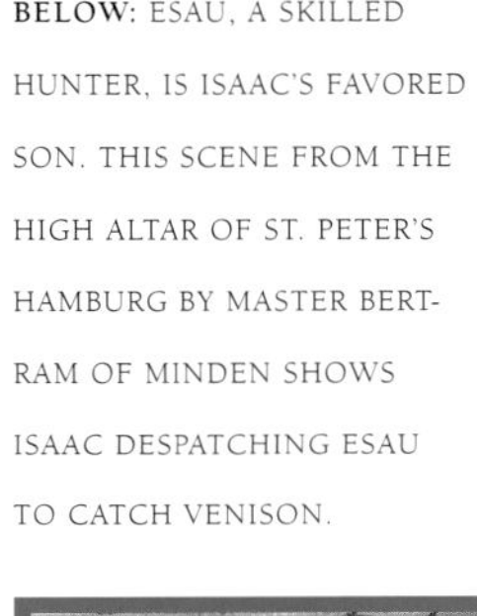

Those lessons are underlined in the telling of Jacob's story. It is to Rebekah, not Isaac, that God reveals the future of their offspring: "Two nations are in your womb, and two peoples born of you shall be divided; the one shall be stronger than the other, the elder shall serve the younger" (Genesis 25:23). The name "Jacob" is also appropriate. It echoes the word for "heel," because he is born immediately after Esau and clutching his heel, but it is also related to words meaning deceive, supplant, overreach, and the like!

BELOW: ESAU, A SKILLED HUNTER, IS ISAAC'S FAVORED SON. THIS SCENE FROM THE HIGH ALTAR OF ST. PETER'S HAMBURG BY MASTER BERTRAM OF MINDEN SHOWS ISAAC DESPATCHING ESAU TO CATCH VENISON.

BIRTHRIGHT AND DECEPTION

As the boys grow, Rebekah remembers God's statements and she loves Jacob, though Isaac loves the hunter, Esau. One day Esau, famished, returns to the camp to smell the fine stew Jacob is cooking. Jacob reveals his opportunistic streak, and offers to sell the food in exchange for his brother's birthright. Esau agrees, and the scene seems set for the next stage of the brothers' rivalry.

However, the next chapter tells of how Isaac (like his father) causes confusion by presenting his wife as his sister, yet grows rich and prosperous in the foreign land. By the time chapter 26 ends, the boys are forty years old and Isaac seems astoundingly inactive, having failed to find a wife for Jacob. Meanwhile, Esau has compensated for his father's inaction by marrying two Hittite women, who cause trouble in the family.

When Isaac is old and ready to die (Genesis 27:1), he orders a final meal from Esau before he passes on the blessing. Rebekah, however, is still determined to organize things so that God's words become true. She takes the initiative, and instructs Jacob to deceive his father and claim the blessing. She has solutions for the problem her son raises, which concerns the practical issue of presenting his smooth skin as Esau's hairiness, rather than moral scruples about lying to his father.

When Isaac greets Jacob with his goatskin disguise, his question is pointed: "who are you, my son?" (Genesis 27:18). As the deceived father passes on the blessing to Jacob, the words he closes with, "Cursed be everyone who curses you, and blessed be everyone who blesses you!" echo God's blessing to Abraham (12:3).

Religious readers are often ready to excuse Jacob, as he is fulfilling the prediction God made to his mother, while Esau has despised his birthright and does not deserve it. It should be noted, however, that not only do Rebekah and Jacob plot to deceive Isaac, but also that Jacob involves God in his lying and deception. When his father asks: "How is it that you have found it so quickly, my son?" Jacob replies: "Because the Lord your God granted me success" (Genesis 27:20).

ESAU'S RESPONSE AND JACOB'S FLIGHT

Having passed on the full divine blessing to his younger son, Isaac can only offer Esau a decidedly mixed blessing (Genesis 27:39–40). The elder brother is so angry that he decides that once Isaac is dead he will kill Jacob (27:41). Rebekah learns of this and once again organizes things. She orders Jacob to flee to her brother in Aram, and convinces Isaac that this move is a good idea, as it will deter Jacob from taking a Hittite wife.

Isaac, as always, does what he is told, and again blesses Jacob. This time, he explicitly passes on to his younger son the blessings first given to his own father, Abraham (Genesis 28:4). It is interesting to contrast chapter 26 with chapter 27. In chapter 26, the Lord instructs Isaac (26:2), blesses him (26:12), and appears to him to renew his ancestral promise (26:24). Here, even the pagans recognize God's role in this family's success (26:28–29). In the following chapter God is spoken about, but does not act, and in Genesis 27:20 he is even lied about! This chapter describes humans taking the divine plan into their own hands.

Naming in Biblical Narratives

Everyone can be identified or named in more than one way. "Jane," "your daughter," and "his teacher" can all identify the same person, but they describe her differently. The telling of Bible stories often chooses how to name people so that important information or emotions are conveyed or underlined. So, in Job 42:7–8, God three times speaks of "my servant Job"; this naming underlines the confidence already signaled as God spoke to "the accuser" in 1:8 and 2:3, thus making the divine evaluation of Job quite clear. Similarly, it should be noted how Isaac addresses Esau as his son (Genesis 27:1) and later Rebekah addresses Jacob in the same way (Genesis 27:8), and there is a reminder too, in Genesis 27:42, that Esau is also Rebekah's child.

BELOW: *ISAAC BLESSING JACOB* BY JEAN-BAPTISTE JOUVENET. DECEPTION AND COLLUSION MARK ISAAC'S BLESSING OF HIS SECOND SON, AS THE AGEING ISAAC IS TRICKED INTO GIVING TO JACOB THE BLESSING THAT RIGHTFULLY BELONGS TO ESAU.

ABOVE: THIS FIFTEENTH-CENTURY C.E. WORK DEPICTS JACOB'S "LADDER" DREAM, IN WHICH GOD PROMISES LAND AND CHILDREN TO JACOB. THE PLACE IS THEN NAMED BETHEL BY JACOB, TO ACKNOWLEDGE GOD'S PRESENCE.

JACOB'S "STAIRWAY"

On the run, Jacob leaves Beer-sheba in the extreme south of the land God had promised to his family, and heads north up the watershed route through the hill country of Canaan. One night he arrives and sleeps at a certain unnamed place, and hearing the story as the Bible tells it, we are struck by how the telling avoids naming this place (Genesis 28:10–11), and the reason will become apparent as the story unfolds.

As he sleeps, Jacob dreams of "a ladder set up on the earth, the top of it reaching to heaven; and the angels of God were ascending and descending on it" (Genesis 28:12). The word used to indicate a "ladder" is a *hapax legomenon* (a word that occurs only once in the Bible), and such words present special difficulty for translators. In this case, related words and the cultural context make it likely that the dream is of a ziggurat. These conical mounds with stairways are described in Mesopotamian sources as temples with their tops reaching to heaven, and priests ascended them to consult the gods. They then descended to earth to make the divine will known.

In this case God is at the human end of the stairway, and blesses Jacob, confirming the promises of land and offspring, repeating that Jacob is blessed, and affirming his continual presence in Jacob's life (Genesis 28:13–15). (God does not require perfection from those who receive the divine blessing.) This is the second time that the Lord appears to humans in Jacob's story. On the first occasion God revealed the twins' future to Rebekah. Jacob renames the place Bethel (meaning "God's house"), and erects the stone he used as a pillow consecrating it as a *massebah*, or memorial pillar.

JACOB AND RACHEL

In dry territory, water sources are natural meeting places. Just as his grandfather's servant, on arriving near Haran, met Rebekah at the well, so Jacob meets Rachel. It is instructive to compare these stories (Genesis 24; 29). It helps also to notice others where meetings at a well result in marriages—such as Moses in Exodus 2:15 and Ruth who meets Boaz over water his servants have drawn (Ruth 2:9). Perhaps even Jesus meeting with the Samaritan woman (John 4:5) echoes some of these elements, though clearly the end result is very different.

In the patriarchal betrothal stories, certain common elements recur:

- the well is in a foreign land (remember that Judah is "foreign" for Ruth);
- water is drawn;
- the girl invites the man to eat at her home (Boaz invites Ruth, again reversing the pattern);
- she hurries home with the news;
- a marriage is arranged.

The characters of both Jacob and Isaac are highlighted by the differences in their stories. Isaac is absent, Abraham's servant takes his place, and Rebekah is the active one watering the servant's camels. By contrast, Jacob single-handedly removes the stone from the well and waters the flock.

As well as revealing the patriarch's character, these stories also hint at providence at work—of all the wells in Aram, Jacob arrives at precisely this one. Biblical narrative often hints at divine action through such coincidences.

RIGHT: *THE MEETING OF JACOB AND RACHEL AT THE WELL* BY NICOLA GRASSI. THE RECURRING THEME OF BOY MEETS GIRL AT A WELL OCCURS AGAIN—THIS TIME WITH JACOB AND RACHEL AS THE LEADING CHARACTERS.

JACOB GETS A FAMILY

Jacob's wedding, however, does not run as smoothly as his betrothal. The trickster who cheated his brother, and, with Rebekah's help, hoodwinked his father, has met his match in uncle Laban. Out of love Jacob agrees to work seven years to pay Rachel's bride price, but ends up married first to her older sister, Leah. Laban's reply highlights the irony: "This is not done in our country—giving the younger before the firstborn" (Genesis 29:26).

He works yet another seven years for Rachel. God gets involved; seeing Leah is unloved in this troubled family, he gives her children. Rachel, however, remains childless. (Always in the Bible, pregnancy and childbirth are the Lord's business.) The rivalry between the sisters extends to using their maids to procure children for Jacob (Genesis 30:1–24). With the names they give the children, the sisters seek to enlist God in their power struggle. Jacob's family, like Jacob, is a contentious group. Through some fast footwork, and using selective breeding techniques on Laban's flocks that he tends, Jacob grows very wealthy at uncle Laban's expense (30:31). In this part of the story, the only time God acts is to provide children for unloved Leah.

LEFT: THIS EIGHTEENTH-CENTURY C.E. ARTWORK BY GIAMBATTISTA TIEPOLO PORTRAYS LABAN, JACOB, AND RACHEL. JACOB IS FINALLY ALLOWED TO MARRY RACHEL AFTER WORKING FOR LABAN FOR MANY YEARS.

BELOW: *JACOB WITH LABAN AND HIS DAUGHTERS* BY CLAUDE LORRAIN. THOUGH A CRAFTY MANIPULATOR HIMSELF, JACOB IS OUTCLASSED BY WILY LABAN, WHO ORCHESTRATES THE MARRIAGE OF BOTH OF HIS DAUGHTERS.

RIGHT: *THE DEPARTURE OF JACOB FROM LABAN* BY ADRIAEN VAN DE VELDE. AFTER 20 YEARS, JACOB ARGUES THAT HIS OBLIGATION TO LABAN HAS BEEN FULFILLED AND TAKES HIS FAMILY TO CANAAN.

BELOW: *FIGHT BETWEEN JACOB AND THE ANGEL* BY EUGENE DELACROIX. JACOB'S STRUGGLE WITH AN UNKNOWN ADVERSARY ENDS WITH JACOB BEING BLESSED AND NAMED ISRAEL.

JACOB'S RETURN TO THE PROMISED LAND

The Lord, however, still has plans for Jacob. In Genesis 31:3 he not only instructs him to return to Canaan, but promises to be with him. Jacob makes a long speech, justifying his wealth at the expense of his father-in-law, even claiming God revealed the trick to him (31:9). In view of his record of dishonesty we may wonder about his truthfulness here. Rachel shows herself to be Laban's daughter and a worthy partner for Jacob—she carries off her father's household gods, as Jacob's family flees Aram. This group of tricksters, liars, and cheats is the family God chooses to bring blessing to all humanity (lest we think humans can bring blessing from our own goodness!).

JACOB AT THE JABBOK

When Jacob is almost "home" (after 20 years away) he sends a message to his brother Esau. The messengers return with ominous news: "Esau is on his way to meet you, and four hundred men are with him!" (Genesis 32:6). Jacob fears that Esau's anger has not cooled with time. He decides to split his wealth in two, in the hope of saving half. He also prays to God, and confesses his unworthiness, asking to be protected from Esau's wrath so that God's promises may be fulfilled.

From his herds Jacob selects hundreds of animals as a rich present for Esau, and sends them ahead. The flocks for Esau are separated into several sections, to impress his brother more. He also sends his wives and children ahead, remaining alone at the camp by the Jabbok. During the night "a man" wrestles with him, and at dawn they are still evenly matched. His opponent dislocates Jacob's hip, and demands to be released. Jacob demands a blessing in return. The man asks his name, and gives him a new name: "You shall no longer be called Jacob, but Israel, for you have striven with God and with humans, and have prevailed" (Genesis 32:28).

Jacob asks the man's name in return. His opponent refuses, but blesses Jacob, who names the place Peniel ("face of God"), claiming he has seen God face-to-face and survived. This story is one of the most puzzling in the Bible. The identity of the man is not given—is he God, as Jacob claims, or, as many interpreters have thought, is he an angel? More psychoanalytically, is he Esau in Jacob's mind, or Jacob's own conscience? The reader is also left to ponder the meaning of the statement: "you have striven with God and with humans, and have prevailed" (Genesis 32:28).

JACOB AND ESAU ARE REUNITED

After the struggle at the Jabbok, and the gift of a new name, we expect Jacob to be a changed man. In the next chapter the brothers at last meet. Jacob has prepared for the meeting not only with his gift, but also by sending the women and children to meet his brother first.

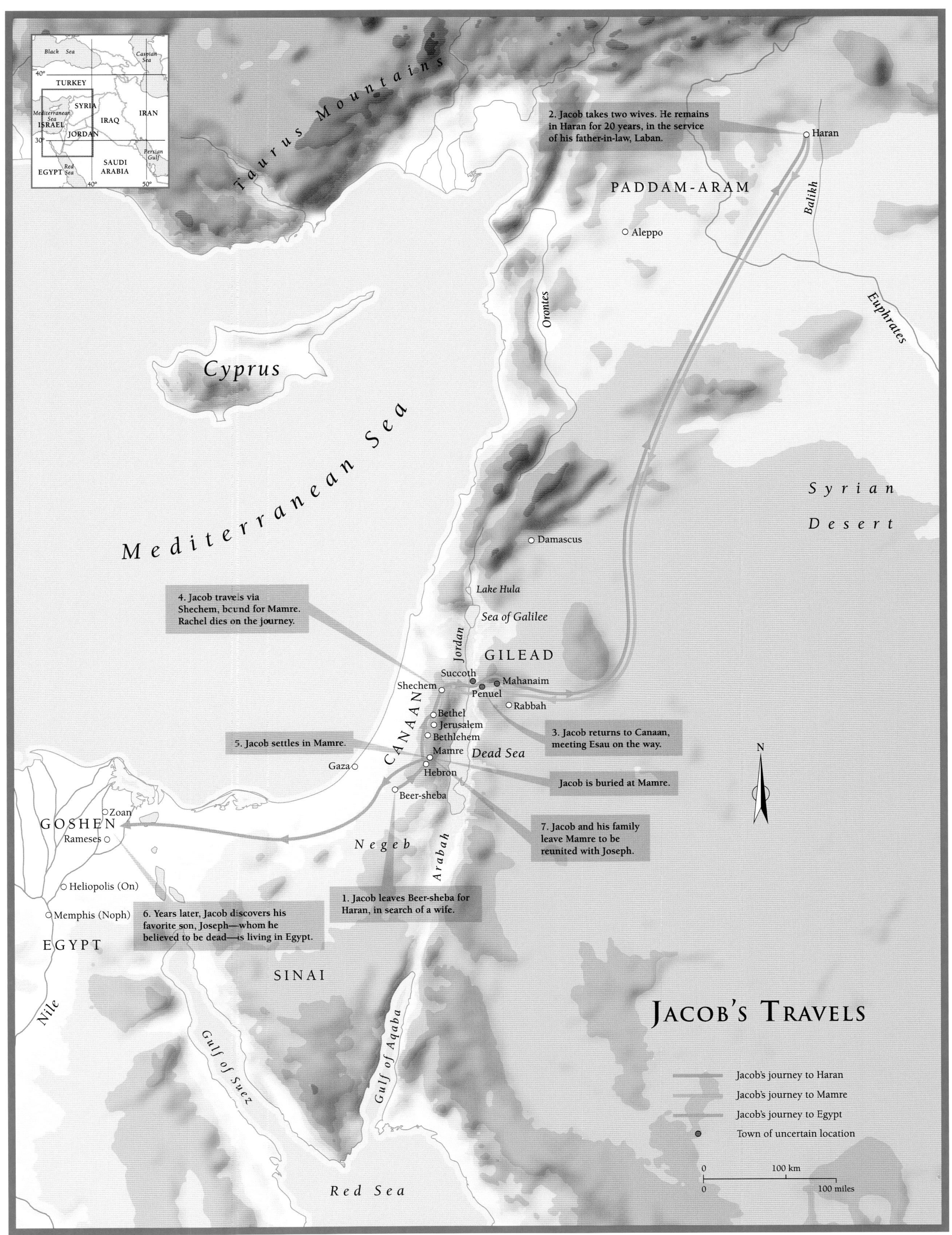
Jacob's Travels
1. Jacob leaves Beer-sheba for Haran, in search of a wife.
2. Jacob takes two wives. He remains in Haran for 20 years, in the service of his father-in-law, Laban.
3. Jacob returns to Canaan, meeting Esau on the way.
4. Jacob travels via Shechem, bound for Mamre. Rachel dies on the journey.
5. Jacob settles in Mamre.
6. Years later, Jacob discovers his favorite son, Joseph—whom he believed to be dead—is living in Egypt.
7. Jacob and his family leave Mamre to be reunited with Joseph.
Jacob is buried at Mamre.
Jacob's journey to Haran
Jacob's journey to Mamre
Jacob's journey to Egypt
Town of uncertain location
Taurus Mountains
Mediterranean Sea
Cyprus
PADDAM-ARAM
Haran
Balikh
Aleppo
Euphrates
Orontes
Syrian Desert
Damascus
Lake Hula
Sea of Galilee
Jordan
GILEAD
Succoth
Mahanaim
Penuel
Rabbah
Shechem
CANAAN
Bethel
Jerusalem
Bethlehem
Mamre
Hebron
Dead Sea
Gaza
Beer-sheba
Negeb
Arabah
GOSHEN
Zoan
Rameses
Heliopolis (On)
Memphis (Noph)
EGYPT
Nile
SINAI
Gulf of Suez
Gulf of Aqaba
Red Sea
N
0
100 km
0
100 miles
Black Sea
Caspian Sea
TURKEY
SYRIA
Mediterranean Sea
ISRAEL
JORDAN
IRAQ
IRAN
Persian Gulf
EGYPT
Red Sea
SAUDI ARABIA
40°
30°
40°
50°

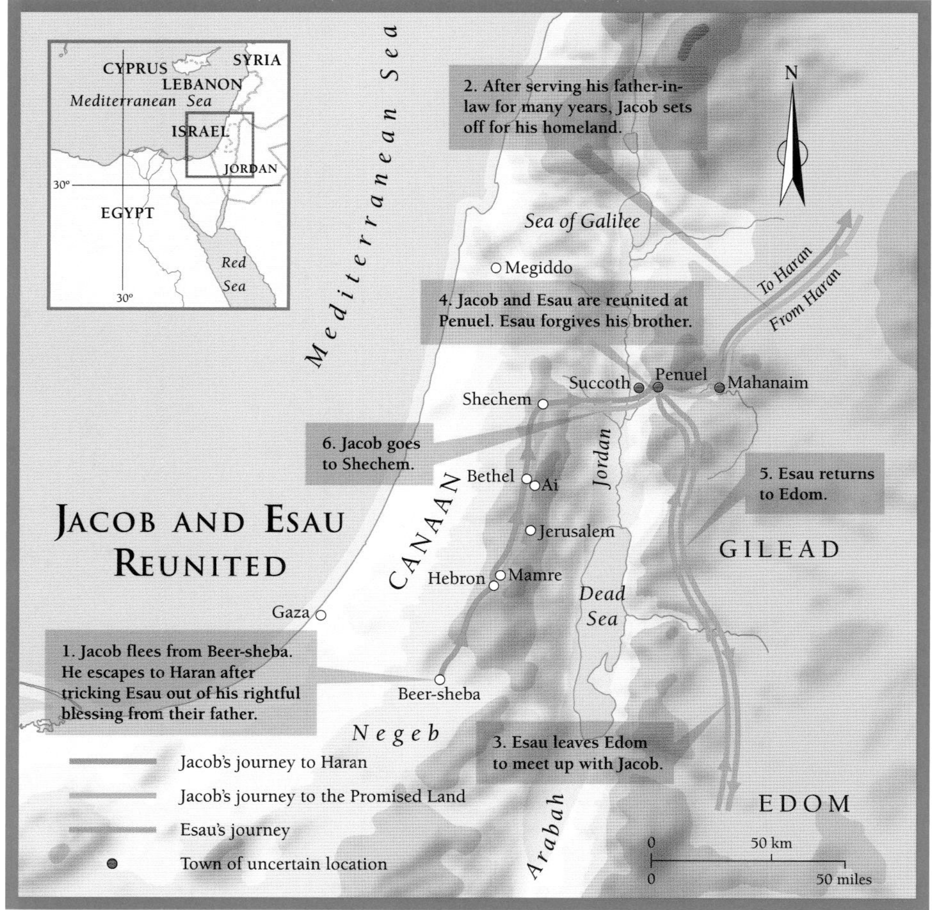

In contrast to Jacob, Esau acts graciously, and though at first Esau refuses Jacob's gift, once again Jacob prevails, and at length he persuades Esau to accept. However, the brothers still seem wary of one another, and when Esau proposes that they travel together, Jacob pleads that the war band will travel too fast for his group. He promises to follow behind, but declines an offer of an armed guard (Genesis 33:15). Now, we learn that Jacob is not entirely renewed after his struggle at the Jabbok. For, instead of heading south, and following his brother to Edom as he promised, he heads west and settles at Shechem, even buying land there.

BELOW: *RECONCILIATION OF ESAU AND JACOB IN CANAAN* BY FRANCESCO HAYEZ. AT PENUEL, TWINS ESAU AND JACOB ARE REUNITED AFTER MANY YEARS. ESAU FORGIVES JACOB FOR PAST WRONGDOINGS.

IMMORALITY IN BIBLE STORIES

A view of Scripture that expects each story to have a "moral" is thwarted by some of the tales in Genesis. These sometimes seem to present people with little sense of morality, let alone a moral to the story! Simple narratives like Aesop's fables present simple messages. Biblical narratives are more complex: the failings of heroes are left visible. In fables, characters are cartoon-like and their "virtue" easily determined. In Dinah's story, by contrast, God is absent, and no one acts well. Chapter 38 of Genesis, about Tamar and Judah, might be entitled "Men Behaving Badly," yet it concerns the ancestor of the tribe from which David and Jesus are descended. This does not, however, mean that Bible stories are (as critics suggest) immoral, or even amoral. We read of the people in such rich narratives as if they were real people. In our responses and judgments on their tales we equip ourselves to judge our own stories.

FAMILY OR COVENANT LOYALTY

The Hebrew word *hesed* describes a complex virtue that was of central importance to the Old Testament, but does not correspond to one idea or term in English. At its core it refers to behaving in ways that are loyal to family or covenant relationships and actions that build up or support the group and its weaker members. This virtue is demonstrated by Ruth, Boaz, and David (and in Genesis by Tamar), but is more often noticeable in its absence, when someone acts in ways that suit them, rather than building up the wider covenant or family community. Throughout the Bible, *hesed* is supremely demonstrated by God. When it describes God, the word is often translated as "loving kindness." In Jacob's story, *hesed* appears only twice—in Jacob's prayer to God (in Genesis 32:10), and when Jacob, from his deathbed, addresses Joseph (47:29).

JACOB'S CHILDREN

Jacob's children prove as turbulent as their father, and the continuing story of this chosen family is marked by strife, treachery, and unfaithfulness in the next generation also. The story of Joseph continues the theme of rivalry and brutality between brothers, which has been prominent in Genesis, and shows this enmity as endemic among Jacob's brood. However, two others of Jacob's children have chapters telling episodes of their stories.

DINAH

The story of Jacob's daughter, Dinah (Genesis 34:1–31), has long been seen as one of rape and revenge, but recently closer examination of the text suggests a more nuanced view. The key is the last verb in verse 2: "lay … by force." Such wording may imply forced intercourse, or it may imply a failure on Shechem's part to take all the required legal formalities beforehand (see also Deuteronomy 21:14b for the same verb), with the ensuing shame Dinah would have to bear.

In any case, Shechem tries to "do the right thing" and marry Dinah. His father, Hamor, begins to negotiate with Jacob. Dinah's brothers

ABOVE: *TAMAR LED TO THE STAKE* BY JACOPO BASSANO. DOUBLE STANDARDS EMERGE AS JUDAH DEMANDS TAMAR'S PUNISHMENT, BELIEVING HER TO BE WANTON—UNAWARE THAT HE IS THE FATHER OF HER UNBORN CHILDREN.

intervene, and trick Hamor and his people into accepting circumcision as the price of intermarriage. While the new covenant partners are still recovering, two of Jacob's sons slaughter the men, while their brothers loot the city.

In view of Jacob's puzzling passivity in this chapter, Dinah's existing relationship with the women of the town, and other details, it has been suggested that what was at stake was the desire by Jacob and Dinah to build community with the Canaanites, and the sons' desire to keep separate. However we interpret this story, it reflects little credit on this dysfunctional family.

TAMAR AND JUDAH

At first, Genesis 38 (which plays a role as foil in Joseph's story) seems like another genealogy of a revered ancestor. However, once Joseph's brother Judah has married his firstborn Er to Tamar (38:6) the story seems to run off the rails. For we are told quite bluntly that Er "was wicked in the sight of the Lord, and the Lord put him to death" (38:7). Er's wickedness is left unspecified, but to understand the fault of his brothers in the succeeding verses we need to know the customs of the time. Deuteronomy 25:5–10 describes a situation where if a man dies childless his brother should marry the widow and raise an heir for the dead brother. The significance of this duty becomes clear in the book of Ruth, and when we remember that offspring were thought of as one's survival and remembrance after death.

Er's brother, Onan, fulfills the letter of the law, but evades its responsibility through coitus interruptus. God therefore kills him too for his wickedness. Judah is fearful that the third brother, Shelah, may suffer the same fate. So he sends Tamar back to her parents, using Shelah's youth as an excuse. Tamar is left as an unwanted barren widow (a primary focus in patriarchal society was on marriage and producing offspring).

When she hears that Judah himself is widowed, and is at Timnah for the sheep shearing, knowing that Shelah is an adult but that she has not been given to him as wife, Tamar takes the initiative. Dressed as a prostitute, she seduces Judah, and accepts his seal and staff as security for her fee.

When Tamar is discovered to be pregnant, Judah is ready to see her punished by gruesome execution (Genesis 38:24). However, when she demonstrates her stratagem and reveals Judah's paternity—coupled with his failure to live up to family loyalty and responsibility as she has done—he is confronted with the truth and admits his fault: "She is more in the right than I, since I did not give her to my son Shelah" (38:26). Twins are born to Tamar, and—like grandfather Jacob and great-uncle Esau—Zerah and Perez are already rivals in the womb.

The story of Canaanite Tamar's family loyalty, and of Judah's lack of family loyalty, contrasts with the story of Joseph and Potiphar in the next chapter. These stories encourage us (even though our social world and family expectations are very different) to reflect on our own lives and decisions.

LEFT: *JUDAH AND TAMAR* BY EMILE JEAN HORACE VERNET. DISGUISED AS A PROSTITUTE, JUDAH'S DAUGHTER-IN-LAW TAMAR BEGUILES HIM—IN A PLAN TO FORCE HIM TO FACE UP TO HIS OBLIGATIONS.

JOSEPH AND HIS FAMILY

NOW ISRAEL LOVED JOSEPH MORE THAN ANY OTHER OF HIS CHILDREN GENESIS 37:3

RIGHT: RELIEF OF JOSEPH GUARDING HIS SHEEP, SAN GENNARO DUOMO, NAPLES. JOSEPH'S BOYHOOD SPENT AS A SIMPLE SHEPHERD WAS IN SHARP CONTRAST TO THE GREATNESS THAT LAY AHEAD.

Genesis 37–50 is often called the "Story of Joseph," but this is something of a misnomer. As the introduction in 37:2 makes clear, this is the story of the family of Jacob (in Hebrew "the generations of Jacob"). Joseph is, of course, a key player in the story, but so are his brothers and his ageing father Jacob. Genesis 37–50 has been called a "short story" or "novella." It has all the ingredients of good storytelling: a cast of characters with good and bad traits, the tale of how an insignificant Israelite achieves success in the international arena (what some call the rags-to-riches plot), plenty of intrigue and dramatic crises, and a powerful ending. But what is most striking about this text is how these elements have been shaped into a powerful theological "Torah" or instruction on the ways of God in our world. The story probably has ancient origins, but the present text reflects careful editorial work by theologically sensitive scribes, who operated at a later date in Israel's preexilic and postexilic periods.

BELOW: FOURTEENTH-CENTURY C.E. FRESCO BY BARTOLO DI FREDI. THOUGH JOSEPH'S DREAMS FORESHADOW THE FUTURE, HIS BROTHERS INTERPRET THEM AS INDICATIONS OF THEIR SUBSERVIENCE TO JOSEPH.

CONFLICT IN THE FAMILY

Genesis 37 introduces the story's key characters in quick succession and, as we are introduced to them, we are left somewhat uncertain as to who is to blame for the troubles that ensue. Verse 2 states that the shepherd boy Joseph brought a bad report about some of his brothers: is Joseph telling the truth about them or telling tales? The text is ambiguous. Verse 3 portrays a doting father Israel (that is, Jacob) making a special robe for his favorite son Joseph. The Hebrew word for this robe is also used in 2 Samuel 13:18 to describe the royal apparel of David's daughters. Modern translations prefer a "robe with long sleeves" to the traditional "coat of many colors." Is this special robe a distant hint of the royal favors that will later be showered on Joseph by Pharaoh? Within the more immediate context, is Jacob being imprudent by favoring Joseph in this way? Verse 4 presents Joseph's brothers as a group united in their hatred of Joseph because of their father's attitude to him. One might expect their anger would be directed against their father rather than Joseph, but perhaps they see his favored status as a threat to their own status within this large family (the 12 sons of Israel). Perhaps too, the content of Joseph's evil report in verse 2 has influenced Jacob to favor him over his brothers.

JOSEPH'S DREAMS

One particular series of events in Joseph's early life is told in three stages. First there was Joseph's evil report, then Jacob's special robe, and now we have Joseph's dreams (Genesis 39:5–11). For ancient peoples, dreams were often seen as a way in which a god communicated his or her purpose. If true, then Joseph's dreams signal God's special purpose for him in contrast to the other members of his family. Joseph's first dream about the sheaves of grain implies his superiority

BRINGING THE WORDS TO LIFE

Biblical texts often record the outline or gist of a story rather than the complete version because it would have been too costly for ancient scribes to record everything verbatim. Writing was an expensive and time-consuming business. Israelite storytellers would bring the written version to life in an actual performance, sometimes by adding details that clarify ambiguities, sometimes by withholding them in order to heighten listeners' interest and involvement. Israelite storytellers liked to develop the plots of their stories in three stages.

BELOW: THIS INTERPRETATION OF JOSEPH'S PIT COMES FROM DOM AUGUSTIN CALMET'S 1732 *DICTIONARY OF THE HOLY BIBLE*. JOSEPH'S BROTHERS THROW HIM IN A PIT WHILE THEY REFINE THEIR PLOT TO RID THEMSELVES OF HIM.

ABOVE: *JACOB PRESENTED WITH JOSEPH'S COAT* BY BALTHASAR BESCHEY. WITH THEIR PLAN GONE WRONG, JOSEPH'S BROTHERS ATTEMPT TO ACCOUNT FOR JOSEPH'S DISAPPEARANCE BY PRODUCING HIS BLOODSTAINED COAT.

over his brothers; the second dream about the sun, moon, and stars implies his superiority over the whole family (although it is uncertain to whom the moon refers because his mother Rachel is dead). In terms of plot, the dreams foreshadow events to come. Relationships between the key characters become more ominous. The brothers are now utterly hostile to Joseph, and even Jacob rebukes him! Something has to give, and the following verses tell how unbridled jealousy leads to plans for murder.

THE ATTEMPT TO ELIMINATE JOSEPH

The brothers' attempt to dispose of Joseph comes badly unstuck. Their initial plan is to kill him but, after interventions by Reuben and Judah, they decide to make some money instead by selling him to passing Ishmaelites. Interpretation of Genesis 37:28 varies, with most suggesting that the brothers sold Joseph to passing Ishmaelite/Midianite traders. More recent theories include the suggestion that passing Midianites beat the brothers to it and snatched Joseph from the pit where he had been thrown. Is Joseph's "escape" by chance or by the mysterious hand of God? As with many biblical stories, some good emerges from human evil. Reuben and Judah display traits of solidarity and compassion for "the persecuted other"—themes that will be developed later in the story.

THE HAUNTING PRESENCE OF JOSEPH

The final episode in Genesis 37:31–35 shows the desperate brothers concocting another scheme to be rid of the bogey of Joseph. Their plan to dispose of Joseph ended in a fiasco, now their plan to erase his memory from the family, by faking his death, fails miserably. In a powerful ironic twist, although Jacob is deceived by the sight of Joseph's special robe stained with goat's blood, his unceasing grieving means that the brothers can never forget Joseph and his exalted position in the family. Even though physically absent, all that he stands for is still present.

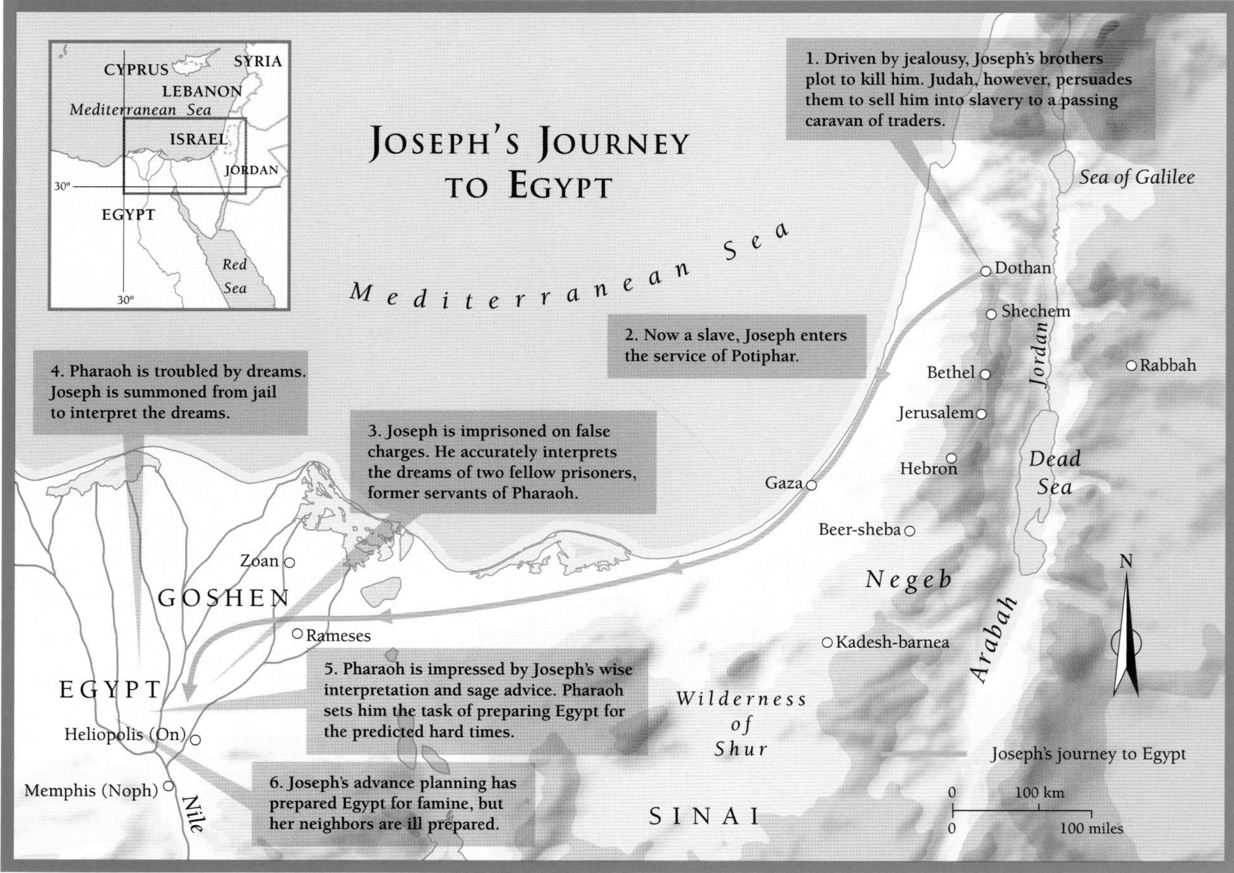

OPPOSITE: *JOSEPH AND POTIPHAR'S WIFE* BY JUAN URRUCHI. POTIPHAR'S WIFE—AS A "WOMAN SCORNED"—FRAMES JOSEPH AFTER HE REJECTS HER ADVANCES.

JUDAH AND JOSEPH: A CONTRAST

Before telling the story of Joseph in Egypt, however, the Old Testament editors have inserted a story of his brother Judah in chapter 38. It is further evidence that Genesis 37–50 is about Jacob's family, not just Joseph. The story of how Judah treats his daughter-in-law Tamar forms a powerful contrast with the way Joseph behaves toward the wife of Potiphar in chapter 39. Where Judah is uncaring and indulgent, Joseph is noble and upright, despite the imprisonment he suffers as a result. But, it is not all bad news about Judah. Tamar eventually brings about a dramatic change in him—perhaps a foreshadowing of his transformation later in Egypt (see 44:18–34). Genesis 39 is important for another reason—for the first time the text emphasizes the guidance of God in Joseph's destiny. What was at most implicit in Genesis 37 here becomes explicit as Joseph enters the most taxing and dangerous part of his adventure. Dumped in a pit by his brothers while they plot his demise, Joseph has now been brought down to Egypt to be dumped in another pit. His journey seems all downward to doom. But, as the text emphasizes, "the Lord was with Joseph" (39:2, 3, 21, 23)—with God on his side and righteous in his conduct, Joseph will ultimately triumph.

JOSEPH IN EGYPT

The next episode in this story focuses on Joseph and his rise to prominence in the great empire of Egypt. As with chapter 37, this part of the plot unfolds in three stages. The first involves Joseph's employment in the house of Potiphar, an officer of Pharaoh (Genesis 39); the second involves his interpretation of the dreams of the chief cupbearer and chief baker, prisoners of Pharaoh (Genesis 40); and the third involves his interpretation of Pharaoh's dreams that no Egyptian could explain (Genesis 41).

BELOW: MOSAIC SHOWING *THE DREAM OF THE VINTNER AND THE BAKER*. JOSEPH'S INTERPRETATION OF THE TWO SERVANTS' DREAMS PREDICTS VERY DIFFERENT OUTCOMES FOR THE TWO MEN.

JOSEPH THE INTERPRETER OF DREAMS

According to Genesis 40, Joseph is appointed to serve the chief cupbearer and baker, who were privileged servants of Pharaoh before their fall from grace and imprisonment. The episode deftly combines two themes. One emphasizes, from a human point of view, the utterly powerless situation of Joseph in Egypt, in the depths of the dungeon, servant to the servants of Pharaoh—the most powerful person in the most powerful country of the ancient world. The future of both cupbearer and baker depends completely on Pharaoh's whim. The other emphasizes the one power that Joseph has and the Egyptians do not—the power to interpret dreams, which, as he says, "belongs to God" (40:8). Joseph's successful interpretation of the servants' dreams is a sign that, as Genesis 39 notes several times, God is with Joseph. The young man whose dreams in Genesis 37 greatly disturbed his family is now portrayed as the interpreter of dreams that greatly disturb Egyptians. Human beings are always seeking to know the one thing that eludes their control—the future. It is Joseph's God-given gift to predict the future and his trust in that gift that brings about a great future for him.

EGYPT AND PALESTINE
IN THE TIME OF JOSEPH
Mediterranean Sea
Damascus
Tyre
Dan
Kedesh
Lake Hula
Hazor
Acco
Chinnereth
Sea of Galilee
Hannathon
Yarmuk
Megiddo
Dor
Taanach
Harod
Beth-shean
Pehel
CANAAN
Dothan
Tirzah
Mt. Ebal
Penuel
Mahanaim
Shechem
Succoth
Jabbok
Mt. Gerizim
Aphek
Joppa
Aijalon
Jordan
Gezer
Bethel
Ai
AMMON
Timnah
Ekron
Gibeon
Jericho
Mt. Pisgah
Mt. Nebo
Ashdod
Jerusalem
Beth-shemesh
Bethlehem
Ashkelon
Lachish
Mamre
Hebron
Dead Sea
Gaza
Arnon
Lake Menzelah
Gerar
Arad
Beer-sheba
Lake Sirbonis
MOAB
Zoan
Negeb
Zoar
Lake Ballah
Tamar
Rameses
Kadesh-barnea
Arabah
EDOM
Lake Timsah
Beer-lahai-roi
Wilderness of Shur
Wilderness of Zin
Heliopolis (On)
Bitter Lakes
EGYPT
Memphis (Noph)
Wilderness of Paran
Ezion-geber
Wilderness of Sin
Gulf of Suez
N
Nile
SINAI
MIDIAN
Gulf of Aqaba
Jebel Musa (Mt. Sinai)
Mountain of uncertain location
Town of uncertain location
0
50 km
0
50 miles
Red Sea
CYPRUS
SYRIA
LEBANON
Mediterranean Sea
ISRAEL
JORDAN
30°
EGYPT
SAUDI ARABIA
Red Sea
30°

JOSEPH'S RISE IN EGYPT

Joseph's opportunity is provided by Pharaoh's troubling dreams about seven cows and seven ears of grain (Genesis 41:1–8). But, even though Joseph enjoys a unique divine gift, his escape from prison and rise to prominence depends, as it does for all, on other human beings—and on God working through them. So it is that the chief cupbearer, restored to his privileged position, remembers or is moved to remember Joseph's service to him (41:9–13). This brings Joseph to the presence of Pharaoh and his interpretation of the two dreams—they portend a calamitous seven-year famine after seven years of plenty. The honest and upright Joseph attributes his interpretation to God (41:16), not to any innate skill he possesses as a human being. In another decisive development of the plot of this story, the authors now portray Joseph not just as a gifted interpreter of dreams, but also as the wise sage who outlines a whole program that will enable Egypt to survive the famine. As Joseph notes in his speech to Pharaoh (41:25–36), a wise and discerning person (41:33) is needed to implement such a program. Pharaoh recognizes, or is moved to recognize, that Joseph is such a man and appoints him to oversee the program. This is not a reward for services rendered but recognition by the most powerful person in the world that the "spirit of God" rests on Joseph (41:38). In order to survive the famine, Pharaoh and Egypt must rely on the guidance of God, manifested in Joseph. As a public sign of this commitment to Joseph, Pharaoh transfers his signet ring to Joseph's hand and gives him Potiphar's daughter, Asenath, as a wife.

LEFT: *EGYPT SAVED BY JOSEPH* BY ALEXANDRE-DENIS ABEL DE PUJOL. PHARAOH'S FAITH IN JOSEPH'S MANAGEMENT AND JUDGMENT IS REWARDED, AS JOSEPH ENSURES EGYPT IS WELL PREPARED FOR THE IMPENDING HARD TIMES.

This raises the question of whether Joseph the Hebrew will, or has already, become Zaphenath-paneah the Egyptian (Genesis 41:45)—an important preparation in the plot of the story for his subsequent encounter with his brothers.

JOSEPH AND THE FAMINE

The future unfolds according to Joseph's interpretation of Pharaoh's dreams. Seven years of plenty are followed by seven years of famine. The number seven is highly significant in biblical and Ancient Near Eastern thought: it symbolizes perfection and completeness. Seven weeks were devoted to the harvest in ancient Israel, to allow enough time for what was hoped would always be the perfect harvest. The great jubilee year that is legislated for in Leviticus takes place in the fiftieth year, after "seven weeks of years, seven times seven years" (Leviticus 25:8). During this year, any Israelite who had suffered loss of property or social dignity would

BELOW: *JOSEPH EXPLAINING PHARAOH'S DREAMS* BY JEAN ADRIEN GUIGNET. PHARAOH IS TROUBLED BY HIS DREAMS AND THEIR MEANING, AND HE CALLS ON JOSEPH TO INTERPRET THE MESSAGE IN THE DREAMS.

have it fully restored. The jubilee aimed to restore all Israel to complete well-being. It is a magnificent ideal that may have been difficult to achieve in reality.

The alternation between good and bad harvests would have been a common experience in Ancient Egypt, which relied on the flow of water in the lower Nile river, itself dependent on rains that fed the headwaters of the White and Blue Niles in the mountains further south. The Nile is the longest river in the world and the soil along its shores, although not wide in many places, is famous for its fertility and produces abundantly in good seasons. All this was known to the Egyptians and to Israel's storytellers. What the number seven brings to the fore is the extraordinary nature of the years of plenty and the years of famine that follow. Today, we might say that perfect abundance was to be followed by the perfect famine.

JOSEPH'S SONS—MANASSEH AND EPHRAIM

As a significant element during these years of God's bounty, the story reports the birth of two sons to Joseph, Manasseh and Ephraim (Genesis 41:50–52). These are the eponymous ancestors of the two major northern tribes of Israel. According to the biblical text (see in particular Deuteronomy 3), half the tribe of Manasseh claimed territory on the western side of the Jordan, and half claimed territory on the eastern side, in company with Reuben and Gad. The tribe of Ephraim's land lay between the great southern tribe of Judah (and Benjamin) and Manasseh on the western side of the Jordan. The presence in the tradition of these two sons of Joseph who was one of the 12 sons of Jacob/Israel, results in the 12 tribes of Israel being listed in two forms. One form lists Joseph and does not mention Manasseh and Ephraim, the other omits Joseph and the priestly tribe of Levi, who had no inheritance of land, in order to include Manasseh and Ephraim and so maintain the number 12 in the process. Examples of the first form occur in Genesis 29–30 and Exodus 1; examples of the second form occur in Numbers 1, 2, 7, 10, and 13. The order of the tribes in the lists varies, with some listing Reuben first (first-born son of Jacob) and others Judah (the dominant tribe of the south and ancestor of David). The differences probably reflect the preferences of different groups in ancient Israel.

JOSEPH AS SAVIOR OF THE WORLD

The onset of the perfect famine is told relatively briefly in Genesis 41:53–57. One might have expected more emphasis, but these few verses are designed to provide a setting for two important developments in the story. The first is the report

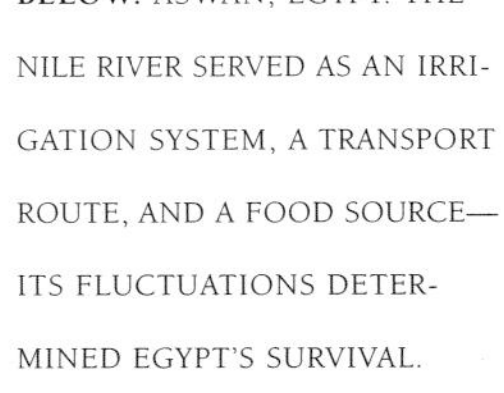

BELOW: ASWAN, EGYPT. THE NILE RIVER SERVED AS AN IRRIGATION SYSTEM, A TRANSPORT ROUTE, AND A FOOD SOURCE—ITS FLUCTUATIONS DETERMINED EGYPT'S SURVIVAL.

that the famine was so terrible that not only the Egyptians but "all the world came to Joseph in Egypt" to obtain food (41:57). There is a distant echo here of the promise to Joseph's ancestor, Abraham, that "in you all the families of the earth shall be blessed" (12:3). Joseph, who in the story now dominates the world stage, becomes the first Israelite in whom this promise is realized. Although the terminology is somewhat different in the two texts (one being a promise, the other part of a narrative), the connection between them seems unmistakable. Through the divine blessing that Joseph, like Abraham, enjoys, the whole world is saved. In making this connection, the reader also becomes aware of a subtle yet powerful irony in the text. The blessing promised to Abraham becomes effective at the point where his descendants, the chosen family of Israel, are wracked by deep division and hatred. The message of the story is that God is able to work his purpose through this chosen family even in the most unlikely circumstances. And that purpose is not just to save a starving humanity that streams to Joseph for food, but also to heal the relationships within his own fragmented family. This is the second important development that unfolds in the following chapters. The famine reaches Joseph's family back in Canaan and Jacob is obliged to send his sons to Egypt to buy food. His decision unwittingly triggers the most dramatic stage in the story of this chosen yet troubled family of Israel, a period that is played out in the setting of the famine.

LEFT: JOSEPH FILLING HIS BROTHERS' SACKS WITH GRAIN, IVORY PANEL FROM MAXIMIAN'S CATHEDRA (THRONE). DESPITE JOSEPH'S POWERFUL POSITION, HE BALANCES HIS BROTHERS' NEEDS WITH HIS OWN INTEREST IN THEIR HONESTY.

JOSEPH'S BROTHERS IN EGYPT

The most dramatic stage of the story of Joseph and his family covers Genesis 42 to the opening verses of Genesis 45, where Joseph reveals his identity to his brothers. The drama unfolds once again in the three stages so favored by Israelite storytellers. Three times the brothers come face-to-face with Joseph in Egypt; three times Joseph tests his brothers' honesty, and the third test produces some surprising, even shocking, results.

THE BROTHERS' FIRST ENCOUNTER WITH JOSEPH

In Israelite thinking, one always goes "down" to Egypt and "up" to the Promised Land and Jerusalem. The different terms are often employed symbolically by Israelite storytellers to evoke faith convictions about God's purpose for Israel. The brothers' first journey down has distinct echoes of Joseph's in the earlier part of the story. They go down as powerless aliens; they encounter a hostile Egyptian overlord (Joseph) who accuses them of criminal intent and throws them into prison. The brothers, of course, know nothing of Joseph's experiences in Egypt and the reader may wonder whether he is being vengeful or does he have some greater purpose in mind? A positive clue is provided by his proposal to test the brothers' honesty, and his weeping as they recall their treatment of him (Genesis 42:18–25). Simeon is kept a prisoner (as Joseph was), while the others are instructed to return home with food but then come "down" again to Egypt, this time bringing young Benjamin (Joseph's brother by Rachel, the favored wife of Jacob).

Money also plays a role in this test—an echo of the money involved in the sale of Joseph. It would be easy for the brothers to take the money returned in their sacks, tell their father that Simeon is dead (as they did in the case of Joseph), and consider the matter closed. But they don't; despite their fears, the brothers report the truth to their father and accept the fearful prospect of having to face up to "the lord of the land" again (42:30). There is hope that the brothers are changed or changing men.

THE BROTHERS' SECOND ENCOUNTER WITH JOSEPH

Their second journey down to Egypt is made in a climate of fear, entrapment, and an emerging solidarity (Genesis 43). Jacob fears to lose Benjamin as he has lost Simeon and, earlier, Joseph. But, both he and his sons realize they are trapped by the famine and the Egyptian overlord's demands. There is no escape. Despite this, Reuben and Judah, the two brothers who deflected their brothers' murderous intent (37:20), display family solidarity by going surety for Benjamin's safe return. The scene is masterfully portrayed and heightens anticipation as to how events will unfold upon their return to Egypt.

In complete contrast to the first encounter, the brothers this time are invited to dine with Joseph, who reassures them about the money that was returned in their sacks and restores Simeon to their company. Joseph maintains his Egyptian identity but arranges the meal in a way that recalls arrangements "at home" with each in his place of seniority and with Benjamin being given favored treatment.

BELOW: *JACOB REFUSING TO RELEASE BENJAMIN* BY ADOLPHE ROGER. JACOB HAS ALREADY LOST ONE SON, POSSIBLY TWO, AND REFUSES TO ALLOW BENJAMIN TO BE TAKEN TO CATER TO THE WHIM OF AN EGYPTIAN LORD.

RIGHT: *JOSEPH RECOGNISED BY HIS BROTHERS* BY BECQUET. OVERWHELMING EMOTION ACCOMPANIES JOSEPH'S REVELATION OF HIS TRUE IDENTITY. HE ABSOLVES HIS BROTHERS OF GUILT, SAYING GOD SENT HIM TO EGYPT.

In contrast to Genesis 37, the brothers display no rancor toward the favored one. It is time for the final stage in Joseph's test—while arranging for the brothers to be given food for their return, he also arranges for Benjamin to be accused of stealing his most precious possession—a silver divining cup. The brothers can escape and leave Benjamin to his fate, but, in a show of genuine solidarity, they return with him to Egypt for the third and final encounter with the Egyptian.

THE BROTHERS' THIRD ENCOUNTER WITH JOSEPH

Joseph offers the brothers an escape—he will keep the alleged thief Benjamin, but the rest can go free. Judah then steps forward and, in words of selfless generosity, offers himself in place of Benjamin. His lengthy speech in Genesis 44:18–34 contains a shocking surprise. So far the story has tended to portray Joseph as the innocent, wronged son in contrast to his deeply flawed brothers. But Judah's report of what has transpired exposes a disturbing side of Joseph. Genesis 44:22–23 reveals that Joseph has knowingly risked his aged father's life in order to see Benjamin and perhaps also to dominate his brothers. Has he taken the dreams of Genesis 37 into his own hands? Rather than Joseph the favored son, it is Judah who now shows filial loyalty by offering himself so that Benjamin can return to his father. It is instructive to note how Old Testament authors avoid portraying their great figures as celebrities. Whether it is Abraham or Sarah, Joseph or Moses, each is in some way flawed and in need of God's healing touch. Old Testament authors display a realistic understanding of the human condition.

The almost palpable tension in the story is released when Joseph reveals his identity to his brothers (Genesis 45:1–3). The text does not explain why Joseph does so at this point: is it because of the impact of Judah's words or because his love for his father triumphs over his desire to pursue his strategy? The reader is left to ponder the options. An Israelite storyteller might have developed one or the other. Perhaps an appropriate conclusion is to echo Joseph's comment that God's purpose in this messy mix of good and evil has been "to preserve life" (45:5).

JACOB AND HIS FAMILY IN EGYPT

Following Joseph's dramatic revelation, the remainder of Genesis draws a number of important items together. The text is somewhat complex and probably reflects the combination of a variety of traditions in ancient Israel.

JACOB AND HIS FAMILY JOURNEY TO EGYPT

The first item, the journey of Jacob to Egypt to see Joseph (Genesis 45:16–47:12), brings the drama of the preceding chapters to a satisfactory close. The troubled and divided members of the family are finally reunited in Egypt where Joseph is able to arrange for them a suitable place to live (Goshen in the northeastern Nile Delta), obtain employment for them, and protect them from the famine. The section climaxes with the impoverished and aged Jacob blessing the all-powerful Pharaoh, a discrete reminder that blessing comes from God through his chosen mediator, not through the power that human beings acquire. With the family of Jacob/Israel safely in Egypt, the stage is set for the story of Israel in the book of Exodus.

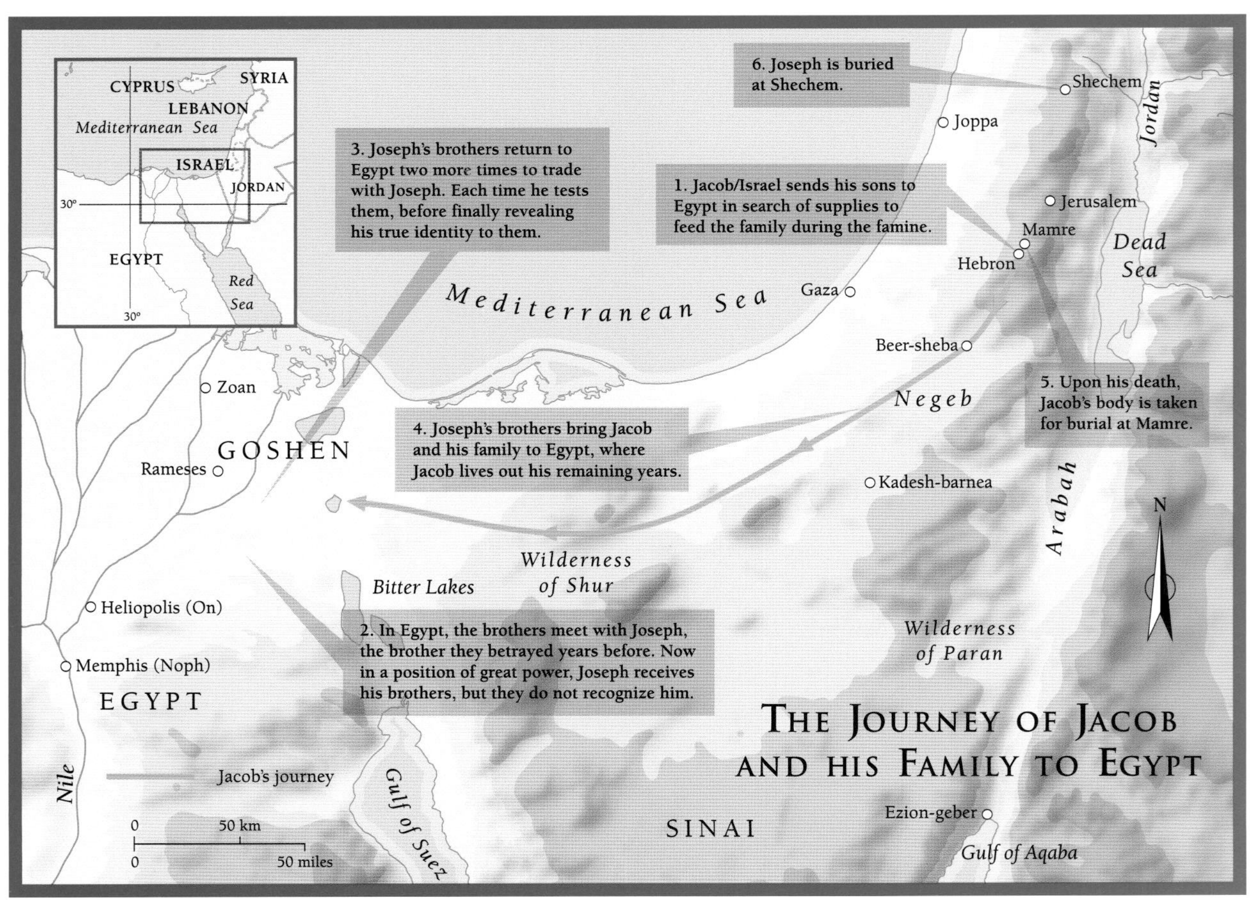

IMPACT OF THE FAMINE ON EGYPT

In Genesis 47:13–26, the text resumes the theme of the famine and, somewhat surprisingly, portrays Joseph acquiring all of Egypt for Pharaoh except for the lands belonging to the priests. To some, Joseph may appear to act like a cunning despot in this passage, but it is the Egyptians who offer to sell themselves as slaves (47:19)—Joseph does not impose slavery on them. He even provides for their

welfare by allowing them to retain four-fifths of the harvest for themselves (47:24). There may be an ironic contrast here with Joseph's earlier status as one sold into slavery in Egypt. Here, the Egyptians sell themselves as slaves to Pharaoh via Joseph, the former slave. There may also be a contrast with the book of Exodus in which Israel is enslaved and oppressed by a Pharaoh whose predecessor was saved by Joseph from famine and enriched beyond measure.

THE SPECIAL STATUS OF EPHRAIM AND MANASSEH

Genesis 47:27–28 serves to conclude the account of Israel's settlement in Egypt and to provide a transition to the next major section, the death of Jacob/Israel and the blessings he bestows on his sons before he dies (47:29–50:14).

Genesis 48 is concerned with the blessing bestowed on Joseph's sons Ephraim and Manasseh. In Genesis 48:5–6, Jacob grants them the same status as his own sons, a unique privilege. In this way, the variant lists of the tribes of Israel in subsequent texts are given the same standing—those that list Ephraim and Manasseh but do not mention Joseph (or Levi) and those that list Joseph (and Levi) but make no mention of Ephraim and Manasseh. In a similar vein, the later prominence of the tribe of Ephraim in relation to Manasseh is explained—it was all foreordained in the blessing bestowed by ancestor Jacob (48:8–22).

JACOB'S FAREWELL AND BLESSING

Genesis 49 deals with another necessary item before the death of the great ancestor Jacob: his farewell address to his sons, ancestors of the 12 tribes of Israel. The prominence of Judah (the dominant tribe of the south) and Joseph (the dominant tribe of the north, bearing in mind that Joseph here stands in place of Ephraim and Manasseh) in this address is understandable. The censuring of Reuben refers to his actions in Genesis 35:22, while that of Simeon and Levi refers to their violent reaction to the rape of their sister Tamar in Genesis 34. The references to the other tribes (Zebulun, Issachar, Dan, Gad, Asher, Naphtali, and Benjamin) are difficult to correlate with Old Testament texts and may be traditional sayings whose precise origin can no longer be determined. Genesis 49:28 appears to distinguish Jacob's preceding words from his blessing, because it stresses that each received a suitable blessing—his censure of Reuben, Simeon, and Levi could hardly be called blessing texts. Jacob then dies and is buried, as he instructed, in the ancestral burial site near Mamre in Canaan (the cave in the field of Machpelah; see Genesis 23).

ABOVE: *JOSEPH RECEIVES HIS FATHER IN EGYPT* BY NICOLAES CORNELISZ MOEYAERT. THE FAMILY OF JACOB ARE REUNITED ONCE MORE, AND ARE ALLOCATED LAND IN THE REGION OF GOSHEN.

THE DEATH OF JOSEPH

The final, rather briefer, section of Genesis records Joseph's own death and burial in Egypt, but with instructions for his bones to be transferred to the Promised Land. However, Joseph is not a patriarch like Abraham, Isaac, and Jacob, and so it is not appropriate for him to be buried in the cave at Machpelah. Joshua 24:32 records that he was eventually buried at Shechem, in a plot bought by his father Jacob, as Abraham had originally bought the cave at Machpelah for his wife Sarah.

ABOVE: COLOR LITHOGRAPH SHOWING THE BURIAL OF JACOB. IN ACCORDANCE WITH HIS LAST WISHES, JACOB'S BODY IS TAKEN TO MACHPELAH NEAR MAMRE IN CANAAN FOR BURIAL.

The account of Joseph's death is preceded by an intriguing little episode that reports the brothers' fear that Joseph will take revenge now that their father is dead. Joseph allays their fears with words that echo his earlier comment that the whole affair has been part of God's purpose to "preserve life" (Genesis 45:5–8). The episode reveals that complete reconciliation between Joseph and his brothers is yet to be achieved; as Genesis draws to a close a measure of tension remains. The episode provides further testimony to the realism and honesty of the Old Testament.

MOSES

THE ISRAELITES WERE FRUITFUL AND PROLIFIC ... SO THAT THE LAND WAS FILLED WITH THEM EXODUS 1:7

RIGHT: THIS CHARCOAL SKETCH OF MOSES AS A YOUNG MAN IS THE WORK OF RAPHAEL. HE IS CAPTURED IN A MOMENT OF DESPAIR, AN EMOTION THAT WILL SURFACE MANY TIMES DURING HIS SERVICE TO GOD.

The second book of the Old Testament is entitled, according to ancient practice, after its opening words—"These are the names" (Exodus 1:1). We know it better as "Exodus"—the "going out" of Israel from Egypt. It was the later translators of the Greek Old Testament, or Septuagint, who applied this more familiar designation to the work. As precise as "exodus" is to describe the central focus of the volume, this experience is not limited to a single, albeit crucial, event, but was all-encompassing, transforming an enslaved and humiliated people into a nation joined together by divine action and purpose. The Bible itself places Israel's journey of liberation within a very specific context.

In Genesis 45–47, the king of Egypt, or pharaoh, allowed Joseph's family to settle in the Nile Delta, supporting them by royal decree, with land and jobs. Historically, the sovereign who would issue this type of charter would personally guarantee its contents. However, these documents were also placed under the abiding protection of the gods of the respective parties. That meant that a divine overseer of the estate could prosecute any infringement of the provisions—even if the violator was a future king. For several generations, this harmonious relationship—guaranteed by legal and religious tradition—prevails. Pharaonic benevolence allows the "sons of Israel" to be "fruitful and prolific; they multiplied and grew exceedingly strong" (Exodus 1:7). Both hosts and guests thrive under the blessing of the god of Jacob. But the situation is not to last. There is a sudden change upon the throne of Egypt, and nothing is the same.

THE BIRTH OF MOSES

"Now a new king arose over Egypt, who did not know Joseph" (Exodus 1:8) describes a dynastic change, marked by the unnamed ruler's annulment of the earlier arrangement with the Israelites. Unbound by law, this pharaoh deigns to speak as if he were God: "Come, let us deal shrewdly with them" (1:10). Without provocation, he decides that this once-welcomed group is a threat. In short order, state terror in the form of forced labor descends into murder. Ironically, the Ancient Egyptians were famed for their medical knowledge—especially their gynecological expertise. But lifesaving skills are now to be employed to bring about death—male children of the Hebrews are to be killed at birth (1:16). Defiantly, the midwives in charge refuse to carry out the inhumane program on ethical and religious grounds ("fearing God"), and they deceive the king (1:17–19). Frustrated, the obsessed tyrant arrives at a final solution: "Every boy ... you shall throw into the Nile" (1:22). The birth of the man whom God chooses to lead Israel out of this pit—Moses—occurs in this crisis-atmosphere. The Bible informs us that his appearance testifies that God's light—though hidden from sight—continues to shine for a people enshrouded by utter darkness. The reaction of Moses' mother to her newborn "that he was a

BELOW: THIS NINETEENTH-DYNASTY PAPYRUS BEARS WITNESS TO EGYPTIAN MIDWIFERY SKILLS—SKILLS THAT PHARAOH INTENDS TO MISUSE TO COMBAT THE PERCEIVED THREAT POSED BY THE HEBREW PEOPLE.

RIGHT: *THE FINDING OF MOSES* BY ADRIAAN VAN DER WERFF. ADRIFT ON THE NILE IN A PAPYRUS BASKET, THE INFANT MOSES IS DISCOVERED BY THE PARTY OF THE PHARAOH'S DAUGHTER. SHE ADOPTS THE CHILD AND ARRANGES FOR HIS UPBRINGING.

fine baby" (2:2) literally means, "he was good"—a phrase that deliberately echoes God's life-affirming benediction over Creation. In the same way, the setting adrift of the child in a basket that had been waterproofed with bitumen and pitch evokes Noah's "ark"—the rare word used to describe the earlier structure is reemployed for Moses' makeshift vessel. God will protect the little craft and its precious contents from being swamped by a "flood" once more unleashed by the arrogance of Man bent on "knowing good and evil" (Genesis 3:5) on its own.

THE BABY IN THE BULRUSHES

Unable to hide her child any longer, Moses' mother seeks to evade the murderous edict issued by the new king. She bundles her infant into a waterproofed container, lodging it amid the reeds of the riverbank (Exodus 2:3). The immediate sequel demonstrates that the site is providentially chosen. It is where Pharaoh's daughter goes to bathe (2:5). The princess's entourage comes across the baby, and brings the child to their mistress. Although she ascertains that he is one of the objects of her father's proscription, she decides to raise him as her own. In effect, the king's daughter will house and support an "enemy of the state." This is nothing less than high treason! It is compounded by the boy's adoption into the royal household (2:10), formally signified by his Egyptian stepmother's naming him as "Moses." The custom of accepting children of foreigners into the palace is documented throughout the New Kingdom, and Moses would probably have been reared in an institution known as the "royal nursery." However, some scholars have noted that the saving of a foundling is attested elsewhere in ancient literature, and have argued that the description of Moses' birth is dependent upon these other accounts. But "exposure" was common in antiquity, and many children must have suffered this cruel fate. More importantly, Moses' career will be in sharp contrast to those of other "orphaned" heroes of lore. Rather than achieving fame as a mighty conqueror—the general thrust of the proposed parallels—he will grow up to be a leader of a very different type.

LEFT: THIS VICTORIAN ILLUSTRATION SHOWS MOSES CAST ADRIFT. TO SAVE HIM FROM PHARAOH'S CRUEL ORDER THAT DEMANDS THE DEATH OF ALL HEBREW BOYS, HIS MOTHER HIDES HIM IN RUSHES ON THE RIVERSIDE.

MOSES KILLS AN EGYPTIAN SLAVEMASTER

Ancient Egyptian society was predicated upon "justice," or what was called *Ma'at*. Its basic expression was the doing of charity—giving bread to the hungry, water to the thirsty, and clothing to the naked. The king was responsible for maintaining this ideal by appointing fair-minded officials to protect the weak from the strong. Ancient texts warn that a monarch's indifference to his duties could lead to national collapse, the telltale sign being civil strife. This social instability is precisely the context for

ABOVE: SISTINE CHAPEL FRESCO, *THE YOUTH OF MOSES* BY BOTTICELLI. UNDER THE PROTECTION OF PHARAOH'S DAUGHTER, MOSES' UPBRINGING WAS FAR MORE COMFORTABLE THAN THAT OF THE ISRAELITES IN EGYPT.

Moses' formative years, most of which seem to have been spent in seclusion from the outside world. Undoubtedly, his education in the palace would have consisted of reading texts on the very subject of *Ma'at*. But, walking one day among his hard-pressed kinsfolk, the blinders fall from Moses' eyes and the gap between ivory-tower abstraction and gritty reality is made clear. Egyptian officials assault Israelites, Hebrews fight Hebrews—the king's sanctioning of violence has unleashed chaos. Moses' reaction is to exact his own brand of justice—he kills an abusive Egyptian, concealing the body in the sand. Although some later traditions saw Moses' act of aggression as heroic, the scene is double-edged. In demonstrating his outrage in this personal manner, he takes on the attributes of the vengeful Lamech who murdered a man for merely "striking me" (Genesis 4:23). The sense of societal anarchy is further heightened when Hebrews coming to blows rebuke Moses for his interference in their squabble: "Who made you a ruler and judge over us? Do you mean to kill me as you killed the Egyptian?" (Exodus 2:14). Order and decency have been swept away—each man would be his own judge, jury, executioner, and, apparently, informer. The news of Moses' action makes its way to Pharaoh, and the once-privileged courtier finds himself driven eastward from what had been a kind of paradise—like Cain, with a bounty on his head.

MOSES IN MIDIAN

The route of Moses' flight is not divulged, other than the Bible's noting that he finally settles "in the land of Midian" (Exodus 2:15b). When considering that the Israelites/Hebrews were dwelling in Goshen (Genesis 45:10), Moses' point of departure likely was from the Wadi Tumilat, in the northeastern Delta. This region was the "gateway" of Egypt, and fortresses and inspection posts were established there to control groups entering and leaving the Nile Valley. The last leg of Moses' journey, Midian, has been located on the

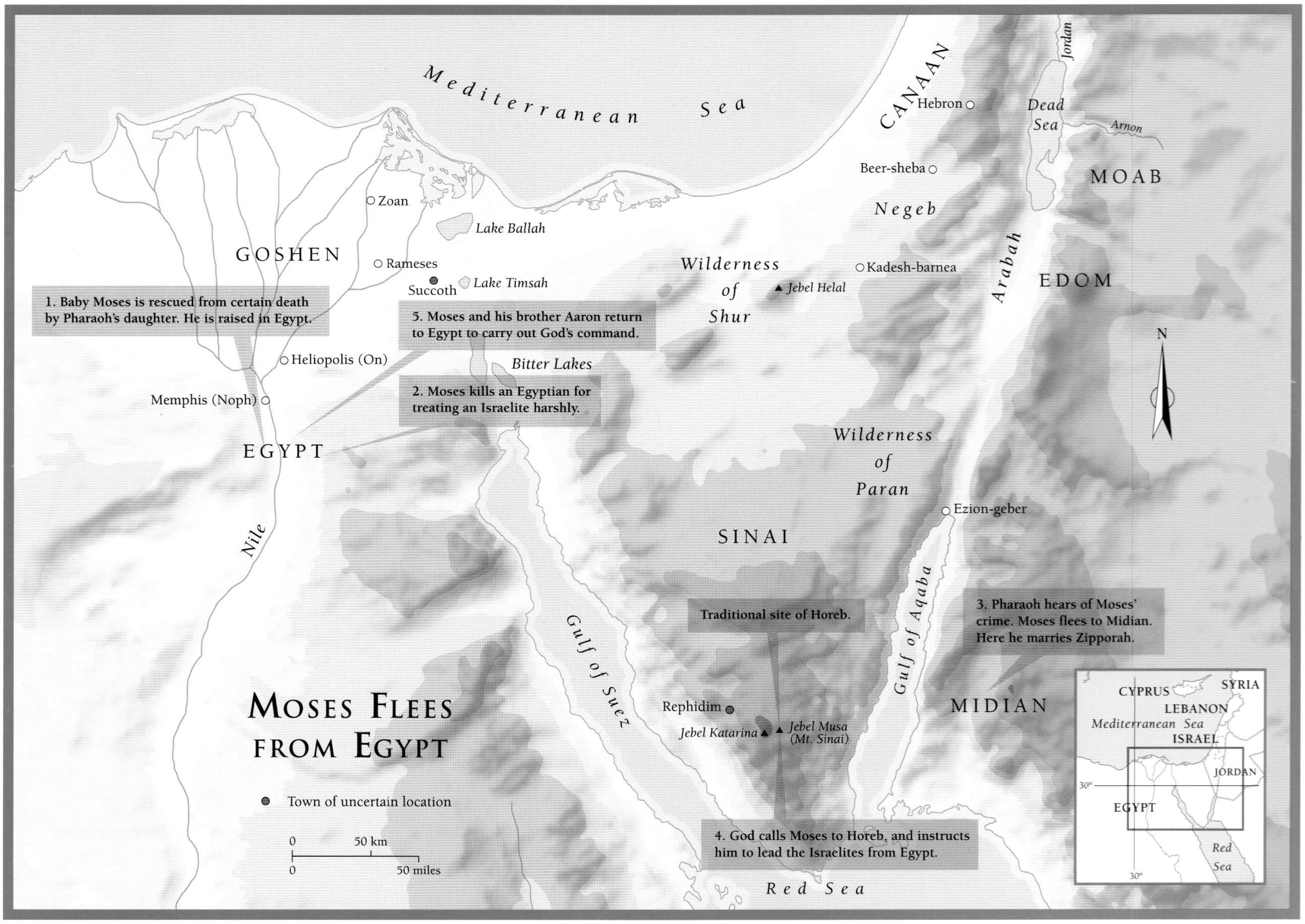

MOSES FLEES FROM EGYPT

1. Baby Moses is rescued from certain death by Pharaoh's daughter. He is raised in Egypt.

2. Moses kills an Egyptian for treating an Israelite harshly.

3. Pharaoh hears of Moses' crime. Moses flees to Midian. Here he marries Zipporah.

4. God calls Moses to Horeb, and instructs him to lead the Israelites from Egypt.

5. Moses and his brother Aaron return to Egypt to carry out God's command.

Traditional site of Horeb.

● Town of uncertain location

0 50 km
0 50 miles

Mediterranean Sea; CANAAN; Hebron; Dead Sea; Arnon; Jordan; Beer-sheba; MOAB; Negeb; Zoan; Lake Ballah; GOSHEN; Rameses; Succoth; Lake Timsah; Wilderness of Shur; Jebel Helal; Kadesh-barnea; Arabah; EDOM; Heliopolis (On); Bitter Lakes; Memphis (Noph); EGYPT; Wilderness of Paran; Ezion-geber; SINAI; Nile; Gulf of Suez; Gulf of Aqaba; Rephidim; Jebel Katarina; Jebel Musa (Mt. Sinai); MIDIAN; Red Sea; N

CYPRUS; SYRIA; LEBANON; Mediterranean Sea; ISRAEL; JORDAN; EGYPT; Red Sea; 30°

northwestern Arabian Peninsula, just east of the Gulf of Aqaba. Excavations in Midian show the emergence of towns in this area from the end of the Late Bronze Age (*c.* 1200 B.C.E.), with evidence of urban development and complex trade connections by the early Iron Age (*c.* 1000 B.C.E.). This period of sophistication, however, would appear to be in the future. Instead, the book of Exodus points to the land of Midian as being a shifting theater of operations for pastoral-nomadic groups, without clear-cut boundaries. In this regard, the Ancient Egyptians referred to land northeast of the Wadi Tumilat as *meten/metenu*. In its spelling, *meten* approximates Midian, and indicated the vast region where Bedouins wandered, encompassing the Sinai and beyond. Moreover, for the Egyptians, *meten* had political and social implications, and basically was a catch-all reference to barbarian territory. A one-time courtier finding himself exiled to such a venue would have regarded it as the equivalent of a death sentence. In a real way, Moses, the erstwhile Egyptian, will "die" in the land of Midian—only to be raised to new life.

ZIPPORAH

Moses makes a swashbuckling entrance among the Midianites, when he rescues daughters of a tribal chief from a group of unruly shepherds at a well. The visitor drives the interlopers off, allowing the daughters to return home earlier than usual. The extra time then is spent in their regaling their father with heroic tales of their savior—an Egyptian—whom they have unthinkingly left behind! Embarrassed, the Midianite patriarch orders the sisters to retrieve the traveler and invite him to a meal. The dinner leads to a permanent agreement, as Moses "contracts" to reside with the clan, and with the eldest of seven girls, Zipporah, meaning "little bird," being given to him in marriage. Despite its compactness, the episode is crammed with information, especially in the way it conveys Moses' changing character. Whereas outrage had led to killing in Egypt, Moses' reaction to injustice is still resolute, but now appropriately measured. Likewise, Moses' drawing water at the well on behalf of the siblings—ostensibly, a "woman's" task—demonstrates that he has acquired

ABOVE: *MOSES AND THE DAUGHTERS OF JETHRO* BY NICOLAS BERTIN. WHEN JETHRO'S DAUGHTERS ARE DRIVEN AWAY FROM A WELL BY A GROUP OF SHEPHERDS, MOSES NOBLY COMES TO THEIR RESCUE.

LEFT: THIS BEAUTIFULLY DETAILED FLEMISH TAPESTRY SHOWS JETHRO'S DAUGHTERS TELLING HIM OF THEIR ORDEAL AT THE WELL AND OF THE STRANGER WHO CAME TO THEIR RESCUE.

humility and charity. In many ways, Moses has come to resemble Joseph—he possesses a basic humanity, which is recognizable anywhere. The ceremonial acts of the "breaking of bread" (Exodus 2:20) and "marriage-pact," which seal the relationship between Moses and the Midianite leader, resemble covenantal practices of the earlier patriarchs. This is hardly surprising, since the Midianites, too, were descendants of Abraham. Moreover, like his ancestor, Moses' father-in-law (called Reuel [2:18] and Jethro [3:1]) serves as a priest of his tribal cult, with the rest of the family assuming religious functions. This will be demonstrated later, when Zipporah herself undertakes the circumcision of her son—a role usually reserved for males (4:24).

RIGHT: SIXTH-CENTURY C.E. ITALIAN MOSAIC SHOWING MOSES SETTLED INTO HIS NEW LIFE IN MIDIAN. HE TAKES JETHRO'S DAUGHTER ZIPPORAH AS HIS WIFE, AND WORKS FOR HIS FATHER-IN-LAW TENDING SHEEP.

BELOW: *MOSES AND THE BURNING BUSH* BY WILLIAM BLAKE. MOSES IS INTRIGUED BY THE BURNING BUSH THAT REMAINS UNSCATHED; GOD APPEARS IN THE FLAMES, TELLING MOSES OF HIS TASK.

THE BURNING BUSH

God's "call" of Moses to be his prophet is a climactic scene in the Bible. After this, nothing is ever the same. Surprisingly, "eternity" breaks through in the middle of daily routine, transforming the mundane into "holy space." Before that jarring moment, however, Moses has long been secure, engaging in husbandry on behalf of his father-in-law (Exodus 3:1). Still, Moses' care of these animals "beyond the wilderness" is laden with deeper significance—it anticipates his summons to herd multitudes across this same formidable terrain as "shepherd of Israel." The site chosen for this commissioning is "Horeb, the mountain of God" (3:1). The locale is not known, and the Bible, tradition, and scholarship are not clear as to whether Horeb and Mt. Sinai were one and the same. Yet, by the fourth century C.E., pilgrims venerated the so-called Jebel Musa, near the southern tip of the Sinai Peninsula, as the spot for the divine revelation.

The precise manner of God's appearance to Moses at Horeb is striking on two counts. Firstly, while fire is often a vehicle for theophany—or "divine appearance"—there is likely an allusion to the fixing of Eden's boundaries by means of a "sword flaming ... to guard the way to the tree of life" (Genesis 3:24). What the event at Horeb and the ensuing exodus will represent is a gateway back to God's original intention for Creation. Secondly, and critically, the manifestation of God, "in a flame of fire out of a bush ... and the bush was blazing, yet it was not consumed" (Exodus 3:2), testifies that God reveals himself by means of paradox—something contrary to human perception, capabilities, and expectations. However, this is only the beginning—God will heap one surprise upon another, including the greatest paradox of all—enslaved Israel is going to be free.

GOD APPEARS TO MOSES

The revelation at Mt. Horeb points to God's advocacy in fulfillment of his promise to Abraham. The divine litany—"I have observed the misery of my people ... I have heard their cry ... I know their sufferings ... I have come down to deliver them" (Exodus 3:7–8)—conveys the idea of a legal investigation. God is going to prosecute Egypt for its "breach of contract." But the outcome of this

God Equips Moses for his Task

Moses' "call" is a model of how a human being becomes a prophet for God. One of the striking features of this process is that the individual tries to get out of his responsibility. Often, resistance arises out of a deep sense of sin and personal inadequacy for the assigned task (Exodus 3:6, 4:10). But Moses is different in his persistent opposition to the divine will. The primary cause of his uneasiness is that his audience might not believe him (4:1)—he questions what authority he has. In response, God enables Moses to perform "signs" and "wonders"—visible indicators of the power behind his claims. One of the signs is in the form of a prophecy fulfilled—when Israel is freed, the people will acknowledge that the God of the patriarchs has been supporting Moses all along (3:12).

However, more immediate proof is to be supplied by three manifestations of God's support. First, his staff will change into a serpent (shown below in this lithograph), then back again (4:2–4). Next, upon placing his hand in his cloak, it will be covered with lesions and then restored to health (4:6–7). Finally, Moses will turn water from the Nile into blood (4:9). Each of these strange actions points to an aspect of the divine power that will be unleashed ahead.

As we shall see, Moses' staff is meant to challenge pharaonic symbols of office—exposing them and the royal post as having no legitimacy whatsoever. The cloaking with leprosy and its reversal is an ancient image of cursing and blessing, pointing to God's covenantal authority to punish and reward. The defilement of the water has a similar function, although it further stresses God's sovereignty over all Creation. Moses' deity is not just limited to a single tribe, but is Lord of the whole earth—Egypt, too, is under his sway.

"lawsuit" will not be a reversion to the *status quo ante*—Pharaoh is to emancipate the Israelites. Moreover, Moses is told that God has chosen him to "sell" this vision on his behalf, to which Moses raises the objection: "If they ask me, 'What is his name?' What should I say to them?" (3:13). In antiquity, a divinity's name conveyed its nature; for example, gods and goddesses were called "Power," "Prosperity," "Fertility," and so on. In essence, Moses says, "What kind of god are you?" The reply sweeps all other concepts away: "I am who I am," (3:14) … "Thus you shall say … 'The Lord … has sent me to you'" (3:15). The defender of Israel cannot be conceived by the human mind. He is the God who defines himself by his own grace and mercy—by his covenantal fidelity.

MOSES RETURNS TO EGYPT

Despite his equipping with signs, Moses continues to hold out, "O my Lord, please send someone else" (Exodus 4:13). This stubbornness provokes God's anger, and the Lord somewhat wearily agrees to dispatch Moses' older brother to do the public speaking! (4:16). The soon-to-appear Aaron will play a vital, and largely cooperative, role in forthcoming events—a vast improvement considering the sibling relationships in Genesis! Chastened, Moses returns to his clan, his staff of office in his possession. With deference, he seeks Jethro's leave to return to the Nile Delta with his own family. The amiable parting observes strict tribal etiquette, preparing us for the "law" as a cornerstone for a blessed society.

Yet assuredly, upon setting out, the Lord warns that trying times lie ahead—Pharaoh will be difficult to persuade. The verse: "but I will harden his heart, so that he will not let the people go" (4:21) has engaged countless theologians over the centuries, including the apostle Paul (Romans 9:17–18). To "harden the heart" can mean to encourage, but also to dull a person's emotions. A parallel expression occurs in Ancient Egyptian, and means "to bolster with bravery" or "make stubborn with pride."

The biblical idiom might well be "playing off" this Egyptian imagery, which was common in royal battle inscriptions. Rulers would boast of "being brave-hearted"—almost to the point of stupidity. So, God declares that he is going to allow "pharaoh to be pharaoh," and in the process expose him for the fool that he is. The ruler's rash policy—and his stubborn refusal to agree to God's request issued via his representatives, Moses and Aaron—will ultimately lead to the loss of what is most precious—his firstborn son (Exodus 4:23).

The family's route back to Egypt and into the arena of royal politics is not described. However, with the death of Moses' persecutor, it is likely that they took the official road along the Sinai coast to Sile—near modern-day Suez—and from there, to Goshen.

BELOW: MOZARABS WERE SPANISH CHRISTIANS LIVING UNDER MUSLIM RULE. THIS TENTH-CENTURY C.E. MOZARABIC BIBLE SHOWS NEGOTIATIONS BETWEEN MOSES AND PHARAOH.

The Plagues of Egypt

NOW YOU SHALL SEE WHAT I WILL DO TO PHARAOH EXODUS 6:1

RIGHT: *MOSES AND AARON*, SCULPTURE BY GIOVANNI BATTISTA TIEPOLO. THE TWO BROTHERS FORM A PARTNERSHIP TO CONVEY GOD'S WORD TO THE ISRAELITES IN EGYPT, AND TO PHARAOH.

Upon their return to Egypt, Moses and Aaron gather together the elders of Israel, who accept their leadership without objection (Exodus 4:29–31). Surely, the next stage of their mission will be just as successful! Unfortunately, Pharaoh is not so easily convinced, and he refuses to acknowledge the existence of Moses' deity. Moreover, while exemption for cultic obligations was normal in Egypt, the king completely disavows the petition of the Israelites to go and offer sacrifice (5:2–3).

PHARAOH'S RESPONSE TO THE APPEAL OF THE ISRAELITES

In reply to the petition of the Israelites, the disdainful monarch issues an onerous decree. Israel is to be penalized merely for its request, and the people must now collect the straw needed for its brick-making, effectively doubling its labor (Exodus 5:4–19). The confrontation ends with the Israelite workforce denouncing Moses and Aaron for bringing it under suspicion of treason (5:21). Moses, rejected, marshals a bitter complaint against God—this is not how things were to turn out! However, the new pharaoh's rejection of Israel's basic right to worship serves an important purpose, in that it publicly exposes the tyrannical nature of his new rule.

GOD SPEAKS TO MOSES

In 1 Kings 19, Elijah seeks an end to his commission as prophet, resulting in his replacement by Elisha (1 Kings 19:16). Moses' cry has a similar intent, but his plea is rejected out of hand. Instead, he is bolstered by the divine assurance that Pharaoh is going to give up all prior claims upon Israel, technically expelling it from his territory (Exodus 6:1). Following this literal "divorce," the Lord promises that he "will take you as my people, and I will be your God" (6:7). The coming release is not just a liberation from tyranny, but a release for a purpose. Israel's full allegiance will be directed to the God "who has freed you from the burdens of the Egyptians" (6:7)—the same deity who had watched over this people from its nomadic days past (6:2–3). There is a meaning and purpose to this group's whole existence. The Lord of all history has vouchsafed its destiny—a future that cannot be prevented by Pharaoh's arrogance, or by Israel's despair (6:9), or even by the tearful excuses of God's spokesman (6:12).

THE TEN PLAGUES AFFLICT EGYPT

Moses' protests (Exodus 6:12, 30) result in an extraordinary declaration: he will be "like God to Pharaoh, and your brother Aaron shall be your prophet" (7:1). Moses will be the visible representative of the divine patron of Israel to an arrogant skeptic. The promotion of Moses contains definite implications of political status. Court protocol required subjects to "kiss the dust at the feet" of the king. This is not the case here, as Moses addresses the monarch as an equal—if not more. Indeed, Aaron's performing of signs at Moses' command further reflects who is really in charge. This is immediately shown by the first wonder at court. Aaron's staff turns into some reptilian form, which destroys the instruments of royal personnel who have sought to replicate the feat (7:10–12). It is likely that the Israelite's implement was originally a shepherd's crook—the same shape as Pharaoh's scepter. When Aaron's "serpent" swallows up the counterfeit objects, it amounts to the annulment of royal authority, pointing to things to come. Nevertheless, despite the graphic warning, Pharaoh "would not listen to them, as the Lord had said" (7:13). Ten more frightening lessons will be necessary.

BELOW: AS SEEN IN THIS HEBREW MANUSCRIPT, MOSES' REQUEST ON BEHALF OF THE ISRAELITES TO WORSHIP THEIR GOD IS DENIED BY PHARAOH, WHO ADDS TO THEIR TROUBLES BY INCREASING THEIR WORKLOAD.

A RIVER OF BLOOD

Ancient texts and the natural world have been seen as providing parallels for the disasters visited upon Egypt. The first of these—water turning to blood—has sometimes been regarded as a metaphor for disaster, as attested in Ancient Egyptian literature. Many scholars, however, have linked it to the problem of a "high Nile." Triggered by excessive rainfall, river water swollen with mud could acquire a blood-red color, accompanied by an explosion of bacteria, triggering disease. Still, the misfortunes striking Egypt and their function need to be considered against the backdrop of Israel's relationship with Pharaoh.

The divine prosecution of the king is the result of his violation of a solemn agreement. The ensuing plagues represent the actualization of the punitive clauses often contained in documents of this type. One contract, in fact, contains the specific injunction that its transgressors are to suffer the loss of offerings to the Nile on their behalf.

LEFT: THIS FOURTEENTH-CENTURY C.E. HEBREW MANUSCRIPT SHOWS THE FIRST DISASTER TO BEFALL THE EGYPTIANS AS A RESULT OF PHARAOH'S OBSTINANCE—THE NILE RIVER IS TURNED TO BLOOD.

Indeed, the king is halted right in the middle of this very sort of ritual. This disruption, signaling divine rejection, would have been regarded as catastrophic. As God now calls upon the king to carry out his legal obligations, Pharaoh's intransigence threatens the entire nation with not just ecological and economic hardships, but utter annihilation.

BELOW: *MOSES AND THE BRAZEN SERPENT* BY NICOLAS POUSSIN. AARON'S STAFF TURNS INTO A SNAKE, WHICH THEN CONSUMES THE SERPENTS PRODUCED IN REPLY BY PHARAOH'S MAGICIANS.

RIGHT: *THE PLAGUE OF FROGS*, EIGHTEENTH-CENTURY C.E. ENGRAVING. IN RESPONSE TO PHARAOH'S PLEA, EGYPT'S PLAGUE OF FROGS IS RESOLVED WHEN MOSES PRAYS FOR THEIR DEPARTURE.

PLAGUE OF FROGS

Some scholars have argued that the natural rubefaction of the Nile nicely accounts for the next trouble to batter the Egyptians—the swarm of frogs. The profusion of microorganisms would affect these amphibians, driving them to abandon their habitat and invade the surrounding terrain. While plausible, especially as frogs are indicators of environmental health, these creatures further serve to remind the king of his disregard of justice. As noted, ancient contracts often ended with threats of punishment. But they also contained "witness-lists" to verify the terms of an agreement. In the Near East, these rosters could include the natural world and its inhabitants—sun, moon, rivers, seas, fields, and mountains. The infestation of the Nile Valley thus represents "accusers" from nature denouncing Pharaoh's infidelity. Their complaint cannot be avoided, as they pervade every aspect of Egypt's private and public life (Exodus 8:3). Curiously, the Egyptian term for frog was the word for "hundreds of thousands." This nuance most likely, and nicely, underlies the Scriptural episode—a myriad of Creation's denizens speaks out on behalf of oppressed Israel.

DUST TURNED TO LICE

In many ways, Moses serves as a lawyer, delivering his divine plaintiff's case against Pharaoh. Importantly, this job as attorney is not intended to be punitive, but instead is to persuade his opponent to repent. When this occurs, another aspect of the prophetic role comes to the fore—that of the intercessor. This is attested by Moses' "crying out" to the Lord regarding the frogs (Exodus 8:12). The same verb expressing Israel's plea for mercy is used for Moses' prayers on Egypt's behalf. Correspondingly, Pharaoh's responsibilities are sharply drawn in these litigious encounters, too. Above all else, the king was to be a possessor of

BELOW: PEN AND INK WORK BY JOSEPH MALLORD WILLIAM TURNER. IN THE FIFTH PLAGUE TO STRIKE EGYPT, LIVESTOCK IS STRUCK DOWN BY PESTILENCE.

wisdom, so as to act as a fair and just arbiter. This was indicated by Pharaoh's willingness to listen to proper counsel. Overrun by frogs, Pharaoh does prudently change policy (8:8). But as soon as the danger passes, his bravado returns, necessitating further indictment from Creation. The "dust of the earth" unleashes gnats (8:16–17), as the very land itself assumes its place on the "witness stand." So overwhelming is the onslaught, that Pharaoh's magicians, who serve as his advisers, recognize the divine charge against them: "This is the finger of God!" (8:19). Stubbornly, Pharaoh declares himself to be his own counselor, demonstrating that he has a fool for a client.

PLAGUE OF FLIES

The rivers and streams, the earth and its creatures protest Pharaoh's criminality. Amazingly, Pharaoh goes about his business, as if nothing had ever happened (Exodus 8:20). Predictably, his headstrong behavior unleashes further pandemonium. Swarms of flies now join their brethren in a chorus of outrage, their witness buzzing in the ears and blanketing the eyes of the king and court (8:21–24). Vermin and noxious insects were common features of life in Egypt, and texts contained prescriptions and incantations to ward off their bites and stings. Undoubtedly, such relief would have been offered to Pharaoh and his administration, but to no avail. Human knowledge and its devices are useless in healing moral infirmities.

THE KILLING OF LIVESTOCK

Pharaoh finds that he is losing complete control over events. Once again, the ruler is reduced to a helpless suppliant, having to beg Moses to intercede. And obligingly, at the prophet's command, the scourge of flies disappears. Almost comically, Pharaoh demonstrates his uncanny ability to misread the signs, as he mistakes divine forbearance for weakness. But the next affliction let loose by royal miscalculation cannot be so easily overlooked as the preceding annoyances. "The hand of the Lord" will weigh heavy on Pharaoh and his land, smiting livestock and beasts of burden with pestilence (Exodus 9:2–4). Cattle were one of the mainstays of the Egyptian economy, and, more importantly, supplied the animals crucial for sacrifice. The country and its cults will grind to a halt.

BOILS

With the debilitation of Egypt's cattle, the contest between Moses and Pharaoh enters into a more frightening stage. While historians have diagnosed the illness as anthrax, pestilence from the hand of a deity indicated that all-out war had been declared from heaven. Typically, such conflict was seen as a legal ordeal, with the contestants being backed by their divine advocates. It is beginning to dawn upon Pharaoh that the Israelites' exemption points to the successful sponsorship of their God. Despite the growing evidence, the king irrationally decides to soldier on. The ruler's misplaced bravery results in the Lord commanding Moses to toss soot into the air. As the dust is dispersed, boils break out over the denizens of the Nile Valley (Exodus 9:8–11). The prophetic action represents the dramatization of a curse, with skin disorders being frequent in maledictions of the Bible and Near East. Importantly, the resulting lesions render those infected as ritually impure. The whole religious machinery of the state is being methodically—and visibly—shut down. Pharaoh has been cut off from his divine patrons, and, more and more, he stands alone.

LEFT: FIFTEENTH-CENTURY C.E. COLOR LITHOGRAPH. THE FOURTH PLAGUE, SWARMS OF FLIES, COVERS THE LAND IN THE WINGED INSECTS—YET PHARAOH REMAINS UNMOVED BY THE ISRAELITE PLEAS.

HAIL AND FIRE

The Ancient Egyptians lived with an eye toward history, and kings would proclaim that what they had done "had never taken place since the founding of the land." This benchmark phrase is used in Exodus 9:18 when Moses relays God's words to Pharaoh. However, this benighted sovereign's tenure is not to be a source of enduring national pride, but shame. The ruler has grown so reckless that the preceding calamities have failed to elicit his remorse, provoking further divine wrath. Hail—the next instrument of divine persuasion—is rare, if nonexistent in the lower Nile Valley, and the accompanying thunder and fire (Exodus 9:23) indicate that this is

BELOW: *THE SEVENTH PLAGUE*, MEZZOTINT BY JOHN MARTIN. HAIL AND THUNDER—THE SEVENTH PLAGUE—OCCUR IN A DOWNPOUR MORE VIOLENT THAN EGYPT HAD EVER EXPERIENCED BEFORE.

ABOVE: *SWARM OF MIGRATORY LOCUSTS* FROM *BREHMS TIERLEBEN: ALLGEMEINE KUNDE DES TIERREICHS.* VORACIOUS LOCUSTS DEVOUR ALL THAT REMAINS FOLLOWING THE SEVEN PREVIOUS PLAGUES TO BEFALL EGYPT.

more than just a storm. The pummeling of Egypt has implications of a literal scourging of the land. Recalcitrant Pharaoh and his minions are being whipped and branded like criminals, which does rouse a belated confession from Pharaoh: "This time I have sinned; the Lord is in the right, and I and my people are in the wrong" (9:27). Pharaoh, at last, acknowledges his guilt in exactly the same language used in an Egyptian court! But upon being "pardoned" through Moses' intervention (9:33–34), the king reverts right back to type—he is beyond rehabilitation.

PLAGUE OF LOCUSTS

Locusts, with their hardened bodies, were often compared in ancient texts to "armed troops." Their immense numbers and their ability to ravage vegetation made them as devastating as any human conqueror. Moses' announcement that Egypt will be invaded by these insect hordes (Exodus 10:3–6) sows panic among Pharaoh's officials.

The continual hammering from heaven, the onslaught of disease, and the accompanying specter of starvation eerily evokes the circumstances of a siege. One of the goals of this type of warfare was to break the opponent's will. With this new threat, the king finds his beleaguered administration calling for unconditional surrender (10:7). This uprising of the courtiers persuades the king to summon Moses and Aaron to parley (10:8). Yes, Pharaoh is willing to accede to some of Moses' requests, agreeing that the men may go to worship, but the women and children are to remain behind as hostages—a common feature of royal policy from the mid-fifteenth century B.C.E. onward. But the intransigence of the monarch to release all the people, as Moses now demands, brings with it a resumption of terrible hostilities. Egypt, often termed "the land of light," becomes "blackened" with the forces of occupation and destruction (10:15). The king refuses to back down, and the siege goes on.

PASSOVER

Some scholars have theorized that the Passover observance—or Feast of Unleavened Bread (shown below in a scene from the fourteenth-century C.E. *Golden Haggadah*)—may have had pre-Exodus roots. That may well be, but its rites are now employed to commemorate the story of Israel's rescue by God. Ultimately joyous, it should not be overlooked that each element in the observance is a sobering reminder that this people's freedom was costly.

Daubing of their houses with blood, a practice that ordinarily would have designated the residents as being liable for condemnation, was carried out by the Hebrews as a sign of occupancy during the latest onslaught. The household will then be spared, while their oppressors will find their injustice has come back upon their own heads, even while ensconced behind palace walls. The actual nature of the divine disaster, which brings Egypt to its knees, is not clear. However, it is worth noting that a medical text of the early to mid-Eighteenth Dynasty does employ the intriguing phrase the "sickness which passes over" in relation to feverish symptoms. Likewise, another document from roughly the same period specifically refers to an outbreak of "the disease of the Semites," which causes the body "to be darkened with lesions." Both conform to ancient epithets and descriptions of plague, with the cause of the outbreak in the second text being attributed to the god of these foreign peoples.

THREE DAYS OF DARKNESS

We know from an Egyptian inscription from the reign of king Merneptah, that Israel was in Canaan by the end of the thirteenth century B.C.E. But is there any written evidence for the events surrounding the Exodus itself? It has been offered that two texts do seem to allude to the Scripture's "dense darkness in all the land" (Exodus 10:22). One document is linked to the departure of the Hyksos from Egypt. The Hyksos were Semitic peoples, who had gained control of Egypt until leaders from Thebes drove them out in the latter part of the sixteenth century B.C.E. In an army diary from that time, a scribe recorded troop movements in pursuit of the Hyksos. He noted that near Suez, the god of these foreigners "gave forth his voice," in other words, thundered. The following day, hail or rain fell. The account abruptly breaks off at this point. Later, an Egyptian king issued a decree concerning a storm, in which there was darkness, tremendous noise, and something falling from the heavens, affecting every household. This, too, is blamed on divine wrath. Both the diary and the official proclamation most likely refer to the same event. Although it has been posited that the phenomenon was a *khamsin*—a sandstorm—a few scholars connect the information to a massive volcanic explosion on the Aegean island of Thira (Santorini). In fact, ash from that locale has been found in the Nile Valley. One thing is for sure—some catastrophe scarred the physical and psychological landscape of the Egyptians at the beginning of the New Kingdom, and was directly linked by them to difficulties with Semitic peoples and their deity.

THE DEATH OF THE FIRSTBORN

Pharaoh is afraid of the dark! And the three-day long nightmare compels him to concede to most, but not all, of Moses' terms. The Israelites' flocks are to remain in Egypt (Exodus 10:24). The tactic is quite shrewd. Without livestock, the Israelites are deprived of the material needed for their rituals, as well as their future security. It will be no time at all before they will turn back to the custody of Pharaoh. Without economic and religious choice there is no real freedom, and Moses' objections on this sticking point (10:25–26), provoke the king to bully his nemesis with petty threats (10:28).

But now, Pharaoh's obstinacy will unleash the thing most feared by an Ancient Egyptian—the death of the firstborn (11:4). It was the firstborn who was responsible for carrying out the rites needed to ensure the deceased's status in the afterlife—the ultimate hope of Ancient Egyptian society. The loss of the eldest child was the most powerful curse in their arsenal of maledictions. This king, suicidal in his obsession with his present prestige, dooms his people and himself to the loss of the future.

LEFT: TWELFTH-CENTURY C.E. BRONZE PORTAL FROM SAN ZENO MAGGIORE, VERONA, ITALY. PHARAOH CAPITULATES AFTER THE FINAL DEVASTATING BLOW TO EGYPT—THE DEATH OF THE FIRSTBORN.

PHARAOH ALLOWS THE ISRAELITES TO LEAVE

Notwithstanding its undoubted extraordinary aspects, Israel's departure from Egypt is also couched as a once-and-for-all release of people from an irrevocably broken—and hence, illegal—contract. This formal juridical aspect would have been of paramount importance in the ancient world. The angry declaration of Pharaoh that Moses and the Israelites are to "rise up, go away ... Take your flocks and herds ... and be gone" (Exodus 12:31–32), is a technical expression for emancipation, verifying that these groups are not fugitive slaves, but had been wrongly enslaved and are now rightfully freed. They are not thieves, but depart with what had been theirs all along. Furthermore, when the Israelites plunder the riches of the indigenous population (12:35–36), this amounts to Egyptian reparations for the suffering of the Hebrews at their hands, and is a public admission of guilt.

The upshot of these details is that Israel has a right to become a nation—a claim supported by human law and divine justification. Incredibly, the body politic that will emerge from pharaonic bondage will be like no other, and its very lifeblood will be the law—not the law of man, but the law of God. Still, before that historical and theological profundity occurs, lawless Pharaoh will attempt one last desperate gambit to hold on to what is no longer—and never was—his.

BELOW: *THE ISRAELITES LEAVING EGYPT* BY JOHANN HEISS. AS THE RULER OF A LAND AND PEOPLE TORN ASUNDER BY THE TEN PLAGUES, PHARAOH ORDERS THE ISRAELITES TO LEAVE EGYPT.

THE FLIGHT OUT OF EGYPT

IN YOUR STEADFAST LOVE YOU LED THE PEOPLE WHOM YOU REDEEMED EXODUS 15:13

RIGHT: THIS SIXTEENTH-CENTURY C.E. STAINED GLASS WINDOW FROM PROVINS, FRANCE, SHOWS THE CELEBRATION OF THE PASSOVER—A FESTIVAL THAT COMMEMORATES THE RELEASE OF THE ISRAELITES FROM EGYPT.

Pharaoh's stubbornness is costing his land and his people dearly. Before his next move is revealed, the focus shifts to the special observances of Passover and the Feast of Unleavened Bread, interrupting the flow of the narrative between the ninth and tenth plagues. The story about the flight from Egypt (Exodus 13:17–14:29) is enclosed by worship rituals (13:1–16 and 15:1–18). Even today a young person will ask the question during the Passover celebration—"Why is this night different from all other nights?"

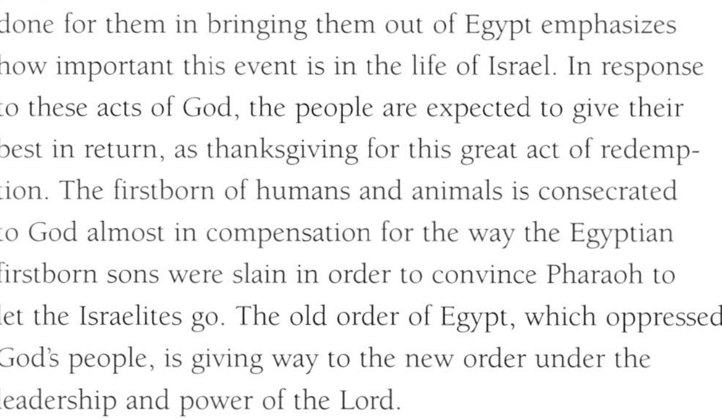

The repetition of the need for the people to remember what God has done for them in bringing them out of Egypt emphasizes how important this event is in the life of Israel. In response to these acts of God, the people are expected to give their best in return, as thanksgiving for this great act of redemption. The firstborn of humans and animals is consecrated to God almost in compensation for the way the Egyptian firstborn sons were slain in order to convince Pharaoh to let the Israelites go. The old order of Egypt, which oppressed God's people, is giving way to the new order under the leadership and power of the Lord.

PROMISE OF LAND ONE STEP CLOSER

Abram (Abraham) was promised that one day his descendants would be in their own land (Genesis 12:1–3), and this long journey is getting closer. God is about to bring the Israelites out of Egypt—a fact that is mentioned six times in just a few verses. Repetition is meant to focus attention on what is important, and these 16 verses certainly do that (Exodus 13:1–16). At the same time there is still the focus on the future and how the Israelites are expected to behave when they enter the Promised Land.

FINALLY THEY BEGIN THE JOURNEY

Earlier in the narrative conversation between Moses and Pharaoh, there was no intention on behalf of Pharaoh to let the Israelites go. Suddenly, without further explanation, there is the simple statement: "When Pharaoh let the people go" (Exodus 13:17). At last they are on their way. However, it seems they are not allowed to go the simple route that leads along the Mediterranean coast and through the Land of the Philistines, but they have to double back into the desert. The coastal route was one of two routes used by traders from the north and Mesopotamia to trade with Egypt. The other route, The King's Highway, came down through Syria, along the east side of the Sea of Galilee, through Moab and Edom to the port at the head of the Gulf of Aqaba. The Egyptians heavily defended the coastal route, because many enemies in previous times had used this route to try to invade Egypt. Therefore, it was not sensible to attempt the obvious route along the coast.

BELOW: *ISRAELITES PASSING THROUGH THE WILDERNESS* BY WILLIAM WEST. GOD USED THE ELEMENTS OF CLOUD AND FIRE TO GUIDE THE ISRAELITES—LED BY MOSES—ON THEIR JOURNEY.

THE WAY IS MARKED

The emphasis on God as leader is stated in four verses enclosing a small section (Exodus 3:17–22). Verses 17–18 state that God will lead them round by the way of the wilderness with no explanation of how this will happen. However, verses 21–22 give us the symbols by which God's presence will lead these people on their perilous journey through the wilderness. During the day, they are guided by a pillar of cloud and at night by a pillar of fire. It is portrayed as part of God's overall purpose that this rather motley crowd will spend a long time in the wilderness—it seems to be a vital part of their training on the way to becoming a nation.

THE WAY OUT

Over the years scholars have debated the exact route by which the Israelites left and arrived in the desert. There are two unrelated pieces of data that strongly suggest Israel moved along an established roadway, rather than setting out on a course of their own or somehow attempting to outmaneuver the pursuing pharaoh and his forces. The Israelites were prevented from taking one particular route, the Way to Land of the Philistines, and were instead led by God by an alternative roundabout route through the wilderness (Exodus 13:17). A second reference, a thirteenth-century B.C.E. Egyptian text, *Papyrus Anastasi V*, tells the tale of runaway slaves who follow a similar route to that recorded in the Bible.

The first stage of the Israelites' journey is from Rameses to Succoth (Exodus 12:37). Rameses is located at modern-day Tell ed-Dab'a; Succoth must be located in the Wadi Tumilat, most plausibly at the site of Tell el-Maskhuta. We are told that the Israelites move from Succoth to "Etham, on the edge of the wilderness" (Exodus 13:20). Etham cannot be located, except broadly—it must be somewhere east, south, or southeast of Succoth (that is, in the direction of the desert). In Exodus 14:2, Israel moves from Etham toward Migdol and "the sea," making camp at Pi-hahiroth.

WHY HAVE YOU BROUGHT US HERE?

The place name Pi-hahiroth, where the Israelites camped, is mentioned twice with two other reference points. Migdol is a name that is used for an Egyptian fortified town, and several towns of this name are attested to in Egyptian sources. The location of Baal-zephon in unknown.

Pharaoh's whole army overtakes them as they are camped at Pi-hahiroth. The sight of this large army with its horses and chariots must have been a terrifying sight to the Israelites. Did they think they had finally got away? Instead they

BELOW: RED SEA, EGYPT. THE PARTING OF THE RED SEA IS ONE OF THE BEST-KNOWN STORIES FROM THE BIBLE, AND SCHOLARS HAVE LONG DEBATED THE POSSIBLE LOCATIONS FOR THE EVENT.

ABOVE: THIS ILLUSTRATION FROM A TENTH-CENTURY C.E. MOZARABIC BIBLE SHOWS MOSES CLOSING THE PASSAGE THROUGH THE RED SEA, THUS DROWNING THE PURSUING EGYPTIAN FORCES.

are facing death in this wilderness—and hold God and Moses responsible. However, Moses calms their fears and is commanded by God to lead the people forward. The sea parts and the Israelites walk across to the other side. One of the best translations of the Hebrew for Red Sea is "sea of the end." It is probable that it was one of the small bodies of water in the Delta region, which needed to be crossed at some point.

Although 600,000 men, together with women and children, are sometimes thought to have fled Egypt, the word here translated "thousand" is elswhere rendered "oxen" (as in Psalms 8:7), "cattle" (as in Deuteronomy 7:13), "leader" (as in Exodus 15:19), or even "clan" (as in Judges 6:15), which makes it just as likely that the figure here refers to 600 clans or families. This group of people, made up of young and old, would take considerable time to cross the path that had opened up. The suspense must have very high as they were hastened on by the leaders, with the might of Pharaoh's army right on their heels. Just as sea mist comes down at night so there appeared a cloud, which prevented the Egyptians following closely.

THE WATERS ROLL BACK

Many people will have a mental image of Moses as he stands there with rod upraised and the waters rolling back into walls on either side. It makes perfect sense that when the Egyptians try to drive their chariots and horses across the same path, not only has it been churned up by many pairs of feet, it is naturally soggy from seepage. They become bogged down, and after the Israelites are safe on the other side, the water returns to normal and the army drowns. We presume that Pharaoh was not one of those who crossed.

ABOVE: CLAY CHARIOT AND HORSES, FOURTH DYNASTY, EGYPT. CHARIOTS—USUALLY MANNED BY A DRIVER AND AN ARCHER—WERE A FAVORED AND EFFECTIVE MILITARY VEHICLE OF THE ANCIENT EGYPTIANS.

This experience was understood by the Israelites to be deliberately manifested by God, as the creator of the world and in control of all nature. Even the Egyptians are recorded as giving credit and power to God for their loss. Oral traditions are valid ways of remembering the past and recognizing its influence on the present. For the Israelites, this extraordinary escape is part of their very psyche. In this narrative, God and Moses are the major actors—God speaks to Moses, who is obedient, and God comes between the Israelites and the pursuing Egyptians. The Israelites trusted God and Moses enough, even after their complaints, to walk through what must have been an awesome and frightening pathway.

EVENTS CAN BE VIEWED THROUGH HUMAN OR DIVINE EYES

Some people prefer to speak of this event—the parting of the sea—as the consequence of perfectly natural causes. The particular tides and wind movements in the Nile Delta region caused the sea to part at exactly the right moment. Others have no difficulty accepting that events occur that they believe are God given.

EGYPTIAN RESPONSE

There is no apparent record of this event—the parting of the sea—in Egyptian annals, but perhaps that is not surprising, since it was such a loss of face to lose a major part of one's slave labor. The debate has centered on the thirteenth century B.C.E. as the probable period, between 1280 B.C.E. and 1230 B.C.E. While this event cannot be proven in the

Western sense of classical theory, it would seem highly likely that some event occurred that gave rise to the memory.

HEBREW RESPONSE: SONG OF PRAISE QUICKLY TURNS TO COMPLAINT

The Israelites were jubilant after they finished their trek through the waters, and they affirmed their faith in God through a song that is attributed to Moses.

There is an important fragment of a song attributed to Miriam, which is said to be one of the earliest recorded (Exodus 15:21). It is quite extraordinary that a tradition that is attributed to a woman is preserved and kept in a written record. Indeed, the role of Miriam begins and finishes the episode of escape from Egypt. Miriam played a role in the rescue of baby Moses—who went on to become the leader acting on behalf of God—and she is the one to sing the final song of praise at their escape and freedom.

However, the relief and joy at their escape from the Egyptian forces soon turns back to fear and complaints when, after only three days traveling, they arrive at Marah and find that the water is bitter. Moses again speaks with God about the situation, and in this instance, the water is made sweet when Moses throws a piece of wood into the water (Exodus 15:25).

LEFT: *THE SONG OF MIRIAM THE PROPHETESS* BY WILLIAM GALE (GAELE). TO CELEBRATE THEIR REMARKABLE ESCAPE, MIRIAM LEADS THE ISRAELITE WOMEN IN DANCING AND PLAYING OF THE TAMBOURINE.

BELOW: *CROSSING THE RED SEA*, FRESCO BY BARTOLO DI FREDI. ONCE THE ISRAELITES WERE SAFELY ASHORE, THE FORCES OF NATURE TURNED, AND A WALL OF WATER ENGULFED PHARAOH'S ARMY.

RIGHT: THIS BEAUTIFUL THIRTEENTH-CENTURY C.E. FRENCH STAINED GLASS WINDOW SHOWS SCENES FROM THE STORY OF THE ISRAELITES IN THE DESERT.

ARRIVAL AT ELIM

What a relief it must have been to arrive at this oasis—12 springs of water and 70 palm trees. Water has played an enormous role in the lives of the Israelites. It was the Nile River that saved the baby Moses. The Nile was involved in the plague sequence and played a role in the progressive fight against Pharaoh. The water of the Red/Reed Sea was both a barrier and a means to freedom. Bitter water at Marah would have meant certain death if it had not been purified by Moses' action. Water is both life-giving and the agent of death.

WILDERNESS OF SIN

It is not known how long the Israelites rested at the oasis of Elim before continuing their journey into the Wilderness of Sin. We are told this lies between Elim and Sinai (Exodus 16:1), which means they are traveling south toward the tip of the Sinai Peninsula. The date in Exodus 16:1 indicates that about six weeks have passed since they began their journey into the Wilderness of Sin. The precise geographic location of the Wilderness of Sin, between the Red Sea and Mt. Sinai, depends on where the other related stopping places and Mt. Sinai are to be located. The location of all of these places is uncertain.

Once more the people "murmur." This word is repeated seven times in the first 12 verses of Exodus 16. In English, this word does not carry the strength it has when used in the Hebrew language. It is far more akin with the English idea of complaint. Indeed, the Hebrew forms used here express resentment, dissatisfaction, anger, and complaint by grumbling in half-muted tones of hostile opposition to God's leaders, and the authority that he has invested in them.

At Marah, the people complained against Moses only, but now, in the Wilderness of Sin, they complain against both Moses and Aaron. As the ancestor of the priestly line who were given so much power and control of the temple duties later in the life of Judah, Aaron is a very important figure in the priestly writings.

We remember the past differently depending on what is happening in the present, and this group of Israelites is no different. At the point when they think they are going to starve, Egypt, by comparison, was heaven. Apparently their memory suggests that they ate to the full, and there is no mention of the slave labor on the Pharaoh's building projects. Aaron and Moses remind the people once more that their murmurings are against God and not themselves.

BELOW: ILLUMINATED PAGE FROM AN EIGHTEENTH-CENTURY C.E. HEBREW BIBLE. MOSES (SHOWN ON RIGHT) AND HIS BROTHER AARON PLAY KEY ROLES IN THE EXODUS. AARON ACTS AS A SPOKESPERSON FOR GOD'S REPRESENTATIVE—MOSES.

UNABLE TO FOLLOW SIMPLE INSTRUCTIONS

God speaks to Moses but Aaron appears to hear the conversation as well, which in turn is relayed to the people. Two assurances are given—firstly, that God has heard their murmurings and doesn't seem to be irritated by their lack of trust and consequent fears, and secondly, that the people will have enough bread given each day for six days. On the sixth day they are to gather twice as much bread, so that they don't have to work on the Sabbath. In this instance, the work involved the need to go out and gather the bread from around the camp. The narrative at this point is demonstrating to us the difficulty these people had in obeying simple instructions. They were told the exact amount to collect each day for their consumption, but some gathered more and it became foul. Others tried to go out on the Sabbath and found there was nothing there. The people had to experience the consequences for themselves; it was only by disobedience that they came to accept the messages from Moses and Aaron. No particular instructions are given about the quails that came around their camp in the evening.

BREAD FROM HEAVEN

The description of this bread, which appeared every morning, was that it was white in color and tasted like wafers with honey. The people named it "man" (the Greeks translated it as manna). There have been many attempts to identify this with some natural edible substance found in western Sinai. The most widely held theory identifies the manna with a secretion from the tamarisk tree. Certain types of insects puncture the bark, and small, sticky, light-colored drops of sap crystallize on the twigs or drop to the ground. In the cool of the morning, before the hot sun melts them, these sweet particles can be gathered and eaten. However, this substance appears only for a few weeks of the year, and hardly seems substantial enough to feed a group of people regularly every day. In this particular event, we need to accept the memory and not try to explain it in naturalistic terms. However, the provision of this sustenance was such an important experience for the Israelites that they had to keep a sample in a jar as a memory of the way God provided in the wilderness.

THE FOURTH COMMANDMENT

The Fourth Commandment states that the Sabbath is to be kept holy (Exodus 20:8–11). Work will be completed in six days, so that the people can concentrate on this day as a Sabbath to the Lord. The journey so far has not reached Mt. Sinai, the place where Moses received the Ten Commandments (20:1–17). The Fourth Commandment became extremely important in the time of the Babylonian Exile (586–538 B.C.E.). It was one of the means by which the Israelite people retained their identity.

ON THE MOVE AGAIN

The people are moving slowly from the Wilderness of Sin toward Rephidim, where again there is a lack of water for them. Rephidim is named as an encampment located between the Wilderness of Sin and the Wilderness of Sinai. Based on the Hebrew text and assuming a southern Exodus route, the location of Rephidim is in the vicinity of Jebel Musa, close to the southern tip of the peninsula. Dating back to Byzantine times, Wadi Feiran has been traditionally identified as the location of Rephidim.

ABOVE: *THE MANNA FROM HEAVEN* BY POMPONIO AMALTEO. WITH MANNA READILY AT HAND AND PLENTIFUL WATER, GOD ENSURED THAT THE ISRAELITES WERE WELL PROVIDED FOR.

LEFT: TAMARISK, *WAYSIDE AND WOODLAND BLOSSOMS* BY MABEL E. STEP. IT HAS BEEN SUGGESTED THAT THE TAMARISK TREE MAY HAVE BEEN THE SOURCE OF THE MANNA THAT NOURISHED THE ISRAELITES.

RIGHT: *VICTORY O LORD* BY JOHN EVERETT MILLAIS. THE ISRAELITES BATTLE WITH THE AMALEKITES. WHILE MOSES' ARMS ARE RAISED, ISRAEL PREVAILS. WHEN HIS ARMS TIRE, THEY ARE HELD ALOFT BY AARON AND HUR.

BELOW: FIFTEENTH-CENTURY C.E. ARTWORK. WHEN THE ISRAELITES COMPLAIN ABOUT THEIR LACK OF WATER, GOD PROVIDES MOSES WITH THE MEANS TO PRODUCE WATER FROM ROCK.

WATER FROM ROCK

The lack of water at Rephidim once again brings forth loud protests from the people. The complaint is centered on Moses, who can sense the hostility of the people to such an extent that he appeals to God to help him. Once more the anger of the Israelites against Moses is appeased when he strikes a rock and water comes forth. Two names are given to this place—Massah and Meribah—meaning "proof and contention" (testing and strife). These names are known in another of the wilderness traditions, which puts the geographic position of Meribah near Kadesh-barnea, north of the Sinai Peninsula. This latter tradition has a slightly different focus to the one in Exodus 17. It is still the case today that water can be divined, and the Bedouin have been known to detect underground springs and break through with a staff to gain access to them.

THE FIRST BATTLE

We suddenly have the appearance of a group of people called the Amalekites, who arrive at the camp at Rephidim to engage in battle with the Israelites. The Amalekites were a nomadic or seminomadic people, descendants of Esau, and one of Israel's traditional enemies. They were scattered across a vast territory, which appeared to cover an area between Sinai and the Arabah of Arabia. Joshua heads up the military part of the operation under Moses' instructions. Many years later, it is Joshua who leads the people across the Jordan and takes the city of Jericho.

The role of Moses appears to be one of constant blessing, with his arms outstretched to ensure the battle was going in favor of the Israelites, but it is hardly surprising to find that his arms get weary. When his arms fall to his sides, the battle turns in favor of the Amalekites. Aaron, his brother, and Hur, who later became a judge in the administrative functions with Moses, held up his arms after providing him with a stone to sit on. Battles, even up to our present day, are not pleasant events to read about. It was the way of the world then and it is only in quite recent decades that we are reconsidering the atrocities of war. Because the Amalekites went into battle with the Israelites, they are condemned for generations to come.

THE FAMILY OF MOSES

Moses' father-in-law, Jethro, was a priest from Midian, the place to which Moses fled after killing an Egyptian. He married the priest's daughter, Zipporah, who had given birth to two sons—Gershom and Eliezer—before Moses was called back to Egypt. Moses' wife and children remained in Midian with Jethro, later traveling with him to join Moses at Mt. Sinai. The Midianites were supposed to be descended from one of Abraham's sons by his second marriage, after Sarah died. The Midianites are named in various places in the Old Testament Scriptures, and the most likely of the settled positions is south of the Transjordan and to the east of the Gulf of Aqaba. Archaeological discoveries suggest that the Midianites were a sophisticated culture that built large cities and existed in the thirteenth century B.C.E. This group of people ceased to exist as a distinct social group, but came to be identified with another ethnic group later called Ishmaelites.

EZEKIEL

The book of Ezekiel relates one of the traditions that places Meribah near Kadesh-barnea, the modern 'Ayn el-Qudeirat (Ezekiel 47:19; 48:28). On the other hand, when we read of this instance in the book of Deuteronomy (Deuteronomy 6:16; 9:22), the preference is to use the name Massah and place it near Mt. Horeb. This is the name that is favored over that of Mt. Sinai by the writer of Deuteronomy. Psalm 95:8 brings both names together—calling the place Meribah, but speaking of "the day of testing" (*massâ*).

We note that marriage to foreigners was not condemned at this stage in the life of the Hebrew people, but certainly became a major issue later. Indeed, we have Jethro, a priest of Midian, who appears to have become a believer in God because of God's role in delivering the Israelites from the hands of Pharaoh. Not only did Jethro become a convert, but he also presided at sacrifices at which Aaron was a participant.

FAMILY ADVICE ON THE WAY TO ORGANIZE COMMUNITY LIFE

The reference to Moses "judging" (Exodus 18) refers to the practice of people bringing any complaints to a "judge," who made legal decisions in civil disputes. It was not the type of judging that we associate with courts, juries, and sentences. The foremost task of the appointed judges was to maintain harmonious relations among the people. The judges often acted as arbitrators, to restore peace in the community. It seems that in those early days of living as a freed people, Moses was attempting to do all the arbitrating himself. Jethro clearly thought this task needed to be shared, and made concrete suggestions about how this might be achieved. Moses would be the person who dealt with the important issues, but others who could be trusted would act in the day-to-day disputes. Moses put this advice into action before his father-in-law departed to his own country of Midian.

ARRIVAL AT MT. SINAI

Often, the reference to the new moon is the Hebrew way of talking about a new month. This means that the Israelites arrived at Mt. Sinai on the first day of the third lunar month after they had fled from Egypt. It seems quite a short period of time when one thinks of the movement of people

ABOVE: THIS EIGHTEENTH-CENTURY C.E. SILK TAPESTRY SHOWS THE ISRAELITES—LED BY JOSHUA—IN BATTLE AGAINST THE AMALEKITES.

LEFT: *MOSES* BY MICHELANGELO BUONARROTI. AS LEADER OF THE ISRAELITES, MOSES ESTABLISHED A JUDICIAL SYSTEM OF SORTS, AIMED AT KEEPING THE PEACE WITHIN THE COMMUNITY.

ABOVE: THIS SEVENTH-CENTURY C.E. ILLUSTRATION FROM *THE HISTORY OF THE HEBREWS (PENTATEUCH OF TOURS)* SHOWS A NUMBER OF SCENES FEATURING THE ISRAELITES AT MT. SINAI.

through desert and the stops associated with setting up encampments. Moses is presented as immediately going up the mountain to speak with God.

Some 60 chapters in the books of Exodus, Leviticus, Numbers, and Deuteronomy are based within the vicinity of the mountain. It is of crucial importance in the life of Israel, because it is the place where the law was revealed to the people through Moses.

LOCATION OF MT. SINAI

Most modern authorities identify Mt. Sinai with Jebel Musa on Egypt's Sinai Peninsula. This particular peak rises to a height of 7,467 ft (2,276 m), and can be scaled with difficulty. Even loftier peaks lie in the region to the south of Jebel Musa, but they, too, are difficult to climb and lack open areas at their bases. The Jebel Musa location is further confirmed by the adjacent plain, which coincides with the encampment area at the base of the mountain of God.

At least a dozen different sites have been proposed for Mt. Sinai, including mountains in the north and west of the Sinai Peninsula, in south Palestine, Transjordan, and Saudi Arabia. In the Bible, Sinai and Horeb are the two names given to this mountain, which for many scholars indicates different traditions. However, there is also the possibility that the names might refer to different places, either close together or far apart. Recently, archaeological and textual evidence has been claimed to support the identification of Sinai with Har Karkom, between Kadesh-barnea and Eilat. The reason for the uncertainty lies partly in the conflicting indications in the biblical evidence and partly in the vagueness of much of the information. The wilderness itinerary (Numbers 33:1–49) seems to point to a mountain in Saudi Arabia, but this view is less likely than that which relates the mountain to routes in the Sinai Peninsula. The most precise indication in the Bible is Deuteronomy 1:2, "By the way of Mount Seir, it takes eleven days to reach Kadesh-barnea from Horeb"—this tends to favor a location in the south of the Sinai Peninsula.

CHRISTIAN/JEWISH SOURCES

From early in the fourth century C.E., Christian tradition has located Mt. Sinai in the south of Sinai Peninsula. The specific identification with Jebel Musa is clearly attested in the *Peregrinatio Egeriae* (C.E. 381–384), and already in that time a monastery that Justinian later rebuilt existed at the foot of the mountain. Possible evidence of this mountain location exists in a second-century C.E. Jewish source, but other early evidence is imprecise or may point to a location closer to Palestine.

UP AND DOWN THE MOUNTAIN

It is very hard to keep track of Moses' journeys up and down the mountain. We presume that Moses returns to the foot of the mountain to relay God's message to the Israelite people (Exodus 19:3–6). They agree to the conditional requirements of the covenant, which demands their obedience and strict adherence to the covenant.

Does Moses return up the mountain to report the people's response or simply speak at the bottom? Again Moses acts as an intermediary and tells the people they have to prepare for God's appearance on the third day.

GOD'S APPEARANCE

Boundaries are set around the mountain, with dire consequences if the boundaries are breached (Exodus 19:12–13). All the natural phenomena, which point to a theophany of God, are present on the third day. Thunder, lightning, thick cloud, smoke, and fire are all signs indicating God's presence. The cloud and fire were the guides given to the Israelites,

RIGHT: *MOSES ON MOUNT SINAI* BY BARTOLO DI FREDI. WHILE SOME OF THE LEADERS OF THE COMMUNITY ARE ALLOWED PARTWAY UP MT. SINAI, ONLY MOSES IS ALLOWED TO REACH THE SUMMIT TO SPEAK WITH GOD.

after they crossed the Red Sea (or Sea of Reeds), to lead them through the wilderness. Again Moses speaks to God and is called up the mountain into God's presence. He then takes another trip down the mountain to collect Aaron and issues a further warning to the people not to come too close. In addition, Exodus 20 sets out the first of the commandments from God. This experience, tied to the freedom from slavery in Egypt, is central to their worship and community life. These events for the Jews parallel what the life, death, and resurrection of Jesus means for Christians.

LEFT: JEBEL MUSA, SINAI PENINSULA, EGYPT. JEBEL MUSA, MEANING "MOUNTAIN OF MOSES," IS BELIEVED TO BE THE SAME MOUNTAIN PEAK AS THE MT. SINAI REFERRED TO IN THE BIBLE.

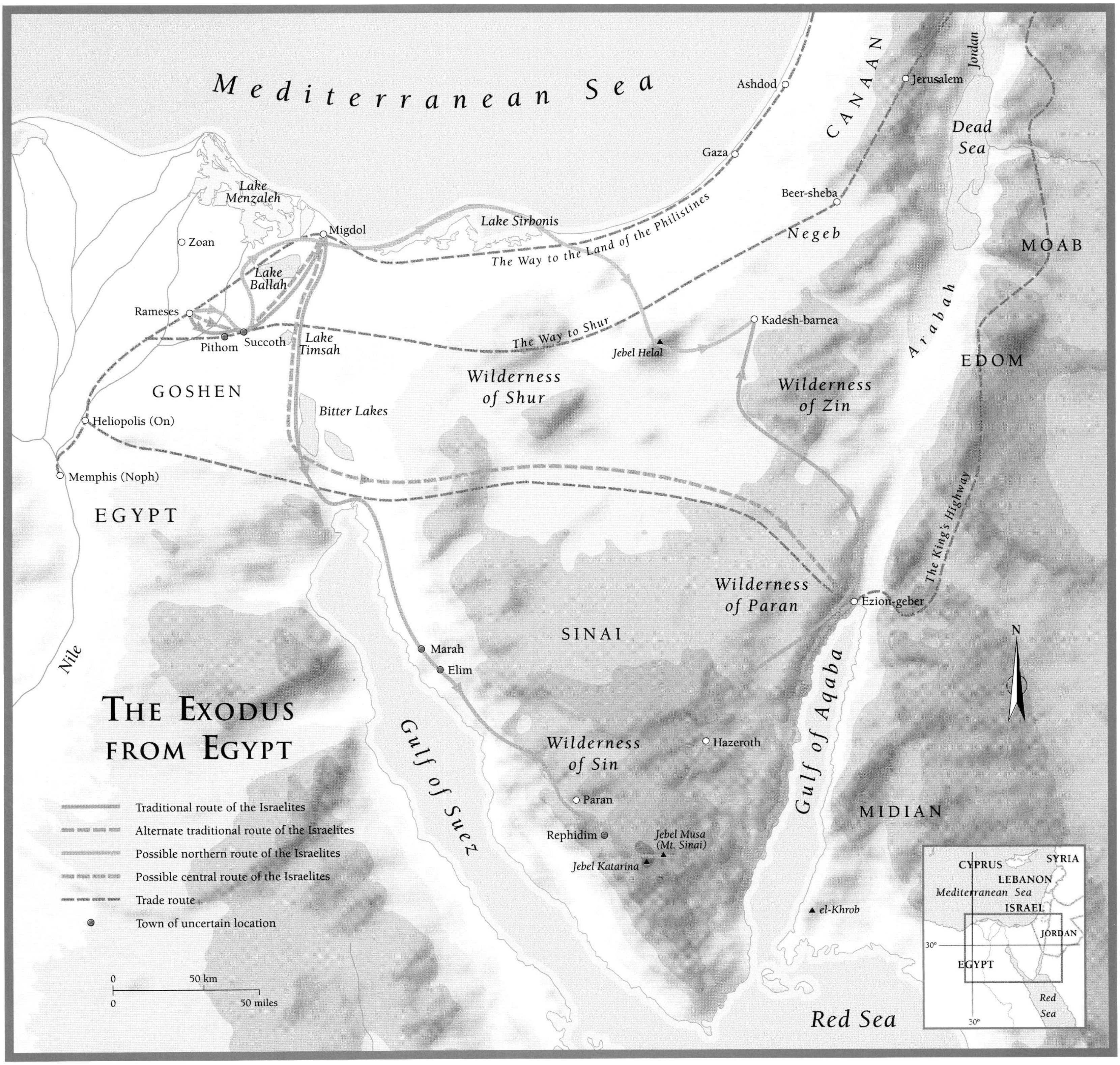

The Exodus from Egypt

- Traditional route of the Israelites
- Alternate traditional route of the Israelites
- Possible northern route of the Israelites
- Possible central route of the Israelites
- Trade route
- Town of uncertain location

0 50 km
0 50 miles

THE GIVING OF THE LAW

I AM THE LORD YOUR GOD, WHO BROUGHT YOU OUT OF THE LAND OF EGYPT EXODUS 20:2

RIGHT: NINTH-CENTURY C.E. BIBLE MANUSCRIPT. AFTER MOSES PASSES 40 DAYS AND NIGHTS ON MT. SINAI, GOD SPEAKS WITH HIM AND HANDS OVER THE TABLETS CONTAINING HIS COMMANDMENTS.

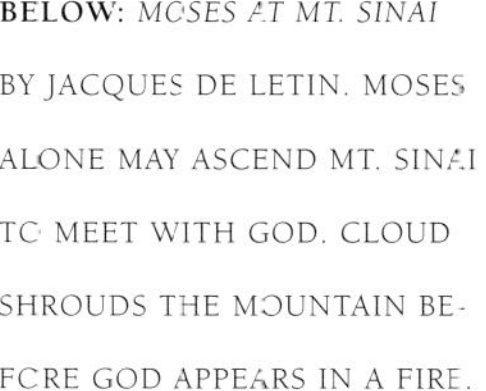

BELOW: *MOSES AT MT. SINAI* BY JACQUES DE LETIN. MOSES ALONE MAY ASCEND MT. SINAI TO MEET WITH GOD. CLOUD SHROUDS THE MOUNTAIN BEFORE GOD APPEARS IN A FIRE.

The narrative breaks off after Exodus 19, and except for a few chapters surrounding the golden calf story (Exodus 32–34), resumes only at Numbers 10. The intervening chapters comprise an anthology of diverse Israelite law. It is all "Mosaic," in the sense that it is understood to derive from the covenant between God and Israel established in Moses' generation, and given to him at Mt. Sinai. Historically speaking, it is a heterogeneous collection, with different parts being compiled over a period of more than 400 years.

THE TEN COMMANDMENTS

The Ten Commandments or Decalogue (known as the "Ten Words" in Jewish tradition) appear in slightly differing forms in Exodus 20:1–17 and Deuteronomy 5:6–21. They constitute the most fundamental guidelines of the ancient Israelite ethical-legal system. The commandments are all apodictic in form. All but two are formulated negatively, employing a linguistic form denoting absolute prohibition.

In Israel's other law collections, there are signs of the socio-historical setting in which they were compiled, for example, the agrarian setting of the Covenant Code against the Deuteronomic Code, which betrays a more developed urban setting with complex financial and social institutions. By contrast, the Decalogue is the most generic—and hence the most undatable—of the biblical collections. It is often claimed that these are the oldest of Israel's laws. This may be so, at least as regards their earliest form. In their present formulation, the commandments clearly show a development in which original, short, peremptory commands have been expanded with explanatory and qualifying phrases. Particularly striking is the Sabbath command, which in Exodus is grounded in the theology of Creation (Exodus 20:8), but in Deuteronomy is rooted in the Exodus (Deuteronomy 5:12).

The precise meaning of the individual commandments is not always self-evident in translation. The prohibition against making images refers to cult objects made as objects of worship, not to all graphic art. The injunction against "wrongful use" of God's name probably refers to the use of the name in magical rituals, not to what we term profanity. The commandment translated as "do not murder" seems to have originated as prohibition of lawless blood vengeance.

A deeply positive theology underlies the negative formulation of most of the commandments. Under Israel's covenant with God, certain specified behaviors are ruled out as unacceptable to the community. Otherwise, the Israelites are free to live as best they can.

MOSES RECEIVES THE STONE TABLETS

Exodus 24:9 describes Moses and the priests and elders ascending the mountain and "seeing" God. The text stresses that, contrary to the usual rule—that no one can see God and live (Exodus 33:20)—they are unharmed; they "ate and

APODICTIC AND CASUISTIC LAW

Scholars of ancient law, both biblical and Near Eastern, distinguish two formal types: casuistic and apodictic. Casuistic laws specify particular circumstances in a conditional clause ("Whoever strikes father or mother …") for which a penalty is then described ("… shall be put to death" [Exodus 21:15]). Apodictic laws are absolute commands ("You shall …," or more commonly "You shall not …"), with no statement of a penalty.

RIGHT: THE CAMP OF THE ISRAELITES, FRENCH COLOR ENGRAVING, EIGHTEENTH CENTURY C.E. THE ISRAELITES CAMPED AT THE BASE OF MT. SINAI. THEY WERE WARNED BY MOSES—CONVEYING GOD'S COMMAND—THAT THEY WOULD DIE IF THEY CLIMBED THE MOUNTAIN.

drank" (24:11), indicating their well-being and perhaps also reflecting a tradition of a covenant meal.

The "glory of God," the palpable presence of the divinity, comes down on Mt. Sinai and settles like a cloud. Moses goes into the cloud to receive the "law and commandments," after which we are told that God gives him "two tablets of the covenant, tablets of stone, written with the finger of God" (Exodus 31:18).

THE TABERNACLE

The description of the Tabernacle may come from the latest layer of the Pentateuch, which dates its probable time of final composition to the period of the Babylonian exile or shortly afterward (or as some scholars have recently argued, to the late period of the Judean monarchy). The account in Exodus is a doublet—almost everything is said twice. In chapters 25–31, Moses receives instructions for making the Tabernacle, and chapters 35–40 describe the execution of the task in almost the same words.

The construction is described in great detail. The structure is made of curtains and entirely covered with red leather, and is supported on a series of wooden frames. It is shaped like three cubes joined together, two being the holy place where the incense altar, table for the bread of the presence (showbread), and golden candlestick are to be placed, and the third, curtained off, the holy of holies ("most holy place"), where the Ark of the Covenant is kept. Every detail is represented—altars, priestly vestments, the bronze basin, and oil. The description climaxes with a dramatic enactment—the "glory of God" comes to the Tabernacle and takes up residence (Exodus 40:34).

Exodus describes the Tabernacle as a portable sanctuary, the place where God's presence is especially focused as the Israelites wander through the wilderness. There are problems in maintaining the precritical view that it was simply this. The text depicts an extremely ornate structure whose construction would have required skilled artisans such as joiners, embroiderers, tanners, and goldsmiths. By one estimate, it would have required 3 tons (3.05 tonnes) of bronze, 4 tons (4.06 tonnes) of silver, $1\frac{1}{4}$ tons (1.27 tonnes) of gold, along with precious stones, fine fabrics, dyes, huge quantities of oil, and so on. According to Numbers 4:28, it took 8,580 Levites to staff. That a group of runaway slaves could produce this in the middle of the desert strains credulity.

The more modest picture in Exodus 33 of a small tent outside the camp, maintained by Joshua and visited by Moses to receive divine revelation is a far more plausible description of the wilderness shrine. But if so, what can the Priestly Tabernacle be? Older scholars suggested it was an imaginary idealized structure that never existed. But this is not so widely accepted now. The picture of the Tabernacle may possibly derive from the tent David is said to have erected in Jerusalem to house the Ark (2 Samuel 6:17), influenced by the appearance of Solomon's Temple.

THE ARK OF THE COVENANT

Exodus 25:10–16 and 37:1–5 describe the Ark of the Covenant. It is a rectangular box of acacia wood measuring approximately $51 \times 31\frac{1}{2} \times 31\frac{1}{2}$ in (around $130 \times 80 \times 80$ cm), overlaid with a layer of gold inside and out. It is designed to be carried, supported on two gilded wooden poles, attached by two golden rings on either side. It is covered with a pure gold *kapporet*, probably a lid (referred to by some sources as the "mercy seat"), flanked by winged sphinxes called cherubim.

It is difficult to determine how the ancient Israelites understood the Ark's function. The oldest tradition (Numbers 10:35–36), mentions it in the story of Israel's pilgrimage through the wilderness. There the Ark is conceived as a throne or footstool from which God goes forth to wage war against the enemies of Israel, returning to it after the battle.

In Exodus 25:10 and in Deuteronomy, the Ark is conceived more modestly as an elaborate box in which the "testimonies" (covenant documents) are stored for safekeeping. But for many, the more theological understanding—linking the Ark of the Covenant to God's presence—must have been dominant.

LEFT: THE ARK OF THE COVENANT, THIRTEENTH-CENTURY C.E. ILLUMINATION FROM A HEBREW TEXT. MOSES WAS GIVEN DETAILED INSTRUCTIONS ON THE CONSTRUCTION OF THE ARK.

RIGHT: ILLUMINATION FROM A THIRTEENTH-CENTURY C.E. HEBREW BIBLE, ILLUSTRATING THE *MENORAH*. GOD COMMANDED THAT THIS SEVEN-BRANCHED LAMPSTAND WAS TO BE CRAFTED FROM GOLD.

As the Ark is the visible symbol of the presence of the invisible God among the the people, this explains why the temporary loss of it during the Philistine Wars (1 Samuel 4) was such a staggering blow, and why its recovery prompted such rejoicing (1 Samuel 6:1–7:2). When David installed the Ark in his new capital of Jerusalem (2 Samuel 6:12–15, 17–19) and when Solomon placed it in the most holy place of the new Temple (1 Kings 8:1–13), these were acts weighted with theological significance.

When the Babylonians conquered Jerusalem in 586 B.C.E., the Ark was apparently captured. Though it was not included in the lists of booty taken by invaders, there is no further mention of it, aside from late speculation on where it might have been hidden. Its loss was surely a key factor in the devastating sense felt by many exiles that God had departed from them.

THE MENORAH

Specifications are given for an elaborate golden lampstand (known in Hebrew as the *menorah*), with two branches and a central shaft, decorated with floral motifs, and supporting seven lamps. The lampstand is to be placed in the Tabernacle opposite the table for the bread of the presence.

Solomon's Temple contained ten lampstands of pure gold, according to 1 Kings 7:49. The postexilic (second) Temple had only one lampstand, which was also true in the Herodian temple. The triumphal Arch of Titus in Rome depicts the *menorah* being carried away with other booty from the Temple after the fall of Jerusalem in C.E. 70.

THE GOLDEN CALF

The narrative resumes briefly in Exodus 31:18–34:35. While Moses is on the mountaintop, the people waiting with Aaron grow impatient and demand new leadership. Aaron melts down their gold rings and casts an image of a calf, which the Israelites acclaim with the astonishing words: "These are your gods, O Israel, who brought you out of the land of Egypt!" (Exodus 32:4).

The next day, while the people are sacrificing and celebrating, God warns Moses what is happening, threatening to obliterate the people. Moses reminds God of ancient divine promises to the ancestors, and points out that if God destroys the people now, it will look bad to the Egyptians!

MOSES' ANGER AND GOD'S PUNISHMENT

Moses returns to the camp, meeting Joshua on the way. Enraged at seeing the Israelites running wild, he shatters the tablets on the ground. He destroys the calf, burning it, pulverizing and mixing the residue with water, and making

LEFT: *ARK OF THE COVENANT SEIZED* BY JEAN FOUQUET FROM *OEUVRE DE JEHAN FOUCQUET*. THE ISRAELITES TOOK THE ARK INTO BATTLE WITH THEM, BUT LOST THIS TREASURE TO THE PHILISTINES.

LEFT: DETAIL FROM *THE ADORATION OF THE GOLDEN CALF* BY NICOLAS POUSSIN. IN MOSES' ABSENCE, THE ISRAELITES FALL INTO BAD WAYS, WORSHIPPING A GOLDEN CALF CREATED BY AARON.

the Israelites drink it. He condemns Aaron, who rationalizes lamely, "I threw it [the gold] into the fire, and out came this calf!" (Exodus 32:24). Thereupon Moses incites the Levites to an orgy of violence, in which they kill 3,000 people, and attempts—with limited success—to atone for the actions of the rest, on whom God sends a plague.

THE COVENANT RENEWED

Moses and the survivors set out again through the wilderness (Exodus 33:1). A tent is pitched outside the camp, where he goes to commune with God, "as one speaks to a friend" (33:11). After further dialog, God commands Moses to make new stone tablets and return to the mountaintop. He receives the law again (34:1), and the covenant is renewed.

MOSES' SHINING FACE

The narrative of Exodus 32–34 concludes with the statement that Moses' face shone when he returned from his mountaintop encounter with God, and subsequently whenever he came out from speaking with God in the tent, so that he had to place a veil over his face.

The meaning is only partly understood. There are no close parallels in ancient literature, but the radiance may be understood as a reflection of the divine "glory," resulting from a close encounter with the divinity.

LITERARY SOURCES OF THE GIVING OF THE LAW

Despite the surface coherence of Exodus 32–34, a careful reading raises a host of questions. The "second" law is not identical with the first, though the text says it is (Exodus 34:1). Chapter 34 is also said to contain ten commandments (34:28), but it does not (seen here is an eighteenth-century C.E. sampler showing the Ten Commandments). Some have suggested that the Decalogue in Exodus 20 (or the Decalogue plus the covenant code) and the laws in Exodus 34 represent two different versions of the covenant-making story, perhaps joined by an editor using the two sets of tablets as a linking motif.

But on the other hand, the antiquity of the golden calf narrative (Exodus 32) has long been recognized and is doubtless echoed in the story of King Jeroboam I (reigned *c.* 931–910 B.C.E.), who is said in 1 Kings 12:28–29 to have set up golden calves in the two sanctuaries of the northern kingdom.

Jeroboam's essential recitation of Aaron's earlier speech at Mt. Sinai (Exodus 32:4) was clearly intended to capitalize upon Israel's earlier cultic traditions and thereby legitimize the new king's actions, reinforced by his choice of Shechem as his capital and Bethel as a place of worship. Both of these places were rich in patriarchal traditions.

FORTY YEARS IN THE DESERT

THE LORD IS WITH US; DO NOT FEAR THEM NUMBERS 14:9

RIGHT: MOSES' DESCENT FROM MT. SINAI SIGNALED THE RECEIPT OF GOD'S COMMANDMENTS, AS SHOWN IN THIS SIXTEENTH-CENTURY C.E. PAINTED ENAMEL DISH BY PIERRE REYMOND.

BELOW: THIS TWELFTH-CENTURY C.E. VELLUM MANUSCRIPT DEPICTS MOSES ON MT. SINAI, AND THE FINISHED ARK AND TABERNACLE, CONSTRUCTED ACCORDING TO GOD'S INSTRUCTIONS.

After the Israelites arrived at Mt. Sinai, they remained there throughout the rest of the events recorded in Exodus 19:1–Numbers 10:10. They were at Mt. Sinai for 11 months and 6 days of their travels, leaving "in the second year, in the second month, on the twentieth day" (Numbers 10:11). The commandments and teachings given in the books of Exodus 19–40, Leviticus 1–27, and Numbers 1:1–10:10, portray them as the words of Moses from God to the people during this stay at Mt. Sinai.

Exodus 19–40 contains God's instructions to Moses, which he has to pass on to the people about the measurements and trappings for the Tabernacle. After the incident with the golden calf and all its consequences, the people obey God's command and build the Tabernacle.

Later, the Tabernacle was the focus of the Temple when it was built in Jerusalem and very special—only the priests could be in its presence. The book of Leviticus sets out precise instructions to the priests on their role, their vestments, a whole range of offerings, and a few chapters to the people about the need for them to be holy and separate from anything that would contaminate them—or entice them to worship other gods.

THE ARK AND THE TABERNACLE

The Ark was probably the forerunner of the Tabernacle and played an integral part in the Israelites' journey through the wilderness. It was light in weight and moved before them to signal that God's presence was with them.

The Ark led the way when the Israelites traveled from Mt. Sinai north through the Wilderness of Paran, which lies to the west of the Gulf of Aqaba, and inland toward Kadesh-barnea. Whenever they set off, the standard of each of the tribes was raised, and they followed the Ark, setting up camp whenever the Ark stopped. When they made camp, the Ark was housed in a tent, which on occasions Moses, Aaron, and Miriam visited when summoned by God.

The Ark was important in the early battles of the Israelites, and on occasions fell into the hands of the Philistines. When this occurred the Israelites were defeated in battle until they recovered the Ark. The significance of the Ark for the Israelites is reinforced throughout their history. David was clever when he installed the Ark in Jerusalem. It indicated that God's presence was in this new city, which he had proclaimed as the political and religious center of his empire.

FISH, CUCUMBERS, MELONS, AND LEEKS

Unlike the complaints prior to the revelation and receiving of the Law at Mt. Sinai, which were answered with compassion and care, the consequences of the complaints in the next few chapters result in punishment.

The memories of good food in Egypt compared with their present deprivation cause the Israelites to complain again. Some of the group are designated as rabble and are blamed for their cravings for more appetizing food. Even Moses has had enough of being blamed for their situation and he, in turn, complains to God, asking why he must bear full responsibility for everything? God answers the complaints in a positive and negative fashion. He gives his Spirit to 70 elders who will help Moses (Jethro also did this in Exodus 18). God provides meat, which is so abundant that it caused them health problems to such an extent that many died. The name given to this place was Kibroth-hattaavah ("graves of craving").

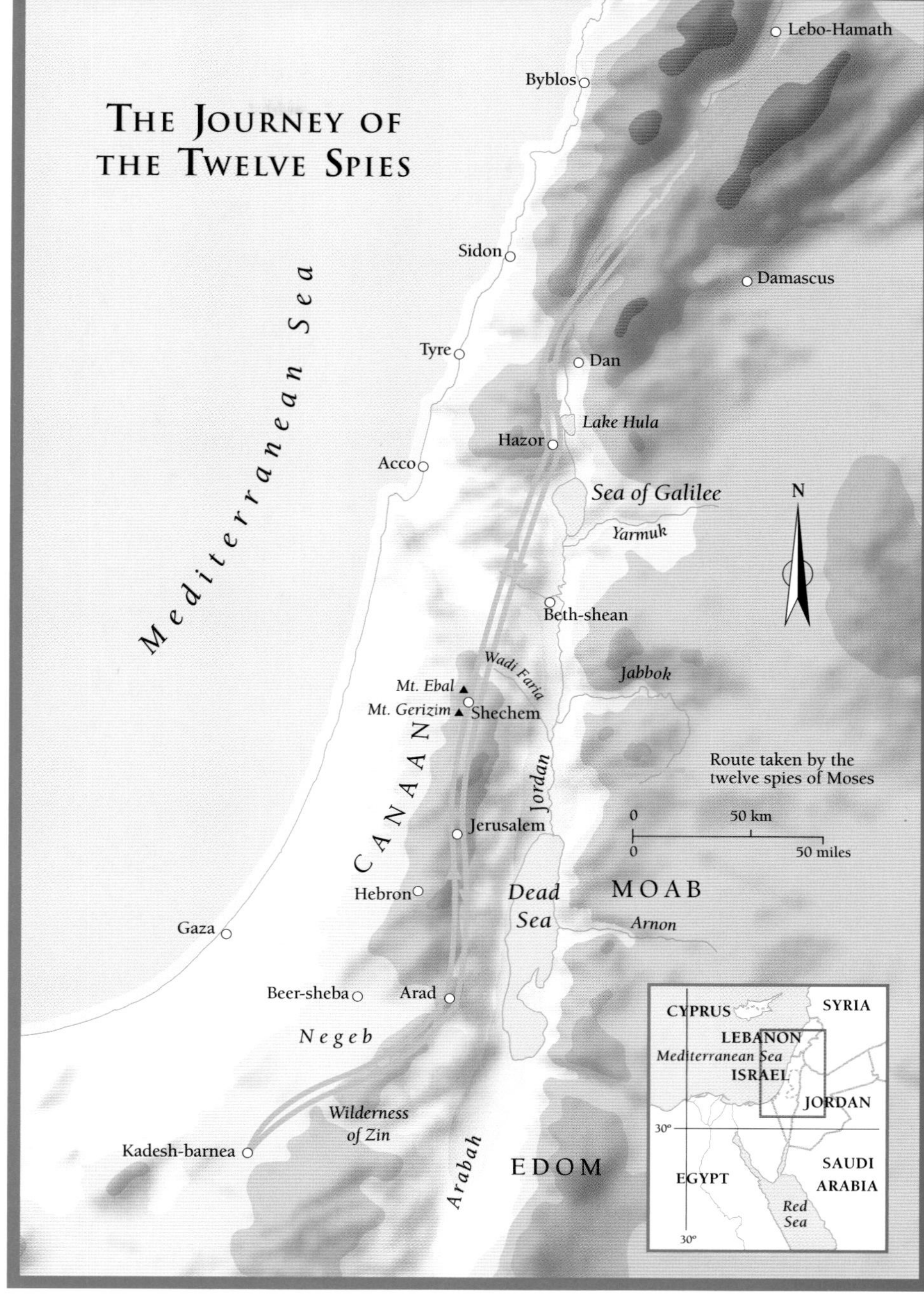

MIRIAM IS PUNISHED

What possessed Miriam to complain against her brother, Moses (Numbers 12:1), especially about his Cushite wife (Cush is known in Egyptian sources as Ethiopia)? His other wife was a foreigner, Zipporah from Midian, and nothing was ever said against her. Nevertheless, this is not the issue for which Miriam suffers a leprosy-like skin disease. She dares to speak against Moses as does her brother, Aaron. However, it is only Miriam who is punished by being excluded from the camp for seven days. It is clear both Aaron and Miriam have the authority to stand in the presence of the Lord, but it is Moses who is the favorite. Even so, the people of the camp refused to move on until Miriam was healed and brought into the camp again (Numbers 12:15). They then moved on from Hazeroth into the Wilderness of Paran.

MEN SENT TO SPY OUT THE LAND

God instructed Moses to send out spies into Canaan. The spies' mission was to assess the strength of the Canaanites who lived in the Negeb, the southernmost part of Canaan. In addition, they were to find out what the land produced and the number of towns in the area. It was meant to be a reasonably comprehensive survey for Moses to assess future actions.

For this mission, one representative was chosen from each of the tribes: Reuben, Simeon, Judah, Issachar, Ephraim, Benjamin, Zebulun, Joseph/Manasseh, Dan, Asher, Naphtali, and Gad. The Levitical tribes are not named as part of the 12 because they do not receive an inheritance of land.

If the men traveled as far north as Lebo-hamath, then the distance they covered was quite considerable. The stated time of their survey was 40 days before they returned and reported back to Moses and Aaron with their findings. Their reports named a number of peoples who lived in the reconnaissance area—the Amalekites, the Hittites, the Jebusites, the Amorites, and the Canaanites.

PEOPLE'S RESPONSE VERSUS THAT OF CALEB

Caleb, the chosen representative of the tribe of Judah, immediately wanted to invade the land, but the other spies instantly said that the strength of the inhabitants was too great and they had giants of men who would crush the Israelites. The people were unhappy and threatened to find another leader who would take them back to Egypt. However, both Caleb and Joshua, who was also on the mission, spoke up to express their faith in the Lord and a willingness to lead the people into Canaan. The people, however, were not convinced and wanted to stone Caleb and Joshua.

ABOVE LEFT: *MOSES MEETS WITH HIS WIFE AND SONS*, ENGRAVING BY W. ARTAUD. MOSES' FIRST WIFE, ZIPPORAH, HIS TWO SONS, GERSHOM AND ELIEZER, AND HIS FATHER-IN-LAW, JETHRO, JOINED HIM AT MT. SINAI.

LEFT: THIS PAGE FROM *BIBLIA SACRA GERMANICA* (KNOWN AS THE NUREMBERG BIBLE) SHOWS THE RETURN OF MOSES' SPIES WITH SPOILS FROM THEIR RECONNAISSANCE MISSION TO CANAAN.

ABOVE: *THE ISRAELITES IN THE DESERT* BY HENDRIK VAN BALEN THE ELDER. AFTER THE ISRAELITES SPEND 40 YEARS IN THE DESERT, THE TIME HAS COME TO MOVE TOWARD THEIR FINAL DESTINATION.

RIGHT: DEATH OF AARON, FROM THE NUREMBERG BIBLE, FIFTEENTH CENTURY. WHEN THE PEOPLE REACH MT. HOR, AARON DIES. THEY MOURN HIS DEATH FOR 30 DAYS.

BELOW: TO REACH THE PROMISED LAND, THE ISRAELITES HAD TO TRAVERSE MANY DIFFICULT TERRAINS, SUCH AS THE ARABAH, LOCATED SOUTH OF THE DEAD SEA.

CALEB'S FAITHFULNESS REWARDED

Caleb will be only one of two people out of the present company who will enter the Promised Land—Joshua is the other. The lack of trust displayed by the remainder of the people resulted in their exclusion from entry into the Promised Land. All those under twenty years of age will be part of the new census that gives the numbers and names of those who will go over the Jordan. Before that occurs they will "wander" around the wilderness for nearly 40 years.

Because the Amalekites and Canaanites occupy the valleys through which the Hebrews would have to travel, they are told to turn south toward the Red Sea. Later, they will turn east to go up the King's Highway. The Israelites cannot help themselves, but again disobey Moses when he tells them to refrain from fighting the Amalekites and Canaanites. Of course they are defeated and chased back to Hormah.

Interspersed at this point in the journey literature are more laws, which spell out the sort of thanksgiving offerings the people are required to make when they do finally settle into their new land.

MOVING ON

The people begin the move from Kadesh-barnea to the Plains of Moab (Numbers 20–21). They have spent nearly 40 years at Kadesh-barnea because they were afraid to trust in God and the spies lied about the situation in Canaan. The story at the beginning of Numbers 20 is a repetition of that told in Exodus 17, except here the wilderness is named as Sin and not Zin. During this part of the journey the King of Edom refused to allow them to pass through his land along the King's Highway. This highway ran all along the east side of Canaan from Syria down through Edom and Moab to the port of the Gulf of Aqaba. Travelers from the Mesopotamia region, where the great civilizations flourished (Assyria and Babylon), would either use this route or the one that ran along the Mediterranean coast and down into Egypt. So, after detouring to avoid Edomite territory, the people arrived at Mt. Hor, where we are told that Aaron was buried (Numbers 20:21–29).

The next king who attempted to obstruct the passage of the Israelites was the Canaanite king of Arad. It is the same name as a place that lies northeast of Kadesh-barnea and west of the Dead Sea. The ensuing battle went in favor of the Israelites who, after the victory, carried out the usual destruction of the enemy towns. The Israelites attempt to go around Edom and at the same time make further complaints against God. The narrative continues with a description of the places at which the

Israelites camped. They headed south from Arad, crossed the Arabah and headed north, either through or around Edom and Moab, to the border with the Amorites. These people were defeated and the Israelites dwelt around this area for a period of time.

Numbers 20 is one of the last stories about the people's complaints against God and Moses. It comes after they have defeated the Canaanite king of Arad. In response to their complaints, the Lord is understood to have sent "fiery serpents" to attack the people. The literary format of this section is structured thus: people complain—people punished—people repent—Moses intercedes—God's response—people saved. Immediately after this incident the Israelites are on the move again to a place called Oboth. It is a curious story in which Moses is instructed to build a "poisonous serpent" but instead builds a bronze serpent. There is an inconsistency about the manner in which this serpent is described—it bites and heals. The Hebrew word *(serapim)* means poisonous and comes from the verb "to burn." In some instances, such as in Isaiah 14:29 and 30:6–7, reference is made to a "flying serpent." We find that the bronze serpent has a literary play on the Hebrew word for bronze, *nehoshet*, and serpent, *nehash*, which is referred to in the later history. King Hezekiah destroyed a bronze serpent referred to as Nehushtan, which was present in the Temple and came to be worshipped as a divine object (2 Kings 18:4). There must be some links other than the literary reference to Moses, but we lack precise details.

In the cultures that surrounded the Israelites as they moved through the desert and gradually settled into the land, the symbol of the serpent was significant in different ways. A serpent could be a symbol of evil power and chaos in some cultures, while in others it was a symbol of life, fertility, and healing. In Numbers 21:4–9 it encompasses both of these extremes—a means of death and a way of healing.

This story is one more in the gradual ending of the old wilderness generation, which came out of Egypt but will not be present as they enter into Canaan.

ABOVE: *MOSES AND THE BRONZE SERPENT*, TAPESTRY DESIGNED BY GIULIO ROMANO. MOSES MADE A BRONZE REPLICA OF A SERPENT—VIEWING THIS WOULD HEAL A SNAKE BITE.

RIGHT: COLOR LITHOGRAPH, *DEAD SEA LOOKING TOWARD MOAB*, FROM *THE HOLY LAND* BY LOUIS HAGHE. MOAB IS YET ANOTHER UNWELCOMING TERRITORY THROUGH WHICH THE ISRAELITES MUST TRAVEL.

BELOW: *BALAAM AND HIS ASS* BY BARTHOLOMEUS BREENBERGH. BALAAM'S DONKEY TURNS FROM AN AVENGING ANGEL THREE TIMES—EFFECTIVELY SAVING BALAAM'S LIFE—BEFORE THE ANGEL BECOMES APPARENT TO BALAAM.

A DONKEY REALIZES THE PRESENCE OF THE LORD

The Israelites arrive in the Plains of Moab, close to the Jordan River, opposite the city of Jericho. After a description of their travels the narrative is interrupted with the story of Balaam and how the king of Moab wanted this non-Israelite seer to curse the Israelites (Numbers 22–24). Balak, the king of Moab, is afraid of the Israelites because he has heard of their victory over the Amorites and wants to prevent a similar defeat. It is a very curious story in which Balaam the seer asks God about going with the king's messengers (Numbers 22–24). He is told to go with the messengers and is then punished for setting out in the morning. The story becomes even more bizarre when an angel prevents the donkey on which Balaam is riding from moving forward. Consequently, the donkey, after being struck three times by Balaam, ends up speaking to his master. Finally, Balaam realizes the presence of the angel. The foreign seer is obedient to the Lord and refuses to curse the Israelites, even when the king of Moab is so desperate that he makes a sacrifice on three occasions. He is unable to persuade Balaam to curse the Israelites, and his desperate measures to have a curse laid on the Israelites are to no avail.

The literary construction of this story has a play on the word "to see." Initially, Balaam was unable to see the angel, but the donkey could see the angel; the king of Moab could see all that Israel had done and was afraid; and later Balaam sees that Israel is blessed. Seeing is an important facet of the relationship between God and the nation, and those who can see will know what God is doing and requiring. One of the confronting truths in this story is the fact that it is a foreign prophet who is obedient to the God of the Israelites, and a donkey that can see the presence of an angel. On many occasions in the past and future, the nation—which knows of God's saving actions in their lives—fails to hear God's word, even from one of their own prophets.

LEFT: THE ISRAELITES SETTLE FOR A WHILE AT SHITTIM, WHERE THE ISRAELITE MEN INDULGE IN DALLIANCES WITH LOCAL AND FOREIGN WOMEN, AS SHOWN IN THIS EXAMPLE FROM THE FOURTEENTH-CENTURY C.E. *BIBLE HISTORY OF THE JEWS.*

THE SEXUAL PROMISCUITY OF THE PEOPLE AND THE REVENGE EXACTED

There is no information about the length of the stay at a place called Shittim near Mt. Nebo in the Plains of Moab. However, it is reported that the men began harassing the daughters of Moab and even worshipped the Moabite idols (Numbers 25:1–2). It appears that the men were bringing women from as far away as Midian, and Zimri (from the tribe of Simeon) had brought Cozbi, a Midianite princess, into the camp. Phinehas, a grandson of Aaron, killed both Zimri and Cozbi, and at the same time a large number of the people were killed by a plague. The consequence was the final deaths of all those people who had begun the journey from Egypt.

Moses, following God's instruction, decrees a final act of revenge on the Midianites before he goes to his grave. Because of the role the foreign women played they all had to be killed, and after the battle all the garments had to be cleansed and all the weapons purified.

The purpose appears to be part of a cleansing process from everything that might contaminate them, including their association with foreign women. They were allowed to keep all the metals as booty, which was distributed among the tribes. Moses has been told that he will be gathered to his forebears after the execution of the Midianites.

ABOVE: *THE PURIFICATION OF THE MIDIANITE VIRGINS* BY TINTORETTO. A HIGH PRICE WILL BE PAID BY THE MIDIANITES FOR THEIR INVOLVEMENT WITH THE ISRAELITES—ALL ARE TO BE KILLED, AND ONLY VIRGINS WILL BE SPARED.

DAUGHTERS OF ZELOPHEHAD MAKE THEIR CLAIM FOR LAND

The story of the daughters of Zelophehad illustrates the progressive nature of law in the Old Testament—the original law (Deuteronomy 21:15–17), augmented by the Old Testament law of Jubilee, bestows inheritance only on male offspring, and land is held by a man and his family/tribe in perpetuity (Leviticus 25:8–12). As Zelophehad had no sons, his death means that his name/estate will be lost, so his daughters appeal for an inheritance in their own right (Numbers 27:1–4). The Lord responds affirmatively (Numbers 27:5–11) and a new law is established. However, as the tribal land would be lost if the daughters married outside their own tribe, the elders from the tribe of Manasseh (that is, Zelophehad's kinsmen) appeal (Numbers 36:1–4)—their concerns are addressed and the law is further revised (Numbers 36:5–10). Now, daughters receiving inheritance are obliged to marry within their own tribe, so that no inheritance transfer occurs. This is a magnificent illustration of the dynamic non-static nature of law and its interpretation in the Old Testament.

MISGUIDED REVENGE?

The region of Midian is below Edom, and the Israelites are now encamped in the north of the Moabite region across the river from Jericho. It is strange that it was the Moabite women whom the Israelite men harassed, and yet the revenge is taken on the Midianites (Numbers 31). Again, this might be an instance of mixed traditions. The description of the revenge reads like modern genocide atrocities.

RIGHT: *MOSES AND JOSHUA DESCEND*, ILLUSTRATION BY ARTHUR A. DIXON FROM *THE CHOSEN PEOPLE*. JOSHUA IS CHOSEN BY GOD TO BE MOSES' SUCCESSOR, AND IT IS HE WHO WILL LEAD THE PEOPLE TO THE PROMISED LAND.

JOSHUA IS COMMISSIONED AS THE NEW LEADER

The time of Moses' death is drawing near and Joshua, who has shown himself obedient to God and a competent leader in battle, is to be commissioned. The ceremony is to take place before the priest Eleazar and all the people. It is a way of ensuring that there are no disruptions to leadership when Moses dies. There is further jockeying for key areas of land such as portrayed in the story of Reuben and Gad, who have great multitudes of cattle and need more grazing land. In return, they have to promise to be in the forefront of the fight when the Israelites cross over the Jordan (Numbers 32).

JOURNEY AND EXTENT OF LAND RECORDED

Numbers 33 and 34 condenses the record of their journey from Egypt to the edge of the Promised Land and names the boundaries after they cross over into the Jordan.

INTERMISSION FOR MORE COMMANDMENTS

Interspersed among their travels are a number of commandments. Some of these relate to the sort of thanksgiving rituals that they need to uphold and many give explicit directions to the priests. However, there are a considerable number of commandments, which are given in order to help the Israelites relate to each other in ways that are fair and just. For example, there are certain cities (six in all) set up that become places of refuge—if a person kills someone without intent, that person may flee there (Numbers 35:9–15). However, they are to stay within the bounds of that city until their case is deliberated upon. There always has to be more than one witness before an accused person can be judged.

There are some commands that show some ecological care for the welfare of the world. If eggs are taken from a nest for food, the parent birds must be left and not taken for food also. If warfare is being waged, the trees that bear fruit in that area are not to be cut down and used for building ramparts.

BELOW: HEAD OF MOSES, SCULPTURE HELD AT THE MUSEE DE L'HOTEL DIEU, MANTES-LA-JOLIE, FRANCE. MOSES' FAITHFULNESS AND LOYALTY ARE THE QUALITIES GOD SOUGHT IN HIS EARTHLY REPRESENTATIVE.

MOSES MAKES A LAST SPEECH

Moses reminds the people of their liberation from Egypt and that he has led them on this journey to the very edge of the Promised Land. It is a clarion call to the people to remain faithful and obedient to God. There is a further promise that if ever they are scattered again among the nations, God will gather them and bring them back again to the land. This time God will work within their hearts and they will love the Lord their God, with all their soul and with all their heart in order that they might live (Deuteronomy 30:6). As a response to this action of God within their hearts, the people will be obedient. Moses calls on heaven and earth to witness these words, which make abundantly clear that the people have a choice—they can choose either life or death. Death occurs when the people betray their relationship with God by worshipping other gods. Life comes from being faithful to their God and remaining in a close relationship.

Care for People

There are a number of commandments regarding care and consideration of the less fortunate. Debts at the end of seven years are totally cleared (Deuteronomy 15:1). If a person's cloak has been taken as part of a debt payment, it has to be handed back at night so the person has covering and doesn't die from cold (24:12–13). If any Hebrews are slaves to their own people, they have to be freed at the end of seven years (15:12). There are clear commands to care for the needy, especially the widow and orphan who have no independent means of support.

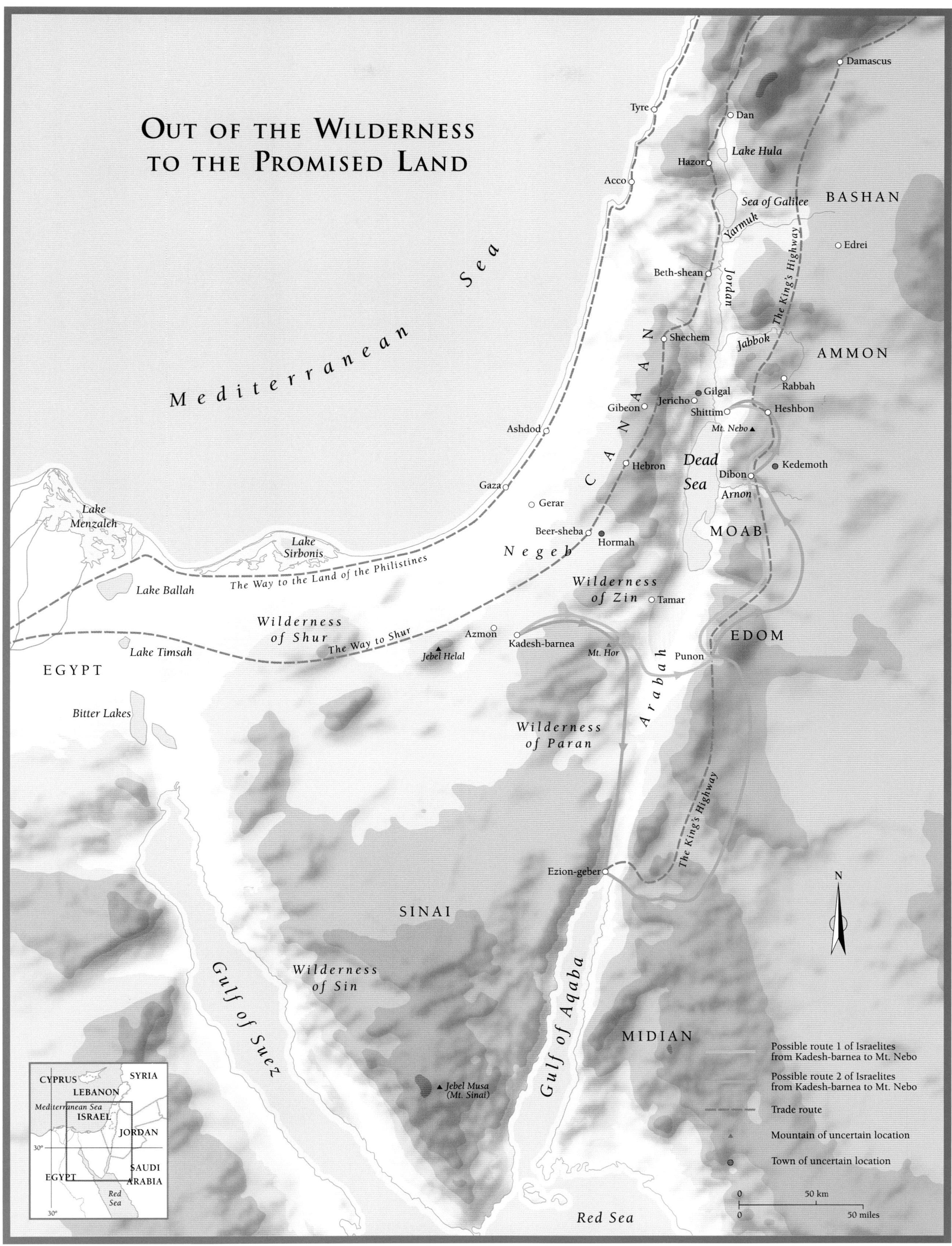
Out of the Wilderness to the Promised Land
Mediterranean Sea
Damascus
Tyre
Dan
Lake Hula
Hazor
Acco
Sea of Galilee
BASHAN
Yarmuk
Edrei
Beth-shean
Jordan
The King's Highway
Shechem
Jabbok
AMMON
CANAAN
Rabbah
Gilgal
Jericho
Gibeon
Shittim
Heshbon
Mt. Nebo
Ashdod
Dead Sea
Hebron
Kedemoth
Dibon
Gaza
Arnon
Gerar
Lake Menzaleh
Lake Sirbonis
Beer-sheba
Hormah
MOAB
Negeb
The Way to the Land of the Philistines
Lake Ballah
Wilderness of Zin
Tamar
Wilderness of Shur
The Way to Shur
Azmon
Kadesh-barnea
EDOM
Lake Timsah
Jebel Helal
Mt. Hor
Punon
EGYPT
Arabah
Bitter Lakes
Wilderness of Paran
The King's Highway
Ezion-geber
N
SINAI
Gulf of Suez
Wilderness of Sin
Gulf of Aqaba
MIDIAN
Jebel Musa (Mt. Sinai)
Possible route 1 of Israelites from Kadesh-barnea to Mt. Nebo
Possible route 2 of Israelites from Kadesh-barnea to Mt. Nebo
Trade route
Mountain of uncertain location
Town of uncertain location
0 50 km
0 50 miles
Red Sea
CYPRUS
SYRIA
LEBANON
Mediterranean Sea
ISRAEL
JORDAN
30°
SAUDI ARABIA
EGYPT
Red Sea
30°

THE DEATH OF MOSES

MOSES, WHOM THE LORD KNEW FACE TO FACE DEUTERONOMY 34:10

RIGHT: *THE SONG OF MOSES,* COLOR LITHOGRAPH FROM THE NUREMBERG BIBLE. AS HIS TIME NEARS ITS END, MOSES RECITES HIS SONG TO THE ISRAELITES TO REAFFIRM THE LAW AS LAID DOWN BY GOD.

The Lord had informed the patriarch Abraham that he would give his descendants the land but first they were to be strangers in a foreign land for 400 years (Genesis 15). He promised Abraham that at some point in the future his children would be oppressed until liberated in the fourth generation. To materialize the assurances the Lord elected Moses to lead Abraham's descendants out of Egypt, through the desert to the Promised Land.

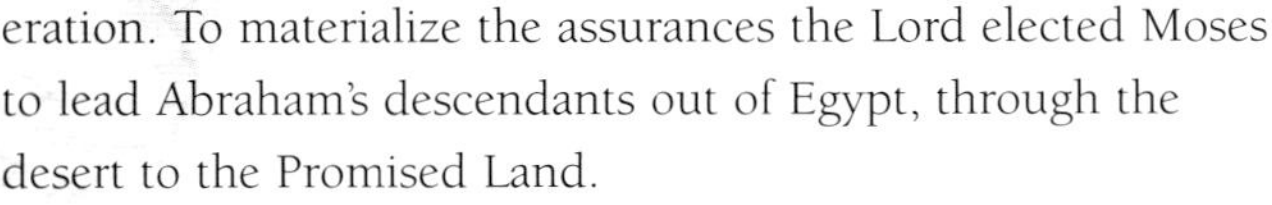

CONTINUITY OF LEADERSHIP

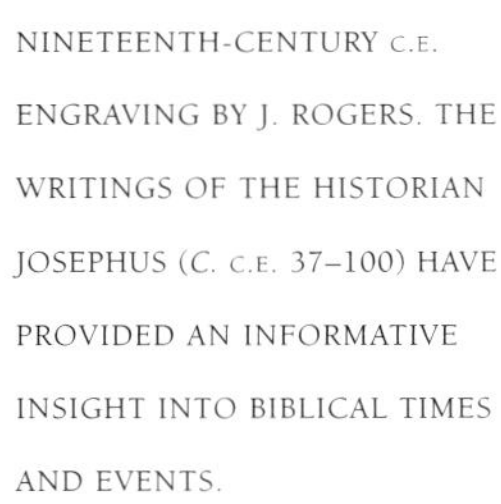

BELOW: *FLAVIUS JOSEPHUS,* NINETEENTH-CENTURY C.E. ENGRAVING BY J. ROGERS. THE WRITINGS OF THE HISTORIAN JOSEPHUS (C. C.E. 37–100) HAVE PROVIDED AN INFORMATIVE INSIGHT INTO BIBLICAL TIMES AND EVENTS.

Moses had little choice but to learn his leadership skills on the job through the power of the divine spirit that he earned by being trustworthy above all others (Exodus 3:12). Moses' disciple, Joshua son of Nun, was groomed by Moses to be the spiritual and military leader of the Children of Israel—a term referring to the descendants of Abraham. Moses transferred to Joshua the spiritual power and physical courage necessary to continue his leadership. Meanwhile, Moses prepared to die. Joshua was to lead the people into the Promised Land and fulfill the Lord's promise to Abraham.

THE SONG OF MOSES

Moses, in a public recitation of the entire Song (Deuteronomy 32) for the whole assembly, then summoned heaven and earth to bear witness to his divinely inspired song of reproof, which outlined the idea that prosperity was dependent on obedience to God's covenant. It was common for Near Eastern rulers to enter into treaties with their subjects ratifying the charter of kingly and subject mutual duties and have gods witness the covenant to bring rewards or punishments to the nation in perpetuity. Moses' song served a similar purpose (Deuteronomy 32:46) but spelled out no obligations explicitly. Instead, nature was the guarantor of Israel's sacred history. The future predictions were to show that prosperity and misfortune would follow Israel's faithfulness, or lack thereof, to God's command. It was understood by the nation that the meaning of the Song foretold that in the end, at the time of the final judgment, God and Israel would be reconciled and the promise to Abraham would be fulfilled. Israel would dwell in security in the Promised Land. God will punish the enemies of Israel for the havoc they wreaked upon his nation. The first-century C.E. writers Josephus and Philo noted the accuracy of the Song in predicting the future.

The Song of Moses has had a special place in the history of Scriptural interpretation. The prophet Hosea made use of it when he warned the Israelites about what they were facing if they continued to flout God's laws and abuse defenseless widows and orphans. Furthermore, Nehemiah 9:25 quotes a version of Deuteronomy 32:15, which includes a phrase about eating to the point of satiation (a concept also preserved in the Samaritan Pentateuch and Old Greek translation, Deuteronomy 32:15, and the Rabbinic commentaries, Sifre Deuteronomy 318). Rebellion against God comes from overindulgence. An interesting split in the versions occurs in Deuteronomy 32:8, where the Hebrew text claims borders were set according to the number of the sons of Israel; the Old Greek version, Ben Sira, a fragment of a Dead Sea Scroll, reads the borders were set according to the number of the sons of angels. The Christian Church Fathers accepted this latter reading and saw here the notion that each of the 70 nations corresponded to a heavenly guardian angel. The Song of Moses deserves careful reading and is written in the Hebrew Torah Scroll according to a fashion reserved for the songs recited by Moses (also Exodus 15).

RIGHT: *THE DEATH OF MOSES* BY ALEXANDRE CABANEL. THROUGH MANY CHALLENGES, MOSES LED THE ISRAELITES TOWARD THEIR FINAL DESTINATION, YET HE DIED WITHOUT SETTING FOOT IN THE PROMISED LAND.

MOSES CONFERS HIS BLESSING

At the age of 120, Moses was about to die, having led the Israelites for 40 years in the desert, and through many trials and tribulations. It was God's will that he did not enter the Promised Land, but was told to climb Mt. Nebo in order to see it all from afar (Deuteronomy 32:49). As the tribes were gathered, Moses bestowed blessings on them. These blessings of bounty began with the tribes of Reuben and Judah. The priestly tribe of Levi received a blessing for the welfare of their oracles and loyalty to God beyond familial ties. They were to instruct the people and atone for sins through sacrificial rites. Benjamin and Joseph, whose territory was divided between Manasseh and Ephraim, were blessed with glory and agricultural plenty. Zebulun and Issachar, Gad, Dan, Naphtali, and Asher were praised with terse, poetic praises of their territories and heroic traits.

DEATH OF THE GREAT PROPHET

Moses was the greatest prophet and his name is mentioned numerous times in the New Testament. Through him God had given his laws and teachings to the world, and now it fell to Joshua to continue the work Moses had begun. While Deuteronomy tells us that Moses was buried in a valley of the Land of Moab such that his grave will never be known (Deuteronomy 34), later traditions came to interpret this to mean that Moses, the Man of God, had in fact never died. Josephus in the first century C.E. describes how Moses departed this world into another plane to serve God. According to the tradition that Josephus is familiar with, Moses himself recorded that he had died since he was so humble, but in fact he had not died at all. Other postbiblical traditions record that Moses was buried by angels. Nonetheless, he was mourned for 30 days (Deuteronomy 34:8), and the memory of his feats has been related worldwide in the ancient and modern worlds. In this manner, the spirit of Moses continues unabated through the teachings of religious believers for all time.

ABOVE: KRONHEIM PRINT OF MOSES ON MT. NEBO. MOSES KNOWS HE IS ABOUT TO DIE. HE CLIMBS TO THE SUMMIT OF MT. NEBO, WHERE HE IS ABLE TO GAZE UPON THE PROMISED LAND.

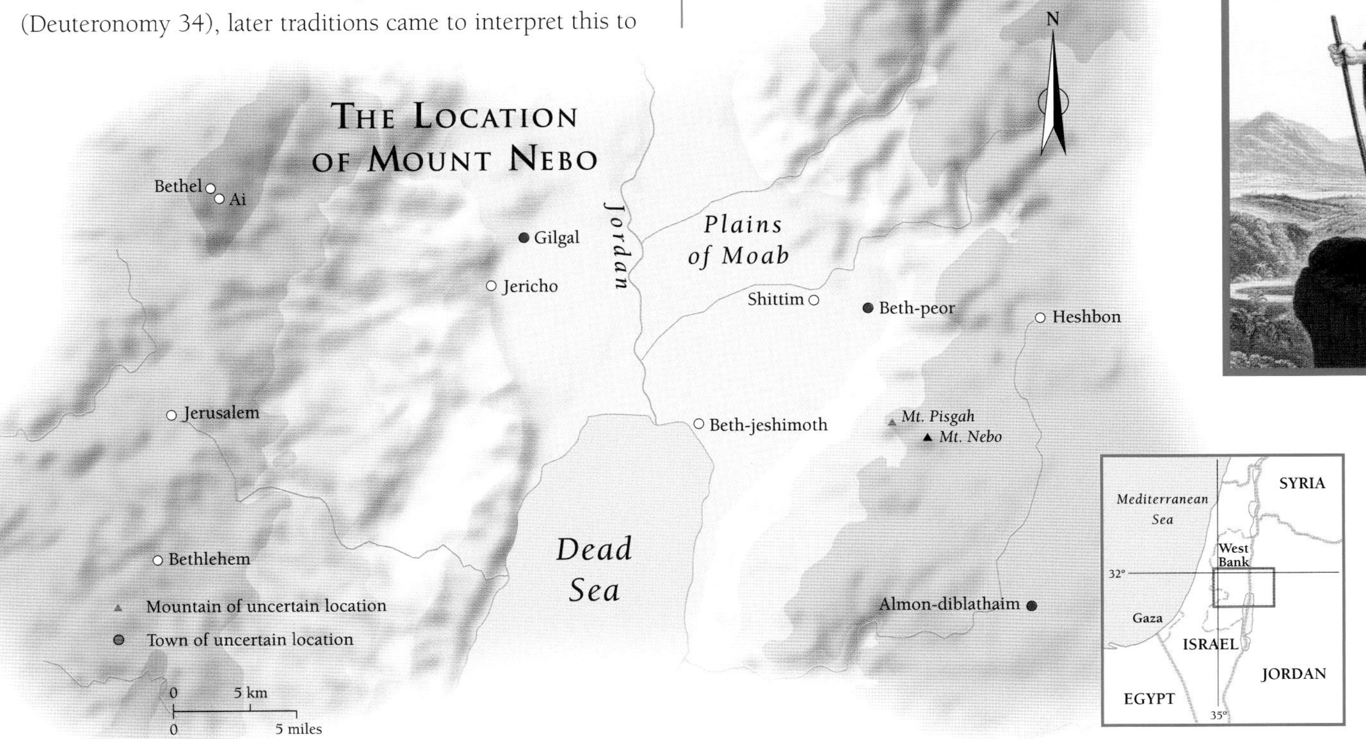

Joshua and the Promised Land

EVERY PLACE ... YOUR FOOT WILL TREAD UPON I HAVE GIVEN TO YOU, AS I PROMISED TO MOSES JOSHUA 1:3

The death of Moses (Deuteronomy 34:5) has left a power vacuum that is to be filled by Joshua, Moses' assistant from the time Israel left Egypt (Exodus 17:9–14). He was present with Moses on the mountain and avoided involvement with the worship of the golden calf (24:13; 23:17). Joshua and Caleb were the only two spies to bring back a good report of Canaan, that indeed Israel could conquer the land (Numbers 13). Now Joshua is to be leader.

RIGHT: EIGHTEENTH-CENTURY C.E. LITHOGRAPH SHOWING THE HANDOVER OF LEADERSHIP. MOSES ENSURES A SMOOTH TRANSITION AFTER HIS DEATH BY PUBLICLY ACKNOWLEDGING JOSHUA AS HIS SUCCESSOR.

GOD COMMANDS JOSHUA

The first nine verses of the book of Joshua record how God speaks to him with promises and encouragements. The promises outline the book. Joshua is to cross the Jordan River along with Israel (Joshua 1:2), something that takes place in chapters 1–5. He receives every part of the land that he travels (1:3), as occurs in chapters 6–12. Joshua maps and distributes the land in chapters 13–21, whose major regions and boundaries are summarized in 1:4 and are identical to the land of Canaan as known in Egyptian records of the second millennium B.C.E. Finally, the reference to the end of Joshua's life (1:5) looks forward to chapters 22–24 and the concluding events of Joshua's human existence.

In Joshua 1:5–9, God encourages Joshua to be a strong and courageous leader, a term reserved for one about to undertake major projects, whether building the Temple of Jerusalem (1 Chronicles 28:20) or fighting the Assyrian superpower (2 Chronicles 32:7). The command to remember God's Word is mentioned several times (Joshua 1:7–8), surrounded on both sides by promises of God's presence with Joshua (1:5, 9). Joshua will be successful as God is present to enable him to understand and obey the divine word.

Although God has recognized Joshua's leadership, will the people of Israel as well? Joshua 1:12–18 tests this question with the two and a half tribes who would have the least to gain by joining him in crossing the Jordan and waging war. The tribes of Reuben, Gad, and eastern Manasseh had already received their land allotments east of the Jordan River. Why should they risk their lives? Yet when Joshua reminds them of their vow to Moses (Deuteronomy 3:18–20; Joshua 1:13–15), they swear allegiance to Joshua. No doubt the other tribes took a similar oath, in a manner resembling the oath made by the Canaanite princes of the land when a new pharaoh ascended the imperial throne in Egypt.

JOSHUA SENDS SPIES TO JERICHO

The act of sending spies had a negative result in Numbers 13–14, when the spies described the strength of Canaan, and the people refused to believe God and were judged with a generation of wandering in the wilderness. It would again create problems when spies sent to Ai bring back advice that leads to Israel's only defeat in the book (Joshua 7:2–3). However, other spies, such as those Moses sent to Jazer (Numbers 21:32) result in successful military operations. In Joshua 2 the spies do not report in a manner that might be expected, with details regarding defenses of the land or its topography or the specifics of Jericho, as Joshua's charge might suggest they should (Joshua 2:1). Instead, their report constitutes a direct quote from Rahab regarding the fear of the Canaanites and the testimony of faith that God has given the land to Israel (2:24). Their actions resemble the "spies" (using the same word) whom Absalom sent through his father David's kingdom to proclaim him (Absalom) as king (2 Samuel 15:10). Joshua's spies also appear to disseminate information with the purpose of seeking supporters among the Canaanites. In this task, they find Rahab.

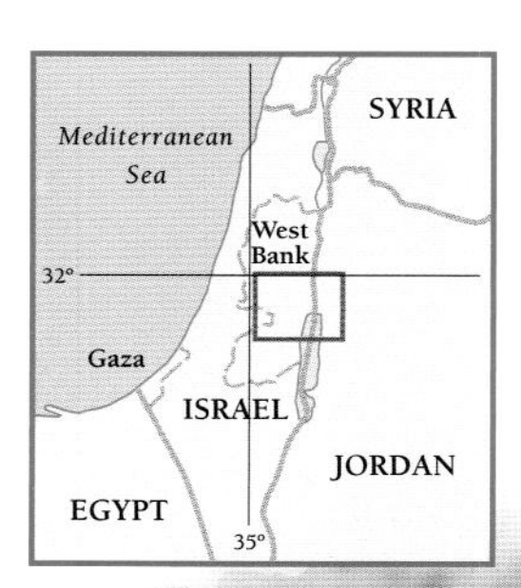

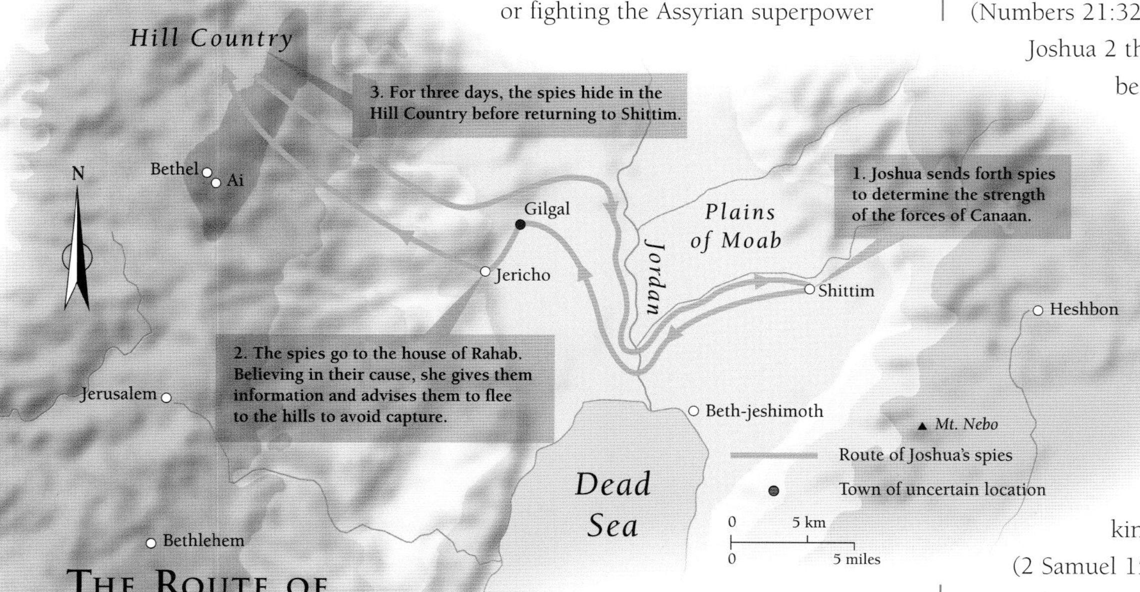

THE ROUTE OF JOSHUA'S SPIES

RAHAB'S KINDNESS

The spies come to Rahab's "house." She is described as a prostitute, which leads some to suppose that the spies had abandoned their mission and were visiting a brothel. However, the evidence from the second millennium B.C.E. suggests that the owner of an inn who was female was expected to be a "prostitute." Thus the instruction to Hittite tower or border commanders, from the mid-second millennium B.C.E., forbids the creation of such places where prostitutes live near the fortress wall. Further, the famous Babylonian laws of Hammurabi, composed centuries before the events of Joshua 2, assume a female innkeeper and warn that, if she hears people plotting conspiracy in her house, she must bring them to the king on pain of death (law 109), as it was assumed that such establishments attracted conspirators. Thus the spies came to the one place in Jericho where they might learn of any supporters, and they found such a supporter in Rahab the innkeeper. Rahab's confession of faith remains a model of what it means to be a believer—whether Old Testament or New Testament. At the heart of Joshua 2:9–11, in verse 10, she bases her faith on God's act of redemption of his people, in delivering them from the Red Sea and preserving them in the wilderness. Her faith will save her and preserve her household.

THE ISRAELITES CROSS THE JORDAN RIVER

In Joshua 3–4, the Israelites leave their camp at Shittim, some miles east of the Jordan River. They move to the bank of the river, a feat in itself as it would have been surrounded on both banks by jungle-like dense growth. In the southern Jordan Valley, the river meanders and, during the spring flood, could reach widths of 100 ft (30 m) and depths of 10 ft (3 m). Although God would fortuitously stop the river, the act of faith of the priests in first stepping (Joshua 3:15) into the river would be a model to the rest of Israel and would signal the blocking of the river, perhaps 17 miles (27 km) north at Adam (Tell ed-Damiyeh).

The whole picture is one of God, as symbolized by the Ark, leading his chosen people safely across the Jordan River. Nothing can stand in their way—neither the natural force of this river in flood, nor the human resistance of Jericho that stands before them.

MEMORIAL STONES

Joshua erects 12 memorial stones (Joshua 4:3–9, 20–23) to represent the 12 tribes who crossed the Jordan River. The site at Gilgal was near the point of crossing. The name Gilgal means "circle" and thus could, and probably did, refer to a number of round sites that were used by the Israelites as camps and as places for worshipping God. The stones would serve as teaching devices and would give new meaning to the Passover that was celebrated at this time. As God led the first generation of Israel through the Red Sea and out of Egypt at Passover, so he led the second generation of Israel into the Promised Land across the Jordan River during the same season of the year.

BELOW: *JOSHUA PASSING THE RIVER JORDAN WITH THE ARK OF THE COVENANT* BY BENJAMIN WEST. THE ARK LEADS THE WAY FOR THE ISRAELITES AS THEY PREPARE TO ENTER CANAAN.

LEFT: *THE FALL OF JERICHO* BY JEAN FOUQUET. THIS VELLUM PAGE FROM A FRENCH TRANSLATION OF FLAVIUS JOSEPHUS'S WORK DEPICTS THE ISRAELITE ATTACK ON JERICHO.

THE FALL OF JERICHO

The story of the battle of Jericho (Joshua 6), perhaps the most famous battle in the Bible, constitutes the first victory of Joshua and Israel in their new land. It therefore has psychological and military importance. This is the reason for the detail. There is nothing in the biblical account to indicate that the site was at this time a large city. Unlike Gibeon (10:2) and especially Hazor (11:10), both of which are identified as cities of some prominence, Jericho is never described as a large city. Indeed, the word for "city" can be used to describe hamlets, villages, and military forts. The last description should probably be applied to Jericho. The site of Tell es-Sultan is universally recognized as Jericho. The absence of clear evidence for much occupation, whenever one dates the Exodus and the entry into the land, suggests that whatever was present was not large nor did the people represent an elite class that preserved special (valuable) pottery whose fragments could be identified with this period. Instead, both the biblical text and the archaeology suggest that Jericho was a fort whose "king," as the usage of the word permits, was not an independent sovereign but a military governor in charge of the fort. This fort would have guarded a number of key east–west trade routes, in addition to the north–south route through the Jordan Valley. These included, among others, routes to Jerusalem (see Luke 10:30–37) and to Bethel (via Ai). The collapse of the walls of Jericho is a remarkable event but not unlike those described by other Ancient Near Eastern military powers who ascribe miraculous victories to their deities. This is not to say God did not act here but rather to recognize that his wondrous actions were intended to let the Canaanites know that he was acting on behalf of his people—the Israelites—and that resistance would be useless.

CIRCUMCISIONS AT GILGAL

Circumcision was a sign of the covenant people from the time of Abraham (Genesis 15). Apparently, Israel had not practiced circumcision in the wilderness. Without a renewal of this rite, Israel would not be the covenant people, faithful to God in his commands and prepared to enter his covenantal gift of the Promised Land. Circumcisions at Gilgal prepared the people for their celebration of Passover on the west bank of the Jordan River (Joshua 5:1–12). The flint knives used would have been made of obsidian and were probably sharper than any metal knife of that period.

With the cessation of the manna, and the eating of the barley grain harvested around them in their new land, Israel brings to an end the experience of the wilderness and begins its new life. The roasted grain was the first fruit of their new land, a token of the greater abundance of a land flowing with (goat) milk and (date) honey (Joshua 5:6). As this was the Passover, the subsequent seven days constituted the Feast of Unleavened Bread and coincided with the march around Jericho.

RIGHT: FLINT KNIFE FROM MIDDLE EGYPT, LATE PREDYNASTIC PERIOD. FLINT KNIVES WOULD HAVE BEEN USED TO PERFORM THE CIRCUMCISIONS REQUIRED TO OBSERVE GOD'S COVENANT.

RAHAB IS SPARED

The rescue of Rahab and her family is a key part of the story of Jericho's defeat. It is interwoven with the battle account in Joshua 6:16–25. In the original Hebrew, of the text devoted to Jericho, more than half concerns

Rahab and her family. Thus the writer of this account considered the salvation of Rahab to be just about as important as the destruction of Jericho.

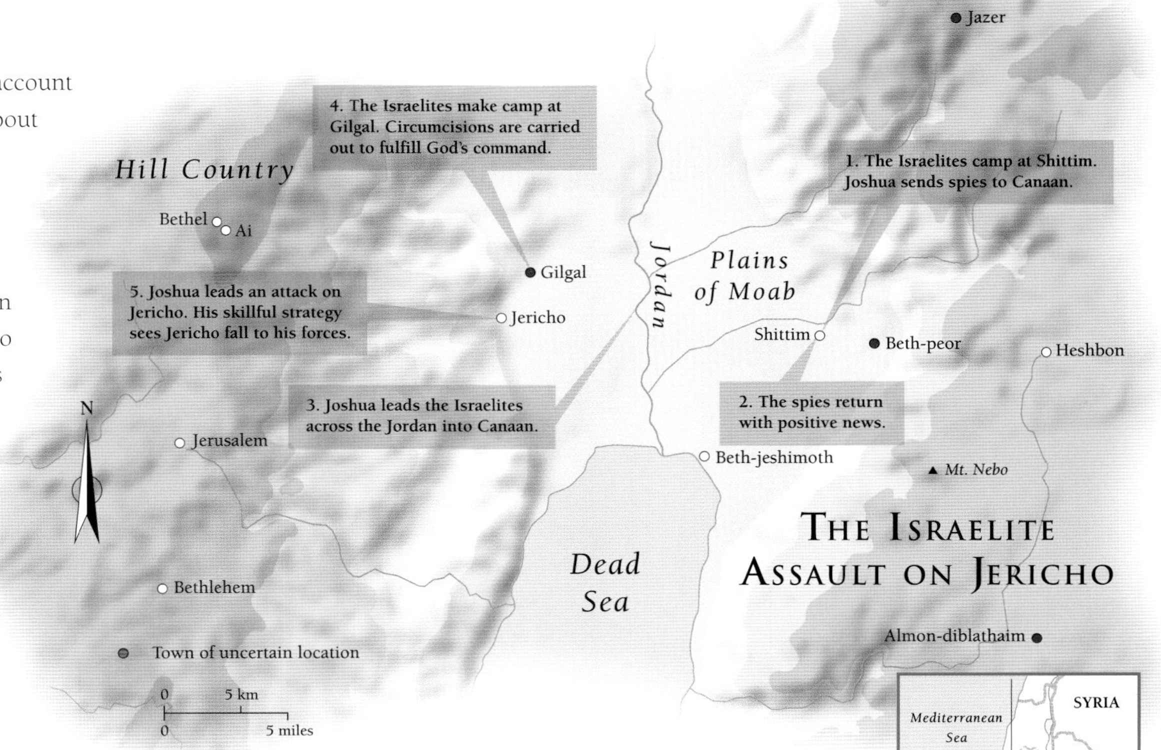

ACHAN'S SIN

With the destruction of the fort of Jericho, the passes to the central hill country were left open to the Israelites. By choosing the central pass to Bethel, Joshua and his army would gain access to the Benjaminite Plateau to the south and the central hill country to the north. These areas constitute the heartland of Canaan and of the region where Israel first settles. Guarding the pass to Bethel was a second fort, Ai, or modern et-Tell. Although other identifications have been proposed and are possible, the chief objection to et-Tell as Ai is the absence of occupation at the time of Israel's entrance into the land. Nevertheless, like Jericho, this site most probably served as a fort that reused some of the earlier (third millennium B.C.E.) walls for purposes of guarding the access to its chief city Bethel, modern Beitin, just a mile or so westward.

The failure of the first assault on Ai (Joshua 7:1–5) is traced to Achan who stole some of the property intended as an offering to God. Such an offering, which is known elsewhere among surrounding countries (see its mention in the ninth-century B.C.E. Moabite stele), is the *herem*. According to Deuteronomy 20:16–18, in general, everything is to be destroyed. All living creatures, human and animal, are to be killed, and all property is to be burnt or (in the case of metals that cannot be so destroyed) dedicated to God's house. Achan's transgression in this matter is identified by lot, and he is taken to the Valley of Achor, likely to be identified with the Buqeiah Valley or one nearby that lies west of the Dead Sea. There he and his family, who would have known of his deed, were stoned to death and a memorial of stones erected to remind Israel of the consequences of willful disobedience of God's commands.

BELOW: ANCIENT JERICHO, LOCATED JUST OUTSIDE MODERN-DAY JERICHO, HAS BEEN A MAGNET FOR ARCHAEOLOGISTS KEEN TO ACCURATELY DATE THE CITY.

ABOVE: *JOSHUA CONQUERING THE CITY OF AI,* MACIEJOWSKI BIBLE. COMMISSIONED BY KING LOUIS IX, THIS BIBLE HAS A HISTORY AS COLORFUL AS ITS PAGES, HAVING PASSED THROUGH VARIOUS ROYAL HANDS THROUGH THE AGES.

OPPOSITE: *JOSHUA COMMANDING THE SUN TO STAND STILL,* NINETEENTH-CENTURY C.E. ARTWORK. EVEN THE SUN AND MOON CAME TO THE AID OF JOSHUA'S SUCCESSFUL DEFENSE OF GIBEON.

THE FALL OF AI

Ai, like Jericho, was a fort that guarded the hill country passes to the east of the important city of Bethel. Therefore, Bethel and its army are also mentioned in this account (Joshua 7:2; 8:9, 12, 16). Joshua 8:1–29 relates the conquest of Ai, using a ruse that would be repeated later against Benjamin (Judges 20:32–35). In the morning, Joshua's main force showed up at Ai's gate. The whole army of Ai rushed forth and pursued the Israelites, chasing them eastward toward the cliffs and steep descents into the Jordan Valley. At the designated moment, Joshua held aloft his curved spear in a manner that reflected the morning sunlight and signaled to the ambush troops, lying west of Ai and the battle. On the night before, the ambush troops had hidden in the valley to the west of Ai. They entered Ai and set it ablaze. At that moment Israel ceased its feigned retreat and turned westward to face the charging army of Ai. Stopped suddenly by this unexpected opposition, and at a disadvantage with the morning sun in their eyes, the army of Ai turned westward to flee back to their fort. When they did so they found their refuge burning and the ambush troops now pursuing them from the west. Caught between the pincers of Israel's army, Ai's forces were completely destroyed. The body of Ai's king was hung on a tree as a humiliation to that army (Joshua 8:29). It was removed at sunset and buried under a pile of stones at Ai's gate, as a memorial to Israel's victory (see the stone memorials at Gilgal in 4:20 and over the body of Achan in 7:26).

Having made their way into the central hill country, the Israelites were able to hold a covenant renewal ceremony at Mt. Ebal (8:30–35) in fulfillment of God's command to Moses (Deuteronomy 11:29; 27:4, 13).

THE GIBEONITES

Joshua 9 describes how one group of Canaanites in the land did not succumb to Israel's military victories. Instead, by means of a ruse they were able to convince the leaders of God's people that they were from a distant country and thus could enter into a peace treaty with Israel. The text describes how the representatives of Gibeon showed up at Israel's camp at Gilgal (here, perhaps a site not far from Mt. Ebal and Shechem as in Joshua 8:30–35). Along with other indications, they appeared with clothes and shoes that were worn out, and with moldy bread (9:4–5). All these were signs of traveling from a long distance away. Soon after the treaty was concluded, Israel learned that their new friends were from Gibeon, a city north of Jerusalem and southwest of Ai, in the center of the land whose inhabitants they were commanded to drive out or destroy, but under no circumstances to make treaties with. The Israelite people were ready to put their own leaders to death for having made this decision. Joshua intervened. The Gibeonites would serve Israel and its sanctuary by chopping wood and carrying water (9:21, 23, 27), an activity appropriate for aliens living in the land with Israel (Deuteronomy 29:11).

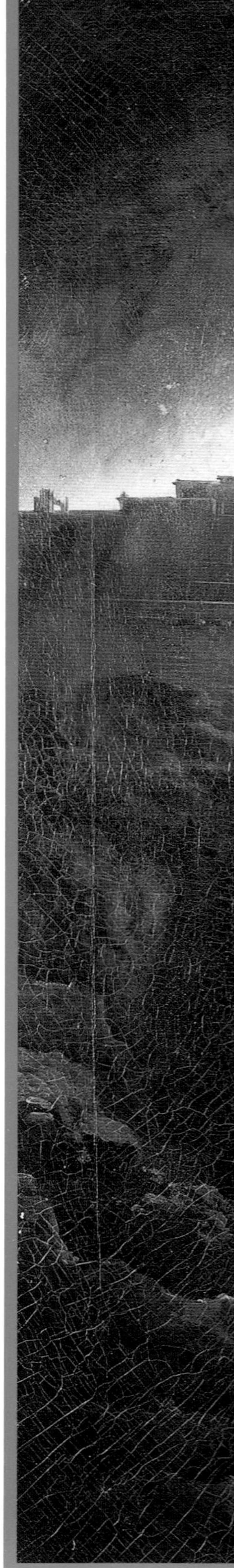

THE CAPTURE OF THE FIVE FUGITIVE KINGS

The treaty between the Gibeonites and Israel led to Israel's battle with the southern coalition in Joshua 10. The Canaanite king of Jerusalem, when he heard of this agreement, summoned four other kings of cities to his south and west. They all joined in battle against Gibeon, who promptly sent for Israel to assist them. Faithful to its treaty, Israel joined in the battle. God's assistance with hailstones and making the sun stand still (Joshua 10:11–14) drove the southern coalition westward though the Aijalon Valley and on past Azekah. At this point the Israelites turned southward and destroyed all the fortified centers of their enemies in an arc sweeping from the northwest to the south and east as far as Hebron and Debir (10:36–39). Meanwhile the leaders of this attack, the five kings who had come together, were put in a cave at Makkedah (Khirbet el-Qom). There the leaders of Israel's army put their feet on the necks of these Canaanite kings. After being killed, the bodies of these enemies were hung on trees until evening. At that point, their bodies were placed into the cave that was sealed with a pile of rocks, not unlike the treatment of Ai's king in 8:29.

JOSHUA EXTENDS HIS LAND

If Joshua 10 describes the victories in the southern part of the Promised Land, the following chapter outlines successes in the northern part. The key city here was Hazor, whose king brought together an army of huge number and possessing many chariots (these functioned as mobile firing platforms for archers and were the most sophisticated and feared examples of military technology in the second millennium B.C.E.). They came to threaten Israel at the Waters of Merom (Joshua 11:7), possibly to be identified with the later Crusader site of the Horns of Hattin. God gave Israel victory and they pursued the remnants of the army clockwise. They moved westward and then north to Sidon. From there they chased their enemies eastward along the

LEFT: *THE EXECUTION OF THE FIVE KINGS*, COLOR LITHOGRAPH, NUREMBERG BIBLE. THE FIVE AMORITE KINGS WERE CAPTURED AND HUNG. THEIR BODIES WERE FINALLY THROWN INTO A CAVE AT MAKKEDAH.

RIGHT: ENGRAVING SHOWING THE 12 TRIBES OF ISRAEL. THE DESCENDANTS OF JACOB AND JOSEPH MAKE UP THE 12 TRIBES WHO WILL SETTLE IN THE LAND OF CANAAN.

BELOW RIGHT: *THE OCCUPATION AND DIVISION OF THE LAND OF CANAAN*, COLOR LITHOGRAPH BY RAPHAEL. THE LAND OF CANAAN WAS DIVIDED AMONG THE 12 TRIBES OF ISRAEL.

Litani Valley that runs north of Galilee into the Valley of Mizpeh, which is perhaps identified with the modern Lebanese Beqa. The army then turned southward through the Hula Basin to Hazor (Tel Hazor). This is the largest second millennium B.C.E. site in the whole of northern Canaan, measuring some 175 acres (about 70 ha). Excavations have revealed a destruction layer from the thirteenth century B.C.E. that may be associated either with this battle or with the second defeat by the Israelites in Judges 4–5. The defaced images found in the temples on the acropolis, as well as the subsequent occupation of a small, possibly Israelite, village, all attest to the fiery destruction described in Joshua 11:13. This verse is important because it suggests that none of the other fortifications that Israel captured and destroyed in its southern and northern campaigns (chapters 10 and 11) were set on fire. This lack of fire is the reason why there is so much difficulty in identifying Israelite destruction layers in other sites throughout the land. Archaeologically, fiery destruction layers are the easiest to identify. Without the fire, it is difficult to identify a destruction layer and therefore to associate the events of Joshua with other sites. Joshua 12 summarizes the victories with a list of fortified centers that resembles many Egyptian conquest lists of Canaan made by pharaohs from the fifteenth through to the tenth centuries B.C.E.

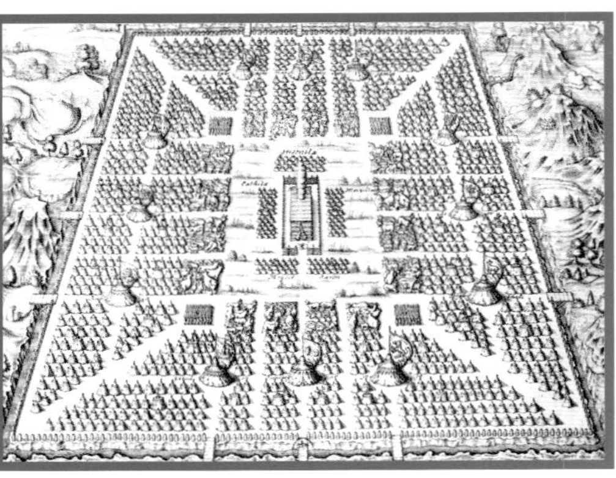

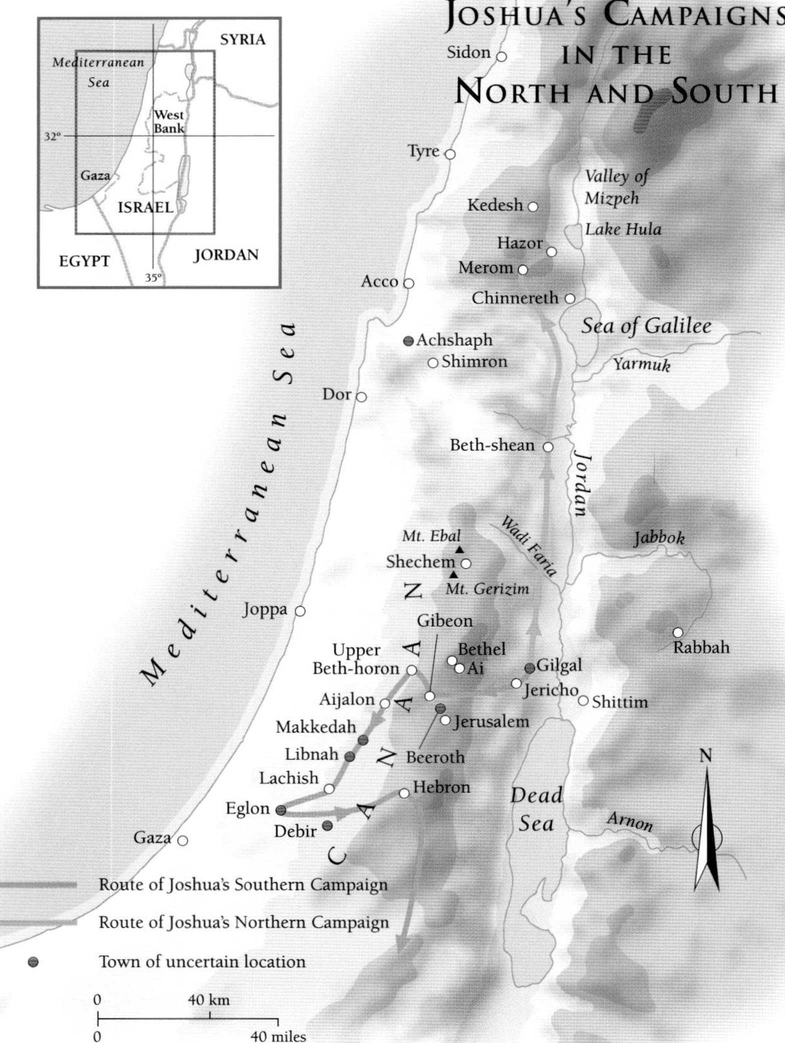

THE DIVISION OF THE LAND

Joshua 13–19 identifies how the land east (chapter 13) and west (chapters 14–19) of the Jordan River were allotted to Israel. East of the Jordan, Reuben, Gad, and East Manasseh received lands that are identified by regions and lists of towns. The tribal allotments given to Israel west of the Jordan River are composed of two types: boundary lists describing the areas at the edge of the allotments or between tribal territories; and town lists that simply identify towns within a region that belong to a particular tribe. Although the tribe of Simeon is described by lists of towns in southern Judah (Joshua 19:1–9) and some towns in Issachar's territory are given to Manasseh (17:11–13), the tribal territorial descriptions are consistent in covering all the area of southern Canaan. They do this by identifying regions contiguous to one another and without any gaps or overlapping. Judah's description (chapter 15) is the most detailed and complete, containing both an exhaustive boundary description and a lengthy and detailed set of town lists that cover the entire region. As one moves northward, the various tribal allotments preserve partial boundary descriptions or none at all. Other tribes are described only in terms of town lists. Some areas, such as the region of Hebron allotted to Caleb, are described in terms of how they were occupied (14:1–15; 15:13–19). Many of the regions were not occupied at the time of the allotments (Joshua 13:2–7; 15:8; 16:10; 17:11–13; 19:47; Judges 1:1–36). Most of the tribal territories were allocated by lot, based on the size of the tribe (Joshua 18:1–10). In many cases they resemble the territories and boundaries controlled by the earlier Canaanite city-states. This is to be expected because the map makers would have identified and defined territories according to the natural topography. Although some areas were not occupied

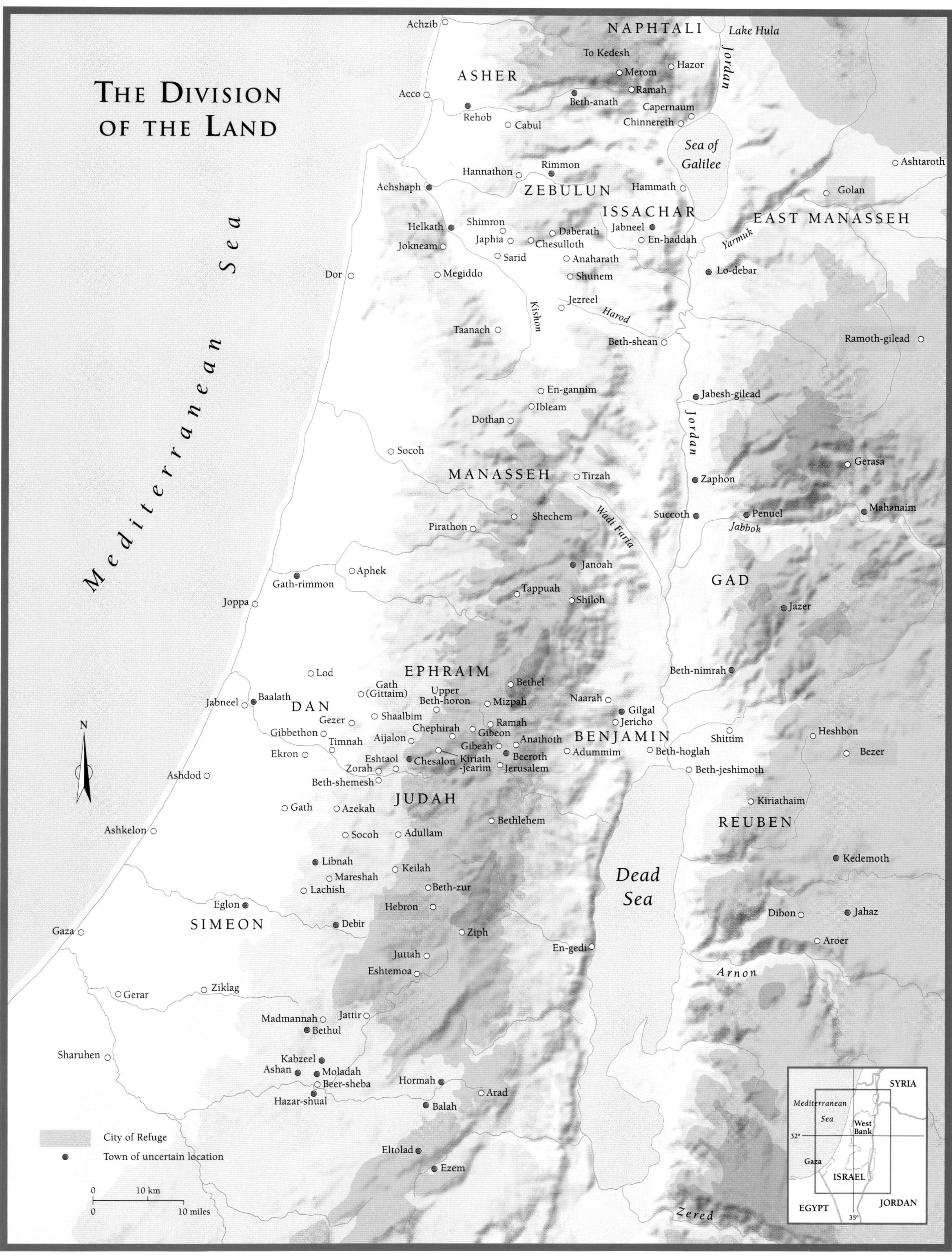
THE DIVISION OF THE LAND
Mediterranean Sea
NAPHTALI
ASHER
ZEBULUN
ISSACHAR
EAST MANASSEH
MANASSEH
EPHRAIM
DAN
BENJAMIN
JUDAH
SIMEON
GAD
REUBEN
Lake Hula
Sea of Galilee
Dead Sea
Jordan
Yarmuk
Kishon
Harod
Wadi Faria
Jabbok
Arnon
Zered
Achzib
Acco
To Kedesh
Merom
Hazor
Ramah
Beth-anath
Capernaum
Chinnereth
Rehob
Cabul
Hannathon
Rimmon
Achshaph
Hammath
Ashtaroth
Golan
Helkath
Shimron
Japhia
Daberath
Chesulloth
Jabneel
En-haddah
Jokneam
Sarid
Anaharath
Dor
Megiddo
Shunem
Lo-debar
Jezreel
Taanach
Beth-shean
Ramoth-gilead
En-gannim
Ibleam
Jabesh-gilead
Dothan
Socoh
Tirzah
Gerasa
Zaphon
Shechem
Succoth
Penuel
Mahanaim
Pirathon
Janoah
Aphek
Gath-rimmon
Tappuah
Shiloh
Joppa
Jazer
Lod
Bethel
Beth-nimrah
Gath (Gittaim)
Upper Beth-horon
Mizpah
Naarah
Jabneel
Baalath
Gilgal
Jericho
Shaalbim
Gezer
Chephirah
Gibeon
Ramah
Shittim
Heshbon
Gibbethon
Aijalon
Timnah
Gibeah
Anathoth
Ekron
Eshtaol
Chesalon
Kiriath-jearim
Beeroth
Adummim
Beth-hoglah
Bezer
Ashdod
Zorah
Jerusalem
Beth-jeshimoth
Beth-shemesh
Kiriathaim
Gath
Azekah
Bethlehem
Ashkelon
Socoh
Adullam
Libnah
Keilah
Kedemoth
Mareshah
Lachish
Beth-zur
Eglon
Hebron
Dibon
Jahaz
Gaza
Debir
Ziph
Aroer
En-gedi
Juttah
Eshtemoa
Gerar
Ziklag
Madmannah
Jattir
Bethul
Sharuhen
Kabzeel
Ashan
Moladah
Beer-sheba
Hormah
Hazar-shual
Arad
Balah
Eltolad
Ezem
City of Refuge
Town of uncertain location
N
0 10 km
0 10 miles
SYRIA
Mediterranean Sea
West Bank
32°
Gaza
ISRAEL
EGYPT
JORDAN
35°

ABOVE: THIS NINETEENTH-CENTURY C.E. ENGRAVING BY A. KRAUSSE SHOWS HEBRON—ONE OF SIX PLACES DESIGNATED AS A CITY OF REFUGE.

RIGHT: *DEATH OF JOSHUA* FROM A MEDIEVAL BIBLE. JOSHUA, THE FAITHFUL AND BRAVE LEADER OF THE ISRAELITES, DIES AT SHECHEM AND IS BURIED AT TIMNATH-SERAH.

BELOW: THE BLESSING MOUNT AT SHECHEM. BEFORE HIS DEATH, JOSHUA GATHERED THE ISRAELITES AT SHECHEM AND REMINDED THEM OF THEIR COVENANT WITH GOD.

during this early period, other areas were heavily occupied. In particular, this was the case in the central hill country. The region around Shechem was given to Manasseh, who nevertheless soon found themselves out of space and in need of additional room. They achieved this by clearing more forest land in their territory (17:14–18). The names of towns in Manasseh's allotment are special because they coincide with the names of early descendants of Manasseh, including the names of the daughters of Zelophehad who were given territory (17:3–6). These same town names appear later on administrative ostraca from the Northern Kingdom capital at Samaria and date to the eighth century B.C.E.

CITIES OF REFUGE

Joshua 20:1–9 recalls the need for cities of refuge to which those who accidentally killed someone might flee and thereby escape blood vengeance from the victim's family. Already envisioned in Exodus 21:13, it was defined in Numbers 35:9–14 as three cities on each side of the Jordan River. Here the towns are identified as strategically placed across the whole land west (Kedesh, Shechem, and Hebron) and east (Bezer, Ramoth-gilead, and Golan) of the Jordan. The same is true of the 48 Levitical cities identified in Joshua 21. These are spaced evenly across the allotments and are given to the various families of Levites who otherwise had no allotment in the Promised Land. Described by some as centers for the teaching of God's Torah or instruction, this would certainly accord with the responsibilities of the priests (Leviticus 10:10–11) and presumably their assistants, the Levites.

Both the cities of refuge and the Levitical cities appear at the end of the allotments for a reason. Although God has given the entire land to Israel, he requests that they return some of it for his purposes. This is similar to the Sabbath and the offerings of the first fruits and first born. In all of these God blesses Israel but expects them to give something back in return, as a token of their confession and acknowledgment that he has given them the blessing.

THE DEATH OF JOSHUA

Joshua's final message to Israel, the covenant that he makes with them, and his death and burial are recorded in Joshua 23–24. In his message, the great leader of Israel emphasizes the importance of remaining loyal to Israel's God alone and of worshipping no other gods. This is especially poignant in Joshua 24:1–28, where at Shechem he

LEFT: ARCHAEOLOGICAL DISCOVERIES ARE HELPING HISTORIANS PIECE TOGETHER THE HISTORY OF BIBLICAL TIMES. JERUSALEM CONTINUES TO PROVIDE A WEALTH OF DISCOVERIES, SUCH AS THE BURNT HOUSE, C. C.E. 70.

rehearses the story of how God led his people from the time of Abraham onward. His warning to the people that they will not be faithful does more than anticipate the failures of the book of Judges. In Joshua 24:23, their leader commands Israel to throw away their foreign gods. Just as their ancestor Jacob, when he came into the Promised Land, commanded his family to get rid of their images and then buried them under the oak tree at Shechem (Genesis 35:2–4), Joshua now commands the same thing to Israel. However, the people respond only by promising to serve God. They do not turn over their images and so they never truly put this behind them. Joshua's death and that of the elders with him mark the end of that faithful generation and the beginning of the problems of the period of the Judges (Joshua 24:29–31; Judges 2:6–13).

ANALYZING THE SETTLEMENT OF CANAAN, INCORPORATING RECENT IRON AGE I ARCHAEOLOGICAL SURVEYS

From 1968 and for decades after that, Israeli archaeologists undertook an intensive survey of the land of Israel, especially of the central hill country where the tribes of Ephraim and Manasseh were given allotments. The science of archaeology, as it has developed in the Middle East, allows experts to identify as centers of habitation places where pottery has worked its way to the surface. Even if these areas were small hamlets occupied for only a generation, it is possible to identify occupation there. Further, because the shapes of pottery change from generation to generation, and because everyone used ceramic vessels in the Ancient Near East, it is possible to examine collections of shards and to determine during which periods the site was settled. Thus, without ever excavating a single shovel of dirt, it is possible for surveys to plot where population centers existed and when they existed throughout the entire region.

Archaeology had long recognized the existence of major centers in the hill country at places such as Shechem, Shiloh, Bethel, and Jerusalem. However, no one had previously undertaken the extensive survey work necessary to obtain an appreciation of the village life, where so many people lived. The results of this survey work began to be published in the 1980s and revealed many surprises, especially for the time of Israel's emergence in the land. It seems that the central hill country region was sparsely settled during the period from 1550–1200 B.C.E. Only a few major city centers, such as those already named, were to be found. However, during the years around 1200 B.C.E. there was a sudden explosion in the settlements of the hill country. In place of a few major urban centers, there appeared perhaps 600–700 identified village sites throughout the region. These were largely unfortified sites in the highlands, exactly where Joshua and early Israel appear to be settling initially (Joshua 17:14–18; 19:49–51). They are concentrated around Shechem, where Joshua and Israel make their earliest covenants with God (8:30–35; 24:1–28). Some of these villages have now been excavated. Their presence, from the Jezreel Valley in the north to the area around Jerusalem in the south, attests to a simple life where all the structures are about the same size. There is no king or special leader. There are no large temples and few small centers for any such worship.

It is true that some of these settlements could be identified with the Hivites, Jebusites, Hittites, Perizzites, and other groups that are described in these regions (Joshua 3:10; 9:1; 11:3; 12:8; 24:11). Many of these groups have associations with people groups to the north of Canaan, and it is possible that they migrated into the region at this time. However, it is surely significant that the earliest extrabiblical mention of Israel, that of Pharaoh Merneptah's victory stele, dates from 1206 B.C.E. and seems to place Israel exactly in this region. It is certainly no accident that many of the biblical stories of early Israel in Judges, Ruth, and 1 Samuel portray a people living in villages and in this central hill region. Their lifestyle does not include kings as is true of the nation in the later monarchy. There are no large palaces or temples, only the portable Tabernacle. The archaeological picture of these village settlements matches that of the biblical texts. Recently, it has been noted that many of these villages were abandoned after being used for only a generation or two. Where did the people go?

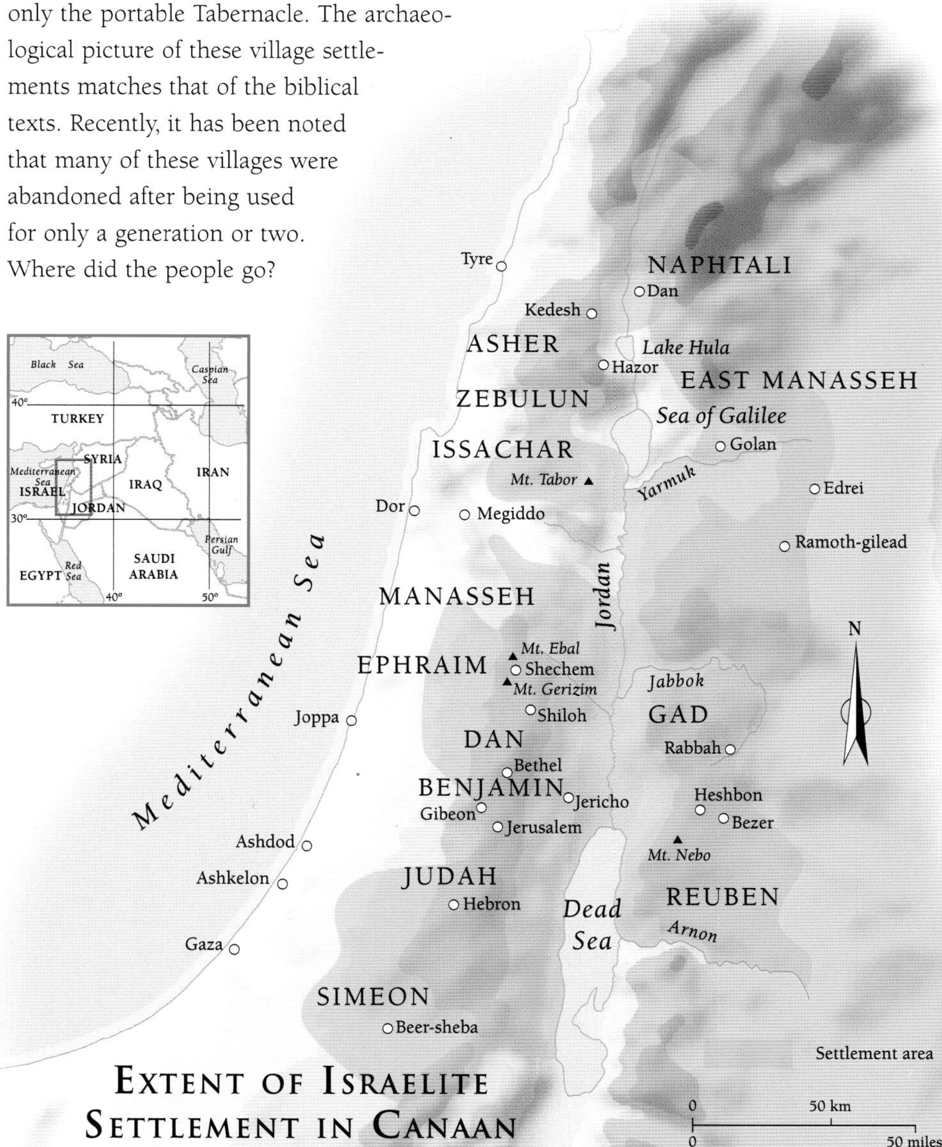

EXTENT OF ISRAELITE SETTLEMENT IN CANAAN

RIGHT: STONE JAR, UGARIT. THE ANCIENT CITY OF UGARIT FLOURISHED FOR MANY CENTURIES, AND WAS AT ITS HEIGHT DURING THE FIFTEENTH AND FOURTEENTH CENTURIES B.C.E.

Could it be that this reflects the progressive movement of Israel into their tribal allotments as the people became more established and secure in the land?

THE MOVEMENT OF THE PHILISTINES FROM THE NORTHWEST OF THE MEDITERRANEAN WORLD, AND HOW THEY GOT TO CANAAN

The Philistines were not indigenous to Palestine, although they gave their name to the land. They came from another place. Amos 9:7 identifies their origins with Caphtor—modern Crete. Indeed, it would appear that these people were originally from the Aegean world of the thirteenth and early twelfth centuries B.C.E. This was the age of the Homeric wars against Troy, perhaps part of conflicts over trade that the Mycenaean warriors and pirates who roamed the Aegean were attempting to control. Some have noted a significant decrease in annual moisture throughout the region around 1200 B.C.E. This itself would have been enough to cause a drought, famine, and migrations. What is certain is that around 1180 B.C.E., Rameses III, Egypt's pharaoh, finds himself battling what he calls "Sea Peoples" who are seeking to encroach on his domain. The fact that this is the same time that the great Hittite empire disappears from the map and that major cities such as Ugarit on the Mediterranean coast of Syria cease to exist, suggests that the pharaoh was locked in a life and death struggle. His reliefs from Medinet Habu in Egypt portray the Sea People warriors with their feathered headdress. More important, however, is the presence of women, children, and ox-drawn carts. This suggests a migration rather than simply an army. The pharaoh's inscriptions designate these people in the consonantal (vowelless) Egyptian hieroglyphs as, among others, *shrdn*, *skl*, and *plst*. It is the latter, the *plst*, whom scholars identify with the Philistines. It seems that these groups traveled both across the seas and overland, as suggested by the reliefs. Overland, they would have passed along modern southern Turkey and followed the coast south toward Egypt. Traveling on the seas,

LEFT: RAMESES III IN BATTLE DRESS, EGYPTIAN WALL PAINTING, TWENTIETH DYNASTY. EGYPTIAN RECORDS FROM THE TIME OF RAMESES III DETAIL CONFLICT WITH THE SEA PEOPLES.

BELOW: *ANCIENT ASHDOD* BY DAVID ROBERTS. THIS ATMOSPHERIC ARTWORK DEPICTS THE TOWN OF ASHDOD, WHICH WAS A PHILISTINE STRONGHOLD.

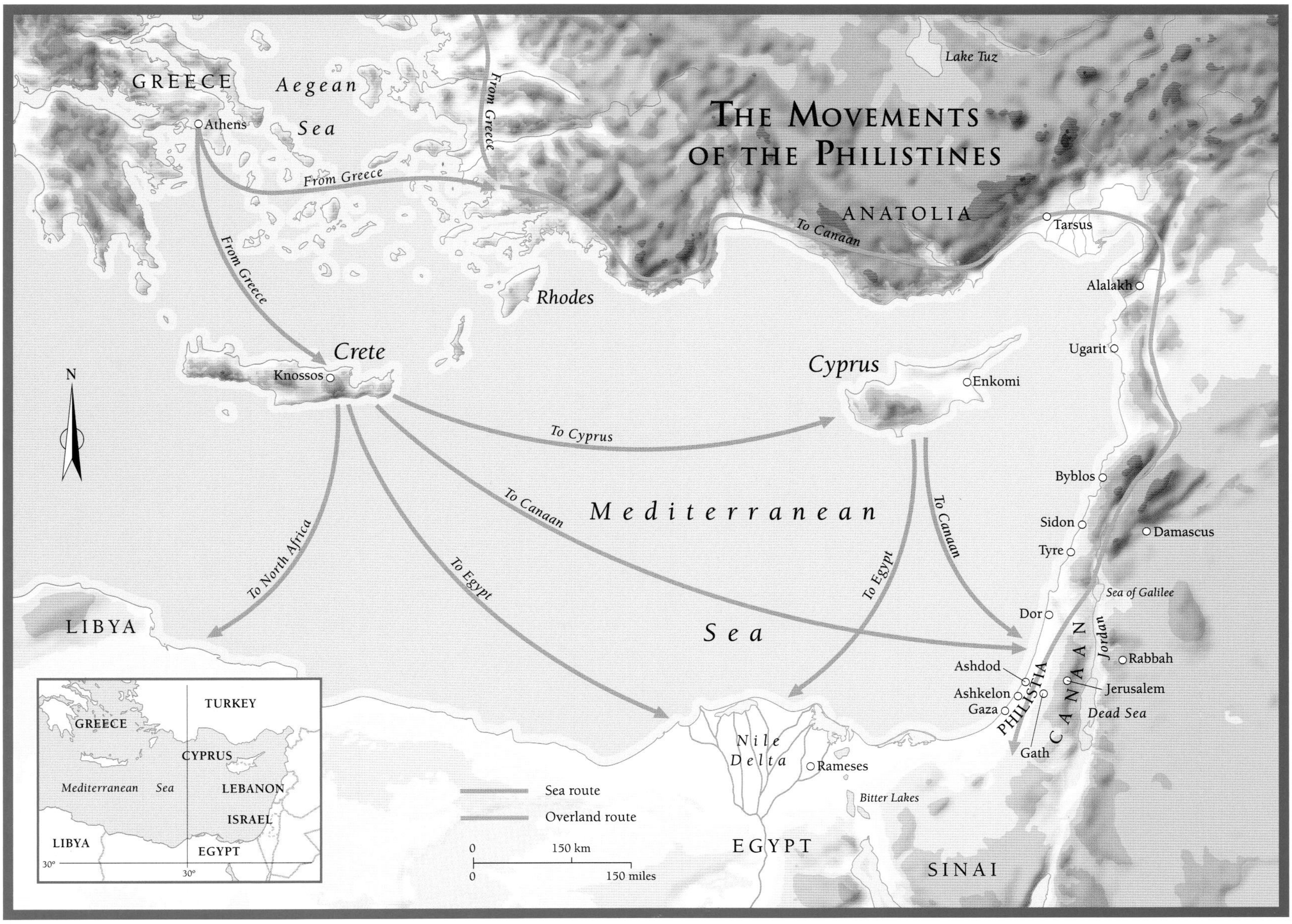

The Movements of the Philistines

GREECE
Athens
Aegean Sea
From Greece
From Greece
From Greece
Lake Tuz
ANATOLIA
To Canaan
Tarsus
Alalakh
Ugarit
Rhodes
Crete
Knossos
Cyprus
Enkomi
To Cyprus
To Canaan
To North Africa
To Egypt
To Egypt
To Canaan
Mediterranean Sea
Byblos
Sidon
Tyre
Damascus
Sea of Galilee
Dor
Jordan
CANAAN
Rabbah
Ashdod
Ashkelon
Gaza
PHILISTIA
Jerusalem
Dead Sea
Gath
LIBYA
Nile Delta
Rameses
Bitter Lakes
EGYPT
SINAI
N
Sea route
Overland route
0 150 km
0 150 miles
TURKEY
GREECE
CYPRUS
Mediterranean Sea
LEBANON
ISRAEL
LIBYA
EGYPT
30°
30°

LEFT: ARCHAEOLOGICAL EXCAVATIONS AT TEL QASILE (NEAR MODERN-DAY TEL AVIV) HAVE REVEALED PHILISTINE STRUCTURES AND AN INSIGHT INTO PHILISTINE CULTURE.

they could have followed a similar route. These Sea Peoples were beaten back by the Egyptians. They settled along the Mediterranean coast of Palestine.

The Philistines appear to have occupied the southwestern coast, where they were first encountered by the Israelites. The five rulers of the Philistines occupied five cities in that region: Ashkelon, Ekron, Ashdod, Gaza, and Gath. They gradually became allies of the Egyptians and seem to have entered their service as mercenaries. Near modern Tel Aviv, the site of Tel Qasile reveals a Philistine center. Unlike the houses of the Israelites, Canaanites, and other Semitic peoples, the houses here have hearths in the center of the room—similar to early Greek architecture. Philistine pottery is also similar to early Greek or Mycenaean pottery. Many biblical customs, such as the fighting of champions like David and Goliath, have parallels in Homeric times, as with Hector and Achilles, but not elsewhere in the Ancient Near East. Linguistically, the Philistine word for leader is preserved in the Bible as *seren*. This has been compared to the Greek *tyrannos*, from which we derive the modern word, tyrant. However, in early Greek it referred merely to the ruler of a city or state. The Philistines would eventually assimilate into their surrounding Semitic culture and come to use a language and script similar to Hebrew. Nevertheless, the Philistines would continue as a distinctive presence in the region for many centuries.

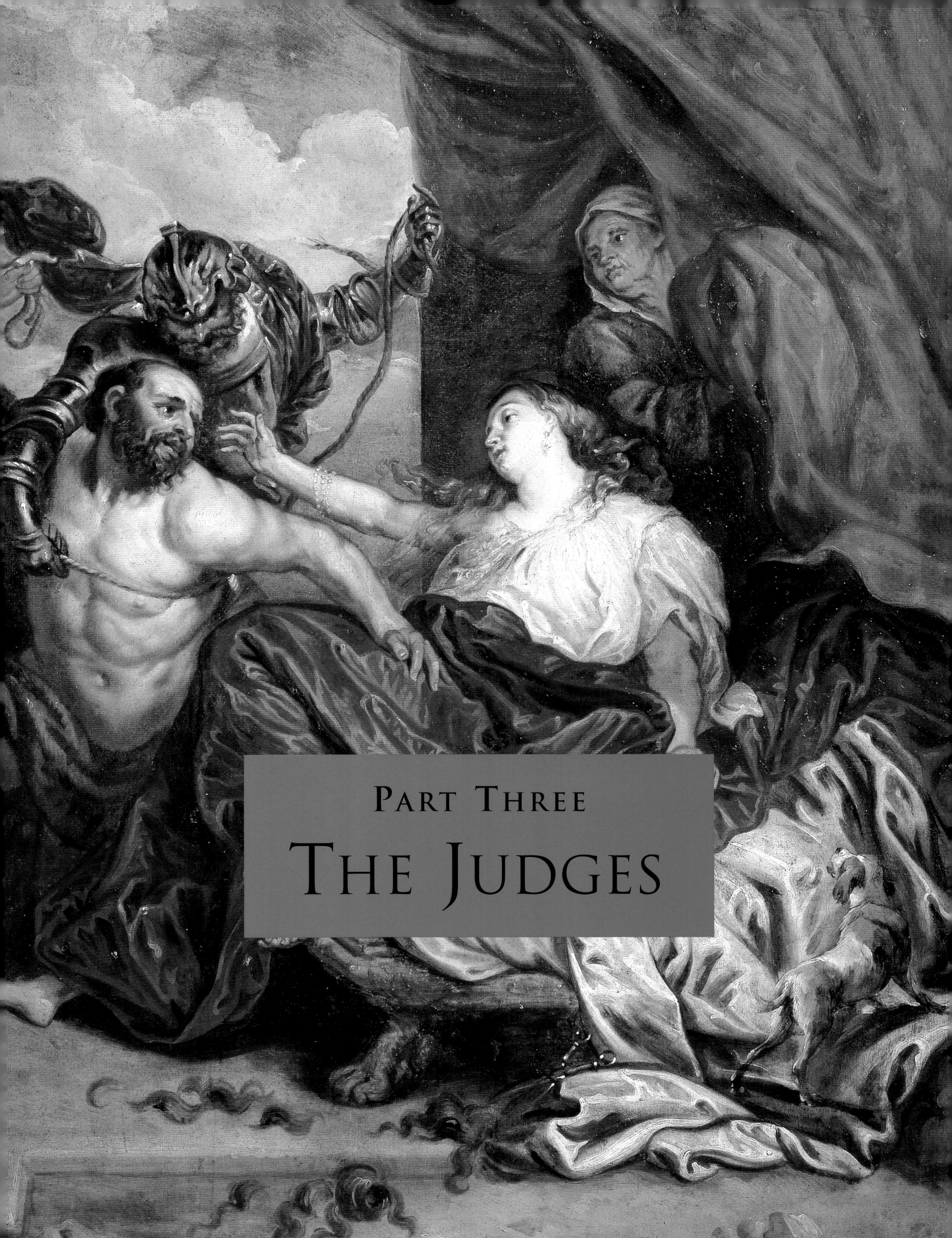

Part Three
The Judges

CLAIMING THE PROMISED LAND

THEN THE LORD RAISED UP JUDGES, WHO DELIVERED THEM JUDGES 2:16

The era of the Judges began in about 1190 B.C.E., when the Israelites started to occupy their Promised Land, and ended in about 1051 B.C.E., when Saul became the first king of Israel. The book of Judges and the opening chapters of 1 Samuel portray this as a turbulent time, shot through with bloodthirsty battles and acts of revolting barbarity: Judges 4 relates how the Kenite woman Jael enticed the Gentile Sisera into her tent and murdered him by driving a tent peg through his temples into the ground.

There are two basic reasons for waging war, and they have not changed in the thousands of years since the time of the Judges. Practically speaking, the motivation is one of economic imperative—the struggle for the control of limited resources. Ideologically, the driving force is a belief system, which is not necessarily religious in nature: wars are still fought in the name of racial supremacy, of the classless society, and of the democratic ideal.

A JEALOUS GOD

For the early Israelites, the ideological reason for taking up arms against the cities and settlements of Canaan was their belief in Yahweh, the one true God—or rather, that was their ostensible reason. The Israelites were frequently disobedient and failed to honor the First Commandment: "you shall have no other gods before me" (Exodus 20:3). The chroniclers of Judges repeatedly record the wrath and vengeance of God when his people turn from him to worship false gods: "So the anger of the Lord was kindled against Israel ... and he sold them into the power of their enemies" (Judges 2:14).

In most ways the history of the early Israelites is no different from that of all the peoples of antiquity. Small wars, minor skirmishes, and cruel murders were all part of the natural order in the struggle to acquire both territory and economic security. It is a struggle that continues in some parts of the world to this day.

But the Israelites were unique in one important respect: theirs was a monotheistic religion. The belief systems of neighboring civilizations, such as Egypt and Assyria, were based on hierarchies of major and minor deities who personified natural forces such as love and war, thunder and fire. They were gods made in the image of humankind, and humans were their playthings. But the Lord God of Israel created humans as beings with free will who would worship God voluntarily or not at all.

God may have been swift to visit retribution on the Israelites when they forsook him, but he was just as swift to forgive them and bring them back into his fold. During the occupation of Canaan, a number of charismatic personalities called "judges" arose under God's guidance. The judges were not the legal luminaries of today but rather militant leaders who spearheaded attacks on the worshippers of false gods, collectively called Baalim, and guided the Children of Israel back to their one true God.

EYELESS IN GAZA

In the early eleventh century B.C.E., disaster struck: Philistia, a small but ambitious nation in the southwestern quadrant of Canaan, beside the Mediterranean Sea, captured the Ark of the Covenant. God intimidated the Philistines into returning the Ark with a heavy tribute of gold, but war between the two nations con-tinued until the legendary judge Samson, though betrayed, blinded, and imprisoned, pulled down the temple of Dagon in Gaza, killing himself and 3,000 Philistines.

The biblical account of the time of the judges is a potent blend of oral history and theology, interlaced with poetic writing of a high order. When considered as history, it relates how a loosely linked group of nomadic tribes took possession of their God-given homeland and moved gradually toward nationhood. Considered as theology, the book affirms the existence of a God who is faithful and just to his chosen people. The concept of a righteous judge—strong and patient—endured and became one of the attributes of God himself: "The Lord judges the peoples; judge me, O Lord, according to my righteousness" (Psalm 7:8).

BELOW: THIS FIFTH-CENTURY MOSAIC DEPICTION OF THE ARK EMPLOYS CHERUBIM AS LATTER-DAY CHRISTIAN ANGELS. IT NOW RESIDES IN THE ORATORY OF THEODULPHUS IN FRANCE.

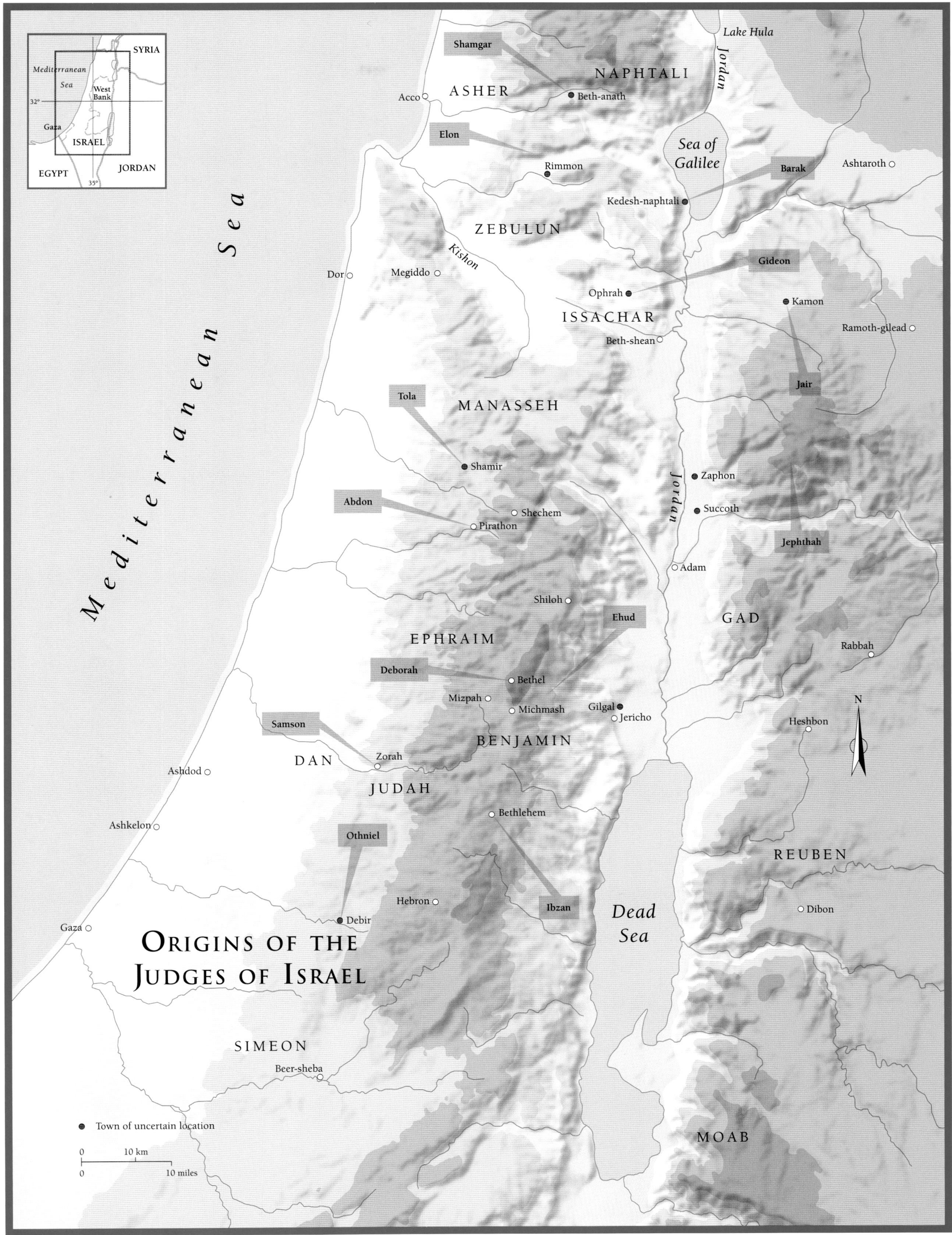

Origins of the Judges of Israel
SYRIA
Mediterranean Sea
West Bank
32°
Gaza
ISRAEL
EGYPT
JORDAN
35°
Mediterranean Sea
Lake Hula
Jordan
Shamgar
NAPHTALI
ASHER
Acco
Beth-anath
Elon
Sea of Galilee
Rimmon
Barak
Ashtaroth
Kedesh-naphtali
ZEBULUN
Kishon
Gideon
Dor
Megiddo
Ophrah
Kamon
ISSACHAR
Beth-shean
Ramoth-gilead
Jair
Tola
MANASSEH
Shamir
Zaphon
Jordan
Abdon
Shechem
Succoth
Pirathon
Jephthah
Adam
Shiloh
Ehud
GAD
EPHRAIM
Rabbah
Deborah
Bethel
Mizpah
Michmash
Gilgal
Jericho
N
Samson
Heshbon
BENJAMIN
Zorah
DAN
Ashdod
JUDAH
Bethlehem
Ashkelon
Othniel
REUBEN
Hebron
Ibzan
Dead Sea
Dibon
Debir
Gaza
SIMEON
Beer-sheba
Town of uncertain location
0 10 km
0 10 miles
MOAB

THE FIRST JUDGES

ANOTHER GENERATION GREW UP ... WHO DID NOT KNOW THE LORD JUDGES 2:10

BELOW: THIS ILLUSTRATION FROM THE *BIBLE RALISEE*, C. C.E. 1235–45, TELLS THE STORY OF THE BOOK OF JUDGES, FROM THE CHILDREN OF ISRAEL FORSAKING GOD FOR THE DEVIL, TO DEBORAH AND BARAK FIGHTING SISERA.

Can a real estate listing be considered as inspiring, spiritual literature? Judges 1 combines two vital Old Testament themes: land and family. The land embodies the promise and will of God for Israel. The tribes, as coalitions of clans made up of extended families, flesh out the promise God made to Abraham. The story of the tribes of Israel gaining possession of their allotted territories demonstrates the fulfillment of God's historic purpose for Israel. Yet, sadly, we could entitle this chapter, "How the West Was Lost." The initial successes of the Israelites in gaining their respective territories following Joshua's death spiral down through decreasing effectiveness and, ultimately, defeat.

THE TRIBES OF JUDAH AND SIMEON

At the beginning, success is the keynote. The question of "Who will go up first?" finds triumphant answer with "Judah," the tribe into whose hands God has given the enemy. Judah shows a cooperating, unifying spirit, calling on Simeon, from within Judah's territory, to join the battle. Judah keeps its promise to repay Simeon's loyalty, demonstrating true solidarity.

Judah's campaign begins in the center of the country. Bezek probably lay between Jerusalem and Shechem (not to be confused with the Bezek of 1 Samuel 11:8), which is north of Judah's territory. Adoni-bezek, the defeated king, confesses the justice of the Judeans' treatment of him before his death. The Judeans' burning of Jerusalem falls short of a full conquest of the city, since a few verses later it still lies in Jebusite hands. From the center of the land the Judeans turn south, capturing cities all the way to Gaza. Apparently they then turn northward, since the only other references to "the plain" in which the enemy's chariots of iron (actually iron axles) provide a legitimate explanation for failing at complete conquest, is the northern Valley of Jezreel. This three-part campaign into the center, south, and north of the land mirrors the three phases of Joshua's campaign, suggesting Judah duplicates Joshua's achievement. The narrative of the Judean campaign also refers to Moses and to the other hero of the conquest generation, Caleb. The overall effect is to present the southern coalition, led by Judah, as fulfilling the divine promise of victory given in Judges 1:2, even extending beyond Judah's boundaries.

OTHNIEL CONQUERS KIRIATH-SEPHER

Few biblical heroes cut so sharp a figure in so few words as Caleb. As an old man, Caleb offers his daughter, Achsah, as wife to the hero who can conquer the city of Kiriath-sepher. Judges 1 essentially reproduces the story of Othniel, who takes the city, verbatim from Joshua, describing Othniel as the "son of Kenaz, Caleb's younger brother." In some translations, however, Judges adds the phrase, "the young one of him," to clarify that Othniel is Caleb's young nephew, and not his youngest brother. Since only Joshua and Caleb survived from the conquest generation, Othniel had to fall into the next generation. This family tie also identifies Othniel with "the elders who outlived Joshua" (Judges 2:7), who were noted for their faithfulness to the Lord, and whose death triggered Israel's later abandonment of faith. Othniel bridges the righteousness of the Joshua-Caleb era and the elders whose death removed the check against this loss of faith.

THE ANGEL AT BOCHIM

After the southern victories the narrative of Judges 1 moves north geographically, but things "go south" militarily. The sequence of the tribes reproduces the order of the tribal allotments in Joshua 13–22, moving from south to north. At the same time, signs of declining effectiveness appear: the "house of Jacob" does not destroy the Canaanite culture of Bethel, but simply relocates it; Manasseh fails to drive out the enemy from the strategic cities of the Valley of Jezreel; Ephraim and Zebulun tolerate Canaanite enclaves. Then the tables are turned. Asher and Naphtali must live among the Canaanites, who remain dominant. Lastly, the Danites, whose inheritance initially fell in the south, are expelled from their territory by the Amorites, with no word about where they ended up until Judges 18. The defeat of the Danites anticipates the abortive efforts of Samson in Judges 13–16, all of which occur in the original, southern, territory of Dan. But the reader of Samson's story already knows the effort will fail. Dan will lose its territory, and the story will take a tragic turn.

The declining fortunes of the tribes in the latter part of Judges 1 reach rock bottom in Judges 2. Throughout Judges 1, the Hebrew term "go up" occurs in the military sense of "move out against." The same sense is hard to resist in Judges 2:1 as the "angel of the Lord went up" from the original base camp of Joshua's conquest, in Gilgal. The location of Bochim remains uncertain, since it seems to be a nickname coined from the Israelites' response to the angel's reproof. Several scholars have suggested Bethel as the location, but the object of the assault this time is Israel. The angel presents a most scouring attack on the tribes, asserting the Lord's covenant and criticizing them for their faithlessness. Thus the military failures of Judges 1 here emerge clearly as spiritual failure. The story is off to a bad start.

KIRIATH-SEPHER

What made Kiriath-sepher so important to Caleb? The name means "City of the Document," and the document was probably a victory stele such as the one of Narim-Sin (right), dated *c.* 2230 B.C.E. Victory steles were inscribed with the name of a conquering king and his patron god, claiming the territory. Such a monument would make the town a target of Israelite hostility since God had commanded the removal of the names of pagan kings and their gods—associated with monuments—from the land in order to assert his ownership and rule (Deuteronomy 7:24, 12:3). The capture of this city with its monument thus destroyed a rival claim of dominion over the land.

OTHNIEL DELIVERS ISRAEL

Othniel's story, and those to follow, make little sense apart from the summary given in Judges 2 and some of Judges 3. The writer repeats almost verbatim Joshua's death and burial from Joshua 24, stressing how Israel faithfully served the Lord not only during Joshua's lifetime but throughout the lifetimes of the elders who survived him—that is, the Israelites born in the wilderness who fought the battles of conquest. This generation was replaced by one that failed to recognize and respond to the Lord, doing instead "what was evil in the sight of the Lord" (Judges 2:11), worshipping the gods of Canaan. This loss of faith by the new generation aroused divine wrath, resulting in oppression by Israel's neighbors.

BELOW: TEMPORARILY TAKEN BY JUDAH IN JUDGES 1, GAZA WAS TO BECOME A PLACE OF STRATEGIC IMPORTANCE. THIS ENGRAVING OF GAZA BY LOUIS HAGHE AND DAVID ROBERTS DATES TO C.E. 1839.

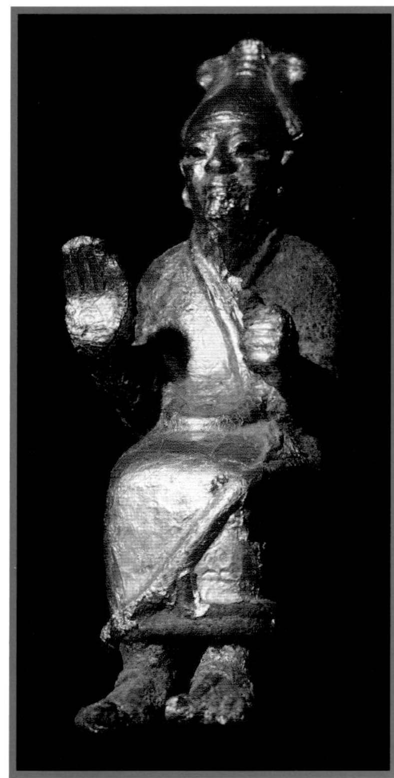

RIGHT: THE FIRST CANAANITE GOD, EL, IS REPRESENTED AS AN AGEING MAN. HE ALSO WORE THE HORNS OF A BULL. THIS PHOENICIAN STATUETTE FROM THE THIRTEENTH CENTURY B.C.E. SHOWS EL SEATED ON HIS THRONE.

This summary mentions neither Israel's cry nor repentance, but moves directly to a description of the judges who arose to deliver Israel, not in response to repentance, but as an expression of divine pity. The real pity, though, was Israel's refusal to heed the judges, continuing in their stubborn rebellion. Thus the judges fail to reverse Israel's loss of faith, and so the Lord's wrath flares anew, but with much graver consequences: the conquest is cancelled. We learn that the nations left behind by Joshua served as a test—one that Israel has failed. Still, a possibility of redemption remains. The catalog of nations that remained in the land notes their function of educating the Israelites in obedience, providing them with the same chance of seeing first-hand the mighty working of God that their forebears knew. Nevertheless, this prolog paints a grim picture of Israel living among the Canaanites, losing their social identity through intermarriage, and ultimately serving the Canaanite gods.

The picture of Israel in Canaan seen in Judges 1–3 fits the archaeological data. The Merneptah inscription, dated to about 1206 B.C.E., denotes "Israel" not as a territory but only as a people group in Palestine, present but by no means dominant. Likewise, while signs of fierce destruction around 1200 B.C.E. exist for cities like Hazor, the settlements and highland villages following those destructions present a much simpler culture than the urban centers. Far from consolidating the initial foothold gained by Joshua, the Israelites start to lose their grip on the land.

Being the first, Othniel establishes a standard for evaluating subsequent judges. A clear sign of Othniel's status as the quintessential judge rises from the name of his adversary, King Cushan-rishathaim. Cushan means "the Great Ethiopian" but rishathaim means "Double Wickedness." In addition, the king's homeland, "Aram-naharaim," is Mesopotamia—a strange home indeed for the Great Ethiopian of Double Wickedness! This name, like so many found in Judges, is an alias typical of chaotic frontier situations such as those that existed in the American West in the eighteenth and nineteenth centuries. Suffice to say, Othniel goes up against the great oppressor and defeats him. Through his deliverance of Israel, Othniel establishes his place as the exemplar judge.

BELOW: MESOPOTAMIA WAS THE HOME OF THE SYRO-MESOPOTAMIAN KING, CUSHAN-RISHATHAIM. HIS OPPRESSION OF ISRAEL LASTED FOR EIGHT YEARS.

EHUD

Ehud at first poses a complete contrast with Othniel. Nowhere said to be anointed by the Spirit, Ehud acts as a ruthless and expert assassin. Yet he receives high accolades from the author of Judges, and his actions bring about 80 years of peace.

The oppressor, Eglon the Moabite, "a very fat man" (Judges 3:17), reoccupies Jericho, the scene of Joshua's most celebrated triumph; this triumph seems undone by the Moabite presence. Ehud, who is to prove Eglon's undoing, possesses certain unique abilities. The text identifies him as "the Benjaminite, a left-handed man" (Judges 3:15). But "left-handed" is a translation of the Hebrew for "bound on his right hand." The Old Testament notes that the tribe of Benjamin had a warrior class of archers and slingers who were ambidextrous (Judges 20, 1 Chronicles 12). Traditionally, the young warrior's right hand was tied until he developed an equal capacity in the left hand. And not only is Ehud ambidextrous, he makes his own sword, at a time when Israel lagged far behind the surrounding nations in metallurgy and sorely lacked weapons (see 1 Samuel 13). That Ehud, in the spirit of heroes of many cultures who customize their weaponry, makes this sword for himself points to his superior abilities.

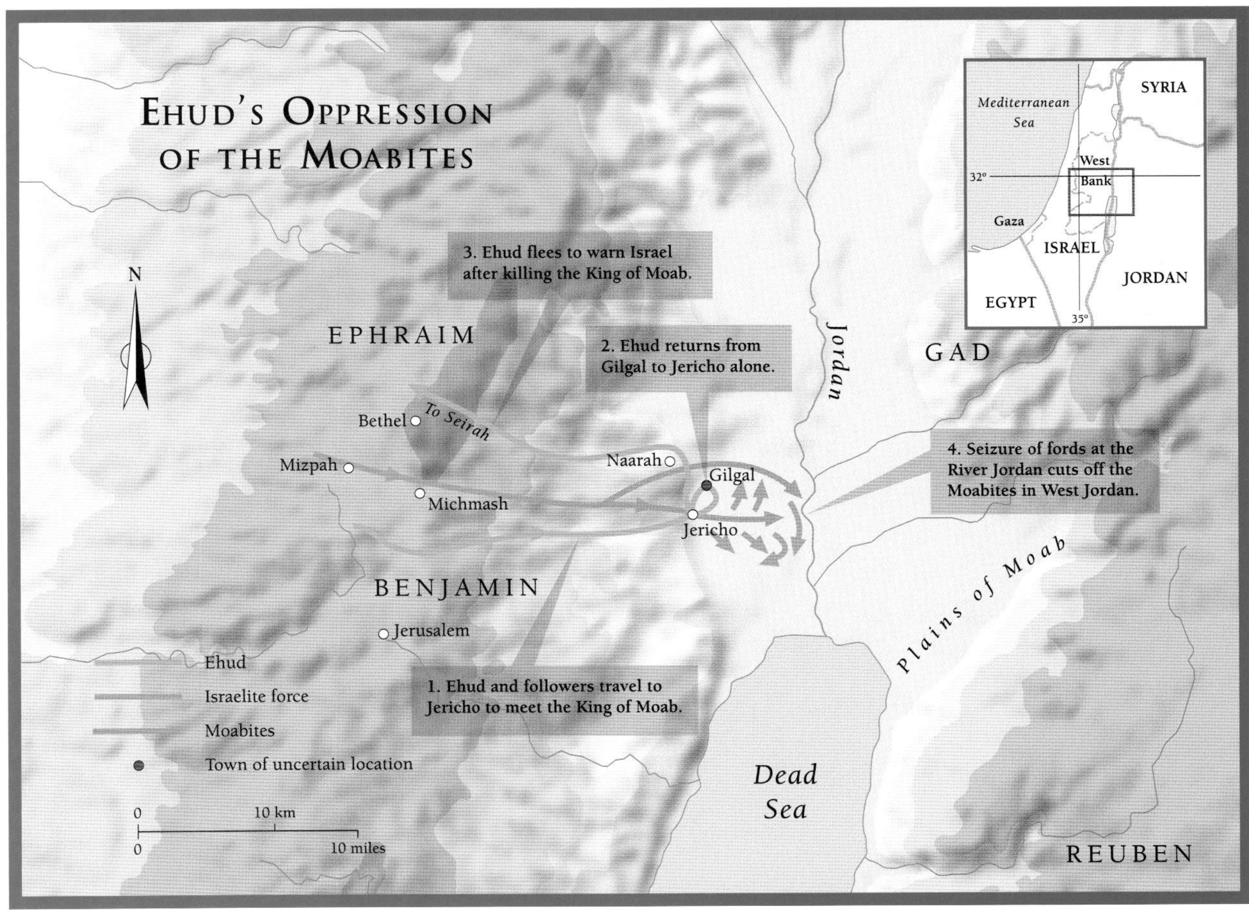

The center of Ehud's story, the assassination of Eglon, makes sense best when seen in the context of the design of ancient palaces. The typical palace of the time was two stories high. On one end both stories were open, creating a high audience chamber. At the other end the stories were enclosed, providing an elevated throne chamber for the king over a maintenance room. To reach the king's throne, one had to ascend a set of steps and pass through a pair of doors. Ehud claims to have a "secret message" for the king, who accordingly dismisses his attendants. At Ehud's announcement of a "message from God," the king stands. Ehud then flashes up the stairs, draws the dagger concealed on his right thigh, and plunges it into the expansive girth of the king. The dagger vanishes into the body of the corpulent monarch, and the "dirt" of his bowels spills on the floor.

Closing and locking the doors, Ehud faces a conundrum. His exit must appear to be normal to the guards or he cannot escape to execute the second stage of his plan, namely the rallying of Benjamin to fight the Moabites. A palace throne chamber often had a toilet, a simple hole opening down into the maintenance room below, with a removable stone seat. In Hebrew, the word for "toilet" sounds suspiciously like the term for the "dirt" that comes out of the slain king, suggesting Ehud escaped by removing the toilet seat and jumping down to the maintenance area. He could then exit the palace normally, with the guards assuming all was as it should be as they moved back into the audience chamber. But the guards observe the locked doors, and, after much delay (not wanting to disturb Eglon at his ablutions), open them to discover their humiliated king. Ironically, the name Eglon means "calf," suggesting the image of a fatted and slaughtered calf. Meanwhile, Ehud escapes, rallies his countrymen, and wins a stunning victory over the Moabites.

LEFT: KAALWEG'S EARLY EIGHTEENTH-CENTURY ENGRAVING CONVEYS THE ANGUISH OF THE MOABITES ON FINDING THE BODY OF THEIR KING, EGLON, WHO HAD BEEN TREACHEROUSLY MURDERED BY EHUD.

BELOW: VICTORY OVER THE CANAANITES IS EVIDENT IN THIS JOYOUS SEVENTEENTH-CENTURY PAINTING OF DEBORAH AND BARAK BY FRANCESCO SOLIMENA.

DEBORAH AND BARAK

The story of Deborah in Judges 4 moves northward to the hill country of Ephraim, where Deborah serves as a judge and prophet. She is the only "major" judge who holds a regular office and functions judicially. The Israelites' abandonment of faith at this time leads to a crisis as a Canaanite coalition led by Jabin, king of Hazor, and his commander, Sisera, threatens Israel. Sisera's "nine hundred chariots of iron" (Judges 4:13) matches the reference to the Canaanite chariot force faced by Thutmose III of Egypt two centuries earlier. This threat in Galilee becomes so grave that Deborah, all the way down in Ephraim, feels called to intervene.

Deborah proposes a bold plan to Barak, the commander of Israel's forces: rally forces from the tribes of Naphtali, Asher, Zebulun, Issachar, Ephraim, and Manasseh to Mt. Tabor, which will lure the Canaanite chariotry onto the slight rise in the Valley of Jezreel over which the main highway runs. This good ground for Canaanite chariots is apparent military suicide for Israel, but God has promised to destroy the enemy. The reliance on divine intervention prompts Barak to request Deborah's presence to ensure the battle's timing is right.

The side note, in Judges 4:11, that Heber the Kenite left the other Kenites, who settled in the far south, and camped in the far north, seems a diversion but is vital to the story. Most scholars suggest that the Kenites (a tribe related to the Israelites) were iron-workers. Later we learn that Heber has a covenant with Sisera, the Canaanite commander. Given the technological backwardness of the Israelites, an iron-worker who made a deal with Sisera and his "chariots of iron" committed high treason! (He might also have been the source of

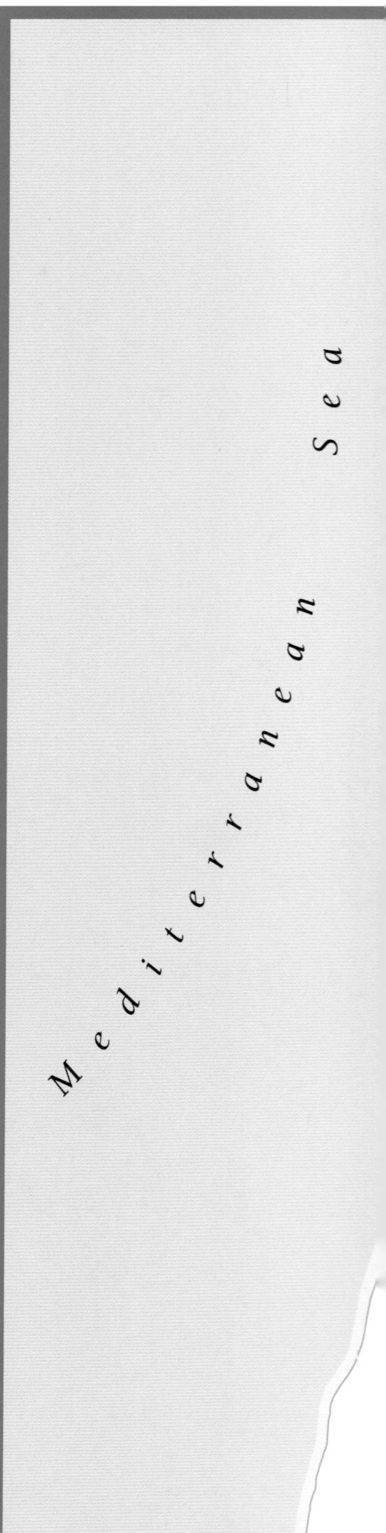

Sisera's tip that the Israelites had mobilized.) We are then told that the Lord threw the Canaanites into a "panic." The Hebrew term used here typically in the Old Testament denotes a divine intervention, often via a thunderstorm or torrent. The Canaanites worshipped Baal, the deity of the thunderstorm, who is often depicted holding a thunderbolt. So the Lord is portrayed crushing Baal's people using Baal's weaponry.

In the poetical celebration of the victory in Judges 5, Deborah extols a creekbed, the Kishon, for its role in the battle. The Valley of Jezreel's red soil becomes a deep, gummy mud when wet. We can imagine the anguish of the Canaanite charioteers as a sudden storm floods the Kishon, turning the battleground into a morass of deep, red mud. The chariot warriors, like tank men of every age, do not take quickly to infantry combat and are slaughtered by the Israelites. Sisera flees on foot straight to the home of his ally, the turncoat Heber. But Heber's wife, Jael, lures Sisera into her tent, gives him creamy curds, and, when he falls asleep, drives a tent peg through his head. Deborah's gleeful celebration of this gruesome act presents a counterpoint to the gloating description of Sisera's mother, unaware her son has met his end.

LEFT: THE CANAANITE CHARIOTS WERE EQUIPPED WITH WHIRLING KNIVES ON THEIR WHEELS. THIS BRONZE CHARIOT, FROM THE TIP OF AN ORNAMENTAL STAFF, DATES FROM AROUND THE FOURTEENTH CENTURY B.C.E.

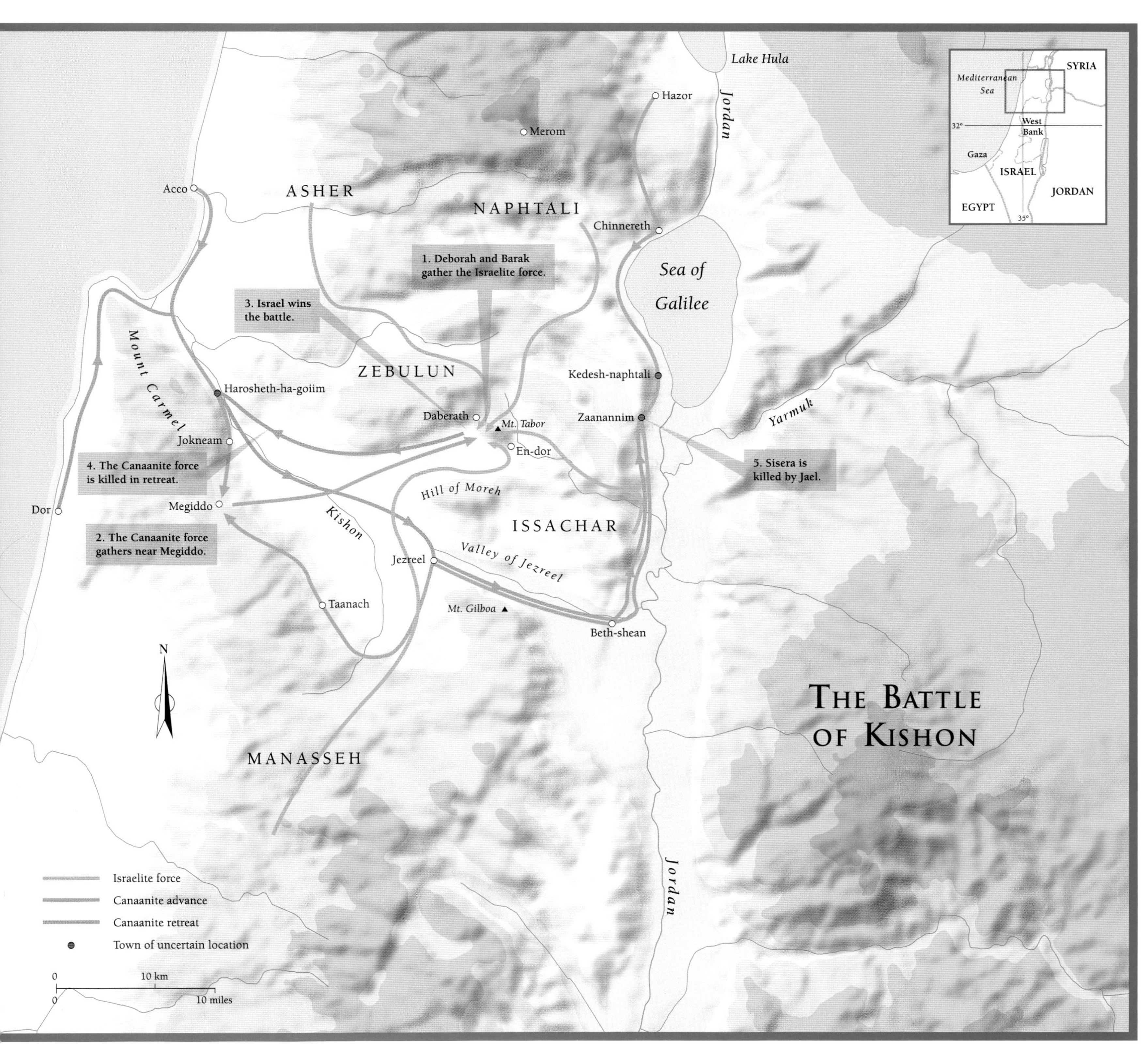

GIDEON

BUT THE SPIRIT OF THE LORD TOOK POSSESSION OF GIDEON; AND HE SOUNDED THE TRUMPET JUDGES 6:34

The repeated pattern of sin and oppression takes a new turn early in Judges 6. The Midianite oppression clearly paralyzes the fragile economy of the Israelite villages in the hills and along the edges of the Valley of Jezreel. The Midianites plunder from Gideon's home region at the southeast end of the Valley of Jezreel all the way to the coast and down to Gaza. In effect, the Midianites control the entire network of roads linking the interior of Israel to the coast and all points south. The text poignantly emphasizes not only the extreme impoverishment caused by the innumerable seasonal plunderers, but highlights a new factor: the camel. Widespread domestication of the camel does not appear in the Ancient Near East until later in the Iron Age, so the use of camels would have been a new and terrifying development, allowing invaders to strike out of the heart of the wilderness, loot their victims, and then retreat back into the wilderness with impunity. Yet the Israelites faced a worse crisis: their cry to the Lord brings not a savior, but a prophet to rebuke their faithlessness. The prophetic invective, "You have not given heed to my voice" (Judges 6:10), casts the story of Gideon into ambiguity.

AN ANGEL APPEARS TO GIDEON

As the book of Judges proceeds, the stories stress increasingly the process by which the heroes prepare for battle. Gideon does not really go into action until the half-way point of the story, which begins with his call. The story opens with a scene of sheer incongruity—Gideon threshing his wheat in a wine press. Threshing required a hard, elevated surface exposed to wind to carry away the chaff. But a wine press was a low, hollowed-out recess, which was hardly a place to thresh wheat. Gideon's fear finds a rebuke in the angelic address of "mighty warrior." The term labels Gideon as a member of the warrior elite, one who should be leading the Israelites against the enemy, and not hiding in a wine press to save his crop. The cynical question from Gideon, "why then has all this happened to us?" (Judges 6:13), ignores the fact of Israel's loss of faith. The angel's reply avoids a debate and simply commissions the hero to come forward and save Israel, promising the divine presence will be with him.

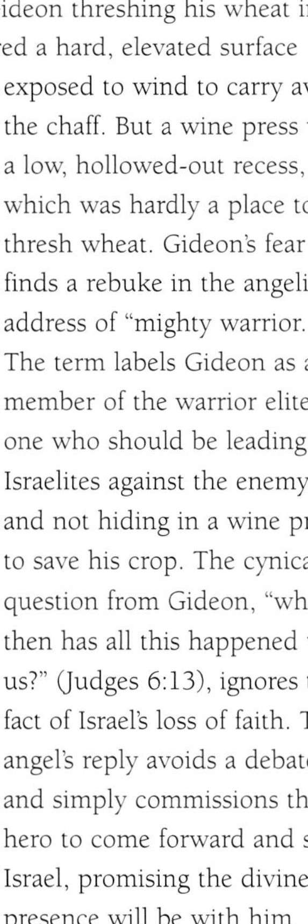

BELOW: IN THIS LITHOGRAPH BY AN UNNAMED FRENCH ARTIST, AN ANGEL SHOWS GIDEON A SACRIFICIAL LAMB, WHICH BURSTS INTO FLAME. IT IS A SIGN THAT HE WILL HAVE HEAVENLY SUPPORT AGAINST THE MIDIANITES.

GIDEON'S OFFERING IS CONSUMED BY FIRE

The story stresses repeatedly the ambiguity and ambivalence that surrounds Gideon. Few heroes witness so many reassuring signs, yet draw so little reassurance from them. Gideon's protest that his family is the least in Manasseh, and that he is the least of his family, does not express humility. In a culture in which one's position in the family structure dictates one's role in life, Gideon is likely to be claiming, in fact, that delivering Israel simply does not fall into his domain of responsibility, which is the equivalent of saying, "Not my job, not my problem!" But the angel insists, so Gideon asks him to wait while he prepares an offering, which the angel then sets ablaze in confirmation of the divine call that Gideon has received. But is he convinced?

GIDEON DESTROYS THE ALTAR TO BAAL

Ironically, when Gideon earlier asked, "why then has all this happened to us?," the answer to his question sat in the middle of his village: in the work of his own father. That Gideon failed to draw reassurance from the angel's incineration of his offering emerges in his response to God's command that Gideon destroy this family shrine to a Canaanite god. Not only would this act publicly repudiate Baal, it would also strike a blow to his family's already fragile economic condition by destroying his father's bull, of which a small villager might only have one or two. The bull was the hope and future of a man's herd. More seriously, Gideon would openly shame his father and thus draw the ire of his townsmen. Not surprisingly, Gideon fears the consequences and performs the deed at night. By doing so, he forfeits the spiritual confrontation and the act looks like mere vandalism. In the ensuing inquiry, it is Gideon's own father who accurately articulates the "message" of the act: if Baal were a real god, he would have defended himself.

THE SIGN OF THE FLEECE

Gideon's ambivalence appears clearly in the fleece affair. Neither a direct appearance by an angel nor the fiery consumption of his offering convinced him of God's presence. Then the spirit of the Lord "took possession of Gideon" (Judges 6:34). Literally, the spirit puts Gideon on like a garment. Even so, he still needs reassurance, which he seeks in the form of a stunt: a fleece that is wet with dew when the ground is dry, and dry when the ground is wet. Ironically, at this point God becomes the one needing reassurance. With an army raised, it might appear that Gideon, in Judges 7, defeats the Midianites by sheer military might. So God thins down the army at the Spring of Harod, within sight of the Hill of Moreh where the battle will transpire. Scholars dispute how the various drinking styles involved indicated readiness for battle, but the most important point is that

all who were afraid or trembling (Hebrew "harod") should leave. We learn that Gideon himself might be afraid. Rather than use another sign, God summons Gideon to a simple act of military intelligence. Gideon overhears a Midianite tell a traumatic dream of being crushed by a giant piece of unleavened bread! With news of the Midianites' fear, Gideon now receives enough courage to launch the attack.

GIDEON DEFEATS THE MIDIANITES

The ambivalence characterizing Gideon in the story continues into the account of the battle. The two-part battle narrative presents the divine-human contrast centering on Gideon. Judges 7 describes the stratagem of a night-ruse with pitchers, torches, trumpets, and war-whoops in which the panicking Midianites attack one another before fleeing. Gideon pursues the Midianites, then musters the Ephraimites, who seize the fords of Jordan against the enemy, exactly as Ehud's troops had done earlier. The Ephraimites protest, having been summoned late to the battle. Gideon's self-effacing tact in answering the Ephraimites' irritation preserves the victory. In this part of the narrative, Gideon appears as the champion of God, who with a clever stratagem and direct divine intervention, defeats the enemy and sweeps Israel to victory despite tribal divisiveness.

ABOVE: IN THIS FIFTEENTH-CENTURY COLOR LITHOGRAPH FROM THE GERMAN SCHOOL, GIDEON PUTS OUT THE FLEECE AND WAITS FOR A SIGN. IF DEW SETTLES ON THE FLEECE AND NOT ON THE LAND, HE IS TO SAVE ISRAEL.

LEFT: IN THIS TRADE CARD ILLUSTRATION FROM FRANCE, GIDEON—THE FIFTH JUDGE OF ISRAEL—EQUIPS HIS ARMY WITH LAMPS COVERED WITH PITCHERS TO FRIGHTEN THEIR MIDIANITE OPPONENTS.

RIGHT: THE ISRAELITES PLEADED WITH GIDEON TO BE THEIR KING BUT HE REFUSED. THIS CERAMIC DEPICTION OF GIDEON IN ARMOR IS BY HAROLD STEWARD RATHBONE AND IS DATED *C.* C.E. 1900.

However, early in Judges 8 a change comes. Readers will note here an abrupt shift. The Midianites flee southeast past Beth-shean, where the Valley of Jezreel joins the Jordan Rift Valley. Heading south, they cross to the east into the valley of the Jabbok River, passing Succoth and Penuel. Gideon still pursues the kings of Midian, but no longer in irresistible triumph. The 300 men in pursuit with him are exhausted and hungry, and Midian seems about to escape. Gideon's men cannot even obtain food, much less military assistance, from the inhabitants of Succoth and Penuel east of Jordan. Gideon shifts from hesitancy to harsh impatience, appearing not as peacemaker and securer of unity, as he had done with the complaining Ephraimites earlier, but as vengeful and threatening. This part of Judges makes no mention of the Lord as the author of victory, and Gideon fulfills his threats to thrash Succoth and Penuel.

Judges 8 also reveals another matter. Gideon, it transpires, had a stake of personal vengeance in the battle: the Midianite princes, Zebah and Zalmunna, had murdered his half-brothers. This revelation throws a new light on his original hesitancy. In a tribal society, the murder of one's kinsmen laid upon one a demand for blood vengeance. Gideon, then, hid not only from the task of liberating his people, but recoiled from his clan obligation to avenge the deaths of his kinsmen. No wonder these men now taunt Gideon, who slays them in his fury. This phase of the story poses a tension centering directly on Gideon. Is he a divinely anointed deliverer or a pursuer of personal revenge? Israel has won deliverance, but, for the first time in the book of Judges, the reader's confidence in the judge is shaken.

BELOW: THIS SEVENTEENTH-CENTURY DEPICTION OF GIDEON PRAYING IS BY JACOB JORDAENS, A FLEMISH ARTIST. GIDEON'S PRAYERS ARE CONSISTENTLY ANSWERED BY GOD.

THE DEATH OF GIDEON

The story comes to a climax in the elders' offer of permanent, hereditary rule to Gideon. Contrary to the Lord's express intention at the beginning of Judges 7, the Hebrews credit victory over the Midianites to Gideon: "you have delivered us out of the hand of Midian" (Judges 8:22). Gideon's response sounds like a pious rejection of kingship based on the belief that God alone is king over Israel, but his response is as flawed as the people's offer. The Old Testament has no objection to human rule. That the Lord is the "judge" (Judges 11:27) does not preclude humans also serving as judges. Also, the Hebrew text does not use the word "king" in this conversation.

Ironically, Gideon offers an alternative to his own rule: namely, his own religion! He collects the gold trinkets taken in battle and fashions an ephod. An ephod was a means by which to learn God's will, thus serving as an instrument of his rule. But Gideon's ephod promotes not God's rule, but spiritual prostitution. The preface to Judges painted Israel's sin as having "lusted after other gods" (Judges 2:17), but this is the first time in the book that the narrator explicitly labels Israel's sin as a form of prostitution. Gideon's ephod marks a significant milestone in Israel's downward plunge.

The conclusion of Judges 8 notes 40 years of peace following Gideon's victory, but goes on to observe that, in his retirement, Gideon did in fact live like a king, even naming one son "Abimelech," which means "My Father is King." Upon Gideon's death, once again the reference to prostitution expresses the intensity of Israel's abandonment of the Lord.

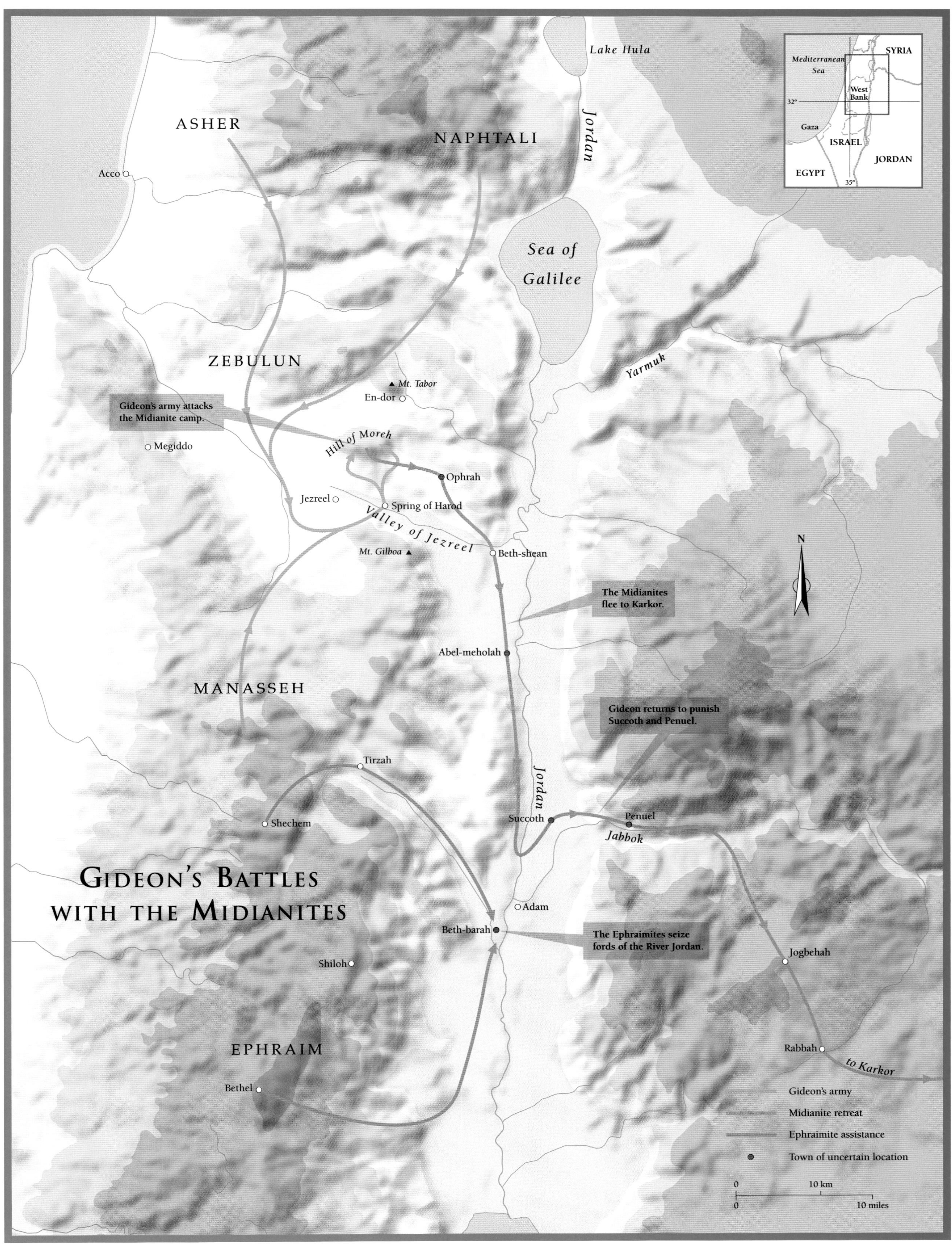
Gideon's Battles with the Midianites
Lake Hula
ASHER
NAPHTALI
Jordan
Acco
Sea of Galilee
ZEBULUN
Yarmuk
Mt. Tabor
En-dor
Gideon's army attacks the Midianite camp.
Megiddo
Hill of Moreh
Ophrah
Jezreel
Spring of Harod
Valley of Jezreel
Mt. Gilboa
Beth-shean
The Midianites flee to Karkor.
Abel-meholah
MANASSEH
Gideon returns to punish Succoth and Penuel.
Tirzah
Jordan
Succoth
Penuel
Jabbok
Shechem
Adam
Beth-barah
The Ephraimites seize fords of the River Jordan.
Shiloh
Jogbehah
EPHRAIM
Rabbah
to Karkor
Bethel
Gideon's army
Midianite retreat
Ephraimite assistance
Town of uncertain location
0
10 km
0
10 miles
N
Mediterranean Sea
SYRIA
West Bank
Gaza
ISRAEL
JORDAN
EGYPT

Abimelech and Jephthah

THUS GOD REPAID ABIMELECH FOR THE CRIME HE COMMITTED JUDGES 9:56

RIGHT: WORSHIP OF THE GOD OR GODS OF BAALIM EXTENDS BACK INTO HIGH ANTIQUITY. THIS IDOL IN BRONZE AND GOLD IS OF THE STORM GOD, BAAL. FROM SYRIA, IT DATES TO C. 1350–1250 B.C.E.

The story of Abimelech is introduced in Judges 8, making it the direct consequence of Israel's treachery and loss of faith. This is the first time Israel's sin is tied directly to the death of a judge, fulfilling the pattern of Judges 2. The striking description of Israel's betrayal of Gideon's family sets the theme of legitimate leadership and possibly even dynastic succession.

ABIMELECH SLAUGHTERS HIS BROTHERS

The story of Abimelech flows relentlessly, from his approach to the lords of Shechem at the beginning of Judges 9, to its conclusion. In this story, actions and their consequences unfold in inexorable sequence. Abimelech's approach is indirect, through the mediation of his mother's family. His overt appeal to order—for one ruler rather than 70—thinly disguises a covert appeal to ethnic prejudice. Ironically, Abimelech's boast of ethnic solidarity with Shechem is in conflict with his own mixed parentage.

The appeal succeeds and Abimelech, bankrolled by the lords of Shechem from the temple treasury of the Canaanite deity Baal-Berith, murders his 70 half-brothers "on one stone" (Judges 9:5). This description portrays the savagery of the deed as an almost ritual execution reminiscent of Athaliah's murder of her grandsons in 2 Kings 11. This usurpation by fratricide triggers a sequence of consequences which unfold over the rest of Judges 9.

The portrayal of Abimelech throughout the story matches up surprisingly well with the portrayal of an earlier ruler in Shechem named Lab'ayu, whom we know from the Amarna Texts, ancient letters written from Palestine to Egypt several centuries earlier. Like Abimelech, Lab'ayu gathered a gang of displaced persons and downright outlaws to take over the city and make it a base of wider operations. Shechem appears to have functioned as a place for diplomatic and political negotations, making it appealing to politicians and thugs alike.

Jotham, who is the sole survivor of Abimelech's purge and the legitimate heir of Jerubbaal (Gideon), directly challenges Abimelech's pretensions to superior fitness to rule. Taking his stand on Mt. Gerizim, Jotham could see Shechem below, and look across to Mt. Ebal, from which the curses of the law were proclaimed. Even the altar constructed by Joshua would be in plain view. Many read Jotham's story as an attack on kingship. The story, however, curses not kingship, but the followers of an unfit ruler. Whoever makes a king out of a bramble should not be surprised when the bramble cannot provide shade. The lords of Shechem have backed an unfit ruler, and perpetrated treachery and violence. To the consequences of folly Jotham adds the curse of faithlessness.

God's actions in the narrative ratify Jotham's curse. Rather than be empowered by God's spirit, an "evil spirit" (Judges 9:23), meaning here a malicious disposition, emerges among Abimelech's former supporters. Divine retribution doesn't hurry, but waits three years, working through the bad spirit to insinuate itself between Abimelech and his co-conspirators.

ABIMELECH DEFEATS GAAL, SON OF EBED

Two threats to Abimelech's rule soon arise. The lords of Shechem begin raiding forays around Shechem and a thug named Gaal, son of Ebed, begins stealing the confidence of the Shechemites. Many drifters

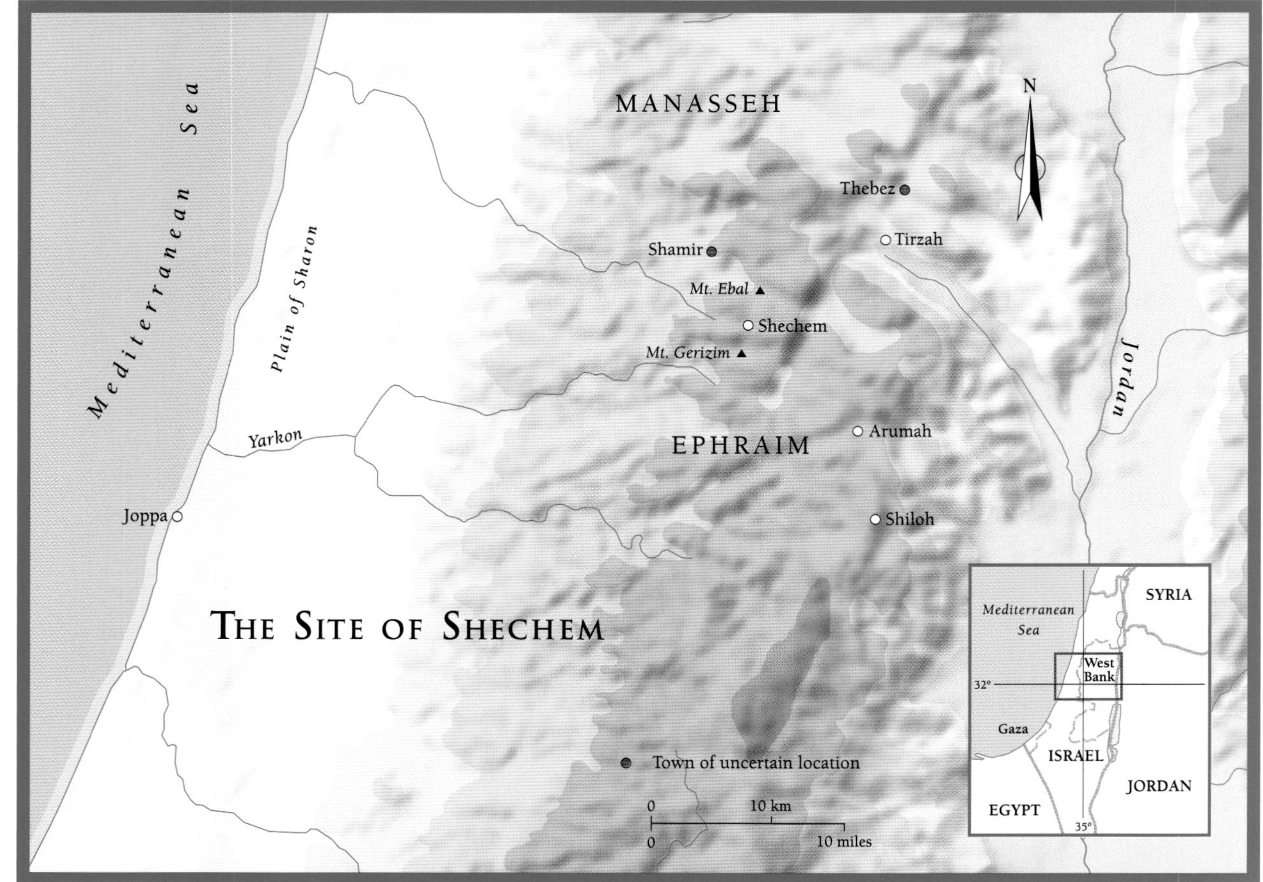

passed through ancient Shechem, and many a drunken malcontent boasted against authority, but Gaal posed a much bigger threat because the Shechemites actually trusted him and he, like Abimelech, resorted to an ugly ethnic appeal: the "sons of Hamor" mentioned by Gaal were the original inhabitants of Shechem described in Genesis 34. Abimelech responds forcefully against the treacherous Shechemite upper class and its popular leader. Aided by the intelligence reports of his henchman Zebul, Abimelech easily overpowers Gaal, whose drunken boast collides with the sobering reality of Abimelech's might.

ABIMELECH DESTROYS SHECHEM

The ambushes set by the lords of Shechem meet their match in a counterstrike by Abimelech, and the lords of Shechem perish, burned alive in the precincts of the very temple from whose treasury they financed Abimelech's ascent to power. Jotham's curse, "let fire come out from Abimelech and devour the lords of Shechem" (Judges 9:20), finds a literal realization. Rather than stop after neutralizing Gaal and then punishing Shechem, Abimelech moves on to Thebez, where he besieges its tower, and prepares to burn it and its occupants as he had at Shechem. This violent excess is his undoing. The gratuitous violence he showed in slaughtering his brothers is now brought forcibly to mind by a Thebezite woman's millstone, which is dropped on Abimelech from a great height. One can only wonder how, in the panic of fleeing from Abimelech's attack, this lady thought to tuck an upper grinding stone weighing several pounds into her gear.

All the events of this story feature human actors living out a scenario that seems to have been common in early Iron Age Canaan prior to the Israelite monarchy: rule by powerful men who organize their outlaw bands and dominate a town and its environs. The biblical narrator penetrates beneath

LEFT: IN THIS ENGRAVING BY M. VANDERGUCHT, ABIMELECH IS FATALLY WOUNDED WHEN A WOMAN DROPS A MILL-STONE ON HIM. RATHER THAN DIE AT THE HANDS OF A WOMAN, ABIMELECH HAS HIS ARMOR-BEARER KILL HIM.

human causes to the vengeance of God, working secretly to redress the evil done to Gideon's family. The story also condemns a whole relationship between leaders and people. By condemning Abimelech's fratricide by means of a speech in the mouth of the sole surviving legitimate heir of Gideon, the story unmistakably endorses inherited or dynastic rule over the "charismatic" model.

LEFT: THIS COLOR LITHOGRAPH BY LOUIS HAGHE AND DAVID ROBERTS, FROM VOLUME I OF *THE HOLY LAND*, PUBLISHED IN C.E. 1842, SHOWS ANCIENT SHECHEM AS LOW AND VULNERABLE.

Shechem—the scene of this story—served as the early capital of the northern Israelite kingdom. In contrast to Judah, which enjoyed an unbroken succession of legitimate Davidic kings, at least seven royal families violently clawed their way to the northern throne, including Athaliah, who murdered all the royal heirs but one. The story of Abimelech and Jotham and that of Athaliah and Joash parallel each other closely, and the Abimelech story clearly mirrors the conviction that rule by popular acclamation, such as the north seemed to favor, easily becomes rule by power-hungry, violent usurpers.

JEPHTHAH

The introduction to the Jephthah story in Judges 10:13–14 unambiguously marks a palpable step down from the preceding stories: Israel actually worships the gods of its oppressors, omitting only the Lord from their worship. Together with the expanded account of Israel's evil comes an enlarged description of their oppression.

JEPHTHAH DELIVERS ISRAEL

The gravity of the oppression Israel suffers appears in the reference to the Ammonites and the Philistines. The loose tribal organization of Israel could not effectually resist the Philistines, whose assaults provoked the transformation of Israel from a tribal confederation into a monarchic state. Israel's outcry also betokens a darkening of the situation. Though Israel confesses its sin, this cry meets a flat divine refusal: "I will deliver you no more. Go and cry to the gods whom you have chosen" (Judges 10:14). Israel's rejoinder betrays its double-mindedness: "do to us whatever seems good to you; but deliver us this day!" (Judges 10:15). In a fleeting fit of foxhole fidelity, not true repentance, Israel hastily gets rid of its false gods. But Israel only rearranges the furniture on its sinking ship. God responds in pity, or possibly exasperation. The Hebrew idiom describing God's motivation at this point translates literally as "his soul became short at Israel's toil." "Shortness of soul" normally denotes in Hebrew the loss of one's temper. (The same idiom describes Samson's exasperated capitulation to Delilah's incessant nagging.) Thus the last utterance of God in this exchange bristles with hostility. The career of Jephthah begins under a cloud of faithlessness, alienation, and divine aggravation.

Jephthah is the first hero not to come into his role by direct divine initiative. To be sure, the text calls him a mighty warrior, in full possession of the "right stuff" to lead Israel. But the taboos of a tribal society and clan solidarity undercut him. His irregular parentage eclipses his potential, and the rejection by his half-brothers consigns him to a brigand's life. When the Ammonite crisis arises, the elders promise to make whoever leads them "head" over Gilead. When the candidate turns out to be Jephthah, they promise him the lesser role of "commander." Knowing he is their only hope, Jephthah demands they keep their original promise and make him head, reminding them of their rejection and ironically echoing God's complaint from the story's introduction. Jephthah coldly clarifies their precise terms and exacts an oath before agreeing in a formal ritual "before the Lord" (Judges 11:11). Jephthah shows himself to be a hard-bitten negotiator who mercilessly tightens the screws to get what he wants. Not one to be rash, he demands a guarantee.

Jephthah's skill in bargaining appears again as he enters into negotiations with the Ammonites. In two exchanges he

BELOW: JEPHTHAH QUITE UNINTENTIONALLY GIVES THE ULTIMATE SACRIFICE—HIS DAUGHTER—IN THIS PAINTING ENTITLED *THE DAUGHTER OF JEPHTHAH* BY ROMBOUT VAN TROYEN, DATED C.E. 1643.

tries to dissuade the Ammonite king from war. He appeals to Israel's originally non-aggressive policy, its right to possession by divinely granted military conquest, and a long period of actual occupation. His concluding charge borders on insult, and the claim "Let the Lord, who is judge, decide today" (Judges 11:27) amounts to a declaration of war. Unintimidated by Jephthah's rhetorical posturing, the Ammonite king refuses to listen. So, Jephthah confronts the necessity of war. Initially, the onrush of the spirit betokens victory, as does the muster-tour of the neighboring territories. The battle, as with most in this story, takes place in the territory east of Jordan, opposite the Ephraimite hill country. The land of Tob, where Jephthah sojourns, probably refers to the vicinity of Ramoth-gilead north of the Jabbok River. Jephthah comes down to encounter the Ammonites just south of the Jabbok. While several of the locations in the story remain uncertain, all point to Jephthah's activities being limited to Gilead.

JEPHTHAH'S DAUGHTER

The coming of the spirit of the Lord on Jephthah is marred by his next act—his notorious vow. Far from rash, Jephthah's vow constitutes a calculated, high-stakes gamble with God. But Jephthah, the victor in battle, loses his gamble. Worse, Jephthah grieves only for himself and blames his daughter for his sorrows. She heroically accepts her fate: death as a human sacrifice. The notion that she became a perpetual virgin comes late in the history of biblical interpretation and cannot translate the Hebrew behind "burnt offering." The daughter, not Jephthah, finds perpetual remembrance in Israel. Jephthah's story has points of contact with other eastern Mediterranean stories featuring a rejected noble hero who prevails over foes only to suffer catastrophic loss. Likewise, Jephthah's daughter has frequently been compared to Iphigenia of early Greek fame.

JEPHTHAH AND THE EPHRAIMITES

Jephthah's final act seals his fate as a disastrous anti-hero. The Ephraimites test Jephthah's leadership. He faces a crisis identical to that faced by Gideon in Judges 7 and 8, both of which contrast with an event in Ehud's career described in Judges 3. Ehud eagerly enlisted the Ephraimites in battle, who then employed a strategy of entrapment at the Jordan. Gideon's call for Ephraimite assistance received the identical response, but was followed by a bitter complaint which Gideon answered with consummate tact. Jephthah, faced with Ephraimite jealousy, responds with bitter recrimination and employs the Ephraimite strategy to destroy 42,000 Israelites! The man who negotiated with Israel's enemy peremptorily slaughters his countrymen. More Israelites die here, at Jephthah's hand, than in all the rest of the book of Judges. The charismatic deliverer has become a destroyer.

The conclusion of the story notes only that Jephthah "judged," conspicuously omitting the reference to Israel "resting" seen earlier in Judges. How could the land rest during the reign of such a leader? The chronological reference also denotes failure. Prior to Jephthah, the periods of peace are at least twice as long as the periods of oppression. Jephthah's career is significantly shorter than the time of oppression. The balance sheet on Israel's judges now registers a loss.

LEFT: IN THIS PAINTING BY EDWIN LONGSDEN LONG, DATED C.E. 1886, JEPHTHAH'S VOW TO SACRIFICE HIS DAUGHTER IS MADE ALL THE MORE POIGNANT BY THE HAPPY FAMILY REUNIONS IN THE BACKGROUND.

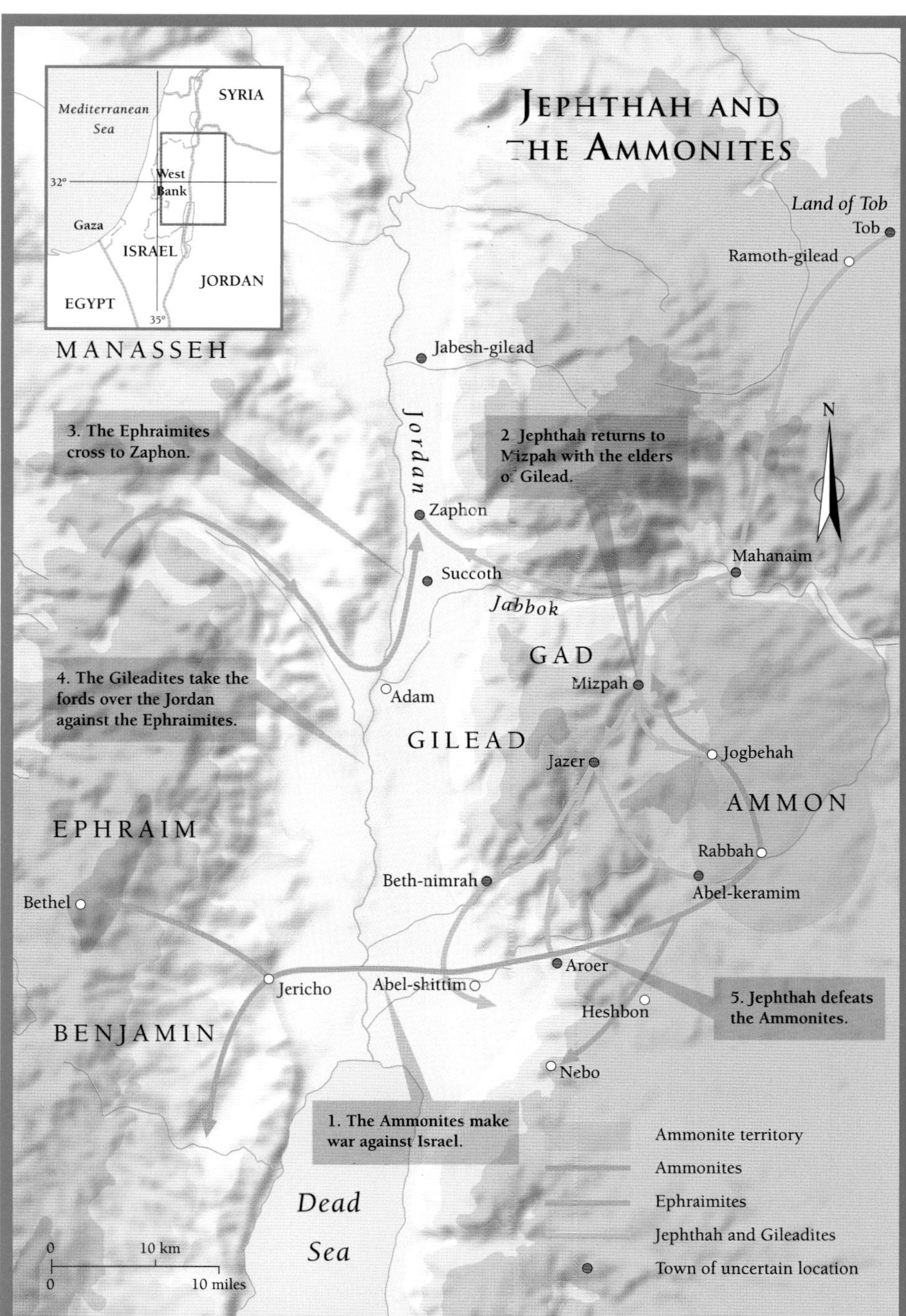

SAMSON AND SAMUEL

BUT HE DID NOT KNOW THAT THE LORD HAD LEFT HIM JUDGES 16:20

The Samson story resumes the story of the tribe of Dan, still living in the southern portion of the Promised Land. Judges 1 indicated that the Danites were ultimately expelled from this territory, so expectations for the story are already low. How, in fact, will the Danites end up abandoning their inherited land? Where will they go after that? These questions find answers in the Samson story in Judges 13–16 and the story of Micah and the Danite migration in Judges 17–18.

The original allotment of land to Dan fell slightly west of Jerusalem, where the Judean highlands, with their steep, V-shaped valleys cut into hard limestone, give way to the broad, flat-bottomed valleys worn into the softer limestone and chalk of the Shephelah. An attacker from the coast could first have control of one of the six valleys that crossed the Shephelah, then gain one of the ridge routes leading into the highland interior. The first attempt by the Philistines, who arrived on the coast of Canaan about the same time as the Israelites, began in the west and moved up the Sorek Valley, directly across the territory of the Danites. Controlling that valley allowed the Philistines to gain the junction of critical roads leading both north and east into the Benjaminite and Judean heartland. If Dan then failed to hold its ground, the way would be left open to the Philistines to expel Israel from their tenuous settlements.

From the mound of Beth-shemesh, one can look northeast across the Sorek Valley to the sites of Zorah and Eshtaol on the opposite ridge, and then sweep westward, observing the route Samson might well have taken on the way down to Timnah in the valley, where he met both the first woman to inspire his impetuous affection and a very unfortunate lion. Further west, down the Sorek, the Shephelah gives way to the coastal plain dominated by the great Philistine cities. Our story transpires on crucial ground, with much at stake.

ABOVE: SAMSON OFTEN USED HIS CONSIDERABLE PHYSIQUE, EVIDENT IN THIS NINETEENTH-CENTURY OIL PAINTING BY GEORGE FREDERICK WATT, TO COMBAT HIS ENEMIES.

THE BIRTH OF SAMSON

Israel's unrelenting loss of faith finally brings on the Philistines, who were to break up Israel's loose tribal confederacy, forcing Israel to choose a king. A sign of the deep alienation between Israel and God comes in Israel's silence: no outcry appears here. Israel stands mute. The book's progressive exposé of the weaknesses of the premonarchic pattern of leadership culminates with Samson, whose birth narrative also brings to a climax the book's increasingly detailed description of each major judge's background. Like Jephthah, Samson lives under a vow, though it is not one of his own making. Samson's mother, who remains anonymous, receives God's promise of a child which decrees that "No razor is to come on his head, for the boy shall be a nazirite" (Judges 13:5). Nazirite status expressed extraordinary devotion to God and required abstinence from alcohol, strict avoidance of contact with the dead, and uncut hair (see Numbers 6). Although most nazirites undertook these obligations voluntarily for a limited period, divine annunciation ordained Samson a lifelong nazirite. Annunciation stories usually herald the arrival of salvation. Samson, however, would barely begin this task. With Jephthah, the deliverance became disaster; with Samson, the deliverance itself slipped away.

The story emphasizes the lack of perception on the part of Samson's father. Rather than receive God's word from his wife, Manoah requires direct confirmation, asking God, "let the man of God whom you sent come to us again" (Judges 13:8). The ensuing encounter brings to light Manoah's spiritually insensitive assertiveness. The word of confirmation emphasizes the primacy of the original word to his wife, but Manoah attempts to fit God's word into a set of religious and traditional expectations: he injects an offering, demands the messenger's name, and fears for his life upon realizing his impertinence. His wife's common-sense approach to simply accepting and believing the divine word is in stark contrast with Manoah's obsessiveness. Samson's birth and blessing fulfills God's promise but also sounds a warning: "The boy grew, and the Lord blessed him. The spirit of the Lord began to stir him" (Judges 13:24–25). The verb "stir" can be translated from the Hebrew in a more forceful sense—strike, harass, hit, plague, or afflict—pointing to Samson's ambition and compulsion.

THE WOMAN FROM TIMNAH

The first phase of Samson's life, as told in Judges 14 and 15, recounts his harassment of the Philistines in a tight sequence, emphasizing riddles and revenge. The narrative opens with Samson's headstrong insistence on marrying a Philistine woman, despite parental protest. The tribal ethos of Israelite society resisted marriage to non-Israelites, not because of racism or prejudice, but because marriage outside the tribe potentially meant inherited land could be transferred to non-Israelites, thus reversing the Lord's promise and gift of the land to Israel. Intermarriage threatened not only Israel's religious identity, but its concrete ability to retain possession of the Promised Land. But the narrator stresses Samson's crush on the Philistine woman as the Lord's opportunity to confront the Philistines. Samson's secret, spirit-energized slaying of a lion inspires the riddle at the heart of the story.

While popular commentary often stresses Samson as either blinded by love, or merely stupid, the story of the wedding banquet reveals Samson's cleverness as he frustrates his cultured, urban Philistine companions. Only threats to burn Samson's wife and her family alive persuade her to extract his secret. Once confronted with humiliation and betrayal, the spirit of the Lord rushes on Samson and he murders 30 Philistines to settle his wager before apparently abandoning his new bride. The Philistines had won their bet, but at a frightening cost to their nation. Ironically, this story portrays Samson already playing fast and loose with his vow. At the wedding banquet, as "toastmaster," Samson likely consumed wine. By eating honey from the body of the lion, Samson certainly violated his vow's prohibition on contact with death. By in turn giving the honey to his mother, he possibly also defiled her.

LEFT: A HERCULEAN FIGURE, SAMSON PERFORMS FEATS UNACHIEVABLE BY ORDINARY MEN, SUCH AS WRESTLING A LION—DEPICTED IN THIS FOLIO FROM A LATIN BIBLE, DATED C.E. 1526–29.

BELOW: *RACHEL'S TOMB AT RAMAH* BY JOSEPH MALLORD WILLIAM TURNER (DATED *C.* C.E. 1835) WRONGLY LOCATES THE TOMB NEAR BETHLEHEM. THE BIBLE PLACES THE TOMB INSIDE SAMSON'S TRIBAL ALLOTMENT OF BENJAMIN.

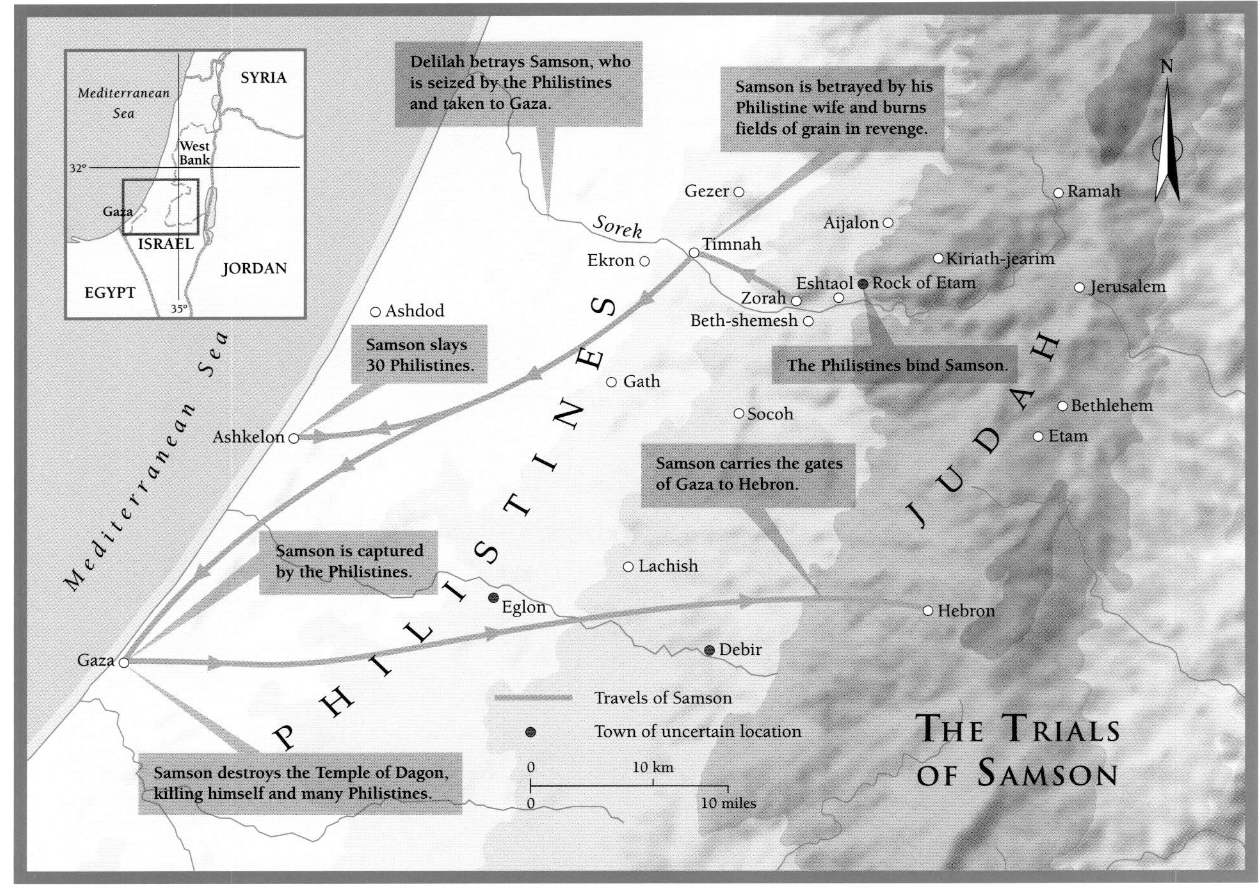

SAMSON DEFEATS THE PHILISTINES

The script for the Samson story appears early in Judges 3, which says the Israelites lived among the Canaanites, intermarried with them, and served their gods. If we substitute "Philistines" for "Canaanites," we have Samson's story. He certainly shows a predilection for Philistine companionship, and the events of Judges 14–15 emanate from Samson's marriage to a Philistine woman. He later dies in a Philistine temple during a celebration of a Philistine god.

After some time, Samson—now the Timnite's "son-in-law"—goes to visit his wife, and he takes with him a peace offering. Full of good intentions, Samson discovers his wife now belongs to another. The offer of a younger and prettier substitute only enrages him. His honor insulted, Samson decides to avenge himself by a prank that brings the entire local economy to its knees. Letting loose 300 foxes with burning tails, he allows them to burn up "the shocks and the standing grain, as well as the vineyards and olive groves" (Judges 15:5). While wheat might grow again the next year, damage to vineyards and olive groves can take years—even generations—to heal. Since wine and olive oil served as the leading trade goods of the immediate area, Samson has exacted an enormous price for his wounded honor.

The enraged Philistines see Samson's reaction as overkill, meriting a comparable response. They answer fire with fire and burn Samson's beloved and her scheming father, presumably hoping to intimidate the long-haired ruffian from the subordinate Israelite community. Both sides might well have spoken Samson's words in Judges 15:7: "If this is what you do, I swear I will not stop until I have taken revenge on you." Samson thinks one more act of vengeance will end the cycle, but what he does not know is that in fact the cycle will only spin faster. He tears into the Philistines, smiting them "hip and thigh with great slaughter" (Judges 15:8) and then fleeing to the Rock of Etam.

As with any good hiding place, the location of Samson's refuge remains obscure. Possibilities include Khirbet el-Khokh, east of the watershed highway just south of Bethlehem, or an unspecified location in the boundary of Simeon. But neither fits the story. Another site, known as Araq Ismain near Zorah, on the northern ridge of the Sorek Valley, could be more likely. But Samson cannot hide from the Philistines' wrath. They raid Lehi and suddenly the Judahites are drawn into the dispute. Locating Lehi poses a challenge. Since the name means "cheek, jawbone," some have thought the Wadi Ismain, noted above, is the place because of rock formations that look, to some, like a jawbone. A better suggestion comes from realizing that the term "cheek" was used in ancient literature to refer to a boundary or edge. Lehi probably just means "the border" between the Philistine and the Israelite territories. Most of the Samson story takes place in these

THE PHILISTINES

Here, for the first time in the story, the Philistines actually appear as a military force. If scholars have correctly identified the Philistines as one of the "Sea Peoples" mentioned in Egyptian and other texts, the Philistines came from the Aegean and sought new homelands all around the eastern Mediterranean. They triggered the collapse of the Hittite Empire, destroyed the coastal city of Ugarit (right), and pressed the Egyptians hard before being repelled and forced to settle for the southern coast of Palestine. Urbanized, technologically astute, and militarily organized under the leadership of "lords," the Philistines were more than raiders or oppressors. Like Israel, they sought to own the territory permanently for themselves. The name "Palestine" itself derives from "Philistine."

border situations, where the aggressive aspirations of the Philistines clash with the persistence of the Israelites.

The men of Judah feel the pressure of Philistine rule, and seem also to know that, despite his divine empowerment, Samson is no deliverer. They simply want to be rid of him, and so turn him over to their Philistine lords. Knowing his strength, Samson allows himself to be bound and handed over, but then explodes in spirit-infused power and breaks free. Seizing the jawbone of a "fresh" dead donkey, Samson kills a thousand Philistines and cannot stop until he has shouted his boast—"I have slain a thousand men" (Judges 15:16)—to the heavens, claiming the victory for himself and never once crediting the "spirit of the Lord" which came upon him, enabling him to break the bonds and fight. But more seriously, the moment he seized his weapon, the jawbone of a donkey, he violated his nazirite vow yet again. His arrogance finds cheeky expression in his prayer, in which he virtually demands that God provide him with water by appealing to God's own honor. The assumption that God and he share the same preoccupation with honor and vengeance is certainly arrogant. God mercifully answers, providing water and sustaining Samson.

LEFT: SAMSON SLAYS A THOUSAND PHILISTINES WITH NOTHING MORE THAN THE JAWBONE OF AN ASS IN THIS ILLUSTRATION FROM *HISTOIRE DE L'ANCIEN ET NOUVEAU TESTAMENT*, DATED C.E. 1724.

SAMSON AND THE WOMAN FROM GAZA

Most readers find an analogy between Samson's careless, frittering away of his divine calling and Israel's behavior in general. Divine mercy only emboldens Samson, who travels all the way down to the coast, to Philistine Gaza, to consort with a prostitute. The terms for prostitution, rare in Judges, are always significant. Israel's loss of faith is described as "lust" in Judges 2:17, and again in the transition from Gideon to Abimelech in Judges 8:27. And just as the time is not expired for Israel, so Samson's time has not yet come. He rises up while the Philistines wait in ambush, wrecks the gateposts of Gaza, and carries them across the Shephelah to deposit them on the ridge near Hebron. But Samson's days of presumption are numbered. His next visit to Gaza will be under vastly changed circumstances.

RIGHT: SAMSON CARRIES THE GATES OF GAZA IN THIS GOLD ALTARPIECE BY NICOLAS DE VERDUN. DATED C.E. 1181, IT IS HOUSED IN THE KLOSTERNEUBURG MONASTERY, AUSTRIA.

BELOW: THIS NINETEENTH-CENTURY ARTWORK IS BY SOLOMON SOLOMON. THE ARTIST DEPARTED FROM THE BIBLE STORY BY DEPICTING SAMSON BEING BOUND BY THE PHILISTINES OF GAZA IN THE PRESENCE OF DELILAH.

SAMSON AND DELILAH

The author of Judges tells the story of Samson and Delilah with artful irony. The third and final woman figuring in Samson's life stands alone. Of the three women, only her name appears in the text. "Delilah" might mean, ironically, "loose hair" but seems to be a pun based on the Hebrew word for "night." Since Samson's name means something like "Little Sun" and many details of his life reflect Ancient Near Eastern imagery surrounding the sun, such as his long locks of hair, the story exploits the interplay between "Sun Man" and "She of the Night." In stories using such motifs, typically the sun vanquishes the night. But this story tells us that Samson "fell in love with the woman" (Judges 16:4). Of the three women, the text speaks of Samson loving only Delilah. Considering his track record, night's victory seems close at hand! While we assume Delilah was a Philistine, the story never betrays her background. Like Rahab in Joshua 2, Delilah maintains her own house independently, a house large enough to conceal Samson's Philistine would-be captors. In a patriarchal society, a woman presiding over such a house would be wealthy, influential, and even high-born. She certainly has an easy rapport with the "lords" of the Philistines—the king-like military rulers of the Philistine cities.

THE WOMAN OF THE SOREK VALLEY

Delilah, we are told, lives in the Sorek Valley. The Sorek is one of the six broad valleys providing access between the coastal plain and the high heartland of Judah, Benjamin, and Ephraim. The red soil—*terra rosa*—which is produced by the hard limestone of the hill country, washes down the seasonal streams called wadis and collects in these broader valleys hewn from the lower, softer rock, thereby producing deep beds of fertile soil. Perhaps even the name "Sorek," which can also denote a fox-red or sorrell color, comes from the color of the soil here. Both the Aijalon Valley to the north of the Sorek and the Elah Valley to the south figure strongly in all the narratives of Judges and 1 Samuel concerning conflicts with the Philistines.

The writer exploits the punning possibilties of "Sorek." Since a very good strain of grape, used in making fine wines, was called sorek, the irony of a wine-refusing nazirite meeting his match in the Sorek would be strong. Sorek also refers to combing, harrowing, or tearing something asunder. Again, the connection with Samson's fate had to provoke a rueful smile from the alert reader. Some have also suggested sorek refers to a particular kind of women's cosmetics, again resonating with our story. The story depicts a certain coldness about Delilah, whose only motive seems to be the 1,100 pieces of silver pledged by the lords of the Philistines. Just one chapter later, 1,100 pieces of stolen silver will be used to construct an illicit idol, again making an ironic connection.

A SECRET REVEALED

The story of Delilah's extraction of Samson's secret unfolds relentlessly. Her approach is direct, even brazen, saying "Please tell me what makes your strength so great" (Judges 16:6). Were the words spoken with arched eyebrows, a sexual undercurrent as part of preconjugal barter? The Philistines had concluded that Samson's strength resulted from some magical feature and not from natural causes. Samson exploits this in his first answer by referring to the number seven, the number of locks of his hair. The use of fresh bowstrings, which would have no natural ability to bind him, points to a magical dimension as well. In round two, Delilah petulantly complains of being mocked, but her words are easily heard as coy. Samson's next answer hearkens back to the attempt by the men of Judah to bind him with "new ropes." Unused ropes carry magical connotations, but also ironically point to virginal purity, as did fresh bowstrings, possibly hinting that Samson's secret is closer to being revealed than even he thinks. In many stories, the third time something happens is the "real" one. Delilah likely thinks that now she will hear the truth. She almost does. Samson daringly approaches the verge of his secret—his hair. The image of shards of Delilah's shattered loom dragging behind Samson as he strides away from the frustrated Philistines must have chagrined and angered them.

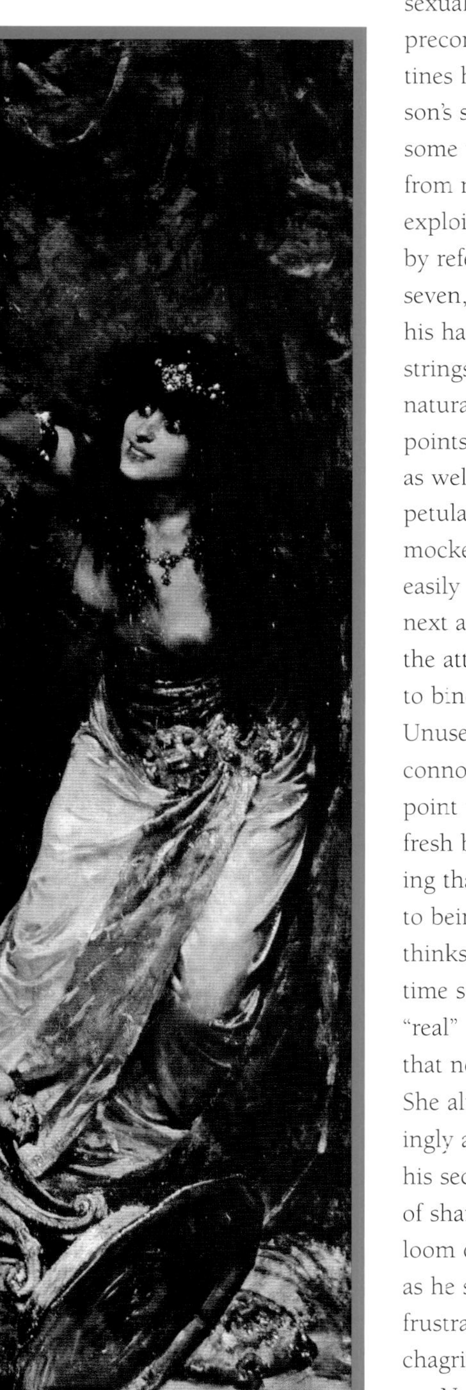

Now Delilah unleashes her strongest appeal yet. She attacks his love for her. The text uses the same idiom for Samson's surrender that was used of God's yielding to Israel's pleading in Judges 10, his "soul became short," meaning "he completely caved in" to her enticements and pleadings. Armed with the certainty of his secret, Delilah lets Samson fall asleep "on her lap." (The expression is literally "on her knees," which might well have a sexual innuendo.) When she awakens the shaven Samson for the fourth time with the cry, "the Philistines are upon you" (Judges 16:20), Samson assumes nothing has changed. But how could he think that? Every time he gave Delilah an answer, she tried it. How could he not expect she would shave his head? His words as he arises suggest that perhaps he believed he was immune. After all, he had already violated the other terms of the nazirite vow with no ill effects. Why was this any different? His whole strength from that point had only been the result of sheer divine mercy. No more tragic words appear in the Bible than, "He did not know that the Lord had left him" (Judges 16:20). Samson's loss of charisma foreshadows the departure of the spirit, and divine blessing, from Saul in 1 Samuel, pointing to the rejection of a leader. Might the abandonment of Samson point to God's rejection of the "charismatic" model of leadership and point the reader toward kingship?

ABOVE: IN THIS DETAIL FROM *THE TRIUMPH OF LOVE* BY THE FIFTEENTH-CENTURY PAINTER GIOVANNI DI APOLLONIO, SAMSON BREAKS THE THIRD LAW OF THE NAZIRITE BY TELLING DELILAH THE SOURCE OF HIS STRENGTH.

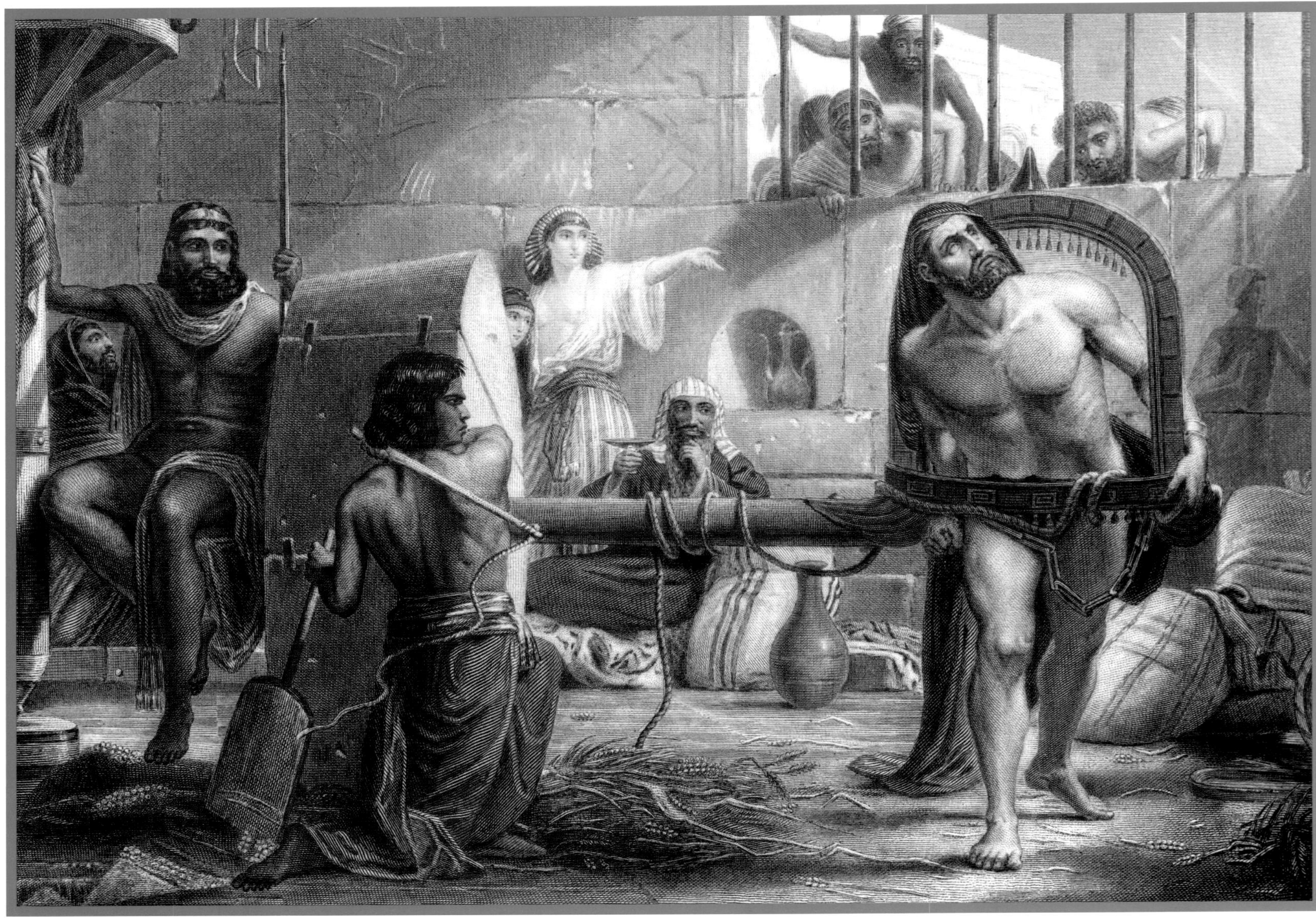

ABOVE: THIS NINETEENTH-CENTURY PRINT OF A BLIND SAMSON AT THE MILL IN GAZA IS BY WILLIAM GREATBACK. IT RECORDS A WELL-KNOWN PAINTING BY THE HISTORY PAINTER EDWARD ARMITAGE, ENTITLED *SAMSON IN PRISON*.

SAMSON'S HUMILIATION

Once captured, Samson finds himself back in Gaza. He had come there once to consort with a prostitute, but now Samson, "eyeless in Gaza" according to Milton, grinds grain in the prison mill. Samson begins to fulfill the final step of the summary for Israel's experience given in Judges 3. He has "lived among" his enemies, and he has intermarried with them. Now, he will serve their gods.

This point in the narrative provides a moment to note just what fierce enemies of Israel the Philistines really were. There are over 900 references in the Old Testament to Israel's various national enemies, but of these almost half specify the Philistines. Often the Bible highlights the fact that the Philistines were uncircumcised to define them as "other" than God's people, but many other cultural differences existed. Philistines had their own styles of pottery, which were distinct from those of the Canaanites and Israelites, making it possible to detect their presence in the sites that dot the landscape. Archaeologists excavating Iron Age sites have discerned another intriguing cultural boundary: those toward the coast that are rich in Philistine pottery also feature pig bones among the remains, thought to be a domesticated food animal. As one moves east, away from the coast and up into the Shephelah, the Philistine pottery thins out, and the pig bones vanish. Clearly a strong sense of difference existed between the Israelites and the Philistines.

Of course, the strongest difference emerged in worship. The Israelites worshipped one sovereign, holy, ungendered creator God, named "Yahweh," who could not be served with images, while the Philistines, in keeping with other ancient cultures, venerated a variety of gods. The god Dagon, mentioned in the text, would not have been the indigenous god of the Philistines from their Aegean homeland, but was a deity well known in the Ancient Near East, the father of Baal in the Ugaritic texts. Other texts associated with the Philistines also identify Baal and Asherah as recipients of Philistine worship, so clearly the Philistines participated in the same polytheistic religious milieu as other ancient cultures. Samson's downfall emerged directly from his failure to take seriously the power of the difference between his identity as an Israelite and the values of the surrounding culture. Even as he said to Delilah, "I have been a nazirite to God from my mother's womb" (Judges 16:17), he seems not fully to grasp that in surrendering his fundamental difference of identity from the Philistines he is surrendering the true source of his strength.

RIGHT: SAMSON'S EXPLOITS INSPIRED MANY ARTWORKS, SUCH AS THIS CERAMIC FROM THE SIXTEENTH CENTURY. IT DEPICTS SAMSON DRINKING FROM THE JAWBONE OF A DONKEY AND DESTROYING THE TEMPLE OF DAGON.

SAMSON'S REVENGE

From grinding in the prison of Gaza, Samson is brought into the temple of Dagon during a great festival. The crowds celebrate the humbling of Samson. Even though Samson did not mount or lead a military campaign of resistance against the Philistines, apparently his constant harassment and disruptions of their economy and social life interfered with and ultimately frustrated the Philistines' attempt to use the Sorek Valley as a staging ground for pressing further into the Judean heartland. Unable to push past the pranks of Samson, their expansionist aspirations had languished. With Samson out of the picture, the Philistines now saw a clear road ahead to blow past the last of the Danites, capture the ridge roads leading up into the highlands, and complete their domination of Canaan. No wonder they were celebrating! And perhaps they were more aware than Samson of the religious distinctions between themselves and Israel. They "gathered to offer a great sacrifice to their god Dagon" (Judges 16:23), just as the Hebrews would celebrate the mighty saving acts of the Lord. And Samson was to entertain them and enhance their worship experience.

The narrative has stressed that, in fact, no automatic connection bound Samson's nazirite regulations to his strength. He violated the first two provisions of the vow with no consequences, even though Numbers 6 requires the nazirite to shave his head the moment any part of the vow is compromised. But Samson's strength continued unabated, broken vow and all, until his encounter with Delilah. Even there, the cause was abandonment by the Lord. Nevertheless, the text points to the silent renewal of Samson's hair. One wonders if the writer wishes to point to the silent, secret working of the same divine mercy that strengthened Samson before.

The Philistines seem uninterested in Samson's growing hair, presuming that, once vanquished, Samson remains impotent. But standing in the temple, blind and humiliated, Samson appeals in prayer not to any provision of a vow, but to a God of justice who hears the cry of his servant: "remember me and strengthen me only this once, O God" (Judges 16:28). As he prays, Samson places his hands on stone columns supporting the temple. Archaeologists excavating the distinctively Philistine Iron Age temples in Ekron and Tel Qasile have found in each site evidence that major structural support came from twin pillars seated in stone sockets on the floor of the temple, placed fairly close together. A man of rather large proportions might be able to unseat the pillars from their bases, thus destabilizing the structure, and with 3,000 people sitting on the roof, the loss of the pillars would literally bring down the house.

Samson's prayer embodies the ethos by which he lived: the tribal ethos of honor, shame, and vengeance. Honor and vengeance drive the story, and finally, even as he turns to God, Samson prays to avenge the loss of his eyes, not for the restoration of God's own honor. Despite his prayer and great finish, killing 3,000 Philistines, Samson in the end champions not God, but himself. The best thing the last charismatic judge does for Israel is to die. Samson remains the emblem of a self-will that denies its addiction to lust, revenge, and power and refuses to face its own bondage.

BELOW: SAMSON BRINGS DOWN THE TEMPLE IN E. S. HARDY'S ILLUSTRATION FROM THE *ALLERS FAMILJ-JOURNAL*, PUBLISHED IN C.E. 1925. THE DEATH OF SAMSON MARKED A MAJOR TURNING POINT IN ISRAEL'S WAR AGAINST THE PHILISTINES.

ABOVE: THIS NINETEENTH-CENTURY ENGRAVING BY HIPPOLYTE LEON BENETT DEPICTS RITUAL MURDER COMMITTED BY THE DANITES, AND SHOWS THE ENDURING DEMONIZATION OF DANITES IN MODERN TIMES.

MICAH AND THE DANITE CONQUEST

The account in Judges 17 and 18 ridicules and castigates the worship, tribe, and city of Dan. Dan later became one of the two shrines established by Jeroboam for the breakaway northern kingdom. The narrative illustrates how the Danite sanctuary originated in theft and violated God's prohibition of images. The thief's ordination of his son as priest also lampoons the northern kingdom's irregular priesthood (see 1 Kings 12). The scene closes by observing that such events could only happen in the absence of a king, where "all the people did what was right in their own eyes" (Judges 17:6). Micah then hires an itinerant Levite to serve as his priest.

The stage being set, the story now returns to the landless Danites of Judges 1, who have also been depicted throughout the Samson story as only tenuously holding on to their territory against the Philistine drive into the Israelite heartland. The Danites' trek northward embarked from precisely the places that witnessed Samson's early deeds, namely from Zorah and from Eshtaol. The great hero Samson left his tribesmen without any inheritance and they must now "Go, explore the land" (Judges 18:2).

Laish, the site the Danites seize upon, lies in the far north of Canaan at the base of Mt. Hermon. A major source of the Jordan River springs from here, producing an enormous quantity of water. Egyptian and Assyrian texts, as well as the Bible, mention Laish. When the Danites confronted Laish, they would have noted to their delight that the city lacked the imposing defense system that characterized cities like Jericho or Hazor. Rather than a wall, the city employed an earthen rampart. A triple-arched mud-brick gate constructed in the 1700s B.C.E. (and recently excavated) would have been covered by the time of our story. While the site has not yielded evidence for a great destruction datable to the time of Judges 18, there is evidence of a new settlement in which the population lived in huts and tents, storing their food in stone-lined pits. Amid the pottery, excavators noted the unusual "collared rim" jar that some consider to be indicative of Israelite presence. If these new settlers are the Danites, they would have arrived in the early twelfth century B.C.E., placing the story of Judges 18 earlier in time than the stories preceding it in the book. The writer of Judges seems to have organized the material thematically rather than chronologically.

Once settled, the Danites appear to have engaged in metallurgy but otherwise, if the *Song of Deborah* in Judges 5 is any indication, they seem to have been somewhat detached from their fellow Israelites. It looks as if the Danites became clients of the surrounding cities, including contracting out to supply crews for shipping (see Judges 5:17) and might have had more of an investment in the stability of Canaanite culture than their farming and herding brethren to the south.

Having failed to occupy the territory assigned to them by God and Joshua, the Danites abandon that assignment, pillage an illegitimate sanctuary, massacre an unsuspecting population, and capture their city with no need of divine intervention. They surpass these dubious achievements by renaming the city for themselves: "They named the city Dan, after their ancestor Dan, who was born to Israel" (Judges 18:29). The story ruthlessly skewers the pretensions of the northern sanctuary, which even claimed a priesthood that was descended from Moses. By the time of Jeroboam, Dan had become an important religious and administrative

FLIGHT OF THE BENJAMINITES

1. The Israelites gather before the Lord.
2. The Benjaminites force the Israelites to retreat to Bethel.
3. The Israelites ambush and destroy the city by fire.
4. The Israelites pursue and smite the Benjaminites.
5. Six hundred Benjaminites flee to the rock of Rimmon.

EPHRAIM
BENJAMIN
JUDAH
Bethel
Rimmon
Mizpah
Ramah
Geba
Gilgal
Jericho
Gibeah
Jerusalem
Bethlehem
Dead Sea

Israelites advance
Israelites retreat
Benjaminites advance
Benjaminites retreat
Town of uncertain location
10 km
10 miles
N

Mediterranean Sea
SYRIA
West Bank
32°
Gaza
ISRAEL
JORDAN
EGYPT
35°

center, with a large sanctuary for Jeroboam's bull image. Today, Dan is the longest continuously excavated site in Israel and it continues to generate valuable data season after season.

OUTRAGE AT GIBEAH: THE LEVITE AND HIS CONCUBINE

Signs of the collapse of Israel as an extended family of tribes appear in the story of the Levite and his concubine. Living in the northern reaches of Ephraim, the Levite travels to Bethlehem to retrieve his wandering mate. The return journey takes him northward on the watershed ridge road from Bethlehem, past Jebus (Jerusalem) and on to Bethel and points north. Owing to a late start, the Levite has to stay for the night in a strange territory. He passes up Jebus in favor of Gibeah, which is an Israelite town. But the Levite fails to find a hospitable reception from the Benjaminites in Gibeah, which later became the capital of Saul, Israel's first king. Gibeah's indifference erupts into outrage in a story manifesting remarkable affinities with the story of Sodom's destruction (Genesis 19), except that Judges 19 ends in a mob's rape of the Levite's concubine.

WAR AGAINST BENJAMIN

The rape of the concubine plunges Israel into war. The Levite's dismemberment of his concubine—another allusion to the Saul story (1 Samuel 11)—energizes the nation's tribal judicial machinery to avenge the crime. Benjamin's refusal to turn Gibeah over to tribal justice prompts an all-Israelite civil war in which a reported 25,000 Benjaminites die and the victorious Israelites subject the territory of Benjamin to burning and annihilation, with only 600 surviving. Israel seeks to restore the tribe it has just annihilated by procuring wives for the few remaining Benjaminites. This ad hoc solution entails yet another atrocity, namely the slaughter of the men and some of the women of Jabesh-gilead, the town later saved from destruction by Saul at the beginning of his reign: "This is what you shall do; every male and every woman that has lain with a male you shall devote to destruction" (Judges 21:11). When this proves inadequate, the elders of Israel authorize the kidnap and coerced marriage of all the maidens of Shiloh—a grim move when one considers how the whole episode began. The narrator's last words recall Israel's true problem: people doing what they chose as "there was no king in Israel" (Judges 19:1). Unfavorable allusions to the Saul story clearly intimate the writer's preference for Davidic kings, preparing the reader for the rise of the monarchy and David in 1 Samuel.

BELOW: THIS PHOTOGRAPH BY RICHARD T. NOWITZ SHOWS THE GOLAN HEIGHTS. HISTORICAL TEXTS REFER TO THE GOLAN HEIGHTS AS THE EXTENSION OF THE SLOPES OF MT. HERMON, NEAR LAISH.

RIGHT: IN ACCORDANCE WITH HER VOW, HANNAH PRESENTS HER SON SAMUEL TO THE HIGH PRIEST ELI IN THIS SEVENTEENTH-CENTURY WORK BY LAMBERT DOORMER.

ELI AT SHILOH

The story of Eli centers around the town of Shiloh. Already, Judges 18 reports a "house of God" in this town. The narrative in 1 Samuel makes it clear that, in fact, the Ark of the Covenant resided for a time in an actual house, with doorposts, rooms, and adequate space for Eli and his assistants to live. This house is even referred to as a "temple of the Lord" (1 Samuel 1:9), even though the Hebrew temple has not yet been constructed. This was probably a Canaanite temple which had been commandeered by the Israelites.

Excavations at Shiloh (Khirbet Seilun) present an unusual picture. The site was not a normal residential community. Finds include broken pottery, ashes, and animal bones, indicating it served as an isolated worship center prior to Israelite occupation. Israelite remains perpetuate this impression. Shiloh would have appealed to the incoming Hebrews. A site with known religious associations, it would have been deserted, with only a scattering of Canaanite settlements in the vicinity. But Israelite villages rapidly popped up all around. In the mid-eleventh century B.C.E., Shiloh underwent destruction by fire. The town that had hosted the Lord's first temple fell into permanent ruin, providing the prophet Jeremiah, 400 years later, with a poignant illustration of divine judgment.

The sanctuary at Shiloh provided a home for the priest Eli, whose lineage continued for centuries through figures such as Abiathar, high priest during David's time, though banished to Anathoth by Solomon. Eli's line possibly reached as far as Jeremiah, who hailed from this same Anathoth. Eli's leadership witnessed serious decline in the

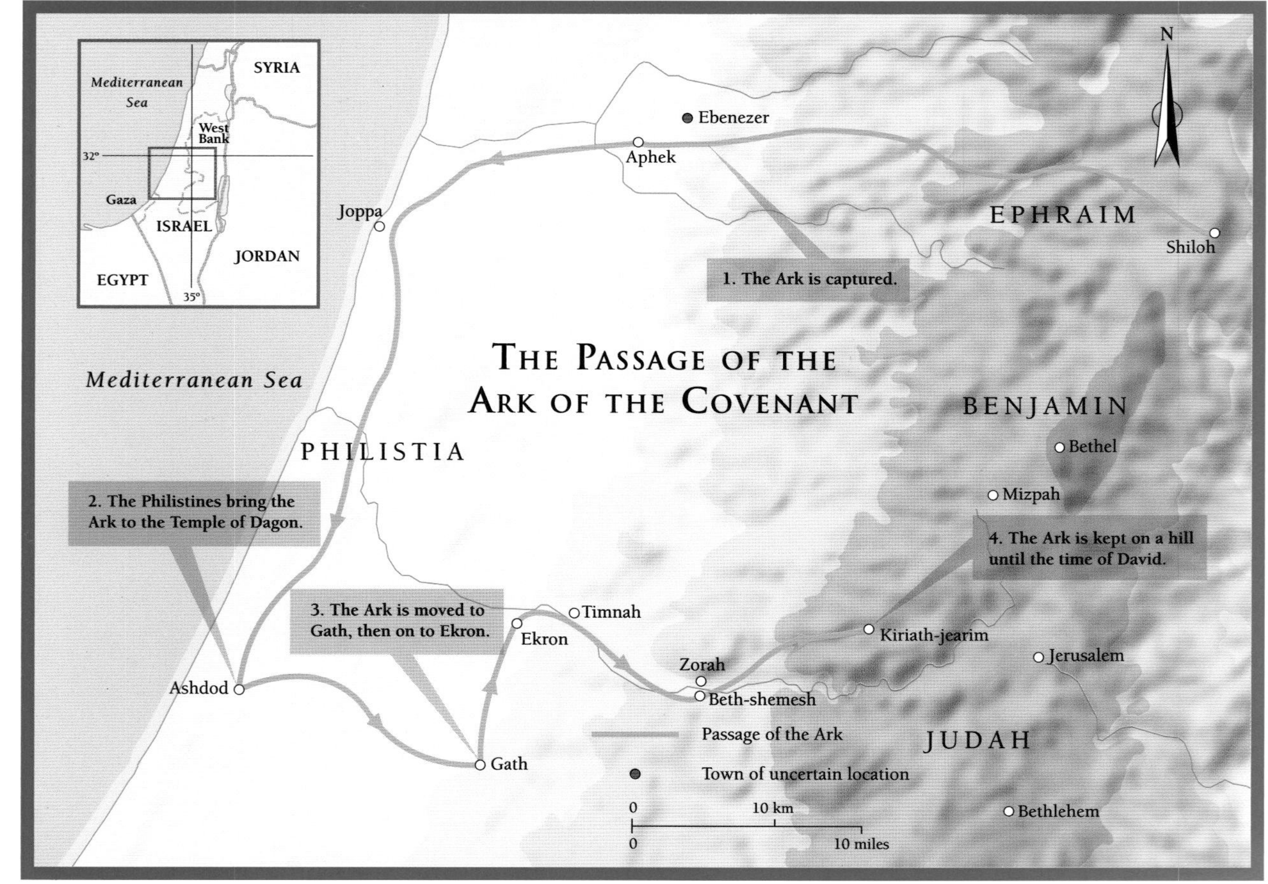

religious life of Israel, his own sons displaying corrupt and immoral behavior (1 Samuel 2).

SAMUEL AND THE PHILISTINE CRISIS

Samuel's conception and birth included the prophetic announcements that he would shape Israel's future, and his calling by God includes a statement of God's rejection of the line of Eli. This prophecy would begin to find immediate fulfillment. Samuel's career opens with a crisis. The Philistines, seeking to push into the Benjaminite heartland from the north, gather at Aphek. The Israelites muster at nearby Ebenezer, likely modern Izbet Sarta. But the battle goes badly, and the Israelites bring up the Ark from Shiloh. Though terrified by the Ark, the Philistines prevail and capture it. When the news reaches Eli at Shiloh, he dies of heart failure. Though the text is silent, this could have been the time when the Philistines destroyed Shiloh. Perhaps they dropped south to the road running from Modein to Lower Beth-horon, swept past Gibeon, up through Mizpah and Bethel to take Shiloh. Such a defeat would have traumatized the Hebrews, quite apart from the loss of the Ark.

THE ADVENTURES OF THE LOST ARK

The Israelite attempt to manipulate the Ark failed, but the Ark itself proved resilient. The Philistines' god Dagon had lost his temple to Samson and now found himself "fallen on his face to the ground before the ark of God" (1 Samuel 5:3), humiliated and mutilated in Ashdod by the ark of the defeated Hebrews. When a plague of tumors struck the Philistines, they decided they had kept the Ark long enough. The people of Gath and Ekron recoiled in horror at the thought of hosting the Israelite artifact, so the Philistines loaded it on a cart with an offering and launched it up the road toward Beth-shemesh, which was the nearest Israelite settlement. Even there, some who did not celebrate the Ark's return perished. The Ark finally found a resting place in Kiriath-jearim, where it remained until the time of David.

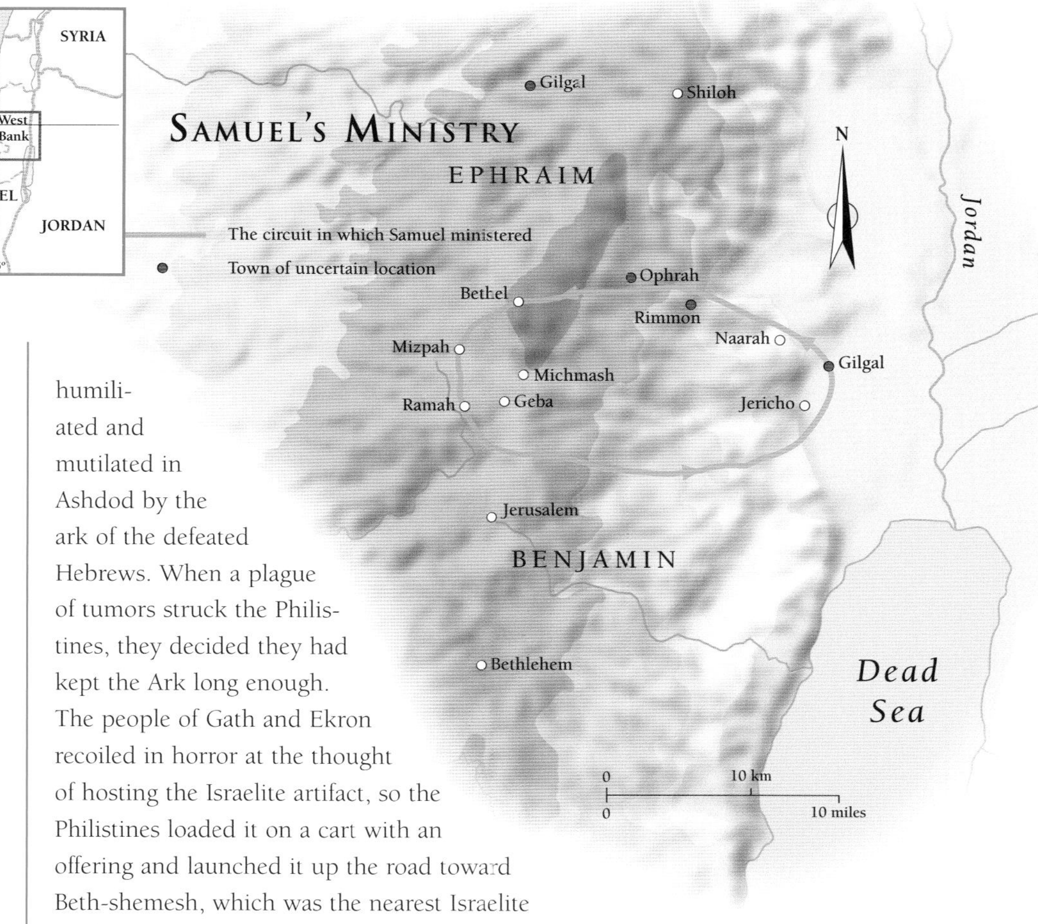

THE BENJAMINITE PLATEAU

A decidedly significant character in this account often goes unmentioned. This character speaks no lines, and "does" nothing, but decisively shapes the story. The character in question is a diamond-shaped area of land with points near Jerusalem in the south, Bethel in the north, Kiriath-jearim in the west, and the descent to Jericho in the east. This area, which is about 25 miles (40 km) from east to west and 15 miles (24 km) from north to south, is known as the central Benjaminite Plateau. It provides the setting for well over half of the events reported in the Old Testament. With the powerful tribes of Judah in the south, and Ephraim in the north, this saddle of lower land between the hills of Ephraim and the Judean hill country became the meeting place, often hostile, between all the forces seeking to control Canaan. The peculiar relationships among valleys, ridges, and seasonal streams force all traffic to move on certain fixed courses, all of which converge on the Benjaminite Plateau. The Philistines, coming from the coast, would move up the Aijalon Valley, the northernmost of six broad valleys providing access to the Shephelah. From there they could move northeast to Lower and Upper Beth-horon, or southeast to Kiriath-jearim and over to Gibeon, just west of the main north-south traffic artery, the watershed ridge route. Gaining this highway, near Samuel's home in Ramah, a military force could move easily south, threatening Jerusalem, Bethlehem, and points farther south still. To the north, an invader could knock off Mizpah, Bethel, and Shiloh, which are located east of the main highway. It's no wonder every clash between the Israelites and Philistines seems to center on this small but crucial region.

SAMUEL RULES ISRAEL

Despite the Ark's return, the Israelites remain demoralized and faithless. To revive them, Samuel calls an assembly in Mizpah. Thinking the Israelites vulnerable, the Philistines attack over their favorite route, the Aijalon Valley. Samuel's prayer, followed by a divinely caused confusion among the Philistines—"a deathly panic throughout the whole city" (1 Samuel 5:11)—rouses the Israelites to counterattack and chase the Philistines back into the valley. With the Philistines temporarily beaten, Samuel establishes a regular pattern of leadership, moving from Ramah to Bethel, Gilgal, and Mizpah.

BELOW: SAMUEL SACRIFICES TO GOD IN THIS ILLUSTRATION TAKEN FROM *HISTOIRE DE L'ANCIEN ET NOUVEAU TESTAMENT,* DATED C.E. 1724. IN RETURN, GOD THANKS SAMUEL BY HELPING HIM TO DEFEAT THE PHILISTINES.

THE MINOR JUDGES

AFTER HIM CAME SHAMGAR ... WHO KILLED SIX HUNDRED OF THE PHILISTINES WITH AN OXGOAD JUDGES 3:31

Readers of Judges often puzzle over the title given to the main characters of the book. Why are they called "judges" when they rarely exercise a judicial role? Typically, the judges are classified as "major" or "minor" judges. The major judges perform mighty acts of deliverance described in colorful narratives, while the minor judges look more like tribal chiefs and appear at the end of Judges 3, and in two lists before and after the Jephthah story in Judges 10 and 12. This distinction only complicates the question further.

One answer might be found in the interpretation of the Hebrew term used, *shophet*. In the cultures surrounding ancient Israel, whose languages were connected to ancient Hebrew, the equivalent term frequently applies to a royal appointee who issues legal decrees and enforces the will of the state. However useful this parallel might be, it describes an institution in the context of an urban monarchy. Since cultural context deeply shapes language usage, applying a word meaning from an urban monarchic culture to a rural, tribal culture poses significant risks. A more effective path would be to explore how the role of the *shophet* unfolds in the context of the tribal society of prestate Israel.

The reference literature on biblical Hebrew notes that the similar-sounding verb *shaphat* carries the notion of restoring balance and equilibrium, denoted by the word *shalom*, to the community. This insight suggests we might learn about the *shophet* by exploring the nature of Israel as a tribal culture. Indeed, the Old Testament and archaeological excavation depict premonarchic Israel as a community based on the image of the extended family, with nested layers of obligation following lines of kinship. The basic unit is the "father's house," presided over by the oldest living male member. In this family unit reside the man's unmarried sons, his married daughters with their families, and other clients. A typical family consisted of about 40 persons on a self-sustaining farm. The head of the family exercised great authority over his household, including the death penalty in some cases. The father's house was the basic unit for land tenure and the heart of the covenant Israel had with the Lord.

BELOW: IN PREMONARCHIC ISRAEL, EXTENDED FAMILIES WERE ON A REASONABLY EQUAL FOOTING IN TERMS OF PRODUCTION AND CONSUMPTION. PEOPLE TRADE ON A STREET IN JERUSALEM IN THIS PAINTING BY WILLIAM J. WEBB, DATED C.E. 1867.

FAMILY UNITS

These family units belonged to larger protective associations, also defined by kinship ties, called "clans." The clan typically coincided with a village. Persons would marry outside their father's house but normally inside the clan, a sensible move considering the role of land in Israelite families. The clan offered the principle protection for the family and its ethos. Central to this ethos was *shalom*. Normally translated as "peace," *shalom* actually refers to the equilibrium and balance of the community resulting from every member observing his or her obligations. Any breach of *shalom* had to be addressed, and the act of restoring the balance was expressed in the term *ga'al*, normally translated "redeem." The redeemer was a kinsman at the clan level who would intervene to restore the equilibrium of the family by fulfilling the threatened or violated kinship obligation. The actions involved included blood vengeance, advocacy for a needy or destitute family member, restoration of forfeited property, or even buying a kinsman out of debt servitude.

Beyond the level of the clan, it is less clear how disturbances of the community's *shalom* were addressed. The tribe functioned as the next level above the clan, but as a regional protective association the tribe might prove an awkward vehicle of conflict resolution. In fact, the book of Judges highlights this problem. In Judges 5, Deborah castigates the tribe of Reuben for not coming to the battle. She notes: "Among the clans [note the plural] of Reuben there were great searchings of heart" (Judges 5:15). Perhaps at the tribal level Reuben just couldn't act decisively enough to enter into battle? Similarly, in Judges 19–21 the tribe of Benjamin does not act decisively to punish the perpetrators of the rape which was recorded in Judges 19. The tribe seems an unwieldy vehicle of restoration.

THE INFLUENCE OF THE JUDGES

Looking at the figures in the book of Judges of whom the term "judge" is actually used, one thing becomes clear. All of them represent persons whose influence reaches far beyond the sphere of normal kinship obligations. This is obvious in the case of the "major" judges, and even Shamgar, who restores *shalom* to a whole region, but the same applies to the other "minor" judges as well. Tola is a "man of Issachar" but "lived in Shamir in the hill country of Ephraim" (Judges 10:1), out of his area.

"Judging" in ancient Israel's tribal culture, in fact, meant the defense of the kinship network and the restoration of its equilibrium by one who is not a near relative and who did not bear the kinsman's obligation. But such a person also lacked the authority inherent in the kinship structure. Such a person would need other authorization. Not surprisingly, therefore, we read of divine calls, dramatic anointings by the spirit of God, and portentous births. Even the massive economic resources noted for the minor judges underwrote their authority. In times of war, the judges would be military leaders, like the major judges, but in other situations they would appear as influential tribal leaders, like the minor judges. Ultimately, though, they were not different roles.

A Growing Family

Many of the minor judges had enormous families by today's standards, but their roles carried their influence far beyond immediate family concerns. Jair is credited with 30 sons, 30 daughters, riding on 30 donkeys, and ruling 30 cities. He is clearly a large-scale operator! The same applies to Ibzan, who also has 30 sons and 30 daughters. Moreover, he "gave his thirty daughters in marriage outside his clan" (Judges 12:9) and imported the same number for his sons, suggesting a move beyond the typical sphere of influence. Abdon also has 70 members of his household on 70 donkeys, stressing his greater influence. Only Elon lacks such a reference, but the location of his home, "Aijalon of Zebulun," might point to activity beyond his normal area.

LEFT: THIS PAINTING BY LEONARDO BELLINI SHOWS A FAMILY AT PRAYER IN THEIR HOME. THE DIVINE CALLS OF ALL MINOR AND MAJOR JUDGES REACHED FAR BEYOND ANY OBLIGATIONS TO FAMILY.

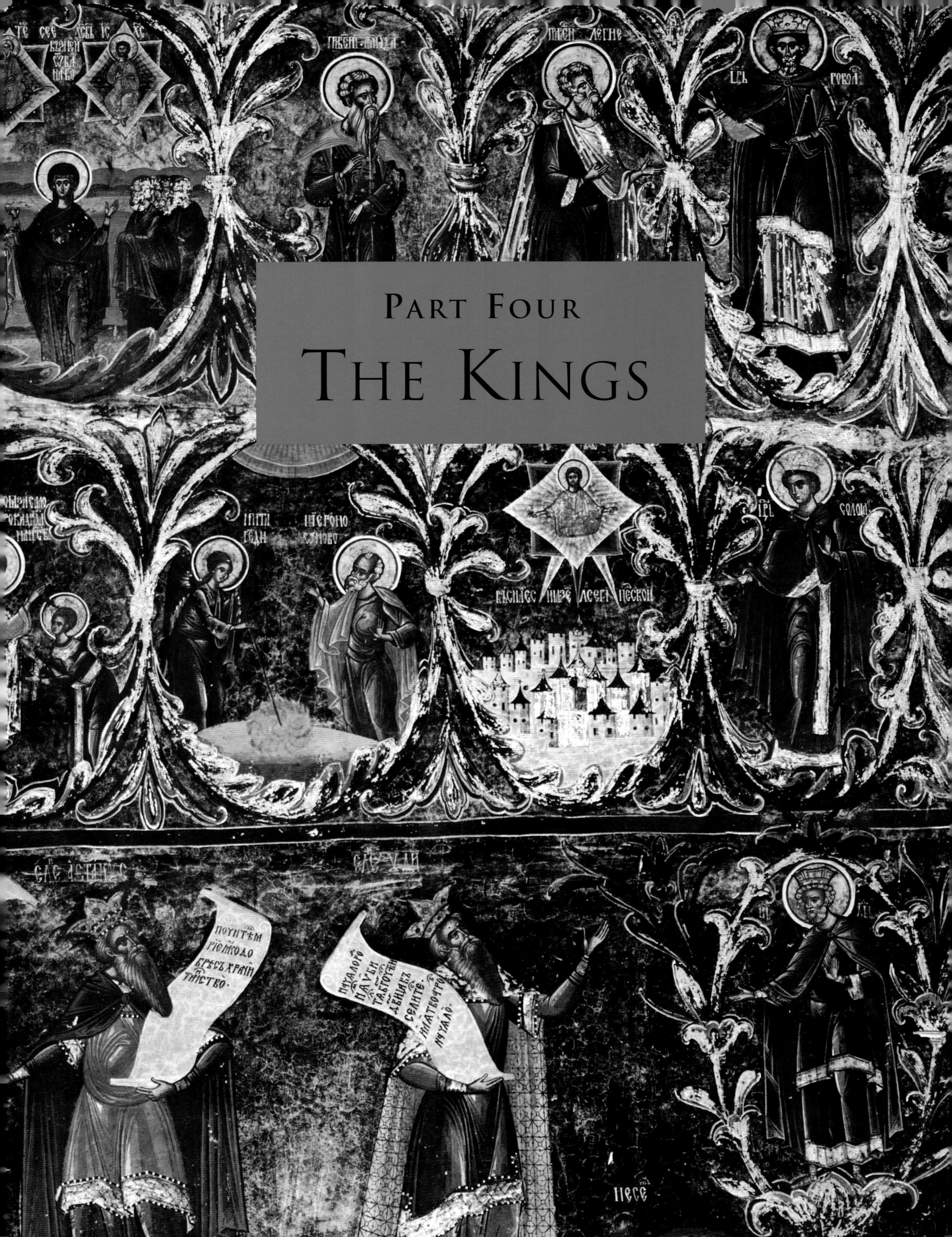

Part Four
The Kings

Kings Over Israel and Judah

THEY SAID, "NO! BUT WE ARE DETERMINED TO HAVE A KING OVER US" 1 SAMUEL 8:19

RIGHT: *KING SOLOMON AND THE QUEEN OF SHEBA,* CHAMPLEVE ENAMELED GOLD, 1181. THE QUEEN OF SHEBA SOUGHT SOLOMON'S GREAT WISDOM, BEARING GIFTS.

BELOW: IVORY PLAQUE DEPICTING KING DAVID ENTHRONED, FROM REIMS, FRANCE, NINTH–TENTH CENTURY C.E. SEVEN YEARS AFTER DAVID BECAME KING OF JUDAH HE WAS ALSO ANOINTED KING OF ISRAEL.

Once the Ark of the Covenant was restored and the Philistines temporarily subdued, the Israelites once more became a power in the land. The books of Samuel and Kings relate how Israel's sense of nationhood flourished after about 1051 B.C.E., when Samuel, the last of the Judges, yielded unwillingly to the people's demands and anointed Saul as Israel's first king. Samuel's reluctance stemmed from his belief that anointing a king would undermine the loyalty of the Israelite people to the one true God, and would lead to a culture of materialism and social inequality.

Saul came from Benjamin, the smallest of the Israelite tribes, and his family was among the humblest of the tribe. He was chosen because "There was not a man among the people of Israel more handsome than he" (1 Samuel 9:2), but it rapidly became apparent that he was an erratic ruler, to say the least. He was brave and idealistic, but his judgment was poor: he waged wars that he could not possibly win, and fell upon his sword after a hopeless battle in 1011 B.C.E. against the Philistines. His three sons died with him.

THE LINE OF DAVID

David, Saul's son-in-law, was the first of the great Israelite kings. He succeeded Saul as king of Judah, and became king over the whole of Israel in *c.* 1004 B.C.E. He ruled for almost 40 years, from about 1011 B.C.E. to 971 B.C.E. He was the first of a long dynasty, and his line would stretch to the first century C.E.: Joseph, the earthly father of Jesus, "was descended from the house and family of David" (Luke 2:4).

David's most important victory was his conquest in about 1000 B.C.E. of Jerusalem, possibly known at that time as Zion and occupied by an insignificant tribe of Gentiles called the Jebusites. David made Jerusalem the capital city of Israel. It was a strategic choice: Jerusalem formed a natural stronghold, protected to the east, the west, and the south by the valleys of Kidron and Hinnom.

The reign of David's son, Solomon, from 971 B.C.E. to 931 B.C.E., saw the kingdom of Israel in full flower. Under Solomon the seven-year construction of the Great Temple of Jerusalem was completed in 950 B.C.E. The Temple was built to house the Ark of the Covenant, and although primarily a shrine to the Lord God of Israel, it also symbolized the wealth and strength of Solomon's kingdom.

At the height of his power King Solomon was a wise, astute, and practical ruler. He consolidated and extended the achievements of his father, King David, overseeing extensive building projects and trading with powerful neighbors for spices and precious metals and stones.

THE FALL OF SOLOMON

Like Saul, Solomon fell from grace and incurred the wrath of the Lord; he took foreign wives who worshipped their own gods and turned his heart away from the one God. And God, as ever, was swift to anger. He caused divisions among the 12 tribes of Israel, and in 931 B.C.E. one kingdom became two: the kingdom of Judah, in the south, consisted of the tribes of Judah and Simeon, and the ten other tribes rebelled and formed the kingdom of Israel in the north.

The tribes were used to conflict with warlike Gentiles, but they were also used to bitter internal strife. The kings of Israel and Judah ruled over a heterogeneous group of tribes,

united only by their faltering obedience to the strict rules of worship and conduct prescribed in the first five books of the Old Testament. Territorial animosities and the proximity of Canaanite tribes meant that it was only too easy for the Israelites to be seduced from their exacting code of belief to the less demanding worship of false gods.

SAMUEL'S DOUBTS JUSTIFIED

Venal kings and queens arose in both Judah and Israel, and under them the people fell into religious hypocrisy and moral corruption. Despite repeated calls to repentance, notably by the prophets Elijah, Isaiah, and Jeremiah, successive rulers forsook the Lord and became cruel and greedy.

Not all the kings were faithless: in 715 B.C.E. Hezekiah of Judah heeded the warnings of Isaiah and instituted extensive religious reforms, but his son, Manasseh, completely undid all his father's good work. In 640 B.C.E. Manasseh's grandson, Josiah, took the throne and tried to bring about reforms, to no permanent avail.

Zedekiah, the last Old Testament king of Judah, came to power in 597 B.C.E. at the age of twenty-one. In 589 B.C.E. he initiated the hopeless revolt of Judea against King Nebuchadnezzar of Babylon. Nebuchadnezzar, in retaliation, "burned the house of the Lord, the king's house, and all the houses of Jerusalem" (2 Kings 25:9). The last remnant of the ancient kingdom of the Israelites was finished.

ABOVE: *JEZEBEL AND AHAB MET BY ELIJAH, C.* 1862–63, BY FREDERIC LEIGHTON. THE PROPHET ELIJAH CONDEMNED THE KING AND QUEEN OF ISRAEL AFTER THEY CAUSED THE DEATH OF NABOTH.

KING SAUL

THE LORD HAS ANOINTED YOU RULER OVER HIS PEOPLE ISRAEL 1 SAMUEL 10:1

Ammonites, Philistines, Amalekites—these enemies of Israel threatened to mutilate, enslave, and kill the fledgling nation of Israel in the twelfth to tenth centuries B.C.E. During these ominous times, three courageous and powerful kings—Saul, David, and Solomon—rallied their people. Although the nation suffered tremendous loss, the Israelites survived and flourished under their leadership. Despite his failures, the first king, Saul, saved his people during crucial battles and left an important legacy for Israel.

RIGHT: WILD DONKEYS ARE NATIVE TO ISRAEL, AND BY THE TIME OF SAUL THEY HAD BEEN DOMESTICATED FOR USE IN PLOUGHING AND LOAD-CARRYING AND FOR RIDING.

SAUL'S LOST DONKEYS

Saul, an unusually handsome yet humble man with an ordinary problem, undergoes an extraordinary transformation. Responding to his father's plea to find his lost donkeys, Saul's journey prompts his encounter with Samuel, the prophet who anoints him as king over Israel.

This dutiful son of Kish, who responds to his father's will and is sensitive to his father's fear about his own safety, is called upon to accept kingship over Israel. As king, he is expected to obey God in all things while saving Israel from the relentless enemies that plague the borders.

The biblical narrative shows that Saul rises to power, in part, because of the sorry state of the tribal leadership under the judges. It is ironic that the judges Joel and Abijah, the sons of the great prophet Samuel, are so corrupt that the elders confront Samuel, demanding a king.

Because he is God's spokesman, Samuel turns to God for instruction. The prophet learns that in demanding a human king, the people are ultimately rejecting God, for they seek a leader who will be like those of other nations, primarily expecting power and privilege. The commandments, however, demand that the people follow the divine word, pursuing God's righteousness and justice. God reluctantly agrees to appoint a king, but emphasizes that if his reign seeks wealth and glory, as do the nations around them, then Israel will fail in its mission to live up to what is required by the covenantal ideal.

Saul's search for his father's lost donkeys throughout the hill country of Ephraim and the region of Zuph (the region of Samuel's home) leads to the meeting of Samuel and Saul. Having been told that the local seer is an honorable man and, more importantly, that his pronouncements will come true, Saul seeks him, even though he does not know his name. Samuel, in the meantime, receives God's word that he is to anoint Saul as king, even before the two meet each other. This revelation signifies that kingship is based on God's sovereignty. Providentially, the first person of whom Saul inquires is Samuel himself.

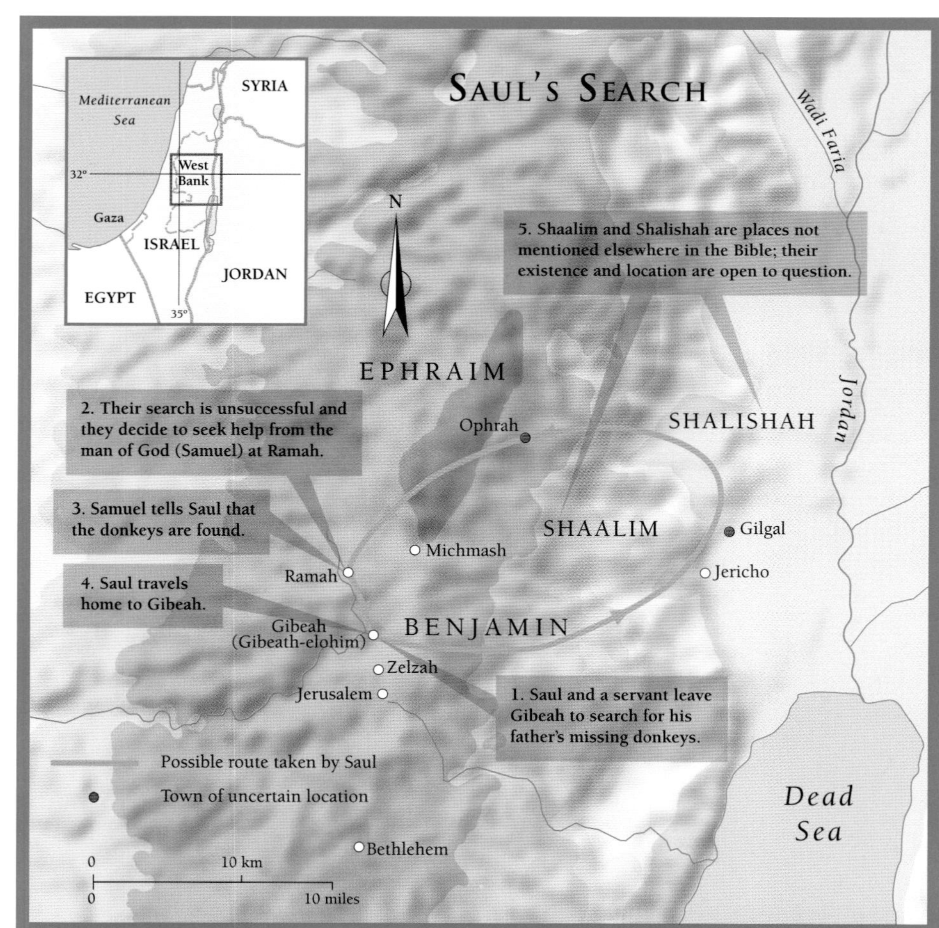

SAUL MEETS SAMUEL

Before even seeing Saul, Samuel receives word from God that this traveler is the one whom God approves to be king, underscoring God's decisive role. Saul learns that Samuel has a plan for him: Saul is to accompany Samuel to the shrine to share in a sacrifice offered to God. Samuel thus establishes that any institution of kingship takes place within the context of doing God's will. Samuel tells Saul that just as he was searching for the donkeys, which in fact have been found, all of Israel appeals to him for his leadership. When Samuel intimates that he will be welcomed by the people as king (1 Samuel 9:20), Saul responds with surprise and humility, protesting that he is from the least significant tribe of Israel and of the lowliest clan within Benjamin.

The first act that Saul and Samuel do together is to share a sacrifice, symbolizing the ideal action of the king who must rely on God and upon the prophet, God's spokesman. It is noteworthy that Samuel ushers Saul to a reserved seat of honor where he is served the choicest parts of the sacrifice normally reserved for the priests. This privilege highlights one of the sacred aspects of the kingly office, for when executed according to God's will, sacrifice is an important commandment that connects the worshipper, in this case the king, with God himself.

SAUL IS MADE KING

Before Saul is publicly acclaimed as king, Samuel anoints him in secret, pouring oil on Saul's head. This method becomes the hallmark to signify the prophet's designation of God's choice and, because of this ceremony, the kings of Israel and the ideal future king (the messiah) are referred to as God's anointed. Samuel explains, moreover, that this human act of anointing with oil is, in truth, a symbol of God's anointing, which will be actualized by three unusual signs. First, Saul will encounter strangers who know of the donkeys' whereabouts; second, Saul will meet pilgrims who will offer him bread; and third, Saul will come upon a band of prophets who will precipitate Saul's spiritual transformation and his ability to receive the spirit of the Lord.

Until Saul is publicly proclaimed as king, however, he remains secretive about the anointing. When his uncle asks about his activities, he demurs; when Samuel initiates a popular acclamation at Mizpah by choosing lots, he hides. Perhaps these actions underscore that God acceded to the people's demand for a king even though their desires were based on a lack of trust in his saving ways. God's hand in choosing Saul, however, is still paramount, for when Saul

ABOVE: *SAUL HIDING AMONG THE STUFF*, 1866, BY JAMES SMETHAM. ALTHOUGH SAUL WAS GIVEN MANY SIGNS THAT HE WAS TO BE ISRAEL'S FIRST KING, HE WAS STILL NOT READY TO ACCEPT KINGSHIP.

RIGHT: STONE HEAD OF A SEMITE CHIEF WITH EGYPTIAN INFLUENCE, FROM AMMAN. ALSO KNOWN AS RABBAH, AMMAN WAS THE CAPITAL CITY OF THE AMMONITE STATE.

cannot be found, God discloses his hiding place. When Saul appears, all seem pleased with this strikingly tall man, and proclaim "Long live the king!" (1 Samuel 10:24). Their accolades are challenged, however, by the remarks of some that follow soon afterward: "How can this man save us?" (1 Samuel 10:27). Indeed, Saul immediately faces terrifying military provocation from the Ammonites.

SAUL AGAINST THE AMMONITES

The biblical account of the origins of the Ammonite people reveals the scorn with which Israel considered their neighbors to the east. Ben-ammi, a child conceived from the incestuous relationship of Lot and his younger daughter, was considered the progenitor of this violent people. In an earlier generation, Israel's judge Jephthah fought against the Ammonites, saving the Israelites of Gilead from their continual raids, yet the aftermath of his victory was tainted by his horrific sacrifice of his daughter. Yet even this fearsome background is not enough to prepare Saul's people for the ghastly tactics of the Ammonite king, Nahash, whose very name means "snake." Having successfully besieged the Israelite city of Jabesh-gilead, Nahash proposes: "On this condition I will make a treaty with you, namely that I gouge out everyone's right eye, and thus put disgrace upon all Israel" (1 Samuel 11:2).

Desperate for deliverance, the Jabesh-gileadites appeal for help throughout Israel. The people of Gibeah, Saul's own city, are distraught, yet helpless. Upon hearing their cries, Saul immediately takes action. Sacrificing a pair of oxen, he sends the pieces throughout the tribes of Israel as a call to war, demanding that men immediately report for duty as he assembles an army. Showing great tactical skill, Saul assembles the troops at the town of Bezek and prepares a successful attack, coming upon the Ammonites unawares.

Saul displays his leadership by quashing internecine threats as well. Being so impressed with his victory, some of the Israelites demand that those groups who earlier had not been supportive of Saul be put to death. Rather than use his success to eliminate the opposition, Saul insists that they be given amnesty. This shrewd move on his part also allows him to capitalize on his victory; he uses it as an opportunity to renew his kingship at Gilgal, taking another step to unify the tribes. Indeed, all come together to offer sacrifice and to thank God for the victory over the Ammonites.

SAUL AGAINST THE PHILISTINES

From the twelfth to tenth centuries B.C.E., Philistia proved to be the most resilient of Israel's enemies and threatened the existence of the nation. Philistia, located on Israel's Mediterranean coast, consisted of a league of five powerful city-states:

BELOW: SAUL AND HIS PEOPLE ANGERED THE LORD SO HE DESTROYED THE WHEAT CROP, ON WHICH THEY DEPENDED FOR THEIR NUTRITIONAL NEEDS, AS A SIGN OF HIS DISPLEASURE.

Gaza, Ashkelon, Ashdod, Ekron, and Gath. Their menacing raids against Israel and their decades of oppression were known to Saul's ancestors from the accounts of the famous judge Samson, who was able to suppress, but not eliminate, their threat. Philistia reached an apex of power during the reigns of Saul and David; both kings were mercilessly tested, and Saul eventually died at their hands.

Before his death, however, the early days of Saul's kingship illustrate that initially he was successful at stemming the tide of the Philistine onslaught into Israelite territory and in preparing the way for David's ultimate victory against them.

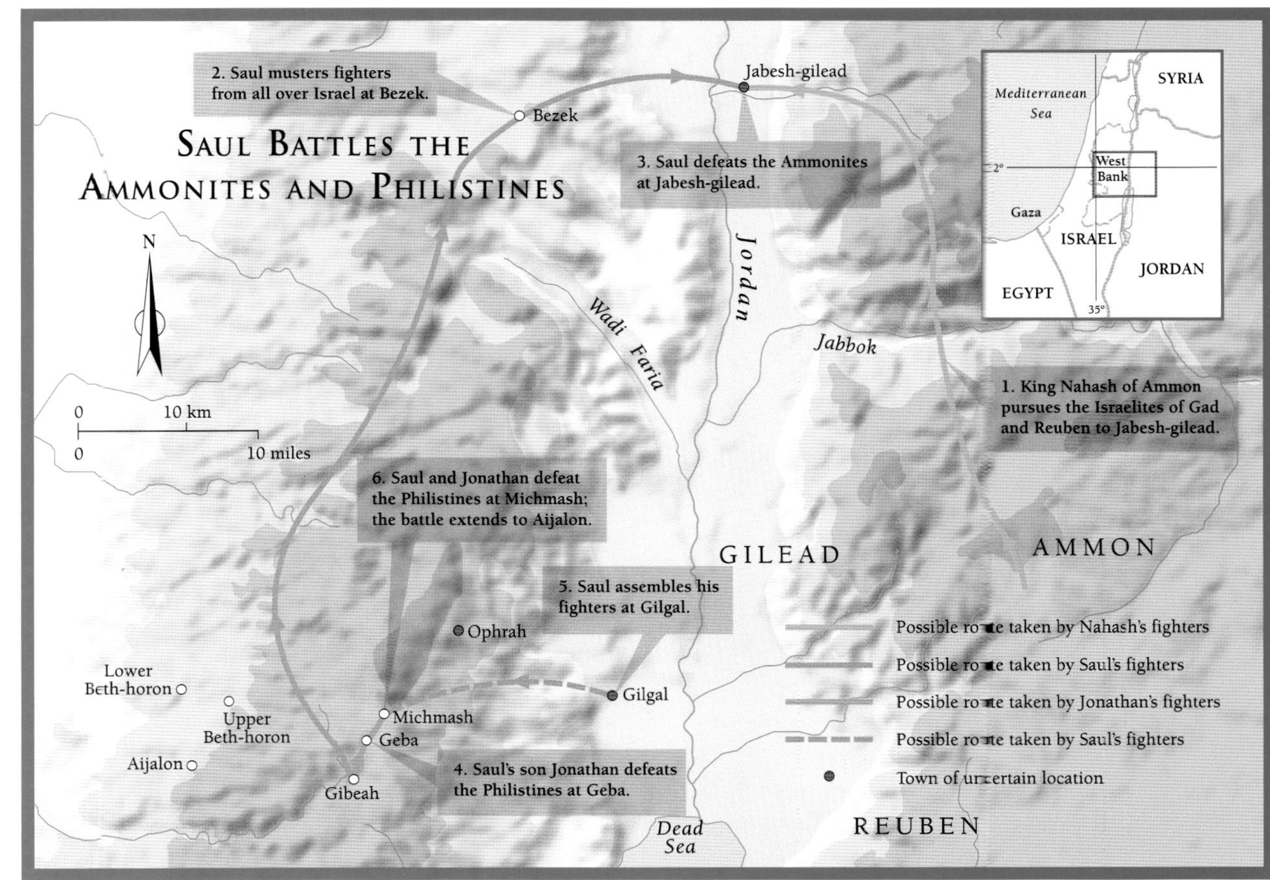

One of Saul's first acts after the defeat of the Ammonites to the east is to organize the Israelites' defense against their western nemesis. While Saul gathers his troops, his son Jonathan advances against the Philistines with his own division, prompting some of the worst of the Philistine retaliation. The Israelites are reduced to hiding "in caves and in holes and in rocks and in tombs and in cisterns" (1 Samuel 13:6). In response, Saul assembles the Israelite army for maneuvers at Gilgal. While the king prepares his demoralized troops, the prophet Samuel instructs Saul to wait for seven days for his arrival before Saul offers sacrifices to God.

These instructions serve as a test of Saul's willingness to accept the prophet as liaison between God and king. Saul is

RIGHT: AFTER THE DEFEAT OF THE AMALEKITES, SAUL SPARED THE BEST OF THE SHEEP AND CATTLE, AGAINST THE EXPLICIT INSTRUCTIONS GIVEN BY SAMUEL BEFORE THE BATTLE.

expected to trust in the word of the prophet when times become most challenging.

While awaiting Samuel's arrival, Saul perceives that the troops are becoming more concerned and that their loyalty to him is diminishing. In an apparent attempt to reinvigorate their allegiance, Saul offers sacrifices before Samuel's return, a breach of God's commandments and of Samuel's expressed instructions. Samuel condemns Saul's actions as showing disloyalty to God, and declares that God's response will be to take away Saul's kingship and dynastic succession over Israel.

Despite the devastating words of God's prophet, Saul continues to deploy his troops. The odds against them seem impossible: the Philistines launch a multi-faceted campaign with three contingents, toward Ophrah, Beth-horon, and the valley of Zeboim. Not only do the Philistines have superior numbers, but their iron monopoly and use of the chariot give them a remarkable advantage in weaponry.

BELOW: THE EARTHQUAKE THAT PANICS THE PHILISTINES AT THE PASS OF MICHMASH IS SENT BY GOD, WHO SHOWS THAT JONATHAN'S FAITH IN THE ASSISTANCE OF THE LORD IS WELL FOUNDED.

JONATHAN

While Saul continues to strategize, Saul's son Jonathan, who has his own loyal contingents, plans an assault against the Philistines at the strategic pass of Michmash. Against all odds, Jonathan has great success at the battle described in language reminiscent of God's deliverance of the Israelites from Pharaoh's troops during the Exodus. Indicative of God's own presence and support of the Israelites who face an intractable enemy, there is an earthquake that throws the Philistines into a panic. Capitalizing on Jonathan's successful rout, Saul adds his own contingent to the battle, which spreads throughout the hill country of Ephraim. The Israelites enjoy an unprecedented victory, having success "from Michmash to Aijalon" (1 Samuel 14:31).

Despite Saul's and Jonathan's victory, however, a vexing problem occurs toward the end of this segment of the Philistine war. Saul vows that his troops will not consume any food before the battle is won. Yet this vow leads to two terrible incidents. Because the Israelites are so weakened, upon their victory against the Philistines they slaughter their cattle without taking the proper steps to follow the food laws, eating the meat with its blood. This was considered a great offense against God. In addition, because Jonathan did not hear of his father's vow, he and his troops eat some honey that they discover. Jonathan unknowingly puts himself, his battalion, and the Israelites in violation of the vow, ultimately because of his father's rash words. In order to rectify the situation, Saul takes draconian measures: he declares that anyone who has eaten in defiance of his vow will be put to death. When the casting of lots shows that the culprit was Jonathan, Saul remains unwavering.

Facing this appalling wrong, Jonathan's supporters do not remain silent. They provide a ransom for him, proving not only their loyalty to their beloved Jonathan, but also displaying a challenge to Saul's own authority.

SAUL AGAINST THE AMALEKITES

The temporary cessation of hostilities between the Philistines and Israelites is not followed by peace. Now Israel must confront its longstanding enemy, the Amalekites and their king, Agag. The Amalekites, the descendants of Esau, were infamous for their unjustified attacks upon the Israelites in the wilderness. In the particularly difficult wilderness wanderings, the prelude to the Israelites' entrance into the Promised Land, the Amalekites preyed upon the helpless, attacking Israel from the rear.

The tumultuous relations between the Israelites and the Amalekites are a prelude to the instructions God gives to Saul. God directly instructs the first king that it is his will for Amalek to come to an end. The Amalekites are to be placed under "the ban," namely, chosen by God for destruction. This means that the Israelites are to carry out the total annihilation of the population and its possessions. This arresting declaration is given for God's expressed purpose: so that Israel does not fall into the abominable practices of the surrounding nations.

The Bible portrays the practice of "the ban" as occurring only under God's directive—it cannot be initiated by humans and cannot be undertaken for personal gain.

Saul once again proves to be an excellent strategist and achieves a great victory, in part by breaking the alliance that the Amalekites had with the Kenites, another mobile people. He warns the Kenites, who had settled among the Amalekites, to separate themselves from this doomed people. It becomes all the more striking that Saul begins by following God's commands in sparing the people whom God did not destine to be destroyed. He nonetheless disobeys God by sparing Agag, the Amalekite king. Saul's victory in this tremendous battle is complete; it stretches "from Havilah as far as Shur" (1 Samuel 15:7). With the exception of Agag, all other Amalekites are placed under the ban; however, all the choice sheep and cattle are spared as well, pointing not only to Saul's disobedience of God, but to his desire to profit from the campaign.

SAUL FAILS AGAIN

It is with this test of following God's command to carry out the ban that Saul fails a second time to do right as king. Because of his disobedience, God tells Samuel, "I regret that I made Saul king, for he has turned back from following me, and has not carried out my commands" (1 Samuel 15:11). Once again, we find that Israel's office of king cannot be like that of other nations. For others, the will of the king reigns supreme. By contrast, in Israel it is God's will that remains paramount and is expressed through the words of the prophets. Samuel must now search for Saul to declare God's judgment. Saul, however, has traveled to Carmel to construct a monument for himself. This act not only expresses his hubris, but may also show Saul's attempt to solidify his rule in this fertile, yet sometimes rebellious region.

It is significant that Saul and Samuel have their final encounter at Gilgal, located within the territory of Benjamin, the land of Saul's own inheritance. This is the third of three crucial encounters that Samuel has with Saul at that location. At the first, Samuel initiated the people's renewal of the kingship with Saul, after his decisive victory against the Ammonites (1 Samuel 11:14). At the second, Samuel condemned Saul for not following God's commands regarding the sacrifice (1 Samuel 13: 13–15). At this third and last encounter, Samuel's repudiation of Saul occurs with stunning drama.

Saul approaches Samuel without any acknowledgment that he has done wrong. In fact, he insists that he carried out God's will! Samuel is not swayed by Saul's feigned innocence. In response, Samuel's words drip with sarcasm: "What then is this bleating of sheep in my ears, and the lowing of cattle that I hear?" (1 Samuel 15:14).

Saul evades the truth, offering two excuses. First, he states that the decision to spare Agag was done by the army. Second, he declares that because the animals are marked for sacrifice, the army did not do anything wrong. Saul's abnegation of responsibility is further underscored by his scornful words to Samuel. The king reports that the animals are to be sacrificed "to the Lord *your God* in Gilgal" (1 Samuel 15:21 [italics added]; see also verse 30). The place where Saul's kingship was renewed, as well as twice taken away, now becomes the location from which Saul distances himself. The Lord now appears foreign to the very man he chose to lead his people; Saul can only refer to him as *Samuel's* God!

SAMUEL DENOUNCES SAUL

In response to Saul's arrogance, Samuel condemns him, reiterating that God has rejected Saul as king over Israel. Echoing a theme found in other prophets, Samuel states that sacrifice without corresponding fidelity to the covenant is not pleasing to God. In Hosea, for example, we find: "For I desire steadfast love and not sacrifice, the knowledge of God rather than burnt offerings" (Hosea 6:6; see also Micah 6:6–8).

ABOVE: *THE PROPHET SAMUEL* BY CLAUDE VIGNON (1593–1670). SAMUEL WAS THE LAST OF THE JUDGES AND BECAME THE INTERMEDIARY BETWEEN THE LORD AND ISRAEL'S FIRST KING, SAUL.

THE AMALEKITES

Throughout the Bible, the Amalekites are portrayed as attempting to annihilate Israel. The Israelites faced their attacks first when they were a fledgling people in the desert, second when they began to establish themselves in the land, and finally, when they were exiled generations later. The book of Judges, for example, reports that the Midianites and Amalekites destroyed the entirety of Israel's food supply: both by wiping out all of the agricultural plantings and by killing the livestock (Judges 6:1–6). In later generations, while living in Persian lands under King Ahasuerus, a certain Haman, the king's administrator, proposed to annihilate the Jewish people. This Haman is identified as a descendant of Agag, the notorious Amalekite king (Esther 3:1). God's response to the Amalekites was to command Israel to destroy them (Deuteronomy 25:17–19); specifically, the Israelites are instructed to wipe them out upon settling the land of Canaan.

Thus, Samuel relates, "Surely, to obey is better than sacrifice, and to heed than the fat of rams" (1 Samuel 15:22). Samuel views Saul's action as the equivalent of rebellion, namely, a rejection of God and God's authority over the king. In addition, Samuel denounces Saul's sin as "divination." Divination, a practice considered characteristic of Israel's neighbors, included attempts to control fate in opposition to God's wishes, false prophecy, and cursing to bring harm upon others. Such practices had the potential to be manipulative of desperate people as well as contrary to God's will. Instead of being the paragon of obedience to God, Saul pursues the practices of the nations that God condemns. God chose Israel to be a people "set apart" to follow his commandments; instead, under Saul's leadership, they are following the practices of the Canaanites. Saul, who was earlier chosen by God, is now "rejected" by him (1 Samuel 15:23). This pronouncement indicates that God's removal of Saul is complete and definitive.

Upon hearing these condemnatory words, Saul attempts to court Samuel's favor and to solicit God's forgiveness. Although he admits that he has sinned, his words ring hollow. Just as he had earlier blamed the army, now he indicts the people, whom he says he feared. Samuel recognizes, however, that Saul's words are self-serving and that he learned nothing from his earlier mistakes; he remains unyielding. In a dramatic scene, Saul grabs onto Samuel's robe as he departs, tearing it. To seize the hem of another's

ABOVE: ISRAEL'S FIRST EXPERIMENT WITH KINGSHIP ENDS BADLY, WITH SAMUEL'S MISGIVINGS PROVING TO HAVE BEEN JUSTIFIED. SAUL COULD NOT OBEY THE WORDS OF THE LORD.

RIGHT: *SAMUEL KILLING AGAG, KING OF THE AMALEKITES* BY ROMBOUT VAN TROYEN (*C.* 1605–1650). FACED WITH SAUL'S FAILURE, SAMUEL CARRIES OUT GOD'S WILL HIMSELF.

garment is suggestive of supplication and deference; here it represents Saul's final appeal for leniency. Samuel sees the tear as representative of Saul's rejection by God. He proclaims, "the Lord has torn the kingdom of Israel from you this very day" (1 Samuel 15:28). The kingship, instead, is to be given to another.

DEATH OF AGAG

In spite of his sin, Saul insists that Samuel return with him to Gilgal (1 Samuel 15:25, 30) so that he may be honored before the elders of Israel. Although Samuel outright refused the first time Saul asked, he assents to this second request. The accompaniment, however, is not what Saul hoped it would be. Rather than using the journey to bring honor to Saul, Samuel uses it to shame him while accomplishing God's will. Although it is true that Saul worshipped the Lord while Samuel was with him in Gilgal, Samuel immediately follows the act of worship with a call to have Agag brought before him. We find this sobering report: "And Samuel hewed Agag in pieces before the Lord in Gilgal" (1 Samuel 15:33). This shameful death is meted out because of Agag's particular defiance against God. God's will is now fulfilled, not by the king, but by the prophet.

SAUL IS REJECTED BY GOD

Samuel and Saul remain estranged, and Samuel grieves over Saul, previewing the extraordinary statement: "And the Lord was sorry that he had made Saul king over Israel" (1 Samuel 15:35). The divine pathos thus expressed, the biblical account now turns to God's new choice for king who, despite his various failures, will remain God's beloved. This man is David.

With the rejection of Saul, Israel learns that their true king is the Lord. It is his plan and his will that they must follow. God has put in place the mechanisms for allowing the king to know what is right. It is God who selects the king. It is he who chooses the prophets who act as his spokesmen. These same prophets anoint the kings of Israel. All of this is clearly presented to Saul, yet Saul fails to appreciate that he is to act in partnership with God and that God's directives, given through the prophets, must be obeyed unfailingly. Saul believes he can supersede God's will as expressed by Samuel; his arrogance not only separates him from God, but removes his posterity from carrying on the dynasty.

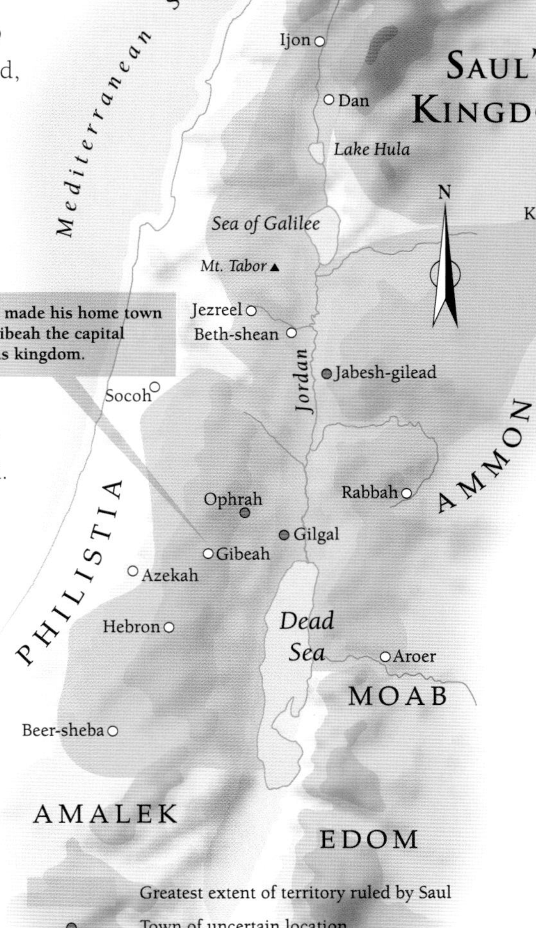

Sadly, Saul never truly accepts God's will. Even after the multiple occasions in which Samuel reveals God's rejection, Saul refuses to relinquish the throne. The humble man who began his journey looking for his father's donkeys is now stubbornly entrenched. His obstinacy causes needless anguish for his family and his people. In his own family, he uses his daughters as pawns while arranging marriages for them with David, all the while plotting to kill his son-in-law. He leads his son Jonathan to his death while battling the Philistines—a struggle that suffers from the divided loyalties of the army (some are devoted to David, others to Saul).

The enormity of the civil war that breaks out between those committed to David and those loyal to Saul has its roots in Saul's hubris and continues for generations after Saul's and David's deaths.

KING DAVID

THE LORD DECLARES TO YOU THAT THE LORD WILL MAKE YOU A HOUSE 2 SAMUEL 7:11

RIGHT: THIS NINETEENTH-CENTURY ILLUSTRATION SHOWS DAVID CARING FOR HIS FATHER'S SHEEP. HOWEVER, HIS LIFE CHANGES WHEN GOD CHOOSES HIM AS SAUL'S SUCCESSOR.

BELOW: *ANOINTING OF DAVID*, 1842, BY FELIX-JOSEPH BARRIAS. SAMUEL ANOINTS DAVID AS THE NEXT KING, BUT SAUL RETAINS THE THRONE FOR QUITE SOME TIME.

The rise and fall of Saul, the first king of Israel, demonstrates what the office ought to be: the king must follow God's will and keep the commandments. These standards must always supersede any quest for human power and glory. With the advent of David as king, Israel finds a brave and dedicated leader, who, although sometimes blinded by personal ambition, nonetheless accepts God's chastisement and unifies the people.

With the story of David, Israel finds a paradigm of justice. This model bolsters the conviction that humanity can hope for a future in which righteous leadership displaces aggrandizement and in which the world becomes a dwelling place for God. Unlike Saul, whose influence over Israel is relatively brief, David becomes the head of "a house"—a dynasty with which God makes an eternal covenant (see 2 Samuel 7).

SAMUEL FINDS DAVID

Saul, having refused God's decision that rejected him as king, stubbornly remains on the throne, thus setting the stage for dividing his people and subjecting the nation to violent conflict. The tension is already felt when the prophet Samuel obeys the divine command to travel to Bethlehem to locate God's choice for the new king, Saul's replacement. Upon seeing Samuel, the elders tremble for fear of ensuing violence. Samuel, however, reassures them that he comes only to offer sacrifice.

The sacrifice becomes the occasion for Samuel to gather the sons of a certain Jesse, as commanded by God. Samuel eyes each son, waiting for God's indication for his chosen one. Struck by the arresting appearance of Jesse's tallest and most handsome son, Eliab, Samuel believes he has found the new king. God, however, declares "the Lord does not see as mortals see; they look on the outward appearance, but the Lord looks on the heart" (1 Samuel 16:7). Thus, the choice of David may be especially indicative of his remarkable character. A further contrast is made between David and Saul by their respective absences when Samuel seeks them. Although both men are missing when Samuel searches each of their families, Saul hides among the baggage, whereas David is absent because he tends to his father's sheep. The image of the devoted shepherd becomes a metaphor for David's care of God's people.

LEFT: A TWELFTH-CENTURY ENGLISH PSALTER (BOOK OF PSALMS), SHOWING THE TREE OF JESSE. ACCORDING TO BIBLICAL TRADITION, JESSE'S FAMILY EXTENDED THROUGH DAVID TO JESUS.

Before returning to Ramah, Samuel anoints David as king with the horn of oil. David is immediately filled with "the spirit of the Lord" (1 Samuel 16:13)—God's presence—that will abide in him, allowing him to defeat Israel's enemies and to lead his people. While this mark of God's presence comes upon David, Saul experiences quite the opposite, for God's spirit departs from the rejected king. Instead, God sends an "evil spirit" that torments Saul (1 Samuel 16:14). This "evil spirit," which may represent Saul's growing insanity, begins to possess him as David becomes king. It accounts for Saul's bizarre behavior that ultimately puts him on a path to his death.

DAVID COMFORTS SAUL

In the early stages of Saul's mental torment, his servants take pity on the obviously troubled king. Their suggestion is that a musician, who plays the lyre, be brought into the palace, providing solace to Saul's tormented soul. The once powerful king is now so desperate that he must rely on the advice of his servants.

One particular servant, not mentioning David's name, reports that he is acquainted with "a son of Jesse the Bethlehemite who is skillful in playing, a man of valor, a warrior, prudent in speech, and a man of good presence; and the Lord is with him" (1 Samuel 16:18).

These words ominously indict Saul, for David's virtues are the characteristics that Saul has spurned. In addition, whereas God is with David, God abandons Saul (1 Samuel 18:12). Curiously, once this son of Jesse is described, Saul refers to him by name, sending word to Jesse, "Send me your son David who is with the sheep" (1 Samuel 16:19). Because these words echo the description of David when he was first introduced (1 Samuel 16:11), it is possible to infer that Saul may have heard about Samuel's anointing of the young David in Bethlehem. Jesse's act of sending David along with generous gifts, namely, a supply of bread and wine as well as a kid, may signal an attempt at appeasement. The tension that will soon exist between David and Saul is thus suggested with this first, deceptively benign introduction.

Desperate for relief, Saul welcomes this musician and shepherd and cannot help but love him. Saul appoints David as his armor-bearer, a position that demonstrates Saul's initial trust in David. David's skilled musicianship is initially effective; Saul's evil spirit departs and the king is relieved whenever David plays. The beginning of the end of Saul's kingship is suggested, nonetheless, not only by the existence of this disorder which continues to plague him, but also because Saul is compelled to ask Jesse that David remain with him in the king's court.

BELOW: *KING DAVID*, 1890, BY SIR EDWARD BURNE-JONES. LIKE THOSE OF MANY OTHER CULTURES, THE ISRAELITES BELIEVED MUSIC COULD DRIVE AWAY EVIL SPIRITS, AND SO DAVID WAS ASKED TO PLAY FOR SAUL.

RIGHT: NINETEENTH-CENTURY PRINT SHOWING DAVID SLAYING A LION. THE LIONS FOUND IN ISRAEL IN THE TIME OF DAVID WERE THE SMALLER ASIATIC TYPE. THEY BECAME EXTINCT DUE TO OVERHUNTING.

DAVID AND GOLIATH

Ominous maneuvers by the army of the Philistines torment the Israelites. Their location between Socoh and Azekah demonstrates their power, for they have moved beyond their own territory on the coast and have infiltrated near the Israelite highlands. The Philistines have been at war with Israel since its tribal period; Saul had been chosen by God to save the Israelites from the sufferings inflicted by their nemesis (1 Samuel 9:16), yet he repeatedly has squandered his responsibility. Saul now faces one of the worst of the Philistine challenges from their mighty leader Goliath, yet all he can do in the face of the giant's demands is tremble.

Goliath's very appearance is petrifying. Besides his enormous height, equivalent to about 10 ft (3 m), his armor and weaponry are unparalleled. His entire body is covered with bronze protection: with a helmet, a coat of mail, and greaves (leg armor). Moreover, his weapons of aggression are fearsomely described, also with outsized proportions: "the shaft of his spear was like a weaver's beam, and his spear's head weighed six hundred shekels [about 20 lbs/9 kg] of iron" (1 Samuel 17:7). Although this sight alone would be enough to completely terrorize the Israelites, his proposal is worse. He demands that they send one man to fight him. The people of the vanquished one would serve the nation of the victor as slaves. Under Saul's leadership, all the Israelites can do is tremble with fear. They are completely paralyzed.

Although the account of Goliath occurs after the narrative about David's introduction to Saul, it may presume a different sequence, as it appears that David is yet completely unknown to the king. In this report, the eldest sons of Jesse, Eliab, Abinadab, and Shammah, serve in Saul's army, whereas David serves as a messenger between his father and brothers while tending sheep. Not only are David's brothers devoted to Saul, but Jesse too shows loyalty by sending provisions to the army. David hardly seems either royal or soldierly in this description. He is, rather, the dutiful son who obeys his father's command. Upon arriving at the army camp, David finds that the army has already been deployed to meet the Philistines. Goliath continues to taunt Israel, insisting that they engage in a decisive, one-on-one battle. Hearing this, David rightly sizes up the situation; it is not just Israel, but God himself whom Goliath defies.

The jealousy that Saul will soon feel toward David is previewed by the scorn of David's brothers who accuse the latter of abandoning his responsibility to the sheep. But it is precisely David's care of these helpless animals that has prepared him for this critical moment.

When Saul is incredulous that a mere shepherd with no army experience volunteers to fight the Philistine, David argues that he has risked his life caring for his sheep. He has slain ferocious bears and lions, rescuing his charges. David reasons that Goliath is like an animal that he will also be able to defeat. David's words are not mere bravado, for he attributes his past successes to God. The one who rescued David "from the paw of the lion and from the paw of the bear" will also not fail to save David "from the hand of this Philistine" (1 Samuel 17:37).

It is not surprising that Saul's attempts to prepare David for battle are hapless. Saul's armor and sword are useless to David. The youth quickly removes them and advances only with his staff, his slingshot, and his pouch containing five stones—the same weapons one would use to protect one's sheep. This is an appropriate metaphor since it is truly the people of Israel—God's sheep—whom David is protecting from the Philistines.

The great Philistine champion, who is accompanied by his shield-bearer, encased in his armor, and protected by his massive armaments, derides the youthful, handsome challenger, cursing him in the name of the Philistine gods and threatening to toss his remains to the wild animals.

David's response is laden with terms that evidence his trust in God and show that the contest is hardly about a battle between Philistia and Israel; it is between those who defy God and God himself. David remarks that he is accompanied by "the Lord of hosts, the God of the armies of Israel" (1 Samuel 17:45), who will deliver Goliath into his hand. This is not all. David recognizes that the purpose of the contest is to defeat the entirety of the Philistines—not just their champion. The victory will be for "all this assembly," friend and foe alike, to testify "that the Lord does not save by sword and spear; for the battle is the Lord's and he will give you into our hand" (1 Samuel 17:47).

Ironically, the Philistine says to David, "Am I a dog, that you come to me with sticks?"

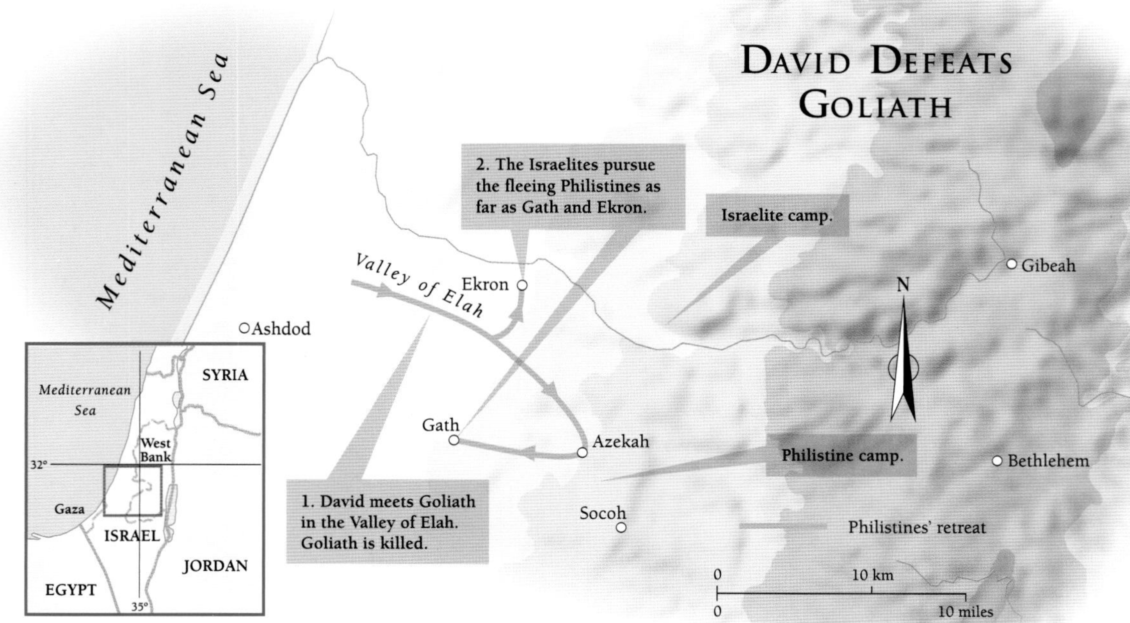

(1 Samuel 17:43). Indeed, the young hero immobilizes Goliath, not as a fearsome warrior, but as an animal. The stone strikes his head and he falls prone to the ground, face first. In another unexpected twist, the youth who shunned Saul's sword as being unwieldy takes Goliath's own sword, and, in a final act of humiliation, slays the tyrant who self-assuredly threatened to enslave an entire people. And although this one who derided Israel promised that his people would serve Israel if he were defeated, the Philistines immediately flee. Israel, to be sure, has no desire to enslave the Philistines; nonetheless, they successfully pursue Goliath's army back to their own territory of Gath and Ekron.

Saul's response to David's victory is curious, pointing to his increasing self-preoccupation and to the deterioration of his mind. Instead of rewarding this young man who saves the people—the one who tried on Saul's very own armor and sword—the king inquires into his identity.

Although Saul's people had earlier promised that whoever could stand up to the challenge of the Philistine and kill him in battle would be rewarded with the hand of the king's daughter and riches, and would be given privileged status for his family, Saul offers David nothing. Instead of rejoicing that his people are saved, Saul's jealousy soon will grow to murderous proportions.

BELOW: *DAVID'S VICTORY OVER GOLIATH* BY TITIAN (TIZIANO VECELLI), *C.* 1488–1576. DAVID BEHEADS GOLIATH AFTER HIS DEATH, PERHAPS TO MAKE DOUBLY SURE THE GIANT IS SLAIN.

RIGHT: JONATHAN USES THE PRETEXT OF ARCHERY PRACTICE TO WARN DAVID OF SAUL'S ENMITY. BOWS AND ARROWS WERE IMPORTANT WEAPONS FOR THE ARMIES OF THESE TIMES.

SAUL'S JEALOUSY

In the aftermath of David's astounding victory, Saul becomes increasingly jealous of the young man who continues to show great success in subsequent battles. With David's popularity ever increasing, Saul reaches a breaking point when he hears the local women's victory songs: "Saul has killed his thousands and David his ten thousands" (1 Samuel 18:7). This king of Israel now plots to murder the hero who has saved the king's very people from slavery, death, and the loss of their nation! No longer does David's music calm Saul's rants. Twice Saul throws his spear at David while David is playing. David, nonetheless, escapes harm.

Failing to spear him, Saul tries to have David killed in battle. Although he promised that anyone who could defeat Goliath would become betrothed to his daughter, he only now offers that David continue leading the army and be rewarded with the marriage to his daughter Merab. The proposal, however, is a ruse, as Saul believes that David will be killed in the fighting. When David proves successful, Saul rescinds his offer; his daughter Merab marries another man. As is the case throughout the account of Saul and David, many elements of the plot occur twice. Again, Saul proposes that David marry his other daughter, Michal. But this time, Saul demands that David bring him 100 Philistine foreskins, thus ensuring David's death as David attempts to retrieve these gruesome tokens. Yet, this plot fails as well, for David returns victorious and marries Michal.

SAUL CONSPIRES, YET DAVID IS SAVED

David's victories only make Saul more enraged; he tries to kill David in three different ways. First, he elicits the support of his staff and his son, Jonathan, to kill David. Unknown to Saul, Jonathan already had made a covenant with David, recognizing that David would be the next king. Saul's son is horrified and pleads for his father to return to reason. Jonathan's appeal works for a time, but David's continuing military victories prompt Saul to attempt to spear God's chosen yet again. David immediately leaves the palace and flees to his own home, unaware that it cannot serve as a refuge. His wife Michal, Saul's own daughter, proves that her loyalty is to her beloved husband. She warns David that her father will kill him if he remains. She helps him escape and prepares his bed with an idol donned with goat's hair, buying time when Saul's second plan is to have his men search for his son-in-law.

Now on the run, David finds refuge with the prophet Samuel. Saul twice sends his henchmen to find him, but the prophetic spirit in the region of Samuel's home is so powerful that both times they fall "into a prophetic frenzy" (1 Samuel 19:20–21), a reference to some sort of overwhelming state that disarms them. Undaunted, Saul himself goes to Ramah, yet he too is overwhelmed by the spirit. Whereas once the spirit empowered him as God's choice to be monarch (1 Samuel 10:5–13), now the "prophetic frenzy," which leaves him undignified and derided, signifies the profound departure of God's presence.

JONATHAN'S CLANDESTINE STRATEGY TO PROTECT DAVID

Jonathan's appeal to reason can no longer bring Saul back from his repeated designs to murder David. The tension between Saul and Jonathan intensifies when Saul, enraged at his son's defense of his friend, not only curses Jonathan by the name of his own mother, but also attempts to spear him in a fit of rage. Jonathan goes to great lengths to save his friend, abandoning his father and thus any hope of inheriting any royal position. He devises a method to communicate with David by code. He pretends to do target practice, followed by specified words given to a boy regarding the retrieval of his arrows. The prearranged formulas indicate whether it is safe for David to reappear. Jonathan is faithful to his plan and not only signals to David to stay hidden, but safely speaks additional code words to stress the urgent need to flee.

Once it is safe for David to begin his flight, the two embrace and weep, swearing loyalty to each other and to each other's descendants. This sad scene previews the tragedy that will ensue between two groups of Israelites—those who are loyal to Saul and those supporting David—as Saul's personal vendetta ultimately prompts a civil war.

BELOW: *SAUL ATTACKING DAVID* BY GIOVANNI FRANCESCO BARBIERI GUERCINO (1591–1666). DAVID'S POPULARITY AROUSES SAUL'S JEALOUSY; SAUL FEARS FOR HIS KINGDOM.

HIGHLIGHTS OF DAVID'S FLIGHT

David's flight takes him throughout the land, from Nob, the city of the priests; to Gath, the hometown of Goliath; to the Cave of Adullam, in the far western regions of Judah; to the land of Moab, on Judah's eastern border; and back to Keilah, again on the western border with Philistia. Additional retreats take him to Ziph, southeast of Keilah; to En-gedi, an oasis on the Dead Sea; and to Maon and Hachilah, towns in Judah. Throughout this time spent in the wilderness, David gathers about him a militia, all the while becoming more threatening to Saul (1 Samuel 22:1–2).

DAVID ELUDES SAUL

1. David flees to Samuel at Ramah.
2. David goes to Nob and finds refuge with Ahimelech.
3. David goes to Adullam via Gath, and gathers followers.
4. David finds refuge for his parents at Mizpeh.
5. David returns from Moab to Israelite territory.
6. David and his followers fight Philistines and save Keilah.
7. Saul tries to take David, who escapes to the Wilderness of Ziph.
8. David flees to the Wilderness of Maon; Saul follows.
9. David goes to En-gedi, pursued by Saul and a large force.
10. David confronts Saul in the Wilderness of Ziph.
11. David escapes to the Philistines at Gath.
12. David becomes ruler of Ziklag and fights for the Philistines.

It is possible that the Dead Sea was low enough to allow crossing by foot.

Mediterranean Sea; Ramah; Gibeah; Nob; Gath; Adullam; Keilah; Wilderness of Ziph; En-gedi; Carmel; Ziklag; Wilderness of Maon; Dead Sea; MOAB; Mizpeh; N

Mediterranean Sea; SYRIA; West Bank; Gaza; ISRAEL; JORDAN; EGYPT; 32°; 35°

David's travels

Town of uncertain location

0 10 km; 0 10 miles

David first finds refuge with Ahimelech, the priest at Nob (1 Samuel 21:1–9). Ahimelech is supportive of the fugitive, allowing David to eat the holy Bread of the Presence, normally reserved for the priests. Lurking at the shrine, however, is a certain Edomite, Doeg, who is loyal to Saul. He betrays Ahimelech's safe haven with disastrous results, for upon hearing of this interlude, Saul assaults the entirety of the house of Ahimelech. This act is so appalling that Saul's own men refuse to slay the priests. Doeg, however, has no scruples and kills all the priests, their families, and their livestock (1 Samuel 22:18–19). Only one soul, Abiathar, escapes to tell David of the massacre. Saul has fallen to his nadir. The one who would not carry out the ban against Amalek, on God's very own command, butchers those holy to the Lord.

Meanwhile, David finds refuge in an unlikely place—with Achish the Philistine, king of Gath. Although Achish's men recognize David and goad the king to have him killed, David acts as though he were mad, thereby rendering himself harmless in the eyes of Achish (1 Samuel 21:13–15). Much later, after being hunted by Saul all over Israel, David eventually ingratiates himself to Achish, and even pretends to go on raids against Judah (while he is actually fighting against Judah's other enemies) in order to court his favor (1 Samuel 27:8–12). David is forced out of Achish's service, however, because the Philistine king's own men do not trust him (1 Samuel 29:3–11). Nonetheless, David wins territory without a fight, as this Achish rewards him with the town of Ziklag (1 Samuel 27:5–7).

David's stay at Keilah is particularly telling of the tragedy that continues to plague Israel because of Saul's refusal to relinquish the office of kingship (1 Samuel 23:1–14). The city of Keilah, located at the foothills of Judah's territory, is continually besieged by its enemy, who is infamous for raiding their harvests. David asks God (the method is not specified) whether he should save the people. Unlike the case with Saul, God communicates with his chosen king, responding affirmatively; indeed, David prevails. Saul, obsessed with finding David, ignores the strategic victory which has delivered his people from a terrible threat and concentrates on finding Keilah's deliverer—to kill him! The struggle between Saul and David has tragic implications for the people of this beleaguered city. Threatened

DAVID'S WIVES

Michal, Saul's daughter, became David's first wife. *The Marriage of Michal to David* (1469) by Jean Colombe is shown here.

Abigail met David while he was hiding from Saul, and she became David's second wife after the Lord struck her husband. Ahinoam of Jezreel married David at about the same time. Maacah, daughter of King Talmai of Geshur, was probably wed for strategic reasons. Little is known of Haggith, Abital, and Eglah. David ensured that Bathsheba's husband was killed in battle so he could marry her.

David married many women (eight were named in the Bible), and it seems polygamy was acceptable. Adultery, however, was not, and David and Bathsheba suffered for their sin.

ABOVE: LATE NINETEENTH-CENTURY ENGRAVING. DAVID BELIEVES THAT HE SHOULD NOT HARM SAUL BECAUSE SAUL IS THE LORD'S ANOINTED, AND SO HE LEAVES SAUL TO SLEEP IN SAFETY.

now, not by the Philistines, but by their very own king, they so fear Saul's retaliation for harboring the fugitive David that they plot to betray the latter. David discovers this by another inquiry to God and flees before it is too late. The greater damage to the loyalties of the unified regions of Judah, however, cannot be undone, and the hunt for the popular hero David will continue to divide the people.

DAVID TWICE SPARES SAUL'S LIFE

Throughout the time that Saul pursues David, David grows in power and in guerrilla tactics. In contrast to Saul's violent designs, David twice abandons opportunities to kill Saul. Although Saul is completely unaware of David's presence alongside him, David is able to prove to his nemesis that he shows mercy. While displaying tokens of his close encounters, namely a piece of Saul's cloak and Saul's own water jar and spear, David appeals to Saul, hoping for a nonviolent conclusion to these wrenching hostilities.

On the first occasion, David serendipitously finds Saul. He and his band of fighters are gathered into the far recesses of a cave near En-gedi. Unaware of their presence, Saul enters alone to relieve himself. Yet, whereas David's men declare to their lord that he now has the opportunity to do whatever "seems good to you" (1 Samuel 24:4), David insists that he will not assault him, "for he is the Lord's anointed" (1 Samuel 24:6). He seizes the opportunity, however, to prove to Saul that he is mistaken in believing that David seeks his life. David surreptitiously cuts off a corner of Saul's cloak. This event contrasts Saul's character with David's. Whereas Saul had no shame when having the priests of Nob slaughtered, when throwing a spear at his own son, when attempting to have David killed, or when using the entirety of the military resources of the state to kill him, David himself feels remorse for the humiliation he caused Saul in ripping his royal cloak!

After exiting the cave, David attempts to persuade Saul to end the pursuit and to find a peaceful resolution. Although this is dangerous, as Saul's troops far outnumber David's, David calls out to him, holding up the corner of the robe. In a moving speech, David deferentially calls Saul "father" and pleads for peace. In an astounding move, Saul addresses him as "my son." For a moment, one may think the war is over, for Saul declares, "Now I know that you shall surely be king, and that the kingdom of Israel shall be established in your hand" (1 Samuel 24:20). This is not to be, however, as Saul cannot sustain his good will. David is wise enough to mistrust Saul, and when Saul departs for home, David goes to his stronghold. Indeed, the next time we see Saul, he is once again in pursuit of David who this time is hiding in the Wilderness of Ziph.

David again has the opportunity to prove to Saul that he could have killed him. While Saul is encamped with his army, God causes a deep sleep to fall upon him and his commander, Abner, so that David and his own captain, Abishai, can approach Saul and abscond with his spear and water jar. When David calls to him from afar, Saul admits that he is in the wrong and promises to never again seek David's harm.

Before the account is over, however, we find that Saul cannot be trusted. When David insists that Saul send a young soldier over to fetch the spear as a sign of good will, Saul never responds.

THE AMALEKITE RAID AT ZIKLAG

The great efforts that David must waste in running from Saul continue to wreak havoc on the people, for David is now unable to defend them. All the while, the security of Israel becomes threatened as never before. On the one hand, the Philistines make their way to Jezreel, located in the coastal plain, and prepare for the decisive battle of

RIGHT: *DAVID*, C. 1408–1411, BY DONATELLO. DONATELLO FOLLOWED THIS EARLY WORK IN MARBLE IN GOTHIC STYLE WITH A NUDE DAVID IN BRONZE IN RENAISSANCE STYLE ABOUT 20 YEARS LATER.

LEFT: ARCHAEOLOGICAL STUDIES OF BETH-SHEAN SHOW IT HAS BEEN POPULATED FOR MORE THAN 6,000 YEARS. IN SAUL'S TIME IT WAS A PHILISTINE TOWN; HIS DEAD BODY WAS NAILED TO ITS WALLS UNTIL ITS RETRIEVAL.

SAUL'S DEATH

Saul's lost opportunities with David are truly tragic, for instead of uniting their military skills and the power of both their armies to fight the Philistines, Saul's personal vendetta leads to unfathomable loss. At the battle of Gilboa, three of his own sons will be slaughtered and Saul himself dies an ignoble death. Moreover, the Israelite army will be destroyed, and the Philistine victory over Israel threatens to annihilate the entire people.

The Philistines gather at Shunem, poised to attack Israel. Overwhelmed by helplessness and by God's silence in the face of his pleas, Saul calls upon the spirit of the deceased prophet Samuel for advice. Although it was forbidden, he consults the medium at Endor. Saul hears what seems to be the voice of the prophet Samuel who speaks to him from beyond the grave.

In a dramatic scene, where the prophet comes up from the ground, Saul hears Samuel's ominous words, "the Lord will give Israel along with you into the hands of the Philistines; and tomorrow you and your sons shall be with me; the Lord will also give the army of Israel into the hands of the Philistines" (1 Samuel 28:19).

Wounded in the terrifying battle of Gilboa, Saul asks his armor-bearer to kill him so that the Philistines do not torture him. Refusing to strike God's anointed, Saul's servant demurs, and thus Saul chooses to fall upon his own sword. The people in the surrounding area, who were without protection, flee their cities. The Philistines take over these abandoned cities, making much greater advances into all of Israel.

The terror the Philistines inflict does not stop with this victory. They return to the battle scene, behead Saul's corpse, and nail his body to the wall of the city of Beth-shean. The people of the town of Jabesh-gilead, however, remember Saul's bravery when he saved them from the mutilation and slavery proposed by the cruel enemy Nahash. Fearless men of the town travel stealthily throughout the night to take down Saul's body for a proper burial. With this report, we are reminded of the tremendous good Saul did in his early days, making his failures all the more tragic.

Gilboa. In addition, the Amalekites terrorize the Israelites in the south, at the town of Ziklag. This city, given to David by the Philistines, is without his protection during the time he is being pursued by Saul.

Undefended, the citizenry of Ziklag are captured as slaves, including David's own two wives, Abigail and Ahinoam. Upon returning to the city, David and his men see a scorched city bereft of people. This description captures their astonishment and sorrow: "Then David and the people who were with him raised their voices and wept, until they had no more strength to weep" (1 Samuel 30:4). The men, blaming David, are so furious that they threaten to kill him. God continues to be with David, however, and while in pursuit of the Amalekites, he discovers that the people of the city were taken alive. He recaptures all of them and strengthens his standing among his makeshift army, paying them all equally with the captured wealth of the Amalekites.

BELOW: *THE SUICIDE AND BEHEADING OF SAUL*, FROM A FIFTEENTH-CENTURY BOOK. SEEING HIS SONS KILLED AND DEFEAT IMMINENT, SAUL DECIDES TO KILL HIMSELF RATHER THAN RISK CAPTURE.

Archaeological Excitement at Jerusalem

Ronny Reich and Eli Shukron (from the Israel Antiquities Authority) have found an Iron Age wall with defensive towers around the outside of the Gihon Spring in Jerusalem. This will have the effect of transforming thinking about how David's men might have gained access to the city and captured it in 1000 B.C.E.

The excavation by Reich and Shukron began in 1997 as a "rescue dig," before the building of a Visitors' Center went ahead. They discovered two huge stone towers (with walls about 10 ft [3 m] thick dating to 3,700 years ago) over a previously unknown pool fed by the Gihon Spring. They also discovered a major city wall about 15 ft (4.5 m) high very close to the Spring, possibly built to protect it.

Their theory proposes that Warren's Shaft (found by Charles Warren of the London-based Palestine Exploration Fund in C.E. 1867) was not used to draw water, and that Joab (the leader of David's forces attacking the city) did not use the shaft to gain access to the city. Instead, a "Middle Bronze Age II Channel" (built about 1800 B.C.E.) from the Gihon Spring to a point near the Pool of Siloam was the subterranean water system that was used in Jebusite Jerusalem.

DAVID, KING OF JUDAH

After the death of Saul, David is accepted as king over Judah and anointed in Hebron of Judah (in the south), but Ishbaal (also known as Ish-bosheth), Saul's son, is simultaneously anointed king of Israel in Mahanaim of Gilead (in the north). Tensions first erupt when the two leaders' military captains, Joab and Abner, challenge each other's soldiers to a military contest. Thus, the early years of David's reign are marked by the tensions between north and south. The real power behind Ishbaal comes from Abner, his commander-in-chief. Abner tries to broker a peace settlement with David, but the attempt is abruptly ended when Joab kills Abner, avenging his brother's death and eliminating any competition for the office of chief commander. Anarchy follows and two renegades murder Ishbaal, leaving the northern tribes without leadership. Yet, all the while, David becomes stronger. After the north is devoid of leadership, David is able to fill the power vacuum; with the lessening of hostilities, all the tribes gather at Hebron, anointing David king over the entire people.

DAVID, KING OF JUDAH AND ISRAEL

David makes a strategic move, establishing Jerusalem as his capital city. Jerusalem was the last of the Canaanite (Jebusite) cities that Israel conquered. Neither belonging to the north nor to the south, it was the ideal place to establish governmental and religious centers.

David's success in unifying the tribes after Ishbaal's death is propitious, for soon the Philistines regroup to threaten the people. In contrast to Saul, David commands a unified army from all the tribes to launch the attack. The victory not only saves Israel, routing the Philistines from Geba to Gezer, but has profound religious significance, for David next brings the Ark of the Covenant to Jerusalem. This Ark, a chest which contained the tablets of the law given to Moses at Mt. Sinai and which symbolized God's very presence, had a history of being captured by the Philistines. It had been placed for safe-keeping in Kiriath-jearim (also known as Baal-judah) in Judah. David's ability to reestablish it as the focal point of a religious center helped him to enhance the reputation of Jerusalem.

RIGHT: *KING DAVID CARRYING THE ARK OF THE COVENANT IN PROCESSION THROUGH JERUSALEM* BY LUIGI ADEMOLLO (1764–1849). THIS JOYFUL OCCASION WAS MARKED WITH SINGING AND DANCING.

DAVID'S KINGDOM
Cyprus
Mediterranean Sea
HAMATH
Hamath
Orontes
Lebo-Hamath
Byblos
ARAM
Sidon
SIDON
Damascus
Tyre
Dan
Lake Hula
Hazor
Acco
Chinnereth
Ashtaroth
Sea of Galilee
Dor
Megiddo
Ramoth-gilead
Tob
Salecah
Beth-shean
Mahanaim
Shechem
Jordan
Joppa
AMMON
Rabbah
Kiriath-jearim
Geba
Ashdod
Ekron
Jerusalem
Medeba
Ashkelon
Gath
PHILISTIA
Hebron
Dead Sea
David made the city of Jerusalem the capital of his kingdom.
Gaza
Raphia
MOAB
Beer-sheba
Kir-hareseth
Zoar
Lake Ballah
Tamar
N
Kadesh-barnea
Lake Timsah
EDOM
AMALEK
EGYPT
Bitter Lakes
Teman
Greatest extent of territory ruled by Saul
Greatest extent of territory conquered by David
Vassal states
Town of uncertain location
Elath
0 50 km
0 50 miles
TURKEY
CYPRUS
SYRIA
Mediterranean Sea
ISRAEL
JORDAN
EGYPT
40°
30°
30°
40°

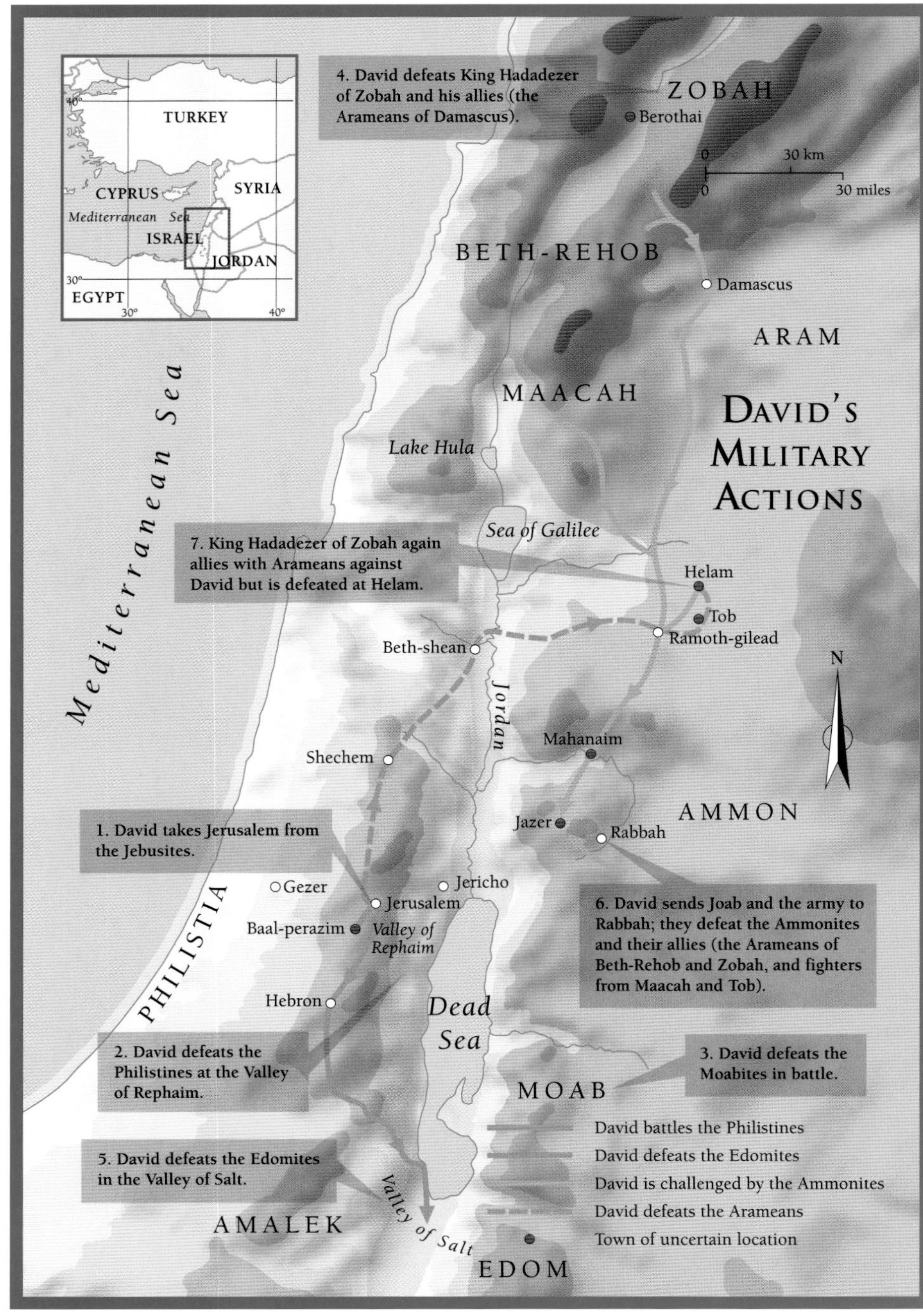

DAVID, HEAD OF A DYNASTY

David's significance in the life of Israel reached far beyond his ability to drive out the Philistines to the west, the Arameans to the north, the Moabites and Ammonites to the east, and the Edomites and Amalekites to the south. In 2 Samuel 7 the encounter that the prophet Nathan has with the king is portrayed, bringing God's message of an eternal covenant with the house of David. Whereas David offers to build God a house, meaning "a temple," God responds that he will build David a house, meaning "a dynasty." God makes a covenant, or binding pact with David, promising that there always will be one of his descendants on the throne. In gratitude, David recognizes that the promise is not only for him, but for the entire people. He declares, "And you established your people Israel for yourself to be your people forever; and you, O Lord, became their God" (2 Samuel 7:24). This promise links Israel's past, present, and future. In the days of Moses, Israel received the covenant at Mt. Sinai; the Lord promised to be Israel's God, and the people agreed to accept his commandments (Exodus 20:2; 24:7). In addition, the covenant with David becomes the cornerstone for the future messianic hope in both Judaism and Christianity. The messiah, or anointed one, is understood as the descendant of David, God's anointed and beloved king who brings all nations to know God (Isaiah 11:10).

RIGHT: *BATHSHEBA AND DAVID* BY NICOLA DA URBINO (1475–1547). AFTER DAVID ARRANGES FOR THE DEATH OF URIAH, BATHSHEBA'S HUSBAND, SHE BECOMES THE LAST OF DAVID'S NAMED WIVES.

TROUBLE IN DAVID'S HOUSE

In the aftermath of David's victories at Israel's borders, he does not know peace. Tragically, violence and civil war rooted in the sins of David and his own sons, Amnon and Absalom, devastate the people. David's sin in taking Bathsheba, another man's wife; Amnon's rape of his sister Tamar; and Absalom's execution of Amnon destroy not only their own lives but the peace of the entire land.

DAVID SINS WITH BATHSHEBA

"I gave you your master's house, and your master's wives into your bosom, and gave you the house of Israel and of Judah; and if that had been too little, I would have added as much more. Why have you despised the word of the Lord, to do what is evil in his sight?" (2 Samuel 12:8–9).

With these words the prophet Nathan condemns David for his appalling failures. The king lays with Bathsheba, a married woman whose husband Uriah is off at war, fighting David's battles. When David learns that Bathsheba is pregnant by him, he first calls Uriah home from the front, hoping that the latter's visit with his wife will hide the paternity of David's child. When this scheme fails, David places Uriah at the forefront of the fighting so that his death appears to be a battle casualty. David marries Bathsheba, but soon learns that he is not excused from following God's laws. David receives a terrible punishment as the prophet declares, "therefore the sword shall never depart from your house" (2 Samuel 12:10). In addition, great personal grief comes to David and Bathsheba as the son born to them dies. (Later, Solomon, who becomes the next king, is born to them.) Unlike Saul, who refused to ever acknowledge that he sinned, David is truly repentant. Sadly, however, the damage cannot be undone, and with the next generation, the devastating words of the prophet come true.

ABSALOM BECOMES ESTRANGED

Another terrible crime involving David's sons precipitates the enmity that will destroy the unity of David's house. Amnon, David's son, rapes his half-sister Tamar and refuses to pay the consequences. According to ancient biblical law, he was required to marry the woman he abused, sparing her a lifetime of shame and desolation. David does nothing to enforce the law, nor does he punish Amnon. Incensed, Absalom, David's son and Tamar's full brother, takes revenge on Amnon, slaying him at a festival. Absalom now becomes a fugitive, echoing the plight of his father who earlier fled from Saul.

After years of estrangement and exile, David finally grants Absalom amnesty and allows him to return. The reconciliation is never complete, however, and Absalom nurses his hurt. He eventually turns to the people, becoming quite popular as an administrator of justice for claims throughout David's kingdom.

Absalom's personal charisma increases his mounting popularity, and eventually he has enough confidence to successfully lead a popular revolt. He becomes so powerful that David relinquishes the throne and leaves the city.

Joined by those loyal to him, David "went up the ascent of the Mount of Olives, weeping as he went, with his head covered and walking barefoot; and all the people who were with him covered their heads and went up, weeping as they went" (2 Samuel 15:30). This sorrowful scene is followed by still worse heartbreak.

Initially successful, Absalom's revolt is undercut when David's adviser, Hushai, infiltrates Absalom's circle, feigning loyalty to the upstart king. Hushai advises Absalom in such a way that Absalom actually falls into David's hand. This becomes the turning point of the war.

Before the great battle at the forest of Ephraim, David warns his fighters that Absalom is not to be killed. The commander Joab, however, insists on taking matters into his own hands, and executes Absalom, who is at his mercy, entangled in a tree (2 Samuel 18:9–15). Hearing the dreadful news from the battlefield, David remains the father, and Absalom remains the son, not the usurper. Inconsolable, David cries, "O my son Absalom, my son, my son Absalom! Would I had died instead of you, O Absalom, my son, my son!" (2 Samuel 18:33).

LEFT: *DAVID MOURNING THE DEATH OF HIS SON ABSALOM, FROM THE BOOK OF HOURS OF LOUIS D'ORLEANS,* 1469, BY JEAN COLOMBE. DAVID IS OVERCOME WITH GRIEF BY ABSALOM'S DEATH.

RIGHT: *ABSALOM'S TOMB, JERUSALEM* BY CHARLES PIERRON (NINETEENTH CENTURY). THIS TOMB HAS BEEN IDENTIFIED AS ABSALOM'S SINCE THE FIRST CENTURY C.E., BUT IT PROBABLY HAS NO CONNECTION WITH HIM.

Rebellions of Absalom and Sheba

Damascus

5. Joab follows Sheba and besieges Abel. The people there kill Sheba to save their city.

Mediterranean Sea

Abel

Lake Hula

Hazor

3. Absalom pursues David and the armies meet at the Forest of Ephraim. Absalom is killed and his forces defeated.

Sea of Galilee

Forest of Ephraim

Jordan

4. David stops at Gilgal on his way back to Jerusalem. Sheba leads his followers from Gilgal to Abel.

Mahanaim

Rabbah

Gilgal

Jerusalem

2. David is warned about Absalom and flees from Jerusalem to Mahanaim.

Hebron

Dead Sea

1. David's son Absalom gathers followers at Hebron.

N

Town of uncertain location

0 50 km

0 50 miles

SHEBA'S REBELLION

Absalom's death gives David the chance to unify the tribes again, but old resentments from the north make the task difficult. One particular challenge to David's attempts at unification comes from Sheba, a Benjaminite who sounds a war cry in order to lead the Israelite tribes in revolt against David (2 Samuel 20). Mindful of Joab's failures to obey him, David appoints Amasa in charge of the army. Amasa, however, proves ineffective against Sheba, opening the door for Joab to return to his position. Joab continues in his duplicitous treachery, killing Amasa before pursuing Sheba. Such posturing and disobedience to David preview the serious threat that Joab presents to David toward the end of David's life when he supports Adonijah as successor instead of David's own choice, Solomon.

Joab's pursuit of Sheba is successful. Believing that he can find refuge among his own clan, Sheba retreats to the city of Abel, among the Bichrites. His presence there threatens the entire city, and the people fear Joab's invasion. One wise woman, acting as peace negotiator, offers terms to Joab—the head of Sheba. Under her leadership, the entirety of the town agrees to execute Sheba; this suffices for Joab to leave in peace. While it is true that with the crushing of this rebellion David's position as king over the northern tribes is more secure, David must fear the continuing power of Joab, whose brutality and duplicity know no boundaries.

THE CENSUS

A fearsome event is recorded at the end of the books of Samuel. God becomes so angry with David that he sends the king a trial. God tests David by making him consider taking a census; the king succumbs to the test. The account is filled with mystery, for God's motivation as well as the reason why a census is considered an offense are unknown. In this regard, the trial is akin to God's request of Abraham to slay Isaac as a sacrifice and to Job's trials of great suffering and the loss of his family.

It may be the case that any taking of a census is considered sinful; scholars suggest it was used for military conscription or for forced labor. Clearly, David feels remorse after the census is completed, and he begs God to forgive his sin, admitting his guilt by echoing the same words that the prophet Samuel used unsuccessfully to have Saul recognize his own sin: "I have done very foolishly" (2 Samuel 24:10; see also 1 Samuel 13:13). God gives David three terrible choices for punishment: to endure three years of famine, three months of flight, or three days of pestilence. Faced with the impossible, David falls on God's mercy; a pestilence follows and thousands of people die. David cries out for his people, "I alone have sinned, and I alone have done

RIGHT: ILLUSTRATION FROM ROYAUMONT'S *HISTOIRE DE L'ANCIEN ET NOUVEAU TESTAMENT* (1724). SHEBA'S HEAD IS THROWN OVER THE WALLS OF ABEL.

wickedly; but these sheep, what have they done? Let your hand, I pray, be against me and against my father's house" (2 Samuel 24:17). Just as Abraham was willing to sacrifice Isaac, the first heir of the covenant promised by God to Abraham (Genesis 22), so too is David, the consummate shepherd, willing to sacrifice the covenantal dynasty if it will spare his beloved people.

It is striking that God does not respond to David directly. The prophet Gad appears and, without citing the authority of God's word, simply states, "Go up and erect an altar to the Lord on the threshing floor of Araunah the Jebusite" (1 Samuel 24:18). These words are presented as another test of obedience. David is careful to purchase the land from its Jebusite owner who offers it *gratis*, thus ensuring that its identification as Israelite land would be incontrovertible. This action parallels that of Abraham, who so carefully purchased the cave of Machpelah to bury Sarah, even though the owner, Ephron, offered to give it to him (Genesis 23). The threshing floor of Araunah, first associated with this horrific story of such suffering and destruction, becomes the holiest land in Israel. In a single generation it becomes the place where Solomon builds the Temple, the meeting ground of heaven and earth, where people could bind themselves to God, receive forgiveness, and be healed from anything that separates them from his grace. David completes the careful transaction, obedient to Gad's brief command. Similar to Abraham's test, in which God accepted the sacrifice of a ram instead of Isaac, David soon discovers that God indeed stops the plague in response.

In addition to its religious significance, this narrative illuminates the extent of David's kingdom, as various regions are listed in the census. Populations are recorded on both sides of the Jordan and from the far northern to the far southern frontiers of Israel and Judah. Indeed, the traversing of the country took the census-takers nine months and 20 days! "They crossed the Jordan, and began from Aroer and from the city that is in the middle of the valley, toward Gad and on to Jazer. Then they came to Gilead, and to Kadesh in the land of the Hittites; and they came to Dan, and from Dan they went around to Sidon, and came to the fortress of Tyre and to all the cities of the Hivites and Canaanites; and they went out to the Negeb of Judah at Beer-sheba" (2 Samuel 24:5–7).

Except for brief accounts of David's final days, with this heartrending but ultimately hopeful account we come to the end of the activities performed by David in his prime. Despite his failures, David, ever repentant, is remembered as God's beloved, the king who ceaselessly risked his life and his legacy in order to save his people and to honor his God.

BELOW LEFT: *KING DAVID*, FOURTEENTH CENTURY, CHURCH OF ST. PETER, LOWICK, NORTHAMPTONSHIRE, UNITED KINGDOM. IMAGES OF DAVID OFTEN DEPICT HIM WITH A LYRE.

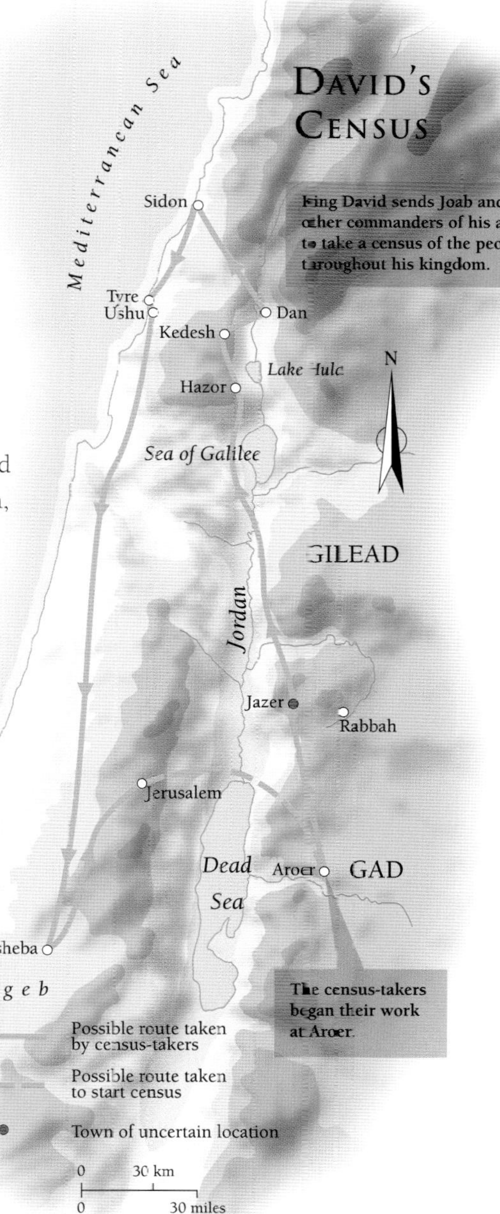

KING SOLOMON

I WILL DWELL AMONG THE CHILDREN OF ISRAEL, AND WILL NOT FORSAKE MY PEOPLE I KINGS 6:13

RIGHT: THE BRASSY TONES OF A TRUMPET ANNOUNCE SOLOMON'S KINGSHIP. MUSIC PLAYED A PART IN ALL ISRAEL'S IMPORTANT OCCASIONS.

BELOW: FOLIO 181V, BIBLE OF GUIARS DE MOULINS AND PIERRE COMESTOR, LATE 1200S–EARLY 1300S. THIS SHOWS DAVID'S OLD AGE AND HIS CHOOSING OF SOLOMON.

The opening chapters of the first book of Kings describe the end of David's reign as he approaches old age and death. At first, David appears sick and irresolute. His own servants take the initiative to bring Abishag of Shunem into David's service as a concubine, lying in his bed to keep him warm. David's infirmity, however, is underscored when the Bible records, "The girl was very beautiful. She became the king's attendant and served him, but the king did not know her sexually" (1 Kings 1:4). Moreover, when Adonijah, his eldest surviving son, begins to act as if he will become the next king, David says nothing to stop him. Adonijah receives the support of Joab, the commander of the army, and Abiathar, one of the priests. Assuming that he will encounter no resistance from David, Adonijah initiates a prestige-enhancing ceremony for himself, offering sacrifice with key royal officials, but avoiding the prophet Nathan; Benaiah, the captain of David's bodyguards; and his brother Solomon.

DAVID'S CHOICE OF SOLOMON AS KING

The prophet Nathan, the messenger of God's dynastic covenant, is the first to act against Adonijah's apparent coup. He

LEFT: *KING SOLOMON* BY JUSTUS VAN GHENT (1410–80?). SOLOMON IS THOUGHT TO BE THE YOUNGEST OF BATHSHEBA'S FOUR CHILDREN, AND SHE URGED DAVID TO CONFIRM HIM AS HEIR.

enlists Bathsheba's help to insist that Solomon, the son she bore to David, be designated as David's successor. With carefully chosen words, both approach David, detailing the threat that Adonijah poses. Poignantly, Bathsheba expresses her concern that upon David's death, "my son Solomon and I will be counted offenders" (1 Kings 1:21), referring to a possible death sentence. This is not all, for Bathsheba also reminds David that Adonijah's acts portend greater violence for the entire nation. She appeals to David's authority: "the eyes of all Israel are on you to tell them who shall sit on the throne of my lord the king after him" (1 Kings 1:20).

With a well-choreographed appearance, Nathan appeals to the king's past strength. He chides David, intimating that Adonijah's self-acclamation could not possibly have happened without David's approval. The prophet cleverly remarks, "Has this thing been brought about by my lord the king and you have not let your servants know who should sit on the throne of my lord the king after him?" (1 Kings 1:27).

With the double appeal by Bathsheba and Nathan, David begins to act decisively. He commands the priest Zadok, the commander Benaiah, and the prophet Nathan to take part in a ceremony at Gihon that will proclaim Solomon as king. David directs Nathan to anoint Solomon with oil, the mark of God's choice. David assigns other public signs to be utilized as well. Solomon is to ride David's own mule, a trumpet must be sounded, and a public acclamation pronounced. David lends his own personal authority as he states that *he* has appointed Solomon king over Israel. David's plan is a success, and so many people participate in the inauguration "that the earth quaked at their noise" (1 Kings 1:40).

The quick action of David is especially noteworthy, for at the same time that Solomon is inaugurated, Adonijah's self-appointment ceremonies continue. While his festivities are still in progress, Adonijah can hear the tumult of Solomon's ceremony, although he does not know what it is. The mystery is soon solved, however, when Jonathan, the son of the priest Abiathar (one of Adonijah's supporters) interrupts with the news that David has made Solomon king.

ADONIJAH'S FALL

Solomon immediately commands respect and fear, for all of Adonijah's supporters abandon their "king," leaving him to fear for his own life for committing treason. Solomon offers the upstart a reprieve, but cautions him that it is conditional on his good behavior. Later, David warns Solomon that others may conspire against him, including David's own commander Joab, whom David regrets not punishing for the murders of two competing army captains, Abner and Amasa.

Immediately after David's death and burial, Adonijah requests that he be given Abishag from Shunem as a wife. To take the wife or concubine of the monarch could readily be interpreted as a claim to the throne. His request remains ambiguous, however, because his motives are not specified. Solomon immediately quashes the claim by having his loyal commander Benaiah execute Adonijah. Solomon also ensures that no one else who supported Adonijah remains to pursue another possible coup. He banishes Abiathar the priest and has Joab executed. Although the beginning of his reign is marked by acts of violence, they may also be understood as preventing the kind of tragedy that marked the competition between Saul and David, and later, David and Absalom.

ABOVE: PARCHMENT ROLL SHOWING KING SOLOMON, NINETEENTH CENTURY, FROM ETHIOPIA, EAST AFRICA. PARCHMENT ROLLS WERE USED UNTIL QUITE RECENTLY IN ETHIOPIA.

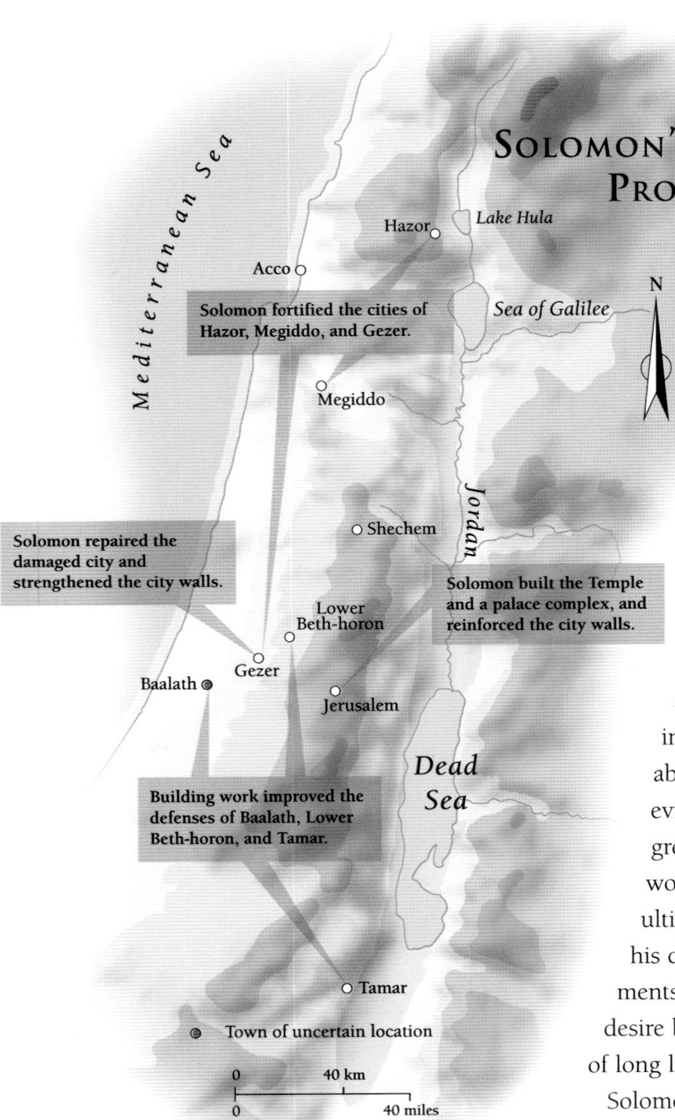

THE WISDOM OF SOLOMON

As Solomon worships God in Gibeon, God appears to him in a dream, offering to fulfill a selected wish. Solomon prays for wisdom, exclaiming, "Give your servant therefore an understanding mind to govern your people, able to discern between good and evil; for who can govern this your great people?" (1 Kings 3:9). These words serve to portray the king's ultimate concern for his people and his desire to keep God's commandments. God not only fulfills the king's desire but also gives to Solomon the gift of long life with riches and honor.

Solomon's wisdom is tested when a most disturbing challenge comes before him. In a famous case, two prostitutes, each of whom has a newborn infant, both come before the king for adjudication. With one infant alive and the other dead, both women claim to be the mother of the living baby. Facing this impossible task, Solomon proposes that the living child be divided in two, thus establishing the truth. The real mother cannot bear the thought of the child's death and thus gives up her claim. The woman who mendaciously claimed to be the mother insists that the child be killed nonetheless. Solomon's wise judgment spreads throughout the land, such that "people came from all the nations to hear the wisdom of Solomon; they came from all the kings of the earth who had heard of his wisdom" (1 Kings 4:34).

SOLOMON AND THE TEMPLE

Solomon proves to be an excellent administrator. One of his first acts as king is to divide the nation into administrative districts that send provisions to the court (the equivalent of taxes) on a rotating basis. His kingdom is thus readily organized into teams that are able to provide the massive labor for building the Temple in Jerusalem. Laborers are sent to Lebanon for timber and to the hill country and quarries for stone. The taxes and labor that these districts provide, however, is a mixed blessing. Late in Solomon's reign, as well as in the reign of his son, the northern tribes express their resentment; a revolt and secession soon follow.

Although David promised to build God "a house," divine instruction insisted that the task be given to David's son. Early in his reign, Solomon begins the construction of the most massive edifice Israel had seen at that time—a 60 × 20 × 30-cubit Temple for sacrifice and worship (a cubit is approximately 1½ ft [45 cm]). The construction takes seven years, and includes striking artistic expressions. Built of stone, the walls are completely lined with cedar and the floor is made of cypress. Inner sections are enhanced with gold, and carved cherubim are placed in the sanctuary. The Temple is filled with carvings and lattice work, including some in the shapes of flowers, palm trees, and pomegranates.

In Israel, the Temple was much more than an amazing building. It was the meeting place of heaven and earth—the very place of God's dwelling. In this holy place people could bind themselves to God, find forgiveness for sin, and thus be reconciled with God, as they promised to obey the covenant given at Mt. Sinai.

SOLOMON'S OTHER BUILDING PROJECTS

Not only did Solomon harness the resources of the state to build the Temple, he undertook massive building projects throughout Israel and Judah in the tenth century B.C.E. Hazor, Megiddo, Gezer, and Jerusalem were some of the major cities altered by his vision. In addition, new cities were constructed for Solomon's expansive growth, including towns for grain storage, chariots, cavalry, "and whatever Solomon desired to build, in Jerusalem, in Lebanon, and in all the land of his dominion" (1 Kings 9:19).

Archaeological digs at these key cities confirm aspects of this biblical record. Hazor, located in the upper Galilee, first appears in the book of Joshua and is identified as one of the fortified cities defeated by Joshua and later by Deborah. The Israeli archaeologist Yigael Yadin detailed the massive walls and gates built during the Solomonic period, including a city gate with six chambers and a casemate wall. Casemate walls, typical of tenth century B.C.E. construction, consisted of two parallels walls, joined at particular intervals; they had the strength of solid walls, but required significantly fewer materials and less labor to build. Hazor served as an important trade-route city, linking Egypt with Babylon.

Megiddo, located in the plain of Esdraelon (in northwest Israel), occupied a strategic location for armies and trade on

RIGHT: *SOLOMON'S DREAM* BY LUCA GIORDANO (1634–1705). THE WISDOM OF SOLOMON IS STILL FAMOUS TODAY, SO IT SEEMS SOLOMON'S DREAM-TIME REQUEST WAS GRANTED IN FULL MEASURE.

LEFT: *SOLOMON BEFORE THE ARK OF THE COVENANT*, 1747, BY BLAISE NICOLAS LE SUEUR. SOLOMON PREPARED A RICHLY DECORATED INNER SANCTUARY OF THE TEMPLE ESPECIALLY FOR THE ARK.

two important routes. One route linked Jerusalem through Shechem and Megiddo along the coast to Acco and Phoenicia. Another linked Egypt with Mesopotamia via the Philistine coast, Megiddo, the plain of Esdraelon, and Damascus. Megiddo is identified as being one of the administrative districts in Solomon's kingdom. Twentieth century archaeological expeditions have identified stratum V-A/IV-B as belonging to the Solomonic period. As is the case with Hazor, it is marked by a casemate wall that fortified the city against attackers, as well as a six-chambered gate. An additional large building from this stratum was identified as a palace or fortress. A narrow passageway marked by ashlar masonry (namely, rectangular or square stones placed horizontally in mortar), which connected the city with a spring, was also documented as coming from the age of Solomon.

Gezer, located in the central foothills near the Shephelah and which linked the Way of the Sea (the International Coastal Highway) and Jerusalem, was partly destroyed by the Egyptian pharaoh around 950 B.C.E., but was then given to Solomon as a dowry upon his marriage to the pharaoh's daughter. The gate for Gezer is marked by four chambers, and this city, too, was fortified with a casemate wall.

The capital city of Jerusalem, conquered by David and chosen as the kingdom's political center—a neutral territory to unify the northern and southern tribes—increased in size, fortification, and importance during Solomon's reign. The threshing floor of Araunah (also identified as Mount Moriah), purchased by David and used as a holy site to offer sacrifice, became the site for the Temple itself. Here Solomon installed the Ark of the Covenant, which contained the two tablets of the law given to Moses at Mt. Sinai. Solomon extended the city walls to include the protection of the Temple Mount. Besides the Temple itself, Solomon built a massive palace and other administrative buildings. One of these structures is identified as "the Millo" (1 Kings 9:15) in the Bible.

The artistic embellishments used in these edifices point to Phoenician artistry and attest to the foreign influences that permeated the expansive Solomonic kingdom. Solomon's increasingly broad world outlook prompted his many foreign alliances made through marriage contracts with Moabites, Ammonites, Edomites, Sidonians, and Hittites. In addition, his reliance on conscripted labor included foreign subjects. These practices, however, were also the cause of his undoing and the eventual break-up of the united kingdom.

TEMPLE TREASURES

Particular features of the Temple are described in detail (1 Kings 7:15–50). They include two bronze pillars with elaborate capitals placed on top, including latticework, lily-work, and pomegranates. The area near these pillars, where the shofar (the ram's horn) is blown, serves as a gathering place on great occasions. Solomon also commissioned the "molten sea"—a 10-cubit-wide cast basin, which rests on 12 decorative bulls. This basin, used for the ceremonial washing of the priests, symbolizes the life-giving aspects of the Temple. Various vessels and instruments for sacrifice are also highlighted. These items of bronze and gold show the priority the king gave to the Temple; no expense was spared. This detail from *Solomon with the Treasure of the Temple of Jerusalem*, 1633, by Frans Francken II, is an example of how the riches described have inspired artists.

SOLOMON'S ECONOMIC ADVENTURES

RIGHT: *SOLOMON RECEIVES GOLD FROM OPHIR*, ENGRAVING BY W. T. GREEN. SOLOMON USED GOLD LAVISHLY IN THE TEMPLE AND HIS PALACE (ALL HIS DRINKING VESSELS WERE MADE OF GOLD).

The growth of the Solomonic kingdom included not only the advancement of cities, but also the development of trade accomplished through both land and sea routes. In addition, successful diplomacy became a chief priority of Solomon, as it was necessary to secure the peace for trading partners to transport their goods in safety.

Biblical locations that preserve a memory of Solomon's trading ventures include the place names Ezion-geber, Tarshish, Ophir, and Sheba.

Ezion-geber, located on the Gulf of Aqaba, served as the point of departure for trade with eastern Africa and southern Arabia. Solomon's ships at Ezion-geber were staffed with sailors from Tyre. Possible locations for Tarshish include Tarsus (in Kue), Rhodes, Sardinia, and coastal Spain. The "ships of Tarshish" transported "gold, silver, ivory, apes, and peacocks" (1 Kings 10:22).

The location of Ophir remains elusive, but several biblical texts acclaim its fame for gold (Isaiah 13:12; Psalms 45:9; Job 22:24; 28:16). In the days of Solomon it was also known for its "almug wood [sandalwood] and precious stones" (1 Kings 10:11). The sandalwood was used for temple supports as well as for musical instruments. Sheba has been variously linked with southwest or northern Arabia, and was known for its exotic wealth.

The visit of the Queen of Sheba may have been prompted, in part, because of Sheba's loss of a trade monopoly after Solomon opened up a successful trading route with the backing of King Hiram of Tyre.

The ships of Hiram were particularly important for Solomon's development of Jerusalem and his kingdom. Hiram's fleet, staffed by his own experienced sailors, was used to bring the construction materials for the Temple (1 Kings 10:11) and his men staffed Solomon's ships which brought the gold from Ophir for Solomon's treasury (1 Kings 9:27–28).

Solomon's payment to Hiram is also indicative of the close political and economic ties Israel and Tyre shared: Solomon delivered wheat and oil to Hiram every year. At one point, to keep up with the necessary payments for the tremendous amount of imports, Solomon gave 20 towns in the Galilee to Hiram. Hiram, however, was dissatisfied with these cities and called them "Cabul," meaning "good for nothing" (1 Kings 9:11–13). Nonetheless the two nations continued as substantial trading partners.

Solomon's imports of chariots and horses from Egypt and Kue and his subsequent exports of this military equipment to the Hittites and Arameans (1 Kings 10:28–29) show that Israel was an important link in exchanges between Egypt, the Middle East, and Anatolia. The land of Kue is identified with Cilicia (present-day Turkey).

The vastness of these trading expanses, their particular association with fantastic wealth, and the recognition that Solomon received visits from famous monarchs underscore the celebrated qualities of this remarkable and sometimes controversial king of the Israelites.

BELOW: *SOLOMON AND THE QUEEN OF SHEBA* BY FRANS FRANCKEN II (1581–1642). ALTHOUGH THE QUEEN OF SHEBA RULED A WEALTHY NATION, RICH IN GOLD AND SPICES, SHE ALSO GREATLY VALUED WISDOM.

THE QUEEN OF SHEBA

The literature of the Ancient Near East often portrays contests of wits between monarchs, used to demonstrate the wealth and superiority of particular nations. The arrival of the Queen of Sheba at Solomon's palace serves to prove that Israel has attained wealth and success. In addition, the account honors the God of Israel and his continuing covenant with Solomon, for the Queen herself acknowledges the Lord and his choice of Solomon.

The battle of wits is indicated by the description of the Queen's questions. Not only are they extensive and difficult, but Solomon answers them with such wisdom that he leaves her awestruck. She admits that his fame has reached her kingdom and that she has wanted to confirm the unbelievable reputation he enjoys in her own realm.

Dazzled by Solomon's material success, she nonetheless recognizes the true purpose of Solomon's kingdom: "Blessed be the Lord your God, who has delighted in you and set you on the throne of Israel! Because the Lord loved Israel forever, he has made you king to execute justice and righteousness" (1 Kings 10:9). Her words point to the covenantal role of the king as the pursuer of justice for all his subjects, and her bequest of an enormous cache of gold, precious stones, and spices portray the united kingdom of Solomon as the equivalent of the great empires of the Ancient Near East.

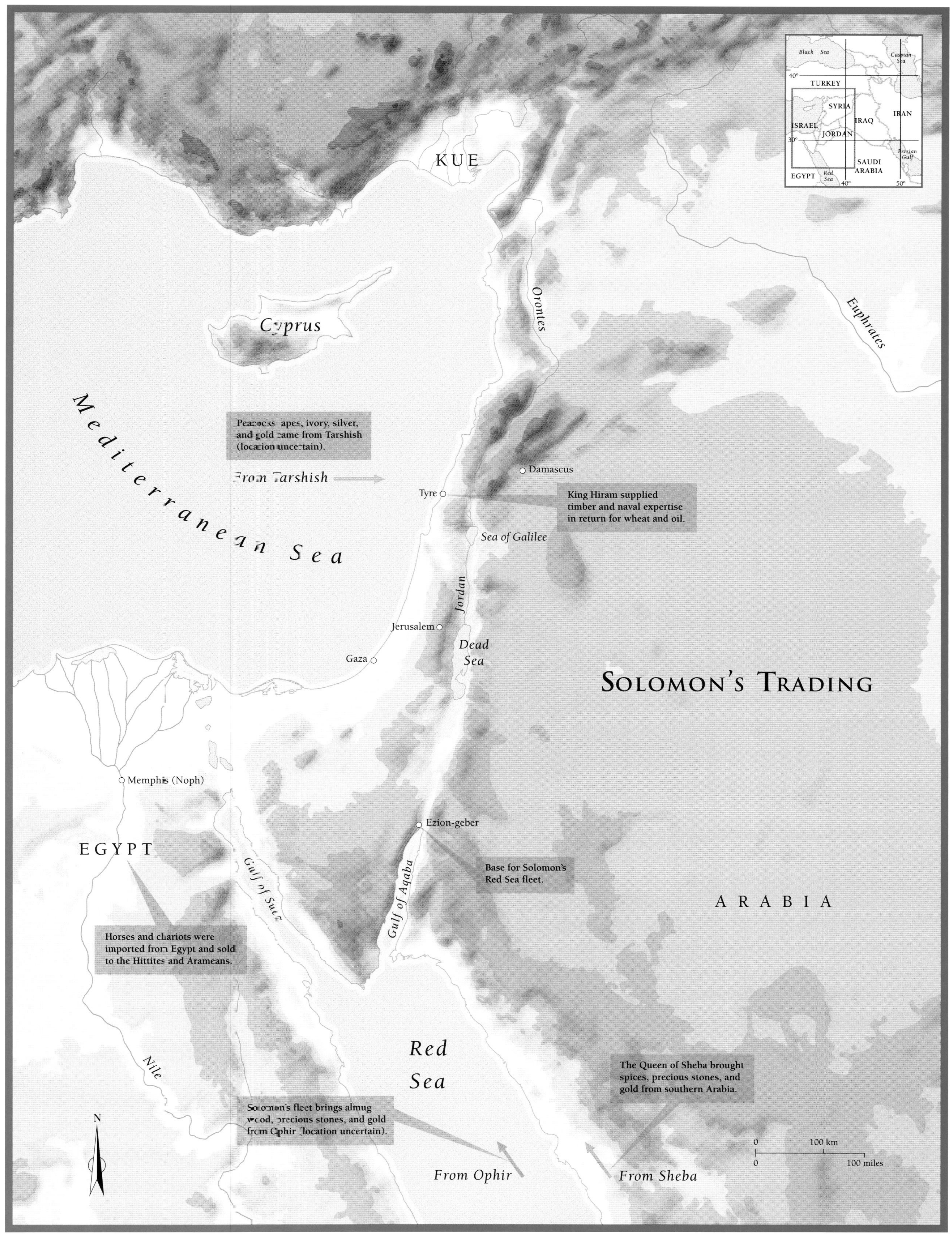
Solomon's Trading
KUE
Cyprus
Mediterranean Sea
Peacocks, apes, ivory, silver, and gold came from Tarshish (location uncertain).
From Tarshish
Orontes
Euphrates
Damascus
Tyre
King Hiram supplied timber and naval expertise in return for wheat and oil.
Sea of Galilee
Jordan
Jerusalem
Dead Sea
Gaza
Memphis (Noph)
EGYPT
Ezion-geber
Base for Solomon's Red Sea fleet.
Gulf of Suez
Gulf of Aqaba
ARABIA
Horses and chariots were imported from Egypt and sold to the Hittites and Arameans.
Nile
Red Sea
The Queen of Sheba brought spices, precious stones, and gold from southern Arabia.
Solomon's fleet brings almug wood, precious stones, and gold from Ophir (location uncertain).
From Ophir
From Sheba
N
0
100 km
0
100 miles
Black Sea
Caspian Sea
40°
TURKEY
SYRIA
IRAQ
IRAN
ISRAEL
JORDAN
30°
Persian Gulf
SAUDI ARABIA
EGYPT
Red Sea
40°
50°

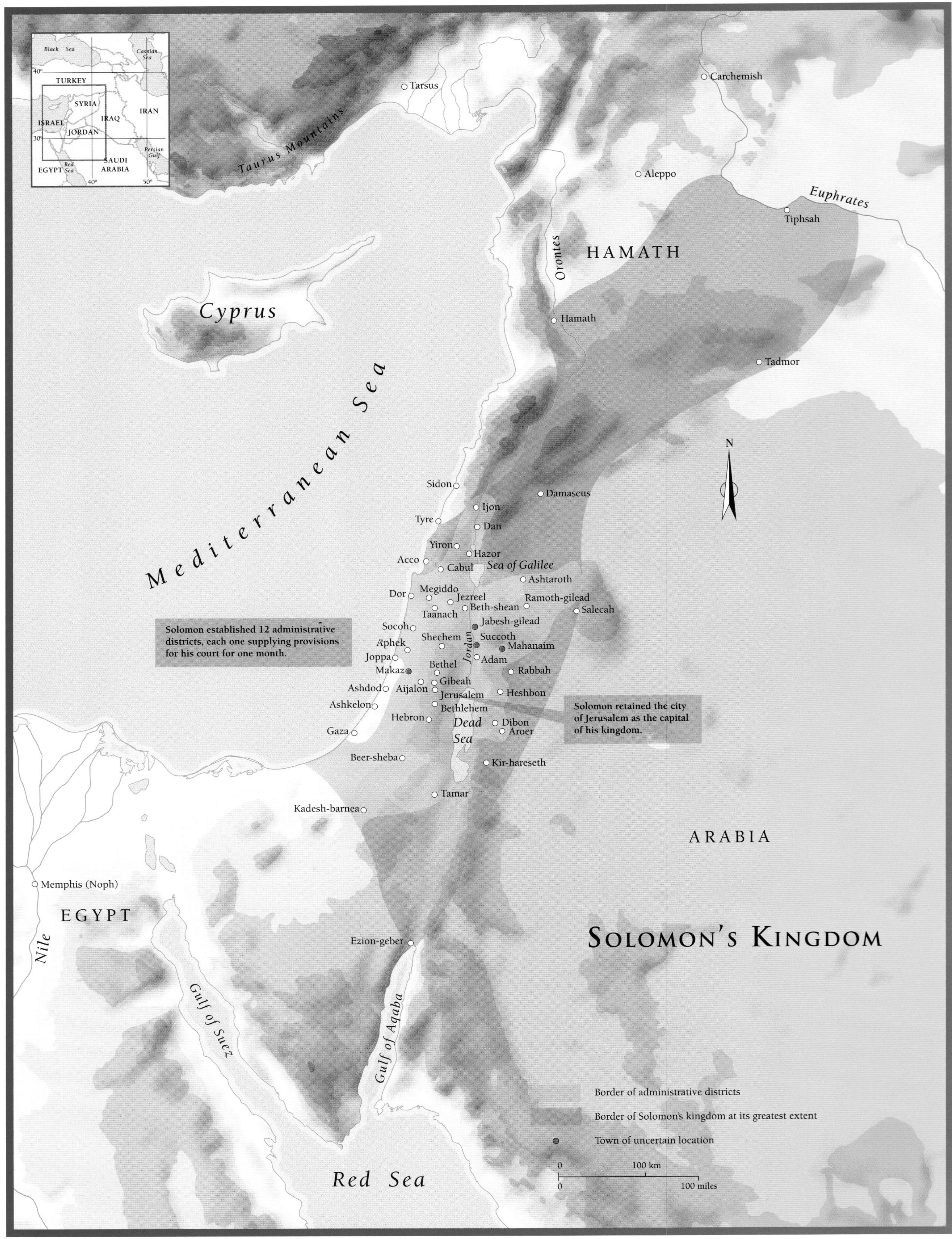
Black Sea
Caspian Sea
TURKEY
SYRIA
IRAN
ISRAEL
IRAQ
JORDAN
Persian Gulf
EGYPT
Red Sea
SAUDI ARABIA
40°
30°
50°
Tarsus
Carchemish
Taurus Mountains
Aleppo
Euphrates
Tiphsah
Orontes
HAMATH
Cyprus
Hamath
Tadmor
Mediterranean Sea
N
Sidon
Damascus
Ijon
Tyre
Dan
Yiron
Hazor
Acco
Cabul
Sea of Galilee
Ashtaroth
Dor
Megiddo
Jezreel
Ramoth-gilead
Taanach
Beth-shean
Salecah
Jabesh-gilead
Solomon established 12 administrative districts, each one supplying provisions for his court for one month.
Socoh
Aphek
Shechem
Succoth
Mahanaim
Jordan
Joppa
Adam
Makaz
Bethel
Rabbah
Ashdod
Aijalon
Gibeah
Jerusalem
Heshbon
Ashkelon
Bethlehem
Solomon retained the city of Jerusalem as the capital of his kingdom.
Hebron
Dead Sea
Dibon
Aroer
Gaza
Beer-sheba
Kir-hareseth
Tamar
Kadesh-barnea
ARABIA
Memphis (Noph)
EGYPT
Nile
Ezion-geber
SOLOMON'S KINGDOM
Gulf of Suez
Gulf of Aqaba
Border of administrative districts
Border of Solomon's kingdom at its greatest extent
Town of uncertain location
0
100 km
0
100 miles
Red Sea

LEFT: *SOLOMON MAKING A SACRIFICE TO THE IDOLS* BY SEBASTIEN BOURDON (1616–1671). IN HIS LATER YEARS, SOLOMON JOINED HIS FOREIGN WIVES IN THEIR ALLEGIANCE TO OTHER GODS.

SOLOMON TURNS FROM GOD

The final years of Solomon's reign are marked by an increasing lack of fidelity to God that leads him astray. His many marriages to foreign women, made for political reasons, have the disastrous effect of encouraging idolatry within his borders. Astarte, Milcom, Chemosh, and Molech are some of the deities whom his wives and concubines follow, and Solomon builds places of worship for them. These deities have had a long reputation of turning Israel away from God. God's response is to turn away from Solomon.

THE END OF THE SOLOMONIC KINGDOM

Responding to Solomon's infidelity, God sends political adversaries to threaten him, namely Hadad of Edom and Rezon of Damascus. With their successful revolts, Solomon's empire begins to crumble. Worse, Solomon faces the loss of his own people. The prophet Ahijah predicts that Jeroboam, one of the supervisors of Solomon's conscripted labor force, will become king of the ten northern tribes.

The scene of Ahijah's encounter with Jeroboam is reminiscent of the time when Saul tore the prophet Samuel's robe in desperation. That rending signified that the kingdom was ripped apart from Saul. This time however, it is the prophet who slashes his own robe. Ahijah tells Jeroboam to retrieve ten pieces, indicating God's choice that he will rule over the ten tribes of Israel. Judah, however, will remain the heir of God's covenant with David, as God remains faithful to his promise.

With the formulaic notice of Solomon's death, we learn that his famous deeds and accounts of his wisdom are also written in the "Book of the Acts of Solomon," a record which no longer exists. This brief death notice (1 Kings 11:41–43) quickly gives way to the account of the revolt of Jeroboam, who leads the ten tribes of Israel to secede from Solomon's son and rightful heir, Rehoboam. With this report, we find that Solomon's glory could not be sustained beyond his own generation.

BELOW: *SOLOMON* BY GUSTAVE DORE (1832–1883). ILLUSTRATOR AND ENGRAVER DORE COMPLETED MORE THAN 200 ILLUSTRATIONS WITH A BIBLICAL THEME.

A Kingdom Divided

MY FATHER DISCIPLINED YOU WITH WHIPS, BUT I WILL DISCIPLINE YOU WITH SCORPIONS 1 KINGS 12:11

RIGHT: *REHOBOAM ILL-ADVISED* BY G. FREEMAN. REHOBOAM'S DECISION NOT TO ALLEVIATE THE EXISTING LOAD OF TAXATION AND FORCED LABOR COSTS HIM THE ALLEGIANCE OF ALL ISRAEL EXCEPTING JUDAH.

King Rehoboam succeeded his father Solomon around 931 B.C.E., but his accession to the throne of David was far from smooth. The decision quoted above, a bold but foolish threat made by Rehoboam to the Israelite people at Shechem, soon proved shortsighted in the extreme.

Solomon, son of David and builder of the Temple in Jerusalem, had presided for some 40 years over one of the larger and stronger empires in the Ancient Near East. Besides the successful administration of all 12 tribes of Israel, Solomon exercised control over much of Transjordania (including Ammon, Moab, and Edom) as well as Aram and Hamath (much of the same territory as present-day Syria) all the way to the Euphrates River. But after Solomon's death this empire was short-lived.

Already by the fifth year of Rehoboam's reign (*c.* 925 B.C.E.) King Shishak of Egypt (Shoshenq I, the founder of the Twenty-second [Bubastite] Dynasty) had conducted a military incursion deep into the land of Palestine. Archaeological and epigraphic evidence both suggest that the pharaoh successfully invaded not only the city of Jerusalem but also much of the rest of Palestine from the southern Negeb desert to the northern valley of Jezreel and even into significant parts of Transjordania. This represented a far different situation to that found in the days of King Solomon.

THE PROBLEM OF FORCED LABOR

This Egyptian historical connection is an interesting one inasmuch as King Solomon himself had taken on some of the less attractive attributes of a powerful pharaoh like the one Moses had to contend with. Like that pharaoh, King Solomon's building projects were indeed impressive. Besides the Temple, they included his own palace complex in Jerusalem, as well as the store-cities of Hazor, Megiddo, Gezer, and elsewhere (see 1 Kings 9:15–19). But these great building projects required much forced labor—virtual slavery of captured foreigners and even some

BELOW: MT. GERIZIM IS ONE OF TWO MOUNTAINS THAT NESTLE PROTECTIVELY AROUND SHECHEM, THE CITY WHERE ALL ISRAEL HAD GATHERED TO MAKE REHOBOAM KING.

members of the northern tribes of Israel (see 1 Kings 5:13; 9:20–22; and also 11:28 where Jeroboam was given charge "over all the forced labor of the house of Joseph"). This, along with Solomon's large and impressive harem, with all the cost required to subsidize their retinues, led naturally to much native unhappiness, and even open rebellion soon after Solomon's death.

Solomon had been styled King of Israel and Judah, a grand title with much historical truth to it. Even during King David's reign the relationship between (north) Israel and (south) Judah had been at times quite strained (see 2 Samuel 2:1–4 for David's original coronation over his home tribe of Judah, and 2 Samuel 5:1–5 for his Israelite coronation some seven years later). Later, during Solomon's reign, we find further references to the separate tribal or national entities Judah and Israel. So we are not surprised to read about the traditional schism reappearing in 1 Kings chapter 12, where the tribal leaders of Israel say they will break away from the Judean king unless he moderates the harsh labor policy of his father. It is after consultation with his peers, who had grown up with him in the luxurious palace, that Rehoboam gave the ignominious statement found at the beginning of this chapter. Yet we soon read that even this obtuseness represented "a turn of affairs brought about by the Lord" (1 Kings 12:15) to fulfill the prophetic word spoken by one Ahijah the Shilonite (see below for the nature of this prophetic word).

THE END OF THE UNITED MONARCHY

When the tribal leaders saw that King Rehoboam would not listen to their complaints, they erupted in open rebellion. "What share do we have in David? We have no inheritance in the son of Jesse" (see 1 Kings 12:16) they remonstrated, and they soon went home. When Rehoboam sent Adoram, his overseer of the forced labor, into Israelite territory, he was stoned to death. Rehoboam himself had to mount his chariot hurriedly and flee to his Judean capital of Jerusalem in disgrace. Instead of one large, powerful, and wealthy United Monarchy of Israel and Judah under King Solomon, we soon find two states: Judah, under his son Rehoboam, and Israel, with newly elected king, Jeroboam (see 1 Kings 12:20, where Jeroboam had returned from his exile in Egypt).

A later attempt by Rehoboam to restore the northern territory to his kingdom by military means was also thwarted, this time peacefully. One Shemaiah, the man of God, spoke up in opposition to this course of action to reestablish the larger Davidic kingdom; for as the Lord commanded, "you shall not go up or fight against your kindred the people of Israel" (see 1 Kings 12:22–24).

Thus in summary, sometimes at war, other times in uneasy political alliance, these two lesser kingdoms of Israel and Judah would never again regain the prominence they enjoyed as a single united Davidic empire during the first two-thirds of the tenth century B.C.E. The rest of the books of Kings, as well as the parallels in 1 and 2 Chronicles, explore at length the vicissitudes of these divided kingdoms of God's people Israel. The northern kingdom will last some 210 years until its demise to the Assyrians in 722 B.C.E., and, more impressively, the southern kingdom with its Davidic dynasty will endure for nearly three and a half more centuries, until its eventual fall to Babylonia in 586 B.C.E.

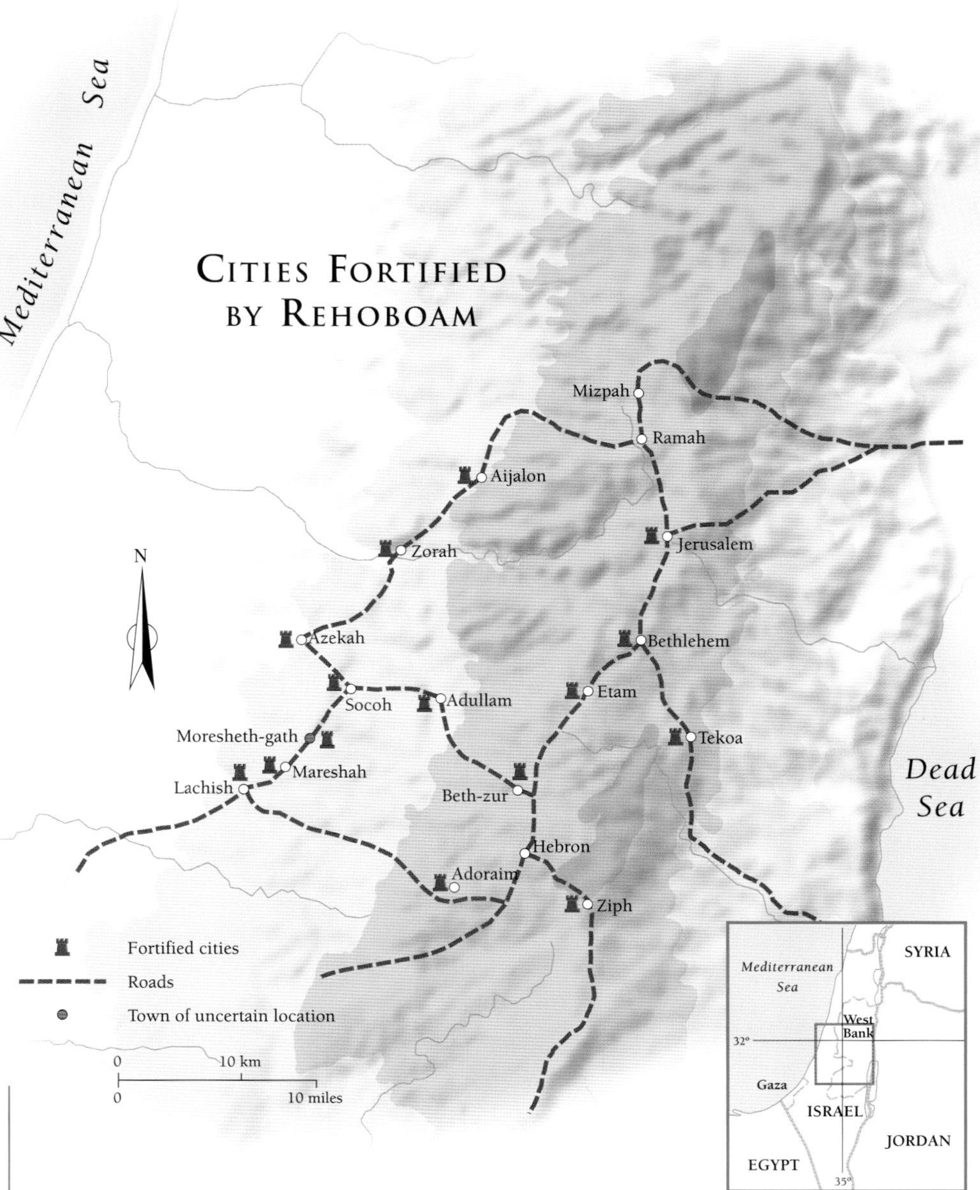

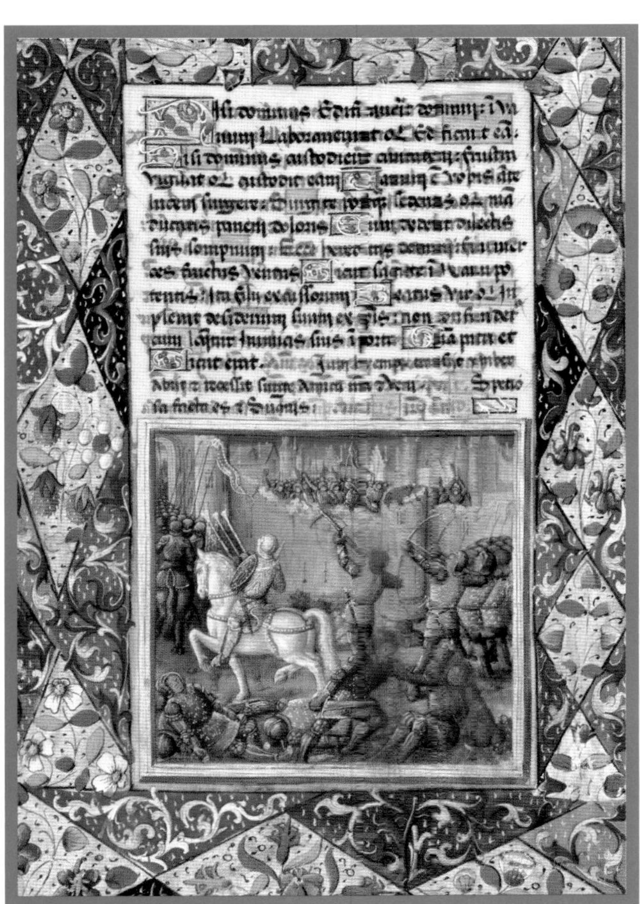

LEFT: *REHOBOAM WAGING WAR AGAINST JEROBOAM,* FROM *THE BOOK OF HOURS OF LOUIS D'ORLEANS,* 1490, BY JEAN COLOMBE. ALTHOUGH AT FIRST THERE WAS PEACE, JUDAH AND ISRAEL WERE AT WAR FOR MUCH OF REHOBOAM'S REIGN.

RIGHT: *JEROBOAM*, ENGRAVING BY WHITE. THE PROPHET AHIJAH USES A TORN GARMENT TO ILLUSTRATE HIS PROPHECY, WHICH IS A NOT UNCOMMON BIBLICAL SYMBOL.

JEROBOAM MADE KING OVER THE NORTHERN TRIBES OF ISRAEL

There is more than a little irony in the fact that the ten northern tribes who had rebelled against King Rehoboam of Judah quickly embraced Jeroboam. Jeroboam, a native Ephraimite, had been forced to seek asylum in Egypt during the reign of King Solomon, inasmuch as he was recognized as potentially an able rival to the king (see 1 Kings 11:40), and it was not until the death of that powerful king that Jeroboam could return home. But the irony dwells in the fact that Jeroboam, of all people, had been originally put in charge of the corvée (forced labor) of the house of Joseph early in Solomon's reign. Solomon had seen that Jeroboam was very competent and hard working (see 1 Kings 11:28), a good choice to head the construction crew closing up the gaps in the wall of the city of David (that is, the city of Jerusalem south of the Temple Mount).

This strategic area was otherwise known as the Millo, of the massive Stepped Stone Structure on the east side of biblical Mount Zion (the term *Millo* in Hebrew in this context probably means filling). Both British Dame Kathleen Kenyon and Israeli archaeologist Yigal Shiloh conducted excavations in this area of Jerusalem, uncovering what is now the most impressive architectural find of First Temple Jerusalem: a sloping terraced wall some 65 ft (20 m) high.

So Jeroboam the Ephraimite was an appropriate choice as leader, both for King Solomon, and after his death, for the seceding Israelite tribes. But the main reason why these tribes rebelled in the first place—to bring to an end the continuing harsh forced-labor policies of Solomon's son Rehoboam—does make their enthusiastic choice of former corvée leader Jeroboam an ironic one indeed.

AHIJAH THE SHILONITE

In Jeroboam's day (before his flight into Egypt), a prophet named Ahijah from Shiloh met him in the countryside near Jerusalem. Ahijah was wearing a new cloak, and he ceremoniously removed it (such prophetic sign actions were commonly part of the prophet's repertoire), and ripped it into 12 pieces, giving ten of them to Jeroboam. The word of the Lord soon followed: "See, I am about to tear the kingdom from the hand of Solomon, and will give you ten tribes. One tribe will remain his, for the sake of my servant David and for the sake of Jerusalem, the city that I have chosen out of all the tribes of Israel" (1 Kings 11:31–32).

Later on, when Rehoboam responded so harshly and so foolishly to the northerners frustrated by his labor policies, his response is described as being caused by the Lord to fulfill this very prophecy (see 1 Kings 12:15). Incidentally, while many would identify the two remaining tribes as Judah and Benjamin, a more likely identification could well be Judah and Simeon, the latter a southern tribe eventually subsumed entirely by Judah.

THE END OF JEROBOAM'S REIGN

If Jeroboam's accession to the throne of Israel was largely effected by prophetic influence, it may be appropriate to recognize that his eventual demise owed much to this influence as well. In one of the strangest prophetic narratives in the Old Testament, an unnamed prophet from Judah came to Jeroboam's new altar at Bethel and denounced it. In a stunning prediction over three centuries before its fulfillment, the prophet proclaimed, "O altar, altar … 'A son shall be born to the house of David, Josiah by name; and he shall sacrifice on you the priests of the high places who offer incense on you, and human bones shall be burned on you'" (1 Kings 13:2). Most prophetic predictions are short-term in nature, easily seen to be true or false by the contemporary audience (see Deuteronomy 18:21–22), and this remarkable long-term prophecy has naturally led some scholars to suggest it was a later interpolation into the text. Be that as it may, the reference is to King Josiah, the great reformer king of the late Judean monarchy (see 2 Kings chapters 22–23), whose reforms in the eighteenth year of his reign (622 B.C.E.) are said to be some of the most radical ever made.

THE PROPHETIC IMPETUS

Some preliminary observations about the nature of prophecy in Israel are in order. The prophet (*nabhi* in Hebrew) was the called-out one, the one designated to be the spokesman (or spokeswoman—for women could be, and were, prophets, too) for God. When the prophet spoke, he or she declared "thus says the Lord," and the penalties for inaccuracy in this area were severe indeed (see, for example, Deuteronomy 18:14–22).

More to the point, the relationship between king and prophet proved to be a vexed one repeatedly throughout the United and Divided Monarchies of Israel and Judah, from the onset of the United Monarchy around the beginning of the first millennium B.C.E. down to the early sixth century B.C.E. (where, famously, the major prophets Jeremiah and Ezekiel sharply criticized the actions of the last several kings of Judah). Indeed, the institution of the prophet was probably established as an effective counterweight to the institution of the monarchy in the first place, presumably by the hereditary priesthood against the tribal elders who wanted a king.

This balance of power would apply especially to the area of "Holy War," which could only take place after an initial oracle of victory was given by the prophet (see, for example, 1 Kings chapter 22). No wonder there would be frequent conflict between the official prophets of Yahweh and the current king of the land throughout most of the four centuries of the monarchy. Ironically, the *Prophet* shown here is from the tomb of Frederick III, Holy Roman Emperor and German King, sculpted by Niclas Gerhaert van Leyden (*c.* 1430–1473).

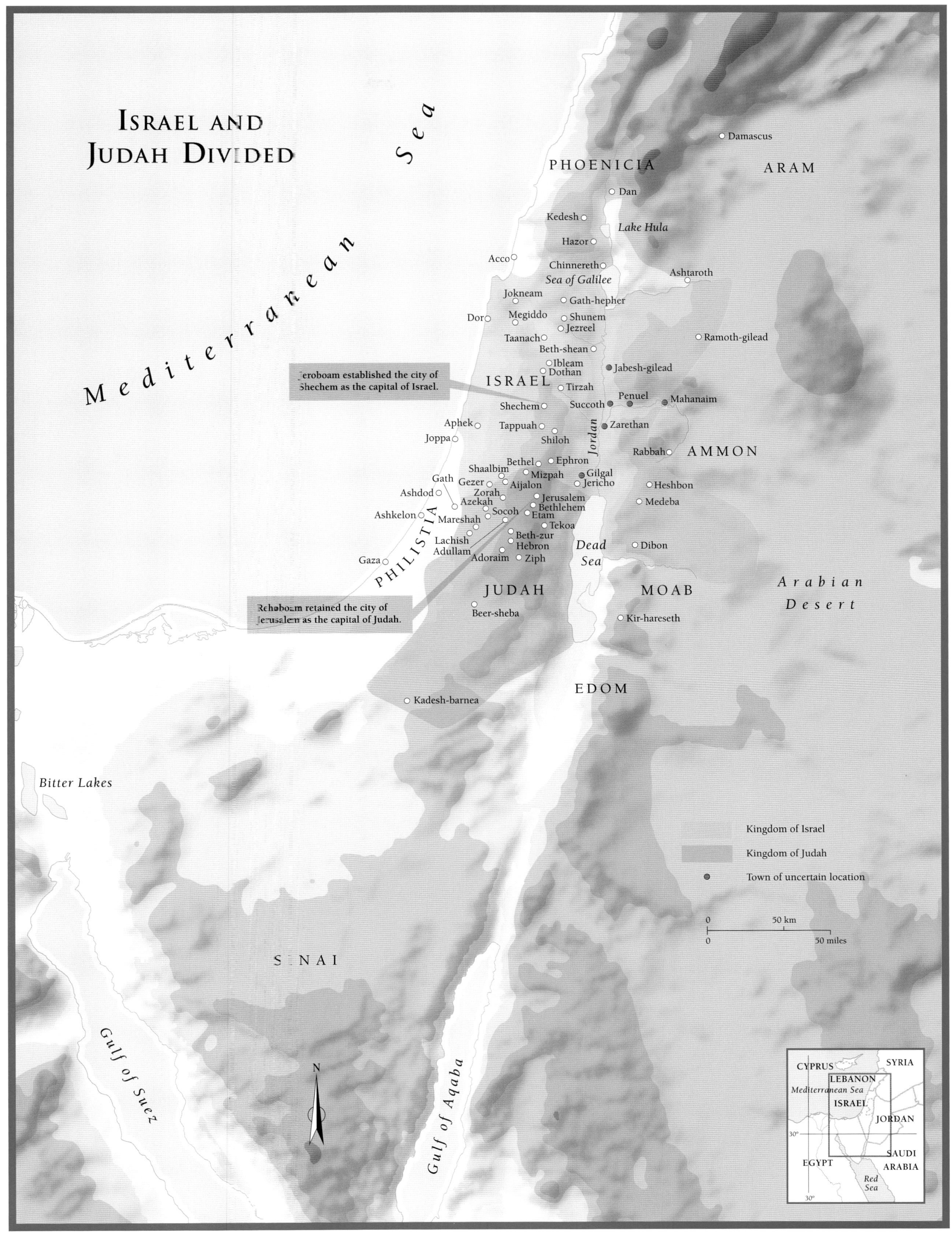
Israel and Judah Divided
Mediterranean Sea
Jeroboam established the city of Shechem as the capital of Israel.
Rehoboam retained the city of Jerusalem as the capital of Judah.
PHOENICIA
ARAM
ISRAEL
AMMON
JUDAH
MOAB
PHILISTIA
EDOM
SINAI
Arabian Desert
Damascus
Dan
Kedesh
Lake Hula
Hazor
Acco
Chinnereth
Sea of Galilee
Ashtaroth
Jokneam
Gath-hepher
Dor
Megiddo
Shunem
Jezreel
Taanach
Ramoth-gilead
Beth-shean
Ibleam
Dothan
Jabesh-gilead
Tirzah
Penuel
Shechem
Succoth
Mahanaim
Aphek
Tappuah
Zarethan
Joppa
Shiloh
Jordan
Rabbah
Bethel
Ephron
Shaalbim
Mizpah
Gilgal
Gath
Gezer
Aijalon
Jericho
Heshbon
Ashdod
Zorah
Azekah
Jerusalem
Medeba
Bethlehem
Ashkelon
Socoh
Etam
Mareshah
Tekoa
Lachish
Beth-zur
Adullam
Hebron
Dead Sea
Dibon
Gaza
Adoraim
Ziph
Beer-sheba
Kir-hareseth
Kadesh-barnea
Bitter Lakes
Gulf of Suez
Gulf of Aqaba
N
Kingdom of Israel
Kingdom of Judah
Town of uncertain location
0
50 km
0
50 miles
CYPRUS
SYRIA
LEBANON
Mediterranean Sea
ISRAEL
JORDAN
EGYPT
SAUDI ARABIA
Red Sea
30°
30°

ABOVE: *JEROBOAM SACRIFICING TO THE GOLDEN CALF*, 1752, BY JEAN-HONORE FRAGONARD. JEROBOAM FOLLOWED AARON'S EXAMPLE AND MADE GOLDEN CALVES. HE TOOK THEM TO DAN AND BETHEL.

As for King Jeroboam's response to the prophet, he "stretched out his hand from the altar, saying, 'Seize him!' But the hand that he stretched out against him withered so that he could not draw it back to himself" (1 Kings 13:4–5)—a stunning sign indicating the authenticity of the prophetic message of condemnation. The king must entreat the prophet to heal his hand—again a reminder that even kings must bow down to the prophetic word. (The chapter continues with a most disturbing story about an old Bethelite prophet deceiving this young Judean prophet, leading to his death, tragically confirming the authenticity of his message.)

This prophetic denunciation of Jeroboam will become a refrain throughout both books of Kings, with nearly every northern king negatively evaluated in connection with the sin of Jeroboam, namely encouraging worship on the high places and appointing priests for these high places "from among the people" (see 1 Kings 13:33–34, and repeated refrains throughout the books of Kings). But the prophet Ahijah once again will have a say in Jeroboam's life as well. By now the aged Ahijah was nearly blind, but when Jeroboam sent his wife in disguise to seek healing for their sick son Abijah, the Lord informed the prophet of her mission and identity (1 Kings 14:5). Again, the prophetic message for Jeroboam was ominous: because of his sins of idolatry and syncretism, his son will soon die; indeed his own dynasty will be short-lived, and the Lord will raise up a king "who shall cut off the house of Jeroboam today, even right now" (see 1 Kings 14:12–14). The story then concludes with the sad death of the son, and the death and burial notice of Jeroboam himself.

Nadab, another son, will succeed him as king over Israel, but Nadab will be assassinated after only two years (see 1 Kings 15:25–30). All of Jeroboam's family also will be killed.

RIGHT: *WAR BETWEEN ASA AND BAASHA*, FIFTEENTH-CENTURY COLOR LITHOGRAPH. THE RULERS CHANGE, BUT THE ENMITY BETWEEN ISRAEL AND JUDAH CONTINUES.

ATTACKS ON JUDAH AND ISRAEL

As already noted, the era of the powerful United Monarchy of David and Solomon had abruptly come to an end (*c.* 931 B.C.E.) with the rise of the Divided Kingdoms of Israel (under Jeroboam) and Judah (under Solomon's son Rehoboam). Jeroboam proved to be an effective and innovative king, but one remembered as irretrievably unorthodox from the point of view of the prophets, and thus worthy of sharp and repeated condemnation throughout the texts of 1 and 2 Kings. Rehoboam on the other hand proved to be an insensitive and incompetent leader, clearly unworthy of retaining the large empire which Solomon his father had possessed.

Warfare between the two kingdoms was averted for a time by prophetic intervention (see 1 Kings 12:21–24), but the conditions for strife between the two neighboring states persisted (and eventually erupted into open invasion during the reigns of King Asa of Judah and King Baasha of Israel, as described in 1 Kings 15:16–22).

LEFT: CARTONNAGE OF SHOSHENQ I, *C.* 945–924 B.C.E. THIS "SECOND SKIN" WAS STUCK ON TO SHISHAK'S MUMMY AND THEN RICHLY DECORATED, WITH A FALCON HEAD AS ONE OF THE MOTIFS.

Both the repeated summary statements "there was war between Rehoboam and Jeroboam continually" (1 Kings 14:30; see also 15:6), and "there was war between Abijam [son of Rehoboam, known elsewhere as Abijah] and Jeroboam" (1 Kings 15:7) in the Kings accounts imply what the Chronicler (see 2 Chronicles chapter 13) spells out in more detail: intermittent conflict throughout the last part of the tenth century B.C.E. took place repeatedly between these two petty kingdoms. The results were essentially an uneasy stalemate.

PHARAOH SHISHAK'S INVASION OF THE LAND

But it was outside pressure from Shishak, king of Egypt, which dominated this period of time. The founder of the Twenty-second (Bubastite) Dynasty, Shishak (Shoshenq I) was quite familiar with the land of Syria–Palestine; he was the pharaoh who had harbored the fleeing Jeroboam during Solomon's reign (1 Kings 11:40). Scholars point out that this was probably meant to undermine Solomon's power, or at least to embarrass him publicly. It will be recalled that King Solomon had established friendly relations with the preceding weak Twenty-first Dynasty, including marrying one of the daughters of the pharaoh (the identity of the pharaoh is not mentioned but scholars presume he was either Siamun or Psusennes II, the two latter kings of the dynasty). A noble from a line of Lybian chieftains, Shishak served as the commander-in-chief of the Egyptian army.

A stela dated sometime after Psusennes's fifth year (*c.* 954 B.C.E.) is our first reference to Shishak; by the close of Psusennes's reign (*c.* 945 B.C.E.) he was a mature man with grown children and was well connected by marriage, with his son Osorkon married to one of Pharaoh Psusennes's daughters. Shishak himself took the throne after Psusennes's death presumably without a male heir.

Shishak's 21-year reign (*c.* 945–924 B.C.E.) inaugurated a brief resurgence in Egyptian political and military power, and eventually led to a remarkable two-and-a-half centuries of Lybian rule. He undertook major building projects especially in the Delta area, and he established his son Yewepet as high priest of Thebes. And of course he marched into Syria–Palestine in his fifth year of reign. Probably spurred on by increased Israelite trade with the southern Arabic tribes, Shishak apparently exploited a minor border incident as an excuse to attack the region. Numerous destruction levels found in excavations throughout the entire region attest to his ferocity, and his own commemorative relief at Karnak lists some 154 towns which he said he destroyed. A careful study of this list leads to the following reconstruction of his campaign: a direct attack on Jerusalem from the west, coupled with further campaigns northward throughout the hill country of Israel, and even a flanking attack eastward on Mahanaim in Transjordania. An extensive southern campaign in the Negeb desert all the way to Ezion-geber, the seaport on the Red Sea, also took place. Shishak's triumphal stela found at Megiddo attests his boast that as the result of this victorious campaign all Palestine was now under imperial control.

Jerusalem itself escaped major damage, but only as the result of Rehoboam's payment of an enormous tribute, including all the shields of gold Solomon had made for his palace complex (see 1 Kings 10:17; 14:26). There is no indication that Shishak was able to follow up on his victorious campaign, and once again the kingdoms of Israel and Judah were largely left to their own petty disputes.

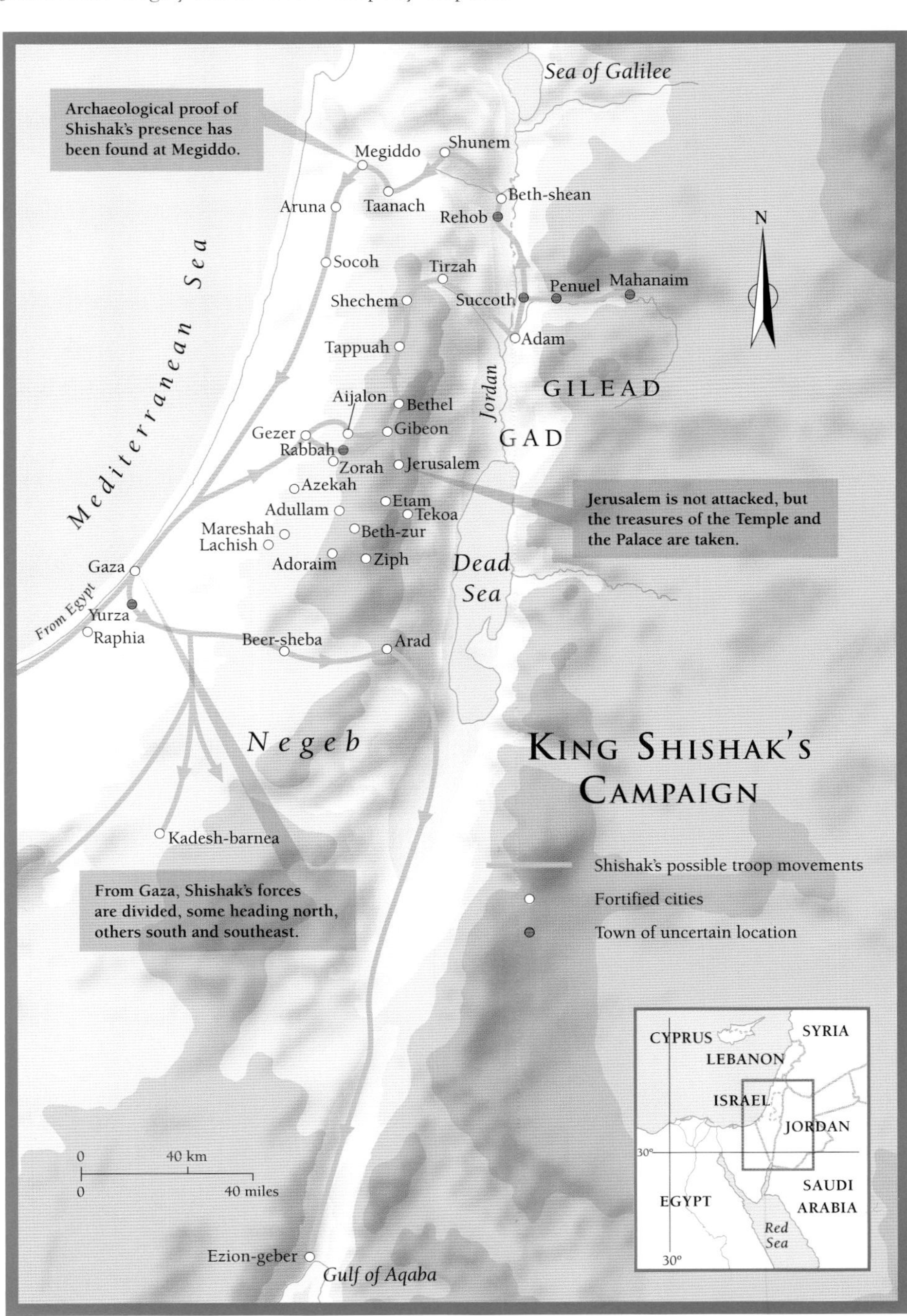

THE KINGS OF ISRAEL

THE LORD HAD NOT SAID THAT HE WOULD BLOT OUT THE NAME OF ISRAEL ... SO HE SAVED THEM 2 KINGS 14:27

RIGHT: *ZIMRI'S REVOLT*, FROM ROYAUMONT'S *HISTOIRE DE L'ANCIEN ET NOUVEAU TESTAMENT* (1724). ZIMRI'S REIGN LASTS ONLY AS LONG AS TIRZAH STANDS AGAINST THE SIEGE; THEY FALL TOGETHER.

For two centuries, the Divided Monarchies of Israel and Judah coexisted, side by side. From the division of the kingdom of David and Solomon in *c.* 931 B.C.E. down to the fall of Samaria in *c.* 722 B.C.E., the Davidic dynasty survived in the south, but in the north, the kingdom of Israel also represented the people of the Lord. This will be neither the first nor the last time that the Lord's people are found in separate groups.

The quotation above, in specific reference to the reign of Jeroboam II of Israel, illustrates the dilemma, as it were, that the Lord faced: he was the God of both the northern and the southern kingdoms, of the ten tribes of Israel who broke away from the house of David, and of the tribe of Judah who retained the Solomonic Temple and the Davidic dynasty.

In both kingdoms, the Lord raised up leaders to bless and protect his people, and he was loath to bring either kingdom into defeat and exile. But, alas, eventually both kingdoms had to confront those very sobering realities. Meanwhile, the ninth and eighth centuries B.C.E. represented exciting historical times for both of the kingdoms of God's people.

THE DYNASTY OF OMRI (*C.* 885–841 B.C.E.)

Even the so-called biblical "minimalists," who discount the historicity of Moses, David, and Solomon, must concede the existence of the dynasty of Omri. For we have incontrovertible extrabiblical evidence for this dynasty from the Assyrian cuneiform records (indeed, the standard Neo-Assyrian term for Israel is the "house/dynasty of Omri" [bīt Humri], which continued to be used until the fall of Samaria over a century after Omri's dynasty formally came to an end). Another, probably better-known, attestation is found in the famous "Moabite Stone" (*c.* 830 B.C.E.), where Mesha, king of Moab, complains, "Omri, king of Israel, oppressed Moab many years." So the existence of King Omri of Israel and his dynasty is beyond dispute.

BELOW: *ELIJAH BY THE BROOK CHERITH*, *C.* 1700, TEMPERA ON PANEL. THE LORD PROTECTS THE PROPHET ELIJAH FROM DROUGHT BY DIRECTING HIM TO WATER AND SENDING RAVENS TO FEED HIM.

However, the rise of the Omride dynasty came as the result of much dispute. Baasha's dynasty had lasted some 26 years, with Baasha himself on the throne in the northern capital at Tirzah for 24 of those years, and his son Elah only lasting two years. Zimri, one of Elah's chariot commanders, conspired against him, and struck him down while drunk at a party (see 1 Kings 16:9–10). In grim poetic justice, perhaps, just as Baasha had previously killed all of Jeroboam's family, Zimri put to death all of Baasha's household.

But Zimri's "reign," if we can style it as such, only lasted seven days. On hearing of Zimri's conspiracy, Omri, commander of Israel's army, led all Israel to besiege Tirzah the capital city (see 1 Kings 16:15–17). When Zimri saw the city was about to fall, he fled into the citadel, set it on fire, and perished in the flames. But Omri still had to contend for the throne. An otherwise unknown individual named Tibni son of Ginath was supported by half the people; Omri by the other half. Some have hypothesized that since there was no clear prophetic successor to Elah, this crisis in the government led to an interregnum of at least two years. In any case, Omri eventually prevailed, and Tibni died.

Omri's reign lasted some 12 years, with six of them in Tirzah, and the other six in his new capital city of Samaria in the western foothills of Manasseh. Samaria indeed will remain the capital city of the kingdom of Israel until its fall in 722 B.C.E. Excavations of the site show that the city was beautifully designed and magnificently constructed, with some of its walls among the finest ever built in Palestine.

KING AHAB OF ISRAEL

Perhaps the most infamous king of Israel from the point of view of the Kings texts, Ahab son of Omri reigned some 22 years (*c.* 874–853 B.C.E.), and his infamous wife Jezebel perhaps surpasses his own dismal reputation in the popular mind. But this is rather unfair, and largely a product of the unforgettable Elijah narratives of 1 Kings chapter 17 through 2 Kings chapter 2. On the other hand, some scholars have made a serious case for taking Psalm 45, the great wedding psalm, as originally composed for Ahab and Jezebel's wedding!

For a more neutral presentation of the political and military ability of King Ahab, one should consult 1 Kings chapter 20, where we find his brilliant riposte to King Ben-hadad II of Aram (present-day Syria), "One who puts on armor should not brag like one who takes it off" (verse 11). King Ahab is able to hold his own against the superior army of Aram, and the narrator of the book of 1 Kings even includes references to an unnamed prophet advising King Ahab on military strategy!

Although the chapter does end on a judgmental note (see 1 Kings 20: 35–43), the overall effect is still to enhance the effectiveness of this otherwise much maligned king. Of course, the Elijah material in 1 Kings chapters 17–19, the Naboth incident in chapter 21, and the Micaiah debacle in chapter 22 contribute to the more familiar picture of Ahab as weak, self-centered, and ineffective. But even in his death on the battlefield as described in the Micaiah account, Ahab does appear in a heroic, if tragic light.

EXCESSES OF THE OMRIDE DYNASTY

As previously noted, King Ahab, son of Omri, as well as his Phoenician wife Jezebel, have come to be characterized in popular thought as cruel, arrogant, and self-serving. Although this impression is not supported by all the biblical texts, it is of course largely from those texts that we tend to characterize Ahab as weak-willed and petulant, and his wife Jezebel as imperious and overbearing. So a quick survey of these texts is in order here.

The continuing conflict between prophet and king has already been discussed. But it is surely in the Elijah and the Elisha cycles (roughly 1 Kings chapter 17 through 2 Kings chapter 9), that one gains the impression that prophet versus king seems fated to be a never-ending struggle.

Whether it be Elijah's calling down fire from heaven against the 450 prophets of Baal, only to be chased away entirely from the land of Israel by Jezebel's later imperious threat to kill him (see 1 Kings chapters 18 and 19); or his rebuke of Ahab's and Jezebel's conniving to steal Naboth's vineyard for their own use, with the result that Naboth the Jezreelite is unjustly stoned to death (1 Kings chapter 21); or, later on, the impetuous reformer King Jehu calling for the bloody death of Jezebel the Queen Mother (2 Kings 9:30–37), with stray dogs chewing on the corpse of Jezebel (according to the word of Elijah the prophet); the impression remains unforgettable that this evil couple deserve nothing but contempt on our part. Once again, it is king (and queen) versus prophet, and one knows who will win that battle!

And that is rightly so, for both Ahab and Jezebel, like King Solomon before them and King Manasseh of Judah after them, blithely assumed all the rights and privileges of absolute monarchs, of Oriental potentates—and that will not be tolerated for long by the God of the Israelites, or by his servants the prophets.

ABOVE: *THE DEATH OF JEZEBEL* BY G. COLI (1643–1681) AND F. GHERARDI (1643–1704). JEZEBEL'S TERRIBLE FATE IS FORETOLD BY ELIJAH, EVEN TO BEING EATEN BY DOGS.

Jehu's Tribute

One of the most dramatic finds in the Ancient Near East must surely be the Black Obelisk of Shalmaneser III found at his capital city of Nimrud, where Jehu or his representative is pictured on his knees before the Assyrian monarch, with the tribute bearers in his train. The inscription reads: "I receive the tribute of Jehu 'son of Omri,' silver, gold [etc.]." (As already noted, the Assyrians tended to label every later king of Israel as from the dynasty of Omri.) The obelisk stands over 6 ft 3 in high (nearly 200 cm); it is now found in the British Museum. Jehu's registry is the second from the top, out of a total of five such scenes of tribute. Scholars date this event to 841 B.C.E.

ABOVE: *JEHU & HEADS OF STATE*, 1904, BY A. HOFFMANN VON VESTENHOF. THIS MACABRE IMAGE COMMUNICATES THE RUTHLESSNESS OF JEHU'S ELIMINATION OF THE HOUSE OF AHAB.

OPPOSITE: *THE ENTRY OF JEHU INTO JEZREEL* BY EDWARD HENRY CORBOULD (1815–1905). JEHU'S DESPERATE RIDE IS INSPIRED BY THE LORD'S CALL FOR VENGEANCE.

THE DYNASTY OF JEHU (*C.* 841–745 B.C.E.)

Already in 1 Kings 19:16–17 the Lord announced to the fugitive prophet Elijah that he should anoint Jehu son of Nimshi to be king over Israel. This did not take place, however, until an unnamed servant of Elisha ran into the military encampment at Ramoth-gilead in Transjordania and poured the anointing oil over Jehu's head (Jehu the commander of the army) and then ran away. But before he fled, he announced, "I anoint you king over the people of the Lord, over Israel. You shall strike down the house of your master Ahab, so that I may avenge on Jezebel the blood of my servants the prophets" (see 2 Kings 9:1–10).

Jehu first laughed off the action as that of a madman, but not much later, after his troops recognize him as king, Jehu himself drives his chariot furiously to confront King Joram (son of Ahab), who lay ill in the winter palace at Jezreel, with King Ahaziah of Judah attending him. By the end of the chapter both kings are dead, as well as the Queen Mother Jezebel. Seventy sons of Ahab in Samaria were killed by the frightened elders of Samaria, with their heads brought in baskets to Jehu in Jezreel, and some 42 royal friends and relatives of the Queen Mother were killed as well (see 2 Kings 10:1–14).

What a bloodthirsty usurper Jehu proved to be. But such was deemed necessary to avenge the blood of the prophets of the Lord, and the blood of Naboth the Jezreelite. Indeed, the Lord commends Jehu as follows: "Because you have done well in carrying out what I consider right, and in accordance with all that was in my heart have dealt with the house of Ahab, your sons of the fourth generation shall sit on the throne of Israel" (2 Kings 10:30). And indeed, Jehu's dynasty by far was the longest one in the relatively short history of the northern kingdom of Israel—nearly 100 years.

KINGS JEHOAHAZ AND JEHOASH OF ISRAEL

A brief reading of 1–2 Kings might lead one to consider all the northern kings of Israel as uniformly wicked, but such is not the case. None of these kings lacks a statement of condemnation: even Jehu is condemned in general terms for not turning away from the "sin of Jeroboam" (see 2 Kings 10:31); and each of the other kings from Jehu's dynasty—Jehoahaz, Jehoash, and Jeroboam II—are evaluated in similar terms. Zechariah, the last king from this dynasty, only lasted six months on the throne, and even he comes under the same condemnation (see 2 Kings 15:9). But these words of condemnation are softened several times by reminders that the Lord saw how his people were suffering and provided some relief: "Jehoahaz entreated the Lord, and the Lord heeded him; for he saw the oppression of Israel.... Therefore the Lord gave Israel a savior" (2 Kings 13:4–5); again, with Jehoash son of Jehoahaz, "The Lord's arrow of victory, the arrow of victory over Aram" (2 Kings 13:17, where the aged and ill prophet Elisha promises Israelite victory over the Arameans, but not complete victory since King Jehoash only struck the ground with the arrows three times, instead of five or six times). The final example, with Jehoash's son Jeroboam II, is quoted at the beginning of this chapter.

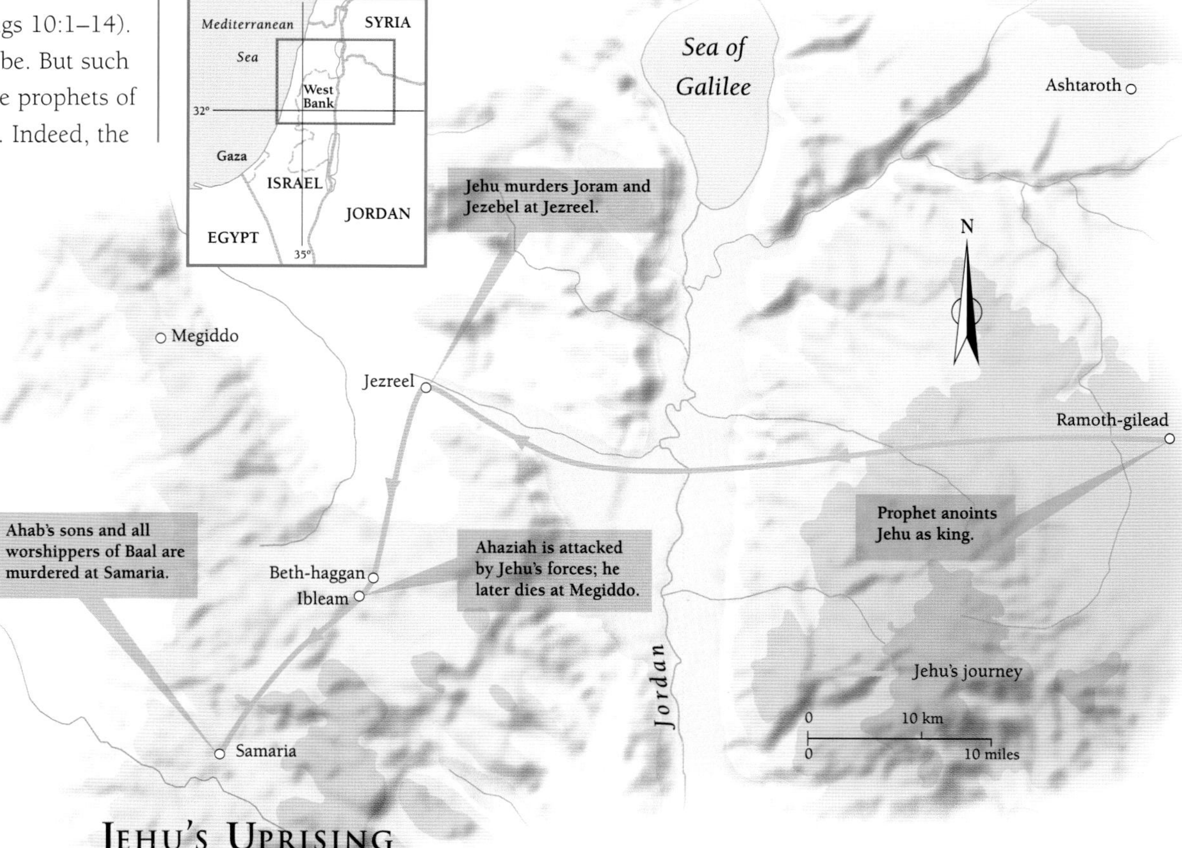

JEHU'S UPRISING

RIGHT: *ICON OF THE FIERY ASCENT OF SAINT ELIJAH WITH SCENES FROM HIS LIFE,* 1647, BY IGNATI PANTELEEV. ELIJAH'S ASCENT IN A FIERY CHARIOT IS THE LAST OF HIS MANY MARVELOUS DEEDS.

THE PROPHETS ELIJAH AND ELISHA

Much has already been said in passing concerning these famous ninth-century Israelite prophets, but a closer look at their lives and careers is most appropriate. After all, their influence has well stood the test of time, with Elijah in particular the quintessential example of a prophet of the Lord, even appearing with Moses on the Mount of Transfiguration in the days of Jesus, and welcomed by observant Jews every Passover Seder (ritual Passover dinner) by a glass of wine poured just for him!

Elijah seems to come out of nowhere, and the confrontation with King Ahab is immediate: "As the Lord the God of Israel lives, before whom I stand, there shall be neither dew nor rain these years, except by my word" (1 Kings 17:1). Elijah's famous contest with the prophets of Baal (the Canaanite and Phoenician god of rain) later on in the next chapter ends with both fire coming down from heaven and the sound of heavy rain (also, alas, with the slaughter of 450 prophets of Baal and the 400 prophets of Asherah supported by Jezebel).

In 2 Kings chapter 19, Elijah is not surprisingly on the run from the vengeful Queen Jezebel, and he spends 40 days and 40 nights on the journey to Mt. Horeb (another name for Mt. Sinai), eventually witnessing the presence of the Lord. He is given further tasks to accomplish: the anointing of Hazael as king over Aram; of Jehu son of Nimshi as king over Israel; and last, but not least, the anointing of Elisha as prophet. This last task is accomplished first, with Elijah throwing his mantle over Elisha, and Elisha leaving his plowing and following his master (1 Kings 19:19–21).

Perhaps the most famous event in Elijah's life is reserved for the end: his amazing ascent to heaven, with his servant and successor Elisha watching, and with horses and a chariot of fire accompanying him in the whirlwind (see 2 Kings chapter 2). Elisha asks for a double share of Elijah's spirit (the share given to the family's firstborn), and his petition is granted.

Elisha, in a literal sense, does receive a double portion of Elijah's spirit, for the wonders he accomplished are roughly double those of Elijah (for example, one resurrection from the dead for Elijah, two for Elisha, including one after his own demise [see 2 Kings 13:20–21]).

Elijah tended to work alone, but Elisha worked with disciples; Elijah is characteristically associated with mountains and fire, but Elisha is associated with rivers and water. But both represented one of the high points of Israelite history, when the Lord worked directly with his wayward people to give evidence of his unmistakable presence and tokens of his deep love.

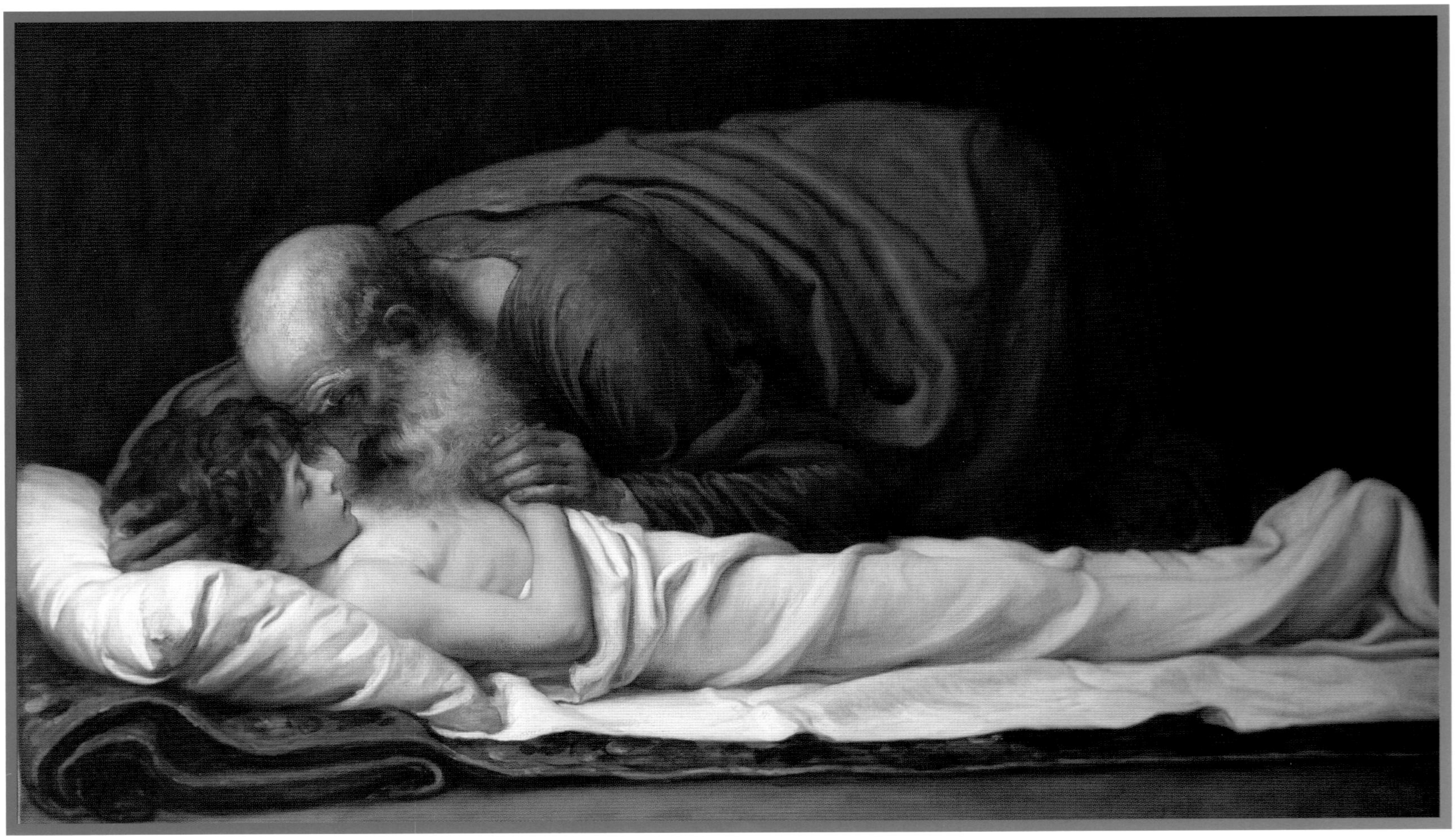

BELOW: *ELISHA RAISING THE SON OF THE SHUNAMITE,* 1881, BY FREDERIC LEIGHTON. ELISHA HAS A SPECIAL BOND WITH THIS CHILD: HE WAS CONCEIVED AFTER THE MOTHER HELPED ELISHA.

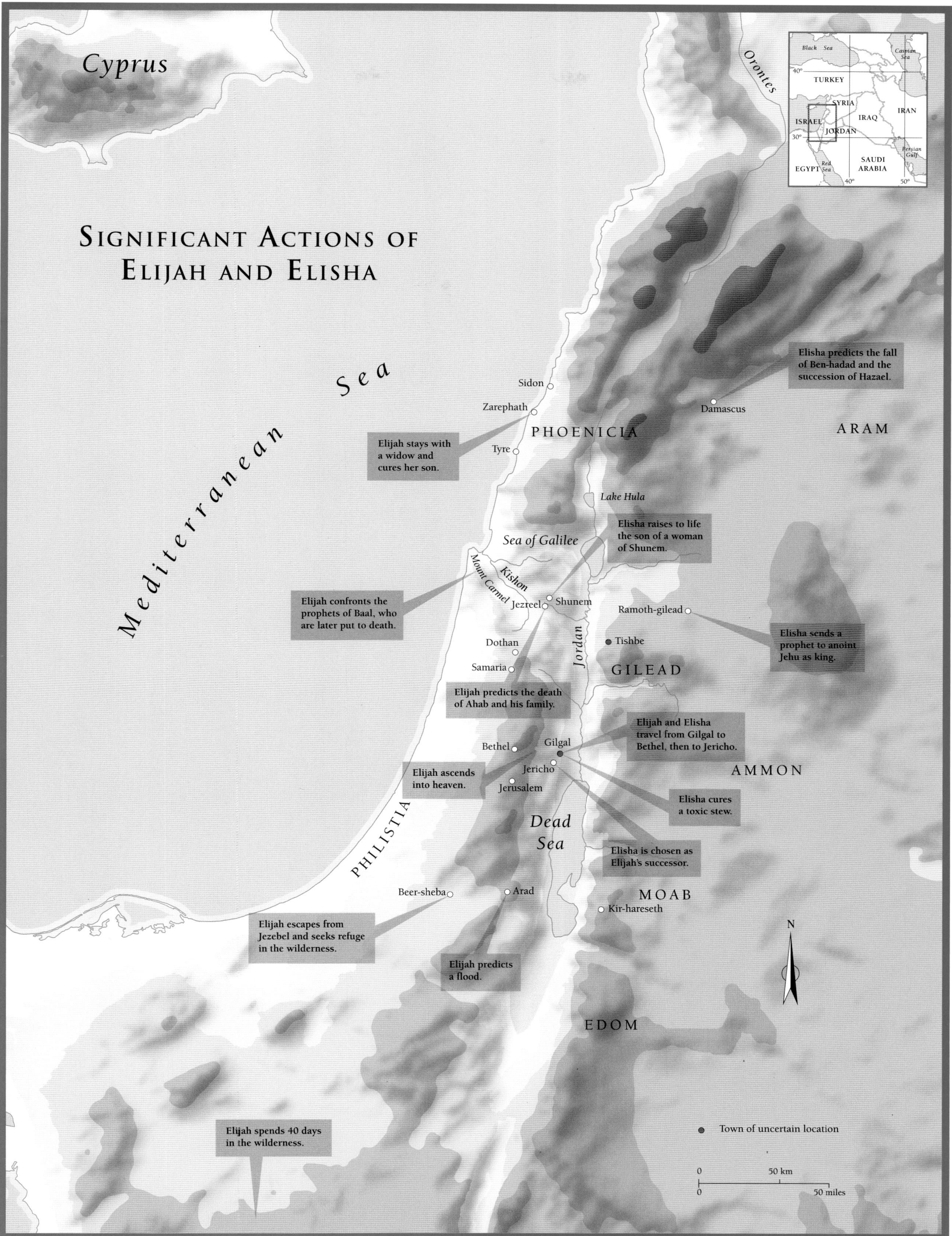
Significant Actions of Elijah and Elisha
Cyprus
Mediterranean Sea
Black Sea
Caspian Sea
TURKEY
SYRIA
IRAQ
IRAN
ISRAEL
JORDAN
SAUDI ARABIA
EGYPT
Red Sea
Persian Gulf
Orontes
Elisha predicts the fall of Ben-hadad and the succession of Hazael.
Damascus
ARAM
Sidon
Zarephath
PHOENICIA
Tyre
Elijah stays with a widow and cures her son.
Lake Hula
Elisha raises to life the son of a woman of Shunem.
Sea of Galilee
Mount Carmel
Kishon
Elijah confronts the prophets of Baal, who are later put to death.
Jezreel
Shunem
Ramoth-gilead
Elisha sends a prophet to anoint Jehu as king.
Dothan
Tishbe
Samaria
Jordan
GILEAD
Elijah predicts the death of Ahab and his family.
Elijah and Elisha travel from Gilgal to Bethel, then to Jericho.
Bethel
Gilgal
Jericho
Elijah ascends into heaven.
Jerusalem
AMMON
Elisha cures a toxic stew.
PHILISTIA
Dead Sea
Elisha is chosen as Elijah's successor.
Beer-sheba
Arad
MOAB
Kir-hareseth
Elijah escapes from Jezebel and seeks refuge in the wilderness.
Elijah predicts a flood.
N
EDOM
Town of uncertain location
Elijah spends 40 days in the wilderness.
0 50 km
0 50 miles

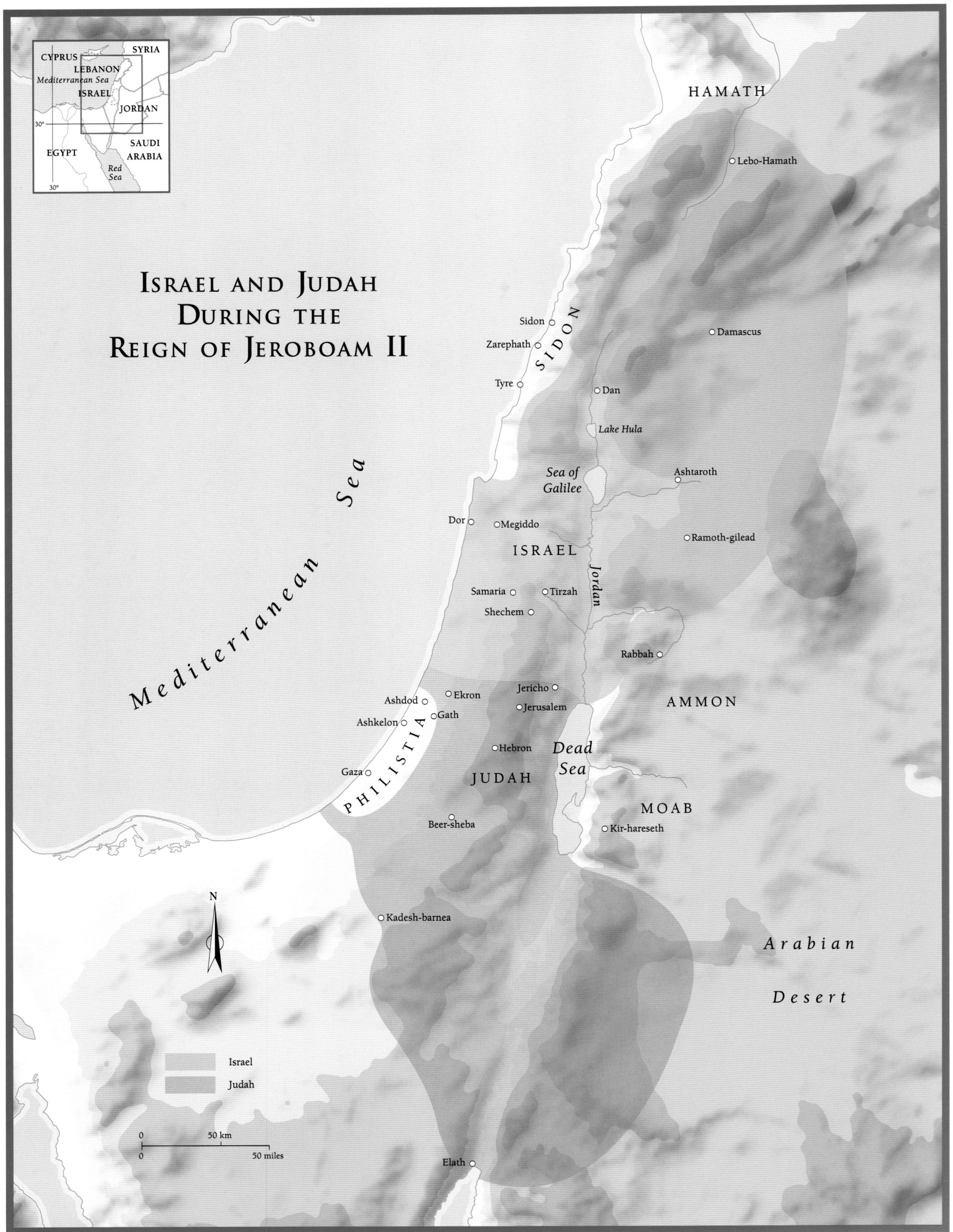
Israel and Judah During the Reign of Jeroboam II
CYPRUS
SYRIA
LEBANON
Mediterranean Sea
ISRAEL
JORDAN
EGYPT
SAUDI ARABIA
Red Sea
HAMATH
Lebo-Hamath
Sidon
Zarephath
SIDON
Damascus
Tyre
Dan
Lake Hula
Mediterranean Sea
Sea of Galilee
Ashtaroth
Dor
Megiddo
Ramoth-gilead
ISRAEL
Jordan
Samaria
Tirzah
Shechem
Rabbah
Jericho
Ashdod
Ekron
Jerusalem
AMMON
Ashkelon
Gath
Hebron
Dead Sea
Gaza
JUDAH
PHILISTIA
MOAB
Beer-sheba
Kir-hareseth
N
Kadesh-barnea
Arabian Desert
Israel
Judah
0
50 km
0
50 miles
Elath

KING JEROBOAM II OF ISRAEL

This, the fourth king in the dynasty of Jehu, may have been the most important king in the history of the Divided Monarchy of Israel. The discussion of Jeroboam II (*c.* 783–745 B.C.E.) does not take much space in the book of 2 Kings (namely seven largely formulaic verses; see 14:23–29), but even there we catch a glimpse of his relative greatness. His remarkable victories restore the ideal borders of the Promised Land, and also of the United Monarchy of David and Solomon.

It is with bitter irony that both the prophecies of Hosea and of Amos at this time show the Lord's extreme displeasure with the prosperous and uncaring Israelites in and around the capital city of Samaria. This time of Israelite prestige and prosperity was also a time of stunning neglect of the poor and worship of idols.

LATER KINGS OF ISRAEL

As already noted, Jeroboam's son Zechariah lasted only six months on the throne before he was assassinated (2 Kings 15:8–12). This event unfortunately proved to be only a foreshadowing of the final 24 years of the Northern Kingdom, where some four additional dynasties (kings from different families) vied for the throne. Of these would-be kings, three of the final five were assassinated (namely, Shallum, Pekahiah, and Pekah); and the last one (Hoshea) was taken into exile. Only Menahem was able to have his son Pekahiah succeed him to the throne (and only for two years, at that). When one realizes the major chronological difficulties attending this era, with possibly more than one king on the throne at any given moment, one can appreciate all the more the prophet Hosea's bitter words: "I [the Lord] gave you a king in my anger, and I took him away in my wrath" (Hosea 13:11).

KING HOSHEA AND THE FALL OF SAMARIA

Perhaps as if to dampen somewhat the horror of what he has to describe, the author of 2 Kings introduces the last Israelite king, Hoshea (no relation to Hosea the prophet), as follows: "He did what was evil in the sight of the Lord, yet not like the kings of Israel who were before him" (2 Kings 17:2). What follows is a final depiction of desperation. Hoshea is exiled, and Samaria captured by the Assyrians by 722 B.C.E. (many suggest that two or three years separate these two dismal events, with the besieged city of Samaria without a king for its last several years). In any case, playing the game of power politics finally caught up with Israel, and the writer of 2 Kings takes nearly an entire chapter (17:7–41) to explain why the Lord finally forsook his people. Some excerpts: "the people of Israel had sinned against the Lord their God … they had worshipped other gods … the people of Israel secretly did things that were not right against the Lord their God … they did wicked things, provoking the Lord to anger; they served idols … they would not listen but were stubborn … they followed the nations that were around them … they made their sons and their daughters pass through fire [probably a euphemism for child sacrifice] … therefore the Lord was very angry with Israel and removed them out of his sight; none was left but the tribe of Judah alone" (excerpts from verses 7–18).

The Assyrians were infamous for their extensive methods of exiling subject peoples, transporting them from ancestral homes to new locations to forestall further rebellion. This was the case with these ten tribes of Israel, and we find that haunting references to the fate of the ten lost tribes remain quite popular even to the present day.

LEFT: *HOSEA*, TWELFTH CENTURY, AT THE ABBEY CHURCH OF STE MARIE, SOUILLAC, FRANCE. GOD CASTIGATES ISRAEL IN THE NATION'S LAST DAYS THROUGH HIS PROPHET HOSEA.

BELOW: *SHALMANESER IN TRIUMPH* BY JEAN FOUQUET (*C.* 1420–*C.* 1481) IN *OEUVRE DE JEHAN FOUCQUET* (*C.* 1866). THE KING OF ASSYRIA BESIEGES SAMARIA AND TAKES THE PEOPLE AWAY FROM ISRAEL.

THE KINGS OF JUDAH

THE LORD HAD PROMISED TO GIVE A LAMP TO HIM [DAVID] AND TO HIS DESCENDANTS FOREVER 2 KINGS 8:19

RIGHT: *JEHOSHAPHAT TRIUMPHS*, IN ROYAUMONT'S *HISTOIRE DE L'ANCIEN ET NOUVEAU TESTAMENT* (1724). THE LORD PROTECTS JEHOSHAPHAT IN BATTLE BY DRAWING HIS ENEMIES AWAY.

After Solomon's death (*c.* 931 B.C.E.), as already noted, the United Monarchy of Israel was divided up into two lesser kingdoms, the so-called Divided Monarchies of Israel and Judah. The northern kingdom (Israel) was able to survive under various dynasties, long or short, for some two centuries, down to the fall of Samaria to the Assyrians in *c.* 722 B.C.E. But the southern kingdom of Judah, which continued to be ruled by the Davidic dynasty, was able to survive for nearly three and a half centuries, until the fall of Jerusalem in 586 B.C.E. to the Babylonians.

Although usually reckoned as representing only one of the original 12 tribes of the patriarch Jacob (also named Israel), the land of Judah did represent nearly the same-sized area as that of northern Israel (although this comparison

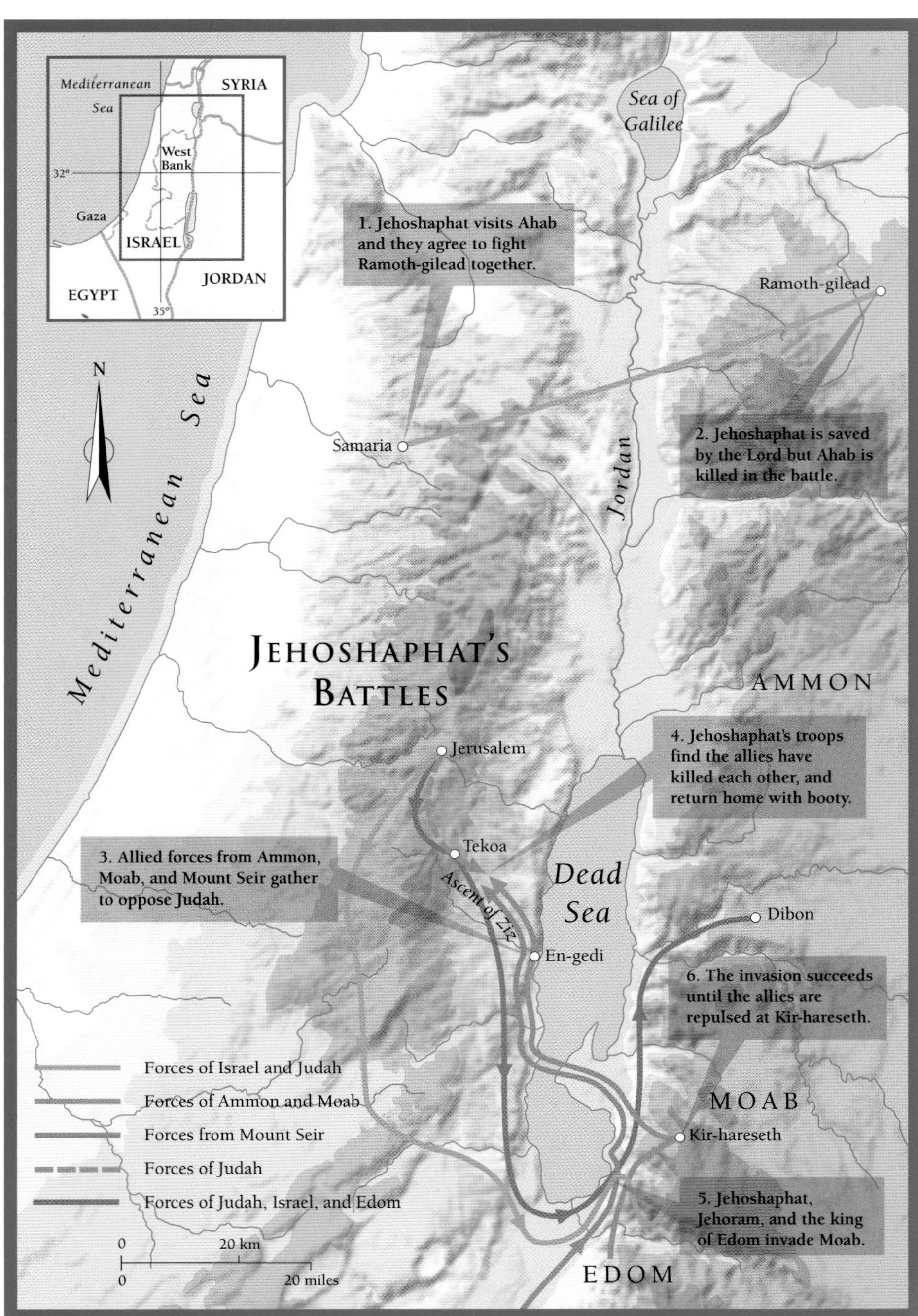

depended on the current size of the northern kingdom, which fluctuated significantly throughout the ninth and eighth centuries B.C.E.). Probably politically, and certainly geographically, the southern tribe of Simeon was also subsumed into "greater Judah" as well.

David's dynasty was meant to be nothing less than forever (see 2 Samuel 7:16), and even though it did last for more than four centuries, a long period of time in comparison to other dynasties in the Ancient Near East, this was far short of forever, as the later prophets Jeremiah and Ezekiel came to recognize. Persistent sin eventually would lead to the downfall of Judah, just as it had for Israel, and David's eternal "lamp," alas, would eventually be extinguished in the debacle of the Babylonian takeover of Judah under King Nebuchadnezzar in *c.* 586 B.C.E.

Indeed, it is the extended description of the systematic looting and destruction of the Solomonic Temple in that year which brings to an end the great literary history book about the Israelite monarchies which we now call 1 and 2 Kings. (To be sure, 2 Kings does end on a note of modest hope, with the release of King Jehoiachin, descendant of David, from Babylonian prison [2 Kings 25:27–30], but never again will we read about a king from the family of David on the throne of any kingdom.)

EARLY NINTH-CENTURY KINGS OF JUDAH

As already noted, Solomon's son Rehoboam represented a significant decline of the Davidic dynasty, for much of the empire was lost to Jeroboam, and Pharaoh Shishak succeeded in invading major portions of the territory of Judah, even ransacking the Temple in Jerusalem. Nonetheless, Rehoboam's son Abijam (also called Abijah) succeeded him on the throne without any difficulty.

In a similar fashion, Abijam's son Asa succeeded him as king in Jerusalem. But by now, the tension between the northern and southern kingdoms led to outright war during Asa's reign, with King Baasha of Israel exerting so much pressure on Judah that Asa had to send tribute to King Ben-hadad I of Aram–Damascus (present-day Syria) to break his non-aggression pact with Israel (see 1 Kings 15:16–20). This strategy proved successful, and both the writers of Kings and Chronicles speak of Asa's lengthy reign of 41 years in largely positive terms.

Jehoshaphat, Asa's son, succeeded him as king in Jerusalem in *c.* 873 B.C.E., and his 25 years of reign were also largely successful. Overshadowed by King Ahab of Israel, Jehoshaphat was able to restore peaceful relations with that Omride king. (The end of hostilities was formally cemented by eventual intermarriage between these two dynasties: Jehoshaphat's son Jehoram married one of Ahab's daughters.)

QUEEN ATHALIAH AND KING JOASH OF JUDAH

The crisis that ended the dynasty of Omri in Israel also proved catastrophic for Judah. For Jehu's slaughter of the descendants and relatives of King Ahab in *c.* 841 B.C.E. also led to the death of King Ahaziah (son of Jehoram and grandson of Jehoshaphat) of Judah, who was visiting Joram (son of Ahab) at the time. Athaliah, the Queen Mother, was able to seize power in Jerusalem for some six years, and she apparently set about to destroy the entire royal family to avenge Ahaziah's death (see 2 Kings 11:1). This is the first substantial threat to the Davidic dynasty.

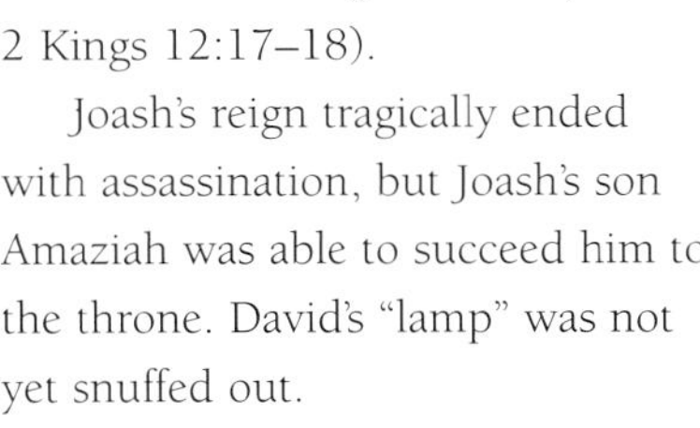

We are relieved to hear about the infant crown-prince Joash being hidden from the wrathful queen, and the intervention of the high priest Jehoiada in restoring the heir to the throne (at seven years of age). All the people rejoiced when they saw the young king "standing by the pillar, according to custom" (2 Kings 11:14), and Queen Athaliah was soon put to death in terms reminiscent of the death of the even more notorious Queen Mother, Jezebel wife of Ahab.

Joash reigned for 40 years in Jerusalem, and both Kings and Chronicles represent his reign as largely successful. His main claim to fame was the restoration of Solomon's Temple. King Joash, in a move reminiscent of Rehoboam, did have to pay off a foreign invader, one King Hazael of Aram; it took the giving of numerous votive offerings, plus gold from both Temple and palace to cause Hazael to withdraw from Jerusalem (see 2 Kings 12:17–18).

Joash's reign tragically ended with assassination, but Joash's son Amaziah was able to succeed him to the throne. David's "lamp" was not yet snuffed out.

ABOVE: *ATHALIAH EXPELLED FROM THE TEMPLE* BY ANTOINE COYPEL (1661–1722). THE PRIESTS DID NOT WANT ATHALIAH TO BE KILLED IN THE TEMPLE, BUT SHE DIED ONCE SHE LEFT THE HOUSE OF THE LORD.

LEFT: *ATHALIAH*, SIXTEENTH-CENTURY FRENCH VELLUM. ATHALIAH DOES HER RUTHLESS BEST TO KILL ALL THE ROYAL FAMILY AFTER THE DEATH OF HER SON AHAZIAH.

ABOVE: *THE PROPHET ISAIAH*, FRESCO BY TOMMASO MASOLINO DA PANICALE, (1383–C. 1447), CASTIGLIONE OLONA, ITALY. ISAIAH SERVED AS PROPHET IN JUDAH FOR MORE THAN 40 YEARS.

KING UZZIAH (AZARIAH) OF JUDAH

We are told in 2 Kings 15:1–2 that King Uzziah (also called Azariah), son of Amaziah, of Judah began to reign while Jeroboam II of Israel was on the throne, and that his reign spanned 52 years. Yet we find only seven verses in 2 Kings devoted to his reign, and part of that focused on his infamous bout with leprosy (see 2 Kings 15:5, and the more expansive account found in 2 Chronicles 26:16–23). And we are then told that, presumably because of the leprosy, his son Jotham was put "in charge of the palace, governing the people of the land" (2 Kings 15:5). What a remarkably terse account for what was apparently an important and long-reigning king!

KINGS AHAZ AND HEZEKIAH OF JUDAH

We are told that King Hezekiah "trusted in the Lord the God of Israel; so that there was no one like him among all the kings of Judah after him, or among those who were before him" (2 Kings 18:5–6). Later on, we will read a similar comment about King Josiah, the great reformer king of Judah in the second half of the seventh century B.C.E. But why such high praise of King Hezekiah of Judah?

Hezekiah's father, the notorious King Ahaz, fares poorly in biblical estimation. Whether it be the accounts in Isaiah chapter 7, or 2 Kings chapter 16, or 2 Chronicles chapter 28, little that is good can be said about this timid and idolatrous king. To be fair, he was under much political and military pressure, facing the combined forces of Rezin King of Aram and Pekah King of Israel marching against Jerusalem in *c.* 734 B.C.E. (It is in the light of this enemy pressure that Isaiah the court prophet announces the "Immanuel" sign to reassure King Ahaz that the Lord had not abandoned his city of Jerusalem; see Isaiah 7:1–16).

Ahaz, however, did not seek his God; rather, in melancholy parallel with some of his predecessors, he sought to buy help from a formidable foreign power—this time, the very menacing Tiglath-pileser III, king of Assyria. Once again taking the silver and gold found in the Temple and

COREGENCIES

Biblical chronographers have long recognized the existence of coregencies, or overlapping reigns of both the kings of Israel and of Judah. Critics of these alleged coregencies often see them as desperate attempts to fit the sometimes long reigns of the biblical texts into the historical eras fixed by extrabiblical references (for example, the invasion of Pharaoh Shishak in *c.* 925 B.C.E., or the reference to King Jehu of Israel on the Black Obelisk of Shalmaneser III of Assyria, *c.* 841 B.C.E.). But the reference to Jotham son of Uzziah (also called Azariah) as governing the people while his father still lived is itself a clear reference to a coregency, and thus justifies our overlapping chronologically at least some of the years of the father's reign with those of the son. To be sure, some scholars have overused this method with dubious results, but most scholars have recognized that the notorious issue of seemingly too-large biblical totals for the reigns of the kings of Israel and Judah can often be resolved by recognition of this phenomenon (some scholars, for example, explain Uzziah's 52-year reign as overlapping some of the years of his father Amaziah, all the years of his son Jotham, and some of the years of his grandson Ahaz).

LEFT: *HEZEKIAH AND THE IDOLS*, IN ROYAUMONT'S *HISTOIRE DE L'ANCIEN ET NOUVEAU TESTAMENT* (1724). HEZEKIAH GATHERS PEOPLE FROM ISRAEL AND JUDAH TO CELEBRATE PASSOVER AND THEN DESTROY THE IDOLS.

palace, Ahaz sent a present to the Assyrian king, with predictable results: Tiglath-pileser attacked Damascus, killing King Rezin (2 Kings 16:8–9), and eventually annexed both Transjordania and Galilee (northern provinces of Israel). No wonder the prophet Isaiah declared, "On that day the Lord will shave with a razor hired beyond the River—with the king of Assyria—the head and the hair of the feet, and it will take off the beard as well" (Isaiah 7:20).

Curiously, the good king Hezekiah will eventually do much the same. After telling us how great Hezekiah was, the Kings narrator informs us that King Sennacherib of Assyria marched against Judah and Jerusalem (this event can be firmly dated to 701 B.C.E.), and Hezekiah paid him off with 300 talents of silver and 30 talents of gold (see 2 Kings 18:13–14; Sennacherib's own records mention 800 talents of silver, and 30 of gold). King Hezekiah had to strip the gold from the doors of the Temple to pay off the Assyrian king.

So what made Hezekiah so incomparably great? The end of the Sennacherib account gives the answer. As the results of Hezekiah's earnest prayer "before the Lord" (2 Kings 19:15), Isaiah the prophet brings back a positive word, denouncing the arrogance of the Assyrian king, and predicting the amazing deliverance of the city of Jerusalem. Sure enough, we read of the mysterious death of some 185,000 Assyrian invaders in one night (2 Kings 19:35; Isaiah 37:36), and the quick withdrawal of the Assyrian army. As Isaiah had prophesied, "By the way that he came, by the same he shall return; he shall not come into this city, says the Lord. For I will defend this city to save it, for my own sake and for the sake of my servant David" (2 Kings 19:33–34; see also Isaiah 37:34–35). Yes, Hezekiah's powerful prayer rescued the city. Once again, Jerusalem is saved from the enemy and the Davidic dynasty continues. David's "lamp" is still burning.

KING MANASSEH OF JUDAH

With unintended irony, the writer of 2 Kings tells us that King Manasseh, son of Hezekiah, was on the throne of David in Jerusalem for some 55 years (including about 10 years as co-regent), which is the longest reign of any of the 40 kings who took the throne in either Israel or Judah during the entire monarchic period of the tenth through sixth centuries B.C.E. The writer is quite clear about how evil Manasseh's reign was: "Because King Manasseh … has done things more wicked than all that the Amorites did, who were before him, and has caused Judah also to sin with his idols; therefore thus says the Lord … I will cast off the remnant of my heritage, and give them into the hand of their enemies" (2 Kings 21:11–14).

We find at this point no more discussion about the eternal "lamp" of David's house.

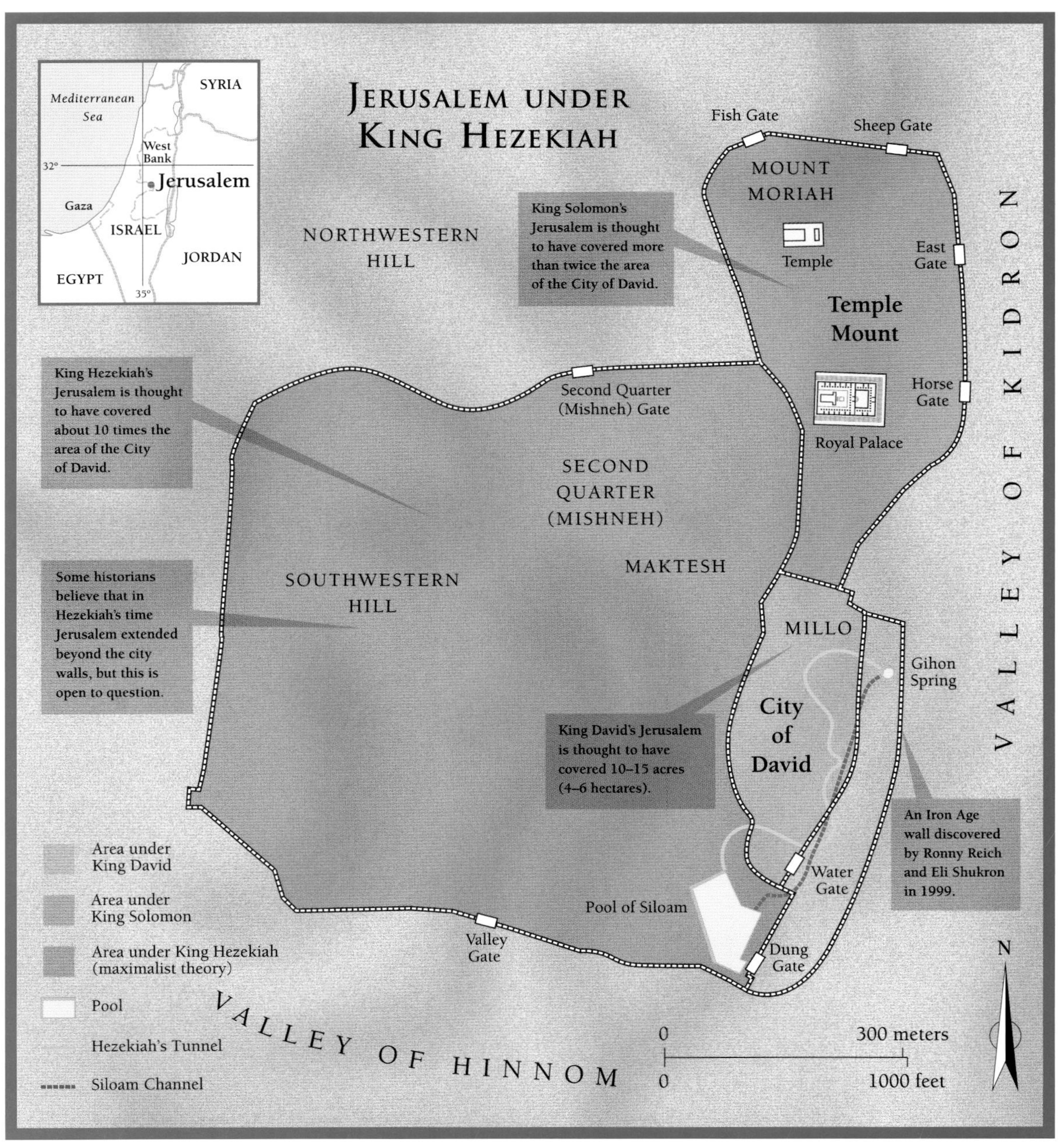

ABOVE: *JOSIAH READS AND REPENTS*, IN ROYAUMONT'S *HISTOIRE DE L'ANCIEN ET NOUVEAU TESTAMENT* (1724). JOSIAH REGARDS THE BOOK OF THE LAW SO HIGHLY HE ARRANGES PUBLIC READINGS SO ALL MAY HEAR ITS WORDS.

KING JOSIAH OF JUDAH, THE HERO OF 1–2 KINGS

The reign of King Josiah can be dated to *c.* 640–609 B.C.E. This king, grandson of the infamous King Manasseh, came to the throne at the age of eight! His father Amon had been assassinated after reigning for only two years (see 2 Kings 21:23–24). But his killers were themselves killed, probably by the conservative aristocracy who more than once had intervened to preserve the Davidic dynasty.

In curious correspondence with his great-grandfather Hezekiah, the writers of 2 Kings unequivocally proclaim King Josiah the best king ever: "Before him there was no king like him, who turned to the Lord with all his heart, with all his soul, and with all his might, according to all the law of Moses; nor did any like him arise after him" (2 Kings 23:25). The reasons for such high praise for King Josiah are not hard to find. In his eighteenth year, he commissioned the high priest Hilkiah to effect much-needed repairs to the Temple. During these repairs, one of the most important discoveries in biblical history was made—the "book of the law" (2 Kings 22:8). Most scholars connect this scroll with most or all of the present-day book of Deuteronomy. Consulting the prophetess Huldah, Josiah learns that Jerusalem's dire fate is sealed, but since "you have torn your clothes and wept before me" (2 Kings 22:19), the Lord would grant King Josiah a peaceful burial and postpone the city's eventual demise.

Furious destruction of idolatrous altars, deposing of idolatrous priests, and desecration of idolatrous tombs ensued, in light of the famous prediction the unnamed Judean prophet gave centuries ago back in the days of Jeroboam I of Israel (see 1 Kings 13:1–2). The most famous Passover celebration "since the days of the judges who judged Israel" also took place (2 Kings 23:21–23).

Josiah himself dies at a relatively young age at the hands of Pharaoh Neco, a tragic and unnecessary death that was publicly lamented at the time by the prophet Jeremiah (see 2 Chronicles 35:20–25). After this, things quickly go downhill for the land of Judah.

THE LAST KINGS OF JUDAH, AND THE EXILE

All in all, Josiah will have three of his sons on the throne of David, but two of them under difficult circumstances. First, the people put Jehoahaz on the throne, but he only lasted three months, being deposed by the same Pharaoh Neco who had killed his father (2 Kings 23:30–34). Judah must then pay an indemnity to the pharaoh, who also installed Jehoahaz's brother Jehoiakim on the throne.

Jehoiakim's 11-year reign was uniformly characterized by extreme wickedness, even to his Egyptian and Babylonian overlords (thus the unanimous testimony of the writers of Kings, Chronicles, and Jeremiah). But in fairness to him, the times were tough, with Egypt itself bowing down to the new Chaldean (Neo–Babylonian) Empire, as well as the Lord himself sending against Jehoiakim "bands of the Chaldeans, bands of the Arameans, bands of the Moabites, and bands of the Ammonites" (2 Kings 24:2; with the next verse again blaming "the sins of Manasseh" for this predicament).

By 598 B.C.E. Jehoiakim is dead (possibly assassinated), and his son Jehoiachin ascends the throne, but only for three months (see 2 Kings 24:6–9). Nebuchadnezzar plunders

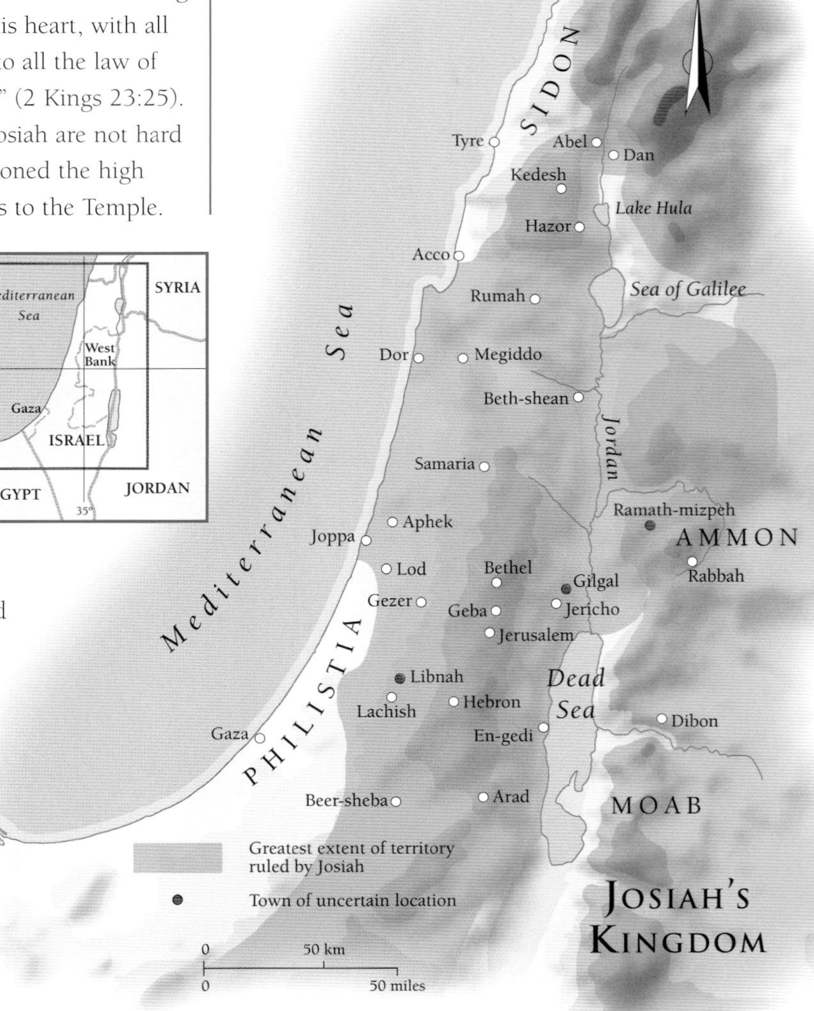

Jerusalem that year, carrying off many of the treasures of the Temple and palace, and installing what would prove to be Judah's last king, Zedekiah, a third son of Josiah. He too rebels against his overlord, and Nebuchadnezzar shows up once again in Jerusalem, besieging it for almost two years until the fall of the city in 586 B.C.E.

The last we read of Zedekiah is his flight toward the plains of Jericho, being captured and taken to Riblah in the land of Hamath (central Syria), and being forced to witness the execution of his children just before his own eyes were put out for covenant violation (2 Kings 25:1–7).

Thus ends the Davidic hope, seemingly, with the Temple ransacked and destroyed and the king exiled to Babylon. But the end of the books of Kings (as well as the book of Jeremiah) reminds us that in the thirty-seventh year of exile of King Jehoiachin (*c.* 561 B.C.E.), in the inaugural year of King Evil-Merodach of Babylon, Jehoiachin is released from prison and given a seat of honor at the king's table. Although the Jeremiah text (52:34) reminds us that Jehoiachin died in exile in Babylon, we are also reminded that in a very real sense the Davidic hope still lives. The "lamp" of David is still not snuffed out.

And for Christians, whose Messiah Jesus is called "the son of David," that hope springs eternal.

ABOVE: *HEBREWS OR ISRAELITES IN CHAINS BEFORE NEBUCHADNEZZAR, FROM BEATAE ELISABETH PSALTER,* THIRTEENTH CENTURY. ALL THE TREASURES OF JERUSALEM AND MANY OF THE PEOPLE WERE CARRIED AWAY.

LEFT: *THE SLAUGHTER OF THE SONS OF ZEDEKIAH* BY GUSTAVE DORE (1832–1883). ZEDEKIAH FAILS TO ESCAPE THE WRATH OF NEBUCHADNEZZAR, WHICH IS ALSO VISITED UPON HIS CHILDREN.

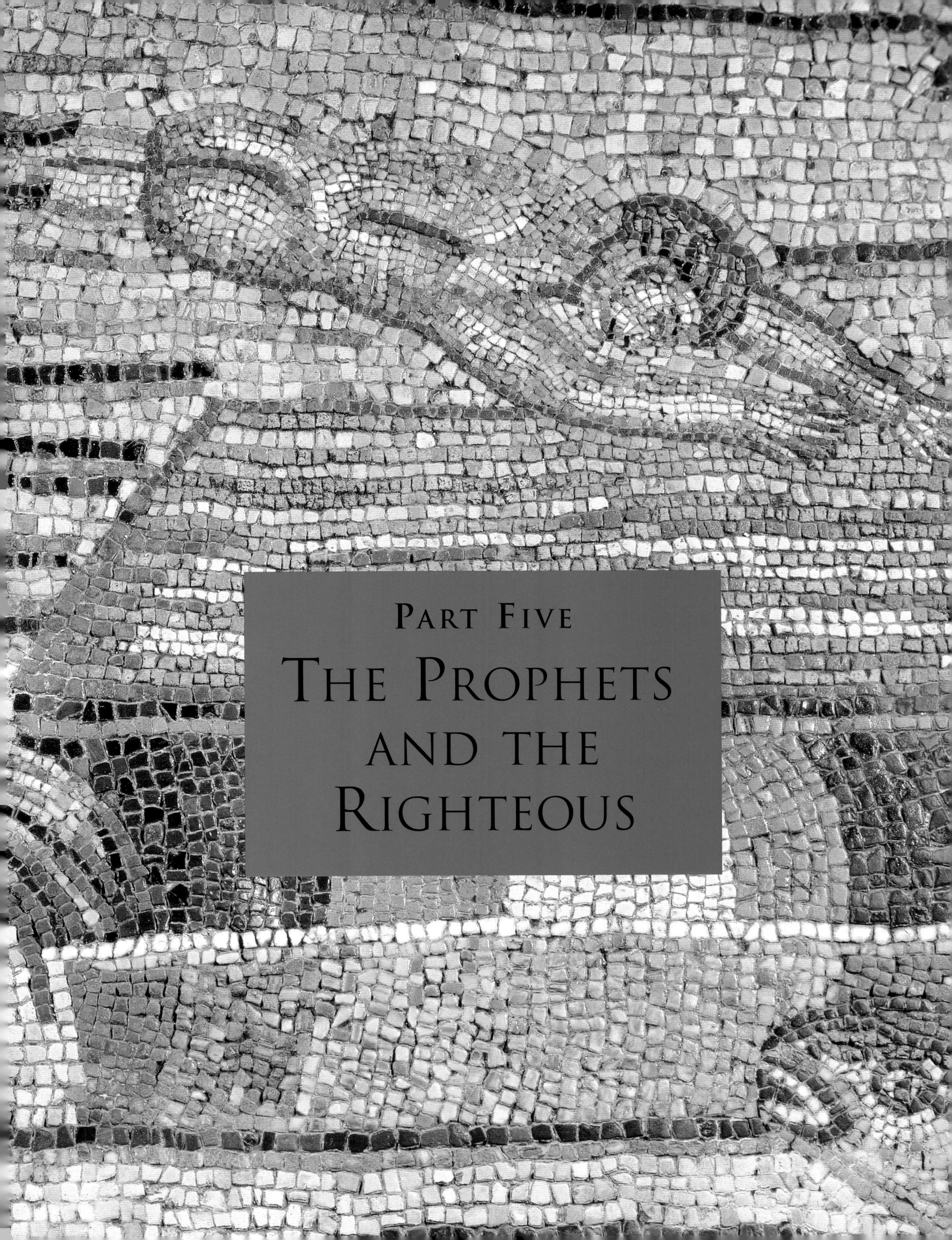

Part Five

The Prophets and the Righteous

Preserving the Faith

BELIEVE IN THE LORD YOUR GOD AND YOU WILL BE ESTABLISHED; BELIEVE HIS PROPHETS 2 CHRONICLES 20:20

After the death of King David, the rulers and the people of Israel and Judah repeatedly forsook the Lord God of Israel, worshipping false gods and abandoning themselves to greed and depravity. So God appointed prophets—visionaries whose vocation was to denounce the wickedness of the Israelites and to warn them of the punishment that God would surely exact. Evil kings were reproved by enlightened men who sought to guide the people back into the Way of the Lord.

JOB AND THE PROBLEM OF EVIL

The book of Job is a unique document, and is possibly the first written statement of the problem of evil: the reconciliation of human suffering with the concept of a just and merciful God. Job was not a prophet; he was a righteous man and a prosperous landowner who became a test case in a strange bargain between God and Satan. God challenged Satan to undermine Job's faith, whereupon Satan took away Job's wealth, killed his family and servants, and afflicted him with agonizing boils. But Job remained steadfast in his faith, and God restored him to health and prosperity.

Scholars have dated the writing of the book of Job to between the tenth and the first centuries B.C.E., but the date scarcely matters. Job's patient endurance of his tribulations and his unshakable faith have become a parable for the Christian paradox: that a good and all-powerful God is capable of inflicting intolerable pain on his subjects.

THE FOUR AND THE TWELVE

When the Greeks edited the Bible, they distinguished between four great prophets and twelve minor prophets. The Four—*hoi tessares*—were Isaiah, Jeremiah, Ezekiel, and Daniel. The Twelve—*to dodekapropheton*—arranged essentially in the Old Testament in a chronological fashion from the Book of Hosea to the Book of Malachi, were called minor because their books were relatively short.

The writings of the prophets cover the period from Isaiah, Hosea, and Amos in the eighth century B.C.E. to Daniel and Malachi in the sixth century B.C.E. under the Babylonian kings Nebuchadnezzar and Belshazzar. God called Isaiah to his prophetic role in 740 B.C.E. In his earthly capacity Isaiah advised the kings of Judah about politics and economics, but his spiritual importance was his messianic vision: "Look, the young woman is with child and shall bear a son, and shall name him Immanuel" (Isaiah 7:14).

RIGHT: AN ELEVENTH-CENTURY FRENCH MANUSCRIPT INCLUDES THIS REPRESENTATION OF JOB. THOUGH AFFLICTED IN MANY WAYS, HE NEVER CEASES TO GIVE PRAISE TO GOD.

SETTING ELIJAH TO MUSIC

Elijah (ninth century B.C.E.) was the earliest and greatest of the Hebrew prophets. He left no writings, but his acts and teachings are recorded in a number of the historical and prophetic books and in the Psalms.

The Old Testament accounts of Elijah's life were the inspiration for Felix Mendelssohn's dramatic oratorio, *Elijah*, which premiered in August 1846 and which contains Mendelssohn's most mature vocal and orchestral inspirations. The libretto, which draws on virtually all the Old Testament sources, is a model of dramatic construction and conciseness. Jewish by ancestry, Mendelssohn clearly responded at a deep emotional level to the prophet's story.

Jeremiah, who was born in about 650 B.C.E., was at once the most human and the most lyrical of all the prophets. He predicted the destruction of Jerusalem and its temple; *The Lamentations of Jeremiah* is an extended poem of grief for the fall of Judah's capital city.

Ezekiel, the third of the great prophets, was imprisoned by Nebuchadnezzar in 597 B.C.E., and probably wrote his prophetic book while he was being held captive in Babylon. The language of the book of Ezekiel is vigorous and muscular; his imagery of the valley of dry bones (Ezekiel 37) is both chilling and powerful.

Daniel was a relative late-comer in the prophetic writings. His book records the persecution of the Jews in the sixth century B.C.E. by the Babylonians, the Medes, and the Persians, but it was probably written by a later scribe. Daniel is perhaps best known for his dramatic preservation from death in the lions' den, but his contribution to prophetic literature was his prevision of the resurrection of the dead: "Many of those who sleep in the dust of the earth shall awake, some to everlasting life, and some to shame and everlasting contempt" (Daniel 12:2).

Most of Israel's prophets died in horrible ways that prefigured the deaths of Christ's messenger, John the Baptist, who was beheaded by Herod Antipas; of Christ himself by crucifixion; and of the followers of Christ who met their deaths by martyrdom, from stoning to beheading. The New Testament Epistle to the Hebrews reports that the prophets were bound, mocked, scourged, tortured, stoned, and even sawn apart (Hebrews 11:36–37). But it was the prophets who managed to sustain the faith of Israel to this day.

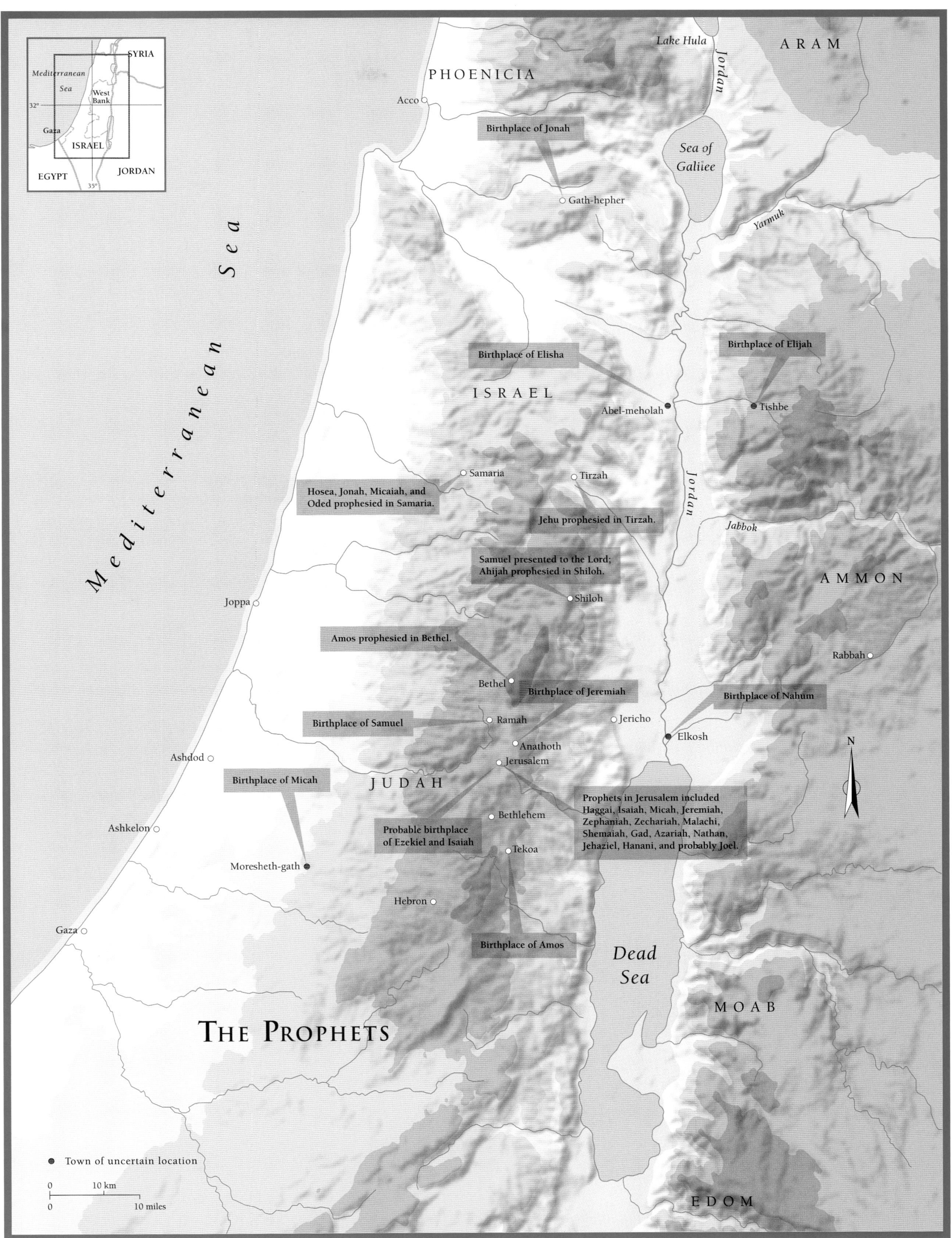

THE PROPHETS
Mediterranean Sea
PHOENICIA
ARAM
ISRAEL
JUDAH
AMMON
MOAB
EDOM
Lake Hula
Jordan
Sea of Galilee
Yarmuk
Jabbok
Dead Sea
Acco
Gath-hepher
Abel-meholah
Tishbe
Samaria
Tirzah
Shiloh
Joppa
Bethel
Ramah
Jericho
Elkosh
Anathoth
Jerusalem
Ashdod
Ashkelon
Bethlehem
Tekoa
Moresheth-gath
Hebron
Gaza
Rabbah
Birthplace of Jonah
Birthplace of Elisha
Birthplace of Elijah
Hosea, Jonah, Micaiah, and Oded prophesied in Samaria.
Jehu prophesied in Tirzah.
Samuel presented to the Lord; Ahijah prophesied in Shiloh.
Amos prophesied in Bethel.
Birthplace of Jeremiah
Birthplace of Nahum
Birthplace of Samuel
Birthplace of Micah
Prophets in Jerusalem included Haggai, Isaiah, Micah, Jeremiah, Zephaniah, Zechariah, Malachi, Shemaiah, Gad, Azariah, Nathan, Jehaziel, Hanani, and probably Joel.
Probable birthplace of Ezekiel and Isaiah
Birthplace of Amos
Town of uncertain location
0
10 km
0
10 miles
N
SYRIA
Mediterranean Sea
West Bank
Gaza
ISRAEL
EGYPT
JORDAN
32°
35°

JOB

THEN SATAN ANSWERED THE LORD, "DOES JOB FEAR GOD FOR NOTHING?" JOB 1:9

The Book of Job tells the story of a righteous man. The first two adjectives used to describe the character of Job are "blameless" and "upright." Next we are told that he "feared God and turned away from evil," as a wise man should. The Book of Job is part of the wisdom literature of the Old Testament, a literature that praises righteousness over wickedness, diligence over laziness, wisdom over folly. Job is a kind of test case of the wisdom worldview.

A BLAMELESS AND UPRIGHT MAN

There is no doubt about Job's integrity and from that has flowed life's blessings. We are told in the prolog of his seven sons and three daughters and then of his great wealth, measured (in patriarchal times in which the scene is set) in numbers of sheep, camels, oxen, and donkeys, all of which need servants to tend them.

Job is described here as "greatest of all the people of the east." This may be a hint as to his location, combined with the reference in Job 1:1 to the land of Uz. The likely position of Uz is to the southeast of Israel, in Edom. This is supported by possible Edomite connections in the names and locations of Job's three friends who appear later in the book. Traditionally, the east was where wisdom was said to reside.

We are then told of the feasting of Job's children—possibly referring to the celebration of birthdays or of other important ceremonial days. This sets the scene for the later calamity which happens during one such feast, but it also serves to show us more about Job's piety. Job used to sacrifice on behalf of his children, in case any of them had sinned. This is to stress the full nature of his righteousness—it is not just for himself that he is concerned, but for others too.

BELOW: JOB'S CLOAK IS KISSED DURING HIS TIME OF PROSPERITY IN THIS ARTWORK BY W. J. MORGAN, PUBLISHED IN *THE FAMILY BIBLE* C. C.E. 1890.

SATAN'S CHALLENGE

The scene now changes from earth to heaven, and we are shown a glimpse of the heavenly council held by the Lord. Among the council members, although not necessarily one of their number, is "Satan." God remarks on how proud he is of Job and describes him as a model of wisdom and piety. Satan questions Job's motivation for being such a God-fearing man. The key phrase is "for nothing." Does Job fear God for nothing? Or does he fear God because he hopes to gain from it? This question raises the theological issue of disinterested righteousness. Why believe in God? Is it for the hope of blessings, or is faith the sole motivation? Satan accuses God of putting a fence around Job and his property and of enumerating his blessings. God has offered such protection to Job that it is no wonder Job fears God! What would happen if all that protection was taken away? What if his children and possessions were all lost? Would Job then maintain his fear of God? This is the challenge that Satan issues to God—take the fence away and see what happens.

So, the scene is set. Satan wagers to God that Job will curse God if all he has is taken away. God is sufficiently trusting of Job's integrity that he is prepared to let Job become the test case. He therefore allows Satan to take away all that Job has, but he makes one proviso and that is not to touch his person. So the heavenly scene ends with the finishing of the interview between God and Satan and we infer that the worst is now going to happen.

SATAN

The Satan figure here in Job is probably one of the earliest depictions of the character that went on to become a personification of evil in later thought. Here he is simply one who challenges God ("the Satan" means "the accuser") but in later thought he becomes God's adversary, even God's antithesis, and the embodiment of evil.

ABOVE: THIS FOURTEENTH-CENTURY FRESCO BY BARTOLO DI FREDI SHOWS THE BRUTAL MASSACRE OF THE SERVANTS AND HERDSMEN OF JOB WHILE GOD AND THE INSTIGATOR, SATAN, LOOK ON.

SCENES OF CATASTROPHE

We are now returned to the earthly scene, and to the feasting of the children of Job. This time they are feasting in the house of Job's eldest brother. Job is not there—he first hears of what happens via four messengers who escape each situation to give him messages of calamity.

First of all, calamity strikes the oxen and donkeys and those tending them. They are attacked by a group of Sabeans (possibly a nomadic tribe from the south), the herds are carried off, and the servants killed. Just as this messenger is relaying his message, another comes, that a natural disaster has struck. This time it is lightning, known as the fire of God, which has consumed the sheep and those tending them. Then the third message comes that more human enemies, this time the Chaldeans (a tribe from the north), came and raided the camels (a source of real wealth in such a culture) and took them away, killing the servants tending them. Finally, the climax comes with the fourth messenger who brings the devastating message that another natural disaster—a great wind from across the desert (probably the sirocco)—caused the house of the eldest brother to fall upon all of Job's children so that all are dead.

RIGHT: IN THIS ILLUSTRATION BY WILLIAM BLAKE, SATAN SMITES JOB WITH BOILS. BLAKE'S BELIEF IN SPIRITUAL AWARENESS DRAWS PARALLELS WITH JOB'S SPIRITUAL AWAKENING.

BELOW: MESSAGES OF BAD TIDINGS ARE DELIVERED ONE AFTER THE OTHER IN THIS FOURTEENTH-CENTURY DEPICTION BY JACOPO DEL CASENTINO. THOUGH VISIBLY OVERWHELMED BY THE NEWS, JOB REFUSES TO CURSE GOD.

Not surprisingly, Job is devastated and he performs a number of mourning rites. He tears his robe, shaves his head, and falls prostrate on the ground. His reaction, in line with the earlier description of his character, is a remarkably accepting one. He realizes that we are born with nothing and we die with nothing. He knows that life does not just consist of blessings from God, despite appearances to the contrary in his own life. He says that the Lord gives his blessings and takes them away, as he wills. It is up to the Lord—human beings cannot "expect" anything from God; all they can do is bless him. We are told at the end of this scene that Job never charged God with wrongdoing; he never blamed God for this misfortune that had come upon him. His reaction to such tragic events is exemplary—he reacts as a righteous man should in accepting his fate, whether good or bad, and continuing to bless God.

IN BONE AND FLESH

The heavenly council is again the center of attention. The scene is again set with God asking Satan where he has come from and Satan replying that he has been walking the earth. Then the exemplary Job comes into the discussion once again. God reveals that Job has maintained his integrity in the face of the unwarranted punishments that Satan persuaded God to inflict upon his righteous servant. Satan's reply now is to challenge God to allow him to afflict Job in the bone and flesh, that is to make him ill with disease. Then, Satan argues, Job will curse God. Satan's theory is that people will do anything to save their own lives—if Job feels that God has abandoned him to death then he will give him up. God allows Satan to afflict Job but with the proviso that Job's life be spared.

Job, of course, does not know that he is the victim of a test or wager. Only the reader is being given an insight into what is going on in heaven, the outcome of which is inevitable. Satan smites Job with sores from head to foot, possibly open sores that never heal, a skin disease that may resemble leprosy. The sores are clearly itchy because Job takes a potsherd with which to scrape away at them.

We are also told that he is sitting among the ashes. This may be because he is still in mourning for the deaths of his children, although it may indicate a heap of burnt ashes (usually dung) just outside the town walls. These heaps would be tall and would be home to outcasts whose uncleanness would not allow them to be a part of town life. However, we don't have any precise location for Job in a town or city, only having been told of the land in which he resided, so we cannot be certain about his location.

ABOVE: THIS ROMANESQUE RELIEF FROM C.E. 1140–1150 SHOWS JOB BEING COUNSELED BY HIS FRIENDS. ULTIMATELY, GOD WILL REWARD JOB AND REBUKE HIS FRIENDS.

JOB'S WIFE HAS HER SAY

At this point we are introduced to Job's wife. Of course, the calamity of losing their children happened to her too. Her character, however, is not developed greatly in the story. She only appears here to advise Job to give up on his integrity and curse God. She is perhaps angry and upset in her bereavement and cannot understand Job's pious attitude toward the misfortune heaped suddenly upon him. She is ready to blame God and to give up on him, and Job rebukes her for it, calling her foolish. He reiterates his belief that one has to accept good and bad alike from God. It is God's will, not ours. Again, we are told that Job did not sin, an important point in maintaining his status as a righteous man.

THREE FRIENDS ENTER INTO DEBATE WITH JOB

Three friends now come from their homes to comfort Job. They are described as being from Teman, Shuhar, and Naaman respectively, all arguably areas in or around Edom. Their names—Eliphaz, Bildad, and Zophar—can be related to Edomite genealogies. They join forces and then go to console Job. We are told that when they saw Job from a distance they did not recognize him—maybe they were too far away, or perhaps the idea is that Job is so changed that they did not realize it was him. On seeing him, they too adopt mourning rituals—they weep, and rend their clothes in sympathy with Job. They sit in comforting silence with Job for seven days and nights out of recognition of the gravity of his suffering. But then a dialog ensues in which the friends speak in turn and are far from silent! This is a curious reversal of their previous forbearance. Each friend speaks to Job in three rounds of speeches which take up the body of the book (Zophar's third speech disappears in the third cycle and scholars have attempted to reconstruct it from some of Job's own words). Job replies to each in turn.

Here, then, the story itself is put on hold as a theological debate ensues on the principle of retribution. This is the belief, from the wisdom tradition, that good people are rewarded by God while the wicked are punished. This principle is the one that Job had also assumed until the calamities struck him. So the friends consistently maintain that the only reason Job is now being treated as a wicked person, with all his sufferings, is because of sins he must have committed. We know (from the heavenly scene), and Job knows because he really is blameless and upright, that this is not the case as he has not sinned. We know that he is the victim of a test, but neither Job nor the friends know this. The friends are individuals, but all three argue the same point of Job's guilt using varying illustrations. Eliphaz claims divine visions in the night for his insight that no one can be innocent before God (Job 4:12–21); Bildad asks if God perverts justice, the answer clearly being no, and he chides Job to seek God and learn from the wisdom of old (Job 8:1–10); and Zophar suggests that Job is actually suffering less than his guilt probably deserves and urges him to repentance (Job 11:1–20). There is a certain amount of banter between the friends and Job—they accuse him of not listening and refusing to see the truth, and Job sees the friends as persecuting him. Their basic argument is

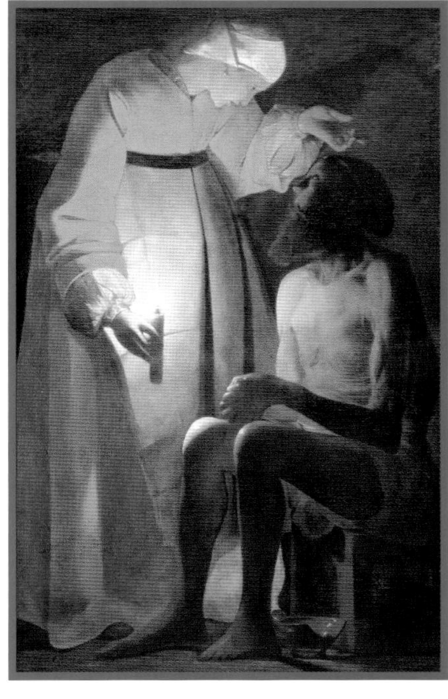

BELOW: IN THIS SEVENTEENTH-CENTURY PAINTING BY GEORGES DE LA TOUR, JOB'S WIFE—WHO SUFFERS ALMOST AS MUCH AS JOB—URGES HIM TO CURSE GOD.

ABOVE: SATAN HOVERS MENACINGLY IN THIS ILLUSTRATION FROM *HISTOIRE DE L'ANCIEN ET NOUVEAU TESTAMENT* (C.E. 1724), WHICH DEPICTS JOB'S INCREASING TORMENT AS HE CURSES THE DAY OF HIS BIRTH.

that God operates according to the principle of retribution and cannot do otherwise. Job, therefore, must have sinned otherwise he wouldn't be suffering, so if Job repents of his sin he will be forgiven by God.

JOB QUESTIONS GOD'S JUSTICE

In the dialog with the friends we are introduced to a rather less accepting Job who questions God on a more profound level than his initial response indicated. Here we find a more realistic description of a person suffering immense torment. A great deal of the dialog is simply lament on Job's part. In chapter 3, for example, Job wishes that he had never been born—then he wouldn't have had to experience such suffering. He tries to wish away the day of his birth and the night of his conception, such is his torment. He would like to wipe the day of his birth from the calendar, so that all memory of him is lost. This contrasts strikingly with his children's celebration of their birthdays.

Babylonian Literature

We find parallels to the laments of Job in Babylonian literature, notably *I Will Praise the Lord of Wisdom* and *The Babylonian Theodicy*, which treat the problem of just retribution. In the first, Ludlul asks why his god Marduk, depicted in this sixth-century B.C.E. bronze (right), allows his servant to suffer when he didn't deserve it. As in Job, restoration eventually follows. *The Babylonian Theodicy* contains an orthodox friend who maintains the traditional view that piety leads to prosperity, against the view of the sufferer, in a similar manner to Job's friends.

Job calls upon evil powers that can evoke the chaos monster, overcome at creation by God. He longs for darkness rather than light in a reversal of creation itself. Job then wishes he had died at birth or been an untimely birth (a miscarriage or abortion) which would not have survived. He is now a man suffering great torment, with old certainties removed. He sees God's protective hedge, as described by Satan earlier, as oppressive. His physical torment means that sighing and groaning are all he can do, and he can't even rest because of the pain. At times Job longs for death as a release, but then he realizes that in death he cannot continue the debate with God and he wants more than anything for his innocence to be vindicated by God himself. He calls for a redeemer or mediator who will judge him independently of God, who appears to have become his prosecutor.

There are moments of optimism, such as a vision of vindication by God (Job 19:23–9) with God on his side, and also moments of despair (Job 14:1–17) in which he reflects on life and its brevity, and on God's oppressive presence. Through this process of lament, despair, and complaint, Job gradually comes to a deeper understanding of his relationship with God. The dialog ends with a final lament (Job 29–31) in which Job, in legal mode, presents his case to God. It is now up to God to reply.

GOD'S APPEARANCE IN A WHIRLWIND

Before we come to God's reply we discover a fourth friend. This is Elihu, a young man who had not liked to speak out before in the face of older wise men, but who now feels it is his moment to speak with Job. Elihu reiterates the friends' repeated point that Job must have sinned and anticipates some of what God goes on to say in his speeches about his greatness and otherness.

Finally, God does appear in a whirlwind, ostensibly to answer Job, although his words do not answer Job's questions directly. Rather, a series of rhetorical questions asking where Job was at creation and describing God's actions in creation and nature have the effect of putting Job in his place. God's power and greatness are stressed here. He is involved in every detail of the creative process; he maintains order against the monsters of chaos that threaten to overcome him; he creates wild animals, each species according to its own type and behavioral patterns. Job's situation seems petty by comparison. Yet, the very fact that God appears to Job is in itself an answer of sorts. It shows that God is not absent for Job or for humanity. The encounter with God is perhaps what influences Job to humble himself before the grandeur of the Almighty.

The relationship between God and man is the main theological issue here—how can human beings relate to God in the face of suffering? Does God care or notice? Does God act according to principles of justice that human beings can know? Or are we in danger of inventing too small a sphere of activity for God? Rather, we need to understand his power and otherness, and accept that he may have his own reasons for acting in ways which we do not understand.

LEFT: THIS ENGRAVING BY WILLIAM BLAKE SHOWS JOB WITH HIS THREE DAUGHTERS. THEIR NAMES WERE SYMBOLIC OF THEIR CHARMS: JEMIMAH, DOVE; KEZIAH, PRECIOUS PERFUME; AND KEREN-HAPPUCH, COSMETIC JAR.

BELOW: THIS NINETEENTH-CENTURY OIL PAINTING BY LEON JOSEPH FLORENTIN BONNAT DEPICTS JOB AT HIS LOWEST POINT OF TORMENT AND UTTER DESPAIR.

RIGHTEOUSNESS REWARDED

The book ends with an epilog that appears to overturn much of the previous debate about whether the righteous and wicked get justice—in the epilog it seems that they do, whereas in the dialog it was far from certain. We are told at the beginning of the epilog that Job was right while the friends were not. Does this refer to Job's protest? Is it better to argue with God than to simply repeat traditional formulas as the friends appeared to do? Or is it Job's initial, more pious reaction in the prolog that is being praised here? Job is then asked by God to offer a sacrifice on behalf of the friends—a sign of forgiveness and healing. He is then restored with a new set of children, camels, sheep, and so on—an exact doubling of numbers of animals as he had before. One might wonder how satisfactory a new set of children might be—not so easily replaced as working animals, perhaps? Job's wife does not reappear at this point, nor, interestingly, does Satan. Rather, the restoration of Job's fortunes is left entirely to God. The message here is that righteousness ultimately has its reward. Job lives to a ripe old age, seeing fresh generations of children descended from his line. His three daughters are known for their beauty and are given an inheritance alongside their brothers (an unusual detail and an uncommon practice at the time). Job has survived his trials, learned from his experience, and been doubly blessed by God.

ISAIAH

FOR ALL THIS HIS ANGER HAS NOT TURNED AWAY, AND HIS HAND IS STRETCHED OUT STILL ISAIAH 5:25

God called Isaiah to be a prophet to Judah during a period of great political and spiritual upheaval. He served as a prophet during the reigns of the Judean kings Uzziah (769–740 B.C.E.), Jotham (740–735 B.C.E.), Ahaz (735–716 B.C.E.), and Hezekiah (716–687 B.C.E.). Most of Isaiah's oracles addressed three critical geo-political situations facing Judah: the Syro-Ephraimite War (735–732 B.C.E.); anti-Assyrian agitation against Sargon II (*c.* 714–711 B.C.E.); and Hezekiah's participation in a revolt against Sennacherib (*c.* 705–701 B.C.E.). Judah was sorely tempted during these crises to look to other nations for assistance instead of looking to God. Isaiah's message focused on trusting in God, the great, holy king of heaven and earth who rules over all the nations—a king who demands absolute allegiance from his people. The prophet's name, Isaiah, meaning "the Lord is salvation," was a very appropriate name given this primary message: that Judah should trust in the Lord for salvation and not in political intrigues with other nations.

Isaiah's call narrative, found in Isaiah 6:1–13, justified his unpopular message, showing that his proclamation of doom came from God, not from his own devising. At the beginning of his call, Isaiah saw the Lord sitting on a throne in the Holy of Holies in the Jerusalem Temple. As Isaiah looked on, the seraphs sang, "Holy, holy, holy is the Lord of hosts" (Isaiah 6:3), stressing God's holiness, his absolute separateness from ordinary humans. This holiness means that God's "thoughts are not your thoughts, nor are your ways [God's] ways" (Isaiah 55:8). After seeing this awe-inspiring sight, Isaiah

BELOW: IN ANTONIO BALESTRA'S EIGHTEENTH-CENTURY PORTRAIT, THE PROPHET ISAIAH WRITES HEBREW WHILE A SERAPH PURIFIES HIS UNCLEAN LIPS.

confessed that he was a man of unclean lips—that is, fallen and profane (just like all people). In order for Isaiah to proclaim the holy words of God, he had to be purified of his unclean state. Isaiah further recognized that God is the king of the whole earth (Isaiah 6:5), that God is the real king of Judah, not the descendant of David who happens to occupy the royal throne in Jerusalem. God is also the king of all the nations. What Isaiah is told to proclaim at the conclusion of his call contains a strange message. He is to tell the people to "Keep listening, but do not comprehend; keep looking, but do not understand" (Isaiah 6:9). Does God really not want the people of Judah to hear his message and return to him? No, God desires that all turn to him and live, but he also knows that the leaders of Judah will refuse to heed the words of the prophet and learn what the Lord requires of them. They will listen but they will not comprehend God's ways; they will look but they will not understand.

THE RISE OF TIGLATH-PILESER III

Isaiah witnessed Ahaz ascend to the throne of Judah at the ripe young age of twenty to face one of the most serious crises of his entire career: the Syro-Ephraimite War—a war fought against a coalition comprised of Rezin, king of Syria, and Pekah, king of Israel. This calamitous situation was precipitated by two factors: first, the rise to power of Tiglath-pileser III in Assyria (744–727 B.C.E.), who created a powerful empire that sought to impose its will on the surrounding lands; and second, the state of anarchy presiding in the northern kingdom of Israel that led to the absence of a coherent Israelite foreign policy that was capable of withstanding Syrian influences.

For about a hundred years prior to the ascendancy of Tiglath-pileser III, Judah and Israel had experienced relative peace and calm. Although Assyria previously had made incursions against Israel, it was now too concerned with both internal and external conflicts to have any resources left to try to influence Israel and Judah. At the same time, the Syrians (a thorn in the flesh for Israel in earlier days) were so busy fighting each other that they could not form a united front that could exert any influence on the lands to the south. Both Israel and Judah were therefore free to go about their economic and political business as they saw fit.

The situation changed with the rise of Tiglath-pileser III in Assyria in 744 B.C.E. For quite some time, Assyria had wanted to secure access to Egypt by controlling Syria-Palestine, but had neither the political unity nor the military resources to accomplish this. Tiglath-pileser III, however, did an outstanding job in controlling the various regions in Assyria and incorporating newly conquered lands, thereby creating internal peace. He also strengthened his military by creating a standing army. So under Tiglath-pileser III Assyria finally had the resources to attempt to secure the route to Egypt. By 738 B.C.E., he had moved militarily on the eastern Mediterranean coast, engaging in several campaigns that enabled him to annex much of northwestern Syria and portions of Phoenicia. Tiglath-pileser III then deported the princes, leaders, and much of the population of the conquered territories and incorporated the lands into his empire, thereby consolidating his power still further.

ABOVE: THIS SIXTH-CENTURY MOSAIC SHOWS THE PROPHET ISAIAH HOLDING A SCROLL OF HIS WRITINGS. ONE GREAT THEME—NAMELY, SALVATION BY FAITH—RUNS THROUGH ALL ISAIAH'S WRITINGS.

ANARCHY IN THE NORTH

At about the same time that Tiglath-pileser III came to power in Assyria, the northern kingdom of Israel had fallen into a state of near anarchy, thus finding itself unable to effectively withstand the onslaughts of foreign powers. During much of Jeroboam II's reign (783–745 B.C.E.), Israel had been militarily and economically sound. Following his death, however, monarchic instability came to Israel, bringing with it increased threats from foreign powers. Jeroboam's son, Zechariah (745 B.C.E.) ruled for a mere six months before he was assassinated by Shallum (745 B.C.E.). Shallum had been on the throne for just one month when he was killed by Menahem (745–736 B.C.E.), who sought to establish a political relationship with Assyria. Menahem gave King Pul (Tiglath-pileser III) a thousand talents of silver in order to "help him [Menahem] confirm his hold on the royal power" (2 Kings 15:19). Menahem's son, Pekahiah, ruled for a scant two years (736–735 B.C.E.) before he was assassinated by Pekah. Nothing is known of

RIGHT: THIS HISTORIATED INITIAL "V" OR "U" DATES FROM THE TWELFTH CENTURY AND DEPICTS THE PROPHECY OF ISAIAH. IN CHAPTERS 1–39 ISAIAH WRITES ABOUT HIS OWN TIME; IN LATER CHAPTERS HE PROPHESIES HUNDREDS OF YEARS INTO THE FUTURE.

Pekahiah's foreign policies, but it is reasonable to assume that he carried on the pro-Assyrian policies of his father. The assassination of Pekahiah may have been an attempt to stir up Israelite resistance to Assyria. It has also been suggested that when Pekah assassinated Pekahiah, he had the support both of an anti-Assyrian faction within Israel and of Rezin.

THE SYRO-EPHRAIMITE LEAGUE

Pekah eventually entered into a full-fledged alliance with Rezin of Syria in order to more adequately resist the advance of Tiglath-pileser III. After Rezin and Pekah joined forces, they tried to persuade Judah to join their alliance, hoping to create an even stronger fighting force. Since Israel had defeated Judah at a battle in Beth-shemesh in the early years of the eighth century B.C.E., reducing Judah to vassal status, Pekah may have assumed that Judah would naturally join the coalition. When Ahaz refused (perhaps for fear of reprisal from Tiglath-pileser III), Pekah may have interpreted this as the action of a rebellious vassal. Ahaz's son and several of his high-ranking officials were killed by Zichri, an Israelite warrior under Pekah's control (2 Chronicles 28:7). Perhaps Ahaz was the intended target of this assassination attempt, but managed to escape. Rezin and Pekah eventually attacked Jerusalem, hoping to depose Ahaz and install the son of Tabeel as king in Jerusalem (Isaiah 7:6) because he was favorably inclined to their policy of resistance to Assyria. This attack worried Ahaz so much that he even sacrificed his own son (2 Kings 16:3) in order to turn away the threat.

Ahaz appealed to Tiglath-pileser III for assistance in 734 B.C.E., believing that this was wiser than trusting in God to save Jerusalem. He sent Tiglath-pileser III a gift of gold and silver and pledged his fealty to Assyria, hoping this would be sufficient to entice the king of Assyria to come to his rescue. No doubt Ahaz did not need to make this request, since Tiglath-pileser III already had plenty of reasons of his own to attack the Syro-Ephraimite League—not the least of which was his desire to crush all resistance to his imperialistic aspirations. The king of Assyria eventually marched against Damascus, deported many of its people, and killed Rezin (2 Kings 16:9). Israel was also attacked, Pekah was assassinated, the people carried captive to Assyria, and Hoshea established as king of Israel, perhaps with the support of Tiglath-pileser III (2 Kings 15:29). The failed Syro-Ephraimite War reduced Israel to a fraction of what it had been, and Judah became for many years a vassal of Assyria.

THE COMING OF THE ASSYRIANS

In the first ten chapters of Isaiah, the prophet frequently referred to Assyria, the enemy from the north, who had been sent by God to punish both Israel and Judah. The prophet proclaimed that the Lord "will shave with a razor hired beyond the River—with the king of Assyria" (Isaiah 7:20). Assyria was the instrument that God would use to punish Israel for its role in the ill-fated alliance with Syria. In fact, Tiglath-pileser III soon did march on Israel to punish Pekah for his part in the coalition, capturing much of the land and reducing the nation basically to the hill country of Samaria. A few years later, in 722 B.C.E., Shalmaneser V of Assyria conquered what was left of Israel. Isaiah indicates in Isaiah 8:5–8 that God will use Assyria to punish Judah because they failed to trust God to deliver them from the Syro-Ephraimite League. In fact, Judah did become a vassal state to Assyria for many years after Ahaz appealed to Tiglath-pileser III for assistance. All of these actions by Assyria, according to Isaiah, were undertaken to fulfill God's plan for Israel and Judah. During Isaiah's call narrative (Isaiah 6:1–13), the prophet saw the Lord sitting on a throne in the Holy of Holies. God, whose glory filled the whole earth, was revealed

BELOW: THIS DETAIL FROM AN ASSYRIAN RELIEF DATES FROM 745–727 B.C.E. AND DEPICTS THE TROOPS OF TIGLATH-PILESER III ATTACKING A PHOENICIAN OR SYRIAN CITY. TIGLATH-PILESER III'S CONQUESTS PAVED THE WAY FOR THE ESTABLISHMENT OF THE SECOND ASSYRIAN EMPIRE.

LEFT: THE KING OF ASSYRIA MARCHED AGAINST DAMASCUS, DEFEATED AND PUT REZIN TO DEATH, AND LAID SIEGE TO THE CITY. THIS FIFTEENTH-CENTURY DEPICTION SHOWS THE PEOPLE OF DAMASCUS TAKEN CAPTIVE.

as the king of the entire earth, of all the nations. Therefore, all nations lay under God's control and they could be used to carry out God's will. They could be, and were, used to punish both Judah and Israel for their sins. The events that happened to Judah, said Isaiah, were determined by God, no matter how painful and destructive they might appear to have been: "until the Lord sends everyone far away, and vast is the emptiness in the midst of the land" (Isaiah 6:12).

ISAIAH SPEAKS TO KING AHAZ

We first encounter Isaiah's prophetic ministry when Rezin of Aram (Syria) and Pekah of Israel confront Ahaz, king of Judah, and demand that he join in their Syro-Ephraimite League, which had been formed to resist Tiglath-pileser III, king of Assyria. Ahaz wants nothing to do with this coalition, preferring instead to request assistance from Assyria (2 Kings 16:7). Isaiah brings his son, Shear-yashub ("a remnant shall return"), to meet Ahaz and tells the king not to worry about Rezin and Pekah because these kings are mere humans and will be defeated before they have a chance to wreak havoc on Jerusalem. All Ahaz needs to do in order to deal with the threat is to trust in God; he does not need to request assistance from Assyria. The choice confronting Ahaz is quite clear: trust in God and live, or go the military route, seek an alliance with Assyria, and perish.

THE SIGN OF IMMANUEL

We know that Ahaz did not believe the initial promises of the prophet because Isaiah once again had to go to Ahaz and offer him further words of assurance. When Ahaz, with false piety, refused to ask for a sign that would confirm the content of Isaiah's prophecy, Isaiah gave him one anyway. Soon, he said, a child named Immanuel ("God-with-us") would be born, whose birth would provide proof that God was going to bring relief from the Syro-Ephraimite threat. While the identity of the young woman in Isaiah 7:14 is uncertain (perhaps the wife of Ahaz, perhaps the wife of Isaiah), we do

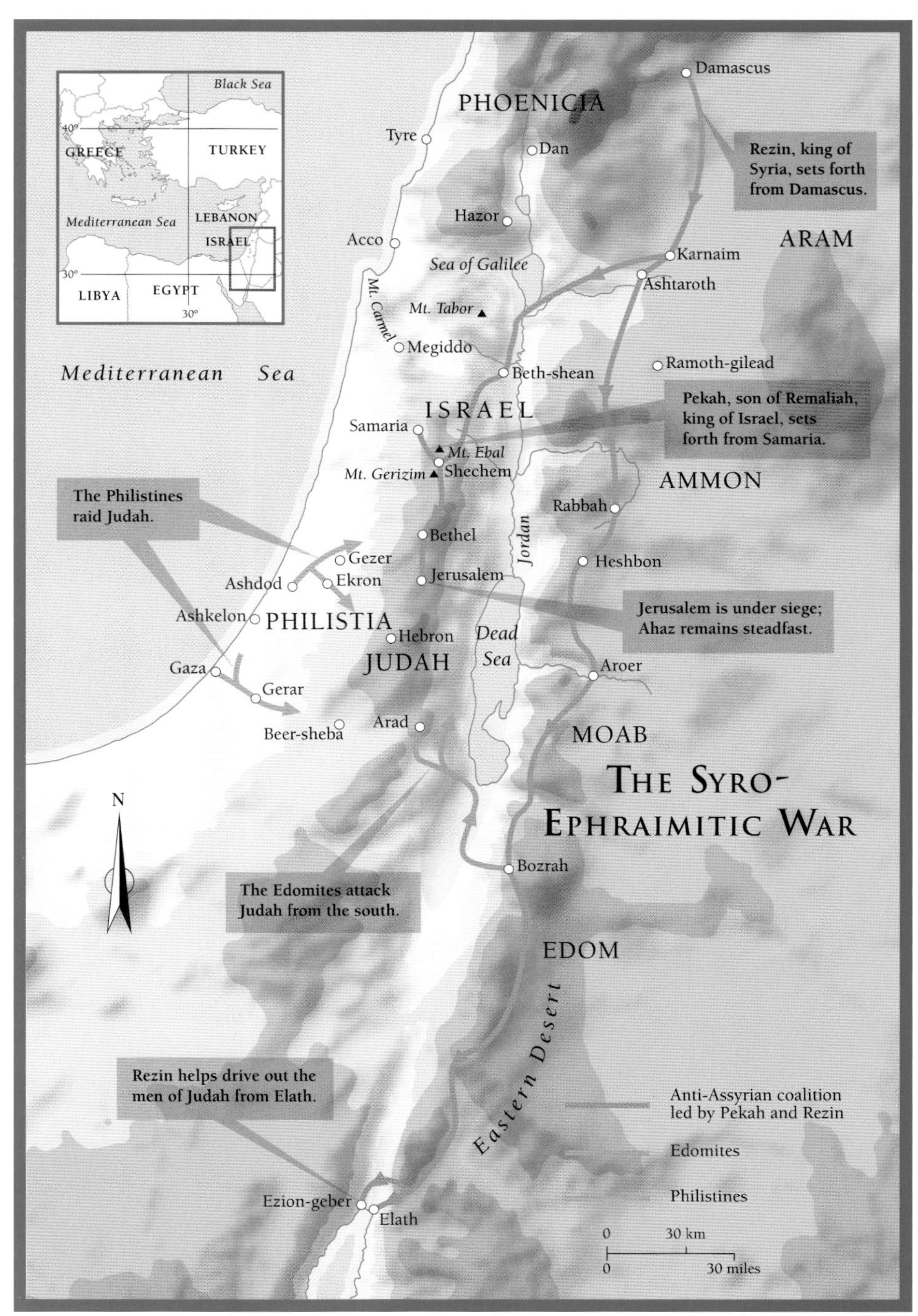

ABOVE: THIS NINETEENTH-CENTURY DEPICTION OF SAVAOPH, GOD THE FATHER, ON HIS THRONE IS BY RUSSIAN ARTIST VICTOR MIKHAILOVICH VASNETSOV.

know two things about her: she was a woman of marriageable age who had not yet had her first child; and also, the woman was someone whom Ahaz already knew and would recognize (since Isaiah said "*the* woman"). She was already, or soon would be, pregnant. The child's birth would provide assurance of God's intention to protect Ahaz and Judah from the Syrians and the Israelites, for before the Immanuel child could choose between good and evil (either before he was weaned at 2–3 years of age or before he reached the age of moral reasoning at 16–20 years), God would bring about the destruction of both Syria and Israel. There was therefore no need to appeal to Assyria for assistance, said Isaiah, since God was in control of the situation and would protect Judah.

It appears Isaiah's Immanuel prophecy did not evoke the necessary act of faith from Ahaz, since the king eventually sent tribute of silver, gold, and other treasures to Tiglath-pileser III in return for protection (2 Kings 16:7–9). Since Ahaz refused to give heed to God's word, Isaiah decided to commit his message to posterity so that future generations could see that God's promise had indeed been fulfilled. According to God's instructions, Isaiah wrote "Belonging to Maher-shalal-hash-baz" (Isaiah 8:1), meaning "the spoil speeds, the prey hastens," on a large tablet, then he went to his wife who conceived and bore a son bearing that name. This child was to serve as a sign that, in spite of Ahaz's lack of belief, God would nevertheless deliver Judah from the siege of Syria and Israel.

The Martyrdom of Isaiah

The Pseudepigrapha of the Old Testament contain an account of the Martyrdom of Isaiah, probably written in the second century B.C.E. According to this text, Isaiah predicted to King Hezekiah that the wicked Manasseh would execute the prophet. After Hezekiah died, Isaiah fled into the desert to escape. Isaiah was eventually captured by Manasseh, then cut in two by a wooden saw, as in this fifteenth-century depiction (left). The prophet felt no pain, however, since he was in communion with the Holy Spirit during his execution.

ritual worship (Isaiah 1:11–14; 29:13); they take advantage of orphans and widows (Isaiah 1:23); they turn to diviners and soothsayers, instead of to God, for information about what they should do (Isaiah 2:6); they are covetous, acquiring great amounts of property by taking advantage of the weak (Isaiah 5:8); they have been drunk from morning until night, thereby not having the presence of mind to know God's will (Isaiah 5:11–13); they mock God (Isaiah 5:18); they reverse revealed morality (Isaiah 5:20); they act arrogantly, relying not on God's instruction but on their own supposed wisdom (Isaiah 5:21); they take bribes (Isaiah 5:21); and they oppress the poor and needy (Isaiah 10:1–2). This behavior offends God's holiness and his desire for justice and righteousness in the land. In the Bible, justice is the social order established by God to bring both benefits and penalties to individuals. Righteousness occurs when one conforms to what God has revealed as the proper way of living. Justice and righteousness result, therefore, from knowing and acting upon God's instruction. This is precisely where, according to Isaiah, the people of Judah have fallen woefully short.

Knowing God involves having a loving and covenantal relationship with God, a relationship that helps one to know the difference between right and wrong, that helps one to become aware of the true meaning of God's laws. When one doesn't know God and his will, however, a person (or even a country) becomes prideful, trusting exclusively in one's own abilities and plans. Pride is precisely what Isaiah sees as the primary sin of Judah because it keeps one from trusting in God. When Ahaz refuses to "test God" (Isaiah 7:12), we see a perfect example of the destructive nature of pride. He didn't want to trust God to deliver Jerusalem from the Assyrians, choosing to rely instead upon his own plans and efforts.

BELOW: ISAIAH DELIVERS A SERIES OF STRONG SERMONS ON THE CONDITION OF SOCIETY, INCLUDING THE PROPHETS, WHO HE SAYS REEL FROM DRINK. THIS MARBLE FIGURE OF A DRUNKARD DATES FROM ROMAN TIMES.

JUDAH'S WILD GRAPES

The Song of the Vineyard, found in Isaiah 5, explains why Isaiah thought God was using Assyria to punish Israel and Judah. In this parable, God likens himself to a vineyard owner who has done everything he can to make the vineyard fruitful. In spite of all the care offered to the vineyard, it does not produce the expected large grapes, but rather small, wild, sour, rotten grapes. This is similar to God's relationship with Israel and Judah. Just as the owner had given the vineyard everything it needed to be successful, God had given Judah everything it needed to be a righteous and faithful people. But just as the vineyard owner harvested rotten grapes, what God received from Judah was likewise disappointing: God looked for justice, but found bloodshed; he looked for righteousness, but found crying (Isaiah 5:7). Just as the protection will be removed from the vineyard so that it becomes a wild pasturage, the Lord will remove his protection from Judah and hand her over to her enemies.

The "wild grapes" that Judah has produced are described clearly in Isaiah's prophecies. The people engage in empty

ISAIAH AND JUDAH'S DRUNKEN PROPHETS

Isaiah is quick to place the blame for this situation, for this pride and lack of knowledge of God, on the poor leadership Judah has received from its priests, prophets, and royal officials. Whereas they were to be the wise ones who gave sound guidance and clear interpretations of God's will, instead they had become like drunkards who could not see straight and think clearly: "the priest and the prophet reel with strong drink, they are confused with wine" (Isaiah 28:7). They rejected the instruction (Torah) of the Lord, became like sleeping men who could not see the reality of God, and thus told only lies. Therefore, all their prophecies

ABOVE: THIS UNATTRIBUTED ENGRAVING FROM SPAMIER WELTGESCHICHTE SHOWS SARGON II OF ASSYRIA. HIS MANY CONQUESTS INCLUDED BABYLONIA, ARMENIA, ISRAEL, AND PHILISTIA.

and instructions were simply human ideas that had no basis in God's will and God's ways. This is what Isaiah meant when he said that what the people call conspiracy is not what God calls conspiracy (Isaiah 8:11–15). The ways of God are quite simply not the ways of humans.

Therefore the Day of the Lord was coming to Judah, but it was not going to be a day of punishment against Judah's enemies, as most people of that time believed. Rather, it was going to be a punishment of Judah for its pride.

THE THREAT FROM ASSYRIA

Ever since Ahaz appealed to Tiglath-pileser III for assistance and paid some form of tribute during the Syro-Ephraimite crisis, Judah had been a vassal state of the Assyrian Empire. After Hezekiah succeeded his father on the Judean throne, he continued paying tribute to the Assyrian rulers. The leaders of Judah no doubt chafed under this arrangement. Sometime during 714–711 B.C.E., another rebellion, again involving various states in southwestern Syria-Palestine, broke out against Sargon II of Assyria. The time seemed ripe for a successful uprising since the Ethiopian Piankhy had, by 716/715 B.C.E., established the twenty-fifth dynasty in Egypt and had control of the entire land, thus returning Egypt to a position where it could again offer support for insurrectionist movements throughout the region. Although Hezekiah considered joining in this rebellion, Isaiah discouraged participation since he knew it would be political suicide, and since God would act against the Assyrians when God so chose. And when God did decide to act, the Assyrians would "be left to the birds of prey of the mountains and to the animals of the earth" (Isaiah 18.6). Isaiah's symbolic act recorded in Isaiah 20:1–6 depicted the fate of anyone who dared engage in this rebellion of 714–711 B.C.E. He walked around Jerusalem naked and barefoot, appearing just like all those who rebelled against Assyria would look when they were taken away into captivity. Hezekiah heeded Isaiah's message and kept Judah out of active involvement in this rebellion. Ashdod, Gath, and other members of the rebellious alliance were besieged, defeated, and looted by Sargon II. Judah, because it had stayed out of this rebellion, was spared from any major reprisals.

THE COALITION AGAINST SENNACHERIB

Another rebellion that began in 704 B.C.E. against Sennacherib, the new king of Assyria, proved more troubling for Hezekiah and Judah. King Merodach-baladan of Babylon, who was a very competent political and military leader, sought to remove Babylon from Assyrian control. He believed he could accomplish this by fomenting revolution throughout the Assyrian empire. With this in mind, he attempted to form a coalition to create disturbances against Assyria. The alliance he formed included Ashkelon and Ekron, as well as the twenty-fifth dynasty of Egypt. At this time, Merodach-baladan sent messengers to Hezekiah to try to enlist him in the coalition (Isaiah 39:1–8). In order to show that Judah had the means necessary to be an active participant in the rebellion, Hezekiah showed the messengers the wealth that he had amassed in his treasure house, armory, and storehouses. Isaiah's response to this was harsh. If Hezekiah pursued this course of action, Isaiah said, Hezekiah's dynasty would eventually be destroyed and its leadership would be taken away to Babylon as a punishment for its lack of faith in God's ability to save. Faith in God, not power politics, was the only way to achieve salvation from foreign threats. Since 2 Kings 18:7 tells us that Hezekiah "rebelled against the king of Assyria [Sennacherib] and would not serve him" it appears he joined the coalition (against Isaiah's advice) and refused to pay his tribute to Sennacherib.

RIGHT: SENNACHERIB WAS KING OF ASSYRIA FROM 704–681 B.C.E. THIS HEXAGONAL CYLINDER IS INSCRIBED WITH AN ACCOUNT OF HIS INVASION OF PALESTINE AND THE SIEGE OF JERUSALEM IN THE REIGN OF HEZEKIAH, KING OF JUDAH. IT IS DATED 686 B.C.E.

Sennacherib defeated Merodach-baladan in 703 B.C.E., then turned his attention toward Syria-Palestine. By 701 B.C.E. Sennacherib had sacked Tyre, Ashdod, Moab, and received tribute from each of them. Ashkelon, Ekron, and Judah held out for a while longer before Sennacherib's forces attacked each of them. Hezekiah took many steps to prepare Jerusalem for the eventual military response of Assyria. The Siloam tunnel was constructed at this time, guaranteeing that Jerusalem would have adequate water supplies within the city in the event of a future siege by the Assyrians (2 Kings 20:20). Hezekiah also took steps to strengthen the army of Judah (2 Chronicles 32:5–6) and established cities to store surplus foods for use in case of any emergency (2 Chronicles 32:28–29). Archaeological discoveries of *lmlk* jar handle seals from this time may indicate administrative planning for taxation—evidence perhaps of Hezekiah's preparation for the storage of food and its eventual distribution during a time of military crisis.

SENNACHERIB SURROUNDS JERUSALEM

Sennacherib marched on Judah in 701 B.C.E., capturing 46 fortified cities, as well as numerous small villages. Finally, he laid siege to Jerusalem. In his *Annals*, Sennacherib tells of how he imprisoned Hezekiah in Jerusalem like a caged bird. At some point during this siege, the Rab-shaqi (a high official of the Assyrian royal court) brought a message from Sennacherib to the leaders of Jerusalem. He mocked them for thinking that the twenty-fifth dynasty of Egypt could provide them any assistance. Then he proceeded to taunt the leaders of Jerusalem for thinking that the God of Israel could help them out of their dire straits: since no other national god had been able to save the lives of their people when Sennacherib attacked, why should the Israelite God be any different? This god was just as weak as all the other gods. The best bet for the people of Jerusalem, the Rab-shaqi announced, would be to surrender to Sennacherib and be deported. Hezekiah, understandably, was disturbed by this message and so sought an audience with Isaiah. The prophet told Hezekiah not to fear, for although God had used Assyria in the past to chastise God's people (Isaiah 37:26), Assyria's current arrogance and blasphemous behavior had led God to make new plans concerning what he should do with Assyria. Assyria's usefulness as a tool of punishment was now at an end. In order to deal with the Assyrian threat posed to Jerusalem, God would cause the king of Assyria to hear some unsettling rumor that would keep him from conquering Jerusalem (Isaiah 37:7). God's promise of deliverance came true when the city was miraculously saved from the Assyrian siege by an angel of the Lord who killed 185,000 Assyrian troops and forced Sennacherib to leave (Isaiah 37:36–37).

BELOW: THIS ILLUSTRATION BY E. WALLCOUSINS SHOWS MERODACH-BALADAN AS HE SETS FORTH IN HIS CHARIOT. HIS EVENTUAL DEFEAT AND THE FALL OF BABYLON INTO THE HANDS OF SARGON HAD BEEN PROPHESIED BY GOD.

JEREMIAH

THE HARVEST IS PAST, THE SUMMER IS ENDED, AND WE ARE NOT SAVED JEREMIAH 8:20

RIGHT: THIS MESOPOTAMIAN ALABASTER FROM MARI DATES FROM THE THIRD MILLENNIUM B.C.E. IT IS A DEPICTION OF THE ANCIENT SUMERO-BABYLONIAN DEITY, ISHTAR—GODDESS OF LOVE AND FERTILITY.

OPPOSITE: JEREMIAH LISTENS TO GOD IN THIS ILLUMINATED LETTER MINIATURE FROM THE FIFTEENTH CENTURY BY BONIFAZIO BEMBO. GOD ASSIGNS JEREMIAH USING SIX VERBS—FOUR SPEAK OF DEMOLITION AND TWO OF RENEWAL.

BELOW: THIS FIFTEENTH-CENTURY DEPICTION OF JEREMIAH IS BY AN ARTIST WHO WENT BY THE TITLE OF MASTER OF THE AIX ANNUNCIATION. HE HAS NEVER BEEN FORMALLY IDENTIFIED.

The prophet Jeremiah, whose name means "the Lord has exalted" or "the Lord has established," prophesied from approximately 626–586 B.C.E. Although we know a great deal about the prophet—that he came from Anathoth (located about 4 miles [6.4 km] from Jerusalem) and that he was of a priestly family—it can still be a daunting task to read through the book that bears his name. This is true for two main reasons. First, many of Jeremiah's oracles are not provided with specific dates, making it difficult to know the precise situation some of his prophecies addressed. Second, the book of Jeremiah does not present us with a chronological order for much of the ministry of Jeremiah. For example, the book begins around 622 B.C.E., moves forward to 605 B.C.E., then back to 609 B.C.E., forward to 594 B.C.E., forward some more to 588 B.C.E., then back again to 605 B.C.E., finally finishing up around 586 B.C.E. With a little guidance, however, the reader should be able to navigate the chronology of the book of Jeremiah, and read and profit from its powerful message.

THE CALL OF JEREMIAH

Since much of Jeremiah's ministry contained a harsh condemnation directed toward the people of Judah, the prophet felt the need to present his credentials at the beginning of his ministry (Jeremiah 1:4–10), showing that God had told him to say these things and that therefore he had the right to proclaim the words of judgment that followed. Jeremiah felt specially chosen by God for this difficult task. Even before he had been formed in the womb, from the very beginning of his existence, the Lord had known Jeremiah—that is, God had a special relationship with him and set him apart for a special task: to be a prophet to the nations. Since the Israelite people believed that the Lord ruled over the entire world, everything that other nations did was according to a divine plan. Prophets therefore had to be concerned with what was happening in these other nations so that they could try to discern God's hand in them and then interpret those events to the people of Judah. Jeremiah initially resisted God's call, however, pleading that he did not have the ability for the challenging work ahead: "I do not know how to speak, for I am only a boy" (Jeremiah 1:6). This wasn't a protest that he was not up to the task because he was just a young child, for the Hebrew word translated as "boy" actually refers to a young man in his twenties. Jeremiah's protest arose because he felt totally unqualified for the task, just as Moses had felt many years earlier (Exodus 3:11). The Lord assured him that he was indeed the person for the job by touching his mouth, assuring Jeremiah that he was going to be with him in his challenging vocation, and then putting the words Jeremiah was to speak into his mouth. It soon becomes clear why Jeremiah was so reluctant to take on the task of prophet: he was told, "to pluck up and to pull down, to destroy and to overthrow, to build and to plant" (Jeremiah 1:10)—that is, he was to correct what was wrong in Judah, to proclaim a message of punishment, so that the people could eventually be restored to wholeness. Judgment had to precede restoration.

JEREMIAH'S TWO VISIONS

To clarify the message Jeremiah was to deliver, God provided him with two visions. The first vision involved a pun—a play on words. The prophet saw an almond branch (in Hebrew, *shaqed*), which reminded him of God's "watching" (in Hebrew, *shoqed*): God was watching over the prophet's proclamation to bring it to completion—the fulfillment of Jeremiah's proclamation of doom was inevitable. In the second vision, Jeremiah saw a pot leaning from the north, indicating that a foe from the north would soon come pouring out over Judah to destroy it. This destruction would be of such catastrophic proportions that the original creation would be reversed (Jeremiah 4:23–26). One particular aspect of this devastation is depicted in Jeremiah 6:1–8, where the prophet saw the enemy besieging the capital and the surrounding cities, forcing the inhabitants to look for a place to flee. This destruction had to happen to Jerusalem: "This is the city that must be punished; there is nothing but oppression within her" (Jeremiah 6:6).

JEREMIAH PREACHES IN THE TEMPLE

Jeremiah elaborated on the reason for this punishment in his Temple Sermon, located in Jeremiah 7:1–15. The sermon, delivered in the first year of Jehoiakim's reign (608 B.C.E.), described the moral and spiritual malaise that had developed in Judah since the death of the reformer Josiah in 609 B.C.E. Everything God expected of his people, they neglected to do. The people of Judah had returned to their old, sinful ways and broken the requirements of their covenant with God: they stole, committed murder, engaged in adultery, swore falsely, and worshipped other gods (Jeremiah 7:9). They failed to observe the divine laws and regulations presented to them by Moses at Sinai (Jeremiah 11:3–4). In addition, the people oppressed the alien, the orphan, and the widow; they engaged in idolatry of the worst sort by worshipping Ishtar, the queen of heaven (Jeremiah 7:18); they even set up idols

PROPHETA
IEREMIAS
p49
VGVSTIE ORA PRO

ABOVE: JEREMIAH SUFFERED PERSECUTION FOR TEACHING GOD'S WORD. BUT EVEN AS A PRISONER HE CONTINUED TO DICTATE THE PROPHECIES, WHICH ARE SPOKEN BY AN ANGEL IN THIS LITHOGRAPH BY A. LEMOINE, DATED C.E. 1843.

BELOW: THE YOKE, DEPICTED IN THIS BRONZE FROM THE SIXTH CENTURY B.C.E., HAS LONG BEEN A SYMBOL OF SUBJECTION AND SERVITUDE. IN THE BOOK OF JEREMIAH, THE BREAKING OF A YOKE DENOTED A DISOWNING OF RIGHTFUL AUTHORITY.

in the Temple (Jeremiah 7:30) and practiced child sacrifice (Jeremiah 7:31). The people thought this kind of behavior was acceptable as long as they worshipped in the traditional way, by offering sacrifices to the Lord (Jeremiah 7:21–22). They also believed that since the Lord had chosen Zion as his dwelling place, it could never be defeated and they would be safe as long as they worshipped at the Temple. Jeremiah knew he had to convince the people that, although they were God's chosen people, there were responsibilities that went along with this—they could not simply trust in the Temple to protect them regardless of what they did. That is what Jeremiah meant when he told them that they shouldn't trust in the phrase "This is the temple of the Lord" (Jeremiah 7:4). This was, argued Jeremiah, a false belief that would lead to certain death. Instead of exhibiting sincere devotion to God, however, the people of Judah had "stiffened their necks" (Jeremiah 7:26) and stubbornly continued on in their evil ways. For this, they had to be punished. Jeremiah's task of plucking up and breaking down was the focus of his Temple Sermon—the rebuilding of the nation would come only later.

THE DROUGHT

One of the first calamities the Lord visited upon Judah was a severe drought (Jeremiah 14:1–10). The drought had come, said Jeremiah, because the people "loved to wander" (Jeremiah 14:10), either creating sanctuaries for alien gods, or else entering into alliances with foreign nations. In either case, they failed to recognize the Lord's demand upon their lives for complete commitment and faithfulness. The people lamented God's abandonment of them, arguing that because they had shown allegiance to the Lord in the past, he ought to take care of them in the present. Instead, the Lord said that he would "remember their iniquity" (Jeremiah 14:10). There was to be no deliverance for the nation: they would certainly be punished. Nevertheless, Jeremiah pleaded for Judah, arguing that the reason the people had sinned was because they had been led astray by false prophets—the false prophets were to blame, Jeremiah suggested, not the people. But God was not moved to mercy. Since God hadn't sent the prophets, the people were responsible for their own actions.

The Judean people continued to reject Jeremiah's message because they could not believe that God would punish his own chosen people. So Jeremiah performed a symbolic act to try to get the people to see the truth: he took a pottery jug, went to the valley of the son of Hinnom, then smashed the jug in the presence of some of the elders and senior priests of Judah. God was going to smash the people of Judah, said the prophet, just as the pot had been smashed. Still they did not repent and believe.

JEREMIAH'S LIFE IS THREATENED

Jeremiah's prophecies about the approaching doom aroused great hostility among the people of Judah, so that many eventually persecuted and tried to kill him. As a result of his frustration at this persecution, the prophet uttered several laments. In the first two laments, found in Jeremiah 11:18–12:6, Jeremiah complained that people from his hometown, even his own family, were so upset with him that they wanted to kill him. Jeremiah questioned the justice of God: why would God allow such plots to take place against the life of his chosen prophet? As with Job's complaints, God gave no answer other than to say that greater ordeals lay ahead for the prophet (Jeremiah 12:5). One of these ordeals occurred when Pashhur, the priest and chief officer of the Temple in Jerusalem, became angry at Jeremiah's message because it disheartened the population of Jerusalem. He struck the prophet, then imprisoned him in the stocks at the Benjamin gate. After Jeremiah was released the following day, Jeremiah renamed Pashhur "Terror-all-around" (Jeremiah 20:3). This was yet another symbolic action, setting into motion a curse upon Pashhur: the priest would go into captivity, along with his family, and die in Babylon—truly "Terror-all-around."

JEREMIAH PURCHASES A FIELD

Jeremiah also prophesied that after God's punishment, there was to be a joyous future. To make his point, when Jeremiah was in jail during the Babylonian siege of Jerusalem in 587 B.C.E., he learned that his cousin Hanamel wanted to sell Jeremiah his property in Anathoth. Jeremiah purchased the field, indicating that he expected one day in the future to benefit from it. This meant that God was going to restore the people to the land of Judah some time in the future. By purchasing the field, Jeremiah announced that God's ultimate purpose was not to destroy, but rather to sweep out the bad in Judah and then to rebuild with a new people who would live faithfully.

JEREMIAH IS BROUGHT TO TRIAL

The trouble was not over for Jeremiah. In 608 B.C.E., shortly after he delivered his upsetting sermon in the Jerusalem Temple, the priests, prophets, and other people in attendance sought to put Jeremiah to death: "You shall die!" (Jeremiah 26:8). He was, they said, a false prophet—for how could a true prophet prophesy the destruction of Jerusalem? He was a traitor—for he had "prophesied against this city" (Jeremiah 26:11). The priests and prophets reported Jeremiah's words to royal officials, hoping that they would decide to execute him. This was a very real possibility, since another prophet, Uriah, had been executed just a short time earlier by Jehoiakim (Jeremiah 26:20–23). But Jeremiah did not soften his message in the face of this threat. God had sent him, he said, so this was not some spurious message. Fortunately, Ahikam, a royal official, came to Jeremiah's assistance and saved him from impending death.

JEREMIAH AND HANANIAH

Further trials followed. Around 594 B.C.E., following the first deportation of the Jerusalem leadership to Babylon, many left in the city wanted Judah to rebel against Babylon. Jeremiah condemned the conspiracy, arguing that the only hope for Judah was submission to Babylon. To make his point, he crafted a yoke and put it on his neck, arguing that the Lord wanted Judah to submit to Babylon as an ox submits to its yoke. Since the Lord is the Lord of all history, he has dominion over everything—even Nebuchadnezzar (also spelled Nebuchadrezzar) was doing God's will. To rebel against Babylon was therefore to rebel against God. The prophet Hananiah disagreed vehemently with Jeremiah's message: within two years, he countered, the Lord would break the yoke of Babylon. To illustrate his point, Hananiah broke Jeremiah's yoke. Although Hananiah spoke like a prophet (starting his false prophecies with "Thus says the Lord"), there was one key difference: true prophets in times past prophesied war and famine, not peace. So when Hananiah prophesied peace and freedom from Babylon, the odds were high that he was a false prophet. Jeremiah later returned to Hananiah with an iron yoke that could not be broken—symbolizing the inevitability of Judah's submission to Babylon—and told Hananiah that since he had prophesied without being sent by God, he would die. Two months later Hananiah did die. Indeed, Hananiah was a false prophet.

BELOW: ACCORDING TO JEREMIAH, GOD DELIBERATELY CREATED A SEVERE DROUGHT TO PUNISH THE JUDEANS FOR THEIR MISDEEDS AND FOR THEIR UNFAITHFULNESS.

JEREMIAH AND THE RECHABITES

During Jehoiakim's reign, Jeremiah became so frustrated with the people of Jerusalem that he frequently resorted to extreme measures to illustrate their lack of commitment to God. Several members of the Rechabites, devoted worshippers of the Lord who had helped Jehu destroy the cult of Baal, were in the area. This was an opportunity not to be missed. So Jeremiah invited them into the Temple and offered them some wine to drink, knowing they would refuse because of their devotion to the teachings of their founder, Jonadab, who had taught that drinking wine was wrong. What impressed Jeremiah most was not their refusal to drink the wine, but rather their devotion and obedience to Jonadab's teachings. The faith of the Rechabites was so unlike the faith of the people of Judah that Jeremiah hoped the people would be embarrassed and in turn inspired to increased fidelity to the Lord. Would that Judah were as loyal to their God as the Rechabites were to their leader. Sadly, Jeremiah was to be disappointed in this hope.

THE SCROLL

The year 605 B.C.E. marked a turning point in Jeremiah's ministry. In that year, Jeremiah decided to commit to writing the prophecies he had given so far and have them read in the Jerusalem Temple. Since Jeremiah could no longer go to the Temple because his Temple Sermon (Jeremiah 7:1–15) had infuriated the people, he sent his scribe, Baruch, to read the scroll to the people who had gathered at the Temple on a fast day. Jeremiah must have hoped that the reading of his collected prophecies in public would alarm the people of Judah so much that they would finally take seriously the threat from Babylon and be motivated to turn from their evil ways (Jeremiah 36:3, 7). When Baruch read the scroll the first time in the Temple, the listeners were so troubled that they asked him to read it again in the palace. After that second reading, the audience became even more alarmed. Since the contents seemed treasonous, Jeremiah and Baruch were urged to go into hiding to protect themselves from the wrath of the king. The scroll was then taken to the king and read to him. As sections of the scroll were read, Jehoiakim would cut off a portion and burn it—showing his utter disregard for the words of God's messenger. How different this response was from that of his father, Josiah, when the book of the law found in the Temple was read to him. When Josiah heard the words, he took them seriously, repented, and decided to act upon them—beginning a widespread reform throughout

BELOW: LIKE ALL SERVANTS OF GOD, JEREMIAH HAD CO-WORKERS WHO SHARED HIS BURDEN. SCRIPTURE TELLS OF HIS COMPANION BARUCH, DEPICTED IN THIS FRESCO, *LOGGIA D'ANNUNCIAZIONE,* BY GIUSTO D'ALLAMAGNA DATED C.E. 1451.

Judah (2 Kings 22:8–23:25). Jehoiakim, by contrast, ignored the words he heard read from Jeremiah's scroll and insolently destroyed them, showing that he had no concern for fixing the spiritual and moral decadence in Judah. This was not to be the end of the scroll, however, for Jeremiah went on to dictate another one, this time adding more oracles condemning this hardness of heart.

LEFT: DURING THE SIEGE OF JERUSALEM, JEREMIAH'S PREDICTIONS OF DEFEAT SO ANNOY THE ROYAL OFFICERS THAT THEY THROW HIM INTO A MUDDY PIT, AS DEPICTED IN THIS EIGHTEENTH-CENTURY ENGRAVING BY F. H. VAN HOVE.

JEREMIAH AND ZEDEKIAH

Zedekiah (reigned 597–586 B.C.E.) became king of Judah after the death of Jehoiakim and the deportation of Jehoiachin to Babylon. Regrettably, at a time when Judah needed strong leadership, Zedekiah proved to be a weak, passive king who had difficulty acting decisively and was often manipulated by his royal officials. Zedekiah met secretly with Jeremiah on two or three occasions, hoping to find guidance about what he should do concerning the threat from Babylon. Jeremiah constantly counseled Zedekiah to surrender, for only by doing this could Jerusalem be saved. Babylon was going to defeat Judah and sack Jerusalem—it was inevitable, for God had willed it. At some point during Zedekiah's reign, Jeremiah set out for his hometown of Anathoth, perhaps to take possession of the land he had just purchased from his cousin. Some inhabitants of Jerusalem, however, thought Jeremiah was deserting to the enemy. So he was arrested and beaten. What enraged the officials of Jerusalem so much was that they thought Jeremiah's preaching of surrender to the Babylonians was disheartening to their soldiers. Jeremiah was thought to be so dangerous that eventually he was put in jail (Jeremiah 37:11–15). During this time of imprisonment, Zedekiah continued his secret meetings with Jeremiah, hoping to get some encouragement, but Jeremiah continued to proclaim only doom—there were to be no encouraging words. Thinking that Zedekiah wasn't doing enough to deal with Jeremiah's subversive preaching, some officials in Jerusalem managed to talk Zedekiah into releasing Jeremiah to them, at which time they threw him into a muddy cistern, intending that he should die there. It appeared that the death that Jeremiah had feared for so long was finally going to happen. But it was not to be. Ebedmelech, an Ethiopian eunuch who was serving in the palace, pulled him from the cistern and saved his life.

THE FALL OF JERUSALEM

Jerusalem was sacked for the final time by the Babylonians after Zedekiah joined with Ammon in a rebellion against Babylon. Nebuchadnezzar II, the king of Babylon, responded immediately to the threat, laying siege to Jerusalem in 587 B.C.E. The siege was briefly lifted so that Nebuchadnezzar could fight an advancing Egyptian army. Zedekiah took this as a hopeful sign, so he once again asked Jeremiah about the future of Jerusalem. Jeremiah told the king there was still no hope. The Babylonians were going to return and destroy Jerusalem. The only salvation for the city was to submit to Babylon (Jeremiah 38:17–18). But Zedekiah would not surrender, and soon the walls of the city were breached and the Babylonians came pouring through. The king and some of his soldiers tried to escape the onslaught, but were caught

BELOW: *COMMENTARY ON THE APOCALYPSE* BY THE MONK BEATUS OF LIEBANA, DATED FROM THE TENTH CENTURY. THESE FOLIOS SHOW THE TAKING OF JERUSALEM BY NEBUCHADNEZZAR II.

RIGHT: THIS BASALT FIGURE OF THE STORM GOD, SHIHAN, FROM THE ANCIENT LAND OF MOAB, IS DATED *C.* 1100 B.C.E. IT IS HOUSED IN THE LOUVRE MUSEUM IN FRANCE.

quickly near Jericho and subjected to an act of extreme cruelty. The Babylonians killed Zedekiah's sons in his presence, then gouged out his eyes so that the last thing he ever saw was the execution of his own children. The Babylonians looted the Temple in Jerusalem (Jeremiah 52:17–23) and 745 people were forced into exile (Jeremiah 52:30). The plucking up and pulling down that Jeremiah had prophesied had happened.

GEDALIAH

After the fall of Jerusalem, Gedaliah was appointed by the Babylonians to organize the remaining Judeans into a viable community. In addition, he was given special responsibility to protect Jeremiah. We shall never know why Gedaliah was chosen to be the governor of the towns of Judah. Some have suggested that the Babylonians wanted to reward Gedaliah because he had opposed Zedekiah's rebellion and encouraged submission to the Babylonians. Baalis, king of the Ammonites, for some reason didn't like the idea of Gedaliah serving as governor and urged Ishmael—a member of the royal family—to assassinate Gedaliah. It has been suggested that Baalis had been in an anti-Assyrian coalition and had disliked Gedaliah's advocacy of submission to the Babylonians. In any case, Ishmael and his collaborators came to Mizpah and killed Gedaliah, a number of Judeans living there, and a few Babylonian soldiers. He then treacherously executed pilgrims who had come down to Jerusalem from the north (Jeremiah 41:1–8). Johanan, who had attempted to warn Gedaliah of this threat, tried to avenge the slaughter, but before he could fully accomplish the task, Ishmael and eight of his men escaped.

JEREMIAH IS TAKEN TO EGYPT

The assassination of the governor appointed by the Babylonians—as well as some of the Babylonian soldiers—made those left in Judah afraid of brutal reprisals from Babylon. Johanan and several others planned to go to Egypt to escape the wrath of Babylon. Before they departed for Egypt, however, a number of them decided to ask Jeremiah what God wanted them to do. After praying for ten days about the matter, Jeremiah received a message: God would punish them if the people left for Egypt. They needed to stay in Judah because God would protect them from the Babylonians and use them to renew the nation. If they left, they could not be used for the intended restoration and they would cut themselves off from God's gracious activity. Jeremiah had been appointed to pluck up and pull down Judah, but also to build and to plant. If the people fled the land, they could not be built up and planted. Jeremiah's advice was ignored, and the people (including Jeremiah and Baruch) went to Tahpanhes in the northeast delta of Egypt. When they arrived, Jeremiah performed one last symbolic action: he buried stones and said Nebuchadnezzar would set his throne on that spot. Nebuchadnezzar would conquer Egypt and punish the Judeans who had fled there.

BELOW: THIS BIBLE ILLUSTRATION BY GUSTAVE DORE SHOWS THE FALL OF BABYLON, WHICH WAS TO BECOME THE HOME OF DEVILS, FOUL SPIRITS, AND UNCLEAN BIRDS.

THE ORACLES AGAINST MOAB AND BABYLON

A sure sign that God intended to build up and plant Judah was the punishment that the Lord would visit upon some of Judah's enemies. There are several oracles proclaiming doom against the nations near the end of the book of Jeremiah. Two nations, in particular, were singled out: Moab and Babylon. The extreme vitriol directed against Moab may be due to the fact that in 601–600 B.C.E., Nebuchadnezzar had sent Moabite troops to deal with Jehoiakim's revolt. As a result, Moab was to be totally destroyed. Chemosh, the chief god of the Moabites, would go into exile and be shown to be nothing but empty air, not a real god worthy of worship. The other nation against which a good deal of animosity was directed was Babylon. The oracle against Babylon (Jeremiah 50:1–51:64) anticipated Babylon's downfall. The one who had been used as God's "hammer" against the nations (Jeremiah 50:23) had been too arrogant and had punished Judah too severely. Now it was to be paid back for its excessive cruelty against Judah (Jeremiah 51:24) and Judah redeemed from its bondage (Jeremiah 50:34). With the enemies of God's people destroyed, God could set about creating a new community in the land that would worship him in spirit and in truth.

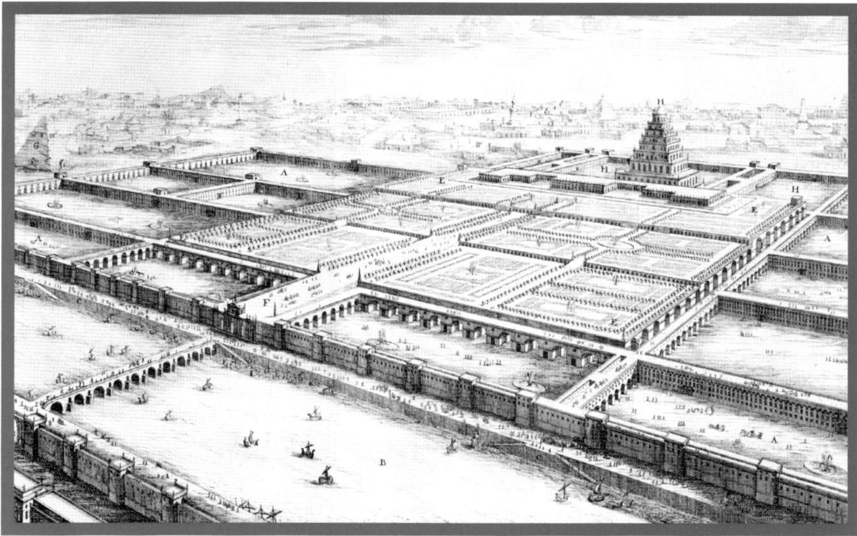

LEFT: THIS EIGHTEENTH-CENTURY ENGRAVING BY FISCHER VON ERLACH AND JOHANN BERNHARD SHOWS A PANORAMIC VIEW OF THE ROYAL PALACE AND HANGING GARDENS OF BABYLON. THE ORACLE AGAINST BABYLON IN JEREMIAH ANTICIPATES BABYLON'S DOWNFALL.

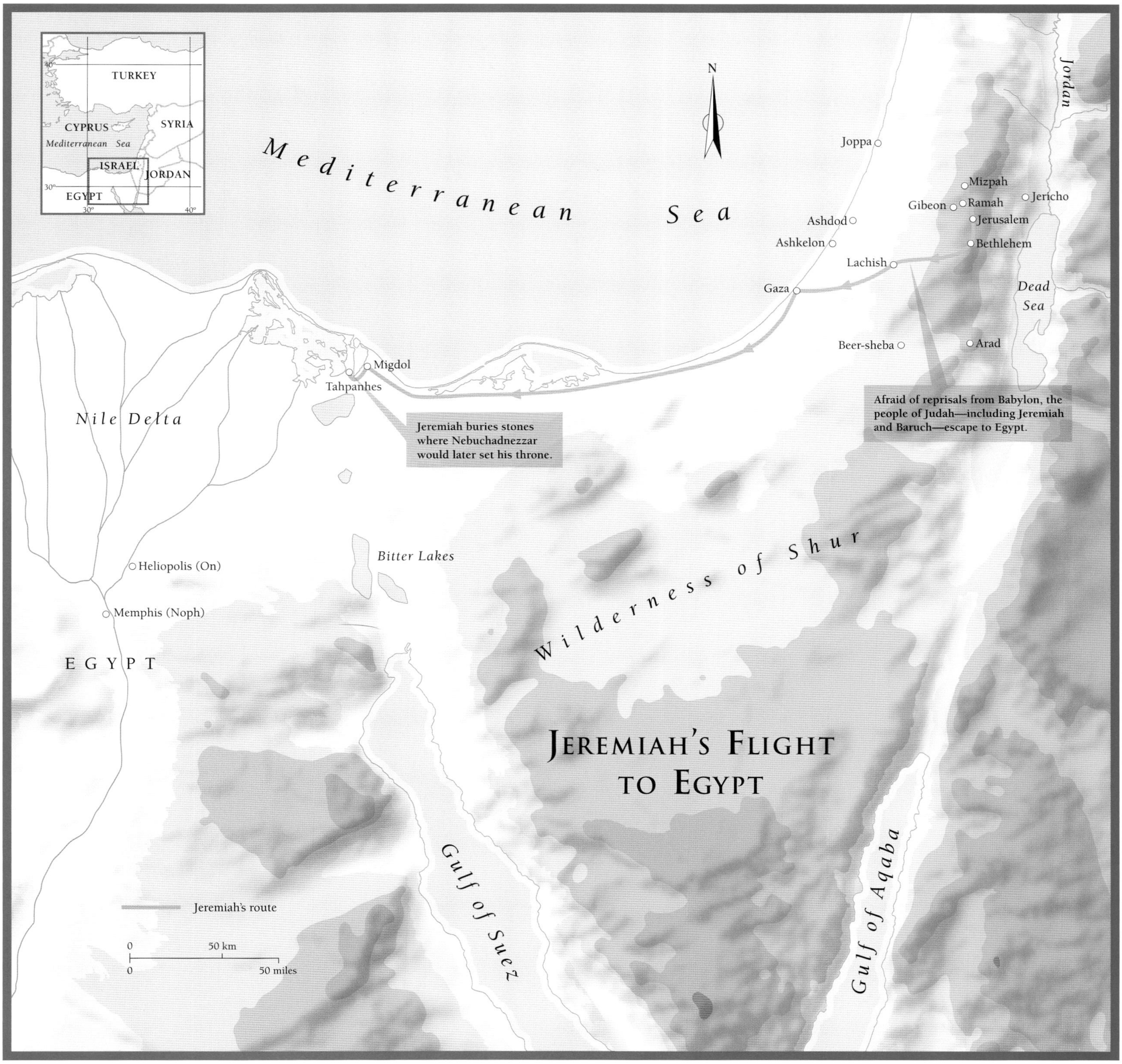

JEREMIAH'S FLIGHT TO EGYPT

TURKEY
CYPRUS
SYRIA
Mediterranean Sea
ISRAEL
JORDAN
EGYPT
N
Mediterranean Sea
Jordan
Joppa
Mizpah
Jericho
Gibeon
Ramah
Jerusalem
Ashdod
Ashkelon
Bethlehem
Lachish
Gaza
Dead Sea
Beer-sheba
Arad
Migdol
Tahpanhes
Nile Delta
Jeremiah buries stones where Nebuchadnezzar would later set his throne.
Afraid of reprisals from Babylon, the people of Judah—including Jeremiah and Baruch—escape to Egypt.
Bitter Lakes
Heliopolis (On)
Memphis (Noph)
EGYPT
Wilderness of Shur
Gulf of Suez
Gulf of Aqaba
Jeremiah's route
0 50 km
0 50 miles

EZEKIEL

THE PARENTS HAVE EATEN SOUR GRAPES, AND THE CHILDREN'S TEETH ARE SET ON EDGE EZEKIEL 18:2

Ezekiel, meaning "God strengthens," served as a priest in Jerusalem until he was exiled to Babylon during the deportation of 597 B.C.E. His ministry in Babylon, as the first exilic prophet, took place from around 593 B.C.E. until 573 B.C.E., with most of his prophetic activity directed toward the Babylonian exiles between the years 593–587 B.C.E. Ezekiel was a contemporary of Jeremiah, and each probably knew of the other's work since they shared many ideas. For example, both opposed Zedekiah's resistance to Babylon. And both emphasized individual, rather than corporate, responsibility for sin.

THE CALL OF EZEKIEL

The book of Ezekiel is presented in a fairly straightforward chronological order, unlike many of the other prophetic books. The first 24 chapters of Ezekiel are from before the fall of Jerusalem in 586 B.C.E. and contain words of judgment against Jerusalem and Judah. Chapters 25–32 contain oracles against the nations, probably written during and after the Babylon siege of Jerusalem that occurred in 587 B.C.E. Chapters 33–48, delivered after the fall of Jerusalem in 586 B.C.E., address the future restoration of Jerusalem and the Temple. These three distinct parts of Ezekiel's book correspond to Ezekiel's understanding of God's dealings with Israel: first, the nation must be punished; then comes the punishment of the nations, a prelude to the eventual restoration of Israel; finally, Jerusalem and Israel will be restored, with the rebuilt Temple the focus of purified worship.

Prior to the destruction of Jerusalem in 586 B.C.E., Ezekiel prophesied doom to his audience in Babylon. This message was necessary because many of the exiles were nationalistic—they wanted King Jehoiachin, who was in Babylon with them, to lead them home from their exile. Several popular prophets in Babylon preached that Babylon would be defeated, encouraging the exiles to rebel against Babylon. Ezekiel tried to quell this dissent: Jerusalem's eventual fall to Babylon was according to God's will. It had to happen as punishment for the sins of the people remaining in Judah. Therefore, to revolt against Babylon was to commit treason against God.

Ezekiel's call to be a prophet to the exiles came when he lived near the river Chebar, a canal close to the Babylonian city of Nippur. He was thus the first prophet to receive his call to prophesy outside Israel. God spoke to him in Babylon. This meant the presence of God was not confined to the land of Israel. In his call vision, the prophet saw a chariot carried by four strange creatures, later identified as cherubim, who were guardians of the Lord's throne. Their four wings enabled them to move in whatever direction they desired. The God whose throne they carried was also mobile and not limited to Jerusalem. Even though the exiles were in Babylon and not near the Temple where the Lord supposedly resided, they

RIGHT: IN HIS FRESCO DATED C.E. 1510, MICHELANGELO SHOWS EZEKIEL CONTORTED BY HIS VISION, AND ENDOWS A SIMPLE HAND GESTURE WITH MANIFOLD MEANING.

were still protected by God: the God of Israel was with the people in their exile. When Ezekiel described the Lord, whom he saw on the throne, he frequently used the word "like" to indicate that he had not actually seen the deity: the Lord was too transcendent for a mere mortal to behold. Also, more than 90 times in the book, the prophet is referred to as "mortal" (literally, "son of man")—pointing to the absolute separation between humans and the transcendent God. In the vision, the Lord told the prophet to go and preach to the people of Israel, a nation that had rebelled against God since its inception. Ezekiel was to warn the people of Jerusalem that they would surely die because of their faithlessness if they did not repent and turn back to God. But if they repented, then they would be saved (Ezekiel 33:2–5). The Lord then gave Ezekiel a scroll containing the message of lamentation and woe that he was to deliver to the people (Ezekiel 2:10). Ezekiel ate the scroll, consuming the message and allowing it to fill his consciousness. Because Ezekiel thought the scroll tasted sweet, it meant that he had accepted the message and made it his own.

EZEKIEL CUTS HIS HAIR

Ezekiel frequently used symbolic actions to warn the people of the divine judgment that was coming against Jerusalem. One time, he took a clay brick and used it to depict the siege of Jerusalem by Nebuchadnezzar. He then lay on his side for 430 days to represent the years of punishment that both Israel and Judah would experience. Later, he dug through a wall and carried baggage out through the hole to represent the fate of the exiles. One of his most poignant acts occurred when he cut his hair with a sword to show what was going to happen to those remaining in Jerusalem. Hair was understood by the people of Ezekiel's time to be a sign of strength and dignity; to have it forcibly cut off was a sign of humiliation and weakness (as when Hanun shaved the beards off David's envoys in 2 Samuel 10:4). This sign act, which is reminiscent of Isaiah's prophecy in Isaiah 7:20 (in which

ABOVE: EZEKIEL'S VISION OF THE CELESTIAL CHARIOT INSPIRED MUCH MYSTICAL SPECULATION AND THEOSOPHY IN LATER WRITINGS. THIS DEPICTION IS FROM *HISTOIRE DE L'ANCIEN ET NOUVEAU TESTAMENT*, C.E. 1724.

LEFT: THIS SEVENTEENTH-CENTURY PORTRAIT OF EZEKIEL FROM THE MOSCOW SCHOOL MAY HAVE BEEN INSPIRED BY THE STORY OF EZEKIEL EATING HIS SCROLL.

ABOVE: THIS SEVENTEENTH-CENTURY WORK BY ROMBOUT VAN TROYEN SHOWS FIGURES WORSHIPPING IDOLS. THE FIRST ABOMINATION EZEKIEL WITNESSED IN THE TEMPLE WAS IDOL WORSHIP.

BELOW: EAGLES WERE COMMON SYMBOLS IN ANCIENT CITY-STATES. THIS BRONZE AQUAMANILE BY MASTER SULEIMAN IS FROM PERSIA, DATED *C.* C.E. 800.

Jerusalem is shaved/punished by the Assyrians), symbolized the humiliation that was going to be visited by the Babylonians upon Jerusalem because of the city's sinfulness. Annihilation awaited Jerusalem. A third of the hair was to be burned in the city; another third was to be struck with a sword; and the last third was to be scattered to the wind. The fate of each portion of the hair revealed what the Lord planned to do to Jerusalem: the part that was burned in the city represented the Babylonian devastation of the holy city, leading to widespread famine and pestilence; the part that was struck with the sword represented the multitudes of residents of Jerusalem who would be killed by the sword; and the part that was scattered to the wind represented those people who would be forced into exile.

EZEKIEL'S SECOND VISION OF GOD

Ezekiel's second vision of the Lord, which took place in 592 B.C.E., revealed the extent of God's anger toward the people in Judah. After the exile, the population remaining in the land thought they would form the basis for the restored Judean community. They also thought that the Jerusalem Temple could never be destroyed, and that the Lord would remain there forever, offering them his protection. Some of the exiles, of whom Ezekiel was one, thought differently. They considered themselves the true Israel—it was the people in the land whose sins had brought destruction upon Judah. The people of Jerusalem needed to be punished before the exiles could return and become the real basis for the restored Israel. Because of the many abominations of the people of Jerusalem, God announced that he was now going to abandon them and use the sword of Babylon to punish them for their disobedience. They had defiled the Lord's sanctuary by placing idols in it and worshipping them. Their Sabbath worship was corrupt and they had broken the laws given to them by God. Therefore the Lord was going to remove his glory, his protective presence, from Jerusalem. Ezekiel 10–11 portrays God's movement away from the Temple and his people in Jerusalem. The prophet saw the glory of the Lord (God's presence) move from atop the cherubim in the Holy of Holies to the threshold of the Temple (Ezekiel 10:4–5), then on to the east gate of the Temple (Ezekiel 10:18–19), before finally leaving the Temple and resting on the nearby Mount of Olives (Ezekiel 11:23). Because of the iniquity of those remaining in Jerusalem, the Lord had chosen to abandon them—he, too, had gone into exile with the rest of his people.

THE EAGLES AND THE VINE

One of the most striking metaphors Ezekiel used to proclaim his message was of the two great eagles and the vine, found in Ezekiel 17:1–21. A great eagle (Nebuchadnezzar) had removed the top of the cedar (Jehoiachin) and taken him to a land of trade (Babylon). He then planted a seed (Zedekiah) in fertile soil where the seed prospered, eventually becoming a strong vine. The vine was not satisfied with the first eagle, however, so it reached out to another eagle (Psammetichus II of Egypt), who transplanted the vine. As a result, the first eagle was going to return and destroy the vine. The actions described in the metaphor relate to events that happened between 598–587 B.C.E. After Zedekiah made a covenant with Nebuchadnezzar and swore an oath of loyalty to him, he became tired of his vassal status, so he forged an alliance with Psammetichus II of Egypt. He hoped that the Egyptian king would assist him in a rebellion against Babylon. As a result, Nebuchadnezzar attacked and laid siege to Jerusalem—eventually uprooting the vine and taking Zedekiah into exile.

SWORDS

Ezekiel 21 contains three sayings about swords that focus on the punishment the Lord planned to send against Jerusalem. Because the sinfulness of Judah was so immense, God would attack both the righteous and the unrighteous in the land, from north to south. The resulting destruction would be total (Ezekiel 21:1–5). The polishing and sharpening of the sword that was to be used against the corrupt princes of the land is described in Ezekiel 21:8–17. The sword would be directed against not

just the princes, however, for all the people of Judah would be slaughtered on account of their idolatry. Finally, in Ezekiel 21:18–27, Babylon is described as marching across Syria while carrying its sword of destruction and trying to decide whether to attack Judah or Ammon first. The sword was coming because the "vile, wicked prince" (Zedekiah) had pursued a political alliance with Egypt.

THE SINFUL SISTERS

Ezekiel used the allegory of two sinful sisters, Oholah ("her own tent") and Oholibah ("my tent is in her"), to explain why Judah deserved its coming punishment. Both sisters, Oholah (Samaria) and Oholibah (Jerusalem), had sinned against the Lord from the beginning of their existence. Oholah had acted like a prostitute (Ezekiel 23:5) when she entered into ill-advised treaties with the Assyrians—treaties where she placed her trust in Assyria and not in the Lord. But her oaths of loyalty to Assyria had not protected her, for she (Samaria) was destroyed by the Assyrians in 722 B.C.E. (Ezekiel 23:9–10). Unfortunately, Oholibah (Jerusalem) did not learn from her sister's experiences. In fact, Oholibah was worse: she had prostituted herself with three nations—Assyria, Babylon, and Egypt—trusting in them, and not the Lord, to bring her to safety. Now Oholibah would be punished by her lovers because of her crimes—especially her attempted alliances which demonstrated a profound lack of faith and trust in God.

EZEKIEL'S PROPHECIES AGAINST THE NATIONS

After the destruction of Jerusalem, Ezekiel began to prophesy against various nations in the vicinity of Judah. These were nations who had once been enemies of Judah. Ammon (Ezekiel 25:1–7) and Edom (Ezekiel 25:12–14) were singled out because they had helped Babylon to destroy Jerusalem in 586 B.C.E. Tyre (Ezekiel 26–28) was mentioned because, unlike Judah, Tyre had been able to resist God's chosen sword, Nebuchadnezzar, and was thus especially deserving of God's wrath. Egypt had often sought to dominate Judah, and Judah at various times had sought to establish alliances with Egypt; therefore Egypt deserved to be punished. Since the

BELOW: ALTHOUGH NOT MENTIONED BY NAME, THE MOUNT OF OLIVES, DEPICTED IN THIS EARLY TWENTIETH-CENTURY ILLUSTRATION BY MORTIMER MENPES, IS REFERRED TO IN EZEKIEL 11.

Lord controlled the fate of all nations, they would be held accountable for their actions against Judah. Ezekiel demonstrated by the placement of these oracles after Ezekiel 1–24 that following the punishment of Judah, its restoration would begin with the punishment of the ungodly nations who had formerly harmed God's chosen people.

EZEKIEL BECOMES A WATCHMAN

The final section of the book of Ezekiel, focused on the restoration of Israel, begins with the prophet's second commissioning to be a sentinel (or "watchman"). The prophet was to warn the people of the approaching threat he had seen so that they had a chance to change their sinful ways. If the prophet fulfilled his task and the people did not repent, then they would be responsible for their punishment. But if the watchman did not warn the people, he would be responsible. It was incumbent upon the watchman to proclaim the message of warning that God had shown him.

THE GOOD SHEPHERD

Ezekiel placed the blame for the exile on the shoulders of corrupt shepherds, the rulers of Judah who had led the people astray. These false shepherds had not strengthened the weak or healed the sick (Ezekiel 34:4). Instead, they had looked out only for their own gain. As a result, their flock was scattered throughout the nations. Because these shepherds were so ineffective in caring for their people, God would begin to serve as their good shepherd. God would return the people from their exile and enable them to live in peace (Ezekiel 34:25). This would prepare the way for a member of the Davidic line in the future to shepherd Judah with justice (Ezekiel 34:23–24).

GOG

The restoration of Israel would take place after God defeated all Israel's enemies. After Israel was returned from its captivity (Ezekiel 38:8), a battle was going to take place between God and the evil nations, with Israel joining in on God's side. In an extended allegory, Ezekiel used Gog to represent all the enemies of Israel who had opposed God's plans throughout history. Ezekiel may have had Nebuchadnezzar in mind when he told the tale of Gog's defeat. After God dragged Gog out to fight (Ezekiel 38:4), God and Israel would fight against many nations (Ezekiel 38:5). Gog's forces—all the enemies of God's people—would be totally defeated, in the process making the Lord's name more clearly known among the people of Judah (Ezekiel 39:7). In particular, the victory would reveal the return of God's glory to the Promised Land. After the battle, the nations surrounding Israel would understand why so many bad things had happened to Israel (Ezekiel 39:23). It was not because of God's weakness, but because of Israel's sinfulness.

THE VALLEY OF BONES

In one of Ezekiel's visions he saw a valley of dry bones, shaking and coming back together as in this nineteenth-century engraving by Charles Laplante. When the skeleton was formed the muscles appeared, and finally the skin. This vision is thought to be symbolic of the rebirth of Israel: "Thus says the Lord God: I am going to open your graves, and bring you up from your graves, O my people; and I will bring you back to the land of Israel" (Ezekiel 37:12).

BELOW: GOG AND MAGOG, DEPICTED HERE BY GEORGE SHEPHERD, C.E. 1809, LATER APPEAR IN THE LEGENDS OF ALEXANDER THE GREAT AND IN THE QUR'AN, WHICH TELLS ITS OWN GOG/MAGOG STORY.

EZEKIEL'S VISION OF THE TEMPLE

In 573 B.C.E., 14 years after the destruction of the Temple, Ezekiel was returned in a vision to Jerusalem, where he received a tour of the ideal Temple. There he saw the glory of the Lord returning to the Temple, and promising to never again leave (Ezekiel 43:1–12). The people, who were now restored to the land, which was once more divided among the tribes, would never again defile God's holy name (Ezekiel 43:7). For Ezekiel, a restored Jerusalem and rebuilt Temple were of the utmost importance, for he knew that only in Jerusalem at the Temple could Israel worship God in spirit and in truth.

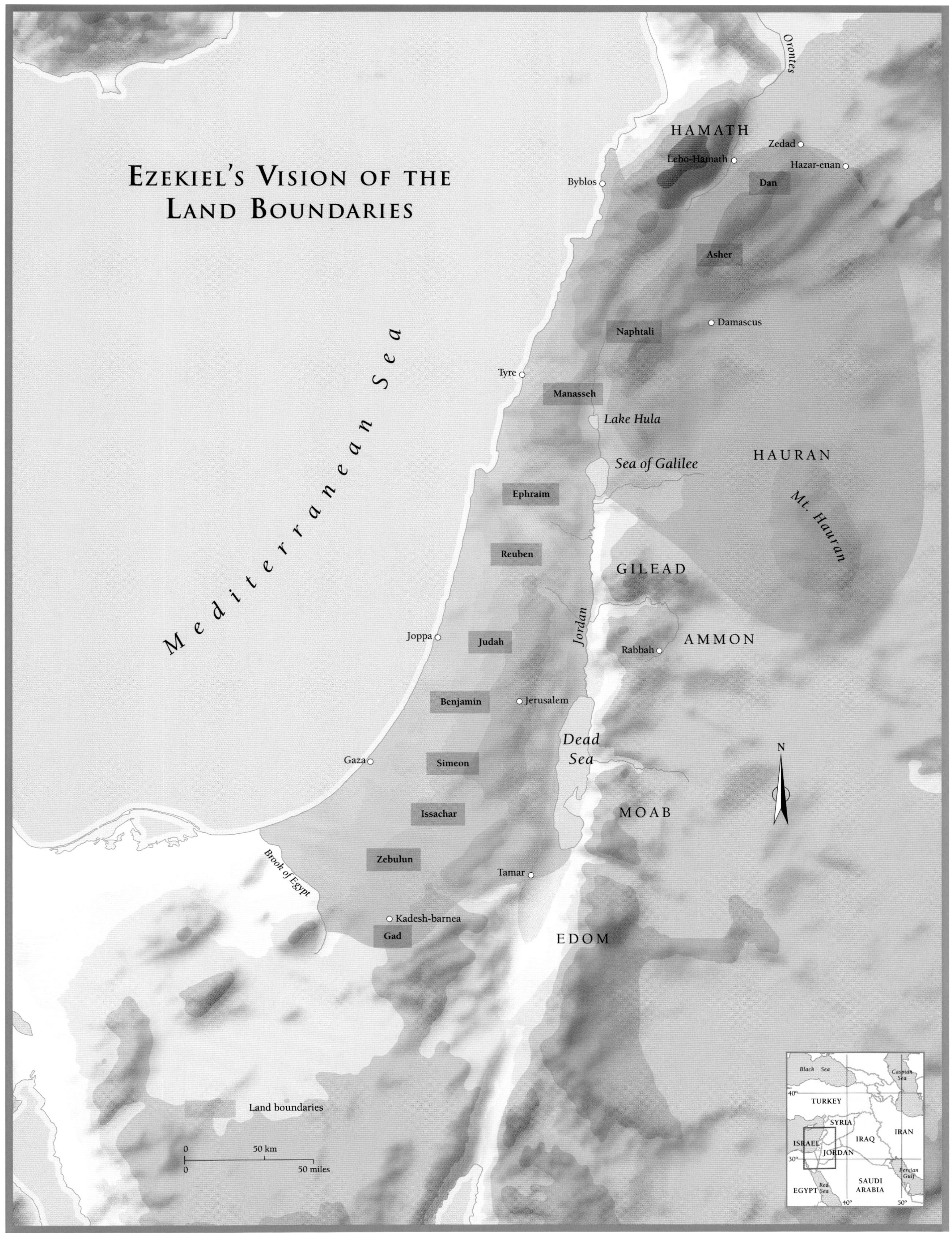
Ezekiel's Vision of the Land Boundaries
Mediterranean Sea
Orontes
HAMATH
Zedad
Lebo-Hamath
Hazar-enan
Byblos
Dan
Asher
Damascus
Naphtali
Tyre
Manasseh
Lake Hula
Sea of Galilee
HAURAN
Ephraim
Mt. Hauran
Reuben
GILEAD
Jordan
Joppa
Judah
AMMON
Rabbah
Benjamin
Jerusalem
Dead Sea
Gaza
Simeon
N
Issachar
MOAB
Zebulun
Brook of Egypt
Tamar
Kadesh-barnea
Gad
EDOM
Land boundaries
0
50 km
0
50 miles
Black Sea
Caspian Sea
TURKEY
SYRIA
IRAQ
IRAN
ISRAEL
JORDAN
SAUDI ARABIA
EGYPT
Red Sea
Persian Gulf
40°
30°
40°
50°

DANIEL

THE GOD OF HEAVEN WILL SET UP A KINGDOM THAT SHALL NEVER BE DESTROYED DANIEL 2:44

In 586–587 B.C.E., the unstoppable army of the Babylonian king Nebuchadnezzar II invaded the tiny nation of Judah, burned its Temple, destroyed its land, and exiled its people. Such unfathomable losses form the background to the book of Daniel. Daniel, one of the Judean exiles, along with his three friends, Hananiah, Mishael, and Azariah, must forge a new life at Nebuchadnezzar's court, where the king's values are pitted against their humble, yet steadfast faith (Daniel 1:1–21). Nebuchadnezzar's court is a microcosm of his regime, having all the trappings of a great power, yet it is marked by an idolatry that supports its tyranny and oppression of vanquished people.

It is from this great court, manned by Nebuchadnezzar's palace master and guards, that two crucial tests are presented to Daniel and his friends. First, by proposing to have them educated in Babylonian curricula, Nebuchadnezzar implicitly seeks their acculturation to his own faith and values. Second, by offering them food contrary to Jewish law, Nebuchadnezzar challenges them to defy a sacred precept. Despite these challenges, Daniel and his friends evidence the firm belief that God is sovereign even while they are exiled from their own land.

BELOW: THIS SEVENTEENTH-CENTURY MARBLE SCULPTURE DEPICTS DANIEL STRETCHED UP TOWARD GOD. THE WORK OF GIOVANNI LORENZO BERNINI, IT IS HOUSED IN THE CHIGI CHAPEL IN ROME.

DANIEL AND HIS FRIENDS

The very alteration of the names of Daniel and his companions Hananiah, Mishael, and Azariah to Belteshazzar, Shadrach, Meshach, and Abednego, respectively, shows the power of Nebuchadnezzar as these names honor the king's gods. In addition, the tests of compliance with Babylonian curricula and of eating the king's portions are crucial for their self-understanding. While in the Diaspora, will they remain Jews, or will they assimilate? With both of these tests, Nebuchadnezzar expects that they will capitulate. Daniel, however, takes the initiative to refuse the food, convincing Nebuchadnezzar's servant that he and his friends will thrive. Indeed, not only do they appear robust to the king after only eating vegetables, but because God has instilled them with "knowledge and skill in every aspect of literature and wisdom" (Daniel 1:17), they have a depth of discernment that impresses their overlord. Far from failing their ordeals, they so impress Nebuchadnezzar that he appoints them as supervisors throughout the empire. With this advancement, Daniel and his friends prove that God's wisdom, to which they hold fast, supersedes any of Babylon's achievements.

DANIEL AND THE KING'S FIRST DREAM

Displays of Nebuchadnezzar's tyranny continue in the account of his first dream (Daniel 2:1–49). Disturbed by the dream, he demands that his diviners both disclose its contents and give its interpretation. When they respond that such a task is impossible, his rage condemns all the wise men to death, including Daniel and his friends. Nevertheless, Daniel solicits his friends' solidarity in prayer and courageously approaches the king. Successfully identifying the

dream's content and providing its interpretation, Daniel declares that the purpose of his instruction is to show the king that "there is a God in heaven who reveals mysteries, and he has disclosed to King Nebuchadnezzar what will happen at the end of days" (Daniel 2:28).

Babylonian Gods

The most famous of the Babylonian gods was Marduk (Bel), the champion of the pantheon. Other deities included Nabu (Nebo), the god of scribes and education; Shamash, the sun god; and Ishtar, the goddess of love. Biblical authors mock the pretensions of Babylonian power and materialism by disparaging these divinities, but their persistent references attest to the attraction they held for the captive people.

Nebuchadnezzar's dream of the great statue with the head of gold, torso of silver, legs of bronze, and feet of iron and clay represents four empires, including Nebuchadnezzar's Babylonia (the head of gold), which are all destined to fall to a fifth kingdom, supported by divine favor. Daniel's dream interpretation shows that the disintegration of the statue, which represents the destruction of the empires, and their replacement by a final, righteous kingdom, is part of God's plan for humanity. Daniel shows that no emperor, no injustice, no cruelty remains ignored by God.

DANIEL IS REWARDED

Although Nebuchadnezzar had threatened a purge, Daniel's successful interpretation staves off the tyrant's murderous designs against the wise men. Instead, the king rewards

ABOVE: A CONFIDENT DANIEL INTERPRETS KING NEBUCHADNEZZAR'S FIRST DREAM TO THE ASTONISHMENT OF ONLOOKING COURTIERS IN THIS SEVENTEENTH-CENTURY DEPICTION BY FLEMISH ARTIST ERASMUS QUELLINUS.

ABOVE: THIS BRONZE PORTAL SHOWS KING NEBUCHADNEZZAR OF BABYLON SITTING ON HIS THRONE. THIS REPRESENTATION DATES FROM THE TWELFTH CENTURY AND IS HOUSED IN SAN ZENO MAGGIORE IN VERONA, ITALY.

Daniel and his companions by promoting them as prefects of Babylon. Nebuchadnezzar, nonetheless, remains obtuse in the face of Daniel's dream interpretation. Despite his acknowledgment of God's sovereignty with the declaration, "Truly, your God is God of gods and Lord of kings" (Daniel 2:47), Nebuchadnezzar worships Daniel and brings sacrifice to him—acts that ought to be given to God alone. In addition, although it may at first seem that Daniel and his friends have reached a pinnacle of success, they must continue to tread carefully in this foreign land ruled by despots, as the subsequent chapters in the book of Daniel illustrate.

NEBUCHADNEZZAR'S GOLD STATUE

In the Ancient Near East, the construction of enormous statues of a king or his god was a testimony to his power and authority and was used to both impress and instill fear in his subjects. This context forms the background of the account of Nebuchadnezzar's construction of the gold statue (Daniel 3:1–30). The identity of the statue is unspecified; it is most likely to be understood as Nebuchadnezzar himself, or one of his patron gods. Its outlandish proportions, 60 cubits tall by 6 cubits wide (corresponding to approximately 90 ft × 9 ft [27.3 m × 2.7 m]), and its solid gold construction attest to the outlandish ways of the profligate king. Nebuchadnezzar utilizes the entirety of the state's resources to enforce his demand that all his subjects prostrate themselves before the great statue. What is seen by the state as an act of loyalty, however, is understood by the faithful to be an act of idolatry. The law serves as a test of ultimate significance, for those who would not comply would be sentenced to a tormenting death: being cast into a fiery furnace.

DANIEL'S FRIENDS ARE SENTENCED TO DEATH

Hananiah, Mishael, and Azariah, who are called by their imposed Babylonian names Shadrach, Meshach, and Abednego, remain steadfast, refusing to compromise their faith. "The Chaldeans" (Daniel 3:8), namely, Nebuchadnezzar's enforcers, waste no time in denouncing them, hastily reporting to the king, "certain Jews … pay no heed to you, O King. They do not serve your gods and they do not worship the golden statue that you have set up" (Daniel 3:12). These carefully chosen words imply that all Jews in the empire are disregarding the entirety of the king's laws. Only as the Chaldeans continue their accusations does the reader discover that Shadrach, Meshach, and Abednego alone are singled out, and their refusal to bow to the idol is their singular offense. This presentation shows that, ultimately, all Jews are at risk from the tyranny of Nebuchadnezzar's regime. An accusation against one may just as easily modulate into a threat against the entire community.

Nebuchadnezzar's rage intensifies when his final offer of compliance is met with refusal. He continues to taunt the Jews with a question he believes is only rhetorical, saying, "who is the god that will deliver you out of my hands?" (Daniel 3:15). With these words, a contest is now set up—not between Nebuchadnezzar and the three condemned men, but between Nebuchadnezzar and the God of Israel. It is one that Nebuchadnezzar cannot win. For Daniel's companions there is no ambiguity as to whether there is a saving God; neither is there any question that they will do the right thing, regardless of how God responds.

Continuing to feel threatened, Nebuchadnezzar has the compliant Jews bound before he has his strongest guards cast them into the flames, which have been heated to seven times their normal state. Before we discover their fate, a dramatic reversal occurs: the guards (perhaps complicit in the injustice or perhaps additional victims of Nebuchadnezzar's rage) are killed by the tremendous heat of the furnace.

THE BLAZING FURNACE

Despite Nebuchadnezzar's expectation that his three defiant subjects would suffer and perish, he instead witnesses that a fourth being, which he first perceives as a god and later as an angel, appears with the men as their protector. Thus humbled, the king declares that the three may exit the furnace. The entirety of Nebuchadnezzar's court witnesses that they are completely unharmed. Nebuchadnezzar's ultimate response, however, still attests to his cruelty. Although he promotes the three, he never rescinds his initial decree and instead adds another. Now, anyone who does not worship the God of these three will also be sentenced to a horrible death: "[they] shall be torn limb from limb, and their houses laid in ruins" (Daniel 3:29).

DANIEL AND THE KING'S SECOND DREAM

Nebuchadnezzar's final appearance in the book of Daniel occurs in the account of his second dream, the dream of the great tree (Daniel 4:1–37). Nebuchadnezzar writes to his entire realm to tell all peoples that he had a dream of an enormous tree which reached to the heights of heaven and which provided shade for birds and animals. A holy watcher (an angel) appears in the dream, however, who warns that the tree must be chopped down and, with the image modulating from tree to human, must be punished. The angel states, "Let him be bathed with the dew of heaven, and let his lot be with the animals of the field in the grass of the earth. Let his mind be changed from that of a human, and let the mind of an animal be given to him. And let seven times pass over him … in order that all who live may know that the Most High is sovereign over the kingdom of mortals; he gives it to whom he will and sets over it the lowliest of human beings" (Daniel 4:15–17).

Until Daniel appears and interprets the dream for the king, however, Nebuchadnezzar is blind to its meaning, not recognizing that the tree represents himself. Daniel reiterates the angel's warning and admonishes Nebuchadnezzar to "atone for your sins with righteousness, and your iniquities with mercy to the oppressed, so that your prosperity may be prolonged" (Daniel 4:27). Rather than acting on Daniel's advice, Nebuchadnezzar continues to boast, not recognizing that his ascendancy comes from God. The divine punishment is immediately enacted, and Nebuchadnezzar is degraded, just as the dream promised: "He was driven away from human society, ate grass like oxen, and his body was bathed with the dew of heaven, until his hair grew as long as eagles' feathers and his nails became like birds' claws" (Daniel 4:33).

LEFT: THIS FIFTEENTH-CENTURY INTERPRETATION OF SHADRACH, MESHACH, AND ABEDNEGO IN THE FIERY FURNACE IS HOUSED IN THE BARNES FOUNDATION IN THE U.S. STATE OF PENNSYLVANIA.

BELOW: THIS ILLUSTRATION FROM *HISTOIRE DE L'ANCIEN ET NOUVEAU TESTAMENT* (C.E. 1724) SHOWS NEBUCHADNEZZAR AS A WILD ANIMAL. MANY BELIEVE THIS AFFLICTION WAS ACTUALLY SUFFERED BY NABONIDUS, A LATER KING OF BABYLON.

ABOVE: A HUMAN HAND DELIVERS A MESSAGE TO STILL THE REVELERS IN THIS NINETEENTH-CENTURY OIL PAINTING OF BELSHAZZAR'S FEAST BY JOHN MARTIN.

The scene of Daniel's interpretation and warning, as well as Nebuchadnezzar's punishment, is not included in the king's letter to his subjects. Rather, the letter continues with a description of Nebuchadnezzar's glory. While it is true that Nebuchadnezzar praises God and acknowledges God's sovereignty, his continual boasting allows the readers of this account to doubt his sincerity. Indeed, he disappears from the narrative at this point, which continues with the account of King Belshazzar and the end of the Babylonian Empire.

THE WRITING ON THE WALL

Daniel 5 portrays Belshazzar, a successor of Nebuchadnezzar, as a profligate ruler who learned nothing from God's response to the earlier king's cruelty. In a stylized portrayal of a powerful, yet pathetic king, the account of Belshazzar's banquet and the writing on the wall illustrates that God's demand for justice supersedes any earthly ruler's quest for power. Either a coronation ceremony, a new year's or traditional festival, or an occasion to encourage the Babylonians to resist the Persians, are all possible backgrounds for the context of Belshazzar's feast, an occasion which showcases Belshazzar's debauchery and immorality. A scene of extreme wealth and power as well as the sacrilegious use of holy vessels from the Temple are portrayed in order to highlight the king's end, for the lavish displays serve as Daniel's stage to announce the destruction of the kingdom of Babylon.

Belshazzar's feasting turns to fear when a disembodied hand mysteriously appears and inscribes baffling writing on a wall, which none of the king's advisers can interpret. The queen prompts Belshazzar to call upon Daniel for assistance, but before Daniel interprets the words, he admonishes the king for his sins against God. Daniel proclaims: "And this is the writing that was inscribed: MENE, MENE, TEKEL, and PARSIN. This is the interpretation of the matter: MENE, God has numbered the days of your kingdom and brought it to an end; TEKEL, you have been weighed on the scales and found wanting; PERES, your kingdom is divided and given to the Medes and Persians" (Daniel 5:25–28).

Belshazzar does not respond to these words. Instead, he promotes Daniel to high office, signifying that Daniel's wisdom surpasses that of the sages of Babylon and, perhaps unwittingly, acknowledging the sovereignty of God. God's words, indeed, come to pass: Belshazzar is killed that same night, and the Babylonian Empire is replaced by the kingdom of Darius the Mede.

DANIEL IN THE LIONS' DEN

Daniel's trials are not over once Darius the Mede comes to power. Although Darius himself never actively threatens Daniel, his very failure to act when his own officials conspire to have Daniel killed proves equally dangerous. These conspirators initiate a test that no prayer should be offered to anyone except Darius himself and claim that once such a decree has been made it can never be altered. Thus, they entrap Daniel as he insists on fulfilling his obligations to pray to God. Confronted with the officials' accusations, Darius, despite his feelings of concern for Daniel, capitulates to their demands that this hero be thrown into a pit of lions. The capriciousness of this action underscores that no exile—not even a respected man such as Daniel—can feel totally at home in the Diaspora. God alone will prove to be Daniel's protector.

In contrast to Darius, who spends a night in torturous waiting, Daniel is unharmed, having been protected by an

RIGHT: DANIEL INTERPRETS THE WRITING ON THE WALL IN THIS NINETEENTH CENTURY DEPICTION BY WASHINGTON ALLSTON. THE DRINKING VESSELS ON THE RIGHT REPRESENT THE GOLD AND SILVER STOLEN FROM THE TEMPLE OF SOLOMON.

angel. Upon exiting, Daniel proclaims to Darius that he has done him no harm. The happy Darius immediately sentences the conspirators to the same fate they had intended for Daniel. In keeping with the theme of God's defeat of arrogant world powers, Daniel's victory in the lions' den previews God's destruction of evil and paves a path for the kingdom of God. Darius himself proclaims, "His kingdom shall never be destroyed, and his dominion has no end. He delivers and rescues, he works signs and wonders in heaven and on earth" (Daniel 6:26–27).

DANIEL'S VISIONS

Chapters 7–12 of the book of Daniel are comprised primarily of apocalyptic visions. Daniel becomes a recipient of mystifying and frightening visions that both reveal and conceal God's future plan. These visions confirm that suffering awaits Daniel's people, yet they also provide assurance that hope for the future and expectations of God's victory are not in vain.

Daniel's visions consist of the One like a Son of Man who prevails over the great beast; the ram and the he-goat who vie for power only to be crushed "not by human hands" (Daniel 8:25); and a sweep of history, which details the schemes of competing governments that only come to naught. In all of these, the message of the interpreting angel to Daniel is consistent—wait for the everlasting kingdom of the holy ones of the Most High: "Happy are those who persevere and attain the thousand three hundred thirty-five days. But you, go your way, and rest; you shall rise for your reward at the end of days" (Daniel 12:12–13). With this paradigm, the book of Daniel encourages people to hope in God's ultimate plan while continuing to live lives of holiness. In times of persecution and community upheaval, these acts become heroic. They are profoundly significant because they allow for the continuation of faith in impossible times and serve as testimony to the God of Israel who demands justice.

The Historicity of Daniel

Although the setting of Daniel 7–12 remains within Daniel's lifetime (*c.* 550 B.C.E.), historical-critical scholarship sees the visions as coming from the time of Antiochus IV Epiphanes (175–164 B.C.E.). Apocalypses are typically characterized by details of the oppressive reign of the author's time presented in symbolic language, with predictive schemas of sequential kings and empires (Babylon, Media, Persia, and Greece), *ex eventu* prophecies, and authorship attributed to a pious sage. Such conventions were not an attempt at deception; rather, they served to honor the tradition of a particular sage, showing that even the most outrageous acts of cruelty are under the watchful plan of God, who brings an end to suffering. In addition, apocalyptic texts may showcase a future cosmological judgment in which the righteous are vindicated. This carved Romanesque (right) shows Daniel between two lions.

BELOW: IN HIS DEPICTION OF THE LIONS' DEN DATED C.E. 1872, BRITON RIVIERE PAINTS DANIEL AS A MODEL OF LIFE WITHOUT FEAR AS HE STANDS BEFORE SEVEN LIONS.

The Minor Prophets

SEE, I AM SENDING MY MESSENGER TO PREPARE THE WAY BEFORE ME MALACHI 3:1

Hosea, perhaps the only known prophet from the northern kingdom, was active during a tumultuous period in Israel's history. After the death of Jeroboam II in 745 B.C.E., political life in Israel deteriorated greatly, with six kings in 23 years. Israel tried to achieve a semblance of security by making political alliances with various nations. Sadly, this led to the worship of other deities. As a consequence, Israel's covenant with the Lord began to deteriorate, leading the Lord to break off his covenant with Israel. Hosea used his own marriage and family life to demonstrate God's word of judgment in this painful situation.

HOSEA'S MARRIAGE AND FAMILY

Hosea married a prostitute, just as the Lord had "married" unfaithful Israel, who had left the Lord and pursued relationships with other gods and nations. After Hosea's wife Gomer "bore him" (Hosea) their first child, Gomer "conceived again and bore a daughter" (Hosea 1:6). The absence of "him" following "bore" (as in Hosea 1:3) suggests to some scholars that Hosea was not the girl's father. However, what is apparent in context is that the name given to this second child, Lo-ruhamah ("not loved" or "not pitied") is a clear indication of the Lord's rejection of his covenant with Israel: he would no longer love or pity Israel.

It has been suggested that the third child, a son named Lo-ammi ("not my people" or "not my kindred"), was also not born to Hosea (Hosea 1:8), but again, the name is also likely to reflect the Lord's repudiation of his covenant with Israel. The relationship that had been established between the Lord and Israel in Exodus 6:7 ("I will take you as my people, and I will be your God") had been undone: Israel was no longer the people of the Lord, and the Lord was no longer their God (Hosea 1:9).

The story of Hosea's marriage to a prostitute was shocking to his listeners. Those who thought that Israel had been a faithful covenant partner to the Lord received the disturbing news that Israel had behaved just like a prostitute. God would thus have to punish Israel, using Assyria to chastise "her" (Hosea 11:5–6). But if the nation repented and returned to the Lord, he would once again love them (Hosea 14:4).

JOEL

Joel ("the Lord is God") was an unknown prophet active sometime between 539–331 B.C.E. Joel began with the description of an invasion of four different kinds of locusts (Joel 1:2–2:27). Such natural disasters were often thought to be the work of God. One cannot be certain if the locusts were real, or if they referred symbolically to invasions of Judah by foreign armies. In either case, the invasion represented the Day of the Lord when God would judge and punish his people for their sins. God hoped the punishment would encourage Judah to repent and return to him (Joel 2:12–17). But this was not God's final word. God heard the cries of his people and had compassion for them (Joel 2:18–27): God would restore the fortunes of Judah and would defeat her enemies (Joel 3:1–8). God had not abandoned his people, but only chastened them for a while so that they would eventually return to him as a purified nation. To seal this promise, the Lord would send his spirit upon all the people, rich and poor alike, to assure them that he had not forsaken them (Joel 2:28–29).

AMOS

Amos, who was from Tekoa in Judah, was active as a prophet in Israel during the reign of Jeroboam II of Israel (783–745 B.C.E.). In the half century before Amos's ministry began, Israel had known great material prosperity. Unfortunately, both social and religious corruption had also become rampant during this time. The number

BELOW: THE MARRIAGE OF HOSEA TO THE PROSTITUTE SYMBOLIZED GOD'S MARRIAGE TO UNFAITHFUL ISRAEL. THIS TWELFTH-CENTURY DEPICTION IS TAKEN FROM *THE BIBLE OF ST. ANDRE AUX-BOIS.*

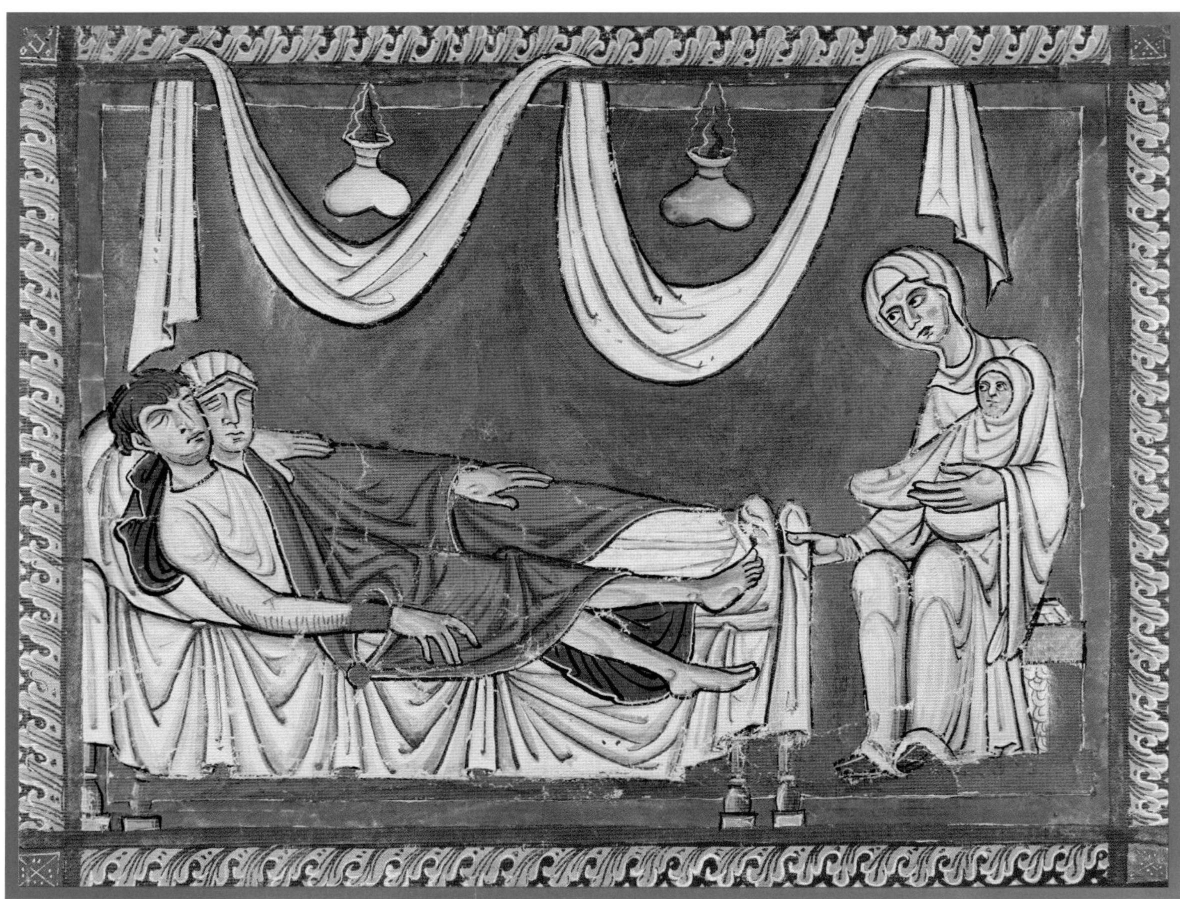

of both wealthy and impoverished citizens had increased greatly, as had the practice of morally bankrupt worship.

Amos was concerned that the Israelites did not take their election as God's chosen people seriously enough. They thought that because God had chosen them, their worship could be superficial and they could engage in destructive social relationships. Without justice and righteousness in their dealings with other people, however, all their religious festivals and sacrifices to God were of absolutely no value (Amos 5:21–24). The quality of one's relationship to God, Amos stated, depended upon how one treated other members of the community (Amos 2:6–8). But the Israelites had failed miserably in this regard: they denied legal rights to the afflicted; they oppressed the poor and needy; they took bribes; and they lived in luxurious houses while others starved. And yet the Israelite people thought that it was all acceptable as long as they brought their tithes to God (Amos 4:4–5). But what good was all the worship in the world if the heart was sick? The Lord was therefore going to send an enemy from the north to punish Israel, with the hope that this would rid the people of their sickness (Amos 6:14). Amos hoped his prophecies would show Israel how dire its future was and inspire the people to repent and take their covenant with the Lord more seriously.

ABOVE: INSPIRATION TAKES THE PLACE OF ACQUIRED KNOWLEDGE IN MICHELANGELO'S SIXTEENTH-CENTURY FRESCO OF JOEL FROM THE SISTINE CHAPEL. THE GENII APPEAR TO BE REENACTING THE PROCESS.

LEFT: THIS SIXTEENTH-CENTURY DEPICTION OF THE PROPHET AMOS BY JUAN DE BORGONA IS HOUSED IN THE MUSEO CATEDRALICIO IN CUENCA, SPAIN.

OBADIAH

The book of Obadiah ("servant of the Lord") was probably composed shortly after the fall of Jerusalem in 586 B.C.E. Prior to this, there had been constant conflict between Judah and the nation of Edom, with the Edomites often blamed for atrocious behavior directed against Judah (Psalms 137:7; Lamentations 4:21–22; Ezekiel 35:12–14). In fact, Judah's final destruction occurred when Edom enticed Judah to join in an anti-Babylonian coalition. The book of Obadiah hints that Edom then participated with Babylon in the destruction of Jerusalem that followed: "For the slaughter and violence done to your brother Jacob, shame shall cover you [Edom], and you shall be cut off forever" (Obadiah 1:10). The imminent demise of Edom was to be the first step in God's restoration of his own people (Obadiah 1:15–17).

RIGHT: CONSISTING OF ONE CHAPTER, OBADIAH'S IS THE SHORTEST BOOK OF THE OLD TESTAMENT. THE PROPHET IS DEPICTED IN THIS STAINED GLASS WINDOW FROM THE THIRTEENTH CENTURY.

JONAH

Jonah is more a story about a prophet than a collection of his oracles. When Jonah was first told to go to Nineveh, he did not act as a faithful prophet should have done: instead of going to Nineveh to deliver his message, he fled in the opposite direction to Tarshish. When the Lord raised a great storm against the Tarshish-bound ship, threatening to sink it, Jonah finally admitted that he was the cause of the storm. The reluctant sailors then threw him overboard, whereupon a great fish swallowed him and saved him from drowning. During the storm, the pagan sailors were more pious than Jonah since they prayed to their gods while Jonah slept. Only when he was in the belly of the great fish did Jonah offer a prayer to the Lord. After Jonah had spent three days and nights in its belly, the fish finally spat Jonah out. The Lord then told Jonah again to go to Nineveh. This time he went and informed the inhabitants that "'Forty days more, and Nineveh shall be overthrown'" (Jonah 3:4). Remarkably, the people of that evil city believed and repented. Because of their sincere repentance, God was merciful and spared their city. But God's mercy upset Jonah greatly because he did not want the Lord to save Nineveh, which had so long dominated and brutalized Judah. In fact, Jonah was more upset about the destruction of a mere plant that provided him shade than about the potential annihilation of the 120,000 people of Nineveh (Jonah 4:8–10).

The great irony in the story is that the people of Nineveh—a symbol of Assyria's cruelty toward Judah—expressed piety and repentance for their deeds, while God's prophet, who should have rejoiced in their repentance, lacked compassion. Jonah did everything a prophet should not do: he refused to proclaim the message God had given him, and he complained about God's mercy when Nineveh was saved. Evil Nineveh, on the other hand, did what it was not expected to do: it believed and repented.

Prophets regularly announced judgment against Assyria, but the book of Jonah shows the nation in a very different light, as repenting and turning to the Lord. It is most unlike

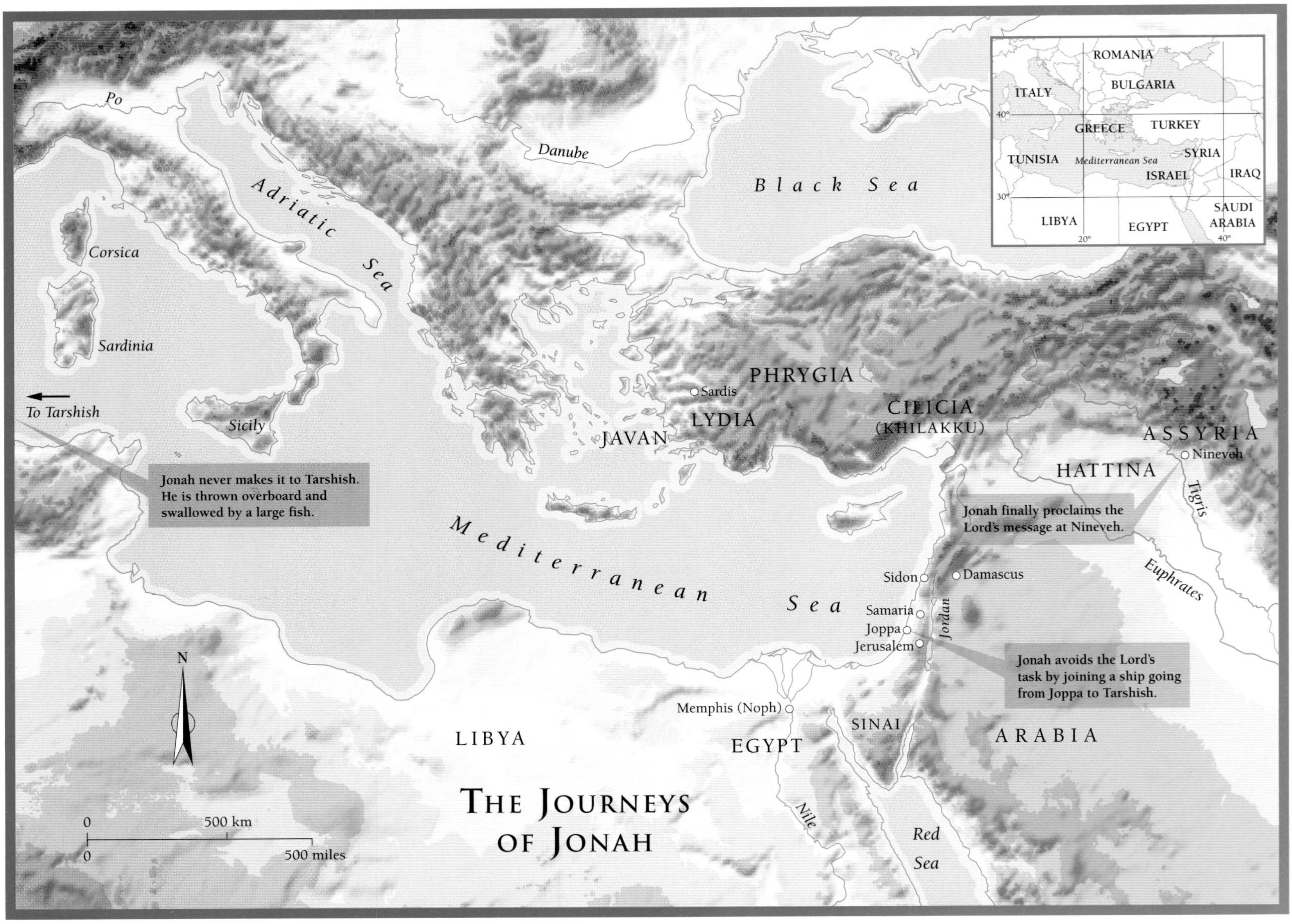

THE JOURNEYS OF JONAH

Jonah never makes it to Tarshish. He is thrown overboard and swallowed by a large fish.

Jonah finally proclaims the Lord's message at Nineveh.

Jonah avoids the Lord's task by joining a ship going from Joppa to Tarshish.

Nahum, which glories in the imminent demise of Assyria. Jonah presents a critique of the nationalism that was rampant in much of Judah, a nationalism that said God loved only the chosen people and not "the other." The book of Jonah challenges the exclusivity and intolerance toward foreign peoples that is found in the books of Ezra and Nehemiah. God can and does extend his mercy to all peoples. Sometimes this mercy seems to contradict God's justice: the Assyrians had brutalized Judah, so where was the justice in God showing mercy to those who deserved death and destruction? But that is the point: sinners don't always get what they deserve. If they repent and turn to God, then God's love and mercy is available to them.

ABOVE: AS JONAH FLEES, GOD CREATES A SERIES OF EVENTS TO BRING JONAH BACK TO HIS CALLING. IN THIS EIGHTEENTH-CENTURY LITHOGRAPH BY BECQUET, JONAH IS THROWN OVERBOARD AND THE STORM IMMEDIATELY STOPS.

MICAH

Micah ("who is like the Lord?") prophesied during the reigns of Jotham (740–735 B.C.E.), Ahaz (735–716 B.C.E.), and Hezekiah (716–687 B.C.E.). During this period, the land of Judah was filled with much sin and injustice: prophets, priests, and judges accepted bribes; merchants cheated their customers; and cults to foreign deities existed alongside the ones that worshipped the Lord. It is likely that Micah was a farmer, since he was from Moresheth-gath, a small village in the Shephelah in the southwestern part of Judah. This could be why he was so concerned with issues of economic unfairness and exploitation, since these issues would have directly affected his rural peasant friends.

With the introduction of the monarchy in Israel and Judah, the tribal ideal of equality was forgotten and separations began to develop between the rich and the poor, between city dwellers and rural farmers, and between the leaders and the ordinary people. Soon there were people in Judah who were unconcerned with the well-being of their neighbors. The mighty took the farms and homes of the weakest members of society (Micah 2:2)—fields that kept the farmers alive. The wealthy committed acts of violence against the poor (Micah 6:12) and businessmen cheated their customers by using dishonest measurements (Micah 6:10–11).

This social injustice in the land was an indication that the people had rejected God. A false sense of security among people had replaced genuine allegiance to God (Micah 3:11). In particular, Micah was upset that the people of Judah had forgotten all the wonderful things God had done for them in the past: how he had delivered them out of their slavery in Egypt, forged a covenant with them, and established them as a nation (Micah 6:3–5). In response, God did not want mere sacrifices and empty rituals. Rather, the Lord wanted his people to show their love and gratitude to him by acting justly and with loving kindness toward others (Micah 6:8). But because of their evil deeds of greed and oppression, Judah would be ruined (Micah 2:3–4). The covenant had been ignored, and so God was going to turn away from his people and abandon them to their approaching punishment. The doom, described vividly in Micah 1–3, was to persuade

LEFT: THE PROPHET MICAH LOOKS DOWN ON THE VIRGIN ANNUNCIATE IN THIS PAINTING BY HUBERT AND JAN VAN EYCK. DATING FROM C.E. 1432, IT IS HOUSED IN THE ST. BAVO CATHEDRAL IN BELGIUM.

ABOVE: HABAKKUK'S PSALM OF PRAISE IN CHAPTER 3 IS A GREAT TESTIMONY OF FAITH. THIS SIXTEENTH-CENTURY RELIEF OF THE PROPHET IS BY PIETRO LOMBARDO AND HIS SONS, TULLIO AND ANTONIO.

the people to acknowledge their responsibility before God and to repent of their sins. After the punishment, a purified and faithful remnant would remain, from whom the Lord would establish a new nation.

The ones Micah saw as most responsible for this dire state of affairs were the religious and political leaders of the land. They knew what was right and what God expected them to do—but all they cared about was tearing down the weak and taking advantage of them (Micah 3:1–4). Even the prophets were culpable. They did not give God's true words to the people, instead leading them astray with false words of comfort and peace (Micah 3:5–8). The leaders, priests, and prophets spoke false words for profit, not out of concern for doing God's will (Micah 3:9–12). As a result, Jerusalem was going to be devastated.

NAHUM

Nahum prophesied shortly before 612 B.C.E. His prophecy celebrates the destruction of the city of Nineveh, long a symbol of Assyrian dominance and cruelty. When Ashurbanipal was king of Assyria (668–627 B.C.E.), he had exacted heavy tribute from Judah, destroyed many of Judah's towns, and treated his victims with extreme brutality (Nahum 2:11–12). But now God planned to execute vengeance on Nineveh (Nahum 2:8–10), bringing joy to God's people and all who had suffered under Assyrian domination (Nahum 1:6–8, 1:15). Assyria was under assault from the Medes and the Babylonians and its imminent demise was apparent, so the enemy once used by God to discipline Israel was now going to be punished for its excesses. The destruction of Assyria would make clear to all that the Lord was the all-powerful God of the universe who protected his people and punished his enemies (Nahum 1:2–3).

HABAKKUK

Habakkuk was active between 612 and 605 B.C.E. He questioned God's justice and treatment of the wicked. He even accused the Lord of appearing indifferent to evil (Habakkuk 1:1–4). Why, he asked, did the Lord remain silent while the unrighteous prospered (Habakkuk 1:13)? Could God remain faithful to his covenant with Israel when the evil empires of the world were so strong? If God was just, how could God allow so much injustice in the world? The response the prophet received from the Lord was not what he expected: instead of words of comfort, Habakkuk was told there would be further reason for dismay—the Lord was going to raise up the Babylonians to punish the wicked leaders of Judah. But, wondered Habakkuk, doesn't God's use of a ruthless people to punish his chosen people contradict God's own holiness? The Lord responded by telling Habakkuk that the people of Judah must wait in faith for the Lord to do the right thing and punish the unjust (Habakkuk 2:4). The Babylonians—the source of so much suffering in Judah—would eventually be punished for their exploitation, gluttony, idolatry, pride, and arrogance (Habakkuk 2:6–20).

ZEPHANIAH

Zephaniah ("the Lord hides") was active as a prophet from 640–622 B.C.E., before the reforms of 622 B.C.E., when Josiah attempted to undo the apostasy of Manasseh (697–642 B.C.E.). Manasseh had adopted many aspects of Assyria's religion, including their preoccupation with astrology and the use of

THE SPOKEN WORD

The Minor and Major Prophets together comprise the literary prophets, as opposed to the "oral" prophets who left no written record bearing their names. The oral prophets include Samuel, Nathan, Elijah (right), and Elisha. It is interesting that we often know more about the lives of the oral prophets than we do the literary prophets, with the exception of Daniel and Jonah.

diviners. Zephaniah prophesied against these practices. Because of this idolatry (Zephaniah 1:4–6), Judah would be punished on the Day of the Lord, a day when creation would be undone (Zephaniah 1:2–3). Because of the magnitude of its evil and immorality, Judah would become a sacrifice offered by God. This sacrifice would not lead to the ultimate destruction of Judah, however, for a righteous remnant—a small, purified people pleasing to the Lord (Zephaniah 3:9–13)—would remain. Judah would not be the only one to be punished, for the Lord would also destroy the old vassals of Israel (Zephaniah 2:4–11), and then Assyria (Zephaniah 2:13–15).

HAGGAI

The prophet Haggai ("my feasts") was active in Jerusalem in 522–515 B.C.E. Those living in Jerusalem were led by a governor, Zerubbabel, and a priest, Joshua. Shortly after the return of some of the exiles to Jerusalem in 537 B.C.E., work began on rebuilding the Jerusalem Temple. When Darius I succeeded Cambyses II as ruler of Persia in 521 B.C.E., revolts broke out throughout Persian provinces. This, along with droughts and disease that afflicted the residents of Judah, caused work on rebuilding the Temple to come to a halt. Haggai was distressed by the cessation of work on the Temple, for he saw the Temple as necessary for the survival of the new community in Jerusalem. The misfortune facing the people, he said, was the result of their failure to finish the building project (Haggai 1:9–11). If only they would finish restoring the Temple and properly perform their religious rituals, then life in Judah would return to normal (Haggai 2:7). It was up to Zerubbabel and Joshua to lead the way or else the project would never be finished. Once the Temple was finished, God would use Zerubbabel to bring a new age of peace and well-being to Judah and destroy all her enemies (Haggai 2:20–23).

ZECHARIAH

The prophet Zechariah ("the Lord has remembered") was part of the postexilic community in Judah from 522–515 B.C.E. Like his contemporary Haggai, he was concerned with rebuilding the Temple in Jerusalem: since Jerusalem was the place where God had chosen to dwell, it was important to rebuild his home. At the time, however, Israel was poverty-stricken and dispirited. Although the returned exiles initially had great zeal for rebuilding the Temple, this zeal had lapsed. Zechariah encouraged the rebuilding project, for he believed that a rebuilt temple would help to initiate the messianic kingdom.

Zechariah received eight night visions (Zechariah 1:7–6:8) that demonstrated that God's plan was being carried out in the world: Babylon was going to be destroyed, the Temple would be restored, and the Lord had chosen two leaders to lead the newly restored nation of Israel—Joshua the priest and Zerubbabel the prince. They were "the two anointed ones" (Zechariah 4:14) who were to lead the Temple rebuilding project (Zechariah 6:12–13). Two messages were at the core of Zechariah's preaching: encouragement to continue with the rebuilding of the Temple, and assurance that the messianic age was about to begin with Zerubbabel.

LEFT: THIS EIGHTEENTH-CENTURY PAINTING BY AMBROISE CROZAT DEPICTS A VISION OF ZECHARIAH'S IN WHICH THE SEVEN EYES OF THE LORD GLADLY OBSERVE ZERUBBABEL IN THE TEMPLE.

MALACHI

Malachi ("my messenger") was active in Judah some time after 515 B.C.E., when the Temple was finished being rebuilt. The new age prophesied by Zechariah and Haggai had not yet arrived, so many in Judah were disillusioned. Malachi argued that the reason for this delay of the new age was because of three abuses taking place in Jerusalem: the priests in the Temple were offering unacceptable sacrifices (Malachi 1:7); the people married foreign wives (Malachi 2:11–12); and the people failed to give God a tithe of their wealth. When the people repented, Malachi said, God would return to be with them (Malachi 3:7). Malachi still held out hope for a new age, but it was not as imminent as Zechariah and Haggai had suggested—it would take time to arrive, so the people had to be prepared to wait.

BELOW: A FRESCO OF MALACHI, FROM THE *LOGGIA D'ANNUNCIAZIONE*, C.E. 1451, BY GIUSTO D'ALLAMAGNA. MALACHI REVEALED THE COMING OF JOHN THE BAPTIST, WHO WOULD PREPARE THE WAY FOR JESUS.

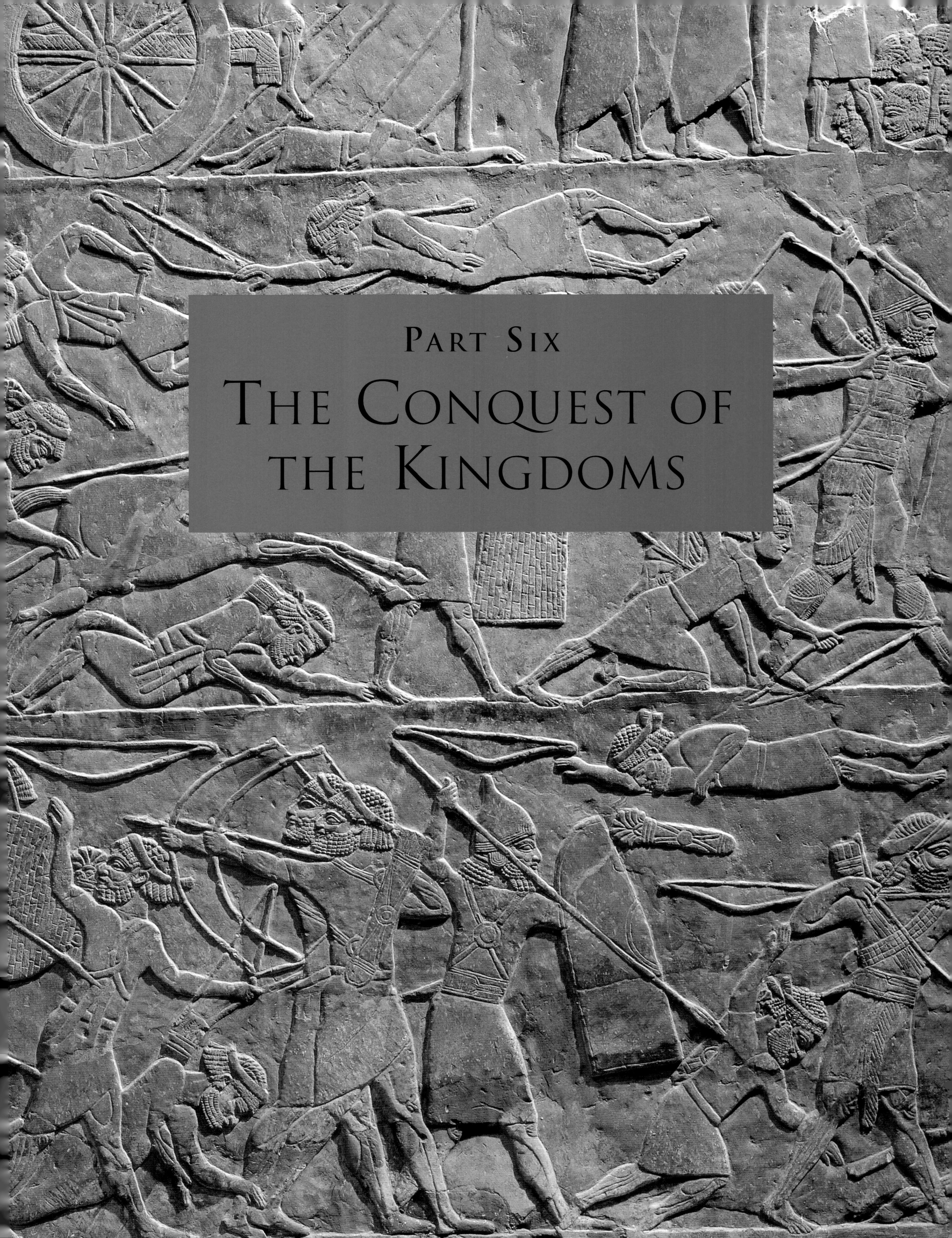

Part Six
The Conquest of the Kingdoms

A PEOPLE BELEAGUERED

IF I FORGET YOU, O JERUSALEM, LET MY RIGHT HAND WITHER! PSALM 137:5

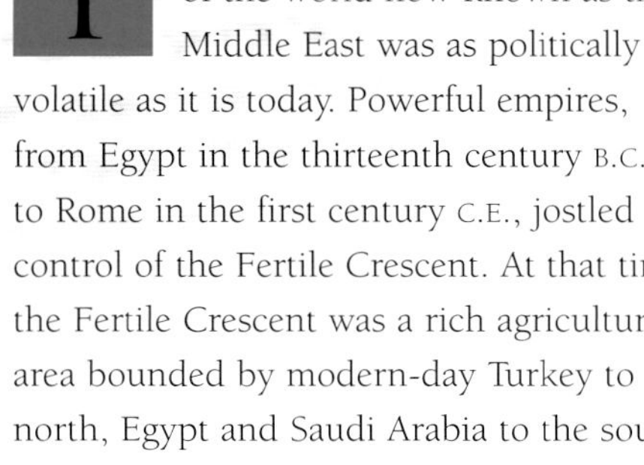

RIGHT: THIS ASSYRIAN IVORY RELIEF OF WINGED GENII IS DATED TO ABOUT 750 B.C.E. AT AROUND THIS TIME, THE ASSYRIANS, THE FIRST OF THE POWER-HUNGRY EMPIRE-BUILDERS, INVADED ISRAEL AND JUDAH.

In Old Testament times, the part of the world now known as the Middle East was as politically volatile as it is today. Powerful empires, from Egypt in the thirteenth century B.C.E. to Rome in the first century C.E., jostled for control of the Fertile Crescent. At that time the Fertile Crescent was a rich agricultural area bounded by modern-day Turkey to the north, Egypt and Saudi Arabia to the south, Iran to the east, and the Mediterranean Sea to the west.

In this political climate the tiny kingdoms of Israel and Judah, lying between the Jordan River and the Mediterranean Sea, became the prey of ambitious empire-builders. Some were cruel and bloodthirsty, others comparatively merciful, but all were charismatic leaders, hungry for power and of undoubted military prowess.

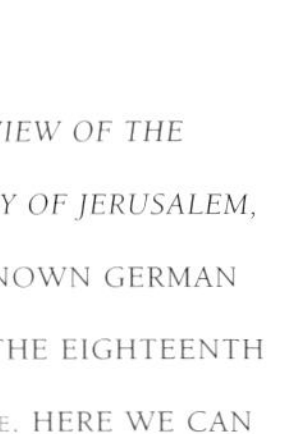

THE FIRST TEMPLE

Early in the tenth century B.C.E., around 250 years after the Israelites had escaped from captivity in Egypt and settled in Canaan, King David captured and fortified Jerusalem—the City of David. Solomon, David's successor, turned his attention to building a Temple to house the Israelites' most precious religious symbol, the Ark of the Covenant, which contained the stone tablets handed down by God to Moses on Mt. Sinai.

Solomon completed the First Temple in about 950 B.C.E.; however, the peace and prosperity that God had promised the Israelites did not eventuate. The first setback was internal strife; the ten northern tribes rebelled from Judah after Solomon's death in 931 B.C.E. and formed the kingdom of Israel. Meanwhile, the Assyrians to the northeast were mustering, and in 722 B.C.E. Shalmaneser V attacked Israel and deported some of its people. In 701 B.C.E. King Sennacherib of Assyria made an assault on Jerusalem and its ruler, Hezekiah, but was driven back by God: "Therefore thus says the Lord concerning the king of Assyria: He shall not come into this city" (2 Kings 19:32).

The Neo-Assyrian Empire collapsed in 609 B.C.E., but the Babylonians to the east were waiting in the wings. In 598 B.C.E. King Nebuchadnezzar II invaded Jerusalem; 12 years later he savagely suppressed a revolt in Judah, seized the Ark of the Covenant, destroyed Solomon's Temple, and drove the inhabitants of Jerusalem into captivity in Babylon. The City of David had become "the abomination that makes desolate" (Daniel 13:31) of which Daniel the prophet had spoken. Henceforth, the Israelites would be known as the Jews—the people of Judea.

BELOW: *A VIEW OF THE WALLED CITY OF JERUSALEM,* BY AN UNKNOWN GERMAN ARTIST OF THE EIGHTEENTH CENTURY C.E. HERE WE CAN SEE SOLOMON'S TEMPLE IN THE FOREGROUND.

LEFT: *BY THE WATERS OF BABYLON*, BY EVELYN DE MORGAN. ALTHOUGH THE EXILES WERE DISTRESSED TO BE AWAY FROM THEIR HOMELAND, THEIR JEWISH IDENTITY WAS STRENGTHENED DURING THEIR TIME IN BABYLON.

STRANGERS IN A STRANGE LAND

The exiled Jews mourned the loss of their native land and vowed to remain faithful to their God and their stronghold. Paradoxically, however, it was the Exile in Babylon that gave definitive shape to the religious and national identity of the Jewish people: their destroyed city and their lost Ark took on an importance that transcended any kind of attachment to the material world and became symbols of the Jews' perception of themselves as the chosen people of the Lord.

Deliverance came in 539 B.C.E., when Cyrus the Great, the founder of the Empire of Persia, conquered Babylon. Cyrus was a benevolent dictator whose policy was to grant religious autonomy to subject nations. Under his rule the Jews were permitted to return to Jerusalem to rebuild their Temple and their city, and to worship the Lord God of Israel without fear of persecution.

THE SECOND TEMPLE

More tribulations lay ahead. In 331 B.C.E., Alexander the Great of Macedonia conquered Babylon, and Judea became part of his huge empire. In the squabbles for supremacy after Alexander's death in 323 B.C.E., Ptolemy I became ruler of Egypt, and the Seleucid dynasty of Antiochus took control of Judea. Antiochus IV savagely suppressed Judaism and defiled the Temple, but Judas Maccabeus, scion of an influential Jewish family, "cleansed the sanctuary and removed the defiled stones to an unclean place" (1 Maccabees 4:43). At last, in 142 B.C.E., Judea became an independent state governed by the Maccabees.

By about 60 B.C.E. the Jews were under Roman domination, and in 37 B.C.E. Marcus Antonius appointed Herod King of Judea. Herod, a ruthless but able ruler who became known as Herod the Great, came from Idumea, south of Judea. One of his projects was the restoration and extension of the Temple of Jerusalem. Herod died in 4 B.C.E., but his Temple remained the focus of the Jewish religion until C.E. 70 when it was destroyed by Titus.

EMPIRES OF THE BIBLICAL WORLD

3000–525 B.C.E.	PHARAOHS AND KINGS
C. 1280–1230 B.C.E.	The Israelites escape from Egypt
C. 1000 B.C.E.	David fortifies Jerusalem
C. 950 B.C.E.	Solomon completes the First Temple
934–609 B.C.E.	THE ASSYRIANS
722 B.C.E.	Shalmaneser V conquers Israel and banishes its ten tribes
701 B.C.E.	Sennacherib attacks Jerusalem but is driven back
626–539 B.C.E.	THE BABYLONIANS
598 B.C.E.	Nebuchadnezzar II invades Jerusalem
586 B.C.E.	Nebuchadnezzar destroys the First Temple and drives the Israelites into exile
559–330 B.C.E.	THE PERSIANS
539 B.C.E.	Cyrus defeats Babylon and repatriates the Jews
515 B.C.E.	The Second Temple is completed
444–397 B.C.E.	Nehemiah and Ezra rebuild Jerusalem and reform Judaism
C. 400–148 B.C.E.	THE MACEDONIANS
332 B.C.E.	Alexander the Great becomes king of Egypt
331 B.C.E.	Alexander conquers Babylon
323 B.C.E.	Alexander dies and his empire is divided
323–30 B.C.E.	THE PTOLEMIES
323 B.C.E.	Ptolemy I succeeds Alexander as ruler of Egypt
204 B.C.E.	Egypt begins to decline under Ptolemy V
164 B.C.E.	Egypt becomes a Roman protectorate under Ptolemy VI
312–63 B.C.E.	THE SELEUCIDS
170 & 168 B.C.E.	Antiochus IV attacks Egypt
167 B.C.E.	Antiochus IV defiles the Temple by constructing a pagan altar there
165 B.C.E.	Judas Maccabeus purifies the Temple
142 B.C.E.	Judea becomes independent under the Maccabees
63 B.C.E.–C.E. 476	THE ROMANS
22 B.C.E.	Herod the Great begins restoration work on the Temple
C.E. 27	Jesus of Nazareth begins his ministry
C.E. 66–70	The Jews revolt against Vespasian and Titus
C.E. 70	Titus destroys Jerusalem and the Temple
C.E. 132–135	The Jews revolt against Hadrian
C.E. 135	Hadrian finishes rebuilding Jerusalem as a Roman city, Aelia Capitolina

THE ASSYRIANS

AH, ASSYRIA, THE ROD OF MY ANGER—THE CLUB IN THEIR HANDS IS MY FURY! ISAIAH 10:5

RIGHT: THIS GERMAN CARD SHOWS FOURTEENTH-CENTURY B.C.E. ASSYRIANS ENJOYING A MEAL. THIS WOULD HAVE BEEN AROUND THE TIME ASSYRIA BECAME AN INDEPENDENT STATE.

During the early first millennium B.C.E. (about 934–609 B.C.E.), Assyria was the largest and most powerful state in southwest Asia, ranging from Persia to Egypt and from Babylonia to Anatolia and the Mediterranean Sea.

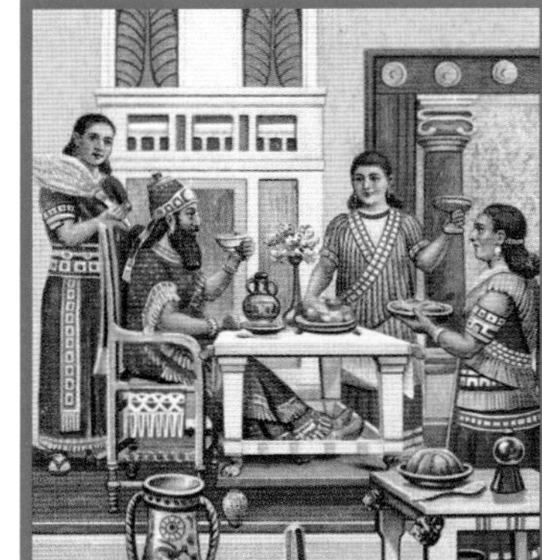

THE RISE OF THE NEO-ASSYRIAN EMPIRE

In its long history, Assyria oscillated between periods of military expansion and relative obscurity. Though the early kings of Assyria (*c.* 1900–1750 B.C.E.) concentrated on mercantile activity, they apparently did not expand militarily, except for Shamshi-adad, who carved out a large state in the Assyrian heartland (*c.* 1814–1782 B.C.E.). Soon thereafter, the Assyrian city-states lapsed into obscurity and were later controlled by the Syrian-based Mitanni Empire (1600–1350 B.C.E.). Assyria became an independent unified state during the reign of Ashuruballit I (*c.* 1363–1328), who established Assyria as one of the major powers of the Near East. Military expansion began with Shalmaneser I (reigned 1273–1244 B.C.E.), who expanded west into Syria. However, Shalmaneser's successor, Tukulti-ninurta I (reigned 1244–1208 B.C.E.) attacked Babylon, a military effort which diverted Assyrian energies and resources from the task of securing other areas, and thus Assyria declined once again. Assyrian military prestige was reasserted by Tiglath-pileser I (reigned 1114–1076 B.C.E.), who campaigned across the Euphrates River to fight against the Semitic-speaking Arameans. Within a century, the Aramean tribes had begun to infiltrate the Assyrian state, forcing the Assyrians into an offensive militarism in order to survive. Once again, however, the Assyrians had overextended themselves and were weakened until the reign of Ashur-dan II (reigned *c.* 934–912 B.C.E.) and Adad-nirari II (reigned *c.* 911–891 B.C.E.), both of whom campaigned extensively against the Arameans, pushing the tribes further west.

ASHURNASIRPAL II

Ashurnasirpal II (reigned 883–859 B.C.E.) is responsible for molding Assyria into one of the dominant powers in the Near East. Though this king's annals are in a poor state of preservation, it is clear that he campaigned continuously during his reign, directing his efforts to the north against the Aramean states of Bit-zamani and Bit-adini (biblical Beth-eden), the Neo-Hittite states located in Anatolia, and the coastal Syrian Phoenician states. Moreover, Ashurnasirpal II established a line of fortresses to protect Assyrian trade routes. He also collected luxury items, exotic goods, and even native troops from the Neo-Hittite state of Carchemish. Ashurnasirpal II used deportees from these campaigns to populate the new Assyrian capital of Calah. He also created a large bureaucracy, and claimed in his annals to have used psychological warfare on his enemies by performing public displays of cruelty, mass executions, and the burning of disloyal vassals.

SHALMANESER III

Though Ashurnasirpal II's successor, Shalmaneser III (reigned 858–824 B.C.E.), inherited a powerful military state, he was beset with internal problems because of the difficulties of keeping together his predecessor's conquests. Thus, he was

BELOW: *ASHURNASIRPAL THANKS THE GODS AFTER A SUCCESSFUL MILITARY CAMPAIGN,* BY AN UNKNOWN ARTIST. ASHURNASIRPAL II CAMPAIGNED RELENTLESSLY FOR MORE THAN A QUARTER OF A CENTURY.

forced to campaign often, and over 30 military ventures are recorded for his reign. A number of these trips were to the west of the Euphrates River, where he first faced a north Syrian coalition that included Ahab of Israel and Hadadezer (also known as Ben-hadad II) of Damascus.

Shalmaneser III also fought against Urartu (biblical Ararat) on Assyria's northern frontier, and intervened in Babylonian politics on several crucial occasions. He conducted (or completed) many building projects at the Assyrian capital, Calah, including the ziggurat, the temples of Ninurta and Nabu, and a fortress. Shalmaneser III restored the temples of Asshur and Anu-adad at the ancient Assyrian center of Asshur.

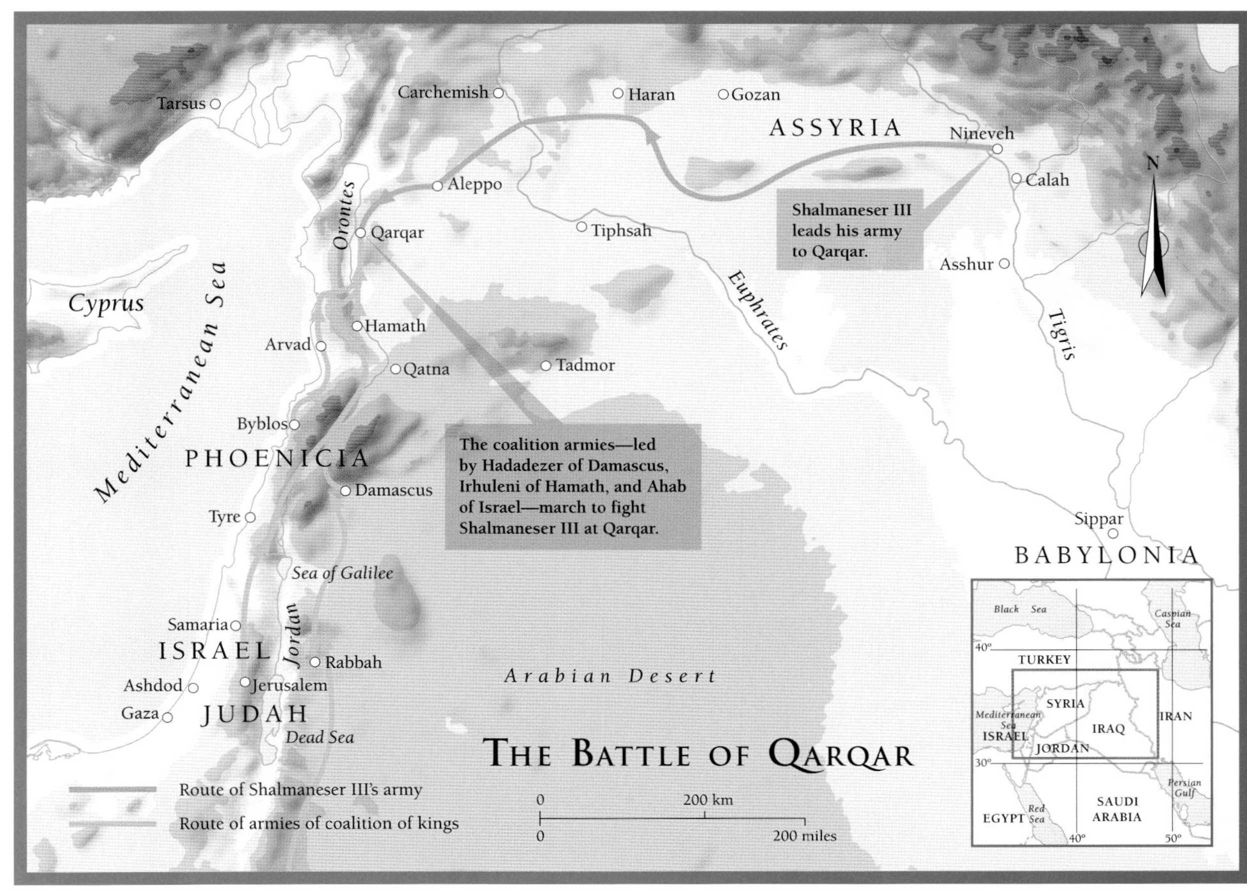

THE BATTLE OF QARQAR

Shalmaneser III's most notorious campaign in the west was against a large coalition led by Hadadezer of Damascus, Irhuleni of Hamath, and Ahab of Israel. According to Shalmaneser III's annals, the armies met at Qarqar (modern Tell Qarqur) in the Orontes River valley during the Assyrian king's sixth regnal year (853–852 B.C.E.). The Assyrians claimed a victory, boasting that 25,000 people were killed. However, the Assyrians did not capitalize on the "victory," as they did not move any further west. In fact, they were forced to face the same coalition on at least three more occasions. In the end, the north Syrian coalition weakened by 841 B.C.E., and the Assyrians were successful in receiving tribute from the individual states. The reception of tribute is portrayed on some of the 20 panels of the Black Obelisk of Shalmaneser III. Even Jehu of Israel is among those shown bringing gifts and bowing down to the Assyrian monarch.

ASSYRIA'S SHORT DECLINE

Late in the reign of Shalmaneser III, campaigns were led, not only by the king, but also by the Turtanu (biblical Tartan), a high official. In fact, several powerful provincial governments emerged and their leaders acted as virtual monarchs in their own districts, although professing allegiance to the Assyrian crown. The concentration of wealth and power in the hands of a few dignitaries weakened the monarchy, eventually leading to an insurrection. Externally, the kingdom displayed the usual trappings of success, but the authority of the monarchy had been eroded. Some nobles actually left their own records of campaigns and deeds. This insurrection continued into the reign of Shalmaneser III's successor, Shamshi-adad V (reigned 823–811 B.C.E.). This Assyrian monarch faced a succession struggle that lasted for four years, and except for some campaigning in the south against Babylon, Assyria was militarily weak.

Though he inherited a state weakened by civil war in the previous generation, Adad-nirari III (reigned 810–783 B.C.E.) had some success in Babylonia subjugating the Chaldean tribes. Moreover, he campaigned in Syria and claimed in his annals to have split a coalition centered at Damascus, which he successfully captured. Among the vassal kings listed is Joash of Israel. Adad-nirari III may have been the "savior" of Israel mentioned in 2 Kings 13:5. After this king's death, however, the Assyrians were once again weak for about 40 years.

THE ASSYRIANS RISE AGAIN

Assyria was able to reassert itself once again during the reign of Tiglath-pileser III (reigned 744–727 B.C.E.), who prepared the way for the Assyrian world state that lasted for over a century. This Assyrian king enacted major changes in Assyria by doubling the size of the army, putting the provincial administration under the direct control of the monarchy, and continuing the policy of deporting conquered peoples to other regions of the empire. He also created a rapid communication and intelligence system which was inherited by the Persian Empire. The Assyrian king-list claims this Assyrian king was the son of Ashur-nirari V,

LEFT: *THE BLACK OBELISK OF SHALMANESER III*, UNATTRIBUTED NINETEENTH-CENTURY C.E. ENGRAVING. THE OBELISK SHOWS (AMONG OTHER THINGS) THE KING COLLECTING TRIBUTE FROM HIS VASSAL STATES.

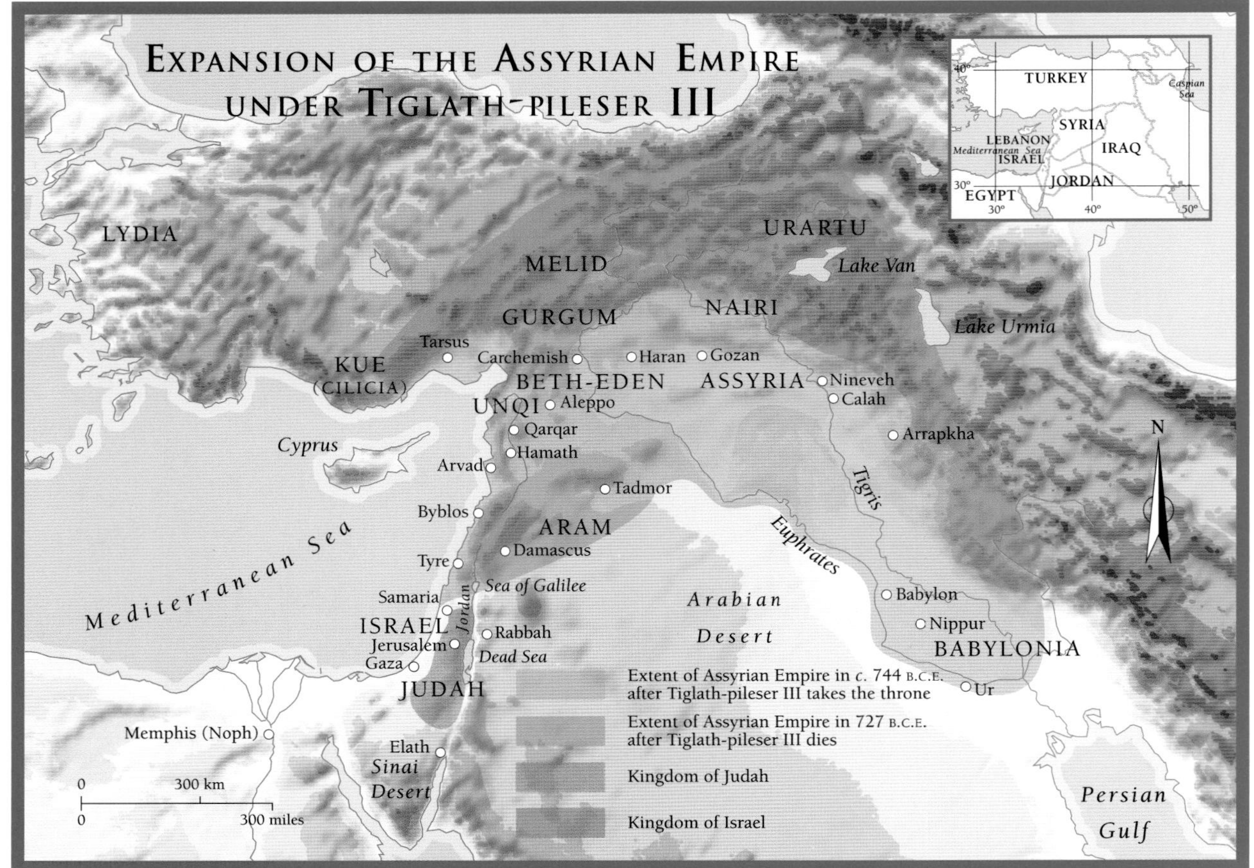

him tribute (including the cities of Damascus, Tyre, and Byblos). He moved west in 738 B.C.E. against a Syrian coalition headed by a certain Azriyau, who might possibly have been Uzziah (or Azariah) of Judah (see 2 Kings 15:1). Tiglath-pileser III took the coastal Philistine city of Gaza in 734 B.C.E., and two years later he conquered Damascus and its king, Rezin, and turned the region into a province.

On at least two occasions Tiglath-pileser III invaded northern Israel, and both Israelite and Judahite kings are listed in Assyrian sources as paying tribute to Assyria in this period. Both Menahem and Pekah of Israel are mentioned in the Assyrian annals of Tiglath-pileser III as paying a large amount of tribute to the Assyrians. The enormous sum of 1,000 talents paid by Menahem to the Assyrian king is proportionate to what was extracted from other Levantine monarchs, according to the Assyrian annals. Ahaz of Judah also paid a large tribute to the Assyrians, and even visited the Assyrian monarch at Damascus, the newly conquered city. The fact that Ahaz copied an altar should be considered a desire of the Judahite king to imitate the Damascus altar, probably for artistic purposes. There is no evidence that the Assyrians forced vassals to adopt Assyrian religious practices: "When King Ahaz went to Damascus to meet King Tiglath-pileser of Assyria, he saw the altar that was at Damascus. King Ahaz sent to the priest Uriah a model of the altar, and its pattern, exact in all its details" (2 Kings 16:10).

but Tiglath-pileser III was likely a usurper who came to the throne during a period of decline and unrest in the Assyrian state. He was able to drive out the Urartians (a powerful state from roughly the region of present-day Armenia) from northern Mesopotamia and invaded Urartu itself. There he faced the king of Urartu, Sarduri II, who was allied with Mati-ilu, the king of Arpad. After a long siege, Tiglath-pileser III took coastal Arpad in 740 B.C.E.

This Assyrian king also was very involved in Babylonian political problems and took the Babylonian throne himself (apparently using the throne name of Pulu, or Pul; see also 2 Kings 15:19), although there was continued resistance during his reign. For centuries it was assumed that Pul and Tiglath-pileser III of Assyria were separate kings, as implied by the account in 2 Kings. It is now known that "Pul" is a diminutive form of Tiglath-pileser (Akkadian, Tukulti-apil-esharra), presumably from the middle portion of the name from where it may have been associated in folk etymology. Pul, or Pulu (in the Akkadian from Assyria) is a well-known Assyrian name, meaning "limestone (or block of limestone)." Of course, it is not clear why the biblical source used both names; the authors may have been unaware of the connection or assumed that the connection was to be understood by the reader: "King Pul of Assyria came against the land; Menahem gave Pul a thousand talents of silver, so that he might help him confirm his hold on the royal power" (2 Kings 15:19); "In the days of King Pekah of Israel, King Tiglath-pileser of Assyria came and captured Ijon, Abel-beth-maacah, Janoah, Kedesh, Hazor, Gilead, and Galilee, all the land of Naphtali; and he carried the people captive to Assyria" (2 Kings 15:29).

In addition to his other conquests, Tiglath-pileser III also encroached upon the territories of Syro–Palestine and caused many Aramean, Neo-Hittite, and Phoenician states to pay

RIGHT: ANCIENT ASSYRIAN WARRIORS ARE DEPICTED WITH THEIR WEAPONRY AND WEARING PROTECTIVE CLOTHING, IN AN ENGRAVING FROM THE GERMAN BOOK *ZUR GESCHICHTE DER COSTUME.*

Information concerning Tiglath-pileser III's reign comes from his annals, which comprised 17 regnal years. Though the texts were inscribed on stone slabs in the palace at Calah (Nimrud), the palace was never completed and Esarhaddon dismantled them and reused some of the slabs in his southwest palace. Moreover, many of the slabs were lost, damaged, or destroyed in antiquity or even in the nineteenth century C.E. excavations of Nimrud. Thus, it has been difficult, not only to reconstruct the texts themselves, but also their chronological order. Similar to other Assyrian kings, most of the annals concern the king's military campaigns, although there is some mention of his building exploits, such as his palace at Nimrud.

ABOVE: ONE OF MANY RELIEFS FOUND AT THE ASSYRIAN PALACE AT NIMRUD. THIS DETAIL SHOWS ASSYRIAN ARCHERS AIMING AT A FORTRESS, WITH A BATTERING RAM IN THE BACKGROUND.

THE ASSYRIAN ARMY

The Assyrian army comprised mainly conscripted native agricultural workers, hillsmen, and seminomads. Foreigners were used early on as royal bodyguards, and by the time of Sargon II were employed in infantry units. The king often went into the field to lead the army, but a military commander is often mentioned in the annals. It is estimated that the Assyrians were able to field an army of over 100,000 men. Furthermore, there appears to have been a quite sophisticated military chain of command, as large units marched under standards that bore different divine emblems, and there are military names for commanders of 1,000, 100, and even 50 men.

The military strength of the army was in part because of its chariotry, which had been invented in the Near East early in the second millennium B.C.E. By the ninth century B.C.E., the Assyrians used a light wooden-framed vehicle with a rear-wheel axis, allowing for more maneuverability. It contained three riders: an archer/lancer, a driver, and a shield bearer. The chariots were used in the center of attack as shock troops. Although stirrups were not yet invented, horses were used for both chariots and horsemen who rode bareback. Since horses were not in good supply in northern Iraq, the Assyrians often raided the Iranian plateau to replenish their stock. The bow was used in all aspects of Assyrian warfare and was effective over 820–2,130 ft (250–650 m). By the time of Tiglath-pileser III, infantry, chariotry lancers, and slingers formed a large part of the army. Defensive clothing included individual armor, which were small metal links sewn on leather. The army was fed on the march with "travel rations" or at provincial centers that supplied food; in hostile territory, the soldiers were trained to live off the land. Communication between units was by messengers and runners.

SHALMANESER V

Little is known of Shalmaneser V (reigned 726–722 B.C.E.) other than the fact that he ruled for a short period and that the Bible and the Babylonian Chronicle give him credit for carrying out the siege of Samaria. Like his father, Tiglath-pileser III, he also was the king of Babylon, although later period sources imply that there were problems with Assyrian rule in this southern kingdom. Perhaps his reign ended because of his imposition of taxes on exempt cities in the Assyrian heartland, causing a rebellion.

Assyrian Siege Techniques

Special siege techniques, which were developed in the mid-second millennium B.C.E., were often employed by the Assyrians. A ramp of piled up earth was used to gain access to the upper walls of an enemy city or fortress. A battering ram was then used to smash down gateways. However, the Assyrians acknowledged that many of their sieges were very long; Israelite Samaria took nearly three years to conquer.

RIGHT: AFTER A SUCCESSFUL CAMPAIGN, SHALMANESER V LEADS AWAY MANY CAPTIVES. THIS PAINTING DEPICTS THE BIBLICAL VERSION OF THE SIEGE OF SAMARIA, WHICH GIVES SHALMANESER V RATHER THAN SARGON II CREDIT FOR THE ATTACK.

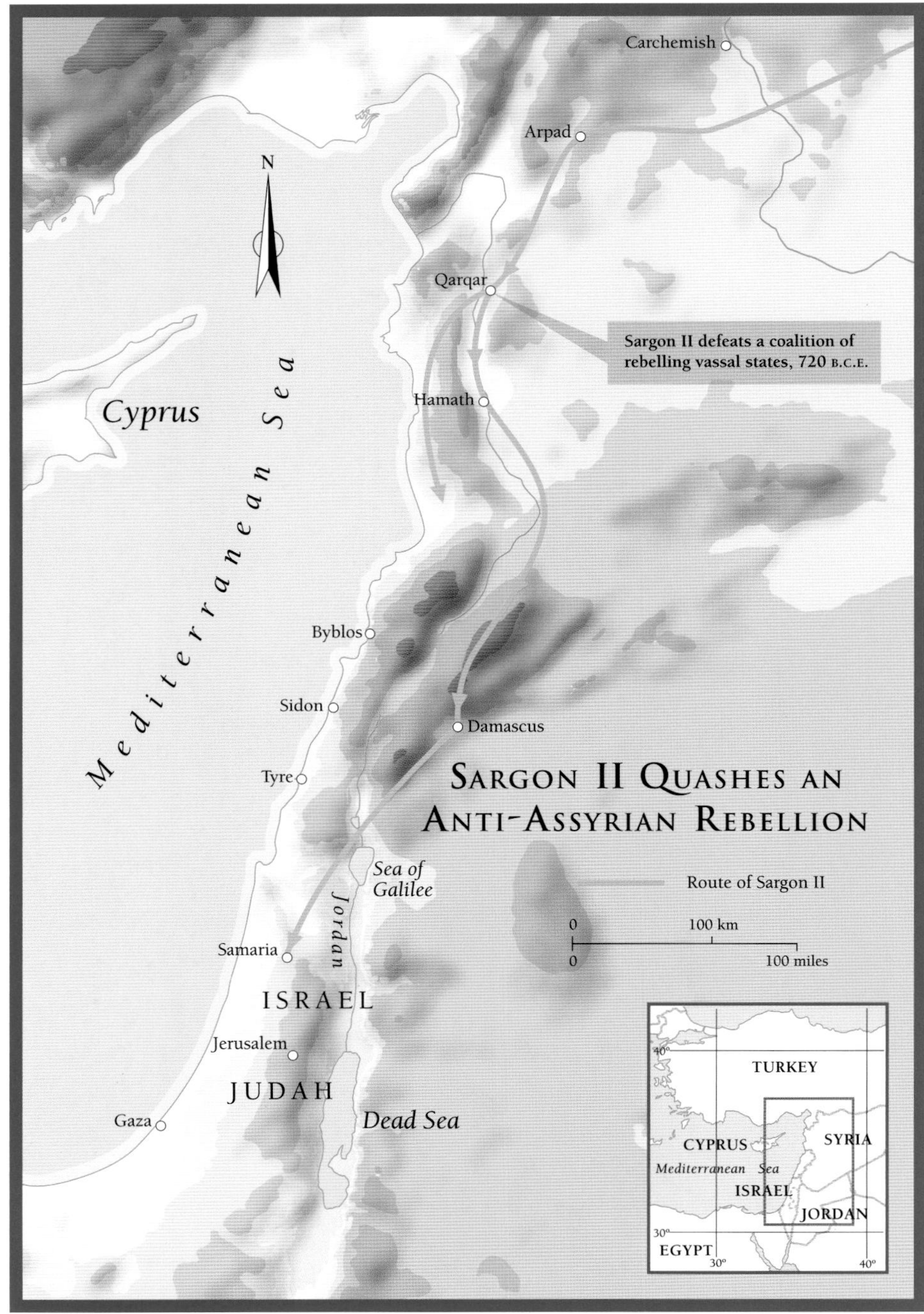

SARGON II

Sargon II (reigned 721–705 B.C.E.) took the throne of Assyria when his predecessor (and likely half-brother) Shalmaneser V was killed. He was apparently a usurper, a fact probably shown by his throne name, Sargon (Akkadian, Sharru-kin, "true king"). He also left an account of his own accession to the throne, justifying the removal (or possibly, murder) of Shalmaneser V. At any rate, Sargon II's accession was no doubt a violent one, and it took him about one year to quell opposition in Assyria and solidify his position as king. Although it appears that he was a son of Tiglath-pileser III, Sargon did not take advantage of this relationship; however, he did include his patrimony in his inscriptions, a typical practice of Assyrian kings.

Because of the violent death of Shalmaneser V, vassal states in Syro–Palestine rebelled against Assyria. Sargon II quickly met a coalition (which included the cities of Damascus, Hamath, Samaria, and Arpad) at Qarqar in 720 B.C.E., which he defeated. He subsequently marched through Palestine and claimed to have defeated an Egyptian army near the Egyptian border. In the wake of this campaign, Sargon II deposed numerous rulers and deported large numbers of the local populations from this area. He is mentioned only once in the Old Testament (Isaiah 20:1), although it is clear that he played a major role in Israelite affairs. He subsequently deported large numbers of important Israelite families to other parts of the empire.

Sargon II also campaigned in eastern Anatolia against Mita (the Classical Midas) of Phrygia and against Urartu, successfully weakening both of these states and creating a peaceful frontier. Like his predecessors, Sargon II continued to have problems with Assyria's southern neighbor, Babylon. The Chaldean, Merodach-baladan II (mentioned in the Bible in three places—2 Kings 20:12, Isaiah 39:1, and 2 Chronicles 32:31—as either Merodach-baladan or Berodach-baladan), seized the Babylonian throne during the succession problem in Assyria in 721 B.C.E. and held it until Sargon II deposed him in 710 B.C.E. Like his predecessor Tiglath-pileser III, Sargon II took the title of king of Babylon, although Merodach-baladan II was able to flee to Elam in the east.

In spite of numerous military campaigns during his reign, Sargon II managed to find the time to build a new capital, Dur-sharrukin, near Nineveh, and repopulated it with many of the deported peoples. Sargon II died in battle in 705 B.C.E. while campaigning in the north. Since the death of the king in battle was considered an evil omen, Sargon II's successor, Sennacherib, was forced to endure a major revolt throughout the whole of the empire.

THE FALL OF SAMARIA

The biblical account of the fall of Samaria is a theological reflection of the incident written by a Judahite source well over a century after the fact. Unlike the annals of Sargon II, where the Assyrian king claims the conquest of Samaria and the deportation of a significant number of its inhabitants, the biblical source attributes the feat to Sargon II's predecessor, Shalmaneser V, whose annals are in very poor condition. Sargon II also claims to have rebuilt the city of Samaria. It is likely that the siege began during the reign of Shalmaneser V,

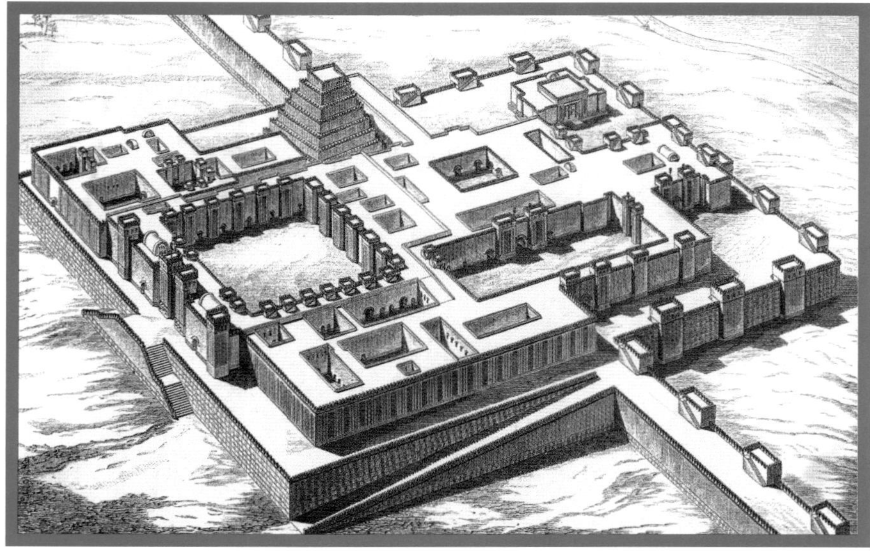

LEFT: A NINETEENTH-CENTURY C.E. RECONSTRUCTION BY PERROT OF DUR-SHARRUKIN (MODERN-DAY KHORSABAD, IRAQ). THE WALLS WERE SAID TO BE 16,280 ASSYRIAN UNITS LONG, WHICH CORRESPONDED TO THE NUMERICAL VALUE OF SARGON II'S NAME.

who died during the three-year military operation. His successor, Sargon II, took credit for the entire siege. He also claims to have rebuilt the city and reorganized the territory in surrounding regions: "King Shalmaneser of Assyria came up against him; Hoshea became his vassal, and paid him tribute.... Then the king of Assyria invaded all the land and came to Samaria; for three years he besieged it. In the ninth year of Hoshea, the king of Assyria captured Samaria; he carried the Israelites away to Assyria" (2 Kings 17:3–6).

THE ASSYRIANS SETTLE IN ISRAEL

Assyrian deportation policies are well known from the Neo-Assyrian annals. Sargon II claims to have repopulated Samaria with other deportees, although Tiglath-pileser III appears not to have repopulated the area of Galilee after his conquest of 733 B.C.E. The places Israelites were taken to, as noted in 2 Kings 17:6, are Assyrian territories in northern inland Syria, along the Habor River. The deportation policy was intended to remove the possibility of future rebellion by means of confusing the ethnic identity of the inhabitants of the land through the mixing of different groups. Assyrian inscriptions state that Sargon II imposed taxes on the new settlers as if they were Assyrians. According to 2 Kings 17:25–29, the Assyrians themselves encouraged the new settlers in Israel to learn the local customs and worship the God of Israel: "The king of Assyria brought people from Babylon, Cuthah, Avva, Hamath, and Sepharvaim, and placed them in the cities of Samaria in place of the people of Israel; they took possession of Samaria and settled in its cities" (2 Kings 17:24).

BELOW: *SAMARIA UNDER SIEGE*, FROM A MEDIEVAL COPY OF THE LUTHER BIBLE. VARIOUS TEXTS TELL DIFFERENT VERSIONS OF HOW SAMARIA WAS BESIEGED.

RIGHT: MERODACH-BALADAN II (THE DRAGON) FIGHTING A FEATHER-ROBED ARCHER (THE ENEMY, ASSYRIA), ILLUSTRATION OF PART OF A RELIEF FOUND AT NIMRUD IN MODERN-DAY IRAQ.

ASSYRIAN EXILES AND DEPORTATIONS

When Sargon II claimed to have deported 27,290 people from Samaria, Assyrian deportation policies were already notorious, as they had been in effect since the Middle Assyrian period and Tiglath-pileser I (reigned 1114–1076 B.C.E.). Sargon II also claimed to have taken enough deportees to make a military regiment of 50 chariots. One cannot be certain from the Assyrian annals whether the number of deportees was only referring to males. Moreover, it is not certain whether deportees from towns other than Samaria were counted. A generation later, Sennacherib claimed to have taken over 200,000 prisoners from Judah, dwarfing the number listed in his father's annals. As stated before, the Assyrians also relocated peoples into conquered lands. Thus, Samaria was repopulated with foreigners. The Assyrian policy in general was probably intended to discourage groups from engaging in further rebellion, as the group's ethnic identity had been merged and therefore confused with other groups.

SENNACHERIB

Sennacherib, who reigned from 704–681 B.C.E., succeeded his father Sargon II (who died in battle) as king of Assyria. The most serious issue Sennacherib confronted during his reign was the unstable situation with Assyria's neighbor to the south, Babylon, which had been a tributary to Assyria for the past half-century. The Chaldean chieftain of Babylon, Merodach-baladan II, rebelled against Assyria at Sennacherib's accession and enlisted Hezekiah of Judah's support, which he received, according to 2 Kings 20. However, the revolt culminated in Babylon's utter destruction by the Assyrians in 689 B.C.E.

Sennacherib conducted many urban renewal projects in Nineveh, including a new palace complex, parks, irrigation projects, and massive fortifications. The Assyrian king was murdered by two of his sons in 681 B.C.E. and was succeeded by another son, Esarhaddon.

Merodach-baladan II's rebellion was part of a larger insurrection that Sennacherib was confronted with at the outset of his reign. Apparently it was led by Hezekiah of Judah and other Syro–Palestinian vassals of Assyria. This rebellion is known from Assyrian and biblical sources (2 Kings 18–19, 2 Chronicles 32, and various portions of Isaiah): "In the fourteenth year of King Hezekiah, King Sennacherib of Assyria came up against all the fortified cities of Judah and captured them. King Hezekiah of Judah sent to the king of Assyria at Lachish, saying, 'I have done wrong; withdraw from me; whatever you impose on me I will bear.'" (2 Kings 18:13–14).

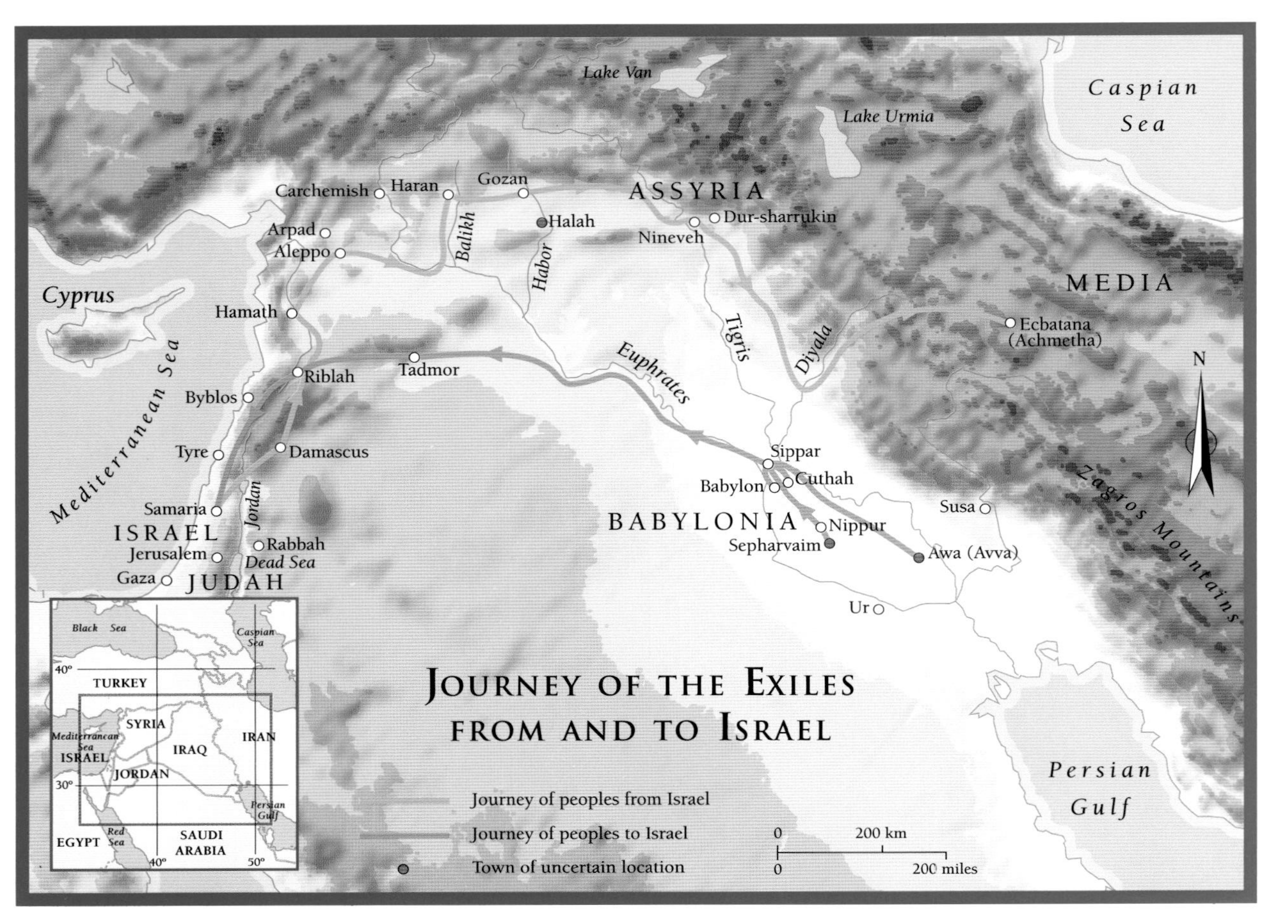

THE ASSYRIAN THREAT TO JUDAH

Sennacherib invaded Judah in 701 B.C.E., claiming to have "caged Hezekiah in Jerusalem like a bird." There is archaeological evidence of massive destruction by the Assyrians in Judah, especially at the Judahite fortress city of Lachish, where an Assyrian siege ramp has been uncovered. The speech of the Assyrian Rabshakeh (the cupbearer for the Assyrian king) at one of the Jerusalem gates was recounted in 2 Kings 18:17–37.

His associates, the Tartan and Rabsaris, were both more military in nature, while the Rabshakeh was primarily domestic and normally did not take part in military campaigns. The Rabshakeh spoke at the gates, likely because of his knowledge of Judahite or because he was the herald. The Rabshakeh's speech was more likely based not on biblical parallels, but rather on the Assyrian annals. There is a parallel account of such a custom in the Nimrud letters found in the excavations in the 1950s. These are letters of the Assyrian royal archive of Tiglath-pileser III concerning the Chaldean tribe of the Bit-amukanni, whom the Assyrians hoped to enlist in order to cause problems for the tribe's overlord, Ukinzer the Chaldean. Some of the letters (dated to 731 B.C.E.) described an Assyrian representative taking a stand at the city gate and "disputing with the man of Babylon." The representative employed reason and diplomacy and is said to have used "many arguments with them." The Assyrians offered tax exemptions to any in the tribe who would desert to the Assyrian camp, but they were unable to gain admission into the city, and ultimately could not persuade them to revolt. Apparently, the Assyrians had no interest in a long, drawn-out siege of Babylon, and used propaganda as an alternative. The Assyrian officer evidently had great freedom to achieve his goal, and was not merely a messenger. He sought to divide the loyalties by offering exemptions. He also stated that the Chaldeans were guilty of breaking treaty obligations, something that was also claimed of Hezekiah. The archives of Esarhaddon also exhibit this situation. There are 15 letters to various population groups (not just foreign rulers) that are similar to the Nimrud letters. There had apparently been a change in the function of the imperial messenger. It was no longer sufficient to have a note read to the king and court; the entire population was to be made aware of the situation.

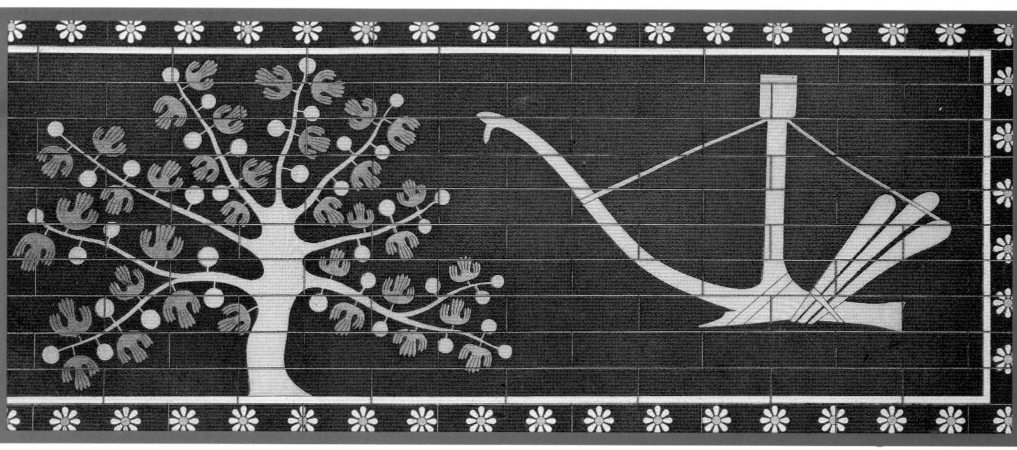

ABOVE: THESE BRILLIANTLY COLORED ENAMEL TILES ARE COPIES OF THOSE FOUND AT THE PALACE OF NINEVEH. FROM THE 1840S ONWARD, BRITISH AND FRENCH ARCHAEOLOGISTS DUG THE SITES OF THE RUINED ASSYRIAN PALACES AT NINEVEH AND NIMRUD.

LEFT: THIS UNATTRIBUTED ENGRAVING FROM AROUND 1850 RECONSTRUCTS THE ELABORATE STAIRCASE LEADING OUT OF THE KING'S PALACE AT NINEVEH, WHICH MAY HAVE BELONGED TO EITHER SENNACHERIB OR ASHURBANIPAL.

ABOVE: *GOD'S VENGEANCE ON ASSYRIA*, A COLORED LITHOGRAPH IN A COPY OF THE NUREMBERG BIBLE. ACCORDING TO 2 KINGS 19:35, AN ANGEL OF THE LORD KILLED 185,000 ASSYRIANS AT NIGHT.

There is also evidence in a Sargon II relief of an Assyrian reading a scroll in the middle of a battle scene. The language used by the Rabshakeh has numerous Neo-Assyrian parallels. There are some references that are similar to biblical passages, for example, the title of the Assyrian king (2 Kings 18:18)—"the great king"—although not exactly attested, has been found with many combinations in Assyrian sources.

RIGHT: EIGHTH-CENTURY B.C.E. FRAGMENT OF ENAMELED TERRACOTTA, DEPICTING TWO MEN WALKING, FOUND AT THE SITE OF THE ANCIENT ASSYRIAN CAPITAL NINEVEH.

THE SIEGE OF JERUSALEM

The Assyrians may have been diverted from capturing Jerusalem by an Egyptian army led by Taharqa. Therefore, Sennacherib demanded harsh terms from Judah, and thus all fortified cities and outlying areas (including some cities in Philistia and Phoenicia) were seized, Hezekiah's treasury was emptied, and some of his daughters were sent as concubines to Nineveh, Sennacherib's capital. However, the biblical writers claimed that the Assyrian army was destroyed by divine intervention: "That very night the angel of the Lord set out and struck down one hundred eighty-five thousand in the camp of the Assyrians; when morning dawned, they were all dead bodies. Then King Sennacherib of Assyria left, went home, and lived at Nineveh" (2 Kings 19:35–36).

ESARHADDON

Esarhaddon (reigned 680–669 B.C.E.) became king of Assyria after the murder of his father Sennacherib (see 2 Kings 19:37). He was immediately confronted with a rebellion which he quelled after six weeks. After restoring Babylon, which his father had destroyed, Esarhaddon turned his attention to the affairs in the west in Syro–Palestine and Egypt. Continuing Sennacherib's policies, he collected heavy tribute from vassal kings in Syro–Palestine, including the rulers of Edom, Moab, Ammon, Tyre, and Sidon, as well as King Manasseh of Judah. Since Egypt was still a threat to Assyrian control of the Levantine coast, Esarhaddon, after a brief failure, became the first Assyrian king to enter and conquer Egypt (671 B.C.E.). Esarhaddon's annals give a detailed description of the capture and looting of Memphis, Egypt's primary city. As soon as the Assyrian king left, the Egyptians under Taharqa revolted, thereby precipitating another campaign by Esarhaddon, who died, however, before he was able to return.

Although not mentioned in the Assyrian annals, there is evidence that Esarhaddon sent deportees into Judah. Ezra 4:2 states during the Achaemenid Period (mid-fifth century B.C.E.) that the enemies of Judah asked to help the exiles in rebuilding the Temple, since they had been sacrificing to God "since the days of King Esarhaddon of Assyria, who had brought us here." It seems probable that this deportation may have come about because of Sennacherib's major campaign in the west (*c.* 701 B.C.E.) and continued during the reign of Esarhaddon.

KING MANASSEH BOWS TO ASSYRIA

Manasseh succeeded Hezekiah as king of Judah and reigned for about 55 years (*c.* 697–642 B.C.E.), the first ten years as co-regent with Hezekiah. According to Assyrian sources, Manasseh was listed as a loyal vassal to Assyria in the reigns of Esarhaddon and Ashurbanipal. According to 2 Chronicles 33, Manasseh was sent by the Assyrians to Babylon in chains. Perhaps this was during the reign of Esarhaddon, who required his vassals to send building materials to Assyria and Babylonia, and to also sign a treaty ensuring the orderly succession of his son Ashurbanipal to the throne.

ASHURBANIPAL

Esarhaddon died in 669 B.C.E. en route to Egypt, and his younger son, Ashurbanipal (reigned 668–627 B.C.E.), became king. The Egyptian monarch, Taharqa, quickly attacked the Assyrian garrison in Memphis. However, Ashurbanipal was able to recapture the fortress. By 663 B.C.E., Ashurbanipal was successful in capturing the Upper Egypt capital of Thebes, thereby expanding the Assyrian Empire to its greatest extent. But Ashurbanipal's successes in Egypt were short lived, and the Assyrian military presence was removed only a few years later in 655 B.C.E.

Although the Assyrians had a relatively quiet northern border during Ashurbanipal's reign, the southern border with Elam (southwestern Iran) and Babylonia was another story. Ashurbanipal attempted to place a pro-Assyrian on the throne of Elam. Although he attacked and destroyed the Elamite capital of Susa, it was a costly victory, limiting the Assyrian resources and thus contributing to Assyria's downfall.

CULTURAL PRESERVATION PROJECTS

There was another side to Ashurbanipal. The Assyrians, like their Babylonian counterparts to the south, took an active role in preserving Mesopotamian civilization by the creation of massive libraries that housed many traditional and canonical texts, some of which had been composed over 1,000

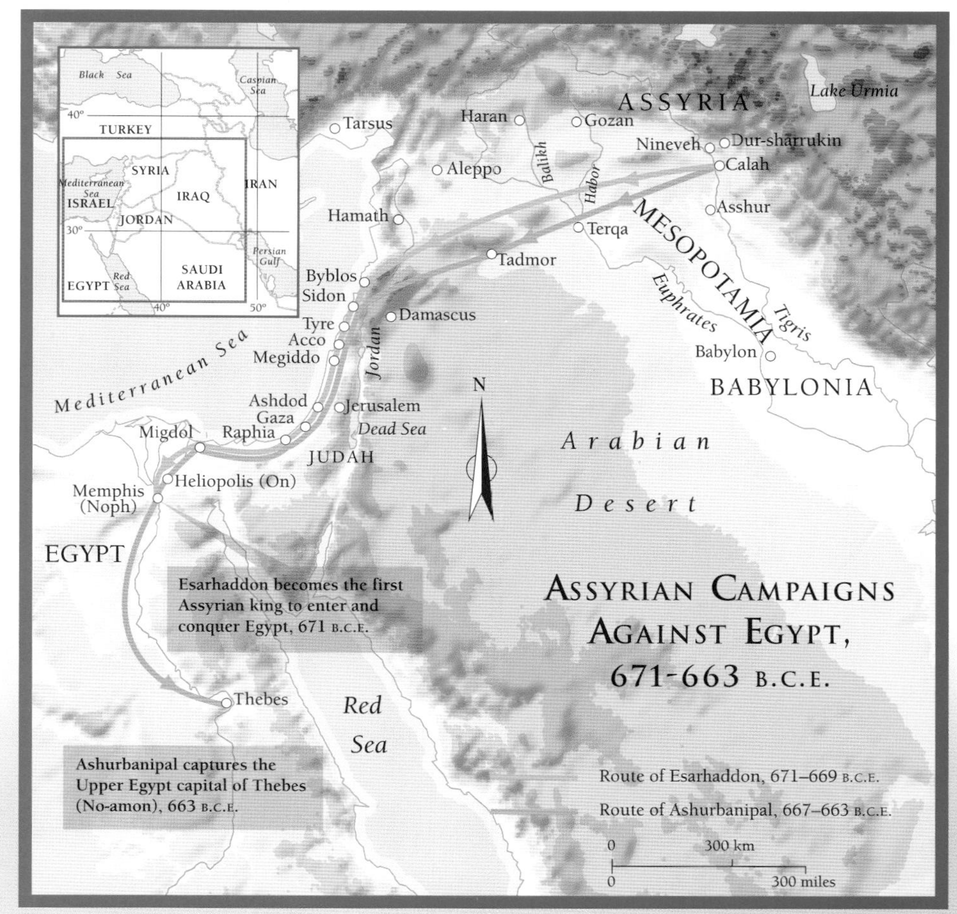

BELOW: AN AERIAL PHOTOGRAPH OF SUSA IN MODERN-DAY IRAN. ONCE THE CAPITAL OF THE ELAMITE KINGDOM, SUSA WAS DESTROYED BY THE ASSYRIANS UNDER ASHURBANIPAL IN AROUND 646 B.C.E.

ABOVE: *THE PALACES OF NIMRUD RESTORED, FROM DISCOVERIES IN THE RUINS OF NINEVEH AND BABYLON* BY AUSTEN HENRY LAYARD, 1853. ASHURBANIPAL BUILT HIS IMPRESSIVE PALACES ON THE BANKS OF THE TIGRIS RIVER.

years earlier. Tukulti-ninurta I (reigned 1244–1208 B.C.E.) actually plundered tablets in Babylon when he sacked that city, and took the documents back to Assyria where they were placed in libraries. Like his predecessor six centuries earlier, Ashurbanipal helped create a magnificent library at Nineveh. In fact, over 80,000 tablets and fragments were discovered by the British excavators of Nineveh in the mid-nineteenth century C.E. Ashurbanipal also claimed to have had a scribal education and stated that he was literate, a rarity among monarchs, as only a handful in all of Mesopotamian history had this training. He took a special interest in the collection of tablets, making certain that texts came from a great variety of disciplines (including magic, omens, literature, religious texts, astrological texts, and even medical texts). Ashurbanipal also engaged in several building projects at Nineveh.

This Assyrian king also restored a number of temples at Babylon, which had been destroyed by his grandfather, Sennacherib, in 689 B.C.E. Of course, this happened before Ashurbanipal's destruction of the city in 648 B.C.E. Moreover, many of the sculptured reliefs discovered at Nineveh were from his reign. Many depict the king in a military context: that is, leading the army, or going on a hunt. However, Ashurbanipal was quick to show himself in a relaxed, cultural context. In fact in one scene, the king dines with his queen in a beautiful garden, while the severed head of Teuman, a rebel Elamite king, hangs from a tree behind the queen (no doubt so she would not have her meal spoiled!).

RIGHT: THE ASSYRIAN KING ASHURBANIPAL, ONE OF THE MANY MAGNIFICENT STONE SCULPTURES UNEARTHED AT THE SITE OF NIMRUD (FORMERLY CALAH).

THE ASSYRIAN EMPIRE IS THREATENED

The most serious problem Ashurbanipal had to face was in the south, in Babylonia. Esarhaddon had established Ashurbanipal's brother, Shamash-shuma-ukin, as king of Babylon, albeit subordinate to the Assyrian monarch. Although the Assyrian records document good relations between the two brothers, Shamash-shuma-ukin rebelled against Ashurbanipal in 652 B.C.E., encouraging many other subject states to rebel as well. The civil war lasted for more than four years, and Babylon was sacked and burned, resulting in the end of Shamash-shuma-ukin's reign. This was the second destruction of Babylon in 40 years, as Sennacherib had destroyed the city in 689 B.C.E.

Though the Assyrians were successful in quelling the rebellion, the stress of a long civil war began to take its toll on the empire. The sources are not clear as to what happened in the next years. There are no royal records after 641 B.C.E., and no economic texts were generated from the capital city of Nineveh after 631 B.C.E. It is unclear when Ashurbanipal died, but it must have been between 631 and 627 B.C.E. By 626 B.C.E., Nabopolassar, a Chaldean, had declared his independence from Assyria and was crowned king in Babylon. And to make matters worse, there was a succession crisis in Assyria following Ashurbanipal's death that lasted for at least three years. The penultimate Assyrian king, Sinsharishkun (reigned 623–612 B.C.E.), had to endure a Babylonian invasion in 616 B.C.E., and a combined Medo-Chaldean invasion just two years later, culminating in the destruction of the ancient capital of Asshur in 614 B.C.E. and the present capital of Nineveh in 612 B.C.E. The last Assyrian king, Ashuruballit II, fled and held camp in the northwest in Haran, only to lose that stronghold in 609 B.C.E., thereby ending the Assyrian Empire.

THE FALL OF NINEVEH

The Babylonian Chronicle claims that the Median siege of Nineveh lasted less than three months. Nahum, listed among the Minor Prophets in the Old Testament, was a seventh-century B.C.E. prophet from Judah, who composed a brief three-chapter work on the subject of the fall of Nineveh. Scholars have been divided as to whether the source wrote after the event itself, or whether or not Nahum was proclaiming the inevitable end of the Assyrian Empire. The mention of Thebes in Nahum 3:8 provides the earliest date for the Nahum source, as this Egyptian city fell to the Assyrians in 663 B.C.E. Nahum writes as if he were present for the destruction, probably for dramatic effect.

Similarly to the Classical writer Diodorus (who employed Ktesias as his source), Nahum attributes the fall of Nineveh to a flood that washed away the city's defensive structures. Nowhere, however, in the Babylonian Chronicle is there mention of flooding, nor has recent archaeological research found any evidence of flood damage, although fire damage is rampant. It is certainly possible that Nahum used metaphorical imagery to describe the attack of the enemy army.

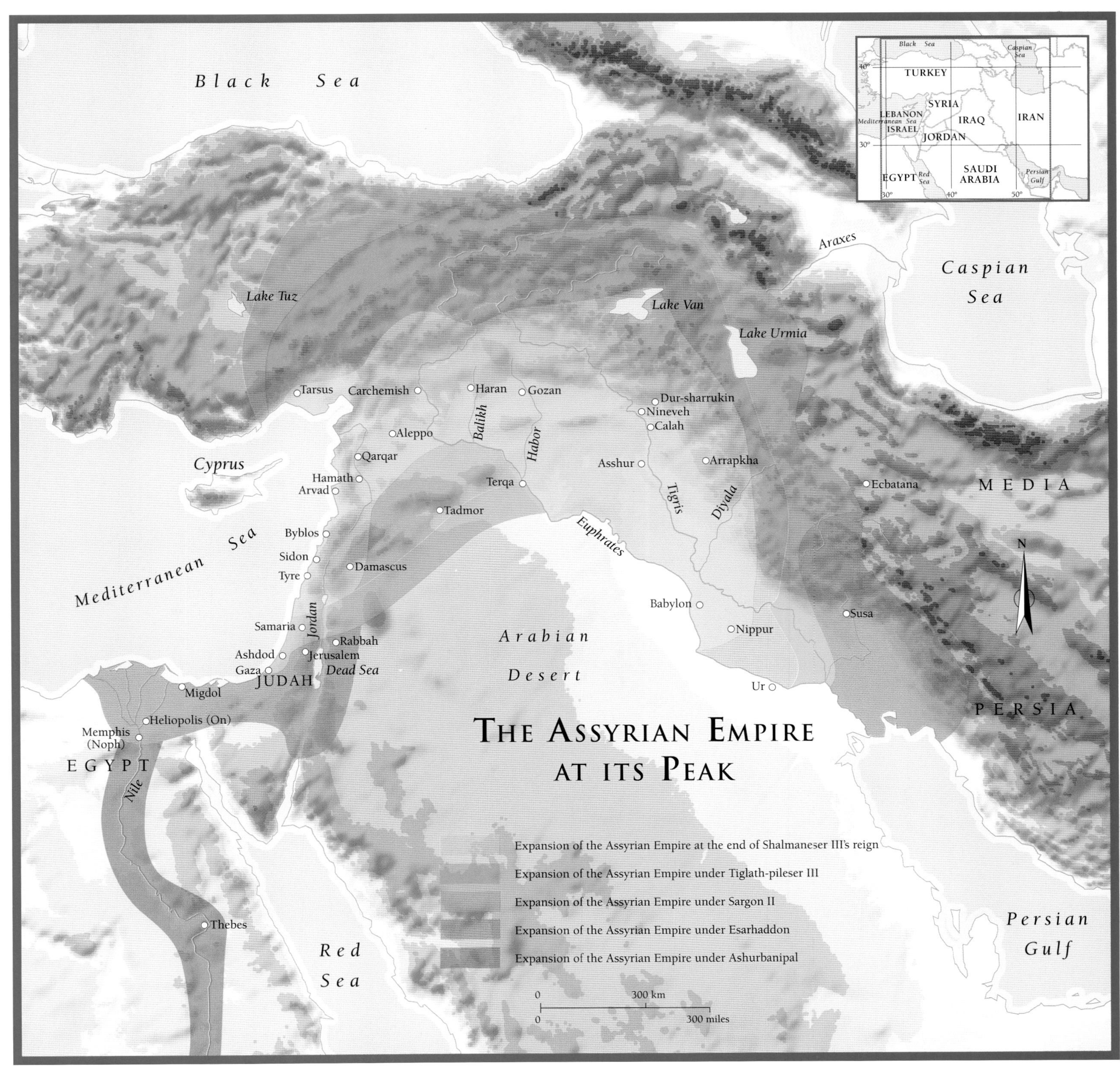

ABOVE: A NINETEENTH-CENTURY RECONSTRUCTION OF AN ASSYRIAN KING'S PALACE. WHEN ASSYRIA FELL, MOST OF THE ONCE GREAT EMPIRE'S RICHES AND PALACES WERE DESTROYED.

END OF THE ASSYRIAN EMPIRE

The end of the Assyrian Empire was a central theme in the book of Zephaniah. The superscription in this book provides the clue that proves that he prophesied in Judah during the reign of Josiah (reigned 640–609 B.C.E.), roughly contemporary with the prophets Nahum and Jeremiah. Most have argued that Zephaniah prophesied before Josiah's reform in the eighteenth year of his reign (*c.* 621 B.C.E.), as the oracles make no mention of the king himself, let alone anything about the reforms during Josiah's reign. Furthermore, the description of Nineveh's doom found in Zephaniah 2:13–15 would probably not have been relevant after 625 B.C.E. (and certainly not after its demise in 612 B.C.E.), when Assyrian power was clearly on the wane.

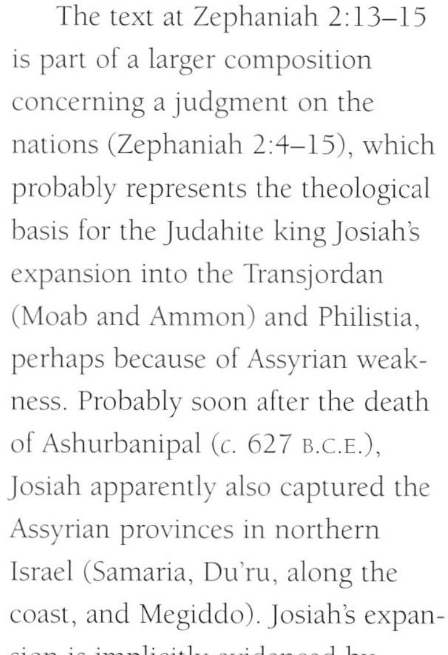

The text at Zephaniah 2:13–15 is part of a larger composition concerning a judgment on the nations (Zephaniah 2:4–15), which probably represents the theological basis for the Judahite king Josiah's expansion into the Transjordan (Moab and Ammon) and Philistia, perhaps because of Assyrian weakness. Probably soon after the death of Ashurbanipal (*c.* 627 B.C.E.), Josiah apparently also captured the Assyrian provinces in northern Israel (Samaria, Du'ru, along the coast, and Megiddo). Josiah's expansion is implicitly evidenced by pottery from Tel Qasile in Philistia from the seventh century B.C.E. that has been considered Judahite.

Since Assyrian kings had terrorized Judah for more than a century, this oracle is not unusual. In fact, the destruction of Nineveh is portrayed in language similar to Ancient Near Eastern treaty curses. Ashurbanipal's annals describe curses against his enemies who violated the terms of his treaties. And so Zephaniah has reversed the "terms" of the treaty, since Assyria was now the weaker party, and Judah, along with its God Yahweh, was the superior party.

Zephaniah's description of the destruction of Assyria was indirectly confirmed by the fourth-century B.C.E. Classical Greek historian Xenophon, whose *Anabasis* appears to be a sensible description of the travel of the 10,000 Greek mercenaries back to Europe from Persia (*c.* 399 B.C.E.). Xenophon was meticulous in this work concerning his geographic descriptions of the regions the army traversed. However, while describing travel through northern Mesopotamia, he omitted to mention (or was largely unaware of) the city of Nineveh, which had fallen a little over two centuries before. Moreover, he was apparently ignorant of the fact that the Assyrians had once controlled this area, and he merely mentioned that the Medes inhabited the region.

RIGHT: IN THIS FIFTEENTH-CENTURY C.E. FRENCH ARTWORK ON VELLUM, NAHUM PROPHESIES THE DESTRUCTION OF NINEVEH, WHICH LEADS TO THE END OF THE ASSYRIAN EMPIRE.

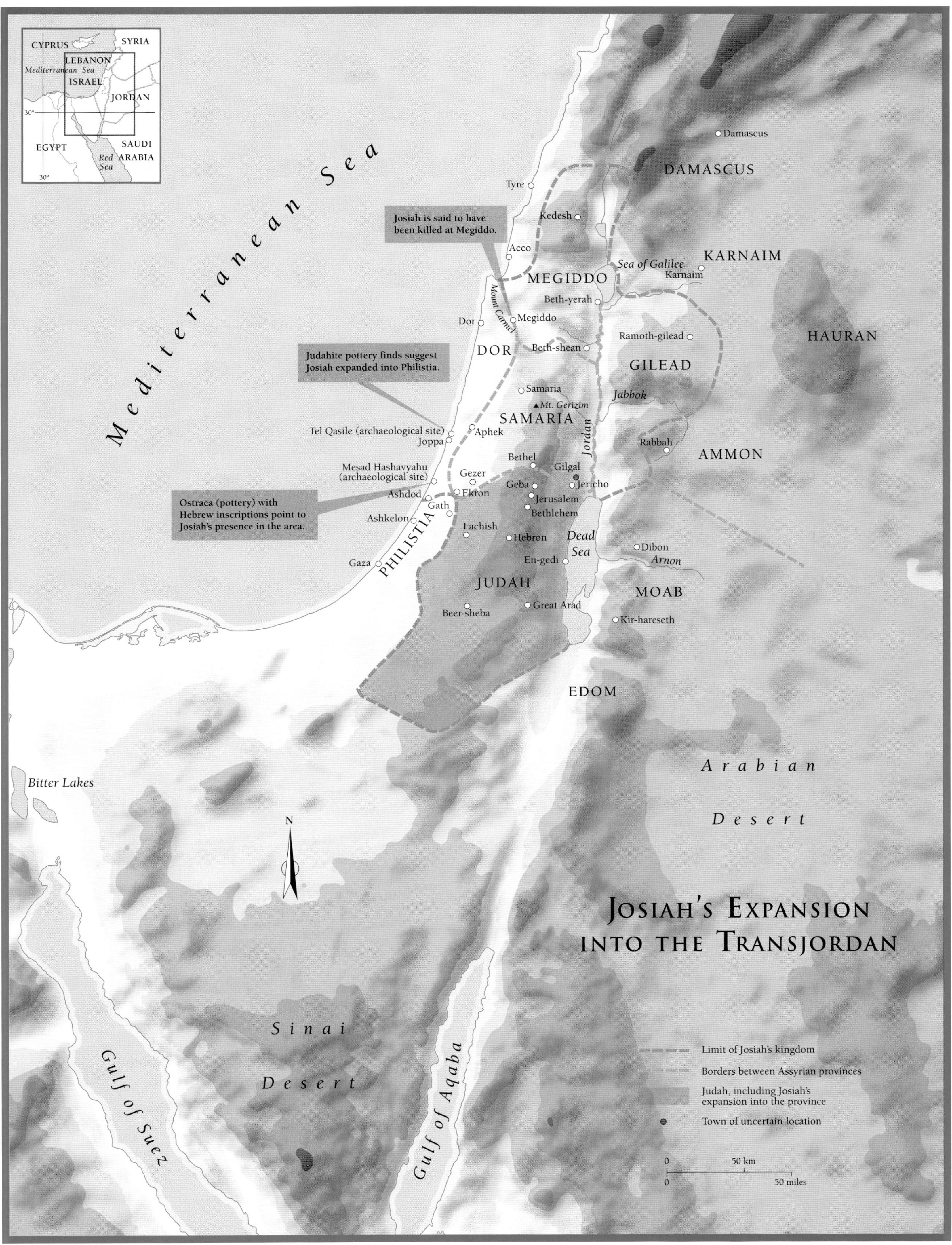

CYPRUS
SYRIA
LEBANON
Mediterranean Sea
ISRAEL
JORDAN
EGYPT
SAUDI ARABIA
Red Sea
30°
Mediterranean Sea
Josiah is said to have been killed at Megiddo.
Judahite pottery finds suggest Josiah expanded into Philistia.
Ostraca (pottery) with Hebrew inscriptions point to Josiah's presence in the area.
Damascus
DAMASCUS
Tyre
Kedesh
Acco
KARNAIM
Sea of Galilee
Karnaim
MEGIDDO
Beth-yerah
Mount Carmel
Megiddo
Dor
Ramoth-gilead
HAURAN
DOR
Beth-shean
GILEAD
Samaria
Jabbok
Mt. Gerizim
SAMARIA
Jordan
Tel Qasile (archaeological site)
Aphek
Joppa
Rabbah
AMMON
Bethel
Mesad Hashavyahu (archaeological site)
Gilgal
Gezer
Geba
Jericho
Ashdod
Ekron
Jerusalem
Gath
Bethlehem
Ashkelon
Lachish
PHILISTIA
Hebron
Dead Sea
Dibon
Arnon
Gaza
En-gedi
JUDAH
MOAB
Beer-sheba
Great Arad
Kir-hareseth
EDOM
Bitter Lakes
Arabian Desert
N
JOSIAH'S EXPANSION INTO THE TRANSJORDAN
Sinai Desert
Gulf of Suez
Gulf of Aqaba
Limit of Josiah's kingdom
Borders between Assyrian provinces
Judah, including Josiah's expansion into the province
Town of uncertain location
0
50 km
0
50 miles

THE BABYLONIANS

AND BABYLON SHALL BECOME A HEAP OF RUINS ... AN OBJECT OF HORROR AND OF HISSING JEREMIAH 51:37

Though the city of Babylon is attested in sources by the end of the Mesopotamian Early Dynastic Period (*c.* 2300 B.C.E.), the city did not become preeminent in southern Mesopotamia until the migration of the Amorites from the northwest (*c.* 1900 B.C.E.). Early in his reign, the Amorite lawgiver Hammurabi was successful in consolidating control of central Mesopotamia. However, in the remaining 15 years of his reign, this king was able to subdue the city-states of Larsa, Uruk, Isin, Mari, and Eshnunna. Thus, at his death, all of Mesopotamia proper was under the control of Babylon. However, the large empire was short lived, and the remaining rulers of the Old Babylonian Kingdom (*c.* 1750–1595 B.C.E.) were little more than rulers of the city of Babylon itself.

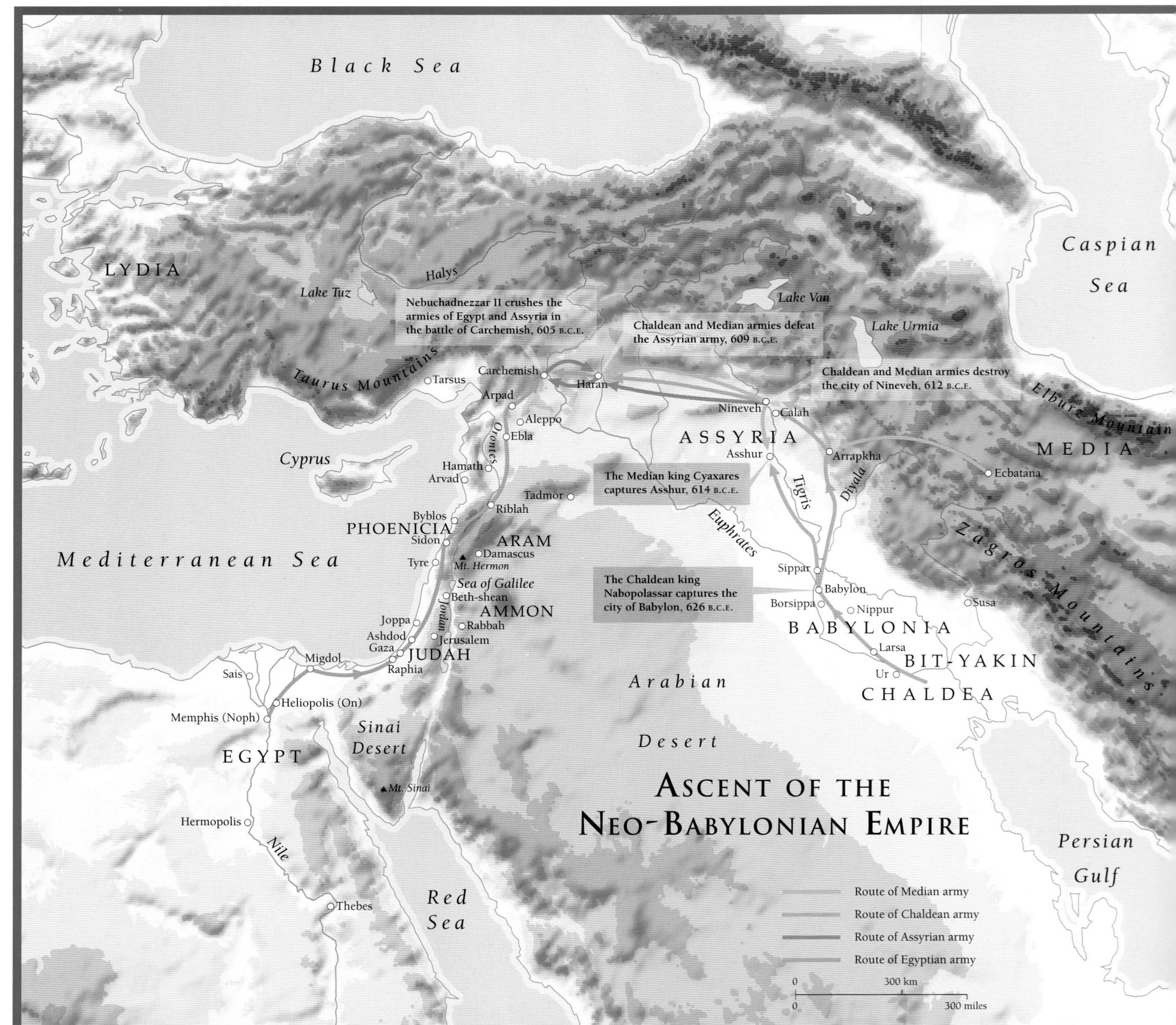

The next major political dynasty of Babylon was that of the Kassites, an ethnic group of unknown origin who ruled Babylon for over four centuries (*c.* 1570–1155 B.C.E.). For most of this period, Babylon controlled a great deal of southern Mesopotamia. Although a series of relatively minor dynasties followed the Kassites, one ruler stood out as a military strategist—Nebuchadnezzar I (reigned 1124–1103 B.C.E.) of the Second Dynasty of Isin. He avenged a previous sack of Babylon by the Elamites (from southwestern Iran) by launching a surprise attack against Susa, the Elamite capital, in the middle of summer, in which he recovered the statue of the patron deity of Babylon, Marduk.

LEFT: BABYLON IS SHOWN IN THE VERY CENTER OF THIS MESOPOTAMIAN MAP OF THE WORLD. THIS TABLET WITH CUNEIFORM INSCRIPTION, HELD IN THE BRITISH MUSEUM, IS DATED TO AROUND 700–500 B.C.E.

THE RISE OF THE NEO-BABYLONIAN EMPIRE

Babylonian political and military power was not again apparent until the rise of the Chaldeans, a tribal group that emerged as the dominant player in Babylonia and competed with Assyria for control of central Mesopotamia. Although Mukin-zeri (*c.* 731–721 B.C.E.) and Merodach-baladan II (*c.* 721–703 B.C.E.) were somewhat successful in keeping an Assyrian military presence out of Babylonia, Sennacherib of Assyria sacked Babylon in 689 B.C.E., and destroyed the city. Assyrian annals describe many of these campaigns in some detail, but one does not get a clear picture of the nature of the Chaldean military tactics, except that they often engaged in guerrilla warfare against their more powerful enemy to the north. With the decline of Assyria (626–612 B.C.E.), the Chaldeans achieved political autonomy under Nabopolassar (reigned 626–605 B.C.E.), who founded the Neo-Babylonian Empire. The Chaldeans and Medians were successful in ending the Assyrian state and destroying the city of Nineveh in 612 B.C.E. (some would say, in part by diverting the Tigris River into the city). However, in 609 B.C.E. Egypt marched through Palestine to assist the remnants of the Assyrian army at Carchemish in northern Syria, where Nebuchadnezzar II, Nabopolassar's crown prince, crushed the enemy and created the largest-ever Babylonian Empire, ranging from the borders of Iran in the east to the borders of Egypt in the west.

NEBUCHADNEZZAR II

Nebuchadnezzar II, who reigned from 605–562 B.C.E., was the greatest ruler and builder of all the Chaldean kings of the Neo-Babylonian Empire. He is also well known as the destroyer of Jerusalem and the kingdom of Judah.

When Nebuchadnezzar II succeeded his father Nabopolassar as Babylonian monarch in 605 B.C.E., he had already established his reputation as a great military commander by his victory over the Egyptians at the decisive battle of Carchemish in the same year. As with his Assyrian predecessors, Nebuchadnezzar II was preoccupied with his western border in Syro–Palestine. In 601 B.C.E. he campaigned against Egypt, a war which ended in a draw, with severe losses on both sides. He also invaded Jerusalem four times.

THE LAST KING OF BABYLON

After Nebuchadnezzar II's death in 562 B.C.E., the Chaldean Empire suffered through six years of minor rulers. Nabonidus was the last king of Babylon (reigned 555–539 B.C.E.).

BELOW: *THE BABYLONIAN MARRIAGE MARKET*, FROM *MYTHS OF BABYLONIA AND ASSYRIA*, BY DONALD A. MACKENZIE. THERE IS NO DIRECT REFERENCE TO A BABYLONIAN MARRIAGE-BY-AUCTION CUSTOM IN HAMMURABI'S CODE.

ABOVE: *THE CITY OF BABYLON,* AN UNATTRIBUTED ENGRAVING IN CALMET'S *DICTIONARY OF THE BIBLE,* PUBLISHED IN 1732. THE FAMOUS HANGING GARDENS ARE IN THE CENTER.

He was apparently not from the royal line, but was the son of a priest of the moon god Sin from Haran in upper Mesopotamia. In a pseudo-autobiographical account of her life, his mother, Adad-guppi (who lived for more than 100 years), claimed to have been instrumental in Nabonidus's rise to power. Nabonidus favored the Sin cult over the cult of Marduk, the chief god of Babylon, and thus caused a certain amount of friction between himself and the religious establishment in Babylon.

THE FALL OF BABYLON

For some unknown reason, Nabonidus left Babylon for the oasis of Tema in the Arabian Desert, and stayed there for approximately ten years (*c.* 553–543 B.C.E.). In his place, his son Belshazzar ruled Babylon, taking care of administrative and military duties. During this time, Nabonidus was not present to fulfill his role as king in the New Year festivals of Marduk, thus incurring the wrath of the Marduk priests. Nabonidus had only returned to Babylon for a short period before his kingdom was attacked by Cyrus II of Persia, who captured the city of Babylon in 539 B.C.E. According to the Babylonian writer Berossus (*c.* 250 B.C.E.), Cyrus II later made Nabonidus a governor in Carmania.

Later historical traditions presented Nabonidus as an "evil king." The Verse Account of Nabu-na'id was a propagandistic text composed by the Marduk priests to justify the takeover of Babylon by the Persians. They asserted that Nabonidus's crime was his ignoring of the Marduk cult. The priests even claim to have helped the Persian cause. The Cyrus Cylinder was a Persian text that extolled the greatness of Cyrus II, while it listed the sins of Nabonidus.

Although Nabonidus is not mentioned in the Bible, he is found in the folkloristic Prayer of Nabonidus, a first-century B.C.E. text written in Aramaic. The depiction there of the Babylonian king is similar to that in the Verse Account.

RIGHT: NEBUCHADNEZZAR II ORDERED THE BUILDING OF THE ISHTAR GATE, THE EIGHTH GATE TO THE INNER CITY OF BABYLON. THE GATE FEATURES GLAZED TILES SHOWING THE CHALDEAN GOD ADAD (YOUNG BULL) AND THE BABYLONIAN GOD MARDUK (DRAGON).

ABOVE: *THE FALL OF BABYLON*, A NINETEENTH-CENTURY C.E. PAINTING BY JOHN MARTIN. THIS DRAMATIC EVENT HAS BEEN THE SUBJECT OF MANY A ROMANTIC PAINTING.

Furthermore, Nabonidus was said to have had a bad inflammation which caused him to be "put away from men" for seven years, not unlike the description of Nebuchadnezzar II in the book of Daniel. The marked similarities between the two Babylonian kings in later traditions has been the subject of much scholarly discussion, but there has been no consensus as to the reason for this.

Why the writer of Daniel ignores Nabonidus and only describes Belshazzar as the ruler of Babylon is not known. According to the Bible, Belshazzar was killed when the city was captured by the Medians and Persians in 539 B.C.E.: "That very night Belshazzar, the Chaldean king, was killed. And Darius the Mede received the kingdom, being about sixty-two years old" (Daniel 5:30–31).

Nabonidus had entrusted the army and kingship to his son, who was apparently considered a co-regent, which would have been a unique case in Mesopotamian history. Belshazzar, however, was never referred to as king, nor did he take part in the New Year festival. Akkadian texts describe Belshazzar's tenure in Babylon until the twelfth year of his father's reign (*c.* 543 B.C.E.). There are a number of legal texts, contracts, and letters that describe Belshazzar as the crown prince. Moreover, they also delineate his duties as co-ruler, including overseeing the temple estates of Uruk and Sippar, and leasing out temple land. His name abruptly disappears from records in 543 B.C.E., which may have been when his father returned. According to the Nabonidus Chronicle, Belshazzar was a grandson of Nebuchadnezzar II (reigned 605–562 B.C.E.), but this may have been an attempt to justify his father Nabonidus's reign, since he was not a member of the royal family.

No sources describe what became of Belshazzar after his father's return in 543 B.C.E. He may have in fact been captured in Babylon in 539 B.C.E. or was commanding the Babylonian forces at Opis when they were defeated by Cyrus II the Persian, who was then successful in taking Babylon.

NEBUCHADNEZZAR II THE GREAT BUILDER

Nebuchadnezzar II was renowned as a prolific builder in the city of Babylon itself. He conducted extensive renovation projects, rebuilt the city walls, constructed a bridge to bring together the two halves of the city separated by the Euphrates River, and restored the Babylonian temple tower (ziggurat) as well as other holy places.

At the end of Nebuchadnezzar II's reign of 43 years, the Babylonian Empire was virtually the same size as was its predecessor, Assyria. Although cuneiform sources give a fragmented picture of Nebuchadnezzar II's reign, he appears in later biblical (e.g., Daniel), rabbinic, and Arabic commentaries, books of the Jewish Apocrypha, and in the works of Classical (e.g., Strabo, Diodorus Siculus, and Berossus, a Babylonian priest of Marduk who wrote the three-volume *Babyloniaca*) and medieval authors. Though the Hebrew sources understandably bemoan his conquest and destruction of Jerusalem and the Temple, other sources describe his great building projects, and some even credit him with superhuman achievements.

THE FIRST TEMPLE DESTROYED

THEY BURNED THE HOUSE OF GOD, BROKE DOWN THE WALL OF JERUSALEM 2 CHRONICLES 36:19

Nebuchadnezzar, who ruled from Babylon for more than 40 years, attacked Jerusalem no fewer than four separate times during his reign. Our information for these campaigns comes from three historical sources: the Old Testament, or Hebrew Bible; the so-called Babylonian Chronicle, which was a contemporary record kept by the Neo-Babylonian priests for each year during much of this period; and Josephus, the Jewish general turned Roman historian who wrote during the reigns of Vespasian and Titus in the first century C.E.

THE CAMPAIGN IN 598 B.C.E.

Jehoiakim, the eighteenth king of Judah, had been a faithful vassal of Nebuchadnezzar for several years. However, in 601 B.C.E., mistakenly thinking that the Neo-Babylonians were weak because they had failed to conquer Egypt, Jehoiakim rebelled and refused to pay Nebuchadnezzar the tribute that he was supposed to pay each year. Jehoiakim evaded payment for three years, but in 598 B.C.E., Nebuchadnezzar decided it was time to recover his money.

Nebuchadnezzar attacked Jerusalem and captured the rebellious king of Judah. Jehoiakim was then either put to death immediately or sent away to exile in Babylon, where he died. The passages in the Bible are rather ambiguous: the book of 2 Chronicles says, "Against him [Jehoiakim] King Nebuchadnezzar of Babylon came up, and bound him with fetters to take him to Babylon" (2 Chronicles 36:6), while the book of 2 Kings says, "In his days King Nebuchadnezzar of Babylon came up … [and] the Lord sent against him [Jehoiakim] bands of the Chaldeans [Neo-Babylonians] … [and] sent them against Judah to destroy it" (2 Kings 24:1–2). It then continues, "So Jehoiakim slept with his ancestors; then his son Jehoiachin succeeded him" (2 Kings 24:6). Either way, Jehoiakim was deposed and his son Jehoiachin

BELOW: MAGNIFICENT TILES FROM NEBUCHADNEZZAR'S ISHTAR GATE. HERE WE SEE THE BABYLONIAN GOD MARDUK. THE JEWISH EXILES MAY HAVE ENTERED BABYLON THROUGH THE ISHTAR GATE.

was placed on the throne of Judah in his place, to rule as a puppet-king on behalf of the Neo-Babylonians.

Nebuchadnezzar also led away many of the citizens of the city, in what would be the first of four deportations that are known collectively as the Babylonian Exile. According to Josephus, Nebuchadnezzar took 3,000 Judahites with him on his journey to Babylon in 598 B.C.E., including the prophet Ezekiel. The worst, however, was yet to come.

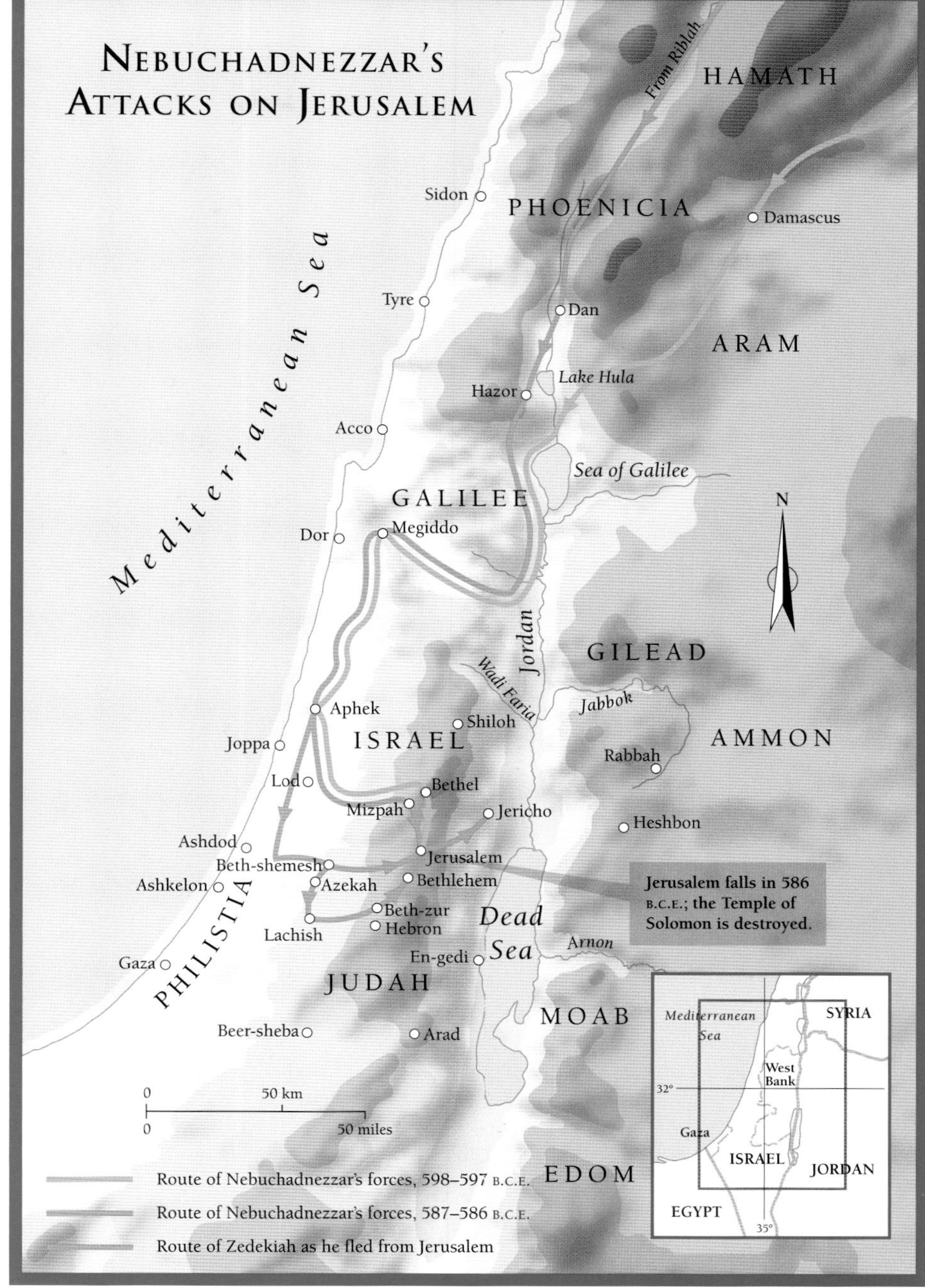

THE CAMPAIGN IN 597 B.C.E.

Jehoiachin was a young man—just eighteen years of age—when he was appointed king of Judah in 598 B.C.E. He didn't rule for very long, however, because Nebuchadnezzar and his army returned within the year, to continue what they had begun. By early March 597 B.C.E., Jerusalem was once again besieged by the Neo-Babylonians.

It was not long before the city and the king capitulated. The book of 2 Kings tells the story concisely: "King Nebuchadnezzar of Babylon came to the city, while his servants were besieging it; King Jehoiachin of Judah gave himself up to the king of Babylon, himself, his mother, his servants, his officers, and his palace officials" (2 Kings 24:11–12). Moreover, we are told that "[Nebuchadnezzar] carried off all the treasures of the house of the Lord, and the treasures of the king's house; he cut in pieces all the vessels of gold in the temple of the Lord, which King Solomon of Israel had made, all this as the Lord had foretold" (2 Kings 24:13). This recounting is confirmed by the Babylonian Chronicle, which records in its entry for Nebuchadnezzar's seventh year that in "the seventh year, the month of Kislev" the Babylonian king was preparing to attack Judah, and on "the second day of the month Adar" he captured the city and arrested Jehoiachin. Nebuchadnezzar then appointed a new king and collected large amounts of tribute, which he took back to Babylon.

This time, in addition to taking Jehoiachin to Babylon with him, Nebuchadnezzar also took 10,000 or more citizens, adding them to the 3,000 he had taken into exile a few months before. The precious vessels that he had looted from Solomon's Temple were placed in a temple in Babylon and rededicated to the god Marduk. And, back in Jerusalem, Zedekiah, the twenty-one-year-old brother of Jehoiakim, was appointed to serve as the new king of

ABOVE LEFT: *JEHOIACHIN RELEASED*, BY G. FREEMAN. FOLLOWING THE DEATH OF NEBUCHADNEZZAR IN 562 B.C.E., THE NEXT BABYLONIAN KING, EVIL-MERODACH, FREED JEHOIACHIN IN 561 B.C.E., ALMOST 40 YEARS AFTER HE HAD BEEN TAKEN PRISONER.

LEFT: BAS RELIEF DEPICTING TRIBUTE FROM THE PALACE OF SARGON II. THE PAYING OF TRIBUTE BY VASSAL STATES CONTINUED TO BE A VITAL SOURCE OF INCOME FOR RULING EMPIRES SUCH AS NEBUCHADNEZZAR'S BABYLONIAN EMPIRE.

ABOVE: *JERUSALEM TAKEN,* AN UNATTRIBUTED ENGRAVING IN CALMET'S EIGHTEENTH-CENTURY C.E. PUBLICATION, *DICTIONARY OF THE BIBLE.* NEBUCHADNEZZAR'S ARMY ENTER JERUSALEM, SACK THE CITY, AND TAKE ITS INHABITANTS INTO EXILE.

NEBUCHADNEZZAR AND THE SACRED TREASURES OF SOLOMON'S TEMPLE

When Nebuchadnezzar took the sacred treasures from Solomon's Temple he was not the first ruler to do so, nor would he be the last. We do know that the treasures of Solomon's Temple were either plundered or used as bribes at least eight different times between *c.* 925 B.C.E. and 586 B.C.E., including during the reigns of the Judahite kings Rehoboam, Asa, Joash, Ahaz, and Hezekiah, in addition to Zedekiah. Below is a fifteenth-century C.E. representation of one of these treasures, the Tabernacle, which was a portable sanctuary for transporting the Ark of the Covenant.

Judah, yet another puppet-king serving at the whim of King Nebuchadnezzar and the Neo-Babylonians.

THE CAMPAIGN IN 587 B.C.E.

It took Zedekiah several years to decide to rebel against the Neo-Babylonian overlords, as his predecessors had done. And, as had happened to his predecessors before him, he soon felt Nebuchadnezzar's wrath as a result.

In January 587 B.C.E., Nebuchadnezzar and his Neo-Babylonian army began destroying the cities of Judah, one by one, in order to suppress the new Jewish rebellion. Soon it was Jerusalem's turn. The siege was long and brutal, with many of the inhabitants facing starvation in the final weeks. The city fell in 586 B.C.E., and soon afterward the Temple of Solomon was destroyed.

Zedekiah fled from Jerusalem, only to be caught near Jericho and brought before Nebuchadnezzar. As his punishment, he was forced to witness the execution of his own sons and was then himself blinded, bound in chains, and taken away as a prisoner to Babylon. More than 800 of Jerusalem's leading citizens were sent with him into exile to Babylon, joining the others who were already living there. Once again Nebuchadnezzar put a puppet-king on the throne of Judah; this time his name was Gedaliah.

THE CAMPAIGN IN 582 B.C.E.

Gedaliah was soon murdered, a deed which set in motion Nebuchadnezzar's final invasion and campaign against the city of Jerusalem, which took place in 582 B.C.E. This time there was virtually no resistance, and another 745 leading citizens were deported to Babylon, in what would turn out to be the last of these deportations.

THE FALL OF JERUSALEM AND JUDAH

As stated earlier, Nebuchadnezzar and his army attacked Judah and Jerusalem in 587 B.C.E. in order to suppress the Jewish rebellion begun by Zedekiah.

The book of 2 Kings tells us that "King Nebuchadnezzar of Babylon came with all his army against Jerusalem, and laid siege to it; they built siegeworks against it all around" (2 Kings 25:1). Jeremiah says that the inhabitants of Jerusalem defended their city by tearing down some of their houses to create a defense against the attack (Jeremiah 33:4).

Josephus agrees with the biblical accounts, telling us in his *Antiquities of the Jews* that when the Neo-Babylonian army reached Jerusalem, after having razed other Judahite cities to the ground, they followed their usual tactics, constructing high towers on top of great mounds of earth that encircled the city. They then attacked the defenders of the city who were standing on top of Jerusalem's walls, by shooting arrows and throwing darts and large stones at them.

Archaeological evidence confirms the biblical descriptions as well as Josephus's account. Neo-Babylonian arrowheads lie on the ground and are embedded in the walls of houses in Jerusalem. Ash, burnt artifacts, and broken bits of pottery are found everywhere in the archaeological excavations within the modern Jewish Quarter of Jerusalem, mixed with huge stones thrown down from the walls by Nebuchadnezzar's men. Fecal matter excavated from the toilets confirms that the inhabitants of the city were starving, reduced to eating dandelions and other plants from their yards and raw or undercooked meat, resulting in tapeworms, whipworms, and other intestinal parasites.

After 18 months, the city fell. This tragic event happened in July 586 B.C.E., during the month of Tammuz in Zedekiah's eleventh year of rule. The inhabitants, greatly reduced by famine and disease, offered little resistance in the end. The book of 2 Kings says simply that the famine was so severe in Jerusalem that the people were starving, then the city wall was breached (2 Kings 25:3–4). The Chronicler says: "Therefore he [the Lord] brought up against them the king of the Chaldeans [Nebuchadnezzar], who killed their youths with the sword in the house of their sanctuary, and had no compassion on young man or young woman, the aged or the feeble; he gave them all into his hand" (2 Chronicles 36:17).

NEBUCHADNEZZAR II OF BABYLON PILLAGES AND DESTROYS THE TEMPLE

Approximately one month after the fall of Jerusalem, Solomon's Temple was destroyed, most likely quite deliberately as a punishment for the Jews' repeated rebellions against Nebuchadnezzar.

The traditional date for the destruction of the Temple of Solomon is the 9th of Ab—August 16, 586 B.C.E. The book of 2 Kings relates the story most succinctly: "In the fifth month, on the seventh day of the month—which was the nineteenth year of King Nebuchadnezzar, king of Babylon—Nebuzaradan, the captain of the bodyguard, a servant of the king of Babylon, came to Jerusalem. He burned the house of the Lord, and the king's house, and all the houses of Jerusalem; every great house he burned down" (2 Kings 25:8–9; see also 2 Chronicles 36:19; Jeremiah 39:8; Jeremiah 52:12–14).

The treasures of the Temple were pillaged and carried off to Babylon, where they were rededicated by Nebuchadnezzar in his own temples, to his own gods. The book of 2 Kings provides us with additional details: "The bronze pillars that were in the house of the Lord, as well as the stands and the bronze sea that were in the house of the Lord, the Chaldeans [Neo-Babylonians] broke in pieces, and carried the bronze to Babylon. They took away the pots, the shovels, the snuffers, the dishes for incense, and all the bronze vessels used in the temple service, as well as the firepans and the basins. What was made of gold the captain of the guard took away for the gold, and what was made of silver, for the silver" (2 Kings 25:13–15; see also Jeremiah 52:17–23).

Josephus tells us a similar story. He relates that Nebuzaradan, the general of the Neo-Babylonian army, came to Jerusalem in the eleventh year of King Zedekiah and pillaged the Temple. Apparently, he took away the treasures and the vessels of God, of both gold and silver, including golden tables and candlesticks, as well as pillars of brass. After his men had carried off the treasures, he set fire to the Temple of Solomon, burnt the palace, and destroyed the rest of the city. This was done, according to Josephus, in the eighteenth year of the reign of Nebuchadnezzar.

BELOW: THIS ILLUSTRATION BY JEAN FOUQUET DEPICTS THE BABYLONIAN ARMY STORMING SOLOMON'S TEMPLE. IT APPEARS IN VOLUME I OF *OEUVRE DE JEHAN FOUCQUET.*

RIGHT: JEWISH EXILES DESPAIR AS THEY ARE BOUND IN CHAINS READY TO BE TRANSPORTED TO BABYLON. FROM THE FRENCH PUBLICATION *HISTOIRE SAINTE EN TABLEAUX*, THIS ILLUSTRATION SHOWS THE AFTERMATH OF NEBUCHADNEZZAR'S ATTACK ON JERUSALEM.

The sacred items taken from the Temple would eventually be returned to Jerusalem, but not for nearly 50 years, when Cyrus the Great and his Persian army overran Babylon in 539 B.C.E. and allowed the Jews to return home to Jerusalem and Judah. In the meantime, the city of Jerusalem lay in ruins, and the population of Judah was affected severely—many of its leading inhabitants had been carted off to Babylon, others had fled to Egypt with Jeremiah, and only the lower classes had remained on the land, under the firm thumb of the Neo-Babylonians.

THE EXILE OF THE JEWS

The so-called Babylonian Exile of the Jews is usually said to have lasted almost 50 years—from 586 B.C.E. until 539 B.C.E. However, the first deportations actually took place 12 years earlier, in 598 B.C.E., and the end of the Exile came about in 538 B.C.E., one year after Cyrus the Great captured Babylon, when he allowed the Jews who had been exiled in Babylon to return to their homeland. Thus, the Babylonian Exile really lasted exactly 60 years, from 598 to 538 B.C.E.

There were four separate deportations of the Jews to Babylon over the course of 16 years, from 598 to 582 B.C.E. Jeremiah reports that 4,600 people were deported (Jeremiah 52:28–30). However, the book of 2 Kings adds another 10,000 to his total, for it seems that Jeremiah omitted those who were exiled in 597 B.C.E.: apparently, the deportations actually consisted of 3,023 people in 598 B.C.E. (Jeremiah 52:28), 10,000 in 597 B.C.E. (2 Kings 24:14–17), 832 in 586 B.C.E. (Jeremiah 52:29), and, finally, 745 in 582 B.C.E. (Jeremiah 52:30).

If these figures are correct, it would mean that a total of at least 14,600 Judahites were deported to Babylon over the course of Nebuchadnezzar's incursions. In addition, there were other Jews who were neither carried off to Babylon nor remained on the land in Judah, but who instead fled to Egypt—including the prophet Jeremiah. As the book of 2 Kings says, "all the people, high and low … went to Egypt" (2 Kings 25:26). Thus, the combined figure of deportees and refugees may actually have been closer to 20,000 people, according to the best estimate from recent archaeological surveys and other relevant data.

In any event, the population of Judah, which probably numbered about 75,000 during that period, and especially the population of Jerusalem, which may have been approximately 15,000 people at the time, would have been radically affected. The fact that it was primarily the upper classes and the craftsmen who were deported, meant that only the peasants and farmers stayed behind in the land. The book of 2 Kings depicts the situation starkly, in describing the deportations of 597 B.C.E.: "He [Nebuchadnezzar] carried away all Jerusalem, and all the officials, and all the warriors, ten thousand captives, and all the artisans and the smiths; no one remained, except the poorest people of the land. He carried away Jehoiachin to Babylon; the

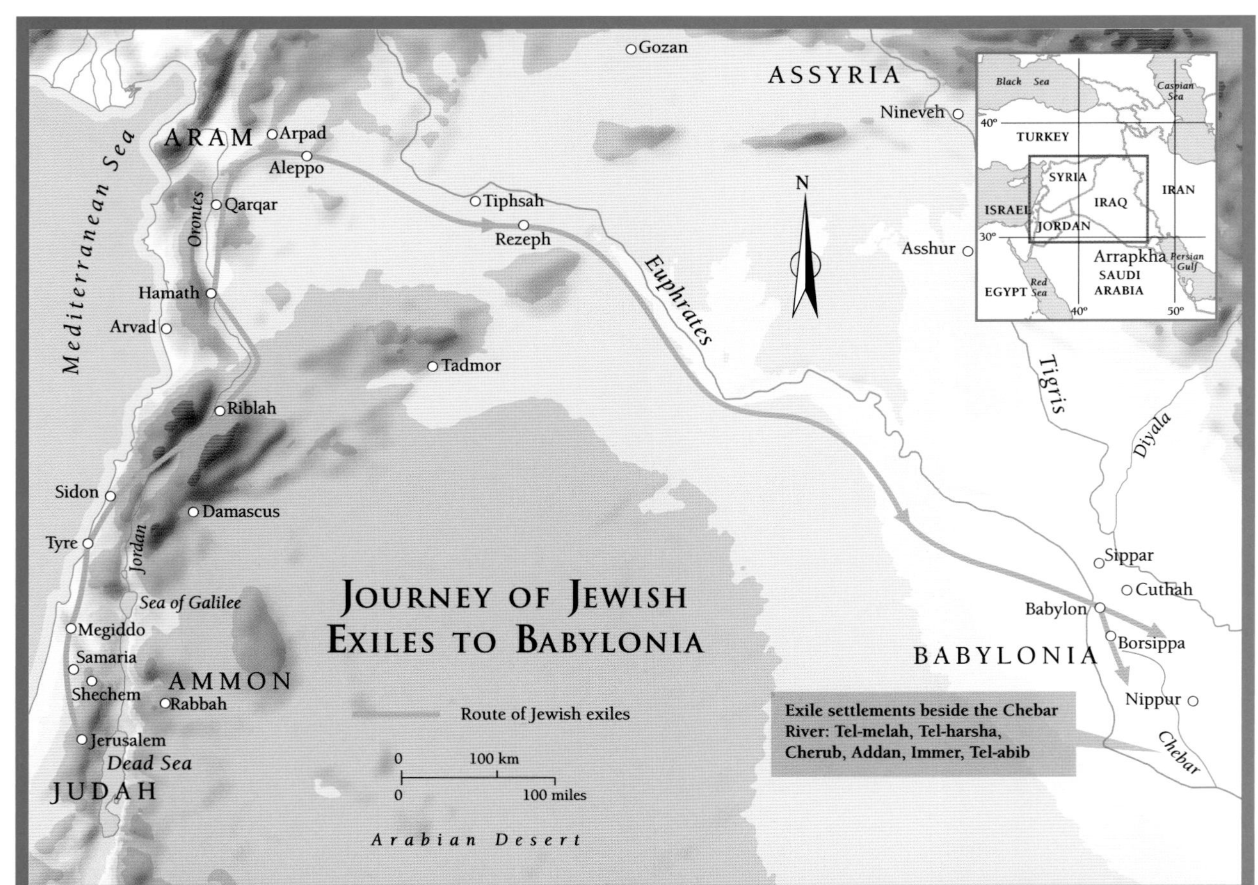

king's mother, the king's wives, his officials, and the elite of the land, he took into captivity from Jerusalem to Babylon" (2 Kings 24:14–15).

Josephus paints a similar picture of the deportations in 586 B.C.E. He says that the city was overthrown to its very foundations and all of the people were removed. He names several priests who were taken away as prisoners, including Seraiah, the high priest. He also notes that various personal friends, and even the personal scribe, of Zedekiah, as well as some 60 unnamed "rulers" from the city and the Temple were led away and appeared before Nebuchadnezzar in the city of Riblah in Syria. There the high priest Seraiah and the various "rulers" were executed, by means of decapitation. The others, including King Zedekiah and the high priest Jehozadak, were then led off into permanent exile in Babylon.

Interestingly, history has remembered best those Jews who were deported to Babylon. Most likely this is because the Babylonian Exile had an enormous impact, not only on the history of the Jewish people but also on the evolution of religious thought in the Western world. Many scholars believe that the Pentateuch and the Deuteronomistic History of the Old Testament were edited into their final form during and immediately after this period.

THE MYTH OF THE EMPTY LAND

It has frequently been said that the land of Judah was left empty by the actions of Nebuchadnezzar and the Neo-Babylonians during the early sixth century B.C.E. Indeed, there are very few archaeological remains that can be definitively dated to the period immediately after Nebuchadezzar's destruction of Jerusalem in 586 B.C.E. The site of Tell en-Nasbeh (biblical Mizpah), located to the north of Jerusalem, is one glaring exception, for this city was apparently thriving during the Neo-Babylonian occupation of Judah. However, recent scholarly investigations, including archaeological surveys, have now shown that it wasn't only biblical Mizpah that was thriving during this period. Despite the severe demographic crisis caused by Nebuchadnezzar's deportations, it is now becoming clear that Judah was left far from empty during the Babylonian Exile.

Nevertheless, although there were Jews left in Judah, they were from the predominantly rural lower classes, for the Babylonians were very selective about those who they chose for exile and those who they left behind. Jeremiah tells us as much, saying: "Nebuzaradan the captain of the guard left in the land of Judah some of the poor people who owned nothing, and gave them vineyards and fields at the same time" (Jeremiah 39:10; see also Jeremiah 40:7–12; Jeremiah 52:16; 2 Kings 25:12, 22).

As a result, when Cyrus the Great allowed the Jews in Babylon to return to Jerusalem and Judah, and those who had fled to Egypt also returned, there were suddenly three very distinct populations of Judahites—those who had been carried off to Babylon, those who had fled to Egypt, and those who had remained behind in Judah. As one might imagine, the three groups had developed in different ways while they were apart, and this led to many questions and problems during the subsequent period of restoration when the Temple was being rebuilt in Jerusalem, including the vexing question of which group of people should be put in charge of the rebuilding.

Eventually the situation was sufficiently resolved so that, although internal squabbling continued for almost another century, the Second Temple was completed under the direction of Zerubbabel in 515 B.C.E. and the gold and silver vessels that had been stolen from the First Temple treasury were once again placed in the Temple, having been returned from Babylon by order of Cyrus the Great.

ABOVE: *THE DAUGHTERS OF JUDAH IN BABYLON*, A NINETEENTH-CENTURY C.E. PAINTING BY HERBERT GUSTAVE SCHMALZ. IN THE FOREGROUND WOMEN WEEP BY THE EUPHRATES RIVER.

The Persians

THUS SAYS THE LORD TO ... CYRUS ... I WILL GO BEFORE YOU AND LEVEL THE MOUNTAINS ISAIAH 45:1-2

RIGHT: A PERSIAN EARTHENWARE BOWL FROM THE NINTH CENTURY B.C.E., NOW HELD IN THE VICTORIA & ALBERT MUSEUM IN LONDON, UNITED KINGDOM.

The Persians were an Indo-European people who were linguistically related to the Medes. Both groups had migrated into the western Iranian plateau in the early first millennium B.C.E. The earliest mentions of the Medes and Persians are in annals of the Assyrian king Shalmaneser III (reigned 858–824 B.C.E.). Apart from the Assyrian sources, our knowledge of the Medes is derived from the Greek historian Herodotus. According to Herodotus, the Medes developed a large empire in southwest Asia during the reign of Cyaxares (reigned 625–585 B.C.E.), who, along with the Chaldeans, helped to end the mighty Assyrian Empire. Herodotus also claimed in his writings that the Persians adopted Median customs during the reign of the Median king Astyages (585–550 B.C.E.). The Persians were playing a subordinate role in a Median state.

The ascension of the Persian Empire is quite explicitly tied to the fortunes of its founder, Cyrus II (reigned 559–530 B.C.E.), who led a successful rebellion against his maternal grandfather, Astyages, defeating him in two battles. This new ruler claimed to have both Median and Persian blood, thus strengthening his claim to unifying the two groups.

BELOW: CYRUS THE GREAT DECREES THAT THE JEWS MAY RETURN TO THEIR HOMELAND. PAINTING FROM JEAN FOUQUET'S *OEUVRE DE JEHAN FOUCQUET*, VOLUME I.

CYRUS II, KNOWN AS CYRUS THE GREAT

Cyrus II thus became founder of the Achaemenid Dynasty (the eponymous ancestor of the Persian royal house) of Persia, which lasted two centuries. He was also the conqueror of a wide expanse from Central Asia to the Mediterranean Sea. The sources for Cyrus II's reign are diverse, ranging from his own inscriptions (such as the Cyrus Cylinder); contemporary Babylonian and biblical historical texts; and later Classical writers, such as Herodotus, Xenophon, and Ctesias [as quoted by Diodorus]). Little is known about Cyrus II's youth, although Xenophon wrote a largely unhistorical account of Cyrus II's childhood and education.

After Cyrus II's great victory over Astyages, he seized the Median capital of Ecbatana, and thereby became the king of the Medes and the Persians, making his capital at Parsagarda (Pasargadae). He promptly began expansion in the west, where he met Croesus of Lydia at the Halys River in Anatolia, and fought to a draw. Soon thereafter, the Achaemenid king attacked Sardis, the Lydian capital; he took the city, and became the undisputed master of nearly all of Anatolia, including a number of the Greek city-states on the western coast. In 539 B.C.E. Cyrus II crossed the Diyala River at Opis in Mesopotamia and attacked the Chaldean Empire of Nabonidus. He defeated a Babylonian force at Opis, and sent a Persian army to capture Babylon itself. He then declared his son, Cambyses II, as king of Babylon. Cyrus II continued to campaign east of Persia in Central Asia, successfully subduing most of southern Central Asia. However, Cyrus II apparently died in Central Asia during a battle against the Massagetae in 530 B.C.E. and was succeeded by Cambyses II.

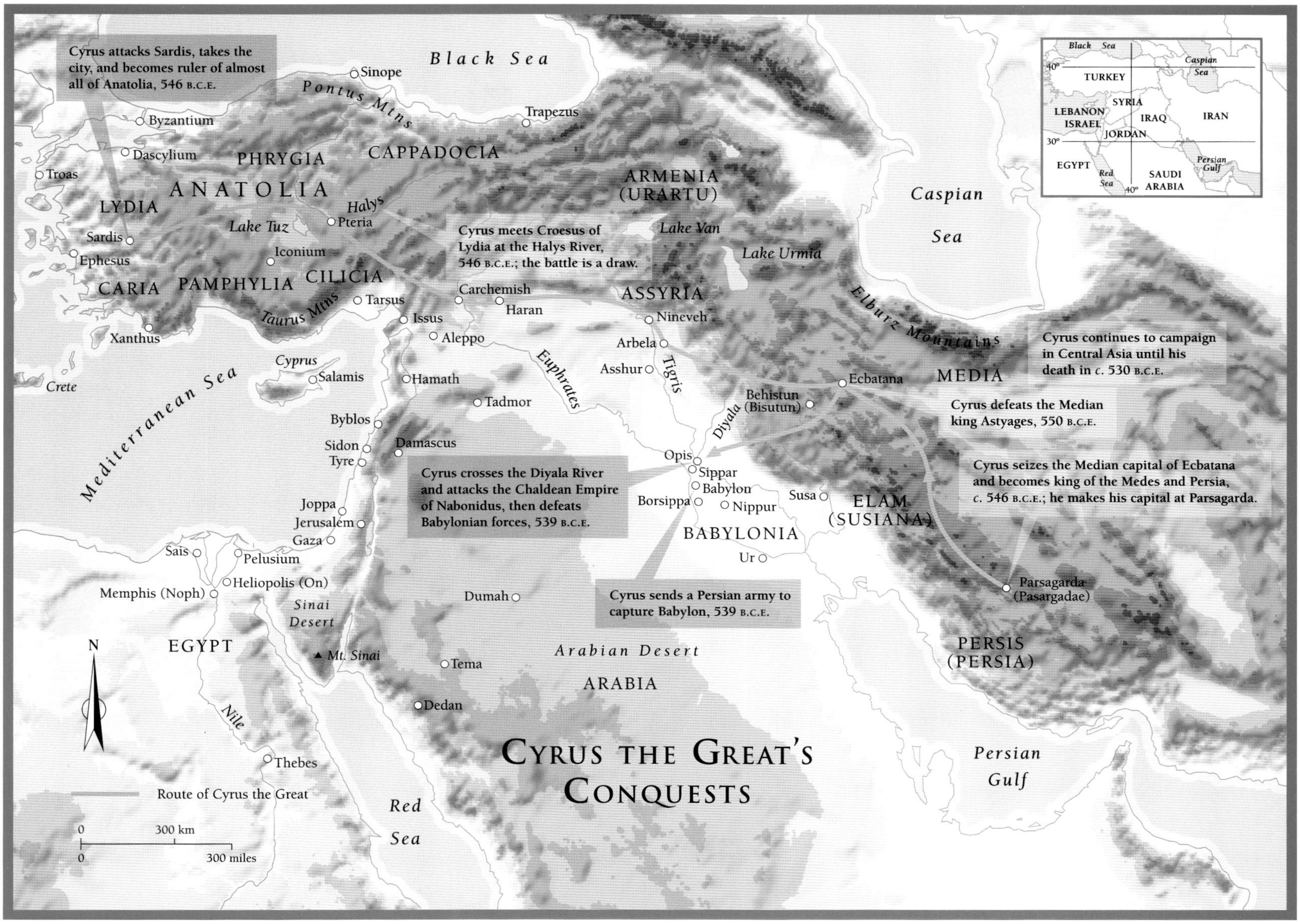

CYRUS THE GREAT'S CONQUESTS

Cyrus attacks Sardis, takes the city, and becomes ruler of almost all of Anatolia, 546 B.C.E.

Cyrus meets Croesus of Lydia at the Halys River, 546 B.C.E.; the battle is a draw.

Cyrus continues to campaign in Central Asia until his death in *c.* 530 B.C.E.

Cyrus defeats the Median king Astyages, 550 B.C.E.

Cyrus seizes the Median capital of Ecbatana and becomes king of the Medes and Persia, *c.* 546 B.C.E.; he makes his capital at Parsagarda.

Cyrus crosses the Diyala River and attacks the Chaldean Empire of Nabonidus, then defeats Babylonian forces, 539 B.C.E.

Cyrus sends a Persian army to capture Babylon, 539 B.C.E.

Route of Cyrus the Great

0 300 km
0 300 miles

CYRUS II AND HIS DECREES

Cyrus II is perhaps best known outside of Scripture for his description in Xenophon's (*c.* 429–357 B.C.E.) *Cyropaedia.* Although apparently historical, this work is not history but in fact historical romance. We glean from it, not so much about Cyrus II and the fall of Babylon, but Xenophon's didactic purpose in exhibiting the ideal virtues of Cyrus II through the use of pseudohistorical narrative. In fact, many have argued that his "biography" of Cyrus II was a vehicle through which Xenophon expounded his views on a variety of topics. Xenophon was not about to allow historical truth to get in the way of his ideal image of Cyrus II. Though it was well known that Cyrus II died in war, Xenophon has him die peacefully in his palace, after a long speech. He also ignores the Medes, who had a large empire before Cyrus II, and gives Cyrus an empire which included Asia and Egypt. He also describes battles that do not appear to have taken place. It seems that the historical Cyrus II was a datum point for which Xenophon created his historical novel. In spite of these concerns, Xenophon's account of the taking of Babylon roughly corresponds to the Herodotean account and the Babylonian inscription known as the Cyrus Cylinder. Interestingly, Xenophon mentions the fact that the attack on Babylon happened at night, a note that Herodotus fails to include.

The text of the Cyrus Cylinder was inscribed on a barrel-shaped clay cylinder. These types of objects were often buried in foundation deposits under walls or buildings and were for posterity. Though the first part of the text is damaged, it seems that first section is a criticism of the last Chaldean king, Nabonidus, aiming to portray him as an enemy of Marduk, the city god of Babylon. The implication is that Cyrus II was a more legitimate ruler for Babylon than Nabonidus, who was an incompetent ruler who had fallen out of divine favor. Marduk then searched the world for a new king to take his place, and found, of course, Cyrus II.

LEFT: THE TOMB OF CYRUS THE GREAT AT PARSAGARDA (PASARGADAE) IN MODERN-DAY IRAN. CYRUS II IS REMEMBERED AS A SOMEWHAT BENEVOLENT RULER.

ABOVE: DARIUS I DEDICATES THE TEMPLE OF JERUSALEM. LITHOGRAPH FROM A COPY OF THE FIFTEENTH-CENTURY C.E. NUREMBERG BIBLE. EZRA 6:16 SAYS THAT: "THE PEOPLE OF ISRAEL ... CELEBRATED THE DEDICATION OF THIS HOUSE OF GOD WITH JOY."

When Cyrus II marched against Babylon, Marduk was on his side. The city thus surrendered without a battle, and the Persians entered in peace and without resorting to the usual plunder. The author of the Cyrus Cylinder claims that Cyrus II was thus different from previous conquerors of the city, as Marduk was with him. It was therefore primarily a propagandistic text that helped to show how Cyrus II went about trying to convince the Babylonian aristocracy of his claims to the throne of Babylon.

RIGHT: ELAMITE SOLDIERS IN THE SERVICE OF DARIUS I. THESE ENAMELED TILES WERE FOUND AT SUSA (IN MODERN-DAY IRAN). THE PERSIAN ARMY HAD AN ELITE CORPS KNOWN AS THE "IMMORTALS."

In sum, the Cyrus Cylinder was not a human rights proclamation, as has traditionally been assumed, but in fact a propagandistic foundation deposit inscription for posterity. However, the Cyrus Cylinder does reflect an allowance of a certain degree of autonomy for the conquered peoples in the empire, and makes mention of repairs made to damaged shrines and temples, and even decreed the return of sacred images (that is, gods) that had been held in Babylon. Captive peoples were allowed to return to their homelands to worship their gods and to serve the Persian king. Although neither the Jews nor the region of Judah are mentioned in the Cyrus Cylinder, it is in this context that one can place the biblical decree of Cyrus II. According to 2 Chronicles 36:22–23, Cyrus II issued a decree allowing deported Jews to return to Palestine to rebuild their temple.

CAMBYSES II

Cambyses II (reigned 529–522 B.C.E.) came to the throne of the Persian Empire after the death of his father Cyrus II in 530 B.C.E. Though Mesopotamian, Egyptian, and Classical sources make mention of this king, there are no contemporary Persian records from his reign. According to the Cyrus Cylinder, Cyrus II placed his son Cambyses II on the throne of Babylon, but he was replaced after less than a year by a certain Gubaru. Classical writers provide a very dark and somewhat maniacal picture of Cambyses II, who was bound to defy religious conventions and to overrun local customs. In 525 B.C.E., Cambyses II was successful in conquering Egypt, which the Persians held (off and on) for two centuries. Herodotus, however, claims that Cambyses II angered the Egyptians by desecrating the Apis Bull, an animal which was considered to be the incarnation of the Egyptian god

Ptah. Diodorus of Sicily mentions the fact that Cambyses II also destroyed and looted some Egyptian temples. The Persian monarch died (either by accident or suicide) in 522 B.C.E. en route to Persia to quell a revolt. The Persian government went into a chaos for the next year or so, culminating in the victory of Darius I, who was the next successful monarch.

Though Cambyses II is not mentioned in the Bible, the books of Haggai and Zechariah are likely to be placed during the period of chaos that followed Cambyses II's death (*c.* 522–521 B.C.E.). Because of the temporary weakness of the Persian throne, both of these prophets had expectations of the return of the Davidic monarchy to Jerusalem. At this time, Zerubbabel (a Davidic descendant) was governor of Judah (see Haggai 2:20–23, and Zechariah 4:6–10; 6:11–13).

LEFT: PERSIAN ARMY PLAQUES FROM THE TIME THE EMPIRE WAS AT ITS PEAK. THE GOLD MEDALLIONS DEPICT FIERCE CREATURES SUCH AS LIONS AND DRAGONS, PROBABLY TO INTIMIDATE THE ENEMY.

DARIUS I

Darius I (reigned 521–486 B.C.E.) came to the Persian throne through very suspicious circumstances. Moreover, his lineage was suspect, although he claimed descent by way of marriage to a daughter of Cyrus II. He defended his legitimacy in the Behistun Inscription, in which he claimed that a usurper (Pseudo-Smerdis) attempted to seize the throne after the death of Cambyses II. The Greek historian Herodotus described a Delphic oracle that appointed Darius I as king, and the Persian nobility supported him. In many respects, Darius I was the administrative founder of the Persian Empire, as he established the satrapies (provinces) and installed Persian nationals as governors. According to Greek sources, he also codified Persian laws, supervised numerous public work projects throughout the empire, established imperial coinage, introduced imperial forms of taxation, and engaged in a great number of building projects at Susa and Persepolis, the Persian capital cities.

Darius I is perhaps best known for his western military campaigns, which became the main theme of Herodotus's *Histories*. Although Darius I successfully quelled an Ionian revolt on the west coast of Turkey (500–494 B.C.E.), he encountered stiff resistance from the Athenians, who burned Sardis, the Persian administrative capital in the region. Darius I responded by sending a reconnaissance force in 490 B.C.E. to the Attic Peninsula of Greece, landing at the Bay of Marathon, where a combined Athenian and Plataean force routed the Persians. The Athenian victory became a symbol of Greek liberty, as they had repelled a foreign tyrant. However, to the Persians, the battle was probably considered a minor setback. Darius I died before a full-scale invasion could be prepared, a task that became the responsibility of his son, Xerxes I.

THE JEWISH BUILDING PROJECT

The book of Ezra portrays Darius I in a positive manner in relation to his dealings with the Jews and their desire to rebuild their Temple in Jerusalem. Although the Jews returned to their land during the reign of Cyrus II, work on the Temple did not commence until the second year of Darius I's reign (*c.* 520 B.C.E.; see Ezra 4:24). Both Haggai and Zechariah recount a successful effort by the local governor, Zerubbabel, to rebuild the Temple, even though some of the local population (that is, non-Jews) petitioned Darius I to stop the building activity (see Ezra 5:6–17).

Like other Ancient Near Eastern kings, Darius I looked to royal precedent to make a determination as to the legitimacy (or lack thereof) of the Jewish building project. According to Ezra 6, Darius found a decree of Cyrus II at Ecbatana (a summer residence of the Persian monarchs) delineating the rebuilding of the Temple at Jerusalem and the orders to

BELOW: INTRICATELY CARVED RELIEF ON THE STAIRCASE OF DARIUS I'S PALACE AT PERSEPOLIS, SHOWING COURT DIGNITARIES IN THE SERVICE OF THE KING. DARIUS I WAS THE FOURTH KING OF THE ACHAEMENID DYNASTY.

RIGHT: GOLDEN RHYTON FROM THE ACHAEMENID PERIOD. DURING THIS TIME, PERSIANS DRANK WINE FROM THESE CEREMONIAL CUPS IN THE SHAPE OF AN ANIMAL'S HEAD OR HORN.

return the Temple utensils that had been sent to Babylon. Darius I implied in his response that the cost of the building program was to be paid out of the royal treasury. It is possible that the Persians levied a special tax to subsidize the project. The Cyrus Cylinder did not delineate any specifics about how and if the Persian government did this type of thing. However, a number of rebuilt temples in Babylon bore bricks stamped with Cyrus II's name, suggesting that the royal treasury financed the project (or at worst, sanctioned it). Furthermore, Darius I's generosity in terms of subject peoples is confirmed by an Egyptian name for him (which translates as "Friend of all the Gods"). The royal request for prayer for the well-being of the king (Ezra 6:10) is paralleled in the Cyrus Cylinder, where Cyrus II asks the gods (through his worshippers, one can presume) to grant Cyrus II and his son Cambyses II long life. In fact, Herodotus noted that every sacrifice had to have a prayer for the king attached to it. Contemporary papyri from Elephantine in Egypt mention prayers to a Persian official if he aided the Elephantine Jews in the rebuilding of their temple. The punishment for disobeying the decree (impalement on a beam from the house of the perpetrator; see Ezra 6:11) is well known from royal inscriptions of Darius I, where Ahura Mazda, the leading Persian god, is asked to kill and destroy the house of those who have been disobedient. Impalement was also known in Persia. The Greek historian Thucydides (*c.* 460–400 B.C.E.) writes that

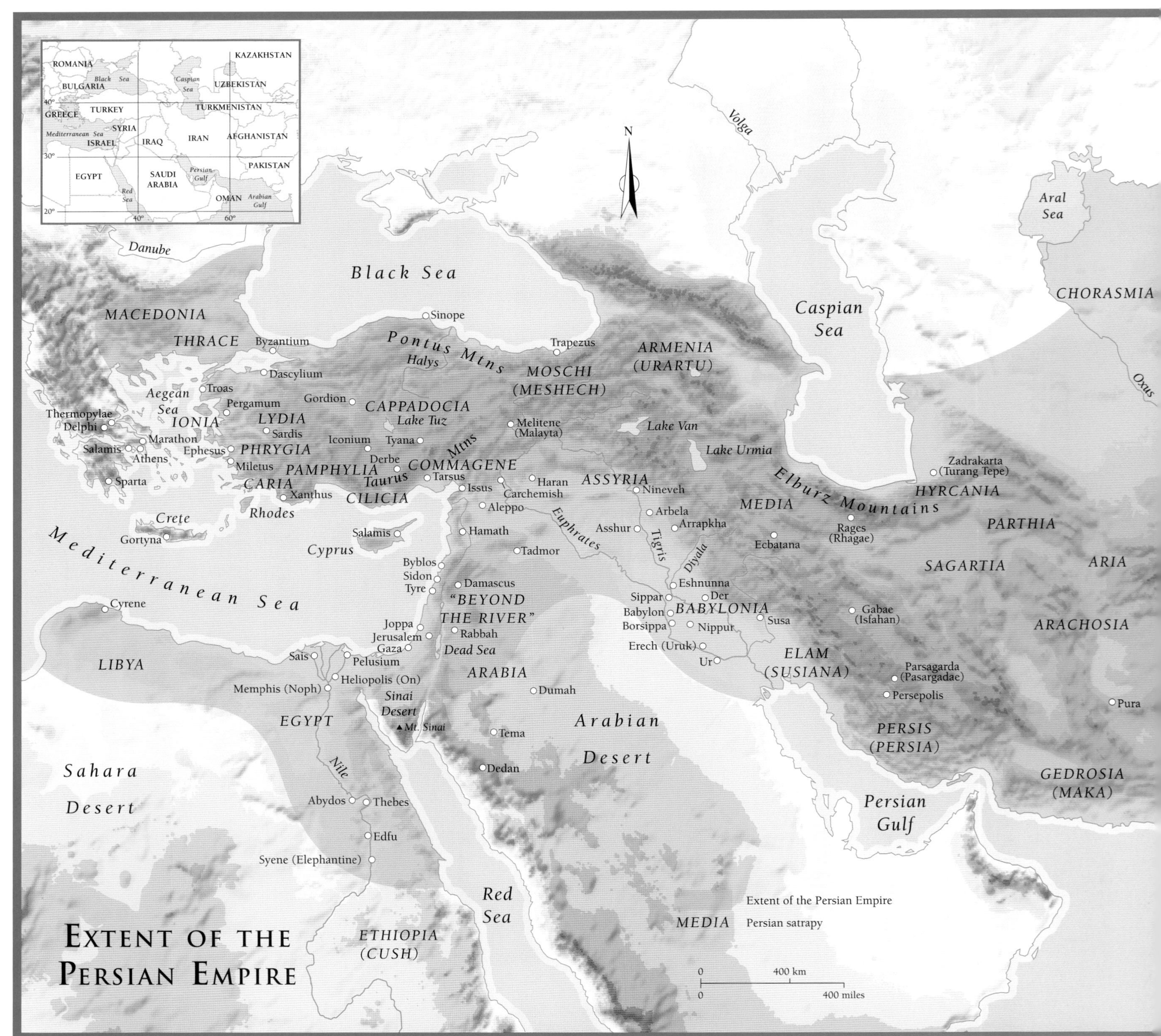

King Inaros of Libya was impaled by the Persians during the reign of Artaxerxes I in about 455 B.C.E.

In sum, because of the many parallels found in Greek and Persian sources, it is reasonable to conclude that the substance of the letter cited in Ezra 6 is historically plausible.

XERXES I

Xerxes I (reigned 485–465 B.C.E.) was king of the Persian Empire when it suffered defeat against the Hellenic coalition in the Greco-Persian wars (480–479 B.C.E.). Knowledge of his reign is derived from antagonistic Greek sources (stemming from Herodotus), Jewish tradition, and scattered Persian inscriptions. Xerxes I succeeded his father Darius I and appears to have continued his policy, at least concerning the western front, where the Persians were attempting to expand into the Balkans and Greece. However, Xerxes I was soon confronted with rebellions in Egypt (486–485 B.C.E., which took a whole year to quell) and in Babylonia (*c.* 481 B.C.E.). Xerxes I failed to control the mainland of Greece, although some Greek city-states did in fact submit to Persian authority (Thessaly and Thebes). Following some early victories in central Greece, Xerxes I's navy lost a decisive battle at Salamis in 480 B.C.E., and the Persian army was defeated on land at Plataea in 479 B.C.E. Xerxes I left abruptly after the naval battle, possibly to successfully quell yet another Babylonian rebellion; control of this centrally located area was crucial for the survival of the empire. The Greeks, however, followed up with a revolt against Persian rule on several Aegean islands, and another Athenian naval victory against Persia in Pamphylia in Asia Minor (in 466 B.C.E.). Xerxes I was murdered along with his crown prince Darius in a palace revolt in 465 B.C.E.

Xerxes I's reputation has suffered more than that of any other Achaemenid king. Plato describes him as raised under the care of women in the royal harem, and thus lacking the same hardened experience of his father Darius I. Furthermore,

LEFT: PERSIAN WARRIORS, FROM THE BOOK *ZUR GESCHICHTE DER COSTUME.* COLORS USUALLY DOMINANT IN PERSIAN MILITARY ROBES WERE PURPLE AND SAFFRON; PURPLE WAS EXTRACTED FROM THE MUREX SHELL, SAFFRON FROM THE PISTILS OF THE CROCUS FLOWER.

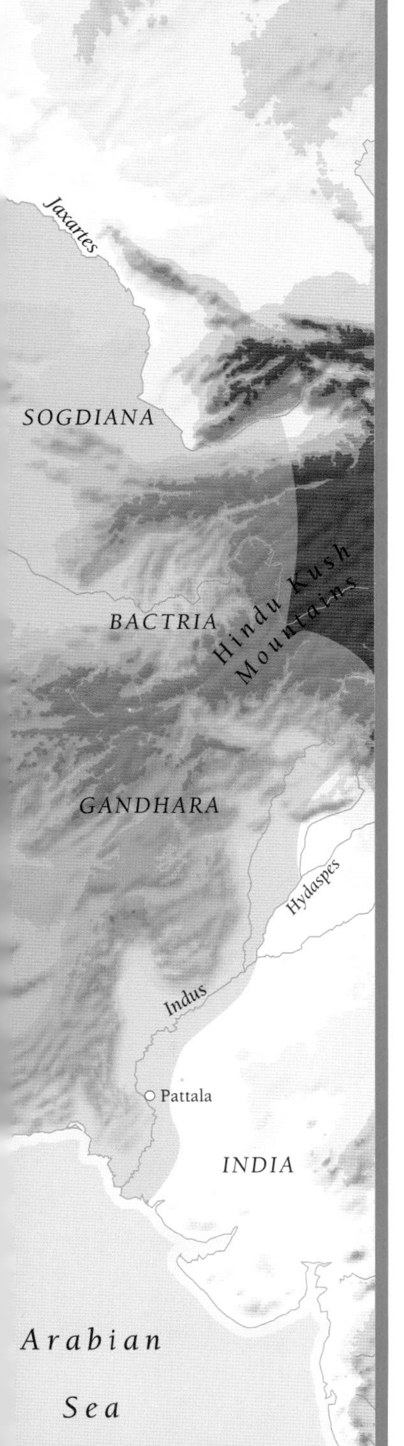

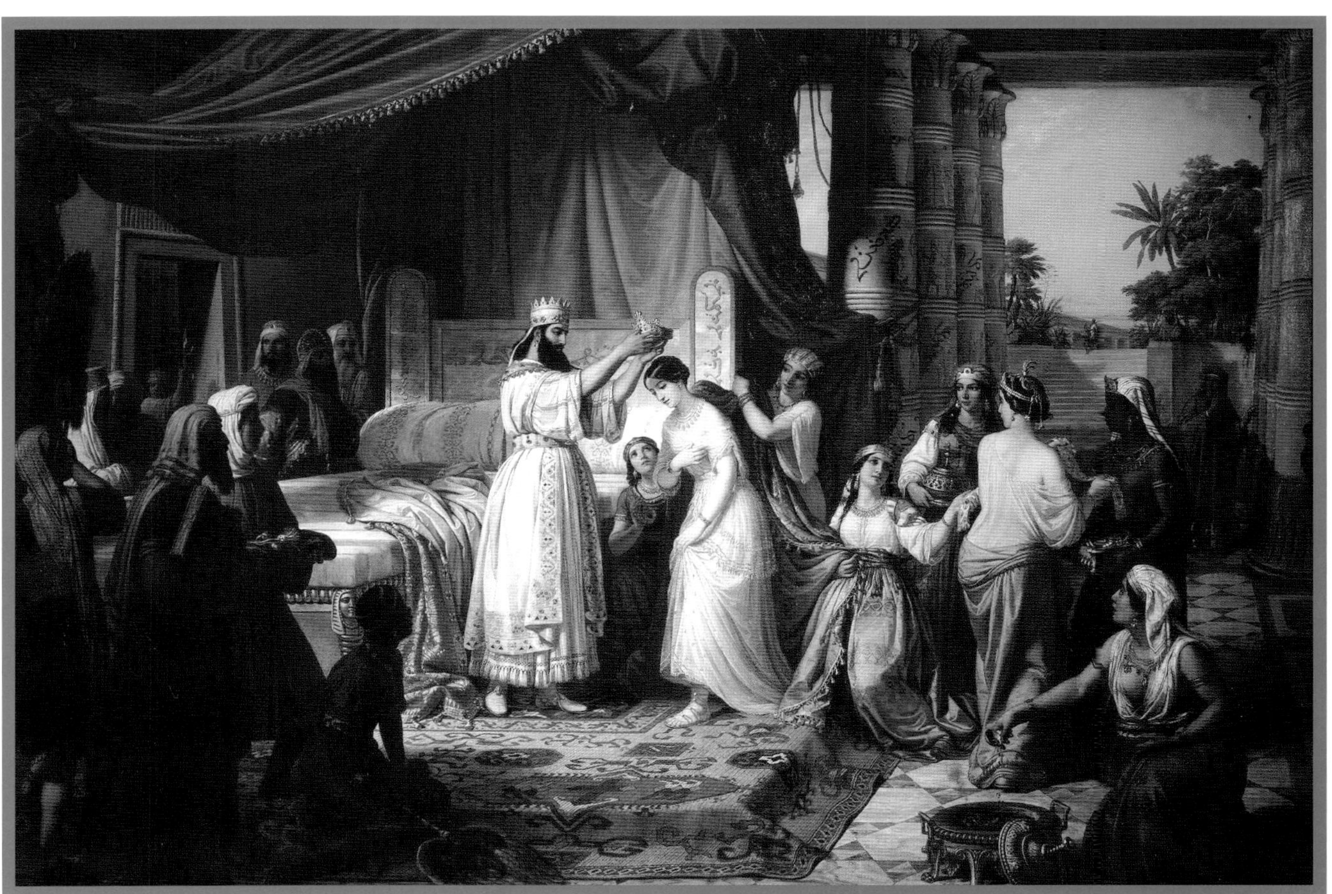

BELOW: *CORONATION OF ESTHER* BY VINCENZO MORANI. THE BOOK OF ESTHER RELATES THE STORY OF HOW QUEEN ESTHER (CROWNED BY XERXES I) AND HER COUSIN MORDECAI FOIL HAMAN'S EVIL PLOT TO EXTERMINATE THE JEWS.

RIGHT: *XERXES (AHASUERUS) AT THE HELLESPONT*, DETAIL OF A PAINTING BY JEAN ADRIEN GUIGNET. THE HELLESPONT IS THE NARROW BODY OF WATER SEPARATING EUROPE AND ASIA.

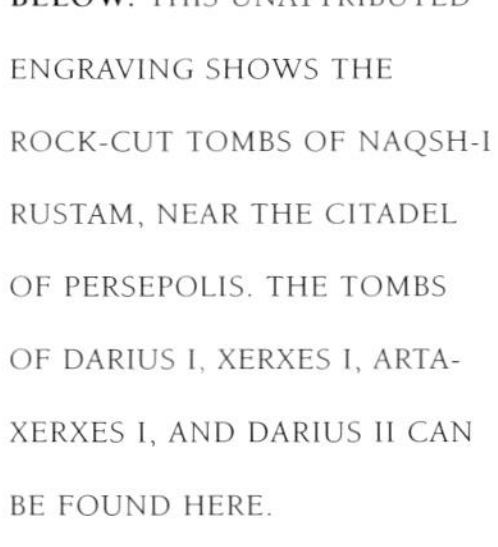

BELOW: THIS UNATTRIBUTED ENGRAVING SHOWS THE ROCK-CUT TOMBS OF NAQSH-I RUSTAM, NEAR THE CITADEL OF PERSEPOLIS. THE TOMBS OF DARIUS I, XERXES I, ARTAXERXES I, AND DARIUS II CAN BE FOUND HERE.

Herodotus claims that he was put in power because of the influence of his mother, Atossa, and allowed himself to be persuaded to undertake the Greek expedition, where he acted with ruthless pride, made many irrational decisions, and angered the gods with his impiety. Both Herodotus and Strabo claim that Xerxes I violated the sanctuaries in Babylonia during the second insurrection, exhibiting a so-called intolerance, which appears to be confirmed by the Persian Daiva Inscription. And in the biblical book of Esther, Xerxes I was satirized as Ahasuerus, a king who makes illogical decisions and is dominated by women.

However, when put in historical perspective, a more balanced estimation of Xerxes I's reign can be made. Herodotus describes Xerxes I as a tragic figure who was divinely fated to fail in the Greek expedition, no matter what decisions he made. His description of Xerxes I as a weakling and a womanizer is found in novelistic sections of Herodotus. Moreover, there is no evidence that Xerxes I discontinued the worship of Marduk at Babylon in this period, or that the king was intolerant of gods other than Ahura Mazda. Xerxes I was also a prolific builder who consolidated the holdings of the empire, although he will forever be tainted by defeat in the Greco-Persian wars.

ARTAXERXES I

Artaxerxes was the name of three Persian monarchs. Artaxerxes I (reigned 464–424 B.C.E.) succeeded his father Xerxes I to the throne. Sources for his reign are very limited. He encountered a number of rebellions during his reign, including one in Egypt in 460 B.C.E., and one from the satrap (provincial governor) Megabysus in 448 B.C.E., both of which he quelled. Although the books of Ezra and Nehemiah do not specify which "King Artaxerxes" they are referring to, most scholars agree that it was Artaxerxes I.

During the time of Artaxerxes I, Judah was still inhabited by those from the lower classes who had not suffered deportation, as well as those Jews who had returned following the decree of Cyrus II. Moreover, Judah was bordered to the north by Jews and other ethnic groups who had been deported to the area by the Assyrians nearly three centuries earlier (see 2 Kings 17:6 and Isaiah 7:8). These northerners (later known as Samaritans) were hostile to the Jews, and thus their offer to help in the Temple rebuilding was not believed to be authentic, and was rebuffed. The northerners then wrote to Artaxerxes I, warning the king of the dangers of allowing the Jews to rebuild the city of Jerusalem, as the Jews had a history of rebellion, and were also prepared to withhold taxes from the king. Though the Persian royal annals have not been rediscovered (unlike their Assyrian and Babylonian predecessors), the writer of Ezra also published the response of Artaxerxes I, who, like other Ancient Near Eastern kings, scanned previous records which provided historical perspective on the "Jewish problem." Though the letter was written in the diplomatic language of Aramaic, the Persian king certainly had the letter translated into Persian. Thus, because of Jerusalem's notorious past history of rebellion, the king decreed that the work on the

The Persian Province "Beyond the River"

The region in the Persian Empire that was west of the Euphrates River (that is, "Beyond the River," except for Babylonia, which was a province of its own) was a very large province, or satrap (see Ezra 4:10–16). Not only was it ruled by an administrative satrap, the province was apparently divided into smaller units, ruled by a *pahat*.

Ezra 5:3 mentions a certain Tattenai, *pahat* under Ushtannu, governor of the "Beyond the River" satrapy. He was responsible for evaluating the progress of the building of the Jewish Temple. The writer of Ezra provides correspondence between Tattenai and Darius I concerning the legitimacy of the building project. Once he received a positive response from the king (Ezra 6), Tattenai carried out the king's orders. A Babylonian source provides evidence that Tattenai was promoted to satrap during the reign of Darius I (*c.* 502 B.C.E.).

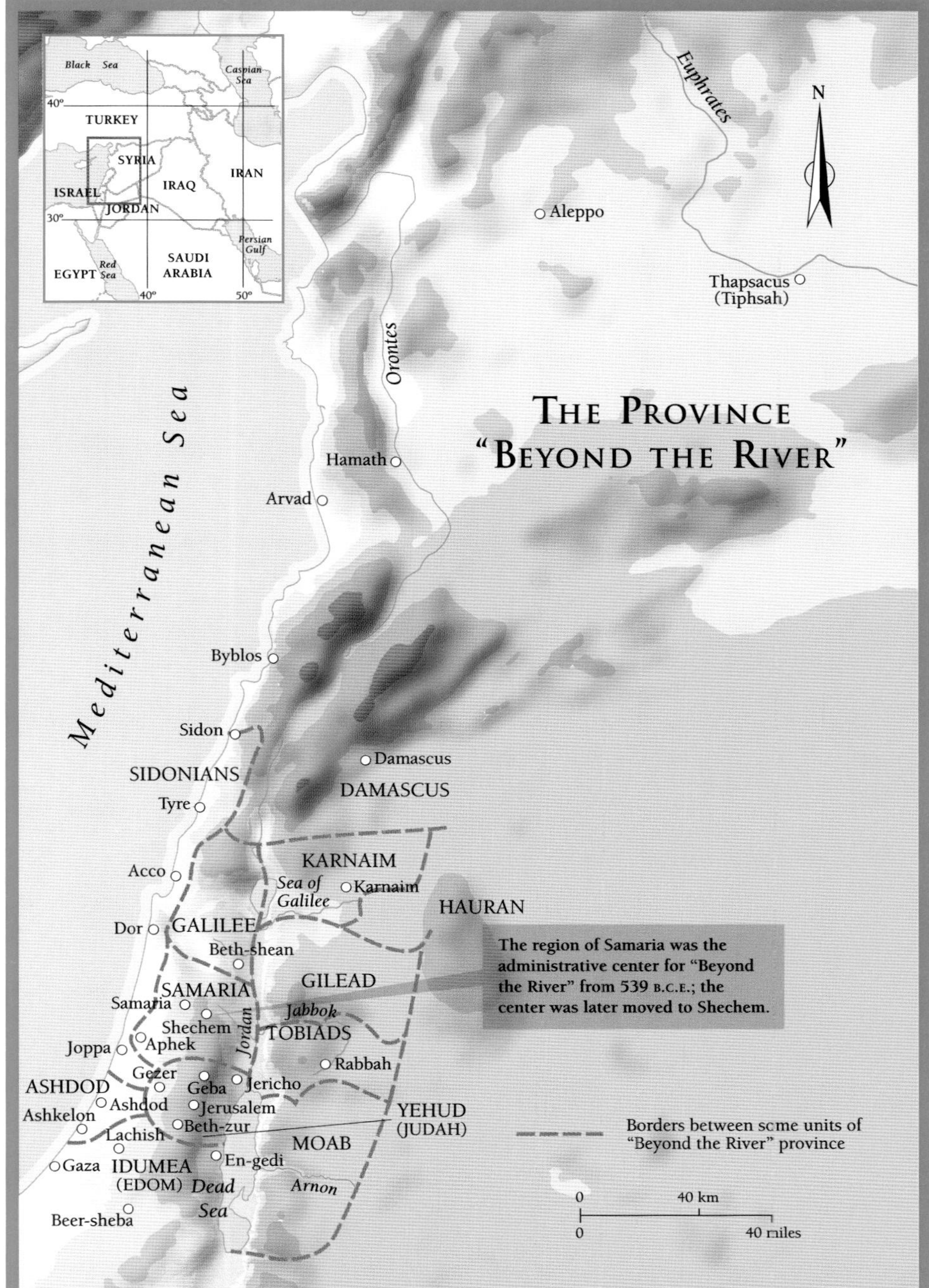

city's rebuilding had to stop. Rehum and Shimshai, representatives of the northerners, went quickly with armed forces to stop the Jewish rebuilding (see Ezra 4:17–22).

THE 127 PERSIAN PROVINCES

The writer of Esther describes the Persian Empire during the reign of Ahasuerus (that is, Xerxes I) as having 127 provinces, or satrapies. However, the number of provinces was usually about 20, according to Herodotus. Each satrapy was given to a Persian noble who was responsible for the defense of the district. The satrap also was required to provide soldiers and taxes to the crown. It is probable that the Esther source is describing smaller administrative districts. It is known that within each satrapy local peoples and even dynastic houses were given a certain measure of autonomy, as long as they contributed their designated quota of soldiers to the Persian armed forces.

PERSIAN PROVINCES IN WHAT HAD BEEN KNOWN AS ISRAEL AND JUDAH

Our primary information concerning Israel and Judah comes from the biblical books of Ezra and Nehemiah. After the conquest of Babylon by the Persians in 539 B.C.E., the region of Samaria in the north of Israel continued as the administrative center of the "Beyond the River" province as it had under the Babylonians. According to Nehemiah, Sanballat was appointed governor of the province (Nehemiah 2:10–19). The region appears to have had wide mercantile relationships and as a result flourished economically, as evidenced by Athenian and Sidonian coins, imported Aegean pottery, and Aramaic ostraca. Furthermore, significant amounts of legal and administrative papyri written in Aramaic from Samaria attest to this economic growth. It is possible that the increased building activity in Jerusalem (as attested in Ezra and Nehemiah) was considered a threat to the resurgence of Samaria. The assassination of Alexander the Great's general, Andromachus, during the succeeding period of Macedonian occupation, was a setback for Samaria. The city of Samaria was attacked and abandoned, and Shechem became the economic and administrative center of this northern area.

The southern province of Judah also retained its provincial status under the Persians, as it had during Babylonian rule. Sheshbazzar, described as a "prince of Judah" (with a Davidic lineage), was commissioned by Cyrus II to return the Temple vessels to Jerusalem (Ezra 1:8–11). He was also appointed governor in the "province of Judah" (Ezra 5:8–14). Zerubbabel (who was also a descendant of David) served as governor under Darius I (Haggai 1:1). Both received credit for laying the foundation of the Second Temple (Ezra 3:8–10, 5:16). It is not certain whether Nehemiah (described as a "cupbearer") or Ezra had any permanent government post in the Persian period. Nehemiah's request to go to Judah and his reliance on the local Palestinian administrators to help in the Jerusalem building project implies that he had no official permanent governmental post in Judah (Nehemiah 1:7–9). However, Nehemiah's labor problems (Nehemiah 5), subjection to constant foreign intrusions (Nehemiah 4), and religious reforms (Nehemiah 13) indicate that he assumed significant authority. It is not certain whether Judah was still considered a "province" during this period.

Building the Second Temple

THE LORD ... HAS CHARGED ME TO BUILD HIM A HOUSE AT JERUSALEM IN JUDAH EZRA 1:2

RIGHT: *CROESUS ON THE FUNERAL PYRE*, AMPHORA, C. 480 B.C.E. IN 546 B.C.E., CYRUS II CONQUERED KING CROESUS'S LYDIA AS PART OF HIS TERRITORIAL EXPANSION, A STEP TOWARD THE FREEING OF THE BABYLONIAN EXILES.

The conquest of Babylon by Cyrus II (Cyrus the Great) brought about profound changes in the Fertile Crescent, and created a new hope for the Jewish exiles. This optimism is vividly portrayed in the oracles contained in chapters 40–55 of the book of Isaiah. There the prophet confidently proclaimed that God had chosen Cyrus II to restore Israel. Cyrus II was God's "anointed" (that is, his "messiah," see Isaiah 45:1), and he would be the agent by whom Jerusalem and the Temple would be rebuilt. This grandiose vision of the role and purpose of the Persian king would do much to restore the confidence of the displaced Jews following the nightmare of the Exile.

THE EXILES RETURN

By 539 B.C.E., the Persians controlled the entire Near East, and their beneficent rule was a most welcome relief from the tyranny of the Babylonians and the Assyrians. Cyrus abandoned the cruel policies of his predecessors, who destroyed cities and towns, stole sacred treasure, and exiled people into captivity. Under Persian rule, territories formerly administered by the other major imperial powers were reorganized into a system of satraps and provinces, and the outlying districts were also granted a reasonable degree of political autonomy. On the whole, peace was established, roads and communication were greatly improved, and the exiled people were given many rights that previously had been denied them under both the Assyrian and the Babylonian rulers.

It is against this background that one should understand the decree that Cyrus issued a year after the fall of Babylon. Cyrus specifically encouraged the cultural autonomy of diverse peoples, and allowed subjected people to return to their homelands, carry on their customs, and worship their gods. This edict had an enormous impact on the Jews who were living in exile: they were released from bondage, encouraged to rebuild their Temple, and given whatever financial assistance they required. So significant was this proclamation that the Bible even records two versions of it, one in Hebrew (Ezra 1:2–4; see also 2 Chronicles 36:22–23) and the other in Aramaic (Ezra 6:3–5), which was at that time the *lingua franca* of international relations. The account written in Hebrew reads: "Thus says King Cyrus of Persia: The Lord, the God of heaven, has given me all the kingdoms of the earth, and he has charged me to build him a house at Jerusalem in Judah. Any of those among you who are of his people—may their God be with them!—are now permitted to go up to Jerusalem in Judah, and rebuild the house of the Lord, the God of Israel—he is the God who is in Jerusalem; and let all survivors, in whatever place they reside, be assisted by the people of their place with silver and gold, with goods and with animals, besides freewill offerings for the house of God in Jerusalem" (Ezra 1:2–4).

Ezra provides specific instructions regarding the building of the Temple: "Its height shall be sixty cubits and its width sixty cubits, with three courses of hewn stones and one course of timber; let the cost be paid from the royal treasury. Moreover, let the gold and silver vessels of the house of God, which Nebuchadnezzar took out of the Temple in Jerusalem, and brought to Babylon, be restored and brought back to the Temple in Jerusalem" (Ezra 6:4–5).

BELOW: CYRUS II IN BABYLON, RETURNING THE TEMPLE VESSELS TO THE JEWISH EXILES. ILLUSTRATION BY GUSTAVE DORE.

SHESHBAZZAR CARRIES THE VESSELS OF PRECIOUS METALS

The first group of exiles to return home carried with them the valuable gold and silver cups and plates that had been looted by King Nebuchadnezzar and the Babylonian army when they sacked Jerusalem back in 586 B.C.E. These vessels, which were once used in the service of the worship of Yahweh, had been under the control of gods worshipped by Nebuchadnezzar II during the Exile. The transference of the vessels back to Jerusalem by the decree of Cyrus reestablished a vital link between the First Temple and the Second Temple, and indicated that the God of Israel was once more about to be worshipped.

The vessels as well as all the silver and gold were to be entrusted to a man called Sheshbazzar, the "prince" *(nasi')* of Judah (Ezra 1:8), and the "governor" *(pehah)* appointed by Cyrus (Ezra 5:14). The term "prince" marks Sheshbazzar as a leader of the Jewish people, and it is likely that Sheshbazzar was of Davidic descent—if, in fact, he is the same person as one of Jehoiachin's sons, called "Shenazzar" and mentioned in the genealogical list in 1 Chronicles 3:17–18. If Sheshbazzar was indeed a member of the Davidic line, his appointment as governor by Cyrus would also be in keeping with the Persian practice of designating a member of the royal house to act as leader for the local state. It is also interesting to note that the Temple artifacts are initially entrusted to a political rather than a religious ruler. Following the building of the Second

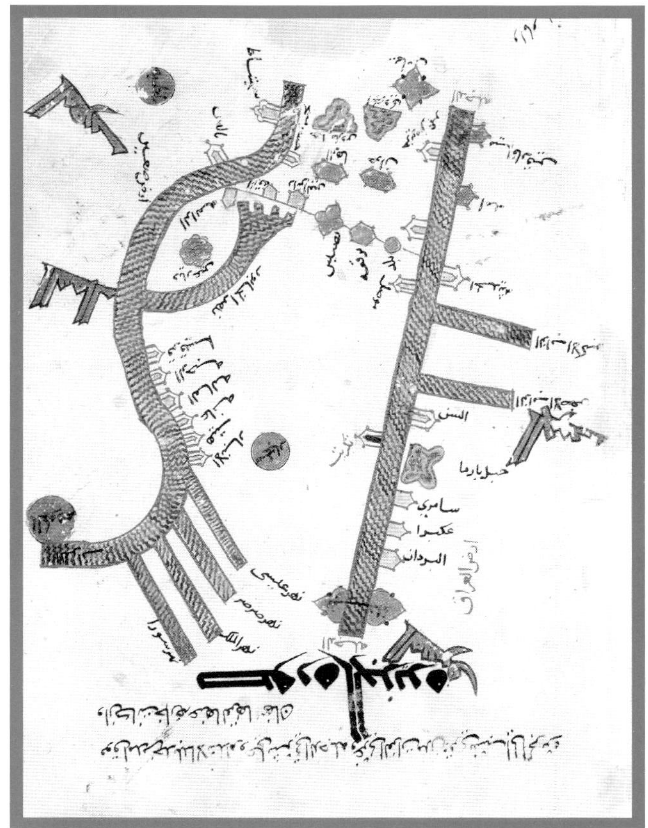

LEFT: THE EUPHRATES AND TIGRIS RIVERS, FROM AN ELEVENTH-CENTURY C.E. ARABIAN MANUSCRIPT (THE MAP IS ORIENTED SOUTH). CYRUS II'S CONTROL OF THIS IMPORTANT REGION ALLOWED THE EXILES SAFE PASSAGE BACK TO JUDAH.

BELOW: *MAP OF JERUSALEM,* FROM *CIVITATES ORBIS TERRARUM* BY GEORG BRAUN AND FRANS HOGENBERG. THIS COLORED ENGRAVING SHOWS THE HOLY CITY BEFORE THE FIRST TEMPLE HAD BEEN DESTROYED.

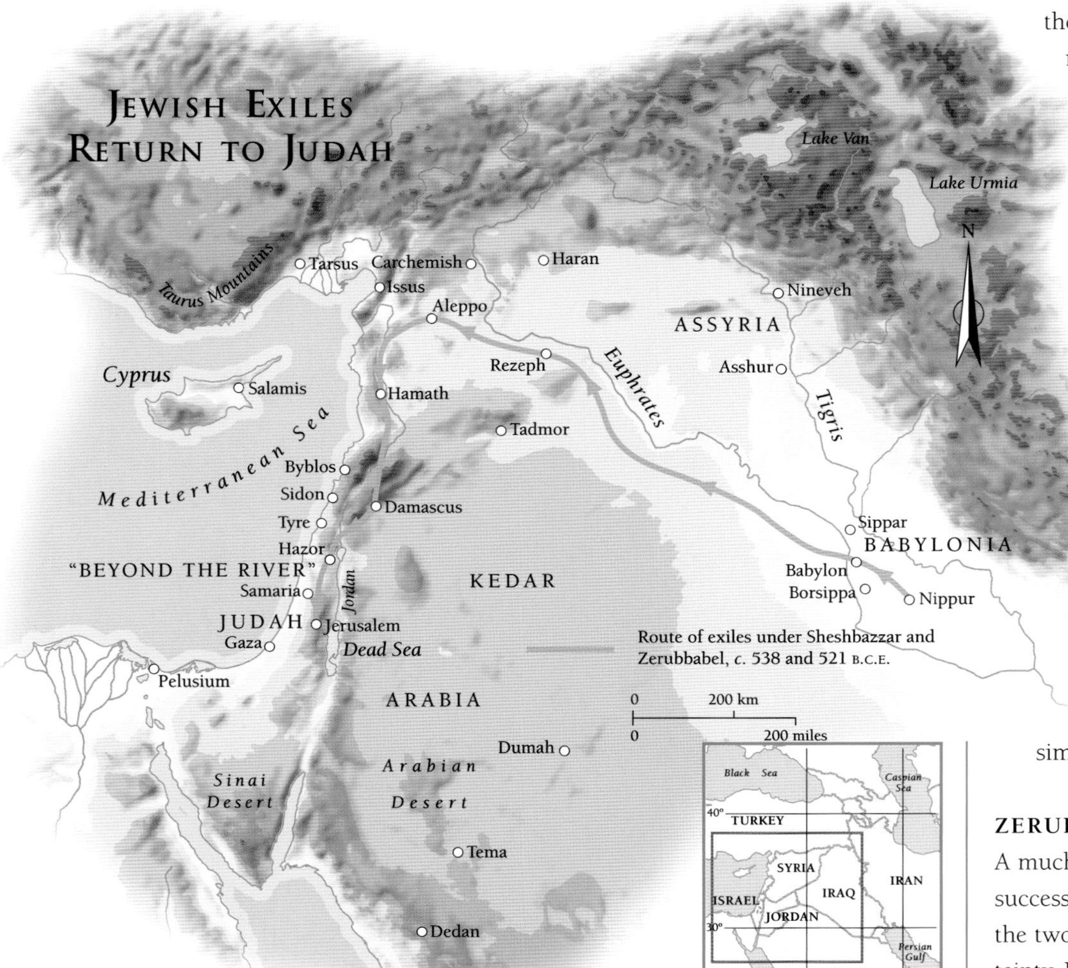

Temple and the establishment of the Second Temple community, however, the religious element would gain supremacy over the political one.

THE EXILES ARRIVE IN JUDAH

Shortly after the decree by Cyrus, Sheshbazzar led a group of exiles home to Judah. Unfortunately, our information regarding the nature and extent of this first contingent is rather vague. No figures are given, and it is probable that many Jews also did not make the trip back. It is likely that they continued to live in Babylon, accounting for a large and thriving community of Jews in Mesopotamia over the next thousand years. This was the community that was responsible for the compilation and the development of the Babylonian Talmud, *c.* 600 C.E. The Jews who remained behind probably assisted the contingent that returned by their many gifts of gold, silver, and freewill offerings.

Although Sheshbazzar is credited as the one who "came and laid the foundations of the house of God in Jerusalem" (Ezra 5:16), not much else is known about his term as governor. He is not mentioned outside the book of Ezra, and he seems to have disappeared sometime after the laying of the foundations. He may have been around when the altar was rebuilt and the official sect was resumed, but these events are not recorded of him. Apparently very little else was accomplished by him, and the work was taken up by Zerubbabel and Joshua. If Sheshbazzar was a son of Jehoiachin, he may have been well advanced in years and may have simply died soon after returning to Judah with the exiles.

ZERUBBABEL

A much more promising start was achieved by Sheshbazzar's successor, Zerubbabel. There are many similarities between the two men, and their relationship is shrouded in uncertainty. Like Sheshbazzar, Zerubbabel is called a governor and is of the royal line and therefore of Davidic descent. He is the son of Shealtiel, who is listed as a son of King Jehoiachin in the genealogical list in Chronicles; see Ezra 3:2 and 1 Chronicles 3:17. Similarly, both Sheshbazzar and Zerubbabel led a group of exiles back home, though it appears that Zerubbabel led a much larger contingent back than did his predecessor. A census of the returnees, recorded in Ezra 2:1–67 and Nehemiah 7:6–73, lists the number of returnees with

JOSHUA THE HIGH PRIEST

Within the party of exiles returning with Zerubbabel was a man called Joshua ben Jehozadak, a priest of the Zadokite lineage who was elevated to the position of "high priest." (The position of high priest during the postexilic period remains hereditary until about 175 B.C.E.) Both the high priest (Joshua) and the governor (Zerubbabel) shared power: Zerubbabel the governor from the line of David had charge over political affairs, whereas Joshua the high priest from the line of Zadok had jurisdiction in spiritual matters. This division of power is clearly seen in the vision of the golden lampstand and the two olive trees in Zechariah 4:1–14. Zerubbabel and Joshua are thus respectively described as the messianic figure and the spiritual leader, and both prince and high priest were to be instrumental in the coming of the kingdom of God.

RIGHT: THE JEWISH EXILES FINALLY RETURN TO THEIR HOMELAND, LITHOGRAPH BY AN UNKNOWN FRENCH ARTIST. THE EXILES TRAVELED FROM BABYLON IN A NUMBER OF SUCCESSIVE GROUPS.

Zerubbabel as 42,360 people, plus 7,337 servants, and 200 singers. Finally, both men are said to have played a part in the laying of the foundation stones of the Second Temple (Ezra 3:8–13 and 5:16).

The figure of Zerubbabel also plays an important role in the work of the postexilic prophets Haggai and Zechariah. In both of these prophetic books, Zerubbabel is the focus of great messianic expectations. According to Haggai, Yahweh is shortly going to "shake the heavens and the earth" (Haggai 2:6), nations would bring their treasures into the new Temple, and Zerubbabel would be established as the new leader. Haggai also declares that Yahweh is soon to "overthrow the throne of kingdoms," and he singles out Zerubbabel as Yahweh's "chosen" and his "signet ring" (Haggai 2:22–23). According to the prophet Zechariah, Zerubbabel is depicted as the Davidic prince who would lead Judah to her destined glory. The sign of Zerubbabel's messianic authority is that he will complete the building of the Temple.

BELOW: GUSTAVE DORE'S DRAMATIC ILLUSTRATION DEPICTS THE JEWISH PEOPLE WORKING HARD TO REBUILD THEIR TEMPLE. THE FOUNDATION STONES OF THE TEMPLE MAY HAVE BEEN LAID TWICE: ONCE BY SHESHBAZZAR, AND ONCE BY ZERUBBABEL.

RIGHT: ERECTING AN ALTAR IN THE SECOND TEMPLE LINKED PAST AND PRESENT. AS WITH THIS IMAGE FROM A TWELFTH-CENTURY C.E. ENGLISH MANUSCRIPT, AN ALTAR IS OFTEN A KEY PART OF A RELIGIOUS SCENE.

WHO LAID THE FOUNDATION STONES FOR THE TEMPLE?

The biblical sources suggest that the laying of the foundations for the Temple took place twice: the first time was after Sheshbazzar returned with a small band of exiles in about 538 B.C.E., as recorded in Ezra 1 and 5:16; the second time was after Zerubbabel and Joshua erected an altar, cleared the rubble and began the preparations for the constructions (Ezra 3). According to the prophets Haggai (1:1–6) and Zechariah (4:9), this event took place in the second year of Darius I (*c.* 520 B.C.E.). Furthermore, Haggai and Zechariah show no awareness of any previous work having been done on laying the foundations or any construction having taken place. It is possible that Ezra, in his desire to show the zeal of the returning exiles in getting on with the business of constructing the Second Temple, places the story of the laying of the foundations immediately after the exiles returned when, in fact, it took place at a later time. According to this theory, Ezra backdates or telescopes Zerubbabel's activity onto the first stage of the return in order to present a more unified account, and conflates the activities of both men. It has also been argued, however, that both Joshua and Zerubbabel had a hand in the laying of the Temple foundations in the time of Cyrus II, but were forced to quit because of strong opposition. Therefore, the reason why neither Haggai nor Zechariah mentions the earlier laying of the foundation stones is because no significant progress had been made. According to this theory, Zerubbabel and Joshua resumed the work of the laying of the Temple foundations during the time of Darius I, and it is this later event to which both Haggai and Zechariah refer, and which is recorded in Ezra 3.

BELOW: LAYING THE TEMPLE FOUNDATIONS REMINDED JEWS OF THE IMPORTANCE OF LOYALTY TO THE ARK OF THE COVENANT. THE ARK, FROM A TENTH-CENTURY C.E. MOZARABIC BIBLE (THE MOZARABS WERE SPANISH CHRISTIANS LIVING UNDER MUSLIM RULE ABOUT 12 CENTURIES AGO).

THE ALTAR IS ERECTED

In the ancient world, altars are found in a variety of religions and come in a range of shapes and sizes. Basically, an altar is any surface on which offerings were made or placed before the deity. Altars are common in the Old Testament, and they were usually built at sacred places, where contact between humans and God could occur. Before the construction of the First Temple, these sites were common enough and associated with Noah, Abraham, and Moses. With the construction of the First Temple, however, only the altar in the Temple was deemed a legitimate place to worship God.

The Old Testament is rife with stories concerning the problems of worshipping outside the Temple and, therefore, the biblical authors warn of the need to tear down these altars to avoid lapsing into idolatrous ways. The most famous example of an illegitimate altar is the establishment of Jeroboam's altars at the towns of Dan and Bethel, an act which becomes known as the "grievous sin of Jeroboam," and leads to the downfall of the northern kingdom of Israel. It is therefore important for the exiles, if they were to reestablish the connection with the past, to erect an altar on the site of the First Temple as one of their first steps in founding the religious community. Such an action would have guaranteed continuity with the preexilic community and lent a great deal of legitimacy to the founding of the religious apparatus of the postexilic or Second Temple community. It also permitted the group of exiles to resume their worship of God without delay, an act essential for the community's well-being. It is possible that the community's actions were meant to reflect those of David, who averted disaster by erecting an altar and offering a sacrifice on the Temple site before it was built (1 Chronicles 21:28–22:1). But, more than likely, Mosaic Law is being recalled here, as the building of the altar should be the community's first act on entering the Promised Land (see also Deuteronomy 27:5–8).

THE TEMPLE DEBRIS IS CLEARED AWAY

After the sack of Jerusalem and the destruction of the First Temple by the Babylonians in 586 B.C.E., the ruins lay desolate on the Temple Mount for the long period of the Babylonian captivity. It is obvious that a great deal of work would be needed before the actual construction of the Temple could begin. To that end, Zerubbabel and Joshua organized a work crew to help clear away the Temple debris and to begin the planning for the building of the Second Temple. They paid money to craftsmen and masons, and they donated food, drink, and oil to the Sidonians and the Tyrians for the transport of lumber to be used in the construction of the Temple (Ezra 3:7). The description of the preparations for the building of the Second Temple—that is, the use of masons and craftsmen as well the Sidonians and Tyrians—recalls the acts preceding the building of the First Temple as described in 1 Chronicles 22:4, 15. That this activity and the preparations took place in the second month of the year (Ezra 3:8), also recalls the fact that Solomon's preparations took place in the second month (2 Chronicles 3:2). In all, the work of clearing the debris and planning for the construction of the Second Temple clearly recalls that of the First Temple, and further stresses the lines of continuity between the preexilic and the postexilic communities.

THE FOUNDATIONS ARE LAID

With the debris cleared away and preparations for the building of the Second Temple progressing well, the way was clear for the laying of the foundation stones for the Temple. This was done with great solemnity and ceremony; priests blew trumpets and the Levites clashed symbols, and there was singing, rejoicing, and the giving of thanks to the LORD to mark the occasion. The Levites sang responsively to the LORD, "For he is good, for his steadfast love endures forever toward Israel" (Ezra 3:11). The goodness and love of God would have recalled the theme of faithfulness to the Covenant, and the phrase is used in a number of Psalms (100:5, 106:1, 118:1–4, 136:1–26).

Yet while there was great rejoicing over the laying of the foundation stones, there was also a contingent of the "old guard," people who had been alive during the time of the First Temple, and who openly wept during the ceremonies. From the book of Haggai we gain some insight into the motivations of this group, as the prophet Haggai reports that the cause of dissatisfaction among the older people was that the Second Temple failed to match the grandeur and magnificence of the First Temple (see Haggai 2:3). This will not be the only opposition to the rebuilding project that will haunt the exiles in the coming years.

ABOVE: *EPHRAIM SON OF JOSEPH CURING A SICK WOMAN,* BY G. DEGLI AVANCINI. ACCORDING TO EZRA, THE RETURNING EXILES BELIEVED CYRUS II'S DECREE DID NOT INCLUDE THE DESCENDANTS OF EPHRAIM AND MANASSEH, THE SAMARITANS.

LEFT: DARIUS I WITH SOME OF HIS DIGNITARIES, FROM A MEDIEVAL ARMENIAN COPY OF AN EARLIER PUBLICATION. THE PROPHETS HAGGAI AND ZECHARIAH SAY THE FOUNDATION STONES FOR THE SECOND TEMPLE WERE LAID EARLY IN DARIUS I'S REIGN.

THE SAMARITANS

Shortly after the work on the Temple started, some "adversaries of Judah and Benjamin" are reported to have contacted Zerubbabel, Joshua, and the elders, and offered to help with the reconstruction of the Temple (Ezra 4:1–2). Who were these adversaries? Most scholars suggest they were people who lived in the northern part of the old kingdom of Israel, in Samaria. These Samaritans were descended from the remnants of the population that were not exiled when Israel was destroyed by the Assyrians in 722 B.C.E., and various foreign nationalities who the Assyrians imported from other provinces. They seemed to have adopted a syncretistic religion that combined the old northern traditions with beliefs from foreign countries. The biblical author elsewhere associates them with idol worshippers (2 Kings 17:24–34). However, the Samaritans regarded themselves as the direct descendants of the Israelite tribes of Ephraim and his brother Manasseh who survived the destruction of Israel.

Initially, at least, the Samaritans appear to be friendly and supportive of the Jews in their building activities. They seem to want to assist with the construction (Ezra 4:2). Nevertheless, the Samaritan offer to help was rejected by Zerubbabel, Joshua, and the elders. This rejection was justified on the technical point that the Samaritans were not included in the original decree of Cyrus II (Ezra 4:3) and, therefore, not

ABOVE: JEAN FOUQUET'S *BUILDING OF THE SECOND TEMPLE*. FOUQUET USED THE TEXT OF A FRENCH ILLUMINATED MANUSCRIPT WRITTEN BY FLAVIUS JOSEPHUS IN THE FIRST CENTURY C.E. TO CREATE HIS ILLUSTRATION.

legally entitled to assist. The real reasons for the rejection, however, were likely quite different. To the exiles (or *golah* community), the Samaritans probably represented an impure or syncretistic form of worship that would have precluded their participation in the building of the Second Temple and their place in a renewed Jewish sect. However, there is probably a political motivation for both the offer and the rejection. The political leaders in Samaria may have felt threatened by the emergence of a new group in Judah who enjoyed the protection of imperial Persian authority. By participating in the reconstruction (and the expense) of the Temple, the Samaritans hoped to secure an interest in its operation and control. The *golah* community, however, would have been wary of such overtures, seeing them as a weakening not only of their religion, but also of their power in the new order.

WORK ON THE TEMPLE IS SUSPENDED

The Samaritan problem is further complicated by an older schism that had occurred many years before. Since the start of the monarchy there had been a long-standing division between the north and the south, a division that led to the creation of the northern state of Israel and the southern state of Judah following the death of Solomon in 931 B.C.E. The northerners probably opposed the centralization of worship in Jerusalem, as they created their own shrines at the towns of Dan and Bethel. Undoubtedly, the attempt by the *golah* community to set up their own altar and Temple may have motivated the northern leaders to hinder the process in any way they could. The book of Ezra reports that "the people of the land [Samaritans] discouraged the people of Judah, and made them afraid to build, and they bribed officials to frustrate their plan throughout the reign of King Cyrus of Persia and until the reign of King Darius of Persia" (Ezra 4:4–5).

Even leaving aside the Samaritan problem, the early years for the fledgling postexilic community must have been difficult ones. In the first place, probably only a small contingent of Jews made the journey and, secondly, Judah had not sufficiently recovered from the terrible destruction caused by King Nebuchadnezzar II's armies to support any significant increase in its population. The economic conditions were severe, discouraging those who returned from life in the well-watered valleys and lavish cities of Babylon. It was probably difficult enough to eke out a living, and work on the restoration of the Temple probably did not take a high priority for most. As a result of these tensions, construction on the Temple ground to a halt shortly after the foundation stones had been laid. The project was eventually resumed some time later, under the auspices of Zerubbabel and the two postexilic prophets Haggai and Zechariah (see Ezra 5:1).

WORK BEGINS AGAIN

In the second year of the reign of Darius I, a major revolt broke out in Babylon. This was the year during which the prophet Haggai was to have so much success in encouraging the Jews to begin their reconstruction work on the Temple. In four short oracles dated in the autumn of 520 B.C.E., Haggai admonished the people to begin the building project. Scarcely a month had passed, however, when the work began to slow down. Apparently, some people were discouraged by the contrast between their Temple and the Temple that Solomon had built. In his second oracle (1:15–2:9), Haggai promised that the Second Temple would surpass the glory of Solomon's, and asserted that Zerubbabel was the anticipated Davidic messiah. Zechariah, a contemporary of Haggai, likewise encouraged the restoration of the nation under the leadership of Zerubbabel and the high priest Joshua. By the time Zechariah gave his final series of oracles (518 B.C.E.), however, the nationalistic spirit had somewhat subsided, and Darius I had once again restored control in Persia. Zechariah, however, still hoped that the Lord would overthrow the nations (see Zechariah 1:18–21), and that Zerubbabel would turn out to be the Davidic prince who would lead Judah to her destined glory (4:6–10).

THE COMPLETION AND CONSECRATION OF THE TEMPLE

The Temple was completed on the third day of the month of Adar, in the sixth year of the reign of Darius I, which, by modern dating, would be March 12, 515 B.C.E. (Ezra 6:13–15). As such, the Second Temple was completed about 70 years after the destruction of the First Temple, which recalls Jeremiah's prophecy that the exile will last for 70 years (Jeremiah 25:11–12, 29:10).

The description of the dedication of the Temple, complete with the sacrifice of animals, as well as the participation of the priests, Levites, and the community (Ezra 6:16–18), recalls the dedicatory celebrations of the First Temple under Solomon (1 Kings 8:62–66). At the end of the consecration, the celebrants held the feast of the Passover, marking a new beginning for the people. The dedication and the celebrations were carried out in accordance with the Law of Moses.

LEFT: *THE HOLY PROPHET ZACHARIAS [ZECHARIAH]*, RUSSIAN ICON, C. 1560, FROM THE ANTONIEV MONASTERY. CHAPTERS 1–8 OF THE BOOK OF ZECHARIAH CONSIST OF ORACLES AND VISIONS RELATING TO THE RESTORATION OF JERUSALEM.

BELOW: *PREPARING FOR PASSOVER*, A NINETEENTH-CENTURY C.E. MINIATURE MODEL BY A. ALOIS AND J. B. PROBST. ONCE THE SECOND TEMPLE HAD BEEN CONSECRATED, THE EXILES CELEBRATED PASSOVER TO MARK THE "REBIRTH" OF THE JEWISH NATION.

ABOVE: *ESDRAS [EZRA] THE SCRIBE*, ILLUSTRATION IN A THIRTEENTH-CENTURY C.E. LATIN MANUSCRIPT. EZRA AND HIS GROUP OF EXILES WOULD HAVE FACED AN ARDUOUS AND LENGTHY JOURNEY ACROSS THE DESERT TO JERUSALEM.

EZRA

Material concerning the work of Ezra himself is contained in Ezra 7–10 and in Nehemiah 8–10. It is likely that sometime in the seventh year of King Artaxerxes I (457 B.C.E.), Ezra led a group of exiles from Babylon to Judah. Like Nehemiah, Ezra was sent to Palestine by the Persian authorities, but whereas Nehemiah's role was that of a political authority or "governor," Ezra was to have authority over religious matters. Ezra is described both as a priest in the line of Aaron, and "a scribe skilled in the law of Moses" (Ezra 7:1–6). He was duly authorized to investigate the religious conditions in Judah and Jerusalem, allocate gifts for the Temple, and install judges and magistrates in accordance with Jewish religious law, but his primary duty was to instruct the people in their religious laws. Thus, not only was he recognized as an authority in religious matters, but his actions in this area would have carried the force of a royal decree (Ezra 7:26). This would have been in agreement with the Persian policy of encouraging local religious and political policies in order to ensure social stability.

On arriving in Jerusalem, one of Ezra's first tasks was to enact strict regulations against intermarriage with foreigners, especially mixed marriages with foreign pagan women. This was not an easy decree to enforce as many people had strong family commitments. Ezra convened an assembly and, in the middle of a driving rainstorm, he admonished the people to give up their foreign wives and to act according to the commandment of God. Though there was initial opposition, the people eventually made a public confession of their sins. As a result, the men agreed to give up their foreign wives, and within three months, this unpopular decree was carried out (Ezra 9:1–10:17). While these measures may look harsh to the modern reader, they were in fact necessary to help maintain the sense of Jewish identity and for preserving the traditions of Israel. These edicts were enforceable because they had the backing of the Persian authorities; furthermore, they would have naturally appealed to the laws and traditions of the Jewish people.

RIGHT: *MOSES WITH THE TABLET OF THE LAW*, BY FLEMISH ARTIST JUSTUS VAN GHENT. EZRA CARRIED WITH HIM TO JERUSALEM A COPY OF THIS VITAL DOCUMENT, WHICH THE LORD HAD GIVEN TO ISRAEL.

EZRA'S BOOK OF THE LAW

Aside from returning with finances and precious goods for the reestablishment of religious rites in the Temple, Ezra carried one very important document with him: a copy of "the book of the law of Moses" (Nehemiah 8:1). In the seventh month, during the autumn Feast of Booths, Ezra convened a second assembly. The people gathered together at the Water Gate of Jerusalem, and Ezra stood on a high, purpose-built wooden platform and read from the book of the law from early morning until midday. The people stood in attention while the Levites gave the "sense" of the passage so that they could understand the reading. According to Nehemiah 8:9, the people were moved to tears by what they heard and, starting the following day, they celebrated the seven-day Feast of Booths according to the directions in the Torah (see Leviticus 23:42–43). Throughout the festival, the people continued to hear readings from the book of the law. The climax of the ceremonies came when the people confessed their sins to Ezra, and he, as the mediator of the Covenant, offered a prayer on behalf of the people. The prayer ended with the official signing of the Covenant by the princes, Levites, and priests (Nehemiah 8:1–9:38). The people vowed to live in accordance with the commandments of Yahweh, to refrain from mixed marriages, to observe the Sabbath, to maintain the Temple, and to render tithes (Nehemiah 10:28–39). Ezra's reading from the law book, the confession of public sins, the series of reforms, and the making of the Covenant, recalls the Covenant ceremony conducted by King Josiah after finding the book of the law during excavations on the First Temple in 622 B.C.E. (see 2 Kings 23). Ezra's Covenant renewal ceremony thus stresses the vital connection between the preexilic and postexilic communities.

It has been widely assumed that Ezra's book of the law was the Pentateuch (the first five books of the Old Testament) or, if not the whole Pentateuch, some version of its law codes such as parts of Deuteronomy, or part of the so-called priestly material of the Pentateuch (that is, the body of legal material found toward the end of Exodus, Leviticus, and the beginning of Numbers), as his reforms are more suggestive of a priestly character. It is difficult to know what exactly Ezra read out, especially because not one of the legal quotations from Ezra and Nehemiah match the law codes from the Pentateuch. Ezra's book of the law, therefore, may have been a summary account of the legal material in the Pentateuch. Regardless of what he actually read out, Ezra was instrumental in organizing the religion around the Torah, a feature that continues in Judaism to this day. If the religion was to survive the difficulties it would face in the ensuing centuries, it needed a center on which to focus. Ezra provided this center. And while it is easy to criticize Ezra for his exclusivism and his emphasis on a written law (therefore running the risk of legalism), Ezra's reforms gave the religion a distinction and dignity that it might not otherwise have enjoyed. It is a tribute to the work of Ezra that the religion of Judaism, which is organized around the principles of Torah obedience, has continued to survive to this day.

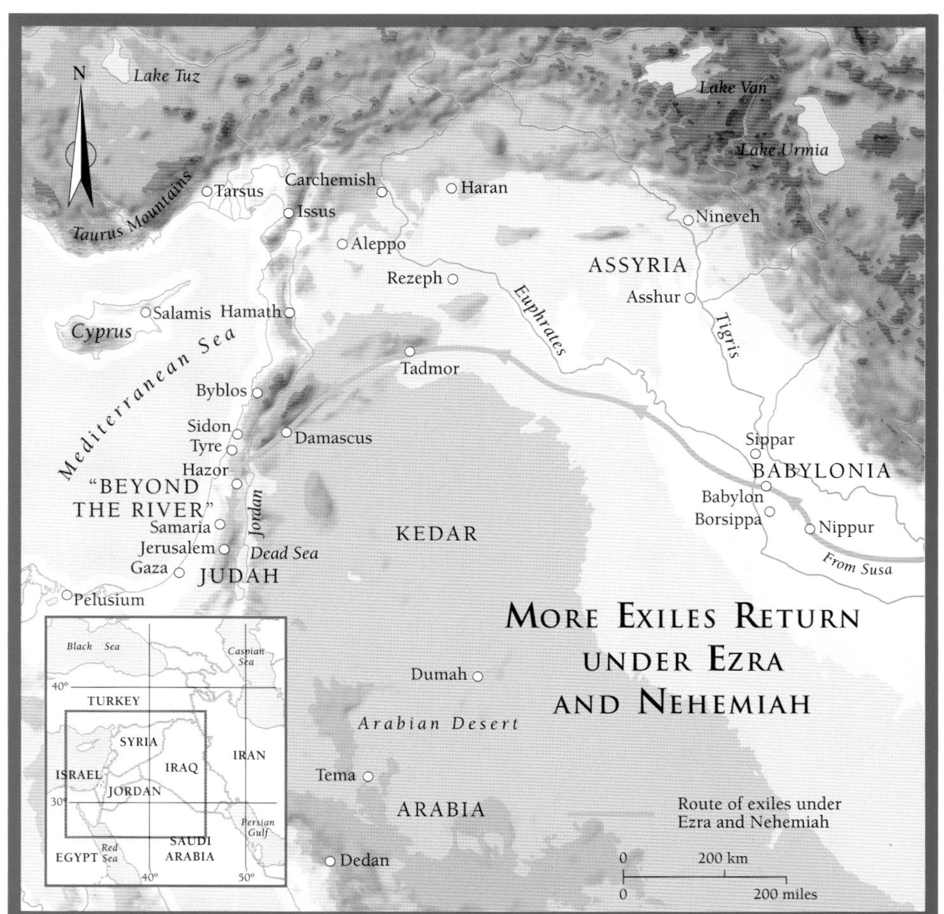

NEHEMIAH

Nehemiah's career was recorded in the "memoirs" of Nehemiah, which, with the exception of chapters 8–10 (which concern Ezra), comprised most of the book of Nehemiah. The memoirs are the only example in the Old Testament of a continuous first-person narrative. As such they provide a

LEFT: THIS FRONTISPIECE OF A FIFTEENTH-CENTURY C.E. COPY OF DEUTERONOMY SHOWS GOD MAKING THE LAWS. SOME SCHOLARS SAY EZRA WAS READING FROM PARTS OF DEUTERONOMY WHEN HE STOOD ON THE PLATFORM (NEHEMIAH 8:4).

ABOVE: *NEHEMIAH REBUILDS JERUSALEM,* UNATTRIBUTED ENGRAVING. IN HIS OLD TESTAMENT BOOK, NEHEMIAH TELLS US THAT WHEN HE HEARD OF THE EXILES' PLIGHT HE "SAT DOWN AND WEPT" (NEHEMIAH 1:4).

wealth of historical detail. Nehemiah's story begins in the twentieth year of King Artaxerxes I's reign (*c.* 444 B.C.E.). It describes a devout Jew, the cupbearer to Artaxerxes I who, when told of the deplorable conditions that existed in Jerusalem, asked the king to send him there as soon as possible. Not only did the king comply with the request, he also appointed Nehemiah governor, furnished him with a royal escort, and gave him official letters that ordered provincial authorities to provide him with timber and other requirements. This indicates that Nehemiah must have been an extremely important and influential man in the Persian court, and also reflects the Persian policy of ensuring they had a man they could trust to rule over their provinces.

REBUILDING THE CITY WALLS

Despite having official backing, Nehemiah's commission was carried out with great secrecy and speed. Nehemiah inspected the city walls during the middle of the night and without the knowledge of the city officials (Nehemiah 2:11–16). The reason for the secrecy was that there was strong opposition to any sort of rebuilding or reconstruction from the officials at Samaria: Sanballat, the governor of Samaria; Tobiah, the governor of Ammon; and Geshem, the governor of Edom. These governors more than likely resented the royal privilege that had been bestowed on Nehemiah, and saw him as a threat to their own power. They claimed that Nehemiah had no right to reconstruct the walls. Nehemiah's reply, that the governors "had no share or claim or historic right in Jerusalem" (Nehemiah 2:20), may have aroused the enthusiasm of the people because a group of volunteer workers accomplished the task of rebuilding the wall in 52 days (Nehemiah 6:15)! This time period is all the more incredible as Nehemiah and his workers had to counter violent opposition from neighboring peoples who tried to prevent the reconstruction of the walls. Apparently, the builders had to work with a tool in one hand and a weapon in the other (Nehemiah 4:17). Eventually the walls were rebuilt, and their completion was officially celebrated with a ceremony of dedication, a procession around the city walls, a sacrificial offering, as well as the singing of psalms (Nehemiah 12:27–43).

Nehemiah also introduced a series of economic reforms to help alleviate the plight of the poor, who had complained that the rich Judeans were driving them into debt (Nehemiah 5:1–5). Nehemiah was successful in getting the wealthy to release the poor from their debts in a manner that resembled

RIGHT: *THE NORTHERN WALL OF JERUSALEM,* WATERCOLOR BY NINETEENTH-CENTURY C.E. ARTIST CARL HAAG. NEHEMIAH INSPECTED JERUSALEM'S BROKEN WALLS ALONE AND UNDER COVER OF DARKNESS.

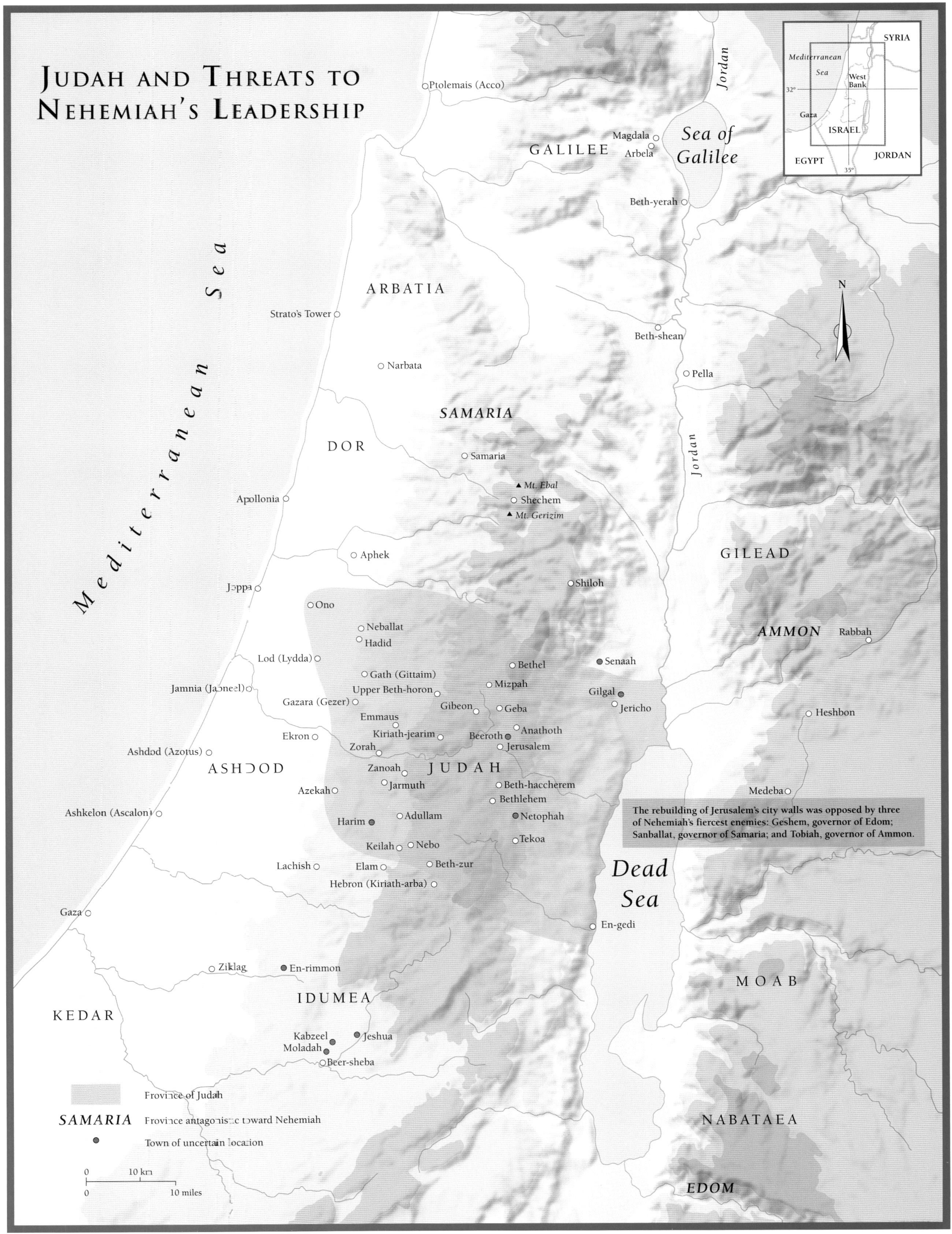
JUDAH AND THREATS TO NEHEMIAH'S LEADERSHIP
Mediterranean Sea
Ptolemais (Acco)
GALILEE
Magdala
Arbela
Sea of Galilee
Jordan
Beth-yerah
SYRIA
Mediterranean Sea
West Bank
Gaza
ISRAEL
EGYPT
JORDAN
ARBATIA
Strato's Tower
Beth-shean
Narbata
Pella
SAMARIA
DOR
Samaria
Mt. Ebal
Shechem
Mt. Gerizim
Apollonia
Aphek
GILEAD
Joppa
Shiloh
Ono
Neballat
Hadid
AMMON
Rabbah
Lod (Lydda)
Bethel
Senaah
Gath (Gittaim)
Mizpah
Jamnia (Jabneel)
Upper Beth-horon
Gilgal
Gazara (Gezer)
Gibeon
Geba
Jericho
Emmaus
Heshbon
Ekron
Kiriath-jearim
Beeroth
Anathoth
Ashdod (Azotus)
Zorah
Jerusalem
ASHDOD
Zanoah
JUDAH
Jarmuth
Beth-haccherem
Medeba
Azekah
Bethlehem
Ashkelon (Ascalon)
Harim
Adullam
Netophah
Keilah
Nebo
Tekoa
Lachish
Elam
Beth-zur
Dead Sea
Hebron (Kiriath-arba)
Gaza
En-gedi
Ziklag
En-rimmon
MOAB
IDUMEA
KEDAR
Kabzeel
Jeshua
Moladah
Beer-sheba
Province of Judah
SAMARIA Province antagonistic toward Nehemiah
Town of uncertain location
0 10 km
0 10 miles
NABATAEA
EDOM
The rebuilding of Jerusalem's city walls was opposed by three of Nehemiah's fiercest enemies: Geshem, governor of Edom; Sanballat, governor of Samaria; and Tobiah, governor of Ammon.

RIGHT: THE ARK OF THE COVENANT, FROM A MEDIEVAL BOOK OF HEBREW TEXTS. THE ARK IS ONE OF THE MISSING TEMPLE TREASURES. SOME DEPICTIONS OF IT SHOW THE CHERUBIM ATTACHED TO THE LID KNEELING, SOME SHOW THEM STANDING.

the remission of debts in the Jubilee year (Leviticus 25). But Nehemiah's reforms also went much deeper. He repopulated the city of Jerusalem by means of a public lottery so that one-tenth of Jewish citizenry was moved into the city (Nehemiah 11), and he established Jewish control over economic life (Nehemiah 13:15–22). He also recalled to Jerusalem the Levites and Temple singers who had moved to the country in order to strengthen the Temple community.

Like Ezra, Nehemiah's great achievement was to help preserve Jewish identity in the midst of great cultural pressures. Nehemiah drew a sharp distinction between Jews and non-Jews, even to the extent of creating a genealogy to verify one's Jewish ancestry. During his second term of office (*c.* 432 B.C.E.), Nehemiah prohibited intermarriage between Jews and Gentiles, and even expelled the son of the high priest, who had married the daughter of his old enemy, Sanballat. He also called upon the Jewish people to keep the Sabbath and to support the Temple worship by tithing their salaries. While a number of these measures may have been severe, Nehemiah's policy of segregation did help to avoid syncretism and to prevent the religion from being swallowed up by other more powerful nations.

WHO WAS FIRST, EZRA OR NEHEMIAH?

One of the perennial problems in biblical studies is in assigning dates for Ezra and Nehemiah. On the surface, the task looks easy: Ezra is said to have arrived in Palestine "in the seventh year of King Artaxerxes" (Ezra 7:7), and Nehemiah is said to have been sent to Palestine as governor in the "twentieth year of King Artaxerxes" (Nehemiah 2:1), and to have had a second term as governor in the "thirty-second year of Artaxerxes" (Nehemiah 13:6–7). Since the dates for the Persian king's rule are 464–424 B.C.E., it would seem a simple matter to determine that Ezra arrived in 457 B.C.E., and that Nehemiah arrived in 444 B.C.E. and again in 432 B.C.E.

Based on internal evidence found in the books of Ezra and Nehemiah themselves, however, the dating of the two men's careers is a little more complicated. The conditions

BELOW: NEHEMIAH INSPIRED THE VOLUNTEERS TO REBUILD THE WALLS IN AN AMAZING 52 DAYS. HOWEVER, EVIDENCE OF THEIR HASTE CAN BE SEEN IN EXCAVATED PARTS OF THE WALLS.

that prevailed in Palestine in Ezra's account indicate that Nehemiah had in fact already arrived. Ezra writes that the walls around Jerusalem had been built and the city had been repopulated, two things which Nehemiah was said to have accomplished. Furthermore, Nehemiah was said to be a contemporary of the High Priest Eliashib, whereas Ezra was a contemporary of the High Priest's grandson. Finally, if Ezra arrived in 457 B.C.E., his reforms had little effect, for when Nehemiah arrived in 444 B.C.E. he had to make similar changes. Given Ezra's prominent role as "reformer" within the Judaic tradition, the fact that his reforms had so little success does seem puzzling.

For these reasons, alternate dates for Ezra's arrival in Palestine have been proposed. Since it seems that Ezra arrived after Nehemiah, the Artaxerxes to whom Ezra referred (see Ezra 7:7) may have been Artaxerxes II, who ruled from 404–359 B.C.E. This would postpone the date of Ezra's arrival in Palestine to 397 B.C.E. The problem with this reconstruction is that for Ezra and Nehemiah to have been contemporaries (see Nehemiah 8:9, 12:36), Nehemiah's second term as governor must have been incredibly long (more than 35 years). A third reconstruction places the date of Ezra's arrival at 427 B.C.E. This date requires changing the chronological notation in Ezra 7:7 from "seventh year" to "thirty-seventh year" of Artaxerxes, the word "thirty" having been omitted due to a scribal error. It should be noted, however, that there is no conclusive evidence for any theory, and the matter is much more complex than we have described here.

DIFFERENCES BETWEEN THE FIRST AND SECOND TEMPLES

Unfortunately, we know little about the exact size of the Second Temple, but given that some of the people apparently were disheartened by its dimensions, many suggest that it is a smaller structure than the First Temple (see Ezra 3:12 and Haggai 2:3). But while it may have been smaller than the Solomonic Temple, it lasted 500 years, over a century longer than its predecessor, and far longer than the 100 years that the Herodian Temple lasted. The fact that Zerubbabel's Temple was built on the same site as the Solomonic building suggests that the former dimensions are comparable to the latter, but the Temple itself was probably not as lavish. It is doubtful whether the carved wood panels overlaid with gold were part of the Second Temple under Zerubbabel, though Zerubbabel, like Solomon, calls for the import of cedar logs from Phoenicia. Nevertheless, the fact that many of the precious Temple vessels found a new home in the Zerubbabel Temple suggests that some of the former glory of the Solomonic one was at least partially restored.

It is curious that Nehemiah later uses the word "fortress" (Nehemiah 2:8) to describe the nearby towers protecting the Temple precinct. Perhaps a military role was part of the function of the Second Temple, which would make sense in light of the opposition that Nehemiah faced.

Nehemiah also describes a chamber prepared for Eliashib the priest in the "courts of the house of God" (see Nehemiah 13:7), which indicates a chamber separate from the Temple building itself, something that was not apparent in the First Temple, which only had an inner court.

ABOVE: WHEN HE SAW THE ROOM BUILT FOR ELIASHIB BESIDE THE TEMPLE, NEHEMIAH WAS SO ANGRY THAT HE ORDERED THE ROOM TO BE CLEANSED. ELIASHIB IS SEEN IN THIS SIXTEENTH-CENTURY C.E. FRENCH BIBLE REBUILDING THE SHEEP GATE IN JERICHO.

MISSING ITEMS OF RELIGIOUS IMPORTANCE

While Sheshbazzar brought several artifacts from Babylon to Jerusalem for use in the Temple service, a number of treasures were either lost or destroyed. Biblical records do not mention what happened to the large basin or "molten sea" after it was broken up by the invading armies (2 Kings 25:13). Likewise, the two cherubim that were placed in the Holy of Holies (the innermost sanctuary of the Temple) have disappeared. Perhaps the most important missing item is the sacred Ark of the Covenant, an artfully constructed wooden chest in which the invisible presence of God, or *shekinah*, was said to dwell. According to one Jewish tradition, Jeremiah removed the Ark before the Babylonians razed the Temple; in another tradition, Jeremiah says that the Ark is gone and will not "be remembered, or missed" (Jeremiah 3:16). According to yet another story, an angel descended from heaven and removed the Ark and other sacred objects before they were destroyed (2 Baruch 6:7). What these stories all indicate is that the Ark disappeared in exilic times and has yet to been found.

ALEXANDER THE GREAT

ALEXANDER ... ADVANCED TO THE ENDS OF THE EARTH, AND PLUNDERED MANY NATIONS 1 MACCABEES 1:1–3

The Kingdom of Macedonia emerged from relative obscurity in the middle of the fourth century B.C.E. to take control of the whole of Greece under its king Philip II and mount a military campaign all the way to India under his son Alexander III (the Great) by 323 B.C.E.

Under Philip II (reigned 359–336 B.C.E.), the Macedonian military was revolutionized with the setting up of a standing army and the introduction of the sarissa-armed phalanx. The sarissa was a spear measuring approximately 18 ft (5 m), and when used in formation was one of the most lethal weapons in the ancient world. Prior to his assassination in 336 B.C.E., Philip was in the beginning stages of a campaign against the Persians; however, it was under his son Alexander III (reigned 336–323 B.C.E.) that the campaign was prosecuted.

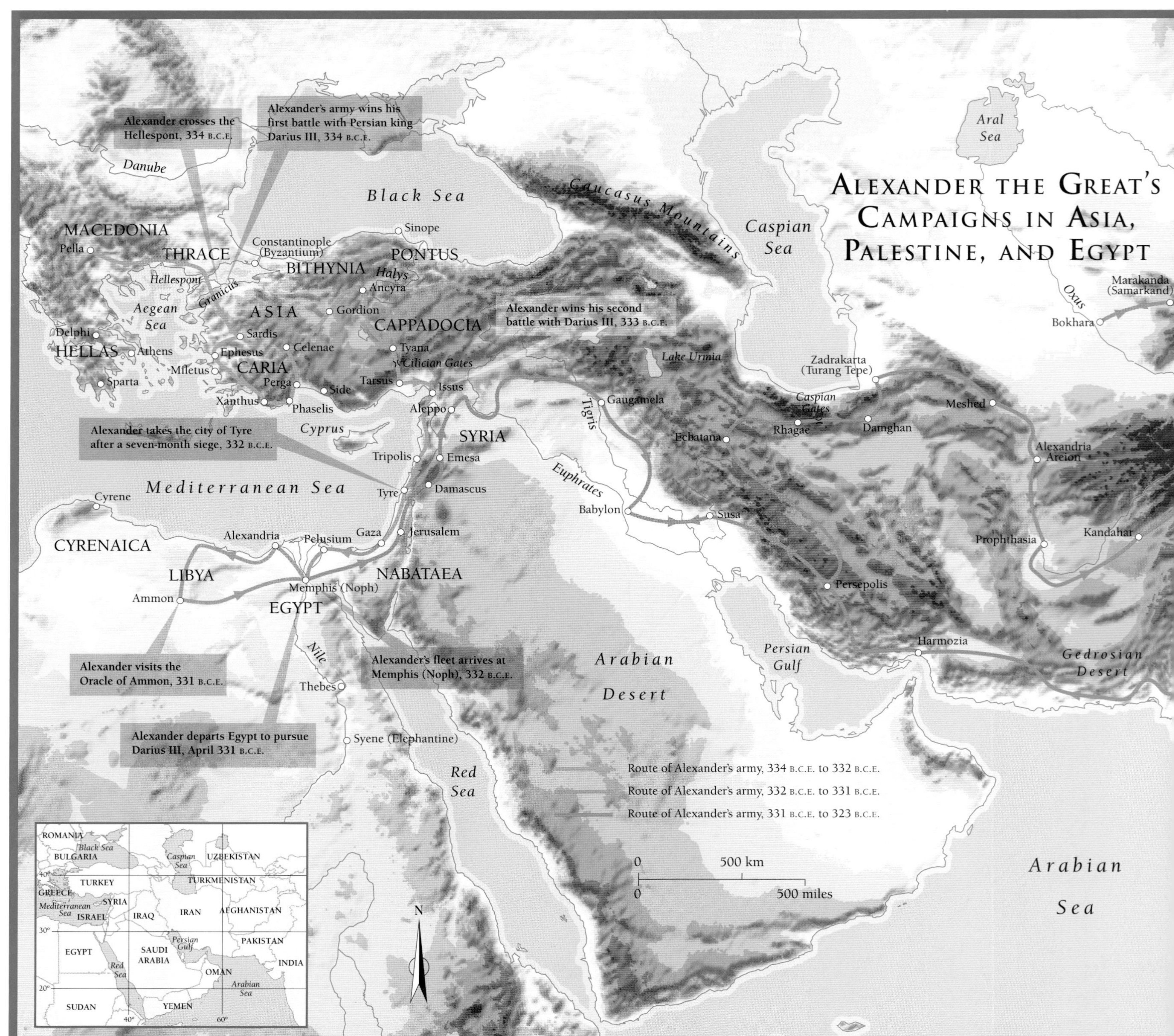

THE GREEKS TAKE ON THE PERSIANS

Alexander was only nineteen years old when he came to power in Macedonia. The treasury appears to have been empty and there were a number of plots against his reign. Despite this situation, or perhaps because of it, Alexander left Macedonia in 334 B.C.E. with an army of approximately 45,000 men to conduct the war against the Persian Empire. The Persian Empire controlled ancient Iran, parts of Central Asia, Mesopotamia, Syria, Asia Minor, and Egypt. Alexander's invasion would change the face of these areas for many centuries by introducing Greek culture to all of these lands.

Alexander's invasion began when his large army crossed the legendary Hellespont, the narrow body of water—measuring around 4 miles (6.4 km) from shore to shore at its widest point—separating the continents of Europe and Asia. Alexander is claimed to have been the first ashore on the eastern side of the Hellespont, symbolically hurling a spear from the prow of his ship onto the beach and claiming Asia as a spear-won land. This was done in conscious emulation of the Greek god Heracles, whose heroic exploits Alexander sought to repeat and outdo throughout his campaigns.

Alexander's army had a major victory in 334 B.C.E. over the forces of the Persian king, Darius III (reigned 335–330 B.C.E.), at the Granicus River in northwest Asia Minor (modern Kocabas, Turkey). This victory allowed Alexander to march along the coast of Asia Minor, taking control of key cities such as Sardis, Ephesus, and Miletus. A number of the cities of Asia Minor were originally founded as Greek trading colonies in the sixth and fifth centuries B.C.E., and by taking control of them Alexander claimed to have liberated them from Persian oppression. Within a few months, a major battle loomed between Alexander's army and the regrouped Persian forces. Following the defeat at the Granicus, Darius III had retreated to Damascus in Syria, where he planned his next move against Alexander's invasion. The battle eventually took place in November 333 B.C.E. at Issus in Cilicia, resulting in another overwhelming victory for Alexander's army. With Darius III again forced to flee, Syria and Egypt lay open to Alexander.

Alexander continued to campaign in early 332 B.C.E., mostly along the Mediterranean coastline of Syria. Many of the cities he encountered in Syria surrendered and were offered friendly terms, which had been the case earlier in Asia Minor, but the ancient city of Tyre was an exception. Tyre was a city of Phoenician origin, which centuries earlier had played a major role in the establishment of trading colonies throughout the Mediterranean. The city was located on an island not far from the Syrian coastline and was well defended. When Tyre refused to accept terms of surrender from Alexander, the Macedonian king ordered the construction of a large ramp to join the island to the mainland. He went on to capture the city and then sold its citizens into slavery. To this very day, the island remains connected to the mainland in modern Lebanon.

ABOVE: ALEXANDER THE GREAT IN A DIVING BELL, FROM A FIFTEENTH-CENTURY C.E. PUBLICATION, *ROMANCE OF ALEXANDER*. ALEXANDER PROMOTED WAR AGAINST PERSIA PARTLY AS RETRIBUTION FOR THE EMPIRE'S ATTACKS ON GREECE UNDER XERXES I 150 YEARS EARLIER.

BELOW: DETAIL OF A FIRST-CENTURY C.E. ROMAN MOSAIC SHOWING ALEXANDER IN THE BATTLE OF ISSUS IN 333 B.C.E. THIS DECISIVE BATTLE PAVED THE WAY FOR ALEXANDER'S CONQUEST OF EGYPT.

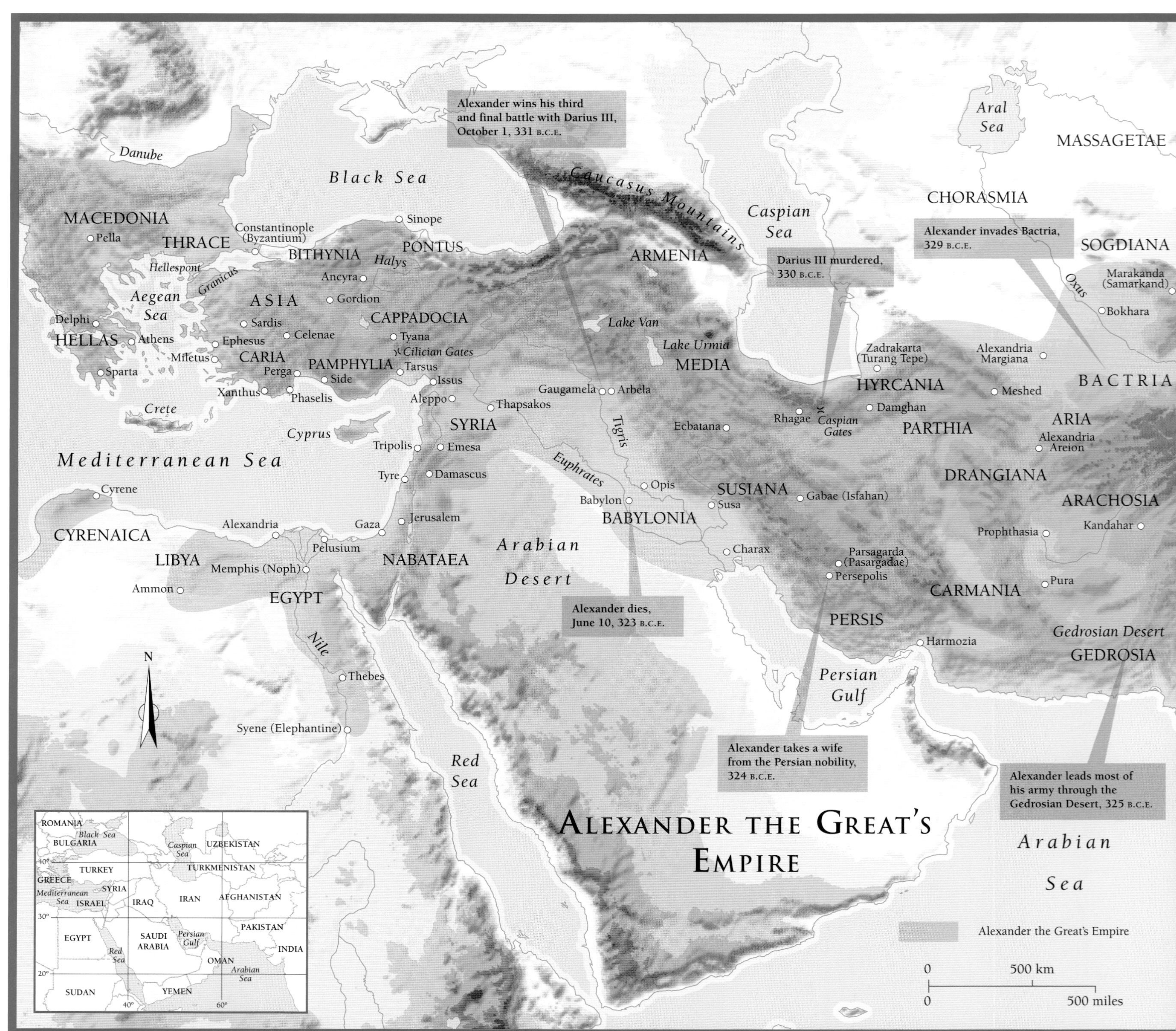

RIGHT: HEAD AND SHOULDERS OF A COLOSSAL STATUE FROM THE PTOLEMAIC PERIOD, FOUND AT KARNAK IN EGYPT. IT DEPICTS ALEXANDER THE GREAT VERY MUCH IN THE STYLE OF AN EGYPTIAN PHAROAH.

ALEXANDER'S EGYPTIAN CAMPAIGN

Following the siege of Tyre, which took seven months to complete, Alexander advanced along the Syrian coastline toward Egypt, meeting with some resistance at Gaza also. The campaign to take control of Egypt began toward the end of 332 B.C.E., but it was barely a campaign at all. Alexander had expected it would take a long time to capture Egypt, but on arriving at Pelusium, the main fortress guarding entry to Egypt, the Macedonian king was welcomed by throngs of Egyptians who greeted him as a liberator. Alexander's reception throughout Egypt was very similar, as the Persian governorship of the country had been unpopular. Alexander's fleet made its way up the Nile, eventually arriving at the capital Memphis, where the city and treasury were surrendered to Alexander by Mazaces, the last Persian satrap of Egypt.

Alexander's experiences in Egypt appear to have profoundly affected his thinking as well as his ability to cultivate images of rulership. It is uncertain as to whether Alexander was actually crowned king of Egypt, but the tradition dating back to early pharaonic times which treated the Egyptian ruler as a living god certainly impressed itself on Alexander. In a similar way, Alexander's visit to the Oracle of Ammon (known to the Egyptians as Amun), in the oasis of Siwa in the desert to the west of the Nile, encouraged his desire to be recognized as a living god. The god Ammon was thought to be a local manifestation of Zeus, the most powerful

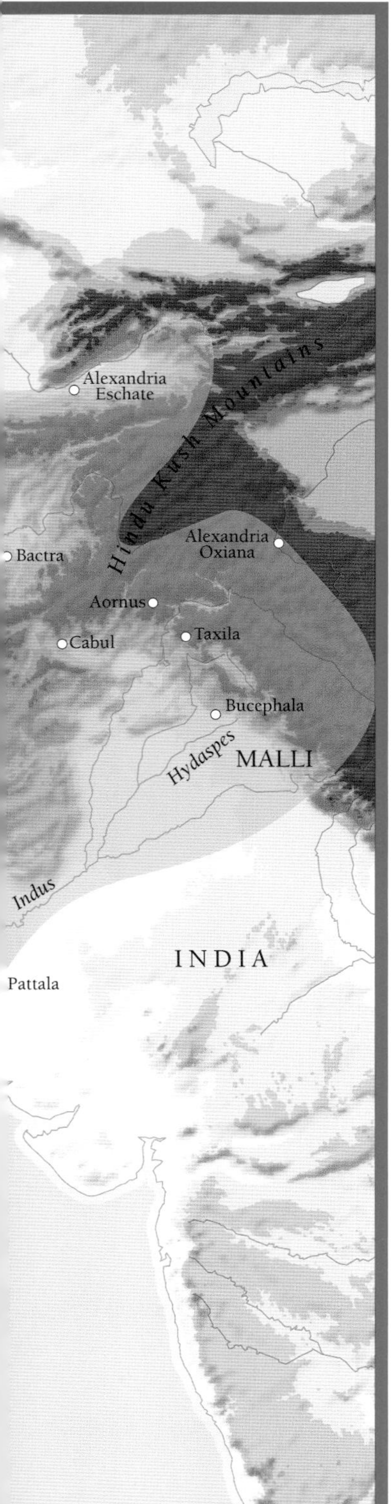

of all the Greek gods. On arrival at the temple which housed the Oracle, Alexander was greeted by the officiating priest as son of Ammon, confirming the idea further in Alexander's mind that he was in fact the son of Zeus. On consulting the Oracle, which effectively spoke for the god, we are told that Alexander was pleased with the responses he received. As the consultation was performed privately, we do not know the questions Alexander put to the god. After returning from Siwa, Alexander and his army departed Egypt in April 331 B.C.E. essentially to pursue the remnants of Darius III's army and to prosecute the campaign to capture Iran and Mesopotamia.

ALEXANDER'S MESOPOTAMIAN CAMPAIGN

On leaving Egypt, Alexander marched across Syria into northern Mesopotamia, where the two largest armies met for the last time. The third and final battle between the forces of Alexander and those of the Persian King Darius III was at Gaugamela in modern northern Iraq in October 331 B.C.E. The victory at Gaugamela saw Darius flee for his life from the battlefield, while the rich cities of Mesopotamia now lay before Alexander. He then easily captured both Babylon and Susa in southern Mesopotamia before marching into the satrapy of Persis and capturing its royal capital Persepolis late in 331 B.C.E. The enormous treasury of the Persian king was held at Persepolis, and its capture by Alexander provided the funds he required to enrich his companions and to take his army further east. Alexander famously burned the royal palace at Persepolis during a drinking party (symposium), an act for which he was widely condemned by later writers.

Meanwhile, following his defeat at Gaugamela, Darius III had fled to Ecbatana in Media. He was betrayed and murdered just east of there by Bessus, the satrap of Bactria (modern Afghanistan), in the summer of 330 B.C.E. Alexander organized for Darius III's body to be sent to Persepolis for proper burial, while Bessus proclaimed himself "King of Kings," the traditional title of the Persian king. Bessus then organized a revolt centered on Bactria and Central Asia, to which Alexander responded by invading Bactria. It was a difficult undertaking due to the mountainous nature of the area and the extreme weather conditions in winter. The invasion began in March 329 B.C.E. and Bessus was unable to rally the Bactrian nobility to his cause, nor could he raise an army to match the size of Alexander's forces. Alexander easily took control of Bactria and its cities while Bessus fled to the north across the Oxus River. Bessus was eventually betrayed by his own entourage and was delivered up to Ptolemy, commander of Alexander's bodyguard and later king of Egypt. Bessus was sent to the city of Bactra, capital of Bactria, where he was mutilated before being sent to Ecbatana in Media to be executed.

ABOVE: *TRIUMPH OF ALEXANDER THE GREAT*, 1665, BY CHARLES LE BRUN SHOWS ALEXANDER'S DRAMATIC ENTRY INTO BABYLON AFTER HIS FINAL BATTLE WITH DARIUS III.

BELOW: THIS SIXTEENTH-CENTURY C.E. CERAMIC PLATE BY GIOVANNI BATTISTA DA FAENZA PORTRAYS DARIUS III AND HIS FAMILY STANDING BEFORE THEIR CONQUEROR, ALEXANDER THE GREAT.

RIGHT: *ISKANDAR OR ALEXANDER AND THE TALKING TREE,* ILLUSTRATION FOR THE EPIC POEM *THE SHAHNAMA,* BY THE PERSIAN POET FIRDAUSI (C.E. 934–1020). BECAUSE HE CONQUERED SUCH VAST TERRITORY, ALEXANDER APPEARS IN THE LITERATURE OF MANY CULTURES.

BELOW: *MOURNING FOR ISKANDAR,* FROM THE PERSIAN MINIATURE MANUSCRIPT *SADD I ISKANDAR* BY NAWA'I. BIBLICAL AND OTHER SOURCES OFFER VARYING ACCOUNTS OF THE CIRCUMSTANCES SURROUNDING ALEXANDER'S DEATH.

Alexander now controlled all the territorial possessions once held by the Persian King of Kings: from Asia Minor, Syria, and Egypt in the west to Mesopotamia, Persis, Media, and Bactria in the east, a distance stretching over 2,200 miles (about 3,500 km). Alexander did not, however, stop at Bactria. The next three and a half years (329–325 B.C.E.) were spent invading Central Asia and India until his troops finally mutinied at the Hyphasis (Beas) River in northern India and refused to continue. Alexander's angry reaction was not enough to dissuade his soldiers from their refusal to go on, and he was forced to turn back. On reaching the Hydaspes River, a fleet of up to 2,000 river craft was assembled to transport the army to the ocean in the vicinity of Karachi in modern-day Pakistan. The army arrived in July 325 B.C.E. and preparations were made for its return to Persia. Part of this return journey involved the army crossing the inhospitable Gedrosian Desert. The march took approximately 60 days, and Alexander came close to losing his entire army due to the harsh nature of the terrain. One source claimed that Alexander lost three-quarters of his whole army, but this is most likely an exaggeration. Nonetheless, the army suffered serious privations, and it is indeed possible that Alexander chose this difficult return route as punishment for the army's mutiny in northern India. The army reached Susa and Persepolis in March 324 B.C.E., arriving back in the cities of Persis which it had captured six years earlier. Alexander and 80 of his companions and generals took wives from the Persian nobility, symbolically setting the scene for Alexander's organization of the government of his vast empire. In the spring of 324 B.C.E. Alexander departed Susa, making his way to the Persian Gulf and then sailing up the Tigris River toward Babylon. He spent the rest of 324 B.C.E. dealing with revolts in the north, particularly in the province of Media. Early in 323 B.C.E., Alexander made his way back to Babylon, where he was greeted by embassies from all over the known world. He then began serious planning for an invasion of Arabia, which had been mooted for some time beforehand.

THE DEATH OF ALEXANDER

Prior to entering Babylon, Alexander received warnings from astrologers that his life was in danger if he entered the city. The motives behind these warnings are disputed, and it is possible that the Babylonian priesthood was concerned that revenues enjoyed by its temples would be diverted for other purposes. Alexander heeded the warnings and attempted to enter the city by its eastern approach rather than the more conventional western one. Much of the time in Babylon was spent preparing for the Arabian expedition before Alexander

RELIGIOUS DEVELOPMENTS UNDER ALEXANDER

Alexander is often attributed with introducing significant religious changes to Egypt, the Near East, and Mesopotamia as a result of his campaigns. In some respects this is true, but religious changes took a considerable period of time to develop and many of these occurred during the reigns of his successors in Egypt, Syria, Greece, and elsewhere.

As Alexander founded a large number of cities across the whole of his empire, Classical Greek gods such as Zeus, Athena, Aphrodite, and Ares were worshipped in these cities. In the religious tradition of Zoroastrianism, the religion of the Persian kings whom Alexander overthrew, Alexander was held to have destroyed many of the religion's sacred texts. However, Zoroastrianism continued as an important religion as did many other indigenous religions.

Alexander's apparent attempts at being recognized as a god while he was still alive had an impact on the development of a ruler cult under his successors. Some rulers, such as the Ptolemies in Egypt and the Antigonids in Greece, followed Alexander's example and were openly worshipped as living gods. This had a far-reaching effect on Roman rulers following Rome's occupation of the various successor kingdoms, as Roman emperors in the first and second centuries C.E. were also honored by some as living gods.

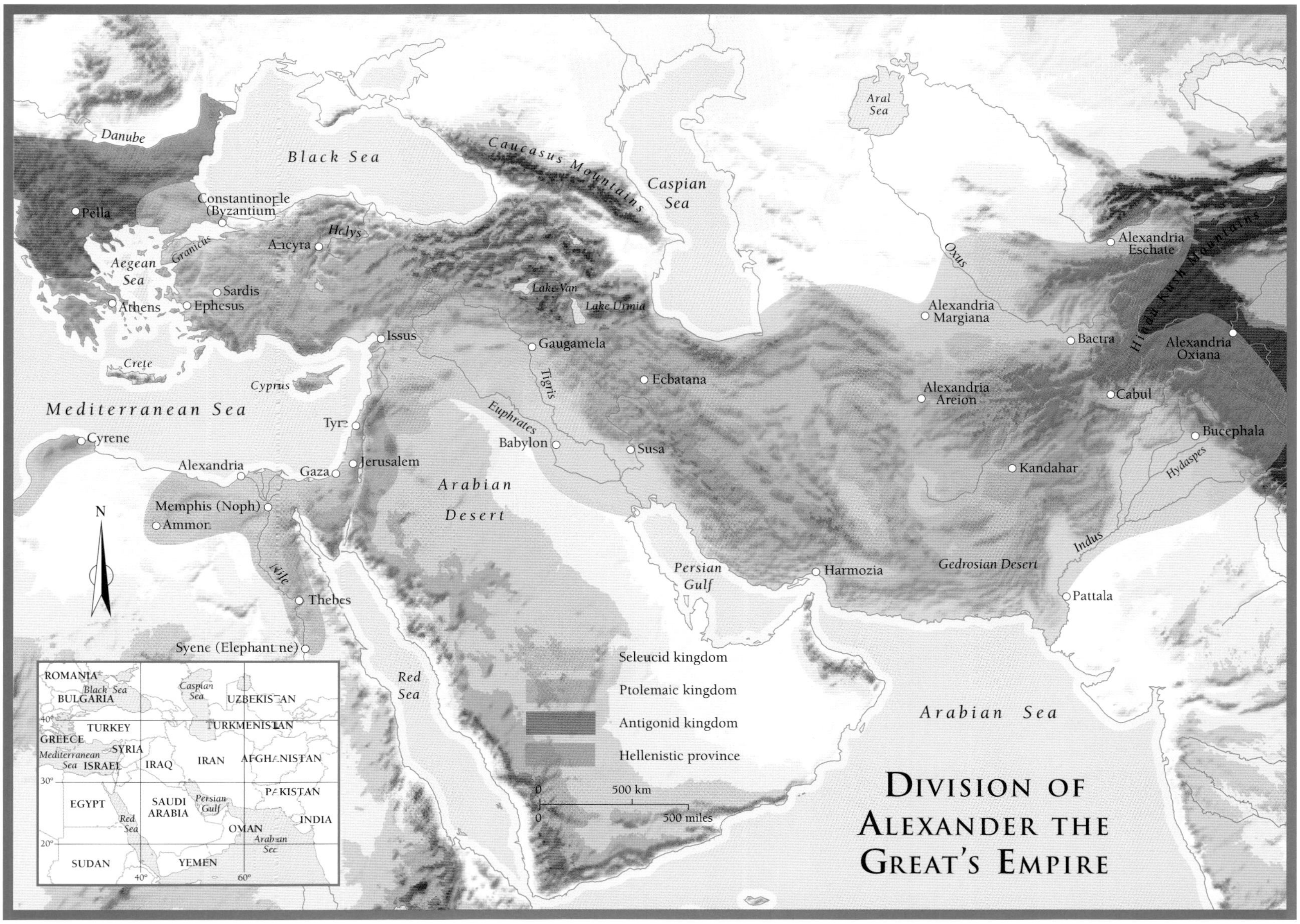

Division of Alexander the Great's Empire

Seleucid kingdom

Ptolemaic kingdom

Antigonid kingdom

Hellenistic province

0 500 km

0 500 miles

unexpectedly fell ill toward the end of May. Two traditions exist as to the cause and progression of the illness. In one he literally drank himself to death, collapsing after drinking 12 pints (about 6 liters) of undiluted wine in one sitting. The other, more accepted tradition is that Alexander developed a fever following a banquet held by one of his close associates. He attempted to maintain his royal duties and continued sacrificing daily to the gods, but by early June 323 B.C.E., Alexander's fever had become so serious that he was confined to bed and unable to speak. Sensing that the end was near, the army filed past the barely conscious king before he finally died in the early evening of June 10, 323 B.C.E.

DIVISION OF ALEXANDER'S EMPIRE

Alexander had not established a succession plan before his death at the young age of thirty-two, leaving his empire it was said "to the strongest." He had no male heir to which his empire might be left, but his Bactrian wife, Rhoxane, was pregnant when Alexander died and some months later gave birth to a son also named Alexander. The only other contender was Alexander's mentally incapacitated half-brother, Philip Arridhaeus. Philip was initially made king under the title Philip III and the child later ruled jointly with him as Alexander IV. However, power really lay with Alexander's generals. Perdiccas initially ruled as regent for the two before his demise in 321 B.C.E. Antipater, the effective ruler of Macedonia, became regent after Perdiccas's death and transferred the joint kings to Macedonia. Philip was murdered in 317 B.C.E. while Alexander IV was killed along with his grandmother, Olympias, by order of Cassander in 311 B.C.E.

The long struggle for power between Alexander's generals and companions after his death is a particularly complex story. It took more than 20 years of conflict characterized by murder and conspiracy before the division of Alexander's empire resembled anything stable or permanent. In short, Ptolemy, one of Alexander's generals, took control of Egypt; another of his generals, Seleucus, emerged to control Syria, Iran, Bactria, and northern India; while Antigonus and his son Demetrius took control of Macedonia and Greece. These rulers established dynasties that ruled over these empires for centuries to come. Numerous cultural changes emerged as a result of Alexander's various conquests, changes that would be fundamental across the region for the next thousand years.

BELOW: THIS BRONZE AND ENAMEL DISH FROM TWELFTH-CENTURY C.E. GREECE DEPICTS ALEXANDER THE GREAT ASCENDING INTO HEAVEN.

THE PTOLEMIES

THEN THE KING OF EGYPT GATHERED GREAT FORCES ... AND MANY SHIPS 1 MACCABEES 11:1

RIGHT: SILVER GREEK COIN WITH PTOLEMY I AS SATRAP OF ALEXANDRIA, READY FOR BATTLE. THE PTOLEMIES RULED EGYPT FOR NEARLY 300 YEARS.

Ptolemy I emerged from obscure origins as the son of a Macedonian noble named Lagos to establish a powerful Greek-speaking dynasty that ruled over Egypt for almost 300 years. Prior to Alexander the Great's capture of Egypt in 332 B.C.E., the country had been governed by the Persians for over 200 years. Alexander's capture of Egypt appears to have been widely popular, as indicated by the public reaction on his arrival at the garrison of the coastal city of Pelusium, where he was welcomed amid scenes of chaotic enthusiasm.

Egypt was a land of great antiquity, as evidenced by the monumental structures such as pyramids and colossal statues that could be found everywhere. The political, cultural, and religious institutions that had developed under the pharaohs over thousands of years also remained and were important. On the whole, however, the Ptolemaic dynasty and the system of government that emerged were Greco-Macedonian and quite exclusive.

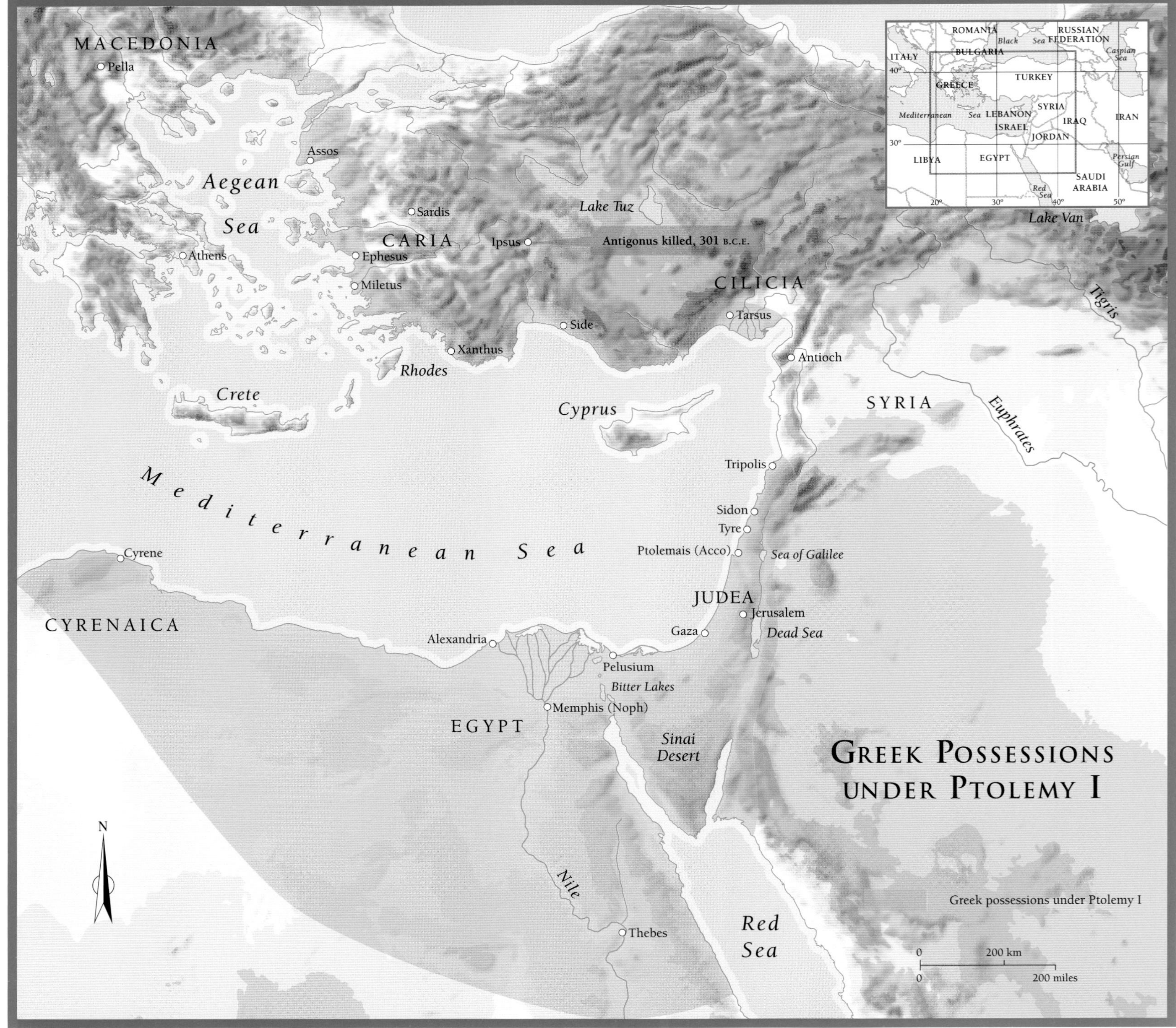

GREEK POSSESSIONS UNDER PTOLEMY I

THE LAND OF EGYPT

Important to any consideration of Ptolemaic rule in Egypt are the geographic and climatic features of the land. Strategically, Egypt was very difficult for the other Hellenistic monarchs to attack. The only route for a land invasion lay to the northeast in the direction of Phoenicia, and this was heavily protected. The Ptolemies were able to use Egypt as a base from which to make assaults by sea on the possessions of the Seleucids along the Syrian coastline and on the islands such as Cyprus and those of the Aegean. The struggle for control of these areas was a feature of relations between the successors of Alexander for much of the third century B.C.E., and the Ptolemies were a key element in this struggle.

Egypt itself is dominated by some significant natural features, which profoundly affect the way that any government controls the land. The Nile River is the most important of these features and has been the lifeblood of Egypt for millennia. The Nile rises in the mountains of modern Sudan (Ancient Upper Egypt) and flows toward the Mediterranean to Ancient Lower Egypt for an amazing distance of 4,160 miles (6,695 km). To the north of the ancient city of Memphis, the Nile breaks up into a myriad of smaller rivers forming the Nile Delta, the most fertile area in the whole of Egypt. The Delta was particularly important for farming, but irrigation was practiced extensively along considerable stretches of the Nile. In the deserts to the west of the Nile lay a series of important oases, which contained significant populations and acted as vital connecting points in overland trade with territories in North Africa further to the west.

The city of Alexandria was the key administrative center under the Ptolemies, and its cultural impact on Egypt and areas outside Egypt was considerable. Located on the Mediterranean just to the west of the Delta and taking advantage of a natural harbor, Alexandria was to become one of the most important cities of the Hellenistic period and also during the Roman period. Alexander the Great had founded Alexandria during his brief six-month stay in Egypt following its capture toward the end of 332 B.C.E. The city quickly grew to prominence under Ptolemy I on the basis of emigration from mainland Greece. It was not until the reign of his son, Ptolemy II Philadelphus (reigned 285–246 B.C.E.), that the city of Alexandria's famed magnificence assumed its essential aspect.

THE EARLY PTOLEMIES

Ptolemy I Soter (Savior), who reigned from 323–285 B.C.E., played an important role in the wars of Alexander's successors that raged for over two decades from the time of the latter's death in 323 B.C.E. The emergence and downfall of important players during this period was often swift, but by the beginning of the third century B.C.E. Ptolemy I came through as one of the significant rulers. Another of those to emerge was Antigonus Monopthalmus ("the one-eyed") who had been appointed satrap of Phrygia in Asia Minor by Alexander. Following Alexander's death, Antigonus took control of Syria and parts of mainland Greece. Of all the contenders for territorial control following Alexander's death, Antigonus was the most intent on reuniting the whole of Alexander's empire under one ruler.

In 301 B.C.E., this eventually led to a combined assault by the surviving successor rulers, including Seleucus I but not Ptolemy I, on Antigonus that saw his army defeated at Ipsus. Antigonus, aged eighty-one, was killed and his territorial possessions were carved up. Ptolemy I occupied territory in southern Syria, but this territory would be fought over with the Seleucids in a tug-of-war that lasted for the next hundred years.

At this time, Ptolemy I also occupied Palestine, together with parts of what we now know as Jordan. At modern-day Acre (at one time Acco), a fortress town called Ptolemais was built; Rabbah was the site of a Ptolemaic city called Philadelphia, after Ptolemy II.

LEFT: A PAGE FROM A FRENCH MEDIEVAL MANUSCRIPT BY BOCCACCIO. IT ILLUSTRATES THE STORY OF SELEUCUS I AND HIS SON ANTIOCHUS I, SUCCESSIVE KINGS OF SYRIA.

BELOW: *PTOLEMY AT GAZA,* BY AN UNKNOWN GERMAN ARTIST. PTOLEMY I DEFEATED ANTIGONUS MONOPTHALMUS AND HIS SON, DEMETRIUS POLIORCETES, IN 306 B.C.E.

RIGHT: THE THIRD-CENTURY B.C.E. GONZAGA CAMEO SHOWS PTOLEMY II AND HIS WIFE ARSINOE II AS GREEK GODS. AFTER ABOUT 10 YEARS OF MARRIAGE, ARSINOE II WAS EXILED TO KOPTOS, POSSIBLY FOR PLOTTING AGAINST HER HUSBAND.

BELOW: THESE RUINS ATTEST TO THE ONCE-THRIVING LIFE OF THE FAIYUM OASIS WEST OF THE NILE. PTOLEMY II ENCOURAGED RENEWED SETTLEMENT HERE IN ORDER TO STRENGTHEN HIS HOLD OVER EGYPT. MANY GREEKS AND JEWS LIVED HERE.

Ptolemy I also took a number of important steps designed to secure control over Egypt. He carefully and skillfully set out to cultivate an image as the legitimate successor of Alexander. All of the successors attempted to do this; however, Ptolemy I was perhaps the most successful. He attempted to link himself to the family of Alexander by inventing an ancestral connection with his own family. Ptolemy I also succeeded in capturing the body of Alexander as it was on its way back to Macedonia. He conveyed the king's body first to Memphis, the Ancient Egyptian capital, before transferring it to Alexandria where an enormous funerary monument was erected for the purpose of housing it. To further link himself with the great conqueror, Ptolemy I minted coins of himself that evoked Alexander's portrayals of himself as Heracles. He wrote a history of Alexander's reign and campaigns, which was relied on considerably by later writers on Alexander. Ptolemy I's history has not survived, but it was influential in the Roman imperial period from which the most complete histories and biographies of Alexander written in antiquity originate. The most celebrated of these surviving accounts is that of the second-century C.E. historian Arrian, whose account relied heavily on Ptolemy I. So Ptolemy I has been particularly successful in establishing a literary representation of Alexander as well as his own part in the conqueror's exploits that has prevailed for well over 2,000 years.

It was due to the efforts of Ptolemy I that a hereditary dynasty was established, one that would continue for more than 250 years after his death. In 285 B.C.E., Ptolemy I elevated his son, Ptolemy II, to the position of co-regent. As an indication of the exclusive nature of Ptolemaic family rule in Egypt, Ptolemy II was married to his sister Arsinoe II. Ptolemy II became known as Philadelphus, which means "brother/sister-loving," a term not insulting or derogatory as it may appear today. The rule of Ptolemy II Philadelphus lasted until 246 B.C.E., and his long reign saw the consolidation of much that his father had established. The early Ptolemies also ensured that the temples and priests of the Ancient Egyptian cults were loyal to them. The temples were often large complexes which had extensive tracts of land attached to them. They were economically and agriculturally very important, providing taxation revenue to the imperial treasury as well as large amounts of food to local populations.

THE SYRO–EGYPTIAN WARS

A feature of Ptolemaic rule in the third century B.C.E. was the ongoing conflict between Egypt and the Seleucids based in Syria. We have already seen that Ptolemy I took control of territory in Palestine and southern Syria after Antigonus's defeat in 301 B.C.E. Further to this, he succeeded in capturing territory in southeast Asia Minor and in the 290s B.C.E. took

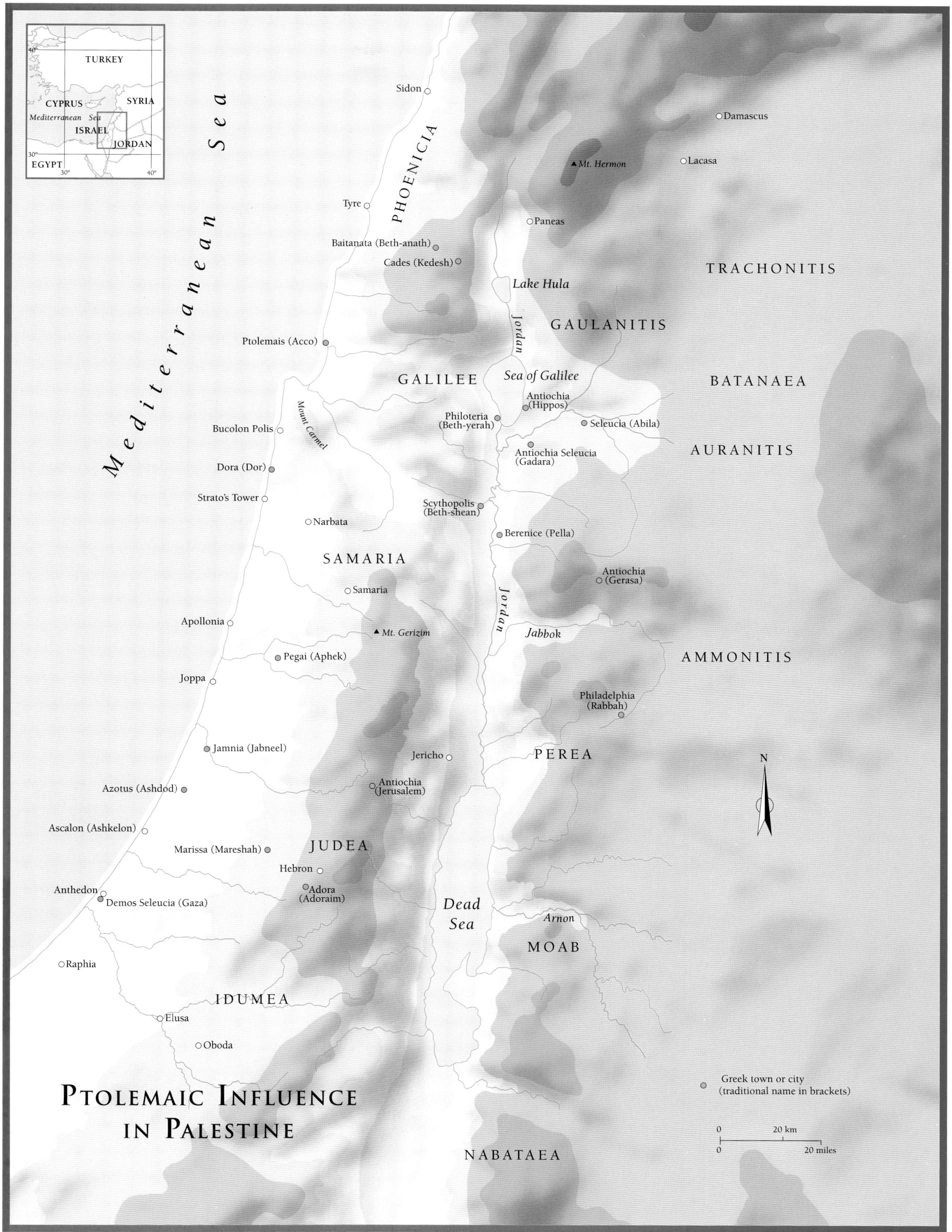

Ptolemaic Influence in Palestine

RIGHT: ROMAN MARBLE BUST OF PTOLEMY III. AFTER ONLY A YEAR ON EGYPT'S THRONE, PTOLEMY SET OUT WITH HIS ARMY TO CONQUER THE SELEUCID KINGDOM.

control of many of the islands of the Aegean Sea. It is interesting to note that Egyptian attempts to take control of Palestine, southern Syria, and other areas in the eastern Mediterranean stretched back to the period of pharaonic rule. A notable example is the campaigns of Rameses II in the thirteenth century B.C.E. It was not long, however, before Ptolemaic territorial expansion was challenged by the Seleucids, who had taken control of Antigonus's possessions in Syria. Early in the sole reign of Ptolemy II, the Seleucids went to war over attempted Ptolemaic expansion in Asia Minor. This was known as the First Syrian War (274–271 B.C.E.), but it led to little change in the balance of power between the Ptolemies and Seleucids in Asia Minor.

Only a decade later the Seleucids were successful in their attempts to regain some of their possessions in Asia Minor while strengthening their power over the islands of the Aegean. This took place as a result of the Second Syrian War (261–253 B.C.E.). This war was concluded by a peace agreement between Ptolemy II and Antiochus II. The agreement included a provision that Ptolemy II's daughter, Berenice, was to be given in marriage to Antiochus II. The eventual breakdown of this marriage was one of the causes of the Third Syrian War between the Ptolemies and the Seleucids. Ptolemy II and Antiochus II both died in 246 B.C.E., and the succession crisis in the Seleucid Empire led to a Ptolemaic invasion of Syria. The marriage between Antiochus II and Berenice had produced a son, but the estrangement of Antiochus II and Berenice saw Antiochus II promote Seleucus II, his son by his former marriage, as the heir to his empire. With Seleucus II successfully taking power following his father's death, the new Ptolemaic king, Ptolemy III Euergetes I (reigned 246–221 B.C.E.), invaded the Seleucid Empire in an attempt to save his sister, Berenice, and to have her son (Ptolemy III's nephew) made king. The war lasted from 246–241 B.C.E., and Ptolemy III succeeded in invading as far as Babylon, deep within the Seleucid Empire. He was unable to secure the safety of his sister or the succession of his nephew; both were murdered soon after the invasion began, and he was also unable to hold any territorial gains.

In the reign of Ptolemy IV Philopator (221–205 B.C.E.), yet another war was fought between the Seleucids and Ptolemies, with a major battle fought at Raphia near Gaza in 217 B.C.E. in which Ptolemy IV was victorious. The success at Raphia came largely as a result of reliance on indigenous Egyptian forces, and their newly discovered importance led them to revolt. This meant that large sections of Lower Egypt were out of Ptolemaic control for the next 25 years. In the reign of Ptolemy V Epiphanes (204–180 B.C.E.), the fortunes of the Ptolemaic kingdom took a turn for the worse. Ptolemaic possessions in Asia Minor and the Aegean were lost, while the defeat of Egyptian troops at Paneas in Palestine in 200 B.C.E. saw the permanent end of Ptolemaic imperialistic activity in Syria. The early decades of the second century B.C.E. saw the rise of Roman power in the eastern Mediterranean, and the Ptolemies benefited from this to an extent as Rome's main

THE BATTLES OF RAPHIA AND PANEAS

The site of the final battle in the Fifth Syrian War.

The site of the final battle in the Fourth Syrian War.

BELOW RIGHT: THE GODDESS ISIS, PAINTED LIMESTONE DECORATION FROM THE TOMB OF HOREMHEB, VALLEY OF THE KINGS, THEBES. THE CULT OF ISIS TOOK HOLD AND EVOLVED ACROSS THE HELLENISTIC WORLD IN THE TIME OF PTOLEMAIC RULE.

focus was on curtailing Seleucid and Antigonid territorial ambitions. The expansion of Roman power in the eastern Mediterranean was the most significant feature on the political landscape during the following two hundred years.

ABOVE: THIS RELIEF AT THE KOM OMBO TEMPLE SHOWS THE EGYPTIAN GOD HORUS WISHING LONG LIFE TO ONE OF THE PTOLEMIES. IN ORDER TO SOLIDIFY THEIR KINGLY POSITION, THE PTOLEMIES SOUGHT DIVINE HONORS IN THE EGYPTIAN TRADITION.

RELIGIOUS DEVELOPMENTS UNDER THE PTOLEMIES

In pharaonic Egypt, the Egyptian king was believed to be a living god, and this was held to guarantee the safety and prosperity of the kingdom. It appears that Alexander the Great sought divine honors before his death in 323 B.C.E.; his experiences in Egypt in 332/331 B.C.E. probably contributed to this desire. The kings who emerged as Alexander's successors—notably the Antigonids, Seleucids, and Ptolemies—all sought divine honors in their own lifetimes in emulation of Alexander the Great as a means of strengthening their claims to legitimacy in the territories they controlled.

There were also some significant religious developments early in the Ptolemaic dynasty, which had an impact in Egypt and across the Hellenistic world. The cults of Isis and Sarapis developed out of earlier indigenous Egyptian cults, but were also novel in a number of ways. In pharaonic Egypt, Isis was the wife of Osiris, the god of the dead, and in Ptolemaic times worship of this goddess spread from Egypt to mainland Greece and the islands of the Aegean. Isis was often worshipped in Greek terms, but she was not without her indigenous Egyptian characteristics as well. The statues and temples of Isis that have survived are often Greek in form, and Greek is often the language of the cult, but she was still portrayed with the Ancient Egyptian headdress. Isis was identified with Demeter and Aphrodite by Greeks, and in Egypt itself the goddess was often directly linked with the Ptolemaic queen. The wife and sister of Ptolemy II, Arsinoe II, appears to have been the first Ptolemaic queen to have identified herself with Isis, and this identification was associated with living kings receiving divine honors. The cult of Isis became increasingly popular across the Hellenistic world, and the goddess also emerged as important in the development of mystery cults. When the Roman Empire took control of the Hellenistic kingdoms in the second and first centuries B.C.E., the cult of Isis became popular throughout the Empire and it continued to develop and change.

Closely linked to Isis and her cult was the cult of the god Sarapis. This god was developed into a particularly Ptolemaic deity who, like Isis, spread throughout the Hellenistic world and was soon widely favored in the Roman Empire. Sarapis was a syncretistic god who had the attributes of a number of Greek gods such as Zeus, Asclepius, and Hades. Sarapis also assumed a number of the characteristics of the Egyptian god of the dead, Osiris. In statues his head is crowned with a *modius* (a vessel used to pour out corn), which is representative of fertility. At his feet, Cerberus, the three-headed dog of Hades, is often seated, thus linking him with the underworld; Sarapis often holds a staff in his left hand, which is symbolic of Asclepius, the god of healing. The cult's importance at the Ancient Egyptian capital city of Memphis and also at Alexandria grew quite significantly throughout the Ptolemaic period. The importance of the cults of both Isis and Osiris to the imperial family is reflected in the fact that by the end of the third century B.C.E., both deities had been included in the royal oath.

THE CULT OF SARAPIS

There is some debate regarding the origins of Sarapis; however, Roman writers claimed that Ptolemy I was responsible for bringing the cult of Sarapis to Egypt. Apparently, Ptolemy I had a dream in which he was told to get a statue of Sarapis and place it in its own temple in Alexandria. This was no easy task but Ptolemy I achieved it. Tacitus, a Roman historian, says that due to lengthy administrative delays the statue got up, walked down to the harbor, and boarded Ptolemy I's ship to go to Egypt. Plutarch, somewhat less fancifully, says the Ptolemaic officials stole it.

THE SELEUCIDS

THE KING OF THE NORTH SHALL COME AND ... TAKE A WELL-FORTIFIED CITY DANIEL 11:15

RIGHT: BRONZE BUST OF SELEUCUS I, FROM VILLA DEI PISONI HERCULANEUM. FOUNDER OF THE SELEUCID DYNASTY, SELEUCID I WAS AROUND FORTY-FIVE YEARS OF AGE WHEN HE RETOOK BABYLONIA IN 312 B.C.E.

The Seleucid dynasty was founded by the son of a Macedonian noble named Seleucus I. Like Ptolemy I in Egypt, Seleucus I's origins were relatively obscure, but he became prominent in the later campaigns of Alexander the Great. In the period following Alexander's death in which his generals fought for control over sections of his vast empire, Seleucus I received the satrapy of Babylonia in 321 B.C.E. He lost the satrapy to Antigonus in 316 B.C.E. and fled to Egypt, where he served as one of Ptolemy I's generals. With the assistance of Ptolemy I, Seleucus I succeeded in regaining Babylonia from Antigonus in 312 B.C.E., and he also took Media and Susiana. This marked the beginning of the Seleucid Empire and the dating system known as the Seleucid era, which was used for centuries afterward.

In the wake of Antigonus's defeat at Ipsus in 301 B.C.E., Seleucus I gained the Antigonid possessions of northern Syria and eastern Asia Minor. At around the same time he took control of eastern Iran and invaded northwestern India, waging war against the Indian emperor Chandragupta. In the end, Seleucus I emerged in control of almost all of Alexander's conquests outside Greece except Egypt and parts of southern Syria under Ptolemaic control. The Ptolemies and Seleucids were serious rivals throughout the third century B.C.E., fighting over territory in southern Syria, coastal Asia Minor, as well as the many Greek islands of the Aegean Sea.

Like the Ptolemies in Egypt and the Antigonids in mainland Greece, the Seleucids established a dynasty that would last for centuries. Seleucus I elevated his son Antiochus I to the position of co-ruler in 292 B.C.E. and even gave his young wife to Antiochus I before his own death in 281 B.C.E. as a sign of dynastic continuity. The fortunes of the Seleucid Empire and the dynasty that ruled it fluctuated throughout the third century B.C.E., and by the last decades of that century the Seleucid Empire faced some serious problems. The enormous and diverse territory over which the Seleucids ruled made controlling it very difficult. There were also considerable difficulties at times in dealing with widely diverse cultural issues, which would be a particular feature of the reign of Antiochus IV in the second century B.C.E.

ANTIOCHUS III AND IV

Following the assassination of Seleucus III in 223 B.C.E., Antiochus III came to power at the age of nineteen. He ruled for almost 40 years (he died in 187 B.C.E.) and succeeded in strengthening the Seleucid Empire in the first half of his reign. For this reason, Antiochus III became known as Megas "the Great." Another feature of Antiochus III's reign, however, was to antagonize the Romans and lose a major battle against them.

As a result of their victory in the battle of Paneas in 200 B.C.E., the Seleucids took control of coastal and southern Syria (Palestine, Coele-Syria) from the Ptolemies. The Ptolemies were never able to regain this territory, and this effectively ended the struggle between the Seleucids and the Ptolemies which had raged during the previous century for control of territory in southern Syria. This meant that Jerusalem and Palestine were under Seleucid control. Antiochus III reached an agreement with the Jews, giving tax concessions to the Temple administration and guaranteeing the Jews the right to live under their own laws. Antiochus III also gave funds for building projects in Jerusalem. The Tobiad family,

BELOW: ANTIOCHUS III OF SYRIA IS SEEN HERE IN THIS UNATTRIBUTED ENGRAVING, CARRYING OUT AN ACT OF COMPASSION. ANTIOCHUS III WAS IN FACT KNOWN AS AN AGGRESSIVE KING.

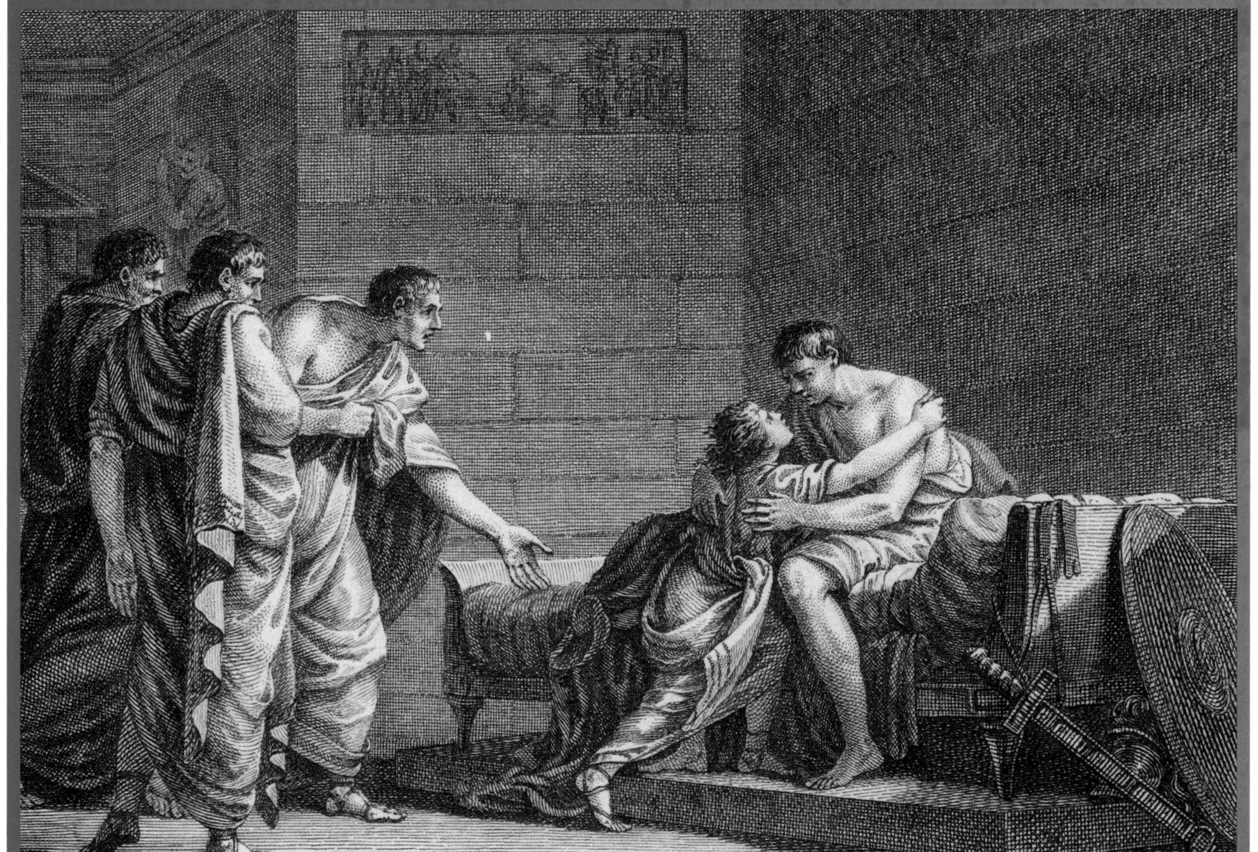

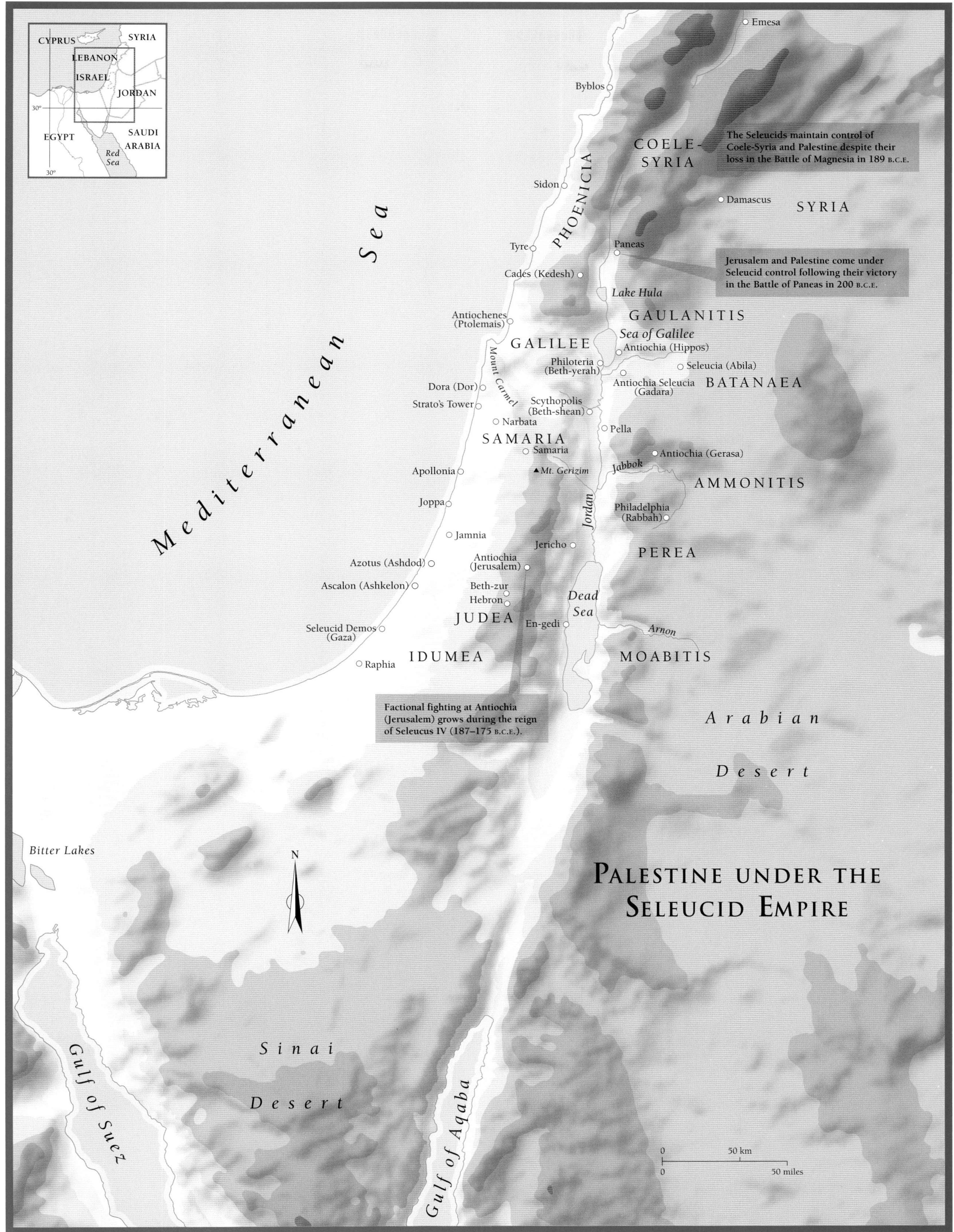
Palestine under the Seleucid Empire
The Seleucids maintain control of Coele-Syria and Palestine despite their loss in the Battle of Magnesia in 189 B.C.E.
Jerusalem and Palestine come under Seleucid control following their victory in the Battle of Paneas in 200 B.C.E.
Factional fighting at Antiochia (Jerusalem) grows during the reign of Seleucus IV (187–175 B.C.E.).
CYPRUS
SYRIA
LEBANON
ISRAEL
JORDAN
EGYPT
SAUDI ARABIA
Red Sea
Mediterranean Sea
Emesa
Byblos
COELE-SYRIA
Sidon
PHOENICIA
Damascus
SYRIA
Tyre
Paneas
Cades (Kedesh)
Lake Hula
Antiochenes (Ptolemais)
GAULANITIS
GALILEE
Sea of Galilee
Antiochia (Hippos)
Mount Carmel
Philoteria (Beth-yerah)
Seleucia (Abila)
Dora (Dor)
Antiochia Seleucia (Gadara)
BATANAEA
Strato's Tower
Scythopolis (Beth-shean)
Narbata
Pella
SAMARIA
Samaria
Antiochia (Gerasa)
Apollonia
Mt. Gerizim
Jabbok
AMMONITIS
Joppa
Jordan
Philadelphia (Rabbah)
Jamnia
Jericho
PEREA
Azotus (Ashdod)
Antiochia (Jerusalem)
Ascalon (Ashkelon)
Beth-zur
Hebron
Dead Sea
JUDEA
En-gedi
Arnon
Seleucid Demos (Gaza)
IDUMEA
MOABITIS
Raphia
Arabian Desert
Bitter Lakes
N
Sinai Desert
Gulf of Suez
Gulf of Aqaba
0 50 km
0 50 miles

ABOVE: *THE EXPULSION OF HELIODORUS FROM THE TEMPLE*, BY B. CAVALLINO. A MINISTER OF SELEUCUS IV, HELIODORUS TRIED TO STEAL THE TEMPLE TREASURES, BUT WAS SET UPON BY THREE GODS IN THE FORM OF A HORSE AND TWO STRONG MEN.

who had collected taxes on behalf of the Ptolemies, continued to do so under the Seleucids. As a result of these moves, Antiochus III received widespread respect from the Jews.

In 191 B.C.E. war broke out between Antiochus III and Rome, with Antiochus III losing at the Battle of Magnesia in 189 B.C.E. In 188 B.C.E., the Peace of Apamea was signed between Antiochus III and Rome. This resulted in heavy financial penalties and the requirement that Antiochus III should send one of his sons, the future Antiochus IV, as a hostage to Rome. He would remain there for 13 years. Significantly, however, the Seleucids did not lose control of Coele-Syria and Palestine, which the Roman treaty guaranteed them.

The need to raise taxes in order to pay the indemnity resulting from the Peace of Apamea placed considerable pressure on communities across the whole empire, including Jerusalem. When Antiochus III was killed attempting to rob a temple in Babylon in June 187 B.C.E., Seleucus IV came to the throne. Seleucus IV reigned until 175 B.C.E., and during his reign factional fighting increased significantly in Jerusalem. Antiochus IV succeeded Seleucus IV in 175 B.C.E. and reigned until 164 B.C.E. Antiochus IV's reign became famous for his confrontation with Rome over attempts to invade Egypt, and particularly for the way he was increasingly drawn into the complex political situation in Jerusalem. This came about as a result of petitions from the most powerful families in Jerusalem for appointment to the High Priesthood. The issue of Greek culture and its influence in Jerusalem was also important in Antiochus IV's relationship with the Jews.

JASON AND MENELAUS

An important issue to emerge in Antiochus IV's dealings with Jerusalem was the political struggle between families and individuals for appointment to the High Priesthood of the Temple and the confirmation of this appointment by the Seleucid king. While Antiochus III had initially earned the admiration of many in Jerusalem, his necessity to raise taxes to pay tribute to the Romans following the Peace of Apamea had made him increasingly unpopular. His two successors,

RIGHT: THIS PAGE FROM A MEDIEVAL FRENCH MANUSCRIPT DEPICTS MENELAUS DELIVERING TRIBUTE MONEY TO ANTIOCHUS IV IN ORDER TO SECURE FOR HIMSELF THE HIGH PRIESTHOOD.

Seleucus IV and Antiochus IV, faced similar difficulties and it appears that some people in Jerusalem began to agitate for a return to Ptolemaic rule. This raised the political stakes in terms of who was appointed to the High Priesthood. Whomever the appointed ones were, they would need to demonstrate pro-Seleucid sympathies, and any bribes they might offer to the Seleucid king would assist in raising funds for the payment of tribute. In turn, however, they ran the risk of losing the support they needed from the elite families in Jerusalem.

LEFT: IN THIS DETAIL FROM A CLASSICAL GREEK RELIEF WE SEE TWO MEN WRESTLING. SPORTING CONTESTS WERE ONE OF THE MANY ASPECTS OF GREEK CULTURE IMPOSED ON JERUSALEM'S CITIZENS.

Onias III was the High Priest at the time Antiochus IV came to power in 175 B.C.E. Onias III was from the family of Zadok who claimed to have ruled as the dynasty of the High Priesthood since the time of King David. Another family, the Tobiads, had been responsible for the collection of taxes under the Ptolemies, and they were confirmed in this role when Antiochus III took control of Judea and Jerusalem from the Ptolemies. The High Priest Onias III had traveled to the court of Seleucus IV in 175 B.C.E. to be confirmed in his position, but arrived just after Seleucus IV's assassination and the elevation of Antiochus IV. Antiochus IV appears to have suspected Onias III of having Ptolemaic sympathies, and he appointed Onias III's brother, Jason, to the High Priesthood instead. At Jason's request a program of Hellenization began in Jerusalem. This meant that the political institutions of a Greek city were established there, and important elements of Greek culture were promoted (see 2 Maccabees 3:40–4:22). The High Priest, Jason, was instrumental in this program and many of the elite Jewish families appear to have embraced Hellenistic culture and institutions. The language, culture, and political institutions of the Greeks were greatly appreciated and sought after in many cities of the Seleucid Empire and also in Ptolemaic Egypt. Jerusalem adopted the name of Antiochia, as did many other cities in Syria, and its citizens were enrolled as Antiochenes. The city was probably constituted as a Greek polis (city-state) at this time.

The impact of the Hellenization program was significant, with the building of a gymnasium, a school for young aristocrats that was modeled on Classical Greek lines, which would have required royal permission to build. It may also have received royal funds for its construction. Some young Jewish aristocrats attempted to hide their circumcision, and others even attempted to have their circumcisions reversed. Antiochus IV visited Jerusalem in 173 B.C.E. and was well received. Jewish participants also took part in the Quinquennial Games at Tyre, yet another indicator of the extent to which Hellenistic culture had been embraced by the Jewish elite.

In a significant development in 172 B.C.E., the head of the Tobiad family, Menelaus, used the tribute he was delivering to Antiochus IV to outbid Jason for the High Priesthood. Though the tribute the Seleucids were responsible for paying to the Romans had been fully paid by 173 B.C.E., they were still desperate for revenue as the tribute had significantly reduced their income. The success Menelaus had in deposing the traditional priestly family is indicative of this. Menelaus further increased taxes and was an even more enthusiastic supporter of the Hellenization program in Jerusalem. Reaction to Menelaus's appointment in Jerusalem led to an escalation in violence, with the murder of Jason's brother Onias III in 170 B.C.E.; Lysimachus, the brother of Menelaus, was murdered in riots in Jerusalem after taking Temple treasures.

Politicization of the High Priesthood in Jerusalem during the reign of Antiochus IV had important ramifications politically and culturally for the Jews. The High Priest became increasingly concerned with maintaining good relations with Antiochus IV so as to secure his own position. This resulted in a greater cultural and political alignment with the Hellenistic world, of which many of the elite at Jerusalem were happy to be a part. When Jason was replaced by Menelaus, however, the High Priest also became the tax collector, and the difficulties Antiochus IV had in raising the necessary revenue to run his kingdom and pay tribute to the Romans led to a significant increase in taxes levied on the people of Judea; this in turn led to increased disgruntlement, not only with the High Priesthood but also with Hellenistic culture itself. One group, known as the Maccabees and led by

BELOW: BATTLE SCENE FROM A FRENCH MANUSCRIPT BIBLE, 1526. IT DEPICTS ONE OF SEVERAL BATTLES BETWEEN THE SELEUCIDS AND THE MACCABEES DESCRIBED IN THE BOOK 1 MACCABEES.

Judas Maccabeus, who for religious reasons had resisted the process of Hellenization, was now able to muster greater support for a full-scale rebellion.

ANTIOCHUS IV'S PLAN TO DESTROY JUDAISM

From 170–168 B.C.E., the Seleucids and the Ptolemies fought over southern Syria once again. Due to Jerusalem's location, Antiochus IV passed through the city on his way to campaign against the Ptolemies on a number of occasions. In 169 B.C.E., following a successful battle with Ptolemy VI at Pelusium, Antiochus IV returned to Syria and on the way plundered the Temple in Jerusalem with the assistance of Menelaus. In the process he entered the Holy of Holies, which was strictly forbidden. In 168 B.C.E., again on the way home to Syria following an engagement with the Egyptians, Antiochus IV passed through Jerusalem and this time suppressed a revolt by Jason. Due to the revolt, Jerusalem received a military colony in 167 B.C.E., the city's fortifications were destroyed, and a Seleucid garrison was installed. A new tax system was introduced in which taxes were collected by royal agents rather than the High Priesthood. Toward the end of the year, religious reforms were instituted including the construction of a pagan altar in the Temple. This altar became known as the Abomination of Desolation and represented the ultimate desecration of a Temple to a monotheistic god.

In 167/166 B.C.E. the Maccabean revolts began. They were a reaction to the Hellenizing process that had been taking place for almost a decade at this point and to the more recent actions of Antiochus IV that so affronted an increasing number of Jews. The revolts were led by Judas Maccabeus, who claimed to be acting to save the Jewish religion from destruction. The movement appears to have begun in rural areas but it became increasingly popular in the cities, particularly in Jerusalem. The books of 1 and 2 Maccabees are a later, sympathetic account of the Maccabean struggle. They indicate that an element of the Jewish elite favored the Hellenization process, and they attribute the hardships experienced under Antiochus IV to the rebellion against Jewish religious traditions that the Hellenizing process represented to the Maccabees. The revolt became so serious that Antiochus IV rescinded his religious reforms in Jerusalem and attempted to return the political and administrative situation to the way it had been prior to his reforms. Because the revolt was so widespread, Antiochus IV was unable to achieve this. The example of the Maccabees as an uncompromising and zealous movement remained a very important element in the way that Jews would later deal with other foreign powers, particularly the Romans.

BELOW: *ANTIOCHUS IN JERUSALEM*, BY FRENCHMAN JEAN FOUQUET, IN *OEUVRE DE JEHAN FOUCQUET*. ANTIOCHUS IV RIDES TRIUMPHANTLY INTO THE CITY, SLAYING SOME RESIDENTS ALONG THE WAY.

AT WAR WITH ROME

The ongoing dispute with the Ptolemies over southern Syria and Palestine was the catalyst for conflict between Antiochus IV and Rome. In 170 B.C.E., both Ptolemy VI and Antiochus IV sent embassies to the Romans in an attempt to justify their positions on who should control the region. This action reflected Rome's increasingly powerful position in the

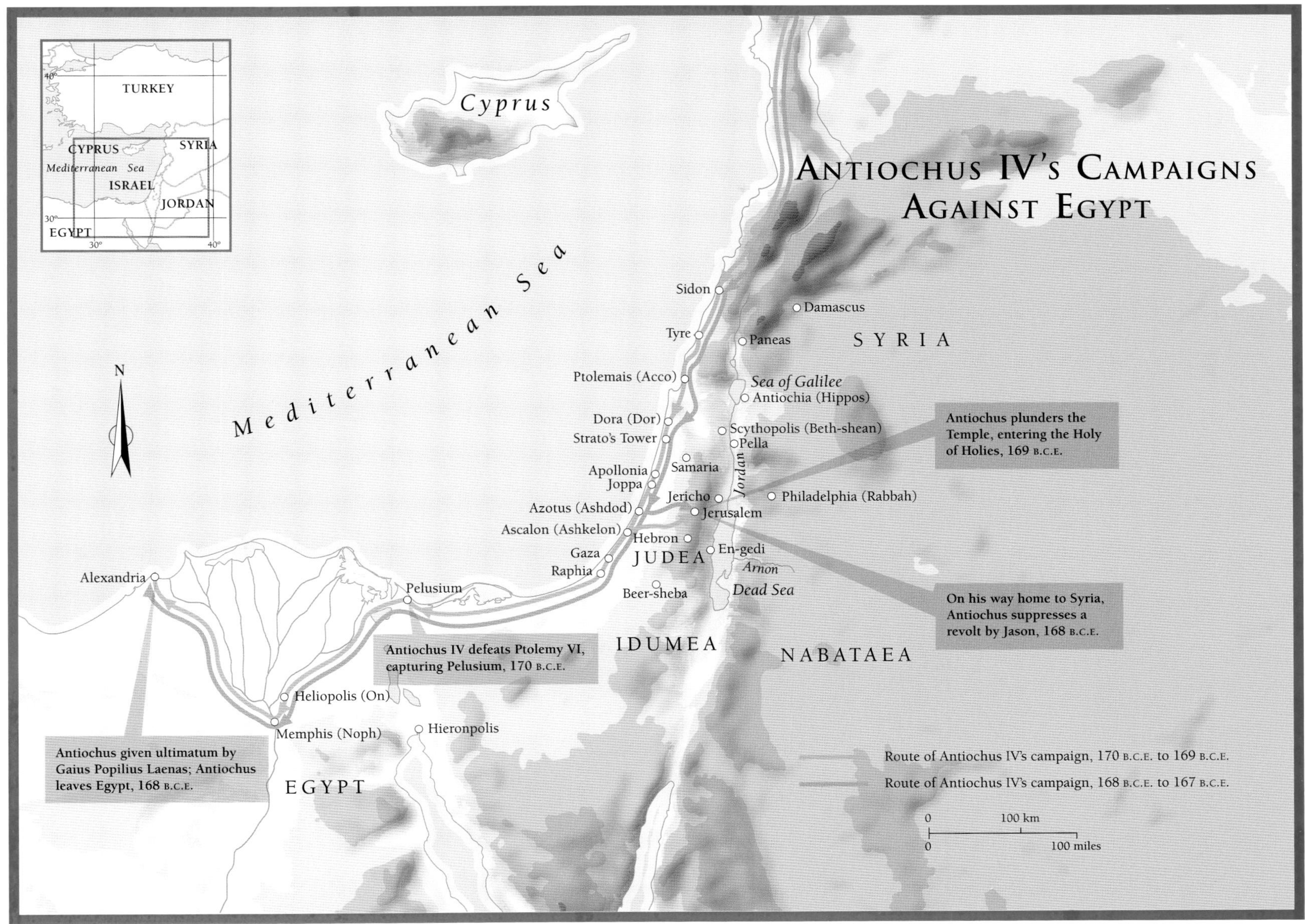

eastern Mediterranean following the defeat of Ptolemy V of Egypt in 196 B.C.E. and Antiochus III of Syria in 189 B.C.E. The Romans were at this stage prosecuting a major campaign against the Macedonians and refused to become involved. Antiochus IV made the first move, and in October/November 170 B.C.E. invaded Egypt and won a major battle, capturing Pelusium in the process. In 169 B.C.E., Antiochus IV came to terms with Ptolemy VI, who virtually accepted him as his guardian, but the conflict escalated again later. While the Romans were still occupied with the war against Macedonia, they nevertheless sent an ambassador insisting on negotiations but it was too late. Antiochus IV was already victorious and seems to have been officially crowned king of Egypt.

After this, the Egyptians decided to renounce the agreement with Antiochus IV and also requested Roman assistance. This led to Antiochus IV's second invasion in 168 B.C.E. While initially successful, Antiochus IV faced a new problem, as the Romans were victorious over the Macedonians in 167 B.C.E. and were now able to lend some practical support to Egypt. When Antiochus IV arrived in Alexandria, he was met by the Roman envoy, Gaius Popilius Laenas, whom he had known during the 13 years in which he was a hostage in Rome as part of Antiochus III's agreement at the Peace of Apamea in 188 B.C.E. Popilius informed Antiochus IV that he should leave Egypt and Antiochus IV responded by saying that he would think about it. In an act of high theater, Popilius took his sword and drew a circle in the sand around Antiochus IV, demanding that he respond before stepping out of the circle. Antiochus IV had no choice but to leave Egypt. From that point any dispute between the Seleucids and the Ptolemies was decided by the Romans. Toward the end of 164 B.C.E., Antiochus IV died in Babylon. Three years later a formal treaty was struck between the Maccabees and Rome. For the Maccabees, this represented protection from future Seleucid actions such as those of Antiochus IV; for the Romans, it provided them with a pretext for intervention in the Seleucid kingdom.

LEFT: TWO LEGIONNAIRES DURING BATTLE, DETAIL FROM A ROMAN RELIEF. WITH THE HELP OF THE ROMANS, EGYPT FORCED ANTIOCHUS IV TO LEAVE ALEXANDRIA.

A MACCABEAN JEWISH STATE

[JUDAS] WAS LIKE A LION IN HIS DEEDS, LIKE A LION'S CUB ROARING FOR PREY 1 MACCABEES 3:4

BELOW: ANTIOCHUS IV TAKES AND PILLAGES THE CITY AND TEMPLE OF JERUSALEM, FROM *HISTORY OF THE JEWS* BY JEWISH HISTORIAN JOSEPHUS. ANTIOCHUS IV PREVENTED THE JEWS FROM PRACTICING THEIR OWN FAITH.

The Jewish presence in Palestine under the leadership of the Maccabees represents the last time an independent Jewish state existed until the founding of the modern state of Israel in 1948. In the second century B.C.E. Judea was able to emerge as the regional power in Palestine largely due to the decline of the Greek Seleucid dynasty's power at that time, and because Rome had not yet come into control of western Asia. This period of Maccabean rule is a most crucial time because its political and religious dynamics significantly shaped the Judaism that followed.

The external influence of Greek culture and religion challenged traditions of Jewishness and instigated a range of responses, from acceptance and adoption, to adaptation and accommodation, to resistance and rejection. In particular, positions taken on the shape of civil rule in its relation to the priesthood prompted a variety of advocacy groups to emerge, groups that would shape Jewish religion and politics for centuries until rabbinic Judaism emerged in the second century C.E. as the carrier of the tradition. The parties of Judaism that later gain clearer definition, including Pharisees, Essenes, Sadducees, and Zealots, can be identified in the history of this period.

WHO WERE THE MACCABEES?

The Maccabees, also known as the Hasmonean dynasty in rabbinic literature and the writings of the Jewish historian Josephus, initially were the leaders of the resistance to Seleucid rule and then served as the heads of the state of Judea from 167 to 63 B.C.E. The Maccabees are the family of Mattathias, who is credited with being the instigator of Jewish resistance to Greek efforts to force Jews in Judea to accept Hellenistic religious and civic practices. Josephus indicates that Mattathias was the great-grandson of Asamoneus, a Greek name from which the designation Hasmonean derives. Other sources suggest that the name derives from a place name, either Heshmon or Hashmonah.

The major historical sources for this period are the first two books of the Maccabees in the Apocrypha. Both books were written toward the end of the second century B.C.E. The first book, called 1 Maccabees, was composed in Hebrew but survives only in a Greek translation. It summarizes the events from Alexander's defeat of Darius III at Issus in 333 B.C.E. down to the beginning of the reign of Antiochus IV in 175 B.C.E., and then it details the events to the death of Simon and the accession of John Hyrcanus I in 134 B.C.E.

The book of 1 Maccabees is written as documentary history in the same style as the biblical books of Samuel and Kings. It approves of the Maccabees and clearly views them as upholding Israel's covenant with Yahweh. The writer generously includes direct quotations from the historical figures whose stories are told, projecting the impression that it is a firsthand account. Another characteristic is the use of poetic encomia or praise as commentary in the style of Samuel and Kings, as in the praise of Judas Maccabeus (1 Maccabees 3:3–9). The writer of 1 Maccabees provides year references throughout the book that enable the reader to establish an absolute chronology; they are based on the beginning of Greek Seleucid rule in 312 B.C.E. (see 1 Maccabees 1:10, 20, and so on).

The second book, called 2 Maccabees, was written in Greek by Jason of Cyrene and covers a 20-year period from 180–160 B.C.E. It encompasses the years immediately before and after the Maccabean revolt against the Seleucids, and describes the persecutions and martyrdoms of the Jews. The tales of Maccabean suffering are so graphic and gruesome in this book that they gave rise to the term *macabre*, from Maccabee. The books of 1 and 2 Maccabees can be supplemented by Josephus's *Antiquities of the Jews*, Books 12–13, written around C.E. 94, and *The Histories* by Polybius.

From the time that Alexander the Great gained control until the beginning of the second century B.C.E., the political climate in Palestine was generally calm for the Jews, and they could practice their own religion as they saw fit. This changed with the reign of Antiochus IV Epiphanes, who ruled from 175–164 B.C.E. After this Seleucid king achieved victory over Egypt and its Ptolemaic ruling dynasty, he imposed himself on Jerusalem and set about remodeling it as a Greek polis or city-state by building a gymnasium and imposing Greek religious and cultural practices. This was just one expression of the very aggressive position he took on coercing peoples throughout his empire to adopt Hellenistic systems. He also plundered the Temple treasury and defiled the sanctuary. According to 1 Maccabees 1:39 and 54, this action made the Temple a desolate place, meaning it lacked the presence of the Lord; the description echoes the language of Daniel 12:11's predicted "abomination that desolates."

Reaction to Antiochus IV's program was mixed. The book of 1 Maccabees reports that Gentiles and many Jews approved of his imposition of Greek practice and outlawing of Jewish Torah and ritual sacrifice. But as the program reached beyond Jerusalem and into rural villages, resistance also stiffened.

MATTATHIAS AND HIS SUPPORTERS

The story of the Maccabean revolt against Antiochus IV starts in Modein, northwest of Jerusalem. An envoy from Antiochus IV commanded Mattathias, a civic leader in Modein and a priest, to offer a sacrifice in the Greek style. Not only would this be a betrayal of Yahweh, it would challenge the centrality of the Temple in Jerusalem which, after the reform of Josiah, was the only place sacrifice could officially be conducted. When Mattathias refused to comply, another Jew rushed forward to offer the sacrifice, but before he could do it, Mattathias killed him along with the king's officer, then he tore down the altar.

ABOVE: MATTATHIAS KILLS THE JEW WHO ATTEMPTED TO OBEY THE ORDER TO OFFER A SACRIFICE IN THE GREEK MANNER AT MODEIN. THIS ENGRAVING BY AN UNKNOWN ARTIST DEPICTS AN ANGRY MATTATHIAS BEFORE HE FLEES INTO THE MOUNTAINS.

Mattathias issued a call for all faithful Jews in the town to follow him, and he led them into the wilderness to find refuge in advance of the king's expected retaliation. Mattathias was accompanied by his five sons: in birth order they were John, Simon, Judas, Eleazar, and Jonathan. Each had a nickname (see 1 Maccabees 2:2–5), but only that of Judas became famous. Judas was labeled the "Maccabee," a term meaning "hammer," referring either to his power or, as some believe, the shape of his head. The label eventually came to be applied to the entire family of "the Maccabees."

Jewish groups from other places had also taken refuge in the wilderness. The king's forces soon learned of their vulnerability. The Greek forces waited to attack the Jews until the Sabbath, on which day the Jews would not take up arms to defend themselves or flee, lest they break the holy day's rules regarding labor and rest. After all, they were in rebellion against Antiochus IV for the very purpose of preserving the Torah and their Jewishness. This situation presented a dilemma for the Jews, however, and the choice was clear now that the Greeks had identified their

LEFT: A SCENE OF MARTYRDOM FROM 2 MACCABEES, IN A MEDIEVAL BIBLE. WRITTEN TO ELICIT AN EMOTIONAL RESPONSE FROM THE READER, 2 MACCABEES DESCRIBES THE RELIGIOUS PERSECUTION THE JEWS ENDURED UNDER ANTIOCHUS IV.

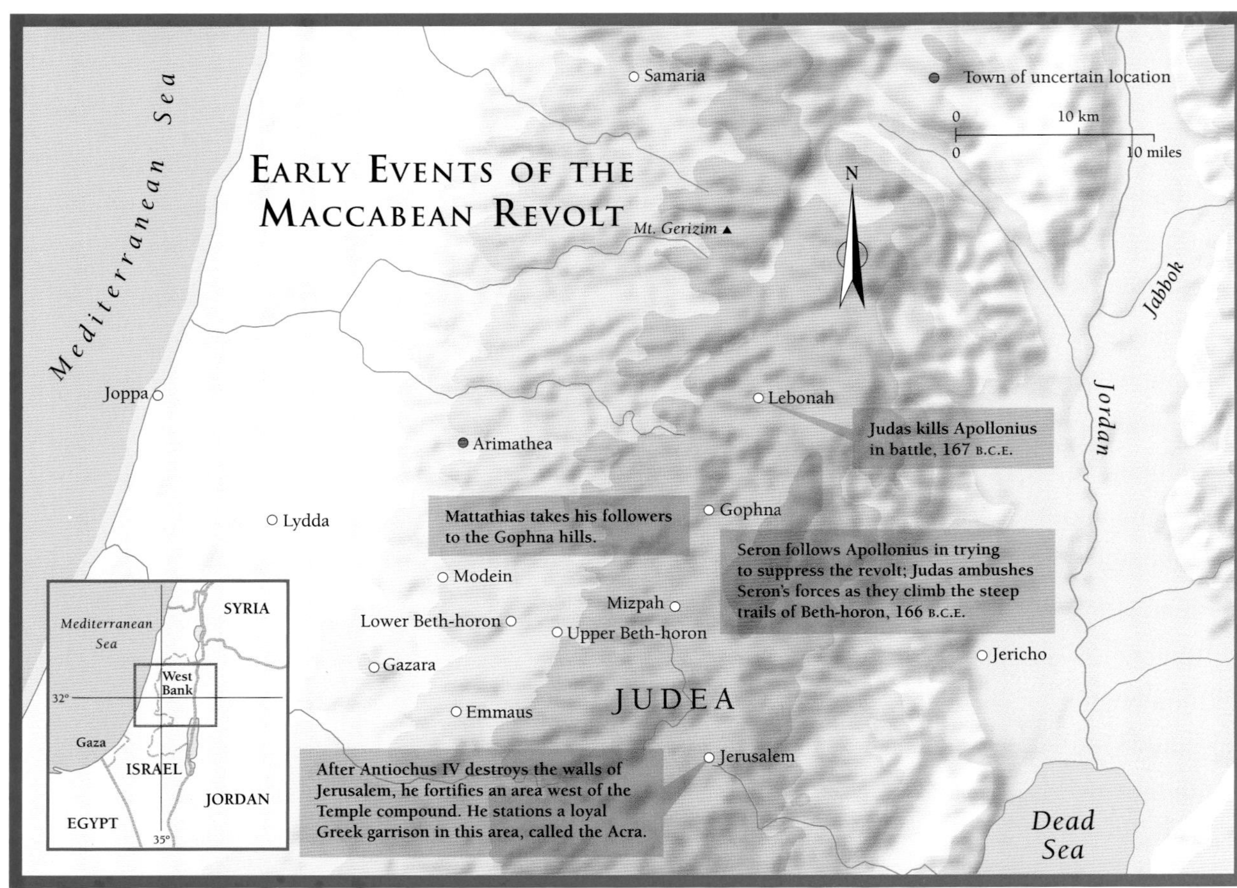

in this case, the direct threat of extinction by their Greek challengers. Together they formed a vigilante force that traveled throughout the countryside demanding strict compliance with the Torah when it came to certain matters, but being able to rationalize noncompliance under certain conditions. These "guardians" of the Torah compelled Jews who were avoiding traditional Jewish practices to circumcise their sons. The very fact that they felt the need to do this is a clear indication that there was a range of Jewish responses to Antiochus IV's efforts to civilize the Jews along the lines of the Greek model: from those who welcomed Hellenism, to those who accepted and accommodated it, to those who fought it by force of arms.

weakness: the Jews must either strictly uphold the Torah and traditions regulating the Sabbath day, or relax the Sabbath laws under this emergency and live to fight the battle another day. Mattathias and his followers chose the latter course of action.

At this point in time a Jewish group called the Hasidim (or Hasideans, "faithful ones") joined Mattathias and his outlaw band. The Hasidim who joined forces with the Maccabees are generally considered to be the prototype of what would be identified later (*c.* 135 b.c.e.) as the Pharisees, a group who were zealous about upholding the Mosaic Torah but able to adjust its application to changed circumstances:

RIGHT: JUDAS MACCABEUS, DETAIL FROM THE FIFTEENTH-CENTURY FRESCO *THE NINE WORTHIES AND THE NINE WORTHY WOMEN* BY GIACOMO JAQUERIO. JUDAS WAS DETERMINED TO REINSTATE JEWISH LAW IN JUDEA.

JUDAS OPPOSES APOLLONIUS AND SERON

It became clear to local Greek authorities that Judas and his followers must be dealt with. Apollonius, commander of the Seleucid troops of the Samaria region, sought out the rebel group. Judas Maccabeus, now the leader of the dissidents after the death of Mattathias, attacked the royal Greek contingent and killed Apollonius, probably near Lebonah. Judas took the sword of Apollonius as a battle prize, and used it for the remainder of his fighting career.

Seron, another Seleucid commander, stepped in to try to suppress the Jewish rebellion. Judas's men attacked Seron's

The Feast of Hanukkah

The restoration of the Temple was celebrated with great festivities and sacrifices (as reported in 1 Maccabees 4 and 2 Maccabees 10), with the Temple decorated for the occasion with crowns and shields. The inaugural Hanukkah, a Hebrew term meaning "dedication," was celebrated on the twenty-fifth day of the month Kislev in 165 B.C.E.—exactly two years to the day after the Gentiles had profaned the Temple. The centerpiece of the celebration was the ceremonial lighting of the Temple menorah. Tradition has it that there was only a one-day supply of ritually pure oil for fuel, yet the menorah stayed lit for eight days. It was then decreed that each year the days of dedication should be celebrated, and Jews celebrate them to this day.

The occasion, sometimes also called the Festival of Lights, is a felicitous confluence of the winter solstice season, the victory of Judaism over Hellenistic worldliness, and the nationalistic freedom and independence that the Maccabean kingdom signifies. The menorah too has become a modern symbol both of Judaism and Jewish nationalism, and has many Israeli manifestations, including as an adornment on the Knesset (parliament) building in Jerusalem.

forces as they were climbing the steep trails at Beth-horon. Seron was caught by surprise and 800 of his men died. He and the other survivors fled to the Mediterranean coast. These two encounters with Seleucid forces demonstrated that the Jews had been seriously underestimated, and they now finally had the attention of Antiochus IV. The king dug deep into his coffers in order to fund a campaign against the Jews, but this only served to bankrupt him. He then decided to take most of his army and campaign further east into Persia in order to raise the revenue he needed. He left Lysias, Seron's commander, in charge of his affairs west and south of the Euphrates River.

LEFT: *SIEGE OF JERUSALEM BY JUDAS MACCABEE AND THE HASIDIM,* FROM A MEDIEVAL LATIN BIBLE HELD IN THE ABBEY OF MONT ST. ELOI IN FRANCE. THE JEWS BELIEVED THEY HAD DIVINE SUPPORT FOR THEIR ACTIONS TO DEFEND THEIR TEMPLE.

JUDAS ATTACKS THE SYRIANS AT EMMAUS

Lysias assembled an army and placed it under the authority of the Seleucid generals Ptolemy, Dorimenes, Nicanor, and Gorgias. Antiochus IV was preoccupied elsewhere, warring against Persia and Media in the east. Lysias's generals camped their army near Emmaus. Gorgias's men constituted a fighting force of 5,000 foot soldiers and 1,000 horsemen from the larger group, and they headed in the direction of Mizpah, where the army of Judas Maccabeus was reportedly headquartered. However, when Judas heard of Gorgias's advance, he left Mizpah and headed to Emmaus. The Jewish rebel force routed the main Seleucid army there and pursued it to Gazara (or Gezer), which was a fortress that protected one of the approach paths to Jerusalem. Meanwhile, when Gorgias found that the Jewish camp was deserted, he returned to Emmaus. At a distance, and from an overlook, he could see that the main camp had been destroyed. By now his troops were exhausted from their fruitless chase to Mizpah and back, so he gathered his troops and retreated to the Mediterranean coast rather than engage in a battle with Judas and his Jewish army.

Lysias again attempted to destroy the Jewish resistance. In 165 B.C.E. he marched his army to Marisa and then to Beth-zur, which guarded a southern advance to Jerusalem. Judas and his army repulsed Lysias at Beth-zur, and after Lysias retreated Judas ascended to Jerusalem. Although Judas did not gain control of the Acra from the Seleucids and Hellenists, he did secure control of the Temple Mount, called Mount Zion. He successfully restored and ritually cleansed the Temple itself for reuse as Yahweh's sanctuary. After the rededication, Judas fortified the Temple Mount. He also fortified Beth-zur in the south to provide protection from the Idumeans, who were supporting the Seleucids against Judas.

BELOW: DOME OF THE ROCK ON TEMPLE MOUNT, JERUSALEM. JUDAS GAINED CONTROL OF THE TEMPLE MOUNT AND FORTIFIED IT AGAINST FURTHER ATTACKS BY THE SELEUCIDS AND HELLENISTS.

RIGHT: THIS INTERPRETATION OF THE DEATH OF JUDAS MACCABEUS IN BATTLE COMES FROM THE MEDIEVAL *BIBLE OF ETIENNE HARDING*. ACCORDING TO 1 MACCABEES 9:7, JUDAS CHOSE TO "DIE BRAVELY" RATHER THAN SURRENDER.

JUDAS'S MILITARY CAMPAIGNS

After securing Jerusalem, Judas undertook numerous military campaigns in order to defend Jews throughout Palestine against their detractors. He attacked the Idumeans at Acrabetene, then came to the rescue of various Jewish towns in Gilead east of the Jordan River. Timothy, the Seleucid commander of Gilead, was killed in a battle against Judas's rebels at Jazer near Philadelphia. Meanwhile Simon, the brother of Judas, conducted a campaign with another 3,000-strong Jewish army against the sea coast cities of Ptolemais (Acco), Tyre, and Sidon, all of which were persecuting Torah-observant Jews. When Judas returned from Gilead he attacked Hebron, Marisa, Joppa, and Jamnia in a campaign to control Idumea.

Still, Jerusalem was divided. Judas's group controlled the Temple Mount on the east side, and the Hellenizers allied with the Seleucids controlled the Acra and Antiochia, the Greek-styled polis, on the west side. Judas again tried to oust the Hellenizers, but they appealed to Antiochus V, who had succeeded Antiochus IV after his death while on campaign in Persia in 164 B.C.E. So Judas decided to confront the army of Antiochus V along the southern route into Jerusalem, rather than in Jerusalem itself. In the ensuing battle near Beth-zechariah in 162 B.C.E., Judas's younger brother Eleazar was killed, and Judas retreated back to the Gophna hills north of Jerusalem. Antiochus V and Lysias entered Jerusalem and gained access to the Temple Mount.

Then followed a struggle for control within the Seleucid family itself. Demetrius I, the son of Seleucus IV, killed Antiochus V and sent his general Bacchides to take charge of Judea. Bacchides installed Alcimus as High Priest in Jerusalem. As Alcimus had an Aaronic pedigree (though he was not a Zadokite), he was accepted by observant Jews including the Hasidim. However, Alcimus turned against these "faithful ones" and slew many of them, prompting Judas to renew the struggle against the Seleucid factions. Demetrius I sent general Nicanor to counter Judas, but in the battle at Adasa north of Jerusalem, Judas surprised Nicanor and defeated the Greeks, even killing Nicanor. This became a celebrated victory and in Jewish tradition has become memorialized as "the Day of Nicanor," although it is no longer generally celebrated.

Judas now formed an alliance with the Romans against the Seleucids. The death of Nicanor gave Demetrius I renewed energy to put down the Jewish revolt. In 160 B.C.E. he sent Bacchides with a large and well-equipped army from Damascus through the region of Galilee into Judea and Jerusalem. Judas elected not to challenge this superior fighting force at that time but instead remained in his Gophna encampment. When Bacchides's army was maneuvering for position, Judas attacked near Elasa; however, he and his forces then became surrounded by Bacchides. Judas was killed in the battle. His brothers Simon and Jonathan carried his body back to Modein, where they buried him in the family tomb of Mattathias.

BELOW: JEAN FOUQUET'S ILLUSTRATION FROM *OEUVRE DE JEHAN FOUCQUET* TELLS THE STORY OF THE JEWS LED BY JONATHAN BEING ATTACKED BY BACCHIDES'S FORCES AT BETH-BASI. JONATHAN HAD BEEN ELECTED LEADER AFTER THE DEATH OF JUDAS.

JONATHAN AND SIMON

Following the death of Judas, the Jewish rebel force chose Jonathan to be their leader. Under pressure from the Seleucid army, he moved the rebel encampment from the Gophna hills to the Judean desert south of Jerusalem near Tekoa. Meanwhile, Bacchides fortified various towns to create a ring of security around Jerusalem: they are Bethel, Pharathon and Jericho, Tekoa,

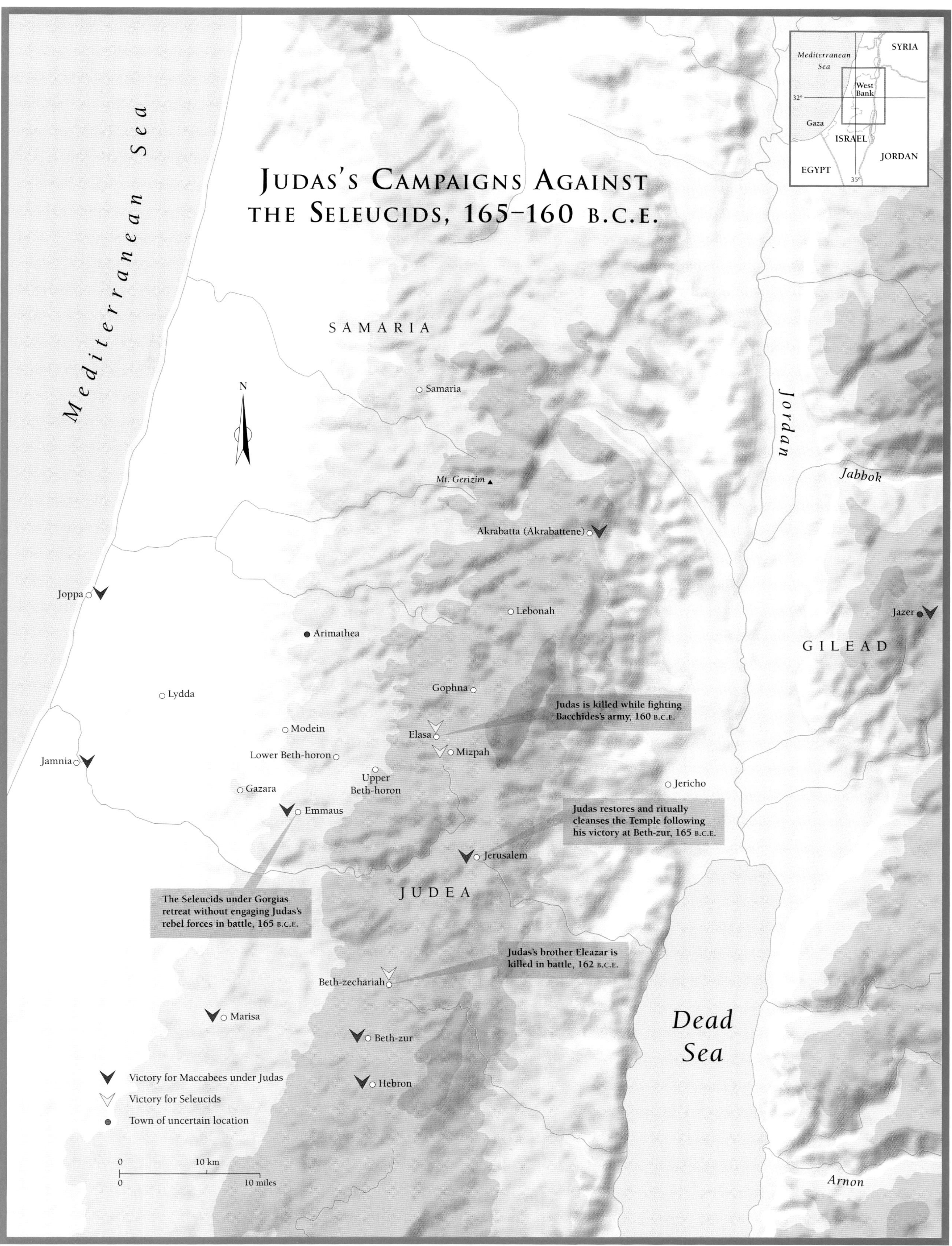

Judas's Campaigns Against the Seleucids, 165–160 B.C.E.
Mediterranean Sea
SYRIA
Mediterranean Sea
West Bank
32°
Gaza
ISRAEL
JORDAN
EGYPT
35°
SAMARIA
Samaria
N
Jordan
Mt. Gerizim
Jabbok
Akrabatta (Akrabattene)
Joppa
Lebonah
Jazer
Arimathea
GILEAD
Lydda
Gophna
Judas is killed while fighting Bacchides's army, 160 B.C.E.
Modein
Elasa
Jamnia
Lower Beth-horon
Mizpah
Upper Beth-horon
Jericho
Gazara
Emmaus
Judas restores and ritually cleanses the Temple following his victory at Beth-zur, 165 B.C.E.
Jerusalem
The Seleucids under Gorgias retreat without engaging Judas's rebel forces in battle, 165 B.C.E.
JUDEA
Judas's brother Eleazar is killed in battle, 162 B.C.E.
Beth-zechariah
Marisa
Beth-zur
Dead Sea
Victory for Maccabees under Judas
Victory for Seleucids
Town of uncertain location
Hebron
0
10 km
0
10 miles
Arnon

RIGHT: THIS NINETEENTH-CENTURY C.E. VIEW OF PTOLEMAIS (ACCO) WAS ENGRAVED BY LOUIS HAGHE AFTER A DRAWING BY DAVID ROBERTS. JONATHAN REFUSED A BRIBE FROM DEMETRIUS I THAT WOULD GIVE HIM THE REVENUE FROM PTOLEMAIS.

Beth-zur, Thamna, Emmaus and Gazara, Tappuah, and Beth-horon.

Alcimus the High Priest continued to provoke the Hasidim in Jerusalem. He removed the screen that separated the inner court of the Temple from the outer courtyard, effectively giving Gentiles access to the sanctuary. Shortly after this, in 159 B.C.E., Alcimus died. Meanwhile Bacchides had left Judea and taken up residence in Antioch, and Palestine remained in relative peace. This lasted for approximately two years until Jonathan and the rebels took control of Beth-basi near Bethlehem; Bacchides returned and attacked Beth-basi. Jonathan and Simon counterattacked, forcing Bacchides to negotiate a peace. Jonathan was allowed to settle in Michmash north of Jerusalem, and Bacchides left Judea with his army.

Gradually, Jonathan extended his influence throughout Judea and this went unchallenged, largely because the Seleucid dynasty was receiving pressure from other directions, as well as from within. Among other things, Alexander Balas laid claim to lineage from Antiochus IV and thus rivaled Demetrius I for the Seleucid throne. After Alexander Balas occupied Ptolemais on the coast, Demetrius I extended privileges to Jonathan to win his support, including jurisdiction over the Temple Mount in Jerusalem and permission to keep an army. This gave Jonathan effective control over the totality of Judea, except for the Acra district in Jerusalem and Beth-zur on the Idumean border to the south.

Alexander Balas competed with Demetrius I for the good will and attention of Jonathan in order to gain his support against Demetrius I. Alexander did this most remarkably by appointing Jonathan the Jewish High Priest in 152 B.C.E. during the festival of Succoth. The office had remained vacant for seven years, following the death of Alcimus. Jonathan served in this capacity until 142 B.C.E., but it became a source of serious discontent among observant Jews, because he was of the Hasmonean line, and not the Levitic-Aaronic-Zadokite one, from which legitimate priests must descend. Demetrius I countered by offering Jewish territory in Samaria. Jonathan remained supportive of Alexander, which was a good choice since Alexander defeated Demetrius I in 150 B.C.E., putting Jonathan in his good graces. Later Alexander also appointed him the commander and governor of Judea, and Jonathan was eventually given control of the four districts of Lydda, Arimathea, Apherema, and Perea.

When Demetrius II ousted Alexander Balas to take the Seleucid throne in 145 B.C.E., he told Apollonius, his general, to take control of Judea from Jonathan. However, when the Seleucid army did face the Maccabean Jewish army, which now included both Jonathan and Simon's forces, near Jamnia, the Maccabees were victorious. The Jewish forces had proved their superiority and were now in total control of Palestine.

As a measure of the dominance of the Jews, Demetrius II called Jonathan to his aid when he was besieged within his own palace in Antioch. The Jews rescued him. But when Antiochus VI and his regent Trypho, rivals to Demetrius II, extended their sphere of influence, they gave Simon jurisdiction over the coastal plain from Tyre to Egypt, effectively winning the support of the Maccabees, and by extension the Maccabees gained more power. Jonathan led the Maccabean army against Demetrius II's Seleucid army at Cadasa (Kedesh) in upper Galilee in 144 B.C.E., and then at Hamath in Coele-Syria (Lebanon) in 143 B.C.E. On both occasions the Jews bettered the Greeks.

Trypho, however, sought an opportunity to humble the Maccabees, who were, in his view, becoming too powerful. He and his army met the Maccabean force in Beth-shean. Although Trypho was not strong enough militarily to defeat Jonathan, he tricked him into dispersing his troops under the promise that he would be allowed to rule Ptolemais. Once in the city, Trypho trapped Jonathan and the contingent of bodyguards that were with him. Jonathan was taken captive

Jonathan and the Fortifications of Bacchides

SAMARIA
Samaria
Pharathon
Tappuah
Lebonah
Joppa
Thamna
Gophna
Lydda
Modein
Bethel
Mizpah
Jamnia
Upper Beth-horon
Gazara
Jericho
Pharathon
Emmaus
Jerusalem
Judean Desert
JUDEA
Jonathan's new rebel encampment in the Judean Desert.
Jordan
Dead Sea
Beth-zechariah
Tekoa
Marisa
Beth-zur
Hebron
IDUMEA
Town fortified by Bacchides
Town of uncertain location
0 10 km
0 10 miles
N
Mediterranean Sea
SYRIA
West Bank
Gaza
ISRAEL
JORDAN
EGYPT
32°
35°

and the soldiers were put to death. Hearing of this, Simon took command of the Jewish army. Later, Trypho also put Jonathan to death. This deception drove Simon into alliance with Demetrius II, and the latter granted formal recognition to an independent Judea in 142 B.C.E. Thus Simon and the dynasty of Hasmon became the official leadership of the Jews, and Simon also assumed the office of High Priest.

Not only was Judea and its surrounding districts under Hasmonean control, even surrounding non-Jewish territories were under their influence. Throughout the Maccabean wars the Acra and western Jerusalem remained under Seleucid control. Jonathan and Simon had besieged the Acra to force the capitulation of its defenders through starvation. Eventually, in 141 B.C.E., it was taken and its defensive walls were dismantled. The Hasmoneans built a Maccabean palace atop the Acra ruins and fortified the larger city of Jerusalem, thus establishing for themselves a defensible location from which to rule their new Israel. Simon continued to rule an independent Jewish state for eight years.

QUMRAN AND THE DEAD SEA SCROLLS

The discovery of the Dead Sea Scrolls, beginning in 1947, is arguably the most famous textual discovery of the modern age. This collection of texts was brought to world attention after a Bedouin shepherd found a group of large clay jars in a cave near the northwestern shoreline of the Dead Sea. In those jars were stored texts written on calf-skin parchment that date to as early as the second century B.C.E. The first discovery prompted further searching of caves in the vicinity, eventually identifying ten more caves that contained textual material, and many more that gave evidence of human activity during the Maccabean period and after that time. It is generally inferred that the texts were hidden in the caves in anticipation of an attack by the Romans in connection with the First Jewish Revolt of 66–70 C.E.

The text caves are sited in the vicinity of the ruins of an ancient settlement called Khirbet Qumran. The discovery of the texts prompted archaeological work on the site, which uncovered occupation layers from the Hasmonean period of the Hellenistic era (150–31 B.C.E.) and the Roman period through to the Second Jewish Revolt (27 B.C.E.–C.E. 135).

LEFT: *THE DECAPITATION OF ALEXANDER I BALAS*, FROM A FIFTEENTH-CENTURY C.E. FRENCH PUBLICATION. AFTER DEMETRIUS II EXPELLED ALEXANDER, HE FLED TO A NABATAEAN PRINCE, WHO MURDERED HIM.

BELOW: CAVES AT KHIRBET QUMRAN, WHERE SOME OF THE DEAD SEA SCROLLS WERE DISCOVERED. THE CAVES ARE SITED ON THE SHORES OF THE DEAD SEA, ABOUT 12 MILES (20 KM) SOUTH OF JERICHO.

RIGHT: THE SAMARITAN DECALOGUE, CARVED LIMESTONE, C. SECOND CENTURY C.E., FOUND AT SHECHEM, ANCIENT CAPITAL OF SAMARIA. JOHN HYRCANUS I REGAINED CONTROL OF SAMARIA AND DESTROYED THE SAMARITANS' TEMPLE.

The identity of the occupants of ancient Qumran and the function of the settlement remains somewhat disputed among scholars, though the majority position is that Jewish Essenes lived there and were in some way responsible for sequestering the scrolls in the caves. The site is notable for the water collection system that is extensive and well preserved. Coins found on the site indicate that the buildings were occupied during the reign of Alexander Jannaeus (103–76 B.C.E.), and possibly during the preceding reign of John Hyrcanus I (134–104 B.C.E.), as well as later.

The work of assembling the fragments and restoring the Dead Sea Scrolls has resulted in a library of more than 500 separate texts, though many remain incomplete. The manuscripts are written in Hebrew, Aramaic, and Greek; and they represent a substantial variety of text categories. Copies and translations of what are now canonical biblical books were found, though there is nothing to indicate that the Old Testament canon was itself fixed at this early time. Every book of the Old Testament is attested in at least one fragment, with the exception of Esther; some books exist in multiple copies. The most complete manuscript is the book of Isaiah, which survived virtually intact in a single scroll measuring approximately 40 ft (12 m) in length. These manuscripts attest the state of the biblical text at the end of the first millennium B.C.E., and represent a Hebrew text that is a thousand years closer to the original than the traditional Masoretic text found in modern Hebrew bibles. Apocryphal texts were also found, including multiple copies of the book of Enoch. But no copies of any New Testament books were found among the Dead Sea Scrolls.

In addition to biblical manuscripts, the Essenes themselves authored a variety of works. The Damascus Document describes the origins of the group: they were dissidents who rejected the leadership of the "wicked priest," whose identity is left unspecified in the text but presumed to be a Maccabee, either Jonathan or Simon. The group expected a cataclysmic battle between the forces of good and evil, detailed in the War Scroll. They had a handbook for the administration of the community, called Community Rule. They made a hymnbook of liturgical and praise poems very similar to the biblical Psalter. And they creatively interpreted and applied biblical prophetic texts in reference to events in their day; these commentaries are called Pesharim.

JOHN HYRCANUS I

When Antiochus VII succeeded Demetrius II as Seleucid ruler, he continued the latter's hands-off policy regarding Judea, and even extended it the privilege of minting its own coinage. But in time Antiochus VII became distrustful of the independent power of the Hasmoneans and tried various means to undermine it. Simon's son-in-law Ptolemy engineered the murder of Simon and Simon's sons Judas and Matthias in a ploy to gain favor with Antiochus VII. Simon's remaining son John, known also as Hyrcanus, survived and took action against Ptolemy, and sought an alliance with the Romans to do so. Ptolemy had the support of Antiochus VII, who besieged Jerusalem with John and his supporters inside. John surrendered and was spared only after paying a heavy tribute.

Antiochus VII died in 129 B.C.E., while campaigning in the east, and Demetrius II retook the throne. Meanwhile, John Hyrcanus I had eliminated the threat of Ptolemy, which, combined with the weakness of Demetrius II at this time, allowed John to reextend Hasmonean control beyond Judea into Idumea, Moab, and Samaria. He destroyed the Samaritan temple on Mt. Gerizim near Shechem, Samaria's holy city. John extended the privilege of Jewish citizenship to the Idumeans at this time as the condition for allowing them to remain in their territory. Along with citizenship came the obligation to follow the Torah, which included forcing the males of these annexed territories to be circumcised. This is the background against which the Idumean Herod the Great would later be able to assume the throne as King of the Jews, and claim himself to be one of them.

John Hyrcanus I sent a delegation to Rome where he received official confirmation of Hasmonean independence. He ruled as a High

BELOW: AFTER HOSTING A BANQUET FOR HIS FATHER-IN-LAW SIMON AND TWO OF HIS BROTHERS-IN-LAW, PTOLEMY TREACHEROUSLY MURDERED THEM ALL. THIS SEVENTEENTH-CENTURY C.E. DRAWING BY JAN LUYKEN WAS ENGRAVED BY GOLDER.

Priest and Jewish king from 134 to 104 B.C.E. Coins minted during his reign read "John the high priest and the congregation of the Jews" on one side, and picture a cornucopia with a poppy head on the other—both are appropriated Greek symbols of fertility and prosperity that indicate a measure of Jewish–Hellenistic syncretism.

ARISTOBULUS I AND ALEXANDER JANNAEUS

Aristobulus I succeeded his father John Hyrcanus I, but ruled for only a year (104–103 B.C.E.). His one accomplishment was the defeat of the Arab Itureans and conversion of the Galilee region into Jewish territory through the circumcision of their men. This effectively finalized the incorporation of all the hill country west of the Jordan River into the Maccabean kingdom, from the Dead Sea in the south to what is now Lebanon in the north.

Aristobulus I was followed by his brother Alexander Jannaeus, who further extended the Maccabean kingdom by finalizing Hasmonean control over the Mediterranean coastland, Idumea, Samaria, Perea, Gaulanitis, and Moab. Under Jannaeus, the Maccabean state reached its greatest extent. However, at the same time internal sectarian dissension grew. The Pharisee party, which first took shape under John Hyrcanus I, rebelled against the Sadducee party, which supported the Hasmoneans, and they were mercilessly defeated.

THE NABATAEANS

The Nabataeans occupied parts of Syria, the steppe between the Jordan River and the Arabian Desert, the Negeb, and the Sinai west to Egypt. More than 1,000 archaeological sites have been associated with the Nabataeans, as well as thousands of Nabataean Aramaic inscriptions, mostly of a funerary memorial nature. The most well-known Nabataean settlement is Petra in modern-day Jordan.

Kings of the Nabataeans had various relationships with the Hasmoneans. Aretas I (170–160 B.C.E.) supported Judas and Jonathan (see 1 Maccabees 5:24–28, 9:35, 15:22) against the Seleucids. During the reign of Aretas II (*c.* 100 B.C.E.), the Nabataeans came into conflict with Alexander Jannaeus, who

ABOVE: *PETRA, JORDAN, 1839,* WATERCOLOR BY DAVID ROBERTS. THE NABATAEANS INCORPORATED THE WAVES AND WHORLS OF COLOR FOUND IN THE LANDSCAPE INTO THEIR ARCHITECTURE.

LEFT: RUINS OF THE THEATER AT PETRA, A NINETEENTH-CENTURY C.E. ENGRAVING BY W. FINDEN. THE SANDSTONE HILLS THAT SURROUNDED PETRA OFFERED THE NABATAEANS PROTECTION FROM INVADERS.

ABOVE: THE URN TOMB, ONE OF THE THREE ROYAL TOMBS CARVED INTO THE ROCK FACE AT PETRA. THE FRIABLE SANDSTONE ALLOWED THE NABATAEANS TO CARVE THEIR TOMBS AND TEMPLES INTO THE CRUMBLING ROCK FACE.

RIGHT: THIS NABATAEAN SCULPTURE IS NOW HELD IN A MUSEUM AT BOSRA IN SYRIA. IT IS DATED TO THE FIRST CENTURY B.C.E., ABOUT 500 YEARS AFTER NOMADIC ARABS ESTABLISHED PETRA AS A COMMERCIAL CENTER.

captured the port city of Gaza from them. Aretas II's successor, Obodas I (*c.* 93–85 B.C.E.), defeated Alexander Jannaeus and gained control of territory in Moab and Galaaditis (Gilead). Obodas I's successor, Aretas III (85–62 B.C.E.), continued the struggle against Alexander Jannaeus for control of Moab and Gilead, and succeeded in expanding the reach of Nabataean control into southern Syria. In 63 B.C.E. Aretas III joined forces with Antipater, the ruler of Idumea and father of Herod the Great, to support the Hasmonean dynasty against the Roman general Pompey. Nonetheless, Nabataea was eventually brought under the control of Rome.

JOHN HYRCANUS II AND ARISTOBULUS II

After Alexander Jannaeus's death, his widow Salome Alexandra ruled in his place. While she reigned over Judea from 76 to 67 B.C.E., her son John Hyrcanus II held the position of High Priest in Jerusalem. After Salome died, John also assumed the civil throne, but his kingship was challenged by his younger brother Aristobulus II. This factionalized Judea and drove the Hasmonean kingdom into civil war. John Hyrcanus II had the weaker position. On the advice of Antipater the Idumean, he asked Aretas III, the Nabataean king, for assistance, and they besieged Jerusalem with their combined forces.

THE ARRIVAL OF THE ROMANS

All the while the Romans had been annexing Seleucid territory. By 64 B.C.E. the Roman General Pompey had finally defeated Mithradates, king of Pontus, and he took possession of Damascus, thus securing the Seleucid kingdom for Rome. Pompey forced a truce between John Hyrcanus II and Aristobulus II. Aristobulus II eventually surrendered his forces to Pompey, who then advanced his army toward Jerusalem, along the way capturing Jericho. When he arrived in Jerusalem, those loyal to John Hyrcanus II opened the gates of the upper city to Pompey. But those loyal to Aristobulus II took refuge on the Temple Mount. The Romans built a ramp and proceeded to destroy the walls and towers that separated the Temple area from the city proper. The assault was successful, and 12,000 Jews died in the aftermath. Once the Romans took full control of Judea in 63 B.C.E., Pompey reinstalled John Hyrcanus II as High Priest and used him to administer Judea. He served from 63 to 40 B.C.E., only later to be executed by Herod the Great.

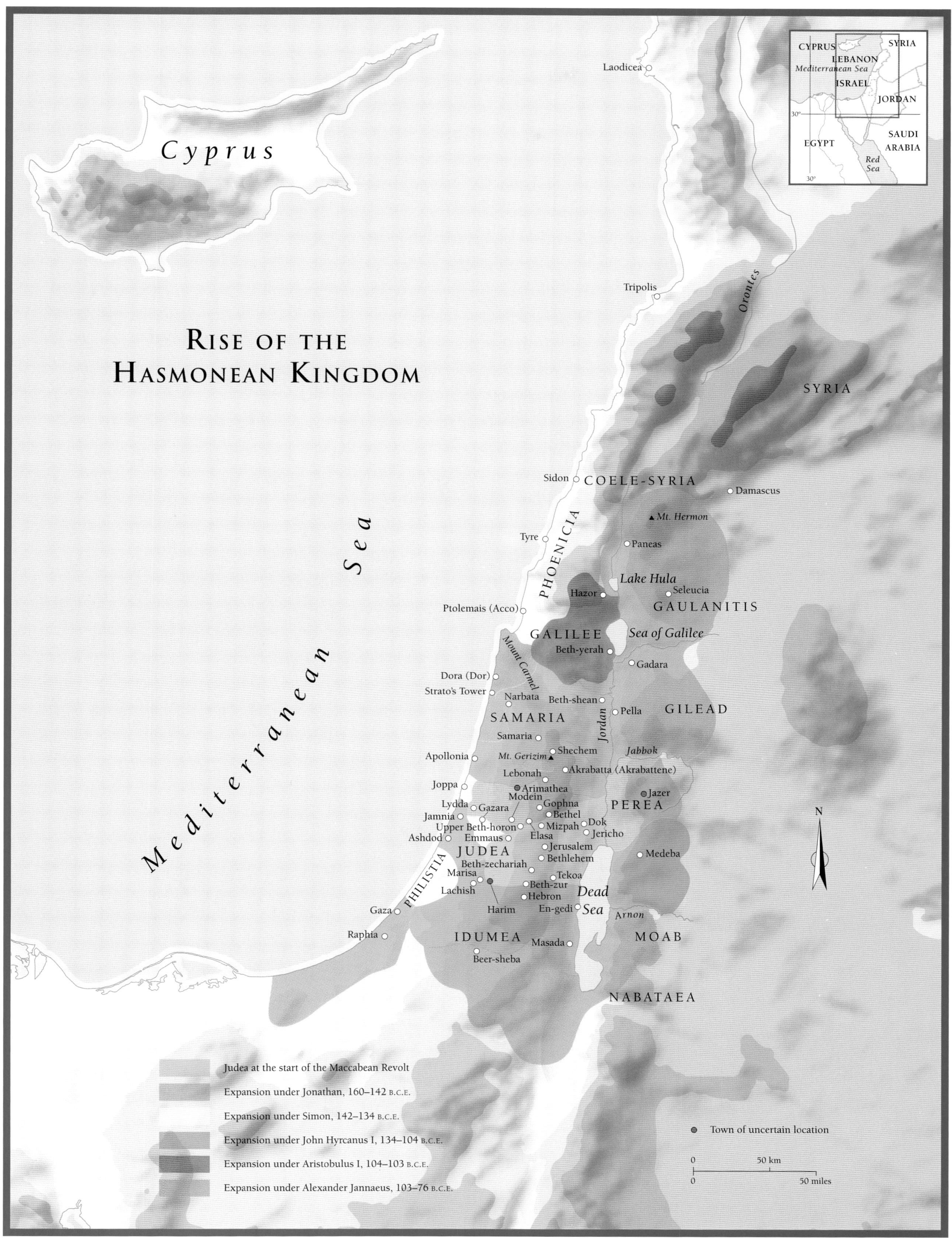

Rise of the Hasmonean Kingdom
Cyprus
Mediterranean Sea
CYPRUS
SYRIA
LEBANON
Mediterranean Sea
ISRAEL
JORDAN
EGYPT
SAUDI ARABIA
Red Sea
Laodicea
Tripolis
Orontes
SYRIA
Sidon
COELE-SYRIA
Damascus
Mt. Hermon
Tyre
PHOENICIA
Paneas
Lake Hula
Hazor
Seleucia
Ptolemais (Acco)
GAULANITIS
GALILEE
Sea of Galilee
Mount Carmel
Beth-yerah
Gadara
Dora (Dor)
Strato's Tower
Narbata
Beth-shean
Pella
GILEAD
SAMARIA
Jordan
Samaria
Apollonia
Mt. Gerizim
Shechem
Jabbok
Lebonah
Akrabatta (Akrabattene)
Joppa
Arimathea
Jazer
Modein
Lydda
Gazara
Gophna
PEREA
Jamnia
Bethel
Upper Beth-horon
Mizpah
Dok
Ashdod
Emmaus
Elasa
Jericho
JUDEA
Jerusalem
Medeba
Beth-zechariah
Bethlehem
Marisa
Tekoa
Lachish
Beth-zur
Hebron
Dead Sea
PHILISTIA
Gaza
Harim
En-gedi
Arnon
Raphia
IDUMEA
Masada
MOAB
Beer-sheba
NABATAEA
N
Judea at the start of the Maccabean Revolt
Expansion under Jonathan, 160–142 B.C.E.
Expansion under Simon, 142–134 B.C.E.
Expansion under John Hyrcanus I, 134–104 B.C.E.
Expansion under Aristobulus I, 104–103 B.C.E.
Expansion under Alexander Jannaeus, 103–76 B.C.E.
Town of uncertain location
0
50 km
0
50 miles

THE ROMANS

OUR SANCTUARY HAS BEEN LAID WASTE, OUR ALTAR THROWN DOWN, OUR TEMPLE DESTROYED 2 ESDRAS 10:21

In Roman historical legend, the city of Rome was founded in 753 B.C.E. by Romulus. This was held to be the commencement date of the Roman state for the whole of its existence. Rome was then ruled by kings until 510 B.C.E., when the last of the kings, Tarquinius Superbus, was expelled from Rome. The Republic was born the following year and two consuls, who could only serve annually, became the senior rulers in the new system. Politically, the Republic comprised a Senate and other voting assemblies. Politics was dominated by the aristocracy, and to serve as senior politicians, individuals needed to have spent at least ten years in the army. For election to the consulship, military success was usually required, because it was the only way that aristocrats could fund election campaigns and gain the popularity required to win. The military nature of Roman politics and society was an early feature of the Roman system, and it remained so throughout the history of the Roman Empire. In the second half of the second century B.C.E., the intensely competitive nature of Roman politics and society saw the Republican system begin to break down. Following the assassination of Julius Caesar in 44 B.C.E., the system broke down completely.

THE ROMAN EMPIRE

With the disintegration of the Republican system due to intense factional fighting, the adopted son of Julius Caesar, Octavian, emerged as the first Roman emperor, Augustus, in 27 B.C.E. Octavian was actually Caesar's great-nephew, and he was adopted by Caesar because Caesar had no male heir. The emperors would rule in the western provinces of the empire until C.E. 476 and in the eastern provinces until C.E. 1453. The empire of the Romans developed outside of Italy during the Republican period when, at the end of the third century B.C.E., Scipio Africanus succeeded in capturing Spain from the Carthaginians under Hannibal. Over the next 170 years Rome came to dominate the lands of the Mediterranean and western Europe. The kingdom of the Macedonians was captured in 167 B.C.E., Carthage and North Africa in 147 B.C.E., and Greece was taken over in the following year. Julius Caesar led the expansion of Roman power into Gaul (modern France and parts of Germany) in the fifties B.C.E. and Pompey formed the province of Syria in 64 B.C.E. Egypt was added to the Roman Empire in 31 B.C.E. after Octavian's defeat of Antony and the Egyptian queen, Cleopatra. The empire continued to expand under the emperors, reaching its greatest extent under the emperor Trajan (reigned C.E. 98–117).

BELOW: RUINS OF A SECOND-CENTURY C.E. ACROPOLIS AT PERGAMON IN MODERN-DAY TURKEY. THE DEATH OF THE KING OF PERGAMON IN 133 B.C.E. WAS PIVOTAL IN THE EXPANSION OF THE ROMAN EMPIRE IN THE EASTERN MEDITERRANEAN.

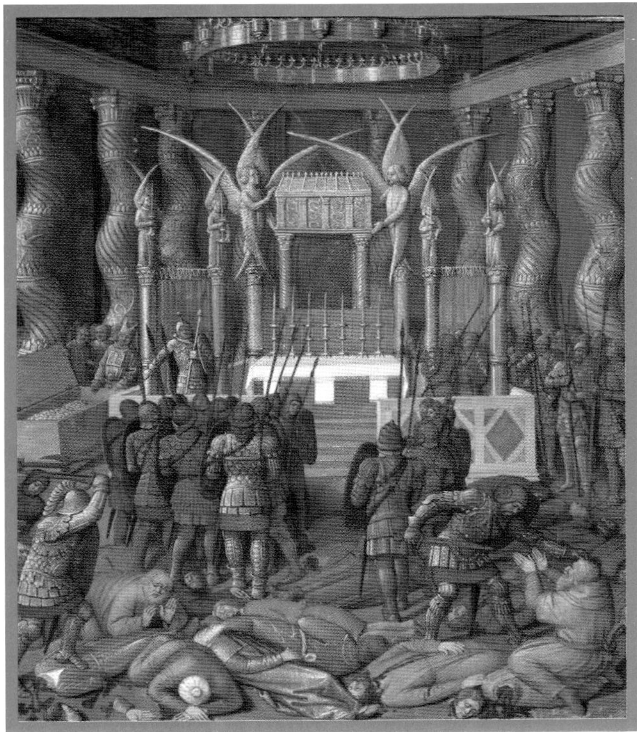

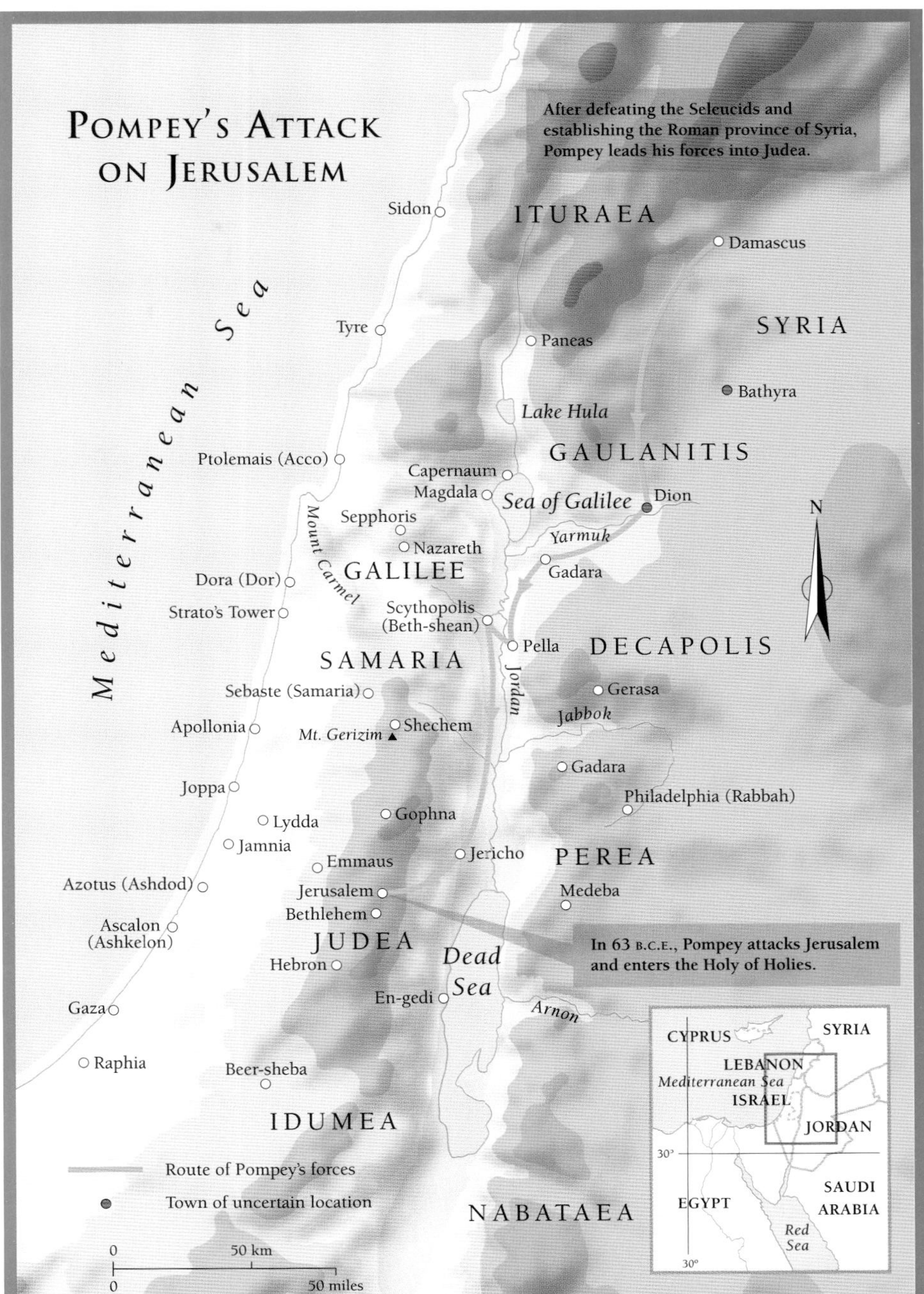

THE ROMANS HEAD EAST

Rome's presence in the eastern Mediterranean came as a result of its intervention in disputes between the Hellenistic kingdoms in the second century B.C.E. The first involvement came about as a result of the Macedonian King Philip V's alliance with Hannibal of Carthage during the war between Rome and Carthage known as the Second Punic War (218–202 B.C.E.). Hannibal almost succeeded in capturing Rome, but the Romans were ultimately victorious over him. Following their defeat of Hannibal, the Romans turned their attention to the Macedonians, eventually capturing the kingdom in 167 B.C.E. Rome's initial involvement was essentially punitive in its intentions, but the increasingly competitive nature of Roman politics motivated Roman politicians to become interested in exploiting Roman influence in the eastern Mediterranean. The Romans also went to war with the Seleucids of Syria, defeating their king Antiochus III in 189 B.C.E. Rome's presence in the east became more significant when the king of Pergamon in Asia Minor died in 133 B.C.E. without an heir, leaving the kingdom to Rome. When Pompey was given a command to deal with King Tigranes of Armenia in 64 B.C.E., he brought what remained of the Seleucid Empire to an end and defeated Tigranes, forming the Roman province of Syria as a result.

POMPEY IN JERUSALEM

Roman control over southern Syria and Palestine took time to establish. The labels Syria and Palestine are broader regional terms when discussed in this context. Judea, Perea, and Samaria, which comprised the bulk of the Jewish kingdom or province in the Roman period, sit broadly within the region of Palestine, and Palestine lies within southern Syria. There was considerable dispute between Rome and the Nabataeans over control of this region during the next century. The Nabataeans, with their capital at Petra in Arabia, had considerable influence in Palestine and southern Syria until the middle of the first century C.E. As had been the case before Pompey's arrival, deep divisions existed within the ruling Jewish elite in Jerusalem and three rival Jewish factional

Early Roman Rule in Palestine

The Romans first became involved with the Jews in Palestine due to the actions in Jerusalem of the Seleucid King Antiochus IV in the first half of the second century B.C.E. The Maccabean rebellion that eventually resulted saw its leaders appeal to the Romans for support, and in 160 B.C.E., Rome obliged. The protection Rome gave the Maccabees provided it with another pretext for intervention in the increasingly troubled Seleucid kingdom. If the Seleucid king caused problems in the way Antiochus IV had for the Jews, Rome would intervene on their behalf. In 139 B.C.E., the Romans renewed their agreement with the Maccabees, who had by this time emerged as the leaders of a state independent of the Seleucids. Rome continued to intervene on behalf of the kingdom, however, warning both the Seleucids and the Ptolemies on numerous occasions that they should not attempt to annex Judea. Pompey's destruction of the Seleucid dynasty was to have significant ramifications for Judea over the next two centuries.

ABOVE LEFT: AFTER CAPTURING JERUSALEM IN 63 B.C.E., POMPEY DESECRATED THE TEMPLE, FROM A FIFTEENTH-CENTURY C.E. FRENCH TRANSLATION OF THE WORK OF FLAVIUS JOSEPHUS.

ABOVE: E. HILLEMACHER'S NINETEENTH-CENTURY C.E. PAINTING DEPICTS ANTONY BEING BROUGHT DYING TO CLEOPATRA. BELIEVING THAT CLEOPATRA HAD ALREADY KILLED HERSELF, ANTONY SUICIDED IN 30 B.C.E.

leaders now appealed to Pompey for support to rule legitimately in Jerusalem. One group, led by Aristobulus II, became hostile to Pompey and made an attack by the Roman general on the Nabataeans difficult to prosecute. In response, Pompey attacked Jerusalem, capturing the Temple. Like Antiochus IV, Pompey entered the Holy of Holies, by Jewish custom accessible only to the High Priest. Pompey's actions offended many Jewish people.

ANTIPATER AND THE INVASION OF THE PARTHIANS

Following the attack on Jerusalem, Pompey reinstated John Hyrcanus II as *ethnarch* (prince) and considerably reduced the territory under his control. John Hyrcanus II was effectively a Roman client-king and much of the territory he had previously controlled now became part of the province of Syria. John Hyrcanus II's most important counselor was Antipater, who came from Idumea, a territory that had been only recently added to the Jewish kingdom. Pompey's harsh dealings with the Jews had convinced Antipater that the Romans were to be placated and supported. In order to secure his own future, Antipater encouraged support for a Roman attack on the Nabataeans in 62 B.C.E. The attack was only partially successful; nevertheless, the Romans were pleased with Antipater's support.

The civil war between Pompey and Julius Caesar, which began in 49 B.C.E., resulted in Pompey's eventual defeat and assassination in Egypt. Caesar had followed him to Egypt but faced a serious rebellion in Alexandria on attempting to place Cleopatra on the throne. Antipater and John Hyrcanus II gave military support to Caesar, who eventually won the day. Caesar in turn extended protection and privileges to the Jews both in Judea and throughout the empire. He also strengthened the positions of John Hyrcanus II and Antipater in Judea itself. Under Caesar, Antipater's sons emerged in positions of power also. One of them, Herod (later known as Herod the Great), would become very important in the later history of Judea. In the upheaval following Caesar's murder in 44 B.C.E., instability in Judea increased and Antipater was killed.

In 40 B.C.E., Rome's eastern enemy, Parthia, invaded Syria and captured Judea. They replaced John Hyrcanus II with his old rival, Antigonus, whom Pompey had driven out. The Parthians encouraged anti-Roman sentiment, and Antigonus found much support in Judea for a nationalist revival. John Hyrcanus II was deported to Babylonia, while the eldest son of Antipater, Phasael, was murdered and Herod was forced to flee from the region.

ANTONY

Herod had gone to Cleopatra in Egypt, and then traveled to Rome in order to gather support from Marcus Antonius (Antony). Herod's refusal of an advisory position in Cleopatra's palace had irritated Cleopatra, and she sought to discredit him to Antony. In the wake of the assassination

THE DECAPOLIS

Created under Pompey in about 64 B.C.E., the Decapolis was a federation of ten Greco-Roman cities in northeastern Palestine. It was created to enhance trade and for mutual protection. The cities most often cited were: Scythopolis, Hippos, Gadara, Pella, Philadelphia, Gerasa, Dion, Canatha, Damascus, and Raphana.

of Julius Caesar, his main supporter, Antony, his great-nephew and adopted son, Octavian, and another powerful politician, Lepidus, formed a triumvirate through which the whole of the empire was governed. Antony had assumed control of the eastern provinces, and he convinced Octavian, Lepidus, and the Roman Senate to recognize Herod as king of Judea and as a friend of the Roman people. Herod returned east with an army under the leadership of Ventidius, one of Antony's most highly regarded generals. Ventidius drove the Parthians out of Syria in 38 B.C.E., and Antigonus was defeated in the following year by Sosius, another of Antony's generals. Herod was then installed in Jerusalem as a client-king of the Romans.

OCTAVIAN (AUGUSTUS)

Antony continued to support Herod despite Cleopatra's regular encouragement of Antony to destroy him. Serious strains also developed in the triumvirate, which eventually saw Octavian (later Augustus) and Antony embark on civil war. Herod needed to read the changing situation carefully if he was to survive. Antony's liaison with Cleopatra, which began in 41 B.C.E., turned into a permanent alliance in 37 B.C.E. The eventual success of Octavian over Antony and Cleopatra in 31 B.C.E. saw the political and military situation in Syria and the Near East change once again. Herod, along with other client-kings in the Near East, joined the cause of Octavian against his old supporter, Antony. Herod

LEFT: OCTAVIAN WAS THIRTY-TWO YEARS OLD WHEN HE CONQUERED EGYPT. AFTER THAT HE TOOK THE NAME AUGUSTUS. THIS MARBLE STATUE IS NOW HELD IN THE LOUVRE MUSEUM IN PARIS.

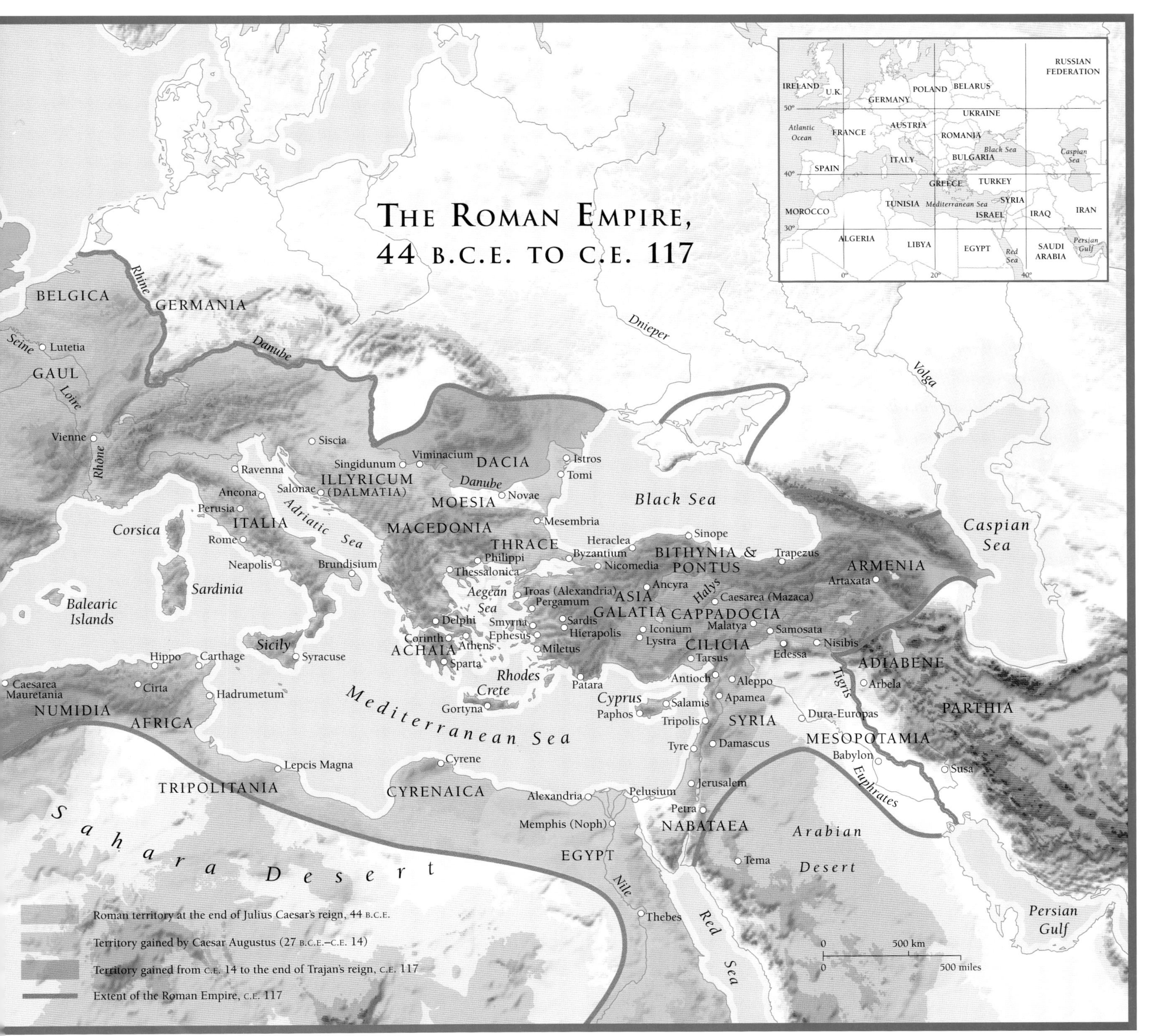

met Octavian in Rhodes, following Antony's defeat, and Octavian rewarded him with a considerable extension in territorial control. He was now given command of the coastal strip of Phoenicia and cities in southern Syria. This was effectively the territory that the Judean king had ruled prior to Pompey's arrival.

RIGHT: THIS NINETEENTH-CENTURY C.E. ILLUSTRATION SHOWS A MENACING HEROD THE GREAT. HEROD DID NOT HESITATE TO HAVE KILLED ANYONE HE PERCEIVED TO BE A THREAT TO HIS POSITION AS KING OF JUDEA, INCLUDING SEVERAL FAMILY MEMBERS.

HEROD

Despite being instated as king of Judea by Antony and having his power confirmed and his territory enlarged by Octavian (Augustus), Herod still faced many problems in maintaining his power. He was, after all, from Idumea, a region only recently added to the Judean kingdom, and his family was of Arabian origin. This was not viewed well by the elite in Jerusalem, as Herod was in many ways an outsider to the elite, and he was also considered wholly unsuited for the position of High Priest. John Hyrcanus II, who was removed by the Parthians, had been both *ethnarch* and High Priest, and the family of the Hasmoneans, from which John Hyrcanus II came, had been well qualified for the High Priesthood. Herod's lack of qualification for the office meant that the kingship and High Priesthood would now be split. The potential political ramifications of Herod's inability to hold the High Priesthood were serious, as it indicated very clearly that his Jewish credentials were not as strong as those of other rivals.

Herod also faced the difficult problem of needing to deal with powerful anti-Hellenizing/anti-Romanizing Jewish groups, particularly in Jerusalem, while at the same time appearing to be a supporter of Augustus and the influence of Romanization on the Near East. The example of the hostile reaction to Hellenization by the Maccabees in the reign of Antiochus IV Epiphanes would have been fresh in Herod's mind, and the Maccabean party was still powerful in Jerusalem during his reign. Faced with all of these problems, Herod needed to tread very carefully indeed. This resulted in some important and quite significant changes in the kingdom of Judea under the rule of Herod and his sons.

HEROD'S JERUSALEM

As a result of Herod's desire and necessity to appeal to the Romans and Roman culture, he staged the Actian games at Jerusalem in 30 B.C.E. to celebrate Octavian's victory over Antony at Actium in northern Greece the year before. In order to stage the games, however, Herod needed to construct a theater and amphitheater at Jerusalem. Included in the games were events such as gymnastics and wrestling. These were all important aspects of conducting the games in Greco-Roman fashion, however, they were a particular problem for the powerful anti-Hellenizing factions in Judea, particularly those residing in Jerusalem.

BELOW: *THE TEMPLE OF HEROD IN OUR LORD'S TIME,* NINETEENTH-CENTURY C.E. PAINTING BY JAMES JACQUES JOSEPH TISSOT. WORK ON THE TEMPLE STARTED AROUND 22 B.C.E.

HEROD THE GREAT'S KINGDOM
Cyprus
Mediterranean Sea
Laodicea
Orontes
CYPRUS
LEBANON
SYRIA
Mediterranean Sea
ISRAEL
JORDAN
EGYPT
SAUDI ARABIA
Red Sea
ABILENE
ITURAEA
Damascus
Sidon
Sarepta
Tyre
Mt. Hermon
SYRIA
Caesarea Philippi (Paneas)
GAULANITIS
Bathyra
Lake Hula
Raphana
GALILEE
TRACHONITIS
Ptolemais (Acco)
Capernaum
Bethsaida
Magdala
Sea of Galilee
Canatha
Sepphoris
Arbela
Hippos
Dion
Mount Carmel
Yarmuk
Abila
BATANAEA
Dora (Dor)
Gabae
Nazareth
Gadara
Caesarea Maritima (Strato's Tower)
Scythopolis (Beth-shean)
AURANITIS
SAMARIA
Pella
DECAPOLIS
Jordan
Sebaste (Samaria)
Gerasa
Mt. Ebal
Apollonia Sozusa
Shechem
Mt. Gerizim
Jabbok
Antipatris
Alexandrium
Gadara
Joppa
Lydda
Gophna
Philadelphia (Rabbah)
Jamnia
JUDEA
Jericho
PEREA
Emmaus
Cyprus
Azotus (Ashdod)
Jerusalem
Bethlehem
Hyrcania
Medeba
Ascalon (Ashkelon) (Free City)
Betogabri
Herodium
Machaerus
Marisa
Hebron
Dead Sea
Adora
En-gedi
Gaza
Arnon
Raphia
Masada
Beer-sheba
Malatha
IDUMEA
NABATAEA
N
Herodian fortress
Herod's kingdom at the beginning of his reign, 37 B.C.E.
Territory added by 30 B.C.E.
Territory added by 23 B.C.E.
Territory added by 20 B.C.E.
Territory conquered from the Nabataean kingdom
Decapolis
Decapolis city
Decapolis city (uncertain location)
Town of uncertain location
0
50 km
0
50 miles

ABOVE: THE THEATER AT CAESAREA MARITIMA. HEROD HAD THIS NEW PORT CITY CONSTRUCTED TO FURTHER SECURE HIS POSITION IN THE REGION.

The construction of the theater and amphitheater at Jerusalem was also undertaken so that Herod's capital might compete architecturally with other prominent Greco-Roman cities in the Near East. This was reminiscent of the construction of the gymnasium during the reign of Antiochus IV. A particular problem also was that Jews of more orthodox interpretations of Scripture were concerned that buildings such as the amphitheater might include images of animals and gladiators, which they interpreted as being forbidden in the Ten Commandments. Herod's response was to convert the capital of Samaria into a new city, which he called Sebaste. The Greek word *sebastos* is the equivalent of the Latin term *augustus*. Herod was clearly advertizing his gratefulness to Augustus for his patronage.

The new city of Sebaste was populated by Samaritans and Greeks (that is, non-Jews), and as a result Herod was able to undertake a significant building program at Sebaste that did not offend them. This included a temple to Roma and Augustus. In an attempt to placate the Jewish elite at Jerusalem, Herod undertook an enlargement and reconstruction program of the Jerusalem Temple in 22 B.C.E. The Wailing Wall, as it is called today in Jerusalem, represents the remains of an enclosure wall west of Herod's reconstructed Temple, which was destroyed by Titus in C.E. 70.

THE ORGANIZATION OF HEROD'S KINGDOM

The establishment of Sebaste as a new city was an indication of the nature of Herod's military strategy for the organization and preservation of his kingdom. Sebaste was constructed with strong walls, and a number of other fortresses were built at strategic locations throughout the kingdom at the same time. These included the fortification of ancient cities such as Jericho, and the construction of other new cities such as Herodium and the magnificent palace complex at Masada, a site of particular importance a century later when the Jews were in open rebellion against Roman rule. Further to this, Herod constructed another city, which was named in honor of Augustus, Caesarea Maritima. As the adopted son of Julius, Augustus had taken the name Caesar as part of his own name. The construction of Caesarea Maritima began in the same year that the reconstruction project started on the Temple in Jerusalem, 22 B.C.E. The city of Caesarea Maritima was designed to act as the main port of Herod's kingdom and to secure the territorial gains that Octavian had granted to him in coastal Syria.

Herod's construction program significantly strengthened the kingdom, and allowed Herod to compete for the favor and ongoing recognition of Augustus. Indeed, Augustus continued to exercise great confidence in Herod by extending his territory even further. In 23 B.C.E., Herod received control of an important section of southern Syria, and in 21 B.C.E., his territory was extended further north again.

BELOW: *THE ENTRANCE OF ANCIENT SAMARIA*, 1870, BY CARL HAAG. HEROD REBUILT SAMARIA AND RENAMED IT SEBASTE TO HONOR THE EMPEROR AUGUSTUS.

THE POWER AND INFLUENCE OF HEROD AND HIS KINGDOM

Herod's ability to collect taxes, together with the increase in trade that the new port city of Caesarea Maritima stimulated, meant that the financial position of the client-kingdom was generally strong throughout his reign. This allowed Herod to finance a variety of building projects in Judea and also to exercise a certain amount of influence outside of the kingdom. Herod became something of a financier in the region and even advanced loans to the Nabataean king. One particularly favorable outcome for Herod and his financial situation was a deal he did with Augustus in 12 B.C.E., in which he paid Augustus a large sum of money in return for half of the revenue of the copper mines on the island of Cyprus. The name of the island comes from the Greek word *kupros*, which means copper. Cyprus was the major supplier of copper to the lands of the Mediterranean and traded its copper over extensive distances.

In a development that saw Herod tied even more closely to the regime of Augustus, Herod won the support and patronage of Marcus Agrippa. Augustus's most trusted and successful general, Agrippa was brought into the imperial family by Augustus when he married him to his daughter Julia. When Agrippa was sent on an official visit to the east by Augustus in 15 B.C.E., he visited Herod's kingdom and made a lavish sacrifice outside the Jerusalem Temple. Herod responded by naming one of the gates of the Temple after Agrippa. When Agrippa moved north to the Black Sea to deal with a usurpation that had taken place in Crimea, Herod accompanied him and provided a fleet that had been constructed at Caesarea Maritima.

On Agrippa and Herod's return through the region of Asia Minor, Agrippa was presented with a number of grievances from Jews living in the cities of the province, whose councils they claimed were not treating them fairly. Herod intervened on their behalf and pleaded their cases before Agrippa. The Jews in Asia Minor had fled Judea in previous times of trouble and were part of what later became known as the Diaspora (or Dispersion). The guarantees of freedom of worship given to the Jews under Julius Caesar still held and were confirmed by Agrippa on behalf of Augustus. Herod had clearly been influential in this respect. Herod also remained popular in the Greek cities of Asia Minor and the Near East; this was reflected in his confirmation as President of the Olympic Games in 12 B.C.E.

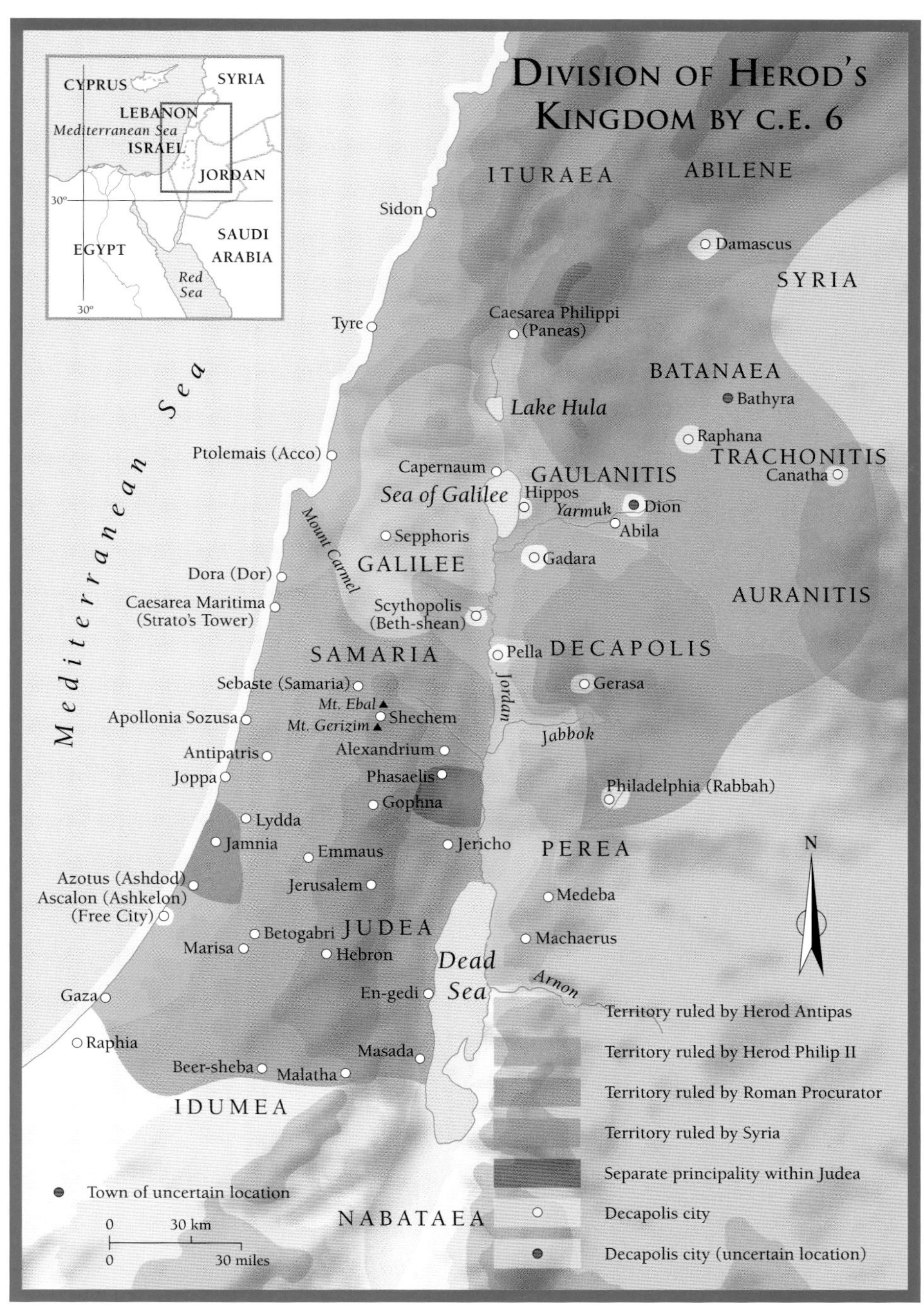

HEROD'S SUCCESSORS

Herod's notable success had come about partly as a result of the patronage he had received from Antony, Augustus, and Agrippa, but it was also the consequence of Herod's own energy and ability to deal successfully with the various factions and groups within his expanding kingdom. The factional disputes that dominated the scene at Jerusalem when Herod was first appointed king by Antony became less of a problem over time and remained settled for much of Herod's reign. However, Herod became increasingly beset by major problems within his own family. Part of the problem came from the fact that his first wife, Mariamne, was related to the family of the last Hasmonean king, John Hyrcanus II. Herod had continued to face opposition from the Hasmoneans in the wake of his appointment as king. Mariamne had been murdered at Herod's instigation long before, but his sons by her came under his suspicion as did the son of another of his ten wives. All three were murdered along with other relatives, and Augustus became increasingly concerned about Herod's succession plan. In 9 B.C.E., Herod made a particularly grave error when he invaded the Nabataean kingdom because of the forfeit of a loan he had made to the

RIGHT: HEROD ANTIPAS, FROM A TENTH-CENTURY C.E. FRENCH MANUSCRIPT. LIKE HIS FATHER, ANTIPAS WAS A GREAT BUILDER. HE IS MOST WELL KNOWN FOR BUILDING TIBERIUS AS HIS CAPITAL ON THE WESTERN SHORE OF THE SEA OF GALILEE.

Nabataean king. As a client-king of the Romans, Herod could only take such action with the permission of Augustus or the Governor of Syria. Herod's position had been seriously weakened as a result, and his ongoing family crisis gave those who still opposed him in Jerusalem an opportunity to destabilize him.

Intrigue and suspicion continued to bedevil the family of Herod, but prior to his death in 4 B.C.E. he established a succession plan that was probably approved by Augustus. His eighteen-year-old son, Archelaus, was to succeed him as king of Judea, but two separate principalities would also exist. This arrangement was known as the Tetrarchy. The territories of Galilee and Perea were to be ruled by Herod Antipas, Archelaus's brother, while Gaulanitis, Trachonitis, Batanaea, and Auranitis were to be ruled by their half-brother, Herod Philip II. All three leaders attempted to undermine each other by petitioning Augustus separately, and after ten years of Archelaus's rule in Judea, the situation became so bad that Augustus received petitions of complaint from representatives of a number of different factions in Judea. In C.E. 6, Augustus banished Archelaus and ordered that Judea be annexed. It became a Roman province governed by a procurator who would work in close connection with the legates (governors) of Syria.

THE FIRST JEWISH REVOLT

Following the annexation of Judea and its formation as a Roman province in C.E. 6, Roman procurators faced considerable difficulty in governing the province. Pontius Pilate was one such procurator, governing the province from C.E. 26–37. The factional and divided nature of Jewish religion and politics at the time Pilate dealt with Jesus is a good example. Eventually a client-kingdom was reestablished under Herod Agrippa I during the reign of Claudius (C.E. 41–54). Though Herod Agrippa I's kingdom was actually more extensive than that of his grandfather, Herod the Great, it was not to last. Judea was once again placed under a procurator when Herod Agrippa I died in C.E. 44. This instability in the leadership and lack of coherent political organization contributed to an increase in the intensity of factionalism in Judea, particularly in Jerusalem. The Roman procurators found it increasingly difficult to deal with the Jews, and the numerous problems in Judea, including the changing nature of its government, saw the emergence of more extreme levels of resistance against Roman rule. Roman emperors required worship of the cult of Roma and Augustus across the empire, but this was particularly unpalatable to the Jewish population. Under Pontius Pilate and other earlier procurators, Jews who refused to partake in such sacrifice were not always dealt with harshly and the policy was not enforced rigidly, but later procurators were more forceful in their requirements. This led to an escalation in opposition and violence.

Problems with famine, overtaxation, as well as the fact that 18,000 workers on Herod's Great Temple became unemployed when the project was completed around C.E. 60 meant that Judea was facing particularly troublesome times. Jewish groups who had resisted Hellenization and Romanization now became more popular, as their more orthodox theological positions provided some answers as to why the situation appeared so unstable and difficult. There was a marked increase in prophecies of an imminent messiah emerging in Judea. One procurator of Judea, Gessius Florus, was labeled as being particularly unable to deal with the problems in his province, and in C.E. 66 a serious disturbance broke out in Caesarea in which Greek and Jewish populations attacked each other. Even more seriously, this led to a full-scale revolt in Jerusalem. The revolt included a general refusal to sacrifice to Roma and Augustus, and the insult that this represented to the Romans, combined with all of the instability that had come before, led to a war with Rome that would change the face of the province of Judea forever.

BELOW: *JOTAPATA BESIEGED,* UNATTRIBUTED ENGRAVING IN *CALMET'S DICTIONARY OF THE BIBLE,* 1732. THIS GRAPHIC IMAGE SHOWS JOSEPHUS AND HIS MEN DEFENDING THEMSELVES AGAINST VESPASIAN'S ATTACK AROUND C.E. 67.

THE CAMPAIGNS OF VESPASIAN AND HIS SON TITUS

In C.E. 67, Vespasian was given command of the Jewish war by Emperor Nero. Vespasian himself later emerged as emperor at the end of C.E. 69. The Jewish historian Josephus, whose writings provide important information on Rome's first war with the Jews, was one of the Judean generals who faced Vespasian's attack. Josephus succeeded in fending off an attack by Vespasian's army at Jotapata, and Vespasian was himself wounded in this engagement. Vespasian was eventually successful over Josephus, who surrendered but was befriended by Vespasian when he prophesied the Roman general's elevation to the Principate.

The Campaigns of Vespasian and Titus
Cyprus
Mediterranean Sea
Vespasian is wounded, but wins his battle with Josephus.
Titus besieges Jerusalem, destroying the Temple and much of the city.
From Antioch
Orontes
From Alexandria
ABILENE
ITURAEA
SYRIA
TRACHONITIS
GAULANITIS
BATANAEA
GALILEE
AURANITIS
DECAPOLIS
SAMARIA
PEREA
JUDEA
IDUMEA
NABATAEA
Sidon
Damascus
Tyre
Caesarea Philippi (Paneas)
Bathyra
Cadasa
Lake Hula
Gischala (Gush Halav)
Raphana
Ptolemais (Acco)
Meroth
Capernaum
Sea of Galilee
Sogane
Taricheae
Jotapata
Gamala
Canatha
Arbela
Garis
Tiberias
Yarmuk
Dion
Sepphoris
Abila
Mount Carmel
Dora (Dor)
Japhia
Gadara
Caesarea Maritima (Strato's Tower)
Narbata
Scythopolis (Beth-shean)
Jordan
Pella
Gerasa
Sebaste (Samaria)
Alexandrium
Apollonia Sozusa
Neapolis
Mt. Ebal
Mt. Gerizim
Jabbok
Antipatris
Gadara
Joppa
Gerasa
Thamna
Philadelphia (Rabbah)
Lydda
Adida
Gophna
Jamnia
Bethennabris
Upper Beth-horon
Jericho
Betharamphtha (Livias Julias)
Emmaus
Cyprus
Azotus (Ashdod)
Jerusalem
Qumran
Medeba
Bethlehem
Ascalon (Ashkelon) (Free City)
Caphartobas
Machaerus
Herodium
Betogabri
Hebron
Dead Sea
Adora
En-gedi
Arnon
Gaza
Raphia
Masada
Beer-sheba
Malatha
CYPRUS
SYRIA
LEBANON
Mediterranean Sea
ISRAEL
JORDAN
EGYPT
SAUDI ARABIA
Red Sea
30°
N
Vespasian's C.E. 67 campaign
Vespasian's C.E. 68 campaign
Titus's C.E. 69–70 campaign
Town of uncertain location
0 50 km
0 50 miles

RIGHT: TITUS FLAVIUS VESPASIANUS [VESPASIAN], ROMAN EMPEROR AND FOUNDER OF THE SHORT-LIVED THOUGH INFLUENTIAL FLAVIAN DYNASTY, BY J. GILBERT, COPIED FROM AN ANTIQUE COIN.

The aftermath of the death of Nero in C.E. 68 meant that Vespasian was distracted for much of C.E. 69 with the civil wars that beset the Roman Empire. There were four emperors during the course of C.E. 69; three only ruled for a few months at a time before Vespasian emerged at the end of the year as emperor. Vespasian had left his son Titus in charge of the Jewish war before heading west to play his part in the complicated proceedings in C.E. 69. The seriousness of Rome's Jewish war was reflected in the legions that were under Titus's command. Vespasian had left three legions, and Titus added another three from Syria and Egypt while also levying troops from client-kingdoms such as Emesa and others in the region. The total number of soldiers Titus had under his command was in the vicinity of 40,000 men. In C.E. 70, this force besieged Jerusalem. The siege was carried out from February to August C.E. 70. When Jerusalem fell, the Temple and much of the city was razed to the ground. Many of the city's inhabitants were sent to Rome to be killed in the arenas as part of the triumphal celebrations associated with the Roman victory. Sacred symbols of the Temple were also taken to Rome, including the great Menorah and the sacred books. In all, it has been estimated that 220,000 people died in the siege. The Jewish revolt was not yet over as other areas in Judea held out. The most famous of these was Masada, which did not fall until late C.E. 73. Formerly a palace complex of Herod the Great, Masada became a symbol of Jewish resistance as approximately 1,000 Jews held out the siege of a Roman legion under the command of Flavius Silva. All but three of the stalwarts committed suicide before the Romans captured the complex after constructing an enormous ramp via which they attacked it.

THE SECOND JEWISH REVOLT

The catastrophic events at Jerusalem in C.E. 70 resulted in many Jews fleeing from Judea to other parts of the Mediterranean. Some of these communities had existed for a long period of time and originated with those who fled Judea in earlier times of trouble, such as during the reign of Antiochus IV. These Diaspora communities could be found in cities such as Antioch, Alexandria, and Rome, but there were communities of Jews all over the Mediterranean at this time. In the aftermath of Titus and Vespasian's attack on Judea there was no active suppression of Judaism by the Romans; however, the seriousness of the revolt in C.E. 66 meant that Roman emperors kept a close watch on events in Judea. More revolts followed, and Roman responses to them, but they were not as serious and widespread as the events of C.E. 66–70.

In C.E. 115–117, there were some disturbances among Jewish communities in Alexandria, Cyrene in North Africa, and also on the island of Cyprus, but the most serious revolt that the Romans had to deal with was one led by Simon Bar Kochba in Jerusalem during the reign of Emperor Hadrian (reigned C.E. 117–138). As part of his extensive tour of the eastern provinces, Hadrian visited Jerusalem in C.E. 130 and began construction of a city to replace the one that had been destroyed in C.E. 70. The city would be a Roman colony,

BELOW: RUINS OF HEROD THE GREAT'S PALACE COMPLEX AT MASADA. AFTER THE FAMOUS SIEGE OF MORE THAN 1,000 JEWISH MEN AND WOMEN IN C.E. 73, MASADA BECAME A SYMBOL OF THE JEWS' DETERMINATION TO BE FREE IN THEIR HOMELAND.

and it included a Roman temple to Jupiter. The city was called Aelia Capitolina after its founder, the name Aelius coming from Hadrian's family name. As was the case with earlier Greco-Roman building activity in Jerusalem, the Jewish response was divided. Some Jews were angry at the idea of a foreign, pagan god being the main focus of the new city's religion; however, other Jews adopted a more moderate line. In C.E. 132, when Hadrian outlawed both castration and circumcision, the Jewish reaction became more militant and widespread. A Jewish national leader called Simon Bar Kochba emerged and received widespread support. He was held by many Jews to be the Messiah, and he led a revolt that would last for the next three years. The rebellion began in rural areas to the south of Jerusalem, and much of the countryside came under Simon Bar Kochba's control. The rebels were unable to capture the city of Jerusalem, but their control of agricultural land, on which the city was dependent, caused considerable problems for the Romans.

ABOVE: *THE DESTRUCTION OF THE TEMPLE IN JERUSALEM BY TITUS*, BY THE SEVENTEENTH-CENTURY C.E. FRENCH ARTIST NICOLAS POUSSIN. TITUS HAD AMASSED A HUGE ARMY FOR HIS ATTACK ON JERUSALEM, WHICH LASTED FOR ABOUT SEVEN MONTHS.

HADRIAN CRUSHES THE REVOLT

The governor of the province of Judea, Tineius Rufus, called for reinforcements to deal with the revolt, and Hadrian took the revolt so seriously that he sent some of his best generals to deal with the crisis. Among them were the governors of Syria, Arabia, and Britain. The rebels, under Simon Bar Kochba's leadership, had learned some lessons from the war of C.E. 66–70 and did not attempt to engage the Roman forces in open battle. Instead, they undertook a guerrilla war, which was very effective. They were so determined to defeat the Romans and to survive the Roman military response that they resorted to digging extensive tunnels from which the war could be conducted and which were large enough to live in. Archaeological discoveries have confirmed this. Early in C.E. 134, the province of Judea was placed under the governorship of Julius Severus, who commanded three legions, 17 auxiliary units, and detachments from other legions. The Roman force numbered around 25,000–30,000 men. One of the legions, Legio XXII Deiotarna, appears to have been wiped out in the course of the struggle as no trace of it appears in documents or literature after the war. Eventually the emperor himself went to Judea and took command.

Roman armies were not used to fighting wars against small bands of guerrillas with the keen religious motivations of those under Simon Bar Kochba. The Roman forces also suffered considerably from famine and disease. Famine was a particular problem as the Jewish forces remained in control of large portions of the countryside. The Romans began to resort to cruel punishments and torture in an effort to wear down the resistance of the rebels. Eventually the Roman forces gained the upper hand. They systematically starved out and attacked the numerous guerrilla bands of Simon Bar Kochba's army. By the end of C.E. 135, the guerrillas had been all but destroyed and a final siege by the Romans took place at Bethar. The Bar Kochba rebels did not surrender, but died of disease and lack of water. When the siege was finally over, Simon Bar Kochba's body was found among the dead and his head was taken to the emperor. Hadrian now dealt ruthlessly with Judaism and Judean nationalism. He forbade the teaching of Mosaic Law, and renamed the province of Judea as Syria Palaestina.

LEFT: *RETURN OF HADRIAN*, RELIEF FROM A TRIUMPHAL ARCH ERECTED IN HADRIAN'S HONOR BY HIS ADOPTED SON AND SUCCESSOR, ANTONNUS PIUS, IN THE SECOND CENTURY C.E. ANTONNUS ALSO FORCED THE ROMAN SENATE TO DEIFY HADRIAN.

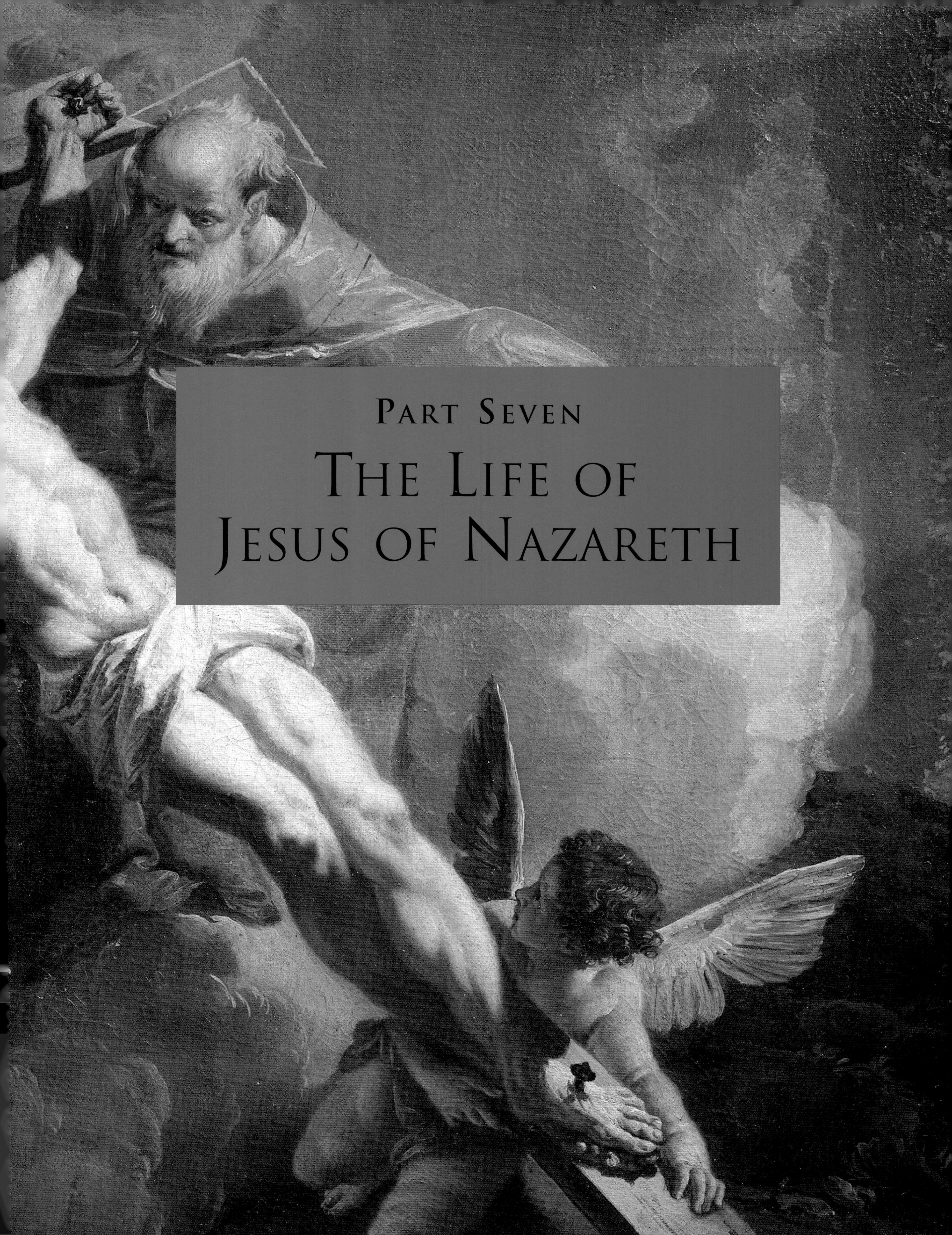

Part Seven
The Life of Jesus of Nazareth

Behold the Man

AND THE WORD BECAME FLESH AND LIVED AMONG US JOHN 1:14

RIGHT: OVER THE CENTURIES, THE HOLY FAMILY HAS BEEN A SOURCE OF INSPIRATION FOR ARTISTS AND CRAFTSMEN, WITH EXAMPLES SUCH AS THIS SIXTEENTH-CENTURY CARVING BY DIEGO DE SILOE.

Since Jesus of Nazareth died, countless words have been written about his life and teachings, by believers and unbelievers, by scholars and lay people. Approaches to the study of his extraordinary personality range from unquestioning acceptance of the Gospel accounts and their supernatural elements, through reasoned attempts to disentangle matters of fact from matters of faith, to radical theories suggesting cultic practices such as the use of mind-altering drugs to induce visions.

THE WORLD OF JESUS

Part Seven of *Biblica* places Jesus within the geographic, historical, political, and social context of the small area of the Near East where he lived and taught. It charts the journey of the Holy Family to Bethlehem, where Jesus was born; the flight into Egypt to escape Herod's Massacre of the Innocents; the return from Egypt to Nazareth and the Sea of Galilee, where Jesus began his ministry; and finally, the journey of Jesus and his followers to Jerusalem, where he would be crucified by the Romans.

Apart from his babyhood in Egypt and a brief sojourn in the Gentile settlements of Tyre and Sidon (now in modern-day Lebanon), Jesus spent the whole of his short life in the narrow strip of land bordering the western shore of the Jordan River, bounded to the north by Galilee and its sea and to the south by Jerusalem, situated at the northernmost end of the Dead Sea. The whole distance from north to south was only about 70 miles (110 km).

THE GOSPELS

Virtually everything we know about the Jesus of history comes from the four Gospels, and to a lesser extent from the Acts of the Apostles and the Epistles of St. Paul. These authors, however, were not writing biography as we understand it, but rhetoric designed to persuade readers of the truth of their belief that Jesus was both human and divine: the Son of Man and the Son of God. Their writings contain scarcely any information about what Jesus was like as a man. What did he look like? What sort of home did he come from? We can speculate about these questions, but we can never know.

Nevertheless, the writings do afford glimpses of the essential humanity of Jesus, and of the world in which he lived. The traditional image of the boy Jesus helping Joseph in a humble carpenter's workshop comes from Mark (6:3), and its corroboration by Matthew (13:55) suggests that Jesus did indeed grow up as the son of an artisan—a skilled workman, but presumably not a learned man. His changing of water into wine at the wedding in Cana provides, with admirable economy of words, a vivid picture of a country wedding and an embarrassed host who has failed to provide enough wine for the celebration (John 2:1–10).

Modern commentators adopt a more critical position, pointing out that the Jesus of the Gospels is an enigmatic and disturbing figure. It has been noted that he was wild-looking, rude to his mother, occasionally violent, and given to inexplicable rages and cryptic utterances. It is an extreme view, but perhaps closer to the truth than the "gentle Jesus, meek and mild" of the child's prayer: "Do not think that I have come to bring peace to the earth; I have not come to bring peace, but a sword" (Matthew 10:34).

HISTORICAL EVIDENCE

Nonbiblical information about Jesus is sparse. Minor Jewish rebellions against Roman rule were too common to be recorded in detail, and crucifixion was the standard Roman penalty for serious crimes; one such execution among thousands would not rate a mention in a factual

Two Great Teachers

Of those who have shaped the history of ideas in the Western world, two of the most influential were the Greek philosopher Socrates (fifth century B.C.E.) and Jesus Christ (first century C.E.). Ironically, neither of these seminal thinkers and teachers lived in what is now known as the West, but in the Near East. (Although politically part of Western Europe, Greece is spiritually and culturally closer to Ankara than to Rome.)

The two men had more in common than their provenance. Neither committed a single word to paper; it was their disciples—Plato in the case of Socrates, and the Apostles in the case of Jesus—who disseminated their teachings through the written word. Finally, both were killed because of perceived subversive activities.

OPPOSITE: VIEW OF MAGDALA AND SEA OF GALILEE FROM MT. ARBEL. THE REGION AROUND THE SEA OF GALILEE WAS JESUS' LOCALE FOR THE MAJORITY OF HIS TIME SPENT PRACTICING HIS MINISTRY.

history. One contemporary source is Flavius Josephus, born Joseph ben Matthias (C.E. 37–c.100), a Jewish historian and general, and, for a time, Governor of Galilee. Despite his part in the Jewish revolt (C.E. 66), he managed to impress his Roman captors, and after the fall of Jerusalem (C.E. 70) moved to Rome, where he wrote, in Greek, his comprehensive histories of the Jewish peoples.

Josephus reported that both the Jews and the Romans saw Jesus as a focus of disaffection and a rabble-rouser—a capital offense—and he recorded the trial and the sentencing but made no mention of the Resurrection. He must be taken seriously as an intelligent, dispassionate observer: his account of the trial is convincingly consistent and rich in circumstantial detail. His omission of the Resurrection means only that he wanted to stick to verifiable facts.

LEFT: THE MEDEBA MAP, A SIXTH-CENTURY BYZANTINE MOSAIC DISCOVERED IN THE CHURCH OF ST. GEORGE AT MEDEBA, DEPICTS PALESTINE IN ITS INTRICATE TILEWORK.

VIRTUE AND FAITH

The Gospel evidence for the divine nature of Jesus resides primarily in his remarkable works. Commentators sometimes try to explain the works of Jesus naturalistically—thus the feeding of the multitude (Matthew 15:32–39; Mark 8:1–9) on a mountain in the wilderness west of the Sea of Galilee happened because the people were shamed into producing their own hoards of food. Possibly so, but it misses the point. Christ's message is spiritual, not moral—not virtue but faith will save. "Blessed are those who have not seen, and yet have come to believe" (John 20:29).

THE BIRTH OF JESUS

TO YOU IS BORN THIS DAY IN THE CITY OF DAVID A SAVIOR, WHO IS THE MESSIAH, THE LORD LUKE 2:11

The "Christmas story"—Mary, Joseph, babe in a manger, angels, shepherds, star, magi—is so familiar it might be presumed to be a single narrative. Yet, of the four Gospels, only Matthew and Luke include an account of the birth of Jesus, and the familiar details are actually spread across their two accounts.

THE ACCOUNTS OF MATTHEW AND LUKE

To get the most out of the story, it helps to read the two "infancy narratives" separately (Matthew 1–2 and Luke 1–2). This is because the audience for whom each author wrote his Gospel came from different religious and cultural backgrounds. Matthew's readers were primarily Jewish Christians while Luke's were essentially Gentile Christians. In addition, as can be seen in Luke's stated purpose in writing, that his readers may "know the truth" as it has been handed down by eyewitnesses (Luke 1:1–4), both Gospels were written several decades after the events described actually took place. Once we recognize this, many of the details emphasized by each author make more sense.

THE ANNUNCIATION AS TOLD BY LUKE

In Luke's account, there are two "annunciations"—announcements made by an angel heralding the birth of a significant person. These are not visitations by God himself as narrated in the Jewish scriptures (Genesis 16, 21, 22; Exodus 3); rather, God speaks to the person of faith through a heavenly messenger (Greek, *angelos*).

The first annunciation (Luke 1:5–25) is the lesser of the two, but sets the scene for what is to come. The reader encounters Zechariah, a Jewish priest whose wife Elizabeth is unable to bear a child. An "angel of the Lord" appears to Zechariah to announce that God has seen fit to remove this shame from Elizabeth. They are to have a child whom they will name John, he will be "filled with the Holy Spirit," (Luke 1:15) and his mission will be to prepare the people to welcome the Messiah. This is too much for the cynical old priest; as a result, he is struck dumb. Only when the baby is born and Zechariah insists he be called John is his speech restored (Luke 1:57–66). Now he recognizes the hand of God, and praises God's goodness in the words of the *Benedictus*—"Blessed be the Lord God of Israel, for he has looked favorably on his people and redeemed them" (Luke 1:67–79).

Situated in the middle of this account, but far surpassing it in importance, is the Annunciation—the appearance by the angel Gabriel to the virgin, Mary of Nazareth (Luke 1:26–38)—a scene that has been made famous by centuries of artistic interpretations. The Annunciation is linked to the preceding narrative with the introductory words "In the sixth month …," that is, of Elizabeth's pregnancy. There are several parallels—the messenger is the angel Gabriel, the event is in the plan of God, the person is reassured with the words "do not

BELOW: THIS IVORY RELIEF CARVING DEPICTS THE STORY OF THE NATIVITY. THE HOLY FAMILY FIGURE PROMINENTLY, SURROUNDED BY THE CHARACTERS ASSOCIATED WITH THE STORY OF JESUS' BIRTH.

be afraid," the Holy Spirit is to be with the child, his unique mission is outlined, and the name chosen by God is stated.

But this time, the message is delivered to the woman herself who is described as having "found favor with God" (Luke 1:30), and whose child will be known as "the Son of God" (Luke 1:35). Unlike Zechariah, Mary's question is for guidance, and her response is one of total obedience: "Here I am, the servant of the Lord, let it be with me according to your word" (Luke 1:38). To the news of Elizabeth's pregnancy she is likewise utterly accepting, as witnessed by her immediate practical response in going to visit her kinswoman. As both women greet one another with mutual faith and understanding, their respective unborn babies are symbolically linked—as they will be in the future mission of both for the redemption of the world. Mary's concluding hymn of praise parallels that of Zechariah as she raises her voice in the *Magnificat* (Luke 1:46–55): "My soul magnifies the Lord, and my spirit rejoices in God my Savior." Luke has now set the scene for the birth of the Savior.

THE ANNUNCIATION AS TOLD BY MATTHEW

Meanwhile, how does the Gospel of Matthew reach this point? The opening verses could not be more different: they trace Jesus' family tree beginning with Abraham (Matthew 1:1–17), the father of the Jewish people. While Luke also provides a genealogy, his does not appear until the beginning of Jesus' public ministry and shows Jesus in direct line back to Adam and the origin of humankind (Luke 3:23–38).

The account of the lead-up to Jesus' birth in Matthew (1:18–25) is much shorter than in Luke, but again it takes the form of an "annunciation," with a similar pattern. The angel's reassurance "do not be afraid" addresses Joseph's confusion. He is engaged to Mary but, as they have not yet lived together, how is it that she is pregnant? The angel explains that Mary has conceived through "the Holy Spirit" and the child will be called "Jesus" because, like his ancestor David (Matthew 1:1; Luke 1:32), he will be the "savior" of God's people (Matthew 1:22–23). But, whereas for Luke the angel engages in dialog with a person fully conscious, Matthew says that the angel appeared in a dream (Matthew 1:20). This notion of God guiding a person in their sleep occurs another three times in Matthew's infancy narrative (2:12, 13, 19).

The section is rounded off with a feature that is repeated by the evangelist Matthew over and over again in his gospel. For his Jewish-Christian readers, he is at great pains to show that everything that happens is in fulfillment of God's plan for his people. Matthew therefore constantly refers back to the Old Testament with a phrase such as: "All this took place to fulfill what was spoken by the Lord through the prophet: 'Look, the virgin shall conceive and bear a son, and they shall name him Emmanuel,' which means 'God is with us'" (Matthew 1:22).

ABOVE: *THE BIRTH OF ST. JOHN THE BAPTIST* BY LUCA SIGNORELLI. JOHN'S BIRTH BORE SIMILARITIES TO THE BIRTH OF CHRIST—THE ANNUNCIATION TO ZECHARIAH PROMISED THE BIRTH OF A SON.

LEFT: EUSTACHE LE SUEUR'S *ANNUNCIATION* CAPTURES THE INTENSITY OF THE MOMENT WHEN A DIVINE MESSENGER CONVEYS GOD'S MESSAGE TO MARY ON HER FUTURE ROLE.

ABOVE: BIRTHPLACE OF KING DAVID AND JESUS—THE TOWN OF BETHLEHEM HAS PLAYED A SIGNIFICANT ROLE IN A NUMBER OF BIBLE STORIES.

RIGHT: THE FUTILE SEARCH TO FIND LODGING IN A TOWN OVERFLOWING WITH PEOPLE IS CAPTURED IN THIS WORK—*THE ARRIVAL AT BETHLEHEM* BY LUC-OLIVER MERSON.

THE JOURNEY TO BETHLEHEM

Matthew makes no mention of a journey to Bethlehem; he seems to presume that Mary and Joseph live there. For Luke, however, the well-established tradition that Jesus was born in Bethlehem requires getting his parents there for the birth. Luke achieves this by constructing a story that inserts this significant event into the world scene.

In the earlier story of Zechariah and Elizabeth, the historical setting was during Herod's reign of Judea (Matthew 1:5). But, for Luke, the birth of the Savior is of world importance. Hence, he expands the context to that of the Roman Empire, setting it at the time of the reign of Emperor Augustus, and when Quirinius was governor of Syria (Luke 2:1–2). Since Augustus ruled from 27 B.C.E. to C.E. 14, but Quirinius governed Syria in C.E. 6–7, this would seem to place the birth of Jesus as C.E. 6–7. But the reign of Herod the Great was from 37 to 4 B.C.E. As Herod is mentioned in both Gospel accounts, the weight of evidence is that the reference to Quirinius is inaccurate or that the census referenced occurred before another census taken when Quirinius became governor of Syria; in either event, Jesus was born around 7–6 B.C.E.

The important thing for Luke is not the detail, but to establish that Jesus' salvation is for the whole known world. This broadening of the historical context also provides a reason for the journey of Mary and Joseph from Nazareth to Bethlehem, in the city of David (Luke 2:4, 11). According to Luke, Augustus issued an edict that all those under Roman rule had to travel to their "home city" for a census (Luke 2:1). Being of "the house of David" (Luke 1:27, 32; 2:4), this meant a trek south to the city of Bethlehem for Mary and Joseph.

As the crow flies, the distance is approximately 70 miles (110 km), but even today the normal route along the Jordan Valley then west via Jerusalem to Bethlehem is somewhat further. The normal method of travel was to join a caravan (an image not unlike that of the American western migration).

NO ROOM AT THE INN

Given such a crowd making its way to Judea, it is not surprising that, on arriving in Bethlehem, "there was no place for them in the inn" (Luke 2:7). But again, while this may be a viable explanation, Luke's main concern is to show that, from his very birth, Jesus is in solidarity with the poor, a central theme highlighted by the simplicity with which his birth is described—Luke's account states that Mary "gave birth to her firstborn son and wrapped him in bands of cloth, and laid him in a manger" (Luke 2:7). Throughout Luke's Gospel, the poor are presented as the preferred object of God's love and concern. While not rejecting the rich minority, Luke's appeal to them is to live in a spirit of inclusiveness and generosity toward those of little or no means.

THE SHEPHERDS AND THE ANGELS

In keeping with this spirit of predilection for the poor, Luke gives to simple shepherds the honor of being the first witnesses to Jesus' birth. Mary's prophecy that he will "lift up the lowly" (Luke 1:52) is already being fulfilled.

It is to such shepherds that yet another angel of the Lord appears. This angel is accompanied by "the glory of the Lord," apparently in the form of a great light (Luke 2:9).

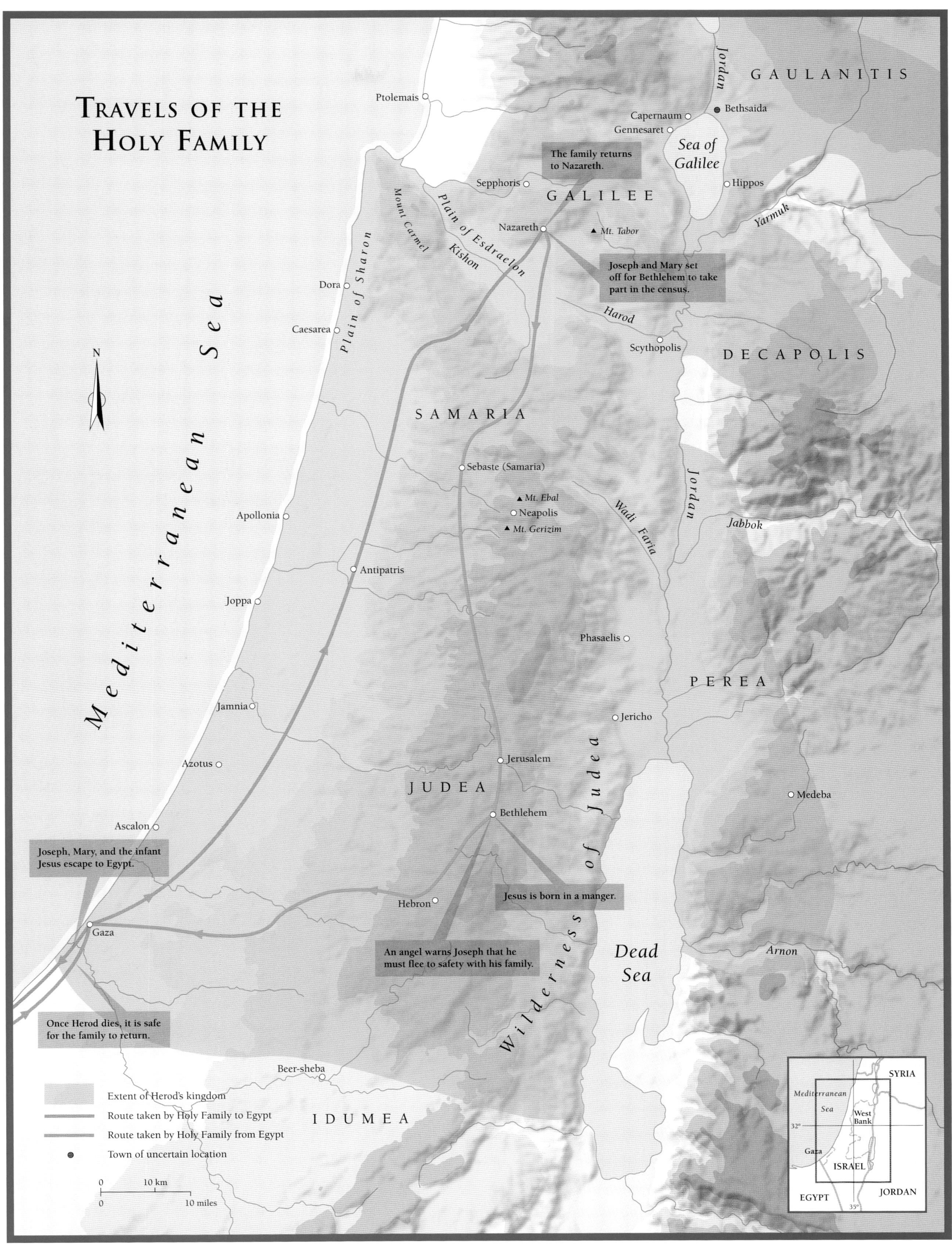

Travels of the Holy Family
The family returns to Nazareth.
Joseph and Mary set off for Bethlehem to take part in the census.
Jesus is born in a manger.
An angel warns Joseph that he must flee to safety with his family.
Joseph, Mary, and the infant Jesus escape to Egypt.
Once Herod dies, it is safe for the family to return.
GAULANITIS
GALILEE
DECAPOLIS
SAMARIA
PEREA
JUDEA
IDUMEA
Mediterranean Sea
Sea of Galilee
Dead Sea
Ptolemais
Capernaum
Bethsaida
Gennesaret
Hippos
Sepphoris
Nazareth
Mt. Tabor
Mount Carmel
Plain of Esdraelon
Kishon
Plain of Sharon
Dora
Caesarea
Harod
Scythopolis
Jordan
Yarmuk
Sebaste (Samaria)
Mt. Ebal
Neapolis
Mt. Gerizim
Wadi Faria
Jabbok
Apollonia
Antipatris
Joppa
Phasaelis
Jamnia
Jericho
Azotus
Jerusalem
Bethlehem
Ascalon
Medeba
Hebron
Gaza
Wilderness of Judea
Arnon
Beer-sheba
N
Extent of Herod's kingdom
Route taken by Holy Family to Egypt
Route taken by Holy Family from Egypt
Town of uncertain location
0 10 km
0 10 miles
SYRIA
Mediterranean Sea
West Bank
32°
Gaza
ISRAEL
EGYPT
JORDAN
35°

RIGHT: VIVID COLOR IS USED TO GREAT EFFECT IN THIS FOURTEENTH-CENTURY GERMAN STAINED GLASS WINDOW, BRINGING TO LIFE THE STORY OF THE ANNUNCIATION TO THE SHEPHERDS.

The idea of glory as light in the Old Testament is associated with the *Shekina*, the presence of God (Numbers 14:21; Ezekiel 43:2; Exodus 33:18–22). It is a divine presence not visible to the human eye, but symbolized by the light that can be seen. Luke is saying that God is now present among his people, in the person of a newborn baby lying in a manger!

Having experienced this presence symbolically, the shepherds now hear it described in words. The angel reassures the shepherds, telling them not to be afraid, followed by the announcement of "good news of great joy for all the people" (Luke 2:10). This phrase is rich in Lukan themes.

CHRIST IS BORN

It is "good news," a word that is at the root of our English word "Gospel." And the good news is this: "to you is born this day in the city of David, a Savior who is the Messiah" (Luke 2:11). In the very city on whose outskirts the shepherds stand, is born the Christ, the Messiah for whom every devout Jew had longed, the Savior who would bring eternal justice and peace for his people. As such, it is an occasion of "great joy" (Luke 1:14, 41, 44, 47, 58). For Luke, the whole Gospel story is a cause for rejoicing, not least because it is for everyone. "All people"—women and men, Jew and Gentile, rich and poor—are invited to participate in the celebration of God's presence in the world in the person of Jesus. God's grace is no longer to be considered as some far-off future event; it is inaugurated "today," a word to which Luke will return many times in the Gospel.

As if to confirm this amazing announcement, there now appears a whole host of heavenly beings (Luke 2:13) who raise their voices in praise of God: "Glory to God in the

BELOW: THE EVENTS LEADING UP TO THE BIRTH OF JESUS ARE DEPICTED IN THIS TWELFTH-CENTURY FRESCO, FOUND IN THE CHURCH OF ST. MARTIN IN ZILLIS, SWITZERLAND.

highest heaven, and on earth peace among those whom he favors!" (Luke 2:14). It is as though the whole of creation is bearing witness to the truth of this event. By contrast, there is an appealing earthiness to the simple language and response of the shepherds (Luke 2:15) who, like Mary before them, hurry away to find everything just as the angel had said (Luke 2:16). Their simple faith is rewarded and, as they return to their ordinary humdrum life, they are transformed. It is now their turn to replicate the heavenly host by "glorifying and praising God" (Luke 2:20).

Luke concludes this section with three responses. For the shepherds, it is immediately to share the good news (Luke 2:17); for those who hear the account, they are filled with wonder (Luke 2:18); and for Mary, it is to ponder these things in her heart (Luke 2:19). There is much more to this simple birth account than meets the eye! The "sign" may be the swaddling clothes and the manger as a birthplace (Luke 2:7, 16), but the reality to which it points is one of enormous significance. For Luke, the truly fitting response by the reader is to be open in faith to what is revealed, to share the good news, and to ponder it in one's heart.

ABOVE: *THE CIRCUMCISION* BY WILLIAM BLAKE. IN KEEPING WITH JEWISH TRADITION, EIGHT DAYS AFTER HIS BIRTH, JOSEPH AND MARY PRESENT THE INFANT JESUS AT THE TEMPLE TO BE CIRCUMCISED.

THE CIRCUMCISION AND PRESENTATION OF JESUS IN THE TEMPLE

Immediately, the Gospel provides as an example the response of two pairs of faith-filled people. This child may indeed be Christ the Lord (Luke 2:11), but, as a fully human baby, it is fitting that his parents carry out all the normal responsibilities of Jewish parents. They therefore arrange that eight days after his birth, he is circumcised and given the name of Jesus (Luke 2:21).

The second phase of fulfilling "the law of Moses" requires them to present the infant to the Lord in the Temple in Jerusalem (Luke 2:22). Their obedience is rewarded when two further witnesses affirm Jesus' true identity. Simeon and Anna are genuine wisdom figures, devout people who have spent a lifetime listening to the Holy Spirit. Both immediately recognize the light of the glory of God in this small child (Luke 2:32) and give thanks and praise to God (Luke 2:38). However, Simeon adds a warning note to Mary, prophesying that salvation will come about through conflict: Jesus' ministry will bring "a sign that will be opposed" (Luke 2:34) and "a sword that will pierce her own soul" for herself (Luke 2:35). But that is for the future.

In the words of Simeon (Luke 2:29–32), Luke presents a third hymn, the *Nunc Dimittis*, echoing the hymns of Mary (Luke 1:46–55) and Zechariah (Luke 1:68–79).

These beautiful poetic prayers have become permanently embedded in the daily worship of millions of Christians who are indebted to the Lukan author each time they pray in thanksgiving for "a light for revelation to the Gentiles and for glory to your people Israel" (Luke 2:32).

MARY AND MARIOLOGY

While Matthew and Luke give accounts of Jesus' conception and birth, only Luke focuses on the role of Mary. In his description of her obedient and generous response to God (Luke 1–2), he portrays her as the perfect disciple. In the fourth Gospel, she is referred to not by name but by the title "the mother of Jesus" in important incidents at both the beginning and end of the Gospel (John 2:1–11; 19:25–27).

Yet Mary's significance has been enormous as demonstrated in many works of art, such as *Coronation of the Virgin* (c. 1642) by Diego Velazquez (right). The early Christian church debated the precise nature of her relationship with God and her role in the story of salvation. Over time, the Catholic and Orthodox traditions developed a strong practice of devotion to Mary; on the other hand, Protestants came to view this devotion as somewhat extreme and taking away from the central figure of Jesus as the unique Son of God and Savior. With the ecumenical document *Mary: Grace and Hope in Christ* (2005), such divisions have moved several steps toward resolution and ultimate unity.

RIGHT: IN THE TWELFTH CENTURY, BONANUS OF PISA CREATED THIS BRONZE RELIEF OF THE THREE WISE MEN ON A DOOR AT PISA CATHEDRAL.

BELOW: RICH IN DETAIL AND COLOR, THIS MOSAIC—FOUND AT SAN APOLLINAIRE NUOVO IN RAVENNA, ITALY—SHOWS THE THREE WISE MEN PRESENTING THEIR GIFTS TO THE NEWBORN KING.

THE THREE WISE MEN

Matthew's description of Jesus' birth is brief, simply stating that Mary gave birth to a son who was named Jesus (Matthew 1:25), and that he was born in Bethlehem during Herod's reign of Judea (Matthew 2:1). This first mention of Bethlehem serves two purposes: to demonstrate the fulfillment of another biblical prophecy, "you, O Bethlehem … from you shall come forth for me one who is to rule in Israel" (Micah 5:2), and to set the scene for the forthcoming visit of the magi.

The reader is now introduced to the wise men from the east (Matthew 2:1), who inquire about the newborn "king of the Jews" whose star they have seen in the east (Matthew 2:2). No mention here of "three" or "kings"! Presumably the number three arose from their three gifts (Matthew 2:11), while the idea that they were kings probably came from reflection on Psalm 72 and Isaiah 63, which both make reference to visits by kings. Although the names of the wise men are not mentioned, later tradition attributed variations of Balthasar, Melchior, and Casper.

So who were the "magi"? The word was borrowed by the Greeks from the Old Persian *magus*, meaning rich, gifted, or powerful. The Greek historian Herodotus uses it of a Zoroastrian priest who had the ability to interpret dreams. As a group, the magi were a priestly sect. Apart from the book of Jeremiah (39:3, 13), the only Old Testament references occur in the book of Daniel. King Nebuchadnezzar's daughter-in-law reminds her husband about Daniel, saying "your father, King Nebuchadnezzar, made him chief of the magicians, enchanters, Chaldeans, and diviners, because an excellent spirit, knowledge, and understanding to interpret dreams, explain riddles, and

Modern Astronomical Evidence for the Star of Bethlehem

In Matthew's account of the story of the magi, the guidance of a "star" is mentioned four times (Matthew 2:2, 7, 9, 10). Its purpose in terms of the narrative is clear—to guide the wise men to the newborn King. But what scientific validity is there for such a phenomenon?

Given that the magi were almost certainly astrologers, the kind of phenomena familiar to them would have included comets, supernova (though not the term), and a conjunction of planets, all of which are consistent with modern scientific observation. While open to modern refinement, the definition of a comet given by the Roman poet Virgil in the *Aenid* is still valid: "a star leading a meteor flew with much light." Likewise, records of the conjunction of planets were carefully kept; there was a conjunction of Jupiter and Saturn in 7 B.C.E. and of Jupiter and Venus in 6 B.C.E.

The modern term supernova, a star that suddenly increases in size and brilliance then fades away, may not occur in ancient documentation, but this does not mean the phenomenon was unknown.

Where modern science would differ is in the interpretation held among the ancients. What was important to the astrologer was not only to notice the phenomena, but to search for their meaning. They would have concurred with the statement of Tacitus in his *Annals* that "the general belief is that a comet means a change of emperor," and that the conjunction of planets is associated with the birth of a king. In fact, a common role for such wise men was to discern the rise of a new king.

If we accept some element of historicity in Matthew's account, then any number of combinations is possible and consistent with modern astronomical understanding. The star first sighted by the wise men (Matthew 2:2) could be explained as a supernova. Then the "star that they had seen at its rising" might be a comet that "stopped over the place where the child was" (Matthew 2:9). Alternately, it could have been a reflection from a planetary conjunction; two of which occurred in 7 B.C.E. and 6 B.C.E.—the most likely years of Jesus' birth.

The occurrence of these phenomena is plausible in terms of modern astronomy, and their coincidence of time and place is not impossible. At some point, it comes down to a belief that it was God who guided the wise men by utilizing the ordinary processes of creation. The event, therefore, is not a violation of nature nor a contradiction of modern science, but the way in which nature allows for such coincidences to occur. Ultimately, their importance for the Gospel is that God uses them to witness to the truth of Jesus' identity on behalf of the Gentile world.

solve problems were found in this David" (Daniel 5:11). This background suggests that these visitors from the east (Matthew 2:1) came from Persia or, more likely, from Babylon.

During their exile in Babylon (586–538 B.C.E.), the Jews produced the final version of their scriptures. When the Persian king Cyrus overtook the country and permitted the Jews to return to Judea, many of them chose to remain. With the Greek conquest two centuries later, Babylon lost its earlier importance. But, at the time of Jesus' birth, it remained a key center for the study of astrology. The wise men must have learned something of the Jewish messianic expectation, perhaps even the astral link: "a star shall come out of Jacob, and a scepter shall rise out of Israel" (Numbers 24:17). How they decided this was "his star" (Matthew 2:2) is impossible to know, but it was enough to convince them to make the long journey to Judea to acknowledge his birth.

Continuing toward Bethlehem, they are rewarded with the reappearance of the star providing them with the exact location. They find the infant and his mother and, true to their stated intentions, fall to their knees to worship him. While they may not be kings, they offer him gifts of gold, frankincense, and myrrh (Matthew 2:11).

THE FLIGHT INTO EGYPT

With all this talk of a newborn "king of the Jews" (Matthew 2:2) and "a ruler who is to shepherd my people Israel" (Matthew 2:6), it is not surprising that the incumbent king, Herod, is getting anxious. He now moves into trickery mode. First, he tries to wangle information out of the wise men by implying that he shares their motives in wanting to worship Jesus (Matthew 2:7–8). When this fails, because the wise men are "warned in a dream not to return to Herod" (Matthew 2:12), he plans to search out and kill Jesus. At this point, an angel warns Joseph in a dream that, in order to escape this imminent threat, he is to take Mary and the child and flee into the safety of Egypt (Matthew 2:13). Without hesitation, they depart as instructed and remain there until Herod's death (Matthew 2:14–15).

As we have seen, Matthew constantly draws links with the Jewish scriptures. In this third example of dream-warnings (Matthew 2:13), there is a hint of comparison

BELOW: *REST ON THE FLIGHT INTO EGYPT* BY CARAVAGGIO. A HEAVENLY WARNING IN A DREAM ALERTS JOSEPH TO THE DANGER POSED TO HIS FAMILY, SO THEY FLEE TO EGYPT.

ABOVE: HEROD FEELS HIS GRASP ON POWER UNDER THREAT AND ORDERS THE "MASSACRE OF THE INNOCENTS," SEEN IN THIS FOURTEENTH-CENTURY FRESCO.

with the Joseph of the Old Testament. Joseph's dream that he will rise to be leader (Genesis 37:5–11) is fulfilled when he becomes an important figure in Egypt and ultimately saves his brothers from starvation. There is an even clearer link being made with Moses, who is rescued as an infant by being taken to Egypt (Exodus 1:22–2:10) and who then saves his people by leading them out of Egypt into the safety of the Promised Land. The Moses story is the context of the quote that the evangelist uses to round off with his usual "fulfillment saying"—again taken from one of the prophets (Hosea 11:1): "This was to fulfill what had been spoken by the Lord through the prophet, 'Out of Egypt I have called my son'" (Matthew 2:15).

KING HEROD'S DEADLY DECREE

Herod the Great (reigned 37–4 B.C.E.) had every reason to be nervous, but not because Jesus would prove to be a threat in any political sense. Herod was hated by the Jews, who resented his power over them, gained by having schemed to win the grace and favor of the Roman Emperor, Caesar Augustus. He was not truly Jewish since his mother was an Idumean princess, and he had little interest in the religious beliefs or practices of Judaism.

At the same time, he achieved an extraordinary cultural and building program throughout the country. Within Jerusalem itself, he created parks and gardens, theaters, a palace for himself and his entourage, and the Fortress of Antonia. In particular, he undertook a magnificent reconstruction of the Temple in Jerusalem, hoping in this way to finally win the approval of his Jewish subjects, but to no avail. Further north, he rebuilt a major city in Samaria. Throughout the land, he established fortresses to help preserve his power and control those of his people who might challenge his authority. Worse still, he gained a reputation for murdering anyone, including members of his own family, who seemed to him to endanger his absolute authority.

Within this context, eliminating some Jewish infants in order to ensure the disappearance of a potential challenger was not likely to cause him too much remorse. Enraged by his failure to dupe the wise men, he attempts to ensure the death of Jesus by ordering the killing of all children two

RIGHT: RUINS OF THE PALACE AT HERODIAN (BUILT 42 B.C.E.). THOUGH HISTORY REMEMBERS HEROD FOR HIS BARBARIC ACTS, HE INITIATED EXTENSIVE BUILDING WORKS.

years old and under (Matthew 2:16). As there is no evidence from extra-biblical sources that such a massacre took place, it is not possible to claim historicity—but, given Herod's track record, it is entirely possible. Once again, the evangelist identifies a link with one of the prophets: "Then was fulfilled what had been spoken through the prophet Jeremiah: 'A voice was heard in Ramah, wailing and loud lamentation, Rachel weeping for her children; she refused to be consoled because they are no more …'" (Matthew 2:17–18).

The reference to Jeremiah 31:15 is precise. The original reference was to Rachel's loss of her sons into exile (Genesis 30:22; 35:16–20). But where there was hope both in the original context and in Jeremiah's application to the imminent new covenant (Jeremiah 31:31–34), the scene depicted by Matthew is one of unmitigated grief. Yet, in spite of the horror, there is an ironic ray of hope. The reader knows that God has intervened to save the infant king, as even the most powerful earthly rulers are unable to thwart the divine plan.

THE RETURN FROM EGYPT

So God uses a fact of history, Herod's death in 4 B.C.E., to bring Jesus back to the land of Israel and his future mission (Matthew 2:19–20). Once again an angel assures Joseph in a dream that it is now safe to return (Matthew 2:20), but his fear of staying in Judea is well-founded. In the terms of Herod's will, the kingdom had been divided among his three sons. Judea came under Archelaus, who shared his father's appalling wickedness but none of his talent or competence. By C.E. 6, even Rome was pleased to banish him, after which Judea was administered by a Roman procurator.

Acting on advice received in a further dream, Joseph takes his small family to Nazareth in Galilee (Matthew 2:22). As before, Matthew combines historical and religious explanations. Given that the title "Jesus of Nazareth" was recognized from the earliest Christian communities, it seems gratuitous for Matthew to provide the usual Old Testament link, "that what was spoken by the prophets might be fulfilled: 'He will be called a Nazorean'" (Matthew 2:23), especially as the reference is not known today. But Matthew's community was under pressure to defend their claims for Jesus' identity, so the evangelist calls on all his resources to defend Jesus' origins in such an insignificant city.

THE CHILDHOOD OF JESUS

One of the surprising things in the New Testament is that there is very little reference to Jesus' childhood. The Gospels of Mark and John make no reference to Jesus' birth, opening their accounts of his earthly life with the beginning of his public ministry. Even Matthew says nothing of the years following the family's return from Egypt. So it is left to the Gospel of Luke to supply the reader with any knowledge of Jesus' childhood and youth.

ABOVE: *THE RETURN FROM EGYPT* BY JAMES JACQUES JOSEPH TISSOT. ONLY AFTER THE DEATH OF HEROD (IN 4 B.C.E.) DOES IT BECOME SAFE FOR THE HOLY FAMILY TO RETURN HOME TO NAZARETH.

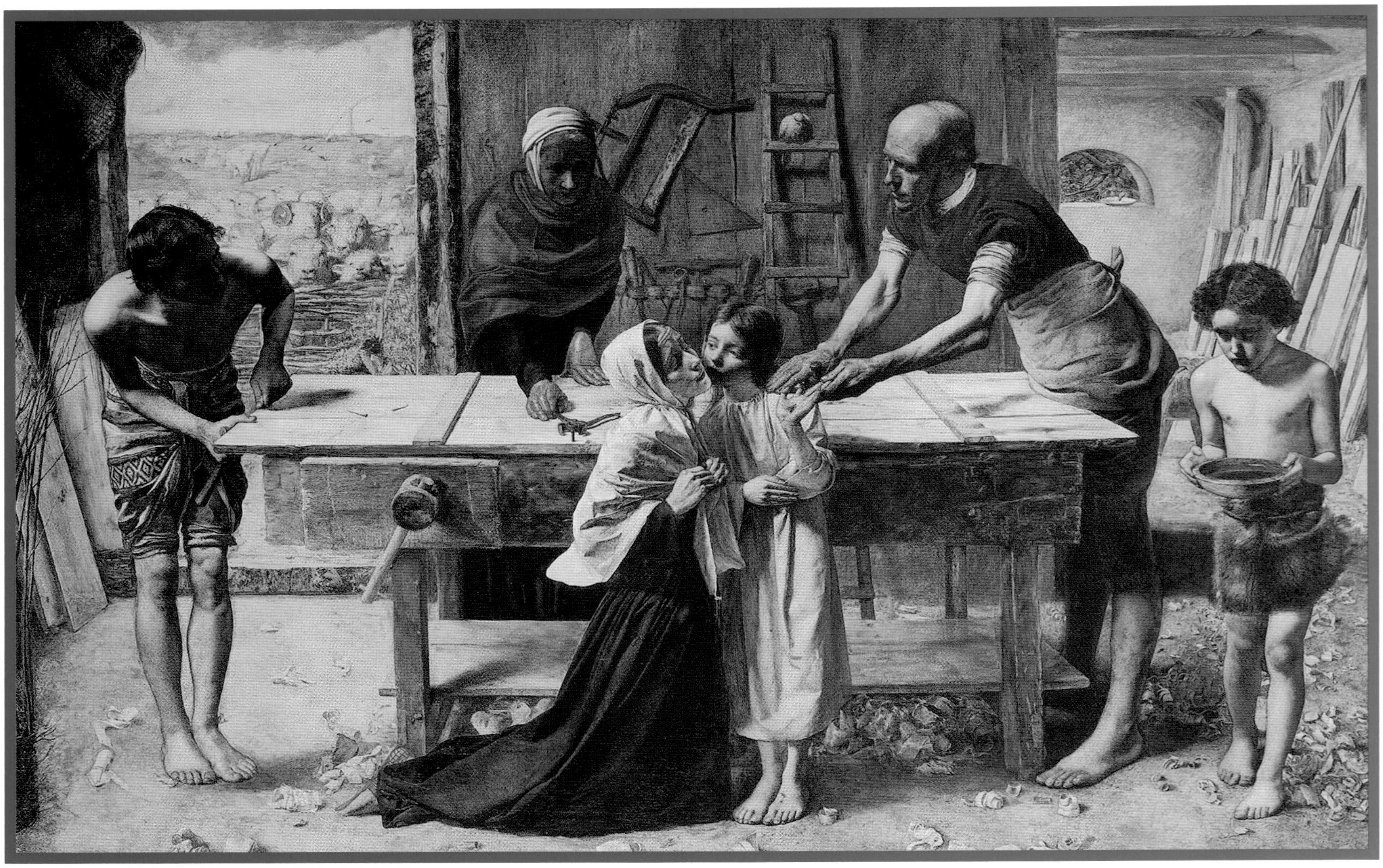

ABOVE: *CHRIST IN THE HOUSE OF HIS PARENTS* BY JOHN EVERETT MILLAIS. LITTLE IS KNOWN OF JESUS' BOYHOOD IN NAZARETH—IT IS BELIEVED THAT HE LEARNED JOSEPH'S TRADE OF CARPENTRY.

Given the paucity of Gospel evidence, two "infancy Gospels" were written to fill in the gaps. *The Protoevangelium of James* was in circulation by the second century and *The Infancy Gospel of Thomas* by the fourth century. They contain further details about Mary's background and fanciful stories about wondrous works carried out by the child Jesus. Like many other such works, they were excluded from the final version of the New Testament.

Luke's narrative includes just two verses (Luke 2:39–40) on Jesus' childhood in Nazareth. Around that time, Herod Antipas, son of Herod the Great and tetrarch of Galilee, was rebuilding the city of Sepphoris, north of Nazareth, and founding a new city, Tiberias, on the western shore of the Sea of Galilee. It seems reasonable to suggest that Joseph, an artisan (Matthew 13:55), would have found ample work on such projects. Perhaps, at times, the child Jesus accompanied him. What a climate of male rough and tumble this would have offered, supplementing his undoubtedly pious formation by his parents as reflected in Luke's simple but rich description: "The child grew and became strong, filled with wisdom; and the favor of God was upon him" (Luke 2:40).

RIGHT: *DARSTELLUNGEN AUS DEN EVANGELIEN* (PLATE 10) BY FRIEDRICH OVERBECK. THIS WORK SHOWS THE BOY JESUS AT THE TEMPLE, IN DISCUSSION WITH LEARNED MEN.

JESUS IN THE TEMPLE

The single incident with which Luke illustrates this development occurs when Jesus is twelve years old. Unknown to his parents, Jesus stays behind in Jerusalem after the Passover. Returning, they find him holding his own in dialog with the Temple elders who are said to be "amazed at his understanding and his answers" (Luke 2:47). Their consternation is met with the response "Did you not know that I must be in my Father's house?" (Luke 2:49). Enigmatic as this may be, it directs the reader to the most important part of Jesus' life: his unique future mission as Son of God and savior of the world.

The next 20 years or so of Jesus' life are only of importance to Luke as preparation for this mission. So it is sufficient to summarize this period of Jesus' life by saying that he lived obediently with his parents, increasing "in wisdom and in years, and in divine and human favor" (Luke 2:52).

Like Mary, the reader can only wonder (Luke 2:51) at the depth of God-given grace and personal formation that produced the Jesus whose demonstration of spiritual perception, compassion, and single-minded commitment make up the rest of the Gospel story.

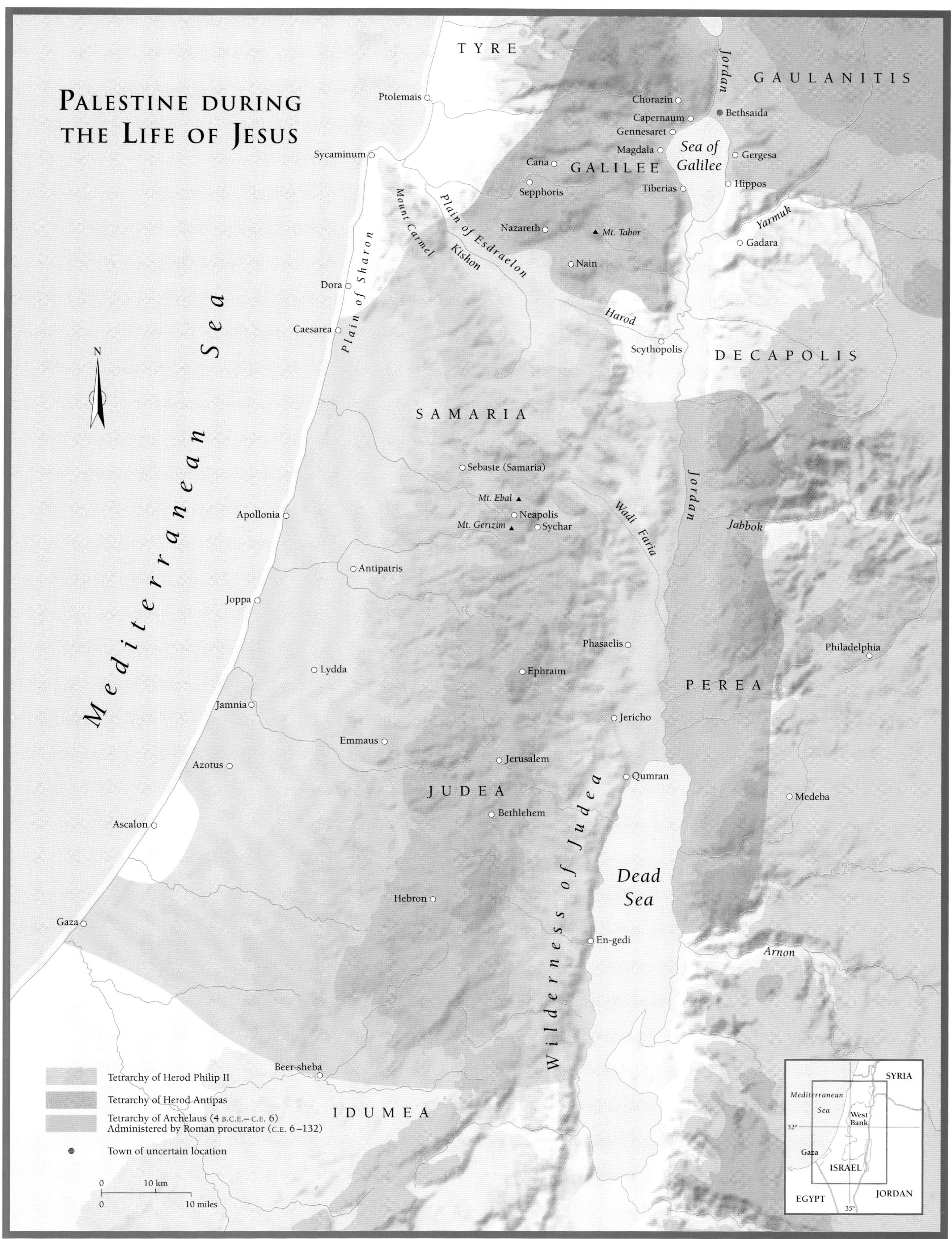
PALESTINE DURING THE LIFE OF JESUS
TYRE
GAULANITIS
Jordan
Ptolemais
Chorazin
Bethsaida
Capernaum
Gennesaret
Magdala
Sea of Galilee
Sycaminum
Cana
GALILEE
Gergesa
Sepphoris
Tiberias
Hippos
Mount Carmel
Plain of Esdraelon
Yarmuk
Nazareth
Mt. Tabor
Gadara
Plain of Sharon
Kishon
Nain
Dora
Harod
Caesarea
Scythopolis
DECAPOLIS
N
Mediterranean Sea
SAMARIA
Sebaste (Samaria)
Mt. Ebal
Jordan
Wadi Faria
Apollonia
Neapolis
Mt. Gerizim
Sychar
Jabbok
Antipatris
Joppa
Phasaelis
Philadelphia
Lydda
Ephraim
PEREA
Jamnia
Jericho
Emmaus
Jerusalem
Azotus
Qumran
JUDEA
Medeba
Bethlehem
Ascalon
Wilderness of Judea
Dead Sea
Hebron
Gaza
En-gedi
Arnon
Beer-sheba
Tetrarchy of Herod Philip II
Tetrarchy of Herod Antipas
Tetrarchy of Archelaus (4 B.C.E.–C.E. 6)
Administered by Roman procurator (C.E. 6–132)
IDUMEA
Town of uncertain location
0 10 km
0 10 miles
SYRIA
Mediterranean Sea
West Bank
32°
Gaza
ISRAEL
EGYPT
JORDAN
35°

THE BAPTISM OF JESUS

REPENT, FOR THE KINGDOM OF HEAVEN HAS COME NEAR MATTHEW 3:2

RIGHT: AS A LEADER IN FINANCE AND BANKING DURING THE RENAISSANCE, THE REPUBLIC OF FLORENCE MINTED CURRENCY DEPICTING ST. JOHN THE BAPTIST.

These words constitute the mission-statement of John the Baptist. Later, they are also the opening words of Jesus' ministry (Matthew 4:17). For John the Baptist, they are the reason he started up a movement directed at his fellow Jews, requiring them to confess their sins, and to be baptized by him in the Jordan River.

John's mission was obviously a highly successful religious activity, and one that operated outside the official religious practices of the Temple and well away from Jerusalem. Crowds came from the cities to John in the wilderness to answer his call. Other groups at that time also performed baptisms. The Dead Sea community at Qumran had regular ceremonial lustrations. Converts to Judaism were admitted through a proselyte baptism. John, however, was different: he baptized Jews in a once-and-for-all rite.

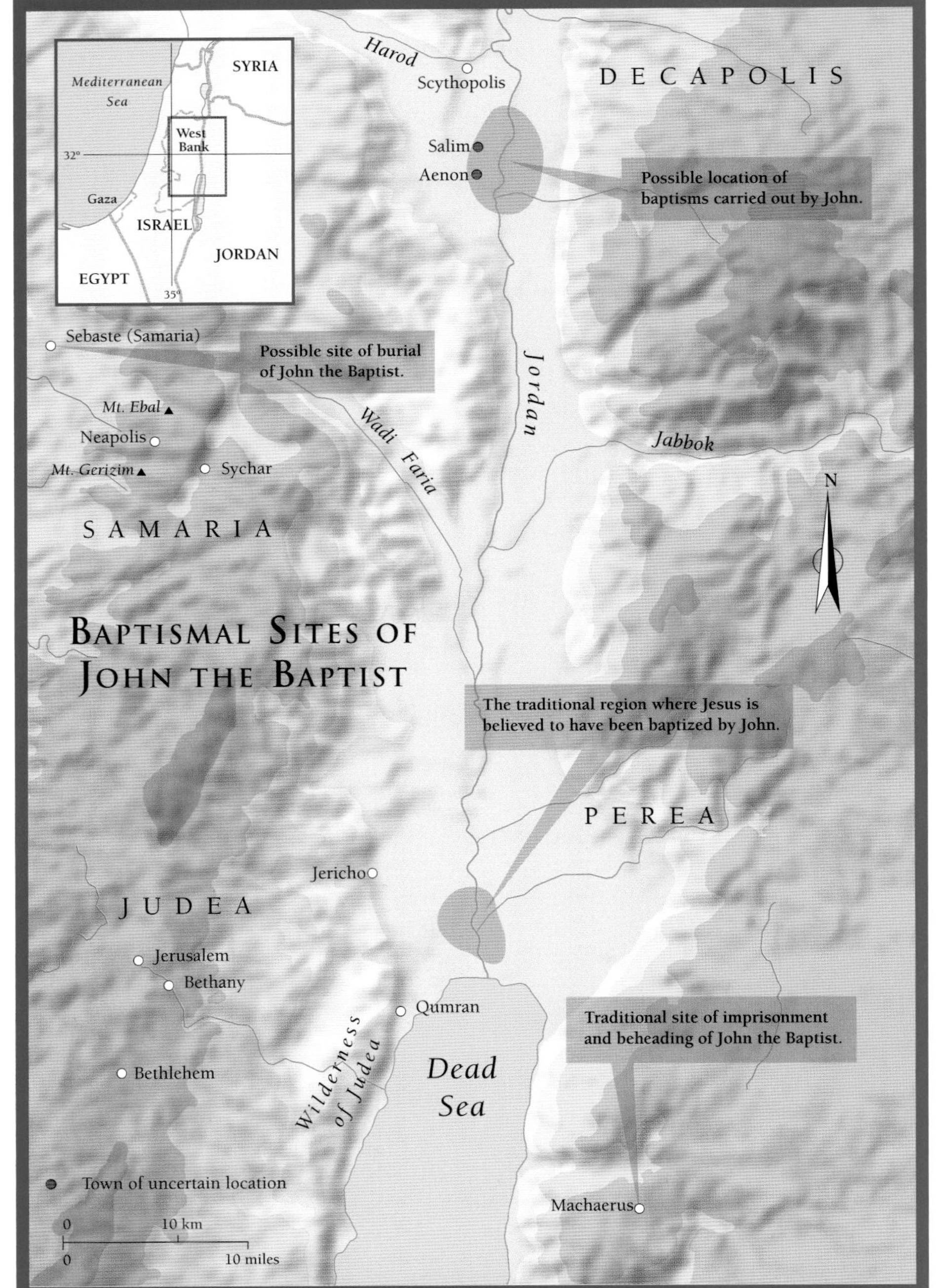

JOHN THE BAPTIST

John became so famous through his distinctive baptism that a new word was coined—baptist—to describe him. Before John, this noun did not exist. John's fame was so great that he appears in all four Gospels, and not only in the story of his encounter with Jesus immediately before Jesus' ministry; there are other places in the Gospel narratives when he and his followers appear, often in contexts where they have questions and doubts about the nature of the ministry and person of Christ. John's influence was still being felt 20 years after his death, according to the Acts of the Apostles. And the first-century Jewish historian Flavius Josephus, in his *The Antiquities of the Jews*, has more to say about John the Baptist than he does about Jesus.

JOHN'S APPEARANCE AND ROLE

John's clothing (dressed in a camel-hair coat), diet (locusts and wild honey), and his base in the wilderness, as well as his uncompromising message and ascetic habits, ensured that he would be identified and recognized as an archetypal prophet in the Old Testament mold. His teaching would have reminded the Jews of Elijah, and it is not surprising that that title was given to him by Jesus (Matthew 11:14). The earliest Gospels locate his activities in the Jordan, which would remind readers of Israel's history and Joshua's crossing of the Jordan before the nation entered its Promised Land. Also, the link to Elijah was strong here too: the Jordan was the scene of Elijah's ascent to heaven (2 Kings 2:11). The significance of these events would not have been lost on those responding to John's call.

Although the reference to the Jordan had these clear symbolic and historical resonances, an exact place for John's activities is not recorded in the earliest three Gospels (Matthew, Mark, and Luke). It is only in the Gospel of John (John 1:28) that the locale is specified—Bethany—but that identification is unhelpful as a Bethany near the Jordan is unknown. Some copyists of this Gospel even altered the text to Bethabara, (meaning "the place of crossing over") which recalls the Jesus/Joshua parallelism, but is likely to have been a later scribal change, encouraged by pilgrim tradition. Later in John's Gospel, John continues baptizing, now at Aenon near Salim (John 3:23), even though in one sense his work was complete—he had already pointed to the arrival of the Christ. The location of these places is unclear. The Medeba map shows two sites named Aenon and both seem to have

RIGHT: HEROD SUCCUMBS TO THE WHIM OF A DANCING GIRL AND ORDERS THE BEHEADING OF JOHN THE BAPTIST. CARAVAGGIO SKILLFULLY DEPICTS THIS DARK EVENT IN *BEHEADING OF ST. JOHN THE BAPTIST.*

been well-watered places. A Salim near Perea is also known—but it is not clear which specific locations the Gospel of John had in mind.

A prophecy from Isaiah 40 accompanies the first mention of John in the Gospels of Matthew, Mark, and Luke, and it is also quoted by the Baptist in John 1:20—John has a divine destiny to fulfill, namely to be the voice of that prophecy, that is the one crying in the wilderness to prepare the people for the coming of God. Eventually the Christian church canonized John. As St. John he was remembered and venerated, not as much as the man who had baptized Jesus, but as the one who pointed out and recognized Christ, the Lamb of God. To identify Christ was something the church itself also claimed to do—hence St. John was a pioneering role model.

JOHN'S CAREER

John's fame was such that he, like Jesus, has his own infancy narrative—these are the only two characters in the New Testament whose details of parentage and birth are recorded. Luke's Gospel reports the remarkable birth of John whose mother, the old barren Elizabeth, conceives; his story parallels the virgin birth of Jesus (Luke 1:5–25, 57–60). Also like Jesus, John's death is described: his preaching denouncing the legitimacy of Herod Antipas's marriage resulted in his arrest and ultimate beheading. The oriental tale of Herod's feast during which he promised the dancing girl whatever she wished and her choice, prompted by her mother, of John's head on a platter is well known. Then, like Jesus, John had his own loyal disciples on hand ready to bury him, and to perpetuate his memory. Some people thereafter were prepared even to speak of John's resurrection. The traditional place of John's imprisonment and death is the fortress of Machaerus at the Dead Sea. His burial-place was believed to have been at Sebaste in Samaria.

JOHN'S TEACHING

Apart from his proclamation about the imminent coming of the Kingdom of God, other preaching by John the Baptist is recorded in the New Testament, most prominently in Matthew 3. There he is reported as vilifying the Jewish groups—the Pharisees and the Sadducees—addressing them as a "brood of vipers" (Matthew 3:7). His uncompromising denunciation of such people is that trees that do not bear good fruit will be destroyed (Luke 3:8–9). His eschatological message is severe: "the chaff will be burned up in unquenchable fire" (Luke 3:8–10). This hell-fire preaching, although sharing some parallels with Jesus' own teaching later in that Gospel, is nevertheless intended to focus on the difference between John's teaching rooted in the old covenant, and Jesus' new message of hope for salvation.

BELOW: THIS AERIAL VIEW SHOWS SEBASTE'S NABI YAHYA MOSQUE (MOSQUE OF ST. JOHN THE BAPTIST). THE TOWN OF SEBASTE IS SAID TO BE THE FINAL RESTING PLACE OF JOHN THE BAPTIST.

RIGHT: THE CONTINUING IMPORTANCE OF JOHN THE BAPTIST TO CHRISTIANS IS EVIDENCED IN THIS EARLY CHRISTIAN TOMBSTONE, WHICH IS ENGRAVED WITH JOHN'S BAPTISM OF CHRIST.

THE BAPTISM OF JESUS

"You are my Son, the Beloved; with you I am well pleased" (Luke 3:22)—these are the words of the divine voice from the heavens proclaiming to the world that Jesus is God's Son and that this is an immediate consequence of his having been baptized. Even though for the Christians Jesus was deemed to be sinless, it was believed that he identified himself with and approved of John's baptism of repentance for sinners. Later, his death too was to be described vicariously: Jesus "died on behalf of sinners." Matthew dispels the evident difficulty felt in some quarters that Jesus, of all people, was seemingly submitting himself to John's baptism for sinners, by including a dialog between the two men. During the exchange, John's reluctance to baptize Jesus is answered by Jesus' telling him that he must be baptized by John (Matthew 3:14–17). Luke and John transfer the earlier record of Jesus' baptism to a report and a reminiscence respectively (Luke 3:21, John 1:26–34), without repeating the earlier vivid narrative. The baptizing of Jesus gets only an oblique reference in John—in his account, it is John the Baptist's role as the forerunner that is emphasized (John 1:32–33). But even in those Gospels that relate the encounter of Jesus and John at the time of Jesus' baptism, the main message from the Baptist minimizes his own act by stating that Jesus will be baptizing in the Spirit, whereas John merely baptized with water.

In Matthew's and Mark's story of Jesus' baptism (Matthew 3:13–17; Mark 1:9–11), the defining moment for Jesus is the descent of God's Spirit onto him and the heavenly proclamation that he is God's Son. This public recognition and announcement mean that, after a period of reflection (the temptations), he can commence his own public teaching. Convinced that he was the Coming One of whom John had preached, Jesus could now begin his own distinctive ministry, inaugurating the Kingdom.

CHRISTIAN BAPTISM

Just as the Gospels recorded that Jesus' ministry began after his baptism by John, new converts to Christianity were admitted to the church by their being baptized into Jesus' name. Primarily this was because the Christians were sharing an experience that their Lord had undertaken, even though

BELOW: THIS MAGNIFICENT SCULPTURE BY MELCHIORE GAFA, A SEVENTEENTH-CENTURY MALTESE SCULPTOR, EXUDES THE POWER AND DRAMA OF JOHN'S BAPTISM OF CHRIST.

JESUS AND JOHN

The two men, John the Baptist and Jesus, share so many common characteristics that observers of the two at the time were confused: when people were asked who John was and who Jesus was, the same answers occur—both are variously called "Christ," "the prophet," or "Elijah" (Matthew 16:14; Mark 6:14–16; John 1:20–21). Herod even thought Jesus was the dead John reincarnated, saying "John, whom I beheaded, has been raised" (Mark 6:16). Obviously, the Christian authors of the New Testament had to make crystal clear throughout that Jesus alone is the Christ and the "Stronger One" of John's preaching. John is made to say that he is unworthy to loosen the Coming One's sandals. The Baptist's swansong is that he, John, will decrease but Jesus will increase in stature (John 3:30); that epitaph should be remembered as the preferred way of judging and differentiating between the two men.

In the account of the Transfiguration (Matthew 17:1–8), Jesus outlives both Elijah, the representative of the prophets, and Moses, the personification of the Jewish Law. Of the three who appear together on the Mount—Jesus, Elijah, and Moses—only Jesus remains at the end. The prophetic forerunner has finished his work, and the Law has been superseded. Luke states that the Law and the Prophets, the key scriptures for the Jews, existed only until John (Luke 16:16). The message is: John the Baptist may well have been considered by his followers as the greatest of the prophets, but for the Christians he is the last in the old dispensation. For them John has a unique role as the forerunner, but once Jesus arrives, John's work is over; Jesus starts the new covenant. With him Christianity is born.

LEFT: A DESOLATE ENVIRONMENT AND A HUMBLE CONTEMPLATIVE MAN ARE THE KEY ELEMENTS IN THIS POIGNANT AND TOUCHING PORTRAYAL OF CHRIST IN *THE TEMPTATION IN THE WILDERNESS* BY BRITON RIVIERE.

for them the significance of the act was imbued with theological teachings, as Paul was to make clear in his letter to the Romans. But also, Christians baptized because they were obeying the risen Christ's final words found in Matthew's post-Easter story, when he commands his followers to "make disciples of all nations, baptizing them in the name of the Father and of the Son and of the Holy Spirit" (Matthew 28:19). Partly also, early Christianity would have embraced baptism as its rite of initiation, because in at least John's Gospel we learn that Jesus, like John, was also a Baptist (John 3:22); as the ones following in his footsteps, Christians too wished to be baptizers.

JESUS' TEMPTATIONS

Immediately after his baptism, Jesus retreats alone into the wilderness, where he is "tempted" for a 40-day period. Mark's Gospel does not try to describe what the temptations were but Matthew and Luke offer three samples of what Jesus must have gone through as he assessed his coming role and destiny (Matthew 4:1–11, Luke 4:1–13). For them the temptation to satisfy his own needs, to employ cheap tricks to gain an audience, and to deviate from following God are doubtless pedagogic messages directed at the readers of the Gospel, but they also serve to show that Jesus was indeed very probably meditating on matters such as those, and he was likely to have undertaken a time of contemplation as he planned his ministry.

The 40-day period for these temptations was clearly intended to recall the 40-year sojourn of the people of Israel, also in the wilderness, prior to their entering the Promised Land. Jesus in the New Testament was about to inaugurate the new Kingdom. The story was not intended to be only an historic record but a theological statement. Jesus' baptism was, above all, a rite of passage for him just as, later, his followers made it the initiation ceremony for Christians as they were entering into a new life.

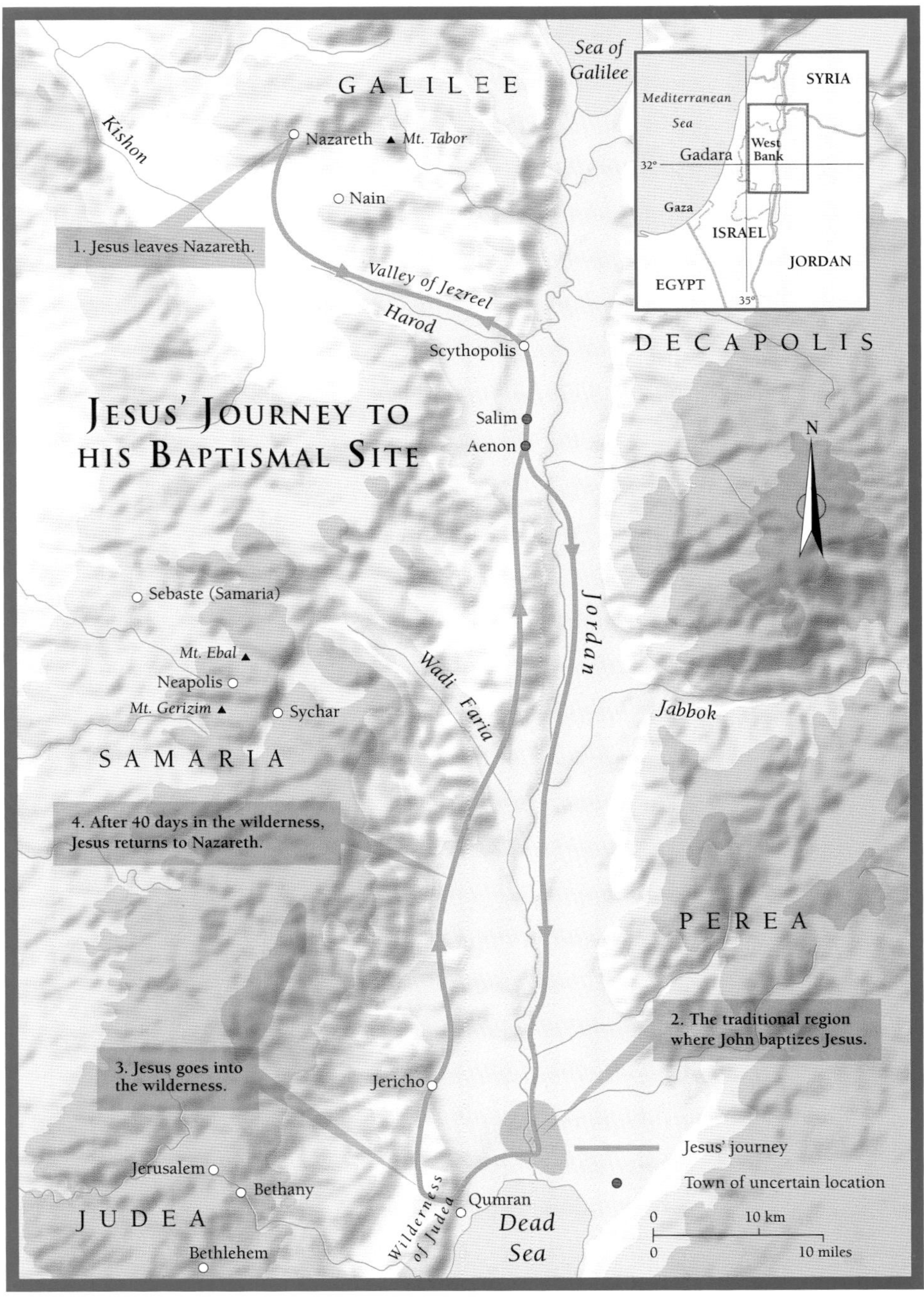

THE MINISTRY OF JESUS

GALILEE OF THE GENTILES—THE PEOPLE WHO SAT IN DARKNESS HAVE SEEN A GREAT LIGHT MATTHEW 4:15

Unlike Bethlehem—a place pregnant with symbolism and history as the City of David—Nazareth in Galilee was free from such associations. It is not even mentioned in the Old Testament. The Gospels say it was Jesus' childhood hometown and Jesus is regularly known as Jesus of Nazareth. Galilee (one of the four administrative districts of Roman Palestine) had a reputation for being more liberal than Jerusalem. Hellenism took root more easily there than in Judea. There was a significant cosmopolitan atmosphere.

JESUS' MINISTRY IN GALILEE

Although much of Jesus' early ministry was concentrated in Galilee, there are very few accounts of his contact with foreigners or Roman officials. Only occasionally did he stray outside its borders, to the Decapolis or to Tyre and Sidon. His milieu was that of the synagogue and his fellow Galilean Jews. The Gospel of John records that Jesus made several visits to Jerusalem, usually for Jewish festivals (e.g., John 2:13; 5:1; 10:22); the other Gospels record only one journey to Jerusalem—Jesus' final and fateful visit.

"Can anything good come out of Nazareth" is a jibe made by Nathanael (John 1:45–46). For the Christians of course this was ironic—their Lord was Jesus from Nazareth. The term "Galilee of the nations" (Isaiah 9:1) or "Galilee of the Gentiles" (Matthew 4:15) is used because the universal Christian message sprang from there. Thus it is contrasted with Jerusalem, which is condemned as the place where Jesus died (Matthew 23:37).

Jesus is reported to have been rejected in his hometown (Luke 4:16–30). The townspeople try to kill him. Even his family rejects him, thinking he is mad (Mark 3:21), and his brothers have no faith in him (John 7:5). Perhaps that is why Jesus decided to settle in Capernaum on the Sea of Galilee (Matthew 4:13). There are several references to Jesus "entering his home" there. Nonetheless, in his list of woes in

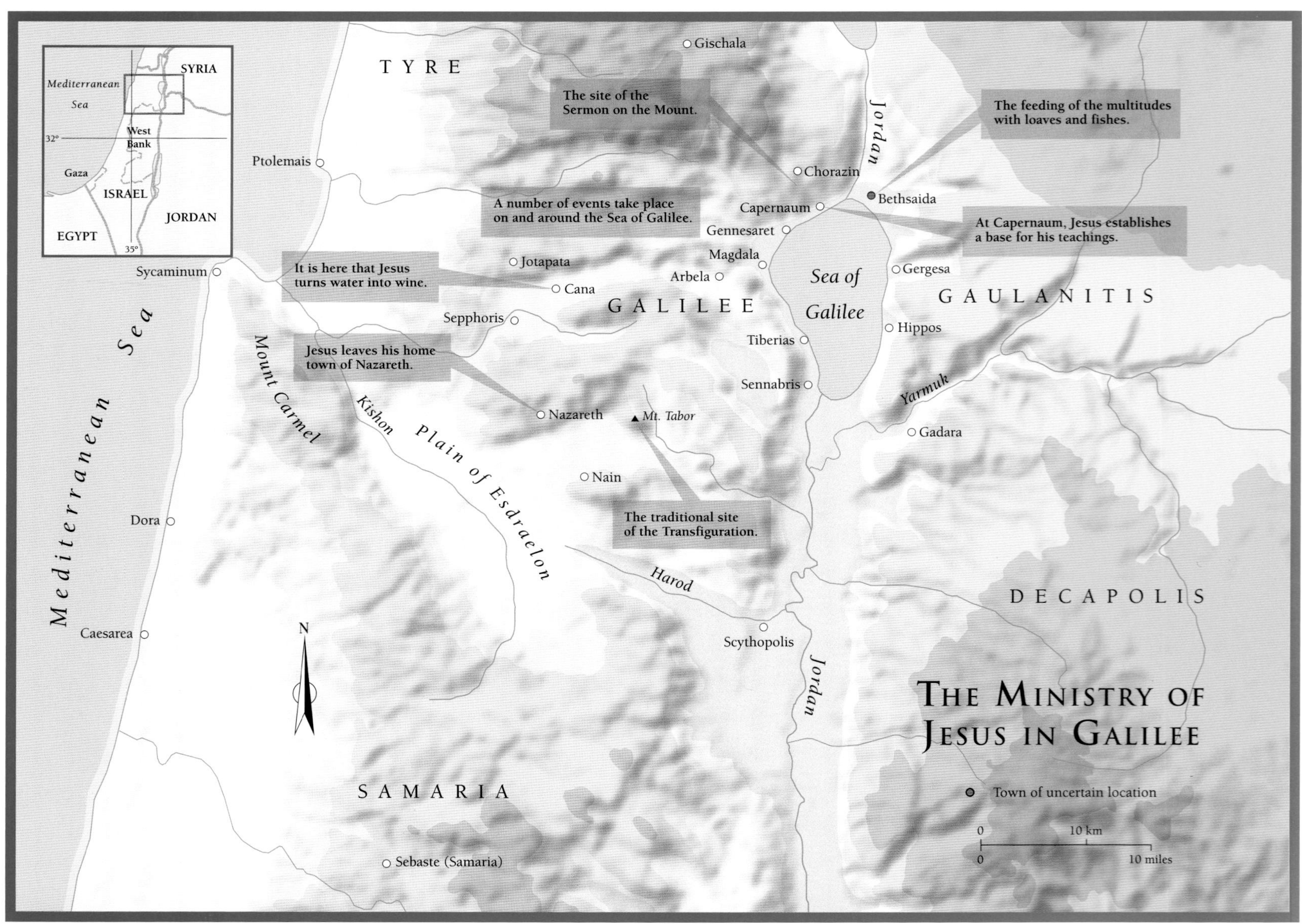

RIGHT: JESUS' BASE FOR HIS MINISTRY—CAPERNAUM—WAS LOCATED ON A MAJOR TRADE ROUTE, AND SERVED AS A CHECKPOINT BETWEEN NEIGHBORING TETRARCHIES.

Matthew 11:23, Capernaum is condemned by Jesus for being even worse than Sodom. Recent excavations have uncovered a synagogue at the site of Capernaum.

Another town in Galilee referred to in the New Testament is Bethsaida. The town was built up by Herod the Great and became a predominantly Gentile city. It was, however, the hometown of three of the disciples (Philip, Peter [also referred to as Simon Peter], and Andrew according to John 1:44; 12:21), and is mentioned several times in the Gospels. Its residents are denounced by Jesus for their unbelief (Matthew 11:21).

WATER TO WINE AT CANA IN GALILEE

The first of Jesus' wondrous works took place at Cana. Several sites have been proposed but the one that seems to fit the context is Khirbet Qana (9 miles [14.5 km] north of Nazareth) and now in ruins. The only Gospel to report this episode is John's (John 2:1–11) where the event is called, characteristically, a "sign," meaning that it is no mere remarkable happening but an event that reveals something about the character and person of Jesus. Seven such signs occur in John's Gospel, and it may be argued that that total is significant because the number seven signifies perfection.

This first sign is intended to show Jesus' divine power. But it could be that the story has symbolic meaning too. Jesus uses water poured into six jars reserved, significantly, for the Jewish rites of purification, and changes it into wine. The wine Jesus produces is said to be superior to the wine previously served during the wedding feast. He brings new wine (his message) that requires a new (religious) container; it cannot be contained in the old wineskins of Judaism (see Mark 2:22).

The joy of the End Time is characterized by a superfluity of wine in Amos 9:13–14; Jeremiah 31:12. For Jewish readers familiar with the Old Testament, such allusions would be significant. Also, Elijah's supplying of meal and oil in 1 Kings 17:1–16, or his successor Elisha's parallel supplying of oil in 2 Kings 4:1–7, would be remembered. In those stories the event served to satisfy an unexpected need, as in the Cana story. For John's Gentile audience, stories about Dionysius transforming water into wine (as in *Bacchae* by Euripides) would doubtless be recalled. The symbolism of the event in Cana would not be lost on the readers.

The Cana story introduces Jesus' mother. This is her only appearance in John's Gospel until she stands at the foot of Jesus' cross (John 19:25–27). Her role in the Cana story is ambiguous. Jesus does not instantly react to the lack of wine to which she draws attention—he does not address the situation at her behest. When he responds to the need she has identified, it is in his own way and his own time, to indicate that the "sign" he is to perform is an anticipation of his own death, his "hour," and his resurrection (see John 7:30; 8:20). For Christians that is the ultimate sign, and one anticipated here from the beginning of Jesus' ministry.

LEFT: SEVENTEENTH-CENTURY BOHEMIAN CARVING DEPICTING THE WEDDING AT CANA. INSUFFICIENT WINE WAS PROVIDED BY THE HOST FOR THE CELEBRATION, AND JESUS WAS CALLED UPON TO TRANSFORM WATER INTO WINE.

ABOVE: TWO FISHERMEN BASED AT CAPERNAUM—ANDREW AND SIMON PETER—WERE JESUS' FIRST DISCIPLES, AS SEEN HERE IN *THE CALLING OF ANDREW AND SIMON PETER*, A FRESCO BY ITALIAN PAINTER GIUSTO DE MENABUOI.

THE CALLING OF THE DISCIPLES

The accounts of the call of the earliest followers (Matthew 4:18–22) are obviously not just intended to be historical, because the readers of the Gospels are also summoned to follow Christ. The responses to Jesus' summons are meant to be exemplary. In John, as in the other Gospels, the first two to answer Jesus' call are Andrew and Simon Peter. In John alone we are informed that these two had previously been disciples of John the Baptist. It is not surprising that they are described as transferring their allegiance to the inaugurator of the new dispensation. Again, the evangelist's motive is one of encouragement. John then goes on to tell of the call of Philip and Nathanael (John 1:35–51). The other Gospels tell of the commissioning of James and John. There are also stories of subsequent calls—Matthew tells of the tax collector (Matthew 9:9), and Mark has the call of Levi (Mark 2:14).

THE MISSION OF THE DISCIPLES

Jesus tells the disciples: "I will make you fish for people" (Matthew 4:19, Mark 1:17). Despite the negative meaning of this expression, implying a deceitful entrapment of people for hostile intent, the context (the calling of Andrew and Simon Peter to be Jesus' disciples) makes it clear that the purpose of the call is for them to abandon their erstwhile profession as fishermen for a greater outreach to attract mankind to Jesus.

References to fish and fishing, as well as stories involving an incredible catch of fish (Luke 5:1–11; John 21:4–14) are inevitable in narratives that originated in Galilee where fish was a staple foodstuff of the local community.

RIGHT: FROM *EVERYDAY LIFE IN THE HOLY LAND* BY JAMES CLARK. FISHING WAS A SIGNIFICANT INDUSTRY AROUND THE SEA OF GALILEE, WITH FISH BEING A MAJOR DIETARY STAPLE IN BIBLICAL TIMES.

In Matthew, there is a parable telling that the Kingdom of Heaven is like a net cast into the sea. The fish caught are judged and divided, the rejects are cast into a great fire, when there will be weeping and gnashing of teeth (Matthew 13:47–50). This uncompromising message, similar to John the Baptist's condemnatory speech (Matthew 3:10–12), is eschatological. So here too, the command to "fish for people" (Matthew 4:19) carries with it a message about the looming End Time—the disciples are to prepare people for the final judgment. The scriptural background of so much in Jesus' teaching and the New Testament makes it likely that Jeremiah's judgment on Judah: "I am now sending for many fishermen says the Lord and they shall catch them (law-breakers)" (Jeremiah 16:16), lies behind the imagery here. The disciples are primarily charged with such a mission. Later Christian iconography used the image of the fisherman as a symbol for baptism, the initiatory rite for converts to Christianity, and that is consistent with the imagery used here as Jesus commissions his first disciples to make converts to Christ.

SERMON ON THE MOUNT

Much in the Gospels' accounts of Jesus' ministry concerns teaching. Some teaching occurs in an isolated verse; sometimes it is found at the end of a story of an inspirational act. Occasionally it occurs in a longer passage such as a parable or a sermon like the passage on inner cleanliness in Mark 7. There are long sections on the future doom (Matthew 24; Mark 13; Luke 21); John 14–17 is an extended farewell discourse. One of the most significant collections of teaching by Jesus occurs in the Sermon on the Mount in Matthew's Gospel (Matthew 5–7). There is a comparable narrative in Luke—a Sermon on the Plain (Luke 6:17–49).

Matthew's great sermon is set up a mountain; that seems especially significant. It is in his Gospel that Jesus is the "one called out of Egypt" (see Matthew 2:15), thus making Jesus parallel to Moses. And, like Moses descending from Mt. Sinai with the tablets of stone containing the Ten Commandments, Jesus' great sermon begins with a Christian counterpart, namely the Beatitudes (Matthew 5:3–12). Matthew's sermon then goes on to have Jesus reinterpret the Jewish Law. By quoting several of the precepts from the Ten Commandments, Jesus uses his own authority to press home their fundamental meaning. It will be seen that Jesus' interpretation is noticeably rigorous and uncompromising. For Matthew's Christian readership, the teachings of Jesus are not the mere pronouncements of an ordinary rabbi—they are the words of the man who is their universal risen savior. They know that the words they report from his ministry are the teachings of the man who is to be raised from the dead.

The sermon also contains shorter sayings on topics as diverse as almsgiving, fasting, anxiety about the future, passing judgment, God, and mammon and the nature of true treasures. Jesus also teaches on prayer, and introduces the Lord's Prayer. Much of his teaching here, as elsewhere, is made up of pithy epigrams, memorable, even humorous sometimes; some teaching is also poetic and designed to be readily memorized.

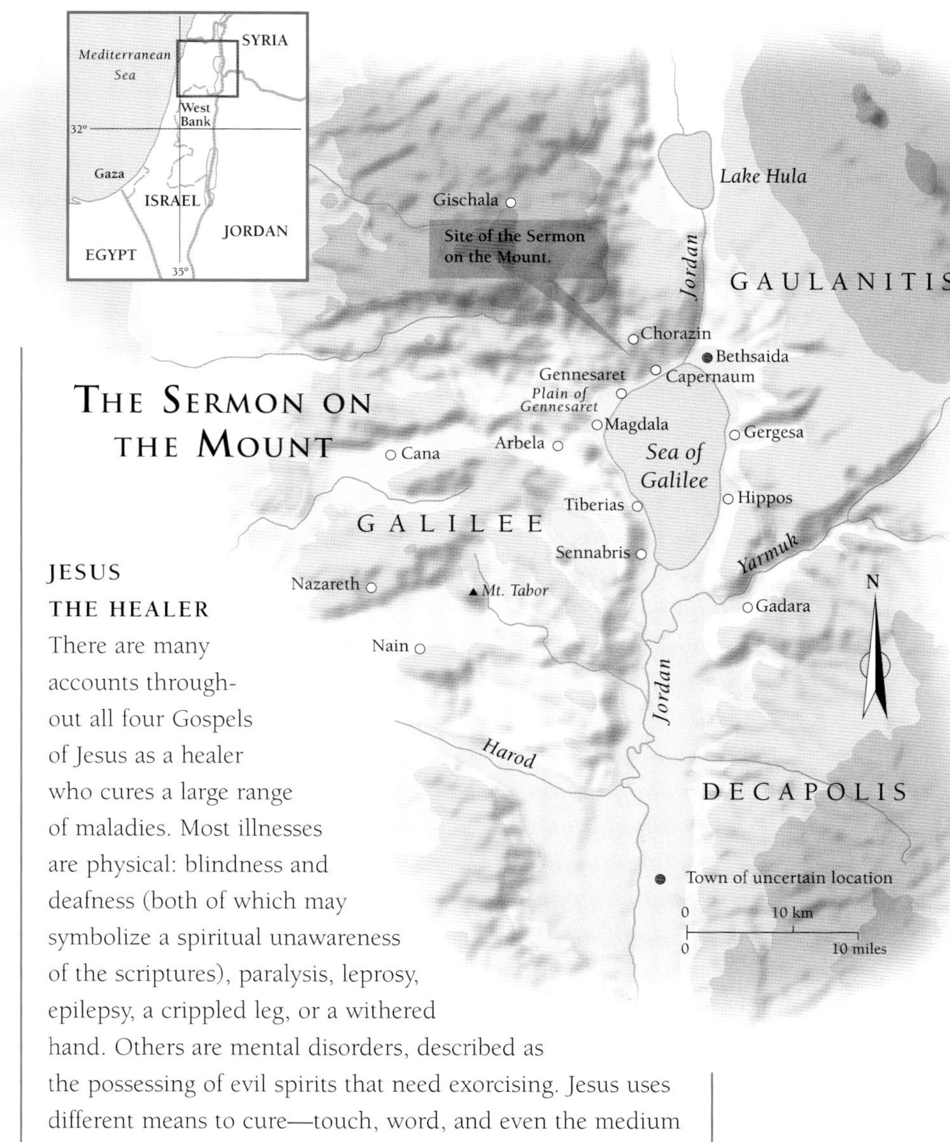

JESUS THE HEALER

There are many accounts throughout all four Gospels of Jesus as a healer who cures a large range of maladies. Most illnesses are physical: blindness and deafness (both of which may symbolize a spiritual unawareness of the scriptures), paralysis, leprosy, epilepsy, a crippled leg, or a withered hand. Others are mental disorders, described as the possessing of evil spirits that need exorcising. Jesus uses different means to cure—touch, word, and even the medium of spittle. The cures are always efficacious, although in one

LEFT: THIS FRESCO BY FRA ANGELICO DEPICTS THE SERMON ON THE MOUNT, WHEN JESUS GAVE HIS MOST FAMOUS SERMON—A MORAL CODE BY WHICH TO LIVE IN RIGHTEOUSNESS.

RIGHT: THIS PLATE FROM WILLIAM HOLE'S *THE LIFE OF JESUS* SHOWS JESUS HEALING A LEPER. QUITE A COMMON DISEASE AT THE TIME, LEPROSY SUFFERERS WERE CONSIDERED "UNCLEAN" AND WERE SHUNNED BY SOCIETY.

BELOW: *THE SWINE DRIVEN INTO THE SEA* BY JAMES JACQUES JOSEPH TISSOT. JESUS' EMPATHY FOR THE DEMONIACS REINFORCES HIS WORDS—THAT IT IS NOT THE RIGHTEOUS, BUT THE SINNERS, THAT HE HAS COME TO SAVE.

case the remedy is at first only partially successful (Mark 8:22–26). Usually Jesus responds to requests for a cure by seeing a demonstration of faith either by the sufferer or by the parent or friend of the sick person. Occasionally the healing is performed at a distance. In one case, a cure is effected without Jesus' prior knowledge (Mark 5:25–34).

There is no healing if there is no faith. Thus in Nazareth, after Jesus had been rejected, he "could do no deed of power there" (Mark 6:5). For the Christian evangelists all the cures effected by Jesus are equivalent to his casting out evil, it being commonly believed that those suffering were afflicted because of their own, or their parents' sins. The healing stories in the New Testament are thus, in effect, a forgiving of sin.

JESUS HEALS A PARALYZED MAN

The healing of a paralyzed man (Mark 2:3–12) is a good example of a story in which Jesus the healer is portrayed as the one who, in introducing the Kingdom of God by removing sins, is thereby reversing the age-old cycle of suffering, sin, and death that had started at the Fall. Jesus' pronouncing that the man's sins are removed is tantamount to his curing him. In this story, Jesus recognizes the faith of the four stretcher-bearers (and, presumably, the paralytic himself). In Mark and in Luke (Luke 5:18–26), the men gain access to Jesus, trapped by throngs surrounding him in the middle of a house, by uncovering the roof of the room where he is and lowering the stretcher through the gap they make. That ingenuity is interpreted as their faith. The objection that the words of forgiveness alone do not give the visible proof of the cure that the crowd needs in order to test Jesus' authority causes him to command the man to rise from his bed before their very eyes.

THE HEALING OF THE LEPER

Among the groups and individuals that Jesus seems to have made deliberate attempts to approach are those outside normal society such as tax collectors and sinners. To justify this, he claims (Matthew 9:12–13) that he has come to call sinners; the righteous do not need a physician. His contact with lepers is of the same type. In the story of the leper (Matthew 8:2–4), the sufferer beseeches Jesus to cure him. The man is aware of Jesus' authority. In agreeing to do so, Jesus touches the man, thereby making himself unclean. Leviticus 13–14 brands leprosy, whatever that term would have then implied, as ritually impure. Jesus then commands the man to go to the Temple and make the required sacrifice as an offering of thanks. Jesus' attitude to Jewish ceremony and to the institution of the Temple portrays him here as a loyal observant Jew. By asking the man to make this public affirmation of his cure, Jesus knows that this will guarantee the man's reacceptance into Jewish society.

JESUS HEALS TWO DEMONIAC MEN

This strange exorcism story of a demon-possessed man occurs with much elaborate detail in Mark 5:2–20. In Matthew 8:28–34, the account is shorter but instead of one demoniac we have two, who act and speak in unison. The incident takes place in Gentile territory insofar as the expelled demons are sent by Jesus into pigs who rush over a cliff to be drowned in the sea. The episode is said to take place in Gadara. Some manuscripts say instead it is in the land of the Gerasenes and yet others have the land of the Gergesenes. The reason for this textual uncertainty is that the place must fit the requirements of the story that the locality is near the Sea of Galilee. Gerasa and Gadara are too far away, so Gergesa was proposed. In Mark's account, Jesus then tells the exorcised man to "Go home to your friends, and tell them how much the Lord has done for you, and what mercy he has shown you" (Mark 5:19). The use of the name "Lord" here is especially significant—either Jesus is, uncharacteristically, referring to himself by the title commonly used of God in the Old Testament, or is drawing attention to what God himself has done through Jesus. Either way, Mark emphasizes the divine nature and origin of the healing.

THE 12 DISCIPLES

The significance of Jesus' having 12 close followers is obvious—the number recalls the 12 tribes of Israel. Jesus set out to inaugurate a new Kingdom, and, like Moses, is leading the whole nation with him. This analogy is made within the Gospels when Jesus tells his 12 disciples that they will "sit on twelve thrones, judging the twelve tribes of Israel" (Matthew 19:28). The 12 disciples are also called apostles, especially by Luke. This is a title applied more widely to cover early church missionaries like Paul, because all are sent out (which is what *apostello* means) to serve as Jesus' envoys. The mission charge to the 12 occurs at Luke 9:1–6, where the disciples are sent out to preach, to heal, and to exercise some of Jesus' functions during his lifetime and beyond.

Among the 12 disciples are Simon the Zealot (meaning a fanatical nationalist), according to Luke 6:15 and Acts 1:13; James and John, the two "sons of thunder"—which sounds like a *nom de guerre*; and Judas Iscariot (a name that may be translated as "assassin"). On the basis of these sobriquets, the 12 disciples are seemingly not as pacific a group as church tradition has sometimes implied.

Before Jesus' arrest and death, when the 12 desert him and escape, the prophecy "for it is written, 'I will strike the shepherd, and the sheep of the flock will be scattered'" is pointed to in Matthew 26:31. However, the group reassembled after Easter, and formed the nucleus of the Jerusalem-based church that exercised a successful missionary activity, related in the Acts of the Apostles.

ABOVE: *CHRIST WITH THE APOSTLES* BY JAMES JACQUES JOSEPH TISSOT. THE 12 CHOSEN DISCIPLES OF JESUS ARE ENTRUSTED WITH SPREADING HIS MESSAGE—BEFORE AND AFTER HIS DEATH.

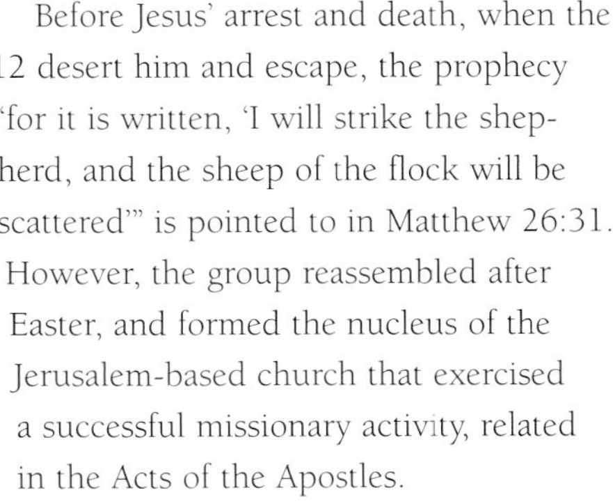

LEFT: THE 12 APOSTLES SEEN HERE ARE CARVED IN GRANITE, FORMING PART OF AN EIGHTH-CENTURY CELTIC CROSS—THE MOONE HIGH CROSS—FOUND IN IRELAND IN THE NINETEENTH CENTURY.

RIGHT: THE SIXTH-CENTURY CATHEDRA (THRONE) OF MAXIMIAN IS ONE OF THE GREATEST IVORY WORKS IN EXISTENCE. THIS PANEL OF THE THRONE DEPICTS JESUS AND A SAMARITAN WOMAN MEETING AT A WELL.

PARABLES

One of the most characteristic and alluring features of Jesus' teaching is the profusion of homely analogies or metaphors and folk tales that he uses, typically to explain the nature of the Kingdom of Heaven or God's character. These parables, as they are described, are found in the Gospels of Matthew, Mark, and Luke. Many are popular vignettes of religious writing and, as such, they have entered our literature (and three are depicted in Sir John Everett Millais's work below). Some are short sayings such as the Parable of the Mustard Seed (Matthew 13:31–32), the Parable of the Leaven (Matthew 13:33), or the Pearl of Great Value (Matthew 13:45–46)—others are lengthier. Stories like the Parable of the Good Samaritan or the Parable of the Prodigal Son are well known. Others among the nearly 40 parables in the New Testament include the parables of the Talents, the Wicked Tenants, and the Ten Maidens. Jesus' penchant for using this teaching method is, according to Matthew 13:35, another example of his career fulfilling a divinely orchestrated path—here in fulfillment of Psalm 78:2. He uses only parables when addressing "the crowds."

The difficult saying in Mark 4:10–12 seems to imply that only insiders are able to really perceive and understand the true underlying meaning of his parables—for the *hoi polloi* the stories remain on the level of parable. In practice, as a popular and engaging speaker, Jesus must have found that his broadly based audiences could all learn something from his analogies drawn from everyday life and experience.

The evangelists, like Jesus himself, obviously used parables with the intention that their hearers ponder and reflect upon the hidden religious meaning behind the simple tales.

Usually parables are left without interpretation, but Luke 18:1 opens with the words: "Then Jesus told them a parable about their need to pray always and not to lose heart."

Generally, it is wrong or unnecessary to allegorize Jesus' parables but one—The Sower—is interpreted to the disciples and other companions (Mark 4:3–20) as if it were an allegory. Parallels between the different soils of the parable, and the different responses to the Christian message, are drawn.

THE DISCOURSE BETWEEN JESUS AND THE SAMARITAN WOMAN AT THE WELL

Among the significant groups targeted by Jesus and later by the church are women, Samaritans, the Jewish establishment, and the followers of John the Baptist. The Samaritans were not accepted as true Jews and hence were ostracized by the Jerusalem establishment.

The discussion between Jesus and a Samaritan woman at Jacob's well (John 4) combines two of those targets at once. This woman's receptiveness to Jesus' teaching enables her immediately to cause many of her countrymen to become believers. The main discussion hinges on the woman's accepting that Jesus is able to provide the water of eternal life, like that in Isaiah 12:3, 55:1, and Zechariah 14:8.

The regular motif in the New Testament, comparing Jesus and his movement with Moses and the Israelites in the wilderness, surfaces yet again here as readers of John's account would recall the giving of water by the Lord through Moses at Exodus 17 and Numbers 21:16. Jesus' superiority to the Jewish patriarch, Jacob, is also apparent in the story, as the water provided by Jesus is superior to the water extracted from Jacob's well.

John 3 contains a comparable long dialog between Jesus and another representative of a target group—Nicodemus from the Sanhedrin. This learned Pharisee is at first unable to understand what Jesus means by his requirement that believers must be reborn through the Spirit, but later on (John 7:50; 19:39) Nicodemus is gradually enlightened.

THE LOAVES AND THE FISHES

All four Gospels tell of an incredible feeding in which Jesus distributes a small quantity of bread and fish among a huge crowd—5,000 people in one account and 4,000 in another (Mark 6:34–44; 8:1–19). It is significant that in John's Gospel the story leads into a discussion of the Eucharist (John 6), and the whole of that chapter becomes in effect a meditation on the significance of this new rite instituted by Jesus. As there is no account of the Institution of the Last Supper in the upper room in John's Gospel, this story serves as its replacement. The feedings not only fully satisfy the participants, but there is ample food left over for others in the future. That is clearly one of the theological messages behind the narratives; the numbers used are also important to the writer, especially in Mark 8:19–20, where the two separate feedings with their differing numbers are pointed to in order to show that there are symbolic interpretations behind both. The Passover, which is clearly present in the accounts of the Last Supper, is also alluded to in the great feedings. The green grass of Mark's story of the 5,000 tells us it is spring, the season of Passover. John 6 refers to the story of the manna from the Exodus narrative.

In the great feedings, Jesus provides sustenance in the wilderness, just as God did through Moses in the Old Testament when the Israelites were in the wilderness prior to their entering the Promised Land. In addition, the Gospels perhaps also have in mind not just that historic parallel, but a future event: the contemporary and popular belief that at the End Time the Messiah would preside over a banquet. Certainly John's Gospel is alert to the eschatological significance

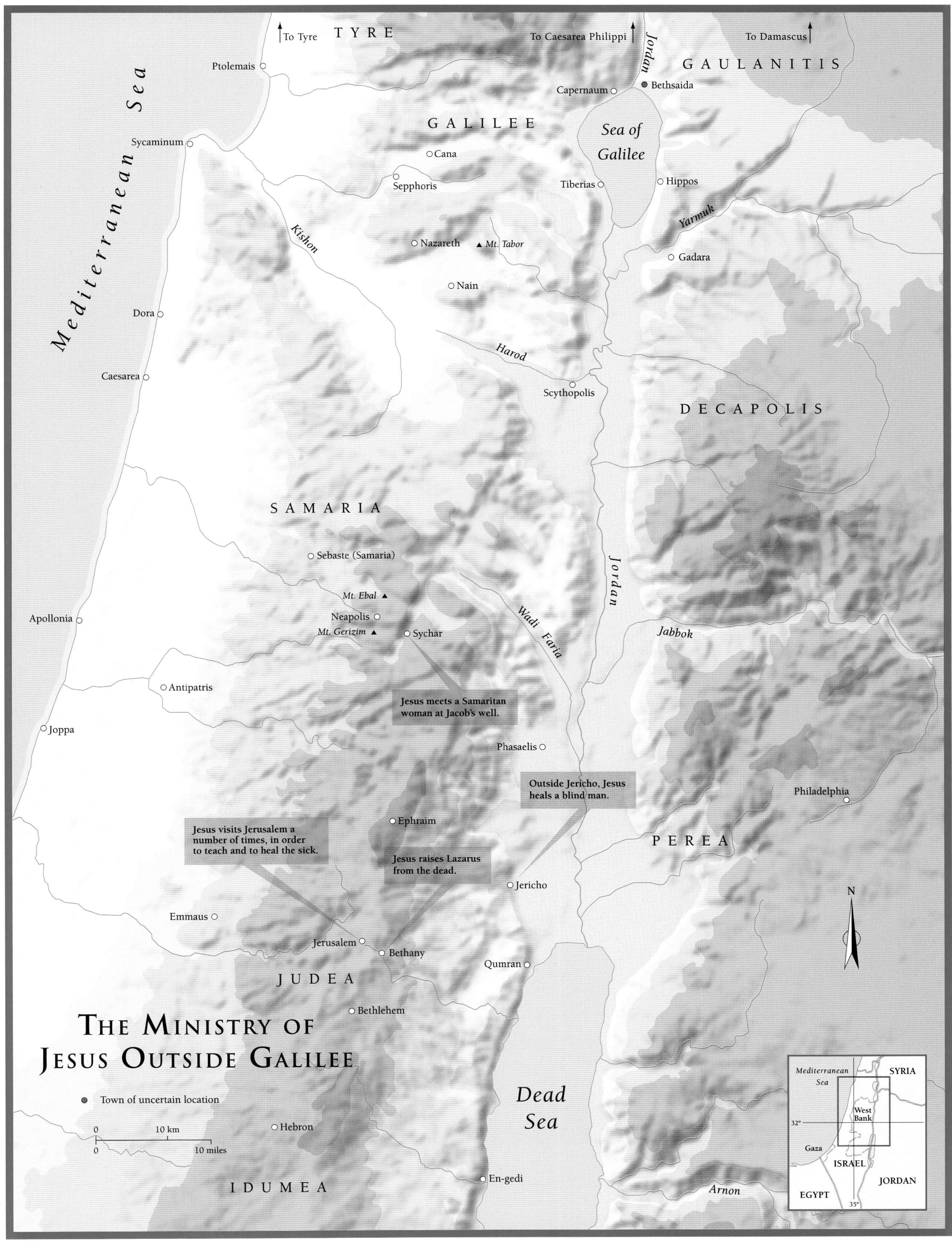

To Tyre
TYRE
To Caesarea Philippi
Jordan
To Damascus
GAULANITIS
Ptolemais
Mediterranean Sea
Capernaum
Bethsaida
GALILEE
Sea of Galilee
Sycaminum
Cana
Sepphoris
Tiberias
Hippos
Yarmuk
Kishon
Nazareth
Mt. Tabor
Gadara
Nain
Dora
Harod
Caesarea
Scythopolis
DECAPOLIS
SAMARIA
Sebaste (Samaria)
Jordan
Mt. Ebal
Wadi Faria
Neapolis
Apollonia
Mt. Gerizim
Sychar
Jabbok
Antipatris
Jesus meets a Samaritan woman at Jacob's well.
Joppa
Phasaelis
Outside Jericho, Jesus heals a blind man.
Philadelphia
Jesus visits Jerusalem a number of times, in order to teach and to heal the sick.
Ephraim
PEREA
Jesus raises Lazarus from the dead.
Jericho
N
Emmaus
Jerusalem
Bethany
Qumran
JUDEA
Bethlehem
THE MINISTRY OF JESUS OUTSIDE GALILEE
Town of uncertain location
Dead Sea
0
10 km
0
10 miles
Hebron
IDUMEA
En-gedi
Arnon
Mediterranean Sea
SYRIA
West Bank
32°
Gaza
ISRAEL
JORDAN
EGYPT
35°

of participating in the Eucharist: "those who eat my flesh and drink my blood have eternal life" (John 6:54). For John, Jesus is the "bread of life" (John 6:48), just as elsewhere he is also the Way, the Truth, and the Life.

LEFT: *THE FEEDING OF THE FIVE THOUSAND* BY JOACHIM PATENIER. THIS SWEEPING PANORAMA CAPTURES THE MAGNITUDE OF THE OCCASION WHEN JESUS PROVIDES FOR HIS FOLLOWERS.

JESUS WALKS ON WATER

Just as Jesus provides sustenance in a way similar to God's distribution of the manna, the episode of Jesus' walking on water shows his divinity (Matthew 14:25–27, Mark 6:48–52). God the Creator in the Old Testament exercises authority over the waters, as is frequently to be seen, for example in Exodus 14:10–15:21, Psalm 107:23–32, and Jonah 1:1–16. Here, Jesus has mastery over natural elements by his word, using the phrase "it is I" to describe himself (Matthew 14:27; Mark 6:50). That term is found elsewhere (such as John 8:24, 28, 13:19, and also probably 6:20; 18:5–6, 8). It is a title that is a euphemism for God, recalling Exodus 3:14, Deuteronomy 32:39, and Isaiah 43:10; 52:6. The two episodes, the Feeding of the Five Thousand and the Walking on the Water, are significantly linked. The disciples do not understand the significance of the great feeding; thus it is not surprising that they are "astonished" by the other manifestation of Jesus' powers. In Matthew's account, Jesus' walk on the water is contrasted with Peter's inability to walk on the water without faltering, due to a lack of faith.

ABOVE: CHRIST TAKES ON AN ETHEREAL APPEARANCE IN THIS WORK BY TISSOT PORTRAYING CHRIST WALKING ON WATER, FROM HIS SERIES OF ILLUSTRATIONS TITLED *THE LIFE OF CHRIST*.

JESUS CALMS A STORM

There are parallels between this story in Matthew 8:23–27 or Mark 4:35–41 and the account of Jesus' Walking on the Water. This time though, Jesus is with the disciples in the boat. He is asleep on a cushion in the stern, according to Mark—he is oblivious of the storm, such is his faith in God. Significantly, the frightened disciples, who do not share his faith, ask him to help them using the words "Lord save us." Again, the title "Lord," comparatively rare in the Gospels, seems to be an address to Jesus in recognition of his divine status. It is comparable to the Aramaic formula, *Marana tha* ("Come, Lord!"), found at the end of 1 Corinthians and apparently used even in Greek-speaking Christian communities from the earliest times in recognition of him as their savior. Jesus duly calms the storm; the danger is averted. The disciples are saved. Once again, Jesus, like God in the Old Testament, has the authority, ability, and power to subdue the waves. The question asked at the end of the story "What sort of man is this?" (Matthew 8:27) or "Who then is this" (Mark 4:41) is intended by the Gospel-writer to be addressed to his readership, requiring here, as elsewhere, the Christian response recognizing the source of Jesus' power.

ABOVE: *SUFFER THE LITTLE CHILDREN TO COME UNTO ME* BY JUAN URRUCHI. THE UNWAVERING TRUST, BELIEF, AND ACCEPTANCE FOUND IN CHILDREN ARE QUALITIES JESUS SEEKS IN ALL HUMANKIND.

JESUS BLESSES LITTLE CHILDREN

The scene in Mark 10:13–16 and its parallels in Luke and Matthew has Jesus surrounded by small children; he blesses them and proclaims that the Kingdom of God is made up of such as these. It is a living parable, explaining, as Jesus frequently does in the parables themselves, the nature of his Kingdom. The scene needs to be understood alongside Mark 9:36–37 when Jesus, touching a child, says to the 12 disciples: "Whoever welcomes one such child in my name welcomes me." The nature of this new Kingdom requires those seeking entry to be like children or servants, presumably in their humility and receptiveness—earthly rankings are reversed, and hindrances like wealth or family ties must be avoided. The 12, and their successors as church leaders, are therefore given this criterion for accepting converts.

RIGHT: SIXTEENTH-CENTURY OAK CARVING DEPICTING JESUS' TRIUMPHAL ENTRY INTO JERUSALEM. HE IS GREETED BY CROWDS WHO LINE HIS PATH WITH CLOAKS AND WAVE PALM FRONDS IN HIS HONOR.

JESUS COMES TO JERUSALEM

Jesus' final visit to Jerusalem took place on the Sunday preceding his death on Good Friday; this is Palm Sunday in the Christian calendar. A disproportionate amount of the narratives found in the Gospels is concerned with the last week in Jesus' life. A third of Mark's Gospel tells what happens between Jesus' arrival in Jerusalem and Easter Day one week later. This is understandable because the evangelists are determined to describe how and why Jesus died, and the events leading up to his crucifixion. The triumphal entry on Palm Sunday is when Jesus overtly acts out a Messianic prophecy by entering Jerusalem astride a foal. This gesture was readily understood by crowds alert to the prophecy in Zechariah 9:9: they clothed his path with garments, waved palms of victory, and proclaimed him King. Clearly his entry was significant to the populace, and at the time he was seen as a liberator of Israel when he entered Jerusalem, as Cleopas's reported expectations make clear in Luke 24:21.

ANOINTING AT BETHANY

According to the chronology of events in John's Gospel, the event immediately preceding the entry is the Anointing of Jesus in Bethany. This Bethany lies on the southeastern slopes of the Mount of Olives, about 5 miles (8 km) southeast of Jerusalem, and therefore a probable resting place for Jesus prior to his entry to Jerusalem. In Matthew and Mark it also looks as if Jesus made Bethany his headquarters during his final week on earth, returning there even after his triumphal entry; the anointing in those Gospels takes place in Bethany two, not six, days before his death. In these three Gospels, as also in Luke (who puts his anointing story in chapter 7, that is, well away from Bethany and a long time before his last week), the basic story is the same: a woman pours oil on Jesus' body; objections are raised by those present but Jesus explains the woman's motive. In Luke, the scene becomes a typical tale of forgiveness—the woman is a prostitute, but she is forgiven through her act of devotion to Jesus, and the Parable of the Two Debtors accompanies his explanation of her devotion. In the other Gospels, the woman's act is explained as rendering unnecessary the need later to anoint Jesus' dead body, this anointing in Bethany being interpreted prophetically by Jesus as anticipating his burial. Whatever the woman's own motive, onlookers would have seen the act as the moment when Jesus is declared literally to be the Christ (Messiah), which means the "Anointed One."

But as anointing was also closely associated with kingship, doubtless the crowds, hearing that Jesus had allowed himself to be publicly anointed (on the head according to Matthew and Mark), would understand that this was a coronation like that of the ancient Israelite kings. The triumphal entry was then described as if it were a coronation procession, like Jehu's in 2 Kings 9:13. And of course it is as "King of the Jews" that Jesus is to be killed. Earlier in his ministry he avoided such approbation and had prevented any such acknowledgment: at John 6:15, for instance, he escapes from the crowd who wished to "take him by force to make him king"—then the time was not right. Later, in Bethany as he approached Jerusalem for the last time, he was ready to be that Messianic King.

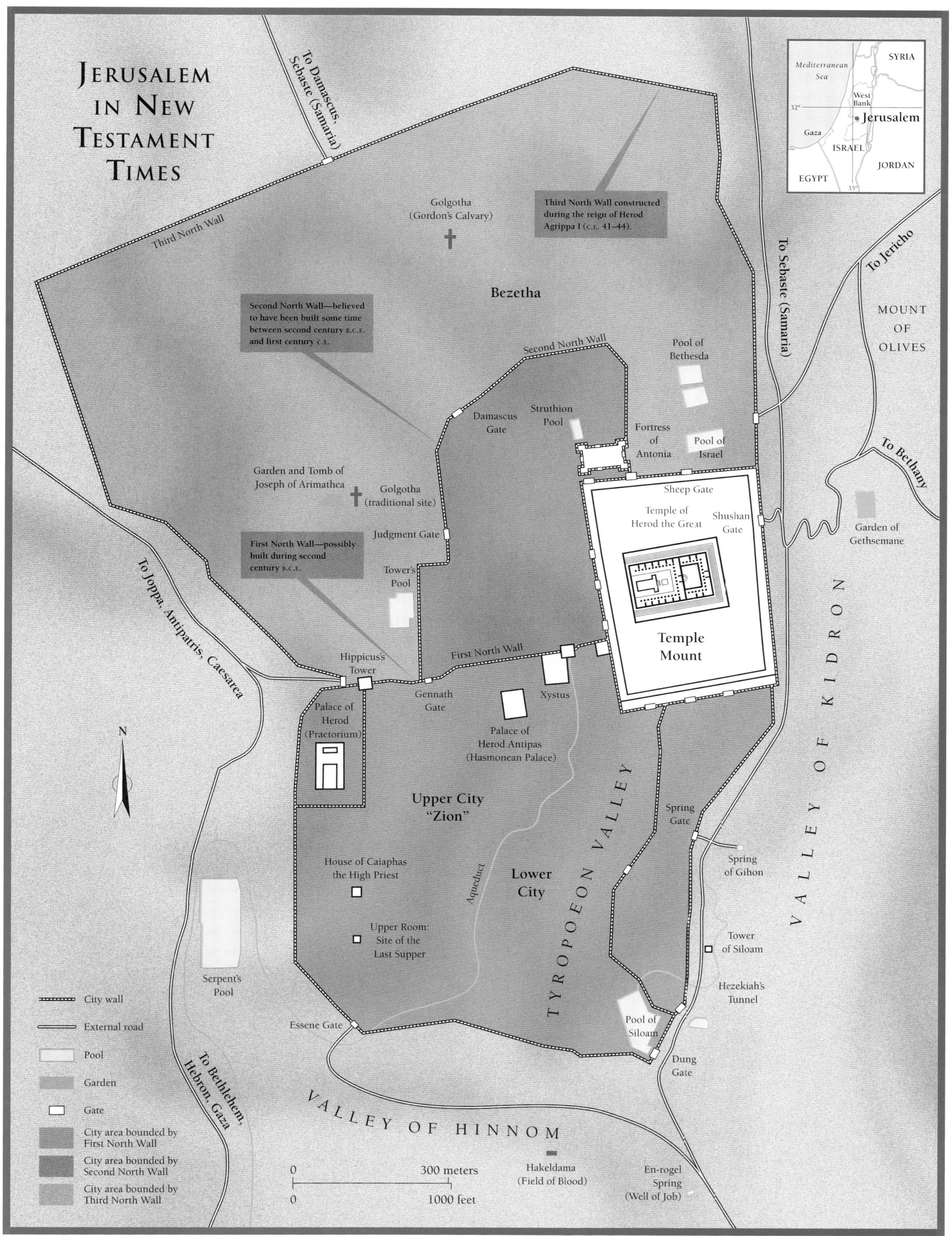

Jerusalem in New Testament Times
To Damascus, Sebaste (Samaria)
Third North Wall
Golgotha (Gordon's Calvary)
Third North Wall constructed during the reign of Herod Agrippa I (C.E. 41–44).
Bezetha
Second North Wall—believed to have been built some time between second century B.C.E. and first century C.E.
Second North Wall
Pool of Bethesda
Damascus Gate
Struthion Pool
Fortress of Antonia
Pool of Israel
Garden and Tomb of Joseph of Arimathea
Golgotha (traditional site)
Sheep Gate
Temple of Herod the Great
Shushan Gate
Judgment Gate
First North Wall—possibly built during second century B.C.E.
Tower's Pool
Temple Mount
First North Wall
Hippicus's Tower
Gennath Gate
Xystus
Palace of Herod (Praetorium)
Palace of Herod Antipas (Hasmonean Palace)
Upper City "Zion"
Tyropoeon Valley
Spring Gate
Spring of Gihon
House of Caiaphas the High Priest
Aqueduct
Lower City
Upper Room: Site of the Last Supper
Tower of Siloam
Serpent's Pool
Hezekiah's Tunnel
Pool of Siloam
Essene Gate
Dung Gate
Valley of Hinnom
Hakeldama (Field of Blood)
En-rogel Spring (Well of Job)
0 300 meters
0 1000 feet
To Joppa, Antipatris, Caesarea
To Bethlehem, Hebron, Gaza
To Sebaste (Samaria)
To Jericho
Mount of Olives
To Bethany
Garden of Gethsemane
Valley of Kidron
N
City wall
External road
Pool
Garden
Gate
City area bounded by First North Wall
City area bounded by Second North Wall
City area bounded by Third North Wall
Mediterranean Sea
SYRIA
West Bank
Jerusalem
Gaza
ISRAEL
JORDAN
EGYPT
32°
35°

RIGHT: *THE RAISING OF LAZARUS* BY LEON JOSEPH FLORENTIN BONNAT. THIS ACT—BRINGING HIS FRIEND BACK FROM THE DEAD—SEALED JESUS' FATE AS THE TEMPLE ELDERS SOUGHT TO BRING HIM DOWN.

THE RAISING OF LAZARUS

This long and convoluted story is peculiar to John's Gospel (11:1–44). It tells of Jesus raising his friend Lazarus from his tomb, and is said by John to be the reason for causing the arrest of Jesus. The incident takes place at Bethany, the venue, later in this Gospel, where Jesus is anointed. Jesus fails to visit the sick Lazarus when he is first informed of his illness. During this delay Lazarus dies, and Jesus hears criticism that, had he not hesitated to visit Lazarus, the death would have been prevented. But Jesus wishes to do more than heal Lazarus; he needs to demonstrate that he has the ability to raise him from the dead because he is "the resurrection and the life" (John 11:25). There is much teaching and symbolism throughout the story, not least the nature of the life that Jesus gives not only here to Lazarus but to all those who are baptized into his name. As such, the story serves as an acted parable or illustration of the Christian's progression from death to life.

This characteristically Johannine account of a raising is comparable in many ways to other stories in which Jesus raises people from the dead (such as the awakening of the young girl in Mark 5:35–43 or the raising of the Widow of Nain's son in Luke 7:11–17). In all of them, Jesus demonstrates his ability to raise the dead here and now—his is no mere promise of a general resurrection at a distant End Time, such as Martha in the Lazarus narrative and many contemporary Jews believed in. With Jesus that End Time is already being inaugurated. (It is worth noting that Matthew dramatizes the belief that the faithful dead will rise as a result of Jesus' death in Matthew 27:52–3.)

THE BEGINNING OF THE LAST WEEK OF JESUS' LIFE

After having triumphantly entered Jerusalem, Jesus embarks on a breathless round of activities and teaching. Most dramatic in Matthew, Mark, and Luke is his overthrowing of the moneychangers' tables in the Temple. That event precipitates plans for his death, and seems to be linked to his prediction (Mark 13:2) that the Temple would be destroyed. Jesus also has conflicts with the authorities over his teaching (Matthew 21:23). He blasts the fig tree; he utters laments over Jerusalem; there are woes over scribes and Pharisees. All these themes of judgment and destruction heighten the tension in the days leading up to Good Friday.

Jesus' teaching includes many parables (the Great Supper, the Two Boys, and others), and there are questions to Jesus about paying taxes to Caesar, his relationship to David, and belief in resurrection. Most noticeable is the extended piece of teaching about the End Time in Matthew 24, Mark 13, and Luke 21. This apocalyptic discourse warns about the events that will announce the Second Coming. Conversely, Jesus also urges caution about misunderstanding disasters that are not eschatological. All of Jesus' teachings about the arrival of God's Kingdom and his actions in Jerusalem hasten the calls for his arrest and death.

BELOW: THIS SECTION OF THE MEDEBA MAP—AN INTRICATE BYZANTINE MOSAIC OF THE HOLY LAND DISCOVERED ON THE FLOOR OF MEDEBA'S CHURCH OF ST. GEORGE—SHOWS JERUSALEM CITY.

OPPOSITE: SUMPTUOUS IN STYLE AND COLOR, JUAN DE JUANES'S MAGNIFICENT WORK, *THE LAST SUPPER*, SHOWS JESUS AND HIS DISCIPLES GATHERED IN JERUSALEM FOR THEIR LAST MEAL TOGETHER.

THE LAST SUPPER

In Mark 14:12–16, Jesus asks his 12 disciples to set in motion the prearranged plan that a Passover meal be made ready in the upper room of a house in Jerusalem. When it is nighttime, they all assemble and celebrate not only the Passover meal, but the last supper that Jesus will share with them. He is aware that his hours are numbered—this is another *memento mori*, showing the reader that Jesus has divine foreknowledge of his fate. After the meal, he distributes the broken bread and the poured wine among the 12 but refuses to eat and drink himself until "that day when I drink it new in the kingdom of God" (Mark 14:25). At that time, he pronounces theologically charged teaching: the wording of the Institution of the Last Supper varies in the four accounts (Matthew 26:26–29; Mark 14:22–25; Luke 22:15–20; 1 Corinthians 11:23–26), but the common denominator is that Jesus links his impending death and resurrection to the participation of his followers in a comparable destiny. The drinking of this wine and the eating of this bread make that link. Paul, in 1 Corinthians 11, makes it plain that the repeating by Christians of the Last Supper is no mere memorial but has contemporary and eschatological significance for them as they await the Second Coming of Christ.

In all the Gospels the proximity of the Passover is underscored and encourages the obvious parallels to be drawn between the "old" Passover of the Jews and the new Passover in which Jesus becomes the paschal lamb (as Paul calls him in 1 Corinthians 5:7). The significance of the salvation and

FOOTWASHING

After the meal in the upper room, John records a footwashing when Jesus washes his disciples' feet (John 13:3–20). This menial task—shown here in a panel from Duccio's *La Maesta* in Siena, Italy—is intended to be another acted parable in which Jesus demonstrates the nature of humility. Several times in the New Testament the role of the self-sacrificing servant is said to be a requirement of Christians as they take up their cross to follow Jesus' example. In addition, with the footwashing, Jesus performs another prophetic action symbolizing his impending death in humiliation for the salvation of others.

ABOVE: TREACHERY AND BETRAYAL MARK JESUS' FINAL WEEK. THIS FIFTEENTH-CENTURY FRESCO SHOWS JUDAS, TEMPTED BY THE OFFER OF 30 PIECES OF SILVER, AGREEING TO LEAD THE ROMAN GUARDS TO JESUS.

rescue of the Jews in the Exodus narrative is now transferred by the Christians to the salvation that they believe came with Christ's sacrificial death. In the changed chronology in John's Gospel, the meal in the upper room takes place one day before the Passover, but John does not lose sight of the symbolism associated with Passover—for him, Jesus now dies at the precise moment when the Jews are slaughtering the lambs in preparation for the forthcoming Passover meal. This too is obviously a significant and comparable theological parallel.

JUDAS

During the Last Supper another prediction made by Jesus is that one of the 12, eating from the common dish, will betray him. He also says that it would have been better for that person had he not been born. Judas is an important pawn in the divinely planned drama that is about to unfold, yet he cannot escape the consequences of the role he must play out. Judas's own motive in fulfilling this role is not clear, although the payment of 30 pieces of silver obviously tempted him (Matthew 26:15). Luke and John give a theological reason for his treachery: Satan has entered Judas (Luke 22:3; John 13:2, 27). After Jesus and his disciples leave the upper room and go to the Mount of Olives, Judas duly leads those seeking Jesus to their quarry, and Jesus is arrested. The inevitable punishment for such treachery is reported in Matthew 27:3–10: Judas, having belatedly regretted his action, commits suicide. Another, and appropriately gory, end to Judas appears in Acts 1:16–20, where his entrails spill out when he dies in the potter's field known as Hakeldama ("Field of Blood"), which had been purchased with the ill-gotten silver. Further polemic against Judas is seen in the Anointing at Bethany in John's Gospel—there the objector to the apparent waste of precious ointment is Judas, described as the 12 disciples' treasurer who pilfered from their common purse (John 12:3–6).

RIGHT: LEADING THE AUTHORITIES TO JESUS IN THE GARDEN OF GETHSEMANE, JUDAS SAYS: "THE ONE I WILL KISS IS THE MAN" (MARK 14:44), AS SEEN IN THIS SIXTEENTH-CENTURY WOOD CARVING.

THE ARREST OF JESUS

After leaving the upper room, Jesus and the disciples made their way to the Mount of Olives. The Gospels of Matthew, Mark, and Luke then place Jesus in the Garden of Gethsemane, separated from his disciples and in prayer to God asking to be released from the ordeal that he, divinely, knows is about to befall him. After praying, Luke 22:43–44 says that Jesus was strengthened and enabled to proceed with his destiny. In some ways that picture of a human Jesus, agonizing about his forthcoming ordeal, is comparable to the parallel period of reflection and self-questioning known as the Temptations, at the beginning of his Ministry.

The sudden arrival of the gang bursting in on that tranquil scene and seeking to arrest Jesus is one of the many dramatic juxtapositions in this narrative. According to the Gospel of John, the party sent to find Jesus was a combined force, comprising a cohort of Roman soldiers plus representatives of the Temple police (John 18:3). The charged political environment and the heightened expectations surrounding Jesus that had accompanied his arrival in Jerusalem obviously alarmed the Roman authorities, who were determined to maintain calm at the busy Passover time; it is not surprising that Romans would be involved in seeking to quell Jesus' activities. The incident in the Temple when Jesus overturned the moneychangers' tables that had also recently happened (in the Gospels of Matthew, Mark, and Luke) would have caused the Jewish authorities also to have been anxious to silence Jesus, and it was inevitable that they too were involved in his arrest, despite the welcoming acclamation of Jesus recently given by the Jewish populace earlier that week.

In order to facilitate the identification of Jesus, Judas was a "guide," as Acts 1:16 summarizes this event. In a poignantly dramatic way, Judas's famous betrayer's kiss is said to have facilitated the arrest according to the Gospels of Matthew, Mark, and Luke.

In John's Gospel, as so often in the Passion, the portrayal of Jesus is somewhat different: John has Jesus in control of the situation (John 18:4–8). There is no kiss; instead Jesus identifies himself twice with the theologically significant words "I am he," anticipating one of Jesus' responses in his trial before the Sanhedrin in Mark 14:62. In John, those who hear this title then fall to the ground in awe (John 18:6). Also, only in John's Gospel, Jesus bargains with his arresters to allow the disciples to escape (John 18:7–8), which is not only a magnanimous gesture, but one that keeps separate the unique fate of Jesus from the destiny of the disciples.

One feature of the arrest common to all four Gospels is the account of a short-lived armed resistance, during which the high priest's servant loses an ear. Simon Peter is named as the swordsman in John 18:10. Jesus condemns this action (and in Luke's Gospel heals the servant)—although armed resistance seems to have been anticipated and prepared for when the disciples and Jesus set off for the Mount of Olives (according to Luke 22:38). Jesus also voices his disapproval that he is arrested by armed police (Matthew 26:55) and is then led away to the High Priest's house.

It is now the appointed time to be arrested. For John's Gospel, where the divine drama has to be fulfilled along predetermined paths, Jesus could not have been arrested earlier in his ministry; previous attempts to capture him had failed on several occasions (John 7:30, 44; 8:20; 10:39), but now the "hour" has arrived.

SIMON PETER DENIES JESUS

Peter is singled out from the 12 for special favor—Jesus tells him (Matthew 16:18–19) that the church will be founded on him, a declaration that has been used to justify the institution of the papacy. Throughout the New Testament, Peter has pride of place, especially as the spokesman of the disciples. But, despite his having been singled out and nicknamed as the rock *(petros)* on which Jesus will found his church, Simon Peter's impulsiveness and lack of comprehension about Jesus' teachings and destiny are prominent through the Gospels. Unlike the idealized but unnamed "beloved disciple" of John's Gospel, Peter, by contrast, is all-too-human a follower. Furthermore, he is even called Satan by Jesus at Mark 8:33. Another low point of his discipleship occurs when he denies his allegiance to Jesus when questioned three times by staff of the High Priest (Matthew 26:69–75). Peter's threefold denial of his being acquainted with Jesus occurs in the courtyard and serves as a counterpoint to his Lord's dignified attitude to his simultaneous questioning in front of the High Priest himself inside the house—such juxtapositions of contrasting stories are characteristic of the Gospels' cinematographic depictions of the last days of Jesus' earthly career. The cock-crowing following the third denial reminds Peter of Jesus' foreknowledge of his denials in an earlier prophecy (John 13:38), and he breaks down in tears. That story of denial has its reversal after Easter, when the risen Jesus confronts Peter—then, according to John 21:15–17, Peter expresses his love for Jesus three times and is thereby rehabilitated. The repetitions here and in other Gospel stories are characteristic of much religious literature; they emphasize the importance of an event—something that occurs twice could be a mere coincidence; a triple occurrence is real and emphatic.

ABOVE: *THE COCK CREW* BY JAMES JACQUES JOSEPH TISSOT. JESUS FORETOLD OF SIMON PETER'S DENIAL—THAT BEFORE THE COCK CROWED, HE WILL DENY JESUS THREE TIMES.

RIGHT: *THE DENIAL OF ST. PETER* BY PENSIONANTE DEL SARACENI. AS JESUS FORETOLD, SIMON PETER DENIES THEIR ASSOCIATION, SAYING "WOMAN, I DO NOT KNOW HIM" (LUKE 22:57).

CRUCIFIXION AND RESURRECTION

HAVING LOVED HIS OWN WHO WERE IN THE WORLD, HE LOVED THEM TO THE END JOHN 13:1

RIGHT: JUDAS IS FILLED WITH REMORSE AFTER HIS BETRAYAL OF JESUS. HE RETURNS THE 30 PIECES OF SILVER AND COMMITS SUICIDE, AS SHOWN IN THIS DETAILED TWELFTH-CENTURY SCULPTURE.

BELOW: *WHAT IS TRUTH?* BY NIKOLAI NIKOLAEVICH GE (GAY). AFTER THE EXCHANGE BETWEEN PILATE AND JESUS, THE ROMAN PROCURATOR ANNOUNCES THAT HE CAN FIND NO CASE AGAINST JESUS.

For centuries the cross has been recognized as the universal symbol of suffering and death. Even those who profess to be non-religious allow it this significance and treat it with respect. For Christians, it is the central reminder of the infinite love of God for humanity, made visible in the life and death of Jesus. As the Gospels of Matthew and Luke echo their Markan source closely, what follows will concentrate on their two accounts and the Gospel of John.

PILATE QUESTIONS JESUS

After Jesus is arrested in Gethsemane, he is taken to Pontius Pilate, procurator of Judea (C.E. 26–36). All four accounts of the trial scene begin with Pilate asking Jesus directly if he is the King of the Jews. In Luke's account, Jesus replies in the affirmative, but in Matthew, Jesus makes no response to any of the accusations.

The conversation as described by John is in two parts (John 18:33–38 and 19:9–11). Jesus accepts the title but only in the sense that his is not an earthly kingdom. His real purpose—"to testify to the truth"—elicits Pilate's famous reply "What is truth?" (John 18:37–38). When Jesus reminds Pilate that whatever power he has is God-given (John 19:11), Pilate is surprisingly accepting and seeks to release him (John 19:12).

THE REPENTANCE AND DEATH OF JUDAS

Despairing at the enormity of his crime, Judas throws back at the chief priests the 30 pieces of silver and goes out and hangs himself (Matthew 27:3–10). Matthew adds his usual "fulfillment prophecy" regarding the bribe and the fact that the field bought by the priests with the blood money is called Hakeldama, the "Field of Blood" (Matthew 27:8).

JESUS IS SENTENCED TO DEATH

Ultimately, Pilate surrenders to the Jews' demands and hands Jesus over to them to be crucified. Essentially the case for the prosecution had no basis and was founded on lies (Luke 23:2). In spite of his cowardly accession to the demands of the crowd, Pilate's own repeated profession of Jesus' innocence supports this claim. So, an innocent and prophetic man is condemned to death out of envy and fear on the part of those in power—they could never have foreseen that their very condemnation ensured his unique place in history as the savior of the world.

THE WAY OF THE CROSS

With the exception of Luke, the Gospels dedicate only one verse to Jesus' actual journey to the place of his crucifixion. The single incident recorded by Matthew is the soldiers' forcing Simon of Cyrene (in modern Libya) to carry Jesus'

TWO SITES FOR GOLGOTHA?

The Way of the Cross route ends at Golgotha. The traditional site (also known as the "Catholic" location) is the ground on which Jerusalem's Church of the Holy Sepulchre currently stands, and there is much hard evidence to support this view. An alternate theory places Golgotha at Gordon's Calvary (known as the "Protestant" location), but this view can only be traced back to the nineteenth century, when General Charles Gordon nominated it as the site of Jesus' crucifixion.

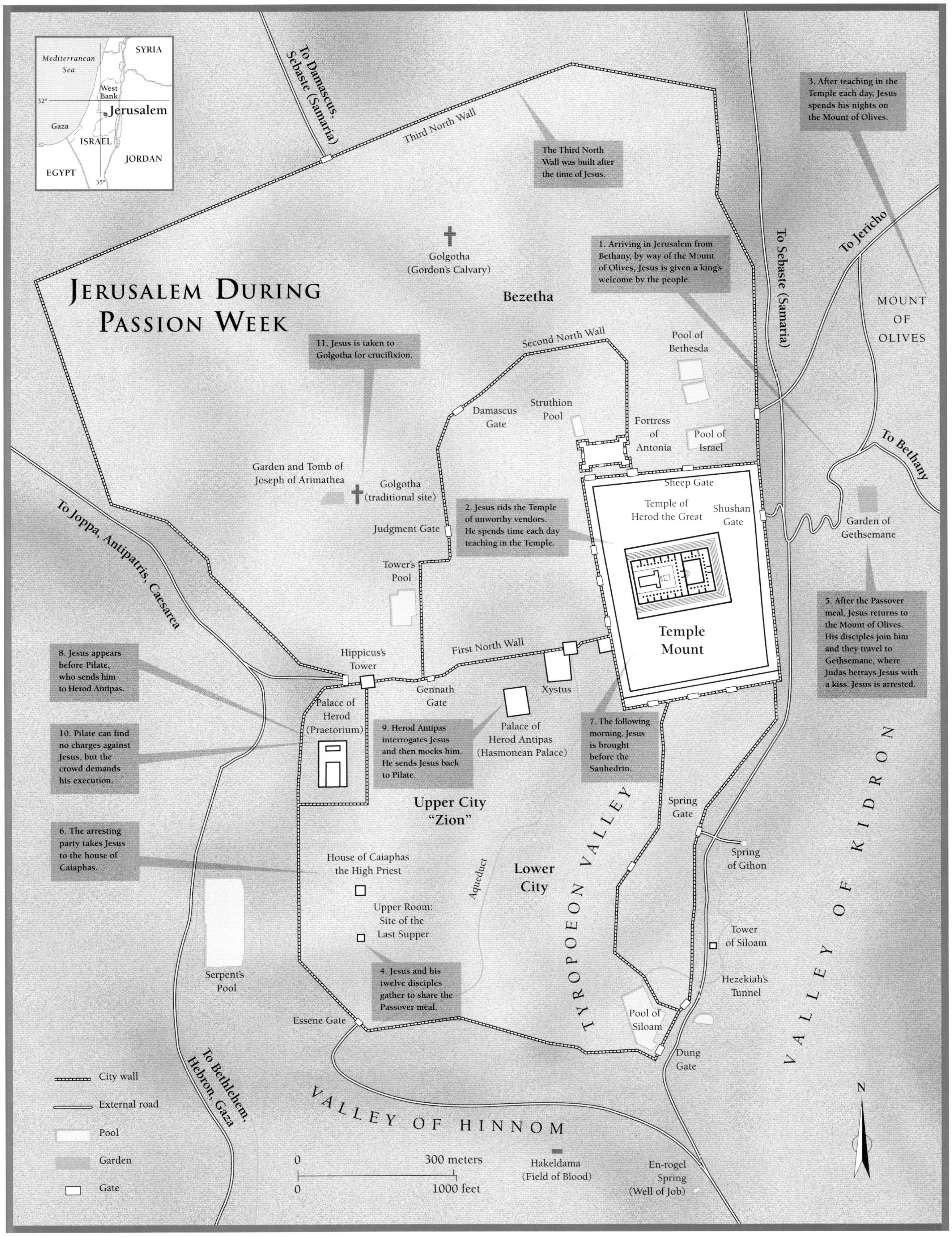

Jerusalem During Passion Week
Mediterranean Sea
SYRIA
West Bank
Jerusalem
Gaza
ISRAEL
JORDAN
EGYPT
To Damascus, Sebaste (Samaria)
Third North Wall
The Third North Wall was built after the time of Jesus.
3. After teaching in the Temple each day, Jesus spends his nights on the Mount of Olives.
Golgotha (Gordon's Calvary)
1. Arriving in Jerusalem from Bethany, by way of the Mount of Olives, Jesus is given a king's welcome by the people.
To Sebaste (Samaria)
To Jericho
Bezetha
MOUNT OF OLIVES
11. Jesus is taken to Golgotha for crucifixion.
Second North Wall
Pool of Bethesda
Damascus Gate
Struthion Pool
Fortress of Antonia
Pool of Israel
To Bethany
Garden and Tomb of Joseph of Arimathea
Golgotha (traditional site)
Sheep Gate
Temple of Herod the Great
Shushan Gate
Garden of Gethsemane
To Joppa, Antipatris, Caesarea
Judgment Gate
2. Jesus rids the Temple of unworthy vendors. He spends time each day teaching in the Temple.
Tower's Pool
Temple Mount
5. After the Passover meal, Jesus returns to the Mount of Olives. His disciples join him and they travel to Gethsemane, where Judas betrays Jesus with a kiss. Jesus is arrested.
8. Jesus appears before Pilate, who sends him to Herod Antipas.
Hippicus's Tower
First North Wall
Gennath Gate
Xystus
Palace of Herod (Praetorium)
10. Pilate can find no charges against Jesus, but the crowd demands his execution.
9. Herod Antipas interrogates Jesus and then mocks him. He sends Jesus back to Pilate.
Palace of Herod Antipas (Hasmonean Palace)
7. The following morning, Jesus is brought before the Sanhedrin.
Upper City "Zion"
Spring Gate
6. The arresting party takes Jesus to the house of Caiaphas.
House of Caiaphas the High Priest
Lower City
Aqueduct
TYROPOEON VALLEY
Spring of Gihon
VALLEY OF KIDRON
Upper Room: Site of the Last Supper
Tower of Siloam
Serpent's Pool
4. Jesus and his twelve disciples gather to share the Passover meal.
Hezekiah's Tunnel
Essene Gate
Pool of Siloam
Dung Gate
To Bethlehem, Hebron, Gaza
VALLEY OF HINNOM
City wall
External road
Pool
Garden
Gate
0 300 meters
0 1000 feet
Hakeldama (Field of Blood)
En-rogel Spring (Well of Job)
N

ABOVE: SECTION OF THE *VIA DOLOROSA*, WHICH IS THE TRADITIONAL ROUTE SAID TO HAVE BEEN TAKEN BY JESUS TO GOLGOTHA FOLLOWING HIS CONDEMNATION.

cross. In John's account, Jesus goes out carrying his own cross.

In contrast to these brief descriptions, Luke adds an account of the women who are wailing loudly as they accompany Jesus (Luke 23:27–28). Using a complex parable, Jesus tells these women to save their grieving for the future disasters that will befall them and their children; if the Romans have done this to him, what will they do to their whole race (Luke 23:29–31)? Although popular piety has added three falls, plus meetings with his mother, and with the woman who wipes his face with a cloth, none of these incidents are mentioned in the actual Gospel account. And so the sad procession makes its way through the narrow jostling streets of the old city of Jerusalem toward Golgotha which, as John explains, is the Hebrew word for "the place of the skull" (John 19:17).

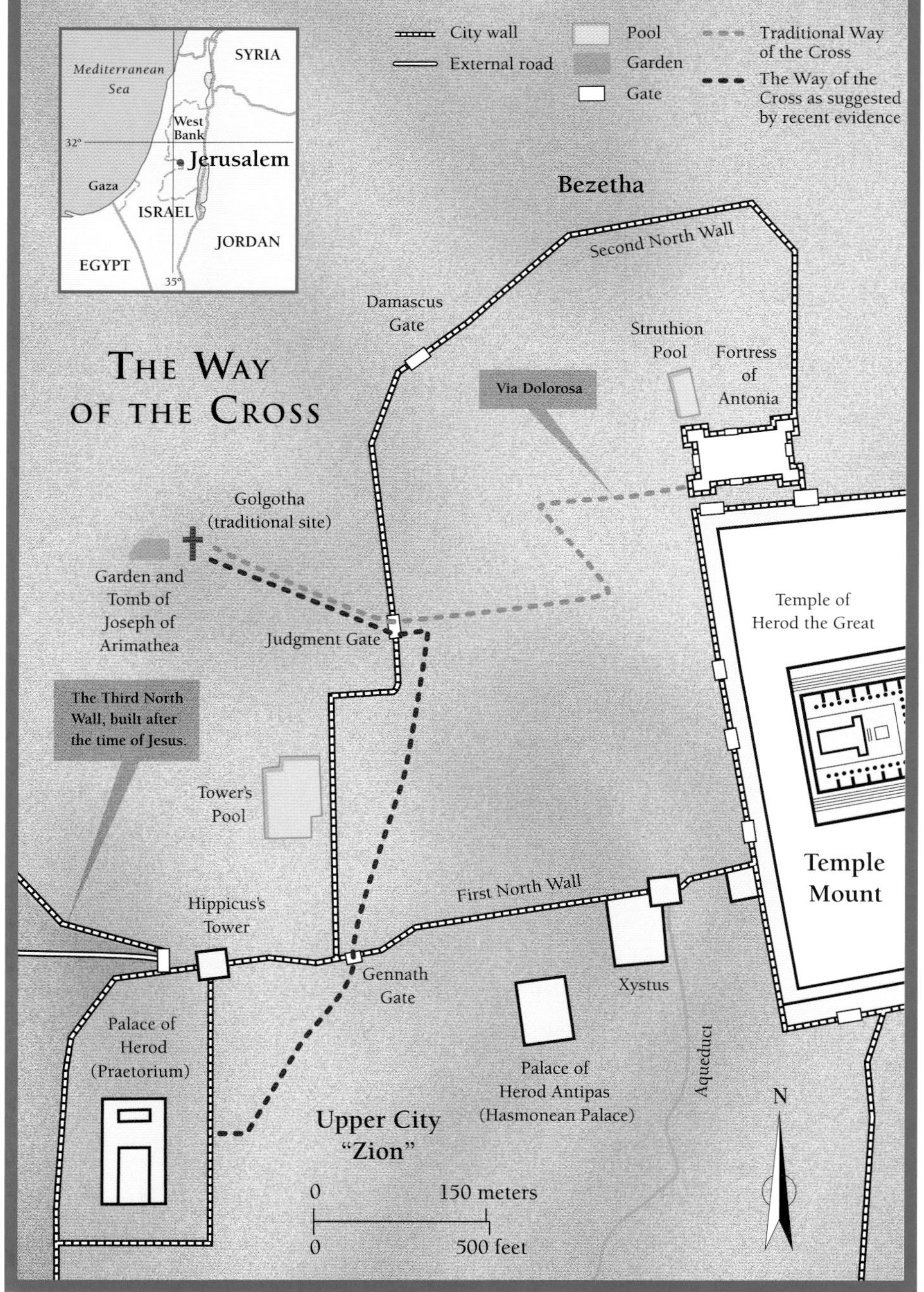

THE SITE OF THE CRUCIFIXION

For the pilgrim, it is not hard to believe that the place now venerated as the site of the crucifixion may well be the actual historical site. On top of the skull-shaped gray stone monolith, is a fissure into which it is thought the cross upright was hammered. One gains access via a staircase to the floor that surrounds the place of the crucifixion. Together with the site of Jesus' grave, this area is now enclosed within the Church of the Holy Sepulchre, a basilica first built by the Christian Emperor Constantine in the fourth century, then twice destroyed and rebuilt. The present edifice was built by the Crusaders in the twelfth century.

THE CRUCIFIXION

None of the Gospels gives any detail about the actual fixing of Jesus to the cross, but the soldiers would probably have followed the Roman custom. The upright remained in the ground; what Jesus carried, and was tied to by ropes, was the horizontal bar. If John's account is historical, the practice of sometimes adding nails was followed in Jesus' case (John 20:25). His bound body is then hoisted up and attached to the upright so that his feet are about 3 ft (1 m) from the ground. Above his head is placed an inscription, not in this case the usual list of crimes, but the title "the King of the Jews" (Matthew 27:37; Luke 23:38). The custom of giving condemned criminals a narcotic drink is mockingly offered to Jesus in the form of a sour wine-soaked sponge, but he rejects it (Matthew 27:34; Luke 23:36). While they sit around, the soldiers toss for items of Jesus' clothing (Matthew 27:35–36; Luke 23:34).

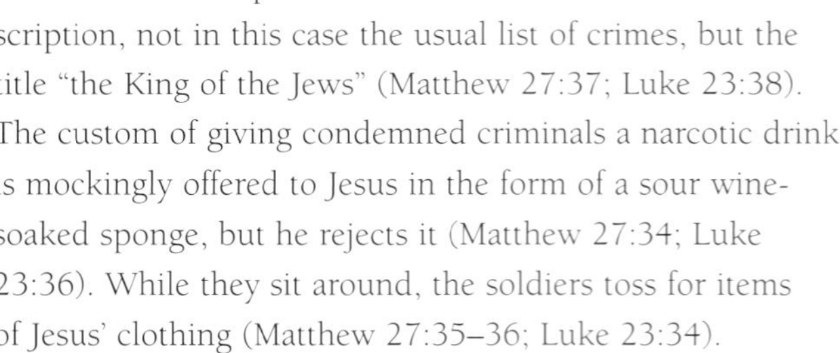

THE TWO THIEVES

All four Gospels mention that Jesus was crucified between two criminals. Luke adds a touching story about one of them who repents and states his acceptance of his situation; unlike that of Jesus, his punishment is justified (Luke 23:41). He then asks to be remembered when Jesus reaches the heavenly kingdom, a request to which Jesus gives a ready promise (Luke 23:43). Earlier, Luke describes Jesus praying for forgiveness for his persecutors (Luke 23:34). As throughout the passion narratives, the reader is being invited to identify with the repentant sinner.

ABOVE: *CHRIST ON THE ROAD TO CALVARY* BY FRANZ FRANCKEN II. JESUS CARRIED THE CROSS TO GOLGOTHA (CALVARY)—THE SITE OF THE CRUCIFIXION.

INSULTS ARE HURLED AT JESUS

By contrast, the other criminal (both, in Matthew's account), the rulers, and bystanders hurl insults at the dying Jesus. While the soldiers and the people are included, each of the accounts emphasizes that it was largely the religious leaders who were responsible for such insults. It is they who repeat the mocking challenge to his claim to be the Son of God. If he is the Messiah, why can't he save himself? Why doesn't God come down and save him (Matthew 27:39–43; Luke 23:35–37)? Embittered by envy of his sheer goodness and their inability to crush him, they go so far as to claim that, were he somehow able to come down from the cross, they would even believe in him.

JOHN'S VIEW OF THE CRUCIFIXION

Although John includes many of the same details as one or more of the other evangelists, he has his own distinct theological interests. For example, in his parallel account of the placing the inscription "the King of the Jews" on the cross, he adds a telling detail. When the chief priests complain to Pilate that he should have made it clear this is only Jesus' claim about himself, Pilate refuses to back down (John 19:22). In doing so, he ironically implies that he accepts Jesus' definition and agrees with the position of the evangelist. Likewise, where the synoptics present Jesus as a victim, the Jesus of John's Gospel is always in control of his decisions and destiny, as exemplified at his arrest (John 18:4–11) and in his dialog with Pilate (John 18:33–19:11).

Basically, the fourth Gospel presents Jesus' crucifixion as a glorious triumph, but not in any worldly way; his is not an earthly kingship (John 18:36). Rather, in his death, Jesus gives glory to the Father by fulfilling his God-given mission and bringing all people to himself (John 12:32–33). This is the unqualified love with

LEFT: THIRTEENTH-CENTURY ITALIAN PANEL SHOWING THE EVENTS OF PASSION WEEK. AFTER THE REFORMATION, CATHOLIC ARTISTS CONTINUED TO PAINT SACRED SCENES, WHILE PROTESTANTS PREFERRED SECULAR SUBJECTS.

which John's passion narrative begins (John 13:1), and which looks forward to a burgeoning of new life for all mankind. In typical Johannine fashion, this is poignantly captured in the image of the cycle of nature: "Unless a grain of wheat falls into the earth and dies, it remains just a single grain of wheat; but if it dies, it bears much fruit" (John 12:24).

BELOW: *CHRIST BETWEEN TWO THIEVES* BY PETER PAUL RUBENS. JESUS WAS PLACED ON THE CROSS BETWEEN TWO COMMON CRIMINALS, WITH THE NOTICE OF HIS ALLEGED CRIME—"KING OF THE JEWS"—AFFIXED TO HIS CROSS.

THE DEATH OF JESUS

The Gospel accounts agree that Jesus' death took place on a Friday, the day of preparation for the Sabbath, at the "ninth hour" or 3 P.M. Those who were crucified usually lasted several days before they ultimately died from exposure, hunger, and thirst. According to the early Markan source (Mark 15:25), Jesus' crucifixion took place at 9 A.M. If so, then Jesus died after hanging on the cross for six hours. These are the bare recorded facts of his death.

Each of the evangelists interprets these details in keeping with the theological interests of his particular community. Matthew's account follows Mark almost exactly. As his death draws near, Jesus is heard to cry out, in Aramaic, his lonely anguished prayer to God (Matthew 27:46); the words are from the opening verse of Psalm 22. Because "Eli" is the word for addressing God, the bystanders' ignorance at claiming he is calling on Elijah to save him is itself being ridiculed (Matthew 27:47–49). Was Jesus simply praying a prayer of trustful surrender or was he genuinely suffering a sense of having been forsaken by God? The combination of physical suffering, humiliation, abandonment by his disciples, and ongoing insults would make anyone's anguish unbearable. But when these are added to the lack of any sensible awareness of his Father's presence, the *cri de coeur* would seem inevitable. Probably the author intends both—a prayer and a painful cry.

Luke's account omits this incident. His Greek Christian readers would miss the Aramaic play on words and be less interested in the references to Elijah. But the significant reason is that Luke tends to present Jesus as so conformed to his Father's will that he is largely beyond human weakness, as indicated earlier when he omits any mention of Jesus' great distress in the Garden of Gethsemane (Matthew 26:37–38).

Where the other Gospels have Jesus dying alone, John places four women at the foot of the cross—Mary, his mother; his mother's sister; Mary, the wife of Clopas; and Mary Magdalene, together with the anonymous "beloved disciple" (John 19:25–26). Jesus commissions his mother and the beloved disciple to be the founding members of the community who will carry on the Father's work after his death (John 19:26–27).

The moment of Jesus' death is described by the synoptic Gospels as a loud cry that accompanies his last breath (Matthew 27:50; Luke 23:46). To this, Luke adds Jesus' final prayer in the words of Psalm 31:5. For John, Jesus' final words and breath have a profound theological meaning. In proclaiming that it is finished, not only does the text mean Jesus' earthly life, but that he has perfectly accomplished his Father's mission and will (John 19:30). Likewise, his last breath is couched in words that mean he hands over the spirit (John 19:30), that is, the Holy Spirit as in this Gospel he had promised would happen when he is glorified, that is, at the moment of his death (John 7:37–39).

LEFT: THIS GERMAN LITHOGRAPH SHOWS THE HAND OF GOD AT WORK, AS THE FULL FORCE OF NATURE COINCIDES WITH JESUS' LAST HOURS—AND DARKNESS FALLS IN THE MIDDLE OF THE DAY.

EVENTS THAT ACCOMPANIED THE DEATH OF JESUS

For the three hours before Jesus' death, the earth is said to be covered in darkness (Matthew 27:45; Luke 23:44). This is an echo of Old Testament prophecies that describe the Day of Judgment as being marked by a sudden darkness (Joel 2:31) that descends at noon (Amos 8:9). Luke's addition of a specific reference from both texts to the sun's decline emphasizes his theme of identifying Jesus as the prophet of God.

The scene portrayed immediately after Jesus dies is one of ritual and cosmic reaction. With the tearing into two of the Temple curtain (Matthew 27:51; Luke 23:45), the message is clear—Jesus' death has overturned the old order. The purpose of the curtain was to keep the people separated from the priests and the inner sanctuary symbolizing God's presence. Salvation and redemption are now open to all without exception so that, in fact, the Temple is no longer needed.

Matthew's account expands the reaction to the natural world with increasing dramatic effect. An earthquake accompanies the tearing of the curtain (Matthew 27:51). This is followed by the opening of graves and the resurrection of some faithful people from the dead (Matthew 27:51–53); it is even claimed that these later appeared to people after Jesus' resurrection. These extraordinary portents are intended to heighten the importance of the event, in the same way as Matthew heralds the birth of Jesus with the appearance of a star (Matthew 2:2, 7, 9, 10).

What Matthew is doing here is called *midrash*, the rabbinical practice of gathering a number of apocalyptic texts and interpreting them in the light of the events being described (see Isaiah 26:19; Ezekiel 37:12; Joel 2:10; Daniel 12:2; and Nahum 1:5–6). Although earthquakes were often regarded as a sign of tragedy, their occurrence as such is not extraordinary. The hand of God is rather in the fact that they should occur precisely at this time. With the portrait of bodies rising from the dead, the evangelist is not necessarily making an historical claim, but is symbolizing the new life with which Jesus' death will be vindicated and to which these faithful ones will be worthy witnesses.

Yet the honor of being the first to see in Jesus' death the verification of his identity is the non-Jewish centurion. In Luke's account, he responds to all he has just experienced by declaring Jesus' innocence (Luke 23:47), but in Matthew he is attributed with the profound faith statement: "Truly this man was God's son!" (Matthew 27:54). This positive note is strengthened even further by the reference to the group of women disciples whose presence is acknowledged, not as in John beneath the cross (John 19:25–26), but from a distance (Matthew 27:55–56; Luke 23:49).

BELOW: ANOTHER SYMBOLIC OCCURRENCE, THIS TIME COINCIDING WITH JESUS' LAST BREATH, IS SEEN IN THIS ENGRAVING BY I. M. PREISSLER, AS THE TEMPLE CURTAIN IS TORN IN TWO.

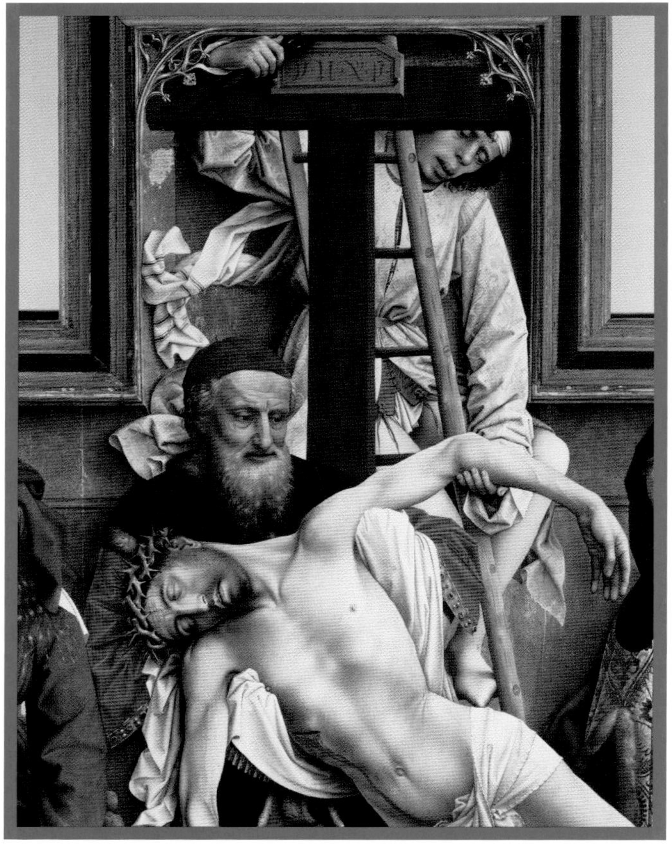

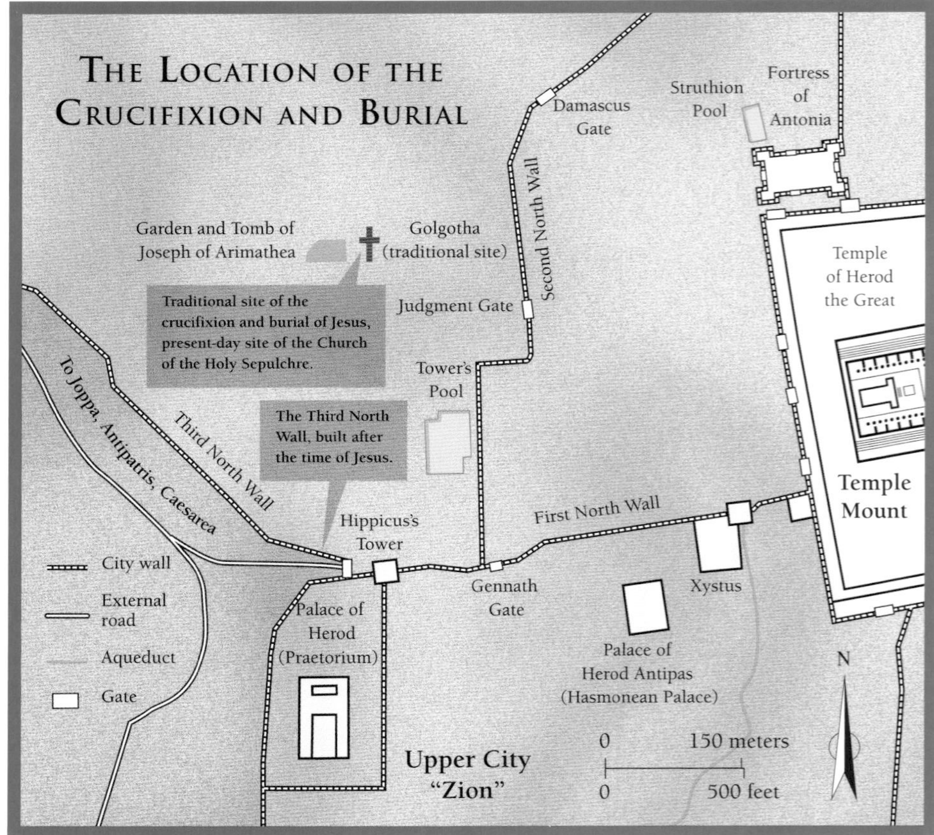

ABOVE: *DESCENT FROM THE CROSS* BY ROGIER VAN DER WEYDEN. THOUGH A MEMBER OF THE COUNCIL THAT CONDEMNED JESUS, JOSEPH OF ARIMATHEA—A FOLLOWER OF JESUS—BOLDLY ASKS FOR THE BODY OF JESUS FOR BURIAL.

JOSEPH BURIES JESUS

Since Jesus' death took place on a Friday, his followers would want to remove his dead body for burial before the Sabbath began at sunset. Criminals were usually interred without ceremony in a common grave, so only someone with sufficient standing could ask for this favor in Jesus' case. At this point, Joseph of Arimathea, a respected member of the Jewish Council, goes to Pilate to ask if he might remove the body of Jesus from the cross (Matthew 27:57–58; Luke 23:50–52; John 19:38).

This is the first and only time the reader encounters Joseph of Arimathea. His name indicates he originally came from the town of Ramathaim, north of Lydda, although in the events recorded he would seem to be living in or near Jerusalem. Luke portrays him as a good and just man, agreeing with Mark that he was a seeker of the kingdom of God and adding that he had challenged the Council's decision to kill Jesus (Luke 23:50–51). Matthew, avoiding any reference to Joseph's being on the Council, presents him as a rich man and a "disciple" of Jesus (Matthew 27:57). The fourth Gospel agrees with the designation "disciple," adding that his discipleship has necessarily been exercised in secret (John 19:38).

Joseph appears to act alone, except in the Gospel of John where he is joined by another interesting character, Nicodemus (John 19:39). Here is a second disciple of Jesus who is a member of the Jewish Council (John 7:50–52) and a Pharisee (John 3:1). As at his first encounter with Jesus, Nicodemus again emerges from the darkness (John 3:2) to share the task of preparing and interring Jesus' body. The enormous quantity and quality of the ointments and spices indicate that he too is a wealthy man (John 19:39). It is important to note that, especially in John's Gospel, discipleship is not limited to the 12 male apostles. The imminent arrival on the scene by Mary Magdalene and other women further confirms the broad range of Jesus' disciples.

Jesus' body is first wrapped in a linen shroud (Matthew 27:59; Luke 23:53) with perfumed spices (John 19:40), then laid in a new tomb hewn out of rock. As so often in John's account, details are included that suggest the author, or his source, had a personal knowledge of Jerusalem. He mentions that the place of the crucifixion is in a garden where there is a new tomb. One possible explanation is that the place was a former quarry; over the ground spread the ubiquitous red poppies and in the remaining outer stone "wall," horizontal graves were hewn out. To this day, one can see a number of first-century graves in the original wall contained within the church of the Holy Sepulchre. Each grave has a tiny vestibule into which a person steps; two or more horizontal slabs are cut into the wall, more or less perpendicular to the entrance. A large rock was placed at the entrance to act as a seal.

RIGHT: *THE ENTOMBMENT*, SIXTEENTH-CENTURY WOOD CARVING. IN OBSERVANCE OF THE APPROACHING SABBATH, JESUS' FOLLOWERS EXPEDITE HIS INTERNMENT IN ACCORDANCE WITH BURIAL CUSTOMS.

MARY MAGDALENE AT THE GRAVE

While all this is taking place, a number of women look on from a distance (Matthew 27:55–56; Luke 23:49). They take careful note of the place and details of Jesus' burial then, according to Luke, go off to prepare spices to anoint his body (Luke 23:55–56). Because of the haste to bury Jesus' body before the Sabbath, the customary Jewish traditions of washing and anointing have to be delayed until the next day, except in John where this service is carried out by the two men at the actual time of Jesus' burial. In Matthew's account, Mary Magdalene and another "Mary" remain sitting at the tomb (Matthew 27:61).

LEFT: FIFTH-CENTURY IVORY RELIEF OF SOLDIERS SLEEPING BEFORE CHRIST'S TOMB. TEMPLE ELDERS DEPLOY GUARDS AT THE TOMB OF CHRIST TO PREVENT TAMPERING WITH THE TOMB.

The names of these women vary in each account, indicating that there were many women who were followers of Jesus. Some were clearly sufficiently wealthy and free from domestic obligations, to follow Jesus from Galilee to Jerusalem and to provide for his temporal needs (Luke 8:3). But the one constant figure mentioned in all four Gospels is Mary Magdalene (Mark 15:40; Matthew 27:56; Luke 23:49, 55; John 19:25).

THE TOMB IS GUARDED

All the accounts mention that a stone is placed across the door of Jesus' tomb (Matthew 27:60; Luke 24:2; John 20:1). Grave robbery was common, but it presumed the custom of interring valuable possessions with the body. As Jesus was crucified as a criminal, the only possible reason for a guard is what is stated—the authorities were anxious that Jesus' disciples might remove his body and pretend he had risen from the dead (Matthew 27:62–64). This is anticipatory defense against the accusation by the chief priests that this is precisely how the tomb came to be empty (Matthew 28:11–15). It is also part of the ongoing apologetic by Matthew's community, who were in constant tension with the Jewish religious authorities especially regarding the core theological premise of Jesus' resurrection.

THE RESURRECTION

In each of the Gospel accounts, Jesus predicts his death and resurrection, either explicitly (Matthew 16:21; Luke 9:22) or by way of using the Temple as an image of his body (John 2:19–22). Yet it is clear from the description of the disciples' reaction to the resurrection that they were not expecting Jesus to rise from the dead. Every incident is marked by some combination of surprise, initial disbelief, questioning, or even skepticism. This suggests that Jesus'

BELOW: *THE ENTOMBMENT* BY ANTONIO CISERI. CHRIST'S FOLLOWERS TAKE HIS BODY DOWN FROM THE CROSS, CARRYING IT TO AN UNUSED TOMB—POSSIBLY THAT OF JOSEPH OF ARIMATHEA.

prediction was probably written with the advantage of hindsight, in order to highlight the central importance of his passion, death, and resurrection.

The actual resurrection is not described. Even the women who take up a position at the tomb (Matthew 27:61) eventually leave the scene and return next morning, apparently to continue their vigil (Matthew 28:1). In this account, a huge earthquake accompanies the arrival of an angel who, as in the infancy narrative, greets them with the assurance that there is no need to be afraid—Jesus has risen from the dead (Matthew 28:5–6). The women are invited to examine the empty tomb and are then commissioned to carry the good news to the other disciples (Matthew 28:7). As they race away to do so, with a mixture of fear and joy, the risen Jesus appears to them and repeats the angel's message that his followers are to return to Galilee where they too will see him (Matthew 28:8–10).

In Luke's version, the women return to the tomb in order to complete the ritual anointing of Jesus' body (Luke 24:1). They find the stone already rolled away, and two angels who give a similar message with a reminder of Jesus' prediction that this would happen (Luke 9:22). Unlike Matthew's account, when the Lukan women obey the injunction to share the good news with the apostles they are treated with total disbelief (Luke 24:11). But the women are vindicated in the section that follows, when the risen Lord appears to two disciples as they return home to Emmaus, and chides them: "Oh, how foolish you are and how slow of heart to believe all that the prophets have declared! Was it not necessary that the Messiah should suffer these things and then enter into his glory?" (Luke 24:25–26).

For John, there are no angels and no statement that Jesus has risen from the dead. Interestingly, the tradition that Jesus predicted the resurrection before his death is disavowed (John 20:9), so no one is given any such reminder. Instead, when Mary Magdalene discovers the empty tomb, she races immediately to tell Simon Peter (also referred to as Peter) and the beloved disciple (John 20:1–2). They, in turn, run to the tomb and, when Peter goes into the entrance, he finds only the grave-cloths and the face cover (John 20:3–5). The beloved disciple then goes in, notices the way in which the cloths have been folded, and takes from this an understanding that only one explanation is possible. The Gospel describes his reaction as that which is to be a model for the reader—having now seen, he believes (John 20:8). What he actually believes is presumed to be that Jesus has risen from the dead, but, in Johannine fashion, the answer is deliberately left open for the reader to ponder.

OPPOSITE: *THE RESURRECTION* BY GIUSEPPE GIOVENONE. THE GOSPELS REPORT THAT ON THE DAY FOLLOWING THE BURIAL, THE BODY OF JESUS WAS GONE, IMPLYING—RATHER THAN DESCRIBING—THE RESURRECTION.

MARY MAGDALENE

The centuries-old reputation of Mary Magdalene (seen here in Titian's work) as a great penitent is without foundation in the New Testament, but is presumably based on the comment that she had been exorcised by Jesus (Luke 8:2). However, these "devils" could well have been any combination of physical or mental illness. When exorcism is carried out on others (Matthew 8:16, 31; 12:22; Luke 4:33–36; 7:21; 8:32; 9:37–43), the symptoms described would be recognized today as a disease like epilepsy or some psychic disorder. Likewise, there is no evidence to identify her with the woman who begs Jesus' forgiveness (Luke 7:39) or anoints his feet (John 12:3). However, that she was recognized as a leader in the early Christian community is beyond question.

In their accounts of the women at Jesus' tomb, the Gospels of Matthew, Luke, and John each mention the presence of Mary Magdalene. The Gospel of John portrays Mary Magdalene as of enormous significance in the early Christian communities. Apart from the books of the New Testament, she is mentioned 11 times in non-canonical texts including *The Gospel of Mary*, *The Gospel of Philip*, and *The Gospel of Peter*. In these works, she is often portrayed as a close companion of Jesus and as a rival to Peter and other male disciples for leadership of the Christian community. It is fascinating to speculate how much of this may be historically accurate and, if so, what may have been the direction of the church if it had not been sidelined as part of the accepted biblical accounts.

JESUS APPEARS TO MARY MAGDALENE

Mary Magdalene is mentioned by name in every account of the women who take the good news of Jesus' Resurrection to the other disciples (Matthew 28:10; Luke 24:9–10). While Luke, unlike Matthew (28:9), does not add that the risen Jesus subsequently appears to the women, he too includes Mary Magdalene in the group (Luke 24:10). Clearly she played a well-attested role in proclaiming the Resurrection to these early Christian communities.

But it is the Gospel of John that attributes to her the role of primary witness to the truth of Jesus' Resurrection. When Simon Peter and the beloved disciple depart from the tomb (John 20:10), Mary Magdalene remains behind. She is crying because she does not know who has removed Jesus' body nor where it has been placed. The two angels who ask the reason for her weeping have no further role (John 20:12–13) Suddenly she sees Jesus but, even though he repeats the angels' question, she does not realize it is him (John 20:14–15) and

LEFT: SIXTEENTH-CENTURY FRESCO ATTRIBUTED TO FRANCESCO AND SPERINDIO CAGNOLA. JESUS APPEARS TO MARY MAGDALENE AS SHE KEEPS HER LONE VIGIL AT THE EMPTY TOMB.

ABOVE: COPTIC ICON, FOURTEENTH CENTURY. THOMAS—SYMBOLICALLY REPRESENTING THOSE WHO DOUBT THE RESURRECTION—IS ALLOWED TO WITNESS JESUS' WOUNDS FROM THE CRUCIFIXION.

thinks he is the gardener. The evangelist is telling the reader that this is no resuscitation as in the case of Lazarus (John 11); in some strange way, the body of the risen Jesus has been transformed. Then, in a most poignant moment, Jesus calls her by her name and the old familiarity returns as she recognizes him (John 20:16). Then he explains to her that their relationship has been transformed and no longer requires his immediate earthly presence; she is not to cling to him, but to carry his message to the rest of the disciples (John 20:17). This she does, utterly believing that it is the risen Lord she has seen, and perhaps understanding something of the profound message she faithfully transmits (John 20:18).

RIGHT: *JESUS ASCENDS* FROM THE *OEUVRE DE JEHAN FOUCQUET* BY JEAN FOUQUET. THE GOSPELS OF MARK AND LUKE INCLUDE REFERENCE TO JESUS' ASCENSION.

JESUS APPEARS TO THE APOSTLES

In Matthew's account, the apostles apparently accept the women's testimony because, as directed, they go to Galilee where Jesus appears to them. The comment that some are still dubious (Matthew 28:17) is intended to encourage the reader—even among the first apostles, some struggled with disbelief. The two disciples who encounter the risen Jesus on the road to Emmaus share their experience (Matthew 24:35) of how Jesus stirred their hearts when he demonstrated how recent events were in accordance with the scriptures (Luke 24:27). As if to confirm this story, the risen Jesus suddenly stands in their midst (Luke 24:36). Recognizing their fear and confusion, he shows them his hands and feet (Luke 24:39) and invites them to touch him and give him something to eat (Luke 24:39, 41–43).

John's account has several similarities. The disciples are huddled together in fear when Jesus suddenly appears in the room and shows them his hands and feet (John 20:19–20). Their response is one of sheer joy (John 20:20).

While doubt is not mentioned, the next verses tell of Thomas, who represents those who demand proof as a condition of belief. Absent when Jesus first appeared, Thomas insists on having his own immediate experience before he will believe (John 20:25). With gracious tolerance, the risen Jesus meets this demand, repeating the same blessing of peace to Thomas (John 20 26–27), who now addresses Jesus as both Lord and God. Jesus' response is the ultimate encouragement to all future disciples: "Have you believed because you have seen me? Blessed are those who have not seen and yet have come to believe" (John 20:29).

THE LAST INSTRUCTIONS OF JESUS

An appendix to John's Gospel relates one further appearance story (John 21:1–23). Otherwise, the evangelists conclude with Jesus' last instructions to his disciples.

For Matthew, these instructions center on their future mission to spread the good news through baptism and teaching (Matthew 28:18–20). In Luke's Gospel, Jesus urges them to preach repentance and forgiveness of sins (Matthew 24:47). In the fourth Gospel, Jesus breathes on the disciples the Holy Spirit, thereby empowering them to continue his mission, including the forgiveness of sins (John 20:22–23).

THE ASCENT INTO HEAVEN

Only Mark (longer version) and Luke include an account of the ascension. For the other evangelists, Jesus' return to the Father is taken for granted, with no hint of a visible sign. Luke wants both to round off his Gospel and to provide the link with his second volume, The Acts of the Apostles. Favorite themes, first appearing in his infancy narrative, are all fitted into these final two verses—journey, Jerusalem, rejoicing, prayers of praise (Luke 24:52–53). Jesus is portrayed as lifting his hands in blessing over the small group of disciples; in Acts 1:6–11, he will commission them to extend this blessing to the entire world and thus throughout the ages.

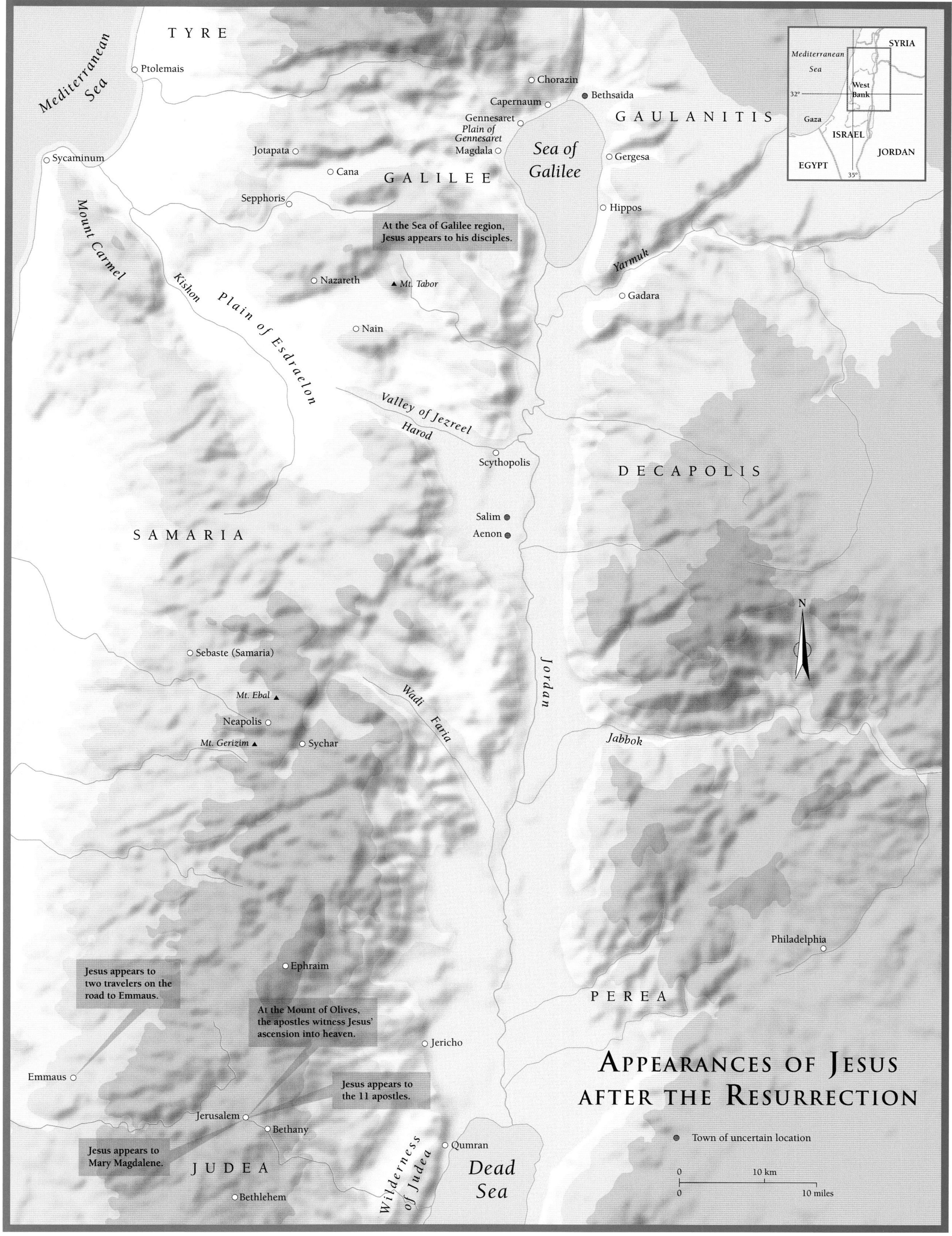

Appearances of Jesus after the Resurrection

Part Eight

Spreading the Word

THE GOSPEL OF TRUTH

THEIR VOICE GOES OUT THROUGH ALL THE EARTH PSALM 19:4

After the Crucifixion and the Resurrection, several decades passed before the teaching took written form, and Christianity as we know it began to take shape. The task of dating and determining the authorship of many of the writings bristles with difficulties; the only certainty is that the Acts and the Epistles of St. Paul—the books that contain the core of Christian teaching—were quite widely known in the world of the Bible by the end of the first century C.E.

Paul was martyred in Rome in about C.E. 65, under Nero, infamous persecutor of Christians; thus the Epistles that are definitively attributed to him—some written from prison—can be dated roughly between C.E. 50 and 65. The Gospels and the Acts were written later, between C.E. 65 and 100, although some scholars believe that Mark's Gospel dates from as early as C.E. 50.

THE APOSTLES GO FORTH

The Acts of the Apostles relates how the disciples of Jesus, by now many more than the original 12, began to disseminate his teachings, beginning with the "speaking in tongues" at the Pentecost. At first they taught only in Jerusalem; then, under the leadership of Paul after his conversion on the road to Damascus, they pushed northwest into Asia Minor, preaching at Antioch in Syria, at Troas and Ephesus in modern-day Turkey, and then thrusting westward to Athens, Corinth, and Rome.

The spreading of the Word of the Lord to Asia Minor and Europe marked the transformation of the disciples into the Apostles, a word that comes from the Greek *apostolos*, a messenger. The backbone of the book of the Acts of the Apostles consists of the three missionary journeys of St. Paul and his various companions. Paul was also known as Saul of Tarsus, his birthplace in Turkey. He was a highly educated Hellenized Jew of the tribe of Benjamin and was brought up a Pharisee and trained in a strict tradition of legalistic Judaism.

Paul encountered the message of Jesus shortly after the Crucifixion. At first he was violently opposed to the Way, as its followers called it, and made it his mission to track down Christians and bring them to trial. After his conversion, he embraced the new faith with the same wholehearted zeal he had employed in stamping it out. His indefatigable efforts to Christianize the known world earned him the title "Apostle to the Gentiles."

Like Christ himself, Paul was not a mild man; his style was confrontational, even militaristic, and his writings abound in the imagery of warfare: "Put on the whole armor

LEFT: THIS FIFTEENTH-CENTURY PAINTING BY TOMMASO MASACCIO SHOWS ST. PETER AND ST. PAUL HEALING THE SICK. IT IS ONE OF COUNTLESS DEPICTIONS OF THE MINISTRY WORK OF THE APOSTLES.

of God.... For our struggle is not against enemies of blood and flesh, but against the rulers, against the authorities, against the cosmic powers of this present darkness, against the spiritual forces of evil in the heavenly places" (Ephesians 6:11–12).

JERUSALEM THE GOLDEN

St. John the Divine, author of Revelation, is traditionally identified with John the Apostle, the "beloved disciple" who was present at the Transfiguration and at the Agony in the Garden. Jesus nicknamed John and his brother James *Boanerges*—meaning sons of thunder—because of their impetuosity.

Revelation was written on Patmos, an Aegean island between Greece and Turkey. Its date is probably no earlier than about C.E. 90, which suggests that the attribution to John the Apostle is reverential rather than accurate. The book opens with messages to the seven churches of Asia, and then becomes an Apocalypse, from the Greek *apokaluptikos*, an uncovering. The author's New Jerusalem glitters with gold and precious jewels, and the Lamb of God reigns there in glory.

Revelation's use of the Greek language has been described as barbarous and its visions as deranged, but the imagery of the book is as powerful as it is surreal. It can be interpreted as an allegory of the history of the world from the Fall in the Garden of Eden to the Redemption on the Cross: "Then I saw a new heaven and a new earth; for the first heaven and the first earth had passed away" (Revelation 21:1).

LEFT: THIS BRONZE STAMP FOR COMMEMORATIVE BREAD DATES FROM THE FOURTH CENTURY C.E. THE PRIMITIVE FORM OF THE CROSS WAS MOST LIKELY THE *SWASTIKA*, A SACRED SIGN IN INDIA.

THE ACTS OF THE APOSTLES

GOD HAS MADE HIM BOTH LORD AND MESSIAH, THIS JESUS WHOM YOU CRUCIFIED ACTS 2:36

RIGHT: SAINTS JOHN, ANDREW, AND PETER ARE REPRESENTED IN THIS GILT AND WOODEN ALTARFRONT FROM DENMARK. ACTS CHARTS THE SUCCESSFUL MINISTRY WORK OF THE APOSTLES AS THEY SPREAD THE WORD AS FAR AS ROME.

BELOW: JOHN FULLEYLOVE'S ILLUSTRATION OF JERUSALEM SHOWS THE HOLY CITY AS IT WAS IN 1912. THE CITY OF THE MOTHER CHURCH IS JUST AS IMPORTANT TODAY AS IT WAS IN THE TIME OF CHRIST.

The Acts of the Apostles provides the New Testament bridge between the Gospels and Paul's letters, and the broad historical framework within which to locate those letters. Written by the same author as Luke's Gospel (traditionally identified as Paul's companion Luke, Colossians 4:14; 2 Timothy 4:11; Philemon 24), it continues that earlier story of the Spirit's activity into the early life of the Church. The author looks back from the later decades of the first century, after many hard-fought battles had been won and the conversion of Gentiles across the Roman Empire had become an established fact. Geographically organized, the book traces the spread of the Gospel stage by stage. The pattern is set by the risen Jesus: "But you will receive power when the Holy Spirit has come upon you; and you will be my witnesses in Jerusalem, in all Judea and Samaria, and to the ends of the earth" (Acts 1:8).

Yet Luke is keen to show that the story of the emerging Church is deeply rooted in the people of Israel, and the fulfillment of God's promises to Israel. Hence the early stages trace the success of the apostolic preaching among fellow Jews in Jerusalem and Judea. This is important, because unless God can be shown not to have gone back on his earlier promises to the Jews, Gentile Christians would understandably lack the confidence that he would remain faithful to them.

CONTINUING THE STORY

When Acts opens in Jerusalem it is continuing the story begun in the life, death, and resurrection of Jesus. For Luke, it was necessary that Christ should suffer in the holy city of Jerusalem (e.g., Luke 9:31, 13:33, 24:26). Now Jerusalem becomes the city of the mother Church, the restored remnant of Israel, to which Gentile converts will look and to which

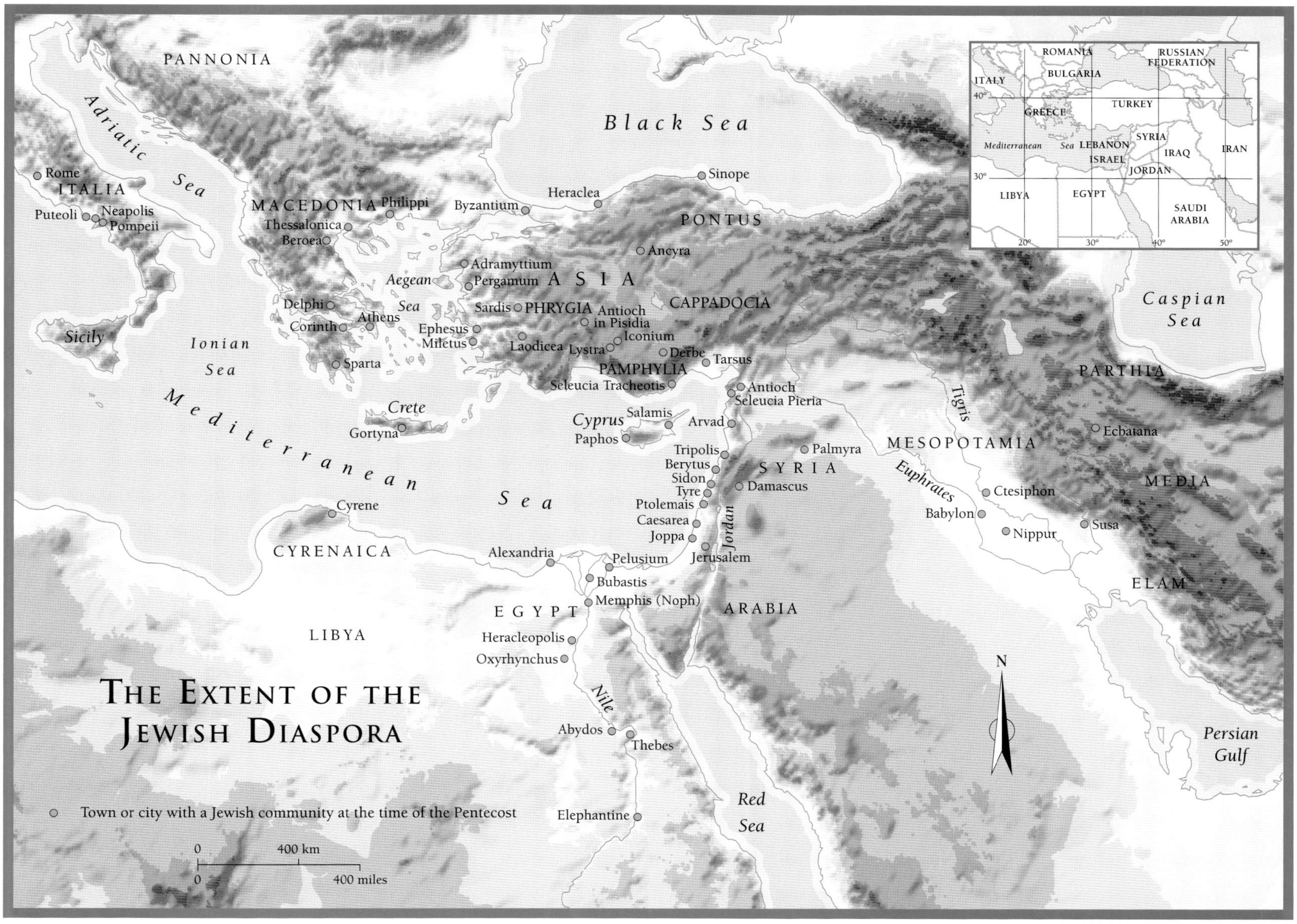

The Extent of the Jewish Diaspora

○ Town or city with a Jewish community at the time of the Pentecost

even Paul will return from time to time (e.g., Acts 9:26, 12:25, 15:2, 18:22, 21:17).

Jerusalem was a splendid city, having benefited from the extensive building projects of Herod the Great (37–4 B.C.E.). Herod built himself a splendid new palace, with three defensive towers named after his brother Phasael, his friend Hippicus, and his favorite wife Mariamne. He also constructed a theater, a stadium, and the Antonia Fortress, which would become the headquarters of the Roman garrison. And he began the massive reconstruction of Jerusalem's Temple and its precincts. Gleaming white and gold in the sun, it would have been an impressive sight indeed to "the tribes of the Lord" as they arrived on pilgrimage (Psalm 122:4).

A GATHERING OF THE SCATTERED TRIBES

By the first century C.E. there were more Jews living outside Palestine than in the Holy Land, because of a number of factors: forced deportation, flight, and voluntary emigration. The Assyrians, for example, deported the northern tribes to Media, while the Judeans had been exiled to Babylonia—or Mesopotamia, the land "between the rivers" of the Tigris and Euphrates—where many chose to remain. There were also substantial Jewish communities within Rome's borders. Some Judeans had fled to Egypt, or subsequently emigrated there and to other parts of North Africa in search of material prosperity. Indeed, the largest Diaspora community was in Alexandria, comprising several hundred thousand by the first century C.E. Finally, there were substantial Jewish communities in Asia Minor (Acts singles out "Cappadocia, Pontus and Asia, Phrygia and Pamphylia") and in Greek cities such as Corinth. Thus, by the time of the Pentecost, about C.E. 30, the Jewish Diaspora covered much of the Mediterranean world, as well as lands well beyond Rome's eastern borders, as far as Parthia (Persia).

LEFT: *LIFE IN MESOPOTAMIA*, MUSEUM OF THE JEWISH DIASPORA, ISRAEL. THIS WALL PAINTING BY AN UNKNOWN ARTIST DEPICTS JEWISH EXILES AS THEY GO ABOUT THEIR DAILY LIFE IN THEIR NEW HOMELAND.

RIGHT: THIS REPRESENTATION OF THE PENTECOST WAS FOUND IN THE MONASTERY OF SANTO DOMINGO DE SILOS IN SPAIN. THE FESTIVAL OF PENTECOST IS ALSO KNOWN AS THE FEAST OF WEEKS.

Despite the Diaspora, Jerusalem was still the center of the Jewish world, as the one place where sacrifices could be offered to God (though it had a rival temple at Leontopolis in Egypt, built by the deposed high priest Onias IV in the second century B.C.E.). Male Jews were expected, where possible, to attend the great pilgrimage festivals. Hence Acts describes among the vast crowd gathered for Pentecost, both Jews and proselytes (converts to Judaism) from the four points of the compass. For Luke, this particular Pentecost will witness the expected ingathering of the scattered tribes of Israel (see Luke 13:29).

A NEW PENTECOST

The Jewish festival of Pentecost (from the Greek word meaning "50") or *Shavuot* occurred 50 days after Passover. An agricultural festival, it originally commemorated God's gift of the land and his blessing upon it (the "Day of First Fruits"). Given that Moses reached Sinai approximately 50 days after the first Passover (Exodus 19:1), it also celebrated the making of the Sinai Covenant, and later the giving of the Law.

For Luke, this celebration of God's covenant relationship with Israel becomes the occasion for a renewal of that covenant. The 12 (complete again with the addition of Matthias) as leaders of the renewed Israel, together with Jesus' mother Mary, his brothers, and other followers, receive the windy, fire-like Spirit in a manner that echoes the manifestation of God on Mt. Sinai. Gathered in a house in the city, the reborn people of God receive the powerful gift promised by Jesus.

Their subsequent preaching, and especially Peter's speech, brings into this remnant some 3,000 people from Israel's scattered tribes, gathered in Jerusalem for the festival. Indeed, in the ability of so many nationalities to understand the apostles in their own languages, Luke may also see a reversal of the tragic story of the tower of Babel (Genesis 11). In the last days, when God pours out his Spirit on all flesh (Acts 2:17–21; see also Joel 2:28–32), the confusion and scattering of humanity is reversed.

BELOW: *SAINT JOHN THE EVANGELIST*, BY AN UNNAMED GERMAN ARTIST. IT IS WIDELY BELIEVED THAT JOHN WAS THE AUTHOR OF THE BOOK OF REVELATION.

A REPLACEMENT FOR JUDAS

Prior to the Pentecost explosion of Spirit, however, one difficulty has to be resolved. The 12, leaders of the renewed tribes, have been fractured by the departure of Judas Iscariot (his name variously interpreted as "man of Qeriot," "the false one," and "assassin" or "dagger-man"). All the evangelists struggle with the person of Judas, and portray him in differing ways. Though one of the chosen 12, he tragically betrayed Jesus to the Jerusalem authorities. Yet paradoxically, that betrayal led to humanity's salvation.

Acts 1:12–26 recounts the replacement of Judas as the twelfth apostle by Matthias. Keen to understand the sad events of Judas's betrayal and demise as according to the divine plan, Luke finds meaning in two psalm passages. The Acts account presents one of two New Testament versions of Judas's death, in which "falling headlong, he burst open in the middle and all his bowels gushed out" (Acts 1:18b; Matthew 27:3–10 describes a suicide). For all their differences, Acts and Matthew do agree that this was a violent event, and it had some association with a field near Jerusalem, still known in their own day as the "Field of Blood" (Aramaic *Hakeldama*).

The grounds on which the number 12 is made up reveals an early Christian definition of apostleship. The suitable candidate needs to have been a companion of Jesus and the apostles, "beginning from the baptism of John until the day when he was taken up from us" (Acts 1:22a), and one who could therefore be a witness to the Resurrection. These qualifications underlie early Christian debates over the status of Paul of Tarsus. Paul did not know Jesus personally, nor was he one of the original disciples. Because of his Damascus Road encounter, however, he was a witness to the Resurrection, and believed himself commissioned as Christ's apostle to the nations (see 1 Corinthians 9:1, 15:8; Galatians 1:15–17).

PETER AND JOHN

In the stories of the early Jerusalem community that follow the Pentecost story, two apostles take particular priority: Simon Peter and John son of Zebedee. This may reflect their subsequent prominence in New Testament Christianity. Later,

ABOVE: THIS SECTION OF A FRESCO BY THE ITALIAN ARTIST MASOLINO DA PANICALE ILLUSTRATES THE BIBLICAL STORY OF ST. PETER HEALING A LAME MAN. MANY VIEW THIS STORY AS AN ALLEGORY FOR THE HEALING OF ALL OF GOD'S CHILDREN.

James the Lord's brother will also come to the fore (Acts 12:17, 15:13, 21:18), and subsequent tradition claims this James and other relatives of Jesus as being among the first bishops of Jerusalem. But for now, attention focuses on these two, with John very much the silent partner. The great set piece speeches of Acts 2–4 are found on Peter's lips, reflecting his role as spokesman for the twelve.

Striking are the parallels between the activity of these apostles and the ministry of Jesus. The risen Christ continues his teaching and healing activity through the Church. Hence much of Peter and John's work occurs in the Temple, echoing Jesus' activity there in Luke 20–21. The healing of the lame man by the Beautiful Gate echoes a similar healing performed by Jesus at Luke 5:18–26. Both are to be seen as part of the healing or restoration of the whole people of God now taking place.

What Happened to Matthias?

In contrast to Paul, whose story will dominate the second half of Acts, once Matthias is chosen as the twelfth apostle (by lot, see Leviticus 16:8; Numbers 26:55), he immediately disappears from Acts' pages. Only later, perhaps unreliable, traditions about Matthias survive. These claim that he continued to preach the faith in Palestine, or alternatively in Ethiopia, and that he eventually died a martyr's death.

The stories take us to the heart of first-century Herodian Jerusalem, especially its Temple. Herod's Temple comprised a series of open courtyards, increasing in holiness as one drew nearer to the actual central sanctuary. This covered building incorporated the Holy Place, where the daily incense offering was made (Luke 1:9); as well as the Holy of Holies, access to which was reserved for the high priest, who entered there only once a year, on Yom Kippur. Luke refers to several locations within the Temple precincts. The "Beautiful Gate" (Acts 3:2) may be the bronze Nicanor Gate, which either marked the boundary between the Court of the Gentiles and the Court of the Women, or provided access from the latter into the Court of Israel. Solomon's Portico (Acts 3:11) was the colonnade skirting the Court of the Gentiles on the east side.

SUFFERING FOR THE NAME

According to Acts, in the earliest years of the Christian movement, persecution came primarily from the religious leaders of Israel rather than Roman authorities. It is yet another motif which connects the experience of Christians with that of Jesus. Named characters allow us to tap into the political intrigue of first-century Jerusalem. Acts 4:6, for example,

RIGHT: THIS MARBLE RELIEF DEPICTS A SERENE SCENE: THE EMPTY THRONE AWAITS THE SECOND COMING OF CHRIST, WHILE TWO LAMBS, SYMBOLIC OF THE APOSTLES, SUGGEST THAT PARADISE IS IMMINENT.

refers to several members of a powerful dynasty of high priests: "Annas the high priest, Caiaphas, John, and Alexander, and all who were of the high-priestly family."

The father of the dynasty, Annas (or Ananus) son of Sethi, was strictly retired by this stage, though he continued to exercise considerable influence, as reflected in his role in Jesus' trial. Joseph Caiaphas was his famous son-in-law, who held the position of high priest between C.E. 18 and 36 (an ossuary bearing the inscription "Joseph son of Caiaphas" has been discovered near Jerusalem). "John" here is possibly Annas's son Jonathan (an alternative reading in one manuscript), who became high priest after Caiaphas in C.E. 36. Alexander is otherwise unknown.

The theme of suffering for the Name will continue throughout Acts. At 5:17–21 Luke recounts the miraculous escape of the apostles from prison, and their bold return to the Temple to continue teaching. A similar event will occur for Peter alone in 12:6–11, while Paul and Silas will experience a miraculous deliverance from jail in Philippi (Acts 16:25–34), resulting in the conversion of the jailer and his household.

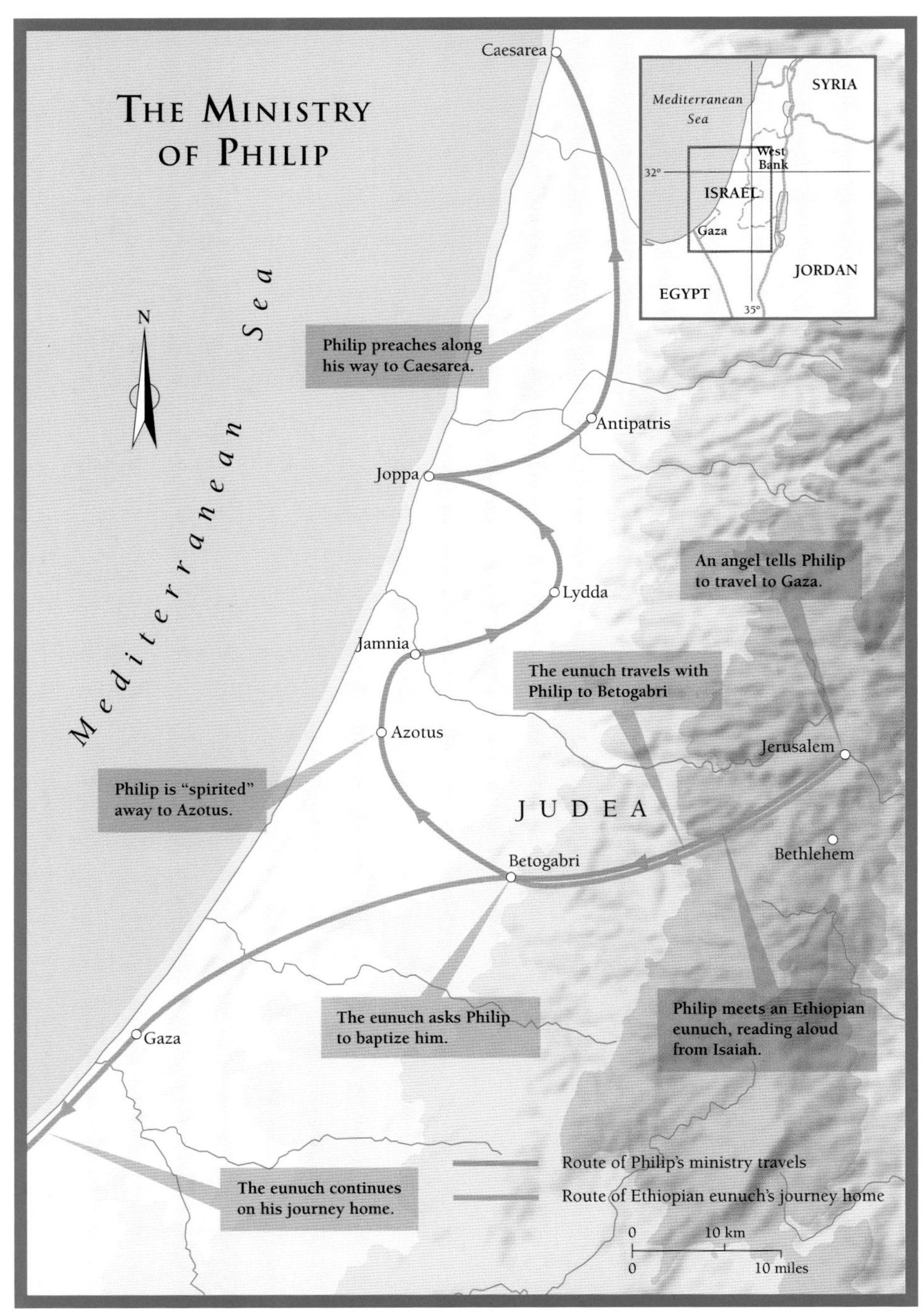

HELLENISTS AND HEBREWS

Although Jesus and his first Galilean disciples were probably Aramaic speakers (with perhaps some Greek for business purposes), Greek language and culture had left its mark on urban Jerusalem. In particular, Diaspora Jews who had settled in the holy city were primarily Greek speakers. Some of these had their own synagogues there: a Greek inscription excavated in Jerusalem refers to a synagogue built by a certain Theodotus son of Vettenus for the benefit of foreign travelers. Acts mentions a "synagogue of the Freedmen" (perhaps descendants of Jews taken as slaves to Rome by Pompey), and synagogues (or possibly the same synagogue) named for Greek-speaking North Africans, Cyrenians, and Alexandrians (Acts 6:9).

This linguistic distinction between Greek-speaking Jews and those whose primary language was Aramaic had an impact on the early Jerusalem Church. Acts refers to tensions between "Hellenists" and "Hebrews" over the daily distribution for one of the most economically vulnerable groups, the widows (Acts 6:1). Seven men are appointed by the apostles to oversee the administration of the community's charitable acts. Their Greek names suggest they are all members of the aggrieved Hellenist group: "Stephen, a man full of faith and the Holy Spirit, together with Philip, Prochorus, Nicanor, Timon, Parmenas, and Nicolaus, a proselyte of Antioch" (Acts 6:5). With the exception of the last, all are probably Christians of Jewish origin. Nicolaus may have been one of the proselytes present in Jerusalem at Pentecost. His city of Antioch on the Orontes in Syria, the third-largest city in the empire, will play an important role in Acts' story of the way the Gospel spread to the wider Gentile world.

Two of these seven, Stephen and Philip, will exercise a more prominent role in the next few chapters of Acts. Indeed, their activity of preaching and performing signs points to their ministry being more than one of practical administration (Acts 6:2: the Greek verb used for waiting on tables, *diakonein*, has led to the later identification of these seven as the first Christian deacons).

THE PASSION OF STEPHEN

Filled with the Spirit, Stephen begins his short-lived preaching ministry. Provoking hostility among some of his fellow Greek-speaking Jews, he finds himself, like Peter and John before him, dragged before the Sanhedrin and interrogated by the high priest. Stephen's ensuing speech (Acts 7:2–53) is sometimes seen as a manifesto of the Hellenists' theology. It retells the history of God's dealings with his chosen people: the call of Abraham, the sojourn in Egypt, the wilderness wanderings under Moses, the settlement and emergence of the monarchy. The emphasis is on the transitory existence of Israel as resident aliens, who worshipped God in a portable Tabernacle, and took that tent into the land. Hence Stephen's

LEFT: THE STONING AND IMPRISONMENT OF ST. STEPHEN IS DEPICTED IN THIS MEDIEVAL PAINTING FROM FRANCE. ACTS TELLS US THAT IMMEDIATELY AFTER STEPHEN'S MURDER, SAUL (PAUL) ABDUCTS MEN AND WOMEN FROM THEIR HOMES AND IMPRISONS THEM.

punchline: "the Most High does not dwell in houses made with human hands" (7:48). Particular similarities have been noted between Stephen's sermon and the theology of the Letter to the Hebrews.

The account of Stephen's martyrdom should be seen as another passion narrative, in which Stephen follows in his master's footsteps. His arrest at Acts 6:11–15 already hints at this: Stephen is accused of blasphemy, while false witnesses charge him with speaking about the Temple's destruction. As Stephen's sermon concludes and the Jerusalem lynch mob surrounds him, Luke reminds us of his own story of Jesus' death. Like Jesus, Stephen prays that his spirit will be received (Acts 7:59; see also Luke 23:46). Again like Jesus, he prays for his persecutors (Acts 7:60; see also Luke 23:34).

The stoning of Stephen marks the discrete entry of Paul of Tarsus onto the stage of Acts. Here he is called by his Jewish name Saul, which he probably received in honor of that other famous Benjaminite (Philippians 3:5), King Saul. Saul plays no part in Stephen's death. He is linked to it indirectly, however, by the laying of Stephen's garments at his feet and the statement that he approved of the killing (Acts 7:58; 8:1). This prepares us for Paul's unfolding role as the Church's persecutor.

FROM JUDEA TO SAMARIA

The second stage in the spread of the Gospel begins in chapter 8, as Stephen's companion Philip moves northward into Samaria. Acts presents this as a consequence of Stephen's martyrdom, and the resulting scattering of disciples. The reading "the city of Samaria" at Acts 8:5 would have Philip visit the town of that name, renamed Sebaste by Herod the Great in honor of the emperor Augustus. Some ancient manuscripts read "a city of Samaria" at Acts 8:5, thus referring to the territory of the Samaritans between Judea in the south and Galilee to the north.

The Samaritans were descendants of the northern tribes, who read their own version of the Pentateuch, and whose worship centered on Mt. Gerizim. There was little love lost between them and the Jews, who disputed their claim to be legitimate Israelites. John's Gospel describes a lengthy encounter between Jesus and a Samaritan woman, resulting in the conversion of a significant number of Samaritans (John 4). Acts, however, restricts the Samaritan mission to the post-Easter period, through the agency of Philip. Philip will go on to push the boundaries even further, baptizing a eunuch from the court of the Ethiopian queen (Acts 8:26–40). Later he will settle with his four prophet daughters at Caesarea Maritima (Acts 21:8; subsequent tradition associates him with Hierapolis in Asia Minor).

But the Samaritan mission is no isolated activity of a maverick evangelist. Acts shows how the ministry of Philip is confirmed by Jerusalem's most prominent apostles, Peter and John, thus rooting the Samaritan venture in the mission of the mother Church. Through their apostolic ministry the converted Samaritans receive the Holy Spirit, validating their earlier baptism at the hands of Philip. The second stage of the spread of the Gospel is now complete.

BELOW: *ST. STEPHEN,* BY ITALIAN ARTIST GIOTTO DI BONDONE. LIKE HIS FELLOW APOSTLES, PETER AND JOHN, BEFORE HIM, STEPHEN HAD TO DEFEND HIS BELIEFS BEFORE THE AUTHORITIES.

PAUL ON THE ROAD TO DAMASCUS

NOW AS HE WAS ... APPROACHING DAMASCUS, SUDDENLY A LIGHT FROM HEAVEN FLASHED AROUND HIM ACTS 9:3

The road from Jerusalem to Damascus owes its fame to an event occurring along it about the year C.E. 34. Acts gives us the most famous account of Paul's "Damascus Road experience." The great persecutor, "still breathing threats and murder against the disciples of the Lord" (Acts 9:1), is on his way to the city, claiming the high priest's authority to arrest any disciples of Jesus he should find there. But this journey will take an unexpected turn.

Roads and journeys are important throughout Luke and the Acts of the Apostles. The Gospel's central section (Luke 9:51–19:27) describes Jesus' last journey to Jerusalem, during which he prepares his disciples for what is to come. But life-changing experiences also happen on roads out of Jerusalem. It is on the road from Jerusalem to Emmaus that Cleopas and his companion encounter the risen Lord (Luke 24:13–35). On the road connecting Jerusalem with Gaza, Philip encounters the Ethiopian eunuch (Acts 8:26–40). Now it is on another road from Jerusalem that the persecutor Saul of Tarsus will be transformed into Paul, Apostle to the Gentiles. Given the significance of journeying, it is not surprising that the earliest followers of Jesus were known as people who belonged to the Way (Acts 9:2).

CONVERSION OR CALL?

Paul most likely followed the major thoroughfare through the Jordan valley, before turning to the northeast from Galilee toward Damascus, the snow-capped Mt. Hermon to the north. As he drew near to Damascus, the dramatic event occurred. Although Christians have come to speak of Paul's conversion, the story told by Acts, and the allusions to it in Paul's letters, suggest another possibility.

In that it was so life changing, shaking the very foundations of his Pharisaic worldview, it is appropriately called a conversion. Yet this did not mean a transfer from one religion to another. Rather, Paul prefers the language of a prophetic call: he is being commissioned for a particular task. He believes, like Jeremiah and Isaiah before him, that he has been prepared for this new role since before birth (Galatians 1:15; see also Isaiah 49:1; Jeremiah 1:5). His call near Damascus is understood to include a direct charge to preach God's Son among the Gentiles (Galatians 1:16).

LEFT: ST. PAUL'S CONVERSION IS SHOWN IN THE TOP PART OF THIS PAGE FROM A BYZANTINE MANUSCRIPT. IN GALATIANS, PAUL ADMITS THAT HE HAD BEEN TRYING TO DESTROY THE CHURCH.

Which is the Real Story?

The three accounts of Paul's "conversion":

Acts 9:1–9: Saul sees a blinding light and hears the voice of Christ, who sends him into Damascus; his companions hear a voice but see no one.

Acts 22:6–21: Saul sees a light and hears a voice; his companions see a light but hear no voice. Later, in a trance in the Jerusalem Temple, he is appointed to go to the Gentiles (verse 21).

Acts 26:12–18: Saul and those with him see a blinding light at midday. The heavenly voice of Christ appoints him to go to the Gentiles.

Acts contains no less than three accounts of this event, retold with varying literary license (two of them reports by Paul himself later in the narrative). It is perhaps not surprising that we have variant attempts to describe the Damascus road event, for how can one describe an encounter with the risen Lord? Readers of Acts may well detect Luke drawing on antecedents: the story of Apollonius, for example, knocked from his horse by angels at 4 Maccabees 4:1–14.

PAUL IN DAMASCUS

Damascus is located in an oasis in southern Syria, approximately 135 miles (217 km) northeast of Jerusalem. The city was completely rebuilt in the Hellenistic period, on a grid system. The one exception to the right-angled layout was the colonnaded "Street called Straight," which crossed the city from east to west. Its name probably reflects a local joke, for it was not straight but slightly crooked. Here Paul will reside with a fellow Jew named Judas.

When Paul finally arrives in Damascus, a Christian Jew, Ananias, seeks him out. Paul later describes him as "a devout man according to the law and well spoken of by all the Jews living" in Damascus (Acts 22:12). Acts does not state how the Christian message reached Damascus, though that might be due to missionaries scattered following Stephen's martyrdom (Acts 8:1). Ananias restores Paul's sight, and brings him by baptism into the messianic community. He boldly addresses as "brother Saul" one who, only days before, was intent on persecuting people such as him. He is another of the unsung heroes of the early Church, who disappears from Luke's story as quickly as he entered it.

ESCAPE FROM DAMASCUS

Apart from describing his synagogue preaching in Damascus, Acts is silent about what happened next. We do know from Galatians, however, that after his call he spent some time in Arabia before returning to Damascus (Galatians 1:17). "Arabia" refers to the area to the south, the kingdom of Nabataea. Its capital was the famous rock-city of Petra. Paul declines to spell out his reason for heading to Arabia/Nabataea. Some have thought that he went in search of a desert retreat, beginning to make sense of his encounter with Christ. Others have believed that the commission to preach to the Gentiles was so strong that he headed to Arabia on an evangelistic mission.

Either way, Paul seems to have made enemies there. Some time after returning to Damascus, he is forced to flee for his life. Under cover of night he is lowered down from the city's wall in a basket (Acts 9:25), and makes his way back to Jerusalem. Although Acts views the Jews of Damascus as the prime movers against him, Paul sees the real threat as "the governor under King Aretas" (2 Corinthians 11:32). The king in question is Aretas IV, king of the Nabataeans from 9 B.C.E. to C.E. 40. Damascus remained firmly under Roman control until Tiberius's death in March C.E. 37; Paul's reference suggests the city then came under Nabataean control, thus giving an approximate date for his escape.

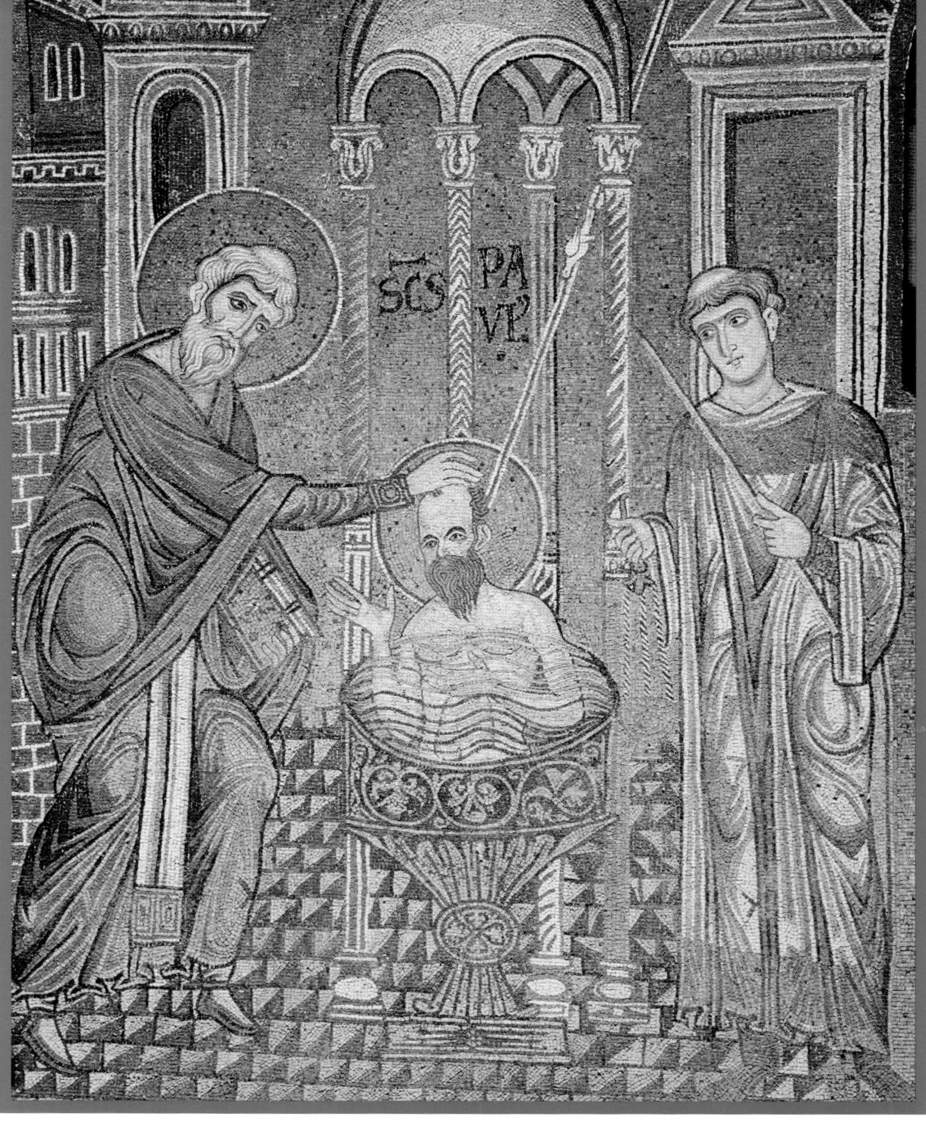

ABOVE: THIS SECTION OF THE ITALIAN MOSAIC *SCENES FROM THE LIFE OF ST. PAUL* SHOWS ANANIAS LAYING HIS HAND ON PAUL. ANANIAS HAD FOLLOWED GOD'S INSTRUCTIONS TO GO AND FIND PAUL AND FILL HIM WITH THE HOLY SPIRIT.

LEFT: PAUL FLEES DAMASCUS, FROM A FRENCH MANUSCRIPT BIBLE. THE METHOD OF PAUL'S ESCAPE VARIES IN THE MANY AVAILABLE REPRESENTATIONS OF THIS BIBLICAL EVENT.

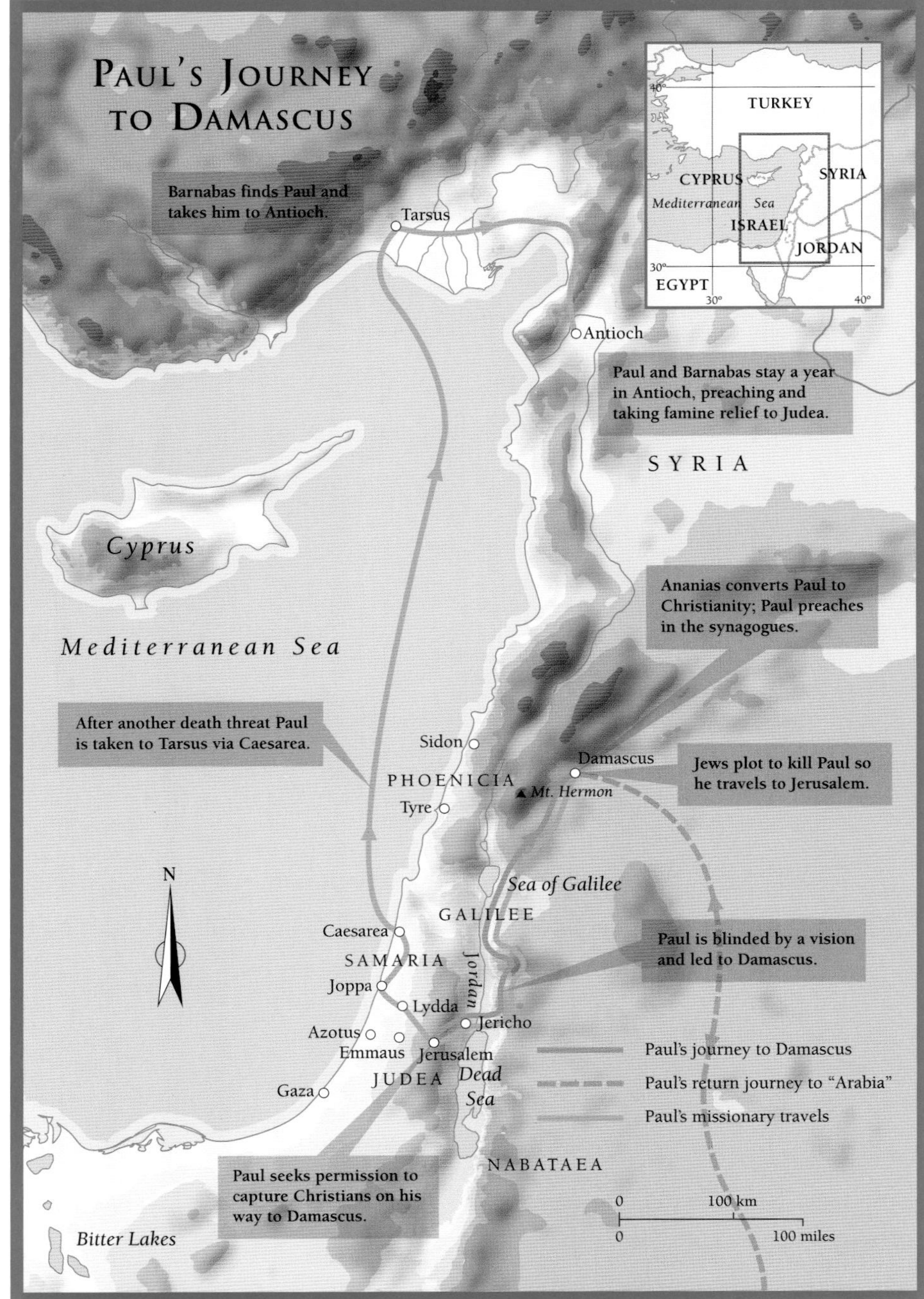

So Saul returns to Jerusalem a changed man. It is not surprising that the Church there suspected a plot to infiltrate their ranks. Later, Paul is insistent that he only met Peter (Cephas) and James the Lord's brother (Galatians 1:18–20); Acts suggests a wider meeting with the Jerusalem apostles. Here the Cypriot Joseph Barnabas emerges out of the shadows to show his worth as a true "son of encouragement" (see Acts 4:36). The stories of Barnabas and Saul will be inextricably linked in the chapters to follow.

OPENING TO THE GENTILES

Having prepared the ground for Paul's future work, Luke now returns to the leader of the Jerusalem apostles, Simon Peter. Although Paul is remembered as the great apostle to the Gentiles, Acts shows how his work is already anticipated in Peter's ministry. Somewhat reluctantly, but in accordance with the divine will, Peter opens a door for the Gentiles; Paul and Barnabas will use this opportunity to great effect, and on a far wider canvas.

HEALING ON THE FRINGES

Peter continues Christ's healing ministry here in two further healings (Acts 9:32–43). Yet as important as continuing Jesus' healing of those "on the margins" is the fact that Peter is also moving to the geographic margins. The locations of the two miraculous events, Lydda and Joppa, are away from Jerusalem on the coastal plain. Beyond them is the Great Sea, the Mediterranean. Soon Paul and Barnabas will sail across that sea to bring the good news to Cyprus and Asia Minor.

Lydda, the ancient Lod, was a large town or city located on the road linking Jerusalem with Joppa, about 10 miles (16 km) inland from Joppa. The port town of Joppa (from a Canaanite word meaning "the beautiful"), although inhabited by Jews, was a Greek city, stressing again Peter's move to the boundaries. Here he resides with Simon the tanner, an occupation despised by many pious Jews.

The story of the healing of Aeneas in Lydda echoes Jesus' healing of a paralytic at Luke 5:18–26. Although Aeneas is not a Jewish name, the fact that Peter's dealings with him are uncontroversial (unlike those with Cornelius) suggests he is a Jew, probably a Christian Jew. Part of Peter's motive in traveling seems to have been to encourage the disciples living on the edge of Judea. Aeneas's healing leads to conversions among the (Jewish) population of Lydda and "the Sharon," the coastal plain located between the sea and the central hill country. Peter's second healing, at Joppa, certainly involves a disciple. When Tabitha, or Dorcas in Greek ("gazelle"), is raised from the dead one is reminded of Jesus' raising of Jairus's daughter (Luke 8:49–56). Acts 8:40 hints that both Lydda and Joppa were evangelized by Philip on his way from Azotus to Caesarea.

GOD-FEARERS CONVERTED

Now that Peter is on the Holy Land's geographic fringes, the stage is set for the next major transition in the spread of the gospel. Cornelius, a Roman centurion of the Italian Cohort stationed at Caesarea, will receive the Holy Spirit and be baptized. Archaeological evidence attests a "Second Italian Cohort" in the area later in the century, though none has been found for Cornelius's time. The Caesarea in question is Caesarea Maritima (distinguishing it from other cities named

RIGHT: THE CENTURION CORNELIUS IS CONVERTED AT THE COASTAL TOWN OF CAESAREA MARITIMA. IN ACTS 10, LUKE ASSERTS THAT PETER BAPTIZED THE FIRST GENTILES WHO HAD BEEN CONVERTED.

after the emperor, such as Caesarea Philippi). Formerly Strato's Tower, it had been magnificently rebuilt by Herod the Great. Ruins have survived of a fine artificial harbor, a Roman theater, and an aqueduct.

LEFT: "THE ANGEL WAKES ST. PETER," FROM THE FRESCO *THE LIBERATION OF ST. PETER.* THE NIGHT BEFORE HEROD WAS GOING TO EXECUTE HIM, AN ANGEL APPEARED BEFORE PETER AND LED HIM OUT OF HIS PRISON CELL.

Luke frequently speaks of Roman officials who are favorable toward the Christian message. Cornelius is described as "a devout man who feared God with all his household" (Acts 10:2). In this, he resembles the centurion who built the synagogue in Capernaum (Luke 7:1–10). The first step toward the Gentiles will be to one who is already on the fringes of the synagogue. Although Peter is instrumental here, what validates this dramatic step is divine revelation. Cornelius's visitation from an angel is followed by a trance-induced vision, in which Peter sees a sheet containing all varieties of creatures. Through this vision, Peter comes to see that God is now overriding the traditional clean/unclean distinction. As he is to learn, this applies not simply to animals and food, but to the distinction between Jews and Gentiles.

Hence, on returning to Jerusalem later (see Acts 11:1–18), he is prepared to justify the action taken at Caesarea. In Cornelius's house, Peter's preaching prompts divine activity, as the Holy Spirit descends even upon the "unclean" Gentiles. The Spirit was the expected gift of the new age, and its possession was a sign of being God's people. Faced with heaven's approval of pious Cornelius and his family, Peter cannot refuse them baptism. Indeed, Luke has him seal this by accepting their hospitality for several days. Nevertheless, the full implications of this are not worked out immediately, either for Peter or for the Church. Later, at Antioch, Paul will challenge Peter over his decision to no longer eat with Gentiles, again treating them as unclean (Galatians 2:11–14).

ANOTHER HEROD PERSECUTES THE CHURCH

Back in Jerusalem, hostility directed toward the Church continues. Now it is associated with King Herod (Acts 12:1–5), who executes James son of Zebedee, and also takes action against Peter. Herod Agrippa I was the grandson of Herod the Great, born in 10 B.C.E. and educated in Rome, where he became friends with the future emperors Gaius and Claudius. He inherited his uncle Philip's tetrarchy in C.E. 38, adding Antipas's Galilee and Perea two years later. He ruled as king of Judea between the years C.E. 41 and 44.

Acts' portrayal of Agrippa is negative, influenced by the memory of his action against the Way. Though a promoter of Hellenism like his grandfather, at home Agrippa was a pious Jew. Acts has a most dramatic account of his untimely death, in which the crowds acclaim him as a god, and he develops a fatal illness. The tragic demise of a figure of royal power (Acts 12:20–23) contrasts powerfully with the escape from prison of the fisherman he sought to destroy, and the inexorable progress of the message he wished to quash.

BELOW: *THE BAZAAR NEAR THE DAMASCUS GATE IN JERUSALEM,* BY CARL HAAG. KNOWING THAT THE JEWISH AUTHORITIES IN JERUSALEM APPROVED OF JAMES'S MURDER INSPIRED HEROD TO ARREST PETER AS WELL.

THE FIRST JOURNEY OF PAUL

THEY WENT DOWN TO SELEUCIA; AND FROM THERE THEY SAILED TO CYPRUS ACTS 13:4

If Peter has labored on the boundaries of the Holy Land, Paul (and initially Barnabas) will be the key players in crossing the geographic boundaries. They will bring the gospel not only to Gentiles already attracted to Judaism, such as Cornelius, but their mission will also embrace worshippers of pagan gods. Furthermore, the center of Luke's story will shift from the mother Church in Jerusalem to a new church in the city of Antioch, which will play the key role in this next stage.

A MISSION FROM ANTIOCH

Antioch on the Orontes in Syria was an impressive city indeed, founded in 300 B.C.E. and by now the third-largest in the whole empire. Its first-century C.E. population has been conservatively estimated at about 100,000. Situated about 15 miles (24 km) from the coast, it had a splendid location in a broad plain, bounded by the Orontes River to the west and Mt. Silpius to the east. Now capital of the Roman province of Syria, Antioch was a flourishing city of commerce and political influence, with a thriving Jewish community. It is not so surprising that it becomes such a crucial center of early Christianity.

According to Acts, the foundation of the Antiochene Church was laid by disciples of Cypriot and Cyrenian origin, who were among those dispersed from Jerusalem during the persecution following Stephen's death (Acts 11:19–30). These seem to have preached in Antioch not simply to fellow Jews but also to non-Jewish Greek speakers (ancient manuscripts read either "Hellenists" or "Greeks" at Acts 11:20). Luke sees this as the logical continuation of Peter's action in Caesarea, preparing the ground for Paul's more robust Gentile mission. By Paul's time, its leaders ("prophets and teachers" Acts 13:1) include his friend the Cypriot Barnabas and Lucius of Cyrene. Two others are also mentioned without reference to their place of origin. Both men have Jewish names: Simeon, nicknamed Niger (from the Latin for "black"), and Manaen (a Greek form of Menahem). The latter is described as a *suntrophos*, perhaps "childhood friend," of Herod the tetrarch, Herod Antipas (reigned 4 B.C.E.–C.E. 39).

ABOVE: *ST. PAUL PREACHING AT ANTIOCH*, BY HAROLD COPPING. OFFICIALS OF THE SYNAGOGUE INVITED PAUL AND BARNABAS TO ADDRESS THE PEOPLE. PAUL DELIVERS A LONG SPEECH.

It is this Church that sponsors the mission to Cyprus and Asia Minor. As a result of divine commissioning through the community's prophets, Barnabas and Saul are sent on their way. While Christians often think of an independent Pauline mission, at this early stage Paul and Barnabas are emissaries, "apostles" of the Antiochene Church. Indeed, Luke's listing of Barnabas first (Acts 13:2) may suggest his more important position.

FROM SELEUCIA TO SALAMIS

Seleucia Pieria was the port town serving the city of Antioch, connected to it by the Orontes River. Named after its founder Seleucus I, and Mt. Pierius on whose slope it was built, the town moved up in tiers from the harbor and lower city, through a terraced residential area, to the most impressive acropolis on the mountain's summit. Seleucia had a Roman fleet stationed in its harbor.

It is from Seleucia that Paul and Barnabas board a vessel sailing to the latter's native island of Cyprus. This sea route reflects the strong trading links between Cyprus and Antioch. They are accompanied on the first stage of their journey by Barnabas's cousin John Mark (Acts 13:5; see also 12:12; Colossians 4:10). Tradition identifies this John Mark with Mark the second evangelist, and companion of Peter (1 Peter 5:13). After some days at sea (a journey of some 130 miles [209 km]), they arrive at the port of Salamis on the eastern coast of Cyprus, 6 miles (10 km) north of the present city of Famagusta.

RIGHT: *THE BLINDING OF ELYMAS* BY RAPHAEL. WHEN THEY REACHED PAPHOS, PAUL AND BARNABAS MET A MAGICIAN CALLED ELYMAS WHO OPPOSED THEM. PAUL TEMPORARILY BLINDS ELYMAS TO PROVE THAT MAGIC IS NO MATCH FOR THE POWER OF GOD.

PAUL AND BARNABAS IN CYPRUS

Salamis was the former capital of the island. Although it ceded this position to Paphos in the Roman period, it still remained an important commercial city. Acts records the preaching activity of Paul, Barnabas, and John in the Jewish synagogues there. Luke does not tell us where Barnabas's native city was located, though it is quite likely he would have wanted to spread the word in his home synagogue. Later traditions in the apocryphal *Acts of Barnabas* locate Barnabas's martyrdom in Salamis.

But the three do not remain in Salamis for long. Their goal is the new center of Roman administration. The missionaries' long journey from Salamis to Paphos in the southwest would have taken them across the vast southern plain, eventually skirting the foothills of the impressive Troodos Mountains (rising to a height of some 4,000 ft [1,220 m]) as they neared their destination.

Two features are worthy of note in Acts' description of their activity in Paphos (Acts 13:6–12). First is the positive reception to the gospel from another Roman official. Cyprus became a Roman senatorial province in 22 B.C.E., and Sergius Paulus is introduced as the current Roman proconsul. An inscription has been found in northern Cyprus referring to a Roman official of this name, though this cannot confidently

LEFT: ANCIENT RUINS OF THE PALESTRA AT SALAMIS, CYPRUS. THIS PUBLIC ARENA FOR THE TRAINING OF ATHLETES WAS BUILT IN THE SECOND CENTURY C.E.

THE "NEW PAPHOS"

The Paphos Acts describes is "New Paphos" (Pliny the Elder, *Natural History* 5.130), so described to distinguish it from the older neighboring city. It had a famous temple to Aphrodite, known locally as the Paphian goddess. Among Roman buildings discovered during excavations are a splendid villa (possibly the palace of the Roman governor) and an amphitheater. Today there is an Aphrodite Beach (below) on Cyprus.

be identified as our Sergius Paulus. What is important for Luke is that he listens eagerly to the message, and that Christianity is thereby introduced into the upper echelons of Roman society. Secondly, the interwoven story of the Jewish magician Elymas or Bar-Jesus ("son of Jesus" or "son of Joshua") proclaims the triumph of Christ over magic, which held so many people in its grip in the ancient world.

Later Christian tradition continues to connect Barnabas with his native island. According to this, he returns to Cyprus some years later with John Mark, and his remains are buried on the island after his martyrdom in the hippodrome in Salamis in about the year C.E. 61.

THE MISSION IN PAMPHYLIA AND SOUTHERN GALATIA

Cyprus was not virgin territory for these Christian missionaries, given the Acts' reference elsewhere to the activity of Christian Jews on the island (e.g., Acts 11:20). Where Paul and Barnabas now head, however, is breaking totally new ground. Leaving Cyprus behind, they head to the mainland of Asia Minor. This vast landmass of Anatolia (present-day Turkey) will feature prominently in Paul's future missionary activity, and will eventually be his gateway into Europe. For the present, however, he and Barnabas will concentrate on cities in the south-central region, located in the territories of Phrygia, Pamphylia, Pisidia, and Lycaonia.

RIGHT: MARBLE STATUE OF ATHENA, SCULPTED IN THE SECOND CENTURY C.E. IT WAS FOUND AT PERGA IN MODERN-DAY TURKEY. ATHENA, GREEK GODDESS OF WISDOM AND WAR, IS THE PATRON DEITY OF ATHENS.

RIGHT: ROMAN RUINS AT PERGA. THE STADIUM WOULD HAVE HAVE BEEN INTACT AND WELL USED AT THE TIME OF PAUL AND BARNABAS'S VISIT TO THIS CITY.

Paul, Barnabas, and John Mark sail to the province of Pamphylia, where John Mark takes leave of them to return to Jerusalem. Their first named destination is Perga. Though Perga is located some miles inland, the navigability of the Kestros River may have enabled them to reach the city's port, rather than docking at the coastal port of Attalia. Perga, or Perge, was a sizable town, with a stadium and theater capable of seating 12,000 and 15,000 people respectively.

The two remaining missionaries do not linger in Perga, however (they will preach the gospel there briefly on their return journey before sailing from Attalia: Acts 14:25). Rather, they take the road northward into the hinterland, crossing into the Roman province of Galatia and eventually arriving at another Antioch, Antioch in Pisidia. There were many towns and cities of this name, dedicated to members of the family of Antiochus, one of Alexander the Great's generals and successors. This Antioch was a Roman colony, populated by veterans from the army, located high on the Anatolian plain. Strictly speaking it was sited in Phrygia near the border with Pisidia: hence it is more correctly called in Greek *Antiocheia pros Pisidian*, "Antioch toward Pisidia." The city was a little piece of Rome in the midst of a very non-Roman territory. One inscription found there refers to a certain "Lucius Sergius Paulus the younger," providing a possible link to Paul's previous activity in Cyprus.

PREACHING IN ANOTHER ANTIOCH

The two Jewish visitors go to the synagogue of Pisidian Antioch on the Sabbath. There Paul preaches a sermon which initiates one of the turning points in the narrative of Acts. In it he rehearses salvation history from the great act of redemption out of Egypt, through the judges to the establishment of the monarchy under Saul and then David, "a man after my heart" (Acts 13:22). In a fine example of the early Christian kerygma (gospel), he then focuses on David's descendant Jesus, highlighting his rejection in Jerusalem, his death, and his resurrection. There are striking similarities with Peter's Pentecost sermon, not least the exegesis of Psalm 16, as well as the speech of Stephen.

Rather like the Nazarenes' reaction to Jesus' synagogue sermon (Luke 4:16–30), the response of the Jews in Antioch is initially favorable. Many of them, including a

number of converts to Judaism, hear the message gladly. Things are quite different the following Sabbath, however, when Paul's preaching is vehemently contradicted by some other Jews. Luke attributes this to jealousy due to the popularity of Paul and Barnabas (Acts 13:45). The response of these two, supported by a quotation from Isaiah 49:6, charts another transition in the story of Acts: "It was necessary that the word of God should be spoken first to you. Since you reject it and judge yourselves to be unworthy of eternal life, we are now turning to the Gentiles" (13:46).

TROUBLE IN ICONIUM

This dramatic statement does not mean an end to the mission among fellow Jews, however. While Luke emphasizes the impressive success of their preaching among Gentiles in the district, Paul and Barnabas's first port of call in the next town they visit, Iconium, is the Jewish synagogue. Indeed, they are successful among both Greeks and Jews in that Greek city (Iconium did not become a Roman colony until the reign of Hadrian). Nor will this dual mission stop here: to the very end of Acts, Paul will continue to preach the Christian message to all who are prepared to listen, including leaders of the Jewish community.

LEFT: *THE MIRACLE OF ST. BARNABAS*, BY PAOLO CALIARI. AS THEY WENT ON THEIR MISSIONARY JOURNEY, PAUL AND BARNABAS PREACHED AND HEALED IN THE SYNAGOGUE AND IN THE STREETS.

RIGHT: THE HEAD OF ZEUS, ETRUSCAN TERRACOTTA BUST. THE PEOPLE OF LYSTRA BELIEVED BARNABAS TO BE ZEUS, THE CHIEF GOD.

BELOW: PAUL AND BARNABAS HEALING IN LYSTRA. THE PIVOTAL STORY CONTAINED IN ACTS 14 IS THAT OF PAUL CURING A MAN WHO HAD BEEN CRIPPLED FROM BIRTH.

Iconium, now modern Konya, was located approximately 80 miles (129 km) southeast of Pisidian Antioch. The two cities were connected by the *Via Sebaste,* the road completed in 6 B.C.E. to link Roman colonies in southern Anatolia. Some ancient writers locate it, like Antioch, in Phrygia, others in Lycaonia. Built on a plateau nearly 4,000 ft (1,220 m) high, it was very much a border town between the mountainous region of the former and the broad plain of the latter. Its origins go back at least into the third millennium B.C.E. Indeed, according to local legends it was the first city to be built after a great flood, and derived its name from the "icons" of human beings made by Prometheus and Athena when the floodwaters subsided. Though not as important in the Roman period as Pisidian Antioch, it was still a significant and strategically located city, the kind favored by Paul for the establishment of his churches.

Although they are at first successful in Iconium, their preaching soon provokes division among the people, both Jewish and Gentile. Discovering an attempt to have them mistreated and stoned, they are forced to flee again, this time to the nearby Lycaonian cities of Lystra and Derbe. The epistle 2 Timothy 3:11 also attests to the difficulties faced by Paul in this stage of his missionary activity: "Now you have observed my persecutions, and my suffering the things that happened to me in Antioch, Iconium, and Lystra." It is a pattern that is played out in Acts again and again as Paul gradually pushes back the boundaries of the Gentile mission as far as Rome itself.

ACTIVITY IN LYSTRA

Lystra, a market town of the Lycaonian region (and the home town of Paul's companion Timothy: Acts 16:1), was situated 25 miles (40 km) southwest of Iconium. The town was on the *Via Sebaste,* about a day's travel from the main road crossing Asia Minor from east to west. Another Roman colony, founded by Augustus in 26 B.C.E., its inscriptions tended to be in Latin rather than Greek. Nevertheless, there remained a strong indigenous population with its distinctive dialect, as a story recounted by Luke reveals (Acts 14:8–18).

Acts' description of this visit to Lystra focuses on the healing of a lame man. Just as Peter performed healings that closely pattern those of Jesus, so too does Paul. There are strong similarities between this miracle in Lystra, and the one performed by Peter at Jerusalem's Beautiful Gate (Acts 3:1–10). Moreover, both echo Luke's account of Jesus healing a paralytic (Luke 5:18–26).

The local reaction to this healing provides an interesting glimpse of the indigenous population, who believe the missionaries to be gods. Barnabas, perhaps because he was older or more impressive, they call the great god Zeus; because he did the talking, Paul is mistaken for the gods' spokesman, Hermes. Led by Lystra's priest of Zeus, the people bring bulls and garlands in a thwarted attempt to offer sacrifices to Paul and Barnabas (surviving carvings from Pisidian Antioch show sacrificial bulls with their horns wreathed in flowers). Their response, a strong assertion of their humanity and a proclamation of the one living God, is noticeable for its omission of any reference to Christ.

TO DERBE, AND RETURN TO ANTIOCH

After a violent stoning, Paul leaves with Barnabas for Derbe, some 60 miles (97 km) away. Located on the Anatolian plateau, Derbe was an ancient city, whose name possibly derives from the local word for "juniper tree." It became part of the Roman province of Galatia in 25 B.C.E., and later was closely linked with the emperor Claudius, earning it the name Claudio-Derbe.

The description of Paul and Barnabas's visit here is brief. They appear to have been successful, and there is no hint of antagonism from the Jewish community. Later we shall hear of a disciple called Gaius from Derbe, who becomes a companion of Paul (Acts 19:29, 20:4). But now Luke is impatient to reconnect the two missionaries with their sponsoring church. A brief summary of their return journey brings them back to Perga, and so to the Mediterranean port of Attalia. This critical new stage in the early Christian mission is at an end. Now, with Antioch's support, Paul and Barnabas will have to defend this development before the Church in Jerusalem.

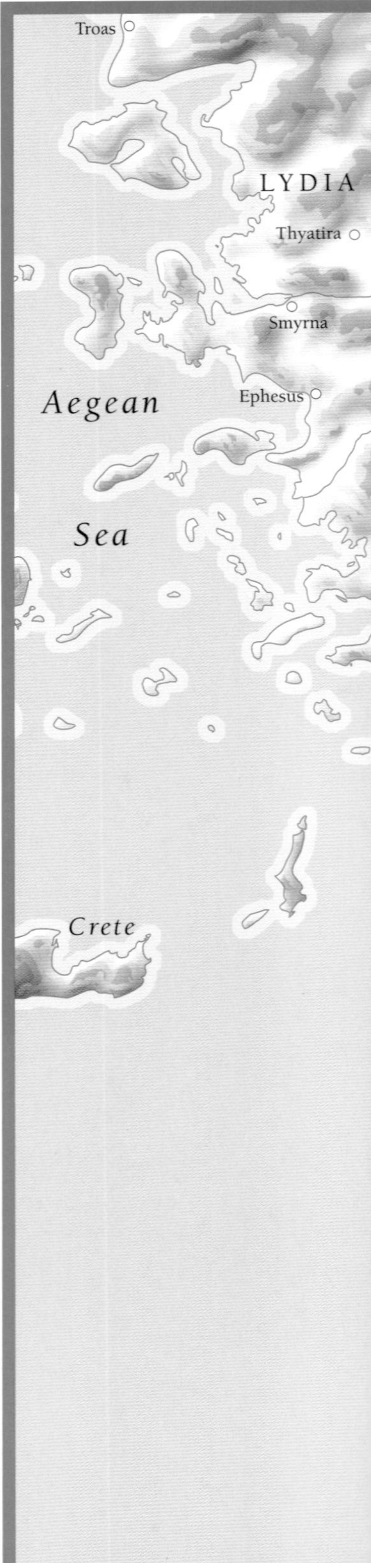

LEFT: ATTALIA, THE SEAPORT OF PERGA, IS TODAY KNOWN AS ANTALYA. NAMED BY ATTALUS II, A KING OF PERGAMON, IN THE SECOND CENTURY B.C.E., THE TOWN HAS BEEN CONTINUOUSLY INHABITED SINCE THEN.

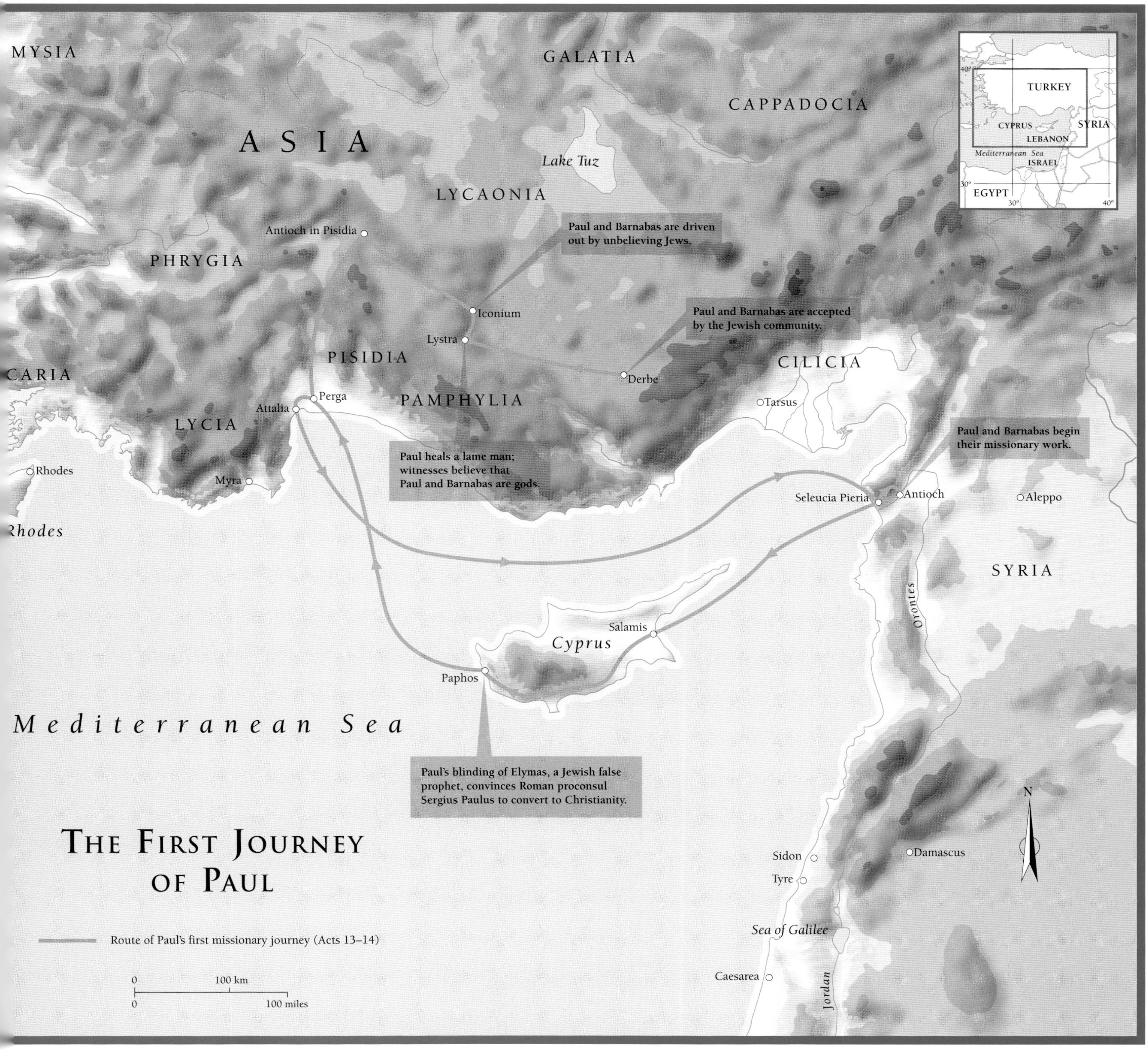

THE FIRST JOURNEY OF PAUL

MYSIA
GALATIA
CAPPADOCIA
ASIA
Lake Tuz
LYCAONIA
PHRYGIA
Antioch in Pisidia
Paul and Barnabas are driven out by unbelieving Jews.
Iconium
Lystra
Paul and Barnabas are accepted by the Jewish community.
PISIDIA
Derbe
CILICIA
CARIA
Perga
Attalia
PAMPHYLIA
Tarsus
LYCIA
Paul heals a lame man; witnesses believe that Paul and Barnabas are gods.
Paul and Barnabas begin their missionary work.
Rhodes
Myra
Seleucia Pieria
Antioch
Aleppo
Rhodes
SYRIA
Salamis
Cyprus
Orontes
Paphos
Mediterranean Sea
Paul's blinding of Elymas, a Jewish false prophet, convinces Roman proconsul Sergius Paulus to convert to Christianity.
Sidon
Tyre
Damascus
Sea of Galilee
Caesarea
Jordan
N
TURKEY
CYPRUS
SYRIA
LEBANON
Mediterranean Sea
ISRAEL
EGYPT

Route of Paul's first missionary journey (Acts 13–14)

0 100 km
0 100 miles

THE SECOND JOURNEY OF PAUL

SO THE CHURCHES WERE STRENGTHENED IN THE FAITH AND INCREASED IN NUMBERS DAILY ACTS 16:5

RIGHT: THIS CHRISTIAN OR JEWISH BRONZE STAMP FROM THE THIRD OR FOURTH CENTURY C.E. FEATURES A SEVEN-BRANCHED CANDLESTICK OR MENORAH, ONE OF THE OLDEST SYMBOLS OF JEWISH FAITH.

In this wonderful section of the Acts of the Apostles we read about the pivotal Jerusalem conference and the beginning of the heart of Paul's missionary work in important Greek cities such as Philippi, Thessalonica, and especially Corinth. Information from this section often corresponds directly with information from Paul's letters, which makes it even more interesting from a historical perspective.

Key to our understanding of this section of Acts is the fact that at this early stage in the Christian movement, its members were largely Jewish and had been since birth. Moreover, in the period from Jesus' death (*c.* C.E. 30) until C.E. 70, the center of the early Church was Jerusalem, not Rome. Only with Paul and the missionaries who, like him, took the message beyond Judea did the issue of non-Jews becoming Christians become important.

MEETING IN JERUSALEM

Chapter 15 of Acts opens by describing the confusion that arose in the early Church when some church leaders from Judea said that unless Christians were circumcised as prescribed by God in the Jewish Law (the Torah) they could not be saved. When strong dissension arose over this issue, it was decided that Paul and Barnabas would go to Jerusalem to discuss this matter with the leaders there.

The meeting in Jerusalem represents a watershed in the early Christian movement. Paul mentions his attendance at the Jerusalem conference in his epistle to the Galatians (2:1–10). Paul's efforts to draw converts and to establish churches were beginning to bear fruit. Paul did not require converts to be circumcised as Jewish men had been commanded by God (Genesis 17:11). However, some of the Jerusalem leadership, who had formerly been Pharisees like Paul himself (Philippians 3:5), felt it was important to keep with tradition and circumcise non-Jewish converts. This question may seem odd to us today, but it was of great significance to the early Christians, who sought to carry out the will of God. Many felt that this meant continuing to be faithful to ancient traditions, such as circumcision, while others, such as Paul, thought that in Jesus, God had done something new, which meant letting go of older traditions.

Luke tells us that the outcome of the Jerusalem conference was that non-Jewish converts would be asked only to "abstain from what has been sacrificed to idols and from blood and from what is strangled and from fornication" (Acts 15:29). This is similar to what Paul outlines in Galatians 2:7–10 as the result of the conference. The decision of the Jerusalem conference defined the way Christianity would look from that point forward. Its

RIGHT: *JERUSALEM*, WATERCOLOR BY KARL FRIEDRICH WERNER. ALTHOUGH GENTILES HAD ALREADY BEEN ADMITTED INTO THE CHURCH, THE MEETING IN JERUSALEM DISCUSSED CONDITIONS THAT MIGHT APPLY TO SUCH ADMISSION, SUCH AS CIRCUMCISION.

members would not be circumcised, nor in large part would they keep the Torah. Instead, baptism would be the primary marker of entry into the community, and new rules of conduct based on the life and teachings of Jesus would guide the movement.

PAUL AND SILAS ENCOUNTER TIMOTHY

At the end of chapter 15, we learn that Paul and Barnabas seem to have had a disagreement over who should travel with them. Acts 15:39 says there arose "a sharp contention." In the end, Barnabas chooses Mark (see also John Mark in Philemon 24; Colossians 4:10) and departs for the island of Cyprus, while Paul chooses Silas and departs for Syria and Cilicia.

LEFT: PAUL ON HIS TRAVELS WITH SILAS AND TIMOTHY, FROM A THIRTEENTH-CENTURY FRENCH MANUSCRIPT. ACTS 16 TELLS US THAT PAUL HAD TIMOTHY CIRCUMCISED TO APPEASE THE JEWISH AUTHORITIES IN LYSTRA AND ICONIUM.

Silas, a co-worker of Paul, is mentioned only in this particular section of Acts (chapters 15–18). He is likely the same individual mentioned by Paul (as Silvanus) in 2 Corinthians 1:19 and in 1 Thessalonians 1:1 (see also 2 Thessalonians 1:1) and also perhaps is the referent in 1 Peter 5:12. He appears to have been Paul's close associate during his most important missionary work.

At the beginning of Acts 16, Paul and Silas meet Timothy in the region of Derbe and Lystra. Timothy becomes perhaps Paul's most important co-worker. Paul mentions him in virtually all of his undisputed letters (Romans 16:21; 1 Corinthians 4:17, 16:10; 2 Corinthians 1:1, 1:19; Philippians 1:1, 2:19; 1 Thessalonians 1:1, 3:2, 3:6). Timothy represents the very type of person about whom Paul and the Jerusalem leaders were concerned. Timothy's mother was Jewish, while his father was a Greek; therefore, Timothy was not originally Jewish and thus not circumcised, but he became a believer in Jesus Christ.

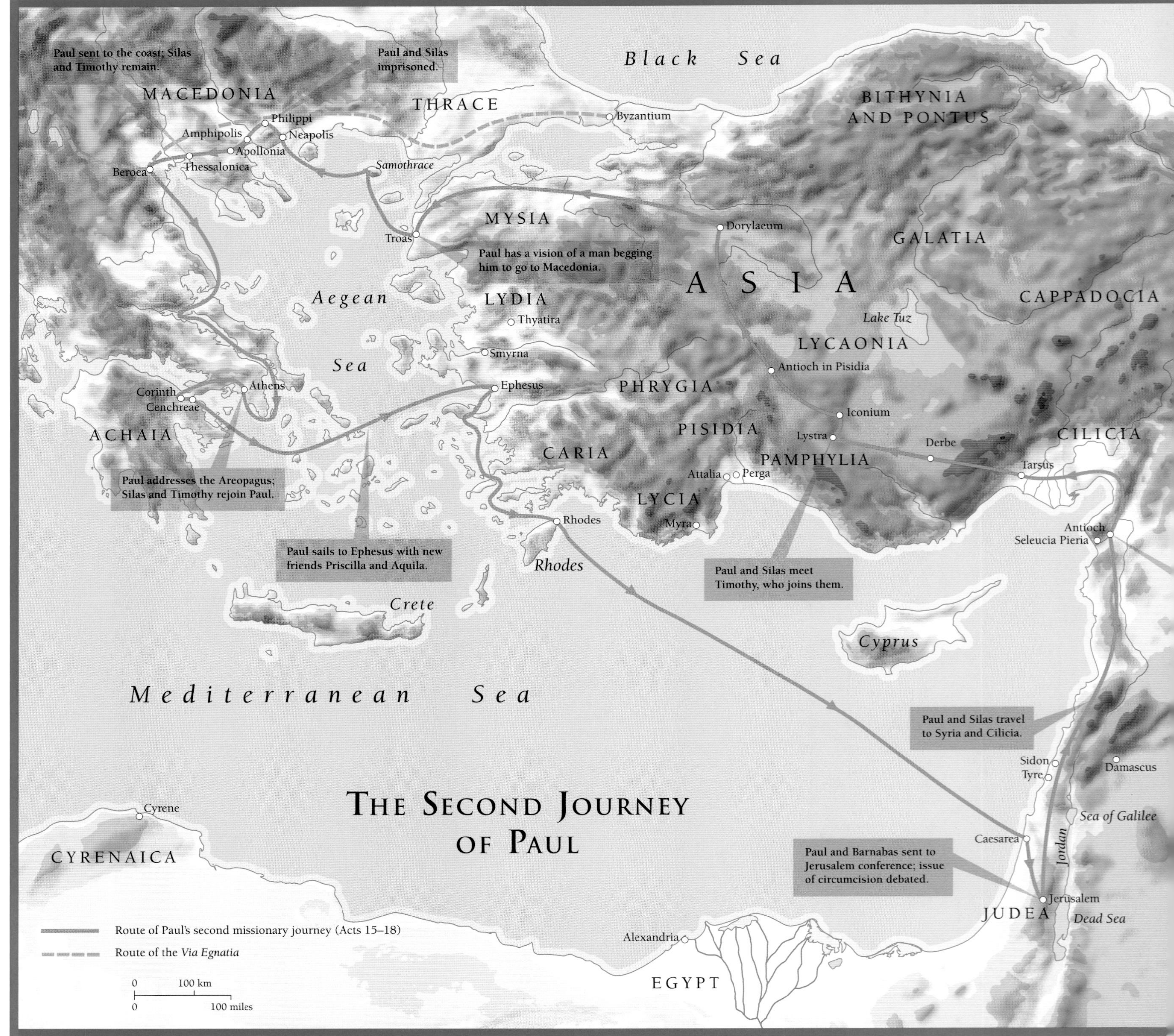

TROAS

Acts 16:10–17 is noteworthy for its important shift from the third person ("they") to the first person ("we"). It represents the first of the so-called "we" sections of Acts. The nature of these "we" sections of Acts is unclear. They are suggestive in that they appear—via either Luke or perhaps another eyewitness—to record moments when the narrator was actually in Paul's company.

The city of Troas is only mentioned a few other times in the New Testament. It appears again in Acts 20:5–6, but also in 2 Corinthians 2:12, where Paul mentions his brief visit there (it also appears in 2 Timothy 4:13). It does not appear to have become an important city for Paul, but it was an important travel city, since it was from there that Paul would cross over from Asia Minor to Greece.

PAUL AND SILAS ARE IMPRISONED IN PHILIPPI

In a lengthy narrative (Acts 16:16–40) we hear about Paul and Silas's experience in Philippi. Philippi was located on the important Roman road called the *Via Egnatia* (the Egnatian Way), making it a good place for meeting a variety of people and for communication. Thus, a strong Roman presence would have been likely, as we see in the Acts narrative. After Paul exorcises a demon from a woman, some Thessalonians take exception and turn Paul and Silas over to the Roman authorities for allegedly disturbing the peace. Paul and Silas are imprisoned. About midnight, as they were praying, an earthquake frees them from their bonds and breaks open their cell. Rather than fleeing, however, they remain in their cell. On seeing this, the guard decides to convert himself and his family to the teachings of Paul and Silas.

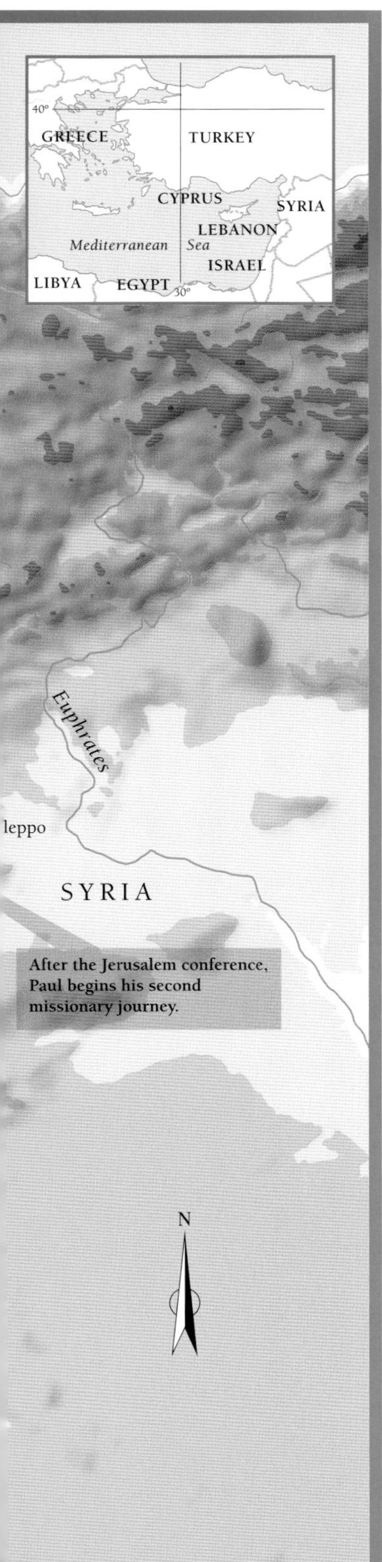

After the Jerusalem conference, Paul begins his second missionary journey.

The next day word comes from the local Roman magistrates that Paul and Silas should be freed. Paul refuses to depart, however, noting his ill-treatment despite the fact that he is a Roman citizen. Nowhere in his epistles does Paul mention the fact that he is a Roman citizen, but it is mentioned again in Acts 22:25. Eventually, the Roman officials placate Paul and convince him to leave.

Years later, in his letter to the Philippians, Paul writes with fond memories of his time with them (Philippians 1:3–5), but also with stern warnings not to fall away to those who promote circumcision (Philippians 3:2). So it appears that while an important decision was reached at the Jerusalem conference, the issue was not entirely settled. We should note that while Paul mentions in his epistle to the Philippians that he is imprisoned (Philippians 1:7, 13–14), he is not referring to the same imprisonment that is recorded in Acts, since it would have been long in the past. Instead, it is likely that Paul was imprisoned when he wrote this letter.

TRAVELS TO THESSALONICA AND BEROEA

At the beginning of Acts 17, we learn that Paul and Silas travel on to Thessalonica via the cities of Amphipolis and Apollonia. Thessalonica was the capital city of the Roman province of Macedonia (northern Greece). Paul wrote at least once (1 Thessalonians) and likely a second time to the Thessalonians (2 Thessalonians). The letter known as 1 Thessalonians is the oldest surviving letter of Paul. Some scholars believe it is also the oldest book in the New Testament (*c.* C.E. 50).

In the story, Paul and Silas enter the Jewish synagogue. This seems to have been a regular practice for Paul. Why would he do this? There are a number of reasons. First, the synagogue was a meeting place, so in an age before any type of mass media, the best way to reach a lot of people quickly was to find them where they congregated (note, for example, how Jesus would gather crowds or teach at the Temple). Next, Paul himself was a Jew and had been a Pharisee. He was thus well versed in the Torah. He was able to debate with other Jews from their sacred text. Moreover, other Jews would have been ready to discuss the topic of the messiah, even if they disagreed as to the messiah's actual identity. Additionally, Paul would have likely made at the synagogue important social contacts such as people that would house him and help him to find work. This makes it quite likely that Paul did begin his work in new cities at the synagogue. This being the case, we can also see why another trend in Paul's missionary work emerged. Paul's mission was an urban one; that is, Paul went to *cities*. Most often, Paul went to cities that were capitals of their respective Roman provinces. Why would Paul have done this? In such cities Paul would have found the most people, synagogues, more potential for work, more means of communication, more food, and so on. It comes as no surprise then that most of Paul's work occurred in, and most of his letters were written to the churches in, major urban areas.

Beroea (Acts 17:10 and 13) is not mentioned elsewhere in Paul's letters and is mentioned only once more in the New Testament at Acts 20:4. It does not appear to have become an important city for Paul and is likely only mentioned because it was on the road from Thessalonica to Athens.

ABOVE: THIS STELE FROM THESSALONICA IS EVIDENCE OF THE CO-EXISTENCE OF GREEK AND ROMAN CULTURES AT THE TIME OF PAUL'S MINISTRY. IT DEPICTS A ROMAN FAMILY, BUT THE INSCRIPTION BENEATH IT IS IN THE GREEK LANGUAGE.

BELOW: RUINS OF A FORUM AT PHILIPPI, BUILT BY THE ROMAN EMPEROR MARCUS AURELIUS. PAUL FOUNDED A CHRISTIAN COMMUNITY HERE IN ABOUT C.E. 50.

Dating Paul's Missions

Perhaps no unit of information is more important in dating Paul and his journeys than the reference in Acts 18:12 that suggests Paul was in Corinth when Gallio was proconsul. This of itself is not terribly useful, but when connected to an inscription discovered in Corinth that outlines the specific time that Gallio was proconsul in the city, it means we can date the time of Paul's visit to Corinth with amazing precision to around the year C.E. 51. This crucial bit of information helps scholars to create a timeline for Paul's missionary activities.

PAUL SPEAKS TO THE ATHENIANS

In Acts 17:16–34 we read of Paul's time in Athens. In verses 22–31, Paul makes an impassioned speech in the Areopagus of Athens. The Areopagus was the Council of Athens where important civic matters were adjudicated. Other than this story in Acts, we have virtually no record of Paul's mission in Athens (see 1 Thessalonians 3:1), and given the fact that Acts records Paul's relative lack of success there, this is not too surprising. The portrayal is an interesting one in that the philosophical schools mentioned in 17:18 (the Epicureans and Stoics) were contemporary to Paul's time and proponents might well have reacted with great skepticism to Paul's teachings about resurrection, as is portrayed in Acts 17.

PAUL'S TIME IN CORINTH

In one of the most interesting sections of Acts, chapter 18, we learn about Paul's stay in Corinth. Paul wrote at least two epistles to the Corinthian Church that appear in the New Testament, and he may have written others (see 1 Corinthians 5:9 and 2 Corinthians 2:3) that do not remain as independent texts. The city of Corinth was ancient; however, it had been destroyed in the second century B.C.E. and was rebuilt by Julius Caesar (*c.* 50 B.C.E.). This meant that when Paul was there the new city of Corinth was less than 100 years old. It was the capital of the Roman province of Achaia (southern Greece), and it had developed into an important port city where goods from the East would cross on their way to Rome (and vice versa). Thus, the city had a burgeoning population of what we might in modern terms call a middle class: that is, people whose initiative and hard work were allowing them to gain some ground socially and economically. It is likely that some of the people with whom Paul interacted in Corinth were from among this class of people.

Acts 18:3 is the only place in the New Testament where we learn of Paul's occupation—a tentmaker. Paul speaks of working with his hands (1 Thessalonians 4:11; 1 Corinthians 4:12). Moreover, it is plausible (and we might even say likely) that Paul would have needed a skill that allowed him to find work wherever he went; tentmaking, which would have meant primarily working with leather, skins, and ropes, would have been such an occupation. Tents were used by a variety of people, especially travelers, not only for lodging on land but also as a shield from the sun and elements when traveling by sea on the deck of ships. Having such a skill would have proven very valuable to an itinerant missionary such as Paul.

Crispus, an official of the synagogue in Corinth (Acts 18:8), is said to have converted to Christianity along with his entire household. Interestingly, Crispus is also mentioned by Paul in 1 Corinthians as one of the only people that Paul himself baptized (1 Corinthians 1:14). While Paul rarely speaks about baptism, it ultimately replaced circumcision as the mark of entry into the new Christian community.

Toward the end of Acts 18, Paul sails to Ephesus with his new companions Priscilla and Aquila (Acts 18:18). He leaves his friends there and sails on to Caesarea, then returns to Jerusalem. Before leaving Ephesus, Paul talks with the Jews in the synagogue; when they ask him to stay, he promises them: "I will return to you, if God wills" (Acts 18:21).

BELOW: AN ANCIENT GREEK COIN, FEATURING THE SYMBOLS OF ATHENS. PAUL WAS UPSET TO FIND ATHENS FILLED WITH IDOLS.

BELOW: *ST. PAUL PREACHING AT ATHENS*, BY RAPHAEL. SOME ATHENIANS INSISTED PAUL SPEAK AT THE AREOPAGUS TO EXPLAIN THE NEW TEACHINGS HE HAD BEEN PRESENTING IN THE SYNAGOGUE AND IN THE MARKETPLACE.

LEFT: THE ROMAN LECHAION ROAD IN CORINTH. THIS ROAD WAS CONSTRUCTED IN THE FIRST CENTURY C.E. AND USED FOR 12 CENTURIES. IT WOULD HAVE BEEN QUITE NEW WHEN PAUL WAS IN CORINTH.

THE THIRD JOURNEY OF PAUL

THE HOLY SPIRIT TESTIFIES TO ME ... THAT IMPRISONMENT AND PERSECUTIONS ARE WAITING FOR ME ACTS 20:23

After visiting the church in Jerusalem, Paul travels by land to Antioch in Syria. It is from here that he begins his third missionary journey: "After spending some time there he departed and went from place to place through the region of Galatia and Phrygia, strengthening all the disciples" (Acts 18:22).

EPHESUS

Ephesus, positioned at the mouth of the Cayster River, was the fourth-greatest city of the first century C.E. after Rome, Alexandria, and Antioch. Although the archaeological remains of Ephesus date from the mid-second century B.C.E., Lysimachus, one of Alexander's generals, established the city at its present site around 286 B.C.E. When Attalus III left the kingdom of Pergamum in his will to Rome (133 B.C.E.), Ephesus became part of the Roman province of Asia. After a troubled period, Octavian (the emperor Augustus) subdued the city (31 B.C.E.), placing the proconsul of Asia permanently in the city (Acts 19:38).

Many buildings in Ephesus are datable to Augustus's reign. The double temple to Rome and Augustus was built and enclosed within the precincts of the temple of Artemis. The theater could seat 24,000 people (Acts 19:29). There were also baths, gymnasia, a stadium, and a medical school in Roman times. But the most famous building was the temple of Artemis (Acts 19:35), begun at the end of the eighth century B.C.E., and one of the seven wonders of the ancient world. It measured 425 ft by 225 ft (about 130 m by 70 m). The 127 columns in a double row surrounding the building were 60 ft (18 m) high, and adorned with works by the famous sculptor Praxiteles, among others. The temple functioned as a bank, acquiring vast wealth because of the donations made to Artemis (Acts 19:24, 25b, 27a).

Ephesus was proud of its reputation as the "Temple Warden of Artemis" (Acts 19:27, 34–35). Artemis, the mistress and protectress of wildlife, was worshipped as the virgin huntress throughout Greece (Acts 19:27b). The temple of Artemis housed her image with many breasts (or are they fruits?), believed to have fallen from the sky (Acts 19:35). Although Ephesus had many magicians (Acts 19:18–20), Artemis was considered a goddess of great occult power. Six magical "Ephesian Letters" were inscribed on her image and she wore a zodiac necklace.

The Artemis cult was marked by strong missionary zeal and spread as far west as Massilia and Carthage. The goddess competed with early Christianity in its universal mission, providing dream revelations for the extension of her own cult. It is little wonder that Luke depicts God directing the Christian mission by means of Spirit-inspired dreams and visions (Acts 2:17, 9:10, 10:10, 16:9, 18:9, 23:11).

Paul arrives at Ephesus in C.E. 54, stays there for the best part of three years (Acts 20:31; see also 18:8, 10), and directs the evangelism of Ephesus as well as the wider province (19:19; see also Colossians 1:6–7; 4:12–13; Revelation 2–3). Upon Paul's arrival, 12 disciples of John, not knowing about the Spirit, respond to the Gospel (Acts 19:1–6; see also 18:25). The Jews of Ephesus possessed citizenship alongside their Gentile contemporaries, but we are unable to determine

BELOW: *MIRACLES OF ST. PAUL AT EPHESUS*, BY JEAN RESTOUT. THE MERE TOUCH OF PAUL'S SKIN ON A SICK PERSON'S HANDKERCHIEF WAS SAID TO CURE THEM.

RIGHT: *THE CITY OF EPHESUS FROM MOUNT CORESSUS*, COLOR LITHOGRAPH BY T. PICKEN. IT SHOWS THE HARBOR, CITY WALLS, AMPHITHEATER, AND FORTIFICATIONS OF THE CITY.

just how many converts there were in the Church from the synagogue (Acts 19:8–9a). Clearly the Gospel affected Jew and Gentile alike (Acts 19:8–10, 17; see also Ephesians 2:11–18). Traveling Jewish exorcists tried vainly to compete with Paul (Acts 19:14–16), as did the Ephesian silversmiths and magicians, who incited worshippers of Artemis to riot against Paul's teachings (19:19–20, 23–27, 38), but Jesus' power and authority in word and deed outstripped them all (19:11, 15, 20, 27).

While at Ephesus Paul determines to revisit the areas in Greece he had already evangelized, namely "Macedonia and Achaia" (Acts 19:21), drop off the Jerusalem collection (Acts 24:17a; see also Romans 15:25–26 and 1 Corinthians 16:3), and, after its delivery, visit Rome with a view to a mission in Spain (Romans 1:19–15; 15:24, 28). Paul sends Timothy and Erastus on an advance mission to Macedonia (Acts 19:22a; see also 1 Corinthians 16:5), perhaps in order to organize the collection. However, Paul continues to minister at Ephesus (Acts 19:22b: "in Asia"), having already written 1 Corinthians (*c.* C.E. 55) while he was in the city (1 Corinthians 16:8).

PAUL RETURNS TO MACEDONIA AND ACHAIA

Having adopted a low profile after the riot (Acts 20:1, 3), Paul returns for three months in the winter of C.E. 57–58 to strengthen some of the Macedonian and Achaian churches he had founded (20:1–5). This journey had been precipitated by an earlier "painful visit" Paul had made to Corinth (2 Corinthians 2:1)—unrecorded in Acts but occurring during Paul's stay at Ephesus—where he had been opposed by "false apostles … disguising themselves as apostles of Christ" and by a Corinthian leader (2 Corinthians 2:5, 3:1, 7:12, 10:12, 11:13, 22).

LEFT: CLASSICAL GREEK BRONZE STATUE OF ARTEMIS. A SILVERSMITH BY THE NAME OF DEMETRIUS WAS THE RINGLEADER IN THE REBELLION OF ARTEMIS-WORSHIPPERS AGAINST PAUL'S TEACHINGS IN EPHESUS.

ABOVE: ONE OF THE MOST IMPORTANT STORIES IN THIS PART OF ACTS IS THAT OF PAUL RESTORING LIFE TO EUTYCHUS, A BOY WHO HAD DIED AFTER A FALL. THIS DEPICTION WAS DRAWN BY PAUL LASINIO AND ENGRAVED BY CAROL LASINIO.

BELOW: RUINS OF AN ANCIENT TEMPLE ON SAMOS, ENGRAVING BY LUIGI MAYER. PAUL TRAVELED TO THIS GREEK ISLAND ON HIS JOURNEY TO MILETUS.

Humiliated, Paul leaves Corinth, writes the (now lost) "letter of tears" to the Corinthians (2 Corinthians 2:4, 7:8), and sends it off with Titus to effect reconciliation (2:12, 7:8, 12). Paul finds out about the letter's success when he meets Titus again at Macedonia (2 Corinthians 7:5, 13). He sends off 2 Corinthians upon his impending third visit to Corinth (2 Corinthians 12:14; see also Acts 20:1–2a), in order to finalize the collection (2 Corinthians 8:1–9), and to ensure the sincerity of the Corinthians' repentance, probably completing the letter after fresh news arrived about some residual problems (2 Corinthians 13:1). Paul arrives in Corinth (Acts 20:3) and stays for three months; while he is there he writes his letter to the Romans (Romans 16:1–2, 23).

PAUL IN TROAS

Paul's decision to sail from Philippi to Troas in the spring of C.E. 58 *after* the Feast of Unleavened Bread (Acts 20:5b–6a) illustrates his Jewish piety (see also 13:13–14, 14:1, 18:7, 18b, 21:23–26, 27:9), though the Feast was transformed by the tradition of the Lord's Supper (Acts 2:42; see also Luke 22:14, 24:30; 1 Corinthians 11:23). The commencement of another "we" section (Acts 20:5–15; see also 16:10–17) indicates that Luke has again joined Paul's traveling party. When Eutychus (or "lucky one") falls from the window of an apartment building (the ancient *insula*: Acts 20:9–12), Luke highlights Elijah–Elisha parallels when Paul resuscitates the youth (20:10; see also Acts 9:36–41, 17:21–22, 24:34–35), underscoring the continuity of the Gospel with the Old Testament.

THE JOURNEY TO MILETUS

Paul's companions sail from Troas to Assos (20 miles [32 km] away), whereas Paul travels overland by foot to meet them there (Acts 20:13–17a). We do not know the reason for Paul's decision, but perhaps he wanted to avoid a potentially stormy trip along a treacherous coastline (see 2 Corinthians 11:25b, 26b). From Assos they proceed south to Mitylene (44 miles [71 km] away), the main city of the island of Lesbos. Then, in a series of day trips, they travel to Chios and Samos and arrive at Miletus, a substantial seaport with four harbors, 31 miles (approximately 50 km) south of Ephesus (Acts 20:14–15).

The reason for bypassing Ephesus was Paul's determination to reach Jerusalem before the Feast of Pentecost (Acts 20:16). Again, we see evidence of Paul's Jewish piety, though the Spirit's outpouring had dramatically transformed the meaning of the Feast for believers (Acts 2:14–39). But, undoubtedly, the danger posed by the riot of the Ephesian silversmiths was still fresh in Paul's mind (Acts 19:23; see also 2 Corinthians 1:8–9; 1 Corinthians 15:22). Nor could Paul count this time on the intervention of his powerful friends, the *asiarchs* (Acts 19:31), who, according to the Ephesian inscriptions, were a powerful elite of city office-bearers and benefactors.

Consequently, Paul summoned the Ephesian elders to meet him at Miletus (Acts 20:16), where the apostle delivered his moving "farewell" address (20:21–35), a well-known "type" of speech in antiquity (e.g., Genesis 49). Paul reminds them of what they have already learned from his ministry (Acts 20:18, 31, 34), focusing on his example and message as a pastor-evangelist (20:18–27), and alerting them to the dangers they would face in the future (20:28–35).

We might ask whether this speech is Luke's composition rather than an accurate rendering of what Paul said. Certainly, some ancient historians invented speeches for their main characters. But others, while adding creative touches, tried to render the thrust of what was originally said.

ABOVE: ANCIENT GREEK ARCHWAY, MILETUS. PAUL'S "FAREWELL" ADDRESS TO THE EPHESIAN ELDERS, MADE AT MILETUS, IS THE ONLY SPEECH IN ACTS THAT IS CLEARLY AIMED AT A CHRISTIAN AUDIENCE.

What is impressive about Luke's presentation of Paul's speech is how closely it aligns with Paul's portrait of ministry in his letters. It emphasizes Paul's servant role (Acts 20:19), humility (20:19), self-support (20:33–34), athletic metaphors (20:24), theology of redemption and church (20:28), gospel of grace (20:24, 32), ministry in local house churches (20:20), appointment of elders (20:17, 28), as well as his outreach to Jew and Gentile alike (20:21). Luke's speech graphically captures the authentic Paul.

The Jerusalem Collection

The men accompanying Paul (Acts 20:4–5a; see also 1 Corinthians 16:3; 2 Corinthians 8:19) are the Gentile church delegates bringing the collection for the Jerusalem poor (Acts 24:17; Galatians 2:10; 1 Corinthians 16:1–4; 2 Corinthians 8–9; Romans 15:25–28). The collection expressed Jew–Gentile unity and equality (2 Corinthians 8:13–15, 9:13–14), thankfulness for God's overflowing grace (2 Corinthians 8:9, 8–12, 14b–15), and Gentile gratitude to the Jerusalem Church for the Gospel (Romans 15:27).

Paul appeals to a saying of Jesus which is unrecorded in the Gospels (Acts 20:35). The saying undermines the Greco-Roman "payback system" where benefactors gave gifts in order to secure favors and honors in return, or to place the recipient under obligation. In emphasizing giving without any expectation of return (see also Luke 6:32, 14:13–14), Jesus exposes the self-interest underlying first-century social relationships and transforms the understanding of the idea of giving in antiquity.

JERUSALEM

A travelog of sea voyages from Cos to Caesarea—the trip to Jerusalem being by land—introduces another "we" section (Acts 21:1–18). The prominence of Spirit-inspired prophetic media in early Christianity (Acts 2:17; 13:1; 15:28, 32; 16:6; 20:32) is seen in the prophetic gifting of Philip's daughters (21:9; see also 1 Corinthians 11:5) and in the prophecies of Agabus (21:10–11; see also 11:27–28). Luke highlights Paul's Spirit-guided return to Jerusalem (see Acts 19:21; 20:22–23; 21:4, 10–11, 13).

Members of the Jerusalem church are again disturbed by Paul's law-free gospel (Acts 21:20–21; see also Acts 15:1);

RIGHT: AFTER HIS ARREST, PAUL WAS BOUND IN CHAINS AND TAKEN TO THE BARRACKS. PAUL THEN SPENT TWO YEARS IN PRISON UNDER ANTONIUS FELIX AT CAESAREA. THIS ILLUSTRATION BY HAROLD COPPING IS FROM *NEW TESTAMENT PICTURES*.

they remind Paul and his Gentile delegates of the decisions of the Jerusalem council (21:25; see also 15:20, 28–29), and they encourage them to undertake a temporary Nazarite vow in order to calm Jewish sensitivities (21:23–24, 26). Paul may have felt that if he undertook the vow along with the Gentile delegates he would secure the acceptance of the Jerusalem collection among Jewish believers, an issue about which Paul was very worried (Romans 15:30–32). The silence of Acts about a positive reception to the collection is probably ominous (see Acts 24:17), unless Paul's reference to his "ministry" (*diakonia*: Acts 21:19: see also *diakonia*: Romans 15:31; 2 Corinthians 8:4; 9:12, 13) among the Gentiles indirectly refers to the collection (Acts 21:20a).

Finally, Acts 21:20b points to the evangelistic success of the Jerusalem church and of the Maccabean "zeal" traditions underlying its law-affirming piety (1 Maccabees 2:27; see also 2:24; 26, 50).

PAUL IS ARRESTED

When Paul's purification vow is almost over, Asian Jews stir up their compatriots, alleging that Paul had taught against the Jewish nation, law, and Temple (Acts 21:28a). This charge echoes the charges brought against Jesus and Stephen (Mark 14:57; Luke 23:1–5; Acts 6:11–14). That the Jews are from "Asia" clears the Jewish Christians at Jerusalem of complicity in Paul's arrest and lays the blame at the feet of Diaspora Jews from Ephesus (see also Acts 19:9a, 13, 23:19), present in Jerusalem for the Feast of Weeks (see also 2:1, 20:16).

The critical charge was that Paul had (allegedly) defiled the Temple by bringing Trophimus the Ephesian beyond the court of the Gentiles into the sacred precincts of the inner courts (Acts 21:28b–29). A stone balustrade had been erected to mark off the inner courts. Slabs inscribed in Greek and Latin warned Gentiles they would receive the death penalty if they proceeded further. Two such inscriptions have been found.

The tribune of the cohort, Claudius Lysias (Acts 23:26), of the nearby Fortress Antonia in the northwest corner of the Temple precincts, intervened before Paul was killed (Acts 21:31–40). That Paul is confused with the Egyptian "sign prophet" (Acts 21:38) and "assassins" (*sicarii* or "dagger men," political assassins of the Jews who were collaborating with the Romans) points to the social chaos engulfing Judea before the Jewish revolt.

BELOW: *ARREST OF SAINT PAUL*, BY LUCA DI TOMME. AFTER THE UPROAR IN THE TEMPLE, PAUL WAS SAVED FROM BEING BEATEN TO DEATH WHEN ROMAN AUTHORITIES ARRESTED HIM.

PAUL DEFENDS HIMSELF

In Acts 22:1–24 Paul defends his Gospel in front of the Jewish crowd at the Temple courts (22:3–21), the Jewish Sanhedrin the next day (23:1–7), and the Roman procurator of Judea, Antonius Felix (24:2–21), at Caesarea several days later. Several notable features emerge from Luke's narrative. Paul's account of his vision in the Jerusalem temple (Acts 23:17–21), after his Damascus road vision (9:1–18, 26:12–19), expands our knowledge of his conversion. The respect given to Paul because of his Roman citizenship (Acts 22:25–29; see also 21:39) fits the first-century historical context where possession of Roman citizenship in the province was rare. The vow to kill Paul by certain Jews (Acts 23:12–35), exposed by Paul's nephew (23:16) and necessitating a military guard for Paul's journey to Caesarea (23:23), points to continued social and political breakdown. Paul exploits the disagreement between the Pharisees and the Sadducees over the Resurrection (Acts 23:6) to divide his accusers.

The result of these defenses was Paul's imprisonment under Felix at Caesarea for two years (Acts 24:27: C.E. 57–59). This ex-slave, who had risen to be a procurator under Claudius, was famous for his corruption (Acts 24:26–27) and savagery in crushing and collaborating with the *sicarrii*. When Porcius Festus succeeded Felix (C.E. 59 or 60: Acts 24:27–25:12), Paul delivered a further defense before Herod Agrippa II (25:13–26:32), emphasizing the continuity of Christianity with Judaism (26:1–29). It is ironic that Festus, who slaughtered a messianic pretender, lost the opportunity of responding to the real Messiah when he sent Paul to Rome upon his appeal to Caesar (Acts 25:10–12, 27:32).

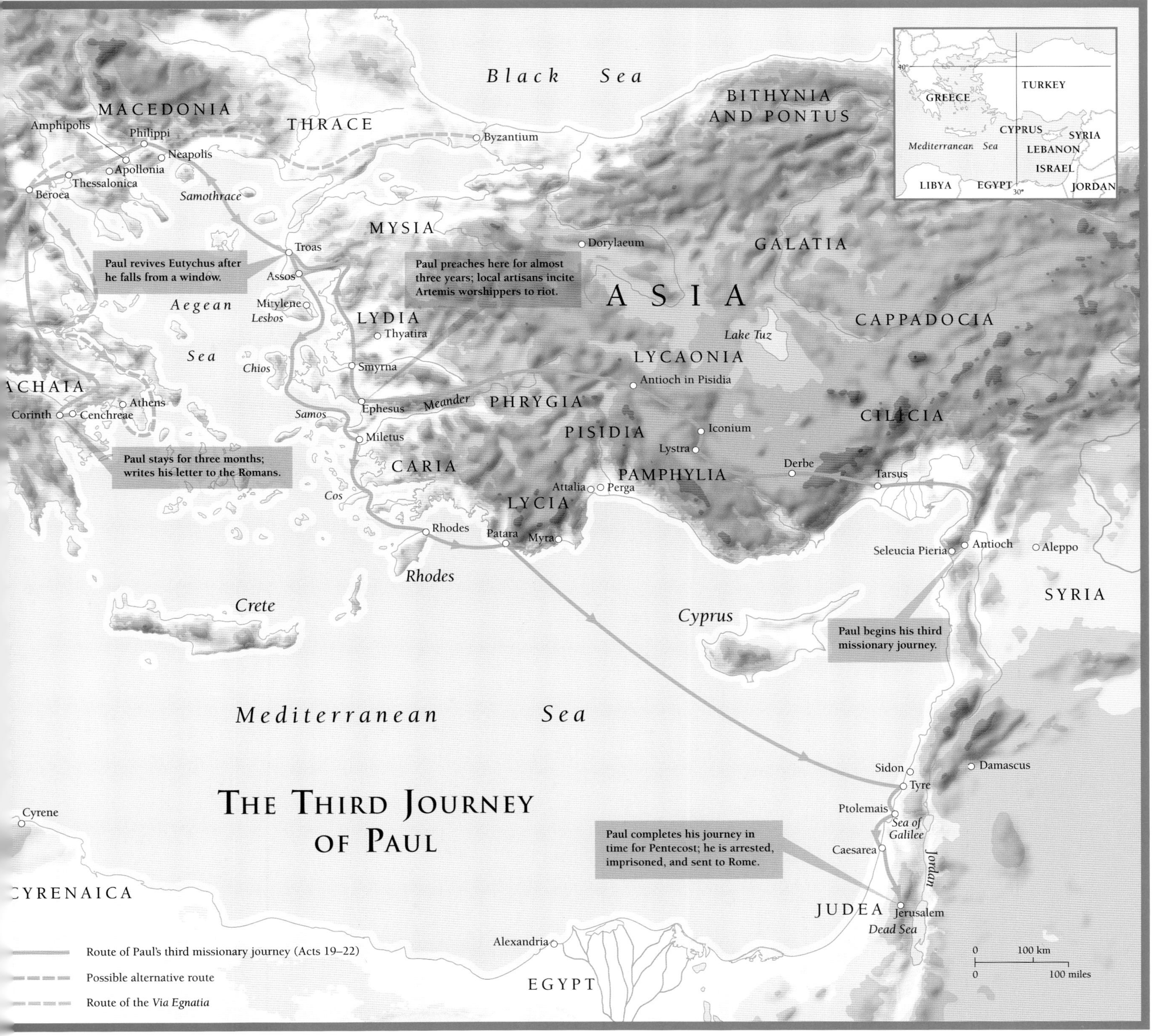

PAUL GOES TO ROME

DO NOT BE AFRAID, PAUL; YOU MUST STAND BEFORE THE EMPEROR ACTS 27:24

RIGHT: THIS IVORY PANEL FROM A SIXTH-CENTURY GALLIC DIPTYCH SHOWS PAUL ON HIS TRAVELS, DELIVERING THE CHRISTIAN MESSAGE.

Another "we" section (Acts 27:1–28:10) commences Paul's sea voyage to Rome. Here Luke draws on his own "eyewitness" traditions for his narrative (Luke 1:2). We do not know, however, where Luke has been in the interim since his last "we" section (Acts 21:1–18). The first part of Paul's voyage comprises a travelog of the places visited before the sea storm (Acts 27:1–8). There are echoes in chapters 27–28 of motifs from ancient literary voyages (e.g., Lucian, Achilles Titus, Petronius, Charition). The literary conventions of the "storm" and "shipwreck" were so well known that many ancient writers (e.g., Juvenal and Lucian) mocked and parodied them. Ancient historians (e.g., Thucydides, Herodotus) also included sea voyages in their narratives. Luke, a versatile historian and theologian, imitated the traditional openings of ancient historians (e.g., Luke 1:1–4; Acts 1:1). However, Luke also added novelistic touches to his narrative of Paul's sea voyage so that he might bring Acts to a resounding and entertaining conclusion.

A high-status Roman citizen of the provinces, Paul is transferred to the command of Julius, the centurion of the Augustan Cohort (Acts 28:1). Syrian mercenaries made up this well-known cohort mentioned in first-century inscriptions. At Caesarea Maritima, Paul boards a trading vessel from Adramyttium destined for the coastal ports of Asia (Acts 27:2). Apart from Luke, Paul's only traveling companion is Aristarchus, a Macedonian from Thessalonica (Acts 27:3; see also 19:29, 20:4; Colossians 4:10; Philemon 24). The next day the trading vessel puts in at Sidon (Acts 27:3a), a Phoenician town famous for its purple dyeing and glass blowing, as well as for its double harbor. Julius acts humanely toward Paul, allowing him access to local believers for the provision of his needs (Acts 27:3b). The Church at Sidon probably arose from the persecution that followed Stephen's death (Acts 11:19).

The vessel hugs the shoreline under the lee of Cyprus (Acts 28:4) so that it would be protected from the autumnal western winds. Then it strikes out westward across the open sea until it reaches Myra in Lycia (Acts 27:5). Julius finds a replacement Alexandrian ship belonging to the grain fleet that serviced Asia Minor and Italy from Egypt, the granary of the Roman Empire (Acts 27:6). Because of adverse wind conditions, the trip to Cnidus is difficult. The vessel again hugs the coastline, this time under the lee of Crete off Salmone, until it comes to Fair Havens and Lasea (Acts 27:7).

BELOW: ROCK TOMBS AT THE SITE OF THE ANCIENT TOWN OF MYRA, ON THE SOUTHERN COAST OF ASIA MINOR. EGYPTIAN SHIPS CARRYING GRAIN TO ITALY REGULARLY STOPPED AT MYRA.

STORM AT SEA

Paul warns the centurion about the dangers of traveling in the severe Mediterranean weather of winter (Acts 27:9–10). However, the enormous bonuses that would accrue if the cargo were safely delivered during the winter months clouds the common sense of the pilot and captain. Consequently, the vessel strikes out for Phoenix, a harbor of Crete (Acts 27:11–12). A "violent wind," a "northeaster" from Crete, is the vessel's undoing (Acts 27:13–15). This particular wind, named "Euraquilo" (Greek: *Eurakulon*), was notorious in antiquity. Its name was inscribed on a 12-point wind-rose on a pavement at Thugga in Africa. No amount of tactical maneuvering by these seasoned seafarers could deliver the vessel and its crew from impending peril (27:16–20). Adrift for 14 tedious days and nights, only the appearance of an angel standing near Paul enables the apostle to deliver words of reassurance to the terrified crew (Acts 27:21–26; see also 23:11).

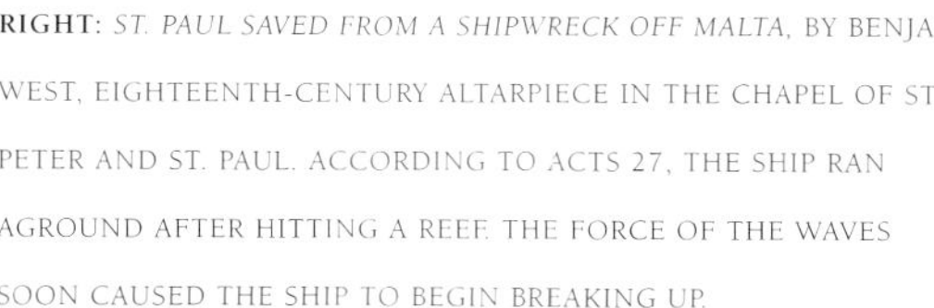

RIGHT: *ST. PAUL SAVED FROM A SHIPWRECK OFF MALTA*, BY BENJAMIN WEST, EIGHTEENTH-CENTURY ALTARPIECE IN THE CHAPEL OF ST. PETER AND ST. PAUL. ACCORDING TO ACTS 27, THE SHIP RAN AGROUND AFTER HITTING A REEF. THE FORCE OF THE WAVES SOON CAUSED THE SHIP TO BEGIN BREAKING UP.

PAUL'S VESSEL IS SHIPWRECKED

After drifting in the Adriatic Sea, the sailors take soundings of the water's depth, using a line and a lead weight for the task (Acts 27:27–28). The danger of running aground was real. The sailors attempt to abandon the vessel in a small boat. But on Paul's warning, the centurion and soldiers listen to the apostle on this occasion and cut loose the boat, thwarting the sailors' scheme. Throughout the entire crisis, Paul functions as a prophet, a pointer to the Pentecost outpouring of the Spirit of prophecy (Acts 27:10, 21, 24–25, 31; see also 2:17–18). Moreover, Paul acts as a Christian pastor to the crew, selflessly modeling care for his neighbor and piety toward God in a time of crisis (Acts 27:33–38). With their spirits lifted by a meal of bread, the crew lightens the ship by discarding the cargo of wheat into the sea (Acts 27:38).

Noticing a bay with a beach, the crew releases its stone anchors and the ropes. They hoist the sail, make for the beach, and ground the vessel on a reef (Acts 27:39–41). Again, God intervenes because of Paul's presence on the vessel, sparing the prisoners from execution (Acts 27:42–43), and landing the entire crew safely in modern St. Paul's Bay (27:43b–44).

PAUL'S TIME ON MALTA

Paul and the others had landed on the small island of Malta (Acts 28:1), 18 miles long and 8 miles wide (29 by 13 km), and located 58 miles (93 km) south of Sicily. This Phoenician colony was founded from North Africa (*c.* 1000 B.C.E.), but from 218 B.C.E. the Romans had controlled it. The "natives" (Acts 28:2: *barbaroi*) spoke a Phoenician dialect and thus were, like all other non-Greeks, labeled by the Greeks as the "*bar-bar*" people because of their incomprehensible language and different culture. The Maltese showed the stranded party "kindness" (Acts 28:2: *philanthropia*), a term used for hospitality and beneficence.

Miraculous events accompany Paul's stay at Malta. A viper, fleeing from a bundle of brushwood collected for a fire, latches onto Paul's hand, but with no deleterious effects. The islanders temporarily regard Paul as a murderer pursued

THE "VIPER INCIDENT"

Some scholars remain skeptical about the historicity of the "viper incident" (depicted in the twelfth-century English mural below), arguing that there are no vipers or poisonous snakes on Malta today. But in an age of unparalleled species extinction, we should not be surprised about the viper's disappearance from such a small island over time.

by *Nemesis* (or Divine Retribution). But when Paul does not die as expected, the islanders believe Paul to be a god instead (Acts 28:3–6; see also 14:8). Luke provides us here with a sympathetic insight into the religious belief systems of the Gentiles to whom Paul ministers (see 14:8, 16:16, 19:23). But he also establishes that Paul, the servant of the risen and triumphant Jesus, had the "authority to tread on snakes and scorpions" (Luke 10:19). Moreover, he demonstrates in a memorable manner that Paul was innocent of any charge worthy of death (Acts 23:29, 25:25, 26:31).

While in Malta, Paul also heals the father of Publius, "the leading man *[protos]* of the island," from fever and dysentery. As a result, many other islanders seek a cure for their diseases from Paul (Acts 28:7–9). Significantly, the term for this official *(protos)* is found on Maltese inscriptions. Once again Luke displays historical accuracy in his use of contemporary inscriptional terminology for officials, family names, as well as the names of deities and civic institutions (e.g., Acts 13:7; 14:12; 17:6; 18:12; 19:9, 31, 35, 39).

FROM MALTA TO ROME

Luke resumes his coverage of the last leg of Paul's journey to Rome with another travelog (Acts 28:11–16; see also 27:1–8). Having spent the three months of winter in Malta, Paul and his entourage are able to recommence their sea trip for Syracuse in Sicily (Acts 28:12) when the westerly winds arrive from early February onward. The Alexandrian ship, part of the grain fleet between Egypt and Rome, had as its figurehead the "Twin Brothers," Castor and Pollux, the sons of Zeus (Acts 28:11). Seneca observes that their constellation, Gemini, gave good fortune in a storm. The irony of this would not have been lost on Paul, who knew that only God and his son Jesus could save voyagers from sea disasters (Jonah 1:4–2:10; Psalm 107:23–30; Mark 4:35, 6:47; Acts 27:21).

RIGHT: FUNERARY ALTAR OF A ROMAN CENTURION, NOW HELD IN THE MUSEO DELLA CIVITTA, ROME. WHILE UNDER HOUSE ARREST IN ROME, PAUL IS GUARDED BY A LOWER-RANKING SOLDIER.

The ship stops at the twin-harbored town of Syracuse for three days (Acts 28:12), undoubtedly to load food supplies. Syracuse, Strabo informs us, was the storehouse of Rome. From there Paul sails to Rhegium, situated in the toe of Italy, with the help of a southerly wind (Acts 28:13). The trip from Rhegium to Puteoli (Acts 28:13) across the Straits of Messina is about 220 miles (350 km). Puteoli declined as the most important Italian port for seafaring traffic, being eventually supplanted by the port of Ostia, which was refurbished in the reign of the emperor Claudius. Since the ship had to unload its precious cargo of food supplies for Rome, Paul is allowed to stay with the believers of Puteoli for seven days (Acts 28:14). Since the service of ancient inns was poor and their reputation for immorality notorious, Paul would have appreciated the hospitality of local believers. Whether these believers were products of the original Pentecost event (Acts 2:10) or were the inevitable result of the mobility of first-century converts (e.g., Priscilla and Aquila), we cannot say.

OPPOSITE: *ST. PAUL IN PRISON* (1627) BY REMBRANDT VAN RIJN. ON PAUL'S ARRIVAL IN ROME HE IS IMPRISONED IN A "HIRED DWELLING" RATHER THAN A TRADITIONAL PRISON. IT IS LIKELY THAT DURING THIS TIME HE WROTE MANY OF HIS EPISTLES.

Luke, anticipating Paul's arrival in Rome (Acts 28:14b), notes that some believers of Rome had come along the Appian Way as far as the Forum of Appius, 43 miles (69 km) from Rome, to meet the apostle (Acts 28:15). Others had traveled as far as the Three Taverns, 33 miles (48 km) from Rome. Paul's controversial reputation would certainly have preceded him (Romans 3:8), as well as his status as the Apostle to the Gentiles (15:15–19), even though he was not the founder of the Church at Rome (Acts 15:20). But Roman believers had been expecting the apostle's arrival for some time now (Romans 1:10–13, 15:22), notwithstanding the fact that God had delayed Paul's trip for two years at Caesarea and had brought about its culmination in a most unexpected way. We do not know who precisely these Roman believers were, but presumably they would have passed on the greetings of the many believers in Romans 16:3–15, including Priscilla and Aquila (16:3–4; see also Acts 18:2–3, 18–19). The pastoral effect of this meeting for Paul is exhilarating (Acts 28:15b), and he proceeds confidently to Rome.

PAUL IN ROME

When Paul arrives in Rome, he is placed under house arrest for two years (Acts 28:16, 23, 30). He lives in a "hired dwelling" (Acts 28:29), probably an apartment in a Roman tenement, paid at "his own expense" (28:30), and large enough to accommodate "great numbers" (28:23). Paul is under the care of one "soldier" (Acts 28:16; see also 12:6), and is chained to his guard (28:20). He was probably near the Praetorian barracks beyond the city walls northeast of Rome. This soldier, however, did not belong to the higher ranked centurions who had guarded Paul at Jerusalem and Caesarea (Acts 21:32, 22:25, 24:23). The change to a low-ranking guard was most likely because Paul's status as a Roman citizen was more common in Rome, whereas it was rare in the provinces (Acts 22:25–29).

Unashamed of his bonds, Paul preaches the kingdom of God boldly at Rome (Acts 28:31). He calls together the Jewish local leaders (Acts 28:17), presumably the elders, scribes, and rulers of the four or five mid-first-century C.E. Roman synagogues. (Paul continues his habit of speaking with the Jews first when he arrives at a new town or city.) Synagogue inscriptions reveal that the Jews had sought out powerful Roman patrons (e.g., Agrippa, Augustus). Paul lays the groundwork for a favorable response to his upcoming legal examination by establishing his Jewish credentials in front of the powerful Roman Jews (Acts 28:17, 20; see also 23:6). He also underscores that his appeal to Caesar did not imply any charge against Israel (Acts 28:19).

Given the recent expulsion of Jews from Rome (C.E. 49: Acts 18:2), it is not surprising that the Roman Jews knew little of the Roman believers (Acts 28:21–22). A later meeting of Paul with the Roman Jews produces another divided response (Acts 28:24–25; see also 13:40–47, 18:5–8, 19:8). In citing Isaiah 6:9–10 (Acts 28:26–28), Paul emphasizes God's transfer of his offer of salvation to the Gentiles (28:30, 13:46–47). However, the apostle did not thereby exclude the Jews from a continuing experience of divine grace, either in the present or in the future (Romans 11:1, 25). The response of a Jewish remnant to the Gospel throughout Acts affirms this, as does Paul's welcome of "all who came to him" (Acts 28:30), whether Jew or Gentile. Finally, the Captivity epistles (Ephesians, Philippians, Colossians, and Philemon) were probably written during this period of Paul's house arrest at Rome in C.E. 61–62.

WHAT WAS PAUL'S FATE?

We are left with a puzzle. Why doesn't Luke indicate what happened to Paul after his two-year detention? What was the result of Paul's trial before Caesar, assuming that it went to court? If Paul was acquitted before Nero, where did Paul go afterward and what happened to him? What did Luke know about Paul's fate? And if Luke was aware that his audience knew about the apostle's fate, is this cryptic conclusion to Luke–Acts satisfying (Luke 1:1–4; Acts 1:1–11)?

Some scholars have argued that Luke died before he finished Acts or before he commenced a projected third volume. Both options are unsatisfactory explanations of the problem of Acts' ending. Verse 31 is typical of the six summary statements throughout Acts regarding the Gospel's continuous progress (Acts 6:7, 9:31, 12:24, 16:5, 19:20, 28:31). The ending appears to be deliberate. Regarding a projected third volume, some scholars have proposed that Luke's use of *protos* in Acts 1:1 does not mean "former" (implying only two volumes, Luke and Acts) but "first" (implying a "third" volume after the "first" and "second"). However, this is an unlikely interpretation of *protos*. Rather than hypothesizing Luke's premature death, it is safer to conclude that Acts 28:30–31 is Luke's intended ending.

Luke gives clear indications of Paul's death (Acts 20:22–24, 29a, 38; 21:10–14), as well as of his impending trial before the emperor (27:24). What Luke does not indicate is whether this took place immediately after his account breaks off (C.E. 62) or occurs at a later date. Paul may have been acquitted, or released when his accusers did not appear due to the prohibitive cost of mounting a prosecution (see Acts 28:21). Either way, if Luke's audience knew of Paul's execution under Nero some time before June 9, C.E. 68, the date of Nero's suicide, Luke could safely omit reference to Paul's fate. This is especially the case if Luke wrote his two-volumed work after the sack of Jerusalem (Luke 21:20: C.E. 70).

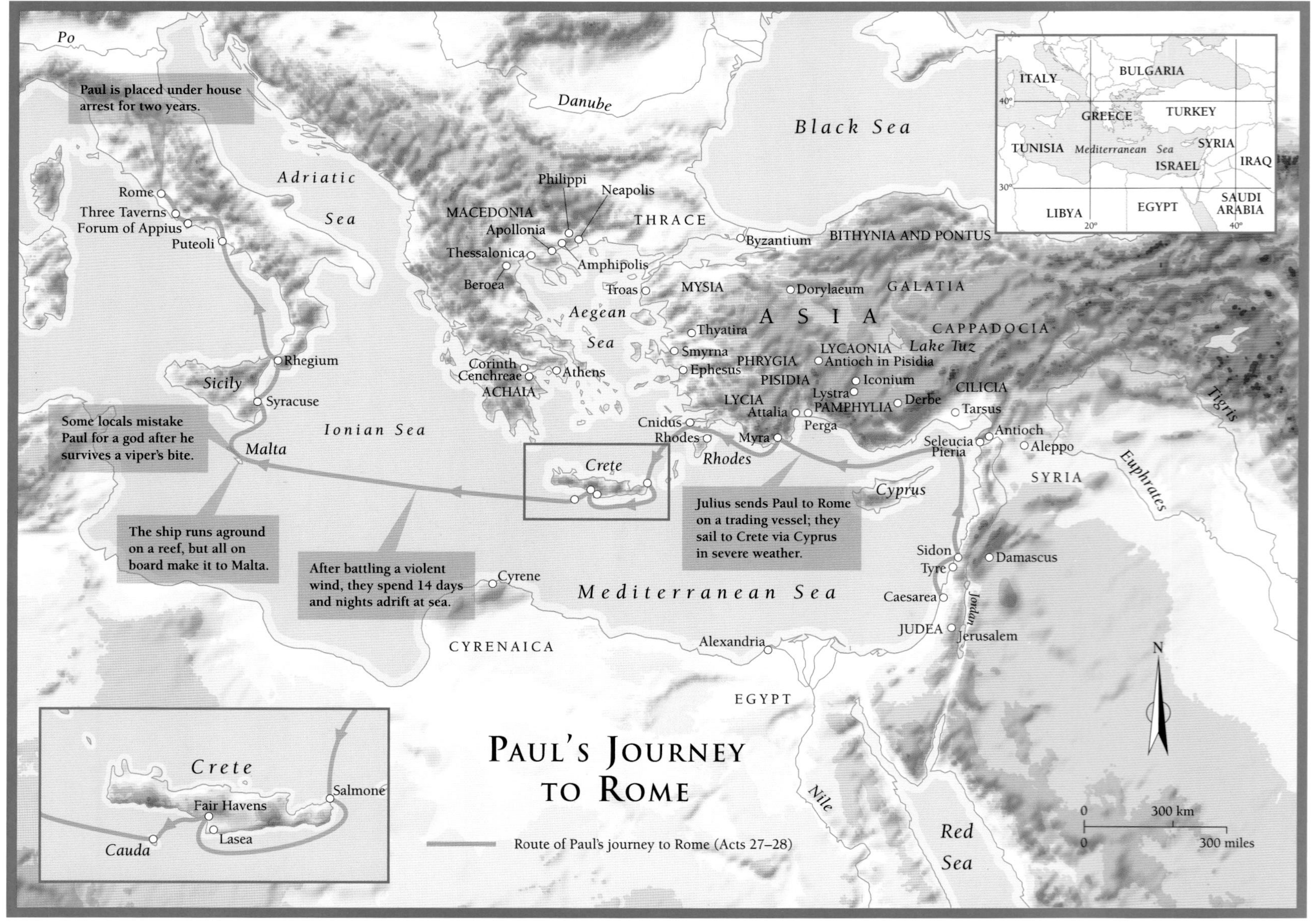

The most likely solution to our puzzle is that Luke brings his two works to a *theological* climax, focusing on how the Gospel spread from Jerusalem to the ends of the earth (Acts 1:8, 13:47, 28:28; see also Luke 24:47), symbolized by Rome as the empire's capital. Luke is not a first-century "Eusebius" writing a universal history on the expansion of the apostolic Church. He leaves out too much that is important. How did the Church at Rome (see Acts 2:10) and Colossae start (see 19:10)? What happened to James, the Lord's brother and leader of the Jerusalem Church? Why does Luke leave out specific mention of Titus, the well-known co-worker of Paul's letters? Nor is Luke writing a multi-volumed historical monograph, but a more narrowly focused work.

Instead, Luke charts the progress of the Gospel from Jerusalem to Rome, with a strong biographical interest in its main proponents (e.g., Peter, Stephen, Philip, Paul, Barnabas, Timothy, James). Luke also concentrates on the two main churches that launched its missionary expansion (Jerusalem and Antioch). He displays encouraging, apologetic, and evangelistic purposes in his "case-studies" of how the Gospel was defended before Jews, Greeks, and Romans. He defends the fulfillment of God's covenantal promises to Israel (Luke 1:1, 24:44; Acts 2:30, 3:18, 7:1, 13:16, 15:15, 26:6–7), but which were rejected by many first-century Jews (Acts 4:1–3, 5:17, 6:9, 7:54, 11:19, 13:50, 14:2, 19, 17:5, 13, 19:9, 20:19, 22:30, 24:1, 28:24b–28). Nonetheless, there were significant examples of Jewish belief in Christ (Acts 2:41, 6:7, 14:1, 16:1, 17:11–12, 18:8, 28:24a). Luke adds novelistic touches that make his narrative vivid and exciting, while maintaining the historical accuracy of his account. In sum, Luke bypasses the fate of Paul for other themes.

What happened to Paul after his Roman imprisonment? The evidence of Titus and 1 and 2 Timothy provides an answer. Many scholars dismiss these letters as the creations of a much later writer who, writing under Paul's name, repackaged the apostle's teaching for believers in the early second century C.E. But if a secretary wrote the Pastorals (is it perhaps Luke? see also 2 Timothy 4:11; Romans 16:22) on behalf of Paul while he was in prison, many of the unusual features pointing to a different author can be accounted for.

Several geographic references contained in the Pastorals (1 Timothy 1:3; 2 Timothy 1:17a; 2:12; 4:13, 20; Titus 1:5; 3:12), not easily reconciled with Acts, point to a fourth missionary journey of Paul upon his release some time after C.E. 62. The earliest evidence that Paul reached Spain, mooted in Romans (15:23, 28), is in Clement of Rome (*Epistle to the Corinthians* 5:5–7: C.E. 95), though this may simply be an inference from Paul's text. By the time of writing 2 Timothy, Paul is again imprisoned in Rome (1:16–18) and awaits execution (4:6–8, 16–18). According to Eusebius, Paul and Peter were martyred in the Neronian persecution in about C.E. 66–67.

ABOVE: THIS TRIPTYCH BY STEFANESCHI ILLUSTRATES THREE IMPORTANT CHRISTIAN THEMES OR EVENTS: THE CRUCIFIXION OF ST. PETER, CHRIST THE REDEEMER, AND THE MARTYDOM OF PAUL.

BELOW: APOSTLES PETER AND PAUL EMBRACE AS THEY SAY FAREWELL. THIS IVORY BUCKLE DATES TO EARLY CHRISTIAN TIMES, THE THIRD OR FOURTH CENTURY C.E.

THE REVELATION OF JOHN

WRITE IN A BOOK WHAT YOU SEE AND SEND IT TO THE SEVEN CHURCHES REVELATION 1:11

The Christian Bible ends with the dramatic book of Revelation. Also referred to as the Apocalypse ("unveiling"), it uses symbolic visions to reveal the truth about the world, especially its future destiny. Revelation invites us to enter another world, in order to see our own world more clearly.

Traditionally dated toward the end of Domitian's reign (*c.* C.E. 96, though by others to the late sixties), Revelation describes visions received by John on Patmos. Since the second century C.E., this prophet-seer has been identified as the apostle John, though he may be another Christian leader such as "John the Elder."

Patmos was a small rocky island, approximately 10 miles (16 km) long, located about 40 miles (64 km) off the coast of Asia (the Roman province of that name, now western Turkey). Scholars regularly claim that Patmos was a Roman penal colony. There is no firm evidence for this; Classical references in Strabo and Pliny simply describe its geographic location. However, it was certainly a suitable place of exile for a troublesome preacher (see Revelation 1:9). Historically connected to the mainland city of Miletus (see Acts 20:17–38), Patmos had a thriving population, a gymnasium, and cults of the god Apollo and the goddess Artemis. A second-century C.E. inscription describes it as "the most august island of the daughter of Leto" (i.e., Artemis), and local tradition places her temple in a prominent location. It is not implausible that John founded a church on the island (as in the fifth-century C.E. *Acts of John by Prochorus*).

SEVEN MESSAGES

Seized by the Spirit on the Lord's day (Sunday, Revelation 1:10), John describes a vision of the exalted Christ (1:12–20). The seven messages that Christ delivers shine a spotlight on their recipients: the seven churches of Asia (1:4, 11), addressed through their angels. An emissary from Patmos could have sailed to Ephesus, and then made a circuit of the remaining churches before returning to his starting point.

These messages encompass the whole of the Christian experience: faithful perseverance, loss of enthusiasm, internal problems caused by rival teachers, complacency. Revelation is especially critical of those Christians who are too closely identified with their cities' political, religious, and economic life: notably the "Nicolaitans," "Balaam" in Pergamum, and "Jezebel" in Thyatira. To these, Revelation's message is not one of comfort but of challenge.

THE LAMB'S SCROLL

John is caught up through an open door into the heavenly throne-room. What he describes would have sounded familiar to Asian Christians. The architecture and statuary of cities like Ephesus or Pergamum proclaimed the universal rule of the emperor in Rome. What John sees in heaven, however, tells a very different story. There is another who controls the world's destiny. God sits emperor-like on a throne, receiving the adoration of all creation.

Most surprising, however, is the appearance of the Lamb (Revelation 5:6). Humans are regularly seen in animal form in apocalypses. This Lamb, who is all seeing and all powerful

LEFT: JOHN THE EVANGELIST AT PATMOS, AN EIGHTEENTH-CENTURY C.E. ICON HELD IN THE ANTALYA MUSEUM, TURKEY. THIS JOHN POSSIBLY ALSO WROTE THE FOURTH GOSPEL.

Allusions Identified?

Archaeology sheds light on some of Revelation's local allusions. "Satan's throne" (Revelation 2:13) may refer to Pergamum's altar to Zeus, its temple to Augustus, or the healing shrine of Asclepius, symbolized by a serpent (see 12:9). The "dead" Christians of Sardis (3:1) might have detected an allusion to the city's striking Lydian rock-cut tombs. The lukewarmness of the Laodiceans (3:16) probably contrasts with the hot thermal baths and cold-water springs of nearby Hierapolis and Colossae respectively.

(symbolized by seven eyes and seven horns), is the victorious Christ. Yet his power lies in having been slaughtered. The sacrificial death of Jesus at the hands of Rome, and his vindication through death, enables him to put into action God's plan to save the world (symbolized by the sealed scroll he now receives). He becomes the Lamb of the new Passover, leading God's people from slavery to freedom.

The scroll he opens, to put into effect "what must soon take place" (Revelation 1:1), is probably the same scroll brought to John by a mighty angel (10:1–2). It has become "little" so that John, like Ezekiel before him (Ezekiel 3:3), can devour its words and prophesy.

THE CHURCH'S BATTLE

Revelation now presents the battle in which all Christians are engaged. Christians living in Asia's cities may not have been experiencing persecution. There is very little evidence that Domitian persecuted the Church; nor did Nero's treatment of Christians in Rome in C.E. 64 extend to the provinces. Indeed, Revelation names only one actual martyr: Antipas of Pergamum (Revelation 2:13). Nevertheless, it expects hostility to be part of the Church's fate.

The vision of the sun-clothed woman and the heavenly dragon (Revelation 12) presents a kaleidoscope of biblical images. The dragon is clearly Satan. Though often identified as Mary, the woman is probably the heavenly counterpart of God's people, threatened by the evil one. Nevertheless, Asian Christians would also recall the pagan story of Leto, mother of Patmos's twin deities, Artemis and Apollo. Leto, pregnant with Apollo, was pursued by the dragon Python. Rescued from Python, Apollo was safely delivered, and went on to defeat the dragon. Emperors like Augustus and Nero were viewed as Apollo-figures, for having brought peace out of disorder. In John's vision, however, it is Jesus who defeats the dragon, not by bloody conquest but by his own blood.

Though the decisive battle has been won, the war is not over. Grotesque monsters often symbolize oppressive kings and empires (e.g., Daniel 7). John's beast from the sea, ably assisted by the beast from the land, continues the dragon's work on earth (Revelation 13), particularly threatening the Church. Ephesian Christians may have recalled the emergence from the sea of the Roman proconsul, personification of imperial power in the province, when he arrived by boat at the city's harbor. From John's perspective, this beast has a name, whose number is 666 (though 616 is also attested). Both numbers may be derived from the name "Nero Caesar," calculated in the Hebrew alphabet.

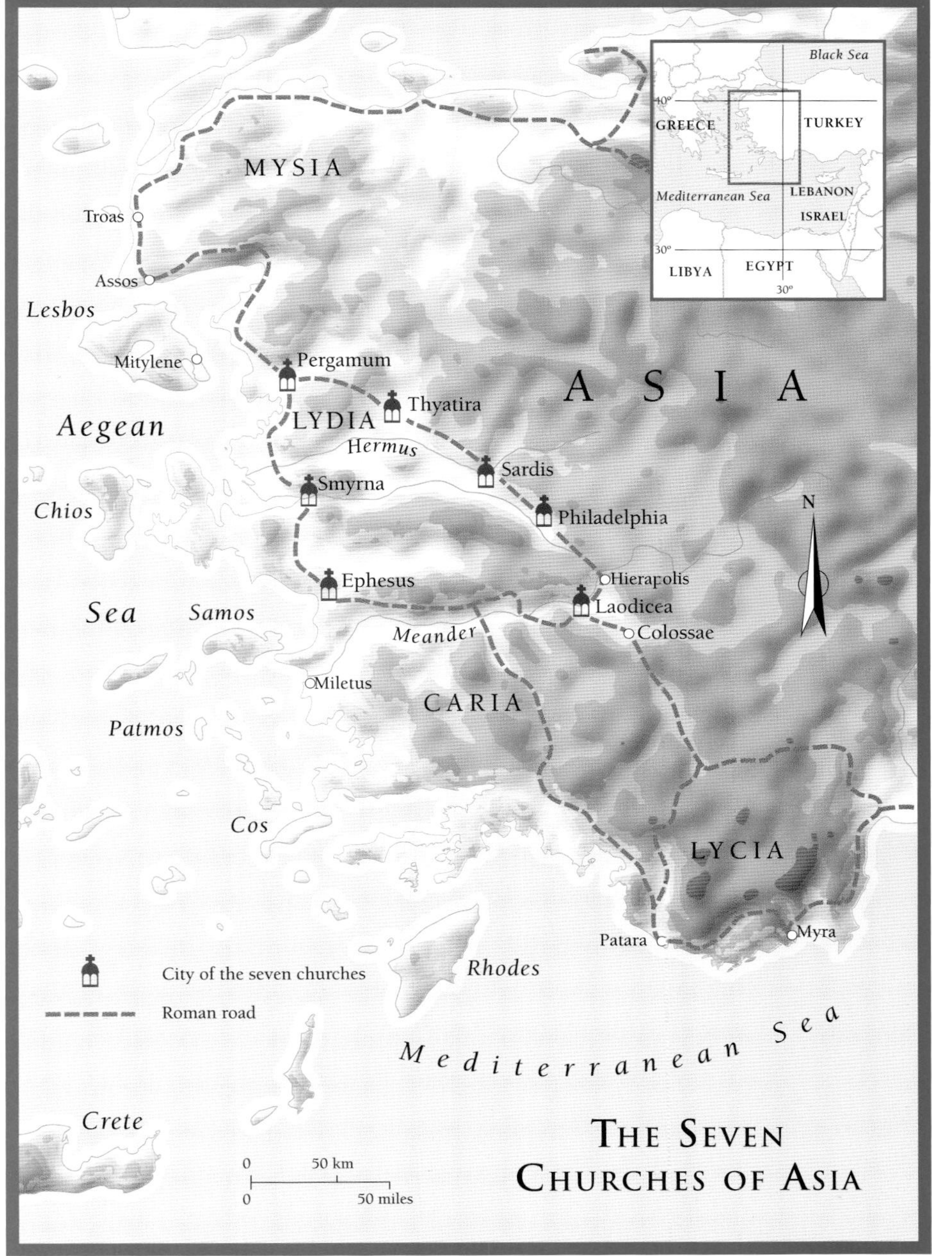

LEFT: THE VISION OF THE WOMAN AND THE DRAGON, FROM THE LATIN MANUSCRIPT *BOOK OF THE APOCALYPSE*. THE WOMAN HAS THE MOON AT HER FEET AND A 12-STAR CROWN ON HER HEAD.

ABOVE: THE FALL OF BABYLON IS ANNOUNCED BY THE SECOND SOUND OF THE TRUMPET. THIS ILLUSTRATION COMES FROM THE LIEBANA BEATUS COMMENTARY ON THE APOCALYPSE.

THE FATE OF BABYLON

The name of Babylon struck fear into many Jewish and Christian hearts. In the Bible, Babylon was remembered as the oppressor of God's people, and the place of exile for deportees from Zion (e.g., Psalm 137). Particularly traumatic was Babylon's destruction of Solomon's Temple. But the woman John is shown by the angel is not historic Babylon on the Euphrates River. Rather, her name is symbolic ("a name, a mystery": Revelation 17:5).

Because she is described as a prostitute, some have identified her as unfaithful Jerusalem (see Ezekiel 16; 23). But first-century Asian Christians would most likely have seen in her a parody of the goddess Roma, who sat on the seven hills by the Tiber (Ezekiel 17:9 identifies the beast's seven heads as seven mountains or hills) and was worshipped throughout the empire. These are the features of first-century imperial Rome; later Protestant identifications of Babylon with the Roman Catholic Church, or with particular Popes, would have been unintelligible to Revelation's first audiences.

RIGHT: THE "WHORE OF BABYLON," FROM A FRENCH MANUSCRIPT. REVELATION 17:1–6 GIVES A DETAILED DESCRIPTION OF THIS SYMBOLIC WOMAN SITTING ON A BEAST.

Nor does Babylon's incarnation in imperial Rome exhaust the meaning of John's vision: Babylon represents the oppressive, idolatrous, rebellious city found in every age. She is "the great city that rules over the kings of the earth" (Revelation 17:18), responsible not only for the blood of Jesus' witnesses (martyrs under Nero may be especially in mind) but for the blood of countless other innocent victims (18:24).

The interpretation of the seven heads as seven kings at Revelation 17:9–10 (often understood as first-century Roman emperors) provides a clue to dating. Given that five kings are said to have fallen, John appears to be writing in the reign of a sixth. But the solution depends on where one starts counting, and whether one omits the short-lived reigns of Galba, Otho, and Vitellius.

Following the heavenly unmasking of Babylon, Revelation 18 presents an evocative combination of lament and exaltation over Babylon's fall. Though echoing Ezekiel's dirge over Tyre (Ezekiel 27), the lists of merchandise accurately reflect imports into first-century Rome. There is particular emphasis on exotic and luxury goods: all the wealth of the nations is sucked into this one city, where it is squandered by a tiny elite group of people.

THE RETURN OF JESUS

The shocking indulgence of Babylon gives way to a joyful vision of another banquet, in which God's people, both rich and poor, may share. A heavenly voice provides the authoritative commentary. Now that Babylon has fallen, heaven rejoices that "the marriage of the Lamb has come, and his bride has made herself ready" (Revelation 19:7). The image of the Messiah's wedding feast is frequent in early Christian thought (e.g., Mark 2:19–20; 2 Corinthians 11:2; Ephesians 5:22–33); the Lamb's bride is the Church, prepared by the faithful witness, righteous deeds, and suffering of her members. It is likely that Christians in the seven churches would have heard Revelation read while gathered for worship, probably the Eucharist. If so, they would already have begun to participate in that wedding banquet during their assemblies in the backstreets of the seven cities of Asia.

The scene now shifts to one of the Apocalypse's most dramatic visions, the rider on the white horse (Revelation 19:11–21). Many Christians find this disturbing, for the returning Christ is a terrifying warrior, with flaming eyes, a sharp sword, and armies of cavalry. Yet this is a symbolic and visionary text, which speaks by its overall effect. Christ is a warrior, because Revelation takes seriously the reality of evil, injustice, and political oppression. The battle between good and evil, truth and falsehood, is only too real. Yet he is no ordinary warrior. He possesses a weapon, but it is not in his hand. Rather, his only means of attack is the double-edged sword coming from his mouth, a symbol of his word (Isaiah 11; Hebrews 4:12–13). His robe is dipped in blood even before the last battle has been engaged. Rather than the blood of his enemies, this may be his own blood, shed on Calvary. In a heavenly vision John witnesses a battle in which Christ's word of truth destroys the lie, in which the blood of the Lamb defeats the forces of evil and chaos.

LEFT: THE RIDER ON THE WHITE HORSE (THE MESSIAH) IS THE ONLY ONE WHO KNOWS HIS NAME, PERHAPS BECAUSE HIS POWER IS LIMITLESS AND SUPREME. AN ILLUSTRATION FROM *BOOK OF THE APOCALYPSE.*

A CITY AND A GARDEN

A sequence of battle and judgment scenes, in which Satan and his accomplices are definitively dealt with, gives way to a glorious vision of a new heaven and a new earth, purged of all evil, chaos, and rebellion. Even the sea is no more, because it has symbolized the presence of evil (Revelation 21:1; see also 13:1).

Paralleling the vision of Babylon is that of another woman-city, the new Jerusalem. John's vision taps into the deepest longings of the human heart. First, it is a perfect city. Its dimensions are multiples of 12, the number of completion (12,000 stadia; 144 cubits), and its length, width, and height are equal. Like the best of ancient cities, it is a place of security from the dangers outside, in which humanity may flourish.

Secondly, it is a temple. Most ancient cities had their temples, Jerusalem being no exception. John's vision sees no temple in the new Jerusalem, because the whole city is a holy place in which all its citizens have direct access to God. Being a perfect cube, the city is like Solomon's Holy of Holies (1 Kings 6:20); its foundations are adorned with 12 precious stones, like the high priest's breastplate (Revelation 21:19–20; see also Exodus 28:17–21). Thirdly, the city is a garden, containing the tree of life and the river of the water of life (22:1–2; see also Genesis 2:8–14). In John's vision, the end is as the beginning. Eden's Paradise, once so tragically lost to humanity, is now regained as humanity finds its true destiny in the purposes of God.

RIGHT: *JUDGMENT DAY,* BY JEAN FOUQUET. REVELATION 20:11–15 DETAILS JOHN'S VISION OF THIS DAY, WHEN THE DEAD WILL BE "JUDGED."

BIBLE REFERENCE

BIBLE TABLES

BOOKS OF THE BIBLE

Section of the Bible	Book Name	Book Abbreviation
Old Testament (Pentateuch)	Genesis	Gen
	Exodus	Ex
	Leviticus	Lev
	Numbers	Num
	Deuteronomy	Deut
Old Testament (Historical Books)	Joshua	Josh
	Judges	Judg
	Ruth	Ruth
	1 Samuel	1 Sam
	2 Samuel	2 Sam
	1 Kings	1 Kings
	2 Kings	2 Kings
	1 Chronicles	1 Chr
	2 Chronicles	2 Chr
	Ezra	Ezra
	Nehemiah	Neh
	Esther	Esth
Old Testament (Wisdom Literature)	Job	Job
	Psalms	Ps (singular) or Pss (plural)
	Proverbs	Prov
	Ecclesiastes	Eccl
	Song of Solomon	Song
Old Testament (Prophetic Books)	Isaiah	Isa
	Jeremiah	Jer
	Lamentations	Lam
	Ezekiel	Ezek
	Daniel	Dan
	Hosea	Hos
	Joel	Joel
	Amos	Am
	Obadiah	Ob
	Jonah	Jon
	Micah	Mic
	Nahum	Nah
	Habakkuk	Hab
	Zephaniah	Zeph
	Haggai	Hag
	Zechariah	Zech
	Malachi	Mal

Section of the Bible	Book Name	Book Abbreviation
Apocrypha/Deuterocanon	Tobit	Tob
	Judith	Jdt
	Additions to Esther	Add Esth
	Wisdom	Wis
	Sirach (Ecclesiasticus)	Sir
	Baruch	Bar
	1 Esdras	1 Esd
	2 Esdras	2 Esd
	Letter of Jeremiah	Let Jer
	Prayer of Azariah/ Song of the Three Jews	Song of Thr
	Susanna	Sus
	Bel and the Dragon	Bel
	1 Maccabees	1 Macc
	2 Maccabees	2 Macc
	3 Maccabees	3 Macc
	4 Maccabees	4 Macc
	Prayer of Manasseh	Pr Man
New Testament (Gospels)	Matthew	Mt
	Mark	Mk
	Luke	Lk
	John	Jn
New Testament (Acts)	Acts of the Apostles	Acts
New Testament (Paul's Epistles)	Romans	Rom
	1 Corinthians	1 Cor
	2 Corinthians	2 Cor
	Galatians	Gal
	Ephesians	Eph
	Philippians	Phil
	Colossians	Col
	1 Thessalonians	1 Thess
	2 Thessalonians	2 Thess
	1 Timothy	1 Tim
	2 Timothy	2 Tim
	Titus	Titus
	Philemon	Philem
	Hebrews	Heb
New Testament (General Epistles)	James	Jas
	1 Peter	1 Pet
	2 Peter	2 Pet
	1 John	1 Jn
	2 John	2 Jn
	3 John	3 Jn
	Jude	Jude
New Testament (Revelation)	Revelation	Rev

ARCHAEOLOGICAL PERIODS FOR THE BIBLE LANDS

Name of Period	Approx. Date of Period
Lower Paleolithic	3,000,000–90,000 B.C.E.
Middle Paleolithic	90,000–40,000 B.C.E.
Upper Paleolithic	40,000–12,000 B.C.E.
Epipaleolithic	12,000–8500 B.C.E.
Early Neolithic	8500–6000 B.C.E.
Late Neolithic	6000–4300 B.C.E.
Chalcolithic	4300–3300 B.C.E.
Early Bronze Age I	3300–3050 B.C.E.
Early Bronze Age II	3050–2600 B.C.E.
Early Bronze Age III	2600–2300 B.C.E.
Early Bronze Age IV	2300–2100 B.C.E.
Middle Bronze Age I	2100–1800 B.C.E.
Middle Bronze Age II	1800–1550 B.C.E.
Late Bronze Age I	1550–1400 B.C.E.
Late Bronze Age II	1400–1200 B.C.E.
Iron Age I	1200–1000 B.C.E.
Iron Age II	1000–586 B.C.E.
Babylonian and Persian Periods	586–332 B.C.E.
Hellenistic Period	332–37 B.C.E.
Roman Period	37 B.C.E.–C.E. 324

THE TEN COMMANDMENTS IN DIFFERENT RELIGIOUS TRADITIONS

Some religious traditions number the commandments differently. This table indicates the traditional numbering system used by Jews, the majority of Protestants, and Roman Catholics (also many Lutherans).

Jewish	Protestant	Catholic	Commandment
1	Prolog	Prolog	"I am the Lord your God, who brought you out of the land of Egypt, out of the house of slavery;"
2a	1	1a	"You shall have no other gods before me."
2b	2	1b	"You shall not make for yourself an idol …"
3	3	2	"You shall not make wrongful use of the name of the Lord your God, for the Lord will not acquit anyone who misuses his name."
4	4	3	"Remember the sabbath day, and keep it holy…."
5	5	4	"Honor your father and your mother, so that your days may be long in the land that the Lord your God is giving you."
6	6	5	"You shall not murder."
7	7	6	"You shall not commit adultery."
8	8	7	"You shall not steal."
9	9	8	"You shall not bear false witness against your neighbor."
10a	10a	9	"You shall not covet your neighbor's wife,"*
10b	10b	10	"You shall not covet your neighbor's house … or anything that belongs to your neighbor."

*This clause comes first in Deuteronomy, but second in Exodus (in the latter, it comes after "your neighbor's house").

THE JUDGES

Name of Judge	Type of Judge	Persecutor	Years of Persecution	Years of Peace (Rest)	Years of Judgment	Scripture Reference
Othniel	Major	Cushan-rishathaim of Aram-naharaim	8	40*	—	Judges 3:8–11
Ehud	Major	Eglon of Moab	18	80	—	Judges 3:12–30
Shamgar	Minor	Philistines	—	—	—	Judges 3:31
Deborah	Major	Jabin and Sisera of Canaan	20	40	—	Judges 4:1–5:31
Gideon	Major	Midianites and Amalekites	7	40	—	Judges 6:1–8:28
Tola	Minor	—	—	—	23	Judges 10:1–2
Jair	Minor	—	—	—	22	Judges 10:3–5
Jephthah	Major	Philistines and Ammonites	18	—	6	Judges 10:6–12:7
Ibzan	Minor	—	—	—	7	Judges 12:8–10
Elon	Minor	—	—	—	10	Judges 12:11–12
Abdon	Minor	—	—	—	8	Judges 12:13–15
Samson	Major	Philistines	40	—	20	Judges 13–16

*The Septuagint accords Othniel 50 years of peace (rest).

RULERS OF THE UNITED KINGDOM

Name of King	Age at Start of Reign	Approx. Date of Reign	Length of Reign*
Saul	—	1051–1011 B.C.E.**	40 years
David	30	1011–971 B.C.E.	40 years
Solomon	—	971–931 B.C.E.	40 years

*The Bible allots Saul, David, and Solomon each a reign of 40 years, which may indicate one generation rather than a particular length of time.

**These dates are open to question, as it is likely that Saul and David ruled as co-regents for ten years.

RULERS OF THE DIVIDED KINGDOM

Rulers of Israel	Age at Start of Reign	Approx. Date of Reign	Length of Reign	Rulers of Judah	Age at Start of Reign	Approx. Date of Reign	Length of Reign
King Jeroboam I	—	931–910 B.C.E.	22 years	King Rehoboam	41	931–915 B.C.E.	17 years
King Nadab	—	910–909 B.C.E.	2 years	King Abijam	—	915–913 B.C.E.	3 years
King Baasha	—	909–886 B.C.E.	24 years	King Asa	—	913–873 B.C.E.	41 years
King Elah	—	886–885 B.C.E.	2 years	King Jehoshaphat	35	873–849 B.C.E.	25 years
King Zimri	—	885 B.C.E.	7 days	King Jehoram	32	849–842 B.C.E.	8 years
King Omri	—	885–874 B.C.E.	12 years	King Ahaziah	22	842–841 B.C.E.	1 year
King Ahab	—	874–853 B.C.E.	22 years	Queen Athaliah	—	841–836 B.C.E.	6 years
King Ahaziah	—	853–852 B.C.E.	2 years	King Joash	7	836–797 B.C.E.	40 years
King Joram	—	852–841 B.C.E.	12 years	King Amaziah	25	797–769 B.C.E.	29 years
King Jehu	—	841–814 B.C.E.	28 years	King Uzziah	16	769–740 B.C.E.	30 years*
King Jehoahaz	—	814–798 B.C.E.	17 years	King Jotham	25	740–735 B.C.E.	6 years
King Jehoash	—	798–783 B.C.E.	16 years	King Ahaz	20	735–716 B.C.E.	19 years
King Jeroboam II	—	783–745 B.C.E.	39 years	King Hezekiah	25	716–687 B.C.E.	29 years
King Zechariah	—	745 B.C.E.	6 months	King Manasseh	12	697–642 B.C.E.	55 years**
King Shallum	—	745 B.C.E.	1 month	King Amon	22	642–640 B.C.E.	2 years
King Menahem	—	745–736 B.C.E.	10 years	King Josiah	8	640–609 B.C.E.	31 years
King Pekahiah	—	736–735 B.C.E.	2 years	King Jehoahaz	23	609 B.C.E.	3 months
King Pekah	—	735–732 B.C.E.	4 years	King Jehoiakim	25	608–598 B.C.E.	11 years
King Hoshea	—	732–722 B.C.E.	10 years	King Jehoiachin	18	598–597 B.C.E.	3 months
				King Zedekiah	21	597–586 B.C.E.	12 years

*In 2 Kings 15:2, the Bible claims that King Uzziah (Azariah) ruled for 52 years, which may indicate a co-regency.

**King Manasseh ruled as co-regent with his father, King Hezekiah, for ten years.

OLD TESTAMENT KINGS IN ANCIENT SECULAR LITERATURE

The following individuals are mentioned by name in both biblical and ancient secular literature. References to biblical characters begin to appear in secular texts and stelae at the time when the Assyrians first marched west to Canaan and came into contact with Israel's Divided Kingdom.

Category of King	Name of King	Approx. Date of Reign	Citation(s)	Bibliographic Source
King of Israel	Omri	885–874 B.C.E. (Mesha: 849–820 B.C.E.) (Shalmaneser III: 858–824 B.C.E.) (Tiglath-pileser III: 744–727 B.C.E.) (Sargon II: 721–705 B.C.E.)	"Omri was the king of Israel" "Jehu, son of Omri" "Land of Omri"	*The Context of Scripture* II, page 137 [Mesha Inscription]; *Ancient Records of Assyria and Babylonia* I, paragraphs 590–591 [Shalmaneser III]; *Ancient Records of Assyria and Babylonia* I, paragraphs 672, 739 [Tiglath-pileser III]; *Ancient Records of Assyria and Babylonia* II, paragraphs 79–80 [Sargon II]
	Ahab	874–853 B.C.E. (Shalmaneser III: 858–824 B.C.E.)	"Ahab the Israelite"	*The Context of Scripture*, page 263 [Shalmaneser III]
	Joram (Jehoram)	852–841 B.C.E.	"[Jeho]ram, son of [Ahab], king of Israel"	*Israel Exploration Journal* 45/1 (1995), pages 9–11 [Tel Dan Inscription]
	Jehu	841–814 B.C.E. (Shalmaneser III: 858–824 B.C.E.)	"Jehu, son of Omri"	*Ancient Records of Assyria and Babylonia* I, paragraphs 590–591 [Shalmaneser III]
	Jehoash (Joash)	798–783 B.C.E. (Adad-nirari III: 810–783 B.C.E.)	"Joash the Samarian"	*Iraq* 30 (1968), pages 142–143 [Adad-nirari III]
	Jeroboam II	783–745 B.C.E.	"Belonging to Shema, servant of Jeroboam"	*The Context of Scripture* II, page 200
	Menahem	745–736 B.C.E. (Tiglath-pileser III: 744–727 B.C.E.)	"Menahem the Samarian"	*Ancient Records of Assyria and Babylonia* I, paragraph 772 [Tiglath-pileser III]
	Pekah	735–732 B.C.E. (Tiglath-pileser III: 744–727 B.C.E.)	"they overthrew king Pekah, and I set Hoshea up as king"	*Ancient Records of Assyria and Babylonia* I, paragraphs 815–816 [Tiglath-pileser III]
	Hoshea	732–722 B.C.E. (Tiglath-pileser III: 744–727 B.C.E.)	"they overthrew king Pekah, and I set Hoshea up as king" "Abdi, servant of Hoshea"	*Ancient Records of Assyria and Babylonia* I, paragraphs 815–816 [Tiglath-pileser III]; *Biblical Archaeology Review* 21/6 (1995), page 49
King of Judah	Ahaziah	842–841 B.C.E.	"[Ahaz]iah son of [Jehoram, k]ing of the House of David"	*Israel Exploration Journal* 45/1 (1995), pages 9–11 [Tel Dan Inscription]
	Uzziah	769–740 B.C.E. (Tiglath-pileser III: 744–727 B.C.E.)	"Shebaniah, servant of Uzziah" "Abiah, servant of Uzziah"	*The Context of Scripture* II, page 200 [Tiglath-pileser III]
	Jotham	740–735 B.C.E.	"Belonging to Ahaz [son of] Jotham, king of Judah"	*Biblical Archaeology Review* 25/2 (1999), page 42
	Ahaz	735–716 B.C.E. (Tiglath-pileser III: 744–727 B.C.E.)	"Ushnu, servant of Ahaz" "Belonging to Ahaz [son of] Jotham, king of Judah" "Belonging to Hezekiah [son of] Ahaz, king of Judah" "[Jeho]ahaz the Judean"	*The Context of Scripture* II, page 200; *Biblical Archaeology Review* 24/3 (1998), pages 54–56, 62; *Biblical Archaeology Review* 25/2 (1999), pages 42–44, 60; *Ancient Records of Assyria and Babylonia* I, paragraphs 815–816 [Tiglath-pileser III]
	Hezekiah	716–687 B.C.E. (Sennacherib: 704–681 B.C.E.)	"Jehozarah, son of Hilkiah, servant of Hezekiah" "Belonging to Hezekiah [son of] Ahaz, king of Judah" "Hezekiah the Judean" "Hezekiah of Judah"	*The Context of Scripture* II, page 200; *Biblical Archaeology Review* 25/2 (1999), pages 42–43; *Ancient Records of Assyria and Babylonia* II, paragraph 240; *The Context of Scripture* II, page 304 [Sennacherib]
	Manasseh	697–642 B.C.E. (Esarhaddon: 680–669 B.C.E.) (Ashurbanipal: 668–627 B.C.E.)	"Manasseh, king of Judah" "Manasseh, king of Judah"	*The Prisms of Esarhaddon and of Ashurbanipal*, page 55, plate 11 [Esarhaddon]; *Ancient Records of Assyria and Babylonia* II, paragraph 876 [Ashurbanipal]
	Jehoiachin	598–597 B.C.E. (Nebuchadnezzar II: 605–562 B.C.E.)	"to Jehoiachin, son of the king of Judah"	*Ancient Near Eastern Texts Relating to the Old Testament*, page 308 [Nebuchadnezzar II]

Bibliographic Sources

Hallo, W. W. and K. L. Younger, Jr. (eds.). *The Context of Scripture*, 3 vols. Brill: Leiden, 1997–2002.
Luckenbill, D. D. (ed.). *Ancient Records of Assyria and Babylonia*, 2 vols. University of Chicago Press: Chicago, 1926–1927.
Pritchard, J. B. (ed.). *Ancient Near Eastern Texts Relating to the Old Testament*. Princeton University Press: Princeton, NJ, 1969.
Thompson, R. C. (ed.). *The Prisms of Esarhaddon and of Ashurbanipal*. Thames & Hudson: London, 1931.

PROPHETS OF THE BIBLE

Name of Prophet	Approx. Dates of Prophesying	Prophesying/ Home Location	Scripture References
Elijah	870–850 B.C.E.	Tishbe	1 Kings 17:1 to 2 Kings 2:18
Elisha	855–800 B.C.E.	Abel-meholah	1 Kings 19:16–21; 2 Kings 2–9:3; 2 Kings 13:14–21
Jonah	785–745 B.C.E.	Gath-hepher	2 Kings 14:25; Jonah 1–4
Hosea	785–745 B.C.E.	Israel	Hosea 1–14
Amos	760–750 B.C.E.	Tekoa	Amos 1–9
Isaiah	740–700 B.C.E.	Jerusalem	2 Kings 19–20; Isaiah 1–66
Micah	735–710 B.C.E.	Moresheth-gath Jerusalem	Jeremiah 26:18; Micah 1–7
Nahum	686–612 B.C.E.	Elkosh	Nahum 1–3
Zephaniah	640–622 B.C.E.	Unknown	Zephaniah 1–3
Jeremiah	626–586 B.C.E.	Anathoth Jerusalem	2 Chronicles 36:12; Jeremiah 1–52
Habakkuk	612–605 B.C.E.	Unknown	Habakkuk 1–3
Ezekiel	593–573 B.C.E.	Babylon	Ezekiel 1–48
Obadiah	586 B.C.E.	Jerusalem	Obadiah 1
Joel	539–331 B.C.E.	Jerusalem	Joel 1–3
Haggai	522–515 B.C.E.	Jerusalem	Ezra 5:1; Ezra 6:14; Haggai 1–2
Zechariah	522–515 B.C.E.	Jerusalem	Ezra 5:1; Ezra 6:14; Zechariah 1–14
Malachi	515–450 B.C.E.	Jerusalem	Malachi 1–4

EGYPTIAN RULERS OF THE NEW KINGDOM

Dynasty	Approx. Date of Reign	Pharaoh/Queen
Eighteenth Dynasty	1550–1525 B.C.E.	Ahmose I
	1525–1504 B.C.E.	Amenhotep I
	1504–1492 B.C.E.	Thutmose I
	1492–1479 B.C.E.	Thutmose II
	1479–1425 B.C.E.	Thutmose III (co-regent)
	1473–1458 B.C.E.	Hatshepsut (co-regent)
	1427–1400 B.C.E.	Amenhotep II
	1400–1390 B.C.E.	Thutmose IV
	1390–1352 B.C.E.	Amenhotep III
	1352–1336 B.C.E.	Amenhotep IV [Akhenaten] (co-regent)
	1338–1336 B.C.E.	Smenkhkare (co-regent)
	1336–1327 B.C.E.	Tutankhamun
	1327–1323 B.C.E.	Ay
	1323–1295 B.C.E.	Horemheb
Nineteenth Dynasty	1295–1294 B.C.E.	Rameses I
	1294–1279 B.C.E.	Seti I
	1279–1213 B.C.E.	Rameses II
	1213–1203 B.C.E.	Merneptah
	1203–1200 B.C.E.	Amenmessu
	1200–1194 B.C.E.	Seti II
	1194–1188 B.C.E.	Siptah
	1188–1186 B.C.E.	Tewosret
Twentieth Dynasty	1186–1184 B.C.E.	Sethnakht
	1184–1153 B.C.E.	Rameses III
	1153–1147 B.C.E.	Rameses IV
	1147–1143 B.C.E.	Rameses V
	1143–1136 B.C.E.	Rameses VI
	1136–1129 B.C.E.	Rameses VII
	1129–1126 B.C.E.	Rameses VIII
	1126–1108 B.C.E.	Rameses IX
	1108–1099 B.C.E.	Rameses X
	1099–1069 B.C.E.	Rameses XI

KINGS OF THE NEO-ASSYRIAN EMPIRE

Name of King	Approx. Date of Reign
Ashur-dan II	934–912 B.C.E.
Adad-nirari II	911–891 B.C.E.
Tukulti-Ninurta II	890–884 B.C.E.
Ashurnasirpal II	883–859 B.C.E.
Shalmaneser III	858–824 B.C.E.
Shamshi-adad V	823–811 B.C.E.
Adad-nirari III	810–783 B.C.E.
Shalmaneser IV	782–773 B.C.E.
Ashur-dan III	772–755 B.C.E.
Ashur-nirari V	754–745 B.C.E.
Tiglath-pileser III	744–727 B.C.E.
Shalmaneser V	726–722 B.C.E.
Sargon II	721–705 B.C.E.
Sennacherib	704–681 B.C.E.
Esarhaddon	680–669 B.C.E.
Ashurbanipal	668–627 B.C.E.
Ashuretililani	626–624 B.C.E.
Sinsharishkun	623–612 B.C.E.
Ashuruballit II	611–609 B.C.E.

KINGS OF THE PERSIAN EMPIRE

Name of King	Approx. Date of Reign
Cyrus II	559–530 B.C.E.
Cambyses II	529–522 B.C.E.
Pseudo-Smerdis	522 B.C.E.
Darius I Hystaspes	521–486 B.C.E.
Xerxes I	485–465 B.C.E.
Artaxerxes I Longimanus	464–424 B.C.E.
Xerxes II	424 B.C.E.
Sogdianus	424 B.C.E.
Darius II Nothus	423–405 B.C.E.
Artaxerxes II Mnemon	404–359 B.C.E.
Artaxerxes III Ochus	358–338 B.C.E.
Arses	337–336 B.C.E.
Darius III Codomannus	335–330 B.C.E.

KINGS OF THE NEO-BABYLONIAN EMPIRE

Name of King	Approx. Date of Reign
Nabopolassar	626–605 B.C.E.
Nebuchadnezzar II	605–562 B.C.E.
Evil-Merodach	561–560 B.C.E.
Neriglissar	559–556 B.C.E.
Labashi-Marduk	556 B.C.E.
Nabonidus	555–539 B.C.E.
Belshazzar	553–543 B.C.E.

RULERS OF THE PTOLEMIES

Name of Ruler	Approx. Date of Rule
Ptolemy I Soter†	323–285 B.C.E.
Ptolemy II Philadelphus	285–246 B.C.E.
Ptolemy III Euergetes I	246–221 B.C.E.
Ptolemy IV Philopator	221–205 B.C.E.
Ptolemy V Epiphanes	204–180 B.C.E.
Ptolemy VI Philometor*	180–145 B.C.E.
Ptolemy VII Neos Philopator	145 B.C.E.
Ptolemy VIII Euergetes II	145–116 B.C.E.
Ptolemy IX Soter II**	116–107 B.C.E.
Ptolemy X Alexander I***	107–88 B.C.E.
Ptolemy IX Soter II	88–81 B.C.E.
Ptolemy XI Alexander II****	80 B.C.E.
Ptolemy XII Neos Dionysus	80–58 B.C.E.
Berenice IV*****	58–55 B.C.E.
Ptolemy XII Neos Dionysus	55–51 B.C.E.
Cleopatra VII Philopator	51–30 B.C.E.

†Satrap 323–305 B.C.E.; king 305–285 B.C.E.
*Co-rule with Ptolemy VIII Euergetes II 170–164 B.C.E.; with Cleopatra II 170–145 B.C.E.
**Co-rule with Cleopatra III
***Co-rule with Cleopatra III 107–101 B.C.E.; with Cleopatra Berenice 101–88 B.C.E.
****Co-rule with Cleopatra Berenice
*****Co-rule with Cleopatra Tryphaena 58–56 B.C.E.; with Archelaus 56–55 B.C.E.

RULERS OF THE SELEUCIDS

Name of Ruler	Approx. Date of Rule
Seleucus I Nicator*	312–281 B.C.E.
Antiochus I Soter	292–261 B.C.E.
Antiochus II Theos	261–246 B.C.E.
Seleucus II Callinicus	246–226 B.C.E.
Seleucus III Soter	226–223 B.C.E.
Antiochus III Megas	223–187 B.C.E.
Seleucus IV Philopator	187–175 B.C.E.
Antiochus IV Epiphanes	175–164 B.C.E.
Antiochus V Eupator	164–162 B.C.E.
Demetrius I Soter	162–150 B.C.E.
Alexander Balas	150–145 B.C.E.
Demetrius II Nicator	145–140 B.C.E.
Antiochus VI Epiphanes	145–142 B.C.E.
Trypho	142–138 B.C.E.
Antiochus VII Sidetes	138–129 B.C.E.
Demetrius II Nicator	129–125 B.C.E.
Cleopatra Thea	125–123 B.C.E.
Antiochus VIII Grypus	125–96 B.C.E.
Seleucus V	125 B.C.E.
Antiochus IX Philopator	114–95 B.C.E.
Seleucus VI	95–94 B.C.E.
Antiochus X Eusebes Philopator	95 B.C.E.
Antiochus XI Epiphanes Philadelphus	95 B.C.E.
Demetrius III Philopator Soter	95–88 B.C.E.
Philip I	95–84 B.C.E.
Antiochus XII Dionysus	87 B.C.E.
Antiochus XIII Asiaticus	87–64 B.C.E.
Philip II	66–63 B.C.E.

*Co-rule with Antiochus I Soter 292–281 B.C.E.

HASMONEAN RULERS

Name of Ruler	Approx. Date of Rule
Mattathias	167–166 B.C.E.
Judas Maccabeus (the Maccabee)	166–160 B.C.E.
Jonathan	160–142 B.C.E.
Simon	142–134 B.C.E.
John Hyrcanus I	134–104 B.C.E.
Aristobulus I	104–103 B.C.E.
Alexander Jannaeus	103–76 B.C.E.
Salome Alexandra	76–67 B.C.E.
Aristobulus II	67–63 B.C.E.
John Hyrcanus II	63–40 B.C.E.
Antigonus	40–37 B.C.E.

ROMAN EMPERORS DURING THE TIME OF THE BIBLE

Name of Emperor	Date of Rule
Caesar Augustus	27 B.C.E.–C.E. 14
Tiberius	C.E. 14–37
Gaius (Caligula)	C.E. 37–41
Claudius	C.E. 41–54
Nero	C.E. 54–68
Galba	C.E. 68–69
Otho	C.E. 69
Vitellius	C.E. 69
Vespasian	C.E. 69–79
Titus	C.E. 79–81
Domitian	C.E. 81–96
Nerva	C.E. 96–98
Trajan	C.E. 98–117
Hadrian	C.E. 117–138

THE WONDROUS ACTS OF JESUS

Wondrous Act	Matthew	Mark	Luke	John
Jesus cleanses a leper	8:2–4	1:40–45	5:12–16	
Jesus heals a centurion's servant	8:5–13		7:1–10	
Jesus heals a disciple's mother-in-law	8:14–15	1:29–31	4:38–39	
Jesus heals the sick and possessed	8:16–17	1:32–34	4:40–41	
Jesus calms the storm	8:23–27	4:35–41	8:22–25	
Jesus sends demons into the swine herd	8:28–32	5:2–13	8:26–33	
Jesus heals a paralyzed man	9:2–8	2:3–12	5:18–26	
Jesus raises the leader's daughter	9:18–19, 9:23–26	5:22–24, 5:35–43	8:40–42, 8:49–56	
Jesus heals the hemorrhaging woman	9:20–22	5:25–34	8:43–48	
Jesus cures a possessed mute	9:32–34			
Jesus heals a man's withered hand	12:9–14	3:1–6	6:6–11	
Jesus heals a possessed blind-mute	12:22–24		11:14–17	
Jesus feeds 5,000 people	14:13–21	6:34–44	9:12–17	6:1–14
Jesus walks on the sea	14:25–27	6:48–52		6:19–21
Jesus heals a woman's daughter	15:22–28	7:24–30		
Jesus feeds 4,000 people	15:32–39	8:1–9		
Jesus heals an epileptic boy	17:14–21	9:17–29	9:38–43	
Jesus sends the tax coin in a fish's mouth	17:24–27			
Jesus heals a blind man/two blind men	9:27–31, 20:30–34	10:46–52	18:35–43	
Jesus makes a fig tree wither	21:18–22	11:12–14		
Jesus casts out an unclean spirit		1:23–28	4:33–37	
Jesus heals a deaf-mute		7:32–37		
Jesus heals a blind man at Bethsaida		8:22–26		
Jesus escapes from the raging crowd			4:27–30	
Jesus commands that fish are caught			5:1–11	
Jesus raises a widow's son			7:11–17	
Jesus heals a crippled woman			13:11–17	
Jesus heals a man suffering from dropsy			14:1–6	
Jesus cleanses ten lepers			17:11–19	
Jesus heals a servant's ear			22:50–51	
Jesus turns water into wine				2:1–11
Jesus heals an official's son				4:46–54
Jesus heals an invalid				5:2–15
Jesus heals a man blind since birth				9:1–41
Jesus raises Lazarus				11:1–44
Jesus commands that fish are caught				21:4–8

THE PARABLES AND OTHER STORIES OF JESUS

Parable/Story	Matthew	Mark	Luke	John*
Lamp under a bushel basket	5:14–16	4:21–22	8:16–17, 11:33–36	
Wise and foolish builders	7:21–27		6:47–49	
Unshrunk cloth on an old cloak	9:16	2:21	5:36	
New wine into old wineskins	9:17	2:22	5:37–39	
The sower	13:3–23	4:3–20	8:4–15	
The weeds	13:24–30			
The mustard seed	13:31–32	4:30–32	13:18–19	
Leavened yeast and flour	13:33		13:20–21	
The hidden treasure	13:44			
The pearl of great value	13:45–46			
The fish net	13:47–50			
The lost sheep	18:12–14		15:3–7	
The unmerciful slave	18:23–35			
The vineyard laborers	20:1–16			
The two sons	21:28–32			
The wicked tenants	21:33–41	12:1–9	20:9–19	
The wedding banquet	22:2–14			
The fig tree	24:32–35	13:28–31	21:29–33	
The thief	24:43–44		12:39–40	
Wise and foolish bridesmaids	25:1–13			
The talents/pounds	25:14–30		19:11–27	
Sheep and goats	25:31–46			
The sprouting seed		4:26–29		
The absent homeowner		13:34–37		
The creditor and his two debtors			7:41–43	
The good Samaritan			10:30–37	

Parable/Story	Matthew	Mark	Luke	John*
A friend at midnight			11:5–13	
The rich fool			12:16–21	
The waiting slaves			12:35–38	
The faithful slaves			12:42–48	
The barren fig tree			13:6–9	
The wedding banquet			14:8–11	
The great dinner			14:16–24	
Building a tower			14:28–30	
The king			14:31–33	
The lost coin			15:8–10	
The lost son			15:11–32	
The shrewd manager			16:1–13	
Lazarus and the rich man			16:19–31	
The worthless slaves			17:7–10	
The persistent widow			18:1–8	
The Pharisee and the tax collector			18:9–14	
The blowing wind				3:8
The bridegroom's friend				3:29
Sowing and reaping				4:35–38
Father and son				5:19–24
The slave and the son				8:35–36
The shepherd				10:1–18
Twelve hours of daylight				11:9–10
The grain of wheat				12:24
Walk in the light				12:35–36
Prepare a place				14:2–7
The vine and the vinegrower				15:1–8
Woman in pain				16:20–24

*The Gospel According to John does not use the word "parable," but the stories told by Jesus in this Gospel are similar in their mode of teaching to the parables in the other Gospels.

APOSTLES OF THE BIBLE

Name of Apostle	Epithet	Also Known As	Symbol
Simon	the fisherman son of John	Peter Simon Peter Simeon	upside down cross with keys
Andrew	brother of Simon son of John	—	X-shaped cross
James	the Great/Greater the Elder son of Zebedee	—	shells
John	brother of James son of Zebedee	—	eagle; snake and chalice
Philip	from Bethsaida	—	basket
Bartholomew	son of Tolmai	Nathanael	knife/knives
Matthew	the tax collector son of Alphaeus	Levi	winged man; purses
Thomas	doubting Thomas the twin	Didymus	spears, stones, and arrows
James	the Less/Lesser the Younger son of Alphaeus	—	saw
Simon	the Zealot the Canaanite	—	fish on a Bible
Judas	the Zealot son of James	Thaddaeus Jude Lebbaeus	ship
Judas Iscariot	the Traitor son of Simon Iscariot	—	noose
Matthias	—	—	sword
Paul	Apostle to the Gentiles Saul of Tarsus	Saul	serpent
Barnabas	the Levite	Joses Joseph	—
Andronicus	—	—	—
Junia	—	—	—

"WE" TEXTS IN ACTS

The three passages of "we" texts found in the Acts of the Apostles lead many scholars to the conclusion that the author of Acts was a traveling companion of Paul at some points in his journeys.

Scripture Reference	Examples
Acts 16:10–18	"… we immediately tried to cross over to Macedonia …" (Acts 16:10)
	"We remained in this city for some days." (Acts 16:12)
	"One day, as we were going to the place of prayer …" (Acts 16:16)
Acts 20:5–21:18	"They went ahead and were waiting for us in Troas …" (Acts 20:5)
	"We went ahead to the ship and set sail for Assos …" (Acts 20:13)
	"When we arrived in Jerusalem, the brothers welcomed us warmly." (Acts 21:17)
Acts 27:1–28:16	"When it was decided that we were to sail for Italy …" (Acts 27:1)
	"… as we were drifting across the sea of Adria …" (Acts 27:27)
	"When we came into Rome, Paul was allowed to live by himself …" (Acts 28:16)

BIBLE FAMILY TREES

FAMILY TREE: ADAM TO ABRAHAM (ABRAM)

FAMILY TREE: TERAH TO MOSES

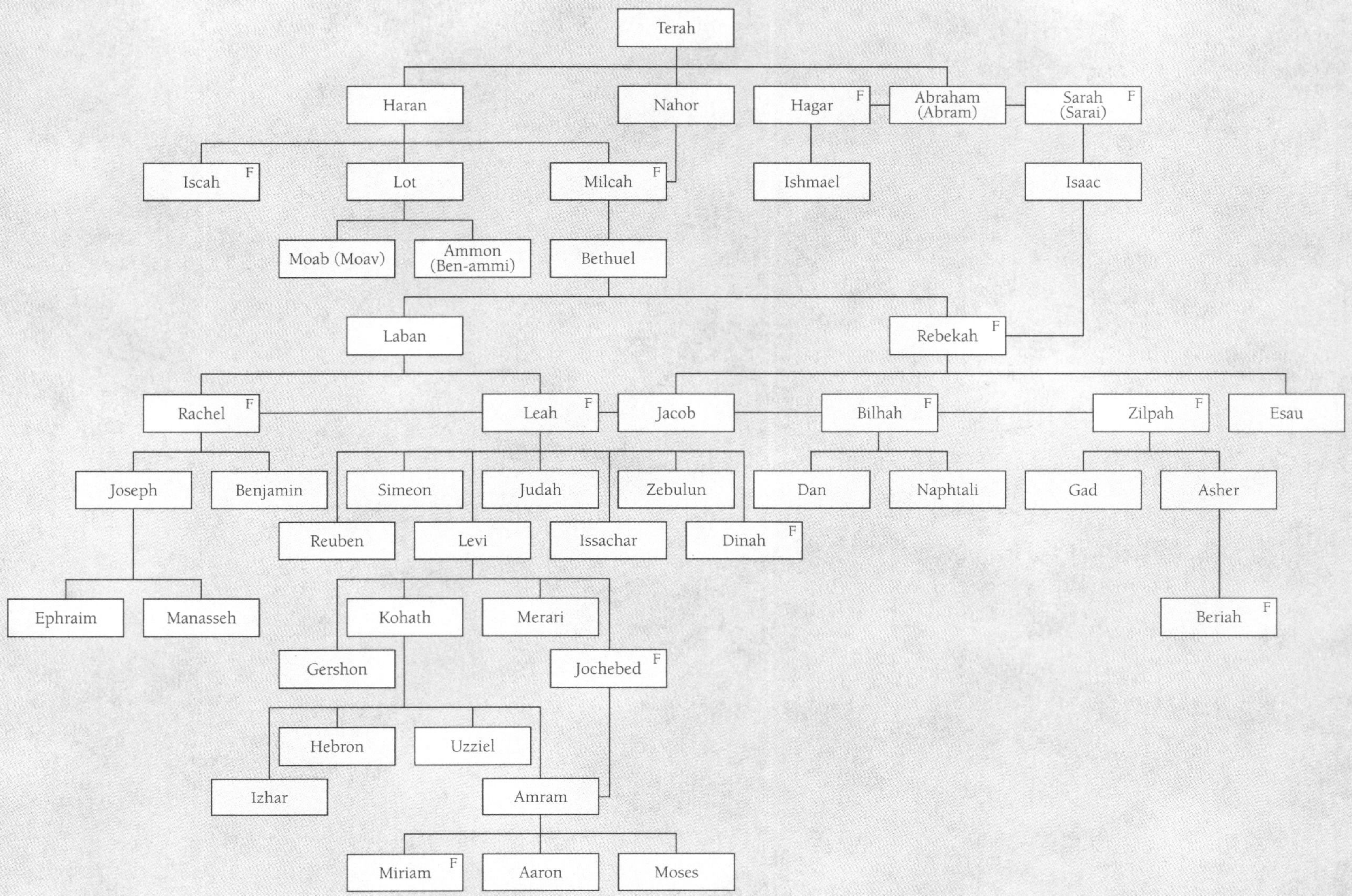

Jacob's Sons

Jacob's two wives (sisters Leah and Rachel) were each given a maid by their father when they married Jacob (see Genesis 29:24, 29:29). Leah was given a woman named Zilpah, and Rachel was given a woman named Bilhah.

When Rachel saw that she was barren and that her sister was fertile, having given birth to Reuben, Simeon, Levi, and Judah, she gave Jacob her maid Bilhah, and it was through that union that Dan and Naphtali were born (Genesis 30:1–8). Probably as an act of emotional retaliation, Leah does the same thing with her maid, and Gad and Asher are born (Genesis 30:9–13).

Accordingly, of the 12 sons born to Jacob, six are born of Leah (Reuben, Simeon, Levi, Judah, Issachar, and Zebulun), two are born of Leah's maid Zilpah (Gad and Asher), two are born of Rachel (Joseph and Benjamin), and two are born of Rachel's maid Bilhah (Dan and Naphtali). There is a direct correlation between the mothers and where the son's tribes were later given land.

FAMILY TREE: BOAZ TO JESUS

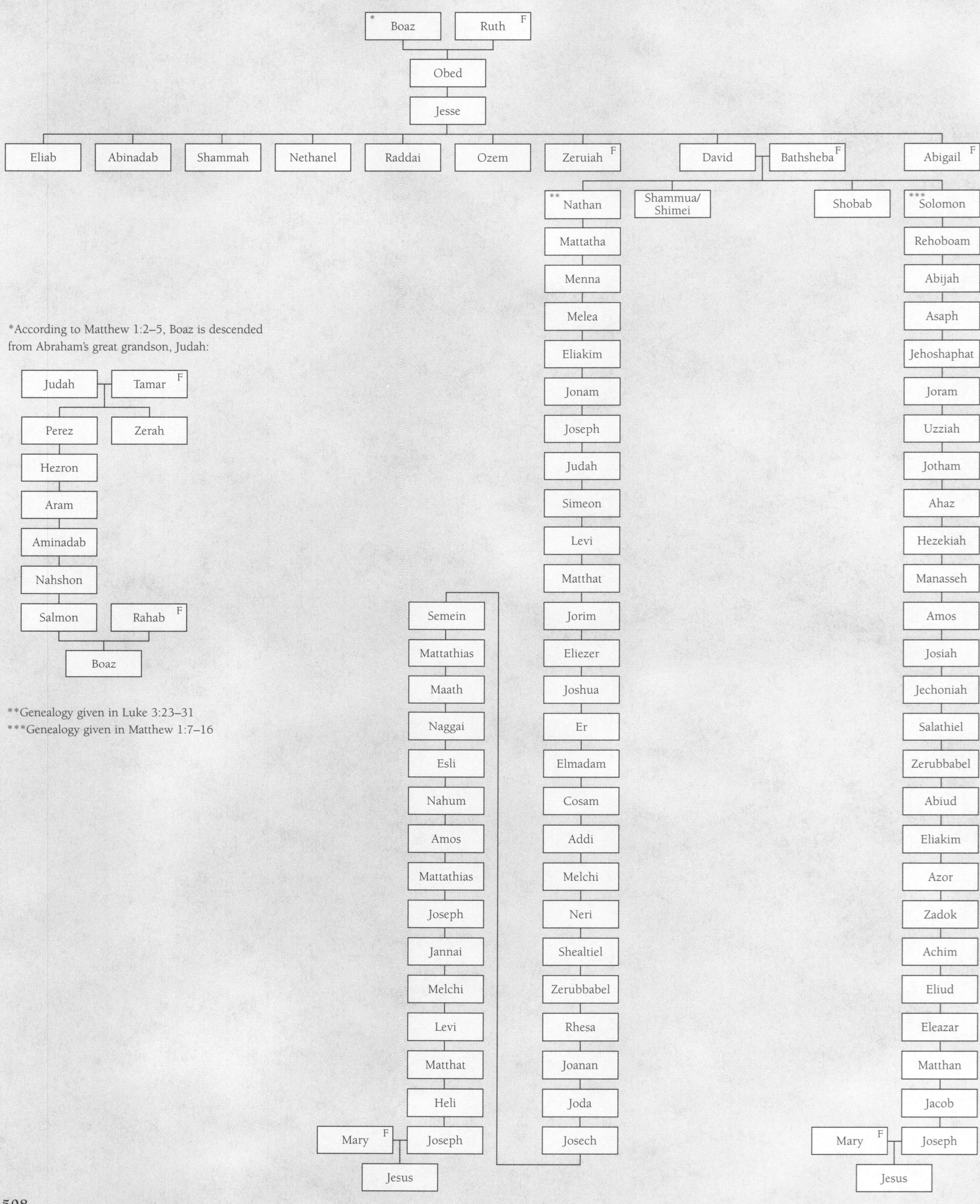

FAMILY TREE: HEROD THE GREAT

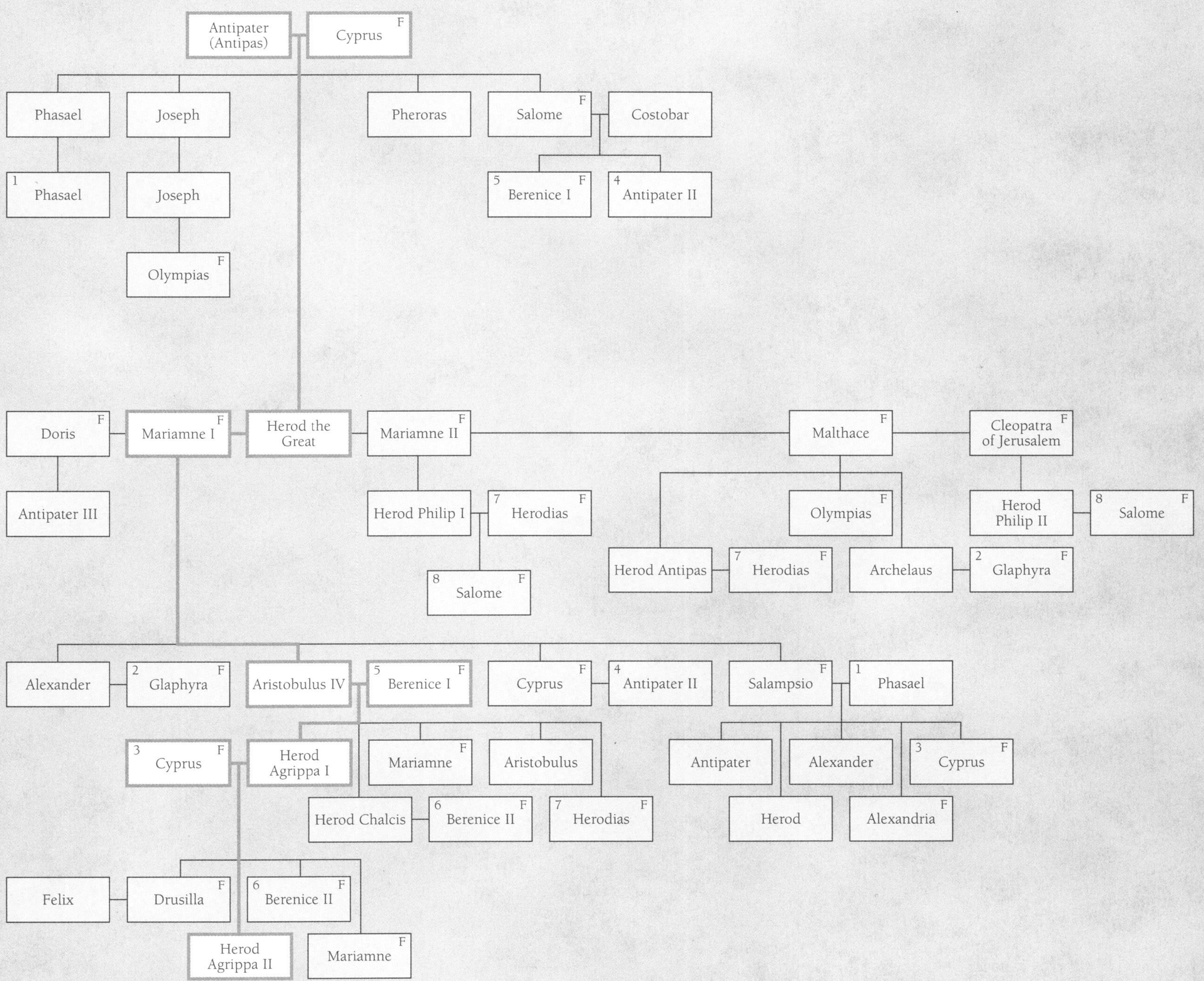

1 Herod's nephew Phasael married his daughter Salampsio.

2 Glaphyra was married to two of Herod's sons: Alexander and Archelaus.

3 Herod's granddaughter Cyprus married his grandson Herod Agrippa I.

4 Herod's nephew Antipater II married his daughter Cyprus.

5 Herod's niece Berenice I married his son Aristobulus IV.

6 Herod's great granddaughter Berenice II married his grandson Herod Chalcis.

7 Herod's granddaughter Herodias was married to two of Herod's sons: Herod Philip I and Herod Antipas.

8 Herod's granddaughter Salome was married to his son Herod Philip II.

— Main "trunk" of Herod's family tree

BIBLIOGRAPHY

INTRODUCTION

Barraclough, Geoffrey (ed.). *The Christian World: A Social and Cultural History of Christianity*. Thames and Hudson: London, 1981.

Blaiklock, E. M. *Commentary on the New Testament*. Hodder and Stoughton: London, 1977.

Chudoba, Bohdan. *Early History and Christ: A Prophetic History of Ancient Times*. Alba House: Staten Island, 1968.

Cross, F. L. (ed.). *The Oxford Dictionary of the Christian Church*. OUP: London, 1961.

Friedman, Richard Elliott. *Who Wrote the Bible?* (Perennial Library). Harper & Row Publishers: New York, 1989.

Guillet, Jacques. *Themes of the Bible*, trans. Albert J. LaMothe. Fides: Indiana, 1960.

Miller, Stephen M. and Robert V. Huber. *The Bible: A History—The Making and Impact of the Bible*. Lion Hudson: Oxford, 2004.

Parry, Melanie (ed.). *Chambers Biographical Dictionary*, 6th edn. Larousse: Edinburgh, 1997.

Patterson, Charles. *Cliff Notes on the Bible*. Wiley: New York, 2003.

Philip, George. *Philip's World Atlas & Gazetteer*, 8th edn. Philip's: London, 2000.

Strong, James. *Strong's Exhaustive Concordance of the Bible*. Thomas Nelson: Nashville, 1979.

Telushkin, Joseph. *Biblical Literacy*. William Morrow: New York, 1997.

Wilson, A. N. *Jesus*. Sinclair–Stevenson: London, 1992.

PART ONE

Avi-Yonah, Michael (ed.). *Encyclopedia of Archaeological Excavations in the Holy Land*. Prentice-Hall: Englewood Cliffs, New Jersey, *c.* 1975.

Beitzel, Barry J. "Exegesis, Dogmatics and Cartography: A Strange Alchemy in Earlier Church Traditions." *Archaeology in the Biblical World* 2/2, 1994, pp8–21.

Beitzel, Barry J. *The Moody Atlas of Bible Lands*. Moody Press: Chicago, 1985.

Ben-Tor, Amnon (ed.). *The Archaeology of Ancient Israel*. Yale University Press: New Haven; Open University of Israel: Tel Aviv, 1992.

Biers, William R. *The Archaeology of Greece: An Introduction*, 2nd edn. Cornell University Press: Ithaca, 1996.

Borowski, Oded. *Agriculture in Iron Age Israel*. Eisenbrauns: Winona Lake, 1987.

Borowski, Oded. *Daily Life in Biblical Times*. Society of Biblical Literature: Atlanta, 2003.

Clayton, Peter A. *Chronicle of the Pharaohs: The Reign-by-Reign Records of the Rulers and Dynasties of Ancient Egypt*. Thames and Hudson: New York, 1994.

Coogan, Michael D. (ed.). *The Oxford History of the Biblical World*. Oxford University Press: Oxford and New York, 2001.

Coogan, Michael D. (ed.). *Stories from Ancient Canaan*. Westminster John Knox Press: Philadelphia, *c.* 1978.

Grant, Michael and Rachel Kitzinger (eds.). *Civilization of the Ancient Mediterranean: Greece and Rome*. Scribner's: New York, *c.* 1988.

Greene, Kevin. *The Archaeology of the Roman Economy*. University of California Press: Berkeley, 1986.

Gurney, O. R. *The Hittites*, 2nd edn. Penguin Books: London and New York, 1990.

Harrison, Roland Kenneth. *Archaeology of the New Testament*. Association Press: New York, 1964.

Hornblower, Simon and Antony Spawforth (eds.). *The Oxford Classical Dictionary*, 3rd edn. (revised). Oxford University Press: Oxford and New York, *c.* 2003.

Hornblower, Simon and Antony Spawforth (eds.). *The Oxford Companion to Classical Civilization*. Oxford University Press: Oxford and New York, 1998.

Jacobsen, Thorkild. *The Harps That Once...: Sumerian Poetry in Translation*. Yale University Press: New Haven, *c.* 1987.

Kramer, Samuel Noah. *From the Tablets of Sumer: Twenty-five Firsts in Man's Recorded History*. Falcon's Wing Press: Indian Hills, *c.* 1956.

Kuhrt, Amélie. *The Ancient Near East*. Routledge: London and New York, 1994.

Levy, Thomas Evan (ed.). *The Archaeology of Society in the Holy Land*. Facts on File: New York, *c.* 1995.

McGeough, Kevin. *The Romans: New Perspectives*. ABC-CLIO: Santa Barbara, 2004.

Mazar, Amihay. *Archaeology of the Land of the Bible, 10,000–586* B.C.E. Doubleday: New York, 1990.

Meyers, Eric M. (ed.). *The Oxford Encyclopedia of Archaeology in the Near East*. OUP: New York, 1996.

Pritchard, James Bennett (ed.). *Ancient Near Eastern Texts Relating to the Old Testament*, 3rd edn. Princeton University Press: New Jersey, 1969.

Redford, Donald B. *Egypt, Canaan, and Israel in Ancient Times*. Princeton University Press: New Jersey, 1992.

Redford, Donald B. (ed.). *The Oxford Encyclopedia of Ancient Egypt*. Oxford University Press: Oxford and New York, 2001.

Roaf, Michael. *Cultural Atlas of Mesopotamia and the Ancient Near East*. Facts on File: New York, *c.* 1990.

Rousseau, John J. and Rami Arav. *Jesus and His World: An Archaeological and Cultural Dictionary*. Fortress Press: Minneapolis, *c.* 1995.

Roux, Georges. *Ancient Iraq*. Penguin Books: Harmondsworth, 1972.

Sasson, Jack M. (ed.). *Civilizations of the Ancient Near East*. Scribner: New York, 1995.

Shanks, Hershel (ed.). *Ancient Israel: A Short History from Abraham to the Roman Destruction of the Temple*. Prentice-Hall: Englewood Cliffs, New Jersey; Biblical Archaeology Society: Washington DC, *c.* 1988.

Shanks, Hershel (ed.). *Christianity and Rabbinic Judaism: A Parallel History of Their Origins and Early Development*. Biblical Archaeology Society: Washington DC, *c.* 1992.

Shanks, Hershel and Dan P. Cole (eds.). *Archaeology and the Bible: the Best of BAR*. Biblical Archaeology Society: Washington DC, *c.* 1990.

Silverman, David P. (ed.). *Ancient Egypt*. Oxford University Press: New York, 1997.

PART TWO

Bailey, Lloyd. "Horns of Moses" in Keith Crim (ed.), *The Interpreter's Dictionary of the Bible* (Supplementary Volume). Abingdon Press: Nashville, 1976, pp419–420.

Brueggemann, Walter. "The Book of Exodus: Introduction, Commentary, and Reflections" in *The New Interpreter's Bible*, vol. 1. Abingdon Press: Nashville, 1994.

Brueggemann, Walter. *Deuteronomy* (Abingdon Old Testament Commentaries). Abingdon Press: Nashville, *c.* 2001.

Cairns, Ian. *Word & Presence: A Commentary on the Book of Deuteronomy*. W. B. Eerdmans: Grand Rapids, Michigan, 1992.

Childs, Brevard S. *The Book of Exodus* (The Old Testament Library). Westminster John Knox Press: Philadelphia, 1974.

Clements, R. E. "The Book of Deuteronomy: Introduction, Commentary, and Reflections" in *The New Interpreter's Bible*, vol. 2. Abingdon Press: Nashville, 1998.

Clements, R. E. *Deuteronomy* (Old Testament Guides). JSOT Press: Sheffield, 1989.

Dozeman, Thomas B. "The Book of Numbers: Introduction, Commentary, and Reflections" in *The New Interpreter's Bible*, vol. 2. Abingdon Press: Nashville, 1998.

Fretheim, Terrence E. *Exodus* (Interpretation series). John Knox Press: Louisville, 1991.

Hess, Richard S. "Achan and Achor: Names and Wordplay in Joshua 7." *Hebrew Annual Review* 14, 1994, pp89–98.

Hess, Richard S. "Asking Historical Questions of Joshua 13–19: Recent Discussion Concerning the Date of the Boundary Lists," pp191-205 in A. R. Millard, J. K. Hoffmeier, and D. W. Baker (eds.), *Faith, Tradition, History: Old Testament Historiography in Its Near Eastern Context*. Eisenbrauns: Winona Lake, 1994.

Hess, Richard S. "The Book of Joshua as a Land Grant." *Biblica* 83, 2002, pp493–506.

Hess, Richard S. "Early Israel in Canaan: A Survey of Recent Evidence and Interpretations," pp492–518 in V. Philips Long (ed.), *Israel's Past in Present Research: Essays on Ancient Israelite Historiography* (Sources for Biblical and Theological Study 7). Eisenbrauns: Winona Lake, 1999. Reprint of "Early Israel in Canaan: A Survey of Recent Evidence and Interpretations" in *Palestine Exploration Quarterly* 126, 1993, pp125–142.

Hess, Richard S. "Joshua 10 and the Sun that Stood Still." *Buried History* 35/1, 1999, pp26–33.

Hess, Richard S. *Joshua: An Introduction and Commentary* (Tyndale Old Testament Commentaries). InterVarsity Press: Leicester and Downers Grove, 1996.

Hess, Richard S. "Late Bronze Age and Biblical Boundary Descriptions of the West Semitic World," pp123–138 in G. Brooke, A. Curtis, and J. Healey (eds.), *Ugarit and the Bible: Proceedings of the International Symposium on Ugarit and the Bible*. Münster: Ugarit-Verlag, 1994.

Hess, Richard S. "A Typology of West Semitic Place Name Lists with Special Reference to Joshua 13–21." *Biblical Archaeologist* 59/3, September 1996, pp160–170.

Hess, Richard S. "West Semitic Texts and the Book of Joshua." *Bulletin for Biblical Research* 7, 1997, pp63–76.

Hillers, Delbert R. *Covenant: The History of a Biblical Idea*. Johns Hopkins. Baltimore, 1969.

Humphreys, W. Lee. *Joseph and his Family: A Literary Study*. University of South Carolina Press: Columbia, 1988.

Lowenthal, E. *The Joseph Narrative in Genesis*. Ktav: New York, 1973.

McConville, J. G. *Deuteronom* (Apollos Old Testament Commentary). InterVarsity Press: Leicester, 2002.

Meeks, Wayne A. (ed.). *The HarperCollins Study Bible*. HarperCollins: New York, 1993.

Mendenhall, George and Gary A. Herion. "Covenant" in David Noel Freedman (ed.), *The Anchor Bible Dictionary*, vol. 1. Doubleday: New York, 1992, pp1179–1202.

Olson, Dennis T. *Numbers* (Interpretation series). John Knox Press: Louisville, 1996.

Roth, Martha T. with Harry A. Hoffner. *Law Collections from Mesopotamia and Asia Minor* (Writings from the Ancient World, vol. 6). Scholars Press: Atlanta, 1995.

Sakenfield, Katharine Doob. *Journeying with God: A Commentary on the Book of Numbers*. W. B. Eerdmans: Grand Rapids, Michigan, 1995.

Sarna, Nahum M. *Exploring Exodus: The Heritage of Biblical Israel*. Schocken Books: New York, 1986.

Wallace, R. S. *The Story of Joseph and the Family of Jacob*. W. B. Eerdmans: Grand Rapids, Michigan, 2001.

Wenham, Gordon J. *Numbers* (Old Testament Guides). Sheffield Academic Press: Sheffield, 1997.

Westbrook, Raymond. "Biblical Law" in N. S. Hecht et al. (eds.), *An Introduction to the History and Sources of Jewish Law*. Clarendon: Oxford, 1996, pp1–17.

Westermann, C. Joseph. *Eleven Bible Studies on Genesis*. Fortress Press: Minneapolis, 1996.

PART THREE

Halpern, Baruch. *The First Historians*. Harper & Row Publishers: New York, 1988.

Matthews, Victor H. *Judges and Ruth* (New Cambridge Bible Commentary). Cambridge University Press: Cambridge, 2004.

Olson, Dennis T. "The Book Of Judges: Introduction, Commentary, and Reflections" in *The New Interpreter's Bible,* vol. 2. Abingdon Press: Nashville, 1998.

Rainey, Anson and Steven Notley. *The Sacred Bridge: Carta's Atlas of the Biblical World*. Carta: Jerusalem, 2005.

Younger, K. Lawson. *Judges, Ruth* (The NIV Application Commentary). Zondervan: Grand Rapids, Michigan, 2002.

PART FOUR

Alter, Robert. *The David Story: A Translation with Commentary of 1 and 2 Samuel*. W. W. Norton: New York, 1999.

Bright, John. *A History of Israel*, 4th edn. Westminster John Knox Press: Louisville, 2000.

Cogan, Mordechai. *I Kings* (Anchor Bible series). Doubleday: New York, 2000.

Cogan, Mordechai and Hayim Tadmor. *II Kings* (Anchor Bible series). Doubleday: New York, 1988.

Coogan, Michael D. (ed.). *The Oxford History of the Biblical World*. Oxford University Press: Oxford and New York, 2001.

DeVries, Simon J. *1 Kings* (Word Biblical Commentary). Word: Dallas, 1985.

Gray, John. *I and II Kings*, 2nd edn. (Old Testament Library). Westminster John Knox Press: Philadelphia, 1970.

Hobbs, T. R. *2 Kings* (Word Biblical Commentary). Word: Dallas, 1985.

Howard, David M., Jr. *An Introduction to the Old Testament Historical Books*. Moody Publishers: Chicago, 1993.

Japhet, Sara. *I & II Chronicles* (Old Testament Library). Westminster John Knox Press: Louisville, 1993.

McCarter, P. Kyle. *I Samuel: A New Translation with Introduction, Notes, and Commentary* (Anchor Bible series). Doubleday: New York, 1980.

McCarter, P. Kyle. *II Samuel: A New Translation with Introduction, Notes, and Commentary* (Anchor Bible series). Doubleday: New York, 1984.

PART FIVE

Blenkinsopp, Joseph. *A History of Prophecy in Israel*, revised edn. Westminster John Knox Press: Philadelphia, 1996.

Bright, John. *A History of Israel*, 3rd edn. Westminster John Knox Press: Philadelphia, 1981.

Brown, Raymond E., Joseph A. Fitzmyer, and Roland E. Murphy (eds.). *The New Jerome Biblical Commentary*. Prentice-Hall: Englewood Cliffs, New Jersey, 1990.

Childs, Brevard S. *Introduction to the Old Testament as Scripture*. Augsburg Fortress Publishers: Philadelphia, 1979.

Collins, John J. *Daniel*, edited by Frank Moore Cross (Hermeneia series). Fortress Press: Minneapolis, 1993.

Coogan, Michael D. *The Old Testament: A Historical and Literary Introduction to the Hebrew Scriptures*. Oxford University Press: New York, 2005.

Dell, Katharine. *Job* (People's Bible Commentary). Bible Reading Fellowship: Oxford, 2002.

Dell, Katharine. *Shaking a Fist at God: Understanding Suffering through the Book of Job*. HarperCollins Publishers: London; Ligouri Publications: Missouri, 1996.

Gordis, Robert. *The Book of God and Man: A Study of Job*. University of Chicago Press: Chicago, 1965.

Habel, Norman. *Job* (Old Testament Library). SCM Press: London; Westminster John Knox Press: Philadelphia, 1985.

PART SIX

Abegg, Martin Jr., Peter Flint, and Eugene Ulrich. *The Dead Sea Scrolls Bible: The Oldest Known Bible Translated for the First Time into English*. HarperCollins: San Francisco, 1999.

Abegg, Martin Jr., Michael Wise, and Edward Cook. *The Dead Sea Scrolls: A New Translation*. HarperCollins: San Francisco, 1996.

Ackroyd, Peter R. *Exile and Restoration*. Westminster John Knox Press: Philadelphia, 1968.

Appian. *The Civil Wars* (Penguin Classics). Penguin Books: Harmondsworth, 1976.

Appian. *Roman History* (Loeb Classical Library), 4 vols. Harvard University Press: Cambridge, Massachusetts.

Arnold, Bill T. *Who Were the Babylonians?* Society of Biblical Literature: Atlanta, 2005.

Arrian. *Anabasis of Alexander* (Loeb Classical Library), vols. V to VII. Harvard University Press: Cambridge, Massachusetts, 1983.

Arrian. *The Campaigns of Alexander* (Penguin Classics). Penguin Books: Harmondsworth, 1976.

Bagnall, R. S. *The Administration of the Ptolemaic Possessions Outside Egypt*. Leiden: The Netherlands, 1976.

Ball, W. *Rome in the East*. Routledge: London, 2000.

Barstad, Hans M. "After the 'Myth of the Empty Land': Major Challenges in the Study of Neo-Babylonian Judah" in Oded Lipschits and Joseph Blenkinsopp (eds.), *Judah and the Judeans in the Neo-Babylonian Period*. Eisenbrauns: Winona Lake, 2003, pp3–20.

Barstad, Hans M. *The Myth of the Empty Land*. Scandinavian University Press: Oslo, 1996.

Blenkinsopp, Joseph. *Ezra–Nehemiah*. Westminster John Knox Press: Philadelphia, 1988.

Bosworth, A. B. *Alexander and the East*. Oxford University Press: Oxford, 1996.

Bosworth, A. B. *Conquest and Empire*. Cambridge University Press: Cambridge, 1988.

Briant, P. *From Cyrus to Alexander: A History of the Persian Empire*, 2 vols. Eisenbrauns: Winona Lake, 2002.

Butcher, K. *Roman Syria and the Near East*. The British Museum Press: London, 2003.

Cahill, Jane M., Karl Reinhard, David Tarler, and Peter Warnock. "It Had to Happen—Scientists Examine Remains of Ancient Bathroom." *Biblical Archaeology Review* 17/3, 1991, pp64–69.

Cassius Dio. *Roman History* (Loeb Classical Library). Harvard University Press: Cambridge, Massachusetts.

Cline, E. H. *Jerusalem Besieged: From Ancient Canaan to Modern Israel*. University of Michigan Press: Ann Arbor, 2004.

Diodorus Siculus. *Library of History* (Loeb Classical Library), 12 vols. Harvard University Press: Cambridge, Massachusetts.

Feldman, Louis H. *Josephus' Interpretation of the Bible*. University of California Press: Berkeley, 1998.

Feldman, Louis H. *Josephus, The Jewish Antiquities*, vol. 9 (Loeb Classical Library). Harvard University Press: Cambridge, 1965.

Feldman, Louis H. *Josephus and Modern Scholarship*, 1937–1980. Walter de Gruyter: Berlin, 1984.

Finkelstein, I. and N. A. Silberman. *The Bible Unearthed: Archaeology's New Vision of Ancient Israel and the Origin of Its Sacred Texts*. The Free Press: New York, 2001.

Fox, R. Lane. *Alexander the Great*. Penguin Books: Harmondsworth, 1973.

Grabbe, Lester L. *A History of the Jews and Judaism in the Second Temple Period*. T&T Clark International: New York, 2004.

Grainger, D. *The Cities of Seleukid Syria*. Oxford University Press: Oxford, 1990.

Grainger, D. *Hellenistic Phoenicia*. Oxford University Press: Oxford, 1991.

Grainger, D. *Seleukos Nikator: Constructing a Hellenistic Kingdom*. Routledge: London, 1990.

Grant, M. *The Jews in the Roman World*. Weidenfeld & Nicholson: London, 1973.

Green, P. *Alexander to Actium: The Hellenistic Age*. Thames & Hudson: London, 1990.

Green, P. *Hellenistic History and Culture*. University of California Press: Berkeley, 1993.

Hallo, William W. "Nebuchadnezzar Comes to Jerusalem" in Jonathan V. Plaut (ed.), *Through the Sound of Many Voices: Writings Contributed on the Occasion of the 70th Birthday of W. Gunther Plaut*. Lester and Orpen Dennys: Toronto, 1982, pp40–57.

Hamilton, J. R. *Alexander the Great*. University of Pittsburgh Press: Pittsburgh, 1974.

Hammond, N. G. L. *Alexander the Great: King, Commander and Statesman*. Noyes: New Jersey, 1980.

Harrington, Daniel J. *The Maccabean Revolt: Anatomy of a Biblical Revolution*. Michael Glazier Books, 1988.

Hayes, John H. and J. Maxwell Miller. *Israelite and Judean History*. Westminster John Knox Press: Philadelphia, 1977.

Josephus. *The Jewish War and Jewish Antiquities* (Loeb Classical Library). Harvard University Press: Cambridge, Massachusetts.

Kuhrt, A. "The Cyrus Cylinder and Achaemenid Imperial Policy." *Journal for the Study of the Old Testament* 25, 1983, pp83–97.

Kuhrt, A. and S. Sherwin-White. *From Samarkand to Sardis: A New Approach to the Seleucid Empire*. Duckworth: London, 1993.

Kuhrt, A. and S. Sherwin-White. *Hellenism in the Greek East*. Duckworth: London, 1987.

Leick, G. *The Babylonians: An Introduction*. Routledge: London, 2002.

Levine, Lee I. *Judaism and Hellenism in Antiquity: Conflict or Confluence?* University of Washington Press: Seattle, 1998.

Lewis, N. *Greeks in Ptolemaic Egypt. Case Studies in the Social History of the Hellenistic World*. Clarendon Press: Oxford, 1986.

Lipschits, Oded. "Demographic Changes in Judah between the Seventh and the Fifth Centuries B.C.E." in Oded Lipschits and Joseph Blenkinsopp (eds.), *Judah and the Judeans in the Neo-Babylonian Period*. Eisenbrauns: Winona Lake, 2003.

Lipschits, Oded. "The History of the Benjamin Region Under Babylonian Rule." *Tel Aviv* 26, 1999b, pp155–190.

Lipschits, Oded. "'Jehoiakim Slept with his Fathers…' (II Kings 24:6)—Did He?" *Journal of Hebrew Scriptures* 4, 2002, pp1–27. Also available online at: www.purl.org/jhs.

Lipschits, Oded. "Judah, Jerusalem and the Temple (586–539 B.C.)." *Ve Colloque International, La Transeuphratene a l'epoque perse: Religions, croyances rites et images*. Institut Catholique: Paris, pp120–134.

Lipschits, Oded. "Nebuchadrezzar's Policy in 'Hattu-Land' and the Fate of the Kingdom of Judah." *Ugarit-Forschungen* 30, 1998, pp467–487.

Lipschits, Oded and Joseph Blenkinsopp (eds.). *Judah and the Judeans in the Neo-Babylonian Period*. Eisenbrauns: Winona Lake, 2003.

Malamat, Avraham. "The Kingdom of Judah between Egypt and Babylon." *Studia Theologica* 44, 1990, pp65–77.

Malamat, Avraham. "The Last Kings of Judah and the Fall of Jerusalem: An Historical-Chronological Study." *Israel Exploration Journal* 18/3, 1968, pp137–155.

Malamat, Avraham. "The Last Wars of the Kingdom of Judah." *Journal of Near Eastern Studies* 9, 1950, pp218–227.

Malamat, Avraham. "The Last Years of the Kingdom of Judah" in Avraham Malamat and Israel Eph'al (eds.), *The Age of the Monarchies: Political History*, vol. 4. Massada Press Ltd: Jerusalem, 1979, pp205–221.

Malamat, Avraham. "A New Record of Nebuchadrezzar's Palestinian Campaigns." *Israel Exploration Journal* 6, 1956, pp246–255.

Malamat, Avraham. "The Twilight of Judah in the Egyptian–Babylonian Maelstrom." *Vetus Testamentum* supp. 28, 1975, pp123–145.

Millar, F. G. B. *The Roman Near East*. Harvard University Press: Cambridge, Massachusetts, 1993.

Miller, J. Maxwell and J. H. Hayes. *A History of Ancient Israel and Judah*. The Westminster John Knox Press: Philadelphia, 1986.

Moerkholm, O. *Antiochus IV of Syria*. Gyldendalske Boghandel: Copenhagen, 1966.

Oates, John. *Babylon*. Thames & Hudson: London, 1986.

Oded, Bustenay. *Mass Deportations and Deportees in the Neo-Assyrian Empire*. Ludwig Reichert: Wiesbaden, 1979.

Peters, F. E. *The Harvest of Hellenism*. Simon & Schuster: New York, 1970.

Plutarch. *The Age of Alexander: Nine Greek Lives* (Penguin Classics). Penguin Books: Harmondsworth, 1973.

Polybius. *The Histories* (Loeb Classical Library), 6 vols. Harvard University Press: Cambridge, Massachusetts.

Polybius. *The Rise of the Roman Empire* (Penguin Classics). Penguin Books: Harmondsworth, 1980.

Postgate, Nicolas. *Taxation and Conscription in the Assyrian Empire*. Pontifical Biblical Institute: Rome, 1974.

Quintus Curtius Rufus. *The History of Alexander* (Penguin Classics). Penguin Books: Harmondsworth, 1984.

Quintus Curtius Rufus. *History of Alexander* (Loeb Classical Library), 2 vols. Harvard University Press: Cambridge, Massachusetts, 1946.

Reinhard, Karl J. and Peter Warnock. "Archaeoparasitology and the Analysis of the Latrine Pit Soils from the City of David" in Ofra Rimon (ed.), *Illness and Healing in Ancient Times*. University of Haifa: Haifa, 1996, pp20–23.

Sacchi, Paolo. *The History of the Second Temple Period*. Sheffield Academic Press: Sheffield, 2000.

Saggs, H. W. F. *Babylonians*. University of California Press: Berkeley, 2000.

Saggs, H. W. F. *Everyday Life in Babylonia and Assyria*. Dorset Press: New York, 1987 (reprint of 1965 edition).

Saggs, H. W. F. *The Might That Was Assyria*. Sidgwick & Jackson: London, 1984.

Scurlock, JoAnn. "Neo-Assyrian Battle Tactics" in Gordon Young, Mark W. Chavalas, and Richard Averbeck (eds.), *Crossing Boundaries and Linking Horizons*. CDL Press: Bethesda, 1997, pp491–517.

Sekunda, N. and S. Chew. *The Persian Army 560–330 B.C.* Osprey: London, 1992.

Shanks, H. (ed.). *Ancient Israel*. Biblical Archaeology Society: Washington, 1999.

Shanks, H. (ed). *Ancient Israel: From Abraham to the Roman Destruction of the Temple*, 2nd edn. (revised). Prentice-Hall: Englewood Cliffs, New Jersey, 1999.

Shipley, G. *The Greek World After Alexander*. Routledge: London, 2000.

Smallwood, E. M. *The Jews Under Roman Rule*. Leiden: The Netherlands, 1976.

Stager, Lawrence E. "The Fury of Babylon: Ashkelon and the Archaeology of Destruction." *Biblical Archaeology Review* 22/1, 1996, pp56–69, pp76–77.

VanderKam, James C. *The Dead Sea Scrolls Today*. W. B. Eerdmans: Grand Rapids, Michigan, 1994. (An authoritative introduction to the Dead Sea Scrolls phenomenon.)

Whiston, William. *The New Complete Works of Josephus* (revised and expanded). Kregel Publications: Grand Rapids, Michigan, 1999.

Wiesehofer, J. *Ancient Persia from 550 B.C.–650 A.D.* I. B. Tauris: London, 1996.

Wiseman, Donald J. *Chronicles of the Chaldean Kings (626–556 B.C.) in the British Museum*. Trustees of the British Museum: London, 1956.

Wiseman, Donald J. *Nebuchadrezzar and Babylon*. Oxford University Press: Oxford, 1985.

Wiseman, Donald J. *Nebuchadrezzar and Babylon: The Schweich Lectures of the British Academy*, 1983. Oxford University Press: Oxford, 1985.

Yamauchi, E. M. *Persia and the Bible*. Baker: Grand Rapids, Michigan, 1990.

PART SEVEN

Beirne, M. M. *Women and Men in the Fourth Gospel: A Genuine Discipleship of Equals* (JSNTSup 242). Sheffield Academic Press: Sheffield, 2003.

Bock, Darrell L. *Jesus According to Scripture: Restoring the Portrait from the Gospel*. Baker: Grand Rapids, Michigan, 2002.

Brown, Raymond E. *The Birth of the Messiah*. Geoffrey Chapman: London, 1977.

Brown, Raymond E. *The Birth of the Messiah: A Commentary on the Infancy Narratives in Matthew and Luke* (revised). Doubleday: New York, 1993.

Brown, Raymond E. *The Death of the Messiah: A Commentary on the Passion Narrative in the Four Gospels*. Doubleday: New York, 1994.

Brown, Raymond E. *The Gospel According to John* (Anchor Bible series), 2 vols. Doubleday: New York, 1970.

Davies, W. D. and D. C. Allison. *Matthew, A Shorter Commentary*. T&T Clark: London, 2004.

Elliott, J. K. *Questioning Christian Origins*. SCM Press: London, 1982.

Freyne, S. *Galilee, Jesus and the Gospels*. Gill and Macmillan: Dublin and Philadelphia, 1988.

Hultgren, Arland J. *The Parables of Jesus*. W. B. Eerdmans: Grand Rapids, Michigan, 2000.

Johnson, L. T. *Luke* (Sacra Pagina series), vol. 3. Liturgical Press: Collegeville, 1991.

Kraeling, C. H. *John the Baptist*. Scribner's: New York, 1951.

Moloney, F. J. *The Gospel of John* (Sacra Pagina series), vol. 4. Liturgical Press: Collegeville, 2005.

Murphy-O'Connor, J. *The Holy Land*, 4th edn. Oxford University Press: Oxford, 1998.

Scobie, C. H. H. *John the Baptist*. Fortress Press: Philadelphia, 1964.

Taylor, Joan E. *The Immerser: John the Baptist within Second Temple Judaism*. W. B. Eerdmans: Grand Rapids, Michigan, 1997.

Throckmorton, B. H. *Gospel Parallels: A Synopsis of the First Three Gospels*, 5th edn. T. Nelson: Nashville, 1992.

Vermes, G. *Jesus the Jew*. SCM Press: London, 1983.

Wink, W. *John the Baptist in the Gospel Tradition*. Cambridge University Press: Cambridge, 1968.

Winter, P. *On the Trial of Jesus*. Walter de Gruyter: Berlin, 1974.

PART EIGHT

Bauckham, R. *The Theology of the Book of Revelation*. Cambridge University Press: Cambridge, 1993.

Boxall, I. *Revelation: Vision and Insight*. SPCK: London, 2002.

Gill, D. W. J. and C. Gempf (eds.). *The Book of Acts in Its First-Century Setting. Volume 2: Graeco-Roman Setting*. Paternoster Press: Carlisle, 1994.

Howard-Brook, W. and A. Gwyther. *Unveiling Empire: Reading Revelation Then and Now*. Orbis: Maryknoll, New York, 1999.

Johnson, L. T. *Acts of the Apostles* (Sacra Pagina series). Liturgical Press: Collegeville, 1992.

Murphy-O'Connor, J. *Paul: His Story*. Oxford University Press: Oxford and New York, 2004.

Rapske, B. *The Book of Acts in Its First-Century Setting. Volume 3: Paul in Roman Custody*. Paternoster Press: Carlisle, 1994.

Rowland, C. *Revelation* (Epworth Commentaries). Epworth Press: London, 1993.

Sherwin-White, A. N. *Roman Society and Roman Law in the New Testament: The Sarum Lectures 1960–1961*. Clarendon Press: Oxford, 1963.

Strelan, R. *Paul, Artemis, and the Jews in Ephesus*. Walter de Gruyter: Berlin–New York, 1995.

Witherington III, B. *The Acts of the Apostles: A Socio-Rhetorical Commentary*. Paternoster Press: Carlisle, 1998.

Yamauchi, E. M. *New Testament Cities in Western Asia Minor*. Baker: Grand Rapids, Michigan, 1980.

Yarbro Collins, A. *Crisis and Catharsis*. The Westminster John Knox Press: Philadelphia, 1984.

GLOSSARY

Absolute law See Apodictic law.

Algum wood See Almug wood.

Almug wood A type of high-quality wood imported by King Hiram of Tyre from a place called Ophir (1 Kings 10:11); the parallel text (2 Chronicles 9:10, see also 2:8) refers to this wood as algum wood (possibly a transposition of the last two consonants), a wood also cited in texts from Ugarit *(almg)* and thought to be red sandalwood *(Pterocarpus santalinus)*, available in antiquity either from the southern Arabian Peninsula or from the Amanus Mountains of southern Turkey.

Annunciation The announcement by the angel Gabriel to Mary of her conception of Christ (Luke 1:26–38).

Apocrypha A term meaning "hidden/secretive," which refers to 14 books not found in the Jewish or Protestant Bibles but included in the Greek translation of the Old Testament (see Septuagint) and therefore added to Roman Catholic and Greek Orthodox Bibles.

Apodictic law Also known as Absolute law, it is a law expressed in absolute terms (i.e., "You shall/You shall not"), as distinguished from Case law (see Casuistic law).

Apostasy The renunciation or abandonment of a prior loyalty to religious faith or to a particular religious tenet.

Aramaic A West Semitic language in the same family as Hebrew, found in Genesis 31:47a; Daniel 2:4–7:28; Ezra 4:8–6:18, 7:12–26; and Jeremiah 10:11; this was the official international diplomatic language *(lingua franca)* across the Middle East from around 800 B.C.E. until the coming of Alexander the Great from Greece in 333–332 B.C.E. (see Semitic languages).

Babylonian Chronicle An historical account of events in Babylonia, primarily related to the king and his military campaigns, written in Akkadian (see Semitic languages) and arranged in order of time (one might consult D. J. Wiseman, *Chronicles of the Chaldean Kings [626–556 B.C.] in the British Museum*, 1956).

Benedictus A term meaning "blessed," which refers to the song/poem of Zacharias, related to the birth of his son John the Baptist (Luke 1:67–79); this prophetic piece is used in the Office of the Lauds in Eastern and Western liturgies.

c. See Circa.

Canon A term meaning "a measuring rod," from which developed the idea of a rule or a norm of faith; in due course this term came to denote the authorized collection of sacred writings recognized by a particular faith community as genuine, being inspired and having special or divine authority (see Scripture).

Case law See Casuistic law.

Casuistic law Also known as Case law, it is a law expressed with modifying clauses, often in an "if … then" format (i.e., "If [this is the situation], then [this shall be the penalty];" e.g., "[If] an ox gores a man or a woman to death, [then] the ox shall be stoned" [Exodus 21:28]), as distinguished from Absolute law (see Apodictic law).

Chaldean A Semitic people who came to control Babylonia by the seventh century B.C.E.; they established the Neo-Babylonian (Chaldean) Empire, of which the most famous king was Nebuchadnezzar II.

Christology Of or pertaining to the study of Jesus Christ and his distinctive person and work, mainly as documented in the writings of the New Testament.

Circa A term meaning "at, in, or approximately" when used with dates; it is abbreviated *c.*

Cuneiform A term meaning "wedge-shaped," which refers to incised pictographic writing, usually on clay or stone, used by the Assyrians, Babylonians, and Persians.

Deuterocanon A term meaning "second canon," which refers to sacred writings by some Christian groups but not found in the Jewish or Protestant Bibles (see Apocrypha; Pseudepigrapha).

Epigraphic Pertaining to an engraved inscription.

Eschatological A Greek term meaning "last" or "the end-times," which refers to the study of ultimate destiny, how and when the end of humankind and the world will occur, and what the end or last period of history will entail.

Evangelist A preacher of the (Christian) gospel.

***Ex eventu* prophecies** Prophecies made "after the fact."

Gentile A term in pre-Christian times referring to non-Jewish peoples; in New Testament times this term is applied to both non-Jewish and non-Christian people and becomes a functional synonym of "pagan."

Gospel The message concerning Jesus Christ, the kingdom of God, and salvation; in canonical terms, Gospel denotes one of the first four books of the New Testament (Matthew, Mark, Luke, John), which tells the story of Christ.

Hasmonean According to Josephus in *Antiquities of the Jews*, (H)asmonaios (or Asamoneus) was the name of the great-grandfather of Mattathias, father of Judas, who led a successful insurrection against the Syrians/Seleucids in the second century B.C.E.; the term came to refer to the Jewish priestly family name, including the Maccabean high priests and kings, who ruled Judea during the first and second centuries B.C.E. (see Maccabean).

Hieroglyphics A term meaning "sacred carving/writing," used originally by early modern Westerners who discovered the pictographic script of the Ancient Egyptians at places thought to be holy (i.e., on temples and at entrances to caves and tombs).

Kerygma A term referring to the proclamation of the Gospel of Christ, especially in the manner of the early church.

King Pul A term used in the Bible (e.g., 2 Kings 15:19) and in Assyrian literature as a nickname for the Assyrian monarch Tiglath-pileser III, who reigned between the years 744 and 727 B.C.E.

Koran See Qur'an.

lingua franca See Aramaic.

***lmlk* jar** A term meaning "belonging to the king," these are royal seal impressions stamped on storage-jar fragments, found among archaeological excavations at various sites within seventh-century B.C.E. Judah; the vessels exhibiting the seals are thought to have contained essential goods—oil, wine, etc.—collected perhaps in the form of taxes and stored by the government for redistribution as needed.

Lustration The act of purification by a propitiatory offering or other religious ceremony.

LXX Abbreviation for the Septuagint (see Septuagint).

Maccabean An adjective referring to the high priests and kings who ruled Judea during the first and second centuries B.C.E. (see Hasmonean).

Maccabees A term meaning "mallet-headed," originally used as a nickname for Judas, who led a Jewish uprising against Syrian/Seleucid oppression; eventually the term was applied almost as a family name to his brothers and successors who served as kings and high priests in Judea throughout the second century B.C.E.

Madaba Map See Medeba Map.

Magnificat A term meaning "magnify," which refers to the song/poem of Mary when she visits Elizabeth (Luke 1:46b–55); this prophetic piece is used in the Office of the Lauds in Eastern and Western liturgies.

Mammon A Hebrew term referring to riches, material wealth, or profit, which is used by Jesus in the New Testament (e.g., Luke 16:9–13).

Manna An expression meaning "What is it?"; the term refers to the food supplied daily by God to the Israelites while they traveled through the wilderness for 40 years (Exodus 16:15–36).

Medeba Map A multicolored mosaic map of Palestine found during restoration on the floor of a Greek Orthodox church in the Jordanian town of Medeba (also known as Madaba). Dating to the sixth century C.E. and probably originating during the reign of Justinian, this approximately 35 × 15 ft (10.7 × 4.6 m) map—discovered in 1884—is the earliest original depiction of Byzantine Palestine in existence.

Midrash A term meaning "exposition" or "commentary," which refers to early forms of rabbinic interpretation and commentary literature on the Old Testament developed in Classical Judaism.

Nebuchadnezzar A name from the Akkadian Nabu-kudurri-usur, which translates to "May (the god) Nabu guard my boundary-stone." Also known as Nebuchadrezzar, this is the monarch who brought about the collapse of the Assyrian Empire in 605 B.C.E. and the full ascendancy of the Neo-Babylonian (Chaldean) Empire, who subsequently invaded Judah and destroyed the city of Jerusalem and its Temple in 586 B.C.E. His name is written Nebuchadnezzar in the books of 2 Kings, 1 Chronicles, 2 Chronicles, Daniel, Ezra, Nehemiah, Esther, and a few times in Jeremiah; his name is written Nebuchadrezzar in Ezekiel and the majority of times in Jeremiah.

Nebuchadrezzar See Nebuchadnezzar.

NRSV An abbreviation for the *Holy Bible: New Revised Standard Version* (Division of Christian Education of the National Council of the Churches of Christ in the United States of America, 1989).

Nunc Dimittis A Latin term meaning "Now lettest thou depart," this is the song/poem of Simeon as he was holding the baby Jesus in the Temple (Luke 2:29–32); since the fourth century C.E. this piece has been used with the Office of Vespers in the Eastern church and the Office of Compline in the Western church.

Ossuary A small box, usually made of limestone, to hold the bones of the dead after the flesh has decayed.

Ostracon A piece/shard of broken pottery with an inscription written on it; the writing was normally in ink but was sometimes incised (plural: ostraca).

Parable A term meaning "to be comparable/similar," which refers to an extended metaphor or a story used to illustrate or teach a moral or religious principle.

Paschal Lamb Originally the term for the lamb that is slaughtered and eaten by the Israelites during the Feast of Passover, this becomes a Pauline designation of Christ and his death in relation to the Passover (1 Corinthians 5:7).

Passover A major annual Jewish Feast celebrating the exodus of the Israelites from Egypt (Exodus 12–13).

Patristics A term meaning "fathers," which refers to the early leaders/fathers of the Christian Church and the sayings, writings, or doctrines attributed to them.

Pentateuch A term meaning "five scrolls/books," which refers to the first five books of the Old Testament traditionally ascribed to Moses—Genesis, Exodus, Leviticus, Numbers, and Deuteronomy (see Torah).

Pharisees A term meaning "separatists," which refers to an early Jewish sect that maintained a strict observance of all religious laws, including oral laws and traditions; in the New Testament, Pharisees are often identified with "scribes" but are consistently distinguished from Sadducees (see Sadducees).

Proconsul A term meaning "for the consul," which refers to an appointed official who acted as a governor or military commander of a Roman province (Acts 13:7, 18:12).

Pseudepigrapha A term meaning "false writings," which refers to Intertestamental literature purported to be written by or about a famous or legendary biblical figure (one might consult James H. Charlesworth, *Old Testament Pseudepigrapha*, 2 vols., 1983–85) (see Deuterocanon).

Ptolemaic See Ptolemy.

Ptolemy A Greek term meaning "warlike," which refers to the dynasty of Greek-speaking kings—beginning with Ptolemy I Soter—whose dynasty came to rule Egypt, Cyrene, Palestine, and Phoenicia in the aftermath of Alexander the Great's death in 323 B.C.E.; Ptolemaic control of Palestine was effectively lost to the Seleucids by around 200 B.C.E.; Ptolemaic kings continued to rule Egypt until it was annexed by Rome in 30 B.C.E.

Pul See King Pul (Tiglath-pileser III).

Qur'an An Arabic term meaning "recitation" or "reading," which refers to the sacred book of the Muslim religion, believed to be the revelations made to Mohammed by Allah. It is also known as the Koran, which is an English spelling based on the sound of the Arabic name.

Rabsaris See Rab-sha-reshi.

Rabshakeh See Rab-shaqi.

Rab-shaqi An Assyrian expression meaning "chief cupbearer"; this high-ranking military position is called Rabshakeh in the Old Testament; together with the Turtanu and the Rab-sha-reshi, the Rab-shaqi was sent to Jerusalem by Assyrian king Sennacherib to negotiate the city's surrender (2 Kings 18:17–19:13).

Rab-sha-reshi An Assyrian expression meaning "commander of the officers"; this high-ranking military position is called Rabsaris in the Old Testament; together with the Turtanu and the Rab-shaqi, the Rab-sha-reshi was sent to Jerusalem by Assyrian king Sennacherib to negotiate the city's surrender (2 Kings 18:17–19:13).

Sadducees A term meaning "(descendant of) Zadok/Zadokite," which refers to an early Jewish sect that recognized as Scripture only the writings of Moses (see Torah and Pentateuch) and that rejected any traditions not directly grounded in Moses. In the New Testament they are consistently distinguished from Pharisees; the group ceased to exist when the Jewish Temple was destroyed by the Romans during the year C.E. 70 (see Pharisees).

Sanhedrin A term meaning "assembly/council," which refers to the ancient Jewish legislative council and secular tribunal during the Intertestamental and New Testament periods (e.g., Matthew 5:22, 26:59).

Satrap The governor of a province/satrapy in ancient Persia, often a close relative of the king himself and usually appointed and removed only by the king (Esther 8:9, 9:3).

Scripture A general term designating canonical or biblical writings (see Canon).

Seleucid A Greek term denoting the dynasty name of Seleucus I Nicator, a distinguished general of Alexander the Great, whose dynasty came to rule Asia Minor, Syria, Mesopotamia, and Iran to the borders of India in the aftermath of Alexander's death in 323 B.C.E.; the Seleucids effectively gained control of Palestine by *c.* 200 B.C.E., which they ruled until the Maccabean revolt.

Semitic languages Languages spoken and written in the biblical world; Semitic languages include Akkadian, Arabic, Aramaic, Canaanite, and Hebrew.

Septuagint A term meaning "(the translation of the) 70," which refers to the Greek translation of the Old Testament, including the 39 books of the Hebrew canon and some 14 books otherwise known as the Apocrypha (see Apocrypha); it is abbreviated LXX.

Shekinah A term meaning "dwelling/settling," which refers to the manifestation of God's presence on earth (e.g., Exodus 24:16; Deuteronomy 12:5; Isaiah 8:18).

Simon Peter/Peter Simon is the original name of Peter ("rock," Matthew 16:18), perhaps the most prominent of the 12 apostles, who is credited with writing the books of 1–2 Peter.

Stele A term meaning "slab/upright stone," which refers to an upright pillar, usually a stone, which is engraved with an inscription or design (plural: stelae).

Syncretism A term meaning "drawing together," which refers to the combining of variegated religious tenets and practices into one system of belief.

Synoptic A term meaning "to view side by side," which refers to the presentation of biblical material in common ways; the term is usually employed when referring to the first three New Testament gospels, but it may also be used to refer to common material in the Old Testament that can be viewed side by side (e.g., books of Kings and Chronicles).

Tartan See Turtanu.

Tel/Tell A term meaning "mound," which refers to an ancient mound containing the remains of successive human settlement; Tel represents the modern Hebrew spelling, and Tell (or Tall) represents the modern Arabic spelling (e.g., Joshua 11:13).

Torah A term meaning "teaching/instruction," which refers more technically to the first five books of the Old Testament (see Pentateuch) and more generally to the entire corpus of Jewish teachings/traditions.

Turtanu An Assyrian term meaning "high-ranking official," this political position is called Tartan in the Old Testament; together with the Rab-shaqi and the Rab-sha-reshi, the Turtanu was sent to Jerusalem by Assyrian king Sennacherib to negotiate the city's surrender (2 Kings 18:17–19:13).

Vulgate A term meaning "common," which refers to the Latin version of the Bible prepared by St. Jerome at the end of the fourth century C.E.

Ziggurat An Assyrian term meaning "temple tower" or "mountain peak," which refers to stepped pyramid-like structures erected as shrines for Mesopotamian deities; the Tower of Babel is thought to be related to this architectural form (Genesis 11:1–9).

NOAH'S ARK BY GUSTAVE DORE. IN GENESIS 6:13–22, GOD REVEALS TO NOAH THAT HE INTENDS TO RID THE WORLD OF CORRUPT AND VIOLENT PEOPLE. HE COMMANDS NOAH TO BUILD AN ARK FROM CYPRESS WOOD, WITH "THE LENGTH OF THE ARK THREE HUNDRED CUBITS, ITS WIDTH FIFTY CUBITS, AND ITS HEIGHT THIRTY CUBITS" (GENESIS 6:15), TO SAVE NOAH AND HIS FAMILY FROM THE FLOOD.

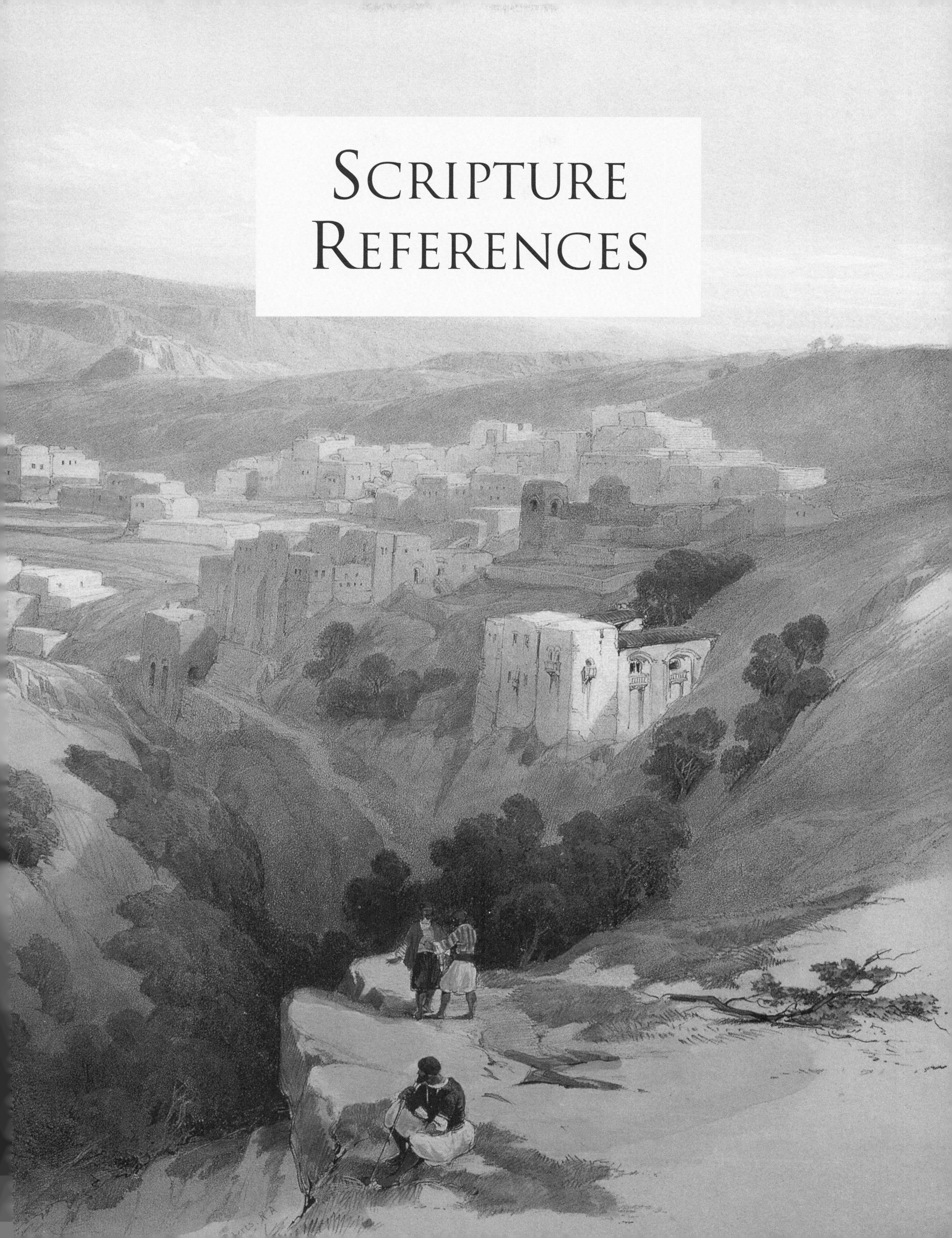

Scripture References

Scripture References

The quotes used in *Biblica: The Bible Atlas* are taken from *The New Oxford Annotated Bible, New Revised Standard Version with the Apocrypha*, Third Edition (2001), and are used by permission of the National Council of the Churches of Christ in the USA. Some quotes appear more than once in *Biblica,* as they illustrate the authors' points on more than one occasion. While the Scripture reference given in *Biblica* may include two or more verses to cover the entire context in which the quote is given, the Scripture references below only relate to the quote itself. The page numbers are in plain text for quotes used in the main body of text and tables, are in **bold** for quotes used in feature boxes, and are in *italics* for quotes used in captions.

OLD TESTAMENT

GENESIS

EXODUS

SIR HENRY CRESWICKE RAWLINSON'S IMPRESSIVE VISION OF THE TOWER OF BABEL WAS DERIVED FROM HIS WORK AS AN ARMY OFFICER AND ASSYRIOLOGIST IN THE NEAR EAST DURING THE NINETEENTH CENTURY. THE TOWER OF BABEL MAY HAVE BEEN A TYPE OF ZIGGURAT, BUILT TO HAVE ITS "TOP IN THE HEAVENS" (GENESIS 11:4).

2 SAMUEL

1 KINGS

2 KINGS

2 CHRONICLES

EZRA

NEHEMIAH

JOB

PSALMS

ISAIAH

JEREMIAH

EZEKIEL

DANIEL

THE DEAD SEA AND JERICHO, NINETEENTH-CENTURY ENGRAVING BY E. FINDEN AFTER A PAINTING BY TURNER. THE DEAD SEA HAS FASCINATED VISITORS TO THE BIBLE LANDS FOR CENTURIES. IT IS THE LOWEST POINT ON LAND AT 1,373 FT (418 M) BELOW SEA LEVEL, AND ITS WATERS ARE RICH IN MINERALS THAT OFFER UNIQUE HEALTH BENEFITS.

HOSEA

OBADIAH

JONAH

MICAH

HAGGAI

MALACHI

2 ESDRAS

1 MACCABEES

NEW TESTAMENT

MATTHEW

MARK

LUKE

JOHN

ACTS OF THE APOSTLES

Gazetteer

Gazetteer

This gazetteer contains all the places (towns, cities, regions, rivers, lakes, seas, oceans, islands, mountain ranges, mountain peaks, and geographic features) that appear on the maps in *Biblica: The Bible Atlas*. All entries are towns or cities unless otherwise designated with italicized text after the name. Alternate place names appear in parentheses after the main name. References to places in the body text of *Biblica* can be found in the Index.

A

THIS ENGRAVING BY AN UNNAMED ARTIST IN CALMET'S *DICTIONARY OF THE BIBLE* (1732) SHOWS JERUSALEM BESIEGED BY THE TROOPS OF THE NEO-BABYLONIAN KING NEBUCHADNEZZAR II IN 587 B.C.E. THE CITY EVENTUALLY FELL IN 586 B.C.E., AND NEBUCHADNEZZAR II EXILED MANY OF JERUSALEM'S WEALTHY AND IMPORTANT RESIDENTS TO BABYLONIA.

F

G

H

I

J

N

O

P

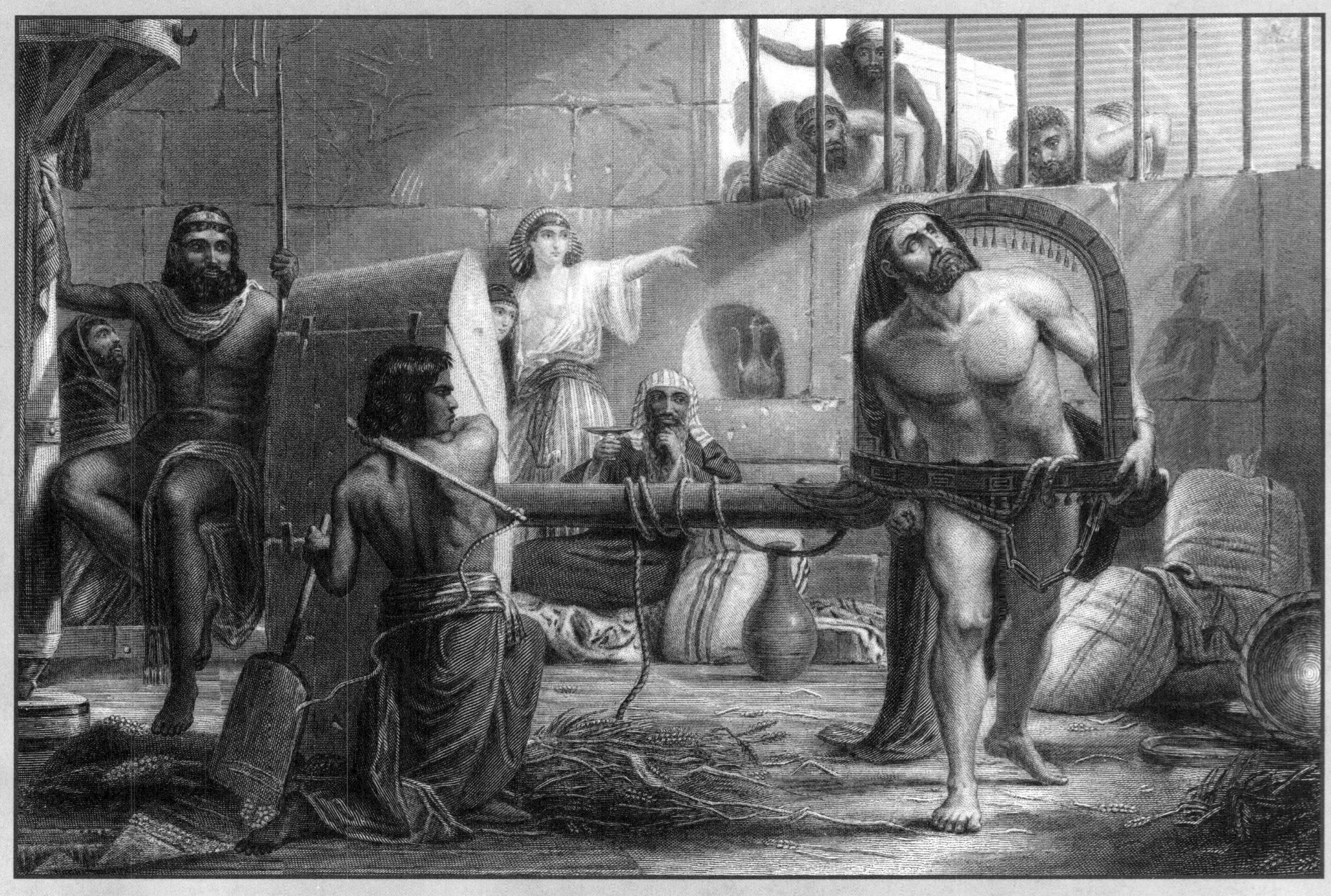

SAMSON IN PRISON, ENGRAVED BY WILLIAM GREATBACK FROM A PAINTING BY EDWARD ARMITAGE. AFTER DELILAH DISCOVERS THE SECRET OF SAMSON'S STRENGTH, HE IS CAPTURED BY THE PHILISTINES AND BROUGHT TO GAZA TO GRIND GRAIN IN THE PRISON. BUT SAMSON HAS NOT YET BEEN ABANDONED BY GOD, WHO GIVES HIM STRENGTH ENOUGH TO BRING DOWN THE TEMPLE OF DAGON.

Q

R

S

T

U

V

W

X

Y

Z

ΗΑΓΙΑΠΟΛΙCΙΕΡΟΥCΑ
ΚΛΗΡ

INDEX

INDEX

Plain numbers indicate references in the body text, family trees, or tables. *Italicized* numbers indicate references in image captions or maps, while **bold** numbers indicate references in feature boxes. For artworks starting with "A," "An," and "The," look under the second word of the title. European surnames prefixed with "di," "de," or "d'" (e.g., Juane de Juane) can be found under D. Surnames beginning with "van" or "von" can be found under V.

A

DAVID PLAYS THE HARP FOR KING SAUL, IN THIS ENGRAVING BY W. HOLL AFTER A PAINTING BY C. VANLOO. THE SWEET MUSIC FROM DAVID'S HARP (ALSO KNOWN AS A BIBLICAL HARP OR KINNOR HARP) SOOTHES SAUL'S TROUBLED SOUL. THE KINNOR HARP IS AN ANCIENT MUSICAL INSTRUMENT AND IS SOMETIMES CALLED THE NATIONAL INSTRUMENT OF ISRAEL.

D

E

F

DANIEL IN THE LIONS' DEN, ENGRAVING BY GUSTAVE DORE. DANIEL SHOWS THAT HE IS A MODEL OF UNQUESTIONING FAITH IN GOD AS HE STANDS AMONG A PRIDE OF SNARLING LIONS. HE IS NOT FEARFUL FOR HIS SAFETY, AS HE IS PROTECTED BY AN ANGEL SENT FROM GOD WHO "SHUT THE LIONS' MOUTHS SO THEY WOULD NOT HURT [HIM]" (DANIEL 6:22).

THE JOURNEY TO EMMAUS BY FLEMISH PAINTER PAUL BRIL (1554–1626). ACCORDING TO LUKE, AFTER THE CRUCIFIXION JESUS APPEARED TO TWO DISCIPLES ON THE ROAD TO EMMAUS, AND CHIDED THEM FOR NOT BELIEVING THAT HE WOULD RETURN. THE EXACT LOCATION OF EMMAUS IS UNCERTAIN; HOWEVER, THE BIBLE STATES THAT IT IS 7 MILES (11 KM) FROM JERUSALEM.

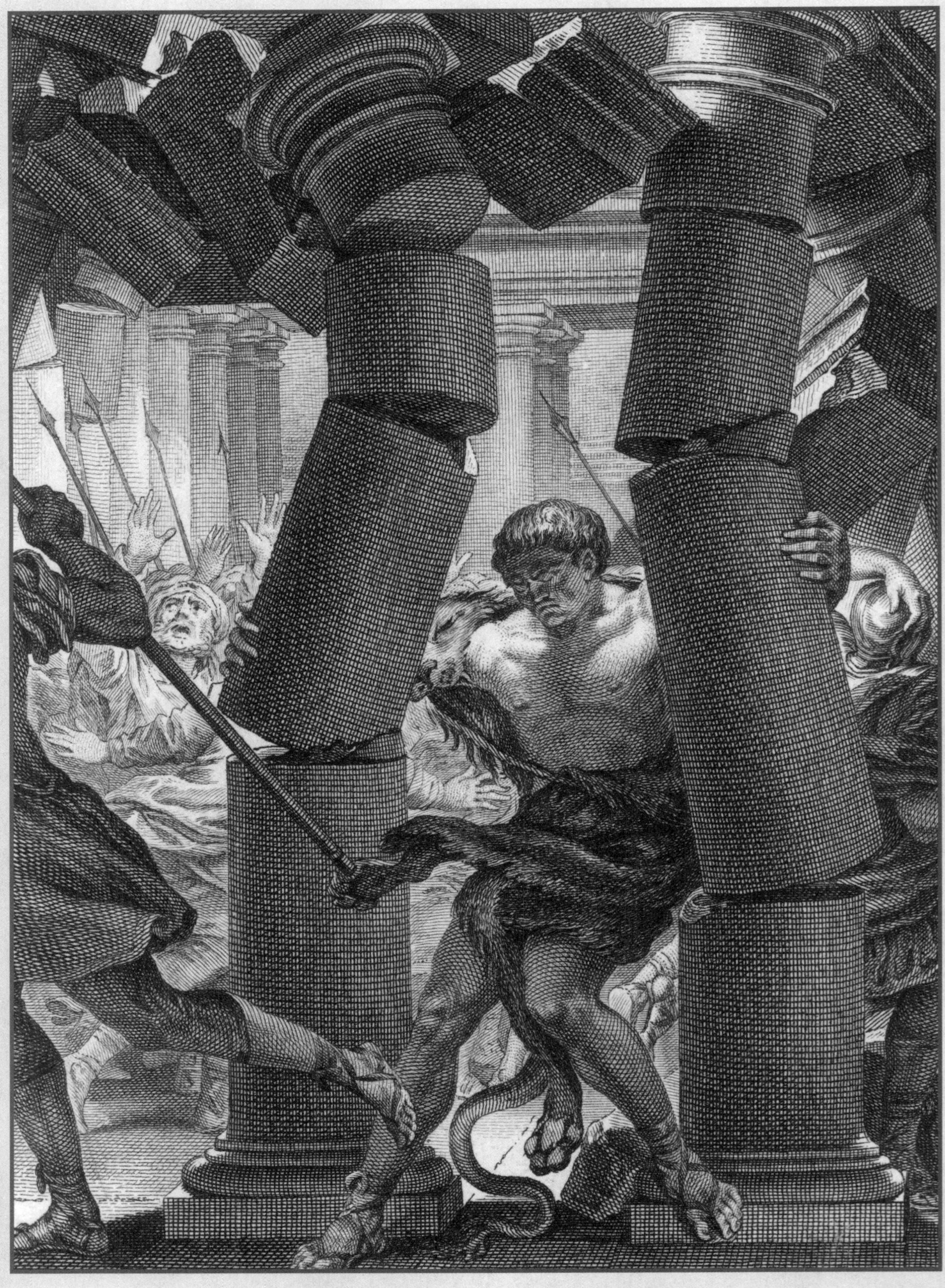

SAMSON IN THE TEMPLE, EIGHTEENTH-CENTURY ENGRAVING BY A. ROMANET. SAMSON PRAYS TO GOD FOR THE STRENGTH TO ATTACK THE PHILISTINES ONE LAST TIME—HE PUSHES WITH ALL HIS GOD-GIVEN MIGHT AND UNSEATS THE PILLARS HOLDING UP THE ROOF OF THE TEMPLE OF DAGON IN GAZA, KILLING HIMSELF AND 3,000 PHILISTINES IN THE PROCESS.

Q

R

JEREMIAH PROPHESYING, NINETEENTH-CENTURY LITHOGRAPH BY A. LEMOINE. JEREMIAH WAS IMPRISONED IN THE STOCKS AT BENJAMIN GATE IN JERUSALEM FOR DISHEARTENING THE POPULATION WITH HIS MESSAGE OF IMPENDING DOOM—DESPITE THIS IMPRISONMENT, AND LATER THREATS TO HIS LIFE, HE WOULD NOT RECANT HIS PROPHECIES.

RUINS OF THE FORTIFIED PALACE AT HERODIAN, LOCATED ON THE EDGE OF THE JUDEAN DESERT, 9 MILES (15 KM) FROM JERUSALEM. BUILT BY HEROD THE GREAT DURING HIS REIGN (37–4 B.C.E.), THE MAIN BUILDING AND ITS FOUR WATCHTOWERS WERE CIRCULAR, AND THE PALACE INCORPORATED A COMPLEX BATH HOUSE WITH A CHOICE OF COLD, WARM, AND HOT POOLS.

Picture Credits

The Publisher would like to thank the following picture libraries and other copyright owners for permission to reproduce their images. Every attempt has been made to obtain permission for use of all images from the copyright owners, however, if any errors or omissions have occurred Global Book Publishing would be pleased to hear from copyright owners.

Key: (t) top of page; (b) bottom of page; (l) left side of page; (r) right side of page; (c) center of page.

The Art Archive, London: 22(l), 84–85(b); Anagni Cathedral Italy/Dagli Orti (A): 31(t), 34(b), 310(b); Antalya Museum Turkey/Dagli Orti (A): 468(b), 468–469(t), 490(b); Antiquarium Castellamare di Stabia Italy/Dagli Orti: 489(b); Archaeological Museum Aleppo Syria/Dagli Orti (A): 16(c); Archaeological Museum Alexandria/Dagli Orti: 38(b); Archaeological Museum Amman Jordan/Dagli Orti: 60(t); Archaeological Museum Baghdad/Dagli Orti: 34(c), 324(b); Archaeological Museum Cividale Friuli/Dagli Orti (A): 267(t); Archaeological Museum Naples/Dagli Orti (A): 363(b); Archaeological Museum Piraeus/Dagli Orti: 479(t); Archaeological Museum Thasos/Dagli Orti (A): 56(c); Archaeological Museum Venice/Dagli Orti (A): 372(t); Archaeological Museum Volos/Dagli Orti: 76(l); Archbishops Palace Ravenna Italy/Dagli Orti (A): 131(t); Autun Cathedral France/Dagli Orti (A): 440(c); Basicilica San Marco Venice/Dagli Orti (A): 99(b); Basilica Aquileia Italy/Dagli Orti (A): 268–9(c); Biblioteca Capitolare di San Giuliano Perugia/Dagli Orti: 156(c); Biblioteca Capitolare Vercelli/Dagli Orti: 461(t); Biblioteca Nacional Lisbon/Dagli Orti: 158(t); Biblioteca Nazionale Marciana Venice/Dagli Orti (A): 42(t); Bibliothèque des Arts Décoratifs Paris/Dagli Orti: 55(t), 323(t), 480(b); Bibliothèque Municipale Arras/Dagli Orti: 356(t), 383(t); Bibliothèque Municipale Dijon/Dagli Orti: 384(t); Bibliothèque Municipale Moulins/Dagli Orti: 1(c); Bibliothèque Municipale Valenciennes/Dagli Orti: 201(t), 361(t), 381(b), 491(b), 493(t); Bibliothèque Municipale Valenciennes/Dagli Orti (A): 377(b), 463(b); Bibliothèque Nationale Paris/Dagli Orti: 154(t); Bibliothèque Universitaire de Mèdecine, Montpellier/Dagli Orti: 240(b); Bodleian Library Oxford: 98(c), 186(b), 366(b), 366(t), 406(b), 462(b); British Library: 31(b), 144(b), 363(t); British Museum/Dagli Orti: 312–313(c), 319(t), 326(b); British Museum/Dagli Orti (A): 64–65(r); Ca Rezzonico Museum Venice/Dagli Orti (A): 111(b); Castello Sforzesco Milan/Dagli Orti: 447(t); Cathedral of Monreale Sicily/Dagli Orti: 19(b); Cenacolo Santa Apollonia Florence/Dagli Orti: 64(l); Church of Saint Barbara, Cairo/Dagli Orti: 450(t); Civiche Raccolte Museo L. Bailo Treviso/Dagli Orti (A): 80(b); Co-Cathedral of Saint John La Valletta Malta/Dagli Orti: 421(t), 422(b); Dagli Orti: 24(b), 30(b), 35(c), 36(t), 37(b), 54(b), 62(b), 62(t), 67(b), 72(b), 74(b), 75(t), 78(t), 83(b), 84(t), 85(t), 87(r), 115(b), 130(b), 202(b), 261(t), 372(b), 383(b), 407(t), 412(b), 414(t), 429(b), 442(t), 449(b), 471(t), 475(b), 476(c), 518–519; Dagli Orti (A): 14–15(c), 50(t), 70(b), 82(b), 86–87(t), 87(b), 110(r), 138(t), 153(b), 279(t), 341(b), 343(b), 370(b), 374(c), 420(c), 458(b), 484(b); Deir-ez-Zor Museum Syria/Dagli Orti (A): 55(b); Duomo di San Gimignano/Dagli Orti: 148–149(r); Duomo Padua/Dagli Orti: 426(t); Eglise Sainte Madeleine Troyes/Dagli Orti: 92(c); Egyptian Museum Cairo/Dagli Orti: 254(b), 364(b); Egyptian Museum Cairo/Dagli Orti (A): 80(t), 89(c); Episcopal Museum Ravenna/Dagli Orti: 430(t); Galleria Borghese Rome/Dagli Orti: 12(c); Galleria d'Arte Moderna Rome/Dagli Orti (A): 345(b); Galleria d'Arte Moderna Trento Italy/Dagli Orti (A): 353(t); Galleria d'Arte Moderna Udine Italy/Dagli Orti (A): 18–19(b), 559; Galleria degli Uffizi Florence/Dagli Orti (A): 110(b); Galleria di Storia ed Arte Udine/Dagli Orti (A): 118(b), 151(t); Galleria Nazionale Parma/Dagli Orti (A): 77(b); Galleria Sabauda Turin/Dagli Orti: Cover(c), 205(t), 448(c); Historical Museum Armenia Erevan/Dagli Orti (A): 191(t); Jan Vinchon Numismatist Paris/Dagli Orti: 71(b); Kanellopoulos Museum Athens/Dagli Orti: 67(r), 72(l), 77(t); Klosterneuburg Monastery Austria/Dagli Orti: 203(b), 216(c); Manuel Cohen: 180(r), 390(b); Mechitarista Congregation Venice/Dagli Orti (A): 353(c); Monastery of Santo Domingo de Silos Spain/Dagli Orti: 458(t); Musée Condé Chantilly/Dagli Orti: 369(t), 380(b); Musée de Cluny Paris/Dagli Orti: 484(r); Musée Départemental des Vosges Epinal/Dagli Orti: 275(b); Musée des Beaux Arts Grenoble/Dagli Orti: 23(c), 394(t); Musée des Beaux Arts Lyons/Dagli Orti: 494–495(c); Musée des Beaux Arts Orléans/Dagli Orti (A): 106–107(r), 210(t); Musée des Beaux Arts Rennes/Dagli Orti: 106(t), 135(r); Musée des Beaux Arts Rouen/Dagli Orti: 116–117(r), 129(b); Musée des Beaux Arts Tours/Dagli Orti: 4–5(r); Musée des Beaux Arts Troyes/Dagli Orti: 156(b); Musée du Château de Versailles/Dagli Orti: 57(c); Musée du Louvre Paris/Dagli Orti: 6–7(l), 82(t), 88(t), 94(b), 101(b), 129(t), 172(b), 243(b), 276(b), 305(t), 348(c), 389(t), 395(t), 409(t); Musée du Louvre Paris/Dagli Orti (A): 28–29(c), 50(b), 335(b), 365(t), 452–3(c); Musée du Petit Palais Avignon/Dagli Orti: 118(t); Musée Rolin Autun France/Dagli Orti : 346(t); Museo Bottacin Padua/Dagli Orti: 2(c); Museo Capitolino Rome/Dagli Orti: 403(b); Museo Civico Cremona/Dagli Orti: 287(c); Museo Civico Modena/Dagli Orti (A): 108(t); Museo Civico Orvieto/Dagli Orti: 470(t); Museo de Arte Antiga Lisbon/Dagli Orti: 111(t); Museo del Duomo Milan/Dagli Orti: 163(r); Museo del Prado Madrid: 413(b), 437(b); Museo dell'Opera del Duomo Siena/Dagli Orti: 437(t); Museo della Civilta Romana Rome/Dagli Orti: 69(t), 74(t), 379(b), 475(t), 486(b); Museo della Civilta Romana Rome/Dagli Orti (A): 422(t); Museo di Capodimonte, Naples/Dagli Orti (A): 68(l); Museo di Castelvecchio Verona/Dagli Orti (A): 278(b); Museo di Navarra Pamplona/Dagli Orti: 275(t); Museo Diocesano Bressanone/Dagli Orti: 355(b); Museo Provincial de Bellas Artes Salamanca/Dagli Orti: 112–113(r); Museo San Marco Florence/Dagli Orti: 360(b); Museo Tosio Martinengo Brescia/Dagli Orti (A): 122(b), 404–405(c); National Archaeological Museum Athens/Dagli Orti: 377(t); National Gallery Budapest/Dagli Orti (A): 103(t), 152(b); National Library Cairo/Dagli Orti: 52(t), 349(t); National Museum Copenhagen/Dagli Orti (A): 456(c); National Museum Damascus Syria/Dagli Orti: 188(t), 286(c); National Museum of Sculpture Valladolid/Dagli Orti: 406(c); Nicolas Sapieha: 258(t); Oldsaksammlung Oslo/Dagli Orti (A): 94(c); Palazzo Barberini Rome/Dagli Orti (A): 230(b); Palazzo dell'Arcivescovado Udine/Dagli Orti: 109(b), 119(t); Palazzo Ducale Urbino/Dagli Orti (A): 241(t), 356(b); Palazzo Pitti Florence/Dagli Orti (A): 234(b); Pinacoteca Nazionale di Siena/Dagli Orti: 482(b); Private Collection/Dagli Orti: 73(t), 132(t), 170(c), 241(r), 309(t); Private Collection Istanbul/Dagli Orti: 150(b), 213(b), 336(b); Queretaro Museum Mexico/Dagli Orti: 127(c), 434(t); Ragab Papyrus Institute Cairo/Dagli Orti: 134(b); Real biblioteca de lo Escorial/Dagli Orti (A): 492(t); Real Collegiata San Isidoro Leon/Dagli Orti: 139(b), 148(t), 352(b); Roger Cabal Collection/Dagli Orti: 19(t), 90–91(c); Royal Palace Madrid: 9(r); Saint Sebastian Chapel Lanslevillard Savoy/Dagli Orti: 438(t); Saint Stephen's Cathedral Vienna/Dagli Orti: 250(b); San Apollinare Nuovo Ravenna/Dagli Orti (A): 414(b); San Carlos Museum Mexico City/Dagli Orti: 182–183(c); San Francesco Assisi/Dagli Orti (A): 416(t); San Gennaro Cathedral Naples/Dagli Orti: 124(c); San Zeno Maggiore Verona Italy/Dagli Orti (A): 145(t), 302(t); Sta Maria del Carmine Florence/Dagli Orti (A): 454(b), 459(c); Stephanie Colasanti: 39(b), 52(b), 70(r), 173(b), 390(t), 468(t), 481(t); Sucevita Monastery Moldavia Romania/Dagli Orti (A): 214–215(c); Tate Gallery London/Eileen Tweedy: 333(t), 418(t); Tiroler Landesmuseum Innsbruck/Dagli Orti (A): 367(b); United Grand Lodge/Eileen Tweedy: 174–175(b); Vatican Museum

Rome/Dagli Orti (A): 489(t); Victoria and Albert Museum London/Graham Brandon: 161(b); Victoria and Albert Museum London/Sally Chappell: 138(b), 472–473(b); Vinchon Numismatist Paris/Dagli Orti (A): 368(c).

Australian Picture Library, Sydney: Richard T. Nowitz: 208–209(b).

BigStockPhoto.com: © Adrian Jones: 300(t); © Andreas Guskos: 362(t); © Asit Jain: 340(t); © Ben Goode: 20(t); © Casey Bishop: 484(t); © Dirk Paessler: 424(t); © Emil Pozar: 289(b); © Ewa Brozek: 124(t); © Fernando Dinis: 368(t); © Heidi Tuller: 24(t); © Howard Sandler: 348(t); © Jeff Gynane: 170(t); © Lee O'Dell: 102(t); © Mari Jensen: 406(t); © Patricia Lampron: 160(t); © Peggi Miller: 94(t); © Ron Hilton: 294(t); © Ronald Hudson: 272(t); © Scott Maxwell: 218(t); © Scott Rothstein: 456(t); © Shawn Kretz: 262(t); © Stasys Eidiejus: 466(t); © Tyler Olson: 38(t); © Vladimir Radosa: 254(t), 440(t); © Xavier Vallet: 34(t); © Yolba Smit: 374(t).

Bridgeman Art Library, London: 604–562 BC (terracotta glazed and moulded bricks), NO_DATA/© The Detroit Institute of Arts, USA, Founders Society purchase, General Membership Fund: 334(b); Achaemenid, (550–330 BC)/Private Collection, © Held Collection: 344(t); Allston, Washington (1779–1843)/© The Detroit Institute of Arts, USA/Gift of the Allston Trust: 304(b); Angelico, Fra (Guido di Pietro) (c. 1387–1455)/Museo di San Marco dell'Angelico, Florence, Italy: 427(b); Arabic School/Archeological Museum, Amman, Jordan, Giraudon: 220(t); Babylonian/British Museum, London, UK: 331(t); Baldung Grien, Hans (1484/5–1545)/Neue Residenz, Bamberg, Germany, Lauros/Giraudon: 98(b); Balen, Hendrik van the Elder (1575–1632)/ Private Collection, © Agnew's, London, UK: 162(t); Barrias, Felix-Joseph (1822–1907)/Musee de la Ville de Paris, Musee du Petit-Palais, France, Giraudon: 226(b); Bartolo di Fredi, also Manfredi de Battilori (1330–1410)/Collegiata, San Gimignano, Italy, Alinari: 106(b), 124(b), 154(b), 273(t); Bassano, Jacopo (Jacopo da Ponte) (1510–92)/Kunsthistorisches Museum, Vienna, Austria: 123(t); Bernini, Giovanni Lorenzo (1598–1680)/Santa Maria del Popolo, Rome, Italy: 300(b); Bertin, Nicolas (c. 1667–1736)/Musee de l'Hotel Sandelin, Saint-Omer, France, Lauros/ Giraudon: 137(t); Beschey, Balthasar (1708–76)/Private Collection: 125(r); Bible Historiale of Guiart des Moulins (vellum), French School, (14th century)/Bibliotheque Sainte-Genevieve, Paris, France, Archives Charmet: 114(t); Blake, William (1757–1827)/© Fitzwilliam Museum, University of Cambridge, UK: 277(t), 413(t); Blake, William (1757–1827)/Pierpont Morgan Library, New York, USA: 274(t); Bohemian School (17th century)/Private Collection/ Joanna Booth: 425(b); Bonnat, Leon Joseph Florentin (1833–1922)/Musee Bonnat, Bayonne, France/Lauros/Giraudon: 277(b); Bonnat, Leon Joseph Florentin (1833–1922)/Musee Bonnat, Bayonne, France: 436(t); Botticelli, Sandro (1444/5–1510)/ Vatican Museums and Galleries, Vatican City, Italy: 136(t); Bourdon, Sebastien (1616–71)/Louvre, Paris, France, Peter Willi: 247(t); Breenbergh, Bartholomeus (1599–1657)/Rafael Valls Gallery, London, UK: 164–165(b); Bridgman, Frederick Arthur (1847–1928)/© Dahesh Museum of Art, New York, USA: 81(t); British Museum, London, UK: 284(b); Brook Cherith, Macedonian, c. 1700 (tempera on panel) by Private Collection/Richard and Kailas Icons, London, UK: 254(b); Brown, Ford Madox (1821–93)/© Bradford Art Galleries and Museums, West Yorkshire, UK: 22(t); Built by the Elaminte King Untash-Gal (1265–46 BC) (photo), NO_DATA/Choga Zambil (ancient Al-Untash), Iran: 51(b), 188(b); Bulgarian School, (19th century)/ Museum of the National Revival Period, Varna, Bulgaria, Lauros/Giraudon: 92(b); Buonarroti, Michelangelo (1475–1564)/ Vatican Museums and Galleries, Vatican City, Italy: 17(b), 294(r), 307(t); Byzantine School, (12th century)/Duomo, Monreale, Sicily, Italy: 463(t); Byzantine, (13th century)/Basilica San Giovanni Evangelista, Ravenna, Italy, Giraudon: 47(b); c. 2250 BC, NO_DATA/British Museum, London, UK: 59(r); c. 750 BC (ivory), NO_DATA/ Louvre, Paris, France: 314(c); Cabanel, Alexandre (1823–89)/© Dahesh Museum of Art, New York, USA: 169(t); Campfield, George (fl.1861)/All Saints Church, Selsley, Gloucestershire, UK, Martyn O'Kelly Photography: 97(r), 104(t); Caravaggio, Michelangelo Merisi da (1571–1610)/ Galleria Doria Pamphilj, Rome, Italy/ Giraudon: 415(b); Casa dei Cervi, Herculaneum, Italy: 283(r); Casentino, Jacopo del (1297–1358)/Musee Marmottan, Paris, France/Giraudon: 274(b); Cavallino, Bernardo (1616–54)/Pushkin Museum, Moscow, Russia: 376(t); Cavalry trumpet, a bugle, a gilt trumpet made by John Harris c. 1730, a trumpet and a silver-mounted trumpet by William Ball c. 1680, from 'Musical Instruments' by Alfred James Hipkins (1826–1903) (litho), NO_DATA/ Stapleton Collection, UK: 240(c); Church of Saint Gaorge, Ma'daba, Jordan: 436(b); Church of St.Peter, Lowick, Northamptonshire, UK: 239(l); Ciseri, Antonio (1821–91)/© Guildhall Art Gallery, City of London: 447(b); Claude Lorrain (Claude Gellee) (1600–82)/© Dulwich Picture Gallery, London, UK: 119(b); Coli, G. (1643–81) & Gherardi, F. (1643–1704) (circle of)/Private Collection, © Bonhams, London, UK: 255(t); Colombe, Jean (c. 1430–c. 93)/National Library, St. Petersburg, Russia: 231(b); Corbould, Edward Henry (1815–1905)/Private Collection, © Christie's Images: 256(c); Coypel, Antoine (1661–1722)/Louvre, Paris, France, Peter Willi: 263(t); Crozat, Ambroise (18th century)/Musee des Augustins, Toulouse, France/Giraudon: 312(t); Delacroix, (Ferdinand Victor) Eugene (1798–1863)/ St. Sulpice, Paris, France, Lauros/Giraudon: 120(b); Donatello, (c. 1386–1466)/Museo Nazionale del Bargello, Florence, Italy, Alinari: 232(r); Dore, Gustave (1832–83) (after)/Private Collection: 247(b), 298(t); Drawn by David and engraved by A. Gusmand (engraving) (b/w photo), Benett, Hippolyte Leon (1839–1917)/Bibliotheque des Arts Decoratifs, Paris, France, Archives Charmet: 208(t); Egyptian, 4th Dynasty (c. 2613–2498 BC)/Louvre, Paris, France, Peter Willi: 148(b); Egyptian, Old Kingdom (c. 2613–2181 BC)/Louvre, Paris, France: 253(t); Elizabeth Coventry, English, 1727 (coloured silks on linen), NO_DATA/© Fitzwilliam Museum, University of Cambridge, UK: 159(b); English School, (12th century)/Canterbury Cathedral, Kent, UK/Paul Maeyaert: 486(l); English School, (16th century)/Church of St. Anietus, St. Neot, Cornwall, UK: 24(r); English School, (19th century)/Private Collection, The Stapleton Collection: 22(r); Engraved by L. Fournier, c. 1868 (engraving), Dore, Gustave (1832–83) (after)/Private Collection: 267(b); Engraved by Louis Haghe (1806–85) pub. 1843 (litho), Roberts, David (1796–1864) (after)/Stapleton Collection, UK: 164(t); Etruscan/Museo Nazionale di Villa Giulia, Rome, Italy: 288(b); Fischer von Erlach, Johann Bernhard (1656–1723) (after)/Private Collection/The Stapleton Collection: 293(t); Flavius Josephus (c. 37–100 AD) c. 1470–76 (vellum), Fouquet, Jean (c. 1420–80)/Bibliotheque Nationale, Paris, France: 100(l); Flemish School, (15th century)/Musee Conde, Chantilly, France/ Lauros/Giraudon: 282(b); Flemish School, (16th century)/Musee des Beaux-Arts, Arras, France/Giraudon: 438(b); Flemish School, (16th century)/Musee Municipal, Cambrai, France/Giraudon: 446(b); Flemish School, (16th century)/Private Collection/Joanna Booth: 417(t); Flemish School/Zaragoza Universidad, Zaragoza, Spain, Paul Maeyaert: 137(b); Found at Nimrud, Iraq, c. 825 BC (black limestone) (see also 128896), Assyrian, (9th century BC)/British Museum, London, UK: 64(b); Fragonard, Jean-Honore (1732–1806)/ Ecole Nationale Superieure des Beaux-Arts, Paris, France, Giraudon: 252(t); Francken, Frans II the Younger (1581–1642)/Musee des Beaux-Arts, Quimper, France: 244(b); Francken, Frans II the Younger (1581–1642)/Musee des Beaux-Arts, Lille, France/ Lauros/Giraudon: 442–443(t); French School, (13th century)/Church of St. Urbain, Troyes, France/Lauros/Giraudon: 308(t), 309(b); French School, (13th century)/Soissons Cathedral, France, Lauros/Giraudon: 150(t); French School, (15th century)/Musee Atger, Faculte de Medecine, Montpellier, France, Giraudon: 328(b), 387(t); French School, (16th century)/Musee Dobree, Nantes, France, Giraudon: 263(b); French School, (16th century)/Musee National de la Renaissance, Ecouen, France, Giraudon: 146(c); French School, (18th century)/Private Collection, The Stapleton Collection: 157(t); From a Bible, 12th–13th century (vellum),

Portuguese School/University Library, Coimbra, Portugal, Giraudon: 178(c); From 'Discoveries in the Ruins of Nineveh and Babylon' by Austen Henry Layard (1817–94) 1853 (colour litho), Fergusson, James (fl.1817–58) (after)/Private Collection: 326(t); From Reims, 9th–10th century (ivory) by French School/Museo Nazionale del Bargello, Florence, Italy, Lauros/Giraudon: 216(b); From the 'Book of Hours of Louis d'Orleans', 1469 (vellum), Colombe, Jean (c. 1430–c. 93)/ National Library, St. Petersburg, Russia: 237(t), 249(b); From the French translation of the work of Flavius Josephus (c. 37–110 AD) c. 1470–76 (vellum), Fouquet, Jean (c. 1420–80)/Bibliotheque Nationale, Paris, France: 393(t), 172(t); From the Pictorial History of the Greek War of Independence, Greek School, (19th century)/Private Collection, The Stapleton Collection: 68(t); From the Souvigny Bible (vellum), French School, (12th century)/ Bibliotheque Municipale, Moulins, France, Lauros/Giraudon: 103(b); From the Tomb of Ramesses III, New Kingdom (wall painting), Egyptian, 20th Dynasty (1200–1085 BC)/Valley of the Kings, Thebes, Egypt, Giraudon: 180(l); From 'The Trias Thaumaturga, or Three Wonder-Working Saints of Ireland', by Mary Cusack (1829–99) published c. 1890s (litho) (b/w photo), Irish School, (19th century)/Private Collection, The Stapleton Collection: 20(c); Gale or Gaele, William (1823–1909)/ Private Collection, © Christie's Images: 149(t); Ge (Gay), Nikolai Nikolaevich (1831–94)/Tretyakov Gallery, Moscow, Russia: 440(b); Georg Braun (1541–1622) and Frans Hogenberg (1535–90), c. 1572 (coloured engraving), Hoefnagel, Joris (1542–1600) (after)/Private Collection, The Stapleton Collection: 349(b); German School, (12th century)/Bibliotheque de l'Ecole des Beaux-Arts, Paris, France/ Giraudon: 306(b); German School, (14th century)/Badisches Landesmuseum, Karlsruhe, Germany: 412(t); German School, (15th century) (after)/Private Collection, The Stapleton Collection: 133(r), 139(t), 143(t), 162(c), 168(c), 175(t), 233(r), 252(b), 279(b), 324(t), 342(t), 357(b); German School, (15th century)/© The Barnes Foundation, Merion, Pennsylvania, USA: 303(t); German School, (18th century)/Private Collection, © Lawrence Steigrad Fine Arts, New York: 314(b); Giordano, Luca (1634–1705)/Prado, Madrid, Spain: 242(b); Giotto di Bondone (c. 1266–1337)/Museo Horne, Florence, Italy/Alinari: 461(b); Giovanni Battista da Faenza (1540–1614), 1563, NO_DATA/Private Collection, Index: 365(b); Giusto d'Allamagna (fl.1451)/Santa Maria di Castello, Genoa, Italy: 290(b), 312(b); Goodall, Frederick (1822–1904)/ Private Collection, © Bonhams, London, UK: 58–59(t); Haag, Carl (1820–1915)/ Private Collection, © Dreweatt Neate Fine Art Auctioneers, Newbury, Berks, UK: 358(b), 398–399(b), 465(b); Heiss, Johann (1640–1704)/Private Collection, © Lawrence Steigrad Fine Arts, New York: 144–145(r); High Altar of St. Peter's in Hamburg, the Grabower Altar, 1383 (tempera on panel), Master Bertram of Minden (c. 1345–c. 1415)/Hamburger Kunsthalle, Hamburg, Germany: 116(b); Illuminated French translation of the original manuscript written by Flavius Josephus (c. 37–100 AD) c. 1470–76 (vellum), Fouquet, Jean (c. 1420–80)/Bibliotheque Nationale, Paris, France: 354(t); Illuminated in Paris and presented to Shah Abbas the Great of Persia by the Papal Mission, NO_DATA/ Pierpont Morgan Library, New York, USA: 174(t); Illumination from a volume of a large selection of Hebrew texts, copied by Benjamin, a pupil of Yehiel of Paris and illuminated by Christian artists from Parisian workshops (vellum), NO_DATA/ British Library, London, UK: 157(b), 360(t); Italian School, (13th century)/ Galleria degli Uffizi, Florence, Italy: 443(b); Italian School, (14th century)/Basilica di San Marco, Venice, Italy, Cameraphoto Arte Venezia: 102(c); Italian School, (14th century)/British Library, London, UK: 165(t); Italian School, (16th century)/ Musee National de Ceramique, Sevres, France/Lauros/Giraudon: 206(b); Italian School, (16th century)/Victoria & Albert Museum, London, UK: 96(b); Italian School, (5th century)/The Oratory of Theodulphus, Germigny-Des-Pres, France/ Peter Willi: 184(b); Italian School/Piazza San Pietro, Rome, Italy: 75(b); Jaquerio, Giacomo, (fl.1403–53)/Castello della Manta, Saluzzo, Italy, Alinari: 382(b); Jordaens, Jacob (1593–1678)/Musee des Beaux-Arts, Arras, France/Giraudon: 194(b); Juan de Borgona, (c. 1470–c. 1535)/Museo Catedralicio, Cuenca, Spain: 307(b); Kennedy, Charles Napier (1852–98)/Private Collection, © Bonhams, London, UK: 96–97(c); Late 13th century (vellum), French School, (13th century)/ British Library, London, UK: 376(b); Le Sueur, Blaise Nicolas (1716–83)/Musee des Beaux-Arts, Caen, France, Giraudon: 243(t); Le Sueur, Eustache (1617–55)/ Louvre, Paris, France/Lauros/Giraudon: 409(b); Leblanc, Theodore (1800–37) (after)/Bibliotheque des Arts Decoratifs, Paris, France, Archives Charmet: 71(r); Leighton, Frederic (1830–96)/© Leighton House Museum and Art Gallery, London, UK: 258(b); Leighton, Frederic (1830–96)/© Scarborough Borough Council, North Yorkshire, UK: 217(t); Lombardo, Pietro (1435–1515) Tullio (1455–1532) & Antonio I/San Francesco della Vigna, Venice, Italy/Cameraphoto Arte Venezia: 310(t); Long, Edwin Longsden (1829–91)/© Russell-Cotes Art Gallery and Museum, Bournemouth, UK: 199(t); Louvre, Paris, France: 292(t); Made by the Bezalel workshop in Jerusalem, before 1914 (cotton and wool), NO_DATA/Private Collection: 93(b); Made in Alexandria, 3rd century BC (sardonyx), Egyptian, Ptolemaic Period (332–30 BC)/Hermitage, St. Petersburg, Russia: 370(t); Mari, Syria: 104(b); Martin, John (1789–1854)/© Yale Center for British Art, Paul Mellon Collection, USA: 304(t); Masolino da Panicale, Tommaso (1383–c. 1447)/Baptistery, Castiglione Olona, Italy, Alinari: 264(l); Master Bertram of Minden (c. 1345–c. 1415)/Hamburger Kunsthalle, Hamburg, Germany: 96(t); Master of the Aix Annunciation, (fl.1442–45)/Musees Royaux des Beaux-Arts de Belgique, Brussels, Belgium/ Giraudon: 286(b); Master Suleiman (fl.800)/Hermitage, St. Petersburg, Russia: 296(b); Merson, Luc-Oliver (1846–1920)/ Musee des Beaux-Arts, France/Giraudon: 410(b); Mesopotamian/Louvre, Paris, France: 187(t); Millais, Sir John Everett (1829–96)/Aberdeen Art Gallery and Museum, Scotland: 430(b); Moeyaert, Nicolaes (Claes) Cornelisz (c. 1592–1655)/ Hamburger Kunsthalle, Hamburg, Germany: 133(t); Morgan, Evelyn De (1855–1919)/© The De Morgan Centre, London: 315(t); Mosaic in the Fourth Cupola of the San Marco Basilica, 13th century, NO_DATA/San Marco, Venice, Italy: 126(b); Moscow School, (17th century)/Private Collection/Mark Gallery, London, UK: 295(b); Murillo, Bartolome Esteban (1618–82)/Gemaeldegalerie Alte Meister, Kassel, Germany, © Staatliche Museen Kassel: 88(b); Museum of the Jewish Diaspora, Tel Aviv, Israel: 457(b); Netherlandish School, (15th century)/Museum Boymans van Beuningen, Rotterdam, The Netherlands: 21(r); Nicola Pellipario of Urbino (fl.1510–42), NO_DATA/Museo Correr, Venice, Italy: 236(b); NO_DATA/© Lambeth Palace Library, London, UK: 160(l); NO_DATA/ Bible Society, London, UK: 321(b); NO_DATA/British Library, London, UK: 17(t), 140(b), 141(t); NO_DATA/Iraq Museum, Baghdad: 332(b); NO_DATA/Kunsthistorisches Museum, Vienna, Austria: 392(t); NO_DATA/Musee de l'Hotel Dieu, Mantes-La-Jolie, France, Peter Willi: 166(l); NO_DATA/Private Collection: 176(t); NO_DATA/Qumran, Israel: 387(b); Orley, Jan van (1665–1735) (after)/© Leeds Museums and Art Galleries (Temple Newsam House) UK: 153(t); Patenier or Patinir, Joachim (1487–1524)/Monasterio de El Escorial, Spain/Giraudon: 432–433(l); Pensionante de Saraceni, (17th century)/Musee de la Chartreuse, Douai, France/Giraudon: 439(b); Persian School, (9th century BC)/ Victoria & Albert Museum, London, UK: 340(c); Persian School/British Museum, London, UK, © Boltin Picture Library: 343(t); Pierron, Charles (19th century)/ Private Collection, © Christie's Images: 237(b); Pittoni, Giovanni Battista (1687–1767)/© Southampton City Art Gallery, Hampshire, UK: 25(b); Plate 65 from Volume II of 'The Holy Land', engraved by Louis Haghe (1806–85) pub. 1843 (litho), Roberts, David (1796–1864) (after)/ Stapleton Collection, UK: 386(t); Plate from "Brehms Tierleben: Allgemeine Kunde des Tierreichs", vol.9, p.592, published by Bibliographisches Institut, 1892 (colour litho), German School, (19th century)/ Private Collection: 144(t); Poussin, Nicolas (1594–1665)/Kunsthistorisches Museum, Vienna, Austria: 403(t); Poussin, Nicolas (1594–1665)/Louvre, Paris, France, Peter Willi: 140–141(r); Poussin, Nicolas (1594–